THE ENGLISH ROMANTICS

THE ENGLISH ROMANTICS
Major Poetry and Critical Theory

With Selected Modern Critical Essays

Edited, with introductions and notes by

JOHN L. MAHONEY
Boston College

WAVELAND
PRESS, INC.
Prospect Heights, Illinois

For information about this book, write or call:
Waveland Press, Inc.
P.O. Box 400
Prospect Heights, Illinois 60070
(847) 634-0081

ACKNOWLEDGMENT

Letters of John Keats reprinted by permission of the publisher from *The Letters of John Keats, 1814–1821*, ed. by Hyder Edward Rollins, Cambridge, Mass.: Harvard University Press, Copyright, 1958, by the President and Fellows of Harvard College.

This book
is dedicated to
Ann, Margaret, and Mildred

Preface

This anthology of major English Romantic literature is the result of the editor's long-standing desire to provide for students and teachers of the first course in the field a collection of representative Romantic poems and critical texts by the major spokesmen of the movement in England. Too many anthologies, geared more to the interests and needs of the specialist, have of necessity included such an abundance of materials that undergraduates just beginning the study of nineteenth-century literature are frequently discouraged from coming to grips with the great works of the age. The long and frequently uninspiring selections from the works of the pre-Romantics and the less important Romantics, although undoubtedly important for a fuller understanding of historical and philosophical backgrounds, are certainly of limited interest to those readers interested in studying the main directions of the movement. Too often, it would seem, unwarranted criticism of the Romantics stems in part from the hodgepodge of materials which swell anthologies and which hide the major achievements of the poets and critics.

With these problems in mind, I have tried to provide a good selection of major works of the outstanding poets and critics of the period—William Blake; William Wordsworth; Samuel Taylor Coleridge; George Gordon, Lord Byron; Percy Bysshe Shelley; William Hazlitt; and John Keats. Wherever feasible, I have printed complete texts of the poetry and criticism. My great hope is that the selections are such that the many and varied facets of the Romantic spirit, its deep faith in man's spirit, its elevation of the imagination and emotions, its great confidence in the power of nature, will be seen and that through them the reader will come to a fuller understanding and appreciation of a great age in English literary history.

The organization of the anthology is straightforward and provides an excellent tool for both student and teacher. Since poetry and criticism are the real objects of attention, the major portion of the book is devoted to the works of the writers. The date of composition, when known, appears to the left following each work, and the date of publication to the right. I have quite deliberately kept editorial machinery to a minimum, injecting comment and explanation only when absolutely necessary. In this connection one cannot help offering thanks to the many editors of these materials who have preceded me; they are obviously present in the background as another editor takes his turn. If I cannot single them out for specific praise, it is only because their influence has by this time become so much a part of my thinking that it is difficult to sort out the different strands.

The general introductory essay is an attempt to set the necessary background for the writers in this volume. There are also introductory essays preceding the selections from each of the writers. All of the introductions include a listing of and commentary on the most important secondary source material. A distinctive feature of this anthology is the inclusion in the final section of a selection of modern critical essays on the Romantics and on the period in general. The approaches and attitudes of critics like M. H. Abrams, W. J. Bate, Harold Bloom, Northrop Frye, Robert Langbaum, and David Perkins should provide the student with a rich body of material for consideration and discussion.

Acknowledgments

It is difficult to single out for special praise all the people who contribute to the making of a book. And yet certain key colleagues and supporters stand out so strikingly that to neglect to thank them would be discourteous. The author is, of course, responsible for whatever shortcomings the anthology may reveal.

For the kind of encouragement and positive help provided by generous and humane administrators, I should like to thank Rev. Charles Donovan, S.J., Dean of Faculties; Donald J. White, Dean of the Graduate School; and Professors Paul Doherty and Robert Reiter, my Department Chairmen during the preparation of this volume, all of Boston College.

For intellectual inspiration and friendship, I have a continuing debt to W. J. Bate of Harvard University and to P. Albert Duhamel, Maurice J. Quinlan, and the late Edward L. Hirsh of Boston College.

My colleagues Robert F. Renehan and Eugene W. Bushala of the Department of Classics at Boston College were most generous in helping me to translate difficult passages from the Latin and Greek.

It is with special warmth and gratitude that I single out the many people who typed the drafts of my manuscript, duplicated materials, and corrected my faulty editing and writing. They are David Anderson, Patricia Davis, Marsha Ludwig, Patricia Mahoney, John L. Mahoney III, William Mahoney, Ann Mahoney, and Bonnie Stevens.

For many services I offer thanks to the staffs of the Boston College Library, Tufts University Library, and the Cary Memorial Library of Lexington.

And what would an anthologist be without an editor. I salute finally Holt

Johnson who, if there were a competition for impeccable method, gentle but firm guidance, and warm counsel, would certainly win first place.

JOHN L. MAHONEY

Contents

William Wordsworth

Samuel Taylor Coleridge

George Gordon, Lord Byron

Percy Bysshe Shelley

William Hazlitt

John Keats

Selected Modern Critical Essays

◆

General Background—Historical, Philosophical, Literary

Blake

General Introduction

DEFINING ROMANTICISM: PROBLEMS
AND APPROACHES

Defining Romanticism has been a favorite preoccupation of students almost from the age in which great writers like Wordsworth and Coleridge provided the impetus and rationale for a new kind of writing. Yet the fascination with definition and description has not always provided illuminating results: indeed, in many cases it has triggered simplistic catalogues of characteristics or long philosophical analyses that seem far removed from the brilliant artistic achievements of the poets, critics, and other artists of the age. The strange irony is that, although many critics and literary historians have tended to think in terms of a revolt or the formation of a movement, the artists themselves rarely, if ever, communicated the sense of unified ideals and common interests that would justify such terms. There is clearly never the feeling of an organized movement like that found in Germany where Friedrich and August Wilhelm Schlegel virtually provided a terminology and a program for a Romantic artistic vision. One cannot, however appealing the prospect, develop the picture of an English literary club, consisting of men like Blake, Wordsworth, Coleridge, Byron, Shelley, Hazlitt, and Keats, meeting regularly to plan a new aesthetic or to organize a common literary response to the culture and art which they had inherited. Such a picture, given the drastic differences in the personalities of the principals and the special ideals, ambitions, and talents of each, can only be a fiction, and, even more distressing, can be the basis for great misunderstanding.

At the same time one must guard against the tendency to abandon the term in a nineteenth-century setting, citing its recurring popularity in classical, medieval, and Renaissance times, its rather loose associations with the remote, the mysterious, and the magical in very different cultures, its ultimate vagueness. Perhaps the strongest variation on this theme has been that of A. O. Lovejoy who argues in his famous essay "On the Discrimination of Romanticisms" that what has come to be called Romanticism is such a varied phenomenon, with different manifestations in England, Germany, France, Italy, Spain, and elsewhere, that any helpful attempt at generalization is almost impossible. This tendency, while informed and properly skeptical, does nevertheless dismiss a little too quickly what students of English literature in the late eighteenth and early nineteenth century observe as a notable drift toward new ideals of the world, of humankind, of nature, of the work of art. It is a drift which, in spite of marvelously individual responses, reveals certain underlying themes and a basic unity.

This sense of a middle ground between the extremes of strict definition and narrow skepticism seems most fruitful for an understanding of those major new developments in English poetry and critical theory that are the stuff of this anthology. This introduction will use the designation English Romanticism, but with this sense in mind and with due modesty and caution, recognizing the danger that, in debunking the weaknesses of fixed interpretations, one can all too easily create still another. Throughout these pages, the controlling purpose will be to look closely at works of art, observe some of their backgrounds, and, most important, to witness and consider the genius that has continued to attract readers.

THE NEOCLASSIC BACKGROUND

A good beginning point would be Restoration and Eighteenth-Century England, again not seen as a monolith called "The Augustan Age" or "The Enlightenment" or "Neoclassicism," but as a time in the nation's history with certain dominant trends that underlie great richness and variety of achievement. It is a good beginning point because so many of the writers included in this anthology so frequently use it as a standard against which to measure their own new and dramatic responses and because it is a time of such innovation and change in so many areas of politics, economics, religion, philosophy and art that it seems to hold within it the seeds of Romanticism. In following such an approach, one hopes to avoid the convention-revolt or cause-effect syndrome, recognizing as always the mystery of human genius and creativity which will often out in spite of everything, and yet at the same time keeping in mind that art is a human endeavor, the work of men and women working at a particular point in time with its peculiar ideals and characteristics.

So much by way of prelude. What can be said of the dominant spirit of the years preceding the work of the Romantics? It is, to be sure, a period of relative stability in many areas. The chaos of political and religious warfare that overshadowed the earlier seventeenth century and that led ultimately to the Puritan Revolution, the execution of Charles I, the strong-man rule of Cromwell, gave way to a new harmony when Charles II was restored to the throne in 1660. The Restoration assumed almost symbolic proportions as intelligent Englishmen, weary of the discord that tore at the foundations of their culture, saw in the return of Charles, who was far from an ideal King, the chance for a new beginning, the opportunity to reestablish life, manners, morals, and art on a new and firmer foundation than the individualism and emotionalism that characterized such features of the early century as Puritan religion, Baroque art, and Metaphysical poetry. Christian Revelation, faith, the belief in the supernatural seemed more and more the specific roots of discord, and the new quest was for a calm, reasoned, sensible approach to the great issues, for a greater emphasis on the empirical and scientific. A new esprit developed, a sense that this was a second Peace of Augustus, a sense of agreement on certain ideas and principles from which one might proceed confidently in any human enterprise.

Perhaps a few of the manifestations of the new consensus will serve to convey some indication of the confidence and optimism of the times. Certainly one dominant idea was that of a demythologised Nature, one no longer seen in relation to some transcendent Deity or realm, but rather eminently understandable by intelligent observers and worthy of admiration in itself as a relatively simple, orderly, and workmanlike universe operating in accordance with never-failing laws. Everything was in its proper place, especially mankind which was, in Pope's words, "Plac'd on this isthmus of a middle state." To maintain a due recognition of this order and of one's place in it was the beginning and end of wisdom. God was a Deistic concept; the Creator to be sure, but now remote and unknowable to creatures who might find abundant evidence of his wisdom in a careful examination of the phenomena which surrounded them. Isaac Newton was, as it were, God's emissary, unfolding in his scientific designs all of Nature's laws. Needless to say, the scorn of metaphysics and abstraction was accompanied by a new and powerful emphasis on the concrete, the actual, the observable. Is it any wonder that books like Hobbes's *Leviathan*, and especially Locke's *Essay Concerning Human Understanding*, strongly empirical in orientation, became Bibles of the age!

A new emphasis on Reason accompanied this idea of Nature, Reason not in the Platonic sense of a repository of innate ideas nor in the Medieval-Renaissance sense of a spiritual power that abstracts ideas from reality, but almost as what we might call common-sense. Locke's notion that all our knowledge results from actual experience or from reflection on that experience is thoroughly representative of this new scientific empiricism. Man possesses within himself the power to know an orderly Nature, to proceed from observation to valid conclusion, to achieve wisdom by a sober understanding of the magnificent regularity of the universe and of his place within it. Pope's famous poetic rendering says it much better than any critic:

> Cease then, nor Order imperfection name:
> Our proper bliss depends on what we blame.
> Know thy own point: This kind, this due degree
> Of blindness, weakness, Heav'n bestows on thee.

Submit.—In this, or any other sphere,
Secure to be as blest as thou canst bear:
Safe in the hand of one disposing Pow'r,
Or in the natal, or the mortal hour.
All Nature is but Art, unknown to thee;
All Chance, Direction, which thou canst not see;
All Discord, Harmony not understood;
All partial Evil, universal Good:
And, spite of Pride, in erring Reason's spite,
One truth is clear, *Whatever is, is Right*.

The great sources of literary and philosophical inspiration, the models of these new ideas, were not Renaissance or medieval figures, often regarded as crude, barbaric, or Gothic, but rather classical, and especially Roman. The Greeks had, of course, come first, had discovered the brilliant order of Nature and rendered it magnificently in the Homeric epics. Homer's genius was so natural and un-tutored that he caught truth in a flash. It remained for the Romans, and Virgil is an oft-cited example, to come to terms with such genius, to reduce it to rules, to provide ideals of imitation for succeeding generations. In a famous section of the *Essay on Criticism,* Pope's version of Virgil's composition of the *Aeneid* is most suggestive:

When first young Maro in his boundless mind
A work t'outlast immortal Rome design'd,
Perhaps he seem'd above the Critic's law,
And but from Nature's fountains scorn'd to draw:
But when t'examine ev'ry part he came,
Nature and Homer were, he found, the same.
Convinc'd, amaz'd, he checks the bold design;
And rules as strict his labour'd work confine,
As if the Stagirite o'erlook'd each line.
Learn hence for ancient rules a just esteem;
To copy nature is to copy them.

To Pope the Ancients had provided what W. J. Bate calls the "burden of the past," a body of literary achievement and critical doctrine so notable and of such wide-ranging application that contemporary writers needed only to study and imi-tate these in order to be in conformity with Nature. Originality is not the greatest ideal, but rather the intelligent, disciplined, and formal expression of the wisdom of the past—a richly denotative language, a clear and decorative imagery, a firm and rhythmic meter. Again Pope comes to mind: "True Wit is Nature to advan-tage dress'd,/What oft was thought, but ne'er so well expressed."

What emerges most clearly is an Horatian, or perhaps Ciceronian, classicism, self-conscious, conservative, traditional, and with a strong emphasis on style. Such a rationalistic outlook pervaded not only the approach to Nature, but also government, religion, morality, the whole spectrum of human endeavor. An ideal and universal standard of taste and behavior developed, a standard best known by the reasoning faculty and best achieved by rules and a method rooted in the practice of the past. The ramifications of such an outlook were many, but only a few need be considered here. Scientific and materialistic conceptions of the universe prevailed. Nature, as Owen Barfield has put it, was "dis-godded," was regarded not so much as the vital and dynamic processes and phenomena that surround us, but as an admirable machine. Human beings are not so much participants in a spiritual and life-giving process as they are spectators at a wonderfully conducted performance. Increasingly man and nature are isolated; the person stirred by the beauty of sea, sky, mountain or flower is regarded as one victimized by some strangely subjective excess. Feeling is the key dimension of this excess and comes increasingly under suspicion as a weak, even destructive, guide to human behavior. Imagination is another, and its creations must constantly be measured against the stern standard of experienced reality.

For the student of literature and of the arts in general, it is interesting to observe how vividly the literature of the age reveals the impact of this Neoclassic world view. The period from roughly 1660–1750 is dominated by prose genres, by the essay, by biography, by literary criticism, by satire, by the rapidly developing novel; and such domination seems to suggest an attitude that prose somehow or other seems to have stronger roots in reality. Yet even the poetry, with its perfectly chiselled couplets and its graceful, elegant, and richly denotative diction, is marked by specific signs of the times. Although there are notable and great exceptions, it is fair to describe the poetry of great writers like Dryden, Pope, and Johnson as one of control and discipline, a poetry of satirical criticism and of moral and philosophical speculation. It is more public and social, keenly aware of an audience and of the need for clear and effective communication. Imagination and imagery are part of it, of course, but they are largely helpmates in the larger process of providing engaging representations of truth. Johnson's criticism of Metaphysical imagery as the "most heterogeneous ideas . . . yoked by violence together," as "combinations of confused magnificence, that not only could not be credited, but could not be imagined" is typical of the larger Neoclassic critique of figurative language. Such language becomes an end in itself, invites the imagination of the reader to ambiguity and vagueness, and hence does not adequately serve its rhetorical function of aiding in the representation of an ordered reality outside the mind. Neither is the direct expression of strong personal emotion a hallmark of the poetry; although there are high moments, they are certainly not typical. One remembers the Zimri portrait in Dryden's *Absalom and Achitophel*, Clarissa's great speech in Pope's *Rape of the Lock*, the moving tone of Johnson's sketches of Wolsey, Charles XII of Sweden, and others in *The Vanity of Human Wishes* not so much for the intensity of the poet's emotions as for his ability to articulate a critique or point up a moral lesson within an overall framework of control.

As already suggested, the abstract order of nature was the ideal. Not the rugged, sublime, unspoiled prospects, but rather those features touched and shaped by human hands, were the special concern of the Neoclassic poet. This is not to say that he did not deal with natural phenomena, but rather that he was seldom engaged by them as vehicles for self-understanding and self-expression, as revelations of profound and transcendent truths about man's relationship with the Divine. All too often in Pope, nature seems formalized; its beauty and harmony are portrayed as the product of human enterprise. Hence the "order in variety," the "peace and plenty" of Windsor Forest are, to the knowing and wise observer, signs that "a Stuart reigns." Hence, although he could admire a grand prospect encountered on his many journeys, Johnson inevitably pointed to London as the center of life, as a microcosm of human action. The "intellectual man," Boswell records him as observing, "is struck with it, as comprehending the whole of human life in all its variety, the contemplation of which is inexhaustible." How often we recall his boisterous and condescending remarks about the untamed glories of the Scottish Highlands, his famous put-down of an enthusiastic Mr. Ogilvie in the midst of his praise of such glories, "But, Sir, let me tell you, the noblest prospect which a Scotsman ever sees, is the high road that leads him to England!"

In general, the Neoclassic poet was less concerned with the transitory delights of the particular, the "pleasures of sudden wonder," than with the persisting truths rooted in the experience of mankind through the centuries. More important than individual artistic ingenuity was the perfect expression of those great truths, that perfect blend of word and idea, image and theme that was the ultimate test of great art.

THE ROMANTIC SPIRIT: FIRST SIGNS AND FULL DEVELOPMENT

We have already alluded to the dangers of generalizing about historical periods or about movements in politics, religion, or any human activity. Men and women resist conformity and categorization. They can agree on certain key aspects of a philosophy or theology and yet guard tenaciously their right to unique and individual variations. Citizens can pledge allegiance to a flag, affirm the wide-ranging tenets of a Constitution, fight to the death for the safety of their land, and yet disagree strongly on their particular interpretations of individual rights, on the ways in which they deem it best to work out their special destinies. What is true in these areas is no less true in the realm of art, the world of poets, painters, musicians; in some ways it is even more so. Genius may find itself sympathetic to the broad outlines of a new trend or an old tradition, yet it is fiercely protective of its own sanctuary and of the need to guard against the incursions of those persons or things that would limit its ultimate autonomy. This maverick quality can be observed in many of the writers of the Neoclassic age which we have been examining as a backdrop for the new spirit of Blake, Wordsworth, Coleridge, and the others. Indeed, one of the great ironies and sources of excitement for students is that, despite the prevailing ideas of the years from the Neoclassic predominance to the publication of the works of the first great Romantics, the seeds of change were always present. The beginnings are unquestionably mild, a new philosophical idea here, an eccentric there, an unruly political movement there, but they seem, especially from about the mid-eighteenth century forward, to intensify instead of flickering and dying. The Neoclassic age had always revealed great variety and resiliency; above and beyond this, however, as the century proceeds, a strong new intellectual, emotional, and spiritual exhilaration becomes increasingly apparent beneath a certain superficial consensus. What we have is something more than variety within unity; there is a decided movement away from older and toward newer ways of looking at life and literature. What is most notable is what can be called a certain gradualism; one senses, in studying the manifold activities of the era, not a sudden revolt, but a gradual erosion of certain tendencies pronounced in the heyday of Neoclassic England and a similarly gradual emergence of new ones.

Philosophical Roots

Where to begin a consideration of this emergence is in itself a major problem, but, for the purpose of this anthology and its readers who are perhaps more interested in suggestions to be followed up at their leisure than in long disquisitions at the expense of the works of art themselves, let us say that philosophy is an interesting and helpful starting-point. One is struck by an irony almost at once, by what might be described not as a dramatic reversal, but rather a continuity inspired by the full evolution of ideas only implicit in earlier ideas, by new interpretations and adaptations quite at variance with earlier formulations of the same philosophical premise. The phenomenon of British empiricism, and of its great manifesto, Locke's *Essay Concerning Human Understanding*, is a fascinating case in point. Published in 1690, it has already been cited in this introduction for its attack on any theory of innate ideas, for its emphasis on the empirical roots of all knowledge and its consequent wariness about the distracting and disruptive powers of imagination associated with so much Neoclassic literary theory. By some eighteenth-century thinkers and writers, however, and Joseph Addison's *Spectator* papers on "The Pleasures of Imagination" come to mind as a stunning early example which openly acknowledges its indebtedness to Locke, new reverberations are felt and expressed. The implications of Locke's stress on the concrete sensation and image, on those secondary qualities in bodies that are the result of the mind's capability to create and bring to reality its own nuances and feelings, on the psychological pleasure to be gained from images linked not so much by a rigorous logic as by a certain set of emotional associations—all of these proved not only intriguing, but supportive of the new attitudes being espoused but somewhat hesitantly expressed by many young artists restless with the prevailing aesthetic.

Clearly another significant force in the realm of philosophy is a now lesser known figure, Anthony Ashley Cooper, the Third Earl of Shaftesbury, an early English anticipation of Rousseau. *Characteristics of Men, Manners, Opinions, Times, etc*, published in 1711 but, because of the religious orthodoxy of the times, not widely known until later in the century, marks him as a great apostle of the gospel of sentimentalism and naturalism. More a poet than a systematic philosopher, Cooper argued for the centrality of feeling in human life. To a generation weary of the Deity as a Great Architect, he offered a Spirit of Benevolence who gently overlooks a world of peace, a Creator whose own essence provides the best model for his creatures. His pictures of nature are not of formal gardens, but of rural things apart from civilization. "Ye fields and woods," he prays in "The Moralists: A Rhapsody," "my refuge from the toilsome world of business, receive me in your quiet sanctuaries, and favor my retreat and thoughtful solitude." To a generation weary of dogmatism and a religion of negatives, he offered the doctrine of the moral sense; human beings have not only an instinctive goodness, but, if properly cultivated, an instinctive taste that, without ratiocination or analysis, will draw them to the virtuous and beautiful and away from the vicious and ugly. In a word, Shaftesbury no longer regards reason as the distinctive guiding principle of human beings; the new emphasis is on their individuality and on the importance of giving full expression to all of their powers.

Later in France Jean-Jacques Rousseau, with the great rallying cry, "Man is born free, and is everywhere in chains," would articulate more fully and more eloquently the philosophy of individualism that served as a major inspiration for the French Revolution and for European Romanticism in general. Rousseau's output, and its variety, is so prodigious that it is difficult for the student to focus on any single idea as the key. There are, of course, overtly political documents like the *Origins of Inequality Among Men* and the *Social Contract*. There are documents of educational and social reform like *Emile*. There are also works more purely literary like the great autobiographical *Confessions*. All of these, however, despite their special concerns, espouse a common view of society, man, and nature that captured the fancy of eighteenth-century intellectuals, but most especially of artists in search of a new credo of freedom. Indeed, the more one examines the broad outlines of what might be called the Rousseau argument, the more one sees its artistic expression in Blake, Wordsworth, Coleridge, and the other Romantics. Man, Rousseau contends, is born noble and good in a state of nature; he is entirely free in this simple, primitive state, free from the ravages of inequality and servitude. Man close to the primitive beauties of nature is at his healthiest and most virtuous; this oneness with the beauties that surround him provides a deep spirituality and a knowledge transcending the merely factual. Only the development of societal structures and the entrapment of men and women therein breed competition, selfishness, inequality, and corruption. An artificial educational system generates hypocrisy, vanity, and, finally, the worst kind of ignorance. Ultimately a government of force supports the new structures, a government not rooted in the consent of the people. This government must be overthrown, and, since the Edenic state of nature can never be recaptured, some form of republic must emerge, a democracy which allows for the full development of the natural man, for his participation in the shaping of his destiny, for the possibility of nourishing himself close to nature and of expressing his deepest feelings.

Later than both Shaftesbury and Rousseau, but of great immediate impact, was William Godwin whose *Inquiry Concerning Political Justice* (1793) caught the attention of the young Wordsworth, Shelley, and a good many others. The book, a curious combination of sentimentalism and rationalism, of anarchism and utopianism, continued the then popular argument for the equality of all men but with a new twist. All men are, for Godwin, when seen through the light of reason, equal. Government, churches, marriage, rank—these, and a multitude of other institutions and customs, are rooted in the selfish emotionalism of men. They need to be swept away and to be replaced by a new altruism. If men can be brought to see things as they are, to recognize the corruption of government, they will come gradually to a new benevolence that will enable them to act for the greatest good of the greatest number. Mankind is not perfect but perfectible; hence, reformation will be a slow process. With characteristic vagueness Godwin envisions a Golden Age of democracy in which goodness and happiness will prevail. For the modern student, it is not difficult to find the appeal of Godwin's communism for the young and naive Samuel Taylor Coleridge and Robert Southey as they planned their ideal community called Pantisocracy which was to be established on the banks of the Susquehanna in remote and idyllic America. Nor is it difficult to see the appeal of Godwin's optimism for a youthful Percy Bysshe Shelley, and for many other kindred spirits, tired of kingly rule, angry with the prejudice that breeds class distinction, and in search of a rationale for their hopes for a better world.

There are, of course, dozens of other intellectual forces at work in the age— the exciting new theories of imagination, sympathy, and taste of the Anglo-Scottish aestheticians and critics; the materialistic philosophies of Helvetius, Holbach, Condorcet; the vibrant political writing of Tom Paine; the dynamic cries for a freedom extended to women of Mary Wollstonecraft—but this brief section should help to point up the kind of ferment that characterized the age and that prepared the way for the full-blown expression of a new Romantic spirit.

Political Drama

Ideas, however, were not the only things that stirred the imaginations of a new generation of artists eager to throw off restraints and to express their vision of the world in fresh and more emotional ways. The eighteenth century, in America and in Europe, was a period of political, social, and economic revolution, and young writers could not help hearing the strong and persuasive music of the heart. The period following 1775 saw the revolt of the American colonies against the tyrannical rule of George III, the stirring spectacle of the underdog slaying the beast of monarchy. The year 1789 brought an even greater Revolution as mobs storm the Bastille with the chant, "Liberty, Fraternity, Equality," topple the Bourbon monarchy, and, for a time at least, begin the march of democracy in Europe. Blake's imagination is so charged by these great events that he incorporates them into his *Prophetic Books* as symbols of a great expression of the human imagination, of a larger evolution of mankind toward divinity. Wordsworth, in that familiar exclamation from *The Prelude*, "Bliss was it in that dawn to be alive, / But to be young was very Heaven!," seems to speak not only for himself and his own exuberant joy at the events in France, but for Coleridge and the other young Romantics. Things were, of course, to change dramatically as new revolutionaries become old tyrants writ large. The savagery of the Reign of Terror, Napoleon's takeover in 1799, the bloodthirsty repression of revolutionaries, England as part of an alliance at war with France, the restoration of the monarchy, and the wave of reaction against liberalism—all of these were to create deep disillusionment among the more contemplative, and vehement opposition among the more hostile and energetic. However, for a rich and rare moment, in Wordsworth's words, "the whole Earth, / The beauty wore of promise." Utopia seemed close, and the poets took on the role of prophets.

Social and Economic Developments

Every schoolchild can recite the basic facts of the Industrial Revolution that developed rapidly in the mid-eighteenth century and that brought with it both good and bad effects. It was a period of great progress, a time of discovery and invention. One thinks of the discovery of coal, of Watts's steam engine, of Whitney's cotton gin, of the development of the factory system as ingredients in a great drama. The drama, however, did not seem to be ending happily. The Parliamentary enclosure of the open fields of the country, so movingly portrayed in Goldsmith's "The Deserted Village," the beginnings of a system of private ownership that drew men and women away from the simplicity and beauty of rural life to the dingy and dehumanizing factories and furnaces, the poverty, the growing influence of the *laissez-faire* economics of Adam Smith's *The Wealth of Nations* (1777)—these and many other developments stirred the minds and hearts of poets and generated, on the one hand, a literature that portrayed the beauty of nature untouched by man and, on the other hand, those angry cries for reform that were to wait until 1832 for some measure of fulfillment.

One could go on in a recital of those new forces at work in the eighteenth century that seem to be preparing the way for the Romantics—the vogue of antiquarianism and primitivism with its nostalgic turning to a strange and exotic past; the great impact of the Wesleys and their emotional, evangelical approach to religion; the growing interest in Platonism, in Neoplatonism, in mystical writing, in German transcendental philosophy—but this would require a much longer introduction than appropriate for an anthology of this kind. Many of these matters will be treated in some depth in the introductions to specific sections on the writers themselves. For now, it is perhaps wise to return to the premise that underlies this section, namely that from roughly 1750 forward new developments in almost every area of human concern seem to be eroding the dominant ideas of Neoclassicism and to be preparing the way, however gradually, for the Romantics.

Literary and Artistic Developments: The Romantic Spirit

A word or two about the artistic side of these often called pre-Romantic years is in order. Wherever one turns in the poetry, the critical theory, the fiction of these years, one finds the same eager and progressive spirit. Poets long before Wordsworth seem increasingly weary of mere regularity and order as ideals. They seem anxious to break out of the confining structure of the couplet, and to utilize the greater freedom of blank verse, with its opportunities for the run-on line that is more faithful to the rhythms of the heart. They seem eager for a more varied metrical pattern that allows for greater freedom for individual expression. The new spirit can be felt in poems like Thompson's *The Seasons*, Young's *Night Thoughts*, Blair's *The Grave*, Akenside's *The Pleasures of Imagination*, and a host of others.

There is also a more personal voice, concerned with the direct expression of feeling, be it joyous or sad, in new and unusual forms. Poems as early as Gray's celebrated *Elegy Written in a Country Churchyard*, Thomas Warton's *The Pleasure of Melancholy*, and Collins's *Ode to Evening*, and as late as Burns's songs and satires and Cowper's magnificent autobiographical *The Castaway* are apt illustrations of this tendency. The imagination, ever so slowly, becomes unshackled from the restraining influence of reason and judgment and unveils in poems like Collins's odes, Akenside's *The Pleasures of Imagination*, and others, a world of concrete natural beauty, a world created by the collaboration of mind and nature. Wild nature, remote from the artificiality of city life, becomes more and more a familiar setting; critics and aestheticians like Burke underline the pleasures of the sublime, the picturesque, the unusual. Joseph Warton's *The Enthusiast: or, The Lover of Nature* scorns the ordered beauty of Versailles for "some Pine-topt Precipice / Abrupt and shaggy" or "some bleak Heath." Gray's *Elegy* celebrates the young swain, untutored in the ways of society, "at the foot of yonder nodding beech / That wreathes its old fantastic roots so high," and meditating "upon the brook that babbles by." So also in the settings of Thomas Warton's *The Pleasures of Melancholy*, of Goldsmith's *The Deserted Village*, of Burns's songs, and others is there found that sense of the spiritual dimension of rural nature, of its power to stir the noblest impulses in human beings.

Most interesting is the search for new ancestors, for new authority to justify the developing primitivism of these years, a search that leads to unusual writers, locales, and epochs. Spenser and Milton are cited increasingly and imitated often; the power of their imagination, the sublimity of their conceptions, the strength of their language hold a greater attraction than the models of Dryden and Pope. Bishop Percy seeks justification in ancient English poetry with its mysterious ambiance, its stark drama, its ballad language and rhythm. Macpherson literally invents stirring tales of ancient heroes of the Scottish Highlands in his *Works of Ossian*. Gray is moved in poems like "The Fatal Sisters" and "The Descent of Odin" by the rousing stories of brave heroes from Old Norse poetry. The vogue of the Gothic, a vogue that persists even today, for those who seek to escape the humdrum reality of everyday life, and the mystery of strange places, mysterious crimes, eerie characters, is seen in novels like Horace Walpole's *The Castle of Otranto* and Ann Radcliffe's *The Mysteries of Udolpho*.

Robert Burns's dramatic scorning of the rules and his turning to the characters, settings, and language of his native Scotland is vivid testimony to a new faith in the impulses of common humanity as a subject matter for poetry and in the poetic possibilities of the language, indeed even the dialects, of rustic people. It is difficult to overestimate the power of "O, My luve is like a red, red rose / That's newly sprung in June" or "I'll ne'er blame my partial fancy, / Naething could resist my Nancy" or "But, Mousie, thou art no thy lane, / In proving foresight may be vain: / The best laid schemes o' mice an men / Gang aft a-gley" on poets and readers, especially on the young Wordsworth and Coleridge, unhappy with the literary inheritance of the eighteenth century and eager to write a series of ballads about "humble and rustic life" in a language close to that of "real men."

In short, there was an enormous change in the literature of the Neoclassic years, a change to a greater extent triggered by new ideas, by political and social upheaval, but most of all by writers restless with the *status quo* and eager to express a new and dynamic vision of themselves and of the world around them. The scene is set as Blake writes his *Songs of Innocence and Experience* and Wordsworth and Coleridge plan the *Lyrical Ballads*. These new poets of the late eighteenth and early nineteenth century are not so much revolutionaries as greater artists who have grown up in the midst of startling change and who can articulate more powerfully the new spirit of freedom and beauty that had been gathering for many years. It is to these poets and to their general contributions to the Romantic mode that we now turn.

THE NEW ROMANTICISM

Although we will have occasion to discuss each of the major Romantics in separate introductions, the closing section of our General Introduction will consider those general themes and techniques that characterize the burgeoning Romantic spirit in England, especially as they are manifested in the work of William Wordsworth; Samuel Taylor Coleridge; George Gordon, Lord Byron; Percy Bysshe Shelley; William Hazlitt; and John Keats. In doing so, the great critical treatises, especially Wordsworth's *Preface to the Lyrical Ballads* (1800), Coleridge's *Biographia Literaria*, Hazlitt's essays on poetry, Shelley's *Defence of Poetry*, and Keats's letters, are extremely helpful, not that they are the only documents to set forth important ideas, but that they stand out as major sources for an understanding of the new poetic theory and practice. In them is a consistent preoccupation with matters like the role and function of the poet and poetry, the language and imagery of poetry, the imagination, and the relationship of poetry and nature. In the following sections we will use these matters, and as many examples from the poetry and critical theory as are feasible, to talk about the new Romanticism.

The Poet and Poetry

One recurring and striking image of the poet is that of a person both like and unlike others. He shares a common humanity, certain hopes and aspirations, but, to use Wordsworth's words from the *Preface*, he is "endowed with more lively sensibility, more enthusiasm and tenderness," a man "who has a greater knowledge of human nature, and a more comprehensive soul, than are supposed to be common among mankind." The more melodramatic Shelley describes poets as "the hierophants of an unapprehended inspiration," as "the unacknowledged legislators of the world." For Coleridge the poet is a figure of greater power who "brings the whole soul of man into activity." The emphasis almost everywhere is on the poet as a private figure deeply concerned with the loss of certain permanent, transcendent values following the demise of the Medieval-Renaissance religious—and the failure of the Neoclassic rationalist-humanist—myths. How to achieve a new sense of communion in an increasingly mechanized and dehumanized world becomes a central question. How to recapture a sense of the unity of things in the midst of growing fragmentation, to restore an almost lost imaginative and emotional approach to life; how, to borrow Whitehead's language, to rediscover value in a fact-oriented culture, become dominant concerns. Wordsworth writes forcefully about the low level of contemporary taste and of those causes which are blunting "the discriminating powers of the mind, . . . unfitting it for all voluntary exertion, to reduce it to a state of almost savage torpor." He writes with equally strong language about the need of the poet to shake the sensibility of audiences, to provoke once again their capacities to feel and to imagine.

There is a note of optimism in the varied answers to the questions and problems raised by the culture and art of the time. Lacking a sense of confidence in external structures like religion, politics, education, and science, artists turn increasingly into themselves to discover sources of value. The poet becomes a pilgrim in what Harold Bloom describes as an internalized quest-romance. The imagination becomes a maker of truth, and metaphor and symbol its vehicles. A new self-consciousness and individualism mark the statements of poets about themselves and their works, a sense that poetry is the new morality, the new religion. In Blake there is the unabashed stance of the *Prophetic Books,* "The Prophets Isaiah and Ezekiel dined with me," the sense that he, like the Old Testament preachers, must prepare the way of the Lord as he sees it; must, through the lyrical *Songs of Innocence and Experience* and the strident prophecies, proclaim the gospel of the imagination, that "all deities reside in the human breast," that "every thing that lives is Holy," that "Energy is Eternal Delight." For Wordsworth the enlargement of the sensibility of an audience is "one of the best services in which, at any period, a writer can be engaged." The poet is special in that he is "a man pleased with his own passions and volitions, and rejoices more than other men in the spirit of life that is in him." Poetry is "the spontaneous overflow of powerful feelings; it takes its origin from emotion recollected in tranquility." Far from merely rehearsing the great truths of the ages in a new form and style, it is the product of genius and originality, of what Rollo May in our day has called "The Courage to Create." The poet, and how often Blake's remarks come to mind, sees what has never been seen before and expresses his vision in ways that touch his audience inwardly. Byron's hero Childe Harold finds meaning only in his creative power; he himself is nothing, "but not so art thou, / Soul of my thought!" His confidence in this power is enormous; for him the power creates a better world:

> 'Tis to create, and in creating live
> A being more intense, that we endow
> With form our fancy, gaining as we give
> The life we image, even as I do now.

The exuberant Hazlitt defines poetry in a way that frees it from all traditional obligations; it is "the language of the imagination and the passions. It relates to whatever gives immediate pleasure or pain to the human mind. It comes home to the bosoms and businesses of men; for nothing but what so comes home to them in the most general and intelligible shape, can be a subject for poetry." Inspiration, not imitation, is the key to Shelley's conception of the poet and his art; planning and rules are secondary to the direct touch of the Divine which stirs the imagination to glimpse and to embody the transcendent and to record it in poetry. Poetry, he proclaims triumphantly, redeems from decay "the visitations of the divinity in man." Even Keats, so often at odds with his contemporaries on the question of subjectivity in poetry and strong in his emphasis on impersonality, nevertheless pays high tribute to its intuitive sources and its power to capture the concrete richness of experience in ways that engage the heart. If it "comes not as naturally as the Leaves to a tree it had better not come at all." The uniqueness of poetry, that which renders it greater than philosophy, and which is most splendidly revealed in *King Lear*, is "its intensity, capable of making all disagreeables evaporate, from their being in close relationship with Beauty & Truth."

Poetry for this new breed of writers is far from a pleasant recreation, a frosting on the cake; it is a deeper and more fertile way of confronting life with all its complexities and of representing it in ways that engage the total personality, blood, intellect, and feeling.

Language and Inquiry: A New Kind of Writing

Wordsworth, more than any other figure of the period, provided not only a critique of the language and imagery of Neoclassic verse, but also a philosophy and a program for what can certainly be called a new kind of writing. His *Preface to the Lyrical Ballads* is, of course, famous for its complaints about "phrases and figures of speech which from father to son have long been regarded as the common inheritance of poets," "personifications of abstract ideas," "falsehood of description," "the gaudiness and inane phraseology of many modern writers." Such stock diction and imagery, such downright bad writing habits reflect again a tradition of imitation, a paralysis in the face of past greatness, a sense that there exists an established body of subject-matter and language which contemporary poets can draw on, and, at least implicitly, a wariness of originality and spontaneity.

Wordsworth straightforwardly expounds his own program. Readers of the *Lyrical Ballads* will, undoubtedly, "frequently have to struggle with feelings of strangeness and awkwardness." His object in these poems has been "to choose incidents and situations from common life, and to relate or describe them, throughout, as far as was possible in a selection of language really used by men." Unlike poets, accustomed to see nature through the eyes of books and to draw their vocabulary from some volume of proper expression, he has tried "to look steadily at my subject," "to keep the Reader in the company of flesh and blood." He has, of course, purified the grosser parts of this language, so that what remains still has a beauty and a naturalness untouched by artificial convention. Indeed, the best of Wordsworth's poems of rustic life have been so touched by his genius as to reveal a natural charm and a sense of direct and personal expression.

One remembers happily the joyous simplicity of the opening of "To My Sister":

> It is the first mild day of March:
> Each minute sweeter than before,
> The redbreast sings from the tall larch
> That stands beside our door.

or the quiet charm of the lines from *Tintern Abbey:*

> Once again I see
> These hedge-rows, hardly hedge-rows, little lines
> Of sportive wood run wild: these pastoral farms
> Green to the very door; and wreaths of smoke
> Sent up, in silence, from among the trees!

or the lilting music of the portrait of "The Solitary Reaper":

> Behold her, single in the field,
> Yon Solitary Highland Lass!
> Reaping and singing by herself;
> Stop here, or gently pass!
> Alone she cuts and binds the grain,
> And sings a melancholy strain,
> O listen! for the Vale profound
> Is overflowing with the sound.

A similar, although much more deceptive and ironic, simplicity marks the brilliant *Songs of Innocence and Experience* of Blake. How vividly he can capture the child's innocence in:

> Little Fly,
> Thy summer's play
> My thoughtless hand
> Has brush'd away.
>
> Am not I
> A fly like thee?
> Or art not thou
> A man like me?

or the primal ferocity of:

> Tyger! Tyger! burning bright
> In the forests of the night,
> What immortal hand or eye,
> Dare frame thy fearful symmetry?

Coleridge, although he complains in the *Biographia Literaria* about Words-worth's "*matter-of-factness* in certain poems," and "a laborious minuteness and fidelity in the representation of objects, and their positions, as they appeared to the poet himself," nevertheless is ringingly positive in his general praise of "an austere purity of language," "the sinewy strength and originality of single lines and paragraphs," "the perfect truth of nature in his images and descriptions, as taken immediately from nature." Indeed his own poetry manifests a similar pre-occupation with the natural and simple, whether in his love of the ballad as re-flected in *The Rime of the Ancient Mariner* and *Christabel,* or in the strong sense of the vernacular, of the rhythms of conversation in great early poems like *The Eolian Harp* or *Frost at Midnight.* It is difficult to make choices, but few would disagree on the rustic beauty of passages like the following from "The Eolian Harp" in which he addresses his wife with clarity and gentleness, evoking the beauty of their cottage and the quiet of their surroundings. Language, imagery, and sound combine to paint a truly Romantic scene:

> My pensive Sara! thy soft cheek reclined
> Thus on mine arm, most soothing sweet it is
> To sit beside our Cot, our Cot o'ergrown
> With white-flower'd Jasmin, and the broad-leav'd Myrtle,
> (Meet emblems they of Innocence and Love!)
> And watch the clouds, that late were rich with light,
> Slow saddening round, and mark the star of eve
> Serenely brilliant (such should Wisdom be)
> Shine opposite! How exquisite the scents
> Snatch'd from yon bean field! and the world *so* hush'd!
> The stilly murmur of the distant Sea
> Tells us of silence.

All of this emphasis on the simple, direct, and spontaneous should not be al-lowed to cloud the obvious examples of a more formal dimension, a more exalted tone in much of the poetry of the Romantics. Wordsworth's *Immortality Ode* and many sections of *The Prelude,* Coleridge's *Dejection: An Ode,* Shelley's *Adonais, Prometheus Unbound,* and *Alastor,* Keats's odes, and many other pieces rise to narrative and dramatic heights in their tone, language, imagery, and situ-ation. They are by no means humble, rustic poems written in the language of real men. And yet, in almost every case, the personal quality of the voices, the natural flow of a language and imagery that seem deeply felt and vividly pic-tured, a looser and more relaxed metrical pattern capture some of the essential spirit behind the Wordsworth program for poetry. Indeed we do a great dis-service to his *Preface* if we regard it only in terms of its emphasis on the primitive and neglect its larger concern with widening the role of the poet and his subject matter, with turning the attention of the artist to a more vital expression of the outer and the inner life, with providing a justification for poetry as a form of knowledge.

M. H. Abrams has offered one of the best descriptions of how so many of the characteristics we have been discussing come together in what he calls the "Greater Romantic Lyric" or what others have called the "conversation poem" or the "poem of experience." The poem, personal in tone, offers a "determinate speaker in a particularized, and usually a localized outdoor setting, whom we overhear as he carries on, in a fluent vernacular which rises easily to a more formal speech, a sustained colloquy, sometimes with himself or with the outer scene, but more frequently with a silent human auditor, present or absent." The poem moves from a description of the setting to a meditative response that brings tranquillity, deeper insight, or even more thoughtful questioning. It is a superb description, with ramifications not just for Wordsworth's *Tintern Abbey* or Coleridge's *Frost at Midnight,* but some of the best sections of Byron's *Childe Harold's Pilgrimage,* for Shelley's *To a Skylark,* and Keats's *Ode to a Nightingale,* a description that points up aptly what we have been attempting to describe as the Romantic's new way of writing.

The Imagination

The use of the term *imagination* to describe the work of the Romantic, while valuable to some extent, has led to such general and vague discussions as to become almost valueless. While it is true that all of the major poets and critics in this anthology consider the imagination as the root of creativity and utilize it in their work, their descriptions vary greatly, and the great challenge for the student is to discover, if possible, a common core of agreement as well as the fascinating individual variations.

For all the Romantics imagination is a central power of the mind, with the ability to order the chaos of experience, to shape and organize, to move beyond the light of sense, to sympathize with reality beyond the self. Its unique power is the discovery of what is essential in the flux of experience and the heightening of that ingredient. Coleridge's oft-quoted definitions are usually the first to come to mind, the famous distinction between the primary imagination, which is "the living Power and prime Agent of all human perception," and, closer to the poet, the secondary, "an echo of the former, coexisting with the conscious will, yet still as identical with the primary in the *kind* of its agency, and differing only in *degree,* and in the *mode* of its operation," a power which "dissolves, diffuses, dissipates in order to recreate." It is, he writes in another context, a "reconciling" and "mediatory" power which "gives birth to a system of symbols, harmonious in themselves, and consubstantial with the truths of which they are conductors."

Wordsworth, although less technical, nevertheless provides in both his poetry and criticism vivid descriptions of his own awareness of a developing power of imagination and later of its decline, a remarkable sense of its workings and especially of those moments of ecstasy when he seems at one with the infinite. On the level of theory, he writes of the poet's delight in discovering manifestations of his own passions and longings "in the goings-on of the Universe," and of how he is "habitually impelled to create them where he does not find them." The great power, he argues, "has no reference to images that are merely a faithful copy, existing in the mind, of absent external objects, but is a word of higher import, denoting operations of the mind upon these objects and processes of creation or of composition governed by certain fixed laws."

Great scenes from the poetry come quickly to mind; they are those wondrous "spots of time" when the mysterious power seems at work. There is the skating scene in Book I of *The Prelude* when the young boy joyously whirls across the ice in the full flush of energy and enthusiasm:

> spinning still
> The rapid line of motion, then at once
> Have I, reclining back upon my heels,
> Stopped short; yet still the solitary cliffs
> Wheeled by me—even as if the earth had rolled
> With visible motion her diurnal round!
> Behind me did they stretch in solemn train,
> Feebler and feebler, and I stood and watched
> Till all was tranquil as a dreamless sleep.

There is the Simplon Pass section in Book VI when the imaginative anticipation of the crossing of the Alps, the "hopes that pointed to the clouds," is greater than the actual crossing and inspires one of his greatest tributes:

> But to my conscious soul I now can say—
> "I recognize thy glory:" in such strength
> Of usurpation, when the light of sense
> Goes out, but with a flash that has revealed
> The invisible world, doth greatness make abode,
> There harbours whether we be young or old.
> Our destiny, our being's heart and home,
> Is with infinitude, and only there;
> With hope it is, hope that can never die,
> Effort, and expectation, and desire,
> And something evermore about to be.

Coleridge, of course, in one of his most movingly ironic passages in *Dejection: An Ode,* mourns his lost creative power, a loss which has left his life bleak and barren. The same poet who could imaginatively identify with and share the joys of a country walk with Charles Lamb and other friends in *This Lime-Tree Bower My Prison,* now laments that he can "see, not feel, how beautiful they are." The imaginative powers, once so vibrantly alive and creative in the conversation poems and the great mystery poems, are now the victims of a killing affliction:

> But oh! each visitation
> Suspends what nature gave me at my birth,
> My shaping spirit of Imagination.

Hazlitt and Keats are most influential in adding the special quality and power of sympathy to the imagination. Hazlitt, the theorist and critic, had from his youthful treatises argued for the natural disinterestedness of the human mind, for the premise that we are healthiest and happiest when we go out of ourselves and become involved in something nobler and greater. "Imagination," he writes, "is, more properly, the power of carrying on a given feeling into other situations, which must be done best according to the hold which the feeling itself has taken of the mind." Keats speaks of the gift as "Negative Capability," the ability to move beyond the special concerns of the ego, to grasp fully reality beyond the mind and to render it concretely. The truly imaginative poet has a special character: "it has no self—it enjoys light and shade; it lives in gusto, be it foul or fair, high or low, rich or poor, mean or elevated." The source of this character is imagination, an "outreaching of mind" as Rollo May has described it, and what it "seizes as Beauty must be truth." The Imagination, says Keats, "may be compared to Adam's dream—he awoke and found it truth."

Imagination, then, not a simple picture-making faculty, is a many-faceted power, one that unifies the many activities of the mind. For the Romantics its creations are greater than human monuments, for they have an immortality rooted in their vital sense of the inner life. Lord Byron, no literary theorist to speak of, but often the world-weary pilgrim who finds his solace in these creations, puts it well in *Childe Harold's Pilgrimage*:

> The beings of the mind are not of clay;
> Essentially immortal, they create
> And multiply in us a brighter ray
> And more beloved existence: that which Fate
> Prohibits to dull life, in this our state
> Of mortal bondage, by these spirits supplied,
> First exiles, then replaces what we hate:
> Watering the heart whose early flowers have died,
> And with a fresher growth replenishing the void.

The Romantic Approach to Nature

We have already considered the Newtonian scientific-rationalistic image of nature inherited by the Romantic writers; we have also considered the restlessness of many of these poets with such a paradigm and their first, faltering steps toward formulating the vision of an animate nature, one in which life breathes through the rugged mountain, the grassy landscape, the stormy ocean, the peaceful stream. Theirs was decidedly a response, but one that lacked a well-formulated rationale. Wherever one turns in the post-1800 period such a rationale, in one form or another, appears. Whether terms like "organicism" or "process" are employed, the fact remains that the Romantics, with Wordsworth and Coleridge certainly the most eloquent spokesmen, rejected the image of a static universe. They described a nature in the process of becoming, a nature inexhaustible in its possibilities in which human beings, through the power of mind, could find meaning and value. Nature was not merely the order of the universe considered as a model for imitation, but the beautiful and awesome phenomena and the presences that lay beyond or behind them. Far from the escapism so often popularly associated with Romantic naturalism is a genuine realism, a sense of the concreteness of natural objects and of their possibilities for stirring the mind. For Wordsworth, the poet "considers men and nature as essentially adapted to each other, and the mind of man as naturally the mirror of the fairest and most interesting properties of nature." Hazlitt speaks of nature having "Her surface and her dark recesses. She is deep, obscure, and infinite. It is only minds on whom she makes her fullest impressions that can penetrate her shrine or unveil her Holy of Holies. It is only those whom she has filled with her spirit that have the boldness or the power to reveal her mysteries to others." Coleridge speaks of the beautiful in nature not as mere facts or things, but as "the unity of the manifold, the coalescence of the diverse; in the concrete, it is the union of the shapely (formosum) with the vital." Shelley's clouds, skylarks, and winds are dynamic forces that move and inspire the poet.

The most moving and engaging expressions of the centrality of nature in Romanticism are not in the critical theory, however, but in the poetry, and in an introduction as short as this all we can do is to note a few examples. Again Wordsworth is very important, for wherever we turn in his poetry, we see the force of nature in his spiritual life, beautiful but fearsome, inspiring yet troubling, "The anchor of my purest thoughts, the nurse, / The guardian of my heart, and soul / Of all my moral being." His earliest poems are dedicated to the principle of the *Preface* that in the life of the country "the essential passions of the heart find a better soul in which they can attain their maturity, are less under restraint, and speak a plainer and more emphatic language," and characters like the old Cumberland beggar, the child in "We Are Seven," "The Idiot Boy," and the unspoiled Lucy are summoned as his chief witnesses.

As a child, Wordsworth recalls in *The Prelude*, he first discovered nature's beauty and wisdom when, hunting at night in the Lake District, he would suddenly stop, "and when the deed was done / I heard among the solitary hills / Low breathings coming after me." Rowing in a stolen boat, under cover of darkness, he is enveloped by the surrounding mountains, and

> after I had seen
> That spectacle, for many days, my brain
> Worked with a dim and undetermined sense
> Of unknown modes of being.

Later, after a period of disillusionment, he finds in Mount Snowdon

> the type
> Of a majestic intellect, its acts
> And its possessions, what it has and craves,
> What in itself it is, and would become.
> There I beheld the emblem of a giant mind
> That feeds upon infinity.

Byron's Childe Harold, ostracized by society and weary of its turbulence and hypocrisy, wanders over Europe, finding refuge only in the remote outposts, gradually to "become / Portion of that around me," and raising the ultimate rhetorical question, "Are not the mountains, waves, and skies, a part / Of me and my soul, as I of them?" Shelley finds in the evanescent clouds symbols of the uncertainty of life, but ultimately of permanence in the midst of change, and in the West Wind he finds a source of strength and inspiration that arouses his most passionate lines:

> Be thou, Spirit fierce,
> My spirit! Be thou me, impetuous one!
>
> Drive my dead thoughts over the universe
> Like withered leaves to quicken a new birth!

Romanticism is a varied phenomenon with many disciples; it is a faith, and literature is its gospel. It is a faith in the natural goodness of human beings, in those inner resources of imagination and feeling which, when nourished by the life-giving forces of nature, can bring joy, "a sense of something evermore about to be." Its exemplars, amply represented in this anthology, produced in the great years from 1789 to 1830 a body of poetry and criticism that remains a vital force in the modern world.

Suggestions for Further Reading

There is an abundance of material on the general backgrounds of Romanticism and a number of excellent general studies on Romantic art. All we can do in a section like this is to highlight some of the more famous and more valuable works and to suggest ways in which they might be useful for the student interested in moving beyond primary sources and in developing special interests. Excellent general guides for anyone doing research in the period are Frank Jordan ed., *The English Romantic Poets: A Review of Research* (1972) and C. W. and L. H. Houtchens, *The English Romantic Poets and Essayists* (1966). The annual bibliography of the *Publications of the Modern Language Association of America* contains all recently published work on the Romantics in its section on the Nineteenth Century, while an annual specialized bibliography of research and publication on the Romantic period can be found in the *Philological Quarterly* for the years through 1964 and in *English Language Notes* for the years thereafter.

Backgrounds of Romanticism and the Spirit of the Age

Useful books for anyone interested in the spirit of the Neoclassic age are Carl Becker's *Heavenly City of the Eighteenth Century Philosophers* (1932); Basil Willey's *The Eighteenth Century Background;* and Peter Gay's comprehensive and authoritative two-volume study, *The Enlightenment: An Interpretation.*

General studies of historical, political, and social backgrounds are Alfred Cobban's *Edmund Burke and the Revolt Against the Eighteenth Century* (1929), which provides a good picture of the setting in which poets like Blake, Wordsworth, and Coleridge started to write; Crane Brinton's helpful *Political Ideas of the English Romanticists;* G. M. Trevelyan's always reliable *British History in the Nineteenth Century* (1922) and *English Social History* (1942); and Carl Woodring's superb study, *Politics in English Romantic Poetry* (1970).

The Literary Setting

W. J. Bate's *From Classic to Romantic* (1946) is still the classic study of the emergence of the Romantic spirit in England; M. H. Abrams, *The Mirror and the Lamp* (1953) is equally important for its painstaking and insightful study of Romantic critical theory and the tradition. Samuel Monk's *The Sublime: A Study of Critical Theories in Eighteenth Century England* (1935) and Kenneth Maclean's *John Locke and English Literature of the Eighteenth Century* (1936) provide important and interesting studies of the connections between poetry and aesthetic and critical theory. Volumes two and three of Hoxie Neale Fairchild's *Religious Trends in English Poetry* (1942, 1949) are a major study of the impact of religion on Romantic poetry.

Important general studies of English Romanticism are Northrop Frye's, *A Study of English Romanticism* (1968); Frank Kermode's *The Romantic Image* (1957); C. M. Bowra's *The Romantic Imagination* (1949); Harold Bloom's *The Visionary Company* (1961); David Perkins' *The Quest for Permanence* (1959); and M. H. Abrams' *Natural Supernaturalism* (1971).

A happy development has been the appearance of a number of anthologies that bring together some of the best critical writings on Romanticism and the Romantic Writers. Especially valuable are M. H. Abrams, *The English Romantic Poets; Modern Essays in Criticism* (1960); Harold Bloom, *Romanticism and Consciousness* (1970) and *The Ringers in the Tower* (1971).

More specific studies of individual writers will follow the introductions to these writers later in the anthology.

William Blake

1757–1827

The poetry of William Blake is for most students a body of art of great complexity and substantial difficulty. This is not to suggest that such complexity and difficulty mar a lyric poetry of great charm and beauty or a series of prophetic books that represents one of the most original and profound efforts to come to terms with the entire situation of humankind from fall to redemption. Indeed, Blake's is the kind of artistry that, while requiring unusual effort from the reader, brings rich dividends of understanding and illumination concerning such themes as human origins and destiny, the evolution of consciousness, the power of imagination, and the greatness of artistic creation.

Blake is certainly, on one level, the least erudite and socially active of the Romantics; his life seems prosaic when compared to the spectacular biography of a Byron or Shelley. Born on November 28, 1757, the year marked by Emanuel Swedenborg as the time of the Last Judgment and the founding of a New Jerusalem on earth, he was from his earliest days a creature of imagination. The stories that most of us have heard about his visionary powers, some well-documented and others not, are exciting. He himself recalls a childhood episode in which he saw God pressing his face against a windowpane. There is also the charming story of his beholding a tree filled with angels as he walked near Peckham Rye in Dulwich. Most touching is George Richmond's account of his death, recorded in Gerald Bentley's *Blake Records:* "He said he was going to that Country he had all His life wished to see & expressed Himself Happy hoping for Salvation through Jesus Christ—Just before he died his Countenance became fair—His eyes brighten'd and He burst out in Singing of the things he Saw in Heaven."

Blake's education was at best informal, largely conducted at home where his parents early recognized his great natural gift for drawing. The Bible was the great textbook for the young man, and the daily reading of its pages, as well as the general religious spirit of his environment, left a pronounced mark on his imagination. Thanks to a concerned father, Blake was at an early age apprenticed to James Basire, an engraver, and he remained with him for several years, studying also at Westminster school, and working rapturously in great Gothic masterpieces like the Abbey. He also studied painting at the Royal Academy, where he first fell under the critical eye of Sir Joshua Reynolds and developed the hostile spirit that was to culminate in his celebrated comment from the annotations to Reynolds's *Discourses* in the *Marginalia,* "To Generalize is to be an Idiot. To Particularize is the Alone Distinction of Merit."

Although Blake made a modest income by engraving for London booksellers, his meeting with three great artists, Thomas Stothard, John Flaxman, and Henry Fuseli, was a great source of inspiration and of professional advancement, and he began a series of exhibitions that continued for a number of years at the Royal Academy. His marriage in 1782 to Catherine Boucher, a simple but totally sympathetic and supportive woman, was from all evidence a happy one. The late 1780s and early 1790s saw him involved in a print-seller's shop, later abandoned, and associated with that legendary circle of radical friends who would congregate at the bookshop of Joseph Johnson. It was here that he met people like Joseph Priestley, Tom Paine, Mary Wollstonecraft, and William Godwin, who stirred his already radical impulses with schemes for equality and plans for a Golden Age of freedom. When the French Revolution broke out, it was as if theory had been translated into practice; the promise of Utopia for all seemed more than a remote possibility.

These were also years of great creativity. *The Songs of Innocence* and *The Book of Thel* appeared in 1789, and *The Marriage of Heaven and Hell,* a savage outburst against the political and religious establishments, in 1790. These were followed by *The French Revolution, Europe: A Prophecy,* and *The Songs of Experience,* all of which begin the formulation of a mythology, the struggle to liberate the individual from artificial restraints and to restore the fragmented human being to unity and holiness. It is, of course, important for the student to keep in mind that Blake's poems and prophecies were engraved by the then new process of illuminated painting which he claimed to have learned from his dead brother Robert in a dream. As more than one critic has observed, word and picture are perfect complements in Blake's work.

Blake continued working feverishly in spite of reversal and poverty, most of his commissions coming from Thomas Butts and William Hayley. It was while working for Hayley at a cottage he rented in Felpham that he became involved in the ill-fated fight with a soldier named Schofield who was trespassing in his garden. Harassment and accusations of treason finally led to his arrest, and, even though he was acquitted, the incident left its mark on his sense of justice and his feelings of oppression. Blake was again victimized by an unscrupulous agent named Cromek, who engaged him to illustrate Robert Blair's poem *The Grave* and then proceeded to cheat him by using his sketches and giving the engraving job to someone else. In spite of all, his confidence in his art was undiminished. These are the years in which he produced the magnificent *Four Zoas* and *Milton*.

A significant turning point for Blake was his meeting in 1818 with a young artist, John Linnell, who admired him greatly and became his angel. After the mystery years from 1811 to 1817, he came alive again, meeting active young artists, receiving commissions, even receiving a grant from the Royal Academy. The great *Jerusalem* was completed around 1820, and the memorable illustrations of the *Book of Job* and Dante followed. Illness plagued him from 1824, however, and he died on August 12, 1827.

Blake's was probably the first total and deliberate reaction against the rationalism and restraint of eighteenth-century Neoclassicism. With all the anti-dogmatism and religious enthusiasm he inherited from a background of dissent, he preached a gospel of unity, of the wholeness and holiness of things, of the power of creation possessed by the human imagination. To him fragmentation was the fundamental curse of his age, the split of God and man, soul and body, male and female. The Newtonian cosmology, the religion of the Deists, had failed to provide a symbolic universe; hence he argues the need to break through the veil of appearance to discover essential reality.

Out of his discontent with the old cosmology comes the formulation of his mythology, not an abstract fable or allegory, but an imaginative vision with overtones from a dozen sources including Swedenborg, Boehme, Plotinus, Plato. The ultimate source is, however, the Bible which, in his famous diabolical reading, is a great inspired and unified poem. Northrop Frye's words in *Fearful Symmetry* are extremely apt: "The Bible is the world's greatest work of art and therefore has primary claim to the title of God's Word. It takes in, in one immense sweep, the entire world of experience from the creation to the final vision of the City of God, embracing heroic saga, prophetic vision, legend, symbolism, the Gospel of Jesus, poetry and oratory on the way." For Blake the Bible becomes his great vehicle for linking a lost Utopia and a new Golden Age.

Behind the notion of a new mythology is, of course, the image of a prophet and mythmaker; and here Blake is typically confident of his special role. He has looked on beauty bare, has seen God's plan, and is now the emissary of the message. Orthodox religion has failed; as he puts it in "Proverbs of Hell," the animate gods of the ancient poets evoked the wonder and reverence of human beings "Till a system was formed, which some took advantage of, & enslav'd the vulgar by attempting to realize or abstract the mental deities from their objects; thus began Priesthood." He, the missionary of a new gospel, has dined with the Old Testament prophets, has learned their power and secrets, has copied as Christ dictated.

Blake's myth sees mankind's fall as one from unity to multiplicity. God and mankind were one in Eternity or Innocence, a condition in which four basic human powers—Urizen (Reason), Urthona (Imagination), Luvah (Emotion), and Tharmas (Instinct)—exist in harmony. Albion is the Divine Man, and there is no sense of fragmentation or discord. Tragically this Golden Age collapses as Urizen, variously regarded as Jehovah or Reason, but consistently as a divisive, mechanistic, analytic spirit, attacks Urthona and inaugurates a destructive war. Blake's portraits of Urizen and his works are savage. Secret, restrictive, uncreative, he is

> Dark, revolving in silent activity:
> Unseen in tormenting passions:
> An activity unknown and horrible,
> A self-contemplating shadow,
> In enormous labours occupied.

His rule is one of domination and restraint: "One command, one joy, one desire, / One curse, one weight, one measure, / One King, one God, one Law." His is an artificial order, one that divides man and creation into neat compartments, the physical universe being the result in Blake's parody of the Divine Creation:

> Six days they shrank up from existence,
> And on the seventh day they rested,
> And they bless'd the seventh day, in sick hope,
> And forgot their eternal life.

Albion, part of the process, falls into a sleep. The Four Zoas separate from themselves and further become separated from their feminine selves or Emanations—Ahania, Enitharmon, Vala, and Enion—who become sinister Spectres. Division is everywhere, soul and body, reason and imagination, male and female. Such oppositions are only apparently true, but they are necessary to the higher vision that will come with spiritual insight. In Blake's famous axiom, "Without Contraries is no progression." *The Songs of Innocence and Experience* explore the division in lyrics of grace and sensitivity, in musical measures and richly concrete language that evokes memories of the Elizabethans. There is, on the one hand, the ringing optimism of the child in "The Lamb," "I a child, & thou a lamb, / We are called by his name"; the naive confidence of "I happy am, / Joy is my name" in "Infant Joy"; the trust and hope of the little black boy for a day of unity when all color will vanish:

> I'll shade him from the heat till he can bear
> To lean in joy upon our father's knee;
> And then I'll stand and stroke his silver hair
> And be like him, and he will then love me.

There is, on the other hand, the stark terror of Experience and of Thel, the overtones of the "dread hand" and "dread feet" of "The Tyger"; the sadness of "Babes reduc'd to misery" in "Holy Thursday"; the cynical words of the pebble in "The Clod and the Pebble":

> Love seeketh only Self to please
> To bind another to Its delight,
> Joys in another's loss of ease,
> And builds a Hell in Heaven's despite.

There is hope, however. In the physical world Urthona becomes Los, the Poetic Genius, the Imagination, and the protector of a humanity lost in the void of Ulro and the physicality of Experience. Los and his emanation Enitharmon generate an abundance of offspring, the most notable of which is Orc, energy, who fights for individual and collective man against the onslaughts of Urizen, and begins the six-thousand-year conflict that will culminate in Albion's reawakening by Jesus and the restoration of unity. The struggle will elevate mankind from the states of Ulro and Experience to Beulah, the imaginative state of love, to the eternal bliss of Jerusalem. There are many great passages in "Night the Ninth" of *The Four Zoas,* but few more powerful in their free-flowing rhythms and provocatively original language and imagery, few more compellingly joyous in their elevation of the Energy and Imagination and Love that are the expression of Jesus and the joy of Paradise than the following:

> The hammer of Urthona sounds
> In the deep caves beneath; his Limbs renew'd his Lions roar
> Around the Furnaces & in Evening sport upon the plains.
> They raise their Faces from the Earth, conversing with the man:
>
> "How is it we have walk'd thro fires & yet are not consum'd?
> How is it that all things are chang'd, even as in ancient times?"
>
> The sun arises from his dewy bed, & the fresh airs
> Play in his smiling beams giving the seeds of life to grow,
> And the fresh Earth beams forth ten thousand thousand springs of life.
> Urthona is arisen in his strength, no longer now
> Divided from Enitharmon, no longer the Spectre Los.
> Where is the Spectre of Prophecy? where the delusive Phantom?
> Departed: & Urthona rises from the ruinous Walls.
> In all his ancient strength to form the golden armour of science
> For intellectual War. The war of swords departed now,
> The dark Religions are departed & sweet Science reigns.

For Blake, when the divinity in mankind emerges, law is superfluous. The full and spontaneous realization and expression of human potential is God. It is this message that Blake preaches.

Suggestions for Further Reading

Blake has been blessed with an abundance of fine critics. Alexander Gilchrist, *The Life of William Blake, Pictor Ignotus* (1863) and Mona Wilson, *The Life of William Blake* (1927) are helpful biographies. S. Foster Damon's *William Blake: His Philosophy and Symbols* (1924) is a wonderfully comprehensive study of Blake's system. For this editor, there is still no more perceptive study of the growth and development of Blake's mythology than Northrop Frye's *Fearful Symmetry* (1947). Also strongly recommended are Max Plowman, *An Introduction to the Study of Blake* (1927); Mark Schorer, *William Blake: The Politics of Vision* (1946); David Erdman, *William Blake: Prophet Against Empire* (1954); George Mills Harper, *The Neoplatonism of William Blake* (1961); Hazard Adams, *William Blake: A Reading of the Shorter Poems* (1963); and Harold Bloom, *Blake's Apocalypse: A Study in Poetic Argument* (1963).

FROM

Poetical Sketches

TO SPRING

O thou, with dewy locks, who lookest down
Thro' the clear windows of the morning, turn
Thine angel eyes upon our western isle,
Which in full choir hails thy approach, O Spring!

The hills tell each other, and the list'ning
Vallies hear; all our longing eyes are turned
Up to thy bright pavillions: issue forth,
And let thy holy feet visit our clime.

Come o'er the eastern hills, and let our winds
Kiss thy perfumed garments; let us taste   10
Thy morn and evening breath; scatter thy pearls
Upon our love-sick land that mourns for thee.

O deck her forth with thy fair fingers; pour
Thy soft kisses on her bosom; and put
Thy golden crown upon her languish'd head,
Whose modest tresses were bound up for thee.

1769–77   *1783*

TO SUMMER

O thou who passest thro' our vallies in
Thy strength, curb thy fierce steeds, allay the heat
That flames from their large nostrils! thou, O Sum-
        mer,
Oft pitched'st here thy golden tent, and oft
Beneath our oaks has slept, while we beheld
With joy thy ruddy limbs and flourishing hair.

Beneath our thickest shades we oft have heard
Thy voice, when noon upon his fervid car
Rode o'er the deep of heaven; beside our springs
Sit down, and in our mossy vallies, on   10
Some bank beside a river clear, throw thy
Silk draperies off, and rush into the stream:
Our vallies love the Summer in his pride.

Our bards are fam'd who strike the silver wire:
Our youth are bolder than the southern swains:
Our maidens fairer in the sprightly dance:

We lack not songs, nor instruments of joy,
Nor echoes sweet, nor waters clear as heaven,
Nor laurel wreaths against the sultry heat.

1769–77   *1783*

TO AUTUMN

O Autumn, laden with fruit, and stained
With the blood of the grape, pass not, but sit
Beneath my shady roof; there thou may'st rest,
And tune thy jolly voice to my fresh pipe,
And all the daughters of the year shall dance!
Sing now the lusty song of fruits and flowers.

"The narrow bud opens her beauties to
The sun, and love runs in her thrilling veins;
Blossoms hang round the brows of morning, and
Flourish down the bright cheek of modest eve,   10
Till clustr'ing Summer breaks forth into singing,
And feather'd clouds strew flowers round her head.

"The spirits of the air live on the smells
Of fruit; and joy, with pinions light, roves round
The gardens, or sits singing in the trees."
Thus sang the jolly Autumn as he sat;
Then rose, girded himself, and o'er the bleak
Hills fled from our sight; but left his golden load.

1769–77   *1783*

TO WINTER

"O Winter! bar thine adamantine doors:
The north is thine; there hast thou built thy dark
Deep-founded habitation. Shake not thy roofs,
Nor bend thy pillars with thine iron car."

He hears me not, but o'er the yawning deep
Rides heavy; his storms are unchain'd, sheathed
In ribbed steel; I dare not lift mine eyes,
For he hath rear'd his sceptre o'er the world.

Lo! now the direful monster, whose skin clings
To his strong bones, strides o'er the groaning
        rocks: 10
He withers all in silence, and his hand
Unclothes the earth, and freezes up frail life.

He takes his seat upon the cliffs; the mariner
Cries in vain. Poor little wretch! that deal'st

With storms, till heaven smiles, and the monster
Is driv'n yelling to his caves beneath mount Hecla.
1769–77   *1783*

FROM
Songs of Innocence

INTRODUCTION

Piping down the valleys wild,
Piping songs of pleasant glee,
On a cloud I saw a child,
And he laughing said to me:

"Pipe a song about a Lamb!"
So I piped with merry chear.
"Piper, pipe that song again",
So I piped: he wept to hear.

"Drop thy pipe, thy happy pipe;
Sing thy songs of happy chear":   10
So I sung the same again,
While he wept with joy to hear.

"Piper, sit thee down, and write
In a book, that all may read."
So he vanish'd from my sight,
And I pluck'd a hollow reed,

And I made a rural pen,
And I stain'd the water clear,
And I wrote my happy songs
Every child may joy to hear.   20
                                              1789

THE SHEPHERD

How sweet is the Shepherd's sweet lot!
From the morn to the evening he strays;
He shall follow his sheep all the day,
And his tongue shall be filled with praise.

For he hears the lamb's innocent call,
And he hears the ewe's tender reply;
He is watchful while they are in peace,
For they know when their Shepherd is nigh.
                                              1789

THE ECCHOING GREEN

The Sun does arise,
And make happy the skies;
The merry bells ring
To welcome the Spring;
The skylark and thrush,
The birds of the bush,
Sing louder around
To the bells' chearful sound,
While our sports shall be seen
On the Ecchoing Green.   10

Old John, with white hair,
Does laugh away care,
Sitting under the oak,
Among the old folk.
They laugh at our play,
And soon they all say:
"Such, such were the joys
When we all, girls & boys,
In our youth time were seen
On the Ecchoing Green."   20

Till the little ones, weary,
No more can be merry;
The sun does descend,
And our sports have an end.
Round the laps of their mothers
Many sisters and brothers,
Like birds in their nest,
Are ready for rest,
And sport no more seen
On the darkening Green.
                                              1789

THE LAMB

Little Lamb, who made thee?
Dost thou know who made thee?
Gave thee life, & bid thee feed
By the stream & o'er the mead;
Gave thee clothing of delight,
Softest clothing, wooly, bright;
Gave thee such a tender voice,
Making all the vales rejoice?
    Little Lamb, who made thee?
    Dost thou know who made thee?   10

Little Lamb, I'll tell thee,
Little Lamb, I'll tell thee:
He is called by thy name,
For he calls himself a Lamb.
He is meek, & he is mild;

He became a little child.
I a child, & thou a lamb,
We are called by his name.
    Little Lamb, God bless thee!
    Little Lamb, God bless thee!   20

1789

THE LITTLE BLACK BOY

My mother bore me in the southern wild,
And I am black, but O! my soul is white;
White as an angel is the English child,
But I am black, as if bereav'd of light.

My mother taught me underneath a tree,
And, sitting down before the heat of day,
She took me on her lap and kissed me,
And, pointing to the east, began to say:

"Look on the rising sun: there God does live,
And gives his light, and gives his heat away;   10
And flowers and trees and beasts and men receive
Comfort in morning, joy in the noonday.

"And we are put on earth a little space,
That we may learn to bear the beams of love;
And these black bodies and this sunburnt face
Is but a cloud, and like a shady grove.

"For when our souls have learn'd the heat to bear,
The cloud will vanish; we shall hear his voice,
Saying: 'Come out from the grove, my love & care,
And round my golden tent like lambs rejoice.'"   20

Thus did my mother say, and kissed me;
And thus I say to little English boy.
When I from black and he from white cloud free,
And round the tent of God like lambs we joy,

I'll shade him from the heat till he can bear
To lean in joy upon our father's knee;
And then I'll stand and stroke his silver hair,
And be like him, and he will then love me.

1789

THE BLOSSOM

Merry, Merry Sparrow!
Under leaves so green
A happy Blossom
Sees you swift as arrow
Seek your cradle narrow
Near my Bosom.

Pretty, Pretty Robin!
Under leaves so green
A happy Blossom
Hears you sobbing, sobbing,   10
Pretty, Pretty Robin,
Near my Bosom.

1789

THE CHIMNEY SWEEPER

When my mother died I was very young,
And my father sold me while yet my tongue
Could scarcely cry " 'weep! 'weep! 'weep! 'weep!"
So your chimneys I sweep, & in soot I sleep.

There's little Tom Dacre, who cried when his head,
That curl'd like a lamb's back, was shav'd: so I said
"Hush, Tom! never mind it, for when your head's
    bare
You know that the soot cannot spoil your white
    hair."

And so he was quiet, & that very night,
As Tom was a-sleeping, he had such a sight!—   10
That thousands of sweepers, Dick, Joe, Ned, &
    Jack,
Were all of them lock'd up in coffins of black.

And by came an Angel who had a bright key,
And he open'd the coffins & set them all free;
Then down a green plain leaping, laughing, they
    run,
And wash in a river, and shine in the Sun.

Then naked & white, all their bags left behind,
They rise upon clouds and sport in the wind;

THE CHIMNEY SWEEPER. 3. 'weep: probably the child's
attempt to say "sweep" as he walks through the streets
in search of work.

And the Angel told Tom, if he'd be a good boy,
He'd have God for his father, & never want joy.   20

And so Tom awoke; and we rose in the dark,
And got with our bags & our brushes to work.
Tho' the morning was cold, Tom was happy &
   warm;
So if all do their duty they need not fear harm.

1789

THE LITTLE BOY LOST

"Father! father! where are you going?
O do not walk so fast.
Speak, father, speak to your little boy,
Or else I shall be lost."

The night was dark, no father was there;
The child was wet with dew;
The mire was deep, & the child did weep,
And away the vapour flew.

1784–85   1789

THE LITTLE BOY FOUND

The little boy lost in the lonely fen,
Led by the wand'ring light,
Began to cry; but God, ever nigh,
Appear'd like his father in white.

He kissed the child & by the hand led
And to his mother brought,
Who in sorrow pale, thro' the lonely dale,
Her little boy weeping sought.

1789

LAUGHING SONG

When the green woods laugh with the voice of joy,
And the dimpling stream runs laughing by;
When the air does laugh with our merry wit,
And the green hill laughs with the noise of it;

When the meadows laugh with lively green,
And the grasshopper laughs in the merry scene,

When Mary and Susan and Emily
With their sweet round mouths sing "Ha, Ha, He!"

When the painted birds laugh in the shade,
Where our table with cherries and nuts is spread,   10
Come live & be merry, and join with me,
To sing the sweet chorus of "Ha, Ha, He!"

c. 1787   1789

A CRADLE SONG

Sweet dreams, form a shade
O'er my lovely infant's head;
Sweet dreams of pleasant streams
By happy, silent, moony beams.

Sweet sleep, with soft down
Weave thy brows an infant crown.
Sweet sleep, Angel mild,
Hover o'er my happy child.

Sweet smiles, in the night
Hover over my delight;   10
Sweet smiles, Mother's smiles,
All the livelong night beguiles.

Sweet moans, dovelike sighs,
Chase not slumber from thy eyes.
Sweet moans, sweeter smiles,
All the dovelike moans beguiles.

Sleep, sleep, happy child,
All creation slept and smil'd;
Sleep, sleep, happy sleep,
While o'er thee thy mother weep.   20

Sweet babe, in thy face
Holy image I can trace.
Sweet babe, once like thee,
Thy maker lay and wept for me,

Wept for me, for thee, for all,
When he was an infant small.
Thou his image ever see,
Heavenly face that smiles on thee,

Smiles on thee, on me, on all;
Who became an infant small.   30
Infant smiles are his own smiles;
Heaven & earth to peace beguiles.

1789

THE DIVINE IMAGE

To Mercy, Pity, Peace, and Love
   All pray in their distress;
And to these virtues of delight
   Return their thankfulness.

For Mercy, Pity, Peace, and Love
   Is God, our father dear;
And Mercy, Pity, Peace, and Love
   Is Man, his child and care.

For Mercy has a human heart,
   Pity a human face,   10
And love, the human form divine;
   And Peace, the human dress.

Then every man, of every clime,
   That prays in his distress,
Prays to the human form divine,
   Love, Mercy, Pity, Peace.

And all must love the human form,
   In heathen, turk, or jew;
Where Mercy, Love, & Pity dwell
   There God is dwelling too.   20

1789

NIGHT

The sun descending in the west,
The evening star does shine;
The birds are silent in their nest,
And I must seek for mine.
The moon like a flower
In heaven's high bower,
With silent delight
Sits and smiles on the night.

Farewell, green fields and happy groves,
Where flocks have took delight.   10
Where lambs have nibbled, silent moves
The feet of angels bright;
Unseen they pour blessing,
And joy without ceasing,
On each bud and blossom,
And each sleeping bosom.

They look in every thoughtless nest,
Where birds are cover'd warm;

They visit caves of every beast,
To keep them all from harm.   20
If they see any weeping
That should have been sleeping,
They pour sleep on their head,
And sit down by their bed.

When wolves and tygers howl for prey,
They pitying stand and weep;
Seeking to drive their thirst away,
And keep them from the sheep;
But if they rush dreadful,
The angels, most heedful,   30
Receive each mild spirit,
New worlds to inherit.

And there the lion's ruddy eyes
Shall flow with tears of gold,
And pitying the tender cries,
And walking round the fold,
Saying "Wrath, by his meekness,
And by his health, sickness
Is driven away
From our immortal day.   40

"And now beside thee, bleating lamb,
I can lie down and sleep;
Or think on him who bore thy name,
Graze after thee and weep.
For, wash'd in life's river,
My bright mane for ever
Shall shine like the gold
As I guard o'er the fold."

1789

A DREAM

Once a dream did weave a shade
O'er my Angel-guarded bed,
That an Emmet lost its way
Where on grass methought I lay.

Troubled, 'wilder'd, and forlorn,
Dark, benighted, travel-worn,
Over many a tangled spray,
All heart-broke I heard her say:

"O, my children! do they cry?
Do they hear their father sigh?   10
Now they look abroad to see:
Now return and weep for me."

Pitying, I drop'd a tear;
But I saw a glow-worm near,
Who replied: "What wailing wight
Calls the watchman of the night?

"I am set to light the ground,
While the beetle goes his round:
Follow now the beetle's hum;
Little wanderer, hie thee home!"   20

1789

ON ANOTHER'S SORROW

Can I see another's woe,
And not be in sorrow too?
Can I see another's grief,
And not seek for kind relief?

Can I see a falling tear,
And not feel my sorrow's share?
Can a father see his child
Weep, nor be with sorrow fill'd?

Can a mother sit and hear
An infant groan, an infant fear?   10
No, no! never can it be!
Never, never can it be!

And can he who smiles on all
Hear the wren with sorrows small,
Hear the small bird's grief & care,
Hear the woes that infants bear,

And not sit beside the nest,
Pouring pity in their breast;
And not sit the cradle near,
Weeping tear on infant's tear;   20

And not sit both night & day,
Wiping all our tears away?
O, no! never can it be!
Never, never can it be!

He doth give his joy to all;
He becomes an infant small;
He becomes a man of woe;
He doth feel the sorrow too.

Think not thou canst sigh a sigh,
And thy maker is not by;   30
Think not thou canst weep a tear,
And thy maker is not near.

O! he gives to us his joy
That our grief he may destroy;
Till our grief is fled & gone
He doth sit by us and moan.

1789

INFANT JOY

"I have no name:
I am but two days old."
What shall I call thee?
"I happy am,
Joy is my name."
Sweet joy befall thee!

Pretty joy!
Sweet joy but two days old.
Sweet joy I call thee:
Thou dost smile,   10
I sing the while,
Sweet joy befall thee!

1789

HOLY THURSDAY

'Twas on a Holy Thursday, their innocent faces
     clean,
The children walking two & two, in red & blue &
     green,
Grey-headed beadles walk'd before, with wands
     as white as snow,
Till into the high dome of Paul's they like Thames'
     waters flow.

O what a multitude they seem'd, these flowers of
     London town!
Seated in companies they sit with radiance all their
     own.
The hum of multitudes was there, but multitudes
     of lambs,
Thousands of little boys & girls raising their inno-
     cent hands.

HOLY THURSDAY. **1. Holy Thursday:** Ascension Day. **4.
Paul's:** St. Paul's Cathedral, London. Every year on
Ascension Day over six thousand children from charity
schools marched to the Cathedral for a service.

Now like a mighty wind they raise to heaven the
    voice of song,
Or like harmonious thunderings the seats of Heav-
    ens among.   10
Beneath them sit the aged men, wise guardians of
    the poor;
Then cherish pity, lest you drive an angel from
    your door.

                1789

FROM
Songs of Experience

INTRODUCTION

Hear the voice of the Bard!
Who Present, Past, & Future, sees;
Whose ears have heard
The Holy Word
That walk'd among the ancient trees,

Calling the lapsed Soul,
And weeping in the evening dew;
That might controll
The starry pole,
And fallen, fallen light renew!   10

"O Earth, O Earth, return!
Arise from out the dewy grass;
Night is worn,
And the morn
Rises from the slumberous mass.

"Turn away no more;
Why wilt thou turn away?
The starry floor,
The wat'ry shore,
Is giv'n thee till the break of day."   20

                1794

EARTH'S ANSWER

Earth rais'd up her head
From the darkness dread & drear.
Her light fled,
Stony dread!
And her locks cover'd with grey despair.

"Prison'd on wat'ry shore,
Starry Jealousy does keep my den:
Cold and hoar,
Weeping o'er,
I hear the father of the ancient men.   10

"Selfish father of men!
Cruel, jealous, selfish fear!
Can delight,
Chain'd in night,
The virgins of youth and morning bear?

"Does spring hide its joy
When buds and blossoms grow?
Does the sower
Sow by night,
Or the plowman in darkness plow?

"Break this heavy chain
That does freeze my bones around.
Selfish! vain!
Eternal bane!
That free Love with bondage bound."

1793   1794

NURSE'S SONG

When the voices of children are heard on the green,
And whisp'rings are in the dale,
The days of my youth rise fresh in my mind,
My face turns green and pale.

Then come home, my children, the sun is gone down,
And the dews of night arise;
Your spring & your day are wasted in play,
And your winter and night in disguise.

1793   1794

THE FLY

Little Fly,
Thy summer's play
My thoughtless hand
Has brush'd away.

Am not I
A fly like thee?

Or art not thou
A man like me?

For I dance,
And drink, & sing,   10
Till some blind hand
Shall brush my wing.

If thought is life
And strength & breath,
And the want
Of thought is death;

Then am I
A happy fly,
If I live
Or if I die.   20

1793

THE TYGER

Tyger! Tyger! burning bright
In the forests of the night,
What immortal hand or eye
Could frame thy fearful symmetry?

In what distant deeps or skies
Burnt the fire of thine eyes?
On what wings dare he aspire?
What the hand dare sieze the fire?

And what shoulder, & what art,
Could twist the sinews of thy heart? 10
And when thy heart began to beat,
What dread hand? & what dread feet?

What the hammer? what the chain?
In what furnace was thy brain?
What the anvil? what dread grasp
Dare its deadly terrors clasp?

When the stars threw down their spears,
And water'd heaven with their tears,
Did he smile his work to see?
Did he who made the Lamb make thee?   20

Tyger! Tyger! burning bright
In the forests of the night,
What immortal hand or eye,
Dare frame thy fearful symmetry?

1793   1794

THE LITTLE GIRL LOST

In futurity
I prophetic see
That the earth from sleep
(Grave the sentence deep)

Shall arise and seek
For her maker meek;
And the desart wild
Become a garden mild.

In the southern clime,
Where the summer's prime   10
Never fades away,
Lovely Lyca lay.

Seven summers old
Lovely Lyca told;
She had wander'd long
Hearing wild birds' song.

"Sweet sleep, come to me
Underneath this tree.
Do father, mother, weep,
Where can Lyca sleep?   20

"Lost in desart wild
Is your little child.
How can Lyca sleep
If her mother weep?

"If her heart does ake
Then let Lyca wake;
If my mother sleep,
Lyca shall not weep.

"Frowning, frowning night,
O'er this desart bright   30
Let they moon arise
While I close my eyes."

Sleeping Lyca lay
While the beasts of prey,
Come from caverns deep,
View'd the maid asleep.

The kingly lion stood
And the virgin view'd,
Then he gamboll'd round
O'er the hallow'd ground.   40

Leopards, tygers, play
Round her as she lay,
While the lion old
Bow'd his mane of gold

And her bosom lick,
And upon her neck
From his eyes of flame
Ruby tears there came;

While the lioness
Loos'd her slender dress,   50
And naked they convey'd
To caves the sleeping maid.

                                        1789

THE LITTLE GIRL FOUND

All the night in woe
Lyca's parents go
Over vallies deep,
While the desarts weep.

Tired and woe-begone,
Hoarse and making moan,
Arm in arm seven days
They trac'd the desert ways.

Seven nights they sleep
Among shadows deep,   10
And dream they see their child
Starv'd in desert wild.

Pale, thro' pathless ways
The fancied image strays
Famish'd, weeping, weak,
With hollow piteous shriek.

Rising from unrest,
The trembling woman prest
With feet of weary woe:
She could no further go.   20

In his arms he bore
Her, arm'd with sorrow sore;
Till before their way
A couching lion lay.

Turning back was vain:
Soon his heavy mane

                                        1793

Bore them to the ground.
Then he stalk'd around,

Smelling to his prey;
But their fears allay   30
When he licks their hands,
And silent by them stands.

They look upon his eyes
Fill'd with deep surprise;
And wondering behold
A spirit arm'd in gold.

On his head a crown,
On his shoulders down
Flow'd his golden hair.
Gone was all their care.   40

"Follow me," he said;
"Weep not for the maid;
In my palace deep
Lyca lies asleep."

Then they followed
Where the vision led,
And saw their sleeping child
Among tygers wild.

To this day they dwell
In a lonely dell;   50
Nor fear the wolvish howl
Nor the lion's growl.

                                        1789

THE CLOD AND THE PEBBLE

"Love seeketh not Itself to please,
Nor for itself hath any care,
But for another gives its ease,
And builds a Heaven in Hell's despair."

So sung a little Clod of Clay,
Trodden with the cattle's feet,
But a Pebble of the brook
Warbled out these metres meet:

"Love seeketh only Self to please,
To bind another to Its delight,   10
Joys in another's loss of ease,
And builds a Hell in Heaven's despite."

                                        1794

THE LITTLE VAGABOND

Dear Mother, dear Mother, the Church is cold,
But the Ale-house is healthy & pleasant & warm;
Besides I can tell where I am used well,
Such usage in Heaven will never do well.

But if at the Church they would give us some Ale,
And a pleasant fire our souls to regale,
We'd sing and we'd pray all the live-long day,
Nor ever once wish from the Church to stray.

Then the Parson might preach, & drink, & sing,
And we'd be as happy as birds in the spring;   10
And modest Dame Lurch, who is always at Church,
Would not have bandy children, nor fasting, nor
    birch.

And God, like a father rejoicing to see
His children as pleasant and happy as he,
Would have no more quarrel with the Devil or the
    Barrel,
But kiss him, & give him both drink and apparel.
1793   1794

A POISON TREE

I was angry with my friend:
I told my wrath, my wrath did end.
I was angry with my foe:
I told it not, my wrath did grow.

And I water'd it in fears,
Night & morning with my tears;
And I sunned it with smiles,
And with soft deceitful wiles.

And it grew both day and night,
Till it bore an apple bright;   10
And my foe beheld it shine,
And he knew that it was mine,

And into my garden stole
When the night had veil'd the pole:
In the morning glad I see
My foe outstretch'd beneath the tree.
1793   1794

HOLY THURSDAY

Is this a holy thing to see
In a rich and fruitful land,
Babes reduc'd to misery,
Fed with cold and usurous hand?

Is that trembling cry a song?
Can it be a song of joy?
And so many children poor?
It is a land of poverty!

And their sun does never shine,
And their fields are bleak & bare,   10
And their ways are fill'd with thorns:
It is eternal winter there.

For where-e'er the sun does shine,
And where-e'er the rain does fall,
Babe can never hunger there,
Nor poverty the mind appall.
1793   1794

THE ANGEL

I dreamt a Dream! what can it mean?
And that I was a maiden Queen,
Guarded by an Angel mild:
Witless woe was ne'er beguil'd!

And I wept both night and day,
And he wip'd my tears away,
And I wept both day and night,
And hid from him my heart's delight.

So he took his wings and fled;
Then the morn blush'd rosy red;   10
I dried my tears, & arm'd my fears
With ten thousand shields and spears.

Soon my Angel came again:
I was arm'd, he came in vain;
For the time of youth was fled,
And grey hairs were on my head.
1793   1794

THE SICK ROSE

O Rose, thou art sick!
The invisible worm,
That flies in the night
In the howling storm,

Has found out thy bed
Of crimson joy,
And his dark secret love
Does thy life destroy.

1793   *1794*

TO TIRZAH *

Whate'er is Born of Mortal Birth
Must be consumed with the Earth
To rise from Generation free:
Then what have I to do with thee?

The Sexes sprung from Shame & Pride,
Blow'd in the morn; in evening died;
But Mercy chang'd Death into Sleep;
The Sexes rose to work & weep.

Thou, Mother of my Mortal part,
With cruelty didst mould my Heart,   10
And with false self-decieving tears
Didst bind my Nostrils, Eyes, & Ears;

Didst close my Tongue in senseless clay,
And me to Mortal Life betray.
The Death of Jesus set me free:
Then what have I to do with thee?

c. 1801

THE VOICE OF THE ANCIENT BARD

Youth of delight, come hither,
And see the opening morn,
Image of truth new born.

----

* TO TIRZAH. A later addition to the *Songs of Experience*. Tirzah, the capital city of Israel, is in Blake's symbolism one of the daughters of Zelopehad. She had no sons and hence sought a separate female inheritance.

Doubt is fled, & clouds of reason,
Dark disputes & artful teazing.
Folly is an endless maze,
Tangled roots perplex her ways.
How many have fallen there!
They stumble all night over bones of the dead,
And feel they know not what but care,   10
And wish to lead others, when they should be led.

1789

MY PRETTY ROSE TREE

A flower was offer'd to me,
Such a flower as May never bore;
But I said "I've a Pretty Rose-tree,"
And I passed the sweet flower o'er.

Then I went to my Pretty Rose-tree,
To tend her by day and by night;
But my Rose turn'd away with jealousy,
And her thorns were my only delight.

1793   *1794*

AH! SUN-FLOWER

Ah, Sun-flower! weary of time,
Who countest the steps of the Sun,
Seeking after that sweet golden clime
Where the traveller's journey is done:

Where the Youth pined away with desire,
And the pale Virgin shrouded in snow
Arise from their graves, and aspire
Where my Sun-flower wishes to go.

1794

THE LILLY

The modest Rose puts forth a thorn,
The humble Sheep a threat'ning horn;
While the Lilly white shall in Love delight,
Nor a thorn, nor a threat, stain her beauty bright.

1793   *1794*

THE GARDEN OF LOVE

I went to the Garden of Love,
And saw what I never had seen:
A Chapel was built in the midst,
Where I used to play on the green.

And the gates of this Chapel were shut,
And "Thou shalt not" writ over the door;
So I turn'd to the Garden of Love
That so many sweet flowers bore;

And I saw it was filled with graves,
And tomb-stones where flowers should be;   10
And Priests in black gowns were walking their
    rounds,
And binding with briars my joys & desires.

1793   *1794*

A LITTLE BOY LOST

"Nought loves another as itself,
Nor venerates another so,
Nor is it possible to Thought
A greater than itself to know:

"And Father, how can I love you
Or any of my brothers more?
I love you like the little bird
That picks up crumbs around the door."

The Priest sat by and heard the child,
In trembling zeal he siez'd his hair: 10
He led him by his little coat,
And all admir'd the Priestly care.

And standing on the altar high,
"Lo! what a fiend is here!" said he,
"One who sets reason up for judge
Of our most holy Mystery."

The weeping child could not be heard,
The weeping parents wept in vain;
They strip'd him to his little shirt,
And bound him in an iron chain;   20

And burn'd him in a holy place,
Where many had been burn'd before:
The weeping parents wept in vain.
Are such things done on Albion's shore?

1793   *1794*

A LITTLE GIRL LOST

Children of the future Age
Reading this indignant page,
Know that in a former time
Love! sweet Love! was thought a crime.

In the Age of Gold,
Free from winter's cold,
Youth and maiden bright
To the holy light,
Naked in the sunny beams delight.

Once a youthful pair,   10
Fill'd with softest care,
Met in garden bright
Where the holy light
Had just remov'd the curtains of the night.

There, in rising day,
On the grass they play;
Parents were afar,
Strangers came not near,
And the maiden soon forgot her fear.

Tired with kisses sweet,   20
They agree to meet
When the silent sleep
Waves o'er heaven's deep,
And the weary tired wanderers weep.

To her father white
Came the maiden bright;
But his loving look,
Like the holy book,
All her tender limbs with terror shook.

"Ona! pale and weak!   30
To thy father speak:
O, the trembling fear!
O, the dismal care!
That shakes the blossoms of my hoary hair."

1794

INFANT SORROW

My mother groan'd! my father wept.
Into the dangerous world I leapt:
Helpless, naked, piping loud:
Like a fiend hid in a cloud.

Struggling in my father's hands,
Striving against my swadling bands,
Bound and weary I thought best
To sulk upon my mother's breast.

1793   *1794*

THE SCHOOLBOY

I love to rise in a summer morn
When the birds sing on every tree;
The distant huntsman winds his horn,
And the sky-lark sings with me.
O! what sweet company.

But to go to school in a summer morn,
O! it drives all joy away;
Under a cruel eye outworn,
The little ones spend the day
In sighing and dismay.   10

Ah! then at times I drooping sit,
And spend many an anxious hour,
Nor in my book can I take delight,
Nor sit in learning's bower,
Worn thro' with the dreary shower.

How can the bird that is born for joy
Sit in a cage and sing?
How can a child, when fears annoy,
But droop his tender wing,
And forget his youthful spring?   20

O! father & mother, if buds are nip'd
And blossoms blown away,
And if the tender plants are strip'd
Of their joy in the springing day,
By sorrow and care's dismay,

How shall the summer arise in joy,
Or the summer fruits appear?
Or how shall we gather what griefs destroy,
Or bless the mellowing year,
When the blasts of winter appear?   30
                                    1789

LONDON

I wander thro' each charter'd street,
Near where the charter'd Thames does flow,

And mark in every face I meet
Marks of weakness, marks of woe.

In every cry of every Man,
In every Infant's cry of fear,
In every voice, in every ban,
The mind-forg'd manacles I hear.

How the Chimney-sweeper's cry
Every black'ning Church appalls;   10
And the hapless Soldier's sigh
Runs in blood down Palace walls.

But most thro' midnight streets I hear
How the youthful Harlot's curse
Blasts the new born Infant's tear,
And blights with plagues the Marriage hearse.

1793   *1794*

THE CHIMNEY SWEEPER

A little black thing among the snow,
Crying "'weep! 'weep!" in notes of woe!
"Where are thy father & mother? say?"
"They are both gone up to the church to pray.

"Because I was happy upon the heath,
And smil'd among the winter's snow,
They clothed me in the clothes of death,
And taught me to sing the notes of woe.

"And because I am happy & dance & sing,
They think they have done me no injury,   10
And are gone to praise God & his Priest & King,
Who make up a heaven of our misery."

1793   *1794*

THE HUMAN ABSTRACT

Pity would be no more
If we did not make somebody Poor;
And Mercy no more could be
If all were as happy as we.

And mutual fear brings peace,
Till the selfish loves increase:
Then Cruelty knits a snare,
And spreads his baits with care.

He sits down with holy fears,
And waters the ground with tears;   10
Then Humility takes its root
Underneath his foot.

Soon spreads the dismal shade
Of Mystery over his head;
And the Catterpiller and Fly
Feed on the Mystery.

And it bears the fruit of Deceit,
Ruddy and sweet to eat;
And the Raven his nest has made
In its thickest shade.   20

The Gods of the earth and sea
Sought thro' Nature to find this Tree;
But their search was all in vain:
There grows one in the Human Brain.

1793   1794

FROM

Prophecies

THERE IS NO NATURAL RELIGION

[FIRST SERIES]

The Argument. Man has no notion of moral fitness but from Education. Naturally he is only a natural organ subject to Sense.

I. Man cannot naturally Percieve but through his natural or bodily organs.

II. Man by his reasoning power can only compare & judge of what he has already perciev'd.

III. From a perception of only 3 senses or 3 elements none could deduce a fourth or fifth.

IV. None could have other than natural or organic thoughts if he had none but organic perceptions.

V. Man's desires are limited by his perceptions, none can desire what he has not perciev'd.

VI. The desires & perceptions of man, untaught by any thing but organs of sense, must be limited to objects of sense.

Conclusion. If it were not for the Poetic or Prophetic character the Philosophic & Experimental would soon be at the ratio of all things, & stand still, unable to do other than repeat the same dull round over again.

c. 1788

THERE IS NO NATURAL RELIGION

[SECOND SERIES]

I. Man's perceptions are not bounded by organs of perception; he percieves more than sense (tho' ever so acute) can discover.

II. Reason, or the ratio of all we have already known, is not the same that it shall be when we know more.

III. [*This proposition has been lost.*]

IV. The bounded is loathed by its possessor. The same dull round, even of a universe, would soon become a mill with complicated wheels.

V. If the many become the same as the few when possess'd, More! More! is the cry of a mistaken soul; less than All cannot satisfy Man.

VI. If any could desire what he is incapable of possessing, despair must be his eternal lot.

VII. The desire of Man being Infinite, the possession is Infinite & himself Infinite.

Application. He who sees the Infinite in all things, sees God. He who sees the Ratio only, sees himself only.

Therefore God becomes as we 'are, that we may be as he is.

c. 1788

ALL RELIGIONS ARE ONE

THE VOICE OF ONE CRYING IN THE WILDERNESS

The Argument. As the true method of knowledge is experiment, the true faculty of knowing must be the faculty which experiences. This faculty I treat of.

PRINCIPLE 1st. That the Poetic Genius is the true Man, and that the body or outward form of Man is derived from the Poetic Genius. Likewise that the forms of all things are derived from their

Genius, which by the Ancients was call'd an Angel & Spirit & Demon.

PRINCIPLE 2ᵈ. As all men are alike in outward form, So (and with the same infinite variety) all are alike in the Poetic Genius.

PRINCIPLE 3ᵈ. No man can think, write, or speak from his heart, but he must intend truth. Thus all sects of Philosophy are from the Poetic Genius adapted to the weakness of every individual.

PRINCIPLE 4ᵗʰ. As none by travelling over known lands can find out the unknown, So from already acquired knowledge Man could not acquire more: therefore an universal Poetic Genius exists.

PRINCIPLE 5ᵗʰ. The Religions of all Nations are derived from each Nation's different reception of the Poetic Genius, which is every where call'd the Spirit of Prophecy.

PRINCIPLE 6ᵗʰ. The Jewish & Christian Testaments are An original derivation from the Poetic Genius; this is necessary from the confined nature of bodily sensation.

PRINCIPLE 7ᵗʰ. As all men are alike (tho' infinitely various), So all Religions &, as all similars, have one source.

The true Man is the source, he being the Poetic Genius.

c. 1788

The Book of Thel

Thel's Motto

Does the Eagle know what is in the pit,
Or wilt thou go ask the Mole?
Can Wisdom be put in a silver rod?
Or Love in a golden bowl?

I

The Daughters of Mne Seraphim led round their
    sunny flocks,
All but the youngest: she in paleness sought the
    secret air,
To fade away like morning beauty from her mortal
    day:

THE BOOK OF THEL. 1. Mne: probably a misprint; "the" makes better sense.

Down by the river of Adona her soft voice is heard,
And thus her gentle lamentation falls like morning
    dew:

"O life of this our spring! why fades the lotus of the
    water?   10
Why fade these children of the spring, born but to
    smile & fall?
Ah! Thel is like a wat'ry bow, and like a parting
    cloud;
Like a reflection in a glass; like shadows in the
    water;
Like dreams of infants, like a smile upon an infant's
    face;
Like the dove's voice; like transient day; like music
    in the air.
Ah! gentle may I lay me down, and gentle rest my
    head,
And gentle sleep the sleep of death, and gentle hear
    the voice
Of him that walketh in the garden in the evening
    time."

The Lilly of the valley, breathing in the humble
    grass,
Answer'd the lovely maid and said: "I am a wat'ry
    weed,   20
And I am very small and love to dwell in lowly
    vales;
So weak, the gilded butterfly scarce perches on my
    head.
Yet I am visited from heaven, and he that smiles on
    all
Walks in the valley and each morn over me spreads
    his hand,
Saying, 'Rejoice, thou humble grass, thou new-born
    lilly flower,
Thou gentle maid of silent valleys and of modest
    brooks;
For thou shalt be clothed in light, and fed with
    morning manna,
Till summer's heat melts thee beside the fountains
    and the springs
To flourish in eternal vales.' Then why should Thel
    complain?

Why should the mistress of the vales of Har utter
    a sigh?"   30

30. Har: the state of Innocence.

She ceas'd, & smil'd in tears, then sat down in her silver shrine.

Thel answer'd: "O thou little virgin of the peaceful valley,
Giving to those that cannot crave, the voiceless, the o'ertired;
Thy breath doth nourish the innocent lamb, he smells thy milky garments,
He crops thy flowers while thou sittest smiling in his face,
Wiping his mild and meekin mouth from all contagious taints.
Thy wine doth purify the golden honey; thy perfume,
Which thou dost scatter on every little blade of grass that springs,
Revives the milkèd cow, & tames the fire-breathing steed.
But Thel is like a faint cloud kindled at the rising sun: 40
I vanish from my pearly throne, and who shall find my place?"

"Queen of the vales," the Lilly answer'd, "ask the tender cloud,
And it shall tell thee why it glitters in the morning sky,
And why it scatters its bright beauty thro' the humid air.
Descend, O little Cloud, & hover before the eyes of Thel."

The Cloud descended, and the Lilly bow'd her modest head
And went to mind her numerous charge among the verdant grass.

II

"O little Cloud," the virgin said, "I charge thee tell to me
Why thou complainest not when in one hour thou fade away:
Then we shall seek thee, but not find. Ah! Thel is like to thee: 50
I pass away: yet I complain, and no one hears my voice."

36. meekin: gentle.

The Cloud then shew'd his golden head & his bright form emerg'd,
Hovering and glittering on the air before the face of Thel.

"O virgin, know'st thou not our steeds drink of the golden springs
Where Luvah doth renew his horses? Look'st thou on my youth,
And fearest thou, because I vanish and am seen no more,
Nothing remains? O maid, I tell thee, when I pass away
It is to tenfold life, to love, to peace and raptures holy:
Unseen descending, weigh my light wings upon balmy flowers,
And court the fair-eyed dew to take me to her shining tent: 60
The weeping virgin, trembling, kneels before the risen sun,
Till we arise link'd in a golden band and never part,
But walk united, bearing food to all our tender flowers."

"Dost thou, O little Cloud? I fear that I am not like thee,
For I walk thro' the vales of Har, and smell the sweetest flowers,
But I feed not the little flowers; I hear the warbling birds,
But I feed not the warbling birds; they fly and seek their food:
But Thel delights in these no more, because I fade away;
And all shall say, 'Without a use this shining woman liv'd,
Or did she only live to be at death the food of worms?' "   70

The Cloud reclin'd upon his airy throne and answer'd thus:

"Then if thou art the food of worms, O virgin of the skies,
How great thy use, how great thy blessing! Every thing that lives

55. Luvah: One of the four creatures in Blake's epic *The Four Zoas*, Luvah is love. See the editor's general introduction to Blake for a full discussion of Blake's mythology.

Lives not alone nor for itself. Fear not, and I will
call
The weak worm from its lowly bed, and thou shalt
hear its voice.
Come forth, worm of the silent valley, to thy pensive queen."

The helpless worm arose, and sat upon the Lilly's
leaf,
And the bright Cloud sail'd on, to find his partner
in the vale.

III

Then Thel astonish'd view'd the Worm upon its
dewy bed.

"Art thou a Worm? Image of weakness, art thou
but a Worm?   80
I see thee like an infant wrapped in the Lilly's leaf.
Ah! weep not, little voice, thou canst not speak, but
thou canst weep.
Is this a Worm? I see thee lay helpless & naked,
weeping,
And none to answer, none to cherish thee with
mother's smiles."

The Clod of Clay heard the Worm's voice & rais'd
her pitying head:
She bow'd over the weeping infant, and her life
exhal'd
In milky fondness: then on Thel she fix'd her humble eyes.

"O beauty of the vales of Har! we live not for our-
selves.
Thou seest me the meanest thing, and so I am in-
deed.
My bosom of itself is cold, and of itself is dark;   90
But he, that loves the lowly, pours his oil upon my
head,
And kisses me, and binds his nuptial bands around
my breast,
And says: 'Thou mother of my children, I have
loved thee,
And I have given thee a crown that none can take
away.'
But how this is, sweet maid, I know not, and I can-
not know;
I ponder, and I cannot ponder; yet I live and love."

The daughter of beauty wip'd her pitying tears
with her white veil,
And said: "Alas! I knew not this, and therefore did
I weep.
That God would love a Worm I knew, and punish
the evil foot
That wilful bruis'd its helpless form; but that he
cherish'd it   100
With milk and oil I never knew, and therefore did
I weep;
And I complain'd in the mild air, because I fade
away,
And lay me down in thy cold bed, and leave my
shining lot."

"Queen of the vales," the matron Clay answer'd, "I
heard thy sighs,
And all thy moans flew o'er my roof, but I have
call'd them down.
Wilt thou, O Queen, enter my house? 'Tis given
thee to enter
And to return: fear nothing, enter with thy virgin
feet."

IV

The eternal gates' terrific porter lifted the northern
bar:
Thel enter'd in & saw the secrets of the land unknown.
She saw the couches of the dead, & where the
fibrous roots   110
Of every heart on earth infixes deep its restless
twists:
A land of sorrows & of tears where never smile was
seen.

She wander'd in the land of clouds thro' valleys
dark, list'ning
Dolours & lamentations; waiting oft beside a dewy
grave
She stood in silence, list'ning to the voices of the
ground,
Till to her own grave plot she came, & there she
sat down,
And heard this voice of sorrow breathed from the
hollow pit.

"Why cannot the Ear be closed to its own destruction?
Or the glist'ning Eye to the poison of a smile?

Why are Eyelids stor'd with arrows ready
    drawn,   120
Where a thousand fighting men in ambush lie?
Or an Eye of gifts & graces show'ring fruits & coinèd
    gold?
Why a Tongue impress'd with honey from every
    wind?
Why an Ear, a whirlpool fierce to draw creations
    in?
Why a Nostril wide inhaling terror, trembling, &
    affright?
Why a tender curb upon the youthful burning boy?
Why a little curtain of flesh on the bed of our
    desire?"

The Virgin started from her seat, & with a shriek
Fled back unhinder'd till she came into the vales
    of Har.

                                                    1789

The Marriage of Heaven and Hell

THE ARGUMENT

Rintrah[1] roars & shakes his fires in the burden'd air;
Hungry clouds swag on the deep.

Once meek, and in a perilous path,
The just man kept his course along
The vale of death.
Roses are planted where thorns grow,
And on the barren heath
Sing the honey bees.

Then the perilous path was planted,
And a river and a spring   10
On every cliff and tomb,
And on the bleachèd bones
Red clay brought forth;

Till the villain left the paths of ease,
To walk in perilous paths, and drive
The just man into barren climes.

Now the sneaking serpent walks
In mild humility,

THE MARRIAGE OF HEAVEN AND HELL. **1. Rintrah:** an
angry prophet in Blake's prophetic works.

And the just man rages in the wilds
Where lions roam.   20

Rintrah roars & shakes his fires in the burden'd air;
Hungry clouds swag on the deep.

As a new heaven is begun, and it is now thirty-three
years since its advent, the Eternal Hell revives. And
lo! Swedenborg[2] is the Angel sitting at the tomb:
his writings are the linen clothes folded up. Now
is the dominion of Edom,[3] & the return of Adam
into Paradise; see Isaiah xxxiv & xxxv Chap.

Without Contraries is no progression. Attraction
and Repulsion, Reason and Energy, Love and Hate,
are necessary to Human existence.

From these contraries spring what the religious
call Good & Evil. Good is the passive that obeys
Reason. Evil is the active springing from Energy.

Good is Heaven. Evil is Hell.

THE VOICE OF THE DEVIL

All Bibles or sacred codes have been the causes of
the following Errors:

1. That Man has two real existing principles:
Viz: a Body & a Soul.

2. That Energy, call'd Evil, is alone from the
body; & that Reason, call'd Good, is alone from the
Soul.

3. That God will torment Man in Eternity for
following his Energies.

But the following Contraries to these are True:

1. Man has no Body distinct from his Soul; for
that call'd Body is a portion of Soul discern'd by
the five Senses, the chief inlets of Soul in this age.

2. Energy is the only life, and is from the Body;
and Reason is the bound or outward circumference
of Energy.

3. Energy is Eternal Delight.

2. Swedenborg: Emanuel Swedenborg (1688–1772), the
Swedish philosopher who greatly influenced the young
Blake. According to Swedenborg, the Last Judgment
started in 1757, the year of Blake's birth. **3. Edom:** Esau,
brother of Jacob. In the Old Testament story Jacob
gained the blessing of his father Isaac by a ruse. Isaac
prophesied the eventual domination of Esau.

Those who restrain desire, do so because theirs is weak enough to be restrained; and the restrainer or reason usurps its place & governs the unwilling.

And being restrain'd, it by degrees becomes passive, till it is only the shadow of desire.

The history of this is written in Paradise Lost, & the Governor or Reason is call'd Messiah.

And the original Archangel, or possessor of the command of the heavenly host, is call'd the Devil or Satan, and his children are call'd Sin & Death.

But in the Book of Job, Milton's Messiah is call'd Satan.

For this history has been adopted by both parties.

It indeed appear'd to Reason as if Desire was cast out; but the Devil's account is, that the Messiah fell, & formed a heaven of what he stole from the Abyss.

This is shewn in the Gospel, where he prays to the Father to send the comforter, or Desire, that Reason may have Ideas to build on; the Jehovah of the Bible being no other than he who dwells in flaming fire.

Know that after Christ's death, he became Jehovah.

But in Milton, the Father is Destiny, the Son a Ratio[4] of the five senses, & the Holy-ghost Vacuum!

Note: The reason Milton wrote in fetters when he wrote of Angels & God, and at liberty when of Devils & Hell, is because he was a true Poet and of the Devil's party without knowing it.

A MEMORABLE FANCY

As I was walking among the fires of hell, delighted with the enjoyments of Genius, which to Angels look like torment and insanity, I collected some of their Proverbs; thinking that as the sayings used in a nation mark its character, so the Proverbs of Hell show the nature of Infernal wisdom better than any description of buildings or garments.

When I came home: on the abyss of the five senses, where a flat sided steep frowns over the present world, I saw a mighty Devil folded in black clouds, hovering on the sides of the rock: with corroding fires he wrote the following sentence now

4. Ratio: creation.

percieved by the minds of men, & read by them on earth:

> How do you know but ev'ry Bird that cuts the
>   airy way,
> Is an immense world of delight, clos'd by your
>   senses five?

PROVERBS OF HELL

In seed time learn, in harvest teach, in winter enjoy.

Drive your cart and your plow over the bones of the dead.

The road of excess leads to the palace of wisdom.

Prudence is a rich, ugly old maid courted by Incapacity.

He who desires but acts not, breeds pestilence.

The cut worm forgives the plow.

Dip him in the river who loves water.

A fool sees not the same tree that a wise man sees.

He whose face gives no light, shall never become a star.

Eternity is in love with the productions of time.

The busy bee has no time for sorrow.

The hours of folly are measur'd by the clock; but of wisdom, no clock can measure.

All wholesom food is caught without a net or a trap.

Bring out number, weight & measure in a year of dearth.

No bird soars too high, if he soars with his own wings.

A dead body revenges not injuries.

The most sublime act is to set another before you.

If the fool would persist in his folly he would become wise.

Folly is the cloke of knavery.

Shame is Pride's cloke.

Prisons are built with stones of Law, Brothels with bricks of Religion.

The pride of the peacock is the glory of God.

The lust of the goat is the bounty of God.

The wrath of the lion is the wisdom of God.

The nakedness of woman is the work of God.

Excess of sorrow laughs. Excess of joy weeps.

The roaring of lions, the howling of wolves, the

raging of the stormy sea, and the destructive sword, are portions of eternity, too great for the eye of man.

The fox condemns the trap, not himself.

Joys impregnate. Sorrows bring forth.

Let man wear the fell of the lion, woman the fleece of the sheep.

The bird a nest, the spider a web, man friendship.

The selfish, smiling fool, & the sullen, frowning fool shall be both thought wise, that they may be a rod.

What is now proved was once only imagin'd.

The rat, the mouse, the fox, the rabbet watch the roots; the lion, the tyger, the horse, the elephant watch the fruits.

The cistern contains: the fountain overflows.

One thought fills immensity.

Always be ready to speak your mind, and a base man will avoid you.

Every thing possible to be believ'd is an image of truth.

The eagle never lost so much time as when he submitted to learn of the crow.

The fox provides for himself, but God provides for the lion.

Think in the morning. Act in the noon. Eat in the evening. Sleep in the night.

He who has suffer'd you to impose on him, knows you.

As the plow follows words, so God rewards prayers.

The tygers of wrath are wiser than the horses of instruction.

Expect poison from the standing water.

You never know what is enough unless you know what is more than enough.

Listen to the fool's reproach! it is a kingly title!

The eyes of fire, the nostrils of air, the mouth of water, the beard of earth.

The weak in courage is strong in cunning.

The apple tree never asks the beech how he shall grow; nor the lion, the horse, how he shall take his prey.

The thankful reciever bears a plentiful harvest.

If others had not been foolish, we should be so.

The soul of sweet delight can never be defil'd.

When thou seest an Eagle, thou seest a portion of Genius; lift up thy head!

As the catterpiller chooses the fairest leaves to lay her eggs on, so the priest lays his curse on the fairest joys.

To create a little flower is the labour of ages.

Damn braces: Bless relaxes.

The best wine is the oldest, the best water the newest.

Prayers plow not! Praises reap not!

Joys laugh not! Sorrows weep not!

The head Sublime, the heart Pathos, the genitals Beauty; the hands & feet Proportion.

As the air to a bird or the sea to a fish, so is contempt to the contemptible.

The crow wish'd every thing was black, the owl that every thing was white.

Exuberance is Beauty.

If the lion was advised by the fox, he would be cunning.

Improvement makes strait roads; but the crooked roads without Improvement are roads of Genius.

Sooner murder an infant in its cradle than nurse unacted desires.

Where man is not, nature is barren.

Truth can never be told so as to be understood, and not be believ'd.

Enough! or Too much.

The ancient Poets animated all sensible objects with Gods or Geniuses, calling them by the names and adorning them with the properties of woods, rivers, mountains, lakes, cities, nations, and whatever their enlarged & numerous senses could perceive.

And particularly they studied the genius of each city & country, placing it under its mental deity;

Till a system was formed, which some took advantage of, & enslav'd the vulgar by attempting to realize or abstract the mental deities from their objects: thus began Priesthood;

Choosing forms of worship from poetic tales.

And at length they pronounc'd that the Gods had order'd such things.

Thus men forgot that All deities reside in the human breast.

A MEMORABLE FANCY

The Prophets Isaiah and Ezekiel dined with me, and I asked them how they dared so roundly to assert that God spoke to them; and whether they did not think at the time that they would be misunderstood, & so be the cause of imposition.

Isaiah answer'd: "I saw no God, nor heard any, in a finite organical perception; but my senses discover'd the infinite in every thing, and as I was then perswaded, & remain confirm'd, that the voice of honest indignation is the voice of God, I cared not for consequences, but wrote."

Then I asked: "does a firm perswasion that a thing is so, make it so?"

He replied: "All poets believe that it does, & in ages of imagination this firm perswasion removed mountains; but many are not capable of a firm perswasion of any thing."

Then Ezekiel said: "The philosophy of the east taught the first principles of human perception: some nations held one principle for the origin, & some another: we of Israel taught that the Poetic Genius (as you now call it) was the first principle and all the others merely derivative, which was the cause of our despising the Priests & Philosophers of other countries, and prophecying that all Gods would at last be proved to originate in ours & to be the tributaries of the Poetic Genius; it was this that our great poet, King David, desired so fervently & invokes so pathetic'ly, saying by this he conquers enemies & governs kingdoms; and we so loved our God, that we cursed in his name all the deities of surrounding nations, and asserted that they had rebelled: from these opinions the vulgar came to think that all nations would at last be subject to the jews."

"This," said he, "like all firm perswasions, is come to pass; for all nations believe the jews' code and worship the jews' god, and what greater subjection can be?"

I heard this with some wonder, & must confess my own conviction. After dinner I ask'd Isaiah to favour the world with his lost works; he said none of equal value was lost. Ezekiel said the same of his.

I also asked Isaiah what made him go naked and barefoot three years? he answer'd: "the same thing that made our friend Diogenes, the Grecian."

I then asked Ezekiel why he eat dung, & lay so long on his right & left side? he answer'd, "the desire of raising other men into a perception of the infinite: this the North American tribes practise, & is he honest who resists his genius or conscience only for the sake of present ease or gratification?"

The ancient tradition that the world will be consumed in fire at the end of six thousand years is true, as I have heard from Hell.

For the cherub with his flaming sword is hereby commanded to leave his guard at tree of life; and when he does, the whole creation will be consumed and appear infinite and holy, whereas it now appears finite & corrupt.

This will come to pass by an improvement of sensual enjoyment.

But first the notion that man has a body distinct from his soul is to be expunged; this I shall do by printing in the infernal method, by corrosives, which in Hell are salutary and medicinal, melting apparent surfaces away, and displaying the infinite which was hid.

If the doors of perception were cleansed every thing would appear to man as it is, infinite.

For man has closed himself up, till he sees all things thro' narrow chinks of his cavern.

A MEMORABLE FANCY

I was in a Printing house in Hell, & saw the method in which knowledge is transmitted from generation to generation.

In the first chamber was a Dragon-Man, clearing away the rubbish from a cave's mouth; within, a number of Dragons were hollowing the cave.

In the second chamber was a Viper folding round the rock & the cave, and others adorning it with gold, silver and precious stones.

In the third chamber was an Eagle with wings and feathers of air: he caused the inside of the cave to be infinite; around were numbers of Eagle-like men who built palaces in the immense cliffs.

In the fourth chamber were Lions of flaming fire, raging around & melting the metals into living fluids.

In the fifth chamber were Unnam'd forms, which cast the metals into the expanse.

There they were reciev'd by Men who occupied the sixth chamber, and took the forms of books & were arranged in libraries.

The Giants who formed this world into its sensual existence, and now seem to live in it in chains, are in truth the causes of its life & the sources of all activity; but the chains are the cunning of weak and tame minds which have power to resist energy; according to the proverb, the weak in courage is strong in cunning.

Thus one portion of being is the Prolific, the other the Devouring: to the Devourer it seems as if the producer was in his chains; but it is not so, he only takes portions of existence and fancies that the whole.

But the Prolific would cease to be Prolific unless the Devourer, as a sea, recieved the excess of his delights.

Some will say: "Is not God alone the Prolific?" I answer: "God only Acts & Is, in existing beings or Men."

These two classes of men are always upon earth, & they should be enemies: whoever tries to reconcile them seeks to destroy existence.

Religion is an endeavour to reconcile the two.

Note: Jesus Christ did not wish to unite, but to separate them, as in the Parable of sheep and goats! & he says: "I came not to send Peace, but a Sword."

Messiah or Satan or Tempter was formerly thought to be one of the Antediluvians who are our Energies.

A MEMORABLE FANCY

An Angel came to me and said: "O pitiable foolish young man! O horrible! O dreadful state! consider the hot burning dungeon thou art preparing for thyself to all eternity, to which thou art going in such career."

I said: "Perhaps you will be willing to shew me my eternal lot, & we will contemplate together upon it, and see whether your lot or mine is most desirable."

So he took me thro' a stable & thro' a church & down into the church vault, at the end of which was a mill: thro' the mill we went, and came to a cave: down the winding cavern we groped our tedious way, till a void boundless as a nether sky appear'd beneath us, & we held by the roots of trees and hung over this immensity; but I said: "if you please, we will commit ourselves to this void, and see whether providence is here also: if you will not, I will:" but he answer'd: "do not presume, O

young man, but as we here remain, behold thy lot which will soon appear when the darkness passes away."

So I remain'd with him, sitting in the twisted root of an oak; he was suspended in a fungus, which hung with the head downward into the deep.

By degrees we beheld the infinite Abyss, fiery as the smoke of a burning city; beneath us, at an immense distance, was the sun, black but shining; round it were fiery tracks on which revolv'd vast spiders, crawling after their prey, which flew, or rather swum, in the infinite deep, in the most terrific shapes of animals sprung from corruption; & the air was full of them, & seem'd composed of them: these are Devils, and are called Powers of the air. I now asked my companion which was my eternal lot? he said: "between the black & white spiders."

But now, from between the black & white spiders, a cloud and fire burst and rolled thro' the deep, black'ning all beneath, so that the nether deep grew black as a sea, & rolled with a terrible noise; beneath us was nothing now to be seen but a black tempest, till looking east between the clouds & the waves, we saw a cataract of blood mixed with fire, and not many stones' throw from us appear'd and sunk again the scaly fold of a monstrous serpent; at last, to the east, distant about three degrees, appear'd a fiery crest above the waves; slowly it reared like a ridge of golden rocks, till we discover'd two globes of crimson fire, from which the sea fled away in clouds of smoke; and now we saw it was the head of Leviathan; his forehead was divided into streaks of green & purple like those on a tyger's forehead: soon we saw his mouth & red gills hang just above the raging foam, tinging the black deep with beams of blood, advancing toward us with all the fury of a spiritual existence.

My friend the Angel climb'd up from his station into the mill: I remain'd alone; & then this appearance was no more, but I found myself sitting on a pleasant bank beside a river by moonlight, hearing a harper, who sung to the harp; & his theme was: "The man who never alters his opinion is like standing water, & breeds reptiles of the mind."

But I arose and sought for the mill, & there I found my Angel, who, surprised, asked me how I escaped?

I answer'd: "All that we saw was owing to your

metaphysics; for when you ran away, I found my-self on a bank by moonlight hearing a harper. But now we have seen my eternal lot, shall I shew you yours?" he laugh'd at my proposal; but I by force suddenly caught him in my arms, & flew westerly thro' the night, till we were elevated above the earth's shadow; then I flung myself with him di-rectly into the body of the sun; here I clothed my-self in white, & taking in my hand Swedenborg's volumes, sunk from the glorious clime, and passed all the planets till we came to saturn: here I stay'd to rest, & then leap'd into the void between saturn & the fixed stars.

"Here," said I, "is your lot, in this space—if space it may be call'd." Soon we saw the stable and the church, & I took him to the altar and open'd the Bible, and lo! it was a deep pit, into which I descended, driving the Angel before me; soon we saw seven houses of brick; one we enter'd; in it were a number of monkeys, baboons, & all of that species, chain'd by the middle, grinning and snatching at one another, but withheld by the shortness of their chains: however, I saw that they sometimes grew numerous, and then the weak were caught by the strong, and with a grinning aspect, first coupled with, & then devour'd, by plucking off first one limb and then another, till the body was left a helpless trunk; this, after grinning & kissing it with seeming fondness, they devour'd too; and here & there I saw one savourily picking the flesh off his own tail; as the stench terribly annoy'd us both, we went into the mill, & I in my hand brought the skeleton of a body, which in the mill was Aristotle's Analytics.

So the Angel said: "thy phantasy has imposed upon me, & thou oughtest to be ashamed."

I answer'd: "we impose on one another, & it is but lost time to converse with you whose works are only Analytics."

Opposition is true Friendship.

I have always found that Angels have the vanity to speak of themselves as the only wise; this they do with a confident insolence sprouting from system-atic reasoning.

Thus Swedenborg boasts that what he writes is new; tho' it is only the Contents or Index of al-ready publish'd books.

A man carried a monkey about for a shew, & because he was a little wiser than the monkey,

grew vain, and conciev'd himself as much wiser than seven men. It is so with Swedenborg: he shews the folly of churches, & exposes hypocrites, till he imagines that all are religious, & himself the single one on earth that ever broke a net.

Now hear a plain fact: Swedenborg has not writ-ten one new truth. Now hear another: he has written all the old falsehoods.

And now hear the reason. He conversed with Angels who are all religious, & conversed not with Devils who all hate religion, for he was incapable thro' his conceited notions.

Thus Swedenborg's writings are a recapitulation of all superficial opinions, and an analysis of the more sublime—but no further.

Have now another plain fact. Any man of me-chanical talents may, from the writings of Para-celsus or Jacob Behmen,[5] produce ten thousand volumes of equal value with Swedenborg's, and from those of Dante or Shakespear an infinite num-ber.

But when he has done this, let him not say that he knows better than his master, for he only holds a candle in sunshine.

A MEMORABLE FANCY

Once I saw a Devil in a flame of fire, who arose before an Angel that sat on a cloud, and the Devil utter'd these words: "The worship of God is: Honouring his gifts in other men, each according to his genius, and loving the greatest men best: those who envy or calumniate great men hate God; for there is no other God."

The Angel hearing this became almost blue; but mastering himself he grew yellow, & at last white, pink, & smiling, and then replied:

"Thou Idolater! is not God One? & is not he visible in Jesus Christ? and has not Jesus Christ given his sanction to the law of ten command-ments? and are not all other men fools, sinners, & nothings?"

The Devil answer'd: "bray a fool in a morter with wheat, yet shall not his folly be beaten out of

---

5. References to Paracelsus (c. 1490–1541), the cele-brated German alchemist and Neoplatonic philosopher, and to Jakob Böhme (1575–1624), mystic and religious philosopher.

him; if Jesus Christ is the greatest man, you ought to love him in the greatest degree; now hear how he has given his sanction to the law of ten commandments: did he not mock at the sabbath, and so mock the sabbath's God? murder those who were murder'd because of him? turn away the law from the woman taken in adultery? steal the labor of others to support him? bear false witness when he omitted making a defence before Pilate? covet when he pray'd for his disciples, and when he bid them shake off the dust of their feet against such as refused to lodge them? I tell you, no virtue can exist without breaking these ten commandments. Jesus was all virtue, and acted from impulse, not from rules."

When he had so spoken, I beheld the Angel, who stretched out his arms, embracing the flame of fire, & he was consumed and arose as Elijah.

Note: This Angel, who is now become a Devil, is my particular friend; we often read the Bible together in its infernal or diabolical sense, which the world shall have if they behave well.

I have also The Bible of Hell, which the world shall have whether they will or no.

One Law for the Lion & Ox is Oppression.

A SONG OF LIBERTY

I

1. The Eternal Female[6] groan'd! it was heard over all the Earth.
2. Albion's coast is sick silent; the American meadows faint!
3. Shadows of Prophecy shiver along by the lakes and the rivers and mutter across the ocean: France, rend down thy dungeon!
4. Golden Spain, burst the barriers of old Rome!
5. Cast thy keys, O Rome, into the deep down falling, even to eternity down falling.
6. And weep and bow thy reverend locks.
7. In her trembling hands she took the new born terror,[7] howling:
8. On those infinite mountains of light, now barr'd

out by the atlantic sea, the new born fire stood before the starry king![8]
9. Flag'd with grey brow'd snows and the thunderous visages, the jealous wings wav'd over the deep.
10. The speary hand burned aloft, unbuckled was the shield; forth went the hand of jealousy among the flaming hair, and hurl'd the new born wonder thro' the starry night.
11. The fire, the fire is falling!
12. Look up! look up! O citizen of London, enlarge thy countenance! O Jew, leave counting gold! return to thy oil and wine. O African! black African! (go, winged thought, widen his forehead.)
13. The fiery limbs, the flaming hair, shot like the sinking sun into the western sea.
14. Wak'd from his eternal sleep, the hoary element roaring fled away:
15. Down rush'd, beating his wings in vain, the jealous king; his grey brow'd councellors, thunderous warriors, curl'd veterans, among helms, and shields, and chariots, horses, elephants, banners, castles, slings, and rocks,
16. Falling, rushing, ruining! buried in the ruins, on Urthona's[9] dens;
17. All night beneath the ruins; then, their sullen flames faded, emerge round the gloomy King.
18. With thunder and fire, leading his starry hosts thro' the waste wilderness, he promulgates his ten commands, glancing his beamy eyelids over the deep in dark dismay,
19. Where the son of fire in his eastern cloud, while the morning plumes her golden breast,
20. Spurning the clouds written with curses, stamps the stony law to dust, loosing the eternal horses from the dens of night, crying:

EMPIRE IS NO MORE! AND NOW THE LION & WOLF SHALL CEASE.

CHORUS

Let the Priests of the Raven of dawn, no longer in deadly black, with hoarse note curse the sons of joy. Nor his accepted brethren—whom, tyrant, he calls free—lay the bound or build the roof. Nor

---

6. **Eternal female:** Enitharmon, pregnant with Orc by Los. 7. **new born terror:** the rebellious Orc.

8. **starry king:** Urizen, reason and restraint. 9. **Urthona:** imagination. All of these characters will play major roles in the unfolding of Blake's prophecies. See the editor's introduction.

pale religious letchery call that virginity that wishes but acts not!

For every thing that lives is Holy.

c. 1790–93

AMERICA: A PROPHECY

PRELUDIUM

The shadowy Daughter of Urthona stood before
    red Orc,
When fourteen suns had faintly journey'd o'er his
    dark abode:
His food she brought in iron baskets, his drink in
    cups of iron:
Crown'd with a helmet & dark hair the nameless
    female stood;
A quiver with its burning stores, a bow like that
    of night,
When pestilence is shot from heaven: no other arms
    she need!
Invulnerable tho' naked, save where clouds roll
    round her loins
Their awful folds in the dark air: silent she stood
    as night;
For never from her iron tongue could voice or
    sound arise,
But dumb till that dread day when Orc assay'd his
    fierce embrace.   10

"Dark Virgin," said the hairy youth, "thy father
    stern, abhorr'd,
Rivets my tenfold chains while still on high my
    spirit soars;
Sometimes an eagle screaming in the sky, sometimes
    a lion
Stalking upon the mountains, & sometimes a whale,
    I lash
The raging fathomless abyss; anon a serpent folding
Around the pillars of Urthona, and round thy dark
    limbs
On the Canadian wilds I fold; feeble my spirit folds,
For chain'd beneath I rend these caverns: when
    thou bringest food
I howl my joy, and my red eyes seek to behold thy
    face—
In vain! these clouds roll to & fro, & hide thee from
    my sight."   20

Silent as despairing love, and strong as jealousy,
The hairy shoulders rend the links; free are the
    wrists of fire;
Round the terrific loins he siez'd the panting,
    struggling womb;
It joy'd: she put aside her clouds & smiled her
    first-born smile,
As when a black cloud shews its lightnings to the
    silent deep.

Soon as she saw the terrible boy, then burst the
    virgin cry:

"I know thee, I have found thee, & I will not let
    thee go:
Thou art the image of God who dwells in darkness
    of Africa,
And thou art fall'n to give me life in regions of dark
    death.
On my American plains I feel the struggling
    afflictions   30
Endur'd by roots that writhe their arms into the
    nether deep.
I see a Serpent in Canada who courts me to his
    love,
In Mexico an Eagle, and a Lion in Peru;
I see a Whale in the South-sea, drinking my soul
    away.
O what limb rending pains I feel! thy fire & my
    frost
Mingle in howling pains, in furrows by they light-
    nings rent.

This is eternal death, and this the torment long
    foretold."
The stern Bard ceas'd, asham'd of his own song;
    enrag'd he swung
His harp aloft sounding, then dash'd its shining
    frame against
A ruin'd pillar in glitt'ring fragments; silent he
    turn'd away,   40
And wander'd down the vales of Kent in sick &
    drear lamentings.

A PROPHECY

The Guardian Prince of Albion burns in his nightly
    tent:

AMERICA: A PROPHECY. 1. **Guardian Prince:** King George III of England, for Blake a symbol of tyrannical power and control.

Sullen fires across the Atlantic glow to America's
    shore,
Piercing the souls of warlike men who rise in silent
    night.
Washington, Franklin, Paine & Warren, Gates,
    Hancock & Green
Meet on the coast glowing with blood from Albion's
    fiery Prince.

Washington spoke: "Friends of America! look over
    the Atlantic sea;
A bended bow is lifted in heaven, & a heavy iron
    chain
Descends, link by link, from Albion's cliffs across
    the sea, to bind
Brothers & sons of America till our faces pale and
    yellow,
Heads deprest, voices weak, eyes downcast, hands
    work-bruis'd,   10
Feet bleeding on the sultry sands, and the furrows
    of the whip
Descend to generations that in future times forget."

The strong voice ceas'd, for a terrible blast swept
    over the heaving sea:
The eastern cloud rent: on his cliffs stood Albion's
    wrathful Prince,
A dragon form, clashing his scales: at midnight he
    arose,
And flam'd red meteors round the land of Albion
    beneath;
His voice, his locks, his awful shoulders, and his
    glowing eyes
Appear to the Americans upon the cloudy night.

Solemn heave the Atlantic waves between the
    gloomy nations,
Swelling, belching from its deeps red clouds &
    raging fires.   20
Albion is sick! America faints! enrag'd the Zenith
    grew.
As human blood shooting its veins all round the
    orbed heaven,
Red rose the clouds from the Atlantic in vast wheels
    of blood,
And in the red clouds rose a Wonder o'er the
    Atlantic sea,
Intense! naked! a Human fire, fierce glowing, as
    the wedge

4. **Washington . . . Green:** heroes in the American struggle for independence.

Of iron heated in the furnace: his terrible limbs
    were fire
With myriads of cloudy terrors, banners dark &
    towers
Surrounded: heat but not light went thro' the
    murky atmosphere.

The King of England looking westward trembles at
    the vision.

Albion's Angel stood beside the Stone of night, and
    saw   30
The terror like a comet, or more like the planet red
That once enclos'd the terrible wandering comets in
    its sphere.
Then, Mars, thou wast our center, & the planets
    three flew round
Thy crimson disk: so e'er the Sun was rent from
    thy red sphere.
The Spectre glow'd, his horrid length staining the
    temple long
With beams of blood; & thus a voice came forth,
    and shook the temple:

"The morning comes, the night decays, the watch-
    men leave their stations;
The grave is burst, the spices shed, the linen
    wrapped up;
The bones of death, the cov'ring clay, the sinews
    shrunk & dry'd
Reviving shake, inspiring move, breathing, awaken-
    ing,   40
Spring like redeemed captives when their bonds &
    bars are burst.
Let the slave grinding at the mill run out into the
    field,
Let him look up into the heavens & laugh in the
    bright air;
Let the inchained soul, shut up in darkness and in
    sighing,
Whose face has never seen a smile in thirty weary
    years,
Rise and look out; his chains are loose, his dungeon
    doors are open;
And let his wife and children return from the
    oppressor's scourge.

They look behind at every step & believe it is a
    dream,

30. **Stone of night:** the first of several references to the
tablets on which the "Thou shalt nots" of the Ten Commandments were engraved.

Singing: 'The Sun has left his blackness & has found
 a fresher morning,
And the fair Moon rejoices in the clear & cloudless
 night;   50
For Empire is no more, and now the Lion & Wolf
 shall cease.' "

In thunders ends the voice. Then Albion's Angel
 wrathful burnt
Beside the Stone of Night, and like the Eternal
 Lion's howl
In famine & war, reply'd: "Art thou not Orc, who
 serpent-form'd
Stands at the gate of Enitharmon to devour her
 children?
Blasphemous Demon, Antichrist, hater of Dignities,
Lover of wild rebellion, and transgressor of God's
 Law,
Why dost thou come to Angel's eyes in this terrific
 form?"

The Terror answer'd: "I am Orc, wreath'd round
 the accursed tree:
The times are ended; shadows pass, the morning
 'gins to break;   60
The fiery joy, that Urizen perverted to ten com-
 mands,
What night he led the starry hosts thro' the wide
 wilderness,
That stony law I stamp to dust; and scatter religion
 abroad
To the four winds as a torn book, & none shall
 gather the leaves;
But they shall rot on desart sands, & consume in
 bottomless deeps,
To make the desarts blossom, & the deeps shrink to
 their fountains,
And to renew the fiery joy, and burst the stony
 roof;
That pale religious letchery, seeking Virginity,
May find it in a harlot, and in coarse-clad honesty
The undefil'd, tho' ravish'd in her cradle night and
 morn;   70
For everything that lives is holy, life delights in life;
Because the soul of sweet delight can never be
 defil'd.
Fires inwrap the earthly globe, yet man is not
 consum'd;
Amidst the lustful fires he walks; his feet become
 like brass,

His knees and thighs like silver, & his breast and
 head like gold."

"Sound! sound! my loud war-trumpets, & alarm my
 Thirteen Angels!
Loud howls the eternal Wolf! the eternal Lion
 lashes his tail!
America is darken'd; and my punishing Demons,
 terrified,
Crouch howling before their caverns deep, like
 skins dry'd in the wind.
They cannot smite the wheat, nor quench the
 fatness of the earth;   80
They cannot smite with sorrows, nor subdue the
 plow and spade;
They cannot wall the city, nor moat round the
 castle of princes;
They cannot bring the stubbed oak to overgrow the
 hills;
For terrible men stand on the shores, & in their
 robes I see
Children take shelter from the lightnings: there
 stands Washington
And Paine and Warren with their foreheads rear'd
 toward the east.
But clouds obscure my aged sight. A vision from
 afar!
Sound! Sound! my loud war-trumpets, & alarm my
 thirteen Angels!
Ah vision from afar! Ah rebel form that rent the
 ancient
Heavens! Eternal Viper, self-renew'd, rolling in
 clouds,   90
I see thee in thick clouds and darkness on America's
 shore,
Writhing in pangs of abhorred birth; red flames the
 crest rebellious
And eyes of death; the harlot womb, oft opened in
 vain,
Heaves in enormous circles: now the times are
 return'd upon thee,
Devourer of thy parent, now thy unutterable torment renews.
Sound! sound! my loud war trumpets, & alarm my
 thirteen Angels!
Ah terrible birth! a young one bursting! where is
 the weeping mouth,
And where the mother's milk? instead, those ever-
 hissing jaws

And parched lips drop with fresh gore: now roll
    thou in the clouds;
Thy mother lays her length outstretch'd upon the
    shore beneath.   100
Sound! sound! my loud war-trumpets, & alarm my
    thirteen Angels!
Loud howls the eternal Wolf! the eternal Lion
    lashes his tail!"

Thus wept the Angel voice, & as he wept, the
    terrible blasts
Of trumpets blew a loud alarm across the Atlantic
    deep.
No trumpets answer; no reply of clarions or of fifes:
Silent the Colonies remain and refuse the loud
    alarm.

On those vast shady hills between America &
    Albion's shore,
Now barr'd out by the Atlantic sea, call'd Atlantean
    hills,
Because from their bright summits you may pass to
    the Golden world,
An ancient palace, archetype of mighty Em-
    peries,   110
Rears its immortal pinnacles, built in the forest of
    God
By Ariston, the king of beauty, for his stolen bride.

Here on their magic seats the thirteen Angels sat
    perturb'd,
For clouds from the Atlantic hover o'er the solemn
    roof.

Fiery the Angels rose, & as they rose deep thunder
    roll'd
Around their shores, indignant burning with the
    fires of Orc;
And Boston's Angel cried aloud as they flew thro'
    the dark night.

He cried: "Why trembles honesty, and like a
    murderer
Why seeks he refuge from the frowns of his im-
    mortal station?
Must the generous tremble & leave his joy to the
    idle, to the pestilence,   120

108. Atlantean hills: the legendary lost continent of
Atlantis, Sir Francis Bacon's utopia. The continent, according to speculation, would have joined England and
America. **112. Ariston:** a king of Sparta, whose name is
translated as "the best."

That mock him? who commanded this? what God?
    what Angel?
To keep the gen'rous from experience till the
    ungenerous
Are unrestrain'd performers of the energies of
    nature;
Till pity is become a trade, and generosity a
    science
That men get rich by; & the sandy desert is giv'n
    to the strong?
What God is he writes laws of peace & clothes him
    in a tempest?
What pitying Angel lusts for tears and fans himself
    with sighs?
What crawling villain preaches abstinence & wraps
    himself
In fat of lambs? no more I follow, no more obedi-
    ence pay!"

So cried he, rending off his robe & throwing down
    his scepter   130
In sight of Albion's Guardian; and all the thirteen
    Angels
Rent off their robes to the hungry wind, & threw
    their golden scepters
Down on the land of America; indignant they
    descended
Headlong from out their heav'nly heights, descend-
    ing swift as fires
Over the land; naked & flaming are their lineaments
    seen
In the deep gloom; by Washington & Paine &
    Warren they stood;
And the flame folded, roaring fierce within the
    pitchy night
Before the Demon red, who burnt towards America,
In black smoke, thunders, and loud winds, rejoicing
    in its terror,
Breaking in smoky wreaths from the wild deep, &
    gath'ring thick   140
In flames as of a furnace on the land from North
    to South,
What time the thirteen Governors that England
    sent, convene
In Bernard's house; the flames cover'd the land,
    they rouze, they cry;
Shaking their mental chains, they rush in fury to
    the sea

143. Bernard: tyrannical governor of Massachusetts from
1760 to 1769. For Blake a symbol of tyranny.

To quench their anguish; at the feet of Washington down fall'n
They grovel on the sand and writhing lie, while all
The British soldiers thro' the thirteen states sent up a howl
Of anguish, threw their swords & muskets to the earth, & ran
From their encampments and dark castles, seeking where to hide
From the grim flames, and from the visions of Orc, in sight   150
Of Albion's Angel; who, enrag'd, his secret clouds open'd
From north to south and burnt outstretch'd on wings of wrath, cov'ring
The eastern sky, spreading his awful wings across the heavens.
Beneath him roll'd his num'rous hosts, all Albion's Angels camp'd
Darken'd the Atlantic mountains; & their trumpets shook the valleys,
Arm'd with diseases of the earth to cast upon the Abyss,
Their numbers forty millions, must'ring in the eastern sky.

In the flames stood & view'd the armies drawn out in the sky,
Washington, Franklin, Paine, & Warren, Allen, Gates, & Lee,
And heard the voice of Albion's Angel give the thunderous command;   160
His plagues, obedient to his voice, flew forth out of their clouds,
Falling upon America, as a storm to cut them off,
As a blight cuts the tender corn when it begins to appear.
Dark is the heaven above, & cold & hard the earth beneath:
And as a plague wind fill'd with insects cuts off man & beast,
And as a sea o'erwhelms a land in the day of an earthquake,
Fury! rage! madness! in a wind swept through America;
And the red flames of Orc, that folded roaring, fierce, around
The angry shores; and the fierce rushing of th' inhabitants together!

The citizens of New York close their books & lock their chests;   170
The mariners of Boston drop their anchors and unlade;
The scribe of Pensylvania casts his pen upon the earth;
The builder of Virginia throws this hammer down in fear.

Then had America been lost, o'erwhelm'd by the Atlantic,
And Earth had lost another portion of the infinite,
But all rush together in the night in wrath and raging fire.
The red fires rag'd! the plagues recoil'd! then roll'd they back with fury
On Albion's Angels: then the Pestilence began in streaks of red
Across the limbs of Albion's Guardian; the spotted plague smote Bristol's
And the Leprosy London's Spirit, sickening all their bands: 180
The millions sent up a howl of anguish and threw off their hammer'd mail,
And cast their swords & spears to earth, & stood, a naked multitude:
Albion's Guardian writhed in torment on the eastern sky,
Pale, quiv'ring toward the brain his glimmering eyes, teeth chattering,
Howling & shuddering, his legs quivering, convuls'd each muscle & sinew:
Sick'ning lay London's Guardian, and the ancient miterd York,
Their heads on snowy hills, their ensigns sick'ning in the sky.
The plagues creep on the burning winds driven by flames of Orc,
And by the fierce Americans rushing together in the night,
Driven o'er the Guardians of Ireland, and Scotland and Wales.   190
They, spotted with plagues, forsook the frontiers; & their banners, sear'd
With fires of hell, deform their ancient heavens with shame & woe.
Hid in his caves the Bard of Albion felt the enormous plagues,

186. **York:** the Bishop of York. **193. Bard of Albion:** William Whitehead, the poet laureate.

And a cowl of flesh grew o'er his head, & scales on
 his back & ribs;
And, rough with black scales, all his Angels fright
 their ancient heavens.
The doors of marriage are open, and the Priests in
 rustling scales
Rush into reptile coverts, hiding from the fires of
 Orc,
That play around the golden roofs in wreaths of
 fierce desire,
Leaving the females naked and glowing with the
 lusts of youth.

For the female spirits of the dead, pining in bonds
 of religion,   200
Run from their fetters reddening, & in long drawn
 arches sitting,
They feel the nerves of youth renew, and desires of
 ancient times
Over their pale limbs, as a vine when the tender
 grape appears.

Over the hills, the vales, the cities, rage the red
 flames fierce:
The Heavens melted from north to south: and
 Urizen, who sat
Above all heavens, in thunders wrap'd, emerg'd his
 leprous head
From out his holy shrine, his tears in deluge piteous
Falling into the deep sublime; flag'd with grey-
 brow'd snows
And thunderous visages, his jealous wings wav'd
 over the deep;
Weeping in dismal howling woe, he dark descended,
 howling   210
Around the smitten bands, clothed in tears & trem-
 bling, shudd'ring cold.
His stored snows he poured forth, and his icy
 magazines
He open'd on the deep, and on the Atlantic sea
 white shiv'ring
Leprous his limbs, all over white, and hoary was
 his visage,
Weeping in dismal howlings before the stern
 Americans,
Hiding the Demon red with clouds & cold mists
 from the earth;
Till Angels & weak men twelve years should govern
 o'er the strong;
And then their end should come, when France
 reciev'd the Demon's light.

Stiff shudderings shook the heav'nly thrones!
 France, Spain, & Italy
In terror view'd the bands of Albion, and the an-
 cient Guardians,   220
Fainting upon the elements, smitten with their own
 plagues.
They slow advance to shut the five gates of their
 law-built heaven,
Filled with blasting fancies and with mildews of
 despair,
With fierce disease and lust, unable to stem the
 fires of Orc.
But the five gates were consum'd, & their bolts and
 hinges melted;
And the fierce flames burnt round the heavens, &
 round the abodes of men.

                                                    c. 1790–1793

THE BOOK OF URIZEN

PRELUDIUM TO THE FIRST BOOK
OF URIZEN

Of the primeval Priest's assum'd power,
When Eternals spurn'd back his religion
And gave him a place in the north,
Obscure, shadowy, void, solitary.

   Eternals! I hear your call gladly.
Dictate swift winged words & fear not
To unfold your dark visions of torment.

CHAP: I

1. Lo, a shadow of horror is risen
In Eternity! Unknown, unprolific,
Self-clos'd, all-repelling: what Demon
Hath form'd this abominable void,
This soul-shudd'ring vacuum? Some said
"It is Urizen." But unknown, abstracted,
Brooding, secret, the dark power hid.

2. Times on times he divided & measur'd
Space by space in his ninefold darkness,
Unseen, unknown; changes appear'd   10
Like desolate mountains, rifted furious
By the black winds of perturbation.

222. five gates: familiar Blake image of the five senses.

3. For he strove in battles dire,
In unseen conflictions with shapes
Bred from his forsaken wilderness
Of beast, bird, fish, serpent & element,
Combustion, blast, vapour and cloud.

4. Dark, revolving in silent activity:
Unseen in tormenting passions:
An activity unknown and horrible,   20
A self-contemplating shadow,
In enormous labours occupied.

5. But Eternals beheld his vast forests;
Age on ages he lay, clos'd, unknown,
Brooding shut in the deep; all avoid
The petrific, abominable chaos.

6. His cold horrors silent, dark Urizen
Prepar'd; his ten thousands of thunders,
Rang'd in gloom'd array, stretch out across
The dread world; & the rolling of wheels,   30
As of swelling seas, sound in his clouds,
In his hills of stor'd snows, in his mountains
Of hail & ice; voices of terror
Are heard, like thunders of autumn
When the cloud blazes over the harvests.

CHAP: II

1. Earth was not: nor globes of attraction;
The will of the Immortal expanded
Or contracted his all flexible senses;
Death was not, but eternal life sprung.

2. The sound of a trumpet the heavens   40
Awoke, & vast clouds of blood roll'd
Round the dim rocks of Urizen, so nam'd
That solitary one in Immensity.

3. Shrill the trumpet: & myriads of Eternity
Muster around the bleak desarts,
Now fill'd with clouds, darkness, & waters,
That roll'd perplex'd, lab'ring; & utter'd
Words articulate bursting in thunders
That roll'd on the tops of his mountains:

4. "From the depths of dark solitude, From   50
The eternal abode in my holiness,
Hidden, set apart, in my stern counsels,
Reserv'd for the days of futurity,
I have sought for a joy without pain,
For a solid without fluctuation.

Why will you die, O Eternals?
Why live in unquenchable burnings?

5. "First I fought with the fire, consum'd
Inwards into a deep world within:
A void immense, wild, dark & deep,   60
Where nothing was: Nature's wide womb;
And self balanc'd, stretch'd o'er the void,
I alone, even I! the winds merciless
Bound; but condensing in torrents
They fall & fall; strong I repell'd
The vast waves, & arose on the waters
A wide world of solid obstruction.

6. "Here alone I, in books form'd of metals,
Have written the secrets of wisdom,
The secrets of dark contemplation,   70
By fightings and conflicts dire
With terrible monsters Sin-bred
Which the bosoms of all inhabit,
Seven deadly Sins of the soul.

7. "Lo! I unfold my darkness, and on
This rock place with strong hand the Book
Of eternal brass, written in my solitude:

8. "Laws of peace, of love, of unity,
Of pity, compassion, forgiveness;
Let each chuse one habitation,   80
His ancient infinite mansion,
One command, one joy, one desire,
One curse, one weight, one measure,
One King, one God, one Law."

CHAP: III

1. The voice ended: they saw his pale visage
Emerge from the darkness, his hand
On the rock of eternity unclasping
The Rock of brass. Rage siez'd the strong,

2. Rage, fury, intense indignation,
In cataracts of fire, blood, & gall,   90
In whirlwinds of sulphurous smoke,
And enormous forms of energy,
All the seven deadly sins of the soul
In living creations appear'd,
In the flames of eternal fury.

3. Sund'ring, dark'ning, thund'ring,
Rent away with a terrible crash,
Eternity roll'd wide apart,

Wide asunder rolling;
Mountainous all around   100
Departing, departing, departing,
Leaving ruinous fragments of life
Hanging, frowning cliffs, &, all between,
An ocean of voidness unfathomable.

4. The roaring fires ran o'er the heav'ns
In whirlwinds & cataracts of blood,
And o'er the dark desarts of Urizen
Fires pour thro' the void on all sides
On Urizen's self-begotten armies.

5. But no light from the fires: all was
        darkness   110
In the flames of Eternal fury.

6. In fierce anguish & quenchless flames
To the desarts and rocks he ran raging
To hide; but he could not: combining,
He dug mountains & hills in vast strength,
He piled them in incessant labour,
In howlings & pangs & fierce madness,
Long periods in burning fires labouring
Till hoary, and age-broke, and aged,
In despair and the shadows of death.   120

7. And a roof vast, petrific around
On all sides he fram'd, like a womb,
Where thousands of rivers in veins
Of blood pour down the mountains to cool
The eternal fires, beating without
From Eternals; & like a black globe,
View'd by sons of Eternity standing
On the shore of the infinite ocean,
Like a human heart, strugling & beating,
The vast world of Urizen appear'd.   130

8. And Los, round the dark globe of Urizen,
Kept watch for Eternals to confine
The obscure separation alone;
For Eternity stood wide apart,
As the stars are apart from the earth.

9. Los wept, howling around the dark Demon,
And cursing his lot; for in anguish
Urizen was rent from his side,
And a fathomless void for his feet,
And intense fires for his dwelling.   140

10. But Urizen laid in a stony sleep,
Unorganiz'd, rent from Eternity.

11. The Eternals said: "What is this? Death.
Urizen is a clod of clay."

12. Los howl'd in a dismal stupor,
Groaning, gnashing, groaning,
Till the wrenching apart was healed.

13. But the wrenching of Urizen heal'd not.
Cold, featureless, flesh or clay,
Rifted with direful changes   150
He lay in a dreamless night,

14. Till Los rouz'd his fires, affrighted
At the formless, unmeasurable death.

CHAP: IV[a]

1. Los, smitten with astonishment,
Frighten'd at the hurtling bones

2. And at the surging, sulphureous,
Perturbed Immortal, mad raging

3. In whirlwinds & pitch & nitre
Round the furious limbs of Los.

4. And Los formed nets & gins   160
And threw the nets round about.

5. He watch'd in shudd'ring fear
The dark changes, & bound every change
With rivets of iron & brass.

6. And these were the changes of Urizen:

CHAP: IV[b]

1. Ages on ages roll'd over him;
In stony sleep ages roll'd over him,
Like a dark waste stretching, chang'able,
By earthquakes riv'n, belching sullen fires:
On ages roll'd ages in ghastly   170
Sick torment; around him in whirlwinds
Of darkness the eternal Prophet howl'd,
Beating still on his rivets of iron,
Pouring sodor of iron; dividing
The horrible night into watches.

2. And Urizen (so his eternal name)
His prolific delight obscur'd more & more
In dark secresy, hiding in surgeing
Sulphureous fluid his phantasies.
The Eternal Prophet heav'd the dark bellows, 180

And turn'd restless the tongs, and the hammer
Incessant beat, forging chains new & new,
Numb'ring with links hours, days & years.

3. The Eternal mind, bounded, began to roll
Eddies of wrath ceaseless round & round,
And the sulphureous foam, surging thick,
Settled, a lake, bright & shining clear,
White as the snow on the mountains cold.

4. Forgetfulness, dumbness, necessity,
In chains of the mind locked up,   190
Like fetters of ice shrinking together,
Disorganiz'd, rent from Eternity,
Los beat on his fetters of iron,
And heated his furnaces, & pour'd
Iron sodor and sodor of brass.

5. Restless turn'd the Immortal inchain'd,
Heaving dolorous, anguish'd unbearable;
Till a roof, shaggy wild, inclos'd
In an orb his fountain of thought.

6. In a horrible, dreamful slumber,   200
Like the linked infernal chain,
A vast Spine writh'd in torment
Upon the winds, shooting pain'd
Ribs, like a bending cavern;
And bones of solidness Froze
Over all his nerves of joy.
And a first Age passed over,
And a state of dismal woe.

7. From the caverns of his jointed Spine
Down sunk with fright a red   210
Round Globe, hot burning, deep,
Deep down into the Abyss;
Panting, Conglobing, Trembling,
Shooting out ten thousand branches
Around his solid bones.
And a second Age passed over,
And a state of dismal woe.

8. In harrowing fear rolling round,
His nervous brain shot branches
Round the branches of his heart   220
On high into two little orbs,
And fixed in two little caves,
Hiding carefully from the wind,
His Eyes beheld the deep.
And a third Age passed over,
And a state of dismal woe.

9. The pangs of hope began.
In heavy pain, striving, struggling,
Two Ears in close volutions
From beneath his orbs of vision   230
Shot spiring out and petrified
As they grew. And a fourth Age passed,
And a state of dismal woe.

10. In ghastly torment sick,
Hanging upon the wind,
Two Nostrils bent down to the deep.
And a fifth Age passed over,
And a state of dismal woe.

11. In ghastly torment sick,
Within his ribs bloated round,   240
A craving Hungry Cavern;
Thence arose his channel'd Throat,
And like a red flame, a Tongue
Of thirst & of hunger appear'd.
And a sixth Age passed over,
And a state of dismal woe.

12. Enraged & stifled with torment,
He threw his right Arm to the north,
His left Arm to the south
Shooting out in anguish deep,   250
And his feet stamp'd the nether Abyss
In trembling & howling & dismay.
And a seventh Age passed over,
And a state of dismal woe.

CHAP: V

1. In terrors Los shrunk from his task:
His great hammer fell from his hand.
His fires beheld, and sickening
Hid their strong limbs in smoke;
For with noises, ruinous, loud,
With hurtlings & clashings & groans,   260
The Immortal endur'd his chains,
Tho' bound in a deadly sleep.

2. All the myriads of Eternity,
All the wisdom & joy of life
Roll like a sea around him,
Except what his little orbs
Of sight by degrees unfold.

3. And now his eternal life
Like a dream was obliterated.

4. Shudd'ring, the Eternal Prophet smote   270
With a stroke from his north to south region.
The bellows & hammer are silent now;
A nerveless silence his prophetic voice
Siez'd; a cold solitude & dark void
The Eternal Prophet & Urizen clos'd.

5. Ages on ages roll'd over them,
Cut off from life & light, frozen
Into horrible forms of deformity.
Los suffer'd his fires to decay;
Then he look'd back with anxious desire,   280
But the space, undivided by existence,
Struck horror into his soul.

6. Los wept obscur'd with mourning,
His bosom earthquak'd with sighs;
He saw Urizen deadly black
In his chains bound, & Pity began,

7. In anguish dividing & dividing,
For pity divides the soul
In pangs, eternity on eternity,
Life in cataracts pour'd down his cliffs.   290
The void shrunk the lymph into Nerves
Wand'ring wide on the bosom of night
And left a round globe of blood
Trembling upon the Void.
Thus the Eternal Prophet was divided
Before the death image of Urizen;
For in changeable clouds and darkness,
In a winterly night beneath,
The Abyss of Los stretch'd immense;
And now seen, now obscur'd, to the eyes   300
Of Eternals the visions remote
Of the dark seperation appear'd:
As glasses discover Worlds
In the endless Abyss of space,
So the expanding eyes of Immortals
Beheld the dark visions of Los
And the globe of life blood trembling.

8. The globe of life blood trembled
Branching out into roots,
Fibrous, writhing upon the winds,   310
Fibres of blood, milk and tears,
In pangs, eternity on eternity.
At length in tears & cries imbodied,
A female form, trembling and pale,
Waves before his deathy face.

9. All Eternity shudder'd at sight
Of the first female now separate,
Pale as a cloud of snow
Waving before the face of Los.

10. Wonder, awe, fear, astonishment   320
Petrify the eternal myriads
At the first female form now separate.
They call'd her Pity, and fled.

11. "Spread a Tent with strong curtains around
    them.
Let cords & stakes bind in the Void,
That Eternals may no more behold them."

12. They began to weave curtains of darkness,
They erected large pillars round the Void,
With golden hooks fasten'd in the pillars;
With infinite labour the Eternals   330
A woof wove, and called it Science.

CHAP: VI

1. But Los saw the Female & pitied;
He embrac'd her; she wept, she refus'd;
In perverse and cruel delight
She fled from his arms, yet he follow'd.

2. Eternity shudder'd when they saw
Man begetting his likeness
On his own divided image.

3. A time passed over: the Eternals
Began to erect the tent,   340
When Enitharmon, sick,
Felt a Worm within her womb.

4. Yet helpless it lay like a Worm
In the trembling womb
To be moulded into existence.

5. All day the worm lay on her bosom;
All night within her womb
The worm lay till it grew to a serpent,
With dolorous hissings & poisons
Round Enitharmon's loins folding.   350

6. Coil'd within Enitharmon's womb
The serpent grew, casting its scales;
With sharp pangs the hissings began
To change to a grating cry:
Many sorrows and dismal throes,
Many forms of fish, bird & beast

Brought forth an Infant form
Where was a worm before.

7. The Eternals their tent finished
Alarm'd with these gloomy visions,   360
When Enitharmon groaning
Produc'd a man Child to the light.

8. A shriek ran thro' Eternity,
And a paralytic stroke,
At the birth of the Human shadow.

9. Delving earth in his resistless way,
Howling, the Child with fierce flames
Issu'd from Enitharmon.

10. The Eternals closed the tent;
They beat down the stakes, the cords   370
Stretch'd for a work of eternity.
No more Los beheld Eternity.

11. In his hands he siez'd the infant,
He bathed him in springs of sorrow,
He gave him to Enitharmon.

CHAP: VII

1. They named the child Orc; he grew,
Fed with the milk of Enitharmon.

2. Los awoke her. O sorrow & pain!
A tight'ning girdle grew
Around his bosom. In sobbings   380
He burst the girdle in twain;
But still another girdle
Oppress'd his bosom. In sobbings
Again he burst it. Again
Another girdle succeeds.
The girdle was form'd by day,
By night was burst in twain.

3. These falling down on the rock
Into an iron Chain
In each other link by link lock'd.   390

4. They took Orc to the top of a mountain.
O how Enitharmon wept!
They chain'd his young limbs to the rock
With the Chain of Jealousy
Beneath Urizen's deathful shadow.

5. The dead heard the voice of the child
And began to awake from sleep;

All things heard the voice of the child
And began to awake to life.

6. And Urizen, craving with hunger,   400
Stung with the odours of Nature,
Explor'd his dens around.

7. He form'd a line & a plummet
To divide the Abyss beneath;
He form'd a dividing rule;

8. He formed scales to weigh,
He formed massy weights;
He formed a brazen quadrant;
He formed golden compasses,
And began to explore the Abyss;   410
And he planted a garden of fruits.

9. But Los encircled Enitharmon
With fires of Prophecy
From the sight of Urizen & Orc.

10. And she bore an enormous race.

CHAP: VIII

1. Urizen explor'd his dens,
Mountain, moor & wilderness,
With a globe of fire lighting his journey,
A fearful journey, annoy'd
By cruel enormities, forms
Of life on his forsaken mountains.   420

2. And his world teem'd vast enormities,
Fright'ning, faithless, fawning
Portions of life, similitudes
Of a foot, or a hand, or a head,
Or a heart, or an eye; they swam mischevous,
Dread terrors, delighting in blood.

3. Most Urizen sicken'd to see
His eternal creations appear,
Sons & daughters of sorrow on mountains   430
Weeping, wailing. First Thiriel appear'd,
Astonish'd at his own existence,
Like a man from a cloud born; & Utha,
From the waters emerging, laments:
Grodna rent the deep earth, howling
Amaz'd; his heavens immense cracks
Like the ground parch'd with heat, then Fuzon
Flam'd out, first begotten, last born;
All his eternal sons in like manner;

His daughters from green herbs & cattle,   440
From monsters & worms of the pit.

4. He in darkness clos'd view'd all his race,
And his soul sicken'd! he curs'd
Both sons & daughters; for he saw
That no flesh nor spirit could keep
His iron laws on moment.

5. For he saw that life liv'd upon death:
The Ox in the slaughter house moans,
The Dog at the wintry door;
And he wept & called it Pity,   450
And his tears flowed down on the winds.

6. Cold he wander'd on high, over their cities
In weeping & pain & woe;
And where ever he wander'd, in sorrows
Upon the aged heavens,
A cold shadow follow'd behind him
Like a spider's web, moist, cold & dim,
Drawing out from his sorrowing soul,
The dungeon-like heaven dividing,
Where ever the footsteps of Urizen   460
Walked over the cities in sorrow;

7. Till a Web, dark & cold, throughout all
The tormented element stretch'd
From the sorrows of Urizen's soul.
And the Web is a Female in embrio.
None could break the Web, no wings of fire,

8. So twisted the cords, & so knotted
The meshes, twisted like to the human brain.

9. And all call'd it The Net of Religion.

CHAP: IX

1. Then the Inhabitants of those Cities   470
Felt their Nerves change into Marrow,
And hardening Bones began
In swift diseases and torments,
In throbbings & shootings & grindings
Thro' all the coasts; till weaken'd
The Senses inward rush'd, shrinking
Beneath the dark net of infection;

2. Till the shrunken eyes, clouded over,
Discern'd not the woven hipocrisy;
But the streaky slime in their heavens,   480
Brought together by narrowing perceptions,
Appear'd transparent air; for their eyes
Grew small like the eyes of a man,

And in reptile forms shrinking together,
Of seven feet stature they remain'd.

3. Six days they shrunk up from existence,
And on the seventh day they rested,
And they bless'd the seventh day, in sick hope,
And forgot their eternal life.

4. And their thirty cities divided   490
In form of a human heart.
No more could they rise at will
In the infinite void, but bound down
To earth by their narrowing perceptions
They lived a period of years;
Then left a noisom body
To the jaws of devouring darkness.

5. And their children wept, & built
Tombs in the desolate places,
And form'd laws of prudence, and call'd them   500
The eternal laws of God

6. And the thirty cities remain'd,
Surrounded by salt floods, now call'd
Africa: its name was then Egypt.

7. The remaining songs of Urizen
Beheld their brethren shrink together
Beneath the Net of Urizen.
Perswasion was in vain;
For the ears of the inhabitants
Were wither'd & deafen'd & cold,   510
And their eyes could not discern
Their brethren of other cities.

8. So Fuzon call'd all together
The remaining children of Urizen,
And they left the pendulous earth.
They called it Egypt, & left it.

9. And the salt Ocean rolled englob'd.

1794

THE BOOK OF AHANIA*

CHAP: IST

1. Fuzon on a chariot iron-wing'd
On spiked flames rose; his hot visage

---

* Ahania is Urizen's female emanation.

THE BOOK OF AHANIA. 1. **Fuzon**: a variant of the rebellious Orc.

Flam'd furious; sparkles his hair & beard
Shot down his wide bosom and shoulders.
On clouds of smoke rages his chariot
And his right hand burns red in its cloud
Moulding into a vast Globe his wrath,
As the thunder-stone is moulded.
Son of Urizen's silent burnings:

2. "Shall we worship this Demon of smoke,"   10
Said Fuzon, "this abstract non-entity,
This cloudy God seated on waters,
Now seen, now obscur'd, King of sorrow?"

3. So he spoke in a fiery flame,
On Urizen frowning indignant,
The Globe of wrath shaking on high;
Roaring with fury he threw
The howling Globe; burning it flew
Length'ning into a hungry beam. Swiftly

4. Oppos'd to the exulting flam'd beam,   20
The broad Disk of Urizen upheav'd
Across the Void many a mile.

5. It was forg'd in mills where the winter
Beats incessant: ten winters the disk
Unremitting endur'd the cold hammer.

6. But the strong arm that sent it remember'd
The sounding beam: laughing, it tore through
That beaten mass, keeping its direction,
The cold loins of Urizen dividing.

7. Dire shriek'd his invisible Lust;   30
Deep groan'd Urizen! stretching his awful hand,
Ahania (so name his parted soul)
He siez'd on his mountains of Jealousy.
He groan'd anguish'd, & called her Sin,
Kissing her and weeping over her;
Then hid her in darkness, in silence,
Jealous, tho' she was invisible.

8. She fell down a faint shadow wand'ring
In chaos and circling dark Urizen,
As the moon anguish'd circles the earth,   40
Hopeless! abhorr'd! a death-shadow,
Unseen, unbodied, unknown,
The mother of Pestilence.

9. But the fiery beam of Fuzon
Was a pillar of fire to Egypt
Five hundred years wand'ring on earth,
Till Los siez'd it and beat in a mass
With the body of the sun.

CHAP: IID

1. But the forehead of Urizen gathering,
And his eyes pale with anguish, his lips   50
Blue & changing, in tears and bitter
Contrition he prepar'd his Bow,

2. Form'd of Ribs, that in his dark solitude,
When obscur'd in his forests, fell monsters
Arose. For his dire Contemplations
Rush'd down like floods from his mountains
In torrents of mud settling thick,
With Eggs of unnatural production:
Forthwith hatching, some howl'd on his hills,
Some in vales, some aloft flew in air.   60

3. Of these, an enormous dread Serpent,
Scaled and poisonous horned,
Approach'd Urizen, even to his knees,
As he sat on his dark rooted Oak.

4. With his horns he push'd furious:
Great the conflict & great the jealousy
In cold poisons, but Urizen smote him.

5. First he poison'd the rocks with his blood,
Then polish'd his ribs, and his sinews
Dried, laid them apart till winter;   70
Then a Bow black prepar'd: on this Bow
A poisoned rock plac'd in silence.
He utter'd these words to the Bow:

6. "O Bow of the clouds of secresy!
O nerve of that lust-form'd monster!
Send this rock swift, invisible thro'
The black clouds on the bosom of Fuzon."

7. So saying, In torment of his wounds
He bent the enormous ribs slowly,
A circle of darkness! then fixed   80
The sinew in its rest; then the Rock,
Poisonous source, plac'd with art, lifting difficult
Its weighty bulk; silent the rock lay,

8. While Fuzon, his tygers unloosing,
Thought Urizen slain by his wrath.
"I am God!" said he, "eldest of things."

9. Sudden sings the rock; swift & invisible
On Fuzon flew, enter'd his bosom;

72. A poisoned rock: The Ten Commandments.

His beautiful visage, his tresses
That gave light to the mornings of heaven,   90
Were smitten with darkness, deform'd
And outstretch'd on the edge of the forest.

10. But the rock fell upon the Earth,
Mount Sinai in Arabia.

CHAP: III

1. The Globe shook, and Urizen seated
On black clouds his sore wound anointed;
The ointment flow'd down on the void
Mix'd with blood—here the snake gets her poison.

2. With difficulty & great pain Urizen
Lifted on high the dead corse: 100
On his shoulders he bore it to where
A Tree hung over the Immensity.

3. For when Urizen shrunk away
From Eternals, he sat on a rock
Barren: a rock which himself
From redounding fancies had petrified.
Many tears fell on the rock,
Many sparks of vegetation.
Soon shot the pained root
Of Mystery under his heel: 110

It grew a thick tree: he wrote
In silence his book of iron,
Till the horrid plant bending its boughs
Grew to roots when it felt the earth,
And again sprung to many a tree.

4. Amaz'd started Urizen when
He beheld himself compassed round
And high roofed over with trees.
He arose, but the stems stood so thick
He with difficulty and great pain   120
Brought his Books, all but the Book
Of iron, from the dismal shade.

5. The Tree still grows over the Void
Enrooting itself all around,
An endless labyrinth of woe!

6. The corse of his first begotten
On the accursed Tree of Mystery,
On the topmost stem of this Tree,
Urizen nail'd Fuzon's corse.

CHAP: IV

1. Forth flew the arrows of pestilence   130
Round the pale living Corse on the tree.

2. For in Urizen's slumbers of abstraction
In the infinite ages of Eternity,
When his Nerves of Joy melted & flow'd,
A white Lake on the dark blue air
In perturb'd pain and dismal torment
Now stretching out, now swift conglobing,

3. Effluvia vapor'd above
In noxious clouds; these hover'd thick
Over the disorganiz'd Immortal,   140
Till petrific pain scurf'd o'er the Lakes
As the bones of man, solid & dark.

4. The clouds of disease hover'd wide
Around the Immortal in torment,
Perching around the hurtling bones,
Disease on disease, shape on shape
Winged screaming in blood & torment.

5. The Eternal Prophet beat on his anvils;
Enrag'd in the desolate darkness
He forg'd nets of iron around   150
And Los threw them around the bones.

6. The shapes screaming flutter'd vain;
Some combin'd into muscles & glands,
Some organs for craving and lust;
Most remain'd on the tormented void,
Urizen's army of horrors.

7. Round the pale living Corse on the Tree
Forty years flew the arrows of pestilence.

8. Wailing and terror and woe
Ran thro' all his dismal world;   160
Forty years all his sons & daughters
Felt their skulls harden; then Asia
Arose in the pendulous deep.

9. They reptilize upon the Earth.

10. Fuzon groan'd on the Tree.

148. Eternal Prophet: Los. 158. Forty years: echoes of
the Israelites wandering in search of the Promised Land.

CHAP: V

1. The lamenting voice of Ahania
Weeping upon the void!
And round the Tree of Fuzon,
Distant in solitary night,
Her voice was heard, but no form   170
Had she; but her tears from clouds
Eternal fell round the Tree.

2. And the voice cried: "Ah, Urizen! Love!
Flower of morning! I weep on the verge
Of Non-entity; how wide the Abyss
Between Ahania and thee!

3. "I lie on the verge of the deep;
I see thy dark clouds ascend;
I see thy black forests and floods,
A horrible waste to my eyes!   180

4. "Weeping I walk over rocks,
Over dens & thro' valleys of death.
Why didst thou despise Ahania
To cast me from thy bright presence
Into the World of Loneness?

5. "I cannot touch his hand,
Nor weep on his knees, nor hear
His voice & bow, nor see his eyes
And joy, nor hear his footsteps and
My heart leap at the lovely sound!   190
I cannot kiss the place
Whereon his bright feet have trod,
But I wander on the rocks
With hard necessity.

6. "Where is my golden palace?
Where my ivory bed?
Where the joy of my morning hour?
Where the sons of eternity singing

7. "To awake bright Urizen, my king,
To arise to the mountain sport,   200
To the bliss of eternal valleys;

8. "To awake my king in the morn,
To embrace Ahania's joy
On the bredth of his open bosom?
From my soft cloud of dew to fall
In showers of life on his harvests,

9. "When he gave my happy soul
To the sons of eternal joy,

When he took the daughters of life
Into my chambers of love,   210

10. "When I found babes of bliss on my beds
And bosoms of milk in my chambers
Fill'd with eternal seed.
O eternal births sung round Ahania
In interchange sweet of their joys!

11. "Swell'd with ripeness & fat with fatness,
Bursting on winds, my odors,
My ripe figs and rich pomegranates
In infant joy at thy feet,
O Urizen, sported and sang.   220

12. "Then thou with thy lap full of seed,
With thy hand full of generous fire
Walked forth from the clouds of morning,
On the virgins of springing joy,
On the human soul to cast
The seed of eternal science.

13. "The sweat poured down thy temples;
To Ahania return'd in evening,
The moisture awoke to birth
My mothers–joys, sleeping in bliss.   230

14. "But now alone over rocks, mountains,
Cast out from thy lovely bosom,
Cruel jealousy! selfish fear!
Self-destroying, how can delight
Renew in these chains of darkness,
Where bones of beasts are strown
On the bleak and snowy mountains,
Where bones from the birth are buried
Before they see the light?"

1795

FROM

The Four Zoas

NIGHT THE NINTH

BEING THE LAST JUDGMENT

And Los & Enitharmon builded Jerusalem, weeping
Over the Sepulcher & over the Crucified body
Which, to their Phantom Eyes, appear'd still in the
Sepulcher;

But Jesus stood beside them in the spirit, separating
Their spirit from their body. Terrified at Non Existence,
For such they deem'd the death of the body, Los his vegetable hands
Outstretch'd; his right hand, branching out in fibrous strength,
Siez'd the Sun; His left hand, like dark roots, cover'd the Moon,
And tore them down, cracking the heavens from immense to immense.
Then fell the fires of Eternity with loud & shrill   10
Sound of Loud Trumpet thundering along from heaven to heaven
A mighty sound articulate: "Awake, ye dead, & come
To judgment from the four winds! Awake & Come away!"
Folding like scrolls of the Enormous volume of Heaven & Earth,
With thunderous noise & dreadful shakings, rocking to & fro,
The heavens are shaken & the Earth removed from its place,
The foundations of the Eternal hills discover'd:
The thrones of Kings are shaken, they have lost their robes & crowns,
The poor smite their oppressors, they awake up to the harvest,
The naked warriors rush together down to the sea shore   20
Trembling before the multitudes of slaves now set at liberty:
They are become like wintry flocks, like forests strip'd of leaves:
The oppressed pursue like the wind; there is no room for escape.

The Spectre of Enitharmon, let loose on the troubled deep,
Wail'd shrill in the confusion, & the Spectre of Urthona
Reciev'd her in the darkening south; their bodies lost, they stood
Trembling & weak, a faint embrace, a fierce desire, as when
Two shadows mingle on a wall; they wail & shadowy tears
Fell down, & shadowy forms of joy mix'd with despair & grief—

Their bodies buried in the ruins of the Universe—   30
Mingled with the confusion. Who shall call them from the Grave?

Rahab & Tirzah wail aloud in the wild flames; they give up themselves to Consummation.

The books of Urizen unroll with dreadful noise; the folding Serpent
Of Orc began to Consume in fierce raving fire; his fierce flames
Issu'd on all sides, gathering strength in animating volumes,
Roaming abroad on all the winds, raging intense, reddening
Into resistless pillars of fire rolling round & round, gathering
Strength from the Earths consumed & heavens & all hidden abysses,
Where'er the Eagle has Explor'd, or Lion or Tyger trod,
Or where the Comets of the night or stars of asterial day   40
Have shot their arrows or long beamed spears in wrath & fury.
And all the while the trumpet sounds, "Awake, ye dead, & come
To Judgment!" From the clotted gore & from the hollow den
Start forth the trembling millions into flames of mental fire,
Bathing their limbs in the bright visions of Eternity.
Then, like the doves from pillars of Smoke, the trembling families
Of women & children throughout every nation under heaven
Cling round the men in bands of twenties & of fifties, pale
As snow that falls around a leafless tree upon the green.
Their oppressors are fall'n, they have stricken them, they awake to life.   50
Yet pale the just man stands erect & looking up to heav'n,
Trembling & strucken by the Universal stroke, the trees unroot,

THE FOUR ZOAS. **32. Rahab:** Blake regarded Rahab as the system of morality, as everything that would restrict human freedom.

The rocks groan horrible & run about; the mountains &
Their rivers cry with a dismal cry; the cattle gather together,
Lowing they kneel before the heavens; the wild beasts of the forests
Tremble; the Lion shuddering asks the Leopard: "Feelest thou
The dread I feel, unknown before? My voice refuses to roar,
And in weak moans I speak to thee. This night,
Before the morning's dawn, the Eagle call'd the Vulture,
The Raven call'd the hawk, I heard them from my forests black,   60
Saying: 'Let us go up far, for soon, I smell upon the wind,
A terror coming from the south.' The Eagle & Hawk fled away
At dawn, & e'er the sun arose, the raven & Vulture follow'd.
Let us flee also to the north." They fled. The Sons of Men
Saw them depart in dismal droves. The trumpet sounded loud
And all the Sons of Eternity Descended into Beulah.

In the fierce flames the limbs of Mystery lay consuming with howling
And deep despair. Rattling go up the flames around the Synagogue
Of Satan. Loud the Serpent Orc rag'd thro' his twenty seven
Folds. The tree of Mystery went up in folding flames.   70
Blood issu'd out in rushing volumes, pouring in whirlpools fierce
From out the flood gates of the Sky. The Gates are burst; down pour
The torrents black upon the Earth; the blood pours down incessant.
Kings in their palaces lie drown'd. Shepherds, their flocks, their tents,
Roll down the mountains in black torrents. Cities, Villages,
High spires & Castles drown'd in the black deluge; shoal on shoal

Float the dead carcases of Men & Beasts, driven to & fro on waves
Of foaming blood beneath the black incessant sky, till all
Mystery's tyrants are cut off & not one left on Earth.

And when all Tyranny was cut off from the face of the Earth,   80
Around the dragon form of Urizen, & round his stony form,
The flames rolling intense thro' the wide Universe
Began to enter the Holy City. Ent'ring, the dismal clouds
In furrow'd lightnings break their way, the wild flames licking up
The Bloody Deluge: living flames winged with intellect
And Reason, round the Earth they march in order, flame by flame.
From the clotted gore & from the hollow den
Start forth the trembling millions into flames of mental fire,
Bathing their limbs in the bright visions of Eternity.

Beyond this Universal Confusion, beyond the remotest Pole   90
Where their vortexes began to operate, there stands
A Horrible rock far in the South; it was forsaken when
Urizen gave the horses of Light into the hands of Luvah.
On this rock lay the faded head of the Eternal Man
Enwrapped round with weeds of death, pale cold in sorrow & woe.
He lifts the blue lamps of his Eyes & cries with heavenly voice:
Bowing his head over the consuming Universe, he cried:
"O weakness & O weariness! O war within my members!
My sons, exiled from my breast, pass to & fro before me.
My birds are silent on my hills, flocks die beneath my branches.   100
My tents are fallen, my trumpets & the sweet sound of my harps

---

66. **Beulah**: in Blake's mythology, a state of Innocence, of love not yet tempered by experience.

93. **Luvah**: One of the Four Zoas, Luvah is love before the fall of the divine Albion. Luvah becomes Orc after the Zoas, originally a unity, separate into warring powers.

Is silent on my clouded hills that belch forth storms
& fire.
My milk of cows & honey of bees & fruit of golden
harvest
Are gather'd in the scorching heat & in the driving
rain.
My robe is turned to confusion, & my bright gold to
stone.
Where once I sat, I weary walk in misery & pain,
For from within my wither'd breast grown narrow
with my woes
The Corn is turned to thistles & the apples into
poison,
The birds of song to murderous crows, My joys to
bitter groans,
The voices of children in my tents to cries of help-
less infants,   110
And all exiled from the face of light & shine of
morning
In this dark world, a narrow house, I wander up &
down.
I hear Mystery howling in these flames of Consum-
mation.
When shall the Man of future times become as in
days of old?
O weary life! why sit I here & give up all my
powers
To indolence, to the night of death, when indolence
& mourning
Sit hovering over my dark threshold? tho' I arise,
look out
And scorn the war within my members, yet my
heart is weak
And my head faint. Yet will I look again unto the
morning.
Whence is this sound of rage of Men drinking each
other's blood,   120
Drunk with the smoking gore, & red, but not with
nourishing wine?"

The Eternal Man sat on the Rocks & cried with awful voice:
"O Prince of Light, where art thou? I behold thee
not as once
In those Eternal fields, in clouds of morning stepping forth
With harps & songs when bright Ahania sang before thy face
And all thy sons & daughters gather'd round my
ample table.

See you not all this wracking furious confusion?
Come forth from slumbers of thy cold abstraction!
Come forth,
Arise to Eternal births! Shake off thy cold repose,
Schoolmaster of souls, great opposer of change,
arise!   130
That the Eternal worlds may see thy face in peace
& joy,
That thou, dread form of Certainty, maist sit in
town & village
While little children play around thy feet in gentle
awe,
Fearing thy frown, loving thy smile, O Urizen,
Prince of Light."

He call'd; the deep buried his voice & answer none
return'd.
Then wrath burst round; the Eternal Man was
wrath; again he cried:
"Arise, O stony form of death! O dragon of the
Deeps!
Lie down before my feet, O Dragon! let Urizen
arise.
*O how couldst thou deform those beautiful pro-
portions*
*Of life & person; for as the Person, so is his life
proportion'd.*   140
Let Luvah rage in the dark deep, even to Consum-
mation,
For if thou feedest not his rage, it will subside in
peace.
But if thou darest obstinate refuse my stern behest,
Thy crown & scepter I will sieze, & regulate all my
members
In stern severity, & cast thee out into the indefinite
Where nothing lives, there to wander; & if thou re-
turnest weary,
Weeping at the threshold of Existence, I will steel
my heart
Against thee to Eternity, & never recieve thee more.
Thy self-destroying, beast form'd Science shall be
thy eternal lot.
My anger against thee is greater than against this
Luvah,   150
For war is energy Enslav'd, but thy religion,
The first author of this war & the distracting of hon-
est minds
Into confused perturbation & strife & honour &
pride,
Is a deciet so detestable that I will cast thee out

If thou repentest not, & leave thee as a rotten
   branch to be burn'd
With Mystery the Harlot & with Satan for Ever &
   Ever.
Error can never be redeemed in all Eternity,
But Sin, Even Rahab, is redeem'd in blood & fury
   & jealousy—
That line of blood that stretch'd across the windows
   of the morning—
Redeem'd from Error's power. Wake, thou dragon
   of the deeps!"   160

Urizen wept in the dark deep, anxious his scaly
   form
To reassume the human; & he wept in the dark
   deep,
Saying: "O that I had never drunk the wine nor
   eat the bread
Of dark mortality, or cast my view into futurity, nor
   turn'd
My back, dark'ning the present, clouding with a
   cloud,
And building arches high, & cities, turrets & towers
   & domes
Whose smoke destroy'd the pleasant gardens, &
   whose running kennels
Chok'd the bright rivers; burd'ning with my Ships
   the angry deep;
Thro' Chaos seeking for delight, & in spaces remote
Seeking the Eternal which is always present to the
   wise;   170
Seeking for pleasure which unsought falls round the
   infant's path
And on the fleeces of mild flocks who neither care
   nor labour;
But I, the labourer of ages, whose unwearied hands
Are thus deform'd with hardness, with the sword
   & with the spear
And with the chisel & the mallet, I, whose labours
   vast
Order the nations, separating family by family,
Alone enjoy not. I alone, in misery supreme,
Ungratified give all my joy unto this Luvah & Vala.
Then Go, O dark futurity! I will cast thee forth
   from these
Heavens of my brain, nor will I look upon futurity
   more.   180
I cast futurity away, & turn my back upon that
   void

Which I have made; for lo! futurity is in this moment.
Let Orc consume, let Tharmas rage, let dark Urthona give
All strength to Los & Enitharmon, & let Los self-
   curs'd
Rend down this fabric, as a wall ruin'd & family
   extinct.
Rage, Orc! Rage Tharmas! Urizen no longer curbs
   your rage."

So Urizen spoke; he shook his snows from off his
   shoulders & arose
As on a Pyramid of mist, his white robes scattering
The fleecy white: renew'd, he shook his aged man-
   tles off
Into the fires. Then, glorious bright, Exulting in his
   joy,   190
He sounding rose into the heavens in naked maj-
   esty,
In radiant Youth; when Lo! like garlands in the
   Eastern sky
When vocal May comes dancing from the East,
   Ahania came
Exulting in her flight, as when a bubble rises up
On to the surface of a lake, Ahania rose in joy.
Excess of Joy is worse than grief; her heart beat
   high, her blood
Burst its bright vessels: she fell down dead at the
   feet of Urizen
Outstretch'd, a smiling corse: they buried her in a
   silent cave.
Urizen dropped a tear; the Eternal Man Darken'd
   with sorrow.

The three daughters of Urizen guard Ahania's
   death couch;   200
Rising from the confusion in tears & howlings &
   despair,
Calling upon their father's Name, upon their Rivers
   dark.

And the Eternal Man said: "Hear my words, O
   Prince of Light.
Behold Jerusalem in whose bosom the Lamb of God
Is seen; tho' slain before her Gates, he self-renew'd
   remains
Eternal, & I thro' him awake from death's dark vale.
The times revolve; the time is coming when all
   these delights

Shall be renew'd, & all these Elements that now
  consume
Shall reflourish. Then bright Ahania shall awake
  from death,
A glorious Vision to thine Eyes, a Self-renewing
  Vision: 210
The spring, the summer, to be thine; then sleep the
  wintry days
In silken garments spun by her own hands against
  her funeral.
The winter thou shalt plow & lay thy stores into thy
  barns
Expecting to recieve Ahania in the spring with joy.
Immortal thou, Regenerate She, & all the lovely Sex
From her shall learn obedience & prepare for a win-
  try grave,
That spring may see them rise in tenfold joy &
  sweet delight.
Thus shall the male & female live the life of Eter-
  nity,
Because the Lamb of God Creates himself a bride &
  wife
That we his Children evermore may live in Jeru-
  salem   220
Which now descendeth out of heaven, a City, yet a
  Woman,
Mother of myriads redeem'd & born in her spiritual
  palaces,
By a New Spiritual birth Regenerated from Death."

Urizen said: "I have Erred, & my Error remains
  with me.
What Chain encompasses? in what Lock is the river
  of light confin'd
That issues forth in the morning by measure & in
  the evening by carefulness?
Where shall we take our stand to view the infinite
  & unbounded?
Or where are human feet? for Lo, our eyes are in
  the heavens."

He ceas'd, for riv'n link from link, the bursting Universe explodes.
All things revers'd flew from their centers: rattling
  bones   230
To bones Join: shaking convuls'd, the shivering clay
  breathes:
Each speck of dust to the Earth's center nestles
  round & round
In pangs of an Eternal Birth: in torment & awe &
  fear,

All spirits deceas'd, let loose from reptile prisons,
  come in shoals:
Wild furies from the tyger's brain & from the lion's
  eyes,
And from the ox & ass come moping terrors, from
  the eagle
And raven: numerous as the leaves of autumn,
  every species
Flock to the trumpet, mutt'ring over the sides of
  the grave & crying
In the fierce wind round heaving rocks & mountains
  fill'd with groans.
On rifted rocks, suspended in the air by inward
  fires,   240
Many a woful company & many on clouds & waters,
Fathers & friends, Mothers & Infants, Kings &
  Warriors,
Priests & chain'd Captives, met together in a hor-
  rible fear;
And every one of the dead appears as he had liv'd
  before,
And all the marks remain of the slave's scourge &
  tyrant's Crown,
And of the Priest's o'ergorged Abdomen, & of the
  merchant's thin
Sinewy deception, & of the warrior's outbraving &
  thoughtlessness
In lineaments too extended & in bones too strait
  & long.
They shew their wounds: they accuse: they sieze
  the opressor; howlings began
On the golden palace, songs & joy on the desart;
  the Cold babe   250
Stands in the furious air; he cries: "the children of
  six thousand years
Who died in infancy rage furious: a mighty multitude rage furious,
Naked & pale standing on the expecting air, to be
  deliver'd.
Rend limb from limb the warrior & the tyrant,
  reuniting in pain."

The furious wind still rends around; they flee in
  sluggish effort;
They beg, they intreat in vain now; they listened
  not to intreaty;
They view the flames red rolling on thro' the wide
  universe
From the dark jaws of death beneath & desolate
  shores remote,

These covering vaults of heaven & these trembling
  globes of earth.
One Plant calls to another & one star enquires of
  another: 260
"What flames are these, coming from the South?
  what noise, what dreadful rout
As a battle in the heavens? hark! heard you not the
  trumpet
As of fierce battle?" While they spoke, the flames
  come on intense roaring.
They see him whom they have pierc'd, they wail
  because of him,
They magnify themselves no more against Jerusa-
  lem, Nor
Against her little ones; the innocent, accused before
  the Judges,
Shines with immortal glory; trembling, the judge
  springs from his throne
Hiding his face in the dust beneath the prisoner's
  feet & saying:
"Brother of Jesus, what have I done? intreat thy
  lord for me:
Perhaps I may be forgiven." While he speaks the
  flames roll on,   270
And after the flames appears the Cloud of the Son
  of Man
Descending from Jerusalem with power and great
  Glory.
All nations looks up to the Cloud & behold him who
  was crucified.
The Prisoner answers: "You scourg'd my father to
  death before my face
While I stood bound with cords & heavy chains.
  Your hipocrisy
Shall now avail you nought." So speaking, he
  dash'd him with his foot.

The Cloud is Blood, dazling upon the heavens, &
  in the cloud,
Above upon its volumes, is beheld a throne & a
  pavement
Of precious stones surrounded by twenty-four
  venerable patriarchs,
And these again surrounded by four Wonders of
  the Almighty,   280
Incomprehensible, pervading all, amidst & round
  about,
Fourfold, each in the other reflected; they are
  named Life's—in Eternity—

Four Starry Universes going forward from Eternity
  to Eternity.
And the Fall'n Man who was arisen upon the Rock
  of Ages
Beheld the Vision of God, & he arose up from the
  Rock,
And Urizen arose up with him, walking thro' the
  flames
To meet the Lord coming to Judgment; but the
  flames repell'd them
Still to the Rock; in vain they strove to Enter the
  Consummation
Together, for the Redeem'd Man could not enter
  the Consummation.

Then siez'd the sons of Urizen the Plow, they
  polish'd it   290
From rust of ages; all its ornaments of gold & silver
  & ivory
Reshone across the field immense where all the
  nations
Darken'd like Mould in the divided fallows where
  the weed
Triumphs in its own destruction; they took down
  the harness
From the blue walls of heaven, starry jingling,
  ornamented
With beautiful art, the study of angels, the workmanship of Demons
When Heaven & Hell in Emulation strove in sports
  of Glory.

The noise of rural works resounded thro' the
  heavens of heavens,
The horses neigh from the battle, the wild bulls
  from the sultry waste,
The tygers from the forests, & the lions from the
  sandy desarts.   300
They sing; they sieze the instruments of harmony;
  they throw away
The spear, the bow, the gun, the mortar; they level
  the fortifications.
They beat the iron engines of destruction into
  wedges;
They give them to Urthona's sons; ringing the
  hammers sound
In dens of death to forge the spade, the mattock &
  the ax,
The heavy roller to break the clods, to pass over
  the nations.

The Sons of Urizen shout. Their father rose. The
    Eternal horses

Harness'd, They call'd to Urizen; the heavens
    moved at their call.

The limbs of Urizen shone with ardor. He laid his
    hand on the Plow,

Thro' dismal darkness drave the Plow of ages over
    Cities   310

And all their Villages; over Mountains & all their
    Vallies;

Over the graves & caverns of the dead; Over the
    Planets

And over the void spaces; over sun & moon &
    constellation.

Then Urizen commanded & they brought the Seed
    of Men.

The trembling souls of All the dead stood before
    Urizen,

Weak wailing in the troubled air. East, west &
    north & south

He turn'd the horses loose & laid his Plow in the
    northern corner

Of the wide Universal field, then step'd forth into
    the immense.

Then he began to sow the seed; he girded round
    his loins

With a bright girdle, & his skirt fill'd with immortal
    souls.   320

Howling & Wailing fly the souls from Urizen's
    strong hand,

For from the hand of Urizen the myriads fall like
    stars

Into their own appointed places, driven back by
    the winds.

The naked warriors rush together down to the sea
    shores:

They are become like wintry flocks, like the forests
    strip'd of leaves;

The Kings & Princes of the Earth cry with a feeble
    cry,

Driven on the unproducing sands & on the harden'd
    rocks;

And all the while the flames of Orc follow the
    vent'rous feet

Of Urizen, & all the while the Trump of Tharmas
    sounds.

Weeping & wailing fly the souls from Urizen's
    strong hands—   330

The daughters of Urizen stand with Cups & mea-
    sures of foaming wine

Immense upon the heavens with bread & delicate
    repasts—

Then follows the golden harrow in the midst of
    Mental fires.

To ravishing melody of flutes & harps & softest
    voice

The seed is harrow'd in, while flames heat the black
    mould & cause

The human harvest to begin. Towards the south
    first sprang

The myriads, & in silent fear they look out from
    their graves.

Then Urizen sits down to rest, & all his wearied sons

Take their repose on beds; they drink, they sing,
    they view the flames

Of Orc; in joy they view the human harvest spring-
    ing up.   340

A time they give to sweet repose, till all the harvest
    is ripe.

And Lo, like the harvest Moon, Ahania cast off her
    death clothes;

She folded them up in care, in silence, & her
    bright'ning limbs

Bath'd in the clear spring of the rock; then from
    her darksome cave

Issu'd in majesty divine. Urizen rose up from his
    couch

On wings of tenfold joy, clapping his hands, his
    feet, his radiant wings

In the immense: as when the Sun dances upon the
    mountains

A shout of jubilee in lovely notes responds from
    daughter to daughter,

From son to son: as if the stars beaming innumer-
    able

Thro' night should sing soft warbling, filling earth
    & heaven;   350

And bright Ahania took her seat by Urizen in songs
    & joy.

The Eternal Man also sat down upon the Couches
    of Beulah,

Sorrowful that he could not put off his new risen
    body

In mental flames; the flames refus'd, they drove him
    back to Beulah.

His body was redeem'd to be permanent thro'
    Mercy Divine.

And now fierce Orc had quite consum'd himself in
    Mental flames,
Expending all his energy against the fuel of fire.
The Regenerate Man stoop'd his head over the
    Universe & in
His holy hands reciev'd the flaming Demon &
    Demoness of smoke
And gave them to Urizen's hands; the Immortal
    frown'd, saying,   360

"Luvah & Vala, henceforth you are Servants; obey
    & live.
You shall forget your former state; return, & Love
    in peace,
Into your place, the place of seed, not in the brain
    or heart.
If Gods combine against Man, setting their domin-
    ion above
The Human form Divine, Thrown down from their
    high station
In the Eternal heavens of Human Imagination,
    buried beneath
In dark Oblivion, with incessant pangs, ages on
    ages,
In enmity & war first weaken'd, then in stern repen-
    tance
They must renew their brightness, & their dis-
    organiz'd functions
Again reorganize, till they resume the image of the
    human,   370
Co-operating in the bliss of Man, obeying his Will,
Servants to the infinite & Eternal of the Human
    form."

    Luvah & Vala descended & enter'd the Gates of
    Dark Urthona,
And walk'd from the hands of Urizen in the shad-
    ows of Vala's Garden
Where the impressions of Despair & Hope for ever
    vegetate
In flowers, in fruits, in fishes, birds & beasts &
    clouds & waters,
The land of doubts & shadows, sweet delusions,
    unform'd hopes.
They saw no more the terrible confusion of the
    wracking universe.
They heard not, saw not, felt not all the terrible
    confusion,

361. Luvah & Vala: Orc reborn as Luvah, Love; Vala is
his female emanation.

For in their orbed senses, within clos'd up, they
    wander'd at will.   380
And those upon the Couches view'd them, in the
    dreams of Beulah,
As they repos'd from the terrible wide universal
    harvest,
Invisible Luvah in bright clouds hover'd over Vala's
    head,
And thus their ancient golden age renew'd; for
    Luvah spoke
With voice mild from his golden Cloud upon the
    breath of morning:

"Come forth, O Vala, from the grass & from the
    silent dew,
Rise from the dews of death, for the Eternal Man
    is Risen."

She rises among flowers & looks toward the Eastern
    clearness
She walks yea runs, her feet are wing'd, on the
    tops of the bending grass,
Her garments rejoice in the vocal wind & her hair
    glistens with dew.   390

She answer'd thus: "Whose voice is this, in the
    voice of the nourishing air,
In the spirit of the morning, awaking the Soul from
    its grassy bed?
Where dost thou dwell? for it is thee I seek, & but
    for thee
I must have slept Eternally, nor have felt the dew
    of thy morning.
Look how the opening dawn advances with vocal
    harmony!
Look how the beams foreshew the rising of some
    glorious power!
The sun is thine, he goeth forth in his majestic
    brightness.
O thou creating voice that callest! & who shall
    answer thee?"

"Where dost thou flee, O fair one? where doest
    thou seek thy happy place?"

"To yonder brightness, there I haste, for sure I
    came from thence   400
Or I must have slept eternally, nor have felt the
    dew of morning."

"Eternally thou must have slept, nor have felt the
    morning dew,

But for yon nourishing sun; 'tis that by which thou
    art arisen.
The birds adore the sun: the beasts rise up & play
    in his beams,
And every flower & every leaf rejoices in his light.
Then, O thou fair one, sit thee down, for thou art
    as the grass,
Thou risest in the dew of morning & at night art
    folded up."

"Alas! am I but as a flower? then will I sit me
    down,
Then will I weep, then I'll complain & sigh for
    immortality,
And chide my maker, thee O Sun, that raisedst me
    to fall."   410

So saying she sat down & wept beneath the apple
    trees.

"O be thou blotted out, thou Sun! that raisedst me
    to trouble,
That gavest me a heart to crave, & raisedst me, thy
    phantom,
To feel thy heat & see thy light & wander here
    alone,
Hopeless, if I am like the grass & so shall pass
    away."

"Rise, sluggish Soul, why sit'st thou here? why dost
    thou sit & weep?
Yon sun shall wax old & decay, but thou shalt ever
    flourish.
The fruit shall ripen & fall down, & the flowers
    consume away,
But thou shalt survive; arise, O dry thy dewy
    tears."

"Hah! shall I still survive? whence came that sweet
    & comforting voice?   420
And whence that voice of sorrow? O sun! thou art
    nothing now to me.
Go on thy course rejoicing, & let us both rejoice
    together.
I walk among his flocks & hear the bleating of his
    lambs.
O that I could behold his face & follow his pure
    feet!
I walk by the footsteps of his flocks; come hither,
    tender flocks.
Can you converse with a pure soul that seeketh for
    her maker?

You answer not: then am I set your mistress in this
    garden.
I'll watch you & attend your footsteps; you are not
    like the birds
That sing & fly in the bright air; but you do lick
    my feet
And let me touch your woolly backs; follow me as
    I sing,   430
For in my bosom a new song arises to my Lord:

"Rise up, O sun, most glorious minister & light of
    day.
Flow on, ye gentle airs, & bear the voice of my
    rejoicing.
Wave freshly, clear waters flowing around the
    tender grass;
And thou, sweet smelling ground, put forth thy life
    in fruits & flowers.
Follow me, O my flocks, & hear me sing my rap-
    turous song.
I will cause my voice to be heard on the clouds that
    glitter in the sun.
I will call; & who shall answer me? I will sing; who
    shall reply?
For from my pleasant hills beyond the living, living
    springs,
Running among my green pastures, delighting
    among my trees.   440
I am not here alone: my flocks, you are my
    brethren;
And you birds that sing & adorn the sky, you are
    my sisters.
I sing, & you reply to my song; I rejoice, & you are
    glad.
Follow me, O my flocks; we will now descend into
    the valley.
O how delicious are the grapes, flourishing in the
    sun!
How clear the spring of the rock, running among
    the golden sand!
How cool the breezes of the valley, & the arms of
    the branching trees!
Cover us from the sun; come & let us sit in the
    shade.
My Luvah here hath plac'd me in a sweet &
    pleasant land,
And given me fruits & pleasant waters, & warm
    hills & cool valleys.   450
Here will I build myself a house, & here I'll call on
    his name,

Here I'll return when I am weary & take my
pleasant rest."

So spoke the sinless soul, & laid her head on the
downy fleece
Of a curl'd Ram who stretch'd himself in sleep
beside his mistress,
And soft sleep fell upon her eyelids in the silent
noon of day.

Then Luvah passed by, & saw the sinless soul,
And said: "Let a pleasant house arise to be the
dwelling place
Of this immortal spirit growing in lower Paradise."
He spoke, & pillars were builded, & walls as white
as ivory.
The grass she slept upon was pav'd with pavement
as of pearl.   460
Beneath her rose a downy bed, & a cieling cover'd
all.

Vala awoke. "When in the pleasant gates of sleep
I enter'd,
I saw my Luvah like a spirit stand in the bright air.
Round him stood spirits like me, who rear'd me a
bright house,
And here I see thee, house, remain in my most
pleasant world.
My Luvah smil'd: I kneeled down: he laid his hand
on my head,
And when he laid his hand upon me, from the
gates of sleep I came
Into this bodily house to tend my flocks in my
pleasant garden."

So saying, she arose & walked round her beautiful
house,
And then from her white door she look'd to see her
bleating lambs,   470
But her flocks were gone up from beneath the trees
into the hills.

"I see the hand that leadeth me doth also lead my
flocks."
She went up to her flocks & turned oft to see her
shining house.
She stop'd to drink of the clear spring & eat the
grapes & apples.
She bore the fruits in her lap; she gather'd flowers
for her bosom.
She called to her flocks, saying, "Follow me, O
my flocks!"

They follow'd her to the silent valley beneath the
spreading trees.
And on the river's margin she ungirded her golden
girdle;
She stood in the river & view'd herself within the
wat'ry glass,
And her bright hair was wet with the waters: she
rose up from the river,   480
And as she rose her eyes were open'd to the world
of waters:
She saw Tharmas sitting upon the rocks beside the
wavy sea.
He strok'd the water from his beard & mourn'd
faint thro' the summer vales.

And Vala stood on the rocks of Tharmas & heard
his mournful voice:

"O Enion, my weary head is in the bed of death,
For weeds of death have wrap'd around my limbs
in the hoary deeps.
I sit in the place of shells & mourn, & thou art clos'd
in clouds.
When will the time of Clouds be past, & the dismal
night of Tharmas?
Arise, O Enion! Arise & smile upon my head
As thou dost smile upon the barren mountains and
they rejoice.   490
When wilt thou smile on Tharmas, O thou bringer
of golden day?
Arise, O Enion, arise, for Lo, I have calm'd my
seas."

So saying, his faint head he laid upon the Oozy
rock,
And darkness cover'd all the deep: the light of
Enion faded
Like a faint flame quivering upon the surface of
the darkness.

Then Vala lifted up her hands to heaven to call on
Enion.
She call'd, but none could answer her & the eccho
of her voice return'd:

"Where is the voice of God that call'd me from the
silent dew?
Where is the Lord of Vala? dost thou hide in clefts
of the rock?

482. Tharmas: another of the Four Zoas, perhaps best
described as instinct. Enion is his female emanation.

Why shouldst thou hide thyself from Vala, from
   the soul that wanders desolate?"   500

She ceas'd, & light beamed round her like the glory
   of the morning,
And she arose out of the river & girded her golden
   girdle.
And now her feet step on the grassy bosom of the
   ground
Among her flocks, & she turn'd her eyes toward her
   pleasant house
And saw in the door way beneath the trees two
   little children playing.
She drew near to her house & her flocks follow'd
   her footsteps.
The children clung around her knees, she embrac'd
   them & wept over them.

"Thou, little Boy, art Tharmas, & thou, bright Girl,
   Enion.
How are ye thus renw'd & brought into the Gar-
   dens of Vala?"

She embrac'd them in tears, till the sun descended
   the western hills,   510
And then she enter'd her bright house, leading her
   mighty children.
And when night came, the flocks laid round the
   house beneath the trees.
She laid the children on the beds which she saw
   prepar'd in the house,
Then last, herself laid down & clos'd her Eyelids in
   soft slumbers.

And in the morning, when the sun arose in the
   crystal sky,
Vala awoke & call'd the children from their gentle
   slumbers:

   "Awake, O Enion, awake & let thine innocent
   Eyes
Enlighten all the Crystal house of Vala! awake!
   awake!
Awake, Tharmas! awake, awake thou child of dewy
   tears.
Open the orbs of thy blue eyes & smile upon my
   gardens."   520

The Children woke & smil'd on Vala; she kneel'd
   by the golden couch,
She pres'd them to her bosom & her pearly tears
   drop'd down.

"O my sweet Children! Enion, let Tharmas kiss thy
   Cheek.
Why dost thou turn thyself away from his sweet
   wat'ry eyes?
Tharmas, henceforth in Vala's bosom thou shalt
   find sweet peace.
O bless the lovely eyes of Tharmas & the Eyes of
   Enion!"

They rose; they went out wand'ring, sometimes
   together, sometimes alone
"Why weep'st thou, Tharmas, Child of tears, in the
   bright house of joy?
Doth Enion avoid the sight of thy blue heavenly
   Eyes?
And dost thou wander with my lambs & wet their
   innocent faces   530
With thy bright tears because the steps of Enion
   are in the gardens?
Arise, sweet boy, & let us follow the path of Enion."

So saying, they went down into the garden among
   the fruits.
And Enion sang among the flowers that grew
   among the trees,
And Vala said: "Go, Tharmas; weep not. Go to
   Enion."

He said: "O Vala, I am sick, & all this garden of
   Pleasure
Swims like a dream before my eyes; but the sweet
   smelling fruit
Revives me to new deaths. I fade, even as a water
   lilly
In the sun's heat, till in the night on the couch of
   Enion
I drink new life & feel the breath of sleeping
   Enion.   540
But in the morning she arises to avoid my Eyes,
Then my loins fade & in the house I sit me down
   & weep."

"Chear up thy Countenance, bright boy, & go to
   Enion.
Tell her that Vala waits her in the shadows of her
   garden."

He went with timid steps, & Enion, like the ruddy
   morn
When infant spring appears in swelling buds &
   opening flowers,

Behind her Veil withdraws; so Enion turn'd her
  modest head.

But Tharmas spoke: "Vala seeks thee, sweet Enion,
  in the shades.
Follow the steps of Tharmas, O thou brightness of
  the gardens."
He took her hand reluctant; she follow'd in infant
  doubts.   550
Thus in Eternal Childhood, straying among Vala's
  flocks
In infant sorrow & joy alternate, Enion & Tharmas
  play'd
Round Vala in the Gardens of Vala & by her river's
  margin.
They are the shadows of Tharmas & of Enion in
  Vala's world.

And the sleepers who rested from their harvest
  work beheld these visions.
Thus were the sleepers entertain'd upon the
  Couches of Beulah.

When Luvah & Vala were clos'd up in their world
  of shadowy forms,
Darkness was all beneath the heavens: only a little
  light
Such as glows out from sleeping spirits, appear'd
  in the deeps beneath.
As when the wind sweeps over a corn field, the
  noise of souls   560
Thro' all the immense, borne down by Clouds
  swagging in autumnal heat,
Mutt'ring along from heaven to heaven, hoarse roll
  the human forms
Beneath thick clouds, dreadful lightnings burst &
  thunders roll,
Down pour the torrent floods of heaven on all the
  human harvest.
Then Urizen, sitting at his repose on beds in the
  bright South,
Cried, "Times are Ended!" he exulted; he arose in
  joy; he exulted;
He pour'd his light, & all his sons & daughters
  pour'd their light
To exhale the spirits of Luvah & Vala thro' the
  atmosphere.
And Luvah & Vala saw the Light; their spirits were
  exhal'd
In all their ancient innocence; the floods depart;
  the clouds   570

Dissipate or sink into the Seas of Tharmas. Luvah
  sat
Above on the bright heavens in peace; the Spirits
  of Men beneath
Cried out to be deliver'd, & the spirit of Luvah
  wept
Over the human harvest & over Vala, the sweet
  wanderer.
In pain the human harvest wav'd, in horrible
  groans of woe.
The Universal Groan went up; the Eternal Man
  was darken'd.

Then Urizen arose & took his sickle in his hand.
There is a brazen sickle, & a scythe of iron hid
Deep in the South, guarded by a few solitary stars.
This sickle Urizen took; the scythe his sons
  embrac'd   580
And went forth & began to reap; & all his joyful
  sons
Reap'd the wide Universe & bound in sheaves a
  wondrous harvest.
They took them into the wide barns with loud
  rejoicing & triumph
Of flute & harp & drum & trumpet, horn & clarion.

The feast was spread in the bright South, & the
  Regenerate Man
Sat at the feast rejoicing, & the wine of Eternity
Was serv'd round by the flames of Luvah all day &
  all the Night.
And when Morning began to dawn upon the distant
  hills,
A whirlwind rose up in the Center, & in the whirl-
  wind a shriek,
And in the shriek a rattling of bones & in the
  rattling of bones   590
A dolorous groan, & from the dolorous groan in
  tears
Rose Enion like a gentle light; & Enion spoke,
  saying:

"O Dreams of Death! the human form dissolving,
  companied
By beasts & worms & creeping things, & darkness
  & despair.
The clouds fall off from my wet brow, the dust
  from my cold limbs
Into the sea of Tharmas. Soon renew'd, a Golden
  Moth,

I shall cast off my death clothes & Embrace Tharmas
    again.
For Lo, the winter melted away upon the distant
    hills,
And all the black mould sings." She speaks to her
    infant race; her milk
Descends down on the sand; the thirsty sand drinks
    & rejoices   600
Wondering to behold the Emmet, the Grasshopper,
    the jointed worm.
The roots shoot thick thro' the solid rocks, bursting
    their way
They cry out in joys of existence; the broad stems
Rear on the mountains stem after stem; the scaly
    newt creeps
From the stone, & the armed fly springs from the
    rocky crevice,
The spider, The bat burst from the harden'd slime,
    crying
To one another: "What are we, & whence is our
    joy & delight?
Lo, the little moss begins to spring, & the tender
    weed
Creeps round our secret nest." Flocks brighten the
    Mountains,
Herds throng up the Valley, wild beasts fill the
    forests.   610

Joy thrill'd thro' all the Furious forms of Tharmas
    humanizing.
Mild he Embrac'd her whom he sought; he rais'd
    her thro' the heavens,
Sounding his trumpet to awake the dead, on high
    he soar'd
Over the ruin'd worlds, the smoking tomb of the
    Eternal Prophet.

The Eternal Man arose. He welcom'd them to the
    Feast.
The feast was spread in the bright South, & the
    Eternal Man
Sat at the feast rejoicing, & the wine of Eternity
Was serv'd round by the flames of Luvah all day
    & all the night.

And Many Eternal Men sat at the golden feast to
    see
The female form now separate. They shudder'd at
    the horrible thing   620
Not born for the sport and amusement of Man, but
    born to drink up all his powers.

They wept to see their shadows; they said to one
    another: "This is Sin:
This is the Generative world"; they remember'd the
    days of old.

And One of the Eternals spoke. All was silent at
    the feast.

"Man is a Worm; wearied with joy, he seeks the
    caves of sleep
Among the Flowers of Beulah, in his selfish cold
    repose
Forsaking Brotherhood & Universal love, in selfish
    clay
Folding the pure wings of his mind, seeking the
    places dark
Abstracted from the roots of Science; then inclos'd
    around
In walls of Gold we cast him like a Seed into the
    Earth   630
Till times & spaces have pass'd over him; duly every
    morn
We visit him, covering him with a Veil the im-
    mortal seed;
With windows from the inclement sky we cover
    him, & with walls
And hearths protect the selfish terror, till divided
    all
In families we see our shadows born, & thence we
    know
That Man subsists by Brotherhood & Universal
    Love.
We fall on one another's necks, more closely we
    embrace.
Not for ourselves, but for the Eternal family we
    live.
Man liveth not by Self alone, but in his brother's
    face
Each shall behold the Eternal Father & love & joy
    abound."   640

So spoke the Eternal at the Feast; they embrac'd
    the New born Man,
Calling him Brother, image of the Eternal Father;
    they sat down
At the immortal tables, sounding loud their instru-
    ments of joy,

635–37. **In . . . embrace:** Blake in a marginal comment
connects these lines with St. Paul to the Ephesians
3:10.

Calling the Morning into Beulah; the Eternal Man
    rejoic'd.

When Morning dawn'd, The Eternals rose to labour
    at the Vintage.
Beneath they saw their sons & daughters, wond'ring
    inconcievable
At the dark myriads in shadows in the worlds
    beneath.

The morning dawn'd. Urizen rose, & in his hand
    the Flail
Sounds on the Floor, heard terrible by all beneath
    the heavens.
Dismal loud redounding, the nether floor shakes
    with the sound,   650
And all Nations were threshed out, & the stars
    thresh'd from their husks.

Then Tharmas took the Winnowing fan; the win-
    nowing wind furious
Above, veer'd round by violent whirlwind, driven
    west & south,
Tossed the Nations like chaff into the seas of
    Tharmas.

"O Mystery," Fierce Tharmas cries, "Behold thy
    end is come!
Art thou she that made the nations drunk with the
    cup of Religion?
Go down, ye Kings & Councellors & Giant Warriors,
Go down into the depths, go down & hide your-
    selves beneath,
Go down with horse & Chariots & Trumpets of
    hoarse war.

    "Lo, how the Pomp and Mystery goes down into
    the Caves!   660
Her great men howl & throw the dust, & rend their
    hoary hair.
Her delicate women & children shriek upon the
    bitter wind,
Spoil'd of their beauty, their hair rent & their skin
    shrivel'd up.

"Lo, darkness covers the long pomp of banners on
    the wind,
And black horses & armed men & miserable bound
    captives.
Where shall the graves recieve them all, & where
    shall be their place?
And who shall mourn for Mystery who never loos'd
    her Captives?

"Let the slave, grinding at the mill, run out into
    the field;
Let him look up into the heavens & laugh in the
    bright air.
Let the inchained soul, shut up in darkness & in
    sighing,   670
Whose face has never seen a smile in thirty weary
    years,
Rise & look out: his chains are loose, his dungeon
    doors are open;
And let his wife & children return from the opres-
    sor's scourge.

"They look behind at every step & believe it is a
    dream.
Are these the slaves that groan'd along the streets
    of Mystery?
Where are your bonds & task masters? are these the
    prisoners?
Where are your chains? where are your tears? why
    do you look around?
If you are thirsty, there is the river: go, bathe your
    parched limbs,
The good of all the Land is before you, for Mystery
    is no more."

Then All the Slaves from every Earth in the wide
    Universe   680
Sing a New Song, drowning confusion in its happy
    notes,
While the flail of Urizen sounded loud, & the
    winnowing wind of Tharmas
So loud, so clear in the wide heavens; & the song
    that they sung was this,
Composed by an African Black from the little Earth
    of Sotha:

"Aha! Aha! how came I here so soon in my sweet
    native land?
How came I here? Methinks I am as I was in my
    youth
When in my father's house I sat & heard his
    chearing voice.
Methinks I see his flocks & herds & feel my limbs
    renew'd,
And Lo, my Brethren in their tents, & their little
    ones around them!"

The song arose to the Golden feast; the Eternal
    Man rejoic'd.   690
Then the Eternal Man said: "Luvah, the Vintage
    is ripe: arise!

The sons of Urizen shall gather the vintage with
   sharp hooks,
And all thy sons, O Luvah! bear away the families
   of Earth.
I hear the flail of Urizen; his barns are full; no room
Remains, & in the Vineyards stand the abounding
   sheaves beneath
The falling Grapes that odorous burst upon the
   winds. Arise
My flocks & herds, trample the Corn! my cattle,
   browze upon
The ripe Clusters! The shepherds shout for Luvah,
   prince of Love.
Let the Bulls of Luvah tread the Corn & draw the
   loaded waggon
Into the Barn while children glean the Ears around
   the door.   700
Then shall they lift their innocent hands & stroke
   his furious nose,
And he shall lick the little girl's white neck & on
   her head
Scatter the perfume of his breath; while from his
   mountains high
The lion of terror shall come down, & bending his
   bright mane
And crouching at their side, shall eat from the
   curl'd boy's white lap
His golden food, and in the evening sleep before
   the door."

"Attempting to be more than Man We become
   less," said Luvah
As he arose from the bright feast, drunk with the
   wine of ages.
His crown of thorns fell from his head, he hung his
   living Lyre
Behind the seat of the Eternal Man & took his
   way   710
Sounding the Song of Los, descending to the
   Vineyards bright.
His sons, arising from the feast with golden baskets,
   follow,
A fiery train, as when the Sun sings in the ripe
   vineyards.
Then Luvah stood before the Wine press; all his
   fiery sons
Brought up the loaded Waggons with shoutings;
   ramping tygers play
In the jingling traces; furious lions sound the song
   of joy

To the golden wheels circling upon the pavement
   of heaven, & all
The Villages of Luvah ring; the golden tiles of the
   villages
Reply to violins & tabors, to the pipe, flute, lyre &
   cymbal.
Then fell the Legions of Mystery in madd'ning
   confusion,   720
Down, down thro' the immense, with outcry, fury
   & despair,
Into the wine presses of Luvah; howling fell the
   clusters
Of human families thro' the deep; the wine presses
   were fill'd;
The blood of life flow'd plentiful. Odors of life arose
All round the heavenly arches, & the Odors rose
   singing this song:

"O terrible wine presses of Luvah! O caverns of
   the Grave!
How lovely the delights of those risen again from
   death!
O trembling joy! excess of joy is like Excess of
   grief."

So sang the Human Odors round the wine presses
   of Luvah;

But in the Wine presses is wailing, terror & de-
   spair.   730
Forsaken of their Elements they vanish & are no
   more,
No more but a desire of Being, a distracted,
   ravening desire,
Desiring like the hungry worm & like the gaping
   grave.
They plunge into the Elements; the Elements cast
   them forth
Or else consume their shadowy semblance. Yet
   they, obstinate
Tho' pained to distraction, cry, "O let us Exist! for
This dreadful Non Existence is worse than pains
   of Eternal Birth:
Eternal death who can Endure? let us consume in
   fires,
In waters stifling, or in air corroding, or in earth
   shut up.
The Pangs of Eternal birth are better than the
   Pangs of Eternal death."   740

How red the sons & daughters of Luvah! how they
   tread the Grapes!

Laughing & shouting, drunk with odors, many fall
    o'erwearied:
Drown'd in the wine is many a youth & maiden;
    those around
Lay them on skins of tygers or the spotted Leopard
    or wild Ass
Till they revive, or bury them in cool Grots making
    lamentation.

But in the Wine Presses the Human Grapes sing
    not nor dance,
They howl & writhe in shoals of torment, in fierce
    flames consuming,
In chains of iron & in dungeons circled with cease-
    less fires,
In pits & dens & shades of death, in shapes of
    torment & woe;
The Plates, the Screws & Racks & Saws & cords &
    fires & floods,   750
The cruel joy of Luvah's daughters, lacerating with
    knives
And whips their Victims, & the deadly sport of
    Luvah's sons.
Timbrels & Violins sport round the Wine Presses.
    The little Seed,
The sportive root, the Earthworm, the small beetle,
    the wise Emmet,
Dance round the Wine Presses of Luvah; the
    Centipede is there,
The ground Spider with many eyes, the Mole
    clothed in Velvet,
The Earwig arm'd, the tender maggot, emblem of
    Immortality;
The slow slug, the grasshopper that sings & laughs
    & drinks:
The winter comes; he folds his slender bones with-
    out a murmur.
There is the Nettle that stings with soft down; &
    there   760
The indignant Thistle whose bitterness is bred in
    his milk
And who lives on the contempt of his neighbour;
    there all the idle weeds,
That creep about the obscure places, shew their
    various limbs
Naked in all their beauty, dancing round the Wine
    Presses.
They dance around the dying & they drink the
    howl & groan;

They catch the shrieks in cups of gold; they hand
    them to one another.
These are the sports of love & these the sweet
    delights of amorous play:
Tears of the grape, the death sweat of the Cluster,
    the last sigh
Of the mild youth who listens to the luring songs
    of Luvah.
The Eternal Man darken'd with sorrow & a wintry
    mantle   770
Cover'd the Hills. He said, "O Tharmas, rise! &
    O Urthona!"
Then Tharmas & Urthona rose from the Golden
    feast, satiated
With Mirth & Joy: Urthona, limping from his fall,
    on Tharmas lean'd,
In his right hand his hammer. Tharmas held his
    shepherd's crook
Beset with gold, gold were the ornaments form'd
    by sons of Urizen.
Then Enion & Ahania & Vala & the wife of dark
    Urthona
Rose from the feast, in joy ascending to their
    Golden Looms.
There the wing'd shuttle sang, the spindle & the
    distaff & the Reel
Rang sweet the praise of industry. Thro' all the
    golden rooms
Heaven rang with winged Exultation. All beneath
    howl'd loud;   780
With tenfold rout & desolation roar'd the Chasms
    beneath
Where the wide woof flow'd down & where the
    Nations are gather'd together.

Tharmas went down to the Wine presses & beheld
    the sons & daughters
Of Luvah quite exhausted with the labour & quite
    fill'd
With new wine, that they began to torment one
    another and to tread
The weak. Luvah & Vala slept on the floor, o'er-
    wearied.
Urthona call'd his sons around him: Tharmas call'd
    his sons
Numerous; they took the wine, they separated the
    Lees,
And Luvah was put for dung on the ground by the
    Sons of Tharmas & Urthona.

They formed heavens of sweetest woods, of gold &
  silver & ivory,   790
Of glass & precious stones. They loaded all the
  waggons of heaven
And took away the wine of ages with solemn songs
  & joy.

Luvah & Vala woke, & all the sons & daughters of
  Luvah
Awoke; they wept to one another & they reascended
To the Eternal Man in woe: he cast them wailing
  into
The world of shadows, thro' the air, till winter is
  over & gone;
But the Human Wine stood wondering; in all their
  delightful Expanses
The elements subside; the heavens roll'd on with
  vocal harmony.

Then Los, who is Urthona, rose in all his regenerate
  power.
The Sea that roll'd & foam'd with darkness & the
  shadows of death   800
Vomited out & gave up all; the floods lift up their
  hands
Singing & shouting to the Man; they bow their
  hoary heads
And murmuring in their channels flow & circle
  round his feet.

Then Dark Urthona took the Corn out of the Stores
  of Urizen;
He ground it in his rumbling Mills. Terrible the
  distress
Of all the Nations of Earth, ground in the Mills of
  Urthona.
In his hand Tharmas takes the Storms: he turns the
  whirlwind loose
Upon the wheels; the stormy seas howl at his dread
  command
And Eddying fierce rejoice in the fierce agitation of
  the wheels
Of Dark Urthona. Thunders, Earthquakes, Fires,
  Water floods,   810
Rejoice to one another; loud their voices shake the
  Abyss,
Their dread forms tending the dire mills. The grey
  hoar frost was there,
And his pale wife, the aged Snow, they watch over
  the fires,

They build the Ovens of Urthona. Nature in darkness groans
And Men are bound to sullen contemplation in the
  night:
Restless they turn on beds of sorrow; in their inmost
  brain
Feeling the crushing Wheels, they rise, they write
  the bitter words
Of Stern Philosophy & knead the bread of knowledge with tears & groans.

Such are the works of Dark Urthona. Tharmas
  sifted the corn.
Urthona made the Bread of Ages, & he placed
  it,   820
In golden & in silver baskets, in heavens of precious
  stone
And then took his repose in Winter, in the night
  of Time.

The Sun has left his blackness & has found a
  fresher morning,
And the mild moon rejoices in the clear & cloudless
  night,
And Man walks forth from midst of the fires: the
  evil is all consum'd.
His eyes behold the Angelic spheres arising night
  & day;
The stars consum'd like a lamp blown out, & in
  their stead, behold
The Expanding Eyes of Man behold the depths of
  wondrous worlds!
One Earth, one sea beneath; nor Erring Globes
  wander, but Stars
Of fire rise up nightly from the Ocean; & one
  Sun   830
Each morning, like a New born Man, issues with
  songs & joy
Calling the Plowman to his Labour & the Shepherd
  to his rest.
He walks upon the Eternal Mountains, raising his
  heavenly voice,
Conversing with the Animal forms of wisdom night
  & day,
That, risen from the Sea of fire, renew'd walk o'er
  the Earth;
For Tharmas brought his flocks upon the hills, & in
  the Vales
Around the Eternal Man's bright tent, the little
  Children play

Among the wooly flocks. The hammer of Urthona
    sounds
In the deep caves beneath; his limbs renew'd, his
    Lions roar
Around the Furnaces & in Evening sport upon the
    plains.   840
They raise their faces from the Earth, conversing
    with the Man:

"How is it we have walk'd thro' fires & yet are not
    consum'd?
How is it that all things are chang'd, even as in
    ancient times?"

The Sun arises from his dewy bed, & the fresh airs
Play in his smiling beams giving the seeds of life
    to grow,
And the fresh Earth beams forth ten thousand
    thousand springs of life.
Urthona is arisen in his strength, no longer now
Divided from Enitharmon, no longer the Spectre
    Los.
Where is the Spectre of Prophecy? where the
    delusive Phantom?
Departed: & Urthona rises from the ruinous
    Walls   850
In all his ancient strength to form the golden
    armour of science
For intellectual War. The war of swords departed
    now,
The dark Religions are departed & sweet Science
    reigns.

END OF THE DREAM

c. 1797–1804   1893

MOCK ON, MOCK ON, VOLTAIRE,
ROUSSEAU

Mock on, Mock on, Voltaire, Rousseau:
Mock on, Mock on: 'tis all in vain!
You throw the sand against the wind,
And the wind blows it back again.

And every sand becomes a Gem
Reflected in the beams divine;

MOCK ON, MOCK ON, VOLTAIRE, ROUSSEAU. 1. Voltaire,
Rousseau: materialistic philosophers, and, for Blake,
enemies of vision.

Blown back they blind the mocking Eye,
But still in Israel's paths they shine.

The Atoms of Democritus
And Newton's Particles of light   10
Are sands upon the Red sea shore,
Where Israel's tents do shine so bright.

1800–1803   1863

THE MENTAL TRAVELLER

I travel'd thro' a Land of Men,
A Land of Men & Women too,
And heard & saw such dreadful things
As cold Earth wanderers never knew.

For there the Babe is born in joy
That was begotten in dire woe;
Just as we Reap in joy the fruit
Which we in bitter tears did sow.

And if the Babe is born a Boy
He's given to a Woman Old,   10
Who nails him down upon a rock,
Catches his shrieks in cups of gold.

She binds iron thorns around his head,
She pierces both his hands & feet,
She cuts his heart out at his side
To make it feel both cold & heat.

Her fingers number every Nerve,
Just as a Miser counts his gold;
She lives upon his shrieks & cries,
And she grows young as he grows old.   20

Till he becomes a bleeding youth,
And she becomes a Virgin bright;
Then he rends up his Manacles
And binds her down for his delight.

He plants himself in all her Nerves,
Just as a Husbandman his mould;
And she becomes his dwelling place
And Garden fruitful seventy fold.

An aged Shadow, soon he fades,
Wand'ring round an Earthly Cot,   30

9. Democritus: Greek philospher who argued that
everything was eventually reducible to matter. 10.
Newton: Sir Isaac Newton, another villain in Blake's
drama, advanced a materialistic theory of light.

Full filled all with gems & gold
Which he by industry had got.

And these are the gems of the Human Soul,
The rubies & pearls of a lovesick eye,
The countless gold of the akeing heart,
The martyr's groan & the lover's sigh.

They are his meat, they are his drink;
He feeds the Beggar & the Poor
And the wayfaring Traveller:
For ever open is his door.   40

His grief is their eternal joy;
They make the roofs & walls to ring;
Till from the fire on the hearth
A little Female Babe does spring.

And she is all of solid fire
And gems & gold, that none his hand
Dares stretch to touch her Baby form,
Or wrap her in his swaddling-band.

But She comes to the Man she loves,
If young or old, or rich or poor;   50
They soon drive out the aged Host,
A Beggar at another's door.

He wanders weeping far away,
Until, some other take him in;
Oft blind & age-bent, sore distrest,
Until he can a Maiden win.

And to allay his freezing Age
The Poor Man takes her in his arms;
The Cottage fades before his sight,
The Garden & its lovely Charms.   60

The Guests are scatter'd thro' the land,
For the Eye altering alters all;
The Senses roll themselves in fear,
And the flat Earth becomes a Ball;

The stars, sun, Moon, all shrink away,
A desert vast without a bound,
And nothing left to eat or drink,
And a dark desert all around.

The honey of her Infant lips,
The bread & wine of her sweet smile,   70
The wild game of her roving Eye,
Does him to Infancy beguile;

For as he eats & drinks he grows
Younger & younger every day;

And on the desart wild they both
Wander in terror & dismay

Like the wild Stag she flees away,
Her fear plants many a thicket wild;
While he pursues her night & day,
By various arts of Love beguil'd,   80

By various arts of Love & Hate,
Till the wide desert planted o'er
With Labyrinths of wayward Love,
Where roam the Lion, Wolf & Boar,

Till he becomes a wayward Babe,
And she a weeping Woman Old.
Then many a Lover wanders here;
The Sun & Stars are nearer roll'd.

The trees bring forth sweet Extacy
To all who in the desert roam;   90
Till many a City there is Built,
And many a pleasant Shepherd's home.

But when they find the frowning Babe,
Terror strikes thro' the region wide:
They cry "The Babe! the Babe is Born!"
And flee away on Every side.

For who dare touch the frowning form,
His arm is wither'd to its root;
Lions, Boars, Wolves, all howling flee,
And every Tree does shed its fruit.   100

And none can touch that frowning form,
Except it be a Woman Old;
She nails him down upon the Rock,
And all is done as I have told.
1803   1863

THE CRYSTAL CABINET

The Maiden caught me in the Wild,
Where I was dancing merrily;
She put me into her Cabinet
And Lock'd me up with a golden Key.

This Cabinet is form'd of Gold
And Pearl & Crystal shining bright,
And within it opens into a World
And a little lovely Moony Night.

Another England there I saw,
Another London with its Tower,   10
Another Thames & other Hills,
And another pleasant Surrey Bower,

Another Maiden like herself,
Translucent, lovely, shining clear,
Threefold each in the other clos'd—
O, what a pleasant trembling fear!

O, what a smile! a threefold Smile
Fill'd me, that like a flame I burn'd;

I bent to Kiss the lovely Maid,
And found a Threefold Kiss return'd.   20

I strove to sieze the inmost Form
With ardor fierce & hands of flame,
But burst the Crystal Cabinet,
And like a Weeping Babe became—

A weeping Babe upon the wild,
And Weeping Woman pale reclin'd,
And in the outward air again
I fill'd with woes the passing Wind.

1803   *1863*

William Wordsworth

1770-1850

William Wordsworth is regarded by most students as the father and high-priest of English Romanticism. Less a pure visionary and inspired missionary than Blake, he nevertheless set down in his famous "Preface" to the second edition of the *Lyrical Ballads* of 1800 and in various prefaces and appendices to later editions a program for a new poetry that included quite different concepts of the poet and his role in society, his subject matter, his language, and his imagery. The "Preface," while not a revolutionary document, does even today have the ring of a manifesto as it gathers together many of the developing ideas of the middle and later eighteenth century and gives them a focus and a form that are remarkable for their freshness and originality. It was around this document that many of the new writers gathered, and in its words they found a source of confidence for many of their artistic ambitions and plans.

Wordsworth did not have impressive beginnings. Born at Cockermouth, Cumberland, on April 7, 1770, one of five children, he grew up at the edge of the still beauteous Lake District of Northwest England, in the midst of the lakes, streams, forests, and mountains that were to be so central in the shaping of the child and the man. It was here, as so many beautiful and haunting sections of *The Prelude* attest, that he first learned the many faces of Nature, its beauty and joy as well as its power and fear, first felt its discipline and mastery, first experienced his love for the solitude and solace it provided against the noisy turbulence of urban life. How much more touching and revealing the sentiments of his great autobiographical poem than any biographer's recreation. Everywhere there is a sense of wonder as he writes of his origins: "Fair seed-time had my soul, and I grew up/

Fostered alike by beauty and by fear: / Much favored in my birth-place"; of the mysterious moment of youthful spiritual insight when, while trapping a woodcock, "I heard among the solitary hills / Low breathings coming after me, and sounds / Of undistinguishable motion, steps / Almost as silent as the turf they trod"; of the brilliance of an autumn day "With silver clouds, and sunshine on the grass, / And in the sheltered and the sheltering grove / A perfect stillness."

After the death of his mother in 1778, Wordsworth was sent to Hawkshead Grammar School and remained there until 1787 (his father died in 1783) studying poetry, mathematics, science, and classics. A year later he found himself in the great world of Cambridge at St. John's College, a world which he tolerated but did not like, an academic institution whose routine and dutiful students did little to engage him, but which provided him with a setting and an atmosphere in which he could roam at will and read at leisure. And roam and read he did, graduating from the university in 1791 with a minimal passing grade that hardly revealed the breadth of his self-education and the promise of his first poetry. Once again so many sections of *The Prelude* vividly capture his mood at the time, the feeling of an eighteen year old that academic success, eagerly sought by "loyal students," "hardy rescusants," and "honest dunces," was "little sought by me, / And little won." His was "A feeling that I was not for that hour, / Nor for that place." He recalls how often he would wander through the adjoining fields alone, searching the earth and sky for some deeper meaning. His rewards were inner and spiritual: "To every natural form, rock, fruit or flower, / Even the looser stones that cover the highway, / I gave a moral life." His ultimate triumph transcended any worldly prize: "I had a world about me—'t was my own; / I made it, for it only lived to me, / And to the God who sees into the heart."

Wordsworth left Cambridge with few commitments, but those few seemed most significant. One was his abiding love for and dedication to Nature, his refuge and source of hope whether in the daily routine of his native England or on the summer walking-tours he had taken in France, Switzerland, and Italy while an undergraduate. The other was a deep and growing dedication to the calling of poetry despite the lack of promise in his earliest efforts. In November of 1791, however, his life was touched in dramatic ways. He left for France with the hope of perfecting his French so that he could become a tutor. France, of course, was at that time on fire with Revolution and with radical ardor. At Blois he met Captain Michael Beaupuy and was for a time fully converted to the course of revolt and reform, a cause he was later to detest because of its growing violence and power politics. At Orleans he fell in love with Annette Vallon and fathered a child Caroline; although marriage was never possible and the liaison brought sharp response from his family, the love affair was to be a notable event in his life.

His state of mind on returning to England in December of 1792 was, to put it mildly, depressed. Still sympathetic to the French in the war with England, out of favor with his relatives, in dire financial straits, he moved from place to place, visiting those who would have him, and spending several memorable weeks in the Lake District with his beloved sister Dorothy, his mainstay and source of his slow recovery of confidence and happiness. Indeed, Dorothy's famous *Journals,* with their rich sense of natural beauty and of the poet's many encounters with it, were a great source of inspiration for William and are today a treasury of information about Wordsworth and the Lake poets. Then came a stroke of good fortune; an inheritance of 900 £ on the death of his friend Raisley Calvert provided him with a sense of security, and he and Dorothy settled at Racedown, in Dorsetshire. Another happy turn of events was his meeting with Coleridge at Racedown where Mary Hutchinson, his wife-to-be, was also visiting. That meeting, and the friendship that followed, was to be one of mutual inspiration as both poets entered upon conversations that were to trigger some of the greatest poetry of the age. The Wordsworths moved to Alfoxden in Nether Stowey, near Bristol, where Coleridge lived, and out of many conversations between the poets during the next year came the plan for the great *Lyrical Ballads* of 1798, the pioneering volume of English Romantic poetry.

After the publication of the *Lyrical Ballads,* the Wordsworths and Coleridge took their celebrated trip to Germany, settling in Goslar, where some of Wordsworth's great early poems were produced, especially sections of *The Prelude.* Dorothy and William returned to England in May of 1799, toured the Lake District with Coleridge, and settled in Dove Cottage, Grasmere where they lived until 1808. In 1802 Wordsworth married Mary Hutchinson, and the couple eventually had five children. In 1805 he became Distributor of Stamps for Westmorland. These were productive years for Wordsworth, the years in which he completed *The Prelude* and the memorable two volumes of 1807 which include so many of his best poems. These were also the years in which the tragic drowning of his brother John was to take a heavy toll on the poet's spirit and was, at least in part, to bring on the depression and the search for more objective values that characterize much of the later poetry. Even a poem as early as "Elegiac Stanzas Suggested By a Picture of Peele Castle, In a Storm, Painted By Sir George Beaumont," written in 1805 and published in the 1807 volumes, clearly expresses his doubts about his earlier optimism and faith in Nature's benevolence. Beaumont, a friend and patron of Wordsworth, had painted a turbulent scene that at first view troubled Wordsworth's memories of a youthful vacation-spot where everything seemed tranquil and untouched by sadness. The closing lines of the poem serve as a climax to his growing realization of his own naiveté and the truth of Beaumont's vision. Those lines capture his feelings about the past and the future most dramatically:

> Farewell, farewell the heart that lives alone,
> Housed in a dream, at distance from the Kind!
> Such happiness, wherever it be known,
> Is to be pitied; for 'tis surely blind.
>
> But welcome fortitude, and patient cheer,
> And frequent sights of what is to be borne!
> Such sights, or worse, as are before me here:—
> Not without hope we suffer and we mourn.

Wordsworth did travel a good deal during these and the later years—to France with Dorothy to visit Annette and Caroline and to arrange for their support; to Scotland with Dorothy and Coleridge in 1803; to the Continent with Mary and Dorothy in 1820; to Ireland in 1829; to France and Italy in 1837—but for all intents and purposes, he lived the rest of his life in his beloved Lake District, moving only from Dove Cottage to Allan Bank and to the Rectory in Grasmere, and finally settling at Rydal Mount in 1813. He quarrelled with Coleridge in 1810, and, although reconciled, the two were never really close again.

The post–1810 years were not ones of great poetic creativity. It has become almost a commonplace of Wordsworth criticism that most of the great work was completed earlier, that the last forty years were an "anti-climax" that saw the publication of volumes like *The Excursion* in 1814; *The River Duddon,* a series of sonnets, in 1820; the *Ecclesiastical Sonnets* of 1822; *Yarrow Revisited, and Other Poems* in 1835; and *Poems, Chiefly of Early and Late Years* in 1842. He received an honorary degree from Oxford in 1839, received a Civil List pension of 300£ yearly in 1842, was appointed Poet Laureate in 1843; but these did little for his poetic spirit. Coleridge's brilliant criticism in *Biographia Literaria* made him well known, but his vanity and conservatism, the growing solitude of his life, the illness of Dorothy, and the death of Dora, his daughter, which brought deep sadness, all did little to make him a popular figure. His last years were lonely; he seemed like a man whose predictions about the world being too much with us had come all too true and who could not or would not keep up with the times. He died on April 23, 1850, the most long-lived of the major Romantics, and he lies buried in the beautiful Grasmere churchyard.

Wordsworth's "Preface" to the second edition of the *Lyrical Ballads* in 1800, already cited as a major Romantic manifesto, provides interesting and fruitful ways of talking about his poetry, especially about the work of the so-called Golden Decade. It is true that the "Preface" is remembered for its philosophy of "humble and rustic life," written in "a selection of language of real men." These are, unquestionably, important aspects of the document, significant characteristics of Wordsworth's art. However, to isolate them as the essence of the new program is to lose touch with the larger context of his argument in favor of greater natural-ness in the settings, language, and feelings of poetry, of greater spontaneity, of a more intense way of seeing and writing about experience. Wordsworth addresses himself in the "Preface" to the sterility of taste in the audiences of his time, to the lack of strong emotion, to the artificial diction and imagery that seems to come from a handbook of poetry instead of from direct observation of nature and ex-perience. He will, he contends, "bring my language near to the language of men," will avoid "falsehood of description," will focus on people who live close to the soil because "in that condition, the essential passions of the heart find a better soil in which they can attain maturity," because in such people the "elementary feelings co-exist in a state of greater simplicity, and, consequently, may be more accurately contemplated, and more forcibly communicated"; because "in that condition the passions of men are incorporated with the beautiful and permanent forms of Nature." Yet this purpose underlies his larger attempt to broaden the base of poetry, to make it "the spontaneous overflow of powerful feelings" which "takes its origin from emotion recollected in tranquillity," his desire to stress that in his poems "the feeling therein developed gives importance to the action and situation, and not the action and situation to the feeling." It underlies his developing concept of imagination, not as a picture-making faculty, a mere adjunct of memory, but as a power "of higher import, denoting operations of the mind upon those objects, and processes of creation or of composition, governed by certain fixed laws." It underlies his pioneering concern, a concern shared by all the Romantics, to liberate poetry from ancillary status as a helpmate to philosophy or religion, from its role as a stepsister of the hard knowledge of Science, one a source of pleasant recreation and entertainment, the other the purveyor of truth. His contrast of Poetry and Science is truly a memorable *apologia* for his profession:

> The knowledge both of the Poet and the Man of science is pleasure; but the knowledge of the one cleaves to us as a necessary part of our existence, our natural and unalienable inheritance; the other as a personal and individual acquisition, slow to come to us, and by no habitual and direct sympathy connecting us with our fellow-beings. The Man of science seeks truth as a remote and unknown benefactor; he cherishes it and loves it in his solitude: the Poet, singing a song in which all human beings join with him, rejoices in the presence of truth as our visible friend and hourly companion.

Wordsworth's poetry manifests the narrower and broader concerns of his "Preface." His enthusiasm for and devotion to ordinary experience did mar much of the poetry of the *Lyrical Ballads*. The crudity of language and situation, the redundancy, the melodrama, the preachiness of many of the pieces seem to stem from an excessive devotion to ordinary experience, to journalistic accuracy, almost as if Wordsworth does not yet trust audiences to understand his purposes. Coleridge, always Wordsworth's ardent supporter and perceptive critic, puts it well when he complains in the *Biographia Literaria* of "a laborious minuteness and fidelity in the representation of objects, and their positions, as they appeared to the poet himself," of "the insertion of accidental circumstances, in order to the full explanation of his living characters, their dispositions and actions; which circumstances might be necessary to establish the probability of a statement in real life, where nothing is taken for granted by the hearer; but appear superfluous in poetry, where the reader is willing to believe for his own sake." When Wordsworth fails, he does so dramatically. One remembers painfully the preachy drama of "Goody Blake and Harry Gill," Goody the old dame gathering wood from the hedges of the wealthy landowner, Harry Gill, to warm her cottage on bitter cold winter nights. Caught in the act by Harry, she prays that he may never again be warm, and, try as he may, he cannot escape the curse, "He never will be warm again."

> No word to any man he utters,
> A-bed or up, to young or old;
> But ever to himself he mutters,
> "Poor Harry Gill is very cold."

> A-bed or up, by night or day;
> His teeth, they chatter, chatter still.
> Now think, ye farmers all, I pray,
> Of Goody Blake and Harry Gill.

Or there is the tale of Simon Lee, a dashing huntsman for thirty-five years, but now the sole survivor of the Hall of Ivor, alone with his wife and reduced to digging up tree stumps, but "the more he works, the more / Do his weak ankles swell." There are the anguished cries of Martha Ray, abandoned with child by her lover Stephen Hill, and now sitting beside "The Thorn" and a mossy grave, "Oh misery! Oh misery! / Oh woe is me! oh misery!"

Not all the ballads are so bathetic, however. In poems like "To My Sister"—"It is the first mild day of March: / Each minute sweeter than before, / The redbreast sings from the tall larch / That stands beside our door"—or "We Are Seven" or "Michael" or "Her Eyes are Wild," he becomes less the journalist, less the ventriloquist uttering his own philosophical sentiments through the mouths of unlikely spokesmen and more the partner of natural scenes, the dramatic recorder of spiritual experiences of those who live close to nature and honest living and express their feelings directly and naturally.

The great triumph of the *Lyrical Ballads* is unquestionably "Tintern Abbey," Wordsworth's first great poem, the beginning of the ten years of creative genius, the articulation of the great themes that pervade his best poetry. The manner of this new kind of poem, the greater romantic lyric, the dramatic monologue, has already been described. The themes stand out sharply as the poet returns to the banks of the River Wye after a five-year absence. During the years, time has taken a toll; some of the freshness and vitality of the earlier experience has been lost, but something, a deeper and richer understanding, has been gained that makes him in maturity, through the power of his imagination, able to find a religious meaning in nature, a basis for living. The crucial lines of the poem record that achievement in moving, yet unpretentious, language:

> And I have felt
> A presence that disturbs me with the joy
> Of elevated thoughts; a sense sublime
> Of something far more deeply interfused,
> Whose dwelling is the light of setting suns,
> And the round ocean and the living air,
> And the blue sky, and in the mind of man:
> A motion and a spirit, that impels
> All thinking things, all objects of all thought,
> And rolls through all things. Therefore am I still
> A lover of the meadows and the woods,
> And mountains; and of all that we behold
> From this green earth; of all the mighty world
> Of eye and ear,—both what they half create,
> And what perceive; well pleased to recognize
> In nature and the language of the sense

> The anchor of my purest thoughts, the nurse,
> The guide, the guardian of my heart, and soul
> Of all my moral being.

These lines from "Tintern Abbey" might well serve as a matrix of Wordsworth's credo and its many themes. It is as if he had found in this poem the kind of poet he wanted to be, the kind of personal, expansive, free-flowing poetry he wanted to write. He seldom returned to the narrowly rustic. For the next ten years he was to concern himself with his *magnum opus, The Prelude*; with the Lucy lyrics; the *Immortality Ode*; memorable sonnets like "It Is A Beauteous Evening, Calm and Free," "Composed Upon Westminster Bridge, September 3, 1802," and "The World Is Too Much With Us; Late And Soon"; longer lyrics like "I Wandered Lonely As A Cloud" and "The Solitary Reaper," all a part of *Poems in Two Volumes, 1807,* one of the greatest collections of poetry in the nineteenth century.

A key element of Wordsworth's best poetry is a deep concern with the relationship between the inner life of man and the outer life of nature; indeed, there is a shared life, and the poet "considers man and nature as essentially adapted to each other, and the mind of man as naturally the mirror of the fairest and most interesting properties of nature." De Quincey's observation on his contemporary is a helpful one for the modern reader: "Wordsworth had his passion for nature fixed in his blood; it was a necessity of his being, like that of the mulberry leaf to the silk-worm, and through his commerce with nature did he live and breathe. Hence it was from the *truth* of his love that his knowledge grew." Nature, his "all in all" as he describes it in "Tintern Abbey," was, of course, the brilliant phenomena that surrounded him, but, more important, a presence, a spirit both benevolent and awesome, experienced with a wild enthusiasm and animal-like absorption in his childhood and with a sober wisdom in his maturity. Through nature one can discover those deeper truths about its life and its Creator. The more complete the rapport with nature, the more one can be liberated from the pettiness and materialism of the world. In this process the power of Imagination makes its contribution, shaping the raw materials of experience into a new and deeper unity, molding those "spots of time" of *The Prelude*, those moments when "the light of sense / Goes out," when, with little effort of will, the mind enters into "the life of things" and discovers meaning. In this sense the Imagination is a maker of order and value for a poet who has lost faith in the orthodox dogmas of religion and politics, in the certainties of science. Book II of *The Prelude* carries further the idea of development sketched in "Tintern Abbey." Having paid tribute to the glorious beauty of his childhood dwelling-place, he is quick to warn "That by the regular action of the world / My soul was unsubdued." It is the emergence of a "plastic power" that is so momentous in his life:

> An auxiliar light
> Came from my mind, which on the setting sun
> Bestowed new splendour; the melodious birds,
> The fluttering breezes, fountains that run on
> Murmuring so sweetly in themselves, obeyed

> A like dominion, and the midnight storm
> Grew darker in the presence of my eye:
> Hence my obeisance, my devotion hence,
> And hence my transport.

The drama of Wordsworth's poetry is enhanced not by a sustained optimism, but by a certain ambivalence and tension. First, there are the two sides of nature, one the bounteous and joyous world of "Nutting" and the youthful poetry, the other the seemingly neutral and fearful force that takes Lucy—"No motion has she now, no force; / She neither hears nor sees; / Rolled round in earth's diurnal course, / With rocks, and stones, and trees"; that batters the former tranquillity of the setting of Peele Castle; that snuffs out the life of his brother John; that slowly but surely, in the words of the *Immortality Ode*, loses its vitality to "die away / And fade into the light of common day."

There is also the exhilaration in the great youthful resources of imagination and emotion, the "time when meadow, grove, and stream, / The earth and every common sight, / To me did seem / Apparelled in celestial light, / The glory and the freshness of a dream"; the power "That penetrates, enables us to mount, / When high, more high, and lifts us up when fallen." For Wordsworth, as for Coleridge, imagination is a unifier of all the mind's resources. It "shapes and *creates;* and how? By innumerable processes; and in none does it more delight than in that of consolidating numbers into unity,—alternations proceeding from and governed by, a sublime consciousness of the soul in her own mighty and almost divine powers." It is truly a creative power, "conferring additional properties upon an object, or abstracting from it some of those which it actually possesses, and thus enabling it to act upon the mind which hath performed the process, like a new existence."

However, alternating with the joy of creation and engagement with nature and spirit are reverberations of fear, of loss, of death. Childhood ecstasy is followed by youthful anxiety and self-consciousness, by adult isolation and loneliness. Even in his most confident early poems the clues are present. "Tintern Abbey" speaks of the fading of "aching joys" and "dizzy raptures," although there is still the compensation of "a sense sublime / Of something far more deeply interfused," still the consolation of seeing his former self in Dorothy. The poet of the *Immortality Ode* acknowledges, "The things which I have seen I now can see no more"; sadly realizes "where'er I go, / That there hath past away a glory from the earth." Yet he still rejoices in the power of imaginative recollection, in the power to recapture those visionary moments and to make them reservoirs of strength as the darkness of age approaches. One of Wordsworth's most brilliant symbols, embodied in the rhythms of the irregular Pindaric ode structure, holds out the hope of recapturing something of what was lost:

> Hence in a season of calm weather
> Though inland far we be,
> Our souls have sight of that immortal sea
> Which brought us hither,
> Can in a moment travel thither,

> And see the Children sport upon the shore,
> And hear the mighty waters rolling evermore.

Yet the alternations of sadness and hope give way to greater despair, a greater sense of loss of the power to create and a consequent search for some external prop or support that will bring consolation and the courage to go on. The organ tones of the "Ode to Duty," "Elegiac Stanzas," "The Small Celandine," "Character of the Happy Warrior," communicate vividly the sense of loss, a search for orthodoxy:

> Me this unchartered freedom tires;
> I feel the weight of chance-desires:
> My hopes no more must change their name;
> I long for a repose that ever is the same.

Although the poems of the later years are more sober in tone, more firmly anchored in man's responsibility to the human condition, the Imagination's debt to external reality; although one does not find the same lyric freedom, the same freshness of diction and imagery, the same intense emotion, there is still something uniquely Wordsworthian. There is the sense of the poet as a nobler and wiser human being, the stateliness of setting and language, the lucid appeal to the heart, the confidence in the ultimate triumph of the spirit. There is still the belief articulated early in his career in *The Prelude*:

> Our destiny, our being's heart and home,
> Is with infinitude, and only there;
> With hope it is, hope that can never die,
> Effort, and expectation, and desire,
> And something evermore about to be.

Suggestions for Further Reading

The standard biography is Mary Moorman, *William Wordsworth*, 2 vols., 1957–1965. Emile Legouis, *The Early Life of William Wordsworth*, although written in 1897, is still valuable for one especially interested in the younger Wordsworth, and Willard Sperry, *Wordsworth's Anti Climax* (1935) is a suggestive study of the problem of decline in the later Wordsworth. A good first book for beginning students is H. M. Margoliouth, *Wordsworth and Coleridge 1795–1834* (1953), valuable because it deals with the links between two poets so central to the beginnings of Romantic theory and practice. An invaluable source book is Mark Reed, *Wordsworth: The Chronology of the Early Years 1770–1779* (1967).

Any student would be advised to begin a reading of criticism of Wordsworth with Coleridge's brilliant analysis in the *Biographia Literaria*, a large section of which appears in this anthology. Although written in 1817, it has survived the test of time and still seems to set the pattern for the best criticism of Wordsworth and his work. Matthew Arnold's essay on Wordsworth in *Essays in Criticism: Second Series* (1888) is another great nineteenth-century landmark, offering a view of the poet's strengths and weaknesses.

Strongly recommended are Newton P. Stallknecht, *Strange Seas of Thought* (1945); Raymond D. Havens, *The Mind of a Poet* (1941); a perceptive and provocative essay by Douglas Bush, "Wordsworth: A Minority Report" in *Wordsworth Centenary Studies*, ed. Gilbert Dunklin (1950); Helen Darbishire, *The Poet Wordsworth* (1950); John Jones, *The Egotistical Sublime* (1954); David Ferry, *The Limits of Mortality* (1959); David Perkins's essay on Wordsworth in *The Quest for Permanence* (1959) as well as his full length study, *Wordsworth and the Poetry of Sincerity* (1964); Herbert Lindenberger, *On Wordsworth's Prelude* (1963); Geoffrey Hartman, *Wordsworth's Poetry, 1787–1814* (1964).

PREFACE TO THE SECOND EDITION OF THE *LYRICAL BALLADS* (1800)

The first Volume of these Poems has already been submitted to general perusal. It was published as an experiment, which, I hoped, might be of some use to ascertain how far, by fitting to metrical arrangement a selection of the real language of men in a state of vivid sensation, that sort of pleasure and that quantity of pleasure may be imparted, which a Poet may rationally endeavour to impart.

I had formed no very inaccurate estimate of the probable effect of those Poems: I flattered myself that they who should be pleased with them would read them with more than common pleasure: and, on the other hand, I was well aware, that by those who should dislike them they would be read with more than common dislike. The result has differed from my expectation in this only, that a greater number have been pleased than I ventured to hope I should please.

Several of my Friends are anxious for the success of these Poems, from a belief that, if the views with which they were composed were indeed realised, a class of Poetry would be produced, well adapted to interest mankind permanently, and not unimportant in the quality and in the multiplicity of its moral relations: and on this account they have advised me to prefix a systematic defence of the theory upon which the Poems were

written. But I was unwilling to undertake the task, knowing that on this occasion the Reader would look coldly upon my arguments, since I might be suspected of having been principally influenced by the selfish and foolish hope of *reasoning* him into an approbation of these particular Poems: and I was still more unwilling to undertake the task, because adequately to display the opinions, and fully to enforce the arguments, would require a space wholly disproportionate to a preface. For, to treat the subject with the clearness and coherence of which it is susceptible, it would be necessary to give a full account of the present state of the public taste in this country, and to determine how far this taste is healthy or depraved; which, again, could not be determined without pointing out in what manner language and the human mind act and re-act on each other, and without retracing the revolutions, not of literature alone, but likewise of society itself. I have therefore altogether declined to enter regularly upon this defence; yet I am sensible that there would be something like impropriety in abruptly obtruding upon the Public, without a few words of introduction, Poems so materially different from those upon which general approbation is at present bestowed.

It is supposed that by the act of writing in verse an Author makes a formal engagement that he will gratify certain known habits of association; that he not only thus apprises the Reader that certain classes of ideas and expressions will be found in his book, but that others will be carefully excluded. This exponent or symbol held forth by metrical language must in different eras of literature have excited very different expectations: for example, in the age of Catullus, Terence, and Lucretius, and that of Stratius or Claudian; and in our own country, in the age of Shakespeare and Beaumont and Fletcher, and that of Donne and Cowley, or Dryden, or Pope. I will not take upon me to determine the exact import of the promise which, by the act of writing in verse, an Author in the present day makes to his reader; but it will undoubtedly appear to many persons that I have not fulfilled the terms of an engagement thus voluntarily contracted. They who have been accustomed to the gaudiness and inane phraseology of many modern writers, if they persist in reading this book to its conclusion, will, no doubt, frequently have to struggle with feelings of strangeness and awkwardness: they will look round for poetry, and will be induced to inquire by what species of courtesy these attempts can be permitted to assume that title. I hope, therefore, the reader will not censure me for attempting to state what I have proposed to myself to perform; and also (as far as the limits of a preface will permit) to explain some of the chief reasons which have determined me in the choice of my purpose: that at least he may be spared any unpleasant feeling of disappointment, and that I myself may be protected from one of the most dishonourable accusations which can be brought against an Author; namely, that of an indolence which prevents him from endeavouring to ascertain what is his duty, or, when his duty is ascertained, prevents him from performing it.

The principal object, then, proposed in these Poems, was to choose incidents and situations from common life, and to relate or describe them throughout, as far as was possible, in a selection of language really used by men, and, at the same time, to throw over them a certain colouring of imagination, whereby ordinary things should be presented to the mind in an unusual aspect; and further, and above all, to make these incidents and situations interesting by tracing in them, truly though not ostentatiously, the primary laws of our nature: chiefly, as far as regards the manner in which we associate ideas in a state of excitement. Humble and rustic life was generally chosen, because in that condition the essential passions of the heart find a better soil in which they can attain their maturity, are less under restraint, and speak a plainer and more emphatic language, because in that condition of life our elementary feelings co-exist in a state of greater simplicity, and, consequently, may be more accurately contemplated, and more forcibly communicated; because the manners of rural life germinate from those elementary feelings, and, from the necessary character of rural occupations, are more easily comprehended, and are more durable; and, lastly, because in that condition the passions of men are incorporated with the beautiful and permanent forms of nature. The language, too, of these men has been adopted (purified indeed from what appear to be its real defects, from all lasting and rational causes of dislike or disgust), because such men hourly communicate with the best objects from which the best part of language is originally derived; and because, from their rank in society and the sameness and narrow circle of their intercourse, being less under the influence of social vanity, they convey their feelings and notions in simple and unelaborated expressions. Accordingly, such a language, arising out of repeated experience and regular feelings, is a more permanent, and a far more philosophical language, than that which is frequently substituted for it by Poets, who think that they are conferring honour upon themselves and their art in proportion as they separate themselves from the sympathies of men, and indulge in arbitrary and capricious habits of expression, in order to furnish food for fickle tastes and fickle appetites of their own creation.[1]

I cannot, however, be insensible to the present outcry against the triviality and meanness, both of thought and language, which some of my contemporaries have occasionally introduced into their metrical compositions; and I acknowledge that this defect, where it exists, is more dishonourable to the Writer's own character than false refinement or arbitrary innovation, though I should contend at the same time that it is far less pernicious in the sum of its consequences. From such verses the Poems in these volumes will be found distinguished at least by one mark of difference, that each of them has a worthy *purpose*. Not that I always began to write with a distinct purpose formally conceived, but habits of meditation have, I trust, so prompted and

---

PREFACE, SECOND EDITION OF THE LYRICAL BALLADS. 1. It is worth while here to observe that the affecting parts of Chaucer are almost always expressed in language pure and universally intelligible even to this day. (Wordsworth)

regulated my feelings, that my descriptions of such objects as strongly excite those feelings will be found to carry along with them a *purpose*. If this opinion be erroneous, I can have little right to the nature of a Poet. For all good poetry is the spontaneous overflow of powerful feelings: and though this be true, Poems to which any value can be attached were never produced on any variety of subjects but by a man who, being possessed of more than usual organic sensibility, had also thought long and deeply. For our continued influxes of feeling are modified and directed by our thoughts, which are indeed the representatives of all our past feelings; and as, by contemplating the relation of these general representatives to each other, we discover what is really important to men, so, by the repetition and continuance of this act, our feelings will be connected with important subjects, till at length, if we be originally possessed of much sensibility, such habits of mind will be produced that, by obeying blindly and mechanically the impulses of those habits, we shall describe objects, and utter sentiments, of such a nature, and in such connection with each other, that the understanding of the Reader must necesarily be in some degree enlightened, and his affection strengthened and purified.

It has been said that each of these Poems has a purpose. Another circumstance must be mentioned which distinguishes these Poems from the popular Poetry of the day; it is, this, that the feeling therein developed gives importance to the action and situation, and not the action and situation to the feeling.

A sense of false modesty shall not prevent me from asserting that the Reader's attention is pointed to this mark of distinction, far less for the sake of these particular Poems than from the general importance of the subject. The subject is indeed important! For the human mind is capable of being excited without the application of gross and violent stimulants; and he must have a very faint perception of its beauty and dignity who does not know this, and who does not further know, that one being is elevated above another in proportion as he possesses this capability. It has therefore appeared to me, that to endeavour to produce or enlarge this capability is one of the best services in which, at any period, a Writer can be engaged; but this service, excellent at all times, is especially so at the present day. For a multitude of causes, unknown to former times, are now acting with a combined force to blunt the discriminating powers of the mind, and, unfitting it for all voluntary exertion, to reduce it to a state of almost savage torpor. The most effective of these causes are the great national events which are daily taking place, and the increasing accumulation of men in cities, where the uniformity of their occupations produces a craving for extraordinary incident which the rapid communication of intelligence hourly gratifies. To this tendency of life and manners the literature and theatrical exhibitions of the country have conformed themselves. The invaluable works of our elder writers, I had almost said the works of Shakspeare and Milton, are driven into neglect by frantic novels, sickly and stupid German Tragedies, and deluges of idle and extravagant stories in verse.— When I think upon this degrading thirst after outrageous stimulation, I am almost ashamed to have spoken of the feeble endeavour made in these volumes to counteract it; and, reflecting upon the magnitude of the general evil, I should be oppressed with no dishonourable melancholy, had I not a deep impression of certain inherent and indestructible qualities of the human mind, and likewise of certain powers in the great and permanent objects that act upon it, which are equally inherent and indestructible; and were there not added to this impression a belief that the time is approaching when the evil will be systematically opposed by men of greater powers, and with far more distinguished success.

Having dwelt thus long on the subjects and aim of these Poems, I shall request the Reader's permission to apprise him of a few circumstances relating to their *style*, in order, among other reasons, that he may not censure me for not having performed what I never attempted. The Reader will find that personifications of abstract ideas rarely occur in these volumes, and are utterly rejected as an ordinary device to elevate the style and raise it above prose. My purpose was to imitate, and, as far as is possible, to adopt the very language of men; and assuredly such personifications do not make any natural or regular part of that language. They are, indeed, a figure of speech occasionally prompted by passion, and I have made use of them as such; but have endeavoured utterly to reject them as a mechanical device of style, or as a family language which Writers in metre seem to lay claim to by prescription. I have wished to keep the Reader in the company of flesh and blood, persuaded that by so doing I shall interest him. Others who pursue a different track will interest him likewise; I do not interfere with their claim, but wish to prefer a claim of my own. There will also be found in these volumes little of what is usually called poetic diction; as much pains has been taken to avoid it as is ordinarily taken to produce it; this has been done for the reason already alleged, to bring my language near to the language of men; and further, because the pleasure which I have proposed to myself to impart is of a kind very different from that which is supposed by many persons to be the proper object of poetry. Without being culpably particular, I do not know how to give my Reader a more exact notion of the style in which it was my wish and intention to write, than by informing him that I have at all times endeavoured to look steadily at my subject; consequently there is, I hope, in these Poems little falsehood of description, and my own ideas are expressed in language fitted to their respective importance. Something must have been gained by this practice, as it is friendly to one property of all good poetry, namely, good sense: but it has necessarily cut me off from a large portion of phrases and figures of speech which from father to son have long been regarded as the common inheritance of Poets. I have also thought it expedient to restrict myself still further, having abstained from the use of many expressions, in themselves proper and beautiful, but which have been foolishly repeated by bad Poets, till such feelings of disgust are connected with them as it is scarcely possible by any art of association to overpower.

If in a poem there should be found a series of lines, or even a single line, in which the language, though naturally arranged, and according to the strict laws of metre, does not differ from that of prose, there is a numerous class of critics, who, when they stumble upon these prosaisms, as they call them, imagine that they have made a notable discovery, and exult over the Poet as over a man ignorant of his own profession. Now these men would establish a canon of criticism which the Reader will conclude he must utterly reject, if he wishes to be pleased with these volumes. And it would be a most easy task to prove to him that not only the language of a large portion of every good poem, even of the most elevated character, must necessarily, except with references to the metre, in no respect differ from that of good prose, but likewise that some of the most interesting parts of the best poems will be found to be strictly the language of prose when prose is well written. The truth of this assertion might be demonstrated by innumerable passages from almost all the poetical writings, even of Milton himself. To illustrate the subject in a general manner, I will here adduce a short composition of Gray, who was at the head of those who, by their reasonings, have attempted to widen the space of separation betwixt Prose and Metrical composition, and was more than any other man curiously elaborate in the structure of his own poetic diction.

> In vain to me the smiling mornings shine,
> And reddening Phœbus lifts his golden fire;
> The birds in vain their amorous descant join,
> Or cheerful fields resume their green attire.
> These ears, alas! for other notes repine;
> *A different object do these eyes require;*
> *My lonely anguish melts no heart but mine;*
> *And in my breast the imperfect joys expire;*
> Yet morning smiles the busy race to cheer,
> And new-born pleasure bring to happier men;
> The fields to all their wonted tribute bear;
> To warm their little loves the birds complain.
> *I fruitless mourn to him that cannot hear,*
> *And weep the more because I weep in vain.*

It will easily be perceived, that the only part of this Sonnet which is of any value is the lines printed in Italics; it is equally obvious that, except in the rhyme and in the use of the single word "fruitless" for fruitlessly, which is so far a defect, the language of these lines does in no respect differ from that of prose.

By the foregoing quotation it has been shown that the language of Prose may yet be well adapted to Poetry; and it was previously asserted that a large portion of the language of every good poem can in no respect differ from that of good Prose. We will go further. It may be safely affirmed that there neither is, nor can be, any *essential* difference between the language of prose and metrical composition. We are fond of tracing the resemblance between Poetry and Painting, and, accordingly, we call them Sisters: but where shall we find bonds of connection sufficiently strict to typify the affinity betwixt metrical and prose composition? They both speak by and to the same organs; the bodies in which both of them are clothed may be of the same substance, their affections are kindred, and almost identical, not necessarily differing even in degree; Poetry[2] shed no tears "such as Angels weep," but natural and human tears; she can boast of no celestial ichor that distinguishes her vital juices from those of Prose; the same human blood circulates through the veins of them both.

If it be affirmed that rhyme and metrical arrangement of themselves constitute a distinction which overturns what has just been said on the strict affinity of metrical language with that of Prose, and paves the way for other artificial distinctions which the mind voluntarily admits, I answer that the language of such Poetry as is here recommended is, as far as is possible, a selection of the language really spoken by men; that this selection, wherever it is made with true taste and feeling, will of itself form a distinction far greater than would at first be imagined, and will entirely separate the composition from the vulgarity and meanness of ordinary life; and, if metre be superadded thereto, I believe that a dissimilitude will be produced altogether sufficient for the gratification of a rational mind. What other distinction would we have? Whence is it to come? And where is it to exist? Not, surely, where the Poet speaks through the mouths of his characters: it cannot be necessary here, either for elevation of style, or any of its supposed ornaments; for, if the Poet's subject be judiciously chosen, it will naturally, and upon fit occasion, lead him to passions, the language of which, if selected truly and judiciously, must necessarily be dignified and variegated, and alive with metaphors and figures. I forbear to speak of an incongruity which would shock the intelligent Reader, should

2. I here use the word "Poetry" (though against my own judgment) as opposed to the word Prose, and synonymous with metrical composition. But much confusion has been introduced into criticism by this contradistinction of Poetry and Prose, instead of the more philosophical one of Poetry and Matter of Fact, or Science. The only strict antithesis to Prose is Metre; nor is this, in truth, a *strict* antithesis, because lines and passages of metre so naturally occur in writing prose, that it would be scarcely possible to avoid them, even were it desirable. (Wordsworth)

the Poet interweave any foreign splendour of his own with that which the passion naturally suggests: it is sufficient to say that such addition is unnecessary. And, surely, it is more probable that those passages, which with propriety abound with metaphors and figures, will have their due effect if, upon other occasions where the passions are of a milder character, the style also be subdued and temperate.

But, as the pleasure which I hope to give by the Poems now presented to the Reader must depend entirely on just notions upon this subject, and as it is in itself of high importance to our taste and moral feelings, I cannot content myself with these detached remarks. And if, in what I am about to say, it shall appear to some that my labour is unnecessary, and that I am like a man fighting a battle without enemies, such persons may be reminded that, whatever be the language outwardly holden by men, a practical faith in the opinions which I am wishing to establish is almost unknown. If my conclusions are admitted, and carried as far as they must be carried if admitted at all, our judgments concerning the works of the greatest Poets, both ancient and modern, will be far different from what they are at present, both when we praise and when we censure: and our moral feelings influencing and influenced by these judgments will, I believe, be corrected and purified.

Taking up the subject, then, upon general grounds, let me ask, what is meant by the word Poet? What is a Poet? To whom does he address himself? And what language is to be expected from him?—He is a man speaking to men: a man, it is true, endowed with more lively sensibility, more enthusiasm and tenderness, who has a greater knowledge of human nature, and a more comprehensive soul, than are supposed to be common among mankind; a man pleased with his own passions and volitions, and who rejoices more than other men in the spirit of life that is in him; delighting to contemplate similar volitions and passions as manifested in the goings-on of the Universe, and habitually impelled to create them where he does not find them. To these qualities he has added a disposition to be affected more than any other men by absent things as if they were present; an ability of conjuring up in himself passions, which are indeed far from being the same as those produced by real events, yet (especially in those parts of the general sympathy which are pleasing and delightful) do more nearly resemble the passions produced by real events than anything which, from the motions of their own minds merely, other men are accustomed to feel in themselves:—whence, and from practice, he has acquired a greater readiness and power in expressing what he thinks and feels, and especially those thoughts and feelings which, by his own choice, or from the structure of his own mind, arise in him without immediate external excitement.

But whatever portion of this faculty we may suppose even the greatest Poet to possess, there cannot be a doubt that the language which it will suggest to him must often, in liveliness and truth, fall short of that which is uttered by men in real life under the actual pressure of those passions, certain shadows of which the Poet thus produces, or feels to be produced, in himself.

However exalted a notion we would wish to cherish of the character of a Poet, it is obvious that, while he describes and imitates passions, his employment is in some degree mechanical compared with the freedom and power of real and substantial action and suffering. So that it will be the wish of the Poet to bring his feelings near to those of the persons whose feelings he describes, nay, for short spaces of time, perhaps, to let himself slip into an entire delusion, and even confound and identify his own feelings with theirs; modifying only the language which is thus suggested to him by a consideration that he describes for a particular purpose, that of giving pleasure. Here, then, he will apply the principle of selection which has been already insisted upon. He will depend upon this for removing what would otherwise be painful or disgusting in the passion; he will feel that there is no necessity to trick out or to elevate nature: and the more industriously he applies this principle the deeper will be his faith that no words, which *his* fancy or imagination can suggest, will be to be compared with those which are the emanations of reality and truth.

But it may be said by those who do not object to the general spirit of these remarks, that, as it is impossible for the Poet to produce upon all occasions language as exquisitely fitted for the passion as that which the real passion itself suggests, it is proper that he should consider himself as in the situation of a translator, who does not scruple to substitute excellences of another kind for those which are unattainable by him; and endeavours occasionally to surpass his original, in order to make some amends for the general inferiority to which he feels he must submit. But this would be to encourage idleness and unmanly despair. Further, it is the language of men who speak of what they do not understand; who talk of Poetry, as of a matter of amusement and idle pleasure; who will converse with us as gravely about a *taste* for Poetry, as they express it, as if it were a thing as indifferent as a taste for rope-dancing, or Frontiniac or Sherry. Aristotle, I have been told, has said, that Poetry is the most philosophic of all writing: it is so: its object is truth, not individual and local, but general and operative; not standing upon external testimony, but carried alive into the heart by passion; truth which is its own testimony, which gives competence and confidence to the tribunal to which it appeals, and receives them from the same tribunal. Poetry is the image of man and nature. The obstacles which stand in the way of the fidelity of the Biographer and Historian, and of their consequent utility, are incalculably greater than those which are to be encountered by the Poet who comprehends the dignity of his art. The Poet writes under one restriction only, namely, the necessity of giving immediate pleasure to a human Being possessed of that information which may be expected from him, not as a lawyer, a physician, a mariner, an astronomer, or a natural philosopher, but as a Man. Except this one restriction, there is no object standing between the Poet and the image of things; between this and the Biographer and Historian, there are a thousand.

Nor let this necessity of producing immediate pleasure be considered as a degradation of the Poet's art. It is far otherwise. It is an acknowledgment of the beauty of the universe, an acknowledgment the more sincere because not formal, but indirect; it is a task light and easy to him who looks at the world in the spirit of love: further, it is a homage paid to the native and naked dignity of man, to the grand elementary principle of pleasure, by which he knows, and feels, and lives, and moves. We have no sympathy but what is propagated by pleasure: I would not be misunderstood; but wherever we sympathise with pain, it will be found that the sympathy is produced and carried on by subtle combinations with pleasure. We have no knowledge, that is, no general principles drawn from the contemplation of particular facts, but what has been built up by pleasure, and exists in us by pleasure alone. The Man of science, the Chemist and Mathematician, whatever difficulties and disgusts they may have had to struggle with, know and feel this. However painful may be the objects with which the Anatomist's knowledge is connected, he feels that his knowledge is pleasure; and where he has no pleasure he has no knowledge. What then does the Poet? He considers man and the objects that surround him as acting and re-acting upon each other, so as to produce an infinite complexity of pain and pleasure; he considers man in his own nature and in his ordinary life as contemplating this with a certain quantity of immediate knowledge, with certain convictions, intuitions, and deductions, which from habit acquire the quality of intuitions; he considers him as looking upon this complex scene of ideas and sensations, and finding everywhere objects that immediately excite in him sympathies which, from the necessities of his nature, are accompanied by an overbalance of enjoyment.

To this knowledge which all men carry about with them, and to these sympathies in which, without any other discipline than that of our daily life, we are fitted to take delight, the Poet principally directs his attention. He considers man and nature as essentially adapted to each other, and the mind of man as naturally the mirror of the fairest and most enterprising properties of nature. And thus the Poet, prompted by this feeling of pleasure, which accompanies him through the whole course of his studies, converses with general nature, with affections akin to those which, through labour and length of time, the Man of science has raised up in himself, by conversing with those particular parts of nature which are the objects of his studies. The knowledge both of the Poet and the Man of science is pleasure; but the knowledge of the one cleaves to us as a necessary part of our existence, our natural and unalienable inheritance; the other is a personal and individual acquisition, slow to come to us, and by no habitual and direct sympathy connecting us with our fellow-beings. The Man of science seeks truth as a remote and unknown benefactor; he cherishes and loves it in his solitude: the Poet, singing a song in which all human beings join with him, rejoices in the presence of truth as our visible

friend and hourly companion. Poetry is the breath and finer spirit of all knowledge; it is the impassioned expression which is the countenance of all Science. Emphatically may it be said of the Poet, as Shakspeare hath said of man, "that he looks before and after." He is the rock of defence for human nature; an upholder and preserver, carrying everywhere with him relationship and love. In spite of difference of soil and climate, of language and manners, of laws and customs: in spite of things silently gone out of mind, and things violently destroyed; the Poet binds together by passion and knowledge the vast empire of human society, as it is spread over the whole earth and over all time. The objects of the Poet's thoughts are everywhere; though the eyes and senses of man are, it is true, his favourite guides, yet he will follow wheresoever he can find an atmosphere of sensation in which to move his wings. Poetry is the first and last of all knowledge—it is as immortal as the heart of man. If the labours of Men of science should ever create any material revolution, direct or indirect, in our condition, and in the impressions which we habitually receive, the Poet will sleep then no more than at present; he will be ready to follow the steps of the Man of science, not only in those general indirect effects, but he will be at his side, carrying sensation into the midst of the objects of the science itself. The remotest discoveries of the Chemist, the Botanist, or Mineralogist, will be as proper objects of the Poet's art as any upon which it can be employed, if the time should ever come when these things shall be familiar to us, and the relations under which they are contemplated by the followers of these respective sciences shall be manifestly and palpably material to us as enjoying and suffering beings. If the time should ever come when what is now called science, thus familiarised to men, shall be ready to put on, as it were, a form of flesh and blood, the Poet will lend his divine spirit to aid the transfiguration, and will welcome the Being thus produced as a dear and genuine inmate of the household of man.—It is not, then, to be supposed that any one, who holds that sublime notion of Poetry which I have attempted to convey, will break in upon the sanctity and truth of his pictures by transitory and accidental ornaments, and endeavour to excite admiration of himself by arts, the necessity of which must manifestly depend upon the assumed meanness of his subject.

What has been thus far said applies to Poetry in general, but especially to those parts of compositions where the Poet speaks through the mouths of his characters; and upon this point it appears to authorise the conclusion that there are few persons of good sense who would not allow that the dramatic parts of composition are defective in proportion as they deviate from the real language of nature, and are coloured by a diction of the Poet's own, either peculiar to him as an individual Poet or belonging simply to Poets in general; to a body of men who from the circumstance of their compositions being in metre, it is expected will employ a particular language.

It is not, then, in the dramatic parts of composition that we look for this distinction of language; but still it may be proper and necessary where the Poet speaks to us in his own person and character. To this I answer by referring the Reader to the description before given of a Poet. Among the qualities there enumerated as principally conducing to form a Poet, is implied nothing differing in kind from other men, but only in degree. The sum of what was said is, that the Poet is chiefly distinguished from other men by a greater promptness to think and feel without immediate external excitement, and a greater power in expressing such thoughts and feelings as are produced in him in that manner. But these passions and thoughts and feelings are the general passions and thoughts and feelings of men. And with what are they connected? Undoubtedly with our moral sentiments and animal sensations, and with the causes which excite these; with the operations of the elements, and the appearances of the visible universe; with storm and sunshine, with the revolutions of the seasons, with cold and heat, with loss of friends and kindred, with injuries and resentments, gratitude and hope, with fear and sorrow. These, and the like, are the sensations and objects which the Poet describes, as they are the sensations of other men and the objects which interest them. The Poet thinks and feels in the spirit of human passions. How, then, can his language differ in any material degree from that of all other men who feel vividly and see clearly? It might be *proved* that it is impossible. But supposing that this were not the case, the Poet might then be allowed to use a peculiar language when expressing his feelings for his own gratification, or that of men like himself. But Poets do not write for Poets alone, but for men. Unless, therefore, we are advocates for that admiration which subsists upon ignorance, and that pleasure which arises from hearing what we do not understand, the Poet must descend from this supposed height, and, in order to excite rational sympathy, he must express himself as other men express themselves. To this it may be added, that while he is only selecting from the real language of men, or which amounts to the same thing, composing accurately in the spirit of such selection, he is treading upon safe ground, and we know what we are to expect from him. Our feelings are the same with respect to metre; for, as it may be proper to remind the Reader, the distinction of metre is regular and uniform, and not, like that which is produced by what is usually called POETIC DICTION, arbitrary, and subject to infinite caprices, upon which no calculation whatever can be made. In the one case, the Reader is utterly at the mercy of the Poet, respecting what imagery or diction he may choose to connect with the passion; whereas, in the other, the metre obeys certain laws, to which the Poet and Reader both willingly submit because they are certain, and because no interference is made by them with the passion but such as the concurring testimony of ages has shown to heighten and improve the pleasure which co-exists with it.

It will now be proper to answer an obvious question, namely, Why, professing these opinions, have I written in verse? To this, in addition to such answer as is included in what has been already said, I reply, in the first place, Because, however I may have restricted myself, there is still left open to me what confessedly constitutes the most valuable object of all writing, whether in prose or verse; the great and universal passions of men, the most general and interesting of their occupations, and the entire world of nature before me—to supply endless combinations of forms and imagery. Now, supposing for a moment that whatever is interesting in these objects may be as vividly described in prose, why should I be condemned for attempting to superadd to such description the charm which, by the consent of all nations, is acknowledged to exist in metrical language? To this, by such as are yet unconvinced, it may be answered that a very small part of the pleasure given by Poetry depends upon the metre, and that it is injudicious to write in metre, unless it be accompanied with the other artificial distinctions of style with which metre is usually accompanied, and that, by such deviation, more will be lost from the shock which will thereby be given to the Reader's associations than will be counterbalanced by any pleasure which he can derive from the general power of numbers. In answer to those who still contend for the necessity of accompanying metre with certain appropriate colours of style in order to the accomplishment of its appropriate end, and who also, in my opinion, greatly under-rate the power of metre in itself, it might, perhaps as far as relates to these Volumes, have been almost sufficient to observe, that poems are extant, written upon more humble subjects, and in a still more naked and simple style, which have continued to give pleasure from generation to generation. Now, if nakedness and simplicity be a defect, the fact here mentioned affords a strong presumption that poems somewhat less naked and simple are capable of affording pleasure at the present day; and, what I wished *chiefly* to attempt, at present, was to justify myself for having written under the impression of this belief.

But various causes might be pointed out why, when the style is manly, and the subject of some importance, words metrically arranged will long continue to impart such a pleasure to mankind as he who proves the extent of that pleasure will be desirous to impart. The end of poetry is to produce excitement in co-existence with an overbalance of pleasure; but, by the supposition, excitement is an unusual and irregular state of the mind; ideas and feelings do not, in that state, succeed each other in accustomed order. If the words, however, by which this excitement is produced be in themselves powerful, or the images and feelings have an undue proportion of pain connected with them, there is some danger that the excitement may be carried beyond its proper bounds. Now the co-presence of something regular, something to which the mind has been accustomed in various moods and in a less excited state, cannot but have great efficacy in tempering and restraining the passion by an intertexture of ordinary feeling, and of feeling not strictly and necessarily connected with the passion. This is unquestionably true; and hence, though the opinion will at first appear paradoxical, from the tendency of metre to divest language, in a certain degree, of its reality, and thus to throw a sort of half-consciousness of unsubstantial existence over the whole composition, there can be little doubt but that more pathetic situations and sentiments, that is, those which have a greater proportion of pain connected with them, may be endured in metrical composition, especially in rhyme, than in prose. The metre of the old ballads is very artless, yet they contain many passages which would illustrate this opinion; and, I hope, if the following poems be attentively perused, similar instances will be found in them. This opinion may be further illustrated by appealing to the Reader's own experience of the reluctance with which he comes to the reperusal of the distressful parts of "Clarissa Harlowe," or the "Gamester"; while Shakspeare's writings, in the most pathetic scenes, never act upon us, as pathetic, beyond the bounds of pleasure—an effect which, in a much greater degree than might at first be imagined, is to be ascribed to small, but continual and regular impulses of pleasurable surprise from the metrical arrangement.—On the other hand (what it must be allowed will much more frequently happen), if the Poet's words should be incommensurate with the passion, and inadequate to raise the Reader to a height of desirable excitement, then (unless the Poet's choice of his metre has been grossly injudicious), in the feelings of pleasure which the Reader has been accustomed to connect with metre in general, and in the feeling, whether cheerful or melancholy, which he has been accustomed to connect with that particular movement of metre, there will be found something which will greatly contribute to impart passion to the words, and to effect the complex end which the Poet proposes to himself.

If I had undertaken a SYSTEMATIC defence of the theory here maintained, it would have been my duty to develop the various causes upon which the pleasure received from metrical language depends. Among the chief of these causes is to be reckoned a principle which must be well known to those who have made any of the Arts the object of accurate reflection; namely, the pleasure which the mind derives from the perception of similitude in dissimilitude. This principle is the great spring of the activity of our minds, and their chief feeder. From this principle the direction of the sexual appetite, and all the passions connected with it take their origin: it is the life of our ordinary conversation; and upon the accuracy with which similitude in dissimilitude, and dissimilitude in similitude, are perceived, depend our taste and our moral feelings. It would not be a useless employment to apply this principle to the consideration of metre, and to show that metre is hence enabled to afford much pleasure, and to point out in what manner that pleasure is produced. But my limits will not permit me to enter upon this subject, and I must content myself with a general summary.

I have said that poetry is the spontaneous overflow of powerful feelings: it takes its origin from emotion recollected in tranquillity; the emotion is contemplated till, by a species of re-action, the tranquillity gradually disappears, and an emotion, kindred to that which was before the subject of contemplation, is gradually produced, and does itself actually exist in the mind. In this mood successful composition generally begins, and in a mood similar to this it is carried on; but the emotion, of whatever kind, and in whatever degree, from various causes, is qualified by various pleasures, so that in describing any passions whatsoever, which are voluntarily described, the mind will, upon the whole, be in a state of enjoyment. If Nature be thus cautious to preserve in a state of enjoyment a being so employed, the Poet ought to profit by the lesson held forth to him, and ought especially to take care that, whatever passions he communicates to his Reader, those passions, if his Reader's mind be sound and vigorous, should always be accompanied with an over-balance of pleasure. Now the music of harmonious metrical language, the sense of difficulty overcome, and the blind association of pleasure which has been previously received from works of rhyme or metre of the same or similar construction, an indistinct perception perpetually renewed of language closely resembling that of real life, and yet, in the circumstance of metre, differing from it so widely—all these imperceptibly make up a complex feeling of delight, which is of the most important use in tempering the painful feeling always found intermingled with powerful descriptions of the deeper passions. This effect is always produced in pathetic and impassioned poetry; while, in lighter compositions, the ease and gracefulness with which the Poet manages his numbers are themselves confessedly a principal source of the gratification of the Reader. All that it is *necessary* to say, however, upon this subject, may be effected by affirming, what few persons will deny, that of two descriptions, either of passions, manners, or characters, each of them equally well executed, the one in prose and the other in verse, the verse will be read a hundred times where the prose is read once.

Having thus explained a few of my reasons for writing in verse, and why I have chosen subjects from common life, and endeavoured to bring my language near to the real language of men, if I have been too minute in pleading my own cause, I have at the same time been treating a subject of general interest; and for this reason a few words shall be added with reference solely to these particular poems, and to some defects which will probably be found in them. I am sensible that my associations must have sometimes been particular instead of general, and that, consequently, giving to things a false importance, I may have sometimes written upon unworthy subjects; but I am less apprehensive on this account, than that my language may frequently have suffered from those arbitrary connections of feelings and ideas with particular words and phrases from which no man can altogether protect himself. Hence I have no doubt that, in some instances, feelings, even of the ludicrous, may be given to my Readers by expressions which appeared to me tender and pathetic. Such faulty expressions, were I convinced they were faulty at present, and that they must necessarily continue to be so, I would willingly take all reasonable pains to correct. But it is dangerous to make these alterations on the simple authority of a few individuals, or even of certain classes of men; for where the understanding of an author is not convinced, or his feelings altered, this cannot be done without great injury to himself: for his own feelings are his stay and support; and, if he set them aside in one instance, he may be induced to repeat this act till his mind shall lose all confidence in itself, and become utterly debilitated. To this it may be added, that the critic ought never to forget that he is himself exposed to the same errors as the Poet, and, perhaps, in a much greater degree: for there can be no presumption in saying of most readers, that it is not probable they will be so well acquainted with the various stages of meaning through which words have passed, or with the fickleness or stability of the relations of particular ideas to each other; and, above all, since they are so much less interested in the subject, they may decide lightly and carelessly.

Long as the reader has been detained, I hope he

will permit me to caution him against a mode of false criticism which has been applied to poetry, in which the language closely resembles that of life and nature. Such verses have been triumphed over in parodies, of which Dr. Johnson's stanza is a fair specimen:—

> I put my hat upon my head
> And walked into the Strand,
> And there I met another man
> Whose hat was in his hand.

Immediately under these lines let us place one of the most justly-admired stanzas of the "Babes in the Wood."

> These pretty Babes with hand in hand
> Went wandering up and down;
> But never more they saw the Man
> Approaching from the Town.

In both these stanzas the words, and the order of the words, in no respect differ from the most unimpassioned conversation. There are words in both, for example, "the Strand," and "the Town," connected with none but the most familiar ideas; yet the one stanza we admit as admirable, and the other as a fair example of the superlatively contemptible. Whence arises this difference? Not from the metre, not from the language, not from the order of the words; but the *matter* expressed in Dr. Johnson's stanza is contemptible. The proper method of treating trivial and simple verses, to which Dr. Johnson's stanza would be a fair parallelism, is not to say, this is a bad kind of poetry, or, this is not poetry; but, this wants sense; it is neither interesting in itself, nor can *lead* to anything interesting; the images neither originate in that sane state of feeling which arises out of thought, nor can excite thought or feeling in the Reader. This is the only sensible manner of dealing with such verses. Why trouble yourself about the species till you have previously decided upon the genus? Why take pains to prove that an ape is not a Newton, when it is self-evident that he is not a man?

One request I must make of my Reader, which is, that in judging these Poems he would decide by his own feelings genuinely, and not by reflection upon what will probably be the judgment of others. How common is it to hear a person say, I myself do not object to this style of composition, or this or that expression, but to such and such classes of people it will appear mean or ludicrous! This mode of criticism, so destructive of all sound unadulterated judgment, is almost universal: let the Reader then abide, independently, by his own feelings, and, if he finds himself affected, let him not suffer such conjectures to interfere with his pleasure.

If an author, by any single composition, has impressed us with respect for his talents, it is useful to consider this as affording a presumption that on other occasions where we have been displeased he, nevertheless, may not have written ill or absurdly; and further, to give him so much credit for this one composition as may induce us to review what has displeased us with more care than we should otherwise have bestowed upon it. This is not only an act of justice, but, in our decisions upon poetry especially, may conduce, in a high degree, to the improvement of our own taste: for an *accurate* taste in poetry, and in all the other arts, as Sir Joshua Reynolds has observed, is an *acquired* talent, which can only be produced by thought and a long-continued intercourse with the best models of composition. This is mentioned, not with so ridiculous a purpose as to prevent the most inexperienced Reader from judging for himself (I have already said that I wish him to judge for himself), but merely to temper the rashness of decision, and to suggest that, if Poetry be a subject on which much time has not been bestowed, the judgment may be erroneous; and that, in many cases, it necessarily will be so.

Nothing would, I know, have so effectually contributed to further the end which I have in view, as to have shown of what kind the pleasure is, and how that pleasure is produced, which is confessedly produced by metrical composition essentially different from that which I have here endeavoured to recommend: for the Reader will say that he has been pleased by such composition; and what more can be done for him? The power of any art is limited; and he will suspect that, if it be proposed to furnish him with new friends, that can be only upon condition of his abandoning his old friends. Besides, as I have said, the Reader is himself conscious of the pleasure which he has received from such composition, composition to which he has peculiarly attached the endearing name of Poetry; and all men feel an habitual gratitude, and something of an honourable bigotry, for the objects which have long continued to please them: we not only wish to be pleased, but to be pleased in that particular way in which we have been accustomed to be pleased. There is in these feelings enough to resist a host of arguments, and I should be the less able to combat them successfully, as I am willing to allow that, in order entirely to enjoy the Poetry which I am recommending, it would be necessary to give up much of what is ordinarily enjoyed. But would my limits have permitted me to point out how this pleasure is produced, many obstacles might have been removed, and the Reader assisted in perceiving that the powers of language are not so limited as he may suppose; and that it is possible for poetry to give other enjoyments, of a purer, more lasting, and more exquisite nature. This part of the subject has not been altogether neglected, but it has not been so much my present aim to prove, that the interest excited by some other kinds of poetry is less vivid, and less worthy of the nobler powers of the mind, as to offer reasons for presuming that if my purpose were fulfilled, a species of poetry would be produced which is genuine poetry; in its nature well adapted to interest mankind permanently, and likewise important in the multiplicity and quality of its moral relations.

From what has been said, and from a perusal of the Poems, the Reader will be able clearly to perceive the object which I had in view: he will determine how far it has been attained, and, what is a much more important question, whether it be worth attaining: and upon the decision of these two questions will rest my claim to the approbation of the Public.

AN EVENING WALK

ADDRESSED TO A YOUNG LADY

The young Lady to whom this was addressed was my Sister. It was composed at school, and during my two first College vacations. There is not an image in it which I have not observed; and now, in my seventy-third year, I recollect the time and place where most of them were noticed. I will confine myself to one instance:—

Waving his hat, the shepherd, from the vale,
Directs his winding dog the cliffs to scale,
The dog, loud barking, 'mid the glittering rocks,

Hunts, where his master points, the intercepted flocks

I was an eye-witness of this for the first time while crossing the Pass of Dunmail Raise. Upon second thought, I will mention another image:—

And, fronting the bright west, yon oak entwines
It's darkening boughs and leaves, in stronger lines.

This is feebly and imperfectly expressed, but I recollect distinctly the very spot where this first struck me. It was in the way between Hawkshead and Ambleside, and gave me extreme pleasure. The moment was important in my poetical history; for I date from it my consciousness of the infinite variety of natural appearances which had been unnoticed by the poets of any age or country, so far as I was acquainted with them; and I made a resolution to supply, in some degree, the deficiency. I could not have been at that time above fourteen years of age. The description of the swans, that follows, was taken from the daily opportunities I had of observing their habits, not as confined to the gentleman's park, but in a state of nature. There were two pairs of them that divided the lake of Esthwaite and its in-and-out-flowing streams between them, never trespassing a single yard upon each other's separate domain. They were of the old magnificent species, bearing in beauty and majesty about the same relation to the Thames swan which that does to the goose. It was from the remembrance of those noble creatures I took, thirty years after, the picture of the swan which I have discarded from the poem of Dion. While I was a school-boy, the late Mr. Curwen introduced a little fleet of those birds, but of the inferior species, to the lake of Windermere. Their principal home was about his own island; but they sailed about into remote parts of the lake, and, either from real or imagined injury done to the adjoining fields, they were got rid of at the request of the farmers and proprietors, but to the great regret of all who had become attached to them, from noticing their beauty and quiet habits. I will conclude my notice of this poem by observing that the plan of it has not been confined to a particular walk or an individual place,—a proof (of which I was unconscious at the time) of my unwillingness to submit the poetic spirit to the chains of fact and real circumstance. The country is idealised rather than described in any one of its local aspects.

General Sketch of the Lakes—Author's regret of his youth which was passed amongst them—Short description of Noon—Cascade—Noontide Retreat—Precipice and sloping Lights—Face of Nature as the Sun declines—Mountain-farm, and the Cock—Slate-quarry—Sunset—Superstition of the Country connected with that moment

—Swans—Female Beggar—Twilight-sounds—
Western Lights—Spirits—Night—Moonlight—
Hope—Night-sounds—Conclusion. (Words-
worth)

———

Far from my dearest Friend, 'tis mine to rove
Through bare grey dell, high wood, and pastoral
    cove;
Where Derwent rests, and listens to the roar
That stuns the tremulous cliffs of high Lodore;
Where peace to Grasmere's lonely island leads,
To willowy hedge-rows, and to emerald meads;
Leads to her bridge, rude church, and cottaged
    grounds,
Her rocky sheepwalks, and her woodland bounds;
Where, undisturbed by winds, Winander sleeps
'Mid clustering isles, and holly-sprinkled
    steeps;   10
Where twilight glens endear my Esthwaite's shore,
And memory of departed pleasures, more.
    Fair scenes, erewhile, I taught, a happy child,
The echoes of your rocks my carols wild:
The spirit sought not then, in cherished sadness,
A cloudy substitute for failing gladness.
In youth's keen eye the livelong day was bright,
The sun at morning, and the stars at night,
Alike, when first the bittern's hollow bill
Was heard, or woodcocks roamed the moonlight
    hill.   20
    In thoughtless gaiety I coursed the plain,
And hope itself was all I knew of pain;
For then, the inexperienced heart would beat
At times, while young Content forsook her seat,
And wild Impatience, pointing upward, showed,
Through passes yet unreached, a brighter road.
Alas! the idle tale of man is found
Depicted in the dial's moral round;
Hope with reflection blends her social rays
To gild the total tablet of his days;   30
Yet still, the sport of some malignant power,
He knows but from its shade the present hour.
    But why, ungrateful, dwell on idle pain?
To show what pleasures yet to me remain,
Say, will my Friend, with unreluctant ear,
The history of a poet's evening hear?

AN EVENING WALK. 3. Derwent: river that flows past the
house where Wordsworth was born. 4. Lodore: waterfall at the foot of the Derwent. 9. Winander: Lake
Windemere.

When, in the south, the wan moon, brooding
    still,
Breathed a pale steam around the glaring hill,
And shades of deep-embattled clouds were seen,
Spotting the northern cliffs with lights be-
    tween;   40
When crowding cattle, checked by rails that make
A fence far stretched into the shallow lake,
Lashed the cool water with their restless tails,
Or from high points of rock looked out for fanning
    gales:
When school-boys stretched their length upon the
    green;
And round the broad-spread oak, a glimmering
    scene,
In the rough fern-clad park, the herded deer
Shook the still-twinkling tail and glancing ear;
When horses in the sunburnt intake stood,
And vainly eyed below the tempting flood,   50
Or tracked the passenger, in mute distress,
With forward neck the closing gate to press—
Then, while I wandered where the huddling rill
Brightens with water-breaks the hollow ghyll
As by enchantment, an obscure retreat
Opened at once, and stayed by devious feet.
While thick above the rill the branches close,
In rocky basin its wild waves repose,
Inverted shrubs, and moss of gloomy green,
Cling from the rocks, with pale wood-weeds be-
    tween;   60
And its own twilight softens the whole scene,
Save where aloft the subtle sunbeams shine
On withered briars that o'er the crags recline;
Save where, with sparkling foam, a small cascade
Illumines, from within, the leafy shade;
Beyond, along the vista of the brook,
Where antique roots its bustling course o'erlook,
The eye reposes on a secret bridge
Half grey, half shagged with ivy to its ridge;
There, bending o'er the stream, the listless
    swain   70
Lingers behind his disappearing wain.
—Did Sabine grace adorn my living line,
Blandusia's praise, wild stream, should yield to
    thine!
Never shall ruthless minister of death
'Mid thy soft glooms the glittering steel unsheath;
No goblets shall, for thee, be crowned with flowers,
No kid with piteous outcry thrill thy bowers;
The mystic shapes that by thy margin rove

A more benignant sacrifice approve—
A mind, that, in a calm angelic mood   80
Of happy wisdom, meditating good,
Beholds, of all from her high powers required,
Much done, and much designed, and more de-
        sired,—
Harmonious thoughts, a soul by truth refined,
Entire affection for all human kind.
   Dear Brook, farewell! To-morrow's noon again
Shall hide me, wooing long thy wildwood strain;
But now the sun has gained his western road,
And eve's mild hour invites my steps abroad.
   While, near the midway cliff, the silvered
        kite   90
In many a whistling circle wheels her flight;
Slant watery lights, from parting clouds, apace
Travel along the precipice's base;
Cheering its naked waste of scattered stone,
By lichens grey, and scanty moss, o'ergrown;
Where scarce the foxglove peeps, or thistle's beard;
And restless stone-chat, all day long, is heard.
   How pleasant, as the sun declines, to view
The spacious landscape change in form and hue!
Here, vanish, as in mist, before a flood   100
Of bright obscurity, hill, lawn, and wood;
There, objects, by the searching beams betrayed,
Come forth, and here retire in purple shade;
Even the white stems of birch, the cottage white,
Soften their glare before the mellow light;
The skiffs, at anchor where with umbrage wide
Yon chestnuts half the latticed boat-house hide,
Shed from their sides, that face the sun's slant
        beam,
Strong flakes of radiance on the tremulous stream:
Raised by yon travelling flock, a dusty cloud   110
Mounts from the road, and spreads its moving
        shroud;
The shepherd, all involved in wreaths of fire,
Now shows a shadowy speck, and now is lost entire.
   Into a gradual calm the breezes sink,
A blue rim borders all the lake's still brink;
There doth the twinkling aspen's foliage sleep,
And insects clothe, like dust, the glassy deep:
And now, on every side, the surface breaks
Into blue spots, and slowly lengthening streaks;
Here, plots of sparkling water tremble bright   120
With thousand thousand twinkling points of light;
There, waves that, hardly weltering, die away,
Tip their smooth ridges with a softer ray;
And now the whole wide lake in deep repose

Is hushed, and like a burnished mirror glows,
Save where, along the shady western marge,
Coasts, with industrious oar, the charcoal barge.
   Their panniered train a group of potters goad,
Winding from side to side up the steep road;
The peasant, from yon cliff of fearful edge   130
Shot, down the headlong path darts with his
        sledge;
Bright beams the lonely mountain-horse illume
Feeding 'mid purple heath, "green rings," and
        broom;
While the sharp slope the slackened team con-
        founds,
Downward the ponderous timber-wain resounds;
In foamy breaks the rill, with merry song,
Dashed o'er the rough rock, lightly leaps along;
From lonesome chapel at the mountain's feet,
Three humble bells their rustic chime repeat;
Sounds from the water-side the hammered
        boat;   140
And *blasted* quarry thunders, heard remote!
   Even here, amid the sweep of endless woods,
Blue pomp of lakes, high cliffs, and falling floods,
Not undelightful are the simplest charms,
Found by the grassy door of mountain-farms.
   Sweetly ferocious, round his native walks,
Pride of his sister-wives, the monarch stalks;
Spur-clad his nervous feet, and firm his tread;
A crest of purple tops the warrior's head.
Bright sparks his black and rolling eye-ball
        hurls   150
Afar, his tail he closes and unfurls;
On tiptoe reared, he strains his clarion throat,
Threatened by faintly-answering farms remote:
Again with his shrill voice the mountain rings,
While, flapped with conscious pride, resound his
        wings.
   Where, mixed with graceful birch, the sombrous
        pine
And yew-tree o'er the silver rocks recline;
I love to mark the quarry's moving trains,
Dwarf panniered steeds, and men, and numerous
        wains;
How busy all the enormous hive within,   160
While Echo dallies with its various din!
Some (hear you not their chisels' clinking sound?)

128. panniered: a pannier is a large basket, pairs of
which are hung across the back of a mule or horse for
carrying market produce.

Toil, small as pigmies in the gulf profound;
Some, dim between the lofty cliffs descried,
O'erwalk the slender plank from side to side;
These, by the pale-blue rocks that ceaseless ring,
In airy baskets hanging, work and sing.
   Just where a cloud above the mountain rears
An edge all flame, the broadening sun appears;
A long blue bar its ægis orb divides,   170
And breaks the spreading of its golden tides;
And now that orb has touched the purple steep
Whose softened image penetrates the deep.
'Cross the calm lake's blue shades the cliffs aspire,
With towers and woods, a "prospect all on fire;"
While coves and secret hollows, through a ray
Of fainter gold, a purple gleam betray.
Each slip of lawn the broken rocks between
Shines in the light with more than earthly green:
Deep yellow beams the scattered stems
     illume,   180
Far in the level forest's central gloom:
Waving his hat, the shepherd, from the vale,
Directs his winding dog the cliffs to scale,—
The dog, loud barking, 'mid the glittering rocks,
Hunts, where his master points, the intercepted
     flocks.
Where oaks o'erhang the road the radiance shoots
On tawny earth, wild weeds, and twisted roots;
The druid-stones a brightened ring unfold;
And all the babbling brooks are liquid gold;
Sunk to a curve, the day-star lessens still,   190
Gives one bright glance, and drops behind the hill.
   In these secluded vales, if village fame,
Confirmed by hoary hairs, belief may claim;
When up the hills, as now, retired the light,
Strange apparitions mocked the shepherd's sight.
   The form appears of one that spurs his steed
Midway along the hill with desperate speed;
Unhurt pursues his lengthened flight, while all
Attend, at every stretch, his headlong fall.
Anon, appears a brave, a gorgeous show   200
Of horsemen-shadows moving to and fro;
At intervals imperial banners stream,
And now the van reflects the solar beam;
The rear through iron brown betrays a sullen
     gleam.
While silent stands the admiring crowd below,
Silent the visionary warriors go,
Winding in ordered pomp their upward way
Till the last banner of the long array
Has disappeared, and every trace is fled

Of splendor—save the beacon's spiry head   210
Tipt with eve's latest gleam of burning red.
   Now, while the solemn evening shadows sail,
On slowly-waving pinions, down the vale;
And, fronting the bright west, yon oak entwines
Its darkening boughs and leaves, in stronger lines;
'T is pleasant near the tranquil lake to stray
Where, winding on along some secret bay,
The swan uplifts his chest, and backward flings
His neck, a varying arch, between his towering
     wings:
The eye that marks the gliding creature sees   220
How graceful pride can be, and how majestic, ease.
While tender cares and mild domestic loves
With furtive watch pursue her as she moves,
The female with a meeker charm succeeds,
And her brown little ones around her leads,
Nibbling the water lilies as they pass,
Or playing wanton with the floating grass.
She, in mother's care, her beauty's pride
Forgetting, calls the wearied to her side;
Alternately they mount her back, and rest   230
Close by her mantling wings' embraces prest.
   Long may they float upon this flood serene;
Theirs be these holms untrodden, still, and green,
Where leafy shades fence off the blustering gale,
And breathes in peace the lily of the vale!
Yon isle, which feels not even the milkmaid's feet,
Yet hears her song, "by distance made more sweet,"
Yon isle conceals their home, their hut-like bower;
Green water-rushes overspread the floor;
Long grass and willows form the woven wall,   240
And swings above the roof the poplar tall.
Thence issuing often with unwieldy stalk,
They crush with broad black feet their flowery
     walk;
Or, from the neighbouring water, hear at morn
The hound, the horse's tread, and mellow horn;
Involve their serpent-necks in changeful rings,
Rolled wantonly between their slippery wings,
Or, starting up with noise and rude delight,
Force half upon the wave their cumbrous flight.
   Fair Swan! by all a mother's joy caressed,   250
Haply some wretch has eyed, and called thee
     blessed;
When with her infants, from some shady seat

---

237. "by distance . . . sweet": quoted from "The Passions" by William Collins.

By the lake's edge, she rose—to face the noontide
    heat;
Or taught their limbs along the dusty road
A few short steps to totter with their load.
  I see her now, denied to lay her head,
On cold blue nights, in hut or straw-built shed,
Turn to a silent smile their sleepy cry,
By pointing to the gliding moon on high.
—When low-hung clouds each star of summer
    hide,   260
And fireless are the valleys far and wide,
Where the brook brawls along the public road
Dark with bat-haunted ashes stretching broad,
Oft has she taught them on her lap to lay
The shining glow-worm; or, in heedless play,
Toss it from hand to hand, disquieted;
While others, not unseen, are free to shed
Green unmolested light upon their mossy bed.
  Oh! when the sleety showers her path assail,
And like a torrent roars the headstrong gale; 270
No more her breath can thaw their fingers cold,
Their frozen arms her neck no more can fold;
Weak roof a cowering form two babes to shield,
And faint the fire a dying heart can yield!
Press the sad kiss, fond mother! vainly fears
Thy flooded cheek to wet them with its tears;
No tears can chill them, and no bosom warms,
Thy breast their death-bed, coffined in thine arms!
  Sweet are the sounds that mingle from afar,
Heard by calm lakes, as peeps the folding
    star,   280
Where the duck dabbles 'mid the rustling sedge,
And feeding pike starts from the water's edge,
Or the swan stirs the reeds, his neck and bill
Wetting, that drip upon the water still;
And heron, as resounds the trodden shore,
Shoots upward, darting his long neck before.
  Now, with religious awe, the farewell light
Blends with the solemn colouring of night;
'Mid groves of clouds that crest the mountain's
    brow,
And round the west's proud lodge their shadows
    throw,   290
Like Una shining on her gloomy way,
The half-seen form of Twilight roams astray;
Shedding, through paly loop-holes mild and small,
Gleams that upon the lake's still bosom fall;

291. **Una:** the heroine of Book I of Spenser's *Faerie Queene.*

Soft o'er the surface creep those lustres pale
Tracking the motions of the fitful gale.
With restless interchange at once the bright
Wins on the shade, the shade upon the light.
No favoured eye was e'er allowed to gaze
On lovelier spectacle in faery days;   300
When gentle Spirits urged a sportive chase,
Brushing with lucid wands the water's face:
While music, stealing round the glimmering deeps,
Charmed the tall circle of the enchanted steeps.
—The lights are vanished from the watery plains:
No wreck of all the pageantry remains.
Unheeded night has overcome the vales:
On the dark earth the wearied vision fails;
The latest lingerer of the forest train,
The lone black fir, forsakes the faded plain; 310
Last evening sight, the cottage smoke, no more,
Lost in the thickened darkness, glimmers hoar;
And, towering from the sullen dark-brown mere,
Like a black wall, the mountain-steeps appear.
—Now o'er the soothed accordant heart we feel
A sympathetic twilight slowly steal,
And ever, as we fondly muse, we find
The soft gloom deepening on the tranquil mind.
Stay! pensive, sadly-pleasing visions, stay!
Ah no! as fades the vale, they fade away: 320
Yet still the tender, vacant gloom remains;
Still the cold cheek its shuddering tear retains.
  The bird, who ceased, with fading light, to
    thread
Silent the hedge or steamy rivulet's bed,
From his grey, re-appearing tower shall soon
Salute with gladsome note the rising moon,
While with a hoary light she frosts the ground,
And pours a deeper blue to Æther's bound;
Pleased, as she moves, her pomp of clouds to fold
In robes of azure, fleecy-white, and gold. 330
  Above yon eastern hill, where darkness broods
O'er all its vanished dells, and lawns, and woods;
Where but a mass of shade the sight can trace,
Even now she shews, half-veiled her lovely face:
Across the gloomy valley flings her light,
Far to the western slopes with hamlets white;
And gives, where woods the chequered upland
    strew,
To the green corn of summer, autumn's hue.
  Thus Hope, first pouring from her blessed horn
Her dawn, far lovelier than the moon's own
    morn,   340
Till higher mounted, strives in vain to cheer

The weary hills, impervious, blackening near;
Yet does she still, undaunted, throw the while
On darling spots remote her tempting smile.

Even now she decks for me a distant scene,
(For dark and broad the gulf of time between)
Gilding that cottage with her fondest ray,
(Sole bourn, sole wish, sole object of my way;
How fair its lawns and sheltering woods appear!
How sweet its streamlet murmurs in mine ear!)
Where we, my Friend, to happy days shall rise,
Till our small share of hardly-paining sighs
(For sighs will ever trouble human breath)
Creep hushed into the tranquil breast of death.

But now the clear bright Moon her zenith gains,
And, rimy without speck, extend the plains:
The deepest cleft the mountain's front displays
Scarce hides a shadow from her searching rays;
From the dark-blue faint silvery threads divide
The hills, while gleams below the azure tide;   360
Time softly treads; throughout the landscape
   breathes
A peace enlivened, not disturbed, by wreaths
Of charcoal-smoke, that o'er the fallen wood,
Steal down the hill, and spread along the flood.

The song of mountain-streams, unheard by day,
Now hardly heard, beguiles my homeward way.
Air listens, like the sleeping water, still,
To catch the spiritual music of the hill,
Broke only by the slow clock tolling deep,
Or shout that wakes the ferry-man from
   sleep,   370
The echoed hoof nearing the distant shore,
The boat's first motion—made with dashing oar;
Sound of closed gate, across the water borne,
Hurrying the timid hare through rustling corn;
The sportive outcry of the mocking owl;
And at long intervals the mill-dog's howl;
The distant forge's swinging thump profound;
Or yell, in the deep woods, of lonely hound.

1787–1793   *1793*

THE OLD CUMBERLAND
BEGGAR

Observed, and with great benefit to my own heart,
when I was a child: written at Racedown and Alfoxden in my twenty-third year. The political econ-
omists were about that time beginning their war

upon mendicity in all its forms, and by implication,
if not directly, on alms-giving also. This heartless
process has been carried as far as it can go by the
AMENDED poor-law bill, though the inhumanity
that prevails in this measure is somewhat disguised
by the profession that one of its objects is to throw
the poor upon the voluntary donations of their
neighbours; that is, if rightly interpreted, to force
them into a condition between relief in the Union
poorhouse, and alms robbed of their Christian grace
and spirit, as being *forced* rather from the benevolent than given by them; while the avaricious and
selfish, and all in fact but the humane and chari-
table, are at liberty to keep all they possess from
their distressed brethren.

The class of Beggars, to which the Old Man here
described belongs, will probably soon be extinct. It
consisted of poor, and, mostly, old and infirm persons, who confined themselves to a stated round in
their neighbourhood, and had certain fixed days,
on which, at different houses, they regularly received alms, sometimes in money, but mostly in
provisions. (Wordsworth)

I saw an aged beggar in my walk;
And he was seated, by the highway side,
On a low structure of rude masonry
Built at the foot of a huge hill, that they
Who lead their horses down the steep rough road
May thence remount at ease. The aged Man
Had placed his staff across the broad smooth stone
That overlays the pile; and, from a bag
All white with flour, the dole of village dames,
He drew his scraps and fragments, one by one;   10
And scanned them with a fixed and serious look
Of idle computation. In the sun,
Upon the second step of that small pile,
Surrounded by those wild unpeopled hills,
He sat, and ate his food in solitude:
And ever, scattered from his palsied hand,
That, still attempting to prevent the waste,
Was baffled still, the crumbs in little showers
Fell on the ground; and the small mountain birds,
Not venturing yet to peck their destined meal,   20
Approached within the length of half his staff.

Him from my childhood have I known; and then
He was so old, he seems not older now;
He travels on, a solitary Man,
So helpless in appearance, that for him
The sauntering Horseman throws not with a slack
And careless hand his alms upon the ground,
But stops,—that he may safely lodge the coin
Within the old Man's hat; nor quits him so,

But still, when he has given his horse the rein,   30
Watches the aged Beggar with a look
Sidelong, and half-reverted. She who tends
The toll gate, when in summer at her door
She turns her wheel, if on the road she sees
The aged beggar coming, quits her work,
And lifts the latch for him that he may pass.
The post-boy, when his rattling wheels o'ertake
The aged Beggar in the woody lane,
Shouts to him from behind; and if, thus warned,
The old man does not change his course, the
    boy   40
Turns with less noisy wheels to the roadside,
And passes gently by, without a curse
Upon his lips, or anger at his heart.
   He travels on, a solitary Man;
His age has no companion. On the ground
His eyes are turned, and, as he moves along
They move along the ground; and, evermore,
Instead of common and habitual sight
Of fields with rural works, of hill and dale,
And the blue sky, one little span of earth   50
Is all his prospect. Thus, from day to day,
Bow-bent, his eyes for ever on the ground,
He plies his weary journey; seeing still,
And seldom knowing that he sees, some straw,
Some scattered leaf, or marks which, in one track,
The nails of cart or chariot-wheel have left
Impressed on the white road,—in the same line,
At distance still the same. Poor Traveller!
His staff trails with him; scarcely do his feet
Disturb the summer dust; he is so still   60
In look and motion, that the cottage curs,
Ere he has passed the door, will turn away,
Weary of barking at him. Boys and girls,
The vacant and the busy, maids and youths,
And urchins newly breeched—all pass him by:
Him even the slow-paced waggon leaves behind.
   But deem not this Man useless.—Statesmen! ye
Who are so restless in your wisdom, ye
Who have a broom still ready in your hands
To rid the world of nuisances; ye proud,   70
Heart-swoln, while in your pride ye contemplate
Your talents, power, or wisdom, deem him not
A burthen of the earth! 'Tis Nature's law
That none, the meanest of created things,
Or forms created the most vile and brute,
The dullest or most noxious, should exist
Divorced from good—a spirit and pulse of good,
A life and soul, to every mode of being

Inseparably linked. Then be assured
That least of all can aught—that ever owned   80
The heaven-regarding eye and front sublime
Which man is born to—sink, howe'er depressed,
So low as to be scorned without a sin;
Without offence to God cast out of view;
Like the dry remnant of a garden-flower
Whose seeds are shed, or as an implement
Worn out and worthless. While from door to door,
This old Man creeps, the villagers in him
Behold a record which together binds
Past deeds and offices of charity,   90
Else unremembered, and so keeps alive
The kindly mood in hearts which lapse of years,
And that half-wisdom half-experience gives,
Make slow to feel, and by sure steps resign
To selfishness and cold oblivious cares.
Among the farms and solitary huts,
Hamlets and thinly-scattered villages,
Where'er the aged Beggar takes his rounds,
The mild necessity of use compels
To acts of love; and habit does the work   100
Of reason; yet prepares that after-joy
Which reason cherishes. And thus the soul,
By that sweet taste of pleasure unpursued,
Doth find herself insensibly disposed
To virtue and true goodness.
               Some there are,
By their good works exalted, lofty minds
And meditative, authors of delight
And happiness, which to the end of time
Will live, and spread, and kindle: even such minds
In childhood, from this solitary Being,   110
Or from like wanderer, haply have received
(A thing more precious far than all that books
Or the solicitudes of love can do!)
That first mild touch of sympathy and thought,
In which they found their kindred with a world
Where want and sorrow were. The easy man
Who sits at his own door,—and, like the pear
That overhangs his head from the green wall,
Feeds in the sunshine; the robust and young,
The prosperous and unthinking, they who live   120
Sheltered, and flourish in a little grove
Of their own kindred;—all behold in him
A silent monitor, which on their minds
Must needs impress a transitory thought
Of self-congratulation, to the heart
Of each recalling his peculiar boons,
His charters and exemptions; and, perchance,

Though he to no one give the fortitude
And circumspection needful to preserve
His present blessings, and to husband up   130
The respite of the season, he, at least,
And 'tis no vulgar service, makes them felt.
  Yet further.——Many, I believe, there are
Who live a life of virtuous decency,
Men who can hear the Decalogue and feel
No self-reproach; who of the moral law
Established in the land where they abide
Are strict observers; and not negligent
In acts of love to those with whom they dwell,
Their kindred, and the children of their blood   140
Praise be to such, and to their slumbers peace!
—But of the poor man ask, the abject poor;
Go, and demand of him, if there be here
In this cold abstinence from evil deeds,
And these inevitable charities,
Wherewith to satisfy the human soul?
No—man is dear to man; the poorest poor
Long for some moments in a weary life
When they can know and feel that they have been,
Themselves the father and the dealers-out   150
Of some small blessings; have been kind to such
As needed kindness, for this single cause,
That we have all of us one human heart.
—Such pleasure is to one kind Being known.
My neighbour, when with punctual care, each week
Duly as Friday comes, though pressed herself
By her own wants, she from her store of meal
Takes one unsparing handful for the scrip
Of this old Mendicant, and, from her door
Returning with exhilarated heart,   160
Sits by her fire, and builds her hope in heaven.
  Then let him pass, a blessing on his head!
And while in that vast solitude to which
The tide of things has borne him, he appears
To breathe and live but for himself alone,
Unblamed, uninjured, let him bear about
The good which the benignant law of Heaven
Has hung around him: and, while life is his,
Still let him prompt the unlettered villagers
To tender offices and pensive thoughts.   170
—Then let him pass, a blessing on his head!
And, long as he can wander, let him breathe
The freshness of the valleys; let his blood
Struggle with frosty air and winter snows;
And let the chartered wind that sweeps the heath
Beat his grey locks against his withered face.
Reverence the hope whose vital anxiousness

Gives the last human interest to his heart.
May never HOUSE, misnamed of INDUSTRY,
Make him a captive!—for that pent-up din,   180
Those life-consuming sounds that clog the air,
Be his the natural silence of old age!
Let him be free of mountain solitudes;
And have around him, whether heard or not,
The pleasant melody of woodland birds.
Few are his pleasures: if his eyes have now
Been doomed so long to settle upon earth
That not without some effort they behold
The countenance of the horizontal sun,
Rising or setting, let the light at least   190
Find a free entrance to their languid orbs.
And let him, *where* and *when* he will, sit down
Beneath the trees, or on a grassy bank
Of highway side, and with the little birds
Share his chance-gathered meal; and, finally,
As in the eye of Nature he has lived,
So in the eye of Nature let him die!

1797   *1800*

FROM

Lyrical Ballads

GOODY BLAKE AND
HARRY GILL

A TRUE STORY

Oh! what's the matter? what's the matter?
What is 't that ails young Harry Gill?
That evermore his teeth they chatter,
Chatter, chatter, chatter still!
Of waistcoats Harry has no lack,
Good duffle grey, and flannel fine;
He has a blanket on his back,
And coats enough to smother nine.

In March, December, and in July,
'T is all the same with Harry Gill;   10
The neighbours tell, and tell you truly,
His teeth they chatter, chatter still.
At night, at morning, and at noon,
'Tis all the same with Harry Gill;

THE OLD CUMBERLAND BEGGAR. 179. House . . . Industry: poorhouse.

Beneath the sun, beneath the moon,
His teeth they chatter, chatter still!

Young Harry was a lusty drover,
And who so stout of limb as he?
His cheeks were red as ruddy clover;
His voice was like the voice of three. 20
Old Goody Blake was old and poor;
Ill fed she was, and thinly clad;
And any man who passed her door
Might see how poor a hut she had.

All day she spun in her poor dwelling:
And then her three hours' work at night,
Alas! 'twas hardly worth the telling,
It would not pay for candle-light.
Remote from sheltered village-green,
On a hill's northern side she dwelt, 30
Where from sea-blasts the hawthorns lean,
And hoary dews are slow to melt.

By the same fire to boil their pottage,
Two poor old Dames, as I have known,
Will often live in one small cottage;
But she, poor Woman! housed alone.
'Twas well enough when summer came,
The long, warm, lightsome summer-day,
Then at her door the *canty* Dame
Would sit, as any linnet, gay. 40

But when the ice our streams did fetter
Oh then how her old bones would shake!
You would have said, if you had met her,
'Twas a hard time for Goody Blake.
Her evenings then were dull and dead:
Sad case it was, as you may think,
For very cold to go to bed,
And then for cold not sleep a wink.

O joy for her! whene'er in winter
The winds at night had made a rout; 50
And scattered many a lusty splinter
And many a rotten bough about.
Yet never had she, well or sick,
As every man who knew her says,
A pile beforehand, turf or stick,
Enough to warm her for three days.

Now, when the frost was past enduring,
And made her poor old bones to ache,
Could any thing be more alluring
Than an old hedge to Goody Blake? 60

And, now and then, it must be said,
When her old bones were cold and chill,
She left her fire, or left her bed,
To seek the hedge of Harry Gill.

Now Harry he had long suspected
This trespass of old Goody Blake;
And vowed that she should be detected—
That he on her would vengeance take.
And oft from his warm fire he'd go,
And to the fields his road would take; 70
And there, at night, in frost and snow,
He watched to seize old Goody Blake.

And once, behind a rick of barley,
Thus looking out did Harry stand:
The moon was full and shining clearly,
And crisp with frost the stubble land.
—He hears a noise—he's all awake—
Again?—on tip-toe down the hill
He softly creeps—'t is Goody Blake;
She's at the hedge of Harry Gill! 80

Right glad was he when he beheld her:
Stick after stick did Goody pull:
He stood behind a bush of elder,
Till she had filled her apron full.
When with her load she turned about,
The by-way back again to take;
He started forward, with a shout,
And sprang upon poor Goody Blake.

And fiercely by the arm he took her,
And by the arm he held her fast, 90
And fiercely by the arm he shook her,
And cried, "I've caught you then at last!"—
Then Goody, who had nothing said,
Her bundle from her lap let fall;
And, kneeling on the sticks, she prayed
To God that is the judge of all.

She prayed, her withered hand uprearing,
While Harry held her by the arm—
"God! who art never out of hearing,
O may he never more be warm!" 100
The cold, cold moon above her head,
Thus on her knees did Goody pray;
Young Harry heard what she had said:
And icy cold he turned away.

He went complaining all the morrow
That he was cold and very chill:

His face was gloom, his heart was sorrow,
Alas! that day for Harry Gill!
That day he wore a riding-coat,
But not a whit the warmer he: 110
Another was on Thursday brought,
And ere the Sabbath he had three.

'Twas all in vain, a useless matter,
And blankets were about him pinned;
Yet still his jaws and teeth they clatter,
Like a loose casement in the wind.
And Harry's flesh it fell away;
And all who see him say, 'tis plain,
That, live as long as live he may,
He never will be warm again.   120

No word to any man he utters,
A-bed or up, to young or old;
But ever to himself he mutters,
"Poor Harry Gill is very cold."
A-bed or up, by night or day;
His teeth they chatter, chatter still.
Now think, ye farmers all, I pray,
Of Goody Blake and Harry Gill!

1798   1798

SIMON LEE

THE OLD HUNTSMAN;
WITH AN INCIDENT IN WHICH HE WAS
CONCERNED

In the sweet shire of Cardigan,
Not far from pleasant Ivor-hall,
An old Man dwells, a little man,—
'Tis said he once was tall.
Full five-and-thirty years he lived
A running huntsman merry;
And still the centre of his cheek
Is red as a ripe cherry.

No man like him the horn could sound,
And hill and valley rang with glee   10
When Echo bandied, round and round,
The halloo of Simon Lee.
In those proud days, he little cared
For husbandry or tillage;
To blither tasks did Simon rouse
The sleepers of the village.

He all the country could outrun,
Could leave both man and horse behind;
And often, ere the chase was done,
He reeled, and was stone-blind.   20
And still there's something in the world
At which his heart rejoices;
For when the chiming hounds are out,
He dearly loves their voices!

But, oh the heavy change!—bereft
Of health, strength, friends, and kindred, see!
Old Simon to the world is left
In liveried poverty.
His Master's dead,—and no one now
Dwells in the Hall of Ivor;   30
Men, dogs, and horses, all are dead;
He is the sole survivor.

And he is lean and he is sick;
His body, dwindled and awry,
Rests upon ankles swoln and thick;
His legs are thin and dry.
One prop he has, and only one,
His wife, an aged woman,
Lives with him, near the waterfall,
Upon the village Common.   40

Beside their moss-grown hut of clay,
Not twenty paces from the door,
A scrap of land they have, but they
Are poorest of the poor.
This scrap of land he from the heath
Enclosed when he was stronger;
But what to them avails the land
Which he can till no longer?

Oft working by her Husband's side,
Ruth does what Simon cannot do;   50
For she, with scanty cause for pride,
Is stouter of the two.
And, though you with your utmost skill
From labour could not wean them,
'Tis little, very little—all
That they can do between them.

Few months of life has he in store
As he to you will tell,
For still, the more he works, the more
Do his weak ankles swell.   60
My gentle Reader, I perceive
How patiently you've waited,

And now I fear that you expect
Some tale will be related.

O Reader! had you in your mind
Such stores as silent thought can bring,
O gentle Reader! you would find
A tale in every thing.
What more I have to say is short,
And you must kindly take it: 70
It is no tale; but, should you think,
Perhaps a tale you'll make it.

One summer-day I chanced to see
This old Man doing all he could
To unearth the root of an old tree,
A stump of rotten wood.
The mattock tottered in his hand;
So vain was his endeavour,
That at the root of the old tree
He might have worked for ever.   80

"You're overtasked, good Simon Lee,
Give me your tool," to him I said;
And at the word right gladly he
Received my proffered aid.
I struck, and with a single blow
The tangled root I severed,
At which the poor old Man so long
And vainly had endeavoured.

The tears into his eyes were brought,
And thanks and praises seemed to run   90
So fast out of his heart, I thought
They never would have done.
—I've heard of hearts unkind, kind deeds
With coldness still returning;
Alas! the gratitude of men
Hath oftener left me mourning.

1798   1798

WE ARE SEVEN

Written at Alfoxden in the spring of 1798, under circumstances somewhat remarkable. The little girl who is the heroine I met within the area of Goodrich Castle in the year 1793. Having left the Isle of Wight and crossed Salisbury Plain, as mentioned in the preface to "Guilt and Sorrow," I proceeded by Bristol up the Wye, and so on to North Wales, to the Vale of Clwydd, where I spent my summer under the roof of the father of my friend, Robert Jones. In reference to this Poem I will here mention one of the most remarkable facts in my own poetic history and that of Mr. Coleridge. In the spring of the year 1798, he, my Sister, and myself, started from Alfoxden, pretty late in the afternoon, with a view to visit Lenton and the valley of Stones near it; and as our united funds were very small, we agreed to defray the expense of the tour by writing a poem, to be sent to the New Monthly Magazine set up by Phillips the bookseller, and edited by Dr. Aikin. Accordingly we set off and proceeded along the Quantock Hills towards Watchet, and in the course of this walk was planned the poem of the "Ancient Mariner," founded on a dream, as Mr. Coleridge said, of his friend, Mr. Cruikshank. Much the greatest part of the story was Mr. Coleridge's invention; but certain parts I myself suggested:— for example, some crime was to be committed which should bring upon the old Navigator, as Coleridge afterwards delighted to call him, the spectral persecution, as a consequence of that crime, and his own wanderings. I had been reading in Shelvock's Voyages a day or two before that while doubling Cape Horn they frequently saw Albatrosses in that latitude, the largest sort of sea-fowl, some extending their wings twelve or fifteen feet. "Suppose," said I, "you represent him as having killed one of these birds on entering the South Sea, and that the tutelary Spirits of those regions take upon them to avenge the crime." The incident was thought fit for the purpose and adopted accordingly. I also suggested the navigation of the ship by the dead men, but do not recollect that I had anything more to do with the scheme of the poem. The Gloss with which it was subsequently accompanied was not thought of by either of us at the time; at least, not a hint of it was given to me, and I have no doubt it was a gratuitous after-thought. We began the composition together on that, to me, memorable evening. I furnished two or three lines at the beginning of the poem, in particular:—

And listened like a three years' child;
The Mariner had his will.

These trifling contributions, all but one (which Mr. C. has with unnecessary scrupulosity recorded) slipt out of his mind as they well might. As we endeavoured to proceed conjointly (I speak of the same evening) our respective manners proved so widely different that it would have been quite presumptuous in me to do anything but separate from an undertaking upon which I could only have been a clog. We returned after a few days from a delightful tour, of which I have many pleasant, and some of them droll-enough, recollections. We returned by Dulverton to Alfoxden. The "Ancient Mariner" grew and grew till it became too important for our first object, which was limited to our expectation of five pounds, and we began to talk of a Volume, which was to consist, as Mr. Coleridge has told the world, of poems chiefly on supernatural subjects taken from common life, but looked at, as much as might be, through an imaginative medium. Accordingly I wrote "The Idiot Boy," "Her eyes are wild," etc., "We are seven," "The Thorn," and some others. To return to "We are seven," the piece that called forth this note, I composed it while walking in the grove at Alfoxden. My friends will not deem it too trifling to relate that while walking to and fro I composed the last stanza first, having begun with the last line. When it was all but finished, I came in and recited it to Mr. Coleridge and my Sister, and said, "A prefatory stanza must be added, and I should sit down to our little tea-meal with greater pleasure if my task were finished." I mentioned in substance what I wished to be expressed, and Coleridge immediately threw off the stanza thus:—

A little child, dear brother Jem,—

I objected to the rhyme, "dear brother Jem," as being ludicrous, but we all enjoyed the joke of hitching-in our friend, James T——'s name, who was familiarly called Jem. He was the brother of the dramatist, and this reminds me of an anecdote which it may be worth while here to notice. The said Jem got a sight of the Lyrical Ballads as it was going through the press at Bristol, during which time I was residing in that city. One evening he came to me with a grave face, and said, "Wordsworth, I have seen the volume that Coleridge and you are about to publish. There is one poem in it which I earnestly entreat you will cancel, for, if published, it will make you everlastingly ridiculous." I answered that I felt much obliged by the interest he took in my good name as a writer, and begged to know what was the unfortunate piece he alluded to. He said, "It is called 'We are seven.'" Nay! said I, that shall take its chance, however, and he left me in despair. I have only to add that in the spring of 1841 I revisited Goodrich Castle, not having seen that part of the Wye since I met the little Girl there in 1793. It would have given me greater pleasure to have found in the neighbouring hamlet traces of one who had interested me so much; but that was impossible, as unfortunately I did not even know her name. The ruin, from its position and features, is a most impressive object. I could not but deeply regret that its solemnity was impaired by a fantastic new Castle set up on a projection of the same ridge, as if to show how far modern art can go by surpassing all that could be done by antiquity and nature with their united graces, remembrances, and associations. (Wordsworth)

————

  —A simple Child,
That lightly draws its breath,
And feels its life in every limb,
What should it know of death?

I met a little cottage Girl:
She was eight years old, she said;
Her hair was thick with many a curl
That clustered round her head.

She had a rustic, woodland air,
And she was wildly clad: 10
Her eyes were fair, and very fair;
—Her beauty made me glad.

"Sisters and brothers, little Maid,
How many may you be?"
"How many? Seven in all," she said
And wondering looked at me.

"And where are they? I pray you tell."
She answered, "Seven are we;
And two of us at Conway dwell,
And two are gone to sea.   20

"Two of us in the church-yard lie,
My sister and my brother;
And, in the church-yard cottage, I
Dwell near them with my mother."

"You say that two at Conway dwell,
And two are gone to sea,
Yet ye are seven!—I pray you tell,
Sweet Maid, how this may be."

Then did the little Maid reply,
"Seven boys and girls are we;   30
Two of us in the church-yard lie,
Beneath the church-yard tree."

"You run about, my little Maid,
Your limbs they are alive;
If two are in the church-yard laid,
Then ye are only five."

"Their graves are green, they may be seen,"
The little Maid replied,
"Twelve steps or more from my mother's door,
And they are side by side.   40

"My stockings there I often knit,
My kerchief there I hem;
And there upon the ground I sit,
And sing a song to them.

"And often after sunset, Sir,
When it is light and fair,
I take my little porringer,
And eat my supper there.

"The first that died was sister Jane;
In bed she moaning lay,   50
Till God released her of her pain;
And then she went away.

"So in the church-yard she was laid;
And, when the grass was dry,
Together round her grave we played,
My brother John and I.

"And when the ground was white with snow,
And I could run and slide,
My brother John was forced to go,
And he lies by her side."   60

"How many are you, then," said I,
"If they two are in heaven?"
Quick was the little Maid's reply,
"O Master! we are seven."

"But they are dead; those two are dead!
Their spirits are in heaven!"
'Twas throwing words away; for still
The little Maid would have her will,
And said, "Nay, we are seven!"

1798   1798

THE THORN

Written at Alfoxden. Arose out of my observing, on
the ridge of Quantock Hill, on a stormy day, a
thorn which I had often past, in calm and bright
weather, without noticing it. I said to myself, "Cannot I by some invention do as much to make this
Thorn permanently an impressive object as the
storm has made it to my eyes at this moment?" I
began the poem accordingly, and composed it with
great rapidity. Sir George Beaumont painted a picture from it which Wilkie thought his best. He gave
it me; though when he saw it several times at Rydal
Mount afterwards, he said, "I could make a better,
and would like to paint the same subject over
again." The sky in this picture is nobly done, but
it reminds one too much of Wilson. The only fault,
however, of any consequence is the female figure,
which is too old and decrepit for one likely to frequent an eminence on such a call. (Wordsworth)

"There is a Thorn—it looks so old,
In truth, you'd find it hard to say
How it could ever have been young,

It looks so old and grey.
Not higher than a two years' child
It stands erect, this aged Thorn;
No leaves it has, no prickly points;
It is a mass of knotted joints,
A wretched thing forlorn.
It stands erect, and like a stone   10
With lichens is it overgrown.

"Like rock or stone, it is o'ergrown,
With lichens to the very top,
And hung with heavy tufts of moss,
A melancholy crop:
Up from the earth these mosses creep,
And this poor Thorn they clasp it round
So close, you'd say that they are bent
With plain and manifest intent
To drag it to the ground;   20
And all have joined in one endeavour
To bury this poor Thorn for ever.

"High on a mountain's highest ridge,
Where oft the stormy winter gale
Cuts like a scythe, while through the clouds
It sweeps from vale to vale;
Not five yards from the mountain path,
This Thorn you on your left espy;
And to the left, three yards beyond,
You see a little muddy pond   30
Of water—never dry
Though but of compass small, and bare
To thirsty suns and parching air.

"And, close beside this aged Thorn,
There is a fresh and lovely sight,
A beauteous heap, a hill of moss,
Just half a foot in height.
All lovely colours there you see,
All colours that were ever seen;
And mossy network too is here,   40
As if by hand of lady fair
The work had woven been;
And cups, the darlings of the eye,
So deep is their vermilion dye.

"Ah me! what lovely tints are there
Of olive green and scarlet bright,
In spikes, in branches, and in stars,
Green, red, and pearly white!
This heap of earth o'ergrown with moss,
Which close beside the Thorn you see,   50
So fresh in all its beauteous dyes,

Is like an infant's grave in size,
As like as like can be:
But never, never any where,
An infant's grave was half so fair.

"Now would you see this aged Thorn,
This pond, and beauteous hill of moss,
You must take care and choose your time
The mountain when to cross.
For oft there sits between the heap   60
So like an infant's grave in size,
And that same pond of which I spoke,
A Woman in a scarlet cloak,
And to herself she cries,
'Oh misery! oh misery!
Oh woe is me! oh misery!'

"At all times of the day and night
This wretched Woman thither goes;
And she is known to every star,
And every wind that blows;   70
And there, beside the Thorn, she sits
When the blue daylight's in the skies
And when the whirlwind's on the hill,
Or frosty air is keen and still,
And to herself she cries,
'Oh misery! oh misery!
Oh woe is me! oh misery!' "

"Now wherefore, thus, by day and night,
In rain, in tempest, and in snow,
Thus to the dreary mountain-top   80
Does this poor Woman go?
And why sits she beside the Thorn
When the blue daylight's in the sky,
Or when the whirlwind's on the hill,
Or frosty air is keen and still,
And wherefore does she cry?—
O wherefore? wherefore? tell me why
Does she repeat that doleful cry?"

"I cannot tell; I wish I could;
For the true reason no one knows: 90
But would you gladly view the spot,
The spot to which she goes;
The hillock like an infant's grave,
The pond—and Thorn, so old and grey;
Pass by her door—'tis seldom shut—
And, if you see her in her hut—
Then to the spot away!
I never heard of such as dare
Approach the spot when she is there."

"But wherefore to the mountain-top   100
Can this unhappy Woman go?
Whatever star is in the skies,
Whatever wind may blow?"
"Full twenty years are past and gone
Since she (her name is Martha Ray)
Gave with a maiden's true good-will
Her company to Stephen Hill;
And she was blithe and gay,
While friends and kindred all approved
Of him whom tenderly she loved.   110

"And they had fixed the wedding day,
The morning that must wed them both;
But Stephen to another Maid
Had sworn another oath;
And, with this other Maid, to church
Unthinking Stephen went—
Poor Martha! on that woeful day
A pang of pitiless dismay
Into her soul was sent;
A fire was kindled in her breast,   120
Which might not burn itself to rest.

"They say, full six months after this,
While yet the summer leaves were green,
She to the mountain-top would go,
And there was often seen.
What could she seek?—or wish to hide?
Her state to any eye was plain;
She was with child, and she was mad;
Yet often was she sober sad
From her exceeding pain.   130
O guilty Father—would that death
Had saved him from that breach of faith!

"Sad case for such a brain to hold
Communion with a stirring child!
Sad case, as you may think, for one
Who had a brain so wild!
Last Christmas-eve we talked of this,
And grey-haired Wilfred of the glen
Held that the unborn infant wrought
About its mother's heart, and brought   140
Her senses back again:
And, when at last her time drew near,
Her looks were calm, her senses clear.

"More know I not, I wish I did,
And it should all be told to you;
For what became of this poor child
No mortal ever knew;

Nay—if a child to her was born
No earthly tongue could ever tell;
And if 'twas born alive or dead,   150
Far less could this with proof be said;
But some remember well,
That Martha Ray about this time
Would up the mountain often climb.

"And all that winter, when at night
The wind blew from the mountain-peak,
'Twas worth your while, though in the dark,
The churchyard path to seek!
For many a time and oft were heard
Cries coming from the mountain head: 160
Some plainly living voices were;
And others, I've heard many swear,
Were voices of the dead:
I cannot think, whate'er they say,
They had to do with Martha Ray.

"But that she goes to this old Thorn,
The Thorn which I described to you,
And there sits in a scarlet cloak
I will be sworn is true.
For one day with my telescope,   170
To view the ocean wide and bright,
When to this country first I came,
Ere I had heard of Martha's name,
I climbed the mountain's height:—
A storm came on, and I could see
No object higher than my knee.

" 'Twas mist and rain, and storm and rain:
No screen, no fence could I discover;
And then the wind! in sooth, it was
A wind full ten times over.   180
I looked around, I thought I saw
A jutting crag,—and off I ran,
Head-foremost, through the driving rain,
The shelter of the crag to gain;
And, as I am a man,
Instead of jutting crag, I found
A Woman seated on the ground.

"I did not speak—I saw her face;
Her face!—it was enough for me;
I turned about and heard her cry,   190
'Oh misery! oh misery!'
And there she sits, until the moon
Through half the clear blue sky will go;
And, when the little breezes make
The waters of the pond to shake,

As all the country know,
She shudders, and you hear the cry,
'Oh misery! oh misery!' "

"But what's the Thorn? and what the pond?
And what the hill of moss to her?   200
And what the creeping breeze that comes
The little pond to stir?"
"I cannot tell; but some will say
She hanged her baby on the tree;
Some say she drowned it in the pond,
Which is a little step beyond:
But all and each agree,
The little Babe was buried there,
Beneath that hill of moss so fair.

"I've heard, the moss is spotted red   210
With drops of that poor infant's blood;
But kill a new-born infant thus,
I do not think she could!
Some say, if to the pond you go,
And fix on it a steady view,
The shadow of a babe you trace,
A baby and a baby's face,
And that it looks at you;
Whene'er you look on it, 'tis plain
The baby looks at you again.   220

"And some had sworn an oath that she
Should be to public justice brought;
And for the little infant's bones
With spades they would have sought.
But instantly the hill of moss
Before their eyes began to stir!
And, for full fifty yards around,
The grass—it shook upon the ground!
Yet all do still aver
The little Babe lies buried there,   230
Beneath that hill of moss so fair.

"I cannot tell how this may be,
But plain it is the Thorn is bound
With heavy tufts of moss that strive
To drag it to the ground:
And this I know, full many a time,
When she was on the mountain high,
By day, and in the silent night,
When all the stars shone clear and bright,
That I have heard her cry,   240
'Oh misery! oh misery!
Oh woe is me! oh misery!' "

1798   1798

EXPOSTULATION AND REPLY

This poem is a favourite among the Quakers, as I
have learnt on many occasions. It was composed in
front of the house at Alfoxden, in the spring of
1798. (Wordsworth)

"Why, William, on that old grey stone,
Thus for the length of half a day,
Why, William, sit you thus alone,
And dream your time away?

"Where are your books?—that light bequeathed
To Beings else forlorn and blind!
Up! up! and drink the spirit breathed
From dead men to their kind.

"You look round on your Mother Earth,
As if she for no purpose bore you;   10
As if you were her first-born birth,
And none had lived before you!"

One morning thus, by Esthwaite lake,
When life was sweet, I knew not why,
To me my good friend Matthew spake,
And thus I made reply:

"The eye—it cannot choose but see;
We cannot bid the ear be still;
Our bodies feel, where'er they be,
Against or with our will.   20

"Nor less I deem that there are Powers
Which of themselves our minds impress;
That we can feed this mind of ours
In a wise passiveness.

"Think you, 'mid all this mighty sum
Of things for ever speaking,
That nothing of itself will come,
But we must still be seeking?

"—Then ask not wherefore, here, alone,
Conversing as I may,   30
I sit upon this old grey stone,
And dream my time away."

1798

THE TABLES TURNED

AN EVENING SCENE ON THE SAME SUBJECT

Up! up! my Friend, and quit your books;
Or surely you'll grow double:
Up! up! my Friend, and clear your looks;
Why all this toil and trouble?

The sun, above the mountain's head,
A freshening lustre mellow
Through all the long green fields has spread,
His first sweet evening yellow.

Books! 'tis a dull and endless strife:
Come, hear the woodland linnet,   10
How sweet his music! on my life,
There's more of wisdom in it.

And hark! how blithe the throstle sings!
He, too, is no mean preacher:
Come forth into the light of things,
Let Nature be your teacher.

She has a world of ready wealth,
Our minds and hearts to bless—
Spontaneous wisdom breathed by health,
Truth breathed by cheerfulness.   20

One impulse from a vernal wood
May teach you more of man,
Of moral evil and of good,
Than all the sages can.

Sweet is the lore which Nature brings;
Our meddling intellect
Mis-shapes the beauteous forms of things:—
We murder to dissect.

Enough of Science and of Art;
Close up those barren leaves;   30
Come forth, and bring with you a heart
That watches and receives.

1798   *1798*

1798

LINES

COMPOSED A FEW MILES ABOVE
TINTERN ABBEY, ON REVISITING
THE BANKS OF THE WYE DURING
A TOUR. JULY 13, 1798

———

No poem of mine was composed under circumstances more pleasant for me to remember than
this. I began it upon leaving Tintern, after crossing
the Wye, and concluded it just as I was entering
Bristol in the evening, after a ramble of four or five
days, with my Sister. Not a line of it was altered,
and not any part of it written down till I reached
Bristol. It was published almost immediately after
in the little volume of which so much has been said
in these Notes. (Wordsworth)

———

Five years have past; five summers, with the length
Of five long winters! and again I hear
These waters, rolling from their mountain-springs
With a soft inland murmur.—Once again
Do I behold these steep and lofty cliffs,
That on a wild secluded scene impress
Thoughts of more deep seclusion; and connect
The landscape with the quiet of the sky.
The day is come when I again repose
Here, under this dark sycamore, and view   10
Those plots of cottage ground, these orchard-tufts,
Which at this season, with their unripe fruits,
Are clad in one green hue, and lose themselves
'Mid groves and copses. Once again I see
These hedge-rows, hardly hedge-rows, little lines
Of sportive wood run wild: these pastoral farms,
Green to the very door; and wreaths of smoke
Sent up, in silence, from among the trees!
With some uncertain notice, as might seem
Of vagrant dwellers in the houseless woods,   20
Or of some Hermit's cave, where by his fire
The Hermit sits alone.   These beauteous forms,
Through a long absence, have not been to me
As is a landscape to a blind man's eye:
But oft, in lonely rooms, and 'mid the din
Of towns and cities, I have owed to them
In hours of weariness, sensations sweet,
Felt in the blood, and felt along the heart;

And passing even into my purer mind,
With tranquil restoration:—feelings too   30
Of unremembered pleasure: such, perhaps,
As have no slight or trivial influence
On that best portion of a good man's life,
His little, nameless, unremembered, acts
Of kindness and of love. Nor less, I trust,
To them I may have owed another gift,
Of aspect more sublime; that blessed mood,
In which the burthen of the mystery,
In which the heavy and the weary weight
Of all this unintelligible world,   40
Is lightened:—that serene and blessed mood,
In which the affections gently lead us on,—
Until, the breath of this corporeal frame
And even the motion of our human blood
Almost suspended, we are laid asleep
In body, and become a living soul:
While with an eye made quiet by the power
Of harmony, and the deep power of joy,
We see into the life of things.
                                        If this
Be but a vain belief, yet, oh! how oft—   50
In darkness and amid the many shapes
Of joyless daylight; when the fretful stir
Unprofitable, and the fever of the world,
Have hung upon the beatings of my heart—
How oft, in spirit, have I turned to thee,
O sylvan Wye! thou wanderer thro' the woods,
How often has my spirit turned to thee!
    And now, with gleams of half-extinguished
        thought,
With many recognitions dim and faint,
And somewhat of a sad perplexity,   60
The picture of the mind revives again:
While here I stand, not only with the sense
Of present pleasure, but with pleasing thoughts
That in this moment there is life and food
For future years. And so I dare to hope,
Though changed, no doubt, from what I was when
        first
I came among these hills; when like a roe
I bounded o'er the mountains, by the sides
Of the deep rivers, and the lonely streams,
Wherever nature led: more like a man   70
Flying from something that he dreads, than one
Who sought the thing he loved. For nature then
(The coarser pleasures of my boyish days,
And their glad animal movements all gone by)

To me was all in all.—I cannot paint
What then I was. The sounding cataract
Haunted me like a passion: the tall rock,
The mountain, and the deep and gloomy wood,
Their colours and their forms, were then to me
An appetite; a feeling and a love,   80
That had no need of a remoter charm,
By thought supplied, nor any interest
Unborrowed from the eye.—That time is past,
And all its aching joys are now no more,
And all its dizzy raptures. Not for this
Faint I, nor mourn nor murmur; other gifts
Have followed; for such loss, I would believe,
Abundant recompense. For I have learned
To look on nature, not as in the hour
Of thoughtless youth; but hearing oftentimes   90
The still, sad music of humanity,
Nor harsh nor grating, though of ample power
To chasten and subdue. And I have felt
A presence that disturbs me with the joy
Of elevated thoughts; a sense sublime
Of something far more deeply interfused,
Whose dwelling is the light of setting suns,
And the round ocean and the living air,
And the blue sky, and in the mind of man;
A motion and a spirit, that impels   100
All thinking things, all objects of all thought,
And rolls through all things. Therefore am I still
A lover of the meadows and the woods,
And mountains; and of all that we behold
From this green earth; of all the mighty world
Of eye, and ear,—both what they half create,
And what perceive; well pleased to recognise
In nature and the language of the sense,
The anchor of my purest thoughts, the nurse,
The guide, the guardian of my heart, and soul   110
Of all my moral being.
               Nor perchance,
If I were not thus taught, should I the more
Suffer my genial spirits to decay:
For thou art with me here upon the banks
Of this fair river; thou my dearest Friend,
My dear, dear Friend; and in thy voice I catch
The language of my former heart, and read
My former pleasures in the shooting lights
Of thy wild eyes. Oh! yet a little while
May I behold in thee what I was once,   120
My dear, dear Sister! and this prayer I make,
Knowing that Nature never did betray
The heart that loved her; 'tis her privilege,

Through all the years of this our life, to lead
From joy to joy: for she can so inform
The mind that is within us, so impress
With quietness and beauty, and so feed
With lofty thoughts, that neither evil tongues,
Rash judgments, nor the sneers of selfish men,
Nor greetings where no kindness is, nor all   130
The dreary intercourse of daily life,
Shall e'er prevail against us, or disturb
Our cheerful faith, that all which we behold
Is full of blessings. Therefore let the moon
Shine on thee in thy solitary walk;
And let the misty mountain-winds be free
To blow against thee: and, in after years,
When these wild ecstasies shall be matured
Into a sober pleasure; when thy mind
Shall be a mansion for all lovely forms,   140
Thy memory be as a dwelling-place
For all sweet sounds and harmonies; oh! then,
If solitude, or fear, or pain, or grief,
Should be thy portion, with what healing thoughts
Of tender joy wilt thou remember me,
And these my exhortations! Nor, perchance—
If I should be where I no more can hear
Thy voice, nor catch from thy wild eyes these
   gleams
Of past existence—wilt thou then forget
That on the banks of this delightful stream   150
We stood together; and that I, so long
A worshipper of Nature, hither came
Unwearied in that service: rather say
With warmer love—oh! with far deeper zeal
Of holier love. Nor wilt thou then forget,
That after many wanderings, many years
Of absence, these steep woods and lofty cliffs,
And this green pastoral landscape, were to me
More dear, both for themselves and for thy sake!
1798   *1798*

THERE WAS A BOY

Written in Germany. This is an extract from the
poem on my own poetical education. This practice
of making an instrument of their own fingers is
known to most boys, though some are more skilful
at it than others. William Raincock of Rayrigg, a
fine spirited lad, took the lead of all my schoolfellows in this art. (Wordsworth)

There was a Boy; ye knew him well, ye cliffs
And islands of Winander!—many a time,
At evening, when the earliest stars began
To move along the edges of the hills,
Rising or setting, would he stand alone,
Beneath the trees, or by the glimmering lake;
And there, with fingers interwoven, both hands
Pressed closely palm to palm and to his mouth
Uplifted, he, as through an instrument,
Blew mimic hootings to the silent owls,   10
That they might answer him.—And they would
    shout
Across the water vale, and shout again,
Responsive to his call,—with quivering peals,
And long halloos, and screams, and echoes loud
Redoubled and redoubled; concourse wild
Of jocund din! And, when there came a pause
Of silence such as baffled his best skill:
Then, sometimes, in that silence, while he hung
Listening, a gentle shock of mild surprise
Has carried far into his heart the voice   20
Of mountain-torrents; or the visible scene
Would enter unawares into his mind
With all its solemn imagery, its rocks,
Its woods, and that uncertain heaven received
Into the bosom of the steady lake.
    This boy was taken from his mates, and died
In childhood, ere he was full twelve years old.
Pre-eminent in beauty is the vale
Where he was born and bred: the church-yard
    hangs
Upon a slope above the village school;   30
And, through that church-yard when my way has
    led
On summer-evenings, I believe, that there
A long half-hour together I have stood
Mute—looking at the grave in which he lies!

1799   1800

NUTTING

Written in Germany; intended as part of a poem on
my own life, but struck out as not being wanted
there. Like most of my schoolfellows I was an impassioned nutter. For this pleasure, the vale of
Esthwaite, abounding in coppice-wood, furnished
a very wide range. These verses arose out of the remembrance of feelings I had often had when a boy,
and particularly in the extensive woods that still
stretch from the side of Esthwaite Lake towards
Graythwaite, the seat of the ancient family of
Sandys. (Wordsworth)

———It seems a day
(I speak of one from many singled out)
One of those heavenly days that cannot die;
When, in the eagerness of boyish hope,
I left our cottage-threshold, sallying forth
With a huge wallet o'er my shoulders slung,
A nutting-crook in hand; and turned my steps
Tow'rd some far-distant wood, a Figure quaint,
Tricked out in proud disguise of cast-off weeds
Which for that service had been husbanded,   10
By exhortation of my frugal Dame—
Motley accoutrement, of power to smile
At thorns, and brakes, and brambles,—and, in truth,
More raggèd than need was! O'er pathless rocks,
Through beds of matted fern, and tangled thickets,
Forcing my way, I came to one dear nook
Unvisited, where not a broken bough
Drooped with its withered leaves, ungracious sign
Of devastation; but the hazels rose
Tall and erect, with tempting clusters hung,   20
A virgin scene!—A little while I stood,
Breathing with such suppression of the heart
As joy delights in; and, with wise restraint
Voluptuous, fearless of a rival, eyed
The banquet;—or beneath the trees I sate
Among the flowers, and with the flowers I played;
A temper known to those, who, after long
And weary expectation, have been blest
With sudden happiness beyond all hope.
Perhaps it was a bower beneath whose leaves   30
The violets of five seasons re-appear
And fade, unseen by any human eye;
Where fairy water-breaks do murmur on
For ever; and I saw the sparkling foam,
And—with my cheek on one of those green stones
That, fleeced with moss, under the shady trees,
Lay round me, scattered like a flock of sheep—
I heard the murmur and the murmuring sound,
In that sweet mood when pleasure loves to pay
Tribute to ease; and, of its joy secure,   40
The heart luxuriates with indifferent things,
Wasting its kindliness on stocks and stones,
And on the vacant air. Then up I rose,
And dragged to earth both branch and bough, with
    crash

And merciless ravage: and the shady nook
Of hazels, and the green and mossy bower,
Deformed and sullied, patiently gave up
Their quiet being: and, unless I now
Confound my present feelings with the past;
Ere from the mutilated bower I turned   50
Exulting, rich beyond the wealth of kings,
I felt a sense of pain when I beheld
The silent trees, and saw the intruding sky—
Then, dearest Maiden, move along these shades
In gentleness of heart; with gentle hand
Touch—for there is a spirit in the woods.

1799   *1800*

FROM

The Prelude
or, Growth of a Poet's Mind

AN AUTOBIOGRAPHICAL POEM

BOOK FIRST

INTRODUCTION—CHILDHOOD AND
SCHOOL-TIME

Oh there is blessing in this gentle breeze,
A visitant that while it fans my cheek
Doth seem half-conscious of the joy it brings
From the green fields, and from yon azure sky.
Whate'er its mission, the soft breeze can come
To none more grateful than to me; escaped
From the vast city, where I long had pined
A discontented sojourner: now free,
Free as a bird to settle where I will.
What dwelling shall receive me? in what vale   10
Shall be my harbour? underneath what grove
Shall I take up my home? and what clear stream
Shall with its murmur lull me into rest?
The earth is all before me. With a heart
Joyous, nor scared at its own liberty,
I look about; and should the chosen guide
Be nothing better than a wandering cloud,
I cannot miss my way. I breathe again!
Trances of thought and mountings of the mind
Come fast upon me: it is shaken off,   20
That burthen of my own unnatural self,
The heavy weight of many a weary day
Not mine, and such as were not made for me.

Long months of peace (if such bold word accord
With any promises of human life),
Long months of ease and undisturbed delight
Are mine in prospect; whither shall I turn,
By road or pathway, or through trackless field,
Up hill or down, or shall some floating thing
Upon the river point me out my course?   30

Dear Liberty! Yet what would it avail
But for a gift that consecrates the joy?
For I, methought, while the sweet breath of heaven
Was blowing on my body, felt within
A correspondent breeze, that gently moved
With quickening virtue, but is now become
A tempest, a redundant energy,
Vexing its own creation. Thanks to both,
And their congenial powers, that, while they join
In breaking up a long-continued frost,   40
Bring with them vernal promises, the hope
Of active days urged on by flying hours,—
Days of sweet leisure, taxed with patient thought
Abstruse, nor wanting punctual service high,
Matins and vespers of harmonious verse!

Thus far, O Friend! did I, not used to make
A present joy the matter of a song,
Pour forth that day my soul in measured strains
That would not be forgotten, and are here
Recorded: to the open fields I told   50
A prophecy: poetic numbers came
Spontaneously to clothe in priestly robe
A renovated spirit singled out,
Such hope was mine, for holy services.
My own voice cheered me, and, far more, the
      mind's
Internal echo of the imperfect sound;
To both I listened, drawing from them both
A cheerful confidence in things to come.

Content and not unwilling now to give
A respite to this passion, I pace on   60
With brisk and eager steps; and came, at length,
To a green shady place, where down I sate
Beneath a tree, slackening my thoughts by choice
And settling into gentler happiness.
'Twas autumn, and a clear and placid day,
With warmth, as much as needed, from a sun
Two hours declined towards the west; a day
With silver clouds, and sunshine on the grass,

THE PRELUDE. BOOK I. **46. Friend:** Samuel Taylor Coleridge, to whom *The Prelude* is addressed.

And in the sheltered and the sheltering grove
A perfect stillness. Many were the thoughts   70
Encouraged and dismissed, till choice was made
Of a known Vale, whither my feet should turn,
Nor rest till they had reached the very door
Of the one cottage which methought I saw.
No picture of mere memory ever looked
So fair; and while upon the fancied scene
I gazed with growing love, a higher power
Than Fancy gave assurance of some work
Of glory there forthwith to be begun,
Perhaps too there performed. Thus long I
    mused,   80
Nor e'er lost sight of what I mused upon,
Save when, amid the stately grove of oaks,
Now here, now there, an acorn, from its cup
Dislodged, through sere leaves rustled, or at once
To the bare earth dropped with a startling sound.
From that soft couch I rose not, till the sun
Had almost touched the horizon; casting then
A backward glance upon the curling cloud
Of city smoke, by distance ruralised;
Keen as a Truant or a Fugitive,   90
But as a Pilgrim resolute, I took,
Even with the chance equipment of that hour,
The road that pointed toward the chosen Vale.
It was a splendid evening, and my soul
Once more made trial of her strength, nor lacked
Æolian visitations; but the harp
Was soon defrauded, and the banded host
Of harmony dispersed in straggling sounds,
And lastly utter silence! "Be it so;
Why think of anything but present good?"   100
So, like a home-bound labourer, I pursued
My way beneath the mellowing sun, that shed
Mild influence; nor left in me one wish
Again to bend the Sabbath of that time
To a servile yoke. What need of many words?
A pleasant loitering journey, through three days
Continued, brought me to my hermitage.
I spare to tell of what ensued, the life
In common things—the endless store of things,
Rare, or at least so seeming, every day   110
Found all about me in one neighbourhood—
The self-congratulation, and, from morn
To night, unbroken cheerfulness serene.
But speedily an earnest longing rose

96. Æolian . . . harp: a familiar image in Wordsworth
and Coleridge, the Æolian harp is a stringed instrument
that produces musical sounds when touched by a breeze.

To brace myself to some determined aim,
Reading or thinking; either to lay up
New stores, or rescue from decay the old
By timely interference: and therewith
Came hopes still higher, that with outward life
I might endue some airy phantasies   120
That had been floating loose about for years,
And to such beings temperately deal forth
The many feelings that oppressed my heart.
That hope hath been discouraged; welcome light
Dawns from the east, but dawns to disappear
And mock me with a sky that ripens not
Into a steady morning: if my mind,
Remembering the bold promise of the past,
Would gladly grapple with some noble theme,
Vain is her wish; where'er she turns she finds   130
Impediments from day to day renewed.

    And now it would content me to yield up
Those lofty hopes awhile, for present gifts
Of humbler industry. But, oh, dear Friend!
The Poet, gentle creature as he is,
Hath, like the Lover, his unruly times;
His fits when he is neither sick nor well,
Though no distress be near him but his own
Unmanageable thoughts: his mind, best pleased
While she as duteous as the mother dove   140
Sits brooding, lives not always to that end,
But like the innocent bird, hath goadings on
That drive her as in trouble through the groves;
With me is now such passion, to be blamed
No otherwise than as it lasts too long.

    When, as becomes a man who would prepare
For such an arduous work, I through myself
Make rigorous inquisition, the report
Is often cheering; for I neither seem
To lack that first great gift, the vital soul,   150
Nor general Truths, which are themselves a sort
Of Elements and Agents, Under-powers,
Subordinate helpers of the living mind:
Nor am I naked of external things,
Forms, images, nor numerous other aids
Of less regard, though won perhaps with toil
And needful to build up a Poet's praise.
Time, place, and manners do I seek, and these
Are found in plenteous store, but nowhere such
As may be singled out with steady choice;   160
No little band of yet remembered names
Whom I, in perfect confidence, might hope
To summon back from lonesome banishment,

And make them dwellers in the hearts of men
Now living, or to live in future years.
Sometimes the ambitious Power of choice, mistak-
    ing
Proud spring-tide swellings for a regular sea,
Will settle on some British theme, some old
Romantic tale by Milton left unsung;
More often turning to some gentle place   170
Within the groves of Chivalry, I pipe
To shepherd swains, or seated harp in hand,
Amid reposing knights by a river side
Or fountain, listen to the grave reports
Of dire enchantments faced and overcome
By the strong mind, and tales of warlike feats,
Where spear encountered spear, and sword with
    sword
Fought, as if conscious of the blazonry
That the shield bore, so glorious was the strife;
Whence inspiration for a song that winds   180
Through ever-changing scenes of votive quest
Wrongs to redress, harmonious tribute paid
To patient courage and unblemished truth,
To firm devotion, zeal unquenchable,
And Christian meekness hallowing faithful loves.
Sometimes, more sternly moved, I would relate
How vanquished Mithridates northward passed,
And, hidden in the cloud of years, became
Odin, the Father of a race by whom
Perished the Roman Empire: how the friends   190
And followers of Sertorious, out of Spain
Flying, found shelter in the Fortunate Isles,
And left their usages, their arts and laws,
To disappear by a slow gradual death,
To dwindle and to perish one by one,
Starved in those narrow bounds: but not the soul
Of Liberty, which fifteen hundred years
Survived, and, when the European came
With skill and power that might not be withstood,
Did, like a pestilence, maintain its hold   200
And wasted down by glorious death that race
Of natural heroes: or I would record

How, in tyrannic times, some high-souled man,
Unnamed among the chronicles of kings,
Suffered in silence for Truth's sake: or tell,
How that one Frenchman, through continued force
Of meditation on the inhuman deeds
Of those who conquered first the Indian Isles,
Went single in his ministry across
The Ocean; not to comfort the oppresed,   210
But, like a thirsty wind, to roam about
Withering the Oppressor: how Gustavus sought
Help at his need in Dalecarlia's mines:
How Wallace fought for Scotland; left the name
Of Wallace to be found, like a wild flower,
All over his dear Country; left the deeds
Of Wallace, like a family of Ghosts,
To people the steep rocks and river banks,
Her natural sanctuaries, with a local soul
Of independence and stern liberty.   220
Sometimes it suits me better to invent
A tale from my own heart, more near akin
To my own passions and habitual thoughts;
Some variegated story, in the main
Lofty, but the unsubstantial structure melts
Before the very sun that brightens it,
Mist into air dissolving! Then a wish,
My last and favourite aspiration, mounts
With yearning toward some philosophic song
Of Truth that cherishes our daily life;   230
With meditations passionate from deep
Recesses in man's heart, immortal verse
Thoughtfully fitted to the Orphean lyre;
But from this awful burthen I full soon
Take refuge and beguile myself with trust
That mellower years will bring a riper mind
And clearer insight. Thus my days are past
In contradiction; with no skill to part
Vague longing, haply bred by want of power,
From paramount impulse not to be withstood,   240
A timorous capacity, from prudence,
From circumspection, infinite delay.
Humility and modest awe, themselves
Betray me, serving often for a cloak

187. **Mithridates:** sometimes called Mithradates the Great. King of Pontus, an ancient kingdom on the Black Sea, he extended his empire greatly until he finally came into conflict with Rome. He was defeated by Pompey in 66 B.C. 189. **Odin:** according to legend, the father of the Gothic people who later conquered Rome. 191. **Sertorius:** another freedom fighter. Sertorius was a Roman general who fought against the powerful forces of the Senate. He was assassinated in 72 B.C.

206. **Frenchman:** Dominique de Gourges, the brave Frenchman who avenged the slaughter of French Protestants by the Spanish in Florida in 1567. 212. **Gustavus:** King Gustavus of Sweden (1496–1560), who freed his country from Danish domination. 214. **Wallace:** Sir William Wallace (1272–1305), Scottish patriot who fought against the English who were attempting to conquer his country.

To a more subtle selfishness; that now
Locks every function up in blank reserve,
Now dupes me, trusting to an anxious eye
That with intrusive restlessness beats off
Simplicity and self-presented truth.
Ah! better far than this, to stray about   250
Voluptuously through fields and rural walks,
And ask no record of the hours, resigned
To vacant musing, unreproved neglect
Of all things, and deliberate holiday.
Far better never to have heard the name
Of zeal and just ambition, than to live
Baffled and plagued by a mind that every hour
Turns recreant to her task; takes heart again,
Then feels immediately some hollow thought
Hang like an interdict upon her hopes.   260
This is my lot; for either still I find
Some imperfection in the chosen theme,
Or see of absolute accomplishment
Much wanting, so much wanting, in myself,
That I recoil and droop, and seek repose
In listlessness from vain perplexity,
Unprofitably travelling toward the grave,
Like a false steward who hath much received
And renders nothing back.   Was it for this
That one, the fairest of all rivers, loved   270
To blend his murmurs with my nurse's song,
And, from his alder shades and rocky falls,
And from his fords and shallows, sent a voice
That flowed along my dreams? For this, didst thou,
O Derwent! winding among grassy holms
Where I was looking on, a babe in arms,
Make ceaseless music that composed my thoughts
To more than infant softness, giving me
Amid the fretful dwellings of mankind
A foretaste, a dim earnest, of the calm   280
That Nature breathes among the hills and groves.

When he had left the mountains and received
On his smooth breast the shadow of those towers
That yet survive, a shattered monument
Of feudal sway, the bright blue river passed
Along the margin of our terrace walk;
A tempting playmate whom we dearly loved.
Oh, many a time have I, a five years' child,
In a small mill-race severed from his stream,

Made one long bathing of a summer's day;   290
Basked in the sun, and plunged and basked again
Alternate, all a summer's day, or scoured
The sandy fields, leaping through flowery groves
Of yellow ragwort; or, when rock and hill,
The woods, and distant Skiddaw's lofty height,
Were bronzed with deepest radiance, stood alone
Beneath the sky, as if I had been born
On Indian plains, and from my mother's hut
Had run abroad in wantonness, to sport
A naked savage, in the thunder shower.   300

    Fair seed-time had my soul, and I grew up
Fostered alike by beauty and by fear:
Much favoured in my birth-place, and no less
In that belovèd Vale to which erelong
We were transplanted;—there were we let loose
For sports of wider range. Ere I had told
Ten birth-days, when among the mountain slopes
Frost, and the breath of frosty wind, had snapped
The last autumnal crocus, 'twas my joy
With store of springes o'er my shoulder hung   310
To range the open heights where woodcocks run
Along the smooth green turf. Through half the
          night,
Scudding away from snare to snare, I plied
That anxious visitation;—moon and stars
Were shining o'er my head. I was alone,
And seemed to be a trouble to the peace
That dwelt among them. Sometimes it befell
In these night wanderings, that a strong desire
O'erpowered my better reason, and the bird
Which was the captive of another's toil   320
Became my prey; and when the deed was done
I heard among the solitary hills
Low breathings coming after me, and sounds
Of undistinguishable motion, steps
Almost as silent as the turf they trod.

    Nor less, when spring had warmed the cultured
          Vale,
Moved we as plunderers where the mother-bird
Had in high places built her lodge; though mean
Our object and inglorious, yet the end
Was not ignoble. Oh! when I have hung   330
Above the raven's nest, by knots of grass
And half-inch fissures in the slippery rock
But ill sustained, and almost (so it seemed)

---

275. **Derwent:** river that flows past the house where Wordsworth was born. 283. **towers:** Cockermouth Castle.

295. **Skiddaw:** Mount Skiddaw, east of Cockermouth. 304. **Vale:** the Vale of Esthwaite. 310. **springes:** traps.

Suspended by the blast that blew amain,
Shouldering the naked crag, oh, at that time
While on the perilous ridge I hung alone,
With what strange utterance did the loud dry wind
Blow through my ear! the sky seemed not a sky
Of earth—and with what motion moved the clouds!

Dust as we are, the immortal spirit grows   340
Like harmony in music; there is a dark
Inscrutable workmanship that reconciles
Discordant elements, makes them cling together
In one society. How strange, that all
The terrors, pains, and early miseries,
Regrets, vexations, lassitudes interfused
Within my mind, should e'er have borne a part,
And that a needful part, in making up
The calm existence that is mine when I
Am worthy of myself! Praise to the end!   350
Thanks to the means which Nature deigned to em-
     ploy;
Whether her fearless visitings, or those
That came with soft alarm, like hurtless light
Opening the peaceful clouds; or she would use
Severer interventions, ministry
More palpable, as best might suit her aim.

One summer evening (led by her) I found
A little boat tied to a willow tree
Within a rocky cove, its usual home.
Straight I unloosed her chain, and stepping in   360
Pushed from the shore. It was an act of stealth
And troubled pleasure, nor without the voice
Of mountain-echoes did my boat move on;
Leaving behind her still, on either side,
Small circles glittering idly in the moon,
Until they melted all into one track
Of sparkling light. But now, like one who rows
Proud of his skill, to reach a chosen point
With an unswerving line, I fixed my view
Upon the summit of a craggy ridge,   370
The horizon's utmost boundary; far above
Was nothing but the stars and the grey sky.
She was an elfin pinnace; lustily
I dipped my oars into the silent lake,
And, as I rose upon the stroke, my boat
Went heaving through the water like a swan;
When, from behind that craggy steep till then
The horizon's bound, a huge peak, black and huge,
As if with voluntary power instinct,
Upreared its head. I struck and struck again,   380
And growing still in stature the grim shape

Towered up between me and the stars, and still,
For so it seemed, with purpose of its own
And measured motion like a living thing,
Strode after me. With trembling oars I turned,
And through the silent water stole my way
Back to the covert of the willow tree;
There in her mooring-place I left my bark,—
And through the meadow homeward went, in grave
And serious mood; but after I had seen   390
That spectacle, for many days, my brain
Worked with a dim and undetermined sense
Of unknown modes of being; o'er my thoughts
There hung a darkness, call it solitude
Or blank desertion. No familiar shapes
Remained, no pleasant images of trees,
Of sea or sky, no colours of green fields;
But huge and mighty forms, that do not live
Like living men, moved slowly through the mind
By day, and were a trouble to my dreams.   400

Wisdom and Spirit of the universe!
Thou Soul that art the eternity of thought
That givest to forms and images a breath
And everlasting motion, not in vain
By day or star-light thus from my first dawn
Of childhood didst thou intertwine for me
The passions that build up our human soul;
Not with the mean and vulgar works of man,
But with high objects, with enduring things—
With life and nature—purifying thus   410
The elements of feeling and of thought,
And sanctifying, by such discipline,
Both pain and fear, until we recognise
A grandeur in the beatings of the heart.
Nor was this fellowship vouchsafed to me
With stinted kindness. In November days,
When vapours rolling down the valley made
A lonely scene more lonesome, among woods,
At noon and 'mid the calm of summer nights,
When, by the margin of the trembling lake,   420
Beneath the gloomy hills homeward I went
In solitude, such intercourse was mine;
Mine was it in the fields both day and night,
And by the waters, all the summer long.

And in the frosty season, when the sun
Was set, and visible for many a mile
The cottage windows blazed through twilight
     gloom,
I heeded not their summons: happy time
It was indeed for all of us—for me

It was a time of rapture! Clear and loud   430
The village clock tolled six,—I wheeled about,
Proud and exulting like an untired horse
That cares not for his home. All shod with steel,
We hissed along the polished ice in games
Confederate, imitative of the chase
And woodland pleasures,—the resounding horn,
The pack loud chiming, and the hunted hare.
So through the darkness and the cold we flew,
And not a voice was idle; with the din
Smitten, the precipices rang aloud;   440
The leafless trees and every icy crag
Tinkled like iron; while far distant hills
Into the tumult sent an alien sound
Of melancholy not unnoticed, while the stars
Eastward were sparkling clear, and in the west
The orange sky of evening died away.
Not seldom from the uproar I retired
Into a silent bay, or sportively
Glanced sideway, leaving the tumultuous throng,
To cut across the reflex of a star   450
That fled, and, flying still before me, gleamed
Upon the glassy plain; and oftentimes,
When we had given our bodies to the wind,
And all the shadowy banks on either side
Came sweeping through the darkness, spinning still
The rapid line of motion, then at once
Have I, reclining back upon my heels,
Stopped short; yet still the solitary cliffs
Wheeled by me—even as if the earth had rolled
With visible motion her diurnal round!   460
Behind me did they stretch in solemn train,
Feebler and feebler, and I stood and watched
Till all was tranquil as a dreamless sleep.

Ye Presences of Nature in the sky
And on the earth! Ye Visions of the hills!
And Souls of lonely places! can I think
A vulgar hope was yours when ye employed
Such ministry, when ye, through many a year
Haunting me thus among my boyish sports,
On caves and trees, upon the woods and hills,   470
Impressed, upon all forms, the characters
Of danger or desire; and thus did make
The surface of the universal earth,
With triumph and delight, with hope and fear,
Work like a sea?
                    Not uselessly employed,
Might I pursue this theme through every change
Of exercise and play, to which the year
Did summon us in his delightful round.

We were a noisy crew; the sun in heaven
Beheld not vales more beautiful than ours;   480
Nor saw a band in happiness and joy
Richer, or worthier of the ground they trod.
I could record with no reluctant voice
The woods of autumn, and their hazel bowers
With milk-white clusters hung; the rod and line,
True symbol of hope's foolishness, whose strong
And unreproved enchantment led us on
By rocks and pools shut out from every star,
All the green summer, to forlorn cascades
Among the windings hid of mountain brooks.   490
—Unfading recollections! at this hour
The heart is almost mine with which I felt,
From some hill-top on sunny afternoons,
The paper kite high among fleecy clouds
Pull at her rein like an impetuous courser;
Or, from the meadows sent on gusty days,
Beheld her breast the wind, then suddenly
Dashed headlong, and rejected by the storm.

Ye lowly cottages wherein we dwelt,
A ministration of your own was yours;   500
Can I forget you, being as you were
So beautiful among the pleasant fields
In which ye stood? or can I here forget
The plain and seemly countenance with which
Ye dealt out your plain comforts? Yet had ye
Delights and exultations of your own.
Eager and never weary we pursued
Our home-amusements by the warm peat-fire
At evening, when with pencil, and smooth slate
In square divisions parcelled out and all   510
With crosses and with cyphers scribbled o'er,
We schemed and puzzled, head opposed to head
In strife too humble to be named in verse:
Or round the naked table, snow-white deal,
Cherry or maple, sate in close array,
And to the combat, Loo or Whist, led on
A thick-ribbed army; not, as in the world,
Neglected and ungratefully thrown by
Even for the very service they had wrought,
But husbanded through many a long
          campaign.   520
Uncouth assemblage was it, where no few
Had changed their functions: some, plebeian cards
Which Fate, beyond the promise of their birth,
Had dignified, and called to represent

514. **deal:** fir or pine wood.

The persons of departed potentates.
Oh, with what echoes on the board they fell!
Ironic diamonds,—clubs, hearts, diamonds, spades,
A congregation piteously akin!
Cheap matter offered they to boyish wit,
Those sooty knaves, precipitated down   530
With scoffs and taunts, like Vulcan out of heaven:
The paramount ace, a moon in her eclipse,
Queens gleaming through their splendour's last
    decay,
And monarchs surly at the wrongs sustained
By royal visages. Meanwhile abroad
Incessant rain was falling, or the frost
Raged bitterly, with keen and silent tooth;
And, interrupting oft that eager game,
From under Esthwaite's splitting fields of ice
The pent-up air, struggling to free itself,   540
Gave out to meadow grounds and hills a loud
Protracted yelling, like the noise of wolves
Howling in troops along the Bothnic Main.

    Nor, sedulous as I have been to trace
How Nature by extrinsic passion first
Peopled the mind with forms sublime or fair,
And made me love them, may I here omit
How other pleasures have been mine, and joys
Of subtler origin; how I have felt,
Not seldom even in that tempestuous time,   550
Those hallowed and pure motions of the sense
Which seem, in their simplicity, to own
An intellectual charm; that calm delight
Which, if I err not, surely must belong
To those first-born affinities that fit
Our new existence to existing things,
And, in our dawn of being, constitute
The bond of union between life and joy.

    Yes, I remember when the changeful earth,
And twice five summers on my mind had
    stamped   560
The faces of the moving year, even then
I held unconscious intercourse with beauty
Old as creation, drinking in a pure
Organic pleasure from the silver wreaths
Of curling mist, or from the level plain
Of waters coloured by impending clouds.

    The sands of Westmoreland, the creeks and bays
Of Cumbria's rocky limits, they can tell
How, when the Sea threw off his evening shade,

543. **Bothnic Main**: refers to an area of the Baltic Sea.

And to the shepherd's hut on distant hills   570
Sent welcome notice of the rising moon,
How I have stood, to fancies such as these
A stranger, linking with the spectacle
No conscious memory of a kindred sight,
And bringing with me no peculiar sense
Of quietness or peace; yet have I stood,
Even while mine eye hath moved o'er many a
    league
Of shining water, gathering as it seemed,
Through every hair-breadth in that field of light,
New pleasure like a bee among the flowers.   580

    Thus oft amid those fits of vulgar joy
Which, through all seasons, on a child's pursuits
Are prompt attendants, 'mid that giddy bliss
Which, like a tempest, works along the blood
And is forgotten; even then I felt
Gleams like the flashing of a shield;—the earth
And common face of Nature spake to me
Rememberable things; sometimes, 'tis true,
By chance collisions and quaint accidents
(Like those ill-sorted unions, work supposed   590
Of evid-minded fairies), yet not vain
Nor profitless, if haply they impressed
Collateral objects and appearances,
Albeit lifeless then, and doomed to sleep
Until maturer seasons called them forth
To impregnate and to elevate the mind.
—And if the vulgar joy by its own weight
Wearied itself out of the memory,
The scenes which were a witness of that joy
Remained in their substantial lineaments   600
Depicted on the brain, and to the eye
Were visible, a daily sight; and thus
By the impressive discipline of fear,
By pleasure and repeated happiness,
So frequently repeated, and by force
Of obscure feelings representative
Of things forgotten, these same scenes so bright,
So beautiful, so majestic in themselves,
Though yet the day was distant, did become
Habitually dear, and all their forms   610
And changeful colours by invisible links
Were fastened to the affections.
               I began
My story early—not misled, I trust,
By an infirmity of love for days
Disowned by memory—ere the breath of spring
Planting my snowdrops among winter snows:
Nor will it seem to thee, O Friend! so prompt

In sympathy, that I have lengthened out
With fond and feeble tongue a tedious tale.
Meanwhile, my hope has been, that I might
    fetch   620
Invigorating thoughts from former years;
Might fix the wavering balance of my mind,
And haply meet reproaches too, whose power
May spur me on, in manhood now mature
To honourable toil. Yet should these hopes
Prove vain, and thus should neither I be taught
To understand myself, nor thou to know
With better knowledge how the heart was framed
Of him thou lovest; need I dread from thee
Harsh judgments, if the song be loth to quit   630
Those recollected hours that have the charm
Of visionary things, those lovely forms
And sweet sensations that throw back our life,
And almost make remotest infancy
A visible scene, on which the sun is shining?

    One end at least hath been attained; my mind
Hath been revived, and if this genial mood
Desert me not, forthwith shall be brought down
Through later years the story of my life.
The road lies plain before me;—'tis a theme   640
Single and of determined bounds; and hence
I choose it rather at this time, than work
Of ampler or more varied argument,
Where I might be discomfited and lost:
And certain hopes are with me, that to thee
This labour will be welcome, honoured Friend!

BOOK SECOND

SCHOOL-TIME (continued)

Thus far, O Friend! have we, though leaving much
Unvisited, endeavoured to retrace
The simple ways in which my childhood walked;
Those chiefly that first led me to the love
Of rivers, woods, and fields. The passion yet
Was in its birth, sustained as might befall
By nourishment that came unsought; for still
From week to week, from month to month, we
    lived
A round of tumult. Duly were our games
Prolonged in summer till the daylight failed;   10
No chair remained before the doors; the bench
And threshold steps were empty; fast asleep

The labourer, and the old man who had sate
A later lingerer; yet the revelry
Continued and the loud uproar: at last,
When all the ground was dark, and twinkling stars
Edged the black clouds, home and to bed we went,
Feverish with weary joints and beating minds.
Ah! is there one who ever has been young,
Nor needs a warning voice to tame the pride   20
Of intellect and virtue's self-esteem?
One is there, though the wisest and the best
Of all mankind, who covets not at times
Union that cannot be;—who would not give
If so he might, to duty and to truth
The eagerness of infantine desire?
A tranquillising spirit presses now
On my corporeal frame, so wide appears
The vacancy between me and those days
Which yet have such self-presence in my
    mind,   30
That, musing on them, often do I seem
Two consciousnesses, conscious of myself
And of some other Being. A rude mass
Of native rock, left midway in the square
Of our small market village, was the goal
Or centre of these sports; and when, returned
After long absence, thither I repaired,
Gone was the old grey stone, and in its place
A smart Assembly-room usurped the ground
That had been ours. There let the fiddle
    scream,   40
And be ye happy! Yet, my Friends! I know
That more than one of you will think with me
Of those soft starry nights, and that old Dame
From whom the stone was named, who there had
    sate,
And watched her table with its huckster's wares
Assiduous, through the length of sixty years.

    We ran a boisterous course; the year span round
With giddy motion. But the time approached
That brought with it a regular desire
For calmer pleasures, when the winning forms   50
Of Nature were collaterally attached
To every scheme of holiday delight
And every boyish sport, less grateful else
And languidly pursued.
                    When summer came,
Our pastime was, on bright half-holidays,
To sweep along the plain of Windermere
With rival oars; and the selected bourne
Was now an Island musical with birds

That sang and ceased not; now a Sister Isle
Beneath the oaks' umbrageous covert, sown   60
With lilies of the valley like a field;
And now a third small Island, where survived
In solitude the ruins of a shrine
Once to Our Lady dedicate, and served
Daily with chaunted rites. In such a race
So ended, disappointment could be none,
Uneasiness, or pain, or jealousy:
We rested in the shade, all pleased alike,
Conquered and conqueror. Thus the pride of
       strength,
And the vain-glory of superior skill,   70
Were tempered; thus was gradually produced
A quiet independence of the heart:
And to my Friend who knows me I may add,
Fearless of blame, that hence for future days
Ensued a diffidence and modesty,
And I was taught to feel, perhaps too much,
The self-sufficing power of Solitude.

     Our daily meals were frugal, Sabine fare!
More than we wished we knew the blessing then
Of vigorous hunger—hence corporeal strength   80
Unsapped by delicate viands; for, exclude
A little weekly stipend, and we lived
Through three divisions of the quartered year
In penniless poverty. But now to school
From the half-yearly holidays returned,
We came with weightier purses, that sufficed
To furnish treats more costly than the Dame
Of the old grey stone, from her scant board,
       supplied.
Hence rustic dinners on the cool green ground,
Or in the woods, or by a river side   90
Or shady fountains, while among the leaves
Soft airs were stirring, and the mid-day sun
Unfelt shone brightly round us in our joy.
Nor is my aim neglected if I tell
How sometimes, in the length of those half-years,
We from our funds drew largely;—proud to curb,
And eager to spur on, the galloping steed;
And with the courteous inn-keeper, whose stud
Supplied our want, we haply might employ
Sly subterfuge, if the adventure's bound   100
Were distant: some famed temple where of yore
The Druids worshipped, or the antique walls

THE PRELUDE. BOOK II. 78. Sabine fare: the Sabines
were a people of ancient Italy known for their simple
life-style.

Of that large abbey, where within the Vale
Of Nightshade, to St. Mary's honour built,
Stands yet a mouldering pile with fractured arch,
Belfry, and images, and living trees;
A holy scene!—Along the smooth green turf
Our horses grazed. To more than inland peace,
Left by the west wind sweeping overhead
From a tumultuous ocean, trees and towers   110
In that sequestered valley may be seen,
Both silent and both motionless alike;
Such the deep shelter that is there, and such
The safeguard for repose and quietness.

     Our steeds remounted and the summons given,
With whip and spur we through the chauntry flew
In uncouth race, and left the cross-legged knight,
And the stone-abbot, and that single wren
Which one day sang so sweetly in the nave
Of that old church, that—though from recent
       showers   120
The earth was comfortless, and, touched by faint
Internal breezes, sobbings of the place
And respirations, from the roofless walls
The shuddering ivy dripped large drops—yet still
So sweetly 'mid the gloom the invisible bird
Sang to herself, that there I could have made
My dwelling-place, and lived for ever there
To hear such music. Through the walls we flew
And down the valley, and, a circuit made
In wantonness of heart, through rough and
       smooth   130
We scampered homewards. Oh, ye rocks and
       streams,
And that still spirit shed from evening air!
Even in this joyous time I sometimes felt
Your presence, when with slackened step we
       breathed
Along the sides of the steep hills, or when
Lighted by gleams of moonlight from the sea
We beat with thundering hoofs the level sand.

     Midway on long Winander's eastern shore,
Within the crescent of a pleasant bay,
A tavern stood; no homely-featured house,   140
Primeval like its neighbouring cottages,
But 'twas a splendid place, the door beset
With chaises, grooms, and liveries, and within
Decanters, glasses, and the blood-red wine.

103. abbey: the ruins of Furness Abbey. 116. chauntry:
chapel.

In ancient times, and ere the Hall was built
On the large island, had this dwelling been
More worthy of a poet's love, a hut,
Proud of its own bright fire and sycamore shade
But—though the rhymes were gone that once
    inscribed
The threshold, and large golden characters,   150
Spread o'er the spangled sign-board had dislodged
The old Lion and usurped his place, in slight
And mockery of the rustic painter's hand—
Yet, to this hour, the spot to me is dear
With all its foolish pomp. The garden lay
Upon a slope surmounted by a plain
Of a small bowling-green; beneath us stood
A grove, with gleams of water through the trees
And over the tree-tops; nor did we want
Refreshment, strawberries and mellow cream.   160
There, while through half an afternoon we played
On the smooth platform, whether skill prevailed
Or happy blunder triumphed, bursts of glee
Made all the mountains ring. But, ere night-fall,
When in our pinnace we returned at leisure
Over the shadowy lake, and to the beach
Of some small island steered our course with one,
The Minstrel of the Troop, and left him there,
And rowed off gently, while he blew his flute
Alone upon the rock—oh, then, the calm   170
And dead still water lay upon my mind
Even with a weight of pleasure, and the sky,
Never before so beautiful, sank down
Into my heart, and held me like a dream!
Thus were my sympathies enlarged, and thus
Daily the common range of visible things
Grew dear to me: already I began
To love the sun; a boy I loved the sun,
Not as I since have loved him, as a pledge
And surety of our earthly life, a light   180
Which we behold and feel we are alive;
Nor for his bounty to so many worlds—
But for this cause, that I had seen him lay
His beauty on the morning hills, had seen
The western mountain touch his setting orb,
In many a thoughtless hour, when, from excess
Of happiness, my blood appeared to flow
For its own pleasure, and I breathed with joy.
And, from like feelings, humble though intense,
To patriotic and domestic love   190
Analogous, the moon to me was dear;
For I could dream away my purposes,
Standing to gaze upon her while she hung

Midway between the hills as if she knew
No other region, but belonged to thee,
Yea, appertained by a peculiar right
To thee and thy grey huts, thou one dear Vale!

    Those incidental charms which first attached
My heart to rural objects, day by day
Grew weaker, and I hasten to tell   200
How Nature, intervenient till this time
And secondary, now at length was sought
For her own sake. But who shall parcel out
His intellect in geometric rules,
Split like a province into round and square?
Who knows the individual hour in which
His habits were first sown, even as a seed?
Who that shall point as with a wand and say
"This portion of the river of my mind
Came from yon fountain?" Thou, my Friend! art
    one   210
More deeply read in thy own thoughts; to thee
Science appears but what in truth she is,
Not as our glory and our absolute boast,
But as a succedaneum, and a prop
To our infirmity. No officious slave
Art thou of that false secondary power
By which we multiply distinctions, then
Deem that our puny boundaries are things
That we perceive, and not that we have made.
To thee, unblinded by these formal arts,   220
The unity of all hath been revealed,
And thou wilt doubt, with me less aptly skilled
Than many are to range the faculties
In scale and order, class the cabinet
Of their sensations, and in voluble phrase
Run through the history and birth of each
As of a single independent thing.
Hard task, vain hope, to analyse the mind,
If each most obvious and particular thought,
Not in a mystical and idle sense,   230
But in the words of Reason deeply weighed,
Hath no beginning.
              Blest the infant Babe,
(For with my best conjecture I would trace
Our Being's earthly progress,) blest the Babe,
Nursed in his Mother's arms, who sinks to sleep
Rocked on his Mother's breast; who with his soul

198–265: Running through this section is the anti-
mechanistic strain of Wordsworth's psychology—his
idea that knowledge involves the interplay of mind and
matter. 214. succedaneum: replacement.

Drinks in the feelings of his Mother's eye!
For him, in one dear Presence, there exists
A virtue which irradiates and exalts
Objects through widest intercourse of sense;   240
No outcast he, bewildered and depressed:
Along his infant veins are interfused
The gravitation and the filial bond
Of nature that connect him with the world.
Is there a flower, to which he points with hand
Too weak to gather it, already love
Drawn from love's purest earthly fount for him
Hath beautified that flower; already shades
Of pity cast from inward tenderness
Do fall around him upon aught that bears   250
Unsightly marks of violence or harm.
Emphatically such a Being lives,
Frail creature as he is, helpless as frail,
An inmate of this active universe:
For, feeling has to him imparted power
That through the growing faculties of sense
Doth like an agent of the one great Mind
Create, creator and receiver both,
Working but in alliance with the works
Which it beholds.—Such, verily, is the first   260
Poetic spirit of our human life,
By uniform control of after years,
In most, abated or suppressed; in some,
Through every change of growth and of decay,
Pre-eminent till death.

From early days,
Beginning not long after that first time
In which, a Babe, by intercourse of touch
I held mute dialogues with my Mother's heart,
I have endeavoured to display the means
Whereby this infant sensibility,   270
Great birthright of our being, was in me
Augmented and sustained. Yet is a path
More difficult before me; and I fear
That in its broken windings we shall need
The chamois' sinews, and the eagle's wing:
For now a trouble came into my mind
From unknown causes. I was left alone
Seeking the visible world, nor knowing why.
The props of my affections were removed,
And yet the building stood, as if sustained   280
By its own spirit! All that I beheld
Was dear, and hence to finer influxes
The mind lay open to a more exact
And close communion. Many are our joys

In youth, but oh! what happiness to live
When every hour brings a palpable access
Of knowledge, when all knowledge is delight,
And sorrow is not there! The seasons came,
And every season wheresoe'er I moved
Unfolded transitory qualities,   290
Which, but for this most watchful power of love,
Had been neglected; left a register
Of permanent relations, else unknown.
Hence life, and change, and beauty, solitude
More active ever than "best society"—
Society made sweet as solitude
By silent inobtrusive sympathies,
And gentle agitations of the mind
From manifold distinctions, difference
Perceived in things, where, to the unwatchful
    eye   300
No difference is, and hence, from the same source,
Sublimer joy; for I would walk alone,
Under the quiet stars, and at that time
Have felt whate'er there is of power in sound
To breathe an elevated mood, by form
Or image unprofaned; and I would stand,
If the night blackened with a coming storm,
Beneath some rock, listening to notes that are
The ghostly language of the ancient earth,
Or make their dim abode in distant winds.   310
Thence did I drink the visionary power;
And deem not profitless those fleeting moods
Of shadowy exultation: not for this,
That they are kindred to our purer mind
And intellectual life; but that the soul,
Remembering how she felt, but what she felt
Remembering not, retains an obscure sense
Of possible sublimity, whereto
With growing faculties she doth aspire,
With faculties still growing, feeling still   320
That whatsoever point they gain, they yet
Have something to pursue.

And not alone,
'Mid gloom and tumult, but no less 'mid fair
And tranquil scenes, that universal power
And fitness in the latent qualities
And essences of things, by which the mind
Is moved with feelings of delight, to me
Came strengthened with a superadded soul,
A virtue not its own. My morning walks
Were early;—oft before the hours of school   330
I travelled round our little lake, five miles

Of pleasant wandering. Happy time! more dear
For this, that one was by my side, a Friend,
Then passionately loved; with heart how full
Would he peruse these lines! For many years
Have since flowed in between us, and, our minds
Both silent to each other, at this time
We live as if those hours had never been.
Nor seldom did I lift our cottage latch
Far earlier, ere one smoke-wreath had risen   340
From human dwelling, or the vernal thrush
Was audible; and sate among the woods
Alone upon some jutting eminence,
At the first gleam of dawn-light, when the Vale,
Yet slumbering, lay in utter solitude.
How shall I seek the origin? where find
Faith in the marvellous things which then I felt?
Oft in these moments such a holy calm
Would overspread my soul, that bodily eyes
Were utterly forgotten, and what I saw   350
Appeared like something in myself, a dream
A prospect in the mind.

               'Twere long to tell
What spring and autumn, what the winter snows,
And what the summer shade, what day and night,
Evening and morning, sleep and waking, thought
From sources inexhaustible, poured forth
To feed the spirit of religious love
In which I walked with Nature. But let this
Be not forgotten, that I still retained
My first creative sensibility;   360
That by the regular action of the world
My soul was unsubdued. A plastic power
Abode with me; a forming hand, at times
Rebellious, acting in a devious mood;
A local spirit of his own, at war
With general tendency, but, for the most,
Subservient strictly to external things
With which it communed. An auxiliar light
Came from my mind, which on the setting sun
Bestowed new splendour; the melodious
    birds,   370
The fluttering breezes, fountains that run on
Murmuring so sweetly in themselves, obeyed
A like dominion, and the midnight storm
Grew darker in the presence of my eye:
Hence my obeisance, my devotion hence,
And hence my transport.

333. Friend: The Reverend John Fleming.

              Nor should this, perchance,
Pass unrecorded, that I still had loved
The exercise and produce of a toil,
Than analytic industry to me,
More pleasing, and whose character I deem   380
Is more poetic as resembling more
Creative agency. The song would speak
Of that interminable building reared
By observation of affinities
In objects where no brotherhood exists
To passive minds. My seventeenth year was come
And, whether from this habit rooted now
So deeply in my mind, or from excess
In the great social principle of life
Coercing all things into sympathy,   390
To unorganic natures were transferred
My own enjoyments; or the power of truth
Coming in revelation, did converse
With things that really are; I, at this time,
Saw blessings spread around me like a sea.
Thus while the days flew by, and years passed on,
From Nature and her everflowing soul,
I had received so much, that all my thoughts
Were steeped in feeling; I was only then
Contented, when with bliss ineffable   400
I felt the sentiment of Being spread
O'er all that moves and all that seemeth still;
O'er all that, lost beyond the reach of thought
And human knowledge, to the human eye
Invisible, yet liveth to the heart;
O'er all that leaps and runs, and shouts and sings,
Or beats the gladsome air; o'er all that glides
Beneath the wave, yea, in the wave itself,
And mighty depth of waters. Wonder not
If high the transport, great the joy I felt,   410
Communing in this sort through earth and heaven
With every form of creature, as it looked
Towards the Uncreated with a countenance
Of adoration, with an eye of love.
One song they sang, and it was audible,
Most audible, then, when the fleshly ear,
O'ercome by humblest prelude of that strain,
Forgot her functions, and slept undisturbed.

    If this be error, and another faith
Find easier access to the pious mind,   420
Yet were I grossly destitute of all
Those human sentiments that make this earth
So dear, if I should fail with grateful voice

To speak of you, ye mountains, and ye lakes
And sounding cataracts, ye mists and winds
That dwell among the hills where I was born.
If in my youth I have been pure in heart,
If, mingling with the world, I am content
With my own modest pleasures, and have lived
With God and Nature communing, removed   430
From little enmities and low desires—
The gift is yours; if in these times of fear,
This melancholy waste of hopes o'erthrown,
If, 'mid indifference and apathy,
And wicked exultation when good men
On every side fall off, we know not how,
To selfishness, disguised in gentle names
Of peace and quiet and domestic love
Yet mingled not unwillingly with sneers
On visionary minds; if, in this time   440
Of dereliction and dismay, I yet
Despair not of our nature, but retain
A more than Roman confidence, a faith
That fails not, in all sorrow my support,
The blessing of my life—the gift is yours,
Ye winds and sounding cataracts! 'tis yours,
Ye mountains! thine, O Nature! Thou hast fed
My lofty speculations; and in thee,
For this uneasy heart of ours, I find
A never-failing principle of joy   450
And purest passion.

    Thou, my Friend! wert reared
In the great city, 'mid far other scenes;
But we, by different roads, at length have gained
The selfsame bourne. And for this cause to thee
I speak, unapprehensive of contempt,
The insinuated scoff of coward tongues,
And all that silent language which so oft
In conversation between man and man
Blots from the human countenance all trace
Of beauty and of love. For thou hast sought   460
The truth in solitude, and, since the days
That gave thee liberty, full long desired,
To serve in Nature's temple, thou hast been
The most assiduous of her ministers;
In many things my brother, chiefly here
In this our deep devotion.

     Fare thee well!
Health and the quiet of a healthful mind
Attend thee! seeking oft the haunts of men,
And yet more often living with thyself,
And for thyself, so haply shall thy days   470
Be many, and a blessing to mankind.

from BOOK THIRD

RESIDENCE AT CAMBRIDGE

It was a dreary morning when the wheels
Rolled over a wide plain o'erhung with clouds,
And nothing cheered our way till first we saw
The long-roofed chapel of King's College lift
Turrets and pinnacles in answering files,
Extended high above a dusky grove.

 Advancing, we espied upon the road
A student clothed in gown and tasselled cap,
Striding along as if o'ertasked by Time,
Or covetous of exercise and air;   10
He passed—nor was I master of my eyes
Till he was left an arrow's flight behind.
As near and nearer to the spot we drew,
It seemed to suck us in with an eddy's force.
Onward we drove beneath the Castle; caught,
While crossing Magdalene Bridge, a glimpse of
 Cam;
And at the *Hoop* alighted, famous Inn.

 My spirit was up, my thoughts were full of hope;
Some friends I had, acquaintances who there
Seemed friends, poor simple schoolboys, now hung
 round   20
With honour and importance: in a world
Of welcome faces up and down I roved;
Questions, directions, warnings and advice,
Flowed in upon me, from all sides; fresh day
Of pride and pleasure! to myself I seemed
A man of business and expense, and went
From shop to shop about my own affairs,
To Tutor or to Tailor, as befell,
From street to street with loose and careless mind.

 I was the Dreamer, they the Dream; I
 roamed   30
Delighted through the motley spectacle;
Gowns grave, or gaudy, doctors, students, streets,
Courts, cloisters, flocks of churches, gateways,
 towers:
Migration strange for a stripling of the hills,
A northern villager.

    As if the change

THE PRELUDE. BOOK III. **16. Cam:** the river flowing
through Cambridge.

Had waited on some Fairy's wand, at once
Behold me rich in monies, and attired
In splendid garb, with hose of silk, and hair
Powdered like rimy trees, when frost is keen.
My lordly dressing-gown, I pass it by,   40
With other signs of manhood that supplied
The lack of beard.—The weeks went roundly on,
With invitations, suppers, wine and fruit,
Smooth housekeeping within, and all without
Liberal, and suiting gentleman's array.

The Evangelist St. John my patron was:
Three Gothic courts are his, and in the first
Was my abiding-place, a nook obscure;
Right underneath, the College kitchens made
A humming sound, less tuneable than bees,   50
But hardly less industrious; with shrill notes
Of sharp command and scolding intermixed.
Near me hung Trinity's loquacious clock,
Who never let the quarters, night or day,
Slip by him unproclaimed, and told the hours
Twice over with a male and female voice.
Her pealing organ was my neighbour too;
And from my pillow, looking forth by light
Of moon or favouring stars, I could behold
The antechapel where the statue stood   60
Of Newton with his prism and silent face,
The marble index of a mind for ever
Voyaging through strange seas of Thought, alone.

Of College labours, of the Lecturer's room
All studded round, as thick as chairs could stand,
With loyal students, faithful to their books,
Half-and-half idlers, hardy recusants,
And honest dunces—of important days,
Examinations, when the man was weighed
As in a balance! of excessive hopes,   70
Tremblings withal and commendable fears,
Small jealousies, and triumphs good or bad—
Let others that know more speak as they know.
Such glory was but little sought by me,
And little won. Yet from the first crude days
Of settling time in this untried abode,
I was disturbed at times by prudent thoughts,
Wishing to hope without a hope, some fears
About my future worldly maintenance,
And, more than all, a strangeness in the mind,   80
A feeling that I was not for that hour,

46. **St. John:** Wordsworth was a student at St. John's
College, Cambridge, from 1787 to 1791.

Nor for that place. But wherefore be cast down?
For (not to speak of Reason and her pure
Reflective acts to fix the moral law
Deep in the conscience, nor of Christian Hope,
Bowing her head before her sister Faith
As one far mightier), hither I had come,
Bear witness Truth, endowed with holy powers
And faculties, whether to work or feel.
Oft when the dazzling show no longer new   90
Had ceased to dazzle, ofttimes did I quit
My comrades, leave the crowd, buildings and
          groves,
And as I paced alone the level fields
Far from those lovely sights and sounds sublime
With which I had been conversant, the mind
Drooped not; but there into herself returning,
With prompt rebound seemed fresh as heretofore.
At least I more distinctly recognised
Her native instincts: let me dare to speak
A higher language, say that now I felt   100
What independent solaces were mine,
To mitigate the injurious sway of place
Or circumstance, how far soever changed
In youth, or *to* be changed in after years.
As if awakened, summoned, roused, constrained,
I looked for universal things; perused
The common countenance of earth and sky
Earth, nowhere unembellished by some trace
Of that first Paradise whence man was driven;
And sky, whose beauty and bounty are ex-
          pressed   110
By the proud name she bears—the name of
          Heaven.
I called on both to teach me what they might;
Or, turning the mind in upon herself,
Pored, watched, expected, listened, spread my
          thoughts
And spread them with a wider creeping; felt
Incumbencies more awful, visitings
Of the Upholder of the tranquil soul,
That tolerates the indignities of Time,
And from the centre of Eternity
All finite motions overruling, lives   120
In glory immutable. But peace! enough
Here to record that I was mounting now
To such community with highest truth—
A track pursuing, not untrod before,
From strict analogies by thought supplied
Or consciousness not to be subdued.
To every natural form, rock, fruits, or flower,

Even the loose stones that cover the highway,
I gave a moral life: I saw them feel,
Or linked them to some feeling: the great
    mass   130
Lay imbedded in a quickening soul, and all
That I beheld respired with inward meaning.
Add that whate'er of Terror or of Love
Or Beauty, Nature's daily face put on
From transitory passion, unto this
I was as sensitive as waters are
To the sky's influence in a kindred mood
Of passion; was obedient as a lute
That waits upon the touches of the wind.
Unknown, unthought of, yet I was most
    rich—   140
I had a world about me—'twas my own;
I made it, for it only lived to me,
And to the God who sees into the heart.
Such sympathies, though rarely, were betrayed
By outward gestures and by visible looks:
Some called it madness—so indeed it was,
If child-like fruitfulness in passing joy,
If steady moods of thoughtfulness matured
To inspiration, sort with such a name;
If prophecy be madness; if things viewed   150
By poets in old time, and higher up
By the first men, earth's first inhabitants,
May in these tutored days no more be seen
With undisordered sight. But leaving this,
It was no madness, for the bodily eye
Amid my strongest workings evermore
Was searching out the lines of difference
As they lie hid in all external forms,
Near or remote, minute or vast; an eye
Which, from a tree, a stone, a withered leaf,   160
To the broad ocean and the azure heavens
Spangled with kindred multitudes of stars,
Could find no surface where its power might sleep;
Which spake perpetual logic to my soul,
And by an unrelenting agency
Did bind my feelings even as in a chain.

    And here, O Friend! have I retraced my life
Up to an eminence, and told a tale
Of matters which not falsely may be called
The glory of my youth. Of genius, power,   170
Creation and divinity itself
I have been speaking, for my theme has been
What has passed within me. Not of outward things
Done visibly for other minds, words, signs,

Symbols or actions, but of my own heart
Have I been speaking, and my youthful mind.
O Heavens! how awful is the might of souls,
And what they do within themselves while yet
The yoke of earth is new to them, the world
Nothing but a wide field where they were
    sown.   180
This is, in truth, heroic argument,
This genuine prowess, which I wished to touch
With hand however weak, but in the main
It lies far hidden from the reach of words.
Points have we all of us within our souls
Where all stand single; this I feel, and make
Breathings for incommunicable powers;
But is not each a memory to himself,
And, therefore, now that we must quit this theme,
I am not heartless, for there's not a man   190
That lives who hath not known his god-like hours,
And feels not what an empire we inherit
As natural beings in the strength of Nature

    No more: for now into a populous plain
We must descend. A Traveller I am,
Whose tale is only of himself; even so,
So be it, if the pure of heart be prompt
To follow, and if thou, my honoured Friend!
Who in these thoughts art ever at my side,
Support, as heretofore, my fainting steps.   200

    It hath been told, that when the first delight
That flashed upon me from this novel show
Had failed, the mind returned into herself;
Yet true it is, that I had made a change
In climate, and my nature's outward coat
Changed also slowly and insensibly.
Full oft the quiet and exalted thoughts
Of loneliness gave way to empty noise
And superficial pastimes; now and then
Forced labour, and more frequently forced
    hopes;   210
And, worst of all, a treasonable growth
Of indecisive judgments, that impaired
And shook the mind's simplicity.—And yet
This was a gladsome time. Could I behold—
Who, less insensible than sodden clay
In a sea-river's bed at ebb of tide,
Could have beheld—with undelighted heart,
So many happy youths, so wide and fair
A congregation in its budding-time
Of health, and hope, and beauty, all at once   220
So many divers samples from the growth

Of life's sweet season—could have seen unmoved
That miscellaneous garland of wild flowers
Decking the matron temples of a place
So famous through the world? To me, at least,
It was a goodly prospect: for, in sooth,
Though I had learnt betimes to stand unpropped,
And independent musings pleased me so
That spells seemed on me when I was alone,
Yet could I only cleave to solitude   230
In lonely places; if a throng was near
That way I leaned by nature; for my heart
Was social, and loved idleness and joy.

from BOOK SIXTH

CAMBRIDGE AND THE ALPS

'Tis not my present purpose to retrace
That variegated journey step by step.   490
A march it was of military speed,
And Earth did change her images and forms
Before us, fast as clouds are changed in heaven.
Day after day, up early and down late,
From hill to vale we dropped, from vale to hill
Mounted—from province on to province swept,
Keen hunters in a chase of fourteen weeks,
Eager as birds of prey, or as a ship
Upon the stretch, when winds are blowing fair:
Sweet coverts did we cross of pastoral life,   500
Enticing valleys, greeted them and left
Too soon, while yet the very flash and gleam
Of salutation were not passed away.
Oh! sorrow for the youth who could have seen,
Unchastened, unsubdued, unawed, unraised
To patriarchal dignity of mind,
And pure simplicity of wish and will,
Those sanctified abodes of peaceful man,
Pleased (though to hardship born, and compassed
     round
With danger, varying as the seasons change),   510
Pleased with his daily task, or, if not pleased,
Contented, from the moment that the dawn
(Ah! surely not without attendant gleams
Of soul-illumination) calls him forth
To industry, by glistenings flung on rocks,
Whose evening shadows lead him to repose.

     Well might a stranger look with bounding heart
Down on a green recess, the first I saw

Of those deep haunts, an aboriginal vale,
Quiet and lorded over and possessed   520
By naked huts, wood-built, and sown like tents
Or Indian cabins over the fresh lawns
And by the river side.
                    That very day,
From a bare ridge we also first beheld
Unveiled the summit of Mont Blanc, and grieved
To have a soulless image on the eye
That had usurped upon a living thought
That never more could be. The wondrous Vale
Of Chamouny stretched far below, and soon
With its dumb cataracts and streams of ice,   530
A motionless array of mighty waves,
Five rivers broad and vast, made rich amends,
And reconciled us to realities;
There small birds warble from the leafy trees,
The eagle soars high in the element,
There doth the reaper bind the yellow sheaf,
The maiden spread the haycock in the sun,
While Winter like a well-tamed lion walks,
Descending from the mountain to make sport
Among the cottages by beds of flowers.   540

     Whate'er in this wide circuit we beheld,
Or heard, was fitted to our unripe state
Of intellect and heart. With such a book
Before our eyes, we could not choose but read
Lessons of genuine brotherhood, the plain
And universal reason of mankind,
The truths of young and old. Nor, side by side
Pacing, two social pilgrims, or alone
Each with his humour, could we fail to abound
In dreams and fictions, pensively composed: 550
Dejection taken up for pleasure's sake,
And gilded sympathies, the willow wreath,
And sober posies of funereal flowers,
Gathered among those solitudes sublime
From formal gardens of the lady Sorrow,
Did sweeten many a meditative hour.

     Yet still in me with those soft luxuries
Mixed something of stern mood, an underthirst
Of vigour seldom utterly allayed:
And from that source how different a sadness   560
Would issue, let one incident make known.
When from the Vallais we had turned, and clomb
Along the Simplon's steep and rugged road,

THE PRELUDE. BOOK VI. **563. Simplon:** the Simplon
Pass, a narrow chasm through the Alps.

Following a band of muleteers, we reached
A halting-place, where all together took
Their noon-tide meal. Hastily rose our guide,
Leaving us at the board; awhile we lingered,
Then paced the beaten downward way that led
Right to a rough stream's edge, and there broke off;
The only track now visible was one   570
That from the torrent's further brink held forth
Conspicuous invitation to ascend
A lofty mountain. After a brief delay
Crossing the unbridged stream, that road we took,
And clomb with eagerness, till anxious fears
Intruded, for we failed to overtake
Our comrades gone before. By fortunate chance,
While every moment added doubt to doubt,
A peasant met us, from whose mouth we learned
That to the spot which had perplexed us first   580
We must descend, and there should find the road,
Which in the stony channel of the stream
Lay a few steps, and then along its banks;
And, that our future course, all plain to sight,
Was downwards, with the current of that stream.
Loth to believe what we so grieved to hear,
For still we had hopes that pointed to the clouds,
We questioned him again, and yet again;
But every word that from the peasant's lips
Came in reply, translated by our feelings,   590
Ended in this,—*that we had crossed the Alps.*

Imagination—here the Power so called
Through sad incompetence of human speech,
That awful Power rose from the mind's abyss
Like an unfathered vapour that enwraps,
At once, some lonely traveller. I was lost;
Halted without an effort to break through;
But to my conscious soul I now can say—
"I recognise thy glory:" in such strength
Of usurpation, when the light of sense   600
Goes out, but with a flash that has revealed
The invisible world, doth greatness make abode,
There harbours; whether we be young or old,
Our destiny, our being's heart and home,
Is with infinitude, and only there;
With hope it is, hope that can never die,
Effort, and expectation, and desire,
And something evermore about to be.
Under such banners militant, the soul
Seeks for no trophies, struggles for no spoils   610
That may attest her prowess, blest in thoughts
That are their own perfection and reward,

Strong in herself and in beatitude
That hides her, like the mighty flood of Nile
Poured from his fount of Abyssinian clouds
To fertilise the whole Egyptian plain.

The melancholy slackening that ensued
Upon those tidings by the peasant given
Was soon dislodged. Downwards we hurried fast,
And, with the half-shaped road which we had
         missed,   620
Entered a narrow chasm. The brook and road
Were fellow-travellers in this gloomy strait,
And with them did we journey several hours
At a slow pace. The immeasurable height
Of woods decaying, never to be decayed,
The stationary blasts of waterfalls,
And in the narrow rent at every turn
Winds thwarting winds, bewildered and forlorn,
The torrents shooting from the clear blue sky,
The rocks that muttered close upon our ears,   630
Black drizzling crags that spake by the way-side
As if a voice were in them, the sick sight
And giddy prospect of the raving stream,
The unfettered clouds and region of the Heavens,
Tumult and peace, the darkness and the light—
Were all like workings of one mind, the features
Of the same face, blossoms upon one tree;
Characters of the great Apocalypse,
The types and symbols of Eternity,
Of first, and last, and midst, and without end. 640

That night our lodging was a house that stood
Alone within the valley, at a point
Where, tumbling from aloft, a torrent swelled
The rapid stream whose margin we had trod;
A dreary mansion, large beyond all need,
With high and spacious rooms, deafened and
         stunned
By noise of waters, making innocent sleep
Lie melancholy among weary bones.

Uprisen betimes, our journey we renewed,
Led by the stream, ere noon-day magnified   650
Into a lordly river, broad and deep,
Dimpling along in silent majesty,
Without mountains for its neighbours, and in view
Of distant mountains and their snowy tops,
And thus proceeding to Locarno's Lake,
Fit resting-place for such a visitant.
Locarno! spreading out in width like Heaven,
How dost thou cleave to the poetic heart,

Bask in the sunshine of the memory;
And Como! thou, a treasure whom the earth   660
Keeps to herself, confined as in a depth
Of Abyssinian privacy. I spake
Of thee, thy chestnut woods, and garden plots
Of Indian corn tended by dark-eyed maids;
Thy lofty steeps, and pathways roofed with vines,
Winding from house to house, from town to town,
Sole link that binds them to each other; walks,
League after league, and cloistral avenues,
Where silence dwells if music be not there:
While yet a youth undisciplined in verse,   670
Through fond ambition of that hour I strove
To chant your praise; nor can approach you now
Ungreeted by a more melodious Song,
Where tones of Nature smoothed by learned Art
May flow in lasting current. Like a breeze
Or sunbeam over your domain I passed
In motion without pause; but ye have left
Your beauty with me, a serene accord
Of forms and colours, passive, yet endowed
In their submissiveness with power as sweet   680
And gracious, almost, might I dare to say,
As virtue is, or goodness; sweet as love,
Or the remembrance of a generous deed,
Or mildest visitations of pure thought,
When God, the giver of all joy, is thanked
Religiously, in silent blessedness;
Sweet as this last herself, for such it is.

With those delightful pathways we advanced,
For two days' space, in presence of the Lake,
That, stretching far among the Alps, assumed   690
A character more stern. The second night,
From sleep awakened, and misled by sound
Of the church clock telling the hours with strokes
Whose import then we had not learned, we rose
By moonlight, doubting not that day was nigh,
And that meanwhile, by no uncertain path,
Along the winding margin of the lake,
Led, as before, we should behold the scene
Hushed in profound repose. We left the town
Of Gravedona with this hope; but soon   700
Were lost, bewildered among woods immense,
And on a rock sate down, to wait for day.
An open place it was, and overlooked,
From high, the sullen water far beneath,
On which a dull red image of the moon
Lay bedded, changing oftentimes its form
Like an uneasy snake. From hour to hour

We sate and sate, wondering, as if the night
Had been ensnared by witchcraft. On the rock
At last we stretched our weary limbs for sleep,   710
But *could not* sleep, tormented by the stings
Of insects, which, with noise like that of noon,
Filled all the woods: the cry of unknown birds;
The mountains more by blackness visible
And their own size, than any outward light;
The breathless wilderness of clouds; the clock
That told, with unintelligible voice,
The widely parted hours; the noise of streams,
And sometimes rustling motions nigh at hand,
That did not leave us free from personal fear;   720
And, lastly, the withdrawing moon, that set
Before us, while she still was high in heaven;—
These were our food; and such a summer's night
Followed that pair of golden days that shed
On Como's Lake, and all that round it lay,
Their fairest, softest, happiest influence.

But here I must break off, and bid farewell
To days, each offering some new sight, or fraught
With some untried adventure, in a course
Prolonged till sprinklings of autumnal snow   730
Checked our unwearied steps. Let this alone
Be mentioned as a parting word, that not
In hollow exultation, dealing out
Hyperboles of praise comparative;
Not rich one moment to be poor for ever;
Not prostrate, overborne, as if the mind
Herself were nothing, a mere pensioner
On outward forms—did we in presence stand
Of that magnificent region. On the front
Of this whole Song is written that my heart   740
Must, in such Temple, needs have offered up
A different worship. Finally, whate'er
I saw, or heard, or felt, was but a stream
That flowed into a kindred stream; a gale,
Confederate with the current of the soul,
To speed my voyage; every sound or sight,
In its degree of power, administered
To grandeur or to tenderness,—to the one
Directly, but to tender thoughts by means
Less often instantaneous in effect;   750
Led me to these by paths that, in the main,
Were more circuitous, but not less sure
Duly to reach the point marked out by Heaven.

Oh, most belovèd Friend! a glorious time,
A happy time that was; triumphant looks
Were then the common language of all eyes;

As if awaked from sleep, the Nations hailed
Their great expectancy: the fife of war
Was then a spirit-stirring sound indeed,
A blackbird's whistle in a budding grove.   760
We left the Swiss exulting in the fate
Of their near neighbours; and, when shortening fast
Our pilgrimage, nor distant far from home,
We crossed the Brabant armies on the fret
For battle in the cause of Liberty.
A stripling, scarcely of the household then
Of social life, I looked upon these things
As from a distance; heard, and saw, and felt,
Was touched, but with no intimate concern;
I seemed to move along them, as a bird   770
Moves through the air, or as a fish pursues
Its sport, or feeds in its proper element;
I wanted not that joy, I did not need
Such help; the ever-living universe,
Turn where I might, was opening out its glories,
And the independent spirit of pure youth
Called forth, at every season, new delights,
Spread round my steps like sunshine o'er green
     fields.

from BOOK EIGHTH

RETROSPECT—LOVE OF NATURE
LEADING TO LOVE OF MAN

   But when that first poetic faculty
Of plain Imagination and severe,
No longer a mute influence of the soul,
Ventured, at some rash Muse's earnest call,
To try her strength among harmonious words;
And to book-notions and the rules of art   370
Did knowingly conform itself; there came
Among the simple shapes of human life
A wilfulness of fancy and conceit;
And Nature and her objects beautified
These fictions, as in some sort, in their turn,
They burnished her. From touch of this new power
Nothing was safe: the elder-tree that grew
Beside the well-known charnel-house had then
A dismal look: the yew-tree had its ghost,
That took his station there for ornament: 380
The dignities of plain occurrence then
Were tasteless, and truth's golden mean, a point

764. Brabant: Belgian.

Where no sufficient pleasure could be found.
Then, if a widow, staggering with the blow
Of her distress, was known to have turned her steps
To the cold grave in which her husband slept,
One night, or haply more than one, through pain
Or half-insensate impotence of mind,
The fact was caught at greedily, and there
She must be visitant the whole year through,   390
Wetting the turf with never-ending tears.

   Through quaint obliquities I might pursue
These cravings; when the foxglove, one by one,
Upwards through every stage of the tall stem,
Had shed beside the public way its bells,
And stood of all dismantled, save the last
Left at the tapering ladder's top, that seemed
To bend as doth a slender blade of grass
Tipped with a rain-drop, Fancy loved to seat,
Beneath the plant despoiled, but crested still   400
With this last relic, soon itself to fall,
Some vagrant mother, whose arch little ones,
All unconcerned by her dejected plight,
Laughed as with rival eagerness their hands
Gathered the purple cups that round them lay,
Strewing the turf's green slope.   A diamond light
(Whene'er the summer sun, declining, smote
A smooth rock wet with constant springs) was seen
Sparkling from out a copse-clad bank that rose
Fronting our cottage. Oft beside the hearth   410
Seated, with open door, often and long
Upon this restless lustre have I gazed,
That made my fancy restless as itself.
'Twas now for me a burnished silver shield
Suspended over a knight's tomb, who lay
Inglorious, buried in the dusky wood:
An entrance now into some magic cave
Or palace built by fairies of the rock;
Nor could I have been bribed to disenchant
The spectacle, by visiting the spot.   420
Thus wilful Fancy, in no hurtful mood,
Engrafted far-fetched shapes on feelings bred
By pure Imagination: busy Power
She was, and when her ready pupil turned
Instinctively to human passions, then
Least understood. Yet, 'mid the fervent swarm
Of these vagaries, with an eye so rich
As mine was through the bounty of a grand
And lovely region, I had forms distinct
To steady me: each airy thought revolved   430

Round a substantial centre, which at once
Incited it to motion, and controlled.
I did not pine like one in cities bred,
As was thy melancholy lot, dear Friend!
Great Spirit as thou art, in endless dreams
Of sickliness, disjoining, joining, things
Without the light of knowledge. Where the harm,
If, when the woodman languished with disease
Induced by sleeping nightly on the ground
Within his sod-built cabin, Indian-wise,   440
I called the pangs of disappointed love,
And all the sad etcetera of the wrong,
To help him to his grave? Meanwhile the man,
If not already from the woods retired
To die at home, was haply, as I knew,
Withering by slow degrees, 'mid gentle airs,
Birds, running streams, and hills so beautiful
On golden evenings, while the charcoal pile
Breathed up its smoke, an image of his ghost
Or spirit that full soon must take her flight.   450
Nor shall we not be tending towards that point
Of sound humanity to which our Tale
Leads, though by sinuous ways, if here I show
How Fancy, in a season when she wove
Those slender cords, to guide the unconscious Boy
For the Man's sake, could feed at Nature's call
Some pensive musings which might well beseem
Maturer years.

    A grove there is whose boughs
Stretch from the western marge of Thurstonmere,
With length of shade so thick, that whoso
  glides   460
Along the line of low-roofed water, moves
As in a cloister. Once—while, in that shade
Loitering, I watched the golden beams of light
Flung from the setting sun, as they reposed
In silent beauty on the naked ridge
Of a high eastern hill—thus flowed my thoughts
In a pure stream of words fresh from the heart:
Dear native Regions, wheresoe'er shall close
My mortal course, there will I think on you;
Dying, will cast on you a backward look;   470
Even as this setting sun (albeit the Vale
Is no where touched by one memorial gleam)
Doth with the fond remains of his last power
Still linger, and a farewell lustre sheds,
On the dear mountain-tops where first he rose.

THE PRELUDE. BOOK VIII. **459. Thurstonmere:** another
name for Coniston Lake.

Enough of humble arguments; recall,
My Song! those high emotions which thy voice
Has heretofore made known; that bursting forth
Of sympathy, inspiring and inspired,
When everywhere a vital pulse was felt,   480
And all the several frames of things, like stars,
Through every magnitude distinguishable,
Shone mutually indebted, or half lost
Each in the other's blaze, a galaxy
Of life and glory. In the midst stood Man,
Outwardly, inwardly contemplated,
As, of all visible natures, crown, though born
Of dust, and kindred to the worm; a Being,
Both in perception and discernment, first
In every capability of rapture,   490
Through the divine effect of power and love;
As, more than anything we know, instinct
With godhead, and, by reason and by will,
Acknowledging dependency sublime.

  Ere long, the lonely mountains left, I moved,
Begirt, from day to day, with temporal shapes
Of vice and folly thrust upon my view,
Objects of sport, and ridicule, and scorn,
Manners and characters discriminate,
And little bustling passions that eclipse,   500
As well they might, the impersonated thought,
The idea, or abstraction of the kind.

  An idler among academic bowers,
Such was my new condition, as at large
Has been set forth; yet here the vulgar light
Of present, actual, superficial life,
Gleaming through colouring of other times,
Old usages and local privilege,
Was welcomed, softened, if not solemnised.
This notwithstanding, being brought more
  near   510
To vice and guilt, forerunning wretchedness,
I trembled,—thought, at times, of human life
With an indefinite terror and dismay,
Such as the storms and angry elements
Had bred in me; but gloomier far, a dim
Analogy to uproar and misrule,
Disquiet, danger, and obscurity.

  It might be told (but wherefore speak of things
Common to all?) that, seeing, I was led
Gravely to ponder—judging between good   520
And evil, not as for the mind's delight
But for her guidance—one who was to *act*,
As sometimes to the best of feeble means

I did, by human sympathy impelled:
And, through dislike and most offensive pain,
Was to the truth conducted; of this faith
Never forsaken, that, by acting well,
And understanding, I should learn to love
The end of life, and everything we know.

  Grave Teacher, stern Preceptress! for at
      times   530
Thou canst put on an aspect most severe;
London, to thee I willingly return.
Erewhile my verse played idly with the flowers
Enwrought upon thy mantle; satisfied
With that amusement, and a simple look
Of child-like inquisition now and then
Cast upwards on thy countenance, to detect
Some inner meanings which might harbour there.
But how could I in mood so light indulge,
Keeping such fresh remembrance of the day,   540
When, having thridded the long labyrinth
Of the suburban villages, I first
Entered thy vast dominion? On the roof
Of an itinerant vehicle I sate,
With vulgar men about me, trivial forms
Of houses, pavement, streets, of men and things,—
Mean shapes on every side: but, at the instant,
When to myself it fairly might be said,
The threshold now is overpast, (how strange
That aught external to the living mind   550
Should have such mighty sway! yet so it was),
A weight of ages did at once descend
Upon my heart; no thought embodied, no
Distinct remembrances, but weight and power,—
Power growing under weight: alas! I feel
That I am trifling: 'twas a moment's pause,—
All that took place within me came and went
As in a moment; yet with Time it dwells,
And grateful memory, as a thing divine.

  The curious traveller, who, from open day,   560
Hath passed with torches into some huge cave,
The Grotto of Antiparos, or the Den
In old time haunted by that Danish Witch,
Yordas; he looks around and sees the vault
Widening on all sides; sees, or thinks he sees,
Erelong, the massy roof above his head,
That instantly unsettles and recedes,—

562. **Antiparos:** an island in the Aegean. **562–64. Den
. . . Yordas:** Yordas Cave, near Ingleton in Yorkshire.

Substance and shadow, light and darkness, all
Commingled, making up a canopy
Of shapes and forms and tendencies to shape   570
That shift and vanish, change and interchange
Like spectres,—ferment silent and sublime!
That after a short space works less and less,
Till, every effort, every motion gone,
The scene before him stands in perfect view
Exposed, and lifeless as a written book!—
But let him pause awhile, and look again,
And a new quickening shall succeed, at first
Beginning timidly, then creeping fast,
Till the whole cave, so late a senseless mass,   580
Busies the eye with images and forms
Boldly assembled,—here is shadowed forth
From the projections, wrinkles, cavities,
A variegated landscape,—there the shape
Of some gigantic warrior clad in mail,
The ghostly semblance of a hooded monk,
Veiled nun, or pilgrim resting on his staff:
Strange congregation! yet not slow to meet
Eyes that perceive through minds that can inspire.

  Even in such sort had I at first been moved,   590
Nor otherwise continued to be moved,
As I explored the vast metropolis,
Fount of my country's destiny and the world's;
That great emporium, chronicle at once
And burial-place of passions, and their home
Imperial, their chief living residence.

  With strong sensations teeming as it did
Of past and present, such a place must needs
Have pleased me, seeking knowledge at that time
Far less than craving power; yet knowledge
      came,   600
Sought or unsought, and influxes of power
Came, of themselves, or at her call derived
In fits of kindliest apprehensiveness,
From all sides, when whate'er was in itself
Capacious found, or seemed to find, in me
A correspondent amplitude of mind;
Such is the strength and glory of our youth!
The human nature unto which I felt
That I belonged, and reverenced with love,
Was not a punctual presence, but a spirit   610
Diffused through time and space, with aid derived
Of evidence from monuments, erect,
Prostrate, or leaning towards their common rest
In earth, the widely scattered wreck sublime

Of vanished nations, or more clearly drawn
From books and what they picture and record.

'Tis true, the history of our native land—
With those of Greece compared and popular Rome,
And in our high-wrought modern narratives
Stript of their harmonising soul, the life   620
Of manners and familiar incidents—
Had never much delighted me. And less
Than other intellects had mine been used
To lean upon extrinsic circumstance
Of record or tradition; but a sense
Of what in the Great City had been done
And suffered, and was doing, suffering, still,
Weighed with me, could support the test of
          thought;
And, in despite of all that had gone by,
Or was departing never to return,   630
There I conversed with majesty and power
Like independent natures. Hence the place
Was thronged with impregnations like the Wilds
In which my early feelings had been nursed—
Bare hills and valleys, full of caverns, rocks,
And audible seclusions, dashing lakes,
Echoes and waterfalls, and pointed crags
That into music touch the passing wind.
Here then my young imagination found
No uncongenial element; could here   640
Among new objects serve or give command,
Even as the heart's occasions might require,
To forward reason's else too-scrupulous march.
The effect was, still more elevated views
Of human nature. Neither vice nor guilt,
Debasement undergone by body or mind,
Nor all the misery forced upon my sight,
Misery not lightly passed, but sometimes scanned
Most feelingly, could overthrow my trust
In what we *may* become; induce belief   650
That I was ignorant, had been falsely taught,
A solitary, who with vain conceits
Had been inspired, and walked about in dreams.
From those sad scenes when meditation turned,
Lo! everything that was indeed divine
Retained its purity inviolate,
Nay brighter shone, by this portentous gloom
Set off; such opposition as aroused
The mind of Adam, yet in Paradise
Though fallen from bliss, when in the East he
          saw   660
Darkness ere day's mid course, and morning light

More orient in the western cloud, that drew
O'er the blue firmament a radiant white,
Descending slow with something heavenly fraught.

Add also, that among the multitudes
Of that huge city, oftentimes was seen
Affectingly set forth, more than elsewhere
Is possible, the unity of man,
One spirit over ignorance and vice
Predominant, in good and evil hearts;   670
One sense for moral judgments, as one eye
For the sun's light. The soul when smitten thus
By a sublime *idea*, whencesoe'er
Vouchsafed for union or communion, feeds
On the pure bliss, and takes her rest with God.

Thus from a very early age, O Friend!
My thoughts by slow gradations had been drawn
To human-kind, and to the good and ill
Of human life: Nature had led me on;
And oft amid the "busy hum" I seemed   680
To travel independent of her help,
As if I had forgotten her; but no,
The world of human-kind outweighed not hers
In my habitual thoughts; the scale of love,
Though filling daily, still was light, compared
With that in which *her* mighty objects lay.

BOOK ELEVENTH

FRANCE

From that time forth, Authority in France
Put on a milder face; Terror had ceased,
Yet everything was wanting that might give
Courage to them who looked for good by light
Of rational Experience, for the shoots
And hopeful blossoms of a second spring:
Yet, in me, confidence was unimpaired;
The Senate's language, and the public acts
And measures of the Government, though both
Weak, and of heartless omen, had not power   10
To daunt me; in the People was my trust:
And, in the virtues which mine eyes had seen,
I knew that wound external could not take
Life from the young Republic; that new foes

THE PRELUDE. BOOK XI. 1. In this section Wordsworth
describes the mood in France following the Reign of
Terror.

Would only follow, in the path of shame,
Their brethren, and her triumphs be in the end
Great, universal, irresistible.
This intuition led me to confound
One victory with another, higher far,—
Triumphs of unambitious peace at home,   20
And noiseless fortitude. Beholding still
Resistance strong as heretofore, I thought
That what was in degree the same was likewise
The same in quality,—that, as the worse
Of the two spirits then at strife remained
Untired, the better, surely, would preserve
The heart that first had roused him. Youth
     maintains,
In all conditions of society,
Communion more direct and intimate
With Nature,—hence, ofttimes, with reason
     too—   30
Than age or manhood, even. To Nature then,
Power had reverted: habit, custom, law,
Had left an interregnum's open space
For *her* to move about in, uncontrolled.
Hence could I see how Babel-like their task,
Who, by the recent deluge stupified,
With their whole souls went culling from the day
Its petty promises, to build a tower
For their own safety; laughed with my compeers
At gravest heads, by enmity to France   40
Distempered, till they found, in every blast
Forced from the street-disturbing newsman's horn,
For her great cause record or prophecy
Of utter ruin. How might we believe
That wisdom could, in any shape, come near
Men clinging to delusions so insane?
And thus, experience proving that no few
Of our opinions had been just, we took
Like credit to ourselves where less was due,
And thought that other notions were as sound,   50
Yea, could not but be right, because we saw
That foolish men opposed them.
                              To a strain
More animated I might here give way,
And tell, since juvenile errors are my theme,
What in those days, through Britain, was
     performed
To turn *all* judgments out of their right course;
But this is passion over-near ourselves,
Reality too close and too intense,
And intermixed with something, in my mind,
Of scorn and condemnation personal,   60

That would profane the sanctity of verse.
Our Shepherds, this say merely, at that time
Acted, or seemed at least to act, like men
Thirsting to make the guardian crook of law
A tool of murder; they who ruled the State—
Though with such awful proof before their eyes
That he, who would sow death, reaps death, or
     worse,
And can reap nothing better—child-like longed
To imitate, not wise enough to avoid;
Or left (by mere timidity betrayed)   70
The plain straight road, for one no better chosen
Than if their wish had been to undermine
Justice, and make an end of Liberty.

    But from these bitter truths I must return
To my own history. It had been told
That I was led to take an eager part
In arguments of civil polity,
Abruptly, and indeed before my time:
I had approached, like other youths, the shield
Of human nature from the golden side,   80
And would have fought, even to the death, to attest
The quality of the metal which I saw.
What there is best in individual man,
Of wise in passion, and sublime in power,
Benevolent in small societies,
And great in large ones, I had oft revolved,
Felt deeply, but not thoroughly understood
By reason: nay, far from it; they were yet,
As cause was given me afterwards to learn,
Not proof against the injuries of the day;   90
Lodged only at the sanctuary's door,
Not safe within its bosom. Thus prepared,
And with such general insight into evil,
And of the bounds which sever it from good,
As books and common intercourse with life
Must needs have given—to the inexperienced
     mind,
When the world travels in a beaten road,
Guide faithful as is needed—I began
To mediate with ardour on the rule
And management of nations; what it is   100
And ought to be; and strove to learn how far
Their power or weakness, wealth or poverty,
Their happiness or misery, depends
Upon their laws, and fashion of the State.

74. A retrospective section begins here as Wordsworth
recalls his own responses to the French Revolution.

O pleasant exercise of hope and joy!
For mighty were the auxiliars which then stood
Upon our side, us who were strong in love!
Bliss was it in that dawn to be alive,
But to be young was very Heaven! O times,
In which the meagre, stale, forbidding ways   110
Of custom, law, and statute, took at once
The attraction of a country in romance!
When Reason seemed the most to assert her rights,
When most intent on making of herself
A prime enchantress—to assist the work,
Which then was going forward in her name!
Not favoured spots alone, but the whole Earth,
The beauty wore of promise—that which sets
(As at some moments might not be unfelt
Among the bowers of Paradise itself)   120
The budding rose above the rose full blown.
What temper at the prospect did not wake
To happiness unthought of? The inert
Were roused, and lively natures rapt away!
They who had fed their childhood upon dreams,
The play-fellows of fancy, who had made
All powers of swiftness, subtilty, and strength
Their ministers,—who in lordly wise had stirred
Among the grandest objects of the sense,
And dealt with whatsoever they found there   130
As if they had within some lurking right
To wield it;—they, too, who of gentle mood
Had watched all gentle motions, and to these
Had fitted their own thoughts, schemers more mild,
And in the region of their peaceful selves;—
Now was it that *both* found, the meek and lofty
Did both find, helpers to their hearts' desire,
And stuff at hand, plastic as they could wish,—
Were called upon to exercise their skill,
Not in Utopia,—subterranean fields,—   140
Or some secreted island, Heaven knows where!
But in the very world, which is the world
Of all of us,—the place where, in the end,
We find our happiness, or not at all!

    Why should I not confess that Earth was then
To me, what an inheritance, new-fallen,
Seems, when the first time visited, to one
Who thither comes to find in it his home?
He walks about and looks upon the spot
With cordial transport, moulds it and
        remoulds,   150
And is half-pleased with things that are amiss,
'Twill be such joy to see them disappear.

An active partisan, I thus convoked
From every object pleasant circumstance
To suit my ends; I moved among mankind
With genial feelings still predominant;
When erring, erring on the better part,
And in the kinder spirit; placable,
Indulgent, as not uninformed that men
See as they have been taught—Antiquity   160
Gives rights to error; and aware, no less
That throwing off oppression must be work
As well of License as of Liberty;
And above all—for this was more than all—
Not caring if the wind did now and then
Blow keen upon an eminence that gave
Prospect so large into futurity;
In brief, a child of Nature, as at first,
Diffusing only those affections wider
That from the cradle had grown up with me,   170
And losing, in no other way than light
Is lost in light, the weak in the more strong.

    In the main outline, such it might be said
Was my condition, till with open war
Britain opposed the liberties of France.
This threw me first out of the pale of love;
Soured and corrupted, upwards to the source,
My sentiments; was not, as hitherto,
A swallowing up of lesser things in great,
But change of them into their contraries;   180
And thus a way was opened for mistakes
And false conclusions, in degree as gross,
In kind more dangerous. What had been a pride,
Was now a shame; my likings and my loves
Ran in new channels, leaving old ones dry;
And hence a blow that, in maturer age,
Would but have touched the judgment, struck
        more deep
Into sensations near the heart: meantime,
As from the first, wild theories were afloat,
To whose pretensions, sedulously urged,   190
I had but lent a careless ear, assured
That time was ready to set all things right,
And that the multitude, so long oppressed,
Would be oppressed no more.
                                But when events
Brought less encouragement, and unto these
The immediate proof of principles no more

174. open war: France declared war on England on
February 1, 1793. Wordsworth records in the following
lines his change of attitude toward the Revolution.

Could be entrusted, while the events themselves,
Worn out in greatness, stripped of novelty,
Less occupied the mind, and sentiments
Could through my understanding's natural
        growth   200
No longer keep their ground, by faith maintained
Of inward consciousness, and hope that laid
Her hand upon her object—evidence
Safer, of universal application, such
As could not be impeached, was sought elsewhere.

    But now, become oppressors in their turn,
Frenchmen had changed a war of self-defence
For one of conquest, losing sight of all
Which they had struggled for: up mounted now,
Openly in the eye of earth and heaven,   210
The scale of liberty. I read her doom.
With anger vexed, with disappointment sore,
But not dismayed, nor taking to the shame
Of a false prophet. While resentment rose,
Striving to hide, what nought could heal, the
        wounds
Of mortified presumption, I adhered
More firmly to old tenets, and, to prove
Their temper, strained them more; and thus,
        in heat
Of contest, did opinions every day
Grow into consequence, till round my mind   220
They clung, as if they were its life, nay more,
The very being of the immortal soul.

    This was the time, when, all things tending fast
To depravation, speculative schemes—
That promised to abstract the hopes of Man
Out of his feelings, to be fixed thenceforth
For ever in a purer element—
Found ready welcome. Tempting region *that*
For Zeal to enter and refresh herself,
Where passions had the privilege to work,   230
And never hear the sound of their own names.
But, speaking more in charity, the dream
Flattered the young, pleased with extremes,
        nor least
With that which makes our Reason's naked self
The object of its fervour. What delight!
How glorious! in self-knowledge and self-rule,

223ff.: Wordsworth records the development of rationalistic, materialistic philosophies like that of William
Godwin at this time. Lines 304–305 reveal the climax
of his disillusionment.

To look through all the frailties of the world,
And, with a resolute mastery shaking off
Infirmities of nature, time, and place,
Build social upon personal Liberty,   240
Which, to the blind restraints of general laws,
Superior, magisterially adopts
One guide, the light of circumstances, flashed
Upon an independent intellect.
Thus expectation rose again; thus hope,
From her first ground expelled, grew proud once
        more.
Oft, as my thoughts were turned to human kind,
I scorned indifference; but, inflamed with thirst
Of a secure intelligence, and sick
Of other longing, I pursued what seemed   250
A more exalted nature; wished that Man
Should start out of his earthy, worm-like state,
And spread abroad the wings of Liberty,
Lord of himself, in undisturbed delight—
A noble aspiration! *yet* I feel
(Sustained by worthier as by wiser thoughts)
The aspiration, nor shall ever cease
To feel it;—but return we to our course.

    Enough, 'tis true—could such a plea excuse
Those aberrations—had the clamorous
        friends   260
Of ancient Institutions said and done
To bring disgrace upon their very names;
Disgrace, of which, custom and written law,
And sundry moral sentiments as props
Or emanations of those institutes,
Too justly bore a part. A veil had been
Uplifted; why deceive ourselves? in sooth,
'Twas even so; and sorrow for the man
Who either had not eyes wherewith to see,
Or, seeing, had forgotten! A strong shock   270
Was given to old opinions; all men's minds
Had felt its power, and mine was both let loose,
Let loose and goaded. After what hath been
Already said of patriotic love,
Suffice it here to add, that, somewhat stern
In temperament, withal a happy man,
And therefore bold to look on painful things,
Free likewise of the world, and thence more bold,
I summoned my best skill, and toiled, intent
To anatomise the frame of social life;   280
Yea, the whole body of society
Searched to its heart. Share with me, Friend!
        the wish

That some dramatic tale, endued with shapes
Livelier, and flinging out less guarded words
Than suit the work we fashion, might set forth
What then I learned, or think I learned, of truth,
And the errors into which I fell, betrayed
By present objects, and by reasonings false
From their beginnings, inasmuch as drawn
Out of a heart that had been turned aside   290
From Nature's way by outward accidents,
And which was thus confounded, more and more
Misguided, and misguiding. So I fared,
Dragging all precepts, judgments, maxims, creeds,
Like culprits to the bar; calling the mind,
Suspiciously, to establish in plain day
Her titles and her honours; now believing,
Now disbelieving; endlessly perplexed
With impulse, motive, right and wrong, the
    ground
Of obligation, what the rule and whence   300
The sanction; till, demanding formal *proof*,
And seeking it in every thing, I lost
All feeling of conviction, and, in fine,
Sick, wearied out with contrarieties,
Yielded up moral questions in despair.

    This was the crisis of that strong disease,
This the soul's last and lowest ebb; I drooped,
Deeming our blessèd reason of least use
Where wanted most: "The lordly attributes
Of will and choice," I bitterly exclaimed,   310
"What are they but a mockery of a Being
Who hath in no concerns of his a test
Of good and evil; knows not what to fear
Or hope for, what to covet or to shun;
And who, if those could be discerned, would yet
Be little profited, would see, and ask
Where is the obligation to enforce?
And, to acknowledged law rebellious, still,
As selfish passion urged, would act amiss,
The dupe of folly, or the slave of crime."   320

    Depressed, bewildered thus, I did not walk
With scoffers, seeking light and gay revenge
From indiscriminate laughter, nor sate down
In reconcilement with an utter waste
Of intellect; such sloth I could not brook,
(Too well I loved, in that my spring of life,
Pains-taking thoughts, and truth, their dear
    reward)
But turned to abstract science, and there sought
Work for the reasoning faculty enthroned

Where the disturbances of space and time—   330
Whether in matters various, properties
Inherent, or from human will and power
Derived—find no admission. Then it was—
Thanks to the bounteous Giver of all good!—
That the belovèd Sister in whose sight
Those days were passed, now speaking in a voice
Of sudden admonition—like a brook
That did but *cross* a lonely road, and now
Is seen, heard, felt, and caught at every turn,
Companion never lost through many a
    league—   340
Maintained for me a saving intercourse
With my true self; for, though bedimmed and
    changed
Much, as it seemed, I was no further changed
Than as a clouded and a waning moon:
She whispered still that brightness would return;
She, in the midst of all, preserved me still
A Poet, made me seek beneath that name,
And that alone, my office upon earth;
And, lastly, as hereafter will be shown,
If willing audience fail not, Nature's self,   350
By all varieties of human love
Assisted, led me back through opening day
To those sweet counsels between head and heart
Whence grew that genuine knowledge, fraught
    with peace,
Which, through the later sinkings of this cause,
Hath still upheld me, and upholds me now
In the catastrophe (for so they dream,
And nothing less), when, finally to close
And seal up all the gains of France, a Pope
Is summoned in, to crown an Emperor—   360
This last opprobrium, when we see a people,
That once looked up in faith, as if to Heaven
For manna, take a lesson from the dog
Returning to his vomit; when the sun
That rose in splendour, was alive, and moved
In exultation with a living pomp
Of clouds—his glory's natural retinue—
Hath dropped all functions by the gods bestowed,
And, turned into a gewgaw, a machine,
Sets like an Opera phantom.
                            Thus, O Friend!   370
Through times of honour and through times of
    shame

360. **Emperor:** Napoleon, crowned on December 2,
1804 with Pope Pius VII participating in the ceremony.

Descending, have I faithfully retraced
The perturbations of a youthful mind
Under a long-lived storm of great events—
A story destined for thy ear, who now,
Among the fallen of nations, dost abide
Where Etna, over hill and valley, casts
His shadow stretching towards Syracuse,
The city of Timoleon! Righteous Heaven!
How are the mighty prostrated! They first,　　380
They first of all that breathe should have awaked
When the great voice was heard from out the
　　tombs
Of ancient heroes. If I suffered grief
For ill-requited France, by many deemed
A trifler only in her proudest day;
Have been distressed to think of what she once
Promised, now is; a far more sober cause
Thine eyes must see of sorrow in a land,
To the reanimating influence lost
Of memory, to virtue lost and hope,　　390
Though with the wreck of loftier years bestrewn.

But indignation works where hope is not,
And thou, O Friend! wilt be refreshed. There is
One great society alone on earth:
The noble Living and the noble Dead.

Thine be such converse strong and sanative,
A ladder for thy spirit to reascend
To health and joy and pure contentedness;
To me the grief confined, that thou art gone
From this last spot on earth, where Freedom
　　now　　400
Stands single in her only sanctuary;
A lonely wanderer, art gone, by pain
Compelled and sickness, at this latter day,
This sorrowful reverse for all mankind.
I feel for thee, must utter what I feel:
The sympathies erewhile in part discharged,
Gather afresh, and will have vent again:
My own delights do scarcely seem to me
My own delights; the lordly Alps themselves,
Those rosy peaks, from which the Morning
　　looks　　410
Abroad on many nations, are no more
For me that image of pure gladsomeness
Which they were wont to be. Through kindred
　　scenes,

For purpose, at a time, how different!
Thou tak'st thy way, carrying the heart and soul
That Nature gives to Poets, now by thought
Matured, and in the summer of their strength.
Oh! wrap him in your shades, ye giant woods,
On Etna's side; and thou, O flowery field
Of Enna! is there not some nook of thine,　　420
From the first play-time of the infant world
Kept sacred to restorative delight,
When from afar invoked by anxious love?

Child of the mountains, among shepherds reared,
Ere yet familiar with the classic page,
I learnt to dream of Sicily; and lo,
The gloom, that, but a moment past, was deepened
At thy command, at her command gives way;
A pleasant promise, wafted from her shores,
Comes o'er my heart: in fancy I behold　　430
Her seas yet smiling, her once happy vales;
Nor can my tongue give utterance to a name
Of note belonging to that honoured isle,
Philosopher or Bard, Empedocles,
Or Archimedes, pure abstracted soul!
That doth not yield a solace to my grief:
And, O Theocritus, so far have some
Prevailed among the powers of heaven and earth,
By their endowments, good or great, that they
Have had, as thou reportest, miracles　　440
Wrought for them in old time: yea, not unmoved,
When thinking on my own beloved friend,
I hear thee tell how bees with honey fed
Divine Comates, by his impious lord
Within a chest imprisoned; how they came
Laden from blooming grove or flowery field,
And fed him there, alive, month after month,
Because the goatherd, blessèd man! had lips
Wet with the Muses' nectar.
　　　　　　　　　　Thus I soothe
The pensive moments by this calm fire-side,　　450
And find a thousand bounteous images
To cheer the thoughts of those I love, and mine.
Our prayers have been accepted; thou wilt stand
On Etna's summit, above earth and sea,
Triumphant, winning from the invaded heavens
Thoughts without bound, magnificent designs,
Worthy of poets who attuned their harps
In wood or echoing cave, for discipline
Of heroes; or, in reverence to the gods,

379. Timoleon: the great hero of Syracuse.

420. Enna: In Ovid's *Metamorphoses* Proserpine, gathering flowers in the field of Enna, is carried off by Dis.

'Mid temples, served by sapient priests, and
    choirs   460
Of virgins crowned with roses. Not in vain
Those temples, where they in their ruins yet
Survive for inspiration, shall attract
Thy solitary steps: and on the brink
Thou wilt recline of pastoral Arethuse;
Or, if that fountain be in truth no more,
Then, near some other spring—which, by the name
Thou gratulatest, willingly deceived—
I see thee linger a glad votary,
And not a captive pining for his home.   470

BOOK TWELFTH

IMAGINATION AND TASTE, HOW IMPAIRED
AND RESTORED

Long time have human ignorance and guilt
Detained us, on what spectacles of woe
Compelled to look, and inwardly oppressed
With sorrow, disappointment, vexing thoughts,
Confusion of the judgment, zeal decayed,
And, lastly, utter loss of hope itself
And things to hope for! Not with these began
Our song, and not with these our song must end.
Ye motions of delight, that haunt the sides
Of the green hills; ye breezes and soft airs,   10
Whose subtle intercourse with breathing flowers,
Feelingly watched, might teach Man's haughty race
How without injury to take, to give
Without offence; ye who, as if to show
The wondrous influence of power gently used,
Bend the complying heads of lordly pines,
And, with a touch, shift the stupendous clouds
Through the whole compass of the sky; ye brooks,
Muttering along the stones, a busy noise
By day, a quiet sound in silent night;   20
Ye waves, that out of the great deep steal forth
In a calm hour to kiss the pebbly shore,
Not mute, and then retire, fearing no storm;
And you, ye groves, whose ministry it is
To interpose the covert of your shades,
Even as a sleep, between the heart of man
And outward troubles, between man himself,
Not seldom, and his own uneasy heart:
Oh! that I had a music and a voice
Harmonious as your own, that I might tell   30
What ye have done for me. The morning shines,

Nor heedeth Man's perverseness; Spring returns,—
I saw the Spring return, and could rejoice,
In common with the children of her love,
Piping on boughs, or sporting on fresh fields,
Or boldly seeking pleasure nearer heaven
On wings that navigate cerulean skies.
So neither were complacency, nor peace,
Nor tender yearnings, wanting for my good
Through these distracted times; in Nature still   40
Glorying, I found a counterpoise in her,
Which, when the spirit of evil reached its height,
Maintained for me a secret happiness.

    This narrative, my Friend! hath chiefly told
Of intellectual power, fostering love,
Dispensing truth, and, over men and things,
Where reason yet might hesitate, diffusing
Prophetic sympathies of genial faith:
So was I favoured—such my happy lot—
Until that natural graciousness of mind   50
Gave way to overpressure from the times
And their disastrous issues. What availed,
When spells forbade the voyager to land,
That fragment notice of a pleasant shore
Wafted, at intervals, from many a bower
Of blissful gratitude and fearless love?
Dare I avow that wish was mine to see,
And hope that future times *would* surely see,
The man to come, parted, as by a gulph,
From him who had been; that I could no more   60
Trust the elevation which had made me one
With the great family that still survives
To illuminate the abyss of ages past,
Sage, warrior, patriot, hero; for it seemed
That their best virtues were not free from taint
Of something false and weak, that could not stand
The open eye of Reason. Then I said,
"Go to the Poets, they will speak to thee
More perfectly of purer creatures;   yet
If reason be nobility in man,   70
Can aught be more ignoble than the man
Whom they delight in, blinded as he is
By prejudice, the miserable slave
Of low ambition or distempered love?"

    In such strange passion, if I may once more
Review the past, I warred against myself—
A bigot to a new idolatry—
Like a cowled monk who hath forsworn the world,
Zealously laboured to cut off my heart
From all the sources of her former strength;   80

And as, by simple waving of a wand,
The wizard instantaneously dissolves
Palace or grove, even so could I unsoul
As readily by syllogistic words
Those mysteries of being which have made,
And shall continue evermore to make,
Of the whole human race one brotherhood.

What wonder, then, if, to a mind so far
Perverted, even the visible Universe
Fell under the dominion of a taste   90
Less spiritual, with microscopic view
Was scanned, as I had scanned the moral world?

O Soul of Nature! excellent and fair!
That didst rejoice with me, with whom I, too,
Rejoiced through early youth, before the winds
And roaring waters, and in lights and shades
That marched and countermarched about the hills
In glorious apparition, Powers on whom
I daily waited, now all eye and now
All ear; but never long without the heart   100
Employed, and man's unfolding intellect:
O Soul of Nature! that, by laws divine
Sustained and governed, still dost overflow
With an impassioned life, what feeble ones
Walk on this earth! how feeble have I been
When thou wert in thy strength! Nor this through
        stroke
Of human suffering, such as justifies
Remissness and inaptitude of mind,
But through presumption; even in pleasure pleased
Unworthily, disliking here, and there   110
Liking; by rules of mimic art transferred
To things above all art; but more,—for this,
Although a strong infection of the age,
Was never much my habit—giving way
To a comparison of scene with scene,
Bent overmuch on superficial things,
Pampering myself with meagre novelties
Of colour and proportion; to the moods
Of time and season, to the moral power,
The affections and the spirit of the place,   120
Insensible. Nor only did the love
Of sitting thus in judgment interrupt
My deeper feelings, but another cause,
More subtle and less easily explained,
That almost seems inherent in the creature,
A twofold frame of body and of mind.
I speak in recollection of a time
When the bodily eye, in every stage of life

The most despotic of our senses, gained
Such strength in *me* as often held my mind   130
In absolute dominion. Gladly here,
Entering upon abstruser argument,
Could I endeavour to unfold the means
Which Nature studiously employs to thwart
This tyranny, summons all the senses each
To counteract the other, and themselves,
And make them all, and the objects with which all
Are conversant, subservient in their turn
To the great ends of Liberty and Power.
But leave we this: enough that my delights   140
(Such as they were) were sought insatiably.
Vivid the transport, vivid though not profound;
I roamed from hill to hill, from rock to rock,
Still craving combinations of new forms,
New pleasure, wider empire for the sight,
Proud of her own endowments, and rejoiced
To lay the inner faculties asleep.
Amid the turns and counterturns, the strife
And various trials of our complex being,
As we grow up, such thraldom of that sense   150
Seems hard to shun. And yet I knew a maid,
A young enthusiast, who escaped these bonds;
Her eye was not the mistress of her heart;
Far less did rules prescribed by passive taste,
Or barren intermeddling subtleties,
Perplex her mind; but, wise as women are
When genial circumstance hath favoured them,
She welcomed what was given, and craved no
        more;
Whate'er the scene presented to her view
That was the best, to that she was attuned   160
By her benign simplicity of life,
And through a perfect happiness of soul,
Whose variegated feelings were in this
Sisters, that they were each some new delight.
Birds in the bower, and lambs in the green field,
Could they have known her, would have loved;
        methought
Her very presence such a sweetness breathed,
That flowers, and trees, and even the silent hills,
And everything she looked on, should have had
An intimation how she bore herself   170
Towards them and to all creatures. God delights
In such a being; for, her common thoughts
Are piety, her life is gratitude.

THE PRELUDE. BOOK XII. **151. maid:** probably Mary
Hutchinson.

Even like this maid, before I was called forth
From the retirement of my native hills,
I loved whate'er I saw, nor lightly loved,
But most intensely; never dreamt of aught
More grand, more fair, more exquisitely framed
Than those few nooks to which my happy feet
Were limited. I had not at that time   180
Lived long enough, nor in the least survived
The first diviner influence of this world,
As it appears to unaccustomed eyes.
Worshipping them among the depth of things,
As piety ordained, could I submit
To measured admiration, or to aught
That should preclude humility and love?
I felt, observed, and pondered; did not judge,
Yea, never thought of judging; with the gift
Of all this glory filled and satisfied.   190
And afterwards, when through the gorgeous Alps
Roaming, I carried with me the same heart:
In truth, the degradation—howsoe'er
Induced, effect, in whatsoe'er degree,
Of custom that prepares a partial scale
In which the little oft outweighs the great;
Or any other cause that hath been named;
Or lastly, aggravated by the times
And their impassioned sounds, which well might
     make
The milder minstrelsies of rural scenes   200
Inaudible—was transient; I had known
Too forcibly, too early in my life,
Visitings of imaginative power
For this to last: I shook the habit off
Entirely and for ever, and again
In Nature's presence stood, as now I stand,
A sensitive being, a *creative* soul.

     There are in our existence spots of time,
That with distinct pre-eminence retain
A renovating virtue, whence—depressed   210
By false opinion and contentious thought,
Or aught of heavier or more deadly weight,
In trivial occupations, and the round
Of ordinary intercourse—our minds
Are nourished and invisibly repaired;
A virtue, by which pleasure is enhanced,
That penetrates, enables us to mount,
When high, more high, and lifts us up when fallen.
This efficacious spirit chiefly lurks
Among those passages of life that give   220
Profoundest knowledge to what point, and how,

The mind is lord and master—outward sense
The obedient servant of her will. Such moments
Are scattered everywhere, taking their date
From our first childhood. I remember well,
That once, while yet my inexperienced hand
Could scarcely hold a bridle, with proud hopes
I mounted, and we journeyed towards the hills:
An ancient servant of my father's house
Was with me, my encourager and guide: 230
We had not travelled long, ere some mischance
Disjoined me from my comrade; and, through fear
Dismounting, down the rough and stony moor
I led my horse, and, stumbling on, at length
Came to a bottom, where in former times
A murderer had been hung in iron chains.
The gibbet-mast had mouldered down, the bones
And iron case were gone; but on the turf,
Hard by, soon after that fell deed was wrought,
Some unknown hand had carved the murderer's
     name.   240
The monumental letters were inscribed
In times long past; but still, from year to year
By superstition of the neighbourhood,
The grass is cleared away, and to this hour
The characters are fresh and visible:
A casual glance had shown them, and I fled,
Faltering and faint, and ignorant of the road:
Then, reascending the bare common, saw
A naked pool that lay beneath the hills,
The beacon on the summit, and, more near,   250
A girl, who bore a pitcher on her head,
And seemed with difficult steps to force her way
Against the blowing wind. It was, in truth,
An ordinary sight; but I should need
Colours and words that are unknown to man,
To paint the visionary dreariness
Which, while I looked all around for my lost guide,
Invested moorland waste and naked pool,
The beacon crowning the lone eminence,
The female and her garments vexed and
     tossed   260
By the strong wind. When, in the blessèd hours
Of early love, the loved one at my side,
I roamed, in daily presence of this scene,
Upon the naked pool and dreary crags,
And on the melancholy beacon, fell
A spirit of pleasure and youth's golden gleam;
And think ye not with radiance more sublime
For these remembrances, and for the power
They had left behind? So feeling comes in aid

Of feeling, and diversity of strength   270
Attends us, if but once we have been strong.
Oh! mystery of man, from what a depth
Proceed thy honours. I am lost, but see
In simple childhood something of the base
On which thy greatness stands; but this I feel,
That from thyself it comes, that thou must give,
Else never canst receive. The days gone by
Return upon me almost from the dawn
Of life: the hiding-places of man's power
Open; I would approach them, but they
        close.   280
I see by glimpses now; when age comes on,
May scarcely see at all; and I would give,
While yet we may, as far as words can give,
Substance and life to what I feel, enshrining,
Such is my hope, the spirit of the Past
For future restoration.—Yet another
Of these memorials:—

                        One Christmas-time,
On the glad eve of its dear holidays,
Feverish, and tired, and restless, I went forth
Into the fields, impatient for the sight   290
Of those led palfreys that should bear us home;
My brothers and myself. There rose a crag,
That, from the meeting-point of two highways
Ascending, overlooked them both, far stretched;
Thither, uncertain on which road to fix
My expectation, thither I repaired,
Scout-like, and gained the summit; 'twas a day
Tempestuous, dark, and wild, and on the grass
I sate half-sheltered by a naked wall;
Upon my right hand couched a single sheep,   300
Upon my left a blasted hawthorn stood;
With those companions at my side, I watched,
Straining my eyes intensely, as the mist
Gave intermitting prospect of the copse
And plain beneath. Ere we to school returned,—
That dreary time,—ere we had been ten days
Sojourners in my father's house, he died;
And I and my three brothers, orphans then,
Followed his body to the grave. The event,
With all the sorrow that it brought, appeared   310
A chastisement; and when I called to mind
That day so lately past, when from the crag
I looked in such anxiety of hope;
With trite reflections of morality,
Yet in the deepest passion, I bowed low
To God, Who thus corrected my desires;
And, afterwards, the wind and sleety rain,
And all the business of the elements,

The single sheep, and the one blasted tree,
And the bleak music from that old stone
        wall,   320
The noise of wood and water, and the mist
That on the line of each of those two roads
Advanced in such indisputable shapes;
All these were kindred spectacles and sounds
To which I oft repaired, and thence would drink,
As at a fountain; and on winter nights,
Down to this very time, when storm and rain
Beat on my roof, or, haply, at noon-day,
While in a grove I walk, whose lofty trees,
Laden with summer's thickest foliage, rock   330
In a strong wind, some working of the spirit,
Some inward agitations thence are brought,
Whate'er their office, whether to beguile
Thoughts over busy in the course they took,
Or animate an hour of vacant ease.

from BOOK THIRTEENTH

IMAGINATION AND TASTE, HOW IMPAIRED AND RESTORED (concluded)

From Nature doth emotion come, and moods
Of calmness equally are Nature's gift:
This is her glory; these two attributes
Are sister horns that constitute her strength.
Hence Genius, born to thrive by interchange
Of peace and excitation, finds in her
His best and purest friend; from her receives
That energy by which he seeks the truth,
From her that happy stillness of the mind
Which fits him to receive it when unsought.   10

    Such benefit the humblest intellects
Partake of, each in their degree; 'tis mine
To speak, what I myself have known and felt;
Smooth task! for words find easy way, inspired
By gratitude, and confidence in truth.
Long time in search of knowledge did I range
The field of human life, in heart and mind
Benighted; but, the dawn beginning now
To re-appear, 'twas proved that not in vain
I had been taught to reverence a Power   20
That is the visible quality and shape
And image of right reason; that matures
Her processes by steadfast laws; gives birth
To no impatient or fallacious hopes,
No heat of passion or excessive zeal,
No vain conceits; provokes to no quick turns

Of self-applauding intellect; but trains
To meekness, and exalts by humble faith;
Holds up before the mind intoxicate
With present objects, and the busy dance   30
Of things that pass away, a temperate show
Of objects that endure; and by this course
Disposes her, when over-fondly set
On throwing off incumbrances, to seek
In man, and in the frame of social life,
Whate'er there is desirable and good
Of kindred permanence, unchanged in form
And function, or, through strict vicissitude
Of life and death, revolving. Above all
Were re-established now those watchful
    thoughts   40
Which, seeing little worthy or sublime
In what the Historian's pen so much delights
To blazon—power and energy detached
From moral purpose—early tutored me
To look with feelings of fraternal love
Upon the unassuming things that hold
A silent station in this beauteous world.

Thus moderated, thus composed, I found
Once more in Man an object of delight,
Of pure imagination, and of love;   50
And, as the horizon of my mind enlarged,
Again I took the intellectual eye
For my instructor, studious more to see
Great truths, than touch and handle little ones.
Knowledge was given accordingly; my trust
Became more firm in feelings that had stood
The test of such a trial; clearer far
My sense of excellence—of right and wrong:
The promise of the present time retired
Into its true proportion; sanguine schemes,   60
Ambitious projects, pleased me less; I sought
For present good in life's familiar face,
And built thereon my hopes of good to come.

BOOK FOURTEENTH

CONCLUSION

In one of those excursions (may they ne'er
Fade from remembrance!) through the Northern
    tracts

THE PRELUDE. BOOK XIV. **1. one of those excursions:** the
famous climbing of Mount Snowdon, the highest mountain in England and Wales.

Of Cambria ranging with a youthful friend,
I left Bethgelert's huts at couching-time,
And westward took my way, to see the sun
Rise, from the top of Snowdon. To the door
Of a rude cottage at the mountain's base
We came, and roused the shepherd who attends
The adventurous stranger's steps, a trusty guide;
Then, cheered by short refreshment, sallied
    forth.   10

It was a close, warm, breezeless summer night,
Wan, dull, and glaring, with a dripping fog
Low-hung and thick that covered all the sky;
But, undiscouraged, we began to climb
The mountain-side. The mist soon girt us round,
And, after ordinary travellers' talk
With our conductor, pensively we sank
Each into commerce with his private thoughts:
Thus did we breast the ascent, and by myself
Was nothing either seen or heard that checked   20
Those musings or diverted, save that once
The shepherd's lurcher, who, among the crags,
Had to his joy unearthed a hedgehog, teased
His coiled-up prey with barkings turbulent.
This small adventure, for even such it seemed
In that wild place and at the dead of night,
Being over and forgotten, on we wound
In silence as before. With forehead bent
Earthward, as if in opposition set
Against an enemy, I panted up   30
With eager pace, and no less eager thoughts.
Thus might we wear a midnight hour away,
Ascending at loose distance each from each,
And I, as chanced, the foremost of the band;
When at my feet the ground appeared to brighten,
And with a step or two seemed brighter still;
Nor was time given to ask or learn the cause,
For instantly a light upon the turf
Fell like a flash, and lo! as I looked up
The Moon hung naked in a firmament   40
Of azure without cloud, and at my feet
Rested a silent sea of hoary mist.
A hundred hills their dusky backs upheaved
All over this still ocean; and beyond,
Far, far beyond, the solid vapours stretched,
In headlands, tongues, and promontory shapes,
Into the main Atlantic, that appeared
To dwindle, and give up his majesty,
Usurped upon far as the sight could reach.

4. Bethgelert: a village in Cambria (Wales). **22.
lurcher:** hunting dog.

Not so the ethereal vault; encroachment none   50
Was there, nor loss; only the inferior stars
Had disappeared, or shed a fainter light
In the clear presence of the full-orbed Moon,
Who, from her sovereign elevation, gazed
Upon the billowy ocean, as it lay
All meek and silent, save that through a rift—
Not distant from the shore whereon we stood,
A fixed, abysmal, gloomy, breathing-place—
Mounted the roar of waters, torrents, streams
Innumerable, roaring with one voice!   60
Heard over earth and sea, and, in that hour,
For so it seemed, felt by the starry heavens.

When into air had partially dissolved
That vision, given to spirits of the night
And three chance human wanderers, in calm
     thought
Reflected, it appeared to me the type
Of a majestic intellect, its acts
And its possessions, what it has and craves,
What in itself it is, and would become.
There I beheld the emblem of a mind   70
That feeds upon infinity, that broods
Over the dark abyss, intent to hear
Its voices issuing forth to silent light
In one continuous stream; a mind sustained
By recognitions of transcendent power,
In sense conducting to ideal form,
In soul of more than mortal privilege.
One function, above all, of such a mind
Had Nature shadowed there, by putting forth,
'Mid circumstances awful and sublime,   80
That mutual domination which she loves
To exert upon the face of outward things,
So moulded, joined, abstracted, so endowed
With interchangeable supremacy,
That men, least sensitive, see, hear, perceive,
And cannot choose but feel. The power, which all
Acknowledge when thus moved, which Nature thus
To bodily sense exhibits, is the express
Resemblance of that glorious faculty
That higher minds bear with them as their own.   90
This is the very spirit in which they deal
With the whole compass of the universe:
They from their native selves can send abroad
Kindred mutations; for themselves create
A like existence; and, whene'er it dawns
Created for them, catch it, or are caught
By its inevitable mastery,

Like angels stopped upon the wing by sound
Of harmony from Heaven's remotest spheres.
Them the enduring and the transient both   100
Serve to exalt; they build up greatest things
From least suggestions; ever on the watch,
Willing to work and to be wrought upon,
They need not extraordinary calls
To rouse them; in a world of life they live,
By sensible impressions not enthralled,
But by their quickening impulse made more prompt
To hold fit converse with the spiritual world,
And with the generations of mankind
Spread over time, past, present, and to come,   110
Age after age, till Time shall be no more.
Such minds are truly from the Deity,
For they are Powers; and hence the highest bliss
That flesh can know is theirs—the consciousness
Of Whom they are, habitually infused
Through every image and through every thought,
And all affections by communion raised
From earth to heaven, from human to divine;
Hence endless occupation for the Soul,
Whether discursive or intuitive;   120
Hence cheerfulness for acts of daily life,
Emotions which best foresight need not fear,
Most worthy then of truth when most intense.
Hence, amid ills that vex and wrongs that crush
Our hearts—if here the words of Holy Writ
May with fit reverence be applied—that peace
Which passeth understanding, that repose
In moral judgments which from this pure source
Must come, or will by man be sought in vain.

Oh! who is he that hath his whole life long   130
Preserved, enlarged, this freedom in himself?
For this alone is genuine liberty:
Where is the favoured being who hath held
That course unchecked, unerring, and untired,
In one perpetual progress smooth and bright?—
A humbler destiny have we retraced,
And told of lapse and hesitating choice,
And backward wanderings along thorny ways:
Yet—compassed round by mountain solitudes,
Within whose solemn temple I received   140
My earliest visitations, careless then
Of what was given me; and which now I range,
A meditative, oft a suffering, man—
Do I declare—in accents which, from truth
Deriving cheerful confidence, shall blend
Their modulation with these vocal streams—

That, whatsoever falls my better mind,
Revolving with the accidents of life,
May have sustained, that, howsoe'er misled,
Never did I, in quest of right and wrong,   150
Tamper with conscience from a private aim;
Nor was in any public hope the dupe
Of selfish passions; nor did ever yield
Wilfully to mean cares or low pursuits,
But shrunk with apprehensive jealousy
From every combination which might aid
The tendency, too potent in itself,
Of use and custom to bow down the soul
Under a growing weight of vulgar sense,
And substitute a universe of death   160
For that which moves with light and life informed,
Actual, divine, and true. To fear and love,
To love as prime and chief, for there fear ends,
Be this ascribed; to early intercourse,
In presence of sublime or beautiful forms,
With the adverse principles of pain and joy—
Evil as one is rashly named by men
Who know not what they speak. By love subsists
All lasting grandeur, by pervading love;
That gone, we are as dust.—Behold the fields   170
In balmy spring-time full of rising flowers
And joyous creatures; see that pair, the lamb
And the lamb's mother, and their tender ways
Shall touch thee to the heart; thou callest this love,
And not inaptly so, for love it is,
Far as it carries thee. In some green bower
Rest, and be not alone, but have thou there
The One who is thy choice of all the world:
There linger, listening, gazing, with delight
Impassioned, but delight how pitiable!   180
Unless this love by a still higher love
Be hallowed, love that breathes not without awe;
Love that adores, but on the knees of prayer,
By heaven inspired; that frees from chains the soul,
Lifted, in union with the purest, best,
Of earth-born passions, on the wings of praise
Bearing a tribute to the Almighty's Throne.

This spiritual Love acts not nor can exist
Without Imagination, which, in truth,
Is but another name for absolute power   190
And clearest insight, amplitude of mind,
And Reason in her most exalted mood.
This faculty hath been the feeding source
Of our long labour: we have traced the stream
From the blind cavern whence is faintly heard

Its natal murmur; followed it to light
And open day; accompanied its course
Among the ways of Nature, for a time
Lost sight of it bewildered and engulphed;
Then given it greeting as it rose once more   200
In strength, reflecting from its placid breast
The works of man and face of human life;
And lastly, from its progress have we drawn
Faith in life endless, the sustaining thought
Of human Being, Eternity, and God.

Imagination having been our theme,
So also hath that intellectual Love,
For they are each in each, and cannot stand
Dividually.—Here must thou be, O Man!
Power to thyself; no Helper hast thou here;   210
Here keepest thou in singleness thy state:
No other can divide with thee this work:
No secondary hand can intervene
To fashion this ability; 'tis thine,
The prime and vital principle is thine
In the recesses of thy nature, far
From any reach of outward fellowship,
Else is not thine at all. But joy to him,
Oh, joy to him who here hath sown, hath laid
Here, the foundation of his future years!   220
For all that friendship, all that love can do,
All that a darling countenance can look
Or dear voice utter, to complete the man,
Perfect him, made imperfect in himself,
All shall be his: and he whose soul hath risen
Up to the height of feeling intellect
Shall want no humbler tenderness; his heart
Be tender as a nursing mother's heart;
Of female softness shall his life be full,
Of humble cares and delicate desires,   230
Mild interests and gentlest sympathies.

Child of my parents! Sister of my soul!
Thanks in sincerest verse have been elsewhere
Poured out for all the early tenderness
Which I from thee imbibed: and 'tis most true
That later seasons owed to thee no less;
For, spite of thy sweet influence and the touch
Of kindred hands that opened out the springs
Of genial thought in childhood, and in spite
Of all that unassisted I had marked   240
In life or nature of those charms minute
That win their way into the heart by stealth
(Still to the very going-out of youth)
I too exclusively esteemed *that* love,

And sought *that* beauty, which, as Milton sings,
Hath terror in it. Thou didst soften down
This over-sternness; but for thee, dear Friend!
My soul, too reckless of mild grace, had stood
In her original self too confident,
Retained too long a countenance severe;   250
A rock with torrents roaring, with the clouds
Familiar, and a favourite of the stars:
But thou didst plant its crevices with flowers,
Hang it with shrubs that twinkle in the breeze,
And teach the little birds to build their nests
And warble in its chambers. At a time
When Nature, destined to remain so long
Foremost in my affections, had fallen back
Into a second place, pleased to become
A handmaid to a nobler than herself,   260
When every day brought with it some new sense
Of exquisite regard for common things,
And all the earth was budding with these gifts
Of more refined humanity, thy breath,
Dear Sister! was a kind of gentler spring
That went before my steps. Thereafter came
One whom with thee friendship had early paired;
She came, no more a phantom to adorn
A moment, but an inmate of the heart,
And yet a spirit, there for me enshrined   270
To penetrate the lofty and the low;
Even as one essence of pervading light
Shines, in the brightest of ten thousand stars
And the meek worm that feds her lonely lamp
Couched in the dewy grass.
                                   With such a theme,
Coleridge! with this my argument, of thee
Shall I be silent? O capacious Soul!
Placed on this earth to love and understand,
And from thy presence shed the light of love,
Shall I be mute, ere thou be spoken of?   280
Thy kindred influence to my heart of hearts
Did also find its way. Thus fear relaxed
Her overweening grasp; thus thoughts and things
In the self-haunting spirit learned to take
More rational proportions; mystery,
The incumbent mystery of sense and soul,
Of life and death, time and eternity,
Admitted more habitually a mild
Interposition—a serene delight
In closelier gathering cares, such as become   290
A human creature, howsoe'er endowed,
Poet, or destined for a humbler name;
And so the deep enthusiastic joy,

The rapture of the hallelujah sent
From all that breathes and is, was chastened,
        stemmed
And balanced by pathetic truth, by trust
In hopeful reason, leaning on the stay
Of Providence; and in reverence for duty,
Here, if need be, struggling with storms, and there
Strewing in peace life's humblest ground with
        herbs,   300
At every season green, sweet at all hours.

    And now, O Friend! this history is brought
To its appointed close: the discipline
And consummation of a Poet's mind,
In everything that stood most prominent,
Have faithfully been pictured; we have reached
The time (our guiding object from the first)
When we may, not presumptuously, I hope,
Suppose my powers so far confirmed, and such
My knowledge, as to make me capable   310
Of building up a Work that shall endure.
Yet much hath been omitted, as need was;
Of books how much! and even of the other wealth
That is collected among woods and fields,
Far more: for Nature's secondary grace
Hath hitherto been barely touched upon,
The charm more superficial that attends
Her works, as they present to Fancy's choice
Apt illustrations of the moral world,
Caught at a glance, or traced with curious
        pains.   320

    Finally, and above all, O Friend! (I speak
With due regret) how much is overlooked
In human nature and her subtle ways,
As studied first in our own hearts, and then
In life among the passions of mankind,
Varying their composition and their hue,
Where'er we move, under the diverse shapes
That individual character presents
To an attentive eye. For progress meet,
Along this intricate and difficult path,   330
Whate'er was wanting, something had I gained,
As one of many schoolfellows compelled,
In hardy independence, to stand up
Amid conflicting interests, and the shock
Of various tempers; to endure and note
What was not understood, though known to be;
Among the mysteries of love and hate,
Honour and shame, looking to right and left,
Unchecked by innocence too delicate,

And moral notions too intolerant,   340
Sympathies too contracted. Hence, when called
To take a station among men, the step
Was easier, the transition more secure,
More profitable also; for, the mind
Learns from such timely exercise to keep
In wholesome separation the two natures,
The one that feels, the other that observes.

  Yet one word more of personal concern;—
Since I withdrew unwillingly from France,
I led an undomestic wanderer's life   350
In London chiefly harboured, whence I roamed,
Tarrying at will in many a pleasant spot
Of rural England's cultivated vales
Or Cambrian solitudes. A youth—(he bore
The name of Calvert—it shall live, if words
Of mine can give it life,) in firm belief
That by endowments not from me withheld
Good might be furthered—in his last decay
By a bequest sufficient for my needs
Enabled me to pause for choice, and walk   360
At large and unrestrained; nor damped too soon
By mortal cares. Himself no Poet, yet
Far less a common follower of the world,
He deemed that my pursuits and labours lay
Apart from all that leads to wealth, or even
A necessary maintenance insures,
Without some hazard to the finer sense;
He cleared a passage for me, and the stream
Flowed in the bent of Nature.
                              Having now
Told what best merits mention, further pains   370
Our present purpose seems not to require,
And I have other tasks. Recall to mind
The mood in which this labour was begun,
O Friend! The termination of my course
Is nearer now, much nearer; yet even then,
In that distraction and intense desire,
I said unto the life which I had lived,
Where art thou? Hear I not a voice from thee
Which 'tis reproach to hear? Anon I rose
As if on wings, and saw beneath me stretched   380
Vast prospect of the world which I had been
And was; and hence this Song, which, like a lark,
I have protracted, in the unwearied heavens
Singing, and often with more plaintive voice
To earth attempered and her deep-drawn sighs,
Yet centring all in love, and in the end
All gratulant, if rightly understood.

Whether to me shall be allotted life,
And, with life, power to accomplish aught of worth,
That will be deemed no insufficient plea   390
For having given the story of myself,
Is all uncertain: but, beloved Friend!
When, looking back, thou seest, in clearer view
Than any liveliest sight of yesterday,
That summer, under whose indulgent skies,
Upon smooth Quantock's airy ridge we roved
Unchecked, or loitered 'mid her sylvan combs,
Thou in bewitching words, with happy heart,
Didst chaunt the vision of that Ancient Man,
The bright-eyed Mariner, and rueful woes   400
Didst utter of the Lady Christabel;
And I, associate with such labour, steeped
In soft forgetfulness the livelong hours,
Murmuring of him who, joyous hap, was found,
After the perils of his moonlight ride,
Near the loud waterfall; or her who sate
In misery near the miserable Thorn—
When thou dost to that summer turn thy thoughts,
And hast before thee all which then we were,
To thee, in memory of that happiness,   410
It will be known, by thee at least, my Friend!
Felt, that the history of a Poet's mind
Is labour not unworthy of regard;
To thee the work shall justify itself.

  The last and later portions of this gift
Have been prepared, not with the buoyant spirits
That were our daily portion when we first
Together wantoned in wild Poesy,
But, under pressure of a private grief,
Keen and enduring, which the mind and
                              heart,   420
That in this meditative history
Have been laid open, needs must make me feel
More deeply, yet enable me to bear
More firmly, and a comfort now hath risen
From hope that thou art near, and wilt be soon
Restored to us in renovated health;
When, after the first mingling of our tears,
'Mong other consolations, we may draw
Some pleasure from this offering of my love.

  Oh! yet a few short years of useful life,   430
And all will be complete, thy race be run,
Thy monument of glory will be raised;
Then, though (too weak to tread the ways of truth)
This age fall back to old idolatry,
Though men return to servitude as fast

As the tide ebbs, to ignominy and shame,
By nations, sink together, we shall still
Find solace—knowing what we have learnt to
    know,
Rich in true happiness if allowed to be
Faithful alike in forwarding a day   440
Of firmer trust, joint labourers in the work
(Should Providence such grace to us vouchsafe)
Of their deliverance, surely yet to come.
Prophets of Nature, we to them will speak
A lasting inspiration, sanctified
By reason, blest by faith: what we have loved,
Others will love, and we will teach them how;
Instruct them how the mind of man becomes
A thousand times more beautiful than the earth
On which he dwells, above this frame of
    things   450
(Which, 'mid all revolution in the hopes
And fears of men, doth still remain unchanged)
In beauty exalted, as it is itself
Of quality and fabric more divine.
1798–1805   *1850*

SHE DWELT AMONG THE UNTRODDEN WAYS*

She dwelt among the untrodden ways
    Beside the springs of Dove,
A Maid whom there were none to praise
    And very few to love:

A violet by a mossy stone
    Half hidden from the eye!
—Fair as a star, when only one
    Is shining in the sky.

She lived unknown, and few could know
    When Lucy ceased to be;   10
But she is in her grave, and, oh,
    The difference to me!

1799   *1800*

-----

* This and the following four selections are the so-
called Lucy poems. Although there has been much
speculation on the subject, there is no conclusive evidence as to the identity of Lucy.

STRANGE FITS OF PASSION HAVE I KNOWN

Strange fits of passion have I known:
    And I will dare to tell,
But in the Lover's ear alone,
    What once to me befell.

When she I loved looked every day
    Fresh as a rose in June
I to her cottage bent my way,
    Beneath an evening-moon.

Upon the moon I fixed my eye,
    All over the wide lea;   10
With quickening pace my horse drew nigh
    Those paths so dear to me.

And now we reached the orchard-plot;
    And, as we climbed the hill,
The sinking moon to Lucy's cot
    Came near, and nearer still.

In one of those sweet dreams I slept,
    Kind Nature's gentlest boon!
And all the while my eyes I kept
    On the descending moon.   20

My horse moved on; hoof after hoof
    He raised, and never stopped:
When down behind the cottage roof,
    At once, the bright moon dropped.

What fond and wayward thoughts will slide
    Into a Lover's head!
"O mercy!" to myself I cried,
    "If Lucy should be dead!"

1799   *1800*

THREE YEARS SHE GREW IN SUN AND SHOWER

Three years she grew in sun and shower,
Then Nature said, "A lovelier flower
On earth was never sown;
This Child I to myself will take;
She shall be mine, and I will make
A Lady of my own.

"Myself will to my darling be
Both law and impulse: and with me
The Girl, in rock and plain,
In earth and heaven, in glade and bower,   10
Shall feel an overseeing power
To kindle or restrain.

"She shall be sportive as the fawn
That wild with glee across the lawn,
Or up the mountain springs;
And hers shall be the breathing balm,
And hers the silence and the calm
Of mute insensate things.

"The floating clouds their state shall lend
To her; for her the willow bend;   20
Nor shall she fail to see
Even in the motions of the Storm
Grace that shall mould the Maiden's form
By silent sympathy.

"The stars of midnight shall be dear
To her; and she shall lean her ear
In many a secret place
Where rivulets dance their wayward round,
And beauty born of murmuring sound
Shall pass into her face.   30

"And vital feelings of delight
Shall rear her form to stately height,
Her virgin bosom swell;
Such thoughts to Lucy I will give
While she and I together live
Here in this happy dell."

Thus Nature spake—The work was done—
How soon my Lucy's race was run!
She died, and left to me
This heath, this calm, and quiet scene;   40
The memory of what has been,
And never more will be.

1799   *1800*

A SLUMBER DID MY SPIRIT
SEAL

A slumber did my spirit seal;
    I had no human fears:
She seemed a thing that could not feel
    The touch of earthly years.

No motion has she now, no force;
    She neither hears nor sees;
Rolled round in earth's diurnal course,
    With rocks, and stones, and trees.

1799   *1800*

LUCY GRAY

OR, SOLITUDE

Written at Goslar in Germany. It was founded on
a circumstance told me by my Sister, of a little girl
who, not far from Halifax in Yorkshire, was bewildered in a snow-storm. Her footsteps were traced
by her parents to the middle of the lock of a canal,
and no other vestige of her, backward or forward,
could be traced. The body however was found in
the canal. The way in which the incident was
treated and the spiritualising of the character might
furnish hints for contrasting the imaginative influences which I have endeavoured to throw over
common life with Crabbe's matter of fact style of
treating subjects of the same kind. This is not spoken to his disparagement, far from it, but to direct
the attention of thoughtful readers, into whose
hands these notes may fall, to a comparison that
may both enlarge the circle of their sensibilities,
and tend to produce in them a catholic judgment.
(Wordsworth)

Oft I had heard of Lucy Gray:
And, when I crossed the wild,
I chanced to see at break of day
The solitary child.

No mate, no comrade Lucy knew;
She dwelt on a wide moor,
—The sweetest thing that ever grew
Beside a human door!

You yet may spy the fawn at play,
The hare upon the green;   10
But the sweet face of Lucy Gray
Will never more be seen.

"To-night will be a stormy night—
You to the town must go;
And take a lantern, Child, to light
Your mother through the snow."

"That, Father! will I gladly do:
'Tis scarcely afternoon—

The minster-clock has just struck two,
And yonder is the moon!"   20

And this the Father raised his hook,
And snapped a faggot-band;
He plied his work;—and Lucy took
The lantern in her hand.

Not blither is the mountain roe:
With many a wanton stroke
Her feet disperse the powdery snow,
That rises up like smoke.

The storm came on before its time:
She wandered up and down;   30
And many a hill did Lucy climb:
But never reached the town.

The wretched parents all that night
Went shouting far and wide;
But there was neither sound nor sight
To serve them for a guide.

At day-break on a hill they stood
That overlooked the moor;
And thence they saw the bridge of wood,
A furlong from their door.   40

They wept—and, turning homeward, cried,
"In heaven we all shall meet;"
—When in the snow the mother spied
The print of Lucy's feet.

Then downwards from the steep hill's edge
They tracked the footmarks small;
And through the broken hawthorn hedge,
And by the long stone-wall;

And then an open field they crossed:
The marks were still the same;   50
They tracked them on, nor ever lost;
And to the bridge they came.

They followed from the snowy bank
Those footmarks, one by one,
Into the middle of the plank;
And further there were none!

—Yet some maintain that to this day
She is a living child;
That you may see sweet Lucy Gray
Upon the lonesome wild.   60

O'er rough and smooth she trips along,
And never looks behind;
And sings a solitary song
That whistles in the wind.

1799   *1800*

MICHAEL

A PASTORAL POEM

Written at Town-end, Grasmere, about the same time as "The Brothers." The Sheepfold, on which so much of the poem turns, remains, or rather the ruins of it. The character and circumstances of Luke were taken from a family to whom had belonged, many years before, the house we lived in at Town-end, along with some fields and woodlands on the eastern shore of Grasmere. The name of the Evening Star was not in fact given to this house, but to another on the same side of the valley, more to the north. (Wordsworth)

If from the public way you turn your steps
Up the tumultuous brook of Greenhead Ghyll,
You will suppose that with an upright path
Your feet must struggle; in such bold ascent
The pastoral mountains front you, face to face.
But, courage! for around that boisterous brook
The mountains have all opened out themselves,
And made a hidden valley of their own.
No habitation can be seen; but they
Who journey thither find themselves alone   10
With a few sheep, with rocks and stones, and kites
That overhead are sailing in the sky.
It is in truth an utter solitude;
Nor should I have made mention of this Dell
But for one object which you might pass by,
Might see and notice not. Beside the brook
Appears a straggling heap of unhewn stones!
And to that simple object appertains
A story—unenriched with strange events,
Yet not unfit, I deem, for the fireside,   20
Or for the summer shade. It was the first
Of those domestic tales that spake to me
Of shepherds, dwellers in the valleys, men
Whom I already loved; not verily

MICHAEL. 2. A ghyll is a steep, narrow valley with a stream running through it. (Wordsworth)

For their own sakes, but for the fields and hills
Where was their occupation and abode.
And hence this Tale, while I was yet a Boy
Careless of books, yet having felt the power
Of Nature, by the gentle agency
Of natural objects, led me on to feel   30
For passions that were not my own, and think
(At random and imperfectly indeed)
On man, the heart of man, and human life.
Therefore, although it be a history
Homely and rude, I will relate the same
For the delight of a few natural hearts;
And, with yet fonder feeling, for the sake
Of youthful Poets, who among these hills
Will be my second self when I am gone.

    Upon the forest-side in Grasmere Vale   40
There dwelt a Shepherd, Michael was his name;
An old man, stout of heart, and strong of limb.
His bodily frame had been from youth to age
Of an unusual strength: his mind was keen,
Intense, and frugal, apt for all affairs,
And in his shepherd's calling he was prompt
And watchful more than ordinary men.
Hence had he learned the meaning of all winds,
Of blasts of every tone; and, oftentimes,
When others heeded not, He heard the South   50
Make subterraneous music, like the noise
Of bagpipers on distant Highland hills.
The Shepherd, at such warning, of his flock
Bethought him, and he to himself would say,
"The winds are now devising work for me!"
And, truly, at all times, the storm, that drives
The traveller to a shelter, summoned him
Up to the mountains: he had been alone
Amid the heart of many thousand mists,
That came to him, and left him, on the heights.   60
So lived he till his eightieth year was past.
And grossly that man errs, who should suppose
That the green valleys, and the streams and rocks,
Were things indifferent to the Shepherd's thoughts.
Fields, where with cheerful spirits he had breathed
The common air; hills, which with vigorous step
He had so often climbed; which had impressed
So many incidents upon his mind
Of hardship, skill or courage, joy or fear;
Which, like a book, preserved the memory   70
Of the dumb animals, whom he had saved,
Had fed or sheltered, linking to such acts
That certainty of honourable gain;

Those fields, those hills—what could they less? had
    laid
Strong hold on his affections, were to him
A pleasurable feeling of blind love,
The pleasure which there is in life itself.

    His days had not been passed in singleness.
His Helpmate was a comely matron, old—
Though younger than himself full twenty years.   80
She was a woman of a stirring life,
Whose heart was in her house: two wheels she had
Of antique form; this large, for spinning wool;
That small, for flax; and if one wheel had rest
It was because the other was at work.
The Pair had but one inmate in their house,
An only Child, who had been born to them
When Michael, telling o'er his years, began
To deem that he was old,—in shepherd's phrase,
With one foot in the grave. This only Son,   90
With two brave sheep-dogs tried in many a storm,
The one of an inestimable worth,
Made all their household. I may truly say,
That they were as a proverb in the vale
For endless industry. When day was gone,
And from their occupations out of doors
The Son and Father were come home, even then,
Their labour did not cease; unless when all
Turned to the cleanly supper-board, and there,
Each with a mess of pottage and skimmed
    milk,   100
Sat round the basket piled with oaten cakes,
And their plain home-made cheese. Yet when the
    meal
Was ended, Luke (for so the Son was named)
And his old Father both betook themselves
To such convenient work as might employ
Their hands by the fireside; perhaps to card
Wool for the Housewife's spindle, or repair
Some injury done to sickle, flail, or scythe,
Or other implement of house or field.

    Down from the ceiling, by the chimney's
    edge,   110
That in our ancient uncouth country style
With huge and black projection overbrowed
Large space beneath, as duly as the light
Of day grew dim the Housewife hung a lamp;
An aged utensil, which had performed
Service beyond all others of its kind.
Early at evening did it burn—and late,
Surviving comrade of uncounted hours,

Which, going by from year to year, had found,
And left, the couple neither gay perhaps   120
Nor cheerful, yet with objects and with hopes,
Living a life of eager industry.
And now, when Luke had reached his eighteenth
    year,
There by the light of this old lamp they sate,
Father and Son, while far into the night
The Housewife plied her own peculiar work,
Making the cottage through the silent hours
Murmur as with the sound of summer flies.
This light was famous in its neighbourhood,
And was a public symbol of the life   130
That thrifty Pair had lived. For, as it chanced,
Their cottage on a plot of rising ground
Stood single, with large prospect, north and south,
High into Easedale, up to Dunmail-Raise,
And westward to the village near the lake;
And from this constant light, so regular
And so far seen, the House itself, by all
Who dwelt within the limits of the vale,
Both old and young, was named THE EVENING
    STAR.

    Thus living on through such a length of
    years,   140
The Shepherd, if he loved himself, must needs
Have loved his Helpmate; but to Michael's heart
This son of his old age was yet more dear—
Less from instinctive tenderness, the same
Fond spirit that blindly works in the blood of all—
Than that a child, more than all other gifts
That earth can offer to declining man,
Brings hope with it, and forward-looking thoughts,
And stirrings of inquietude, when they
By tendency of nature needs must fail.   150
Exceeding was the love he bare to him,
His heart and his heart's joy! For often-times
Old Michael, while he was a babe in arms,
Had done him female service, not alone
For pastime and delight, as is the use
Of fathers, but with patient mind enforced
To acts of tenderness; and he had rocked
His cradle, as with a woman's gentle hand.

    And, in a later time, ere yet the Boy
Had put on boy's attire, did Michael love,   160
Albeit of a stern unbending mind,
To have the Young-one in his sight, when he
Wrought in the field, or on his shepherd's stool
Sate with a fettered sheep before him stretched

Under the large old oak, that near his door
Stood single, and, from matchless depth of shade,
Chosen for the Shearer's covert from the sun,
Thence in our rustic dialect was called
The CLIPPING TREE, a name which yet it bears.
There, while they two were sitting in the
    shade,   170
With others round them, earnest all and blithe,
Would Michael exercise his heart with looks
Of fond correction and reproof bestowed
Upon the Child, if he disturbed the sheep
By catching at their legs, or with his shouts
Scared them, while they lay still beneath the shears.

    And when by Heaven's good grace the boy
    grew up
A healthy Lad, and carried in his cheek
Two steady roses that were five years old;
Then Michael from a winter coppice cut   180
With his own hand a sapling, which he hooped
With iron, making it throughout in all
Due requisites a perfect shepherd's staff,
And gave it to the Boy; wherewith equipt
He as a watchman oftentimes was placed
At gate or gap, to stem or turn the flock;
And, to his office prematurely called,
There stood the urchin, as you will divine,
Something between a hindrance and a help;
And for this cause not always, I believe,   190
Receiving from his Father hire of praise;
Though nought was left undone which staff, or
    voice,
Or looks, or threatening gestures, could perform.

    But soon as Luke, full ten years old, could stand
Against the mountain blasts; and to the heights,
Not fearing toil, nor length of weary ways,
He with his Father daily went, and they
Were as companions, why should I relate
That objects which the Shepherd loved before
Were dearer now? that from the Boy there
    came   200
Feelings and emanations—things which were
Light to the sun and music to the wind;
And that the old Man's heart seemed born again?

    Thus in his Father's sight the Boy grew up:
And now, when he had reached his eighteenth year,
He was his comfort and his daily hope.

    While in this sort the simple household lived
From day to day, to Michael's ear there came

Distressful tidings. Long before the time
Of which I speak, the Shepherd had been
     bound   210
In surety for his brother's son, a man
Of an industrious life, and ample means;
But unforeseen misfortunes suddenly
Had prest upon him; and old Michael now
Was summoned to discharge the forfeiture,
A grievous penalty, but little less
Than half his substance. This unlooked-for claim,
At the first hearing, for a moment took
More hope out of his life than he supposed
That any old man ever could have lost.   220
As soon as he had armed himself with strength
To look his trouble in the face, it seemed
The Shepherd's sole resource to sell at once
A portion of his patrimonial fields.
Such was his first resolve; he thought again,
And his heart failed him. "Isabel," said he,
Two evenings after he had heard the news,
"I have been toiling more than seventy years,
And in the open sunshine of God's love
Have we all lived; yet if these fields of ours   230
Should pass into a stranger's hand, I think
That I could not lie quiet in my grave.
Our lot is a hard lot; the sun himself
Has scarcely been more diligent than I;
And I have lived to be a fool at last
To my own family. An evil man
That was, and made an evil choice, if he
Were false to us, and if he were not false,
There are ten thousand to whom loss like this
Had been no sorrow. I forgive him;—but   240
'Twere better to be dumb than to talk thus.

    "When I began, my purpose was to speak
Of remedies and of a cheerful hope.
Our Luke shall leave us, Isabel; the land
Shall not go from us, and it shall be free;
He shall possess it, free as is the wind
That passes over it. We have, thou know'st,
Another kinsman—he will be our friend
In this distress. He is a prosperous man,
Thriving in trade—and Luke to him shall go,   250
And with his kinsman's help and his own thrift
He quickly will repair this loss, and then
He may return to us. If here he stay,
What can be done? Where every one is poor,
What can be gained?"
                At this the old Man paused,

And Isabel sat silent, for her mind
Was busy, looking back into past times.
There's Richard Bateman, thought she to herself,
He was a parish boy   at the church door
They made a gathering for him, shillings,
     pence   260
And halfpennies, wherewith the neighbours bought
A basket, which they filled with pedlar's wares;
And with this basket on his arm, the lad
Went up to London, found a master there,
Who, out of many, chose the trusty boy
To go and overlook his merchandise
Beyond the seas; where he grew wondrous rich,
And left estates and monies to the poor.
And, at his birth-place, built a chapel, floored
With marble which he sent from foreign
     lands.   270
These thoughts, and many others of like sort,
Passed quickly through the mind of Isabel,
And her face brightened. The old Man was glad,
And thus resumed;—"Well, Isabel! this scheme
These two days, has been meat and drink to me.
Far more than we have lost is left us yet.
—We have enough—I wish indeed that I
Were younger;—but this hope is a good hope.
—Make ready Luke's best garments, of the best
Buy for him more, and let us send him forth   280
To-morrow, or the next day, or to-night:
—If he *could* go, the Boy should go tonight."

    Here Michael ceased, and to the fields went forth
With a light heart. The Housewife for five days
Was restless morn and night, and all day long
Wrought on with her best fingers to prepare
Things needful for the journey of her son.
But Isabel was glad when Sunday came
To stop her in her work: for, when she lay
By Michael's side, she through the last two
     nights   290
Heard him, how he was troubled in his sleep:
And when they rose at morning she could see
That all his hopes were gone. That day at noon
She said to Luke, while they two by themselves
Were sitting at the door, "Thou must not go:
We have no other Child but thee to lose—
None to remember—do not go away,
For if thou leave thy Father he will die."
The Youth made answer with a jocund voice;
And Isabel, when she had told her fears,   300
Recovered heart. That evening her best fare

Did she bring forth, and all together sat
Like happy people round a Christmas fire.

With daylight Isabel resumed her work;
And all the ensuing week the house appeared
As cheerful as a grove in Spring: at length
The expected letter from their kinsman came,
With kind assurances that he would do
His utmost for the welfare of the Boy;
To which, requests were added, that forth-
    with
He might be sent to him. Ten times or more   310
The letter was read over; Isabel
Went forth to show it to the neighbours round;
Nor was there at that time on English land
A prouder heart than Luke's. When Isabel
Had to her house returned, the old Man said,
"He shall depart to-morrow." To this word
The Housewife answered, talking much of things
Which, if at such short notice he should go,
Would surely be forgotten. But at length   320
She gave consent, and Michael was at ease.

Near the tumultuous brook of Greenhead Ghyll,
In that deep valley, Michael had designed
To build a Sheepfold; and, before he heard
The tidings of his melancholy loss,
For this same purpose he had gathered up
A heap of stones, which by the streamlet's edge
Lay thrown together, ready for the work.
With Luke that evening thitherward he walked:
And soon as they had reached the place he
    stopped,   330
And thus the old Man spake to him:— "My Son,
To-morrow thou wilt leave me: with full heart
I look upon thee, for thou art the same
That wert a promise to me ere thy birth,
And all thy life has been my daily joy.
I will relate to thee some little part
Of our two histories; 'twill do thee good
When thou art from me, even if I should touch
On things thou canst not know of.—After thou
First cam'st into the world—as oft befalls   340
To new-born infants—thou didst sleep away
Two days, and blessings from thy Father's tongue
Then fell upon thee. Day by day passed on,
And still I loved thee with increasing love.
Never to living ear came sweeter sounds
Than when I heard thee by our own fireside
First uttering, without words, a natural tune;
While thou, a feeding babe, didst in thy joy

Sing at thy Mother's breast. Month followed
    month,
And in the open fields my life was passed   350
And on the mountains; else I think that thou
Hadst been brought up upon thy Father's knees.
But we were playmates, Luke: among these hills,
As well thou knowest, in us the old and young
Have played together, nor with me didst thou
Lack any pleasure which a boy can know."
Luke had a manly heart; but at these words
He sobbed aloud. The old Man grasped his hand,
And said, "Nay, do not take it so—I see
That these are things of which I need not
    speak.   360
—Even to the utmost I have been to thee
A kind and a good Father: and herein
I but repay a gift which I myself
Received at others' hands; for, though now old
Beyond the common life of man, I still
Remember them who loved me in my youth.
Both of them sleep together: here they lived,
As all their Forefathers had done; and when
At length their time was come, they were not loth
To give their bodies to the family mould.   370
I wished that thou should'st live the life they lived:
But, 'tis a long time to look back, my Son,
And see so little gain from threescore years.
These fields were burthened when they came to
    me;
Till I was forty years of age, not more
Than half of my inheritance was mine.
I toiled and toiled; God blessed me in my work,
And till these weeks past the land was free.
—It looks as if it never could endure
Another Master. Heaven forgive me, Luke,   380
If I judge ill for thee, but it seems good
That thou should'st go."

                At this the old Man paused;
Then, pointing to the stones near which they stood,
Thus, after a short silence, he resumed:
"This was a work for us; and now, my Son,
It is a work for me. But, lay one stone—
Here, lay it for me, Luke, with thine own hands.
Nay, Boy, be of good hope;—we both may live
To see a better day. At eighty-four
I still am strong and hale;—do thou thy part;   390
I will do mine.—I will begin again
With many tasks that were resigned to thee:
Up to the heights, and in among the storms,
Will I without thee go again, and do

All works which I was wont to do alone,
Before I knew thy face.—Heaven bless thee, Boy!
Thy heart these two weeks has been beating fast
With many hopes; it should be so—yes—yes—
I knew that thou could'st never have a wish
To leave me, Luke: thou hast been bound to
    me   400
Only by links of love: when thou art gone,
What will be left to us!—But, I forget
My purposes. Lay now the corner-stone,
As I requested; and hereafter, Luke,
When thou art gone away, should evil men
Be thy companions, think of me, my Son,
And of this moment; hither turn thy thoughts,
And God will strengthen thee: amid all fear
And all temptation, Luke, I pray that thou
May'st bear in mind the life thy Fathers
    lived,   410
Who, being innocent, did for that cause
Bestir them in good deeds. Now, fare thee well
When thou return'st, thou in this place wilt see
A work which is not here: a covenant
'Twill be between us; but, whatever fate
Befall thee, I shall love thee to the last,
And bear thy memory with me to the grave."

   The Shepherd ended here; and Luke stooped
    down,
And, as his Father had requested, laid
The first stone of the Sheepfold. At the sight   420
The old Man's grief broke from him; to his heart
He pressed his Son, he kissèd him and wept;
And to the house together they returned.
—Hushed was that House in peace, or seeming
    peace,
Ere the night fell:—with morrow's dawn the Boy
Began his journey, and when he had reached
The public way, he put on a bold face;
And all the neighbours, as he passed their doors,
Came forth with wishes and with farewell prayers,
That followed him till he was out of sight.   430

   A good report did from their Kinsman come,
Of Luke and his well-doing: and the Boy
Wrote loving letters, full of wondrous news,
Which, as the Housewife phrased it, were
    throughout
"The prettiest letters that were ever seen."
Both parents read them with rejoicing hearts.
So, many months passed on: and once again
The Shepherd went about his daily work

With confident and cheerful thoughts; and now
Sometimes when he could find a leisure hour   440
He to that valley took his way, and there
Wrought at the Sheepfold. Meantime Luke began
To slacken in his duty; and, at length,
He in the dissolute city gave himself
To evil courses: ignominy and shame
Fell on him, so that he was driven at last
To seek a hiding-place beyond the seas.

   There is a comfort in the strength of love;
'Twill make a thing endurable, which else
Would overset the brain, or break the heart: 450
I have conversed with more than one who well
Remember the old Man, and what he was
Years after he had heard this heavy news.
His bodily frame had been from youth to age
Of an unusual strength. Among the rocks
He went, and still looked up to sun and cloud,
And listened to the wind; and, as before,
Performed all kinds of labour for his sheep,
And for the land, his small inheritance.
And to that hollow dell from time to time   460
Did he repair, to build the Fold of which
His flock had need. 'Tis not forgotten yet
The pity which was then in every heart
For the old Man—and 'tis believed by all
That many and many a day he thither went,
And never lifted up a single stone.

   There, by the Sheepfold, sometimes was he seen
Sitting alone, or with his faithful Dog,
Then old, beside him, lying at his feet.
The length of full seven years, from time to
    time,   470
He at the building of this Sheepfold wrought,
And left the work unfinished when he died.
Three years, or little more, did Isabel
Survive her Husband: at her death the estate
Was sold, and went into a stranger's hand.
The Cottage which was named the EVENING STAR
Is gone—the ploughshare has been through the
    ground
On which it stood; great changes have been
    wrought
In all the neighbourhood:—yet the oak is left
That grew beside their door; and the remains   480
Of the unfinished Sheepfold may be seen
Beside the boisterous brook of Greenhead Ghyll.

1800   *1800*

TO THE CUCKOO

Composed in the orchard, Town-end, Grasmere.
(Wordsworth)

O blithe New-comer! I have heard,
I hear thee and rejoice.
O Cuckoo! shall I call thee Bird,
Or but a wandering Voice?

While I am lying on the grass
Thy twofold shout I hear;
From hill to hill it seems to pass
At once far off, and near.

Though babbling only to the Vale,
Of sunshine and of flowers,   10
Thou bringest unto me a tale
Of visionary hours.

Thrice welcome, darling of the Spring!
Even yet thou art to me
No bird, but an invisible thing,
A voice, a mystery;

The same whom in my schoolboy days
I listened to; that Cry
Which made me look a thousand ways
In bush, and tree, and sky.   20

To seek thee did I often rove
Through woods and on the green;
And thou wert still a hope, a love;
Still longed for, never seen.

And I can listen to thee yet;
Can lie upon the plain
And listen, till I do beget
That golden time again.

O blessèd Bird! the earth we pace
Again appears to be   30
An unsubstantial, faery place;
That is fit home for Thee!

1802   *1807*

MY HEART LEAPS UP WHEN I BEHOLD

My heart leaps up when I behold
    A rainbow in the sky:
So was it when my life began;
So is it now I am a man;
So be it when I shall grow old,
    Or let me die!
The Child is father of the Man;
And I could wish my days to be
Bound each to each by natural piety.

1802   *1807*

ODE

INTIMATIONS OF IMMORTALITY
FROM RECOLLECTIONS OF
EARLY CHILDHOOD

This was composed during my residence at Town-end, Grasmere. Two years at least passed between the writing of the four first stanzas and the remaining part. To the attentive and competent reader the whole sufficiently explains itself; but there may be no harm in adverting here to particular feelings or *experiences* of my own mind on which the structure of the poem partly rests. Nothing was more difficult for me in childhood than to admit the notion of death as a state applicable to my own being. I have said elsewhere—

A simple child,
That lightly draws its breath,
And feels its life in every limb,
What should it know of death?

But it was not so much from feelings of animal vivacity that *my* difficulty came as from a sense of the indomitableness of the Spirit within me. I used to brood over the stories of Enoch and Elijah, and almost to persuade myself that, whatever might become of others, I should be translated, in something of the same way, to heaven. With a feeling congenial to this, I was often unable to think of external things as having external existence, and I communed with all that I saw as something not apart from, but inherent in, my own immaterial nature. Many times while going to school have I grasped at a wall or tree to recall myself from this abyss of idealism to the reality. At that time I was afraid of such processes. In later periods of life I have deplored, as we have all reason to do, a subjugation of an opposite character, and have rejoiced over the remembrances, as is expressed in the lines—

> Obstinate questionings
> Of sense and outward things,
> Fallings from us, vanishings; etc.

To that dream-like vividness and splendour which invest objects of sight in childhood, every one, I believe, if he would look back, could bear testimony, and I need not dwell upon it here: but having in the poem regarded it as presumptive evidence of a prior state of existence, I think it right to protest against a conclusion, which has given pain to some good and pious persons, that I meant to inculcate such a belief. It is far too shadowy a notion to be recommended to faith, as more than an element in our instincts of immortality. But let us bear in mind that, though the idea is not advanced in revelation, there is nothing there to contradict it, and the fall of Man presents an analogy in its favour. Accordingly, a pre-existent state has entered into the popular creeds of many nations; and, among all persons acquainted with classic literature, is known as an ingredient in Platonic philosophy. Archimedes said that he could move the world if he had a point whereon to rest his machine. Who has not felt the same aspirations as regards the world of his own mind? Having to wield some of its elements when I was impelled to write this poem on the "Immortality of the Soul," I took hold of the notion of pre-existence as having sufficient foundation in humanity for authorising me to make for my purpose the best use of it I could as a poet. (Wordsworth)

> *The Child is Father of the Man;*
> *And I could wish my days to be*
> *Bound each to each by natural piety.*

I

There was a time when meadow, grove, and stream,
The earth, and every common sight,
　　To me did seem
　　Apparelled in celestial light,
The glory and the freshness of a dream.
It is not now as it hath been of yore;—
　　Turn wheresoe'er I may,
　　By night or day,
The things which I have seen I now can see no
　　more.

II

The Rainbow comes and goes,　　　　10
　　And lovely is the Rose,
　　The Moon doth with delight
Look round her when the heavens are bare,
　　Waters on a starry night
　　Are beautiful and fair;
　　The sunshine is a glorious birth;
　　But yet I know, where'er I go,
That there hath past away a glory from the earth.

III

Now, while the birds thus sing a joyous song,
　　And while the young lambs bound　　20
　　As to the tabor's sound,
To me alone there came a thought of grief:
A timely utterance gave that thought relief,
　　And I again am strong:
The cataracts blow their trumpets from the steep;
No more shall grief of mine the season wrong;
I hear the Echoes through the mountains throng,
The Winds come to me from the fields of sleep,
　　And all the earth is gay;
　　　Land and sea　　　　30
　　Give themselves up to jollity,
　　　And with the heart of May
　　Doth every Beast keep holiday;—
　　　Thou Child of Joy,
Shout round me, let me hear thy shouts, thou happy
　　　Shepherd-boy!

IV

Ye blessèd Creatures, I have heard the call
　　Ye to each other make; I see
The heavens laugh with you in your jubilee;
　　My heart is at your festival,　　　40
　　My head hath its coronal,
The fulness of your bliss, I feel—I feel it all.
　　Oh evil day! if I were sullen
　　While Earth herself is adorning,
　　　This sweet May-morning,
　　And the Children are culling
　　　On every side,
　　In a thousand valleys far and wide,
　　Fresh flowers; while the sun shines warm,
And the Babe leaps up on his Mother's arm:—

I hear, I hear, with joy I hear!   50
—But there's a Tree, of many, one,
A single Field which I have looked upon,
Both of them speak of something that is gone:
　　The Pansy at my feet
　　Doth the same tale repeat:
Whither is fled the visionary gleam?
Where is it now, the glory and the dream?

V

Our birth is but a sleep and a forgetting;
The Soul that rises with us, our life's Star,
　　Hath had elsewhere its setting,   60
　　　　And cometh from afar:
　　Not in entire forgetfulness,
　　And not in utter nakedness,
But trailing clouds of glory do we come
　　From God, who is our home:
Heaven lies about us in our infancy!
Shades of the prison-house begin to close
　　Upon the growing Boy,
But He beholds the light, and whence it flows,
　　He sees it in his joy;   70
The Youth, who daily farther from the east
　　Must travel, still is Nature's Priest,
　　And by the vision splendid
　　Is on his way attended;
At length the Man perceives it die away,
And fade into the light of common day.

VI

Earth fills her lap with pleasures of her own
Yearnings she hath in her own natural kind,
And, even with something of a Mother's mind,
　　And no unworthy aim,   80
　　The homely Nurse doth all she can
To make her Foster-child, her Inmate Man,
　　Forget the glories he hath known,
And that imperial palace whence he came.

VII

Behold the Child among his new-born blisses,
A six years' Darling of a pigmy size!
See, where 'mid work of his own hand he lies,
Fretted by sallies of his mother's kisses,

With light upon him from his father's eyes!
See, at his feet, some little plan or chart,   90
Some fragment from his dream of human life,
Shaped by himself with newly-learnèd art;
　　A wedding or a festival,
　　A mourning or a funeral;
　　　　And this hath now his heart,
　　And unto this he frames his song:
　　　　Then will he fit his tongue
To dialogues of business, love, or strife;
　　But it will not be long
　　Ere this be thrown aside,   100
　　And with new joy and pride
The little Actor cons another part;
Filling from time to time his "humorous stage"
With all the Persons, down to palsied Age,
That Life brings with her in her equipage;
　　As if his whole vocation
　　Were endless imitation.

VIII

Thou, whose exterior semblance doth belie
　　Thy Soul's immensity;
Thou best Philosopher, who yet dost keep   110
Thy heritage, thou Eye among the blind,
That, deaf and silent, read'st the eternal deep,
Haunted for ever by the eternal mind,—
　　Mighty Prophet! Seer blest!
　　On whom those truths do rest,
Which we are toiling all our lives to find,
In darkness lost, the darkness of the grave;
Thou, over whom thy Immortality
Broods like the Day, a Master o'er a Slave,
A Presence which is not to be put by;   120
Thou little Child, yet glorious in the might
Of heaven-born freedom on thy being's height,
Why with such earnest pains dost thou provoke
The years to bring the inevitable yoke,
Thus blindly with thy blessedness at strife?
Full soon thy Soul shall have her earthly freight,
And custom lie upon thee with a weight,
Heavy as frost, and deep almost as life!

IX

　　O joy! that in our embers
　　Is something that doth live,   130
　　That nature yet remembers
　　What was so fugitive!

The thought of our past years in me doth breed
Perpetual benediction: not indeed
For that which is most worthy to be blest—
Delight and liberty, the simple creed
Of Childhood, whether busy or at rest,
With new-fledged hope still fluttering in his
      breast:—
    Not for these I raise
    The song of thanks and praise;   140
  But for those obstinate questionings
  Of sense and outward things,
  Fallings from us, vanishings;
  Blank misgivings of a Creature
Moving about in worlds not realised,
High instincts before which our mortal Nature
Did tremble like a guilty Thing surprised:
    But for those first affections,
    Those shadowy recollections,
  Which, be they what they may,   150
Are yet the fountain light of all our day,
Are yet a master light of all our seeing;
  Uphold us, cherish, and have power to make
Our noisy years seem moments in the being
Of the eternal Silence: truths that wake,
    To perish never;
Which neither listlessness, nor mad endeavour,
    Nor Man nor Boy,
Nor all that is at enmity with joy,
Can utterly abolish or destroy!   160
    Hence in a season of calm weather
    Though inland far we be,
Our Souls have sight of that immortal sea
    Which brought us hither,
    Can in a moment travel thither,
And see the Children sport upon the shore,
And hear the mighty waters rolling evermore.

X

Then sing, ye Birds, sing, sing a joyous song!
    And let the young Lambs bound
    As to the tabor's sound!   170
We in thought will join your throng,
    Ye that pipe and ye that play,
    Ye that through your hearts to-day
    Feel the gladness of the May!
What though the radiance which was once so bright
Be now for ever taken from my sight,

Though nothing can bring back the hour
Of splendour in the grass, of glory in the flower;
    We will grieve not, rather find
    Strength in what remains behind;   180
    In the primal sympathy
    Which having been must ever be;
    In the soothing thoughts that spring
    Out of human suffering;
    In the faith that looks through death,
In years that bring the philosophic mind.

XI

And O, ye Fountains, Meadows, Hills, and Groves,
Forebode not any severing of our loves!
Yet in my heart of hearts I feel your might;
I only have relinquished one delight   190
To live beneath your more habitual sway.
I love the Brooks which down their channels fret,
Even more than when I tripped lightly as they;
The innocent brightness of a new-born Day
    Is lovely yet;
The Clouds that gather round the setting sun
Do take a sober colouring from an eye
That hath kept watch o'er man's mortality;
Another race hath been, and other palms are won.
Thanks to the human heart by which we live,   200
Thanks to its tenderness, its joys, and fears,
To me the meanest flower that blows can give
Thoughts that do often lie too deep for tears.
1802–04   1807

TO A BUTTERFLY

I've watched you now a full half-hour,
Self-poised upon that yellow flower,
And, little Butterfly! indeed
I know not if you sleep or feed.
How motionless!—not frozen seas
More motionless! and then
What joy awaits you, when the breeze
Hath found you out among the trees,
And calls you forth again!

This plot of orchard-ground is ours;   10
My trees they are, my sister's flowers;
Here rest your wings when they are weary;

Here lodge as in a sanctuary!
Come often to us, fear no wrong;
Sit near us on the bough!
We'll talk of sunshine and of song,
And summer days, when we were young;
Sweet childish days, that were as long
As twenty days are now.

1802   1807

TO A SKY-LARK

Up with me! up with me into the clouds!
    For thy song, Lark, is strong;
Up with me, up with me into the clouds!
    Singing, singing,
With clouds and sky about thee ringing,
    Lift me, guide me till I find
That spot which seems so to thy mind!

I have walked through wildernesses dreary
And to-day my heart is weary;
Had I now the wings of a Faery,   10
Up to thee would I fly.
There is madness about thee, and joy divine
In that song of thine;
Lift me, guide me high and high
To thy banqueting-place in the sky.

        Joyous as morning
Thou art laughing and scorning;
Thou hast a nest for thy love and thy rest,
And, though little troubled with sloth,
Drunken Lark! thou would'st be loth   20
To be such a traveller as I.
Happy, happy Liver,
With a soul as strong as a mountain river
Pouring out praise to the Almighty Giver,
    Joy and jollity be with us both!

Alas! my journey, rugged and uneven,
Through prickly moors or dusty ways must wind;
But hearing thee, or others of thy kind,
As full of gladness and as free of heaven,
I, with my fate contented, will plod on,   30
And hope for higher raptures, when life's day
    is done.

1802   1807

RESOLUTION AND INDEPENDENCE

Written at Town-end, Grasmere. This old Man I met a few hundred yards from my cottage; and the account of him is taken from his own mouth. I was in the state of feeling described in the beginning of the poem, while crossing over Barton Fell from Mr. Clarkson's, at the foot of Ullswater, towards Askham. The image of the hare I then observed on the ridge of the Fell. (Wordsworth)

There was a roaring in the wind all night;
The rain came heavily and fell in floods;
But now the sun is rising calm and bright;
The birds are singing in the distant woods;
Over his own sweet voice the Stock-dove broods;
The Jay makes answer as the Magpie chatters;
And all the air is filled with pleasant noise of
    waters.

All things that love the sun are out of doors;
The sky rejoices in the morning's birth;
The grass is bright with rain-drops;—on the
    moors   10
The hare is running races in her mirth;
And with her feet she from the plashy earth
Raises a mist, that, glittering in the sun,
Runs with her all the way, wherever she doth run.

I was a Traveller then upon the moor,
I saw the hare that raced about with joy;
I heard the woods and distant waters roar;
Or heard them not, as happy as a boy:
The pleasant season did my heart employ:
My old remembrances went from me wholly;   20
And all the ways of men, so vain and melancholy.

But, as it sometimes chanceth, from the might
Of joy in minds that can no further go,
As high as we have mounted in delight
In our dejection do we sink as low;
To me that morning did it happen so;
And fears and fancies thick upon me came;
Dim sadness—and blind thoughts, I knew not, nor
    could name.

I heard the sky-lark warbling in the sky;
And I bethought me of the playful hare: 30

Even such a happy Child of earth am I;
Even as these blissful creatures do I fare;
Far from the world I walk, and from all care;
But there may come another day to me—
Solitude, pain of heart, distress, and poverty.

My whole life I have lived in pleasant thought,
As if life's business were a summer mood;
As if all needful things would come unsought
To genial faith, still rich in genial good;
But how can He expect that others should   40
Build for him, sow for him, and at his call
Love him, who for himself will take no heed at all?

I thought of Chatterton, the marvellous Boy,
The sleepless Soul that perished in his pride;
Of Him who walked in glory and in joy
Following his plough, along the mountain-side:
By our own spirits are we deified:
We Poets in our youth begin in gladness;
But thereof come in the end despondency and
    madness.

Now, whether it were by peculiar grace,   50
A leading from above, a something given,
Yet it befell, that, in this lonely place,
When I with these untoward thoughts had striven,
Beside a pool bare to the eye of heaven
I saw a Man before me unawares:
The oldest man he seemed that ever wore grey
    hairs.

As a huge stone is sometimes seen to lie
Couched on the bald top of an eminence;
Wonder to all who do the same espy,
By what means it could thither come, and
    whence;   60
So that it seems a thing endued with sense:
Like a sea-beast crawled forth, that on a shelf
Of rock or sand reposeth, there to sun itself;

Such seemed this Man, not all alive nor dead,
Nor all asleep—in his extreme old age:
His body was bent double, feet and head
Coming together in life's pilgrimage;
As if some dire constraint of pain, or rage

RESOLUTION AND INDEPENDENCE. **43. Chatterton:** the
gifted lyric poet Thomas Chatterton (1752–1770).
Charged with forging many of his medieval poems, he
committed suicide at the age of seventeen. **45. Him
who walked:** the great poet of humble and rustic life,
Robert Burns (1759–1796).

Of sickness felt by him in times long past,
A more than human weight upon his frame had
    cast.   70

Himself he propped, limbs, body, and pale face,
Upon a long grey staff of shaven wood:
And, still as I drew near with gentle pace,
Upon the margin of that moorish flood
Motionless as a cloud the old Man stood,
That heareth not the loud winds when they call
And moveth all together, if it move at all.

At length, himself unsettling, he the pond
Stirred with his staff, and fixedly did look
Upon the muddy water, which he conned,   80
As if he had been reading in a book:
And now a stranger's privilege I took;
And, drawing to his side, to him did say,
"This morning gives us promise of a glorious day."

A gentle answer did the old Man make,
In courteous speech which forth he slowly drew:
And him with further words I thus bespake,
"What occupation do you there pursue?
This is a lonesome place for one like you."
Ere he replied, a flash of mild surprise   90
Broke from the sable orbs of his yet-vivid eyes.

His words came feebly, from a feeble chest,
But each in solemn order followed each,
With something of a lofty utterance drest—
Choice word and measured phrase, above the reach
Of ordinary men; a stately speech;
Such as grave Livers do in Scotland use,
Religious men, who give to God and man their
    dues.

He told, that to these waters he had come
To gather leeches, being old and poor: 100
Employment hazardous and wearisome!
And he had many hardships to endure:
From pond to pond he roamed, from moor to moor;
Housing, with God's good help, by choice or
    chance,
And in this way he gained an honest maintenance.

The old Man still stood talking by my side;
But now his voice to me was like a stream
Scarce heard; nor word from word could I divide;
And the whole body of the Man did seem
Like one whom I had met with in a dream;   110
Or like a man from some far region sent,
To give me human strength, by apt admonishment.

My former thoughts returned: the fear that kills;
And hope that is unwilling to be fed;
Cold, pain, and labour, and all fleshly ills;
And mighty Poets in their misery dead.
—Perplexed, and longing to be comforted,
My question eagerly did I renew,
"How is it that you live, and what is it you do?"

He with a smile did then his words repeat;   120
And said, that, gathering leeches, far and wide
He travelled; stirring thus above his feet
The waters of the pools where they abide.
"Once I could meet them on every side;
But they have dwindled long by slow decay;
Yet still I persevere, and find them where I may."

While he was talking thus, the lonely place,
The old Man's shape, and speech—all troubled me:
In my mind's eye I seemed to see him pace
About the weary moors continually,   130
Wandering about alone and silently.
While I these thoughts within myself pursued,
He, having made a pause, the same discourse
    renewed.

And soon with this he other matter blended,
Cheerfully uttered, with demeanour kind,
But stately in the main; and when he ended,
I could have laughed myself to scorn to find
In that decrepit Man so firm a mind.
"God," said I, "be my help and stay secure;
I'll think of the Leech-gatherer on the lonely
    moor!"   140
1802   *1807*

IT IS A BEAUTEOUS EVENING, CALM AND FREE

It is a beauteous evening, calm and free,
The holy time is quiet as a Nun
Breathless with adoration; the broad sun
Is sinking down in its tranquillity;
The gentleness of heaven broods o'er the Sea:
Listen! the mighty Being is awake,
And doth with his eternal motion make
A sound like thunder—everlastingly.

Dear Child! dear Girl! that walkest with me here,
If thou appear untouched by solemn thought,   10
Thy nature is not therefore less divine:
Thou liest in Abraham's bosom all the year;
And worship'st at the Temple's inner shrine,
God being with thee when we know it not.
1802   *1807*

TO TOUSSAINT L'OUVERTURE *

Toussaint, the most unhappy man of men!
Whether the whistling Rustic tend his plough
Within thy hearing, or thy head be now
Pillowed in some deep dungeon's earless den:—
O miserable Chieftain! where and when
Wilt thou find patience? Yet die not; do thou
Wear rather in thy bonds a cheerful brow:
Though fallen thyself, never to rise again,
Live, and take comfort. Thou hast left behind
Powers that will work for thee; air, earth, and
    skies;   10
There's not a breathing of the common wind
That will forget thee; thou has great allies;
Thy friends are exultations, agonies,
And love, and man's unconquerable mind.
1802   *1803*

NEAR DOVER, SEPTEMBER 1802

Inland, within a hollow vale, I stood;
And saw, while sea was calm and air was clear,
The coast of France—the coast of France how near!
Drawn almost into frightful neighbourhood.
I shrunk; for verily the barrier flood
Was like a lake, or river bright and fair,
A span of waters; yet what power is there!
What mightiness for evil and for good!

IT IS A BEAUTIFUL EVENING, CALM AND FREE. **9. Dear Child:** probably Caroline, the daughter of Wordsworth and Annette Vallon. **12. Abraham's bosom:** close to Heaven.

---

* The great Haitian leader in the struggle for freedom from France in the early nineteenth century. He was captured and died in prison.

Even so doth God protect us if we be
Virtuous and wise. Winds blow, and waters
    roll,   10
Strength to the brave, and Power, and Deity;
Yet in themselves are nothing! One decree
Spake laws to *them*, and said that by the soul
Only, the Nations shall be great and free.

1802   *1807*

COMPOSED UPON WESTMINSTER BRIDGE SEPT. 3, 1802

———

Written on the roof of a coach, on my way to
France. (Wordsworth)

———

Earth has not anything to show more fair:
Dull would he be of soul who could pass by
A sight so touching in its majesty:
This City now doth, like a garment, wear
The beauty of the morning; silent, bare,
Ships, towers, domes, theatres, and temples lie
Open unto the fields, and to the sky;
All bright and glittering in the smokeless air.
Never did sun more beautifully steep
In his first splendour, valley, rock, or hill;   10
Ne'er saw I, never felt, a calm so deep!
The river glideth at his own sweet will:
Dear God! the very houses seem asleep;
And all that mighty heart is lying still!

1802   *1807*

LONDON, 1802

Milton! thou should'st be living at this hour:
England hath need of thee: she is a fen
Of stagnant waters: altar, sword, and pen,
Fireside, the heroic wealth of hall and bower,
Have forefeited their ancient English dower
Of inward happiness. We are selfish men;
Oh! raise us up, return to us again;
And give us manners, virtue, freedom, power.
Thy soul was like a Star, and dwelt apart:
Thou hadst a voice whose sound was like the
    sea: 10

Pure as the naked heavens, majestic, free,
So didst thou travel on life's common way,
In cheerful godliness; and yet thy heart
The lowliest duties on herself did lay.

1802   *1807*

GREAT MEN HAVE BEEN AMONG US; HANDS THAT PENNED

Great men have been among us; hands that penned
And tongues that uttered wisdom—better none:
The later Sidney, Marvel, Harrington,
Young Vane, and others who called Milton friend.
These moralists could act and comprehend:
They knew how genuine glory was put on;
Taught us how rightfully a nation shone
In splendour: what strength was, that would not
    bend
But in magnanimous meekness. France, 'tis strange,
Hath brought forth no such souls as we had
    then.   10
Perpetual emptiness! unceasing change!
No single volume paramount, no code,
No master spirit, no determined road;
But equally a want of books and men!

1802   *1807*

THE WORLD IS TOO MUCH WITH US; LATE AND SOON

The world is too much with us; late and soon,
Getting and spending, we lay waste our powers:
Little we see in Nature that is ours;
We have given our hearts away, a sordid boon!
This Sea that bares her bosom to the moon;
The winds that will be howling at all hours,
And are up-gathered now like sleeping flowers;
For this, for everything, we are out of tune;
It moves us not.—Great God! I'd rather be
A Pagan suckled in a creed outworn;   10
So might I, standing on this pleasant lea,

GREAT MEN HAVE BEEN AMONG US. 3–4. Sidney...
Vane: Freedom fighters in the Puritan struggle of the
seventeenth century.

Have glimpses that would make me less forlorn;
Have sight of Proteus rising from the sea;
Or hear old Triton blow his wreathèd horn.

1802–1804   *1807*

SCORN NOT THE SONNET

Scorn not the sonnet; critic, you have frowned,
Mindless of its just honors; with this key
Shakespeare unlocked his heart; the melody
Of this small lute gave ease to Petrarch's wound;
A thousand times this pipe did Tasso sound;
With it Camöens soothed an exile's grief;
The sonnet glittered a gay myrtle leaf
Amid the cypress with which Dante crowned
His visionary brow; a glow-worm lamp,
It cheered mild Spenser, called from Faeryland   10
To struggle through dark ways; and, when a damp
Fell round the path of Milton, in his hand
The thing became a trumpet; whence he blew
Soul-animating strains—alas, too few!

1820–27   *1827*

ODE TO DUTY

———

This ode is on the model of Gray's Ode to Adversity, which is copied from Horace's Ode to Fortune. Many and many a time have I been twitted by my wife and sister for having forgotten this dedication of myself to the stern lawgiver. Transgressor indeed I have been, from hour to hour, from day to day: I would fain hope, however, not more flagrantly or in a worse way than most of my tuneful brethren. But these last words are in a wrong strain. We should be rigorous to ourselves and forbearing, if not indulgent, to others, and, if we make comparisons at all, it ought to be with those who have morally excelled us. (Wordsworth)

———

"Jam non consilio bonus, sed more eò perductus, ut non tantum rectè facere possim, sed nisi rectè facere non possim." °

THE WORLD IS TOO MUCH WITH US; LATE AND SOON. 13–14. Proteus . . . Triton: sea-gods in the mythology of Homer's *Odyssey*.

° See Seneca, *Moral Epistles*, CXX, 10. "Now I am guided not by good counsel, but by habit, so that I am not so much able to act rightly, but cannot act except rightly."

Stern Daughter of the Voice of God!
O Duty! if that name thou love
Who art a light to guide, a rod
To check the erring, and reprove;
Thou, who art victory and law
When empty terrors overawe;
From vain temptations dost set free;
And calm'st the weary strife of frail humanity!

There are who ask not if thine eye
Be on them; who, in love and truth,   10
Where no misgiving is, rely
Upon the genial sense of youth:
Glad Hearts! without reproach or blot
Who do thy work, and know it not:
Oh! if through confidence misplaced
They fail, thy saving arms, dread Power! around
     them cast.

Serene will be our days and bright,
And happy will our nature be,
When love is an unerring light,
And joy its own security.   20
And they a blissful course may hold
Even now, who, not unwisely bold,
Live in the spirit of this creed;
Yet seek thy firm support, according to their need.

I, loving freedom, and untried;
No sport of every random gust,
Yet being to myself a guide,
Too blindly have reposed my trust:
And oft, when in my heart was heard
Thy timely mandate, I deferred   30
The task, in smoother walks to stray;
But thee I now would serve more strictly, if I may.

Through no disturbance of my soul,
Or strong compunction in me wrought,
I supplicate for thy control;
But in the quietness of thought:
Me this unchartered freedom tires;
I feel the weight of chance-desires:
My hopes no more must change their name,
I long for a repose that ever is the same.   40

Stern Lawgiver! yet thou dost wear
The Godhead's most benignant grace;
Nor know we anything so fair
As is the smile upon thy face:
Flowers laugh before thee on their beds

And fragrance in thy footing treads;
Thou dost preserve the stars from wrong;
And the most ancient heavens, through Thee, are
    fresh and strong

To humbler functions, awful Power!
I call thee: I myself commend   50
Unto thy guidance from this hour;
Oh, let my weakness have an end!
Give unto me, made lowly wise,
The spirit of self-sacrifice;
The confidence of reason give;
And in the light of truth thy Bondman let me live!

1804   *1807*

THE SMALL CELANDINE

There is a Flower, the lesser Celandine,
That shrinks, like many more, from cold and rain;
And, the first moment that the sun may shine,
Bright as the sun himself, 'tis out again!

When hailstones have been falling, swarm on
    swarm,
Or blasts the green field and the trees distrest,
Oft have I seen it muffled up from harm,
In close self-shelter, like a Thing at rest.

But lately, one rough day, this Flower I passed
And recognised it, though an altered form,   10
Now standing forth an offering to the blast,
And buffeted at will by rain and storm.

I stopped, and said with inly-muttered voice,
"It doth not love the shower, nor seek the cold:
This neither is its courage nor its choice,
But its necessity in being old.

"The sunshine may not cheer it, nor the dew;
It cannot help itself in its decay;
Stiff in its members, withered, changed of hue."
And, in my spleen, I smiled that it was grey.   20

To be a Prodigal's Favourite—then, worse truth,
A Miser's Pensioner—behold our lot!
O Man, that from thy fair and shining youth
Age might but take the things Youth needed not!

1804   *1807*

I WANDERED LONELY AS A CLOUD

———

Written at Town-end, Grasmere. The Daffodils grew and still grow on the margin of Ullswater, and probably may be seen to this day as beautiful in the month of March, nodding their golden heads beside the dancing and foaming waves. (Wordsworth)

[A poem greatly influenced by Dorothy's *Grasmere Journal*. See the editor's general introduction to Wordsworth.]

———

I wandered lonely as a cloud
That floats on high o'er vales and hills,
When all at once I saw a crowd,
A host, of golden daffodils;
Beside the lake, beneath the trees,
Fluttering and dancing in the breeze.

Continuous as the stars that shine
And twinkle on the milky way,
They stretched in never-ending line
Along the margin of a bay: 10
Ten thousand saw I at a glance,
Tossing their heads in sprightly dance.

The waves beside them danced; but they
Out-did the sparkling waves in glee:
A poet could not but be gay,
In such a jocund company:
I gazed—and gazed—but little thought
What wealth the show to me had brought:

For oft, when on my couch I lie
In vacant or in pensive mood,   20
They flash upon that inward eye
Which is the bliss of solitude;
And then my heart with pleasure fills,
And dances with the daffodils.

1804   *1807*

ELEGIAC STANZAS

SUGGESTED BY A PICTURE OF PEELE CASTLE, IN A STORM, PAINTED BY SIR GEORGE BEAUMONT*

Sir George Beaumont painted two pictures of this subject, one of which he gave to Mrs. Wordsworth, saying she ought to have it; but Lady Beaumont interfered, and after Sir George's death she gave it to Sir Uvedale Price, in whose house at Foxley I have seen it. (Wordsworth)

I was thy neighbour once, thou rugged Pile!
Four summer weeks I dwelt in sight of thee:
I saw thee every day; and all the while
Thy Form was sleeping on a glassy sea.

So pure the sky, so quiet was the air!
So like, so very like, was day to day!
Whene'er I looked, thy Image still was there;
It trembled, but it never passed away.

How perfect was the calm! it seemed no sleep;
No mood, which season takes away, or brings: 10
I could have fancied that the mighty Deep
Was even the gentlest of all gentle Things.

Ah! then, if mine had been the Painter's hand,
To express what then I saw; and add the gleam,
The light that never was, on sea or land,
The consecration, and the Poet's dream;

I would have planted thee, thou hoary Pile
Amid a world how different from this!
Beside a sea that could not cease to smile;
On tranquil land, beneath a sky of bliss.   20

Thou shouldst have seemed a treasure-house divine
Of peaceful years; a chronicle of heaven;—
Of all the sunbeams that did ever shine
The very sweetest had to thee been given.

A Picture had it been of lasting ease,
Elysian quiet, without toil or strife;

No motion but the moving tide, a breeze,
Or merely silent Nature's breathing life.

Such, in the fond illusion of my heart,
Such Picture would I at that time have made: 30
And seen the soul of truth in every part,
A stedfast peace that might not be betrayed.

So once it would have been,—'tis so no more;
I have submitted to a new control:
A power is gone, which nothing can restore;
A deep distress hath humanised my Soul.

Not for a moment could I now behold
A smiling sea, and be what I have been:
The feeling of my loss will ne'er be old;
This, which I know, I speak with mind serene.   40

Then, Beaumont, Friend! who would have been the
      Friend,
If he had lived, of Him whom I deplore,
This work of thine I blame not, but commend;
This sea in anger, and that dismal shore.

O 'tis a passionate Work!—yet wise and well,
Well chosen is the spirit that is here;
That Hulk which labours in the deadly swell,
This ruleful sky, this pageantry of fear!

And this huge Castle, standing here sublime,
I love to see the look with which it braves,   50
Cased in the unfeeling armour of old time,
The lightning, the fierce wind, and trampling waves.

Farewell, farewell the heart that lives alone,
Housed in a dream, at distance from the Kind!
Such happiness, wherever it be known,
Is to be pitied; for 'tis surely blind.

But welcome fortitude, and patient cheer,
And frequent sights of what is to be borne!
Such sights, or worse, as are before me here.—
Not without hope we suffer and we mourn.   60
1805   *1807*

THE SOLITARY REAPER

Behold her, single in the field,
You solitary Highland Lass!
Reaping and singing by herself;
Stop here, or gently pass!
Alone she cuts and binds the grain,

---

* Wordsworth visited a cousin, Elizabeth Wordsworth, at Rampside in August, 1794. Peele Castle is on an island off the coast of Lancashire.

And sings a melancholy strain;
O listen! for the Vale profound
Is overflowing with the sound.

No Nightingale did ever chaunt
More welcome notes to weary bands   10
Of travellers in some shady haunt,
Among Arabian sands:
A voice so thrilling ne'er was heard
In spring-time from the Cuckoo-bird,
Breaking the silence of the seas
Among the farthest Hebrides.

Will no one tell me what she sings?—
Perhaps the plaintive numbers flow
For old, unhappy, far-off things,
And battles long ago: 20
Or is it some more humble lay,
Familiar matter of to-day?
Some natural sorrow, loss, or pain,
That has been, and may be again?

Whate'er the theme, the Maiden sang
As if her song could have no ending;
I saw her singing at her work,
And o'er the sickle bending;—
I listened, motionless and still;
And, as I mounted up the hill   30
The music in my heart I bore,
Long after it was heard no more.

1805   1807

CHARACTER OF THE HAPPY WARRIOR

The course of the great war with the French naturally fixed one's attention upon the military character, and, to the honour of our country, there were many illustrious instances of the qualities that constitute its highest excellence. Lord Nelson carried most of the virtues that the trials he was exposed to in his department of the service necessarily call forth and sustain, if they do not produce the contrary vices. But his public life was stained with one great crime, so that, though many passages of these lines were suggested by what was generally known as excellent in his conduct, I have not been able to connect his name with the poem as I could wish, or even to think of him with satisfaction in reference to the idea of what a warrior ought to be. For the sake of such of my friends as may happen to read this note I will add, that many elements of the character here pourtrayed were found in my brother John, who perished by shipwreck as mentioned elsewhere. His messmates used to call him the Philosopher, from which it must be inferred that the qualities and dispositions I allude to had not escaped their notice. He often expressed his regret, after the war had continued some time, that he had not chosen the Naval, instead of the East India Company's service, to which his family connection had led him. He greatly valued moral and religious instruction for youth, as tending to make good sailors. The best, he used to say, came from Scotland; the next to them, from the North of England, especially from Westmoreland and Cumberland, where, thanks to the piety and local attachments of our ancestors, endowed, or, as they are commonly called, free, schools abound. (Wordsworth)

Who is the happy Warrior? Who is he
That every man in arms should wish to be?
—It is the generous Spirit, who, when brought
Among the tasks of real life, hath wrought
Upon the plan that pleased his boyish thought:
Whose high endeavours are an inward light
That makes the path before him always bright:
Who, with a natural instinct to discern
What knowledge can perform, is diligent to learn;
Abides by this resolve, and stops not there,   10
But makes his moral being his prime care;
Who, doomed to go in company with Pain,
And Fear, and Bloodshed, miserable train!
Turns his necessity to glorious gain;
In face of these doth exercise a power
Which is our human nature's highest dower;
Controls them and subdues, transmutes, bereaves
Of their bad influence, and their good receives:
By objects, which might force the soul to abate
Her feeling, rendered more compassionate;   20
Is placable—because occasions rise
So often that demand such sacrifice;
More skilful in self-knowledge, even more pure,
As tempted more; more able to endure,
As more exposed to suffering and distress;
Thence, also, more alive to tenderness.
—'Tis he whose law is reason; who depends
Upon that law as on the best of friends;
Whence, in a state where men are tempted still
To evil for a guard against worse ill,   30
And what in quality or act is best
Doth seldom on a right foundation rest,
He labours good on good to fix, and owes

To virtue every triumph that he knows:
—Who, if he rise to station of command,
Rises by open means; and there will stand
On honourable terms, or else retire,
And in himself possess his own desire;
Who comprehends his trust, and to the same
Keeps faithful with a singleness of aim;   40
And therefore does not stoop, nor lie in wait
For wealth, or honours, or for worldly state;
Whom they must follow; on whose head must fall,
Like showers of manna, if they come at all:
Whose powers shed round him in the common strife,
Or mild concerns of ordinary life,
A constant influence, a peculiar grace;
But who, if he be called upon to face
Some awful moment to which Heaven has joined
Great issues, good or bad for human kind,   50
Is happy as a Lover; and attired
With sudden brightness, like a Man inspired;
And, through the heat of conflict, keeps the law
In calmness made, and sees what he foresaw;
Or if an unexpected call succeed,
Come when it will, is equal to the need:
—He who, though thus endued as with a sense
And faculty for storm and turbulence,
Is yet a Soul whose master-bias leans
To homefelt pleasures and to gentle scenes;   60
Sweet images! which, wheresoe'er he be,
Are at his heart; and such fidelity
It is his darling passion to approve;
More brave for this, that he hath much to love:—
'Tis, finally, the Man, who, lifted high,
Conspicuous object in a Nation's eye,
Or left unthought-of in obscurity,—
Who, with a toward or untoward lot,
Prosperous or adverse, to his wish or not—
Plays, in the many games of life, that one   70
Where what he most doth value must be won:
Whom neither shape of danger can dismay,
Nor thought of tender happiness betray;
Who, not content that former worth stand fast,
Looks forward, persevering to the last,
From well to better, daily self-surpast:
Who, whether praise of him must walk the earth
For ever, and to noble deeds give birth,
Or he must fall, to sleep without his fame,
And leave a dead unprofitable name—   80
Finds comfort in himself and in his cause;
And, while the mortal mist is gathering, draws
His breath in confidence of Heaven's applause:

This is the happy Warrior; this is He
That every Man in arms should wish to be.
1805–06   *1807*

SURPRISED BY JOY—
IMPATIENT AS THE WIND

This was in fact suggested by my daughter Catherine, long after her death. (Wordsworth)

Surprised by joy—impatient as the Wind
I turned to share the transport—Oh! with whom
But Thee, deep buried in the silent tomb,
That spot which no vicissitude can find?
Love, faithful love, recalled thee to my mind—
But how could I forget thee? Through what power,
Even for the least division of an hour,
Have I been so beguiled as to be blind
To my most grievous loss!—That thought's return
Was the worst pang that sorrow ever bore,   10
Save one, one only, when I stood forlorn,
Knowing my heart's best treasure was no more;
That neither present time, nor years unborn
Could to my sight that heavenly face restore.
1812–15   *1815*

LAODAMIA*

Written at Rydal Mount. The incident of the trees growing and withering put the subject into my thoughts, and I wrote with the hope of giving it a loftier tone than, so far as I know, has been given to it by any of the Ancients who have treated it. It cost me more trouble than almost anything of equal length I have ever written. (Wordsworth)

"With sacrifice before the rising morn
Vows have I made by fruitless hope inspired;
And from the infernal Gods, 'mid shades forlorn
Of night, my slaughtered Lord have I required:
Celestial pity I again implore;—
Restore him to my sight—great Jove, restore!"

---

* The wife of Protesilaus, the first Greek to die in the Trojan war.

So speaking, and by fervent love endowed
With faith, the Suppliant heavenward lifts her
    hands;
While, like the sun emerging from a cloud,
Her countenance brightens—and her eye
    expands;   10
Her bosom heaves and spreads, her stature grows;
And she expects the issue in repose.

O terror! what hath she perceived?—O joy!
What doth she look on?—whom doth she behold?
Her Hero slain upon the beach of Troy?
His vital presence? his corporeal mould?
It is—if sense deceive her not—'tis He!
And a God leads him, wingèd Mercury!

Mild Hermes spake—and touched her with his
    wand
That calms all fear; "Such grace hath crowned thy
    prayer,   20
Laodamía! that at Jove's command
Thy Husband walks the paths of upper air:
He comes to tarry with thee three hours' space;
Accept the gift, behold him face to face!"

Forth sprang the impassioned Queen her Lord to
    clasp;
Again that consummation she essayed;
But unsubstantial Form eludes her grasp
As often as that eager grasp was made.
The Phantom parts—but parts to re-unite,
And re-assume his place before her sight.   30

"Protesiláus, lo! thy guide is gone!
Confirm, I pray, the vision with thy voice:
This is our palace,—yonder is thy throne;
Speak, and the floor thou tread'st on will rejoice.
Not to appal me have the gods bestowed
This precious boon; and blest a sad abode."

"Great Jove, Laodamía! doth not leave
His gifts imperfect:—Spectre though I be,
I am not sent to scare thee or deceive;
But in reward of thy fidelity.   40
And something also did my worth obtain;
For fearless virtue bringeth boundless gain.

"Thou knowest, the Delphic oracle foretold
That the first Greek who touched the Trojan strand
Should die; but me the threat could not withhold:
A generous cause a victim did demand;
And forth I leapt upon the sandy plain;
A self-devoted chief—by Hector slain."

"Supreme of Heroes—bravest, noblest, best!
Thy matchless courage I bewail no more,   50
Which then, when tens of thousands were deprest
By doubt, propelled thee to the fatal shore;
Thou found'st—and I forgive thee—here thou art—
A nobler counsellor than my poor heart.

"But thou, though capable of sternest deed,
Wert kind as resolute, and good as brave;
And he, whose power restores thee, hath decreed
Thou should'st elude the malice of the grave:
Redundant are thy locks, thy lips as fair
As when their breath enriched Thessalian air.   60

"No Spectre greets me,—no vain Shadow this;
Come, blooming Hero, place thee by my side!
Give, on this well-known couch, one nuptial kiss
To me, this day, a second time thy bride!"
Jove frowned in heaven: the conscious Parcæ threw
Upon those roseate lips a Stygian hue.

"This visage tells thee that my doom is past:
Nor should the change be mourned, even if the joys
Of sense were able to return as fast
And surely as they vanish. Earth destroys   70
Those raptures duly—Erebus disdains:
Calm pleasures there abide—majestic pains.

"Be taught, O faithful Consort, to control
Rebellious passion: for the Gods approve
The depth, and not the tumult, of the soul;
A fervent, not ungovernable, love.
Thy transports moderate; and meekly mourn
When I depart, for brief is my sojourn—"

"Ah, wherefore?—Did not Hercules by force
Wrest from the guardian Monster of the tomb   80
Alcestis, a reanimated corse,
Given back to dwell on earth in vernal bloom?
Medea's spells dispersed the weight of years,
And Æson stood a youth 'mid youthful peers.

"The Gods to us are merciful—and they
Yet further may relent: for mightier far
Than strength of nerve and sinew, or the sway

LAODAMIA. **65. Parcæ:** the Fates. **66. Stygian:** black,
hellish. The river Styx flows through the underworld.
71. Erebus: an area of the underworld. **79–82:** In the
ancient Greek myth Admetus, husband of Alcestis, was
doomed to die unless someone were willing to die in
his place. His courageous wife volunteered, only to be
replaced by Hercules, who defeated Death in a wrest-
ling contest. **83–84:** Medea's supernatural power restored Aeson, her father-in-law, to youth.

Of magic potent over sun and star,
Is love, though oft to agony distrest,
And though his favourite seat be feeble woman's
    breast.   90

"But if thou goest, I follow—" "Peace!" he said,—
She looked upon him and was calmed and cheered;
The ghastly colour from his lips had fled;
In his deportment, shape, and mien, appeared
Elysian beauty, melancholy grace,
Brought from a pensive though a happy place.

He spake of love, such love as Spirits feel
In worlds whose course is equable and pure;
No fears to beat away—no strife to heal—
The past unsighed for, and the future sure;   100
Spake of heroic arts in graver mood
Revived, with finer harmony pursued;

Of all that is most beauteous—imaged there
In happier beauty; more pellucid streams,
An ampler ether, a diviner air,
And fields invested with purpureal gleams;
Climes which the sun, who sheds the brightest day
Earth knows, is all unworthy to survey.

Yet there the Soul shall enter which hath earned
That privilege by virtue.—"Ill," said he,   110
"The end of man's existence I discerned,
Who from ignoble games and revelry
Could draw, when we had parted, vain delight,
While tears were thy best pastime, day and night;

"And while my youthful peers before my eyes
(Each hero following his peculiar bent)
Prepared themselves for glorious enterprise
By martial sports,—or, seated in the tent,
Chieftains and kings in council were detained;
What time the fleet at Aulis lay enchained.   120

"The wished-for wind was given:—I then revolved
The oracle, upon the silent sea;
And, if no worthier led the way, resolved
That, of a thousand vessels, mine should be
The foremost prow in pressing to the strand,—
Mine the first blood that tinged the Trojan sand.

"Yet bitter, oft-times bitter, was the pang
When of thy loss I thought belovèd Wife!
On thee too fondly did my memory hang,
And on the joys we shared in mortal life,—   130

120. Aulis: the port in Boetia where the Greek fleet
was becalmed until Agamemnon sacrificed his daughter.

The paths which we had trod—these fountains,
    flowers,
My new-planned cities, and unfinished towers.

"But should suspense permit the Foe to cry,
'Behold they tremble!—haughty their array,
Yet of their number no one dares to die?'
In soul I swept the indignity away:
Old frailties then recurred:—but lofty thought,
In act embodied, my deliverance wrought.

"And Thou, though strong in love, art all too weak
In reason, in self-government too slow;   140
I counsel thee by fortitude to seek
Our blest re-union in the shades below.
The invisible world with thee hath sympathised;
Be thy affections raised and solemnised.

"Learn, by a mortal yearning, to ascend—
Seeking a higher object. Love was given,
Encouraged, sanctioned, chiefly for that end;
For this the passion to excess was driven—
That self might be annulled: her bondage prove
The fetters of a dream, opposed to love."——   150

Aloud she shrieked! for Hermes re-appears!
Round the dear Shade she would have clung—'tis
    vain:
The hours are past—too brief had they been years;
And him no mortal effort can detain:
Swift, toward the realms that know not earthly day,
He through the portal takes his silent way,
And on the palace-floor a lifeless corse She lay.

Thus, all in vain exhorted and reproved,
She perished; and, as for a wilful crime,
By the just Gods whom no weak pity moved,   160
Was doomed to wear out her appointed time,
Apart from happy Ghosts, that gather flowers
Of blissful quiet 'mid unfading bowers.

—Yet tears to human suffering are due;
And mortal hopes defeated and o'erthrown
Are mourned by man, and not by man alone,
As fondly he believes.—Upon the side
Of Hellespont (such faith was entertained)
A knot of spiry trees for ages grew
From out the tomb of him for whom she died;   170
And ever, when such stature they had gained
That Ilium's walls were subject to their view,
The trees' tall summits withered at the sight;
A constant interchange of growth and blight!
1814   *1815*

YARROW REVISITED

The gallant Youth, who may have gained,
   Or seeks, a "winsome Marrow,"
Was but an Infant in the lap
   When first I looked on Yarrow;
Once more, by Newark's Castle-gate
   Long left without a warder,
I stood, looked, listened, and with Thee,
   Great Minstrel of the Border!

Grave throughts ruled wide on that sweet day,
   Their dignity installing   10
In gentle bosoms, while sere leaves
   Were on the bough, or falling;
But breezes played, and sunshine gleamed—
   The forest to embolden;
Reddened the fiery hues, and shot
   Transparence through the golden.

For busy thoughts the Stream flowed on
   In foamy agitation;
And slept in many a crystal pool
   For quiet contemplation: 20
No public and no private care
   The freeborn mind enthralling,
We made a day of happy hours,
   Our happy days recalling.

Brisk Youth appeared, the Morn of youth,
   With freaks of graceful folly,—
Life's temperate Noon, her sober Eve,
   Her Night not melancholy;
Past, present, future, all appeared
   In harmony united,   30
Like guests that meet, and some from far,
   By cordial love invited.

And if, as Yarrow, through the woods
   And down the meadow ranging,
Did meet us with unaltered face,
   Though we were changed and changing;
If, *then*, some natural shadows spread
   Our inward prospect over,
The soul's deep valley was not slow
   Its brightness to recover.   40

Eternal blessings on the Muse,
   And her divine employment!
That blameless Muse, who trains her Sons

For hope and calm enjoyment;
   Albeit sickness, lingering yet,
Has o'er their pillow brooded;
   And Care waylays their steps—a Sprite
Not easily eluded.

For thee, O Scott! compelled to change
   Green Eildon-hill and Cheviot   50
For warm Vesuvio's vine-clad slopes;
   And leave thy Tweed and Tiviot
For mild Sorento's breezy waves;
   May classic Fancy, linking
With native Fancy her fresh aid,
   Preserve thy heart from sinking!

Oh! while they minister to thee,
   Each vying with the other,
May Health return to mellow Age
   With Strength, her venturous brother;   60
And Tiber, and each brook and rill
   Renowned in song and story,
With unimagined beauty shine,
   Nor lose one ray of glory!

For Thou, upon a hundred streams,
   By tales of love and sorrow,
Of faithful love, undaunted truth,
   Hast shed the power of Yarrow;
And streams unknown, hills yet unseen,
   Wherever they invite Thee,   70
At parent Nature's grateful call,
   With gladness must requite Thee.

A gracious welcome shall be thine,
   Such looks of love and honour
As thy own Yarrow gave to me
   When first I gazed upon her;
Beheld what I had feared to see,
   Unwilling to surrender
Dreams treasured up from early days,
   The holy and the tender.   80

And what, for this frail world, were all
   That mortals do or suffer,
Did no responsive harp, no pen,
   Memorial tribute offer?
Yea, what were mighty Nature's self?
   Her features, could they win us,
Unhelped by the poetic voice
   That hourly speaks within us?

Nor deem that localised Romance
   Plays false with our affections;   90

Unsanctifies our tears—made sport
   For fanciful dejections:
Ah, no! the visions of the past
   Sustain the heart in feeling
Life as she is—our changeful Life,
   With friends and kindred dealing.

Bear witness, Ye, whose thoughts that day
   In Yarrow's groves were centred;
Who through the silent portal arch
   Of mouldering Newark entered;   100
And clomb the winding stair that once
   Too timidly was mounted
By the "last Minstrel," (not the last!)
   Ere he his Tale recounted.

Flow on for ever, Yarrow Stream!
   Fulfil thy pensive duty,
Well pleased that future Bards should chant
   For simple hearts thy beauty;
To dream-light dear while yet unseen,
   Dear to the common sunshine,   110
And dearer still, as now I feel,
   To memory's shadowy moonshine!

1831   *1835*

MUTABILITY

From low to high doth dissolution climb,
And sink from high to low, along a scale
Of awful notes, whose concord shall not fail;
A musical but melancholy chime,
Which they can hear who meddle not with crime,
Nor avarice, nor over-anxious care.
Truth fails not; but her outward forms that bear
The longest date do melt like frosty rime,
That in the morning whitened hill and plain
And is no more; drop like the tower sublime   10
Of yesterday, which royally did wear
His crown of weeds, but could not even sustain
Some casual shout that broke the silent air,
Or the unimaginable touch of Time.

1821   *1822*

TEMPTATIONS FROM ROMAN REFINEMENTS

Watch, and be firm! for, soul-subduing vice,
Heart-killing luxury, on your steps await.

Fair houses, baths, and banquets delicate,
And temples flashing, bright as polar ice,
Their radiance through the woods—may yet suffice
To sap your hardy virtue, and abate
Your love of Him upon whose forehead sate
The crown of thorns; whose life-blood flowed, the
   price
Of your redemption. Shun the insidious arts
That Rome provides, less dreading from her
   frown   10
Than from her wily praise, her peaceful gown,
Language, and letters;—these, though fondly
   viewed
As humanising graces, are but parts
And instruments of deadliest servitude!

1821   *1822*

STEAMBOATS, VIADUCTS, AND RAILWAYS

Motions and Means, on land and sea at war
With old poetic feeling, not for this,
Shall ye, by Poets even, be judged amiss!
Nor shall your presence, howsoe'er it mar
The loveliness of Nature, prove a bar
To the Mind's gaining that prophetic sense
Of future change, that point of vision whence
May be discovered what in soul ye are.
In spite of all that beauty may disown
In your harsh features, Nature doth embrace   10
Her lawful offspring in Man's art; and Time,
Pleased with your triumphs o'er his brother Space,
Accepts from your bold hands the proffered crown
Of hope, and smiles on you with cheer sublime.

1833   *1835*

CONCLUSION

TO ———

If these brief Records, by the Muses' art
Produced as lonely Nature or the strife
That animates the scenes of public life
Inspired, may in thy leisure claim a part;
And if these Transcripts of the private heart
Have gained a sanction from thy falling tears;
Then I repent not. But my soul hath fears

Breathed from eternity; for, as a dart
Cleaves the blank air, Life flies: now every day
Is but a glimmering spoke in the swift wheel   10
Of the revolving week. Away, away,
All fitful cares, all transitory zeal!
So timely Grace the immortal wing may heal,
And honour rest upon the senseless clay.

1827   *1827*

FROM

The Excursion

PREFACE TO THE EDITION OF 1814

The Title-page announces that this is only a portion
of a poem; and the Reader must be here apprised
that it belongs to the second part of a long and
laborious Work, which is to consist of three parts.
—The Author will candidly acknowledge that, if
the first of these had been completed, and in such
a manner as to satisfy his own mind, he should
have preferred the natural order of publication, and
have given that to the world first; but, as the second
division of the Work was designed to refer more to
passing events, and to an existing state of things,
than the others were meant to do, more continuous
exertion was naturally bestowed upon it, and
greater progress made here than in the rest of the
poem; and as this part does not depend upon the
preceding to a degree which will materially injure
its own peculiar interest, the Author, complying
with the earnest entreaties of some valued Friends,
presents the following pages to the Public.

It may be proper to state whence the poem, of
which "The Excursion" is a part, derives its Title
of "The Recluse."—Several years ago, when the
Author retired to his native mountains, with the
hope of being enabled to construct a literary Work
that might live, it was a reasonable thing that he
should take a review of his own mind, and examine how far Nature and Education had qualified
him for such employment. As subsidiary to this
preparation, he undertook to record, in verse, the
origin and progress of his own powers, as far as he
was acquainted with them. That Work, addressed
to a dear Friend, most distinguished for his knowledge and genius, and to whom the Author's Intellect is deeply indebted, has been long finished; and
the result of the investigation which gave rise to it
was a determination to compose a philosophical
poem, containing views of Man, Nature, and Society; and to be entitled, "The Recluse"; as having
for its principal subject the sensations and opinions
of a poet living in retirement.—The preparatory

poem is biographical, and conducts the history of
the Author's mind to the point when he was em-
boldened to hope that his faculties were sufficiently
matured for entering upon the arduous labour
which he had proposed to himself; and the two
Works have the same kind of relation to each other,
if he may so express himself, as the ante-chapel
has to the body of a Gothic church. Continuing this
allusion, he may be permitted to add, that his
minor Pieces, which have been long before the
Public, when they shall be properly arranged, will
be found by the attentive Reader to have such connection with the main Work as may give them
claim to be likened to the little cells, oratories, and
sepulchral recesses, ordinarily included in those
edifices.

The Author would not have deemed himself
justified in saying, upon this occasion, so much of
performances either unfinished or unpublished, if
he had not thought that the labour bestowed by
him upon what he has heretofore and now laid
before the Public entitled him to candid attention for such a statement as he thinks necessary to
throw light upon his endeavours to please and, he
would hope, to benefit his countrymen.—Nothing
further need be added, than that the first and third
parts of "The Recluse" will consist chiefly of meditations in the Author's own person; and that in the
intermediate part ("The Excursion") the intervention of characters speaking is employed, and something of a dramatic form adopted.

It is not the Author's intention formally to announce a system; it was more animating to him to
proceed in a different course; and if he shall succeed in conveying to the mind clear thoughts, lively
images, and strong feelings, the Reader will have
no difficulty in extracting the system for himself.
And in the meantime the following passage, taken
from the conclusion of the first book of "The Recluse," may be acceptable as a kind of *Prospectus*
of the design and scope of the whole Poem.
(Wordsworth)

PROSPECTUS

On Man, on Nature, and on Human Life,
Musing in solitude, I oft perceive
Fair trains of imagery before me rise,
Accompanied by feelings of delight
Pure, or with no unpleasing sadness mixed;
And I am conscious of affecting thoughts
And dear remembrances, whose presence soothes
Or elevates the Mind, intent to weigh
The good and evil of our mortal state.
—To these emotions, whencesoe'er they come,   10
Whether from breath of outward circumstance,

Or from the Soul—an impulse to herself—
I would give utterance in numerous verse.
Of Truth, of Grandeur, Beauty, Love, and Hope,
And melancholy Fear subdued by Faith;
Of blessèd consolations in distress;
Of moral strength, and intellectual Power;
Of joy in widest commonalty spread;
Of the individual Mind that keeps her own
Inviolate retirement, subject there   20
To Conscience only, and the law supreme
Of that Intelligence which governs all—
I sing:—"fit audience let me find though few!"

    So prayed, more gaining than he asked, the
        Bard—
In holiest mood. Urania, I shall need
Thy guidance, or a greater Muse, if such
Descend to earth or dwell in highest heaven!
For I must tread on shadowy ground, must sink
Deep—and, aloft ascending, breathe in worlds
To which the heaven of heavens is but a veil.   30
All strength—all terror, single or in bands,
That ever was put forth in personal form—
Jehovah—with his thunder, and the choir
Of shouting Angels, and the empyreal thrones—
I pass them unalarmed. Not Chaos, not
The darkest pit of lowest Erebus,
Nor aught of blinder vacancy, scooped out
By help of dreams—can breed such fear and awe
As fall upon us often when we look
Into our Minds, into the Mind of Man—   40
My haunt, and the main region of my song.
—Beauty—a living Presence of the earth,
Surpassing the most fair ideal Forms
Which craft of delicate Spirits hath composed
From earth's materials—waits upon my steps;
Pitches her tents before me as I move,
An hourly neighbour. Paradise, and groves
Elysian, Fortunate Fields—like those of old
Sought in the Atlantic Main—why should they be
A history only of departed things,   50
Or a mere fiction of what never was?
For the discerning intellect of Man,
When wedded to this goodly universe
In love and holy passion, shall find these
A simple produce of the common day.
—I, long before the blissful hour arrives,

THE EXCURSION. PROSPECTUS. 23. "fit . . . few": an
adaptation from Milton's *Paradise Lost*. 25. Urania:
the Muse of astronomy.

Would chant, in lonely peace, the spousal verse
Of this great consummation:—and, by words
Which speak of nothing more than what we are,
Would I arouse the sensual from their sleep   60
Of Death, and win the vacant and the vain
To noble raptures; while my voice proclaims
How exquisitely the individual Mind
(And the progressive powers perhaps no less
Of the whole species) to the external World
Is fitted:—and how exquisitely, too—
Theme this but little heard of among men—
The external World is fitted to the Mind;
And the creation (by no lower name
Can it be called) which they with blended
    might   70
Accomplish:—this is our high argument.
—Such grateful haunts foregoing, if I oft
Must turn elsewhere—to travel near the tribes
And fellowships of men, and see ill sights
Of madding passions mutually inflamed;
Must hear Humanity in fields and groves
Pipe solitary anguish; or must hang
Brooding above the fierce confederate storm
Of sorrow, barricadoed evermore
Within the walls of cities—may these sounds   80
Have their authentic comment; that even these
Hearing, I be not downcast or forlorn!—
Descend, prophetic Spirit! that inspir'st
The human Soul of universal earth,
Dreaming on things to come; and dost possess
A metropolitan temple in the hearts
Of mighty Poets; upon me bestow
A gift of genuine insight; that my Song
With star-like virtue in its place may shine,
Shedding benignant influence, and secure   90
Itself from all malevolent effect
Of those mutations that extend their sway
Throughout the nether sphere!—And if with this
I mix more lowly matter; with the thing
Contemplated, describe the Mind and Man
Contemplating; and who, and what he was—
The transitory Being that beheld
This Vision; when and where, and how he lived;
Be not this labour useless. If such theme
May sort with highest objects, then—dread
    Power!   100
Whose gracious favour is the primal source
Of all illumination,—may my Life
Express the image of a better time,
More wise desires, and simpler manners;—nurse

My Heart in genuine freedom:—all pure thoughts
Be with me;—so shall thy unfailing love
Guide, and support, and cheer me to the end!

BOOK FIRST

THE WANDERER

Argument

A summer forenoon—The Author reaches a ruined
Cottage upon a Common, and there meets with a
revered Friend, the Wanderer, of whose education
and course of life he gives an account—The Wanderer, while resting under the shade of the Trees
that surround the Cottage, relates the History of its
last Inhabitant.

'Twas summer, and the sun had mounted high:
Southward the landscape indistinctly glared
Through a pale steam; but all the northern downs,
In clearest air ascending, showed far off
A surface dappled o'er with shadows flung
From brooding clouds; shadows that lay in spots
Determined and unmoved, with steady beams
Of bright and pleasant sunshine interposed;
To him most pleasant who on soft cool moss
Extends his careless limbs along the front   10
Of some huge cave, whose rocky ceiling casts
A twilight of its own, an ample shade,
Where the wren warbles, while the dreaming man,
Half conscious of the soothing melody,
With side-long eye looks out upon the scene,
By power of that impending covert, thrown
To finer distance. Mine was at that hour
Far other lot, yet with good hope that soon
Under a shade as grateful I should find
Rest, and be welcomed there to livelier joy.   20
Across a bare wide Common I was toiling
With languid steps that by the slippery turf
Were baffled; nor could my weak arm disperse
The host of insects gathering round my face,
And ever with me as I paced along.

Upon that open moorland stood a grove,
The wished-for port to which my course was
       bound.
Thither I came, and there, amid the gloom

Spread by a brotherhood of lofty elms,
Appeared a roofless Hut; four naked walls   30
That stared upon each other!—I looked round,
And to my wish and to my hope espied
The Friend I sought; a Man of reverend age,
But stout and hale, for travel unimpaired.
There was he seen upon the cottage-bench,
Recumbent in the shade, as if asleep;
An iron-pointed staff lay at his side.

Him had I marked the day before—alone
And stationed in the public way, with face
Turned toward the sun then setting, while that
       staff   40
Afforded, to the figure of the man
Detained for contemplation or repose,
Graceful support; his countenance as he stood
Was hidden from my view, and he remained
Unrecognised; but, stricken by the sight,
With slackened footsteps I advance, and soon
A glad congratulation we exchanged
At such unthought-of meeting.—For the night
We parted, nothing willingly; and now
He by appointment waited for me here,   50
Under the covert of these clustering elms.

We were tried Friends: amid a pleasant vale,
In the antique market-village where was passed
My school-time, an apartment he had owned,
To which at intervals the Wanderer drew,
And found a kind of home or harbour there.
He loved me; from a swarm of rosy boys
Singled out me, as he in sport would say,
For my grave looks, too thoughtful for my years.
As I grew up, it was my best delight   60
To be his chosen comrade. Many a time,
On holidays, we rambled through the woods:
We sate—we walked; he pleased me with report
Of things which he had seen; and often touched
Abstrusest matter, reasonings of the mind
Turned inward; or at my request would sing
Old songs, the product of his native hills;
A skilful distribution of sweet sounds,
Feeding the soul, and eagerly imbibed
As cool refreshing water, by the care   70
Of the industrious husbandman, diffused
Through a parched meadow-ground, in time of
       drought.
Still deeper welcome found his pure discourse;
How precious, when in riper days I learned

To weigh with care his words, and to rejoice
In the plain presence of his dignity!

    Oh! many are the Poets that are sown
By Nature; men endowed with highest gifts,
The vision and the faculty divine;
Yet wanting the accomplishment of verse,   80
(Which, in the docile season of their youth,
It was denied them to acquire, through lack
Of culture and the inspiring aid of books,
Or haply by a temper too severe,
Or a nice backwardness afraid of shame)
Nor having e'er, as life advanced, been led
By circumstance to take unto the height
The measure of themselves, these favoured Beings,
All but a scattered few, live out their time,
Husbanding that which they possess within,   90
And go to the grave, unthought of. Strongest minds
Are often those of whom the noisy world
Hears least; else surely this Man had not left
His graces unrevealed and unproclaimed.
But, as the mind was filled with inward light,
So not without distinction had he lived,
Beloved and honoured—far as he was known.
And some small portion of his eloquent speech,
And something that may serve to set in view
The feeling pleasures of his loneliness,   100
His observations, and the thoughts his mind
Had dealt with—I will here record in verse;
Which, if with truth it correspond, and sink
Or rise as venerable Nature leads,
The high and tender Muses shall accept
With gracious smile, deliberately pleased,
And listening Time reward with sacred praise.

    Among the hills of Athol he was born;
Where, on a small hereditary farm,
An unproductive slip of rugged ground,   110
His Parents, with their numerous offspring, dwelt;
A virtuous household, though exceeding poor!
Pure livers were they all, austere and grave,
And fearing God; the very children taught
Stern self-respect, a reverence for God's word,
And an habitual piety, maintained
With strictness scarcely known on English ground.

    From his sixth year, the Boy of whom I speak,
In summer, tended cattle on the hills;
But, through the inclement and the perilous
    days   120
Of long-continuing winter, he repaired,

Equipped with satchel, to a school, that stood
Sole building on a mountain's dreary edge,
Remote from view of city spire, or sound
Of minster clock! From that bleak tenement
He, many an evening, to his distant home
In solitude returning, saw the hills
Grow larger in the darkness; all alone
Beheld the stars come out above his head,
And travelled through the wood, with no one
    near   130
To whom he might confess the things he saw.

    So the foundations of his mind were laid
In such communion, not from terror free,
While yet a child, and long before his time,
Had he perceived the presence and the power
Of greatness; and deep feelings had impressed
So vividly great objects that they lay
Upon his mind like substances, whose presence
Perplexed the bodily sense. He had received
A precious gift; for, as he grew in years,   140
With these impressions would he still compare
All his remembrances, thoughts, shapes, and forms;
And, being still unsatisfied with aught
Of dimmer character, he thence attained
An active power to fasten images
Upon his brain; and on their pictured lines
Intensely brooded, even till they acquired
The liveliness of dreams. Nor did he fail,
While yet a child, with a child's eagerness
Incessantly to turn his ear and eye   150
On all things which the moving seasons brought
To feed such appetite—nor this alone
Appeased his yearning:—in the after-day
Of boyhood, many an hour in caves forlorn,
And 'mid the hollow depths of naked crags
He sate, and even in their fixed lineaments,
Or from the power of a peculiar eye,
Or by creative feeling overborne,
Or by predominance of thought oppressed,
Even in their fixed and steady lineaments   160
He traced an ebbing and a flowing mind,
Expression ever varying!
                Thus informed,
He had small need of books; for many a tale
Traditionary, round the mountains hung,
And many a legend, peopling the dark woods,
Nourished Imagination in her growth,
And gave the Mind that apprehensive power
By which she is made quick to recognise

The moral properties and scope of things.
But eagerly he read, and read again,   170
Whate'er the minister's old shelf supplied;
The life and death of martyrs, who sustained,
With will inflexible, those fearful pangs
Triumphantly displayed in records left
Of persecution, and the Covenant—times
Whose echo rings through Scotland to this hour!
And there, by lucky hap, had been preserved
A straggling volume, torn and incomplete,
That left half-told the preternaural tale,
Romance of giants, chronicle of fiends,   180
Profuse in garniture of wooden cuts
Strange and uncouth; dire faces, figures dire,
Sharp-kneed, sharp-elbowed, and lean-ankled too,
With long and ghostly shanks—forms which once
    seen
Could never be forgotten!
                In his heart,
Where Fear sate thus, a cherished visitant,
Was wanting yet the pure delight of love
By sound diffused, or by the breathing air,
Or by the silent looks of happy things,
Or flowing from the universal face   190
Of earth and sky. But he had felt the power
Of Nature, and already was prepared,
By his intense conceptions, to receive
Deeply the lesson deep of love which he,
Whom Nature, by whatever means, has taught
To feel intensely, cannot but receive.

   Such was the Boy—but for the growing Youth
What soul was his, when, from the naked top
Of some bold headland, he beheld the sun
Rise up, and bathe the world in light! He
    looked—   200
Ocean and earth, the solid frame of earth
And ocean's liquid mass, in gladness lay
Beneath him:—Far and wide the clouds were
    touched,
And in their silent faces could he read
Unutterable love. Sound needed none,
Nor any voice of joy; his spirit drank
The spectacle: sensation, soul, and form,
All melted into him; they swallowed up
His animal being; in them did he live,

And by them did he live; they were his life.   210
In such access of mind, in such high hour
Of visitation from the living God,
Thought was not; in enjoyment it expired.
No thanks he breathed, he proffered no request;
Rapt into still communion that transcends
The imperfect offices of prayer and praise,
His mind was a thanksgiving to the power
That made him; it was blessedness and love!

   A Herdsman on the lonely mountain tops,
Such intercourse was his, and in this sort   220
Was his existence oftentimes *possessed*.
O then how beautiful, how bright, appeared
The written promise! Early had he learned
To reverence the volume that displays
The mystery, the life which cannot die;
But in the mountains did he *feel* his faith.
All things, responsive to the writing, there
Breathed immortality, revolving life,
And greatness still revolving; infinite:
There littleness was not; the least of things   230
Seemed infinite; and there his spirit shaped
Her prospects, nor did he believe,—he *saw*.
What wonder if his being thus became
Sublime and comprehensive! Low desires,
Low thoughts had there no place; yet was his heart
Lowly; for he was meek in gratitude,
Oft as he called those ecstasies to mind,
And whence they flowed; and from them he
    acquired
Wisdom, which works through patience; thence
    he learned
In oft-recurring hours of sober thought   240
To look on Nature with a humble heart,
Self-questioned where it did not understand,
And with a superstitious eye of love.

   So passed the time; yet to the nearest town
He duly went with what small overplus
His earnings might supply, and brought away
The book that most had tempted his desires
While at the stall he read. Among the hills
He gazed upon that mighty orb of song,
The divine Milton. Lore of different kind,   250
The annual savings of a toilsome life,
His Schoolmaster supplied; books that explain
The purer elements of truth involved
In lines and numbers, and, by charm severe,
(Especially perceived where nature droops
And feeling is suppressed) preserve the mind

THE EXCURSION. BOOK I. **175. Covenant:** a reference to
the National Covenant of 1638, introduced under James
I and Charles I, which guaranteed the rights of Presby-
terianism in Scotland.

Busy in solitude and poverty.
These occupations oftentimes deceived
The listless hours, while in the hollow vale,
Hollow and green, he lay on the green turf   260
In pensive idleness. What could he do,
Thus daily thirsting, in that lonesome life,
With blind endeavours? Yet, still uppermost,
Nature was at his heart as if he felt,
Though yet he knew not how, a wasting power
In all things that from her sweet influence
Might tend to wean him. Therefore with her hues,
Her forms, and with the spirit of her forms,
He clothed the nakedness of austere truth.
While yet he lingered in the rudiments   270
Of science, and among her simplest laws,
His triangles—they were the stars of heaven,
The silent stars! Oft did he take delight
To measure the altitude of some tall crag
That is the eagle's birth-place, or some peak
Familiar with forgotten years, that shows,
Inscribed upon its visionary sides,
The history of many a winter storm,
Or obscure records of the path of fire.

　　And thus before his eighteenth year was
　　　　told,   280
Accumulated feelings pressed his heart
With still increasing weight; he was o'er-powered
By Nature; by the turbulence subdued
Of his own mind; by mystery and hope,
And the first virgin passion of a soul
Communing with the glorious universe.
Full often wished he that the winds might rage
When they were silent: far more fondly now
Than in his earlier season did he love
Tempestuous nights—the conflict and the
　　　　sounds   290
That live in darkness. From his intellect
And from the stillness of abstracted thought
He asked repose; and, failing oft to win
The peace required, he scanned the laws of light
Amid the roar of torrents, where they send
From hollow clefts up to the clearer air
A cloud of mist that, smitten by the sun,
Varies its rainbow hues. But vainly thus,
And vainly by all other means, he strove
To mitigate the fever of his heart.   300

　　In dreams, in study, and in ardent thought,
Thus was he reared; much wanting to assist
The growth of intellect, yet gaining more,

And every moral feeling of his soul
Strengthened and braced, by breathing in content
The keen, the wholesome, air of poverty,
And drinking from the well of homely life.
—But, from past liberty, and tried restraints,
He now was summoned to select the course
Of humble industry that promised best   310
To yield him no unworthy maintenance.
Urged by his Mother, he essayed to teach
A village-school—but wandering thoughts were
　　　　then
A misery to him; and the Youth resigned
A task he was unable to perform.

　　That stern yet kindly Spirit, who constrains
The Savoyard to quit his naked rocks,
The free-born Swiss to leave his narrow vales,
(Spirit attached to regions mountainous
Like their own stedfast clouds) did now
　　　　impel   320
His restless mind to look abroad with hope.
—An irksome drudgery seems it to plod on,
Through hot and dusty ways, or pelting storm,
A vagrant Merchant under a heavy load,
Bent as he moves, and needing frequent rest;
Yet do such travellers find their own delight;
And their hard service, deemed debasing now,
Gained merited respect in simpler times;
When squire, and priest, and they who round them
　　　　dwelt
In rustic sequestration—all dependent   330
Upon the PEDLAR's toil—supplied their wants,
Or pleased their fancies, with the wares he brought.
Not ignorant was the Youth that still no few
Of his adventurous countrymen were led
By perseverance in this track of life
To competence and ease:—to him it offered
Attractions manifold;—and this he chose.
—His Parents on the enterprise bestowed
Their farewell benediction, but with hearts
Foreboding evil. From his native hills   340
He wandered far; much did he see of men,
Their manners, their enjoyments, and pursuits,
Their passions and their feelings; chiefly those
Essential and eternal in the heart,
That, 'mid the simpler forms of rural life,
Exist more simple in their elements,
And speak a plainer language. In the woods,
A lone Enthusiast, and among the fields,
Itinerant in this labour, he had passed

The better portion of his time; and there   350
Spontaneously had his affections thriven
Amid the bounties of the year, the peace
And liberty of nature; there he kept
In solitude and solitary thought
His mind in a just equipoise of love.
Serene it was, unclouded by the cares
Of ordinary life; unvexed, unwarped
By partial bondage. In his steady course,
No piteous revolutions had he felt,
No wild varieties of joy and grief.   360
Unoccupied by sorrow of its own,
His heart lay open; and, by nature tuned
And constant disposition of his thoughts
To sympathy with man, he was alive
To all that was enjoyed where'er he went,
And all that was endured; for, in himself
Happy, and quiet in his cheerfulness,
He had no painful pressure from without
That made him turn aside from wretchedness
With coward fears. He could *afford* to suffer   370
With those whom he saw suffer. Hence it came
That in our best experience he was rich,
And in the wisdom of our daily life.
For hence, minutely, in his various rounds,
He had observed the progress and decay
Of many minds, of minds and bodies too;
The history of many families;
How they had prospered; how they were o'erthrown
By passion or mischance, or such misrule
Among the unthinking masters of the earth   380
As makes the nations groan.
                              This active course
He followed till provision for his wants
Had been obtained;—the Wanderer then resolved
To pass the remnant of his days, untasked
With needless services, from hardship free.
His calling laid aside, he lived at ease:
But still he loved to pace the public roads
And the wild paths; and, by the summer's warmth
Invited, often would he leave his home
And journey far, revisiting the scenes   390
That to his memory were most endeared.
—Vigorous in health, of hopeful spirits, undamped
By worldly-mindedness or anxious care;
Observant, studious, thoughtful, and refreshed
By knowledge gathered up from day to day;
Thus had he lived a long and innocent life.

The Scottish Church, both on himself and those
With whom from childhood he grew up, had held

The strong hand of her purity; and still
Had watched him with an unrelenting eye.   400
This he remembered in his riper age
With gratitude, and reverential thoughts.
But by the native vigour of his mind,
By his habitual wanderings out of doors,
By loneliness, and goodness, and kind works,
Whate'er, in docile childhood or in youth,
He had imbibed of fear or darker thought
Was melted all away; so true was this,
That sometimes his religion seemed to me
Self-taught, as of a dreamer in the woods;   410
Who to the model of his own pure heart
Shaped his belief, as grace divine inspired,
And human reason dictated with awe.
—And surely never did there live on earth
A man of kindlier nature. The rough sports
And teasing ways of children vexed not him;
Indulgent listener was he to the tongue
Of garrulous age; nor did the sick man's tale,
To his fraternal sympathy addressed,
Obtain reluctant hearing.
                           Plain his garb;   420
Such as might suit a rustic Sire, prepared
For sabbath duties; yet he was a man
Whom no one could have passed without remark.
Active and nervous was his gait; his limbs
And his whole figure breathed intelligence.
Time had compressed the freshness of his cheek
Into a narrower circle of deep red,
But had not tamed his eye; that, under brows
Shaggy and grey, had meanings which it brought
From years of youth; which, like a Being
          made   430
Of many Beings, he had wondrous skill
To blend with knowledge of the years to come,
Human, or such as lie beyond the grave.

    So was He framed; and such his course of life
Who now, with no appendage but a staff,
The prized memorial of relinquished toils,
Upon that cottage-bench reposed his limbs,
Screened from the sun. Supine the Wanderer lay,
His eyes as if in drowsiness half shut,
The shadows of the breezy elms above   440
Dappling his face. He had not heard the sound
Of my approaching steps, and in the shade
Unnoticed did I stand some minutes' space.
At length I hailed him, seeing that his hat
Was moist with water-drops, as if the brim

Had newly scooped a running stream. He rose,
And ere our lively greeting into peace
Had settled, " 'Tis," said I, "a burning day:
My lips are parched with thirst, but you, it seems
Have somewhere found relief." He, at the
    word,   450
Pointing towards a sweet-briar, bade me climb
The fence where that aspiring shrub looked out
Upon the public way. It was a plot
Of garden ground run wild, its matted weeds
Marked with the steps of those, whom, as they
    passed,
The gooseberry trees that shot in long lank slips,
Or currants, hanging from their leafless stems,
In scanty strings, had tempted to o'erleap
The broken wall. I looked around, and there,
Where two tall hedge-rows of thick alder
    boughs   460
Joined in a cold damp nook, espied a well
Shrouded with willow-flowers and plumy fern.
My thirst I slaked, and, from the cheerless spot
Withdrawing, straightway to the shade returned
Where sate the old Man on the cottage bench;
And, while, beside him, with uncovered head,
I yet was standing, freely to respire,
And cool my temples in the fanning air,
Thus did he speak. "I see around me here
Things which you cannot see: we die, my
    Friend,   470
Nor we alone, but that which each man loved
And prized in his peculiar nook of earth
Dies with him, or is changed; and very soon
Even of the good is no memorial left.
—The Poets, in their elegies and songs
Lamenting the departed, call the groves,
They call upon the hills and streams, to mourn,
And senseless rocks; nor idly; for they speak,
In these their invocations, with a voice
Obedient to the strong creative power   480
Of human passion. Sympathies there are
More tranquil, yet perhaps of kindred birth,
That steal upon the meditative mind,
And grow with thought. Beside yon spring I stood,
And eyed its waters till we seemed to feel
One sadness, they and I. For them a bond
Of brotherhood is broken: time has been
When, every day, the touch of human hand
Dislodged the natural sleep that binds them up
In mortal stillness; and they ministered   490
To human comfort. Stooping down to drink,

Upon the slimy foot-stone I espied
The useless fragment of a wooden bowl,
Green with the moss of years, and subject only
To the soft handling of the elements:
There let it lie—how foolish are such thoughts!
Forgive them;—never—never did my steps
Approach this door but she who dwelt within
A daughter's welcome gave me, and I loved her
As my own child. Oh, Sir! the good die first   500
And they whose hearts are dry as summer dust
Burn to the socket. Many a passenger
Hath blessed poor Margaret for her gentle looks,
When she upheld the cool refreshment drawn
From that forsaken spring; and no one came
But he was welcome; no one went away
But that it seemed she loved him. She is dead,
The light extinguished of her lonely hut,
The hut itself abandoned to decay,
And she forgotten in the quiet grave.   510

"I speak," continued he, "of One whose stock
Of virtues bloomed beneath this lonely roof.
She was a Woman of a steady mind,
Tender and deep in her excess of love;
Not speaking much, pleased rather with the joy
Of her own thoughts: by some especial care
Her temper had been framed, as if to make
A Being, who by adding love to peace
Might live on earth a life of happiness.
Her wedded Partner lacked not on his side   520
The humble worth that satisfied her heart:
Frugal, affectionate, sober, and withal
Keenly industrious. She with pride would tell
That he was often seated at his loom,
In summer, ere the mower was abroad
Among the dewy grass,—in early spring,
Ere the last star had vanished.—They who passed
At evening, from behind the garden fence
Might hear his busy spade, which he would ply,
After his daily work, until the light   530
Had failed, and every leaf and flower were lost
In the dark hedges. So their days were spent
In peace and comfort; and a pretty boy
Was their best hope, next to the God in heaven.

    Not twenty years ago, but you I think
Can scarcely bear it now in mind, there came
Two blighting seasons, when the fields were left
With half a harvest. It pleased Heaven to add
A worse affliction in the plague of war:
This happy Land was stricken to the heart!   540

A Wanderer then among the cottages,
I, with my freight of winter raiment, saw
The hardships of that season: many rich
Sank down, as in a dream, among the poor;
And of the poor did many cease to be,
And their place knew them not. Meanwhile,
    abridged
Of daily comforts, gladly reconciled
To numerous self-denials, Margaret
Went struggling on through those calamitous
    years
With cheerful hope, until the second autumn,   550
When her life's Helpmate on a sick-bed lay,
Smitten with perilous fever. In disease
He lingered long; and, when his strength returned,
He found the little he had stored, to meet
The hour of accident or crippling age,
Was all consumed. A second infant now
Was added to the troubles of a time
Laden, for them and all of their degree,
With care and sorrow; shoals of artisans
From ill-requited labour turned adrift   560
Sought daily bread from public charity,
They, and their wives and children—happier far
Could they have lived as do the little birds
That peck along the hedge-rows, or the kite
That makes her dwelling on the mountain rocks!

    A sad reverse it was for him who long
Had filled with plenty, and possessed in peace,
This lonely Cottage. At the door he stood,
And whistled many a snatch of merry tunes
That had no mirth in them; or with his knife   570
Carved uncouth figures on the heads of sticks—
Then, not less idly, sought, through every nook
In house or garden, any casual work
Of use or ornament; and with a strange,
Amusing, yet uneasy, novelty,
He mingled, where he might, the various tasks
Of summer, autumn, winter, and of spring.
But this endured not; his good humour soon
Became a weight in which no pleasure was:
And poverty brought on a petted mood   580
And a sore temper: day by day he dropped,
And he would leave his work—and to the town
Would turn without an errand his slack steps;
Or wander here and there among the fields.
One while he would speak lightly of his babes,
And with a cruel tongue: at other times
He tossed them with a false unnatural joy:

And 'twas a rueful thing to see the looks
Of the poor innocent children. 'Every smile,'
Said Margaret to me, here beneath these
    trees,   590
'Made my heart bleed.' "
              At this the Wanderer paused;
And looking up to those enormous elms,
He said, " 'Tis now the hour of deepest noon.
At this still season of repose and peace,
This hour when all things which are not at rest
Are cheerful; while this multitude of flies
With tuneful hum is filling all the air;
Why should a tear be on an old Man's cheek?
Why should we thus, with an untoward mind,
And in the weakness of humanity,   600
From natural wisdom turn our hearts away;
To natural comfort shut our eyes and ears;
And, feeding on disquiet, thus disturb
The calm of nature with our restless thoughts?"

He spake with somewhat of a solemn tone:
But, when he ended, there was in his face
Such easy cheerfulness, a look so mild,
That for a little time it stole away
All recollection; and that simple tale
Passed from my mind like a forgotten sound.   610
A while on trivial things we held discourse,
To me soon tasteless. In my own despite,
I thought of that poor Woman as of one
Whom I had known and loved. He had rehearsed
Her homely tale with such familiar power,
With such an active countenance, an eye
So busy, that the things of which he spake
Seemed present; and, attention now relaxed,
A heart-felt chillness crept along my veins.
I rose; and, having left the breezy shade,   620
Stood drinking comfort from the warmer sun,
That had not cheered me long—ere, looking round
Upon that tranquil Ruin, I returned,
And begged of the old Man that, for my sake,
He would resume his story.
              He replied,
"It were a wantonness, and would demand
Severe reproof, if we were men whose hearts
Could hold vain dalliance with the misery
Even of the dead; contented thence to draw
A momentary pleasure, never marked   630
By reason, barren of all future good.
But we have known that there is often found
In mournful thoughts, and always might be found,

A power to virtue friendly; were't not so,
I am a dreamer among men, indeed
An idle dreamer! 'Tis a common tale,
An ordinary sorrow of man's life,
A tale of silent suffering, hardly clothed
In bodily form.—But without further bidding
I will proceed.

        While thus it fared with them,   640
To whom this cottage, till those hapless years,
Had been a blessèd home, it was my chance
To travel in a country far remote;
And when these lofty elms once more appeared,
What pleasant expectations lured me on
O'er the flat Common!—With quick step I reached
The threshold, lifted with light hand the latch;
But, when I entered, Margaret looked at me
A little while; then turned her head away
Speechless,—and, sitting down upon a chair,   650
Wept bitterly. I wist not what to do,
Nor how to speak to her. Poor Wretch! at last
She rose from off her seat, and then,—O Sir!
I cannot *tell* how she pronounced my name:—
With fervent love, and with a face of grief
Unutterably helpless, and a look
That seemed to cling upon me, she enquired
If I had seen her husband. As she spake
A strange surprise and fear came to my heart,
Nor had I power to answer ere she told   660
That he had disappeared—not two months gone.
He left his house: two wretched days had past,
And on the third, as wistfully she raised
Her head from off her pillow, to look forth,
Like one in trouble, for returning light,
Within her chamber-casement she espied
A folded paper, lying as if placed
To meet her waking eyes. This tremblingly
She opened—found no writing, but beheld
Pieces of money carefully enclosed,   670
Silver and gold. 'I shuddered at the sight,'
Said Margaret, 'for I knew it was his hand
That must have placed it there; and ere that day
Was ended, that long anxious day, I learned,
From one who by my husband had been sent
With the sad news, that he had joined a troop
Of soldiers, going to a distant land.
—He left me thus—he could not gather heart
To take a farewell of me; for he feared
That I should follow with my babes, and sink   680
Beneath the misery of that wandering life.'

This tale did Margaret tell with many tears:
And, when she ended, I had little power
To give her comfort, and was glad to take
Such words of hope from her own mouth as served
To cheer us both. But long we had not talked
Ere we built up a pile of better thoughts,
And with a brighter eye she looked around
As if she had been shedding tears of joy.
We parted.—'Twas the time of early spring;   690
I left her busy with her garden tools;
And well remember, o'er that fence she looked,
And, while I paced along the foot-way path,
Called out, and sent a blessing after me,
With tender cheerfulness, and with a voice
That seemed the very sound of happy thoughts.

    I roved o'er many a hill and many a dale,
With my accustomed load; in heat and cold,
Through many a wood and many an open ground,
In sunshine and in shade, in wet and fair,   700
Drooping or blithe of heart, as might befall;
My best companions now the driving winds,
And now the 'trotting brooks' and whispering trees,
And now the music of my own sad steps,
With many a short-lived thought that passed
    between,
And disappeared.

        I journeyed back this way,
When, in the warmth of midsummer, the wheat
Was yellow; and the soft and bladed grass,
Springing afresh, had o'er the hay-field spread
Its tender verdure. At the door arrived,   710
I found that she was absent. In the shade,
Where now we sit, I waited her return.
Her cottage, then a cheerful object, wore
Its customary look,—only, it seemed,
The honeysuckle, crowding round the porch,
Hung down in heavier tufts; and that bright weed,
The yellow stone-crop, suffered to take root
Along the window's edge, profusely grew,
Blinding the lower panes. I turned aside,
And strolled into her garden. It appeared   720
To lag behind the season, and had lost
Its pride of neatness. Daisy-flowers and thrift
Had broken their trim border-lines, and straggled
O'er paths they used to deck: carnations, once
Prized for surpassing beauty, and no less
For the peculiar pains they had required,
Declined their languid heads, wanting support.

The cumbrous bind-weed, with its wreaths and
    bells,
Had twined about her two small rows of peas,
And dragged them to the earth
                      Ere this an hour   730
Was wasted.—Back I turned my restless steps;
A stranger passed; and, guessing whom I sought,
He said that she was used to ramble far.—
The sun was sinking in the west; and now
I sate with sad impatience. From within
Her solitary infant cried aloud;
Then, like a blast that dies away self-stilled,
The voice was silent. From the bench I rose;
But neither could divert nor soothe my thoughts.
The spot, though fair, was very desolate—   740
The longer I remained, more desolate:
And, looking round me, now I first observed
The corner stones, on either side the porch,
With dull red stains discoloured, and stuck o'er
With tufts and hairs of wool, as if the sheep,
That fed upon the Common, thither came
Familiarly, and found a couching-place
Even at her threshold. Deeper shadows fell
From these tall elms; the cottage-clock struck
    eight;—
I turned, and saw her distant a few steps.   750
Her face was pale and thin—her figure, too,
Was changed. As she unlocked the door, she said,
'It grieves me you have waited here so long,
But, in good truth, I've wandered much of late;
And sometimes—to my shame I speak—have need
Of my best prayers to bring me back again.'
While on the board she spread our evening meal,
She told me—interrupting not the work
Which gave employment to her listless hands—
That she had parted with her elder child,   760
To a kind master on a distant farm
Now happily apprenticed.—'I perceive
You look at me, and you have cause; today
I have been travelling far; and many days
About the fields I wander, knowing this
Only, that what I seek I cannot find;
And so I waste my time: for I am changed;
And to myself,' said she, 'have done much wrong
And to this helpless infant. I have slept
Weeping, and weeping have I waked; my
    tears   770
Have flowed as if my body were not such
As others are; and I could never die.

But I am now in mind and in my heart
More easy; and I hope,' said she, 'that God
Will give me patience to endure the things
Which I behold at home.'
                    It would have grieved
Your very soul to see her. Sir, I feel
The story linger in my heart; I fear
'Tis long and tedious; but my spirit clings
To that poor Woman:—so familiarly   780
Do I perceive her manner, and her look,
And presence; and so deeply do I feel
Her goodness, that, not seldom, in my walks
A momentary trance comes over me;
And to myself I seem to muse on One
By sorrow laid asleep; or borne away,
A human being destined to awake
To human life, or something very near
To human life, when he shall come again
For whom she suffered. Yes, it would have
    grieved   790
Your very soul to see her: evermore
Her eyelids drooped, her eyes downward were cast;
And, when she at her table gave me food,
She did not look at me. Her voice was low,
Her body was subdued. In every act
Pertaining to her house-affairs, appeared
The careless stillness of a thinking mind
Self-occupied; to which all outward things
Are like an idle matter. Still she sighed,
But yet no motion of the breast was seen,   800
No heaving of the heart. While by the fire
We sate together, sighs came on my ear,
I knew not how, and hardly whence they came.

    Ere my departure, to her care I gave,
For her son's use, some tokens of regard,
Which with a look of welcome she received;
And I exhorted her to place her trust
In God's good love, and seek his help by prayer.
I took my staff, and, when I kissed her babe,
The tears stood in her eyes. I left her then   810
With the best hope and comfort I could give:
She thanked me for my wish;—but for my hope
It seemed she did not thank me.
                    I returned,
And took my rounds along this road again
When on its sunny bank the primrose flower
Peeped forth, to give an earnest of the Spring.
I found her sad and drooping: she had learned

No tidings of her husband; if he lived,
She knew not that he lived; if he were dead,
She knew not he was dead. She seemed the
    same   820
In person and appearance; but her house
Bespake a sleepy hand of negligence;
The floor was neither dry nor neat, the hearth
Was comfortless, and her small lot of books,
Which, in the cottage-window, heretofore
Had been piled up against the corner panes
In seemly order, now, with straggling leaves
Lay scattered here and there, open or shut,
As they had chanced to fall. Her infant Babe
Had from his Mother caught the trick of
    grief,   830
And sighed among its playthings. I withdrew,
And once again entering the garden saw,
More plainly still, that poverty and grief
Were now come nearer to her: weeds defaced
The hardened soil, and knots of withered grass:
No ridges there appeared of clear black mould,
No winter greenness; of her herbs and flowers,
It seemed the better part was gnawed away
Or trampled into earth; a chain of straw,
Which had been twined about the slender
    stem   840
Of a young apple-tree, lay at its root;
The bark was nibbled round by truant sheep.
—Margaret stood near, her infant in her arms,
And, noting that my eye was on the tree,
She said, 'I fear it will be dead and gone
Ere Robert come again.' When to the House
We had returned together, she enquired
If I had any hope:—but for her babe
And for her little orphan boy, she said,
She had no wish to live, that she must die   850
Of sorrow. Yet I saw the idle loom
Still in its place; his Sunday garments hung
Upon the self-same nail; his very staff
Stood undisturbed behind the door.
                            And when,
In bleak December, I retraced this way,
She told me that her babe was dead,
And she was left alone. She now, released
From her maternal cares, had taken up
The employment common through these wilds, and
    gained,
By spinning hemp, a pittance for herself;   860
And for this end had hired a neighbour's boy
To give her needful help. That very time

Most willingly she put her work aside,
And walked with me along the miry road,
Heedless how far; and, in such piteous sort
That any heart had ached to hear her, begged
That, wheresoe'er I went, I still would ask
For him whom she had lost. We parted then—
Our final parting; for from that time forth
Did many seasons pass ere I returned   870
Into this tract again.
                    Nine tedious years;
From their first separation, nine long years,
She lingered in unquiet widowhood;
A Wife and Widow. Needs must it have been
A sore heart-wasting! I have heard, my Friend,
That in yon arbour oftentimes she sate
Alone, through half the vacant sabbath day;
And, if a dog passed by, she still would quit
The shade, and look abroad. On this old bench
For hours she sate; and evermore her eye   880
Was busy in the distance, shaping things
That made her heart beat quick. You see that path,
Now faint,—the grass has crept o'er its grey line;
There, to and fro, she paced through many a day
Of the warm summer, from a belt of hemp
That girt her waist, spinning the long-drawn thread
With backward steps. Yet ever as there passed
A man whose garments showed the soldier's red,
Or crippled mendicant in sailor's garb,
The little child who sate to turn the wheel   890
Ceased from his task; and she with faltering voice
Made many a fond enquiry; and when they,
Whose presence gave no comfort, were gone by,
Her heart was still more sad. And by yon gate,
That bars the traveller's road, she often stood,
And when a stranger horseman came, the latch
Would lift, and in his face look wistfully;
Most happy, if, from aught discovered there
Of tender feeling, she might dare repeat
The same sad question. Meanwhile her poor
    Hut   900
Sank to decay; for he was gone, whose hand,
At the first nipping of October frost,
Closed up each chink, and with fresh bands of
    straw
Chequered the green-grown thatch. And so
    she lived
Through the long winter, reckless and alone;
Until her house by frost, and thaw, and rain,
Was sapped; and while she slept, the nightly
    damps

Did chill her breast; and in the stormy day
Her tattered clothes were ruffled by the wind,
Even at the side of her own fire. Yet still   910
She loved this wretched spot, nor would for worlds
Have parted hence; and still that length of road,
And this rude bench, one torturing hope endeared,
Fast rooted at her heart: and here, my Friend,—
In sickness she remained; and here she died;
Last human tenant of these ruined walls!"

The old Man ceased: he saw that I was moved;
From that low bench, rising instinctively
I turned aside in weakness, nor had power
To thank him for the tale which he had told.   920
I stood, and leaning o'er the garden wall
Reviewed that Woman's sufferings; and it seemed
To comfort me while with a brother's love
I blessed her in the impotence of grief.
Then towards the cottage I returned; and traced
Fondly, though with an interest more mild,
That secret spirit of humanity
Which, 'mid the calm oblivious tendencies
Of nature, 'mid her plants, and weeds, and flowers,
And silent overgrowings, still survived.   930
The old Man, noting this, resumed, and said,
"My Friend! enough to sorrow you have given,
The purposes of wisdom ask no more:
Nor more would she have craved as due to One
Who, in her worst distress, had ofttimes felt
The unbounded might of prayer; and learned,
    with soul
Fixed on the Cross, that consolation springs,
From sources deeper far than deepest pain,
For the meek Sufferer. Why then should we read

The forms of things with an unworthy eye?   940
She sleeps in the calm earth, and peace is here.
I well remember that those very plumes,
Those weeds, and the high spear-grass on that wall,
By mist and silent rain-drops silvered o'er,
As once I passed, into my heart conveyed
So still an image of tranquillity,
So calm and still, and looked so beautiful
Amid the uneasy thoughts which filled my mind,
That what we feel of sorrow and despair
From ruin and from change, and all the grief   950
That passing shows of Being leave behind,
Appeared an idle dream, that could maintain,
Nowhere, dominion o'er the enlightened spirit
Whose meditative sympathies repose
Upon the breast of Faith. I turned away,
And walked along my road in happiness."

He ceased. Ere long the sun declining shot
A slant and mellow radiance, which began
To fall upon us, while beneath the trees,
We sate on that low bench: and now we felt,   960
Admonished thus, the sweet hour coming on.
A linnet warbled from those lofty elms,
A thrush sang loud, and other melodies,
At distance heard, peopled the milder air.
The old Man rose, and, with a sprightly mien
Of hopeful preparation, grasped his staff;
Together casting then a farewell look
Upon those silent walls, we left the shade;
And, ere the stars were visible, had reached
A village-inn,—our evening resting-place.   970
1795–1814   *1814*

Samuel Taylor Coleridge

1772-1834

Although William Wordsworth and Samuel Taylor Coleridge shared the general ideals of the "Preface" to the *Lyrical Ballads*, they were clearly very different human beings and artists. It is as if Coleridge desired to begin at the other side of experience, to focus on the psychological, the mysterious, and the supernatural, and, as he says in the *Biographia Literaria*, "so as to transfer from our inward nature a human interest and a semblance of truth sufficient to procure for these shadows of imagination that willing suspension of disbelief for the moment, which constitutes poetic faith." Less interested in the humble and rustic, in the language of real men, he, from early in his poetic career, concerned himself with the delicate, vivid perception and description of natural objects, with the subtle rendering of complex mental states, with finding, as Richard Haven puts it, a way of rendering symbolically patterns of consciousness. His poetry was to include works as diverse as great conversation poems like "The Eolian Harp" and "Frost at Midnight," his own particular variation of what we have considered in the general introduction as the "Greater Romantic Lyric"; the celebrated trilogy of mystery poems, "Christabel," "The Rime of the Ancient Mariner," and "Kubla Khan"; the extraordinary later poems beginning with "Dejection: An Ode" and including "Limbo," "Ne Plus Ultra," "Work Without Hope," and others in which he probes relentlessly the problems of imaginative loss and emotional paralysis.

Yet, despite differences, he shared with Wordsworth, his friend and associate, the common goal of a poetry of freedom and vitality in which the life of the mind was to play a prominent part. His critical theory and practice, in so many ways a pioneering work, was to reverse the mimetic priorities of Neoclassic critics like

Pope and Johnson, and, in his treatment of Shakespeare, Milton, and his own contemporaries, to focus more on the artist himself, on his peculiar imaginative and emotional power. He sought to probe critically the work of art itself, getting inside of it to understand and to feel the roots of its psychological power. Similarly his religious thought and writing, the central concern of his later years, was to test the relative position of faith and reason in belief, to challenge the stern mechanism of eighteenth-century Deism and the intellectual softness and sentimentality of religion in his search for a synthesis worthy of intelligent believers. More about these matters later in the introduction.

Coleridge was born in the village of Ottery, St Mary, Devonshire, on October 21, 1772, the son of Anne Bowdon and the Reverend John Coleridge, vicar of the parish. Almost from the beginning the pattern of his life seemed fixed. The youngest of fourteen children, he was a loner, a precocious, imaginative child who read voraciously in highly imaginative and often difficult works, listened to the tales of wonder recounted by his father, and amazed his elders of house and neighborhood by his brilliance and articulateness. Strikingly a remembrance of his youth underlines the pattern even more: "I never regarded my *senses* in any way as the criteria of my belief. I regulated all my creeds by my conceptions not by my sight—even at that age."

After his father died in 1781, his mother sent him to Christ's Hospital in London, where he studied diligently, especially classical subjects, with a group of bright classmates under the tutelage of that legendary taskmaster, the Reverend James Boyer, and continued to read without interruption. He met his first love, Mary Evans, and experienced the excitement of the people and places of the great city. When he was nineteen he entered Jesus College, Cambridge, where he had success at first but soon lost his initiative and sense of purpose. The dampness of the college rooms intensified a rheumatic condition he had experienced earlier and may have brought on the first stages of his opium addiction. The year was 1791; revolution was in the European air. He associated himself with the radical element at school, abandoned the Church of England, and became a great admirer of the liberal writings of men like David Hartley and William Godwin. He also grew to like the life of food, wine, and conversation. Debts poured in, and the naive young man, in what now seems like a serio-comic episode, enlisted in the Light Dragoons on December 4, 1793, under the magnificent pseudonym of Silas Tomkyn Comberbache. Only the combined efforts of his brothers George and James got him discharged and returned to Cambridge, but the old resolve was gone, and he never finished a degree.

Shortly after this time he met Robert Southey, poet, practicing radical, and later the anti-hero of Byron's wonderful travesty, *The Vision of Judgment*. Together they talked of a utopian community called Pantisocracy, a communistic community of twelve married couples (Coleridge at this time, more with enthusiasm for his political dreams than with love, became engaged to marry Sarah Fricker, the sister of Southey's wife-to-be) that was to be inaugurated on the banks of the Susquehanna in romantic Pennsylvania. The spirit was willing, but the money was lacking, and the entire scheme, a vain dream, collapsed in

1795. Coleridge, almost out of a sense of duty, married Sarah Fricker, but the relationship was not a happy one.

The year 1795 also brought the first meeting with Wordsworth, and since we have already considered the magic of the friendship, the mutual inspiration it provided and the golden years of creativity it seemed to produce, we will not elaborate any further here. For the better part of the next fifteen years the two poets virtually lived and worked together, with the presence of Dorothy always an additional source of strength, and for a spell Coleridge wrote his best poetry, most notably "The Rime of the Ancient Mariner" and the conversation poems included in his *Poems on Various Subjects* of 1796. He also lectured on politics, edited a short-lived periodical called *The Watchman*, and even tried the Unitarian ministry.

Still there was great personal anguish. An unhappy marriage, no regular income, poor health, and a growing problem with opium addiction left him depressed, but a life annuity of £150 from the famous Wedgewoods, Thomas and Josiah, seemed to offer new hope and promise. The *Lyrical Ballads* had been published; his "Frost at Midnight" and "France: An Ode" were written. Financially more secure, he left for Germany with the Wordsworths in September of 1798 and remained for almost a year, learning the language, and, most important, imbibing deeply the German philosophy that was to nourish that ever-present transcendental strain in his thought. Upon returning to England in July of 1799, he settled in Keswick near the Wordsworths, and continued his German studies, especially of the philosophy of Kant. There seemed no end to his anguish, however, for it was at this time that, trapped in his marriage, he met and fell in love with Sara Hutchinson, Wordsworth's sister-in-law. Coleridge could never marry the one great love of his life.

A trip to Malta and Italy in 1804 to restore his health helped little, and he returned to England in 1806 to separate from his wife and to live with the Wordsworths in Grasmere. He had become a hopeless drug addict. For a time he lectured at the Royal Institution, brought out another periodical called *The Friend* from time to time between June 1809 and March 1810, had his play *Remorse* produced, and, most unhappily, quarrelled with Wordsworth, whose well-intentioned remarks about the state of Coleridge's health were exaggerated and repeated by Basil Montagu. It is all the more miraculous that, in the face of such misfortune, he could have begun his flawed masterpiece of autobiography, critical theory, and practical criticism, the *Biographia Literaria*, in 1815.

The year 1816 was a turning point for Coleridge. In April, a pathetic figure physically weakened by drugs and psychologically distraught, he literally committed himself to the care of Dr. James Gillman in his household at Highgate. Here he spent the rest of his life, gained a measure of inner calm and some control of the opium habit, and produced an amazing variety of work: the strange and remarkably modern nightmare poetry, *The Stateman's Manual* in 1816 and 1817, *The Friend* (with the *Treatise on Method*) in 1818, lectures on poetry in 1818 and 1819, *Aids to Reflection* in 1825, and *On the Constitution of Church and State* in 1830. At Highgate he became a kind of guru, visited by peers and disciples and regarded as a source of great wisdom. His health failed in the early 1830s as he continued to work on his great synthesis, the *Opus Maximum,* and he died on July 25, 1834, a major figure of intellectual and artistic range and achievement.

Talking about Coleridge's career is an almost impossible task; it is perhaps best to talk about his several careers, as poet, as philosopher and critic, as religious thinker. His earliest work is poetic, and not especially distinguished, consisting of dreams of romantic love and utopian communities and of philosophical speculations expressed in bad imitations of eighteenth-century verse filled with stock diction and imagery. Who can forget the blissful picture of the Pantisocratic community with its "cottag'd dell / Where Virtue calm with careless step may stray, / And dancing to the moonlight roundelay, / The wizard passions weave an holy spell." Or the bathos of the young radical's poetic tribute to the unity of all living things, even the "Young Ass" of the poem:

> It seems to say, "And have I then *one* friend?"
> Innocent foal! thou poor despis'd forlorn!
> I hail thee *Brother*—spite of the fool's scorn!
> And fain would take thee with me, in the Dell
> Of peace and mild Equality to dwell,
> Where Toil shall call the charmer Health his bride,
> And Laughter tickle Plenty's ribless side!

There is rapid development in the poems of the 1790s, however, and the development assumes a variety of forms. First, Coleridge, through his conversation poems, continues the tradition of the "Greater Romantic Lyric" already discussed, that blend of description and rumination centered around a solitary speaker and usually silent auditor or auditors. The metrical pattern is the freer flowing blank verse; the manner relaxed and idiomatic; the language and imagery precise, delicate, sensuous; the subject matter the revelation of complex psychological states. In "The Eolian Harp," the speaker, in the presence of an orthodox and watchful Sara, moves from a warm and comforting silent cottage setting:

> How exquisite the scents
> Snatch'd from yon bean-field! and the world *so* hush'd!

to a daring speculation on the lute in the casement, "its strings / Boldlier swept, the long sequacious notes / Over delicious surges sink and rise":

> And what if all of animated nature
> Be but organic Harps diversely fram'd,
> That tremble into thought, as o'er them sweeps
> Plastic and vast, one intellectual breeze,
> At once the Soul of each and God of all?

to an awareness of the wife's dissatisfaction with such pantheistic talk, to a final statement of his "unregenerate mind" and a prayer for God's gift of faith to "A sinful and most miserable man, / Wilder'd and dark."

There is the matter-of-factness of the opening of "This Lime-Tree Bower My Prison" as his friends, especially Charles Lamb to whom he addresses the poem, leave his cottage for a walk while he remains at home because of an accident.

> Well, they are gone, and here I must remain,
> This lime-tree bower my prison! I have lost
> Beauties and feelings such as would have been
> Most sweet to my remembrance even when age
> Had dimm'd mine eyes to blindness!

There is also that formal and moving statement of confidence that, even though absent, he can share imaginatively with his sauntering friends the joys of the "walnut tree," the "ancient ivy," the "late twilight":

> Henceforth I shall know
> That Nature ne'er deserts the wise and pure;
> No plot so narrow, be but Nature there,
> No waste so vacant, but may well employ
> Each faculty of sense, and keep the heart
> Awake to Love and Beauty! and sometimes
> 'Tis well to be bereft of promis'd good,
> That we may lift the soul, and contemplate
> With lively joy the joys we cannot share.

One thinks also of a very different kind of poetry conceived and created during Coleridge's magical years of creativity, especially of the great trio, "Ancient Mariner," "Christabel," and "Kubla Khan." Here he seems much closer to the assignment he drew for himself in the *Lyrical Ballads*, the creation of a world of the mysterious, the preternatural, the supernatural made credible by the gift of the artist in securing "that willing suspension of disbelief that constitutes poetic faith." And yet, despite the variety of genres—ballad, Gothic tale, Oriental ode— the poems share a preoccupation with themes of unity and isolation and a power to evoke silence and wonder through special gifts of verbal and musical magic and of a delicate and sensuous rendering of the beauties of nature and the work- ings of the human psyche. Ever since G. Wilson Knight's stimulating essay called "Coleridge's Divine Comedy," one is attracted by a way of looking at the trilogy as moving from the betrayal, loneliness, and blackness of *Christabel*, to the purga- torial motif of the Mariner's sin, punishment, redemption, and penance, to the ecstatic triumph of the poet in "Kubla Khan." There is a tragic paralysis of the innocent Christabel that renders her unable to express her predicament to her father now captivated by the seductive powers of Geraldine:

> The maid, alas! her thoughts are gone,
> She nothing sees—no sight but one!
> The maid, devoid of guile and sin,
> I know not how, in fearful wise,
> So deeply had she drunken in
> That look, those shrunken serpent eyes,
> That all her features were resigned
> To this sole image in her mind:

> And passively did imitate
> That look of dull and treacherous hate!
> And thus she stood, in dizzy trance,
> Still picturing that look askance
> With forced unconscious sympathy
> Full before her father's view——
> As far as such a look could be
> In eyes so innocent and blue!

There is the great moment of imaginative vision when the Mariner, having shot the albatross and brought death and sterility to his world, sees and blesses the water snakes and the oneness of all living things:

> Within the shadow of the ship
> I watched their rich attire:
> Blue, glossy green, and velvet black,
> They coiled and swam; and every track
> Was a flash of golden fire.
>
> O happy living things! no tongue
> Their beauty might declare:
> A spring of love gushed from my heart,
> And I blessed them unaware:
> Sure my kind saint took pity on me,
> And I blessed them unaware.

And finally there is the almost Dionysiac tone of the closing lines of "Kubla Khan," lines which celebrate the visionary poet whose creations can outrival even the greatest of human creations:

> Could I revive within me
> Her symphony and song,
> To such a deep delight 'twould win me,
> That with music loud and long,
> I would build that dome in air,
> That sunny dome! those caves of ice!
> And all who heard should see them there,
> And all should cry, Beware! Beware!
> His flashing eyes, his floating hair!
> Weave a circle round him thrice,
> And close your eyes with holy dread,
> For he on honey-dew hath fed,
> And drunk the milk of Paradise.

There has been a pronounced tendency to neglect the so-called later poems of Coleridge, to regard them as products of a man physically and psychologically drained, as nightmares unworthy of the name of art. And yet, beginning as early as "Dejection: An Ode" (1804), there is in Coleridge's poetry the sense of loss of psychic energy, of joy, a sense sometimes profoundly ironic because it so brilliantly captures the sense of inner anguish, of a nature no longer alive to the poet. One need only examine poems like "Limbo," "Ne Plus Ultra," "Human Life," or "Work Without Hope" to see a modernity that is remarkable as the poet, often through nightmarish situations and gnarled and disconnected imagery, attempts to communicate the agony of the mind diseased.

Coleridge's next career, as it were, is in the field of literary theory and practical criticism, and here again the search for unity stands out sharply. Nature was for him not the static "one, clear, unchanged, and universal light" of Pope's *Essay on Criticism* nor the marvelous machine of eighteenth-century Deistic thought, but a process, a living force in which universal forms and concrete particulars are constantly interacting. Beauty "is that in which the *many,* still seen as many, become one." It is "Multeity in Unity." Coleridge, following a familiar distinction in German philosophy, argues that through reason we can know the universal, the abstract; through the power of understanding we can know the concrete, the particular. Imagination, the root of genius and of greatness in the arts, is the great completing faculty, mediating between and reconciling opposites to create unity and, in the words of his famous definition from *The Statesman's Manual,* giving "birth to a system of symbols, harmonious in themselves, and consubstantial with the truths of which they are the conductors." A symbol, then, is far more than an ordinary image; it is a translation of reality which, by its persuasive force, renders truth realizable to the human mind.

Given these premises, then, art, and specifically poetry, is not merely a vehicle of self-expression, but a vision of experience, an imitation of what is essential in the creative activity of nature. "The artist," says Coleridge, "must imitate that which is within the thing, that which is active through form and figure, and discourses to us by symbols—the *Natur-geist,* or spirit of nature, as we unconsciously imitate those whom we love; for so only can we hope to produce any work truly natural in the object and truly human in the effect." Hence poetry offers an ideal, the eternal in the temporal, the infinite in the finite, the universal in the particular.

The practical criticism is remarkably faithful to the broad principles of the critical theory. Hence, citing Aristotle in Chapter XVII of his *Biographia Literaria,* he finds Wordsworth's *Lyrical Ballads* wanting because of their over-fidelity in the representation of characters and situations, of their preoccupation with accidental circumstances and details that might be needed to establish the probability of a statement in real life, but which are not the proper concern of art. For him, "poetry as poetry is essentially ideal," avoiding and excluding "all accident"; its "apparent individualities of rank, character, or occupation must be *representative* of a class"; the "*persons* of poetry must be clothed with generic attributes, with the *common* attributes of the class: not such as one gifted individual might *possibly* possess, but such as from his situation it is most probable before-hand that he *would* possess."

Shakespeare is everywhere the poet of nature, minimizing self in his search for truths rooted in reality. He consistently adheres to the great law of nature that opposites tend to attract and modify each other. His plays possess organic form, imitating the living process of nature. In Shakespeare, "Such as the life is, such is the form."

Coleridge's later years are devoted increasingly to the development of his religious thought, a subject-matter that is beyond the scope of this anthology. Again, however, the flashes of brilliance are everywhere, as he struggles to reconcile the conflicting claims of faith and reason, and to develop a liberal Christianity that is responsive to the tradition and yet aware of the staggering changes in life and thought that are so much a part of his age.

In Samuel Taylor Coleridge we see something of Johnson's notion of genius as a mind of large general powers. In his life we see the poet, critic, and philosopher at work, but, most of all, the human being in search of synthesis and unity.

Suggestions For Further Reading

Students of Coleridge still await a definitive biography. W. J. Bate's short critical study called *Coleridge* (1968) is the best view of the life and work, and Molly Lefebure's recent *Samuel Taylor Coleridge: The Bondage of Opium* (1974) is an excellent contribution to our understanding of the toll taken by Coleridge's addiction on his life and work. Norman Fruman's highly controversial *Coleridge: The Damaged Archangel* (1971) has renewed interest in the question of Coleridge's plagiarism.

An early but still useful study of the sources of Coleridge's poems, especially of "The Rime of the Ancient Mariner" and "Kubla Khan," is John Livingston Lowes, *The Road to Xanadu* (1927). Other helpful studies of the poems are Humphry House, *Coleridge* (1953); George Watson, *Coleridge as Poet* (1966); Patricia Adair, *The Waking Dream: A Study of Coleridge's Poetry* (1967); and the appropriate sections of Richard Haven's *Patterns of Consciousness* (1969).

J. A. Appleyard's *Coleridge's Philosophy of Literature* (1965) is an excellent study interested in coming to terms with the roots of Coleridge's critical theory and practice. Earlier works like J. H. Muirhead's *Coleridge as Philosopher* (1930) and Rene Wellek's *Immanuel Kant in England* (1931) are still useful as background studies, and more recent studies like Richard Harter Fogle's *The Idea of Coleridge's Criticism* (1962) and Owen Barfield's *What Coleridge Thought* (1971) are valuable in their attempts to confront some of the central premises of the thought and criticism.

James Boulger's *Coleridge as Religious Thinker* (1961) and J. Robert Barth's *Coleridge and Christian Doctrine* (1969) are the best studies of Coleridge's religious concerns.

All students will appreciate the variety and quality of the essays collected by Kathleen Coburn in *Coleridge: A Collection of Critical Essays* (1967).

PANTISOCRACY *

No more my visionary soul shall dwell
On joys that were; no more endure to weigh
The shame and anguish of the evil day,
Wisely forgetful! O'er the ocean swell
Sublime of Hope, I seek the cottag'd dell
Where Virtue calm with careless step may stray,
And dancing to the moonlight roundelay,
The wizard Passions weave an holy spell.
Eyes that have ach'd with Sorrow! Ye shall weep
Tears of doubt-mingled joy, like theirs who start   10
From Precipices of distemper'd sleep,
On which the fierce-eyed Fiends their revels keep,
And see the rising Sun, and feel it dart
New rays of pleasance trembling to the heart.

1794   *1849*

TO A YOUNG ASS

ITS MOTHER BEING TETHERED
NEAR IT

Poor little Foal of an oppressèd race!
I love the languid patience of thy face:
And oft with gentle hand I give thee bread,
And clap thy ragged coat, and pat thy head.
But what thy dulled spirits hath dismay'd,
That never thou dost sport along the glade?
And (most unlike the nature of things young)
That earthward still thy moveless head is hung?
Do thy prophetic fears anticipate,
Meek Child of Misery! thy future fate?   10
The starving meal, and all the thousand aches
"Which patient Merit of the Unworthy takes"?
Or is thy sad heart thrill'd with filial pain
To see thy wretched mother's shorten'd chain?
And truly, very piteous is *her* lot—
Chain'd to a log within a narrow spot,

TO A YOUNG ASS. 12. The quotation is from *Hamlet*, III, i, 74.

* The Utopian communal society which Coleridge and Robert Southey hoped to establish in America. The plan was never realized.

Where the close-eaten grass is scarcely seen,
While sweet around her waves the tempting green!
Poor Ass! thy master should have learnt to show
Pity—best taught by fellowship of Woe!   20
For much I fear me that *He* lives like thee,
Half famish'd in a land of Luxury!
How *askingly* its footsteps hither bend!
It seems to say, "And have I then *one* friend?"
Innocent foal! thou poor despis'd forlorn!
I hail thee *Brother*—spite of the fool's scorn!
And fain would take thee with me, in the Dell
Of Peace and mild Equality to dwell,
Where Toil shall call the charmer Health his bride,
And Laughter tickle Plenty's ribless side!   30
How thou wouldst toss thy heels in gamesome play,
And frisk about, as lamb or kitten gay!
Yea! and more musically sweet to me
Thy dissonant harsh bray of joy would be,
Than warbled melodies that soothe to rest
The aching of pale Fashion's vacant breast!

1794   *1794*

TO THE REV. W. L. BOWLES *

My heart has thank'd thee, BOWLES! for those soft
        strains
    Whose sadness soothes me, like the murmuring
    Of wild-bees in the sunny showers of spring!
For hence not callous to the mourner's pains

Through Youth's gay prime and thornless paths I
        went:
    And when the mightier Throes of mind began,
    And drove me forth, a thought-bewilder'd man,
Their mild and manliest melancholy lent

A mingled charm, such as the pang consign'd
    To slumber, though the big tear it renew'd;   10
    Bidding a strange mysterious PLEASURE brood
Over the wavy and tumultuous mind,

As the great SPIRIT erst with plastic sweep
Mov'd on the darkness of the unform'd deep.

? 1795 or 1796   *1796*

* William Lisle Bowles (1762–1850), a minor poet whose work young Coleridge greatly admired.

THE EOLIAN HARP

COMPOSED AT CLEVEDON, SOMERSETSHIRE

My pensive Sara! thy soft cheek reclined
Thus on mine arm, most soothing sweet it is
To sit beside our Cot, our Cot o'ergrown
With white-flower'd Jasmin, and the broad-leav'd
        Myrtle,
(Meet emblems they of Innocence and Love!)
And watch the clouds, that late were rich with
        light,
Slow saddening round, and mark the star of eve
Serenely brilliant (such should Wisdom be)
Shine opposite! How exquisite the scents
Snatch'd from yon bean-field! and the world *so*
        hush'd!   10
The stilly murmur of the distant Sea
Tells us of silence.
                        And that simplest Lute,
Placed length-ways in the clasping casement, hark!
How by the desultory breeze caress'd,
Like some coy maid half yielding to her lover,
It pours such sweet upbraiding, as must needs
Tempt to repeat the wrong! And now, its strings
Boldlier swept, the long sequacious notes
Over delicious surges sink and rise,
Such a soft floating witchery of sound   20
As twilight Elfins make, when they at eve
Voyage on gentle gales from Fairy-Land,
Where Melodies round honey-dropping flowers,
Footless and wild, like birds of Paradise,
Nor pause, nor perch, hovering on untam'd wing!
O! the one Life within us and abroad,
Which meets all motion and becomes its soul,
A light in sound, a sound-like power in light,
Rhythm in all thought, and joyance every where—
Methinks, it should have been impossible   30
Not to love all things in a world so fill'd;
Where the breeze warbles, and the mute still air
Is Music slumbering on her instrument.

    And thus, my Love! as on the midway slope
Of yonder hill I stretch my limbs at noon,

Whilst through my half-clos'd eye-lids I behold
The sunbeams dance, like diamonds, on the main,
And tranquil muse upon tranquillity;
Full many a thought uncall'd and undetain'd,
And many idle flitting phantasies,   40
Traverse my indolent and passive brain,
As wild and various as the random gales
That swell and flutter on this subject Lute!

    And what if all of animated nature
Be but organic Harps diversely fram'd,
That tremble into thought, as o'er them sweeps
Plastic and vast, one intellectual breeze,
At once the Soul of each, and God of all?

    But thy more serious eye a mild reproof
Dart, O belovèd Woman! nor such thoughts   50
Dim and unhallow'd dost thou not reject,
And biddest me walk humbly with my God.
Meek Daughter in the family of Christ!
Well hast thou said and holily disprais'd
These shapings of the unregenerate mind;
Bubbles that glitter as they rise and break
On vain Philosophy's aye-babbling spring.
For never guiltless may I speak of him,
The Incomprehensible! save when with awe
I praise him, and with Faith that inly *feels;*   60
Who with his saving mercies healèd me,
A sinful and most miserable man,
Wilder'd and dark, and gave me to possess
Peace, and this Cot, and thee, heart-honour'd Maid!

1795   *1796*

REFLECTIONS ON HAVING LEFT A PLACE OF RETIREMENT °

Low was our pretty Cot: our tallest Rose
Peep'd at the chamber-window. We could hear
At silent noon, and eve, and early morn,
The Sea's faint murmur. In the open air
Our Myrtles blossom'd; and across the porch
Thick Jasmins twined: the little landscape round
Was green and woody, and refresh'd the eye.
It was a spot which you might aptly call

THE EOLIAN HARP. 1. Sara: Coleridge's wife-to-be, Sara
Fricker.

° The home at Clevedon where Coleridge lived for a
short time after his marriage.

The Valley of Seclusion! Once I saw
(Hallowing his Sabbath-day by quietness)   10
A wealthy son of Commerce saunter by,
Bristowa's citizen. methought, it calm'd
His thirst of idle gold, and made him muse
With wiser feelings: for he paus'd, and look'd
With a pleas'd sadness, and gaz'd all around,
Then eyed our Cottage, and gaz'd round again,
And sigh'd, and said, it was a Blessèd Place.
And we *were* bless'd. Oft with patient ear
Long-listening to the viewless sky-lark's note
(Viewless, or haply for a moment seen   20
Gleaming on sunny wings) in whisper'd tones
I've said to my Belovèd, "Such, sweet Girl!
The inobtrusive song of Happiness,
Unearthly minstrelsy! then only heard
When the Soul seeks to hear; when all is hush'd,
And the Heart listens!"
                              But the time, when first
From that low Dell, steep up the stony Mount
I climb'd with perilous toil and reach'd the top,
Oh! what a goodly scene! *Here* the bleak mount,
The bare bleak mountain speckled thin with
        sheep;   30
Grey clouds, that shadowing spot the sunny fields;
And river, now with bushy rocks o'er-brow'd,
Now winding bright and full, with naked banks;
And seats, and lawns, the Abbey and the wood,
And cots, and hamlets, and faint city-spire;
The Channel *there*, the Islands and white sails,
Dim coasts, and cloud-like hills, and shoreless
        Ocean—
It seem'd like Omnipresence! God, methought,
Had built him there a Temple: the whole World
Seem'd *imag'd* in its vast circumference: 40
No *wish* profan'd my overwhelmèd heart.
Blest hour! It was a luxury,—to be!

  Ah! quiet Dell! dear Cot, and Mount sublime!
I was constrain'd to quit you. Was it right,
While my unnumber'd brethren toil'd and bled,
That I should dream away the entrusted hours
On rose-leaf beds, pampering the coward heart
With feelings all too delicate for use?
Sweet is the tear that from some Howard's eye
Drops on the cheek of one he lifts from earth: 50
And he that works me good with unmov'd face,
Does it but half: he chills me while he aids,
My benefactor, not my brother man!
Yet even this, this cold beneficence
Praise, praise it, O my Soul! oft as thou scann'st

The sluggard Pity's vision-weaving tribe!
Who sigh for Wretchedness, yet shun the
        Wretched,
Nursing in some delicious solitude
Their slothful loves and dainty sympathies!
I therefore go, and join head, heart, and hand,   60
Active and firm, to fight the bloodless fight
Of Science, Freedom, and the Truth in Christ.

Yet oft when after honourable toil
Rests the tir'd mind, and waking loves to dream,
My spirit shall revisit thee, dear Cot!
Thy Jasmin and thy window-peeping Rose,
And Myrtles fearless of the mild sea-air.
And I shall sigh fond wishes—sweet Abode!
Ah!—had none greater! And that all had such!
It might be so—but the time is not yet.   70
Speed it, O Father! Let thy Kingdom come!

1795   *1796*

THIS LIME-TREE BOWER
MY PRISON

[ADDRESSED TO CHARLES LAMB,
OF THE INDIA HOUSE, LONDON]

———

In the June of 1797 some long-expected friends[*]
paid a visit to the author's cottage; and on the
morning of their arrival, he met with an accident,
which disabled him from walking during the whole
time of their stay. One evening, when they had left
him for a few hours, he composed the following
lines in the garden-bower. (Coleridge)

———

Well, they are gone, and here must I remain,
This lime-tree bower my prison! I have lost
Beauties and feelings, such as would have been
Most sweet to my remembrance even when age
Had dimm'd mine eyes to blindness! They, mean-
        while,
Friends, whom I never more may meet again,
On springy heath, along the hill-top edge,
Wander in gladness, and wind down, perchance,
To that still roaring dell, of which I told;
The roaring dell, o'erwooded, narrow, deep,   10
And only speckled by the mid-day sun;
Where its slim trunk the ash from rock to rock

———

[*] Charles Lamb and Dorothy and William Wordsworth.

Flings arching like a bridge;—that branchless ash,
Unsunn'd and damp, whose few poor yellow leaves
Ne'er tremble in the gale, yet tremble still,
Fann'd by the water-fall! and there my friends
Behold the dark green file of long lank weeds,
That all at once (a most fantastic sight!)
Still nod and drip beneath the dripping edge
Of the blue clay-stone.

               Now, my friends emerge   20
Beneath the wide wide Heaven—and view again
The many-steepled tract magnificent
Of hilly fields and meadows, and the sea,
With some fair bark, perhaps, whose sails light up
The slip of smooth clear blue betwixt two Isles
Of purple shadow! Yes! they wander on
In gladness all; but thou, methinks, most glad,
My gentle-hearted Charles! for thou hast pined
And hunger'd after Nature, many a year,
In the great City pent, winning thy way   30
With sad yet patient soul, through evil and pain
And strange calamity! Ah! slowly sink
Behind the western ridge, thou glorious Sun!
Shine in the slant beams of the sinking orb,
Ye purple heath-flowers! richlier burn, ye clouds!
Live in the yellow light, ye distant groves!
And kindle, thou blue Ocean! So my friend
Struck with deep joy may stand, as I have stood,
Silent with swimming sense; yea, gazing round
On the wide landscape, gaze till all doth seem   40
Less gross than bodily; and of such hues
As veil the Almighty Spirit, when yet he makes
Spirits perceive his presence.

             A delight
Comes sudden on my heart, and I am glad
As I myself were there! Nor in this bower,
This little lime-tree bower, have I not mark'd
Much that has sooth'd me. Pale beneath the blaze
Hung the transparent foliage; and I watch'd
Some broad and sunny leaf, and lov'd to see
The shadow of the leaf, and stem above   50
Dappling its sunshine! And that walnut-tree
Was richly ting'd, and a deep radiance lay
Full on the ancient ivy, which usurps
Those fronting elms, and now, with blackest mass
Makes their dark branches gleam a lighter hue
Through the late twilight: and though now the bat
Wheels silent by, and not a swallow twitters,
Yet still the solitary humble-bee
Sings in the bean-flower! Henceforth I shall know

That Nature ne'er deserts the wise and pure;   60
No plot so narrow, be but Nature there,
No waste so vacant, but may well employ
Each faculty of sense, and keep the heart
Awake to Love and Beauty! and sometimes
'Tis well to be bereft of promis'd good,
That we may lift the soul, and contemplate
With lively joy the joys we cannot share.
My gentle-hearted Charles! when the last rook
Beat its straight path along the dusky air
Homewards, I blest it! deeming its black wing   70
(Now a dim speck, now vanishing in light)
Had cross'd the mighty Orb's dilated glory,
While thou stood'st gazing; or, when all was still,
Flew creeking o'er thy head, and had a charm
For thee, my gentle-hearted Charles, to whom
No sound is dissonant which tells of Life.

1797   *1800*

THE RIME OF
THE ANCIENT MARINER

*Facile credo, plures esse Naturas invisibiles quam
visibiles in rerum universitate. Sed horum omnium
familiam quis nobis enarrabit? et gradus et cogna-
tiones et discrimina et singulorum munera? Quid
agunt? quae loca habitant? Harum rerum notitiam
semper ambivit ingenium humanum, nunquam atti-
git. Juvat, interea, non diffiteor, quandoque in
animo, tanquam in tabulà, majoris et melioris mundi
imaginem contemplari: ne mens assuefacta hodier-
nae vitae minutiis se contrahat nimis, et tota sub-
sidat in pusillas cogitationes. Sed veritati interea
invigilandum est, modusque servandus, ut certa
ab incertis, diem a nocte, distinguamus.*

        —T. BURNET, *Archaeol. Phil.* p. 68.°

° I readily believe that there are more invisible than
visible things in the universe. But who will tell us of
their families, ranks, similarities and differences? What
do they do? Where do they live? Human knowledge
has always circled around the understanding of these
things but has never achieved it. It is pleasant, however, to contemplate at times, as in a picture, the image
of a greater and better world lest the mind, too accustomed to the details of everyday life, become contracted and dwell completely on trivial things. But
meanwhile we must be watchful of truth and keep
within certain limits so that we may distinguish truth
from opinion, day from night.

ARGUMENT

How a Ship, having first sailed to the Equator, was driven by Storms to the cold Country towards the South Pole; how the Ancient Mariner cruelly and in contempt of the laws of hospitality killed a Sea-bird and how he was followed by many and strange Judgements: and in what manner he came back to his own Country. [*Lyrical Ballads*. ed. of 1800.]

PART I

An ancient Mariner meeteth three Gallants bidden to a wedding-feast, and detaineth one.

It is an ancient Mariner,
And he stoppeth one of three.
"By thy long grey beard and glittering eye,
Now wherefore stopp'st thou me?

The Bridegroom's doors are opened wide,
And I am next of kin;
The guests are met, the feast is set:
May'st hear the merry din."

He holds him with his skinny hand,
"There was a ship," quoth he.   10
"Hold off! unhand me, grey-beard loon!"
Eftsoons his hand dropt he.

The Wedding-Guest is spellbound by the eye of the old seafaring man, and constrained to hear his tale.

He holds him with his glittering eye—
The Wedding-Guest stood still,
And listens like a three years' child:
The Mariner hath his will.

The Wedding-Guest sat on a stone:
He cannot choose but hear;
And thus spake on that ancient man,
The bright-eyed Mariner.   20

"The ship was cheered, the harbour cleared,
Merrily did we drop
Below the kirk, below the hill,
Below the lighthouse top.

The Mariner tells how the ship sailed southward with a good wind and fair weather, till it reached the line.

The Sun came up upon the left,
Out of the sea came he!
And he shone bright, and on the right
Went down into the sea.

Higher and higher every day,
Till over the mast at noon—"   30

The Wedding-Guest here beat his breast,
For he heard the loud bassoon.

The Wedding-Guest heareth the bridal music; but the Mariner continueth his tale.

The bride hath paced into the hall,
Red as a rose is she;
Nodding their heads before her goes
The merry minstrelsy.

The Wedding-Guest he beat his breast,
Yet he cannot choose but hear;
And thus spake on the ancient man,
The bright-eyed Mariner.   40

The ship driven by a storm toward the south pole.

"And now the STORM-BLAST came, and he
Was tyrannous and strong:
He struck with his o'ertaking wings,
And chased us south along.

With sloping masts and dipping prow,
As who pursued with yell and blow
Still treads the shadow of his foe,
And forward bends his head,
The ship drove fast, loud roared the blast,
And southward aye we fled.   50

And now there came both mist and snow,
And it grew wondrous cold:
And ice, mast-high, came floating by,
As green as emerald.

The land of ice, and of fearful sounds where no living thing was to be seen.

And through the drifts the snowy clifts
Did send a dismal sheen:
Nor shapes of men nor beasts we ken—
The ice was all between.

The ice was here, the ice was there,
The ice was all around: 60
It cracked and growled, and roared and howled,
Like noises in a swound!

Till a great sea-bird, called the Albatross, came through the snow-fog, and was received with great joy and hospitality.

At length did cross an Albatross,
Thorough the fog it came;
As if it had been a Christian soul,
We hailed it in God's name.

It ate the food it ne'er had eat,

THE RIME OF THE ANCIENT MARINER. 62. swound: swoon.

And round and round it flew.
The ice did split with a thunder-fit;
The helmsman steered us through!   70

And lo! the Albatross proveth a bird of good omen, and followeth the ship as it returned northward through fog and floating ice.

And a good south wind sprung up
    behind;
The Albatross did follow,
And every day, for food or play,
Came to the mariners' hollo!

In mist or cloud, on mast or shroud,
It perched for vespers nine;
Whiles all the night, through fog-
    smoke white,
Glimmered the white Moon-shine."

The ancient Mariner inhospitably killeth the pious bird of good omen.

"God save thee, ancient Mariner!
From the fiends, that plague thee
    thus!—   80
Why look'st thou so?"—With my
    cross-bow
I shot the ALBATROSS.

PART II

The Sun now rose upon the right:
Out of the sea came he,
Still hid in mist, and on the left
Went down into the sea.

And the good south wind still blew
    behind,
But no sweet bird did follow,
Nor any day for food or play
Came to the mariners' hollo!   90

His shipmates cry out against the ancient Mariner, for killing the bird of good luck.

And I had done a hellish thing,
And it would work 'em woe:
For all averred, I had killed the bird
That made the breeze to blow.
Ah wretch! said they, the bird to slay,
That made the breeze to blow!

But when the fog cleared off, they justify the same, and thus make themselves accomplices in the crime.

Nor dim nor red, like God's own head,
The glorious Sun uprist:
Then all averred, I had killed the bird
That brought the fog and mist.   100
'Twas right, said they, such birds to
    slay,
That bring the fog and mist.

75. **shroud:** the rope that supports the masthead.

The fair breeze continues; the ship enters the Pacific Ocean, and sails north-ward, even till it reaches the Line.

The fair breeze blew, the white foam
    flew,
The furrow followed free;
We were the first that ever burst
Into that silent sea.

Down dropt the breeze, the sails dropt
    down,
'Twas sad as sad could be;
And we did speak only to break
The silence of the sea!   110

The ship hath been suddenly becalmed.

All in a hot and copper sky,
The bloody Sun, at noon,
Right up above the mast did stand,
No bigger than the Moon.

Day after day, day after day,
We stuck, nor breath nor motion;
As idle as a painted ship
Upon a painted ocean.

And the Alba-tross begins to be avenged.

Water, water, every where,
And all the boards did shrink;   120
Water, water, every where,
Nor any drop to drink.

The very deep did rot: O Christ!
That ever this should be!
Yea, slimy things did crawl with legs
Upon the slimy sea.

A Spirit had followed them; one of the invisible inhabitants of this planet, neither de-parted souls nor angels; concerning whom the learned Jew, Josephus, and the Platonic Constantino-politan, Michael Psellus, may be consulted. They are very numerous, and there is no climate or element with-out one or more.

About, about, in reel and rout
The death-fires danced at night;
The water, like a witch's oils,
Burnt green, and blue and
    white.   130

And some in dreams assurèd were
Of the Spirit that plagued us so;
Nine fathom deep he had followed us
From the land of mist and snow.

And every tongue, through utter
    drought,
Was withered at the root;
We could not speak, no more than if
We had been choked with soot.

The shipmates, in their sore distress, would fain throw the whole guilt on the ancient Mariner: in sign whereof they hang the dead sea-bird round his neck.

Ah! well a-day! what evil looks
Had I from old and young!   140
Instead of the cross, the Albatross
About my neck was hung.

PART III

There passed a weary time. Each
    throat
Was parched, and glazed each eye.
A weary time! a weary time!

The ancient Mariner beholdeth a sign in the element afar off.

How glazed each weary eye,
When looking westward, I beheld
A something in the sky.

At first it seemed a little speck,
And then it seemed a mist;   150
It moved and moved, and took at last
A certain shape, I wist.

A speck, a mist, a shape, I wist!
And still it neared and neared:
As if it dodged a water-sprite,
It plunged and tacked and veered.

At its nearer approach, it seemeth him to be a ship; and at a dear ransom he freeth his speech from the bonds of thirst.

With throats unslaked, with black lips
    baked,
We could nor laugh nor wail;
Through utter drought all dumb we
    stood!
I bit my arm, I sucked the blood,   160
And cried, A sail! a sail!

With throats unslaked, with black lips
    baked,
Agape they heard me call:

A flash of joy;

Gramercy! they for joy did grin,
And all at once their breath drew in,
As they were drinking all.

And horror follows. For can it be a ship that comes onward without wind or tide?

See! see! (I cried) she tacks no more!
Hither to work us weal;
Without a breeze, without a tide,
She steadies with upright keel!   170

The western wave was all a-flame.
The day was well nigh done!
Almost upon the western wave
Rested the broad bright Sun;
When that strange shape drove sud-
    denly
Betwixt us and the Sun.

It seemeth him but the skeleton of a ship.

And straight the Sun was flecked with
    bars,
(Heaven's Mother send us grace!)
As if through a dungeon-grate he
    peered
With broad and burning face.   180

And its ribs are seen as bars on the face of the setting Sun.

Alas! (thought I, and my heart beat
    loud)
How fast she nears and nears!
Are those *her* sails that glance in the
    Sun,
Like restless gossameres?

The Spectre-Woman and her Death-mate, and no other on board the skeleton ship.

Are those *her* ribs through which the
    Sun
Did peer, as through a grate?
And is that Woman all her crew?
Is that a DEATH? and are there two?
Is DEATH that woman's mate?

Her lips were red, *her* looks were
    free,   190
Her locks were yellow as gold:
Her skin was as white as leprosy,
The Night-mare LIFE-IN-DEATH was
    she,

Like vessel, like crew!

Who thicks man's blood with cold.

Death and Life-in-death have diced for the ship's crew, and she (the latter) winneth the ancient Mariner.

The naked hulk alongside came,
And the twain were casting dice;
"The game is done! I've won! I've
    won!"
Quoth she, and whistles thrice.

No twilight within the courts of the Sun.

The Sun's rim dips; the stars rush out:
At one stride comes the dark;   200
With far-heard whisper, o'er the sea,
Off shot the spectre-bark.

At the rising of the Moon,

We listened and looked sideways up!
Fear at my heart, as at a cup,
My life-blood seemed to sip!
The stars were dim, and thick the
    night,
The steersman's face by his lamp
    gleamed white;
From the sails the dew did drip—
Till clomb above the eastern bar
The hornèd Moon, with one bright
    star   210
Within the nether tip.

One after another,

One after one, by the star-dogged
    Moon,
Too quick for groan or sigh,
Each turned his face with a ghastly
    pang,
And cursed me with his eye.

His shipmates
drop down
dead.

Four times fifty living men,
(And I heard nor sigh nor groan)
With heavy thump, a lifeless lump,
They dropped down one by one.

But Life-in-
Death begins
her work on
the ancient
Mariner.

The souls did from their bodies
    fly,—   220
They fled to bliss or woe!
And every soul, it passed me by,
Like the whizz of my cross-bow!

PART IV

The Wedding-
Guest feareth
that a Spirit
is talking to
him;

"I fear thee, ancient Mariner!
I fear thy skinny hand!
And thou art long, and lank, and
    brown,
As is the ribbed sea-sand.

I fear thee and thy glittering eye,
And thy skinny hand, so brown."—
Fear not, fear not, thou Wedding-
    Guest!   230
This body dropt not down.

But the
ancient Ma-
riner assureth
him of his
bodily life, and
proceedeth to
relate his hor-
rible penance.

Alone, alone, all, all alone,
Alone on a wide wide sea!
And never a saint took pity on
My soul in agony.

He despiseth
the creatures
of the calm,

The many men, so beautiful!
And they all dead did lie:
And a thousand thousand slimy things
Lived on; and so did I.

And envieth
that *they*
should live,
and so many
lie dead.

I looked upon the rotting sea,   240
And drew my eyes away;
I looked upon the rotting deck,
And there the dead men lay.

I looked to heaven, and tried to pray;
But or ever a prayer had gusht,
A wicked whisper came, and made
My heart as dry as dust.

226–27: For the last two lines of this stanza I am
indebted to Mr. Wordsworth. It was on a delightful
walk from Nether Stowey to Dulverton, with him and
his sister, in the Autumn of 1797, that this poem was
planned, and in part composed (Coleridge).

I closed my lids, and kept them close,
And the balls like pulses beat;
For the sky and the sea, and the sea
    and the sky   250
Lay like a load on my weary eye,
And the dead were at my feet.

But the curse
liveth for him
in the eye of
the dead men.

The cold sweat melted from their
    limbs,
Nor rot nor reek did they:
The look with which they looked on
    me
Had never passed away.

In his lone-
liness and
fixedness he
yearneth to-
wards the
journeying
Moon, and the
stars that still
sojourn, yet
still move
onward; and
every where
the blue sky
belongs to
them, and is
their ap-
pointed rest,
and their
native country
and their own
natural homes,
which they
enter unan-
nounced, as
lords that are
certainly ex-
pected and yet
there is a silent
joy at their
arrival.

An orphan's curse would drag to hell
A spirit from on high;
But oh! more horrible than that
Is the curse in a dead man's eye!   260
Seven days, seven nights, I saw that
    curse,
And yet I could not die.

The moving Moon went up the sky,
And no where did abide:
Softly she was going up,
And a star or two beside—

Her beams bemocked the sultry main,
Like April hoar-frost spread;
But where the ship's huge shadow lay,
The charmèd water burnt alway   270
A still and awful red.

By the light
of the Moon
he beholdeth
God's crea-
tures of the
great calm.

Beyond the shadow of the ship,
I watched the water-snakes:
They moved in tracks of shining white,
And when they reared, the elfish light
Fell off in hoary flakes.

Within the shadow of the ship
I watched their rich attire:
Blue, glossy green, and velvet black,
They coiled and swam; and every
    track   280
Was a flash of golden fire.

Their beauty
and their
happiness.

O happy living things! no tongue
Their beauty might declare:
A spring of love gushed from my
    heart,
And I blessed them unaware:
Sure my kind saint took pity on me,
And I blessed them unaware.

He blesseth
them in his
heart.

The self-same moment I could pray;
And from my neck so free
The Albatross fell off, and sank   290
Like lead into the sea.

PART V

Oh sleep! it is a gentle thing,
Beloved from pole to pole!
To Mary Queen the praise be given!
She sent the gentle sleep from Heaven,
That slid into my soul.

By grace of
the holy
Mother, the
ancient
Mariner is
refreshed with
rain.

The silly buckets on the deck,
That had so long remained,
I dreamt that they were filled with
    dew;
And when I awoke, it rained.   300

My lips were wet, my throat was cold,
My garments all were dank;
Sure I had drunken in my dreams,
And still my body drank.

I moved, and could not feel my limbs:
I was so light—almost
I thought that I had died in sleep,
And was a blessèd ghost.

He heareth
sounds and
seeth strange
sights and
commotions
in the sky and
the element.

And soon I heard a roaring wind:
It did not come anear;   310
But with its sound it shook the sails,
That were so thin and sere.

The upper air burst into life!
And a hundred fire-flags sheen,
To and fro they were hurried about!
And to and fro, and in and out,
The wan stars danced between.

And the coming wind did roar more
    loud,
And the sails did sigh like sedge;
And the rain poured down from one
    black cloud;   320
The Moon was at its edge.

The thick black cloud was cleft, and
    still
The Moon was at its side:
Like waters shot from some high crag,
The lightning fell with never a jag,
A river steep and wide.

The bodies of
the ship's crew
are inspired
and the ship
moves on;

The loud wind never reached the ship,
Yet now the ship moved on!
Beneath the lightning and the Moon
The dead men gave a groan.   330

They groaned, they stirred, they all
    uprose,
Nor spake, nor moved their eyes;
It had been strange, even in a dream,
To have seen those dead men rise.

The helmsman steered, the ship moved
    on;
Yet never a breeze up-blew;
The mariners all 'gan work the ropes,
Where they were wont to do;
They raised their limbs like lifeless
    tools—
We were a ghastly crew.   340

The body of my brother's son
Stood by me, knee to knee:
The body and I pulled at one rope,
But he said nought to me.

"I fear thee, ancient Mariner!"
Be calm, thou Wedding-Guest!
'Twas not those souls that fled in pain,
Which to their corses came again,
But a troop of spirits blest:

But not by the
souls of the
men, nor by
daemons of
earth or
middle air, but
by a blessed
troop of
angelic spirits,
sent down by
the invocation
of the guar-
dian saint.

For when it dawned—they dropped
    their arms,   350
And clustered round the mast;
Sweet sounds rose slowly through their
    mouths,
And from their bodies passed.

Around, around, flew each sweet
    sound,
Then darted to the Sun;
Slowly the sounds came back again,
Now mixed, now one by one.

Sometimes a-dropping from the sky
I heard the sky-lark sing;
Sometimes all little birds that
    are,   360
How they seemed to fill the sea and
    air
With their sweet jargoning!

And now 'twas like all instruments,
Now like a lonely flute;
And now it is an angel's song,
That makes the heavens be mute.

It ceased; yet still the sails made on
A pleasant noise till noon,
A noise like of a hidden brook
In the leafy month of June,   370
That to the sleeping woods all night
Singeth a quiet tune.

Till noon we quietly sailed on,
Yet never a breeze did breathe:
Slowly and smoothly went the ship,
Moved onward from beneath.

The lonesome Spirit from the south-pole carries on the ship as far as the Line, in obedience to the angelic troop, but still requireth vengeance.

Under the keel nine fathom deep,
From the land of mist and snow,
The spirit slid: and it was he
That made the ship to go.   380
The sails at noon left off their tune,
And the ship stood still also.

The Sun, right up above the mast,
Had fixed her to the ocean:
But in a minute she 'gan stir,
With a short uneasy motion—
Backwards and forwards half her
          length
With a short uneasy motion.

Then like a pawing horse let go,
She made a sudden bound: 390
It flung the blood into my head,
And I fell down in a swound.

The Polar Spirit's fellow-daemons, the invisible inhabitants of the element, take part in his wrong; and two of them relate, one to the other, that penance long and heavy for the ancient Mariner hath been accorded to the Polar Spirit, who returneth southward.

How long in that same fit I lay,
I have not to declare;
But ere my living life returned,
I heard and in my soul discerned
Two voices in the air.

"Is it he?" quoth one, "Is this the man?
By him who died on cross,
With his cruel bow he laid full
          low   400
The harmless Albatross.

The spirit who bideth by himself
In the land of mist and snow,
He loved the bird that loved the man
Who shot him with his bow."

The other was a softer voice,
As soft as honey-dew:
Quoth he, "The man hath penance
          done,
And penance more will do."

PART VI

FIRST VOICE

"But tell me, tell me! speak
          again,   410
Thy soft response renewing—
What makes that ship drive on so fast?
What is the ocean doing?"

SECOND VOICE

"Still as a slave before his lord,
The ocean hath no blast;
His great bright eye most silently
Up to the Moon is cast—

If he may know which way to go;
For she guides him smooth or grim.
See, brother, see! how graciously   420
She looketh down on him."

FIRST VOICE

The Mariner hath been cast into a trance; for the angelic power causeth the vessel to drive northward faster than human life could endure.

"But why drives on that ship so fast,
Without or wave or wind?"

SECOND VOICE

"The air is cut away before,
And closes from behind.

Fly, brother, fly! more high, more
          high!
Or we shall be belated:
For slow and slow that ship will go,
When the Mariner's trance is abated."

The supernatural motion is retarded; the Mariner awakes, and his penance begins anew.

I woke, and we were sailing on   430
As in a gentle weather:
'Twas night, calm night, the moon was
          high;
The dead men stood together.

All stood together on the deck,
For a charnel-dungeon fitter:
All fixed on me their stony eyes,
That in the Moon did glitter.

The pang, the curse, with which they
    died,
Had never passed away:
I could not draw my eyes from
    theirs,   440
Nor turn them up to pray.

*The curse is
finally ex-
piated.*

And now this spell was snapt: once
    more
I viewed the ocean green,
And looked far forth, yet little saw
Of what had else been seen—

Like one, that on a lonesome road
Doth walk in fear and dread,
And living once turned round walks
    on,
And turns no more his head;
Because he knows, a frightful
    fiend   450
Doth close behind him tread.

But soon there breathed a wind on
    me,
Nor sound nor motion made:
Its path was not upon the sea,
In ripple or in shade.

It raised my hair, it fanned my cheek
Like a meadow-gale of spring—
It mingled strangely with my fears,
Yet it felt like a welcoming.

Swiftly, swiftly flew the ship,   460
Yet she sailed softly too:
Sweetly, sweetly blew the breeze—
On me alone it blew.

*And the
ancient
Mariner be-
holdeth his
native
country.*

Oh! dream of joy! is this indeed
The light-house top I see?
Is this the hill? is this the kirk?
Is this mine own countree?

We drifted o'er the harbour-bar,
And I with sobs did pray—
O let me be awake, my God!   470
Or let me sleep alway.

The harbour-bay was clear as glass,
So smoothly it was strewn!
And on the bay the moonlight lay,
And the shadow of the Moon.

The rock shone bright, the kirk no
    less,
That stands above the rock:
The moonlight steeped in silentness
The steady weathercock.

And the bay was white with silent
    light,   480
Till rising from the same,
Full many shapes, that shadows were,
In crimson colours came.

*The angelic
spirits leave
the dead
bodies,*

*And appear in
their own
forms of light.*

A little distance from the prow
Those crimson shadows were:
I turned my eyes upon the deck—
Oh, Christ! what saw I there!

Each corse lay flat, lifeless and flat,
And, by the holy rood!
A man all light, a seraph-man,   490
On every corse there stood.

This seraph-band, each waved his
    hand:
It was a heavenly sight!
They stood as signals to the land,
Each one a lovely light;

This seraph-band, each waved his
    hand,
No voice did they impart—
No voice; but oh! the silence sank
Like music on my heart.

But soon I heard the dash of
    oars,   500
I heard the Pilot's cheer;
My head was turned perforce away
And I saw a boat appear.

The Pilot and the Pilot's boy,
I heard them coming fast:
Dear Lord in Heaven! it was a joy
The dead men could not blast.

I saw a third—I heard his voice:
It is the Hermit good!
He singeth loud his godly hymns   510
That he makes in the wood.
He'll shrieve my soul, he'll wash away
The Albatross's blood.

PART VII

The Hermit of
the Wood,

This Hermit good lives in that wood
Which slopes down to the sea.
How loudly his sweet voice he rears!
He loves to talk with marineres
That come from a far countree.

He kneels at morn, and noon, and
  eve—
He hath a cushion plump: 520
It is the moss that wholly hides
The rotted old oak-stump.

The skiff-boat neared: I heard them
  talk,
"Why, this is strange, I trow!
Where are those lights so many and
  fair,
That signal made but now?"

Approacheth
the ship with
wonder.

"Strange, by my faith!" the Hermit
  said—
"And they answered not our cheer!
The planks looked warped! and see
  those sails,
How thin they are and sere! 530
I never saw aught like to them,
Unless perchance it were

Brown skeletons of leaves that lag
My forest-brook along;
When the ivy-tod is heavy with snow,
And the owlet whoops to the wolf be-
  low,
That eats the she-wolf's young."

"Dear Lord! it hath a fiendish look—
(The Pilot made reply)
I am a-feared"—"Push on, push
  on!" 540
Said the Hermit cheerily.

The boat came closer to the ship,
But I nor spake nor stirred;
The boat came close beneath the ship,
And straight a sound was heard.

The ship
suddenly
sinketh.

Under the water it rumbled on,
Still louder and more dread:
It reached the ship, it split the bay;
The ship went down like lead.

535. **ivy-tod:** ivy-bush.

The ancient
Mariner is
saved in the
Pilot's boat.

Stunned by that loud and dreadful
  sound, 550
Which sky and ocean smote,
Like one that hath been seven days
  drowned
My body lay afloat;
But swift as dreams myself I found
Within the Pilot's boat.

Upon the whirl, where sank the ship,
The boat spun round and round;
And all was still, save that the hill
Was telling of the sound.

I moved my lips—the Pilot
  shrieked 560
And fell down in a fit;
The holy Hermit raised his eyes,
And prayed where he did sit.

I took the oars: the Pilot's boy,
Who now doth crazy go,
Laughed loud and long, and all the
  while
His eyes went to and fro.
"Ha! ha!" quoth he, "full plain I see,
The Devil knows how to row."

And now, all in my own
  countree, 570
I stood on the firm land!
The Hermit stepped forth from the
  boat,
And scarcely he could stand.

The ancient
Mariner
earnestly en-
treateth the
Hermit to
shrieve him;
and the
penance of
life falls on
him.

"O shrieve me, shrieve me, holy man!"
The Hermit crossed his brow.
"Say quick," quoth he, "I bid thee
  say—
What manner of man art thou?"

Forthwith this frame of mine was
  wrenched
With a woeful agony,
Which forced me to begin my
  tale; 580
And then it left me free.

And ever and
anon through
out his future
life an agony
constraineth
him to travel
from land to
land;

Since then, at an uncertain hour,
That agony returns:
And till my ghastly tale is told,
This heart within me burns.

I pass, like night, from land to land;
I have strange power of speech;
That moment that his face I see,
I know the man that must hear me:
To him my tale I teach.   590

What loud uproar bursts from that
        door!
The wedding-guests are there:
But in the garden-bower the bride
And bride-maids singing are:
And hark the little vesper bell,
Which biddeth me to prayer!

O Wedding-Guest! this soul hath been
Alone on a wide wide sea:
So lonely 'twas that God himself
Scarce seemèd there to be.   600

O sweeter than the marriage-feast,
'Tis sweeter far to me,
To walk together to the kirk
With a goodly company!—

To walk together to the kirk,
And all together pray,
While each to his great Father bends,
Old men, and babes, and loving
        friends
And youths and maidens gay!

And to teach, by his own example, love and reverence to all things that God made and loveth.

Farewell, farewell! but this I tell   610
To thee, thou Wedding-Guest!
He prayeth well, who loveth well
Both man and bird and beast.

He prayeth best, who loveth best
All things both great and small;
For the dear God who loveth us,
He made and loveth all.

The Mariner, whose eye is bright,
Whose beard with age is hoar,
Is gone: and now the Wedding-
        Guest   620
Turned from the bridegroom's door.

He went like one that hath been
        stunned,
And is of sense forlorn:
A sadder and a wiser man,
He rose the morrow morn.

CHRISTABEL

PREFACE

The first part of the following poem was written in the year 1797, at Stowey, in the county of Somerset. The second part, after my return from Germany, in the year 1800, at Keswick, Cumberland. It is probable that if the poem had been finished at either of the former periods, or if even the first and second part had been published in the year 1800, the impression of its originality would have been much greater than I dare at present expect. But for this I have only my own indolence to blame. The dates are mentioned for the exclusive purpose of precluding charges of plagiarism or servile imitation from myself. For there is amongst us a set of critics, who seem to hold, that every possible thought and image is traditional; who have no notion that there are such things as fountains in the world, small as well as great; and who would therefore charitably derive every rill they behold flowing, from a perforation made in some other man's tank. I am confident, however, that as far as the present poem is concerned, the celebrated poets whose writings I might be suspected of having imitated, either in particular passages, or in the tone and the spirit of the whole, would be among the first to vindicate me from the charge, and who, on any striking coincidence, would permit me to address them in this doggerel version of two monkish Latin hexameters.

'Tis mine and it is likewise yours;
But an if this will not do;
Let it be mine, good friend! for I
Am the poorer of the two.

I have only to add that the metre of Christabel is not, properly speaking, irregular, though it may seem so from its being founded on a new principle: namely, that of counting in each line the accents, not the syllables. Though the latter may vary from seven to twelve, yet in each line the accents will be found to be only four. Nevertheless, this occasional variation in number of syllables is not introduced wantonly, or for the mere ends of convenience, but in correspondence with some transition in the nature of the imagery or passion.

PART I

'Tis the middle of night by the castle clock,
And the owls have awakened the crowing cock;
Tu—whit!——Tu—whoo!

And hark, again! the crowing cock,
How drowsily it crew.

Sir Leoline, the Baron rich,
Hath a toothless mastiff bitch;
From her kennel beneath the rock
She maketh answer to the clock,
Four for the quarters, and twelve for the hour;   10
Ever and aye, by shine and shower,
Sixteen short howls, not over loud;
Some say, she sees my lady's shroud.

Is the night chilly and dark?
The night is chilly, but not dark.
The thin gray cloud is spread on high,
It covers but not hides the sky.
The moon behind, and at the full;
And yet she looks both small and dull.
The night is chill, the cloud is gray: 20
'Tis a month before the month of May,
And the Spring comes slowly up this way.

The lovely lady, Christabel,
Whom her father loves so well,
What makes her in the wood so late,
A furlong from the castle gate?
She had dreams all yesternight
Of her own betrothèd knight;
And she in the midnight wood will pray
For the weal of her lover that's far away.   30

She stole along, she nothing spoke,
The sighs she heaved were soft and low,
And naught was green upon the oak
But moss and rarest mistletoe:
She kneels beneath the huge oak tree,
And in silence prayeth she.

The lady sprang up suddenly,
The lovely lady, Christabel!
It moaned as near, as near can be,
But what it is she cannot tell.—   40
On the other side it seems to be,
Of the huge, broad-breasted, old oak tree.

The night is chill; the forest bare;
Is it the wind that moaneth bleak?
There is not wind enough in the air
To move away the ringlet curl
From the lovely lady's cheek—
There is not wind enough to twirl
The one red leaf, the last of its clan,
That dances as often as dance it can,   50

Hanging so light, and hanging so high,
On the topmost twig that looks up at the sky.

Hush, beating heart of Christabel!
Jesu, Maria, shield her well!
She folded her arms beneath her cloak,
And stole to the other side of the oak.
    What sees she there?

There she sees a damsel bright,
Drest in a silken robe of white,
That shadowy in the moonlight shone: 60
The neck that made that white robe wan,
Her stately neck, and arms were bare;
Her blue-veined feet unsandal'd were,
And wildly glittered here and there
The gems entangled in her hair.
I guess, 'twas frightful there to see
A lady so richly clad as she—
Beautiful exceedingly!

Mary mother, save me now!
(Said Christabel,) And who art thou?   70

The lady strange made answer meet,
And her voice was faint and sweet:—
Have pity on my sore distress,
I scarce can speak for weariness:
Stretch forth thy hand, and have no fear!
Said Christabel, How camest thou here?
And the lady, whose voice was faint and sweet,
Did thus pursue her answer meet:—

My sire is of a noble line,
And my name is Geraldine: 80
Five warriors seized me yestermorn,
Me, even me, a maid forlorn:
They choked my cries with force and fright,
And tied me on a palfrey white.
The palfrey was as fleet as wind,
And they rode furiously behind.
They spurred amain, their steeds were white:
And once we crossed the shade of night.
As sure as Heaven shall rescue me,
I have no thought what men they be;   90
Nor do I know how long it is
(For I have lain entranced I wis)
Since one, the tallest of the five,
Took me from the palfrey's back,
A weary woman, scarce alive.
Some muttered words his comrades spoke:
He placed me underneath this oak;

He swore they would return with haste;
Whither they went I cannot tell—
I thought I heard, some minutes past,   100
Sounds as of a castle bell.
Stretch forth thy hand (thus ended she),
And help a wretched maid to flee.

Then Christabel stretched forth her hand,
And comforted fair Geraldine:
O well, bright dame! may you command
The service of Sir Leoline;
And gladly our stout chivalry
Will he send forth and friends withal
To guide and guard you safe and free   110
Home to your noble father's hall.

She rose: and forth with steps they passed
That strove to be, and were not, fast.
Her gracious stars the lady blest,
And thus spake on sweet Christabel:
All our household are at rest,
The hall as silent as the cell;
Sir Leoline is weak in health,
And may not well awakened be,
But we will move as if in stealth,   120
And I beseech your courtesy,
This night, to share your couch with me.

They crossed the moat, and Christabel
Took the key that fitted well;
A little door she opened straight,
All in the middle of the gate;
The gate that was ironed within and without,
Where an army in battle array had marched out.
The lady sank, belike through pain,
And Christabel with might and main   130
Lifted her up, a weary weight,
Over the threshold of the gate:
Then the lady rose again,
And moved, as she were not in pain.

So free from danger, free from fear,
They crossed the court: right glad they were.
And Christabel devoutly cried
To the lady by her side,
Praise we the Virgin all divine
Who hath rescued thee from thy distress!   140
Alas, alas! said Geraldine,
I cannot speak for weariness.
So free from danger, free from fear,
They crossed the court: right glad they were.

Outside her kennel, the mastiff old
Lay fast asleep, in moonshine cold.
The mastiff old did not awake,
Yet she an angry moan did make!
And what can ail the mastiff bitch?
Never till now she uttered yell   150
Beneath the eye of Christabel.
Perhaps it is the owlet's scritch:
For what can ail the mastiff bitch?

They passed the hall, that echoes still,
Pass as lightly as you will!
The brands were flat, the brands were dying,
Amid their own white ashes lying;
But when the lady passed, there came
A tongue of light, a fit of flame;
And Christabel saw the lady's eye,   160
And nothing else saw she thereby,
Save the boss of the shield of Sir Leoline tall,
Which hung in a murky old niche in the wall.
O softly tread, said Christabel,
My father seldom sleepeth well.

Sweet Christabel her feet doth bare,
And jealous of the listening air
They steal their way from stair to stair,
Now in glimmer, and now in gloom,
And now they pass the Baron's room,   170
As still as death, with stifled breath!
And now have reached the chamber door;
And now doth Geraldine press down
The rushes of the chamber floor.

The moon shines dim in the open air,
And not a moonbeam enters here.
But they without its light can see
The chamber carved so curiously,
Carved with figures strange and sweet,
All made out of the carver's brain,   180
For a lady's chamber meet:
The lamp with twofold silver chain
Is fastened to an angel's feet.

The silver lamp burns dead and dim;
But Christabel the lamp will trim.
She trimmed the lamp, and made it bright,
And left it swinging to and fro,
While Geraldine, in wretched plight,
Sank down upon the floor below.

O weary lady, Geraldine,   190
I pray you, drink this cordial wine!

It is a wine of virtuous powers;
My mother made it of wild flowers.

And will your mother pity me,
Who am a maiden most forlorn?
Christabel answered—Woe is me!
She died the hour that I was born.
I have heard the grey-haired friar tell
How on her death-bed she did say,
That she should hear the castle-bell   200
Strike twelve upon my wedding-day.
O mother dear! that thou wert here!
I would, said Geraldine, she were!

But soon with altered voice, said she—
"Off, wandering mother! Peak and pine!
I have power to bid thee flee."
Alas! what ails poor Geraldine?
What stares she with unsettled eye?
Can she the bodiless dead espy?
And why with hollow voice cries she,   210
"Off, woman, off! this hour is mine—
Though thou her guardian spirit be,
Off, woman, off! 'tis given to me."

Then Christabel knelt by the lady's side,
And raised to heaven her eyes so blue—
Alas! said she, this ghastly ride—
Dear lady! it hath wildered you!
The lady wiped her moist cold brow,
And faintly said, " 'tis over now!"

Again the wild-flower wine she drank: 220
Her fair large eyes 'gan glitter bright,
And from the floor whereon she sank,
The lofty lady stood upright:
She was most beautiful to see,
Like a lady of a far countree.

And thus the lofty lady spake—
"All they who live in the upper sky,
Do love you, holy Christabel!
And you love them, and for their sake
And for the good which me befel,   230
Even I in my degree will try,
Fair maiden, to requite you well.
But now unrobe yourself; for I
Must pray, ere yet in bed I lie."

Quoth Christabel, So let it be!
And as the lady bade, did she.
Her gentle limbs did she undress,
And lay down in her loveliness.

But through her brain of weal and woe
So many thoughts moved to and fro,   240
That vain it were her lids to close;
So half-way from the bed she rose,
And on her elbow did recline
To look at the lady Geraldine.

Beneath the lamp the lady bowed,
And slowly rolled her eyes around;
Then drawing in her breath aloud,
Like one that shuddered, she unbound
The cincture from beneath her breast:
Her silken robe, and inner vest,   250
Dropt to her feet, and full in view,
Behold! her bosom and half her side—
A sight to dream of, not to tell!
O shield her! shield sweet Christabel!

Yet Geraldine nor speaks nor stirs;
Ah! what a stricken look was hers!
Deep from within she seems half-way
To lift some weight with sick assay,
And eyes the maid and seeks delay;
Then suddenly as one defied,   260
Collects herself in scorn and pride,
And lay down by the Maiden's side!—
And in her arms the maid she took,
          Ah wel-a-day!
And with low voice and doleful look
These words did say:
"In the touch of this bosom there worketh a spell,
Which is lord of thy utterance, Christabel!
Thou knowest to-night, and wilt know to-
          morrow,   270
This mark of my shame, this seal of my sorrow;
          But vainly thou warrest,
              For this is alone in
              Thy power to declare,
                 That in the dim forest
              Thou heard'st a low moaning,
And found'st a bright lady, surpassingly fair;
And didst bring her home with thee in love and in
          charity,
To shield her and shelter her from the damp air."

THE CONCLUSION TO PART I

It was a lovely sight to see   280
The lady Christabel, when she
Was praying at the old oak tree.
     Amid the jaggèd shadows

Of mossy leafless boughs,
    Kneeling in the moonlight,
    To make her gentle vows;
Her slender palms together prest,
Heaving sometimes on her breast;
Her face resigned to bliss or bale—
Her face, oh call it fair not pale,
And both blue eyes more bright than clear,   290
Each about to have a tear.

With open eyes (ah woe is me!)
Asleep, and dreaming fearfully,
Fearfully dreaming, yet, I wis,
Dreaming that alone, which is—
O sorrow and shame! Can this be she,
The lady, who knelt at the old oak tree?
And lo! the worker of these harms,
That holds the maiden in her arms,
Seems to slumber still and mild,   300
As a mother with her child.

A star hath set, a star hath risen,
O Geraldine! since arms of thine
Have been the lovely lady's prison.
O Geraldine! one hour was thine—
Thou'st had thy will! By tairn and rill,
The night-birds all that hour were still.
But now they are jubilant anew,
From cliff and tower, tu—whoo! tu—whoo!
Tu—whoo! tu—whoo! from wood and fell!   310

And see! the lady Christabel
Gathers herself from out her trance;
Her limbs relax, her countenance
Grows sad and soft; the smooth thin lids
Close o'er her eyes; and tears she sheds—
Large tears that leave the lashes bright!
And oft the while she seems to smile
As infants at a sudden light!

Yea, she doth smile, and she doth weep,
Like a youthful hermitess,   320
Beauteous in a wilderness,
Who, praying always, prays in sleep.
And, if she move unquietly,
Perchance, 'tis but the blood so free
Comes back and tingles in her feet.
No doubt, she hath a vision sweet.
What if her guardian spirit 'twere,
What if she knew her mother near?
But this she knows, in joys and woes,

That saints will aid if men will call: 330
For the blue sky bends over all!

PART II

Each matin bell, the Baron saith,
Knells us back to a world of death.
These words Sir Leoline first said,
When he rose and found his lady dead:
These words Sir Leoline will say
Many a morn to his dying day!

And hence the custom and law began
That still at dawn the sacristan,
Who duly pulls the heavy bell,   340
Five and forty beads must tell
Between each stroke—a warning knell,
Which not a soul can choose but hear
From Bratha Head to Wyndermere.

Saith Bracy the bard, So let it knell!
And let the drowsy sacristan
Still count as slowly as he can!
There is no lack of such, I ween,
As well fill up the space between.
In Langdale Pike and Witch's Lair,   350
And Dungeon-ghyll so foully rent,
With ropes of rock and bells of air
Three sinful sextons' ghosts are pent,
Who all give back, one after t'other,
The death-note to their living brother;
And oft too, by the knell offended,
Just as their one! two! three! is ended,
The devil mocks the doleful tale
With a merry peal from Borodale.

The air is still! through mist and cloud   360
That merry peal comes ringing loud;
And Geraldine shakes off her dread,
And rises lightly from the bed;
Puts on her silken vestments white,
And tricks her hair in lovely plight,
And nothing doubting of her spell
Awakens the lady Christabel.
"Sleep you, sweet lady Christabel?
I trust that you have rested well."

CHRISTABEL. **344. Bratha Head to Wyndermere:** These
and the places referred to in lines 350–59 are in the
Lake District of northern England. **365. plight:** braid.

And Christabel awoke and spied   370
The same who lay down by her side—
O rather say, the same whom she
Raised up beneath the old oak tree!
Nay, fairer yet! and yet more fair!
For she belike hath drunken deep
Of all the blessedness of sleep!
And while she spake, her looks, her air
Such gentle thankfulness declare,
That (so it seemed) her girded vests
Grew tight beneath her heaving breasts.   380
"Sure I have sinn'd!" said Christabel,
"Now heaven be praised if all be well!"
And in low faltering tones, yet sweet,
Did she the lofty lady greet
With such perplexity of mind
As dreams too lively leave behind.

So quickly she rose, and quickly arrayed
Her maiden limbs, and having prayed
That He, who on the cross did groan,
Might wash away her sins unknown,   390
She forthwith led fair Geraldine
To meet her sire, Sir Leoline.

The lovely maid and the lady tall
Are pacing both into the hall,
And pacing on through page and groom,
Enter the Baron's presence-room.

The Baron rose, and while he prest
His gentle daughter to his breast,
With cheerful wonder in his eyes
The lady Geraldine espies,   400
And gave such welcome to the same,
As might beseem so bright a dame!

But when he heard the lady's tale,
And when she told her father's name,
Why waxed Sir Leoline so pale,
Murmuring o'er the name again,
Lord Roland de Vaux of Tryermaine?

Alas! they had been friends in youth;
But whispering tongues can poison truth;
And constancy lives in realms above;   410
And life is thorny; and youth is vain;
And to be wroth with one we love
Doth work like madness in the brain.
And thus it chanced, as I divine,
With Roland and Sir Leoline.

Each spake words of high disdain
And insult to his heart's best brother:
They parted—ne'er to meet again!
But never either found another
To free the hollow heart from paining—   420
They stood aloof, the scars remaining,
Like cliffs which had been rent asunder;
A dreary sea now flows between;—
But neither heat, nor frost, nor thunder,
Shall wholly do away, I ween,
The marks of that which once hath been.

Sir Leoline, a moment's space,
Stood gazing on the damsel's face:
And the youthful Lord of Tryermaine
Came back upon his heart again.   430

O then the Baron forgot his age,
His noble heart swelled high with rage;
He swore by the wounds in Jesu's side
He would proclaim it far and wide,
With trump and solemn heraldry,
That they, who thus had wronged the dame,
Were base as spotted infamy!
"And if they dare deny the same,
My herald shall appoint a week,
And let the recreant traitors seek   440
My tourney court—that there and then
I may dislodge their reptile souls
From the bodies and forms of men!"
He spake: his eye in lightning rolls!
For the lady was ruthlessly seized; and he kenned
In the beautiful lady the child of his friend!

And now the tears were on his face,
And fondly in his arms he took
Fair Geraldine, who met the embrace,
Prolonging it with joyous look,   450
Which when she viewed, a vision fell
Upon the soul of Christabel,
The vision of fear, the touch and pain!
She shrunk and shuddered, and saw again—
(Ah, woe is me! Was it for thee,
Thou gentle maid! such sights to see?)

Again she saw that bosom old,
Again she felt that bosom cold,
And drew in her breath with a hissing sound:
Whereat the Knight turned wildly round,   460
And nothing saw, but his own sweet maid
With eyes upraised, as one that prayed.

The touch, the sight, had passed away,
And in its stead that vision blest,
Which comforted her after-rest
While in the lady's arms she lay,
Had put a rapture in her breast,
And on her lips and o'er her eyes
Spread smiles like light!
                                        With new surprise,
"What ails then my belovèd child?"   470
The Baron said—His daughter mild
Made answer, "All will yet be well!"
I ween, she had no power to tell
Aught else: so mighty was the spell.

Yet he, who saw this Geraldine,
Had deemed her sure a thing divine:
Such sorrow with such grace she blended,
As if she feared she had offended
Sweet Christabel, that gentle maid!
And with such lowly tones she prayed   480
She might be sent without delay
Home to her father's mansion.
                                        "Nay!
Nay, by my soul!" said Leoline.
"Ho! Bracy the bard, the charge be thine!
Go thou, with music sweet and loud,
And take two steeds with trappings proud,
And take the youth whom thou lov'st best
To bear thy harp, and learn thy song,
And clothe you both in solemn vest,
And over the mountains haste along,   490
Lest wandering folk, that are abroad,
Detain you on the valley road.

"And when he has crossed the Irthing flood,
My merry bard! he hastes, he hastes
Up Knorren Moor, through Halegarth Wood,
And reaches soon that castle good
Which stands and threatens Scotland's wastes

"Bard Bracy! bard Bracy! your horses are fleet,
Ye must ride up the hall, your music so sweet,
More loud than your horses' echoing feet!   500
And loud and loud to Lord Roland call,
Thy daughter is safe in Langdale hall!
Thy beautiful daughter is safe and free—
Sir Leoline greets thee thus through me!
He bids thee come without delay
With all thy numerous array
And take thy lovely daughter home:
And he will meet thee on the way

With all his numerous array
White with their panting palfreys' foam: 510
And, by mine honour! I will say,
That I repent me of the day
When I spake words of fierce disdain
To Roland de Vaux of Tryermaine!—
—For since that evil hour hath flown,
Many a summer's sun hath shone;
Yet ne'er found I a friend again
Like Roland de Vaux of Tryermaine.

The lady fell, and clasped his knees,
Her face upraised, her eyes o'erflowing;   520
And Bracy replied, with faltering voice,
His gracious Hail on all bestowing!—
"Thy words, thou sire of Christabel,
Are sweeter than my harp can tell;
Ye might I gain a boon of thee,
This day my journey should not be,
So strange a dream hath come to me,
That I had vowed with music loud
To clear yon wood from thing unblest,
Warned by a vision in my rest!   530
For in my sleep I saw that dove,
That gentle bird, whom thou dost love,
And call'st by thy own daughter's name—
Sir Leoline! I saw the same
Fluttering, and uttering fearful moan,
Among the green herbs in the forest alone.
Which when I saw and when I heard,
I wonder'd what might ail the bird;
For nothing near it could I see,
Save the grass and green herbs underneath the
          old tree.   540

"And in my dream methought I went
To search out what might there be found;
And what the sweet bird's trouble meant,
That thus lay fluttering on the ground.
I went and peered, and could descry
No cause for her distressful cry;
But yet for her dear lady's sake
I stooped, methought, the dove to take,
When lo! I saw a bright green snake
Coiled around its wings and neck.   550
Green as the herbs on which it couched,
Close by the dove's its head it crouched;
And with the dove it heaves and stirs,
Swelling its neck as she swelled hers!
I woke; it was the midnight hour,
The clock was echoing in the tower;

But though my slumber was gone by,
This dream it would not pass away—
It seems to live upon my eye!
And thence I vowed this self-same day   560
With music strong and saintly song
To wander through the forest bare,
Lest aught unholy loiter there."

Thus Bracy said: the Baron, the while,
Half-listening heard him with a smile;
Then turned to Lady Geraldine,
His eyes made up of wonder and love;
And said in courtly accents fine,
"Sweet maid, Lord Roland's beauteous dove,
With arms more strong than harp or song,   570
Thy sire and I will crush the snake!"
He kissed her forehead as he spake,
And Geraldine in maiden wise
Casting down her large bright eyes,
With blushing cheek and courtesy fine
She turned her from Sir Leoline;
Softly gathering up her train,
That o'er her right arm fell again;
And folded her arms across her chest,
And couched her head upon her breast,   580
And looked askance at Christabel—
Jesu, Maria, shield her well!

A snake's small eye blinks dull and shy;
And the lady's eyes they shrunk in her head,
Each shrunk up to a serpent's eye,
And with somewhat of malice, and more of dread,
At Christabel she looked askance!—
One moment—and the sight was fled!
But Christabel in dizzy trance
Stumbling on the unsteady ground   590
Shuddered aloud, with a hissing sound;
And Geraldine again turned round,
And like a thing, that sought relief,
Full of wonder and full of grief,
She rolled her large bright eyes divine
Wildly on Sir Leoline.

The maid, alas! her thoughts are gone,
She nothing sees—no sight but one!
The maid, devoid of guile and sin,
I know not how, in fearful wise,   600
So deeply had she drunken in
That look, those shrunken serpent eyes,
That all her features were resigned
To this sole image in her mind:

And passively did imitate
That look of dull and treacherous hate!
And thus she stood, in dizzy trance,
Still picturing that look askance
With forced unconscious sympathy
Full before her father's view—   610
As far as such a look could be
In eyes so innocent and blue!

And when the trance was o'er, the maid
Paused awhile, and inly prayed:
Then falling at the Baron's feet,
"By my mother's soul do I entreat
That thou this woman send away!"
She said: and more she could not say:
For what she knew she could not tell,
O'er-mastered by the mighty spell.   620

Why is thy cheek so wan and wild,
Sir Leoline? Thy only child
Lies at thy feet, thy joy, thy pride,
So fair, so innocent, so mild;
The same, for whom thy lady died!
O by the pangs of her dear mother
Think thou no evil of thy child!
For her, and thee, and for no other,
She prayed the moment ere she died:
Prayed that the babe for whom she died,   630
Might prove her dear lord's joy and pride!
    That prayer her deadly pangs beguiled,
        Sir Leoline!
    And wouldst thou wrong thy only child,
        Her child and thine?

Within the Baron's heart and brain
If thoughts, like these, had any share,
They only swelled his rage and pain,
And did but work confusion there.
His heart was cleft with pain and rage,   640
His cheeks they quivered, his eyes were wild,
Dishonoured thus in his old age;
Dishonoured by his only child,
And all his hospitality
To the wronged daughter of his friend
By more than woman's jealousy
Brought thus to a disgraceful end—
He rolled his eye with stern regard
Upon the gentle minstrel bard,
And said in tones abrupt, austere—   650
"Why, Bracy! dost thou loiter here?
I bade thee hence!" The bard obeyed;
And turning from his own sweet maid,

The agèd knight, Sir Leoline,
Led forth the lady Geraldine!

THE CONCLUSION TO PART II

A little child, a limber elf,
Singing, dancing to itself,
A fairy thing with red round cheeks,
That always finds, and never seeks,
Makes such a vision to the sight   660
As fills a father's eyes with light;
And pleasures flow in so thick and fast
Upon his heart, that he at last
Must needs express his love's excess
With words of unmeant bitterness.
Perhaps 'tis pretty to force together
Thoughts so all unlike each other;
To mutter and mock a broken charm,
To dally with wrong that does no harm.
Perhaps 'tis tender too and pretty   670
At each wild word to feel within
A sweet recoil of love and pity.
And what, if in a world of sin
(O sorrow and shame should this be true!)
Such giddiness of heart and brain
Comes seldom save from rage and pain,
So talks as it's most used to do.

? 1797–1801   1816

FROST AT MIDNIGHT

The Frost performs its secret ministry,
Unhelped by any wind. The owlet's cry
Came loud—and hark, again! loud as before.
The inmates of my cottage, all at rest,
Have left me to that solitude, which suits
Abstruser musings: save that at my side
My cradled infant slumbers peacefully.
'Tis calm indeed! so calm, that it disturbs
And vexes meditation with its strange
And extreme silentness. Sea, hill, and wood,   10
This populous village! Sea, and hill, and wood,
With all the numberless goings-on of life,
Inaudible as dreams! the thin blue flame
Lies on my low-burnt fire, and quivers not;
Only that film, which fluttered on the grate,

FROST AT MIDNIGHT. **7. cradled infant:** Coleridge's son
Hartley. **15. film:** In all parts of the kingdom these
films are called *strangers* and supposed to portend the
arrival of some absent friend (Coleridge).

Still flutters there, the sole unquiet thing.
Methinks, its motion in this hush of nature
Gives it dim sympathies with me who live,
Making it a companionable form,
Whose puny flaps and freaks the idling Spirit   20
By its own moods interprets, every where
Echo or mirror seeking of itself,
And makes a toy of Thought.

                               But O! how oft,
How oft, at school, with most believing mind,
Presageful, have I gazed upon the bars,
To watch that fluttering *stranger!* and as oft
With unclosed lids, already had I dreamt
Of my sweet birth-place, and the old church-tower,
Whose bells, the poor man's only music, rang
From morn to evening, all the hot Fair-day,   30
So sweetly, that they stirred and haunted me
With a wild pleasure, falling on mine ear
Most like articulate sounds of things to come!
So gazed I, till the soothing things, I dreamt,
Lulled me to sleep, and sleep prolonged my dreams!
And so I brooded all the following morn,
Awed by the stern preceptor's face, mine eye
Fixed with mock study on my swimming book:
Save if the door half opened, and I snatched
A hasty glance, and still my heart leaped up,   40
For still I hoped to see the *stranger's* face,
Townsman, or aunt, or sister more beloved,
My play-mate when we both were clothed alike!

Dear Babe, that sleepest cradled by my side,
Whose gentle breathings, heard in this deep calm,
Fill up the interspersèd vacancies
And momentary pauses of the thought!
My babe so beautiful! it thrills my heart
With tender gladness, thus to look at thee,
And think that thou shalt learn far other lore,   50
And in far other scenes! For I was reared
In the great city, pent 'mid cloisters dim,
And saw nought lovely but the sky and stars.
But *thou*, my babe! shalt wander like a breeze
By lakes and sandy shores, beneath the crags
Of ancient mountain, and beneath the clouds,
Which image in their bulk both lakes and shores
And mountain crags: so shalt thou see and hear
The lovely shapes and sounds intelligible
Of that eternal language, which thy God   60
Utters, who from eternity doth teach
Himself in all, and all things in himself.
Great universal Teacher! he shall mould

Thy spirit and by giving make it ask.

    Therefore all seasons shall be sweet to thee,
Whether the summer clothe the general earth
With greenness, or the redbreast sit and sing
Betwixt the tufts of snow on the bare branch
Of mossy apple-tree, while the nigh thatch
Smokes in the sun-thaw; whether the eave-drops
    fall   70
Heard only in the trances of the blast,
Or if the secret ministry of frost
Shall hang them up in silent icicles,
Quietly shining to the quiet Moon.

1798   *1798*

FRANCE: AN ODE

I

Ye Clouds! that far above me float and pause,
    Whose pathless march no mortal may controul!
    Ye Ocean-Waves! that, wheresoe'er ye roll,
Yield homage only to eternal laws!
Ye Woods! that listen to the night-birds singing,
    Midway the smooth and perilous slope reclined,
Save when your own imperious branches swinging,
    Have made a solemn music of the wind!
Where, like a man beloved of God,
Through glooms, which never woodman trod,   10
    How oft, pursuing fancies holy,
My moonlight way o'er flowering weeds I wound,
    Inspired, beyond the guess of folly,
By each rude shape and wild unconquerable sound!
O ye loud Waves! and O ye Forests high!
    And O ye Clouds that far above me soared!
Thou rising Sun! thou blue rejoicing Sky!
    Yea, every thing that is and will be free!
    Bear witness for me, wheresoe'er ye be,
With what deep worship I have still adored   20
    The spirit of divinest Liberty.

II

When France in wrath her giant-limbs upreared,
    And with that oath, which smote air, earth, and
        sea,
    Stamped her strong foot and said she would be
        free,
Bear witness for me, how I hoped and feared!

With what a joy my lofty gratulation
    Unawed I sang, amid a slavish band:
And when to whelm the disenchanted nation,
    Like fiends embattled by a wizard's wand,
        The Monarchs marched in evil day,   30
        And Britain joined the dire array;
    Though dear her shores and circling ocean,
Though many friendships, many youthful loves
    Had swoln the patriot emotion
And flung a magic light o'er all her hills and groves;
Yet still my voice, unaltered, sang defeat
    To all that braved the tyrant-quelling lance,
And shame too long delayed and vain retreat!
For ne'er, O Liberty! with partial aim
I dimmed thy light or damped thy holy flame;   40
    But blessed the paeans of delivered France,
And hung my head and wept at Britain's name.

III

"And what," I said, "though Blasphemy's loud
    scream
    With that sweet music of deliverance strove!
    Though all the fierce and drunken passions wove
A dance more wild than e'er was maniac's dream!
    Ye storms, that round the dawning East
        assembled,
The Sun was rising, though ye hid his light!"
    And when, to soothe my soul, that hoped and
        trembled,
The dissonance ceased, and all seemed calm and
        bright;   50
    When France her front deep-scarr'd and gory
Concealed with clustering wreaths of glory;
    When, insupportably advancing,
Her arm made mockery of the warrior's ramp;
    While timid looks of fury glancing,
Domestic treason, crushed beneath her fatal
        stamp,
Writhed like a wounded dragon in his gore;
    Then I reproached my fears that would not flee;
"And soon," I said, "shall Wisdom teach her lore
In the low huts of them that toil and groan!   60
And, conquering by her happiness alone,
    Shall France compel the nations to be free,
Till Love and Joy look round, and call the Earth
    their own."

FRANCE: AN ODE. **30–31**: Austria, Prussia, and England
were allied against France in 1793.

IV

Forgive me, Freedom! O forgive those dreams!
 I hear thy voice, I hear thy loud lament,
 From bleak Helvetia's icy caverns sent—
I hear thy groans upon her blood-stained streams!
 Heroes, that for your peaceful country perished,
And ye that, fleeing, spot your mountain-snows
 With bleeding wounds; forgive me, that I
  cherished   70
One thought that ever blessed your cruel foes!
 To scatter rage, and traitorous guilt,
 Where Peace her jealous home had built;
  A patriot-race to disinherit
Of all that made their stormy wilds so dear;
  And with inexpiable spirit
To taint the bloodless freedom of the moun-
  taineer—
O France, that mockest Heaven, adulterous, blind,
 And patriot only in pernicious toils!
Are these thy boasts, Champion of human
  kind?   80
 To mix with Kings in the low lust of sway,
Yell in the hunt, and share the murderous prey;
To insult the shrine of Liberty with spoils
 From freemen torn; to tempt and to betray?

V

 The Sensual and the Dark rebel in vain,
 Slaves by their own compulsion! In mad game
 They burst their manacles and wear the name
  Of Freedom, graven on a heavier chain!
  O Liberty! with profitless endeavour
Have I pursued thee, many a weary hour; 90
 But thou nor swell'st the victor's strain, nor ever
Didst breathe thy soul in forms of human power.
 Alike from all, howe'er they praise thee,
 (Nor prayer, nor boastful name delays thee)
  Alike from Priestcraft's harpy minions,
And factious Blasphemy's obscener slaves.
  Thou speedest on thy subtle pinions,
The guide of homeless winds, and playmate of the
  waves!
And there I felt thee!—on the sea-cliff's verge,
 Whose pines, scarce travelled by the breeze
  above,   100
Had made one murmur with the distant surge!

66. Helvetia: Switzerland.

Yes, while I stood and gazed, my temples bare,
And shot my being through earth, sea, and air,
 Possessing all things with intensest love,
  O Liberty! my spirit felt thee there.

1798   *1798*

KUBLA KHAN

OR, A VISION IN A DREAM.
A FRAGMENT.

———

The following fragment is here published at the request of a poet of great and deserved celebrity [Lord Byron], and, as far as the Author's own opinions are concerned, rather as a psychological curiosity, than on the ground of any supposed *poetic* merits.

In the summer of the year 1797, the Author, then in ill health, had retired to a lonely farm-house between Porlock and Linton, on the Exmoor confines of Somerset and Devonshire. In consequence of a slight indisposition, an anodyne had been prescribed, from the effects of which he fell asleep in his chair at the moment that he was reading the following sentence, or words of the same substance, in "Purchas's Pilgrimage": "Here the Khan Kubla commanded a palace to be built, and a stately garden there-unto. And thus ten miles of fertile ground were inclosed with a wall." The Author continued for about three hours in a profound sleep, at least of the external senses, during which time he has the most vivid confidence, that he could not have composed less than from two to three hundred lines; if that indeed can be called composition in which all the images rose up before him as *things*, with a parallel production of the correspondent expressions, without any sensation or consciousness of effort. On awakening he appeared to himself to have a distinct recollection of the whole, and taking his pen, ink, and paper, instantly and eagerly wrote down the lines that are here preserved. At this moment he was unfortunately called out by a person on business from Porlock, and detained by him above an hour, and on his return to his room, found, to his no small surprise and mortification, that though he still retained some vague and dim recollection of the general purport of the vision, yet, with the exception of some eight or ten scattered lines and images, all the rest had passed away like the images on the surface of a stream into which a stone has been cast, but, alas! without the after restoration of the latter!

     Then all the charm
Is broken—all that phantom-world so fair
Vanishes, and a thousand circlets spread,

And each mis-shape['s] the other. Stay awhile,
Poor youth! who scarcely dar'st lift up thine
    eyes—
The stream will soon renew its smoothness,
    soon
The visions will return! And lo, he stays,
And soon the fragments dim of lovely forms
Come trembling back, unite, and now once
    more
The pool becomes a mirror.*

Yet from the still surviving recollections in his mind, the Author has frequently purposed to finish for himself what had been originally, as it were, given to him. Σαμερον αδιον ασω:** but the tomorrow is yet to come. (Coleridge)

In Xanadu did Kubla Khan
A stately pleasure-dome decree:
Where Alph, the sacred river, ran
Through caverns measureless to man
    Down to a sunless sea.
So twice five miles of fertile ground
With walls and towers were girdled round:
And there were gardens bright with sinuous rills,
Where blossomed many an incense-bearing tree;
And here were forests ancient as the hills,   10
Enfolding sunny spots of greenery.

But oh! that deep romantic chasm which slanted
Down the green hill athwart a cedarn cover!
A savage place! as holy and enchanted
As e'er beneath a waning moon was haunted
By woman wailing for her demon-lover!
And from this chasm, with ceaseless turmoil
    seething
As if this earth in fast thick pants were breathing,
A mighty fountain momently was forced:
Amid whose swift half-intermitted burst   20
Huge fragments vaulted like rebounding hail,
Or chaffy grain beneath the thresher's flail:
And 'mid these dancing rocks at once and ever
It flung up momently the sacred river.
Five miles meandering with a mazy motion
Through wood and dale the sacred river ran,
Then reached the caverns measureless to man,

KUBLA KHAN. 1: Kubla Khan was the Mogul emperor of the thirteenth century, a descendant of Genghis Khan.

---

* Lines from Coleridge's poem "The Picture."
** "To sing a sweeter song tomorrow." (Theocritus, *Idylls*, I, 132.)

And sank in tumult to a lifeless ocean:
And 'mid this tumult Kubla heard from far
Ancestral voices prophesying war!   30
    The shadow of the dome of pleasure
    Floated midway on the waves;
    Where was heard the mingled measure
    From the fountain and the caves.
It was a miracle of rare device,
A sunny pleasure-dome with caves of ice!

    A damsel with a dulcimer
    In a vision once I saw:
    It was an Abyssinian maid,
    And on her dulcimer she played,   40
    Singing of Mount Abora.
    Could I revive within me
    Her symphony and song,
    To such a deep delight 'twould win me,
That with music loud and long,
I would build that dome in air,
That sunny dome! those caves of ice!
And all who heard should see them there,
And all should cry, Beware! Beware!
His flashing eyes, his floating hair!   50
Weave a circle round him thrice,
And close your eyes with holy dread,
For he on honey-dew hath fed,
And drunk the milk of Paradise.
1798   *1816*

DEJECTION: AN ODE

WRITTEN APRIL 4, 1802

Late, late yestreen I saw the new Moon,
With the old Moon in her arms;
And I fear, I fear, my Master dear!
We shall have a deadly storm.

                Ballad of Sir Patrick Spence.

I

Well! If the Bard was weather-wise, who made
    The grand old ballad of Sir Patrick Spence,
    This night, so tranquil now, will not go hence
Unroused by winds, that ply a busier trade
Than those which mould yon cloud in lazy flakes,

Or the dull sobbing draft, that moans and rakes
Upon the strings of this Æolian lute,
   Which better far were mute.
   For lo! the New-moon winter-bright!
   And overspread with phantom light,   10
   (With swimming phantom light o'erspread
   But rimmed and circled by a silver thread)
I see the old Moon in her lap, foretelling
   The coming-on of rain and squally blast.
And oh! that even now the gust were swelling,
   And the slant night-shower driving loud and fast!
Those sounds which oft have raised me, whilst they
      awed,
   And sent my soul abroad,
Might now perhaps their wonted impulse give,
Might startle this dull pain, and make it move and
      live!   20

II

A grief without a pang, void, dark, and drear,
   A stifled, drowsy, unimpassioned grief,
   Which finds no natural outlet, no relief,
      In word, or sigh, or tear—
O lady! in this wan and heartless mood,
To other thoughts by yonder throstle woo'd,
   All this long eve, so balmy and serene,
Have I been gazing on the western sky,
   And its peculiar tint of yellow green:
And still I gaze—and with how blank an eye!   30
And those thin clouds above, in flakes and bars,
That give away their motion to the stars;
Those stars, that glide behind them or between,
Now sparkling, now bedimmed, but always seen:
Yon crescent Moon, as fixed as if it grew
In its own cloudless, starless lake of blue;
I see them all so excellently fair,
I see, not feel, how beautiful they are!

III

   My genial spirits fail;
      And what can these avail   40
To lift the smothering weight from off my breast?
      It were a vain endeavour,
      Though I should gaze for ever
On that green light that lingers in the west:
I may not hope from outward forms to win
The passion and the life, whose fountains are
      within.

IV

O Lady! we receive but what we give,
And in our life alone does Nature live:
Ours is her wedding garment, ours her shroud!
   And would we aught behold, of higher
      worth,   50
Than that inanimate cold world allowed
To the poor loveless ever-anxious crowd,
   Ah! from the soul itself must issue forth
A light, a glory, a fair luminous cloud
      Enveloping the Earth—
And from the soul itself must there be sent
   A sweet and potent voice, of its own birth,
Of all sweet sounds the life and element!

V

O pure of heart! thou need'st not ask of me
What this strong music in the soul may be!   60
What, and wherein it doth exist,
This light, this glory, this fair luminous mist,
This beautiful and beauty-making power.
   Joy, virtuous Lady! Joy that ne'er was given,
Save to the pure, and in their purest hour,
Life, and Life's effluence, cloud at once and shower,
Joy, Lady! is the spirit and the power,
Which wedding Nature to us gives in dower
   A new Earth and new Heaven,
Undreamt of by the sensual and the proud—   70
Joy is the sweet voice, Joy the luminous cloud—
      We in ourselves rejoice!
And thence flows all that charms or ear or sight,
   All melodies the echoes of that voice,
All colours a suffusion from that light.

VI

There was a time when, though my path was rough,
   This joy within me dallied with distress,
And all misfortunes were but as the stuff
   Whence Fancy made me dreams of happiness:
For hope grew round me, like the twining
      vine,   80
And fruits, and foliage, not my own, seemed mine.
But now afflictions bow me down to earth:
Nor care I that they rob me of my mirth;
      But oh! each visitation
Suspends what nature gave me at my birth,
   My shaping spirit of Imagination.

For not to think of what I needs must feel,
   But to be still and patient, all I can;
And haply by abstruse research to steal
   From my own nature all the natural man—   90
This was my sole resource, my only plan:
Till that which suits a part infects the whole,
And now is almost grown the habit of my soul.

VII

Hence, viper thoughts, that coil around my mind,
   Reality's dark dream!
I turn from you, and listen to the wind,
   Which long has raved unnoticed. What a scream
Of agony by torture lengthened out
That lute sent forth! Thou Wind, that rav'st
      without,
   Bare crag, or mountain-tairn, or blasted
      tree,   100
Or pine-grove whither woodman never clomb,
Or lonely house, long held the witches' home,
   Methinks were fitter instruments for thee,
Mad Lutanist! who in this month of showers,
Of dark-brown gardens, and of peeping flowers,
Mak'st Devils' yule, with worse than wintry song,
The blossoms, buds, and timorous leaves among.
   Thou Actor, perfect in all tragic sounds!
Thou mighty Poet, e'en to frenzy bold!
     What tell'st thou now about?   110
     'Tis of the rushing of an host in rout,
   With groans, of trampled men, with smarting
      wounds—
At once they groan with pain, and shudder with
      the cold!
But hush! there is a pause of deepest silence!
   And all that noise, as of a rushing crowd,
With groans, and tremulous shudderings—all is
      over—
   It tells another tale, with sounds less deep and
      loud!
     A tale of less affright,
     And tempered with delight,
As Otway's self had framed the tender lay,—   120
     'Tis of a little child
     Upon a lonesome wild,
Not far from home, but she hath lost her way:

DEJECTION: AN ODE. 121–25: The story of Wordsworth's
"Lucy Gray."

And now moans low in bitter grief and fear,
And now screams loud, and hopes to make her
      mother hear.

VIII

'Tis midnight, but small thoughts have I of sleep:
Full seldom may my friend such vigils keep!
Visit her, gentle Sleep! with wings of healing,
   And may this storm be but a mountain-birth,
May all the stars hang bright above her
      dwelling,   130
   Silent as though they watched the sleeping
      Earth!
     With light heart may she rise,
     Gay fancy, cheerful eyes,
Joy lift her spirit, joy attune her voice;
To her may all things live, from pole to pole,
Their life the eddying of her living soul!
   O simple spirit, guided from above,
Dear Lady! friend devoutest of my choice,
Thus mayest thou ever, evermore rejoice.
1802   *1802*

THE PAINS OF SLEEP

Ere on my bed my limbs I lay,
It hath not been my use to pray
With moving lips or bended knees;
But silently, by slow degrees,
My spirit I to Love compose,
In humble trust mine eye-lids close,
With reverential resignation,
No wish conceived, no thought exprest,
Only a sense of supplication;
A sense o'er all my soul imprest   10
That I am weak, yet not unblest,
Since in me, round me, every where
Eternal Strength and Wisdom are.

But yester-night I prayed aloud
In anguish and in agony,
Up-starting from the fiendish crowd
Of shapes and thoughts that tortured me:
A lurid light, a trampling throng,
Sense of intolerable wrong,
And whom I scorned, those only strong!   20

Thirst of revenge, the powerless will
Still baffled, and yet burning still!
Desire with loathing strangely mixed
On wild or hateful objects fixed.
Fantastic passions! maddening brawl!
And shame and terror over all!
Deeds to be hid which were not hid,
Which all confused I could not know
Whether I suffered, or I did:
For all seemed guilt, remorse or woe,   30
My own or others still the same
Life-stifling fear, soul-stifling shame.

So two nights passed: the night's dismay
Saddened and stunned the coming day.
Sleep, the wide blessing, seemed to me
Distemper's worst calamity.
The third night, when my own loud scream
Had waked me from the fiendish dream,
O'ercome with sufferings strange and wild,
I wept as I had been a child;   40
And having thus by tears subdued
My anguish to a milder mood,
Such punishments, I said, were due
To natures deepliest stained with sin,—
For aye entempesting anew
The unfathomable hell within,
The horror of their deeds to view,
To know and loathe, yet wish and do!
Such griefs with such men well agree,
But wherefore, wherefore fall on me?   50
To be beloved is all I need,
And whom I love, I love indeed.

1803   1816

TO WILLIAM WORDSWORTH

COMPOSED ON THE NIGHT AFTER HIS
RECITATION OF A POEM * ON THE
GROWTH OF AN INDIVIDUAL MIND

Friend of the wise! and Teacher of the Good!
Into my heart have I received that Lay
More than historic, that prophetic Lay
Wherein (high theme by thee first sung aright)
Of the foundations and the building up
Of a Human Spirit thou hast dared to tell
What may be told, to the understanding mind

---

* *The Prelude.*

Revealable; and what within the mind
By vital breathings secret as the soul
Of vernal growth, oft quickens in the heart   10
Thoughts all too deep for words!—

          Theme hard as high!
Of smiles spontaneous, and mysterious fears
(The first-born they of Reason and twin-birth),
Of tides obedient to external force,
And currents self-determined, as might seem,
Or by some inner Power; of moments awful,
Now in thy inner life, and now abroad,
When power streamed from thee, and thy soul
    received
The light reflected, as a light bestowed—
Of fancies fair, and milder hours of youth,   20
Hyblean murmurs of poetic thought
Industrious in its joy, in vales and glens
Native or outland, lakes and famous hills!
Or on the lonely high-road, when the stars
Were rising; or by secret mountain-streams,
The guides and the companions of thy way!

Of more than Fancy, of the Social Sense
Distending wide, and man beloved as man,
Where France in all her towns lay vibrating
Like some becalmed bark beneath the burst   30
Of Heaven's immediate thunder, when no cloud
Is visible, or shadow on the main.
For thou wert there, thine own brows garlanded,
Amid the tremor of a realm aglow,
Amid a mighty nation jubilant,
When from the general heart of human kind
Hope sprang forth like a full-born Deity!
——Of that dear Hope afflicted and struck down,
So summoned homeward, thenceforth calm and sure
From the dread watch-tower of man's absolute
    self,   40
With light unwaning on her eyes, to look
Far on—herself a glory to behold,
The Angel of the vision! Then (last strain)
Of Duty, chosen Laws controlling choice,
Action and joy!—An Orphic song indeed,
A song divine of high and passionate thoughts
To their own music chaunted!

          O great Bard!
Ere yet that last strain dying awed the air,

TO WILLIAM WORDSWORTH. **21. Hyblean:** honeyed. Hybla is a town in Sicily famed for its bees. **45. Orphic:** melodious; pertaining to the musical power of Orpheus.

With stedfast eye I viewed thee in the choir
Of ever-enduring men. The truly great   50
Have all one age, and from one visible space
Shed influence! They, both in power and act,
Are permanent, and Time is not with them,
Save as it worketh for them, they in it.
Nor less a sacred Roll, than those of old,
And to be placed, as they, with gradual fame
Among the archives of mankind, thy work
Makes audible a linked lay of Truth,
Of Truth profound a sweet continuous lay,
Not learnt, but native, her own natural notes!   60
Ah! as I listened with a heart forlorn,
The pulses of my being beat anew:
And even as Life returns upon the drowned,
Life's joy rekindling roused a throng of pains—
Keen pangs of Love, awakening as a babe
Turbulent, with an outcry in the heart;
And fears self-willed, that shunned the eye of Hope;
And Hope that scarce would know itself from Fear;
Sense of past Youth, and Manhood come in vain,
And Genius given, and Knowledge won in vain;   70
And all which I had culled in wood-walks wild,
And all which patient toil had reared, and all,
Commune with thee had opened out—but flowers
Strewed on my corse, and borne upon my bier
In the same coffin, for the self-same grave!

   That way no more! and ill beseems it me,
Who came a welcomer in herald's guise,
Singing of Glory, and Futurity,
To wander back on such unhealthful road,
Plucking the poisons of self-harm! And ill   80
Such intertwine beseems triumphal wreaths
Strew'd before thy advancing!

                              Nor do thou,
Sage Bard! impair the memory of that hour
Of thy communion with my nobler mind
By pity or grief, already felt too long!
Nor let my words import more blame than needs.
The tumult rose and ceased: for Peace is nigh
Where Wisdom's voice has found a listening heart.
Amid the howl of more than wintry storms,
The Halcyon hears the voice of vernal hours   90
Already on the wing.

                         Eve following eve,
Dear tranquil time, when the sweet sense of Home
Is sweetest! moments for their own sake hailed
And more desired, more precious, for thy song,

In silence listening, like a devout child,
My soul lay passive, by thy various strain
Driven as in surges now beneath the stars,
With momentary stars of my own birth,
Fair constellated foam, still darting off
Into the darkness; now a tranquil sea,   100
Outspread and bright, yet swelling to the moon.

And when—O Friend! my comforter and guide!
Strong in thyself, and powerful to give strength!—
Thy long sustained Song finally closed,
And thy deep voice had ceased—yet thou thyself
Wert still before my eyes, and round us both
That happy vision of belovèd faces—
Scarce conscious, and yet conscious of its close
I sate, my being blended in one thought
(Thought was it? or aspiration? or resolve?)   110
Absorbed, yet hanging still upon the sound—
And when I rose, I found myself in prayer.
1807   1817

HUMAN LIFE

ON THE DENIAL OF IMMORTALITY

If dead, we cease to be; if total gloom
   Swallow up life's brief flash for aye, we fare
As summer-gusts, of sudden birth and doom,
   Whose sound and motion not alone declare,
But are their whole of being! If the breath
   Be Life itself, and not its task and tent,
If even a soul like Milton's can know death;
   O Man! thou vessel purposeless, unmeant,
Yet drone-hive strange of phantom purposes!
   Surplus of Nature's dread activity,   10
Which, as she gazed on some nigh-finished vase,
Retreating slow, with meditative pause,
   She formed with restless hands unconsciously.
Blank accident! nothing's anomaly!
   If rootless thus, thus substanceless thy state,
Go, weigh thy dreams, and be thy hopes, thy fears,
The counter-weights!—Thy laughter and thy tears
   Mean but themselves, each fittest to create
And to repay the other! Why rejoices
   Thy heart with hollow joy for hollow good?   20
   Why cowl thy face beneath the mourner's hood?
Why waste thy sighs, and thy lamenting voices,
   Image of Image, Ghost of Ghostly Elf,
That such a thing as thou feel'st warm or cold?
Yet what and whence thy gain, if thou withhold

Those costless shadows of thy shadowy self?
Be sad! be glad! be neither! seek, or shun!
Thou hast no reason why! Thou canst have none;
Thy being's being is contradiction.

? *1815*   *1817*

LIMBO

The sole true Something—This! In Limbo's Den
It frightens Ghosts, as here Ghosts frighten men.
Thence cross'd unseiz'd—and shall some fated hour
Be pulveris'd by Demogorgon's power,
And given as poison to annihilate souls—
Even now it shrinks them—they shrink in as Moles
(Nature's mute monks, live mandrakes of the
    ground)
Creep back from Light—then listen for its sound;—
See but to dread, and dread they know not why—
The natural alien of their negative eye.   10

'Tis a strange place, this Limbo!—not a Place,
Yet name it so;—where Time and weary Space
Fettered from flight, with night-mare sense of
    fleeing,
Strive for their last crepuscular half-being;—
Lank Space, and scytheless Time with branny
    hands
Barren and soundless as the measuring sands,
Not mark'd by flit of Shades,—unmeaning they
As moonlight on the dial of the day!
But that is lovely—looks like Human Time,—
An Old Man with a steady look sublime,   20
That stops his earthly task to watch the skies;
But he is blind—a Statue hath such eyes;—
Yet having moonward turn'd his face by chance,
Gazes the orb with moon-like countenance,
With scant white hairs, with foretop bald and high,
He gazes still,—his eyeless face all eye;—
As 'twere an organ full of silent sight,
His whole face seemeth to rejoice in light!
Lip touching lip, all moveless, bust and limb—
He seems to gaze at that which seems to gaze on
    him!   30
    No such sweet sights doth Limbo den immure,
Wall'd round, and made a spirit-jail secure,
By the mere horror of blank Naught-at-all,
Whose circumambience doth these ghosts enthral.
A lurid thought is growthless, dull Privation,
Yet that is but a Purgatory curse;

Hell knows a fear far worse,
A fear—a future state;—'tis positive Negation!

1817   *1893*

NE PLUS ULTRA

Sole Positive of Night!
Antipathist of Light!
Fate's only essence! primal scorpion rod—
The one permitted opposite of God!—
Condensed blackness and abysmal storm
    Compacted to one sceptre
    Arms the Grasp enorm—
    The Intercepter—
The Substance that still casts the shadow Death!—
    The Dragon foul and fell—   10
    The unrevealable,
And hidden one, whose breath
Gives wind and fuel to the fires of Hell!
    Ah! sole despair
    Of both th' eternities in Heaven!
Sole interdict of all-bedewing prayer,
    The all-compassionate!
    Save to the Lampads Seven
Reveal'd to none of all th' Angelic State,
    Save to the Lampads Seven,   20
    That watch the throne of Heaven!

1826   *1834*

WORK WITHOUT HOPE

LINES COMPOSED 21ST FEBRUARY 1825

All nature seems at work. Slugs leave their lair—
The bees are stirring—birds are on the wing—
And Winter slumbering in the open air,
Wears on his smiling face a dream of Spring!
And I the while, the sole unbusy thing,
Nor honey make, nor pair, nor build, nor sing.

    Yet well I ken the banks where amaranths blow,
Have traced the font whence streams of nectar flow.
Bloom, O ye amaranths! bloom for whom ye may,
For me ye bloom not! Glide, rich streams, away!   10
With lips unbrightened, wreathless brow, I stroll:
And would you learn the spells that drowse my soul?
Work without Hope draws nectar in a sieve,
And Hope without an object cannot live.

1825   *1828*

SELF-KNOWLEDGE

—*E coelo descendit* γνῶθι σεαυτόν—JUVENAL, xi.
27.°

Γνῶθι σεαυτόν!—and is this the prime
And heaven-sprung adage of the olden time!—
Say, canst thou make thyself?—Learn first that
    trade;—
Haply thou mayst know what thyself had made.
What hath thou, Man, that thou dar'st call thine
    own?—
What is there in thee, Man, that can be known?—
Dark fluxion, all unfixable by thought,
A phantom dim of past and future wrought,
Vain sister of the worm,—life, death, soul, clod—
Ignore thyself, and strive to know thy God!   10
1832   *1834*

EPITAPH

Stop, Christian passer-by!—Stop, child of God,
And read with gentle breast. Beneath this sod
A poet lies, or that which once seem'd he.
O, lift one thought in prayer for S. T. C.;
That he who many a year with toil of breath
Found death in life, may here find life in death!
Mercy for praise—to be forgiven for fame
He ask'd, and hoped, through Christ. Do thou the
    same!
1833   *1834*

FROM

Biographia Literaria

From CHAPTER IV.

*The lyrical ballads with the preface—Mr. Words-
worth's earlier poems—On fancy and imagination
—The investigation of the distinction important to
the fine arts.*

    I have wandered far from the object in view, but
as I fancied to myself readers who would respect

° From heaven descends [the adage] *know thyself.*

the feelings that had tempted me from the main
road; so I dare calculate on not a few, who will
warmly sympathize with them. At present it will be
sufficient for my purpose, if I have proved, that
Mr. Southey's writings no more than my own, furnished the original occasion to this fiction of a *new
school* of poetry, and of clamors against its supposed
founders and proselytes.

    As little do I believe that "MR. WORDSWORTH'S
Lyrical Ballads" were in *themselves* the cause. I
speak exclusively of the two volumes so entitled. A
careful and repeated examination of these confirms
me in the belief, that the omission of less than an
hundred lines would have precluded nine-tenths of
the criticism on this work. I hazard this declaration,
however, on the supposition, that the reader had
taken it up, as he would have done any other collection of poems purporting to derive their subjects
or interests from the incidents of domestic or ordinary life, intermingled with higher strains of
meditation which the poet utters in his own person
and character; with the proviso, that they were perused without knowledge of, or reference to, the
author's peculiar opinions, and that the reader had
not had his attention previously directed to those
peculiarities. In these, as was actually the case with
Mr. Southey's earlier works, the lines and passages
which might have offended the general taste, would
have been considered as mere inequalities, and attributed to inattention, not to perversity of judgement. The men of business who had passed their
lives chiefly in cities, and who might therefore be
expected to derive the highest pleasure from acute
notices of men and manners conveyed in easy, yet
correct and pointed language; and all those who,
reading but little poetry, are most stimulated with
that species of it, which seems most distant from
prose, would probably have passed by the volume
altogether. Others more catholic in their taste, and
yet habituated to be most pleased when most excited, would have contented themselves with deciding, that the author had been successful in proportion to the elevation of his style and subject. Not a
few perhaps, might by their admiration of "the lines
written near Tintern Abbey," those "left upon a
Seat under a Yew Tree," the "old Cumberland beggar," and "Ruth," have been gradually led to peruse
with kindred feeling the "Brothers," the "Hart leap
well," and whatever other poems in that collection
may be described as holding a middle place be-

tween those written in the highest and those in the humblest style; as for instance between the "Tintern Abbey," and "the Thorn," or the "Simon Lee." Should their taste submit to no further change, and still remain unreconciled to the colloquial phrases, or the imitations of them, that are, more or less, scattered through the class last mentioned; yet even from the small number of the latter, they would have deemed them but an inconsiderable subtraction from the merit of the whole work; or, what is sometimes not unpleasing in the publication of a new writer, as serving to ascertain the natural tendency, and consequently the proper direction of the author's genius.

In the critical remarks therefore, prefixed and annexed to the "Lyrical Ballads," I believe that we may safely rest, as the true origin of the unexampled opposition which Mr. Wordsworth's writings have been since doomed to encounter. The humbler passages in the poems themselves were dwelt on and cited to justify the rejection of the theory. What in and for themselves would have been either forgotten or forgiven as imperfections, or at least comparative failures, provoked direct hostility when announced as intentional, as the result of choice after full deliberation. Thus the poems, admitted by *all* as excellent, joined with those which had pleased the far *greater* number, though they formed two-thirds of the whole work, instead of being deemed (as in all right they should have been, even if we take for granted that the reader judged aright) an atonement for the few exceptions, gave wind and fuel to the animosity against both the poems and the poet. . . .

During the last year of my residence at Cambridge, I became acquainted with Mr. Wordsworth's first publication entitled "Descriptive Sketches"; and seldom, if ever, was the emergence of an original poetic genius above the literary horizon more evidently announced. In the form, style, and manner of the whole poem, and in the structure of the particular lines and periods, there is an harshness and acerbity connected and combined with words and images all a-glow, which might recall those products of the vegetable world, where gorgeous blossoms rise out of the hard and thorny rind and shell, within which the rich fruit was elaborating. The language was not only peculiar and strong, but at times knotty and contorted, as by its own impatient strength; while the novelty and struggling

crowd of images acting in conjunction with the difficulties of the style, demanded always a greater closeness of attention, than poetry, (at all events, than descriptive poetry) has a right to claim. It not seldom therefore justified the complaint of obscurity. In the following extract I have sometimes fancied, that I saw an emblem of the poem itself, and of the author's genius as it was then displayed.

" 'Tis storm; and hid in mist from hour to hour,
All day the floods a deepening murmur pour;
The sky is veiled, and every cheerful sight:
Dark is the region as with coming night;
And yet what frequent bursts of overpowering
    light!
Triumphant on the bosom of the storm,
Glances the fire-clad eagle's wheeling form;
Eastward, in long perspective glittering, shine
The wood-crowned cliffs that o'er the lake re-
    cline;
Wide o'er the Alps a hundred streams unfold,
At once to pillars turn'd that flame with gold;
Behind his sail the peasant strives to shun
The West, that burns like one dilated sun,
Where in a mighty crucible expire
The mountains, glowing hot, like coals of fire."

The poetic PSYCHE, in its process to full development, undergoes as many changes as its Greek name-sake, the butterfly.* And it is remarkable how soon genius clears and purifies itself from the faults and errors of its earliest products; faults which, in its earliest compositions, are the more obtrusive and confluent, because as heterogeneous elements, which had only a temporary use, they constitute the very *ferment,* by which themselves are carried off. Or we may compare them to some diseases, which must work on the humours, and be thrown out on the surface, in order to secure the patient

---

* The fact, that in Greek Psyche is the common name for the soul, and the butterfly, is thus alluded to in the following stanza from an unpublished poem of the author:

"The butterfly the ancient Grecians made
    The soul's fair emblem, and its only name—
But of the soul, escaped the slavish trade
Of mortal life! For in this earthly frame
Our's is the reptile's lot, much toil, much blame,
Manifold motions making little speed,
And to deform and kill things, whereon we feed."
                                            S.T.C.

[Throughout the selections from the *Biographia Litera-ria,* Coleridge's footnotes are indicated by asterisks, the editor's by Arabic numerals.]

from their future recurrence. I was in my twenty-fourth year, when I had the happiness of knowing Mr. Wordsworth personally, and while memory lasts, I shall hardly forget the sudden effect produced on my mind, by his recitation of a manuscript poem, which still remains unpublished, but of which the stanza, and tone of style, were the same as those of the "Female Vagrant" as originally printed in the first volume of the "Lyrical Ballads." There was here, no mark of strained thought, or forced diction, no crowd or turbulence of imagery, and, as the poet hath himself well described in his lines "on re-visiting the Wye," manly reflection, and human associations had given both variety, and an additional interest to natural objects, which in the passion and appetite of the first love they had seemed to him neither to need or permit. The occasional obscurities, which had risen from an imperfect controul over the resources of his native language, had almost wholly disappeared, together with that worse defect of arbitrary and illogical phrases, at once hackneyed, and fantastic, which hold so distinguished a place in the *technique* of ordinary poetry, and will, more or less, alloy the earlier poems of the truest genius, unless the attention has been specifically directed to their worthlessness and incongruity.* I did not perceive any thing particular in the mere style of the poem alluded to during its recitation, except indeed such difference as was not separable from the thought and manner; and the Spencerian stanza, which always, more or less, recalls to the reader's mind

---

* Mr. Wordsworth, even in his two earliest "the Evening Walk and the Descriptive Sketches," is more free from this latter defect than most of the young poets his contemporaries. It may however be exemplified, together with the harsh and obscure construction, in which he more often offended, in the following lines:—

" 'Mid stormy vapours ever driving by,
  Where ospreys, cormorants, and herons cry;
  Where hardly given the hopeless waste to cheer,
  Denied the bread of life the foodful ear,
  Dwindles the pear on autumn's latest spray,
  And *apple sickens* pale in summer's ray;
  *Ev'n here content has fixed her smiling reign
  With independence, child of high disdain.*"

I hope, I need not say, that I have quoted these lines for no other purpose than to make my meaning fully understood. It is to be regretted that Mr. Wordsworth has not republished these two poems entire.

Spencer's own style, would doubtless have authorized in my then opinion a more frequent descent to the phrases of ordinary life, than could without an ill effect have been hazarded in the heroic couplet. It was not however the freedom from false taste, whether as to common defects, or to those more properly his own, which made so unusual an impression on my feelings immediately, and subsequently on my judgement. It was the union of deep feeling with profound thought; the fine balance of truth in observing with the imaginative faculty in modifying the objects observed; and above all the original gift of spreading the tone, the *atmosphere*, and with it the depth and height of the ideal world around forms, incidents, and situations, of which, for the common view, custom had bedimmed all the lustre, had dried up the sparkle and the dew drops. "To find no contradiction in the union of old and new; to contemplate the ANCIENT of days and all his works with feelings as fresh, as if all had then sprang forth at the first creative fiat; characterizes the mind that feels the riddle of the world, and may help to unravel it. To carry on the feelings of childhood into the powers of manhood; to combine the child's sense of wonder and novelty with the appearances, which every day for perhaps forty years had rendered familiar;

"With sun and moon and stars throughout the
        year,
And man and woman;"[1]

this is the character and privilege of genius, and one of the marks which distinguish genius from talents. And therefore is it the prime merit of genius and its most unequivocal mode of manifestation, so to represent familiar objects as to awaken in the minds of others a kindred feeling concerning them and that freshness of sensation which is the constant accompaniment of mental, no less than of bodily, convalescence. Who has not a thousand times seen snow fall on water? Who has not watched it with a new feeling, from the time that he has read Burns' comparison of sensual pleasure

"To snow that falls upon a river
A moment white—then gone for ever!"[2]

BIOGRAPHIA LITERARIA. CHAPTER IV. **1.** Lines quoted from Milton's "To Mr. Cyriack Skinner." **2.** Lines quoted from Robert Burns's "Tam o'Shanter."

In poems, equally as in philosophic disquisitions, genius produces the strongest impressions of novelty, while it rescues the most admitted truths from the impotence caused by the very circumstance of their universal admission. Truths of all others the most awful and mysterious, yet being at the same time of universal interest, are too often considered as *so* true, that they lose all the life and efficiency of truth, and lie bed-ridden in the dormitory of the soul, side by side, with the most despised and exploded errors." THE FRIEND,* page 76, No. 5.

This excellence, which in all Mr. Wordsworth's writings is more or less predominant, and which constitutes the character of his mind, I no sooner felt, than I sought to understand. Repeated meditations led me first to suspect, (and a more intimate analysis of the human faculties, their appropriate marks, functions, and effects matured my conjecture into full conviction) that fancy and imagination were two distinct and widely different faculties, instead of being, according to the general belief, either two names with one meaning, or at furthest, the lower and higher degree of one and the same power. It is not, I own, easy to conceive a more opposite translation of the Greek *Phantasia*, than the Latin *Imaginatio*; but it is equally true that in all societies there exists an instinct of growth, a certain collective, unconscious good sense working progressively to desynonymize** those words originally of the same meaning, which the conflux of dialects

had supplied to the more homogeneous languages, as the Greek and German: and which the same cause, joined with accidents of translation from original works of different countries, occasion in mixt languages like our own. The first and most important point to be proved is, that two conceptions perfectly distinct are confused under one and the same word, and (this done) to appropriate that word exclusively to one meaning, and the synonyme (should there be one) to the other. But if (as will be often the case in the arts and sciences) no synonyme exists, we must either invent or borrow a word. In the present instance the appropriation had already begun, and been legitimated in the derivative adjective: Milton had a highly *imaginative*, Cowley a very *fanciful* mind. If therefore I should succeed in establishing the actual existences of two faculties generally different, the nomenclature would be at once determined. To the faculty by which I had characterized Milton, we should confine the term *imagination*; while the other would be contra-distinguished as *fancy*. Now were it once fully ascertained, that this division is no less grounded in nature, than that of delirium from mania, or Otway's

"Lutes, lobsters, seas of milk, and ships of   amber," [3]

from Shakespear's

"What! have his daughters brought him to this   pass?" [4]

or from the preceding apostrophe to the elements; the theory of the fine arts, and of poetry in particu-

---

* As "the Friend" was printed on stampt sheets, and sent only by the post to a very limited number of subscribers, the author has felt less objection to quote from it, though a work of his own. To the public at large indeed it is the same as a volume in manuscript.

** This is effected either by giving to the one word a general, and to the other an exclusive use; as "to put on the back" and "to indorse"; or by an actual distinction of meanings as "naturalist," and "physician"; or by difference of relation as "I" and "Me"; (each of which the rustics of our different provinces still use in all the cases singular of the first personal pronoun). Even the mere difference, or corruption, in the *pronunciation* of the same word, if it have become general, will produce a new word with a distinct signification; thus "property" and "propriety"; the latter of which, even to the time of Charles II. was the *written* word for all the senses of both. Thus too "mister" and "master" both hasty pronunciations of the same word "magister," "mistress," and "miss," "if," and "give," &c. &c. There is a sort of *minim immortal* among the animalcula infusoria which has not naturally either birth, or

---

death, absolute beginning, or absolute end: for at a certain period a small point appears on its back, which deepens and lengthens till the creature divides into two, and the same process recommences in each of the halves now become integral. This may be a fanciful, but it is by no means a bad emblem of the formation of words, and may facilitate the conception, how immense a nomenclature may be organized from a few simple sounds by rational beings in a social state. For each new application, or excitement of the same sound, will call forth a different sensation, which cannot but affect the pronunciation. The after recollection of the sound, without the same vivid sensation, will modify it still further; till at length all trace of the original likeness is worn away.

3. *Venice Preserved, V*, ii, 151. 4. *King Lear, III*, iv, 63.

lar, could not, I thought, but derive some additional and important light. It would in its immediate effects furnish a torch of guidance to the philosophical critic; and ultimately to the poet himself. In energetic minds, truth soon changes by domestication into power; and from directing in the discrimination and appraisal of the product, becomes influencive in the production. To admire on principle, is the only way to imitate without loss of originality.

It has been already hinted, that metaphysics and psychology have long been my hobby-horse. But to have a hobby-horse, and to be vain of it, are so commonly found together, that they pass almost for the same. I trust therefore, that there will be more good humour than contempt, in the smile with which the reader chastises my self-complacency, if I confess myself uncertain, whether the satisfaction from the perception of a truth new to myself may not have been rendered more poignant by the conceit, that it would be equally so to the public. There was a time, certainly, in which I took some little credit to myself, in the belief that I had been the first of my countrymen, who had pointed out the diverse meaning of which the two terms were capable, and analyzed the faculties to which they should be appropriated. Mr. W. Taylor's recent volume of synonymes I have not yet seen;* but his specifica-

tion of the terms in question has been clearly shown to be both insufficient and erroneous by Mr. Wordsworth in the preface added to the late collection of his "Lyrical Ballads and other poems." The explanation which Mr. Wordsworth has himself given, will be found to differ from mine, chiefly perhaps, as our objects are different. It could scarcely indeed happen otherwise, from the advantage I have enjoyed of frequent conversation with him on a subject to which a poem of his own first directed my attention, and my conclusions concerning which, he had made more lucid to myself by many happy instances drawn from the operation of natural objects on the mind. But it was Mr. Wordsworth's purpose to consider the influences of fancy and imagination as they are manifested in poetry, and from the different effects to conclude their diversity in kind; while it is my object to investigate the seminal principle, and then from the kind to deduce the degree. My friend has drawn a masterly sketch of the branches with their *poetic* fruitage. I wish to add the trunk, and even the roots as far as they lift themselves above ground, and are visible to the naked eye of our common consciousness.

Yet even in this attempt I am aware, that I shall be obliged to draw more largely on the reader's attention, than so immethodical a miscellany can authorize; when in such a work (*the Ecclesiastical Policy*) of such a mind as Hooker's, the judicious author, though no less admirable for the perspicuity

---

* I ought to have added, with the exception of a single sheet which I accidentally met with at the printers. Even from this scanty specimen, I found it impossible to doubt the talent, or not to admire the ingenuity of the author. That his distinctions were for the greater part unsatisfactory to *my* mind, proves nothing against their accuracy; but it may possibly be serviceable to him in case of a second edition, if I take this opportunity of suggesting the query; whether he may not have been occasionally misled, by having assumed, as to me he appeared to have done, the non-existence of *any* absolute synonymes in our language? Now I cannot but think, that there are many which remain for our posterity to distinguish and appropriate, and which I regard as so much reversionary wealth in our mother-tongue. When two distinct meanings are confounded under one or more words, (and such must be the case, as sure as our knowledge is progressive and of course imperfect) erroneous consequences will be drawn, and what is true in one sense of the word, will be affirmed as true in toto. Men of research startled by the consequences, seek in the things themselves (whether in or out of the mind) for a knowledge of the fact, and having discovered the difference, remove the equivocation either by the substitution of a new word, or by the appropriation of one of the two or more words, that had

before been used promiscuously. When this distinction has been so naturalized and of such general currency, that the language itself does as it were *think* for us (like the sliding rule which is the mechanics safe substitute for arithmetical knowledge) we then say, that it is evident to *common sense*. Common sense, therefore, differs in different ages. What was born and christened in the schools passes by degrees into the world at large, and becomes the property of the market and the tea-table. At least I can discover no other meaning of the term, *common sense*, if it is to convey any specific difference from sense and judgement in genere, and where it is not used scholastically for the *universal reason*. Thus in the reign of Charles II. the philosophic world was called to arms by the moral sophisms of Hobbes, and the ablest writers exerted themselves in the detection of an error, which a school boy would now be able to confute by the mere recollection, that *compulsion* and *obligation* conveyed two ideas perfectly disparate, and that what appertained to the one, had been falsely transferred to the other by a mere confusion of terms.

than for the port and dignity of his language; and though he wrote for men of learning in a learned age; saw nevertheless occasion to anticipate and guard against "complaints of obscurity," as often as he was to trace his subject "to the highest well-spring and fountain." Which, (continues he) "because men are not accustomed to, the pains we take are more needful a great deal, than acceptable; and the matters we handle, seem by reason of newness (till the mind grow better acquainted with them) dark and intricate." I would gladly therefore spare both myself and others this labor, if I knew how without it to present an intelligible statement of my poetic creed; not as my *opinions*, which weigh for nothing, but as deductions from established premises conveyed in such a form, as is calculated either to effect a fundamental conviction, or to receive a fundamental confutation. If I may dare once more adopt the words of Hooker, "they, unto whom we shall seem tedious, are in no wise injured by us, because it is in their own hands to spare that labour, which they are not willing to endure." Those at least, let me be permitted to add, who have taken so much pains to render me ridiculous for a perversion of taste, and have supported the charge by attributing strange notions to me on no other authority than their own conjectures, owe it to themselves as well as to me not to refuse their attention to my own statement of the theory, which I *do* acknowledge; or shrink from the trouble of examining the grounds on which I rest it, or the arguments which I offer in its justification.

From CHAPTER XIII.

On the imagination, or esemplastic power.

O Adam! one Almighty is, from whom
All things proceed, and up to him return
If not depraved from good: created all
Such to perfection, one first nature all
Indued with various forms, various degrees
Of substance, and in things that live, of life;
But more refin'd, more spiritous and pure,
As nearer to him plac'd or nearer tending,
Each in their several active spheres assign'd,
Till body up to spirit work, in bounds
Proportion'd to each kind. So from the root

Springs lighter the green stalk: from thence the
leaves
More airy: last the bright consummate flower
Spirits odorous breathes. Flowers and their fruit,
Man's nourishment, by gradual scale sublim'd,
To vital spirits aspire: to animal:
To intellectual!—*give both life and sense,*
Fancy and understanding: whence the soul
REASON *receives. And reason is her* being,
Discursive or intuitive.

PAR. LOST, b. v.

Des Cartes, speaking as a naturalist, and in imitation of Archimedes, said, give me matter and motion and I will construct you the universe. We must of course understand him to have meant; I will render the construction of the universe intelligible. In the same sense the transcendental philosopher says; grant me a nature having two contrary forces, the one of which tends to expand infinitely, while the other strives to apprehend or *find* itself in this infinity, and I will cause the world of intelligences with the whole system of their representations to rise up before you. Every other science pre-supposes intelligence as already existing and complete: the philosopher contemplates it in its growth, and as it were represents its history to the mind from its birth to its maturity.

The venerable Sage of Koenigsberg has preceded the march of this master-thought as an effective pioneer in his essay on the introduction of negative quantities into philosophy, published 1763. In this he has shown, that instead of assailing the science of mathematics by metaphysics, as Berkley did in his Analyst, or of sophisticating it, as Wolff did, by the vain attempt of deducing the first principles of geometry from supposed deeper grounds of ontology, it behoved the metaphysician rather to examine whether the only province of knowledge, which man has succeeded in erecting into a pure science, might not furnish materials or at least hints for establishing and pacifying the unsettled, warring, and embroiled domain of philosophy. An imitation of the mathematical *method* had indeed been attempted with no better success than attended the essay of David to wear the armour of Saul. Another use however is possible and of far greater promise, namely, the actual application of the positions which had so wonderfully enlarged the discoveries of geometry, mutatis mutandis, to philosophical sub jects. Kant having briefly illustrated the utility of such an attempt in the questions of space, motion, and infinitely small quantities, as employed by the mathematician, proceeds to the idea of negative quantities and the transfer of them to metaphysical investigation. Opposites, he well observes, are of two kinds, either logical, i.e. such as are absolutely incompatible; or real without being contradictory. The former he denominates Nihil negativum irrepræsentabile, the connexion of which produces nonsense. A body in motion is something—Aliquid cogitabile; but a body, at one and the same time in motion and not in motion, is nothing, or at most, air articulated into nonsense. But a motory force of a body in one direction, and an equal force of the same body in an opposite direction is not incompatible, and the result, namely rest, is real and representable. For the purposes of mathematical calculus it is indifferent which force we term negative, and which positive, and consequently we appropriate the latter to that, which happens to be the principal object in our thoughts. Thus if a man's capital be ten and his debts eight, the subtraction will be the same, whether we call the capital negative debt, or the debt negative capital. But in as much as the latter stands practically in reference to the former, we of course represent the sum as 10-—8. It is equally clear that two equal forces acting in opposite directions, both being finite and each distinguished from the other by its direction only, must neutralize or reduce each other to inaction. Now the transcendental philosophy demands; first, that two forces should be conceived which counteract each other by their essential nature; not only not in consequence of the accidental direction of each, but as prior to all direction, nay, as the primary forces from which the conditions of all possible directions are derivative and deductible: secondly, that these forces should be assumed to be both alike infinite, both alike indestructible. The problem will then be to discover the result or product of two such forces, as distinguished from the result of those forces which are finite, and derive their difference solely from the circumstance of their direction. When we have formed a scheme or outline of these two different kinds of force, and of their different results by the process of discursive reasoning, it will then remain for us to elevate the Thesis from notional to actual, by contemplating intuitively this one power with its two inherent indestructible yet counteract-

ing forces, and the results or generations to which their inter-penetration gives existence, in the living principle and in the process of our own self-consciousness. By what instrument this is possible the solution itself will discover, at the same time that it will reveal, to and for whom it is possible. Non omnia possumes omnes.[5] There is a philosophic, no less than a poetic genius, which is differenced from the highest perfection of talent, not by degree but by kind. . . .

The IMAGINATION then I consider either as primary, or secondary. The primary IMAGINATION I hold to be the living Power and prime Agent of all human Perception, and as a repetition in the finite mind of the eternal act of creation in the infinite I AM. The secondary I consider as an echo of the former, co-existing with the conscious will, yet still as identical with the primary in the *kind* of its agency, and differing only in *degree,* and in the *mode* of its operation. It dissolves, diffuses, dissipates, in order to re-create; or where this process is rendered impossible, yet still at all events it struggles to idealize and to unify. It is essentially *vital,* even as all objects (*as* objects) are essentially fixed and dead.

FANCY, on the contrary, has no other counters to play with, but fixities and definites. The Fancy is indeed no other than a mode of Memory emancipated from the order of time and space; and blended with, and modified by that empirical phenomenon of the will, which we express by the word CHOICE. But equally with the ordinary memory it must receive all its materials ready made from the law of association.

Whatever more than this, I shall think it fit to declare concerning the powers and privileges of the imagination in the present work, will be found in the critical essay on the uses of the Supernatural in poetry and the principles that regulate its introduction: which the reader will find prefixed to the poem of The Ancient Mariner.

CHAPTER XIII. 5. Non . . . omnes: "Everyone cannot do all things."

CHAPTER XIV.

Occasion of the Lyrical Ballads, and the objects originally proposed—Preface to the second edition—The ensuing controversy, its causes and acrimony—Philosophic definitions of a poem and poetry with scholia.

During the first year that Mr. Wordsworth and I were neighbours, our conversations turned frequently on the two cardinal points of poetry, the power of exciting the sympathy of the reader by a faithful adherence to the truth of nature, and the power of giving the interest of novelty by the modifying colours of imagination. The sudden charm, which accidents of light and shade, which moonlight or sun-set diffused over a known and familiar landscape, appeared to represent the practicability of combining both. These are the poetry of nature. The thought suggested itself (to which of us I do not recollect) that a series of poems might be composed of two sorts. In the one, the incidents and agents were to be, in part at least, supernatural; and the excellence aimed at was to consist in the interesting of the affections by the dramatic truth of such emotions, as would naturally accompany such situations, supposing them real. And real in *this* sense they have been to every human being who, from whatever source of delusion, has at any time believed himself under supernatural agency. For the second class, subjects were to be chosen from ordinary life; the characters and incidents were to be such, as will be found in every village and its vicinity, where there is a meditative and feeling mind to seek after them, or to notice them, when they present themselves.

In this idea originated the plan of the "Lyrical Ballads"; in which it was agreed, that my endeavours should be directed to persons and characters supernatural, or at least romantic; yet so as to transfer from our inward nature a human interest and a semblance of truth sufficient to procure for these shadows of imagination that willing suspension of disbelief for the moment, which constitutes poetic faith. Mr. Wordsworth, on the other hand, was to propose to himself as his object, to give the charm of novelty to things of every day, and to excite a feeling analogous to the supernatural, by awakening the mind's attention from the lethargy of custom, and directing it to the loveliness and the wonders of the world before us; an inexhaustible treasure, but for which in consequence of the film of familiarity and selfish solicitude we have eyes, yet see not, ears that hear not, and hearts that neither feel nor understand.

With this view I wrote the "Ancient Mariner," and was preparing among other poems, the "Dark Ladie," and the "Christabel," in which I should have more nearly realized my ideal, than I had done in my first attempt. But Mr. Wordsworth's industry had proved so much more successful, and the number of his poems so much greater, that my compositions, instead of forming a balance, appeared rather an interpolation of heterogeneous matter. Mr. Wordsworth added two or three poems written in his own character, in the impassioned, lofty, and sustained diction, which is characteristic of his genius. In this form the "Lyrical Ballads" were published; and were presented by him, as an *experiment*, whether subjects, which from their nature rejected the usual ornaments and extra-colloquial style of poems in general, might not be so managed in the language of ordinary life as to produce the pleasurable interest, which it is the peculiar business of poetry to impart. To the second edition he added a preface of considerable length; in which notwithstanding some passages of apparently a contrary import, he was understood to contend for the extension of this style to poetry of all kinds, and to reject as vicious and indefensible all phrases and forms of style that were not included in what he (unfortunately, I think, adopting an equivocal expression) called the language of *real* life. From this preface, prefixed to poems in which it was impossible to deny the presence of original genius, however mistaken its direction might be deemed, arose the whole long continued controversy. For from the conjunction of perceived power with supposed heresy I explain the inveteracy and in some instances, I grieve to say, the acrimonious passions, with which the controversy has been conducted by the assailants.

Had Mr. Wordsworth's poems been the silly, the childish things, which they were for a long time described as being; had they been really distinguished from the compositions of other poets merely by meanness of language and inanity of thought; had they indeed contained nothing more than what is found in the parodies and pretended imitations of them; they must have sunk at once, a dead weight, into the slough of oblivion, and have dragged the preface along with them. But year after year increased the number of Mr. Wordsworth's admirers. They were found too not in the lower classes of the reading public, but chiefly among young men of strong sensibility and meditative minds; and their admiration (inflamed perhaps in some degree by opposition) was distinguished by its intensity, I might almost say, by its *religious* fervour. These facts, and the intellectual energy of the author, which was more or less consciously felt, where it was outwardly and even boisterously denied, meeting with sentiments of aversion to his opinions, and of alarm at their consequences, produced an eddy of criticism, which would of itself have borne up the poems by the violence, with which it whirled them round and round. With many parts of this preface in the sense attributed to them and which the words undoubtedly seem to authorise, I never concurred; but on the contrary objected to them as erroneous in principle, and as contradictory (in appearance at least) both to other parts of the same preface, and to the author's own practice in the greater number of the poems themselves. Mr. Wordsworth in his recent collection has, I find, degraded this prefatory disquisition to the end of his second volume, to be read or not at the reader's choice. But he has not, as far as I can discover, announced any change in his poetic creed. At all events, considering it as the source of a controversy, in which I have been honored, more than I deserve, by the frequent conjunction of my name with his, I think it expedient to declare once for all, in what points I coincide with his opinions, and in what points I altogether differ. But in order to render myself intelligible I must previously, in as few words as possible, explain my ideas, first, of a POEM; and secondly, of POETRY itself, in *kind,* and in *essence.*

The office of philosophical *disquisition* consists in just *distinction;* while it is the privilege of the philosopher to preserve himself constantly aware, that distinction is not division. In order to obtain adequate notions of any truth, we must intellectually separate its distinguishable parts; and this is the technical *process* of philosophy. But having so done, we must then restore them in our conception to the unity, in which they actually co-exist; and this is the *result* of philosophy. A poem contains the same elements as a prose composition; the difference therefore must consist in a different combination of them, in consequence of a different object proposed. According to the difference of the object will be the difference of the combination. It is possible, that the object may be merely to facilitate the recollection of any given facts or observations by artificial arrangement; and the composition will be a poem, merely because it is distinguished from prose by metre, or by rhyme, or by both conjointly. In this, the lowest sense, a man might attribute the name of a poem to the well known enumeration of the days in the several months;

> "Thirty days hath September,
> April, June, and November, &c."

and others of the same class and purpose. And as a particular pleasure is found in anticipating the recurrence of sounds and quantities, all compositions that have this charm superadded, whatever be their contents, *may* be entitled poems.

So much for the superficial *form.* A difference of object and contents supplies an additional ground of distinction. The immediate purpose may be the communication of truths; either of truth absolute and demonstrable, as in works of science; or of facts experienced and recorded, as in history. Pleasure, and that of the highest and most permanent kind, may *result* from the *attainment* of the end; but it is not itself the immediate end. In other works the communication of pleasure may be the immediate purpose; and though truth, either moral or intellectual, ought to be the *ultimate* end, yet this will distinguish the character of the author, not the class to which the work belongs. Blest indeed is that state of society, in which the immediate purpose would be baffled by the perversion of the proper ultimate end; in which no charm of diction or imagery could exempt the Bathyllus even of an Anacreon, or the Alexis of Virgil, from disgust and aversion! [6]

But the communication of pleasure may be the immediate object of a work not metrically composed; and that object may have been in a high

CHAPTER XIV. **6.** Bathyllus and Alexis were handsome youths in the pastoral poetry of the Greek Anacreon and the Roman Vergil.

degree attained, as in novels and romances. Would then the mere superaddition of metre, with or without rhyme, entitle *these* to the name of poems? The answer is, that nothing can permanently please, which does not contain in itself the reason why it is so, and not otherwise. If metre be superadded, all other parts must be made consonant with it. They must be such, as to justify the perpetual and distinct attention to each part, which an exact correspondent recurrence of accent and sound are calculated to excite. The final definition then, so deduced, may be thus worded. A poem is that species of composition, which is opposed to works of science, by proposing for its *immediate* object pleasure, not truth; and from all other species (having *this* object in common with it) it is discriminated by proposing to itself such delight from the *whole*, as is compatible with a distinct gratification from each component *part*.

Controversy is not seldom excited in consequence of the disputants attaching each a different meaning to the same word; and in few instances has this been more striking, than in disputes concerning the present subject. If a man chooses to call every composition a poem, which is rhyme, or measure, or both, I must leave his opinion uncontroverted. The distinction is at least competent to characterize the writer's intention. If it were subjoined, that the whole is likewise entertaining or affecting, as a tale, or as a series of interesting reflections, I of course admit this as another fit ingredient of a poem, and an additional merit. But if the definition sought for be that of a *legitimate* poem, I answer, it must be one, the parts of which mutually support and explain each other; all in their proportion harmonizing with, and supporting the purpose and known influences of metrical arrangement. The philosophic critics of all ages coincide with the ultimate judgments of all countries, in equally denying the praises of a just poem, on the one hand, to a series of striking lines or distichs, each of which absorbing the whole attention of the reader to itself disjoins it from its context, and makes it a separate whole, instead of an harmonizing part; and on the other hand, to an unsustained composition, from which the reader collects rapidly the general result unattracted by the component parts. The reader should be carried forward, not merely or chiefly by the mechanical impulse of curiosity, or by a restless desire to arrive at the final solution; but by the pleasureable activity of mind excited by the attractions of the journey itself. Like the motion of a serpent, which the Egyptians made the emblem of intellectual power; or like the path of sound through the air; at every step he pauses and half recedes, and from the retrogressive movement collects the force which again carries him onward. Precipitandus est *liber* spiritus,[7] says Petronius Arbiter most happily. The epithet, *liber*, here balances the preceding verb; and it is not easy to conceive more meaning condensed in fewer words.

But if this should be admitted as a satisfactory character of a poem, we have still to seek for a definition of poetry. The writings of PLATO, and Bishop TAYLOR, and the Theoria Sacra of BURNET, furnish undeniable proofs that poetry of the highest kind may exist without metre, and even without the contradistinguishing objects of a poem. The first chapter of Isaiah (indeed a very large proportion of the whole book) is poetry in the most emphatic sense; yet it would be not less irrational than strange to assert, that pleasure, and not truth, was the immediate object of the prophet. In short, whatever *specific* import we attach to the word, poetry, there will be found involved in it, as a necessary consequence, that a poem of any length neither can be, or ought to be, all poetry. Yet if an harmonious whole is to be produced, the remaining parts must be preserved *in keeping* with the poetry; and this can be no otherwise effected than by such a studied selection and artificial arrangement, as will partake of *one*, though not a *peculiar*, property of poetry. And this again can be no other than the property of exciting a more continuous and equal attention, than the language of prose aims at, whether colloquial or written.

My own conclusions on the nature of poetry, in the strictest use of the word, have been in part anticipated in the preceding disquisition on the fancy and imagination. What is poetry? is so nearly the same question with, what is a poet? that the answer to the one is involved in the solution of the other. For it is a distinction resulting from the poetic genius itself, which sustains and modifies the images, thoughts, and emotions of the poet's own

7. **Precipitandus . . . spiritus:** "The free spirit must be hurled forward."

mind. The poet, described in *ideal* perfection, brings the whole soul of man into activity, with the subordination of its faculties to each other, according to their relative worth and dignity. He diffuses a tone, and spirit of unity, that blends, and (as it were) *fuses,* each into each, by that synthetic and magical power, to which we have exclusively appropriated the name of imagination. This power, first put in action by the will and understanding, and retained under their irremissive, though gentle and unnoticed, controul (*laxis effertur habenis*)[8] reveals itself in the balance or reconciliation of opposite or discordant qualities: of sameness, with difference; of the general, with the concrete; the idea, with the image; the individual, with the representative; the sense of novelty and freshness, with old and familiar objects; a more than usual state of emotion, with more than usual order; judgement ever awake and steady self-possession, with enthusiasm and feeling profound or vehement; and while it blends and harmonizes the natural and the artificial, still subordinates art to nature; the manner to the matter; and our admiration of the poet to our sympathy with the poetry. "Doubtless," as Sir John Davies observes of the soul (and his words may with slight alteration be applied, and even more appropriately to the poetic IMAGINATION.)

"Doubtless this could not be, but that she turns
Bodies to spirit by sublimation strange,
As fire converts to fire the things it burns,
As we our food into our nature change.

From their gross matter she abstracts their forms,
And draws a kind of quintessence from things;
Which to her proper nature she transforms
To bear them light, on her celestial wings.

Thus does she, when from individual states
She doth abstract the universal kinds;
Which then re-clothed in divers names and fates
Steal access through our senses to our minds."

Finally, GOOD SENSE is the BODY of poetic genius, FANCY its DRAPERY, MOTION its LIFE, and IMAGINATION the SOUL that is every where, and in each; and forms all into one graceful and intelligent whole.

8. Laxis . . . habenis: "carried forward with loose reins."

CHAPTER XVII.

Examination of the tenets peculiar to Mr. Wordsworth—Rustic life (above all, low *and rustic life) especially unfavorable to the formation of a human diction—The* best *parts of language the product of philosophers, not clowns or shepherds—Poetry essentially ideal and generic—The language of Milton as much the language of* real *life, yea, incomparably more so than that of the cottager.*

As far then as Mr. Wordsworth in his preface contended, and most ably contended, for a reformation in our poetic diction, as far as he has evinced the truth of passion, and the *dramatic* propriety of those figures and metaphors in the original poets, which stript of their justifying reasons, and converted into mere artifices of connection or ornament, constitute the characteristic falsity in the poetic style of the moderns; and as far as he has, with equal acuteness and clearness, pointed out the process in which this change was effected, and the resemblances between that state into which the reader's mind is thrown by the pleasureable confusion of thought from an unaccustomed train of words and images; and that state which is induced by the natural language of empassioned feeling; he undertook a useful task, and deserves all praise, both for the attempt and for the execution. The provocations to this remonstrance in behalf of truth and nature were still of perpetual recurrence before and after the publication of this preface. I cannot likewise but add, that the comparison of such poems of merit, as have been given to the public within the last ten or twelve years, with the majority of those produced previously to the appearance of that preface, leave no doubt on my mind, that Mr. Wordsworth is fully justified in believing his efforts to have been by no means ineffectual. Not only in the verses of those who have professed their admiration of his genius, but even of those who have distinguished themselves by hostility to his theory, and depreciation of his writings, are the impressions of his principles plainly visible. It is possible, that with these principles others may have been blended, which are not equally evident; and some which are unsteady and subvertible from the narrowness or imperfection of their basis. But it is more than possible, that these errors of defect or exaggeration, by kindling and feeding the controversy, may have conduced not only to the wider propagation of the accompanying truths, but that by their frequent presentation to the mind in an excited state, they may have won for them a more permanent and practical result. A man will borrow a part from his opponent the more easily, if he feels himself justified in continuing to reject a part. While there remain important points in which he can still feel himself in the right, in which he still finds firm footing for continued resistance, he will gradually adopt those opinions, which were the least remote from his own convictions, as not less congruous with his own theory, than with that which he reprobates. In like manner with a kind of instinctive prudence, he will abandon by little and little his weakest posts, till at length he seems to forget that they had ever belonged to him, or affects to consider them at most as accidental and "petty annexments," the removal of which leaves the citadel unhurt and unendangered.

My own differences from certain supposed parts of Mr. Wordsworth's theory ground themselves on the assumption, that his words had been rightly interpreted, as purporting that the proper diction for poetry in general consists altogether in a language taken, with due exceptions, from the mouths of men in real life, a language which actually constitutes the natural conversation of men under the influence of natural feelings. My objection is, first, that in *any* sense this rule is applicable only to *certain* classes of poetry; secondly, that even to these classes it is not applicable, except in such a sense, as hath never by any one (as far as I know or have read) been denied or doubted; and lastly, that as far as, and in that degree in which it is *practicable*, yet as a *rule* it is useless, if not injurious, and therefore either need not, or ought not to be practised. The poet informs his reader, that he had generally chosen *low and rustic* life; but not *as* low and rustic, or in order to repeat that pleasure of doubtful moral effect, which persons of elevated rank and of superior refinement oftentimes derive from a happy *imitation* of the rude unpolished manners and discourse of their inferiors. For the pleasure so derived may be traced to three exciting causes. The first is the naturalness, in *fact*, of the things represented. The second is the apparent naturalness of the *representation*, as raised and qualified by an imperceptible infusion of the author's own knowledge and talent, which infusion does, indeed, constitute it an *imitation* as distinguished from a mere *copy*. The third cause may be found in the reader's conscious feeling of his superiority awakened by the contrast presented to him; even as for the same purpose the kings and great barons of yore retained, sometimes *actual* clowns and fools, but more frequently shrewd and witty fellows in that *character*. These, however, were not Mr. Wordsworth's objects. *He* chose low and rustic life, "because in that condition the essential passions of the heart find a better soil, in which they can attain their maturity, are less under restraint, and speak a plainer and more emphatic language; because in that condition of life our elementary feelings coexist in a state of greater simplicity, and consequently may be more accurately contemplated, and more forcibly communicated; because the manners of rural life germinate from those elementary feelings; and from the necessary character of rural occupations are more easily comprehended, and are more durable; and lastly, because in that condition the passions of men are incorporated with the beautiful and permanent forms of nature."

Now it is clear to me, that in the most interesting of the poems, in which the author is more or less dramatic, as the "Brothers," "Michael," "Ruth," the "Mad Mother," &c. the persons introduced are by no means taken *from low or rustic life* in the common acception of those words; and it is not less clear, that the sentiments and language, as far as they can be conceived to have been really transferred from the minds and conversation of such persons, are attributable to causes and circumstances not necessarily connected with "their occupations and abode." The thoughts, feelings, language, and manners of the shepherd-farmers in the vales of Cumberland and Westmoreland, as far as they are actually adopted in those poems, may be accounted for from causes, which will and do produce the same results in *every* state of life, whether in town or country. As the two principal I rank that INDEPENDENCE, which raises a man above servitude, or daily toil for the profit of others, yet not above the necessity of industry and a frugal simplicity of domestic life; and the accompanying unambitious, but solid and religious EDUCATION, which has rendered few books familiar, but the bible, and the liturgy or hymn book. To this latter cause, indeed, which is so far *accidental*, that it is the blessing of particular countries and a particular age, not the product of particular places or employments, the poet owes the shew of probability, that his personages might really feel, think, and talk with any tolerable resemblance to his representation. It is an excellent remark of Dr. Henry More's[9] (Enthusiasmus triumphatus, Sec. xxxv) that "a man of confined education, but of good parts, by constant reading of the bible will naturally form a more winning and commanding rhetoric than those that are learned; the intermixture of tongues and of artificial phrases debasing *their* style."

It is, moreover, to be considered that to the formation of healthy feelings, and a reflecting mind, *negations* involve impediments not less formidable, than sophistication and vicious intermixture. I am convinced, that for the human soul to prosper in rustic life, a certain vantage-ground is pre-requisite. It is not every man, that is likely to be improved by a country life or by country labours. Education, or original sensibility, or both, must pre-exist, if the changes, forms, and incidents of nature are to prove a sufficient stimulant. And where these are not sufficient, the mind contracts and hardens by want of stimulants; and the man becomes selfish, sensual, gross, and hard-hearted. Let the management of the POOR LAWS in Liverpool, Manchester, or Bristol be compared with the ordinary dispensation of the poor rates in agricultural villages, where the *farmers* are the overseers and guardians of the poor. If my own experience have not been particularly unfortunate, as well as that of the many respectable country clergymen with whom I have conversed on the subject, the result would engender more than scepticism concerning the desirable influences of low and rustic life in and for itself. Whatever may be concluded on the other side, from the stronger local attachments and enterprizing spirit of the Swiss, and other mountaineers, applies to a particular mode of pastoral life, under forms of property, that permit and beget manners truly republican, not to rustic life in general, or to the absence of artificial cultivation. On the contrary the mountaineers,

CHAPTER XVII. 9. Henry More (1614–1687) was one of the so-called Cambridge Platonists of seventeenth-century England. Their philosophy of sentiment and feeling appealed greatly to Coleridge.

whose manners have been so often eulogized, are in general better educated and greater readers than men of equal rank elsewhere. But where this is not the case, as among the peasantry of North Wales, the ancient mountains, with all their terrors and all their glories, are pictures to the blind, and music to the deaf.

I should not have entered so much into detail upon this passage, but here seems to be the point, to which all the lines of difference converge as to their source and centre. (I mean, as far as, and in whatever respect, my poetic creed *does* differ from the doctrines promulged in this preface.) I adopt with full faith the principle of Aristotle, that poetry as poetry is essentially* *ideal*, that it avoids and excludes all *accident;* that its apparent individualities of rank, character, or occupation must be *representative* of a class; and that the *persons* of poetry must be clothed with *generic* attributes, with the *common* attributes of the class; not with such as one gifted individual might *possibly* possess, but such as from his situation it is most probable beforehand, that he *would* possess. If my premises are right, and my deductions legitimate, it follows that there can be no *poetic* medium between the swains of Theocritus and those of an imaginary golden age.

The characters of the vicar and the shepherd-

---

* Say not that I am recommending abstractions, for these class-characteristics which constitute the instructiveness of a character, are so modified and particularized in each person of the Shaksperian Drama, that life itself does not excite more distinctly that sense of individuality which belongs to real existence. Paradoxical as it may sound, one of the essential properties of Geometry is not less essential to dramatic excellence; and Aristotle has accordingly required of the poet an involution of the universal in the individual. The chief differences are, that in Geometry it is the universal truth, which is uppermost in the consciousness; in poetry the individual form, in which the truth is clothed. With the ancients, and not less with the elder dramatists of England and France, both comedy and tragedy were considered as kinds of poetry. They neither sought in comedy to make us laugh merely; much less to make us laugh by wry faces, accidents of jargon, *slang* phrases for the day, or the clothing of common-place morals in metaphors drawn from the shops or mechanic occupations of their characters. Nor did they condescend in tragedy to wheedle away the applause of the spectators, by representing before them fac-similes of their own mean selves in all their existing meanness, or to work on their sluggish sympathies by a pathos not a whit more respectable than the maudlin

mariner in the poem of the "brothers," those of the shepherd of Green-head Gill in the "michael," have all the verisimilitude and representative quality, that the purposes of poetry can require. They are persons of a known and abiding class, and their manners and sentiments the natural product of circumstances common to the class. Take "michael" for instance:

"An old man stout of heart, and strong of limb;
His bodily frame had been from youth to age
Of an unusual strength: his mind was keen,
Intense and frugal, apt for all affairs,
And in his shepherd's calling he was prompt
And watchful more than ordinary men.
Hence he had learnt the meaning of all winds,
Of blasts of every tone, and oftentimes,
When others heeded not, he heard the South
Make subterraneous music, like the noise
Of bagpipers on distant highland hills.
The shepherd, at such warning, of his flock
Bethought him, and he to himself would say,
The winds are now devising work for me!
And truly at all times the storm, that drives
The traveller to a shelter, summon'd him
Up to the mountains. He had been alone
Amid the heart of many thousand mists,
That came to him and left him on the heights.
So liv'd he, till his eightieth year was pass'd.
And grossly that man errs, who should suppose
That the green vallies, and the streams and rocks,
Were things indifferent to the shepherd's thoughts.
Fields, where with chearful spirits he had breath'd
The common air; the hills, which he so oft
Had climb'd with vigorous steps; which had impress'd
So many incidents upon his mind
Of hardship, skill or courage, joy or fear;
Which like a book preserved the memory
Of the dumb animals, whom he had sav'd,
Had fed or shelter'd, linking to such acts,
So grateful in themselves, the certainty
Of honorable gains; these fields, these hills

Which were his living being, even more
Than his own blood—what could they less?
      had laid
Strong hold on his affections, were to him
A pleasurable feeling of blind love,
The pleasure which there is in life itself."

On the other hand, in the poems which are pitched at a lower note, as the "harry gill," "idiot boy," &c. the *feelings* are those of human nature in general; though the poet has judiciously laid the *scene* in the country, in order to place *himself* in the vicinity of interesting images, without the necessity of ascribing a sentimental perception of their beauty to the persons of his drama. In the "Idiot Boy," indeed, the mother's character is not so much a real and native product of a "situation where the essential passions of the heart find a better soil, in which they can attain their maturity and speak a plainer and more emphatic language," as it is an impersonation of an instinct abandoned by judgement. Hence the two following charges seem to me not wholly groundless: at least, they are the only plausible objections, which I have heard to that fine poem. The one is, that the author has not, in the poem itself, taken sufficient care to preclude from the reader's fancy the disgusting images of *ordinary, morbid idiocy*, which yet it was by no means his intention to represent. He has even by the "burr, burr, burr," uncounteracted by any preceding description of the boy's beauty, assisted in recalling them. The other is, that the idiocy of the *boy* is so evenly balanced by the folly of the *mother,* as to present to the general reader rather a laughable burlesque on the blindness of anile dotage, than an analytic display of maternal affection in its ordinary workings.

In the "Thorn," the poet himself acknowledges in a note the necessity of an introductory poem, in which he should have pourtrayed the character of the person from whom the words of the poem are supposed to proceed: a superstitious man moderately imaginative, of slow faculties and deep feelings, "a captain of a small trading vessel, for example, who being past the middle age of life, had retired upon an annuity, or small independent income, to some village or country town of which he was not a native, or in which he had not been accustomed to live. Such men having nothing to do become credulous and talkative from indolence." But in a poem, still more in a lyric poem (and the

---

tears of drunkenness. Their tragic scenes were meant to *affect* us indeed; but yet within the bounds of pleasure, and in union with the activity both of our understanding and imagination. They wished to transport the mind to a sense of its possible greatness, and to implant the germs of that greatness, during the temporary oblivion of the worthless "thing we are," and of the peculiar state in which each man *happens* to be, suspending our individual recollections and lulling them to sleep amid the music of nobler thoughts.

(Friend, Pages 251, 252.)

NURSE in Shakspeare's Romeo and Juliet alone prevents me from extending the remark even to dramatic *poetry*, if indeed the Nurse itself can be deemed altogether a case in point) it is not possible to imitate truly a dull and garrulous discourser, without repeating the effects of dulness and garrulity. However this may be, I dare assert, that the parts (and these form the far larger portion of the whole) which might as well or still better have proceeded from the poet's own imagination, and have been spoken in his own character, are those which have given, and which will continue to give universal delight; and that the passages exclusively appropriate to the supposed narrator, such as the last couplet of the third stanza;* the seven last lines of the tenth**; and the five following stanzas, with the exception of the four admirable lines at the commencement of the fourteenth are felt by many unprejudiced and unsophisticated hearts, as sudden and unpleasant sinkings from the height to which the poet had previously lifted them, and to which he again re-elevates both himself and his reader.

If then I am compelled to double the theory, by which the choice of *characters* was to be directed,

not only *a priori*, from grounds of reason, but both from the few instances in which the poet himself *need* be supposed to have been governed by it, and from the comparative inferiority of those instances; still more must I hesitate in my assent to the sentence which immediately follows the former citation; and which I can neither admit as particular fact, or as general rule. "The language too of these men is adopted (purified indeed from what appears to be its real defects, from all lasting and rational causes of dislike or disgust) because such men hourly communicate with the best objects from which the best part of language is originally derived; and because, from their rank in society, and the sameness and narrow circle of their intercourse, being less under the action of social vanity, they convey their feelings and notions in simple and unelaborated expressions." To this I reply; that a rustic's language, purified from all provincialism and grossness, and so far re-constructed as to be made consistent with the rules of grammar (which are in essence no other than the laws of universal logic, applied to Psychological materials) will not differ from the language of any other man of

---

* "I've measured it from side to side;
   'Tis three feet long, and two feet wide."
** "Nay, rack your brain—'tis all in vain,
   I'll tell you every thing I know;
   But to the Thorn, and to the Pond
   Which is a little step beyond,
   I wish that you would go:
   Perhaps, when you are at the place,
   You something of her tale may trace.

   I'll give you the best help I can:
   Before you up the mountain go,
   Up to the dreary mountain-top,
   I'll tell you all I know.

   'Tis now some two-and-twenty years
   Since she (her name is Martha Ray)
   Gave, with a maiden's true good will,
   Her company to Stephen Hill;
   And she was blithe and gay,
   And she was happy, happy still
   Whene'er she thought of Stephen Hill.

   And they had fix'd the wedding-day,
   The morning that must wed them both;
   But Stephen to another maid
   Had sworn another oath;
   And with this other maid to church
   Unthinking Stephen went—

   Poor Martha! on that woeful day
   A pang of pitiless dismay
   Into her soul was sent;
   A fire was kindled in her breast,
   Which might not burn itself to rest.

   They say, full six months after this,
   While yet the summer leaves were green,
   She to the mountain-top would go,
   And there was often seen.
   'Tis said, a child was in her womb,
   As now to any eye was plain;
   She was with child, and she was mad;
   Yet often she was sober sad
   From her exceeding pain.
   Oh me! ten thousand times I'd rather
   That he had died, that cruel father!

   .   .   .

   Last Christmas when we talked of this,
   Old farmer Simpson did maintain,
   That in her womb the infant wrought
   About its mother's heart, and brought
   Her senses back again:
   And when at last her time drew near,
   Her looks were calm, her senses clear.

   No more I know, I wish I did,
   And I would tell it all to you;

common-sense, however learned or refined he may be, except as far as the notions, which the rustic has to convey, are fewer and more indiscriminate. This will become still clearer, if we add the consideration (equally important though less obvious) that the rustic, from the more imperfect development of his faculties, and from the lower state of their cultivation, aims almost solely to convey *insulated facts*, either those of his scanty experience or his traditional belief; while the educated man chiefly seeks to discover and express those *connections* of things, or those relative *bearings* of fact to fact, from which some more or less general law is deducible. For *facts* are valuable to a wise man, chiefly as they lead to the discovery of the indwelling *law*, which is the true *being* of things, the sole solution of their modes of existence, and in the knowledge of which consists our dignity and our power.

As little can I agree with the assertion, that from the objects with which the rustic hourly communicates, the best part of language is formed. For first, if to communicate with an object implies such an acquaintance with it, as renders it capable of being discriminately reflected on; the distinct knowledge of an uneducated rustic would furnish a very scanty vocabulary. The few things, and modes of action, requisite for his bodily conveniences, would alone be individualized; while all the rest of nature would be expressed by a small number of confused, general terms. Secondly, I deny that the words and combinations of words derived from the objects, with which the rustic is familiar, whether with distinct or confused knowledge, can be justly said to form the *best* part of language. It is more than probable that many classes of the brute creation possess discriminating sounds, by which they can convey to each other notices of such objects as concern their food, shelter, or safety. Yet we hesitate to call the aggregate of such sounds a language, otherwise

For what became of this poor child
There's none that ever knew:
And if a child was born or no,
There's no one that could ever tell;
And if 'twas born alive or dead,
There's no one knows, as I have said;
But some remember well,
That Martha Ray about this time
Would up the mountain often climb."

than metaphorically. The best part of human language, properly so called, is derived from reflection on the acts of the mind itself. It is formed by a voluntary appropriation of fixed symbols to internal acts, to processes and results of imagination, the greater part of which have no place in the consciousness of uneducated man; though in civilized society, by imitation and passive remembrance of what they hear from their religious instructors and other superiors, the most uneducated share in the harvest which they neither sowed or reaped. If the history of the phrases in hourly currency among our peasants were traced, a person not previously aware of the fact would be surprized at finding so large a number, which three or four centuries ago were the exclusive property of the universities and the schools; and at the commencement of the Reformation had been transferred from the school to the pulpit, and thus gradually passed into common life. The extreme difficulty, and often the impossibility, of finding words for the simplest moral and intellectual processes in the languages of uncivilized tribes has proved perhaps the weightiest obstacle to the progress of our most zealous and adroit missionaries. Yet these tribes are surrounded by the same nature, as our peasants are; but in still more impressive forms; and they are, moreover, obliged to *particularize* many more of them. When therefore Mr. Wordsworth adds, "accordingly such a language" (meaning, as before, the language of rustic life purified from provincialism) "arising out of repeated experience and regular feelings is a more permanent, and a far more philosophical language, than that which is frequently substituted for it by poets, who think they are conferring honor upon themselves and their art in proportion as they indulge in arbitrary and capricious habits of expression"; it may be answered, that the language, which he has in view, can be attributed to rustics with no greater right, than the style of Hooker or Bacon to Tom Brown or Sir Roger L'Estrange. Doubtless, if what is peculiar to each were omitted in each, the result must needs be the same. Further, that the poet, who uses an illogical diction, or a style fitted to excite only the low and changeable pleasure of wonder by means of groundless novelty, substitutes a language of *folly* and *vanity*, not for that of the *rustic*, but for that of *good sense* and *natural feeling*.

Here let me be permitted to remind the reader, that the positions, which I controvert, are contained in the sentences—*"a selection of the* REAL *language of men"*;—*"the language of these men* (i.e. men in low and rustic life) *I propose to myself to imitate, and as far as possible, to adopt the very langauge of men." "Between the language of prose and that of metrical composition, there neither is, nor can be any essential difference."* It is against these exclusively, that my opposition is directed.

I object, in the very first instance, to an equivocation in the use of the word "real." Every man's language varies, according to the extent of his knowledge, the activity of his faculties, and the depth or quickness of his feelings. Every man's language has, first, its *individualities*; secondly, the common properties of the *class* to which he belongs; and thirdly, words and phrases of *universal* use. The language of Hooker, Bacon, Bishop Taylor, and Burke, differs from the common language of the learned class only by the superior number and novelty of the thoughts and relations which they had to convey. The language of Algernon Sidney differs not at all from that, which every well educated gentleman would wish to write, and (with due allowances for the undeliberateness, and less connected train, of thinking natural and proper to conversation) such as he would wish to talk. Neither one or the other differ half as much from the general language of cultivated society, as the language of Mr. Wordsworth's homeliest composition differs from that of a common peasant. For "real" therefore, we must substitute *ordinary*, or *lingua communis*. And this, we have proved, is no more to be found in the phraseology of low and rustic life, than in that of any other class. Omit the peculiarities of each, and the result of course must be common to all. And assuredly the omissions and changes to be made in the language of rustics, before it could be transferred to any species of poem, except the drama or other professed imitation, are at least as numerous and weighty, as would be required in adapting to the same purpose the ordinary language of tradesmen and manufacturers. Not to mention, that the language so highly extolled by Mr. Wordsworth varies in every county, nay in every village, according to the accidental character of the clergyman, the existence or non-existence of schools; or even, perhaps, as the excise-

man, publican, or barber happen to be, or not to be, zealous politicians, and readers of the weekly newspaper *pro bono publico*. Anterior to cultivation the lingua communis of every country, as Dante has well observed, exists every where in parts, and no where as a whole.

Neither is the case rendered at all more tenable by the addition of the words, *"in a state of excitement."* For the nature of a man's words, when he is strongly affected by joy, grief, or anger, must necessarily depend on the number and quality of the general truths, conceptions and images, and of the words expressing them, with which his mind had been previously stored. For the property of passion is not to *create;* but to set in increased activity. At least, whatever new connections of thoughts or images, or (which is equally, if not more than equally, the appropriate effect of strong excitement) whatever generalizations of truth or experience, the heat of passion may produce; yet the terms of their conveyance must have preexisted in his former conversations, and are only collected and crowded together by the unusual stimulation. It is indeed very possible to adopt in a poem the unmeaning repetitions, habitual phrases, and other blank counters, which an unfurnished or confused understanding interposes at short intervals, in order to keep hold of his subject which is still slipping from him, and to give him time for recollection; or in mere aid of vacancy, as in the scanty companies of a country stage the same player pops backwards and forwards, in order to prevent the appearance of empty spaces, in the procession of Macbeth, or Henry VIIIth. But what assistance to the poet, or ornament to the poem, these can supply, I am at a loss to conjecture. Nothing assuredly can differ either in origin or in mode more widely from the *apparent* tautologies of intense and turbulent feeling, in which the passion is greater and of longer endurance, than to be exhausted or satisfied by a single representation of the image or incident exciting it. Such repetitions I admit to be a beauty of the highest kind; as illustrated by Mr. Wordsworth himself from the song of Deborah. *"At her feet he bowed, he fell, he lay down; at her feet he bowed, he fell; where he bowed, there he fell down dead."* [10]

---

10. *"At . . . dead,"*: a reference to Judges 5:27.

From CHAPTER XXII.

The characteristic defects of Wordsworth's poetry, with the principles from which the judgement, that they are defects, is deduced—Their proportion to the beauties—For the greatest part characteristic of his theory only.

———

[In the section immediately preceding, Coleridge has been discussing problems in the subject matter and style of Wordsworth's poetry.]

———

To these defects which, as appears by the extracts, are only occasional, I may oppose with far less fear of encountering the dissent of any candid and intelligent reader, the following (for the most part correspondent) excellencies. First, an austere purity of language both grammatically and logically; in short a perfect appropriateness of the words to the meaning. Of how high value I deem this, and how particularly estimable I hold the example at the present day, has been already stated: and in part too the reasons on which I ground both the moral and intellectual importance of habituating ourselves to a strict accuracy of expression. It is noticeable, how limited an acquaintance with the master-pieces of art will suffice to form a correct and even a sensitive taste, where none but master-pieces have been seen and admired: while on the other hand, the most correct notions, and the widest acquaintance with the works of excellence of all ages and countries, will not perfectly secure us against the contagious familiarity with the far more numerous offspring of tastelessness or of a perverted taste. If this be the case, as it notoriously is, with the arts of music and painting, much more difficult will it be, to avoid the infection of multiplied and daily examples in the practice of an art, which uses words, and words only, as its instruments. In poetry, in which every line, every phrase, may pass the ordeal of deliberation and deliberate choice, it is possible, and barely possible, to attain that ultimatum which I have ventured to propose as the infallible test of a blameless style; namely, its *untranslatableness* in words of the same language without injury to the meaning.

Be it observed, however, that I include in the *meaning* of a word not only its correspondent object, but likewise all the associations which it recalls. For language is framed to convey not the object alone, but likewise the character, mood and intentions of the person who is representing it. In poetry it *is* practicable to preserve the diction uncorrupted by the affectations and misappropriations, which promiscuous authorship, and reading not promiscuous only because it is disproportionally most conversant with the compositions of the day, have rendered general. Yet even to the poet, composing in his own province, it is an arduous work: and as the result and pledge of a watchful good sense, of fine and luminous distinction, and of complete self-possession, may justly claim all the honor which belongs to an attainment equally difficult and valuable, and the more valuable for being rare. It is at *all* times the proper food of the understanding; but in an age of corrupt eloquence it is both food and antidote.

In prose I doubt whether it be even possible to preserve our style wholly unalloyed by the vicious phraseology which meets us every where, from the sermon to the newspaper, from the harangue of the legislator to the speech from the convivial chair, announcing a *toast* or sentiment. Our chains rattle, even while we are complaining of them. The poems of Boetius rise high in our estimation when we compare them with those of his contemporaries, as Sidonius Apollinaris, &c. They might even be referred to a purer age, but that the prose, in which they are set, as jewels in a crown of lead or iron, betrays the true age of the writer. Much however may be effected by education. I believe not only from grounds of reason, but from having in great measure assured myself of the fact by actual though limited experience, that to a youth led from his first boyhood to investigate the meaning of every word and the reason of its choice and position, Logic presents itself as an old acquaintance under new names.

On some future occasion, more especially demanding such disquisition, I shall attempt to prove the close connection between veracity and habits of mental accuracy; the beneficial after-effects of verbal precision in the preclusion of fanaticism, which masters the feelings more especially by indistinct watch-words; and to display the advantages which language alone, at least which language with incomparably greater ease and certainty than any other means, presents to the instructor of impressing modes of intellectual energy so constantly, so imperceptibly, and as it were by such elements and atoms, as to secure in due time the formation of a second nature. When we reflect, that the cultivation of the judgment is a positive command of the moral law, since the reason can give the *principle* alone, and the conscience bears witness only to the *motive*, while the application and effects must depend on the judgment: when we consider, that the greater part of our success and comfort in life depends on distinguishing the similar from the same, that which is peculiar in each thing from that which it has in common with others, so as still to select the most probable, instead of the merely possible or positively unfit, we shall learn to value earnestly and with a practical seriousness a mean, already prepared for us by nature and society, of teaching the young mind to think well and wisely by the same unremembered process and with the same never forgotten results, as those by which it is taught to speak and converse. Now how much warmer the interest is, how much more genial the feelings of reality and practicability, and thence how much stronger the impulses to imitation are, which a *contemporary* writer, and especially a contemporary *poet,* excites in youth and commencing manhood, has been treated of in the earlier pages of these sketches. I have only to add, that all the praise which is due to the exertion of such influence for a purpose so important, joined with that which must be claimed for the infrequency of the same excellence in the same perfection, belongs in full right to Mr. Wordsworth. I am far however from denying that we have poets whose *general* style possesses the same excellence, as Mr. Moore, Lord Byron, Mr. Bowles, and in all his later and more important works our laurel-honoring Laureate.[11] But there are none, in whose works I do not appear to myself to find *more* exceptions, than in those of Wordsworth. Quotations or specimens would here be wholly out of place, and must be left for the critic who doubts and would invalidate the justice of this eulogy so applied.

The second characteristic excellence of Mr. W's works is: a correspondent weight and sanity of the Thoughts and Sentiments,—won, not from books; but—from the poet's own meditative observation. They are *fresh* and have the dew upon them. His muse, at least when in her strength of wing, and when she hovers aloft in her proper element,

> "Makes audible a linked lay of truth,
> Of truth profound a sweet continuous lay,
> Not learnt, but native, her own natural notes!"
>   S. T. C.

Even throughout his smaller poems there is scarcely one, which is not rendered valuable by some just and original reflection.

See page 25, vol. 2nd: or the two following passages in one of his humblest compositions.

> "O Reader! had you in your mind
> Such stores as silent thought can bring,
> O gentle Reader! you would find
> A tale in every thing."

and

> "I have heard of hearts unkind, kind deeds
> With coldness still returning:
> Alas! the gratitude of men
> Has oftener left *me* mourning."

or in a still higher strain the six beautiful quatrains, page 134.

> "Thus fares it still in our decay:
> And yet the wiser mind
> Mourns less for what age takes away
> That what it leaves behind.
>
> The Blackbird in the summer trees,
> The Lark upon the hill,
> Let loose their carols when they please,
> Are quiet when they will.
>
> With nature never do *they* wage
> A foolish strife; they see
> A happy youth, and their old age
> Is beautiful and free!
>
> But we are pressed by heavy laws;
> And often, glad no more,
> We wear a face of joy, because
> We have been glad of yore.
>
> If there is one, who need bemoan
> His kindred laid in earth,
> The household hearts that were his own,
> It is the man of mirth.
>
> My days, my Friend, are almost gone,
> My life has been approved,
> And many love me; but by none
> Am I enough beloved."

CHAPTER XXII. **11.** Robert Southey.

or the sonnet on Buonaparte, page 202, vol. 2; or finally (for a volume would scarce suffice to exhaust the instances,) the last stanza of the poem on the withered Celandine, vol. 2, p. 212.

> "To be a prodigal's favorite—then, worse truth,
> A miser's pensioner—behold our lot!
> Oh man! that from thy fair shining youth
> Age might but take the things, youth needed
> not."

Both in respect of this and of the former excellence, Mr. Wordsworth strikingly resembles Samuel Daniel, one of the golden writers of our golden **Elizabethan age, now most causelessly neglected:** Samuel Daniel, whose diction bears no mark of time, no distinction of age, which has been, and as long as our language shall last, will be so far the language of the to-day and for ever, as that it is more intelligible to us, than the transitory fashions of our own particular age. A similar praise is due to his sentiments. No frequency of perusal can deprive them of their freshness. For though they are brought into the full day-light of every reader's comprehension; yet are they drawn up from depths which few in any age are priviledged to visit, into which few in any age have courage or inclination to descend. If Mr. Wordsworth is not equally with Daniel alike intelligible to all readers of average understanding in all passages of his works, the comparative difficulty does not arise from the greater impurity of the ore, but from the nature and uses of the metal. A poem is not necessarily obscure, because it does not aim to be popular. It is enough, if a work be perspicuous to those for whom it is written, and,

> "Fit audience find, though few."

To the "Ode on the intimation of immortality from recollections of early childhood" the poet might have prefixed the lines which Dante addresses to one of his own Canzoni—

> "Canzon, io credo, che saranno radi
> Che tua ragione intendan bene:
> Tanto lor sei faticoso alto."

> "O lyric song, there will be few, think I,
> Who may thy import understand aright:
> Thou art for *them* so arduous and so high!"

But the ode was intended for such readers only as had been accustomed to watch the flux and reflux of their inmost nature, to venture at times into the twilight realms of consciousness, and to feel a deep interest in modes of inmost being, to which they know that the attributes of time and space are inapplicable and alien, but which yet can not be conveyed, save in symbols of time and space. For such readers the sense is sufficiently plain, and they will be as little disposed to charge Mr. Wordsworth with believing the platonic pre-existence in the ordinary interpretation of the words, as I am to believe, that Plato himself ever meant or taught it . . .

Third (and wherein he soars far above Daniel) the sinewy strength and originality of single lines and paragraphs: the frequent *curiosa felicitas* of his diction, of which I need not here give specimens, having anticipated them in a preceding page. This beauty, and as eminently characteristic of Wordsworth's poetry, his rudest assailants have felt themselves compelled to acknowledge and admire.

Fourth; the perfect truth of nature in his images and descriptions as taken immediately from nature, and proving a long and genial intimacy with the very spirit which gives the physiognomic expression to all the works of nature. Like a green field reflected in a calm and perfectly transparent lake, the image is distinguished from the reality only by its greater softness and lustre. Like the moisture or the polish on a pebble, genius neither distorts nor false-colours its objects; but on the contrary brings out many a vein and many a tint, which escape the eye of common observation, thus raising to the rank of gems, what had been often kicked away by the hurrying foot of the traveller on the dusty high road of custom.

Let me refer to the whole description of skating, vol. I, page 42 to 47, especially to the lines

> "So through the darkness and the cold we flew,
> And not a voice was idle: with the din
> Meanwhile the precipices rang aloud;
> The leafless trees and every icy crag
> Tinkled like iron; while the distant hills
> Into the tumult sent an alien sound
> Of melancholy, not unnoticed, while the stars
> Eastward were sparkling clear, and in the west
> The orange sky of evening died away."

Or to the poem on the green linnet, vol. I. p. 244. What can be more accurate yet more lovely than the two concluding stanzas?

> "Upon yon tuft of hazel trees,
> That twinkle to the gusty breeze,
> Behold him perched in ecstacies,
> Yet seeming still to hover,
> There! where the flutter of his wings

> Upon his back and body flings
> Shadows and sunny glimmerings
>   That cover him all over.
>
> While thus before my eyes he gleams,
> A brother of the leaves he seems;
> When in a moment forth he teems
>   His little song in gushes:
> As if it pleased him to disdain
> And mock the form when he did feign
> While he was dancing with the train
>   Of leaves among the bushes."

Or the description of the blue-cap, and of the noon-tide silence, p. 284; or the poem to the cuckoo, p. 299; or, lastly, though I might multiply the references to ten times the number, to the poem so completely Wordsworth's commencing

"Three years she grew in sun and shower," &c.

Fifth: a meditative pathos, a union of deep and subtle thought with sensibility; a sympathy with man as man; the sympathy indeed of a contemplator, rather than a fellow-sufferer or co-mate, (spectator, haud particeps)[12] but of a contemplator, from whose view no difference of rank conceals the sameness of the nature; no injuries of wind or weather, of toil, or even of ignorance, wholly disguise the human face divine. The superscription and the image of the Creator still remain legible to *him* under the dark lines, with which guilt or calamity had cancelled or cross-barred it. Here the man and the poet lose and find themselves in each other, the one as glorified, the latter as substantiated. In this mild and philosophic pathos, Wordsworth appears to me without a compeer. Such he *is:* so he *writes.* See vol. I. page 131 to 136, or that most affecting composition, the "Affliction of Margaret———of———," page 165 to 168, which no mother, and if I may judge by my own experience, no parent can read without a tear. Or turn to that genuine lyric, in the former edition, entitled, the "Mad Mother," p. 174 to 178, of which I can not refrain from quoting two of the stanzas, both of them for their pathos, and the former for the fine transition in the two concluding lines of the stanza, so expressive of that deranged state, in which from the increased sensibility the sufferer's attention is abruptly drawn off by every trifle, and in the same instant plucked back again by the one despotic

12. **spectator . . . particeps:** "a spectator, by no means a participant."

thought, and bringing home with it, by the blending, *fusing* power of Imagination and Passion, the alien object to which it had been so abruptly diverted, no longer an alien but an ally and an inmate.

> "Suck, little babe, oh suck again!
> It cools my blood; it cools my brain:
> Thy lips, I feel them, baby! they
> Draw from my heart the pain away.
> Oh! press me with thy little hand;
> It loosens something at my chest;
> About that tight and deadly band
> I feel thy little fingers prest.
> The breeze I see is in the tree!
> It comes to cool my babe and me."
>
> "Thy father cares not for my breast,
> 'Tis thine, sweet baby, there to rest,
> 'Tis all thine own!—and, if it's hue,
> Be changed, that was so fair to view,
> 'Tis fair enough for thee, my dove!
> My beauty, little child, is flown,
> But thou wilt live with me in love,
> And what if my poor cheek be brown?
> 'Tis well for me, thou can'st not see
> How pale and wan it else would be."

Last, and pre-eminently I challenge for this poet the gift of IMAGINATION in the highest and strictest sense of the word. In the play of *Fancy,* Wordsworth, to my feelings, is not always graceful, and sometimes *recondite.* The *likeness* is occasionally too strange, or demands too peculiar a point of view, or is such as appears the creature of predetermined research, rather than spontaneous presentation. Indeed his fancy seldom displays itself, as mere and unmodified fancy. But in imaginative power, he stands nearest of all modern writers to Shakespear and Milton; and yet in a kind perfectly unborrowed and his own. To employ his own words, which are at once an instance and an illustration, he does indeed to all thoughts and to all objects—

> "————————————add the gleam,
> The light that never was on sea or land,
> The consecration, and the poet's dream."

I shall select a few examples as most obviously manifesting this faculty; but if I should ever be fortunate enough to render my analysis of imagination, its origin and characters thoroughly intelligible to the reader, he will scarcely open on a page of this poet's works without recognizing, more or less, the presence and the influences of this faculty.

From the poem on the Yew Trees, vol. I. page 303, 304.

"But worthier still of note
Are those fraternal four of Borrowdale,
Joined in one solemn and capacious grove:
Huge trunks!—and each particular trunk a
　　growth
Of intertwisted fibres serpentine
Up-coiling, and inveterately convolved,—
Not uninformed with phantasy, and looks
That threaten the prophane;—a pillared shade,
Upon whose grassless floor of red-brown hue,
By sheddings from the pinal umbrage tinged
Perennially—beneath whose sable roof
Of boughs, as if for festal purpose decked
With unrejoicing berries, ghostly shapes
May meet at noontide—FEAR and trembling
　　HOPE,
SILENCE and FORESIGHT—DEATH, the skeleton,
And TIME, the shadow—there to celebrate,
As in a natural temple scattered o'er
With altars undisturbed of mossy stone,
United worship; or in mute repose
To lie, and listen to the mountain flood
Murmuring from Glanamara's inmost caves."

The effect of the old man's figure in the poem of
Resignation and Independence, vol. II. page 33.

"While he was talking thus, the lonely place
The old man's shape, and speech, all troubled
　　me:
In my mind's eye I seemed to see him pace
About the weary moors continually,
Wandering about alone and silently."

Or the 8th, 9th, 19th, 26th, 31st, and 33rd, in the
collection of miscellaneous sonnets—the sonnet on
the subjugation of Switzerland, page 210, or the last
ode from which I especially select the two following
stanzas or paragraphs, page 349 to 350.

"Our birth is but a sleep and a forgetting:
The soul that rises with us, our life's star
Hath had elsewhere its setting,
　　And cometh from afar.
Not in entire forgetfulness,
And not in utter nakedness,
But trailing clouds of glory do we come
From God who is our home:
Heaven lies about us in our infancy!
Shades of the prison-house begin to close
　　Upon the growing boy;
But he beholds the light, whence it flows,
　　He sees it in his joy!
The youth who daily further from the east
Must travel, still is nature's priest,
　　And by the vision splendid
　　Is on his way attended;
At length the man perceives it die away,
And fade into the light of common day."

And page 352 to 354 of the same ode.

"O joy in our embers
Is something that doth live,
That nature yet remembers
What was so fugitive!
The thought of our past years in me doth breed
Perpetual benedictions: not in deed
For that which is most worthy to be blest
Delight and liberty the simple creed
Of childhood, whether busy or at rest,
With new-fledged hope still fluttering in his
　　breast:—
Not for these I raise
The song of thanks and praise;
But for those obstinate questionings
Of sense and outward things,
Fallings from us, vanishings;
Blank misgivings of a creature
Moving about in worlds not realized,
High instincts, before which our mortal nature
Did tremble like a guilty thing surprised!
But for those first affections,
Those shadowy recollections,
Which, be they what they may,
Are yet the fountain light of all our day,
Are yet a master light of all our seeing;
Uphold us—cherish—and have power to make
Our noisy years seem moments in the being
Of the eternal silence; truths that wake
　　To perish never:
Which neither listlessness, nor mad endeavour
Nor man nor boy
Nor all that is at enmity with joy
Can utterly abolish or destroy!
Hence, in a season of calm weather,
Though inland far we be,
Our souls have sight of that immortal sea
Which brought us hither,
Can in a moment travel thither—
And see the children sport upon the shore,
And hear the mighty waters rolling evermore."

And since it would be unfair to conclude with
an extract, which though highly characteristic must
yet from the nature of the thoughts and the subject
be interesting, or perhaps intelligible, to but a limited number of readers; I will add from the poet's
last published work a passage equally Wordsworthian; of the beauty of which, and of the imaginative
power displayed therein, there can be but one
opinion, and one feeling. See White Doe, page 5.

"Fast the church-yard fills;—anon
Look again and they are gone;
The cluster round the porch, and the folk
Who sate in the shade of the prior's oak!
And scarcely have they disappear'd
Ere the prelusive hymn is heard:—

With one consent the people rejoice,
Filling the church with a lofty voice!
They sing a service which they feel
For 'tis the sun-rise of their zeal
And faith and hope are in their prime
In great Eliza's golden time."
A moment ends the fervent din
And all is hushed without and within;
For though the priest more tranquilly
Recites the holy liturgy,
The only voice which you can hear
Is the river murmuring near.
When soft!—the dusky trees between
And down the path through the open green,
Where is no living thing to be seen;
And through yon gateway, where is found,
Beneath the arch with ivy bound,
Free entrance to the church-yard ground;
And right across the verdant sod
Towards the very house of God;
Comes gliding in with lovely gleam,
Comes gliding in serene and slow,
Soft and silent as a dream,
A solitary doe!
White she is as lilly of June,
And beauteous as the silver moon
When out of sight the clouds are driven
And she is left alone in heaven!
Or like a ship some gentle day
In sunshine sailing far away—
A glittering ship that hath the plain
Of ocean for her own domain.

. . .

What harmonious pensive changes
Wait upon her as she ranges
Round and round this pile of state
Overthrown and desolate!
Now a step or two her way
Is through space of open day,
Where the enamoured sunny light
Brightens her that was so bright:
Now doth a delicate shadow fall,
Falls upon her like a breath
From some lofty arch or Wall,
As she passes underneath.

The following analogy will, I am apprehensive, appear dim and fantastic, but in reading Bartram's Travels[13] I could not help transcribing the following lines as a sort of allegory, or connected simile and metaphor of Wordsworth's intellect and genius. —"The soil is a deep, rich, dark mould, on a deep stratum of tenacious clay; and that on a foundation of rocks, which often break through both strata,

lifting their back above the surface. The trees which chiefly grow here are the gigantic, black oak; magnolia magnifloria; fraximus excelsior; platane; and a few stately tulip trees." What Mr. Wordsworth *will* produce, it is not for me to prophecy: but I could pronounce with the liveliest convictions what he is capable of producing. It is the FIRST GENUINE PHILOSOPHIC POEM.

The preceding criticism will not, I am aware, avail to overcome the prejudices of those, who have made it a business to attack and ridicule Mr. Wordsworth's compositions.

Truth and prudence might be imaged as concentric circles. The poet may perhaps have passed beyond the latter, but he has confined himself far within the bounds of the former, in designating these critics, as too petulant to be passive to a genuine poet, and too feeble to grapple with him; —"men of palsied imaginations, in whose minds all healthy action is languid;—who, therefore, feel as the many direct them, or with the many are greedy after vicious provocatives."

Let not Mr. Wordsworth be charged with having expressed himself too indignantly, till the wantonness and the systematic and malignant perseverance of the aggressions have been taken into fair consideration. I myself heard the commander in chief [14] of this unmanly warfare make a boast of his private admiration of Wordsworth's genius. I have heard him declare, that whoever came into his room would probably find the Lyrical Ballads lying open on his table, and that (speaking exclusively of those written by Mr. Wordsworth himself), he could nearly repeat the whole of them by heart. *But* a Review, in order to be a saleable article, must be *personal, sharp,* and *pointed*: and, *since then,* the Poet has made himself, and with himself all who were, or were supposed to be, his friends and admirers, the object of the critic's revenge—how? by having spoken of a work so conducted in the terms which it deserved! I once heard a clergyman in boots and buckskin avow, that he would cheat his own father *in a horse*. A moral system of a similar nature seems to have been adopted by too many anonymous critics. As we used to say at school, in reviewing they *make* being rogues: and he, who complains, is to be laughed at for his ignorance of *the game.*

13. a reference to a book by one William Bartram, *Travels Through North and South Carolina and the Cherokee Country* (1792).

14. the infamous Francis Jeffrey (1773–1850), editor of the powerful *Edinburgh Review.*

With the pen out of their hand they are *honorable men.* They exert indeed power (which is to that of the injured party who should attempt to expose their glaring perversions and misstatements, as twenty to one) to write down, and (where the author's circumstances permit) to *impoverish* the man, whose learning and genius they themselves in private have repeatedly admitted. They knowingly strive to make it impossible for the man even to publish[*] any future work without exposing himself to all the wretchedness of debt and embarrassment. But this is all *in their vocation:* and bating what they do in their *vocation, "who can say that black is the white of their eye?"*

So much for the detractors from Wordsworth's merits. On the other hand, much as I might wish for their fuller sympathy, I dare not flatter myself, that the freedom with which I have declared my opinions concerning both his theory and his defects, most of which are more or less connected with his theory either as cause or effect, will be satisfactory or pleasing to *all* the poet's admirers and advocates. More indiscriminate than mine their admiration may be: deeper and more sincere it can not be. But I have advanced no opinion either for praise or censure, other than as texts introductory to the reasons which compel me to form it. Above all, I was fully convinced that such a criticism was not only wanted; but that, if executed with adequate ability, it must conduce in no mean degree to Mr. Wordsworth's *reputation.* His *fame* belongs to another age, and can neither be accelerated or retarded. How small the proportion of the defects are to the beauties, I have repeatedly declared; and that no one of them originates in deficiency of poetic genius. Had they been more and greater, I should still, as a friend to his literary character in the present age, consider an analytic display of them as *pure gain;* if only it removed, as surely to all reflecting minds even the foregoing analysis must have removed, the strange mistake so slightly grounded, yet so widely and industriously propagated, of Mr. Wordsworth's

turn for SIMPLICITY! I am not half as much irritated by hearing his enemies abuse him for vulgarity of style, subject, and conception; as I am disgusted with the gilded side of the same meaning, as displayed by some affected admirers with whom he is, forsooth, a *sweet, simple poet!* and *so* natural, that little master Charles, and his younger sister, are *so* charmed with them, that they play at "Goody Blake," or at "Johnny and Betty Foy!"

Were the collection of poems published with these biographical sketches, important enough, (which I am not vain enough to believe) to deserve such a distinction: EVEN AS I HAVE DONE, SO WOULD I BE DONE UNTO.

For more than eighteen months have the volume of Poems, entitled SIBYLLINE LEAVES, and the present volumes up to this page been printed, and ready for publication. But ere I speak of myself in the tones, which are alone natural to me under the circumstances of late years, I would fain present myself to the Reader as I was in the first dawn of my literary life:

> "When Hope grew round me, like the climbing
> vine,
> And fruits and foliage not my own seem'd
> mine!" [15]

For this purpose I have selected from the letters which I wrote home from Germany, those which appeared likely to be most interesting, and at the same time most pertinent to the title of this work.

1815   *1817*

FROM

The Statesman's Manual

THE IMAGINATION[*]

(1) The histories and political economy of the present and preceding century partake in the general

---

[*] Not many months ago an eminent bookseller was asked what he thought of ————? The answer was: "I have heard his powers very highly spoken of by some of our first-rate men; but I would not have a work of his if any one would give it me: for he is spoken but slightly of, or not at all in the Quarterly Review: and the Edinburgh, you know, is decided, to cut him up!"

15. Coleridge's "Dejection: An Ode," ll. 80–81.

[*] Although several famous considerations of imagination are found in the selections from the *Biographia Literaria,* this one from *The Statesman's Manual* of 1816 is one of Coleridge's clearest and most searching.

contagion of its mechanistic philosophy, and are the product of an unenlivened generalizing understanding. In the Scriptures they are the living educts of the imagination; of that reconciling and mediatory power, which incorporating the reason in images of the sense, and organizing (as it were) the flux of the senses by the permanence and self-circling energies of the reason, gives birth to a system of symbols, harmonious in themselves, and consubstantial with the truths of which they are the conductors. These are the *wheels* which Ezekiel beheld, when the hand of the Lord was upon him, and he saw the the visions of God as he sate among the captives by the river of Chebar. *Whithersoever the Spirit was to go, the* wheels *went, and thither was their spirit to go:—for the spirit of the living creature was in the* wheels *also.*

1816   1816

FROM

Shakespearean Criticism

SHAKESPEARE'S JUDGMENT EQUAL TO HIS GENIUS

Thus then Shakespeare appears, from his Venus and Adonis and Rape of Lucrece alone, apart from all his great works, to have possessed all the conditions of the true poet. Let me now proceed to destroy, as far as may be in my power, the popular notion that he was a great dramatist by mere instinct, that he grew immortal in his own despite, and sank below men of second or third-rate power, when he attempted aught beside the drama—even as bees construct their cells and manufacture their honey to admirable perfection; but would in vain attempt to build a nest. Now this mode of reconciling a compelled sense of inferiority with a feeling of pride, began in a few pedants, who having read that Sophocles was the great model of tragedy, and Aristotle the infallible dictator of its rules, and finding that the Lear, Hamlet, Othello, and other masterpieces were neither in imitation of Sophocles, nor in obedience to Aristotle,—and not having (with one or two exceptions) the courage to affirm, that the delight which their country received from generation to generation, in defiance of the alterations of circumstances and habits, was wholly groundless,

—took upon them, as a happy medium and refuge, to talk of Shakespeare as a sort of beautiful *lusus naturæ,* a delightful monster,—wild, indeed, and without taste or judgment, but like the inspired idiots so much venerated in the East, uttering, amid the strangest follies, the sublimest truths. In nine places out of ten in which I find his awful name mentioned, it is with some epithet of "wild," "irregular," "pure child of nature," &c. If all this be true, we must submit to it; though to a thinking mind it can not but be painful to find any excellence, merely human, thrown out of all human analogy, and thereby leaving us neither rules for imitation, nor motives to imitate;—but if false, it is a dangerous falsehood;—for it affords a refuge to secret self-conceit,—enables a vain man at once to escape his reader's indignation by general swoln panegyrics, and merely by his *ipse dixit* to treat, as contemptible, what he has not intellect enough to comprehend, or soul to feel, without assigning any reason, or referring his opinion to any demonstrative principle; thus leaving Shakespeare as a sort of grand Lama, adored indeed, and his very excrements prized as relics, but with no authority or real influence. I grieve that every late voluminous edition of his works would enable me to substantiate the present charge with a variety of facts, one tenth of which would of themselves exhaust the time allotted to me. Every critic, who has or has not made a collection of black-letter books—in itself a useful and respectable amusement,—puts on the seven-league boots of self-opinion, and strides at once from an illustrator into a supreme judge, and blind and deaf, fills his three-ounce phial at the waters of Niagara; and determines positively the greatness of the cataract to be neither more nor less than his three-ounce phial has been able to receive.

I think this a very serious subject. It is my earnest desire—my passionate endeavor,—to enforce at various times, and by various arguments and instances, the close and reciprocal connection of just taste with pure morality. Without that acquaintance with the heart of man, or that docility and childlike gladness to be made acquainted with it, which those only can have, who dare look at their own hearts—and that with a steadiness which religion only has the power of reconciling with sincere humility;—without this, and the modesty produced by it, I am deeply convinced that no man, however wide his erudition, however patient his antiquarian researches, can possibly understand, or be worthy of understanding, the writings of Shakespeare.

Assuredly that criticism of Shakespeare will alone be genial which is reverential. The Englishman, who, without reverence, a proud and affectionate reverence, can utter the name of William Shakespeare, stands disqualified for the office of critic. He wants one at least of the very senses, the language of which he is to employ, and will discourse at best, but as a blind man, while the whole harmonious creation of light and shade with all its subtle interchange of deepening and dissolving colors rises in silence to the silent *fiat* of the uprising Apollo. However inferior in ability I may be to some who have followed me, I own I am proud that I was the first in time who publicly demonstrated to the full extent of the position, that the supposed irregularity and extravagances of Shakespeare were the mere dreams of a pedantry that arraigned the eagle because it had not the dimensions of the swan. In all the successive courses of lectures delivered by me, since my first attempt at the Royal Institution, it has been, and still remains, my object, to prove that in all points from the most important to the most minute, the judgment of Shakespeare is commensurate with his genius—nay, that his genius reveals itself in his judgment, as in its most exalted form. And the more gladly do I recur to this subject from the clear conviction, that to judge aright, and with distinct consciousness of the grounds of our judgment, concerning the works of Shakespeare, implies the power and the means of judging rightly of all other works of intellect, those of abstract science alone excepted.

It is a painful truth that not only individuals, but even whole nations, are ofttimes so enslaved to the habits of their education and immediate circumstances, as not to judge disinterestedly even on those subjects, the very pleasure arising from which consists in its disinterestedness, namely, on subjects of taste and polite literature. Instead of deciding concerning their own modes and customs by any rule of reason, nothing appears rational, becoming, or beautiful to them, but what coincides with the peculiarities of their education. In this narrow circle, individuals may attain to exquisite discrimination, as the French critics have done in their own literature; but a true critic can no more be such without placing himself on some central point, from

which he may command the whole, that is, some general rule, which, founded in reason, or the faculties common to all men, must therefore apply to each—than an astronomer can explain the movements of the solar system without taking his stand in the sun. And let me remark, that this will not tend to produce despotism, but, on the contrary, true tolerance, in the critic. He will, indeed, require, as the spirit and substance of a work, something true in human nature itself, and independent of all circumstances; but in the mode of applying it, he will estimate genius and judgment according to the felicity with which the imperishable soul of intellect shall have adapted itself to the age, the place, and the existing manners. The error he will expose, lies in reversing this, and holding up the mere circumstances as perpetual to the utter neglect of the power which can alone animate them. For art can not exist without, or apart from, nature; and what has man of his own to give to his fellow-man, but his own thoughts and feelings, and his observations, so far as they are modified by his own thoughts or feelings?

Let me, then, once more submit this question to minds emancipated alike from national, or party, or sectarian prejudice:—Are the plays of Shakespeare works of rude uncultivated genius, in which the splendor of the parts compensates, if aught can compensate, for the barbarous shapelessness and irregularity of the whole? Or is the form equally admirable with the matter, and the judgment of the great poet, not less deserving our wonder than his genius?—Or, again, to repeat the question in other words:—Is Shakespeare a great dramatic poet on account only of those beauties and excellences which he possesses in common with the ancients, but with diminished claims to our love and honor to the full extent of his differences from them?—Or are these very differences additional proofs of poetic wisdom, at once results and symbols of living power as contrasted with lifeless mechanism—of free and rival originality as contra-distinguished from servile imitation, or, more accurately, a blind copying of effects, instead of a true imitation of the essential principles?—Imagine not that I am about to oppose genius to rules. No! the comparative value of these rules is the very cause to be tried. The spirit of poetry, like all other living powers, must of necessity circumscribe itself by rules, were it only to unite power with beauty. It must embody in order to reveal itself; but a living body is of necessity an organized one; and what is organization but the connection of parts in and for a whole, so that each part is at once end and means?—This is no discovery of criticism;—it is a necessity of the human mind; and all nations have felt and obeyed it, in the invention of metre, and measured sounds, as the vehicle and *involucrum*[1] of poetry—itself a fellow-growth from the same life—even as the bark is to the tree!

No work of true genius dares want its appropriate form, neither indeed is there any danger of this. As it must not, so genius can not, be lawless; for it is even this that constitutes it genius—the power of acting creatively under laws of its own origination. How then comes it that not only single *Zoili*,[2] but whole nations have combined in unhesitating condemnation of our great dramatist, as a sort of African nature, rich in beautiful monsters—as a wild heath where islands of fertility look the greener from the surrounding waste, where the loveliest plants now shine out among unsightly weeds, and now are choked by their parasitic growth, so intertwined that we can not disentangle the weed without snapping the flower?—In this statement I have had no reference to the vulgar abuse of Voltaire, save as far as his charges are coincident with the decisions of Shakespeare's own commentators and (so they would tell you) almost idolatrous admirers. The true ground of the mistake lies in the confounding mechanical regularity with organic form. The form is mechanic, when on any given material we impress a pre-determined form, not necessarily arising out of the properties of the material;—as when to a mass of wet clay we give whatever shape we wish it to retain when hardened. The organic form, on the other hand, is innate; it shapes, as it develops, itself from within, and the fulness of its development is one and the same with the perfection of its outward form. Such as the life is, such is the form. Nature, the prime genial artist, inexhaustible in diverse powers, is equally inexhaustible in forms;—each exterior is the physiognomy of the being within—its true image reflected and thrown out from the concave mirror;—and even such is the appropriate excellence of her chosen poet, of our own Shakespeare—himself a nature humanized, a genial understanding directing self-consciously a power and an implicit wisdom deeper even than our consciousness.

I greatly dislike beauties and selections in general; but as proof positive of his unrivalled excellence, I should like to try Shakespeare by this criterion. Make out your amplest catalogue of all the human faculties, as reason or the moral law, the will, the feeling of the coincidence of the two (a feeling *sui generis et demonstratio demonstrationum*[3]) called the conscience, the understanding or prudence, wit, fancy, imagination, judgment—and then of the objects on which these are to be employed, as the beauties, the terrors, and the seeming caprices of nature, the realities and the capabilities, that is, the actual and the ideal, of the human mind, conceived as an individual or as a social being, as in innocence or in guilt, in a play-paradise, or in a war-field of temptation;—and then compare with Shakespeare under each of these heads all or any of the writers in prose and verse that have ever lived! Who, that is competent to judge, doubts the result?—And ask your own hearts—ask your own common-sense—to conceive the possibility of this man being—I say not, the drunken savage of that wretched socialist, whom Frenchmen, to their shame, have honored before their elder and better worthies—but the anomalous, the wild, the irregular, genius of our daily criticism! What! are we to have miracles in sport?—Or, I speak reverently, does God choose idiots by whom to convey divine truths to man?

1818   *1836*

SUMMARY OF THE CHARACTERISTICS OF SHAKESPEARE'S DRAMAS

It seems to me that his plays are distinguished from those of all other dramatic poets by the following characteristics:

1. Expectation in preference to surprise. It is like the true reading of the passage—"God said, Let there be light, and there was *light*";—not there *was* light. As the feeling with which we startle at a

SHAKESPEARE'S JUDGMENT EQUAL TO HIS GENIUS. **1.** involucrum: enclosure. **2.** Zoili: after Zoilus, a classical bad critic.

3. sui ... demonstrationum: "unique and best of the best."

shooting star compared with that of watching the sunrise at the pre-established moment, such and so low is surprise compared with expectation.

2. Signal adherence to the great law of nature, that all opposites tend to attract and temper each other. Passion in Shakespeare generally displays libertinism, but involves morality; and if there are exceptions to this, they are, independently of their intrinsic value, all of them indicative of individual character, and, like the farewell admonitions of the parent, have an end beyond the parental relation. Thus the Countess's beautiful precepts to Bertram, by elevating her character, raise that of Helena her favorite, and soften down the point in her which Shakespeare does not mean us not to see, but to see and to forgive, and at length to justify. And so it is in Polonius, who is the personified memory of wisdom no longer actually possessed. This admirable character is always misrepresented on the stage. Shakespeare never intended to exhibit him as a buffoon; for although it was natural that Hamlet,— a young man of fire and genius, detesting formality, and disliking Polonius on political grounds, as imagining that he had assisted his uncle in his usurpation,—should express himself satirically,—yet this must not be taken as exactly the poet's conception of him. In Polonius a certain induration of character had arisen from long habits of business; but take his advice to Laertes, and Ophelia's reverence for his memory, and we shall see that he was meant to be represented as a statesman somewhat past his faculties—his recollections of life all full of wisdom, and showing a knowledge of human nature, whilst what immediately takes place before him, and escapes from him, is indicative of weakness.

But as in Homer all the deities are in armor, even Venus; so in Shakespeare all the characters are strong. Hence real folly and dulness are made by him the vehicles of wisdom. There is no difficulty for one being a fool to imitate a fool; but to be, remain, and speak like a wise man and a great wit, and yet so as to give a vivid representation of a veritable fool,—*hic labor, hoc opus est*. A drunken constable is not uncommon, nor hard to draw; but see and examine what goes to make up a Dogberry.

3. Keeping at all times in the high road of life. Shakespeare has no innocent adulteries, no interesting incests, no virtuous vice;—he never renders that amiable which religion and reason alike teach us to detest, or clothes impurity in the garb of virtue,

like Beaumont and Fletcher, the Kotzebues[1] of the day. Shakespeare's fathers are roused by ingratitude, his husbands stung by unfaithfulness; in him, in short, the affections are wounded in those points in which all may, nay, must, feel. Let the morality of Shakespeare be contrasted with that of the writers of his own, or the succeeding age, or of those of the present day, who boast their superiority in this respect. No one can dispute that the result of such a comparison is altogether in favor of Shakespeare; —even the letters of women of high rank in his age were often coarser than his writings. If he occasionally disgusts a keen sense of delicacy, he never injures the mind; he neither excites, nor flatters passion, in order to degrade the subject of it; he does not use the faulty thing for a faulty purpose, nor carries on warfare against virtue, by causing wickedness to appear as no wickedness, through the medium of a morbid sympathy with the unfortunate. In Shakespeare vice never walks as in twilight; nothing is purposely out of its place;—he inverts not the order of nature and propriety,—does not make every magistrate a drunkard or glutton, nor every poor man meek, humane, and temperate; he has no benevolent butchers, nor any sentimental ratcatchers.

4. Independence of the dramatic interest on the plot. The interest in the plot is always in fact on account of the characters, not *vice versa*, as in almost all other writers; the plot is a mere canvass and no more. Hence arises the true justification of the same stratagem being used in regard to Benedict and Beatrice,—the vanity in each being alike. Take away from the Much Ado About Nothing all that which is not indispensable to the plot, either as having little to do with it, or, at best, like Dogberry and his comrades, forced into the service, when any other less ingeniously absurd watchmen and nightconstables would have answered the mere necessities of the action;—take away Benedict, Beatrice, Dogberry, and the reaction of the former on the character of Hero,—and what will remain? In other writers the main agent of the plot is always the prominent character; in Shakespeare it is so, or is not so, as the character is in itself calculated, or not

SUMMARY OF THE CHARACTERISTICS OF SHAKESPEARE'S DRAMAS. **1.** August Friedrich Ferdinand von Kotzebue (1761–1819), a German dramatist who wrote over two hundred popular plays, many translated into English.

calculated, to form the plot. Don John is the main-spring of the plot of this play; but he is merely shown and then withdrawn.

5. Independence of the interest on the story as the groundwork of the plot. Hence Shakespeare never took the trouble of inventing stories. It was enough for him to select from those that had been already invented or recorded such as had one or other, or both, of two recommendations, namely, suitableness to his particular purpose, and their being parts of popular tradition,—names of which we had often heard, and of their fortunes, and as to which all we wanted was, to see the man himself. So it is just the man himself, the Lear, the Shylock, the Richard, that Shakespeare makes us for the first time acquainted with. Omit the first scene in Lear, and yet every thing will remain; so the first and second scenes in the Merchant of Venice. Indeed it is universally true.

6. Interfusion of the lyrical—that which in its very essence is poetical—not only with the drama-tic, as in the plays of Metastasio, where at the end of the scene comes the *aria* as the *exit* speech of the character,—but also in and through the dramatic. Songs in Shakespeare are introduced as songs only, just as songs are in real life, beautifully as some of them are characteristic of the person who has sung or called for them, as Desdemona's "Willow," and Ophelia's wild snatches, and the sweet carollings in As You Like It. But the whole of the Midsummer Night's Dream is one continued specimen of the dramatized lyrical. And observe how exquisitely the dramatic of Hotspur;—

> Marry, and I'm glad on't with all my heart;
> I'd rather be a kitten and cry—mew, &c.

melts away into the lyric of Mortimer;—

> I understand thy looks: that pretty Welsh
> Which thou pourest down from these swelling
>   heavens,
> I am too perfect in, &c.
> > Henry IV. part i. act iii. sc. i.

7. The characters of the *dramatis personæ*, like those in real life, are to be inferred by the reader;—they are not told to him. And it is well worth re-marking that Shakespeare's characters, like those in real life, are very commonly misunderstood, and almost always understood by different persons in different ways. The causes are the same in either case. If you take only what the friends of the char-

acter say, you may be deceived, and still more so, if that which his enemies say; nay, even the charac-ter himself sees himself through the medium of his character, and not exactly as he is. Take all to-gether, not omitting a shrewd hint from the clown or the fool, and perhaps your impression will be right; and you may know whether you have in fact discovered the poet's own idea, by all the speeches receiving light from it, and attesting its reality by reflecting it.

Lastly, in Shakespeare the heterogeneous is united, as it is in nature. You must not suppose a pressure or passion always acting on or in the char-acter!—passion in Shakespeare is that by which the individual is distinguished from others, not that which makes a different kind of him. Shakespeare followed the main march of the human affections. He entered into no analysis of the passions or faiths of men, but assured himself that such and such pas-sions and faiths were grounded in our common nature, and not in the mere accidents of ignorance or disease. This is an important consideration and constitutes our Shakespeare the morning star, the guide and the pioneer, of true philosophy.

1812–13   *1840*

ON POESY OR ART

Man communicates by articulation of sounds, and paramountly by the memory in the ear; nature by the impression of bounds and surfaces on the eye, and through the eye it gives significance and ap-propriation, and thus the conditions of memory, or the capability of being remembered, to sounds, smells, &c. Now Art, used collectively for painting, sculpture, architecture and music, is the mediatress between, and reconciler of, nature and man. It is, therefore, the power of humanizing nature, of in-fusing the thoughts and passions of man into every-thing which is the object of his contemplation; color, form, motion, and sound, are the elements which it combines, and it stamps them into unity in the mould of a moral idea.

The primary art is writing;—primary, if we re-gard the purpose abstracted from the different modes of realizing it, those steps of progression of which the instances are still visible in the lower degrees of civilization. First, there is mere gesticu-lation; then rosaries or *wampum;* then picture-language; then hieroglyphics, and finally alphabetic letters. These all consist of a translation of man into nature, of a substitution of the visible for the audible.

The so called music of savage tribes as little deserves the name of art for the understanding, as the ear warrants it for music. Its lowest state is a mere expression of passion by the sounds which the passion itself necessitates;—the highest amounts to no more than a voluntary reproduction of these sounds in the absence of the occasioning causes, so as to give the pleasure of contrast,—for example, by the various outcries of battle in the song of security and triumph. Poetry also is purely human; for all its materials are from the mind, and all its products are for the mind. But it is the apotheosis of the former state, in which by excitement of the associative power passion itself imitates order, and the order resulting produces a pleasureable passion, and thus it elevates the mind by making its feelings the object of its reflexion. So likewise, whilst it recalls the sights and sounds that had accompanied the occasions of the original passions, poetry impregnates them with an interest not their own by means of the passions, and yet tempers the passion by the claiming power which all distinct images exert on the human soul. In this way poetry is the preparation for art, inasmuch as it avails itself of the forms of nature to recall, to express, and to modify the thoughts and feelings of the mind. Still, however, poetry can only act through the intervention of articulate speech, which is so peculiarly human, that in all languages it constitutes the ordinary phrase by which man and nature are contradistinguished. It is the original force of the word "brute," and even "mute" and "dumb" do not convey the absence of sound, but the absence of articulated sounds.

As soon as the human mind is intelligibly addressed by an outward image exclusively of articulate speech, so soon does art commence. But please to observe that I have laid particular stress on the words "human mind,"—meaning to exclude thereby all results common to man and all other sentient creatures, and consequently confining myself to the effect produced by the congruity of the animal impression with the reflective powers of the mind; so that not the thing presented, but that which is represented by the thing, shall be the source of the pleasure. In this sense nature itself is to a religious observer the art of God; and for the same cause art itself might be defined as of a middle quality between a thought and a thing, or, as I said before, the union and reconciliation of that which is nature with that which is exclusively human. It is the figured language of thought, and is distinguished from nature by the unity of all the parts in one thought or idea. Hence nature itself would give us the impression of a work of art, if we could see the thought which is present at once in the whole and every part; and a work of art will be just in proportion as it adequately conveys the thought, and rich in proportion to the variety of parts which it holds in unity.

If, therefore, the term "mute" be taken as opposed not to sound but to articulate speech, the old definition of painting will in fact be the true and best definition of the Fine Arts in general, that is, *muta poesis,* mute poesy, and so of course poesy. And, as all languages perfect themselves by a gradual process of desynonymizing words originally equivalent, I have cherished the wish to use the word "poesy" as the generic or common term, and to distinguish that species of poesy which is not *muta poesis* by its usual name "poetry"; while of all the other species which collectively form the Fine Arts, there would remain this as the common definition,—that they all, like poetry, are to express intellectual purposes, thoughts, conceptions, and sentiments which have their origin in the human mind,—not, however, as poetry does, by means of articulate speech, but as nature or the divine art does, by form, color, magnitude, proportion, or by sound, that is, silently or musically.

Well! it may be said—but who has ever thought otherwise? We all know that art is the imitatress of nature. And, doubtless, the truths which I hope to convey would be barren truisms, if all men meant the same by the words "imitate" and "nature." But it would be flattering mankind at large, to presume that such is the fact. First, to imitate. The impression on the wax is not an imitation, but a copy, of the seal; the seal itself is an imitation. But, further, in order to form a philosophic conception, we must seek for the kind, as the heat in ice, invisible light, &c., whilst, for practical purposes, we must have reference to the degree. It is sufficient that philosophically we understand that in all imitation two elements must coexist, and not only coexist, but must be perceived as coexisting. These two constituent elements are likeness and unlikeness, or sameness and difference, and in all genuine creations of art there must be a union of these disparates. The artist may take his point of view where he pleases, provided that the desired effect be perceptibly produced,—that there be likeness in the difference, difference in the likeness, and a reconcilement of both in one. If there be likeness to nature without any check of difference, the result is disgusting, and the more complete the delusion, the more loathsome the effect. Why are such simulations of nature, as wax-work figures of men and women, so disagreeable? Because, not finding the motion and the life which we expected, we are shocked as by a falsehood, every circumstance of detail, which before induced us to be interested, making the distance from truth more palpable. You set out with a supposed reality and are disappointed and disgusted with the deception; whilst, in respect to a work of genuine imitation, you begin with an acknowledged total difference, and then every touch of nature gives you the pleasure of an approximation to truth. The fundamental principle of all this is undoubtedly the horror of falsehood and the love of truth inherent in the human breast. The Greek tragic dance rested on these principles, and I can deeply sympathize in imagination with the Greeks in this favorite part of their theatrical exhibitions, when I call to mind the pleasure I felt in beholding the combat of the Horatii and Curiatii most exquisitely danced in Italy to the music of Cimarosa.

Secondly, as to nature. We must imitate nature! yes, but what in nature,—all and every thing? No, the beautiful in nature. And what then is the beautiful? What is beauty? It is, in the abstract, the unity of the manifold, the coalescence of the diverse; in the concrete, it is the union of the shapely (*formosum*) with the vital. In the dead organic it depends on regularity of form, the first and lowest species of which is the triangle with all its modifications, as in crystals, architecture, &c.; in the living organic it is not mere regularity of form, which would produce a sense of formality; neither is it subservient to any thing beside itself. It may be present in a disagreeable object, in which the proportion of the parts constitutes a whole; it does not arise from association, as the agreeable does, but sometimes lies in the rupture of association; it is not different to different individuals and nations, as has been said, nor is it connected with the ideas of the good, or the fit, or the useful. The sense of beauty is intuitive, and beauty itself is all that inspires pleasure without, and aloof from, and even contrarily to, interest.

If the artist copies the mere nature, the *natura naturata*, what idle rivalry! If he proceeds only from a given form, which is supposed to answer to the notion of beauty, what an emptiness, what an unreality there always is in his productions, as in Cipriani's pictures! Believe me, you must master the essence, the *natura naturans*, which presupposes a bond between nature in the higher sense and the soul of man.

The wisdom in nature is distinguished from that in man by the co-instantaneity of the plan and the execution; the thought and the product are one, or are given at once; but there is no reflex act, and hence there is no moral responsibility. In man there is reflexion, freedom, and choice; he is, therefore, the head of the visible creation. In the objects of nature are presented, as in a mirror, all the possible elements, steps, and processes of intellect antecedent to consciousness, and therefore to the full development of the intelligential act; and man's mind is the very focus of all the rays of intellect which are scattered throughout the images of nature. Now so to place these images, totalized, and fitted to the limits of the human mind, as to elicit from, and to superinduce upon, the forms themselves the moral reflexions to which they approximate, to make the external internal, the internal external, to make nature thought, and thought nature,—this is the mystery of genius in the Fine Arts. Dare I add that the genius must act on the feeling, that body is but a striving to become mind,—that it is mind in its essence!

In every work of art there is a reconcilement of the external with the internal; the conscious is so impressed on the unconscious as to appear in it; as compare mere letters inscribed on a tomb with figures themselves constituting the tomb. He who combines the two is the man of genius; and for that reason he must partake of both. Hence there is in genius itself an unconscious activity; nay, that is the genius in the man of genius. And this is the true exposition of the rule that the artist must first eloign himself from nature in order to return to her with full effect. Why this? Because if he were to begin by mere painful copying, he would produce masks only, not forms breathing life. He must out of his own mind create forms according to the severe laws of the intellect, in order to generate in himself that co-ordination of freedom and law, that involution of obedience in the prescript, and of the prescript in the impulse to obey, which assimilates him to nature, and enables him to understand her. He merely absents himself for a season from her, that his own spirit, which has the same ground with nature, may learn her unspoken language in its main radicals, before he approaches to her endless compositions of them. Yes, not to acquire cold notions—lifeless technical rules—but living and life-producing ideas, which shall contain their own evidence, the certainty that they are essentially one with the germinal causes in nature,—his consciousness being the focus and mirror of both,—for this does the artist for a time abandon the external real in order to return to it with a complete sympathy with its internal and actual. For of all we see, hear, feel and touch the substance is and must be in ourselves; and therefore there is no alternative in reason between the dreary (and thank heaven! almost impossible) belief that every thing around us is but a phantom, or that the life which is in us is in them likewise; and that to know is to resemble, when we speak of objects out of ourselves, even as within ourselves to learn is, according to Plato, only to recollect;—the only effective answer to which, that I have been fortunate to meet with, is that which Pope has consecrated for future use in the line—

And coxcombs vanquish Berkeley with a grin!

The artist must imitate that which is within the thing, that which is active through form and figure, and discourses to us by symbols—the *Natur-geist*, or spirit of nature, as we unconsciously imitate those whom we love; for so only can he hope to produce any work truly natural in the object and truly human in the effect. The idea which puts the form together cannot itself be the form. It is above form, and is its essence, the universal in the individual, or the individuality itself,—the glance and the exponent of the indwelling power.

Each thing that lives has its moment of self-exposition, and so has each period of each thing, if we remove the disturbing forces of accident. To do this is the business of ideal art, whether in images of childhood, youth, or age, in man or in woman. Hence a good portrait is the abstract of the personal; it is not the likeness for actual comparison, but for recollection. This explains why the likeness of a very good portrait is not always recognized; because some persons never abstract, and amongst these are especially to be numbered the near relations and friends of the subject, in consequence of the constant pressure and check exercised on their minds by the actual presence of the original. And each thing that only appears to live has also its possible position of relation to life, as nature herself testifies, who where she cannot be, prophesies her being in the crystallized metal, or the inhaling plant.

The charm, the indispensable requisite, of sculpture is the unity of effect. But painting rests in a material remoter from nature, and its compass is therefore greater. Light and shade give external, as well as internal, being even with all its accidents, whilst sculpture is confined to the latter. And here I may observe that the subjects chosen for works of art, whether in sculpture or painting, should be such as really are capable of being expressed and conveyed within the limits of those arts. Moreover they ought to be such as will affect the spectator by their truth, their beauty, or their sublimity, and therefore they may be addressed to the judgement, the senses, or the reason. The peculiarity of the impression which they may make, may be derived either from color and form, or from proportion and fitness, or from the excitement of the moral feelings; or all these may be combined. Such works as do combine these sources of effect must have the preference in dignity.

Imitation of the antique may be too exclusive, and may produce an injurious effect on modern sculpture;—1st, generally, because such an imitation cannot fail to have a tendency to keep the attention fixed on externals rather than on the thought within;—2ndly, because, accordingly, it leads the artist to rest satisfied with that which is always imperfect, namely, bodily form, and circumscribes his views of mental expression to the ideas of power and grandeur only;—3rdly, because it induces an effort to combine together two incongruous things, that is to say, modern feelings in antique forms;—4thly, because it speaks in a language, as it were, learned and dead, the tones of which, being unfamiliar, leave the common spectator cold and unimpressed;—and lastly, because it necessarily causes a neglect of thoughts, emotions and images of profounder interest and more exalted dignity, as motherly, sisterly, and brotherly love, piety, devotion, the divine become human,—the Virgin, the Apostle, the Christ. The artist's principle in the statue of a great man should be the illustration of departed merit; and I cannot but think that a skilful adoption of modern habiliments would, in many instances, give a variety and force of effect which a bigoted adherence to Greek or Roman costume precludes. It is, I believe, from artists finding Greek models unfit for several important modern purposes, that we see so many allegorical figures on monuments and elsewhere. Painting was, as it were, a new art, and being unshackled by old models it chose its own subjects, and took an eagle's flight. And a new field seems opened for modern sculpture in the symbolical expression of the ends of life, as in Guy's monument,[1] Chantrey's children[2] in Worcester Cathedral, &c.

Architecture exhibits the greatest extent of the difference from nature which may exist in works of art. It involves all the powers of design, and is sculpture and painting inclusively. It shews the greatness of man, and should at the same time teach him humility.

Music is the most entirely human of the fine arts, and has the fewest *analoga* in nature. Its first delightfulness is simple accordance with the ear; but it is an associated thing, and recalls the deep emotions of the past with an intellectual sense of proportion. Every human feeling is greater and larger than the exciting cause,—a proof, I think, that man is designed for a higher state of existence; and this is deeply implied in music, in which there is always something more and beyond the immediate impression.

With regard to works in all the branches of the fine arts, I may remark that the pleasure arising from novelty must of course be allowed its due place and weight. This pleasure consists in the identity of two opposite elements, that is to say— sameness and variety. If in the midst of the variety there be not some fixed object for the attention, the unceasing succession of the variety will prevent the mind from observing the difference of the individual objects; and the only thing remaining will be the succession, which will then produce precisely the same effect as sameness. This we experience when we let the trees or hedges pass before the fixed eye during a rapid movement in a carriage, or, on the other hand, when we suffer a file of soldiers or ranks of men in procession to go on before us without resting the eye on any one in particular. In order to derive pleasure from the occupation of the mind, the principle of unity must always be present, so that in the midst of the multeity the centripetal force be never suspended, nor the sense be fatigued by the predominance of the centrifugal force. This unity in multeity I have elsewhere stated as the principle of beauty. It is equally the source of pleasure in variety, and in fact a higher term including both. What is the seclusive or distinguishing term between them?

Remember that there is a difference between form as proceeding, and shape as superinduced;— the latter is either the death or the imprisonment of the thing;—the former is its self-witnessing and self-effected sphere of agency. Art would or should be the abridgment of nature. Now the fulness of nature is without character, as water is purest when without taste, smell, or color; but this is the highest, the apex only,—it is not the whole. The object of art is to give the whole *ad hominem;* hence each step of nature hath its ideal, and hence the possibility of a climax up to the perfect form of a harmonized chaos.

To the idea of life victory or strife is necessary; as virtue consists not simply in the absence of vices, but in the overcoming of them. So it is in beauty. The sight of what is subordinated and conquered heightens the strength and the pleasure; and this should be exhibited by the artist either inclusively in his figure, or else out of it, and beside it to act by way of supplement and contrast. And with a view to this, remark the seeming identity of body and mind in infants, and thence the loveliness of the former; the commencing separation in boyhood, and the struggle of equilibrium in youth: thence onward the body is first simply indifferent; then demanding the translucency of the mind not to be worse than indifferent; and finally all that presents the body as body becoming almost of an excremental nature.

ON POESY. **1.** Sir Thomas Guy, founder of the famous Guy's Hospital in London. **2.** a reference to "Sleeping Children" by Sir Francis Chantrey, a contemporary sculptor.

1818

1818

George Gordon, Lord Byron

1788-1824

It is probably fair to say that no nineteenth-century writer embodies more fully in the popular mind the image of the Romantic than Lord Byron. Born in the atmosphere of revolution triggered by the events in France and disillusioned when his hopes for a new era that would see the overthrow of all forms of tyranny were shattered, the young aristocrat saw himself as the prototype of the new modern man. Angry with his family background and with the narrowness of his religious and educational experience, trapped in a marriage that fell far short of his exuberant dreams of love, he turned away from and rejected brashly a society that he considered pretentious and hypocritical when it ostracized him for breaking out of such a marriage. Journeying across Europe in search of some fulfillment of his dreams, a pioneer in his ability to dramatize himself and his predicament and to set a style of behavior and dress for his contemporaries, he truly became the portrait of the artist as a quester for freedom and beauty in a world of tyranny and ugliness. His work, whether the wanderings of Childe Harold, the solitary dreams of Manfred, or the saga of Don Juan, is in many ways the record of a complex and paradoxical life, the story of a pilgrimage that never seems to end, and we read it today with an awareness of its strident subjectivity, but also with a sense that it touches us and our own situation in strangely powerful ways. Is it any wonder that the popular mind looks more to Byron than to Wordsworth or Shelley, for an embodiment of that elusive and difficult-to-define concept of Romanticism. Here is the artist who never seemed to flag in his restlessness with things as they were, who never seemed to abandon his radical commitments, who actually lived what he wrote.

Byron has all too often been victimized by biographical critics who read his work only in terms of the bare details of his life and who consequently engaged in a simplistic process of glorification or vilification. Neither conclusion will do for a man so vital, so complex, so divided. Recent biographies like Leslie Marchand's wonderfully comprehensive account or Elizabeth Longford's shorter, but no less perceptive, book have taught us how biography can be used creatively in studying a man and his work, how the interaction of the details of a life and the breadth of understanding and sympathy of the biographer can produce truly satisfying results. Such biographies allow the life to speak for itself and provoke us to read and think more deeply about an artist and his work.

Born in London on January 22, 1788, Byron seems flawed from the beginning. His father, dubiously remembered as "Mad Jack," a rebellious, egotistical, and self-indulgent rascal, had eloped with the wife of the Marquis of Carmathen and had a child, Augusta, by her in 1783. After the mother died and "Mad Jack" had spent his fortune in France, he returned to marry a well-to-do and high-spirited Scottish maiden, Catherine Gordon, and Byron was the product of this marriage. The marriage was a stormy one, and they soon separated, she with her young son to Aberdeen, and he to France where, described by his son as "born for his own ruin," he died in 1791.

Byron's half-sister Augusta was sent away to live with a relative, and he, living with his mother in Aberdeen, was subject to the whims of her temperament, now tender, loving, even doting; now angry, demanding, and violent. His was at best a strange and unpredictable upbringing.

Byron seemed especially self-conscious about his clubfoot, a physical inheritance that provided feelings of inadequacy and that perhaps contributed to a strong desire to compensate, to assert his virility by leading a life of action. After his uncle's death in 1798, he became at age ten Lord Byron, master of a ruined Newstead Abbey whose Gothic setting and atmosphere stirred the imagination of the young boy. His early Scottish schooling, at Bower's neighborhood school and at Aberdeen Grammar School, provided him with a good knowledge of the Bible but with that bellicose, otherworldly, hell-and-damnation kind of Calvinistic Christianity that seemed to darken his view of the human situation and of the hopes of men and women for happiness and love. He, of course, abandoned any real fidelity to the formalities of such a religion, and became a kind of Romantic Deist, in love with the sublime settings of the Highlands, reading widely in the literature of travel, dreaming intensely of the exotic beauty of the Near East.

His education, despite his voracious reading habits, was irregular. He attended and hated Harrow; and, although he was to receive a degree from Cambridge, he distinguished himself far more for his gambling and general dissipation than for any dedication to the formal business of studies, a preparation for the wild living he was to pursue in London. Byron's sexual education has become legendary; it began early with a boyhood love affair with his cousin Mary Duff, an encounter with his nurse May Gray, and further passionate yearnings for Margaret Parker, and, especially, for Mary Chaworth whose abandonment of him left him disconsolate. In 1802, after a long separation, Byron remet his half-sister Augusta, and was smitten by her although she was engaged to George Leigh. Then he was separated from her for a second time. Elizabeth Longford's words in her new biography, *Byron*, are most apt. "It would have been happier for Augusta and her 'baby Byron,' as she called this brother four years her junior, if their relationship had developed from now on uninterruptedly, and therefore in all probability normally." Instead separation evoked romantic longings in the young man, longings which were later to be acted out in the incestuous relationship that clouded his later life.

After several false starts and private printings, his first volume of poems, the unfortunately titled *Hours of Idleness*, appeared in 1807. It is, with few exceptions, a collection of maudlin, self-indulgent, and poorly structured poems which was savagely reviewed by Henry Brougham in the *Edinburgh Review*, a review which triggered Byron's magnificent *English Bards and Scotch Reviewers*, an iambic pentameter couplet satire in the best tradition of his Neoclassic heroes Dryden and Pope.

On coming of age in 1809, Byron assumed his royal role formally, was seated in the House of Lords, and began the restoration of Newstead Abbey. Always the aristocrat, he nevertheless fought ardently for liberal political causes, for the poor weavers victimized by the Industrial Revolution, for persecuted Catholics, for harassed radicals like Hunt. Byron, however, was the eternal pilgrim, filled with wanderlust, a man eager to act out his dreams. In July of 1809 he sailed with James Hobhouse for Portugal, for the two-year journey that became the subject-matter of the first two cantos of *Childe Harold's Pilgrimage*. From Portugal to Spain, to the magnificent and much admired ruggedness of Albania by way of Malta, to Athens; travel through Greece and Turkey; the spectacular, but typically Byronic swimming of the Hellespont; the return to England in 1811—such was the itinerary, and its love affairs and romantic adventures form the fabric of a work that treads the intriguing twilight zone between life and art. Back in England, and deeply depressed by the death of his mother, he, through his friend and publisher John Murray, brought out the first part of Harold's adventures, with its thinly disguised hero glorifying the simplicity of the Albanians and other primitive societies as compared to the corruptions of English and European civilization. It is, at best, a weak effort, filled with mawkish self-pity and an aggravating affectation of diction and style. Yet, then as now, who can predict the taste of a reading audience? What the critics might deplore, the public welcomed. The first two cantos were an immediate and stunning success as were the so-called Oriental tales, The *Giaour, The Bride of Abydos, The Corsair*, and *Lara*, which followed over the next two years. It is fair to say that a phenomenon had been born that completely captured the popular imagination, the phenomenon of the Byronic hero—a lonely, alienated, primitivistic figure, dwelling in the remote outposts of nature, haunted by a sense of mysterious guilt, and pouring out his emotions for all to share. Women, and Lady Caroline Lamb and Lady Oxford come to mind as notable examples, were wildly attracted to the author-hero, to his physical beauty and to his mysterious melancholy.

Sometime around the middle of 1813 the always close relationship with his half-sister Augusta Leigh developed into something even deeper; and, while the familiar "alleged" is invariably used as a qualifier, it seems clear that it is proper to describe their love as incestuous. It was a deep and mysterious love, one that provided strength and solace for Byron even when it seemed most clearly headed for doom and disaster. In two poems written in 1816, but one of them withheld from publication until 1830 because of Augusta's objections, he shares his passion. Among the most haunting lines are the following:

> For thee, my own sweet sister, in thy heart
> I know myself secure, as thou in mine;
> We were and are—I am, even as thou art—
> Beings who ne'er each other can resign;
> It is the same, together or apart,
> From Life's commencement to its slow decline
>   We are entwined—let Death come slow or fast,
> The tie which bound the first endures the last!

Byron's one venture into marriage was disastrous. An heiress and a classic Bluestocking, Annabella Milbanke fell madly in love with the dashing figure of Byron. As for Byron, he found the young woman attractive, wealthy, maybe even the kind of woman who could turn him from his amours, his vices, and redeem him at last. The wooing was an on-again, off-again affair for some three years, but the couple married on January 2, 1815, and a daughter, Augusta Ada, was born on December 10 of that year. Elizabeth Longford's observation on the strange marriage is an intriguing one: "Byron's attraction to Annabella was the feeling of the eighteenth century for the nineteenth century. Stirred now to admiration, now to cynicism, one moment sympathetic the next critical, he illustrated the transition of an era into its successor." The marriage, given Byron's temperament, his love affairs, his debts, his drinking, lasted a year. Annabella left him, and they were formally separated in April of 1816. Society was rife with rumors of Byron's cruelty, his insanity, his Satanism; indeed, he was virtually ostracized as a result of the separation proceedings. He left England on April 25, never to return.

Now the true expatriate, Byron journeyed through France and Belgium to Switzerland and the famous meeting with Shelley, a poet who was to exert a marked influence on his life and work. He spent the summer of 1816 with Shelley, Mary Godwin, and Claire Clairmont, who was to bear him a child, Allegra. Switzerland was a propitious locale for Byron, and the Byron-Shelley relationship in the midst of the grandeur of the Alps seemed to trigger the best in both poets. Canto III of *Childe Harold's Pilgrimage* is the product of this Swiss summer, and the advance in Byron's thematic and stylistic maturity is truly remarkable. Much of the self-pity and maudlin confessionalism have been mitigated; a great deal of the affected archaism and pretentious language has been eliminated. Instead there is a new freshness and power of diction and imagery, an energy and vitality of expression as the poet-hero, a man of varied and rapidly shifting moods, graphically creates the natural beauties of his travels and the patterns of history.

From Switzerland Byron moved to Italy in 1817, to be joined later by the Shelleys. Although he travelled a great deal, Venice was his home. Here he completed *Childe Harold* with a fourth canto that reveals a still greater sense of freedom, and yet a great awareness of the smallness of the individual when seen against the backdrop of human monuments. The great monodrama *Manfred* was also completed in this year. In Italy the full flowering of his great satiric vein took place; *Beppo* was published in February of 1818, and the first cantos of his monumental essay on man, *Don Juan,* were produced. Here also, living a life of utter depravity, he met and fell in love with the beautiful sixteen-year-old Countess Teresa Giuccioli and gradually isolated himself from Claire Clairmont.

The years 1820–24 were ones of intense activity, artistic and political. Plays like *Cain* and *Sardanapalus* were published; his great travesty *The Vision of Judgment* was written; and *Don Juan* was continued. Through the influence of Teresa's family, the Gambas, he became involved in the revolutionary Carbonari movement to liberate Italy from Austrian domination. He took an even more active role in the Greek struggle for independence from the Turks. Byron, one of the so-called Philhellenes, actually went to Greece to lend his physical and financial support. Here, in the midst of great involvement and activity, he was taken ill and died on April 19, 1824. The outcast to the end, he was refused burial in Westminster Abbey and was laid to rest instead in Hucknell Torkard Church near his beloved Newstead.

There are two distinct manners in Byron's poetry: one the more overtly Romantic and revealed especially in the great long poems like *Childe Harold's Pilgrimage* and *Manfred,* and the other more realistic and satiric and revealed especially in works like *Beppo, The Vision of Judgment,* and *Don Juan.* Wherever one turns in the poetry, there is a great sense of movement and energy, a command of verse forms, language, and imagery that is notable. One develops the sense that technique and style are Byron's servants, that he has the power to turn them to a variety of uses. This great command is at times the source of triumph, at others of self-indulgence, expansiveness, and downright rubbish. Take, for example, the speed conveyed by an early stanza in Canto III of *Childe Harold,* the alternating of short and long vowel sounds, the use of strategic alliteration, the clarity and directness of the language. Harold is again moving:

> Once more upon the waters! yet once more!
>   And the waves bound beneath me as a steed
>   That knows his rider. Welcome to their roar!
>   Swift be their guidance, wheresoe'er it lead!
>   Though the strained mast should quiver as a reed,
>   And the rent canvass fluttering strew the gale,
>   Still must I on; for I am as a weed,
>   Flung from the rock on Ocean's foam, to sail
> Where'er the surge may sweep, the tempest's breath prevail.

Or consider the sheer virtuosity of a satiric stanza like the following, modelled on the *ottava rima* of the Italian comic epic, and yet rendered uniquely Byronic as the speaker of *Don Juan,* taking all society as his target, focuses on Juan's mother and romps through a feast of "classical moan," studied self-abasement, and a comeback rapier-like couplet that hits home with startling vitality:

'Tis pity learned virgins ever wed
  With persons of no sort of education,
Or gentlemen, who, though well born and bred,
  Grow tired of scientific conversation:
I don't choose to say much upon this head,
  I'm a plain man, and in a single station,
But—Oh! ye lords of ladies intellectual,
Inform us truly, have they not hen-pecked you all?

In the best of Byron's poetry there is a great power to evoke the mood of human loneliness, isolation, the turning of mind and feeling away from the specters of an ugly world to its own resources, the quest for an ideal unrealizable except in the creations of the imagination. The blend of nature and personal feeling produces at times moments of psychological power, of both exhilaration and of world-weariness. Manfred, alone on the cliffs of the Jungfrau, is a superb example as he speaks:

The spirits I have raised abandon me,
The spells which I have studied baffle me,
The remedy I recked of tortured me;
I lean no more on superhuman aid;
It hath no power upon the past, and for
The future, till the past be gulfed in darkness,
It is not of my search.—My mother earth!
And thou fresh-breaking day, and you, ye mountains,
Why are ye beautiful? I cannot love ye.
And thou, the bright eye of the Universe,
That openest over all, and unto all
Art a delight—thou shin'st not on my heart.
And you, ye crags, upon whose extreme edge
I stand, and on the torrents brink beneath
Behold the tall pines dwindled as to shrubs
In dizziness of distance; when a leap,
A stir, a motion, even a breath, would bring
My breast upon its rocky bosom's bed
To rest forever—wherefore do I pause?

Harold, exiled from an hypocritical, unforgiving society because of his differentness, finds strength in the power of his imagination to redeem the day:

'Tis to create, and in creating live
  A being more intense that we endow
With form our fancy, gaining as we give
  The life we image, even as I do now—
What am I? Nothing: but not so art thou,
  Soul of my thought! with whom I traverse earth,
Invisible but gazing, as I glow
  Mixed with thy strong spirit, blended with thy birth,
And feeling still with thee in my crushed feelings' dearth.

There is also the half-serious, half-cynical speaker of *Don Juan*, the jaded man of the world, who moves from the high romance of Juan's desert-isle love affair with the beautiful Haidée to a passage of sheer bravado:

> It was such pleasure to behold him, such
>   Enlargement of existence to partake
> Nature with him, to thrill beneath his touch,
>   To watch him slumbering, and to see him wake:
> To live with him for ever were too much;
>   But then the thought of parting made her quake:
> He was her own, her ocean-treasure, cast
> Like a rich wreck—her first love, and her last.
>
>   .   .   .
>
> Man, being reasonable, must get drunk;
>   The best of life is but intoxication:
> Glory, the grape, love, gold, in these are sunk
>   The hopes of all men, and of every nation;
> Without their sap, how branchless were the trunk
>   Of life's strange tree, so fruitful on occasion!
> But to return,—Get very drunk, and when
> You wake with headache, you shall see what then.

Few poets evoke the sense of time and place as well as Byron, a quality called by some critics the historical and geographical imagination. Only a wide-ranging imagination, a mind capable of harmonizing with nature, a poet confident of his linguistic powers could produce the grandeur of Harold's view of the Alps, and of himself:

>   Above me are the Alps,
>   The palaces of Nature, whose vast walls
> Have pinnacled in clouds their snowy scalps,
>   And throned eternity in icy halls
> Of cold sublimity, where forms and falls
>   The avalanche—the thunderbolt of snow!
> All that expands the spirit, yet appals,
>   Gather around these summits, as to show
> How Earth may pierce to Heaven, yet leave vain men below.

Only the poet, charged with a sense of history, could bemoan the present and yet rejoice in the reverberations of the past in Venice:

>   In Venice Tasso's echoes are no more,
>   And silent rows the songless gondolier;
>   Her palaces are crumbling to the shore,
>   And music meets not always now the ear:
>   Those days are gone—but Beauty still is here.
>   States fall, arts fade—but Nature doth not die,
>   Nor yet forget how Venice once was dear,
>   The pleasant place of all festivity,
> The revel of the earth, the masque of Italy!

As suggested throughout this introduction, Byron as man and artist is much more complex than the popularizers would like him to be. A man of contradictions, aristocrat and liberal, libertine and idealist of love and beauty, Romantic poseur and Neoclassic critic, satirist and moralist, he forces us to deal with his reality rather than his image. And that reality is best found in a poetry of enormous variety and vitality, from the lively, sensitive lyrics of *Hebrew Melodies* to the richly exotic world of Childe Harold, Manfred, and the pirate heroes, to the Popean satire of human society in *Don Juan*. Byron loved truth, beauty, and virtue even when he found these ideals difficult to actualize in his own life. A man who delighted in living life to the full, who found freedom in the creations of his mind and in the sublime, lonely outposts of nature, he found the world wanting and society imprisoning the yearnings of the spirit. His poetry is a vivid dramatization of the dream unfulfilled, but of the dream nevertheless, and of the struggle that seeks victory and all too often brings disillusionment. Perhaps his own words speak best:

> Ye, who have traced the Pilgrim to the scene
> Which is his last, if in your memories dwell
> A thought which once was his, if on ye swell
> A single recollection, not in vain
> He wore his sandal-shoon and scallop-shell;
> Farewell! with *him* alone may rest the pain,
> If such there were—with *you*, the moral of his strain.

Suggestions For Further Reading

After many years of gossipy or defensive biographies, students of Byron have occasion to rejoice in a number of superior lives of the poet. The best is Leslie Marchand's wonderfully comprehensive *Byron: A Biography* (1958), a three-volume study that has been skillfully abridged as a one-volume *Byron: A Portrait* (1970). Elizabeth Longford's recent *Byron* (1976) is a short biography, to be sure, but one that cuts through the great mass of materials confronting any scholar and offers a thoroughly accurate and wonderfully vivid portrait of the poet.

Leslie Marchand's *Byron's Poetry: A Critical Introduction* (1965) is a good beginning point for the student of the poetry. Peter Thorslev's *The Byronic Hero: Types and Prototypes* (1962) studies with great care and discrimination the origins and development of a major aspect of Byron's poetry and examines major exemplars like Childe Harold and Manfred. Paul Trueblood's *The Flowering of Byron's Genius: Studies in Don Juan* (1945) is an extremely helpful treatment of the satiric dimension in Byron's work. Also recommended are T. S. Eliot's essay on Byron in *On Poetry and Poets* (1937); G. Wilson Knight, *Lord Byron: Christian Virtues* (1952); Paul West, *Byron and the Spoiler's Art* (1960); W. H. Marshall, *The Structure of Byron's Major Poems* (1962); Robert Gleckner, *Byron and the Ruins of Paradise* (1967); and Michael Cooke,

The Blind Man Traces the Circle: On the Patterns and Philosophy of Byron's Poetry (1968).

Two very useful volumes, which bring together a great deal of scholarly writing on Byron and his work, are Paul West, ed. *Byron: A Collection of Critical Essays* (1963) and Edward Bostetter, ed. *Twentieth Century Interpretations of Don Juan: A Collection of Critical Essays* (1969).

WHEN WE TWO PARTED

When we two parted
 In silence and tears,
Half broken-hearted
 To sever for years,
Pale grew the cheek and cold,
 Colder thy kiss;
Truly that hour foretold
 Sorrow to this.

The dew of the morning
 Sunk chill on my brow—   10
It felt like the warning
 Of what I feel now.
Thy vows are all broken,
 And light is thy fame:
I hear thy name spoken,
 And share in its shame.

They name thee before me,
 A knell to mine ear;
A shudder comes o'er me—
 Why wert thou so dear?   20
They know not I knew thee,
 Who knew thee too well:—
Long, long shall I rue thee,
 Too deeply to tell.

In secret we met—
 In silence I grieve,
That thy heart could forget,
 Thy spirit deceive.
If I should meet thee
 After long years,   30
How should I greet thee?—
 With silence and tears.

1808   *1816*

from
ENGLISH BARDS AND SCOTCH REVIEWERS

A SATIRE

I had rather be a kitten, and cry mew!
Than one of these same metre ballad-mongers.

SHAKSPEARE.

Such shameless bards we have; and yet 'tis true,
There are as mad, abandon'd critics too.

POPE.

PREFACE

All my friends, learned and unlearned, have urged me not to publish this Satire with my name. If I were to be "turned from the career of my humour by quibbles quick, and paper bullets of the brain," I should have complied with their counsel. But I am not to be terrified by abuse, or bullied by reviewers, with or without arms. I can safely say that I have attacked none personally, who did not commence on the offensive. An author's works are public property: he who purchases may judge, and publish his opinion if he pleases; and the authors I have endeavoured to commemorate may do by me as I have done by them. I dare say they will succeed better in condemning my scribblings, than in mending their own. But my object is not to prove that I can write well, but, if possible, to make others write better.

As the poem has met with far more success than I expected, I have endeavoured in this edition to make some additions and alterations, to render it more worthy of public perusal.

In the first edition of this satire, published anonymously, fourteen lines on the subject of Bowles's Pope were written by, and inserted at the request of, an ingenious friend of mine, who has now in the press a volume of poetry. In the present edition they are erased, and some of my own substituted in their stead, my only reason for this being that which I conceive would operate with any other person in the same manner,—a determination not to publish with my name any production, which was not entirely and exclusively my own composition.

With regard to the real talents of many of the poetical persons whose performances are mentioned or alluded to in the following pages, it is presumed by the author that there can be little difference of opinion in the public at large; though, like other sectaries, each has his separate tabernacle of proselytes, by whom his abilities are over-rated, his faults overlooked, and his metrical canons received without scruple and without consideration. But the unquestionable possession of considerable genius by several of the writers here censured renders their mental prostitution more to be regretted. Imbecility may be pitied, or, at worst, laughed at and forgotten; perverted powers demand the most decided reprehension. No one can wish more than the author that some known and able writer had undertaken their exposure; but Mr. Gifford has devoted himself to Massinger, and, in the absence of the regular physician, a country practitioner may, in cases of absolute necessity, be allowed to prescribe his nostrum to prevent the extension of so deplorable an epidemic, provided there be no quackery in his treatment of the malady. A caustic is here offered; as it is to be feared nothing short of actual cautery can recover the numerous patients afflicted with the present prevalent and distressing *rabies* for rhyming.—As to the Edinburgh Reviewers it would indeed require an Hercules to crush the Hydra; but if the author succeeds in merely "bruising one of the heads of the serpent," though his own hand should suffer in the encounter, he will be amply satisfied.

Still must I hear?—shall hoarse Fitzgerald bawl
His creaking couplets in a tavern hall,
And I not sing, lest, haply, Scotch reviews
Should dub me scribbler and denounce my muse?
Prepare for rhyme—I'll publish, right or wrong:
Fools are my theme, let satire be my song.

Oh, nature's noblest gift, my grey goose-quill!
Slave of my thoughts, obedient to my will,
Torn from thy parent bird to form a pen,
That mighty instrument of little men!   10
The pen! foredoom'd to aid the mental throes
Of brains that labour, big with verse or prose,
Though nymphs forsake, and critics may deride,

The lover's solace and the author's pride.
What wits! what poets dost thou daily raise!
How frequent is thy use, how small thy praise,
Condemn'd at length to be forgotten quite,
With all the pages which 'twas thine to write.
But thou, at least, mine own especial pen!
Once laid aside, but now assumed again,   20
Our task complete like Hamet's, shall be free;
Though spurn'd by others, yet beloved by me:
.Then let us soar to-day; no common theme,
No eastern vision, no distemper'd dream
Inspires—our path, though full of thorns, is plain;
Smooth be the verse, and easy be the strain.

When Vice triumphant holds her sov'reign sway,
Obey'd by all who nought beside obey;
When Folly, frequent harbinger of crime,
Bedecks her cap with bells of every clime;   30
When knaves and fools combined o'er all prevail,
And weigh their justice in a golden scale;
E'en then the boldest start from public sneers,
Afraid of shame, unknown to other fears,
More darkly sin, by satire kept in awe,
And shrink from ridicule though not from law.

Such is the force of wit! but not belong
To me the arrows of satiric song;
The royal vices of our age demand
A keener weapon and a mightier hand.   40
Still there are follies, e'en for me to chase,
And yield at least amusement in the race.
Laugh when I laugh, I seek no other fame;
The cry is up, and scribblers are my game.
Speed, Pegasus!—ye strains of great and small,
Ode, epic, elegy, have at you all!
I too can scrawl, and once upon a time
I pour'd along the town a flood of rhyme,
A schoolboy freak, unworthy praise or blame;
I printed—older children do the same.   50
'Tis pleasant, sure, to see one's name in print;
A book's a book, although there's nothing in 't.
Not that a title's sounding charm can save
Or scrawl or scribbler from an equal grave:
This Lambe must own, since his patrican name
Fail'd to preserve the spurious farce from shame.
No matter, George continues still to write,

ENGLISH BARDS AND SCOTCH REVIEWERS. **1.** Fitzgerald: William Thomas Fitzgerald, a contemporary bad poet.

21. Hamet: Cid Hamet promises to abandon writing in the last chapter of *Don Quixote*. **55. Lambe:** George Lambe, cousin of Lady Byron, author of a savagely criticized farce, *Whistle for It*.

Though now the name is veil'd from public sight.
Moved by the great example, I pursue
The self-same road, but make my own review: 60
Not seek great Jeffrey's, yet like him will be
Self-constituted judge of poesy.

. . .

Oh, Southey! Southey! cease thy varied song!
A bard may chant too often and too long:
As thou art strong in verse, in mercy, spare!
A fourth, alas! were more than we could bear.
But if, in spite of all the world can say,
Thou still wilt verseward plod thy weary way;   230
If still in Berkley ballads most uncivil,
Thou wilt devote old women to the devil,
The babe unborn thy dread intent may rue:
"God help thee," Southey, and thy readers too.

Next comes the dull disciple of thy school
That mild apostate from poetic rule,
The simple Wordsworth, framer of a lay
As soft as evening in his favourite May,
Who warns his friend "to shake off toil and trouble,
And quit his books, for fear of growing
        double";   240
Who, both by precept and example, shows
That prose is verse, and verse is merely prose;
Convincing all, by demonstration plain,
Poetic souls delight in prose insane;
And Christmas stories tortured into rhyme
Contain the essence of the true sublime.
Thus, when he tells the tale of Betty Foy,
The idiot mother of "an idiot boy";
A moon-struck, silly lad, who lost his way,
And, like his bard, confounded night with
        day;   250
So close on each pathetic part he dwells,
And each adventure so sublimely tells,
That all who view the "idiot in his glory"
Conceive the bard the hero of the story.

Shall gentle Coleridge pass unnoticed here,
To turgid ode and tumid stanza dear?
Though themes of innocence amuse him best,
Yet still obscurity's a welcome guest.
If Inspiration should her aid refuse
To him who takes a pixy for a muse,   260

Yet none in lofty numbers can surpass
The bard who soars to elegise an ass.
So well the subject suits his noble mind,
He brays, the laureat of the long ear'd kind.

Oh, wonder-working Lewis! monk, or bard,
Who fain wouldst make Parnassus a churchyard!
Lo! wreaths of yew, not laurel, bind thy brow,
Thy muse a sprite, Apollo's sexton thou!
Whether on ancient tombs thou takest thy stand,
By gibb'ring spectres hail'd, thy kindred band;
Or tracest chaste descriptions on thy page,
To please the females of our modest age;
All hail, M. P.! from whose infernal brain
Thin sheeted phantoms glide, a grisly train;
At whose command "grim women" throng in
        crowds,
And kings of fire, of water, and of clouds,
With "small grey men," "wild yagers," and what
        not,
To crown with honour thee and Walter Scott.
Again all hail; if tales like thine may please,
St. Luke alone can vanquish the disease;   280
Even Satan's self with thee might dread to dwell,
And in thy skull discern a deeper hell.

. . .

Truth! rouse some genuine bard, and guide his
        hand
To drive this pestilence from out the land.
E'en I—least thinking of a thoughtless throng,
Just skill'd to know the right and choose the
        wrong,   690
Freed at that age when reason's shield is lost,
To fight my course through passion's countless host,
Whom every path of pleasure's flow'ry way
Has lured in turn, and all have led astray—
E'en I must raise my voice, e'en I must feel
Such scenes, such men, destroy the public weal;
Although some kind, censorious friend will say,
"What art thou better, meddling fool, than they?"
And every brother rake will smile to see
That miracle, a moralist in me.   700
No matter—when some bard in virtue strong,
Gifford perchance, shall raise the chastening song,
Then sleep my pen for ever! and my voice

231–32. Berkley . . . devil: Southey wrote a ballad, *The Old Woman of Berkeley*, in which the old woman is carried away by the devil.

265. Lewis: M. G. Lewis, author of the celebrated Gothic novel, *The Monk* (1796). 277. yagers: hunters. 702. Gifford: William Gifford (1756–1826), poet and critic.

Be only heard to hail him, and rejoice;
Rejoice, and yield my feeble praise, though I
May feel the lash that Virtue must apply.

As for the smaller fry, who swarm in shoals
From silly Hafiz up to simple Bowles,
Why should we call them from their dark abode,
In broad St. Giles's or in Tottenham-road?   710
Or (since some men of fashion nobly dare
To scrawl in verse) from Bond-street or the Square?
If things of ton their harmless lays indite,
Most wisely doom'd to shun the public sight,
What harm? In spite of every critic elf,
Sir T. may read his stanzas to himself;
Miles Andrews still his strength in couplets try,
And live in prologues, though his dramas die.
Lords too are bards, such things at times befall,
And 'tis some praise in peers to write at all.   720
Yet, did or taste or reason sway the times,
Ah! who would take their titles with their rhymes?
Roscommon! Sheffield! with your spirits fled,
No future laurels deck a noble head;
No muse will cheer, with renovating smile,
The paralytic puling of Carlisle.
The puny schoolboy and his early lay
Men pardon, if his follies pass away;
But who forgives the senior's ceaseless verse,
Whose hairs grow hoary as his rhymes grow
          worse!   730
What heterogeneous honours deck the peer!
Lord, rhymester, petit-maître, pamphleteer!
So dull in youth, so drivelling in his age,
His scenes alone had damn'd our sinking stage;
But managers for once cried, "Hold, enough!"
Nor drugg'd their audience with the tragic stuff.
Yet at their judgment let his lordship laugh,
And case his volumes in congenial calf:
Yes! doff that covering, where morocco shines,
And hang a calf-skin on those recreant lines.   740

. . .

Let these, or such as these, with just applause,
Restore the muse's violated laws;
But not in flimsy Darwin's pompous chime,
That mighty master of unmeaning rhyme,
Whose gilded cymbals, more adorn'd than clear,
The eye delighted, but fatigued the ear;
In show the simple lyre could once surpass,
But now, worn down, appear in native brass;
While all his train of hovering sylphs around
Evaporate in similes and sound: 900
Him let them shun, with him let tinsel die:
False glare attracts, but more offends the eye.

Yet let them not to vulgar Wordsworth stoop,
The meanest object of the lowly group,
Whose verse, of all but childish prattle void,
Seems blessed harmony to Lamb and Lloyd.
Let them—but hold, my muse, nor dare to teach
A strain far, far beyond thy humble reach:
The native genius with their being given
Will point the path, and peal their notes to
          heaven.   910

And thou, too, Scott! resign to minstrels rude
The wilder slogan of a border feud:
Let others spin their meagre lines for hire;
Enough for genius if itself inspire!
Let Southey sing, although his teeming muse,
Prolific every spring, be too profuse;
Let simple Wordsworth chime his childish verse,
And brother Coleridge lull the babe at nurse;
Let spectre-mongering Lewis aim, at most,
To rouse the galleries, or to raise a ghost;   920
Let Moore still sigh; let Strangford steal from
          Moore,
And swear that Camoëns sang such notes of yore;
Let Hayley hobble on, Montgomery rave,
And godly Grahame chant a stupid stave;
Let sonneteering Bowles his strains refine,
And whine and whimper to the fourteenth line;
Let Stott, Carlisle, Matilda, and the rest
Of Grub-street, and of Grosvenor-place the best,
Scrawl on, till death release us from the strain,
Or Common Sense assert her rights again.   930
But thou, with powers that mock the aid of praise,
Shouldst leave to humbler bards ignoble lays:
Thy country's voice, the voice of all the nine,

708. **Hafiz:** also known as Stott, a poetaster whose work appeared at times in *The Morning Post.* **717. Miles Andrews:** Member of Parliament for many years, author of farces, one of the heroes of the satiric *Baviad.* **723. Roscommon:** Wentworth Dillon, fourth Earl of Roscommon (1633–1685), who once attempted to found an academy of literature. **Sheffield:** John Sheffield, Duke of Buckingham (1649–1721), author of an *Essay on Poetry.* **726. Carlisle:** Frederick Howard, fifth Earl of Carlisle (1748–1825), Lord Byron's guardian, author of *Tragedies and Poems.*

893. **Darwin:** Erasmus Darwin (1731–1802), physician and poet. **922. Camoëns:** Luiz Camoëns (1524–1580), the great Portuguese poet.

Demand a hallow'd harp—that harp is thine.
Say! will not Caledonia's annals yield
The glorious record of some nobler field
Than the vile foray of a plundering clan,
Whose proudest deeds disgrace the name of man?
Or Marmion's acts of darkness, fitter food
For Sherwood's outlaw tales of Robin Hood?   940
Scotland! still proudly claim thy native bard,
And be thy praise his first, his best reward!
Yet not with thee alone his name should live,
But own the vast renown a world can give;
Be known, perchance, when Albion is no more,
And tell the tale of what she was before;
To future times her faded fame recall,
And save her glory, though his country fall.

Yet what avails the sanguine poet's hope,
To conquer ages, and with time to cope?   950
New eras spread their wings, new nations rise,
And other victors fill the applauding skies;
A few brief generations fleet along,
Whose sons forget the poet and his song:
E'en now, what once-loved minstrels scarce may
    claim
The transient mention of a dubious name!
When fame's loud trump hath blown its noblest
    blast,
Though long the sound, the echo sleeps at last;
And glory, like the phoenix 'midst her fires,
Exhales her odours, blazes, and expires.   960

Shall hoary Granta call her sable sons,
Expert in science, more expert at puns?
Shall these approach the muse? ah, no! she flies,
Even from the tempting ore of Seaton's prize;
Though printers condescend the press to soil
With rhyme by Hoare, and epic blank by Hoyle:
Not him whose page, if still upheld by whist,
Requires no sacred theme to bid us list.
Ye! who in Granta's honours would surpass,
Must mount her Pegasus, a full-grown ass;   970
A foal well worthy of her ancient dam,
Whose Helicon is duller than her Cam.

There Clarke, still striving piteously 'to please,'
Forgetting doggerel leads not to degrees,

A would-be satirist, a hired buffoon,
A monthly scribbler of some low lampoon,
Condemn'd to drudge, the meanest of the mean,
And furbish falsehoods for a magazine,
Devotes to scandal his congenial mind;
Himself a living libel on mankind.   900

Oh! dark asylum of a Vandal race,
At once the boast of learning, and disgrace!
So lost to Phœbus, that nor Hodgson's verse
Can make thee better, nor poor Hewson's worse.
But where fair Isis rolls her purer wave,
The partial muse delighted loves to lave;
On her green banks a greener wreath she wove,
To crown the bards that haunt her classic grove;
Where Richards wakes a genuine poet's fires,
And modern Britons glory in their sires.   990

For me, who, thus unask'd, have dared to tell
My country, what her sons should know too well,
Zeal for her honour bade me her engage
The host of idiots that infest her age;
No just applause her honour'd name shall lose,
As first in freedom, dearest to the muse.
Oh! would thy bards but emulate thy fame,
And rise more worthy, Albion, of thy name!
What Athens was in science, Rome in power,
What Tyre appear'd in her meridian hour,   1000
'Tis thine at once, fair Albion! to have been—
Earth's chief dictatress, ocean's lovely queen.
But Rome decay'd, and Athens strew'd the plain,
And Tyre's proud piers lie shatter'd in the main;
Like these, thy strength may sink, in ruin hurl'd,
And Britain fall, the bulwark of the world.
But let me cease, and dread Cassandra's fate,
With warning ever scoff'd at, till too late;
To themes less lofty still my lay confine,
And urge thy bards to gain a name like
    thine.   1010

Then, hapless Britain! be thy rulers blest,
The senate's oracles, the people's jest!
Still hear thy motley orators dispense
The flowers of rhetoric, though not of sense,

964-966. Seaton ... Hoyle: Rev. Charles Hoare published in 1808 the Shipwreck of St. Paul, a Seatonian prize poem. Rev. Charles Hoyle wrote Exodus, an epic, and several other such prize poems.

983. Hodgson: Francis Hodgson (1781-1852), Byron's close friend, did original work as a writer plus translations of Juvenal. 989. Richards: Rev. George Richards (1769-1835), another example of a good poet for Byron. Richards was the author of a highly regarded poem, The Aboriginal Britons.

While Canning's colleagues hate him for his wit,
And old dame Portland fills the place of Pitt.

Yet once again, adieu! ere this the sail
That wafts me hence is shivering in the gale;
And Afric's coast and Calpe's adverse height,
And Stamboul's minarets must greet my
    sight: 1020
Thence shall I stray through beauty's native clime,
Where Kaff is clad in rocks and crown'd with snows
    sublime.
But should I back return, no tempting press
Shall drag my journal from the desk's recess.
Let coxcombs, printing as they come from far,
Snatch his own wreath of ridicule from Carr:
Let Aberdeen and Elgin still pursue
The shade of fame through regions of virtù;
Waste useless thousands on their Phidian freaks,
Misshapen monuments and maim'd
    antiques;   1030
And make their grand saloons a general mart
For all the mutilated blocks of art:
Of Dardan tours let dilettanti tell,
I leave topography to rapid Gell;
And, quite content, no more shall interpose
To stun the public ear—at least with prose.

Thus far I've held my undisturb'd career,
Prepared for rancour, steel'd 'gainst selfish fear.
This thing of rhyme I ne'er disdain'd to own—
Though not obtrusive, yet not quite
    unknown: 1040
My voice was heard again, though not so loud,
My page, though nameless, never disavow'd;
And now at once I tear the veil away:—
Cheer on the pack! the quarry stands at bay,

Unscared by all the din of Melbourne house,
By Lambe's resentment, or by Holland's spouse,
By Jeffrey's harmless pistol, Hallam's rage,
Edina's brawny sons and brimstone page.
Our men in buckram shall have blows enough,
And feel they too are "penetrable stuff":   1050
And though I hope not thence unscathed to go,
Who conquers me shall find a stubborn foe.
The time hath been, when no harsh sound would
    fall
From lips that now may seem imbued with gall;
Nor fools nor follies tempt me to despise
The meanest thing that crawl'd beneath my eyes:
But now, so callous grown, so changed since youth,
I've learn'd to think and sternly speak the truth;
Learn'd to deride the critic's starch decree,
And break him on the wheel he meant for
    me;   1060
To spurn the rod a scribbler bids me kiss,
Nor care if courts and crowds applaud or hiss:
Nay more, though all my rival rhymesters frown,
I too can hunt a poetaster down;
And, arm'd in proof, the gauntlet cast at once
To Scotch marauder and to southern dunce.
Thus much I've dared; if my incondite lay
Hath wrong'd these righteous times, let others say:
This, let the world, which knows not how to spare
Yet rarely blames unjustly, now declare.   1070
1807–09   *1809*

WRITTEN AFTER SWIMMING FROM SESTOS TO ABYDOS[*]

If, in the month of dark December,
    Leander, who was nightly wont
(What maid will not the tale remember?)
    To cross thy stream, broad Hellespont!

If, when the wintry tempest roared,
    He sped to Hero, nothing loth,

1015. **Canning:** George Canning (1770–1827), appointed Foreign Secretary in 1822. Founder of and contributor to *The Anti-Jacobin*. 1016. **dame Portland:** William Henry Cavendish, third Duke of Portland (1738–1809). 1019. **Calpe:** ancient name for Gibraltar. 1020. **Stamboul:** Istanbul. **minarets:** high, slender towers attached to Moslem mosques. 1022. **Kaff:** Mount Caucasus. 1026. **Carr:** Sir John Carr, a famous contemporary traveller. 1027. **Aberdeen and Elgin:** George Hamilton-Gordon Aberdeen (1784–1860), British statesman. Thomas Bruce, Earl of Elgin (1766–1841), British soldier and diplomat who brought to England the so-called Elgin Marbles. 1033. **Dardan:** Trojan. 1034. **Gell:** author of *Topography of Troy and Ithaca*.

1045. **din . . . house:** a reference to the sound of bad poets at the home of William Lamb, second Viscount Melbourne, Whig statesman.

[*] Byron and a friend swam the Hellespont in imitation of the legendary Leander, who every night swam across the strait to visit his beloved Hero, a priestess of Aphrodite.

And thus of old thy current poured,
    Fair Venus! how I pity both!

For *me*, degenerate modern wretch,
    Though in the genial month of May   10
My dripping limbs I faintly stretch,
    And think I've done a feat to-day.

But since he crossed the rapid tide,
    According to the doubtful story,
To woo,—and—Lord knows what beside,
    And swam for Love, as I for Glory;

'Twere hard to say who fared the best:
    Sad mortals! thus the Gods still plague you!
He lost his labour, I my jest:
    For he was drowned, and I've the ague.   20

1810   *1812*

MAID OF ATHENS, ERE WE PART

Ζώη μοῦ, σᾶς ἀγαπῶ. °

Maid of Athens, ere we part,
Give, oh give me back my heart!
Or, since that has left my breast,
Keep it now, and take the rest!
Hear my vow before I go,
Ζώη μοῦ, σᾶς ἀγαπῶ.

By those tresses unconfined,
Woo'd by each Ægean wind;
By those lids whose jetty fringe
Kiss thy soft cheeks' blooming tinge;   10
By those wild eyes like the roe,
Ζώη μοῦ, σᾶς ἀγαπῶ.

By that lip I long to taste;
By that zone-encircled waist;
By all the token-flowers that tell
What words can never speak so well;
By love's alternate joy and woe,
Ζώη μοῦ, σᾶς ἀγαπῶ.

Maid of Athens, I am gone:
Think of me, sweet! when alone.   20
Though I fly to Istambol,

° "My life, I love you."

Athens holds my heart and soul:
Can I cease to love thee? No!
Ζώη μοῦ, σᾶς ἀγαπῶ.

1810   *1812*

SHE WALKS IN BEAUTY

She walks in beauty, like the night
    Of cloudless climes and starry skies;
And all that's best of dark and bright
    Meet in her aspect and her eyes:
Thus mellow'd to that tender light
    Which heaven to gaudy day denies.

One shade the more, one ray the less,
    Had half impaired the nameless grace
Which waves in every raven tress,
    Or softly lightens o'er her face;   10
Where thoughts serenely sweet express
    How pure, how dear their dwelling-place.

And on that cheek, and o'er that brow,
    So soft, so calm, yet eloquent,
The smiles that win, the tints that glow,
    But tell of days in goodness spent,
A mind at peace with all below,
    A heart whose love is innocent!

1814   *1815*

THE DESTRUCTION OF SENNACHERIB°

The Assyrian came down like the wolf on the fold,
And his cohorts were gleaming in purple and gold;
And the sheen of their spears was like stars on the
    sea,
When the blue wave rolls nightly on deep Galilee.

Like the leaves of the forest when summer is green,
That host with their banners at sunset were seen:
Like the leaves of the forest when autumn hath
    blown,
That host on the morrow lay wither'd and strown.

SHE WALKS IN BEAUTY. **1. She:** Lady Wilmot Horton, a
cousin of Byron. Byron had seen her at a ball the night
before.

° For an account of the episode see II Kings 18–19.

For the Angel of Death spread his wings on the
    blast,
And breathed in the face of the foe as he
    pass'd   10
And the eyes of the sleepers wax'd deadly and chill,
And their hearts but once heaved, and forever grew
    still!

And there lay the steed with his nostril all wide,
But through it there roll'd not the breath of his
    pride;
And the foam of his gasping lay white on the turf,
And cold as the spray of the rock-beating surf.

And there lay the rider distorted and pale,
With the dew on his brow, and the rust on his mail:
And the tents were all silent, the banners alone,
The lances unlifted, the trumpet unblown.   20

And the widows of Ashur are loud in their wail,
And the idols are broke in the temple of Baal;
And the might of the Gentile, unsmote by the
    sword,
Hath melted like snow in the glance of the Lord!
1815   1815

FARE THEE WELL

"Alas! they had been friends in youth;
But whispering tongues can poison truth;
And constancy lives in realms above:
And life is thorny; and youth is vain;
And to be wroth with one we love,
Doth work like madness in the brain;
But never either found another
To free the hollow heart from paining—
They stood aloof, the scars remaining,
Like cliffs which had been rent asunder;
A dreary sea now flows between,
But neither heat, nor frost, nor thunder,
Shall wholly do away, I ween,
The marks of that which once hath been."

               —COLERIDGE's *Christabel.*

Fare thee well! and if forever,
    Still forever, fare *thee well:*
Even though unforgiving, never
    'Gainst thee shall my heart rebel.

Would that breast were bared before thee
    Where thy head so oft hath lain,
While that placid sleep came o'er thee
    Which thou ne'er canst know again:

Would that breast, by thee glanced over,
    Every inmost thought could show!   10
Then thou wouldst at last discover
    'Twas not well to spurn it so.

Though the world for this commend thee—
    Though it smile upon the blow,
Even its praises must offend thee,
    Founded on another's woe:

Though my many faults defaced me,
    Could no other arm be found,
Than the one which once embraced me,
    To inflict a cureless wound?   20

Yet, oh yet, thyself deceive not;
    Love may sink by slow decay,
But by sudden wrench, believe not
    Hearts can thus be torn away:

Still thine own its life retaineth,
    Still must mine, though bleeding, beat;
And the undying thought which paineth
    Is—that we no more may meet.

These are words of deeper sorrow
    Than the wail above the dead;   30
Both shall live, but every morrow
    Wakes us from a widow'd bed.

And when thou wouldst solace gather,
    When our child's first accents flow,
Wilt thou teach her to say "Father!"
    Though his care she must forego?

When her little hands shall press thee,
    When her lip to thine is press'd,
Think of him whose prayer shall bless thee,
    Think of him thy love had bless'd!   40

Should her lineaments resemble
    Those thou never more may'st see,
Then thy heart will softly tremble
    With a pulse yet true to me.

All my faults perchance thou knowest,
    All my madness none can know;
All my hopes, where'er thou goest,
    Wither, yet with *thee* they go.

Every feeling hath been shaken;
   Pride, which not a world could bow,   50
Bows to thee—by thee forsaken,
   Even my soul forsakes me now:

But 'tis done—all words are idle—
   Words from me are vainer still;
But the thoughts we cannot bridle
   Force their way without the will.

Fare thee well! thus disunited,
   Torn from every nearer tie,
Sear'd in heart, and lone, and blighted,
   More than this I scarce can die.   60

1816   *1816*

STANZAS TO AUGUSTA*

When all around grew drear and dark,
   And reason half withheld her ray—
And hope but shed a dying spark
   Which more misled my lonely way;

In that deep midnight of the mind,
   And that internal strife of heart,
When, dreading to be deem'd too kind,
   The weak despair—the cold depart;

When fortune changed—and love fled far,
   And hatred's shafts flew thick and fast,   10
Thou wert the solitary star
   Which rose and set not to the last.

Oh! blest be thine unbroken light,
   That watch'd me as a seraph's eye,
And stood between me and the night,
   For ever shining sweetly nigh.

And when the cloud upon us came,
   Which strove to blacken o'er thy ray—
Then purer spread its gentle flame,
   And dash'd the darkness all away.   20

Still may thy spirit dwell on mine,
   And teach it what to brave or brook—
There's more in one soft word of thine
   Than in the world's defied rebuke.

----

* Augusta Leigh, Byron's half-sister.

Thou stood'st, as stands a lovely tree,
   That still unbroke, though gently bent,
Still waves with fond fidelity
   Its boughs above a monument.

The winds might rend, the skies might pour,
   But there thou wert—and still wouldst be   30
Devoted in the stormiest hour
   To shed thy weeping leaves o'er me.

But thou and thine shall know no blight,
   Whatever fate on me may fall;
For Heaven in sunshine will requite
   The kind—and thee the most of all.

Then let the ties of baffled love
   Be broken—thine will never break;
Thy heart can feel—but will not move;
   Thy soul, though soft, will never shake.   40

And these, when all was lost beside,
   Were found and still are fix'd in thee;—
And bearing still a breast so tried,
   Earth is no desert—ev'n to me.

1816   *1816*

DARKNESS

I had a dream, which was not all a dream.
The bright sun was extinguished, and the stars
Did wander darkling in the eternal space,
Rayless, and pathless, and the icy Earth
Swung blind and blackening in the moonless air;
Morn came and went—and came, and brought no
   day,
And men forgot their passions in the dread
Of this their desolation; and all hearts
Were chill'd into a selfish prayer for light:
And they did live by watchfires—and the
   thrones,   10
The palaces of crowned kings—the huts,
The habitations of all things which dwell,
Were burnt for beacons; cities were consumed,
And men were gather'd round their blazing homes
To look once more into each other's face;
Happy were those who dwelt within the eye
Of the volcanos, and their mountain-torch:
A fearful hope was all the World contain'd;
Forests were set on fire—but hour by hour
They fell and faded—and the crackling trunks   20

Extinguished with a crash—and all was black.
The brows of men by the despairing light
Wore an unearthly aspect, as by fits
The flashes fell upon them; some lay down
And hid their eyes and wept; and some did rest
Their chins upon their clenched hands, and smiled;
And others hurried to and fro, and fed
Their funeral piles with fuel, and looked up
With mad disquietude on the dull sky,
The pall of a past World; and then again   30
With curses cast them down upon the dust,
And gnash'd their teeth and howled: the wild birds
    shrieked
And, terrified, did flutter on the ground,
And flap their useless wings; the wildest brutes
Came tame and tremulous; and vipers crawled
And twined themselves among the multitude,
Hissing, but stingless—they were slain for food:
And War, which for a moment was no more,
Did glut himself again:—a meal was bought
With blood, and each sate sullenly apart   40
Gorging himself in gloom: no Love was left;
All earth was but one thought—and that was Death
Immediate and inglorious; and the pang
Of famine fed upon all entrails—men
Died, and their bones were tombless as their flesh;
The meagre by the meagre were devoured,
Even dogs assailed their masters, all save one,
And he was faithful to a corse, and kept
The birds and beasts and famished men at bay,
Till hunger clung them, or the dropping dead   50
Lured their lank jaws; himself sought out no food,
But with a piteous and perpetual moan,
And a quick desolate cry, licking the hand
Which answered not with a caress—he died.
The crowd was famished by degrees; but two
Of an enormous city did survive,
And they were enemies: they met beside
The dying embers of an altar-place
Where had been heaped a mass of holy things
For an unholy usage; they raked up,   60
And shivering scraped with their cold skeleton
    hands
The feeble ashes, and their feeble breath
Blew for a little life, and made a flame
Which was a mockery; then they lifted up
Their eyes as it grew lighter, and beheld
Each other's aspects— saw, and shrieked, and
    died—

Even of their mutual hideousness they died,
Unknowing who he was upon whose brow
Famine had written Fiend. The World was void,
The populous and the powerful was a lump,   70
Seasonless, herbless, treeless, manless, lifeless—
A lump of death—a chaos of hard clay.
The rivers, lakes, and ocean all stood still,
And nothing stirred within their silent depths;
Ships sailorless lay rotting on the sea,
And their masts fell down piecemeal: as they
    dropped
They slept on the abyss without a surge—
The waves were dead; the tides were in their grave,
The Moon, their mistress, had expired before;
The winds were withered in the stagnant air,   80
And the clouds perished; Darkness had no need
Of aid from them—She was the Universe.
1816   *1816*

PROMETHEUS

Titan! to whose immortal eyes
    The sufferings of mortality,
    Seen in their sad reality,
Were not as things that gods despise;
What was thy pity's recompense?
A silent suffering, and intense;
The rock, the vulture, and the chain,
All that the proud can feel of pain,
The agony they do not show,
The suffocating sense of woe,   10
    Which speaks but in its loneliness,
And then is jealous lest the sky
Should have a listener, nor will sigh
    Until its voice is echoless.

Titan! to thee the strife was given
    Between the suffering and the will,
    Which torture where they cannot kill;
And the inexorable Heaven,
And the deaf tyranny of Fate,
The ruling principle of Hate,   20
Which for its pleasure doth create
The things it may annihilate,
Refused thee even the boon to die:
The wretched gift eternity
Was thine—and thou hast borne it well.

All that the Thunderer wrung from thee
Was but the menace which flung back
On him the torments of thy rack;
The fate thou didst so well foresee,
But would not to appease him tell;   30
And in thy silence was his sentence,
And in his soul a vain repentance,
And evil dread so ill dissembled,
That in his hand the lightnings trembled.

Thy Godlike crime was to be kind,
  To render with thy precepts less
  The sum of human wretchedness,
And strengthen man with his own mind;
But baffled as thou wert from high,
Still in thy patient energy,   40
In the endurance, and repulse
  Of thine impenetrable spirit,
Which Earth and Heaven could not convulse,
  A mighty lesson we inherit:
Thou art a symbol and a sign
  To mortals of their fate and force;
Like thee, man is in part divine,
  A troubled stream from a pure source;
And man in portions can foresee
His own funereal destiny;   50
His wretchedness, and his resistance,
And his sad unallied existence.
To which his spirit may oppose
Itself—and equal to all woes,
  And a firm will, and a deep sense,
Which even in torture can descry
  Its owns concenter'd recompense,
Triumphant where it dares defy,
And making death a victory.

1816   *1816*

PROMETHEUS. 26. Thunderer: Zeus, hurler of thunderbolts. 28. fate ... foresee: Prometheus held the secret of what would ultimately bring about the downfall of Zeus.

FROM
Childe Harold's Pilgrimage

from CANTO III

Afin que cette application vous forçât de penser à autre chose: il n'y a en vérité de remède que celui-là et le temps.—Lettre du Roi de Prusse à D'Alembert, *Sept. 7, 1776.*°

1

Is thy face like thy mother's, my fair child!
Ada! sole daughter of my house and heart?
When last I saw thy young blue eyes they
    smiled,
And then we parted,—not as now we part,
But with a hope.—
            Awaking with a start,
The waters heave around me; and on high
The winds lift up their voices: I depart,
Whither I know not; but the hour's gone by,
When Albion's lessening shores could grieve or glad
    mine eye.

2

Once more upon the waters! yet once more!   10
And the waves bound beneath me as a steed
That knows his rider. Welcome to their roar!
Swift be their guidance, whereso'er it lead!
Though the strained mast should quiver as a
    reed,
And the rent canvas fluttering strew the gale,
Still must I on; for I am as a weed,
Flung from the rock, on Ocean's foam to sail
Where'er the surge may sweep, the tempest's breath
    prevail.

CHILDE HAROLD'S PILGRIMAGE. CANTO III. **2.** Ada: Byron's daughter, Augusta Ada, was scarcely a month old when his wife left him in January, 1816.

° "In order that this work may force you to think of something else: there is in truth no remedy but that and time."

3

In my youth's summer I did sing of One,
The wandering outlaw of his own dark mind;   20
Again I seize the theme, then but begun,
And bear it with me, as the rushing wind
Bears the cloud onwards: in that tale I find
The furrows of long thought, and dried-up tears,
Which, ebbing, leave a sterile track behind,
O'er which all heavily the journeying years
Plod the last sands of life,—where not a flower
      appears.

4

Since my young days of passion—joy, or pain,
Perchance my heart and harp have lost a string,
And both may jar: it may be, that in vain   30
I would essay as I have sung to sing.
Yet, though a dreary strain, to this I cling;
So that it wean me from the weary dream
Of selfish grief or gladness—so it fling
Forgetfulness around me—it shall seem
To me, though to none else, a not ungrateful theme.

5

He, who grown aged in this world of woe,
In deeds, not years, piercing the depths of life,
So that no wonder waits him; nor below
Can love or sorrow, fame, ambition, strife,   40
Cut to his heart again with the keen knife
Of silent, sharp endurance: he can tell
Why thought seeks refuge in lone caves, yet rife
With airy images, and shapes which dwell
Still unimpaired, though old, in the soul's haunted
      cell.

6

'Tis to create, and in creating live
A being more intense that we endow
With form our fancy, gaining as we give
The life we image, even as I do now.
What am I? Nothing: but not so art thou,   50
Soul of my thought! with whom I traverse earth,

Invisible, but gazing, as I glow
Mixed with thy spirit, blended with thy birth,
And feeling still with thee in my crushed feelings'
      dearth.

7

Yet must I think less wildly:—I *have* thought
Too long and darkly, till my brain became,
In its own eddy boiling and o'erwrought,
A whirling gulf of phantasy and flame:
And thus, untaught in youth my heart to tame,
My springs of life were poisoned. 'Tis too
      late!   60
Yet am I changed; though still enough the same
In strength to bear what time cannot abate,
And feed on bitter fruits without accusing Fate.

8

Something too much of this:—but now 'tis past,
And the spell closes with its silent seal.
Long absent Harold reappears at last;
He of the breast which fain no more would feel,
Wrung with the wounds which kill not, but ne'er
      heal;
Yet Time, who changes all, had altered him
In soul and aspect as in age: years steal   70
Fire from the mind as vigor from the limb;
And life's enchanted cup but sparkles near the
      brim.

9

His had been quaffed too quickly, and he found
The dregs were wormwood; but he filled again,
And from a purer fount, on holier ground,
And deemed its spring perpetual; but in vain!
Still round him clung invisible a chain
Which galled forever, fettering though unseen,
And heavy though it clanked not; worn with
      pain,
Which pined although it spoke not, and grew
      keen,   80
Entering with every step he took through many a
      scene.

19. **I did sing:** a reference to the Harold of Cantos I and II, composed in 1809.

74. **wormwood:** a plant with a bitter taste.

10

Secure in guarded coldness, he had mixed
Again in fancied safety with his kind,
And deemed his spirit now so firmly fixed
And sheathed with an invulnerable mind,
That, if no joy, no sorrow lurked behind;
And he, as one, might 'midst the many stand
Unheeded, searching through the crowd to find
Fit speculation; such as in strange land
He found in wonder-works of God and Nature's
    hand. 90

11

But who can view the ripened rose, nor seek
To wear it? who can curiously behold
The smoothness and the sheen of beauty's cheek,
Nor feel the heart can never all grow old?
Who can contemplate Fame through clouds
    unfold
The star which rises o'er her steep, nor climb?
Harold, once more within the vortex, rolled
On with the giddy circle, chasing Time,
Yet with a nobler aim than in his youth's fond
    prime.

12

But soon he knew himself the most unfit   100
Of men to herd with man; with whom he held
Little in common; untaught to submit
His thoughts to others, though his soul was
    quelled
In youth by his own thoughts; still uncompelled,
He would not yield dominion of his mind
To spirits against whom his own rebelled;
Proud though in desolation; which could find
A life within itself, to breathe without mankind.

13

Where rose the mountains, there to him were
    friends;
Where rolled the ocean, thereon was his
    home;   110
Where a blue sky, and glowing clime, extends,

99. **fond**: foolish.

He had the passion and the power to roam;
The desert, forest, cavern, breaker's foam,
Were unto him companionship; they spake
A mutual language, clearer than the tome
Of his land's tongue, which he would oft forsake
For Nature's pages glassed by sunbeams on the
    lake.

14

Like the Chaldean, he could watch the stars,
Till he had peopled them with beings bright
As their own beams; and earth, and earth-
    born jars,   120
And human frailties, were forgotten quite:
Could he have kept his spirit to that flight
He had been happy; but this clay will sink
Its spark immortal, envying it the light
To which it mounts, as if to break the link
That keeps us from yon heaven which woos us to
    its brink.

15

But in man's dwelling he became a thing
Restless and worn, and stern and wearisome,
Drooped as a wild-born falcon with clipt wing,
To whom the boundless air alone were
    home: 130
Then came his fit again, which to o'ercome,
As eagerly the barred-up bird will beat
His breast and beak against his wiry dome
Till the blood tinge his plumage, so the heat
Of his impeded soul would through his bosom eat.

16

Self-exiled Harold wanders forth again,
With nought of hope left, but with less of gloom;
The very knowledge that he lived in vain,
That all was over on this side the tomb,
Had made Despair a smilingness assume,   140
Which, though 'twere wild,—as on the plundered
    wreck
When mariners would madly meet their doom
With draughts intemperate on the sinking
    deck,—
Did yet inspire a cheer, which he forbore to check.

17

Stop!—for thy tread is on an empire's dust!
An earthquake's spoil is sepulchred below!
Is the spot marked with no colossal bust?
Nor column trophied for triumphal show?
None; but *the moral's truth* tells simpler so,
As the ground was before, thus let it be;—   150
How that red rain hath made the harvest grow!
And is this all the world has gained by thee,
Thou first and last of fields! king-making Victory?

18

And Harold stands upon this place of skulls,
The grave of France, the deadly Waterloo!
How in an hour the power which gave annuls
Its gifts, transferring fame as fleeting too!
In "pride of place" here last the eagle flew,
Then tore with bloody talon the rent plain,
Pierced by the shaft of banded nations
        through;   160
Ambition's life and labors all were vain;
He wears the shattered links of the world's broken
        chain.

19

Fit retribution! Gaul may champ the bit
And foam in fetters;— but is Earth more free?
Did nations combat to make *one* submit;
Or league to teach all kings true sovereignty?
What! shall reviving Thraldom again be
The patched-up idol of enlightened days?
Shall we, who struck the Lion down, shall we
Pay the Wolf homage? proffering lowly
        gaze   170
And servile knees to thrones? No; *prove* before ye
        praise!

145. **Stop:** The setting is Waterloo, where Napoleon had been defeated on June 18, 1815. **153. king-making Victory:** Byron is critical here and in the following lines of the restoration of a king in France and the strengthening of the forces of reaction in Europe. **158. "pride of place":** a term from falconry indicating the highest point of flight. The eagle is Napoleon.

20

If not, o'er one fallen despot boast no more!
In vain fair cheeks were furrowed with hot tears
For Europe's flowers long rooted up before
The trampler of her vineyards; in vain, years
Of death, depopulation, bondage, fears,
Have all been borne, and broken by the accord
Of roused-up millions; all that most endears
Glory, is when the myrtle wreathes a sword
Such as Harmodius drew on Athens' tyrant
        lord.   180

21

There was a sound of revelry by night,
And Belgium's capital had gathered then
Her Beauty and her Chivalry, and bright
The lamps shone o'er fair women and brave
        men;
A thousand hearts beat happily; and when
Music arose with its voluptuous swell,
Soft eyes looked love to eyes which spake again,
And all went merry as a marriage bell;
But hush! hark! a deep sound strikes like a rising
        knell!

22

Did ye not hear it?—No; 'twas but the
        wind,   190
Or the car rattling o'er the stony street;
On with the dance! let joy be unconfined;
No sleep till morn, when Youth and Pleasure
        meet
To chase the glowing Hours with flying feet—
But hark!—that heavy sound breaks in once
        more,
As if the clouds its echo would repeat;
And nearer, clearer, deadlier than before!
Arm! Arm! it is—it is—the cannon's opening roar!

180. **Harmodius:** Together with his friend Aristogiton, Harmodius killed the tyrant Hipparchus in Athens in 514 B.C. Their daggers were covered with myrtle. **181. sound of revelry:** the famous ball given by the Duchess of Richmond on June 15, 1815, three days before Waterloo.

23

Within a windowed niche of that high hall
Sate Brunswick's fated chieftain; he did
    hear   200
That sound the first amidst the festival,
And caught its tone with Death's prophetic ear;
And when they smiled because he deemed it
    near,
His heart more truly knew that peal too well
Which stretched his father on a bloody bier,
And roused the vengeance blood alone could
    quell;
He rushed into the field, and, foremost fighting,
    fell.

24

Ah! then and there was hurrying to and fro,
And gathering tears, and tremblings of distress,
And cheeks all pale, which but an hour ago   210
Blushed at the praise of their own loveliness;
And there were sudden partings, such as press
The life from out young hearts, and choking sighs
Which ne'er might be repeated; who could guess
If ever more should meet those mutual eyes,
Since upon night so sweet such awful morn could
    rise!

25

And there was mounting in hot haste: the steed,
The mustering squadron, and the clattering car,
Went pouring forward with impetuous speed,
And swiftly forming in the ranks of war;   220
And the deep thunder peal on peal afar;
And near, the beat of the alarming drum
Roused up the soldier ere the morning star;
While thronged the citizens with terror dumb,
Or whispering, with white lips—"The foe! They
    come! they come!"

26

And wild and high the *Cameron's Gathering*
    rose!
The war-note of Lochiel, which Albyn's hills
Have heard, and heard, too, have her Saxon
    foes:—
How in the noon of night that pibroch thrills,
Savage and shrill! But with the breath which
    fills   230
Their mountain-pipe, so fill the mountaineers
With the fierce native daring which instils
The stirring memory of a thousand years,
And Evan's, Donald's fame rings in each clansman's
    ears!

27

And Ardennes waves above them her green
    leaves,
Dewy with Nature's tear-drops, as they pass,
Grieving, if aught inanimate e'er grieves,
Over the unreturning brave,—alas!
Ere evening to be trodden like the grass
Which now beneath them, but above shall
    grow   240
In its next verdure, when this fiery mass
Of living valor, rolling on the foe
And burning with high hope, shall moulder cold
    and low.

28

Last noon beheld them full of lusty life,
Last eve in Beauty's circle proudly gay,
The midnight brought the signal-sound of strife,
The morn the marshalling in arms,—the day
Battle's magnificently-stern array!
The thunder-clouds close o'er it, which when
    rent
The earth is cover'd thick with other clay,   250

200. **Brunswick's fated chieftain:** The Duke of Brunswick was killed at the Battle of Quatre-Bras.

226. **Cameron's Gathering:** battle-song of the Clan of
Cameron, whose chief was Lochiel. 227. **Albyn:** Scotland. 229. **pibroch:** bagpipe music. 234. **Evan's, Donald's:** The references are to Sir Evan Cameron and his
descendant, Donald. Evan fought for James II against
Cromwell, and Donald had fought for the young Pre-
tender at the Battle of Culloden in 1746. 235. **Ardennes:** the forest in Belgium and northern France.

Which her own clay shall cover, heap'd and pent,
Rider and horse,—friend, foe,—in one red burial
    blent!

29

Their praise is hymn'd by loftier harps than
    mine;
Yet one I would select from that proud throng,
Partly because they blend me with his line,
And partly that I did his sire some wrong,
And partly that bright names will hallow song;
And his was of the bravest, and when shower'd
The death-bolts deadliest the thinn'd files along,
Even where the thickest of war's tempest
    lower'd,   260
They reach'd no nobler breast than thine, young,
    gallant Howard!

30

There have been tears and breaking hearts for
    thee,
And mine were nothing, had I such to give;
But when I stood beneath the fresh green tree,
Which living waves where thou didst cease to
    live,
And saw around me the wide field revive
With fruits and fertile promise, and the Spring
Come forth her work of gladness to contrive,
With all her reckless birds upon the wing,
I turn'd from all she brought to those she could
    not bring.   270

31

I turn'd to thee, to thousands, of whom each
And one as all a ghastly gap did make
In his own kind and kindred, whom to teach
Forgetfulness were mercy for their sake;
The Archangel's trump, not Glory's, must awake
Those whom they thirst for; though the sound
    of Fame
May for a moment soothe, it cannot slake
The fever of vain longing, and the name
So honour'd but assumes a stronger, bitterer claim.

254. one: Frederick Howard, son of the Earl of Carlisle, a target of some of Byron's satire in *English Bards
and Scotch Reviewers.*

32

They mourn, but smile at length; and, smiling,
    mourn: 280
The tree will wither long before it fall;
The hull drives on, though mast and sail be torn;
The roof-tree sinks, but moulders on the hall
In massy hoariness; the ruin'd wall
Stands when its wind-worn battlements are gone;
The bars survive the captive they enthral;
The day drags through though storms keep out
    the sun;
And thus the heart will break, yet brokenly live on:

33

Even as a broken mirror, which the glass
In every fragment multiplies; and makes   290
A thousand images of one that was,
The same, and still the more, the more it breaks;
And thus the heart will do which not forsakes,
Living in shatter'd guise, and still, and cold,
And bloodless, with its sleepless sorrow aches,
Yet withers on till all without is old,
Showing no visible sign, for such things are untold.

34

There is a very life in our despair,
Vitality of poison,—a quick root
Which feeds these deadly branches; for it
    were   300
As nothing did we die; but life will suit
Itself to sorrow's most detested fruit,
Like to the apples on the Dead Sea's shore,
All ashes to the taste. Did man compute
Existence by enjoyment, and count o'er
Such hours 'gainst years of life,—say, would he
    name threescore?

35

The Psalmist numbered out the years of man:
They are enough; and if thy tale be *true*,
Thou, who didst grudge him even that fleeting
    span,
More than enough, thou fatal Waterloo!   310
Millions of tongues record thee, and anew
Their children's lips shall echo them, and say—

"Here, where the sword united nations drew,
Our countrymen were warring on that day!"
And this is much, and all which will not pass away.

36

There sunk the greatest, nor the worst of men,
Whose spirit, antithetically mixt,
One moment of the mightiest, and again
On little objects with like firmness fixt;
Extreme in all things! hadst thou been
    betwixt,   320
Thy throne had still been thine, or never been;
For daring made thy rise as fall: thou seek'st
Even now to re-assume the imperial mien,
And shake again the world, the thunderer of the
    scene!

37

Conqueror and captive of the earth art thou!
She trembles at thee still, and thy wild name
Was ne'er more bruited in men's minds than now
That thou art nothing, save the jest of fame,
Who wooed thee once, thy vassal, and became
The flatterer of thy fierceness, till thou
    wert   330
A god unto thyself! nor less the same
To the astounded kingdoms all inert,
Who deemed thee for a time whate'er thou didst
    assert.

38

Oh, more or less than man—in high or low,
Battling with nations, flying from the field,
Now making monarchs' necks thy footstool, now
More than thy meanest soldier taught to yield;
An empire thou couldst crush, command, rebuild,
But govern not thy pettiest passion, nor,
However deeply in men's spirits skilled,   340
Look through thine own, nor curb the lust of
    war,
Nor learn that tempted fate will leave the loftiest
    star.

327. bruited: sounded.

39

Yet well thy soul hath brooked the turning tide
With that untaught innate philosophy,
Which, be it wisdom, coldness, or deep pride,
Is gall and wormwood to an enemy.
When the whole host of hatred stood hard by,
To watch and mock thee shrinking, thou hast
    smiled
With a sedate and all-enduring eye;—
When fortune fled her spoiled and favorite
    child,   350
He stood unbowed beneath the ills upon him piled.

40

Sager than in thy fortunes; for in them
Ambition steeled thee on too far to show
That just habitual scorn, which could contemn
Men and their thoughts; 'twas wise to feel, not so
To wear it ever on thy lip and brow,
And spurn the instruments thou wert to use
Till they were turned unto thine overthrow:
'Tis but a worthless world to win or lose;
So hath it proved to thee, and all such lot who
    choose.   360

41

If, like a tower upon a headland rock,
Thou hadst been made to stand or fall alone,
Such scorn of man had helped to brave the
    shock;
But men's thoughts were the steps which paved
    thy throne,
Their admiration thy best weapon shone;
The part of Philip's son was thine, not then
(Unless aside thy purple had been thrown)
Like stern Diogenes to mock at men;
For sceptred cynics earth were far too wide a den.

42

But quiet to quick bosoms is a hell,   370
And *there* hath been thy bane; there is a fire

366. Philip's son: Alexander the Great. **368. Diogenes:**
the Greek philosopher famed for his vain quest for an
honest man.

And motion of the soul which will not dwell
In its own narrow being, but aspire
Beyond the fitting medium of desire;
And, but once kindled, quenchless evermore,
Preys upon high adventure, nor can tire
Of aught but rest; a fever at the core,
Fatal to him who bears, to all who ever bore.

. . .

72

I live not in myself, but I become   680
Portion of that around me; and to me
High mountains are a feeling, but the hum
Of human cities torture: I can see
Nothing to loathe in nature, save to be
A link reluctant in a fleshly chain,
Classed among creatures, when the soul can flee,
And with the sky, the peak, the heaving plain
Of ocean, or the stars, mingle, and not in vain.

73

And thus I am absorbed, and this is life:
I look upon the peopled desert past,   690
As on a place of agony and strife,
Where, for some sin, to sorrow I was cast,
To act and suffer, but remount at last
With a fresh pinion; which I feel to spring,
Though young, yet waxing vigorous as the blast
Which it would cope with, on delighted wing,
Spurning the clay-cold bonds which round our
        being cling.

74

And when, at length, the mind shall be all free
From what it hates in this degraded form,
Reft of its carnal life, save what shall be   700
Existent happier in the fly and worm,—
When elements to elements conform,
And dust is as it should be, shall I not
Feel all I see, less dazzling, but more warm?
The bodiless thought? the spirit of each spot?
Of which, even now, I share at times the immortal
        lot?

75

Are not the mountains, waves, and skies, a part
Of me and of my soul, as I of them?
Is not the love of these deep in my heart
With a pure passion? should I not contemn   710
All objects, if compared with these? and stem
A tide of suffering, rather than forego
Such feelings for the hard and worldly phlegm
Of those whose eyes are only turned below,
Gazing upon the ground, with thoughts which dare
        not glow?

76

But this is not my theme; and I return
To that which is immediate, and require
Those who find contemplation in the urn,
To look on one, whose dust was once all fire,
A native of the land where I respire   720
The clear air for a while—a passing guest,
Where he became a being,—whose desire
Was to be glorious; 'twas a foolish quest,
The which to gain and keep, he sacrificed all rest.

77

Here the self-torturing sophist, wild Rousseau,
The apostle of affliction, he who threw
Enchantment over passion, and from woe
Wrung overwhelming eloquence, first drew
The breath which made him wretched; yet he
        knew
How to make madness beautiful, and cast   730
O'er erring deeds and thoughts a heavenly hue
Of words, like sunbeams, dazzling as they past
The eyes, which o'er them shed tears feelingly and
        fast.

78

His love was passion's essence:—as a tree
On fire by lightning, with ethereal flame
Kindled he was, and blasted; for to be
Thus, and enamored, were to him the same.
But his was not the love of living dame,

Nor of the dead who rise upon our dreams,
But of ideal beauty, which became   740
In him existence, and o'erflowing teems
Along his burning page, distempered though it
    seems.

79

This breathed itself to life in Julie, *this*
Invested her with all that's wild and sweet;
This hallowed, too, the memorable kiss
Which every morn his fevered lip would greet,
From hers, who but with friendship his would
    meet;
But to that gentle touch through brain and
    breast
Flashed the thrilled spirit's love-devouring heat;
In that absorbing sigh perchance more
    blest   750
Than vulgar minds may be with all they seek
    possest.

80

His life was one long war with self-sought foes,
Or friends by him self-banished; for his mind
Had grown suspicion's sanctuary, and chose,
For its own cruel sacrifice, the kind,
'Gainst whom he raged with fury strange and
    blind.
But he was phrensied,—wherefore, who may
    know?
Since cause might be which skill could never
    find;
But he was phrensied by disease or woe,
To that worst pitch of all, which wears a reasoning
    show   760

81

For then he was inspired, and from him came,
As from the Pythian's mystic cave of yore,
Those oracles which set the world in flame,
Nor ceased to burn till kingdoms were no more:

743. **Julie:** heroine of Rousseau's *La Nouvelle Héloïse.*
745. **memorable kiss:** In the *Confessions* (Book 9),
Rousseau recounts his love for the Comtesse d'Houdetot
and his daily walk for a morning kiss of greeting. 762.
Pythian's . . . cave: the oracle of Apollo at Delphi.

Did he not this for France? which lay before
Bowed to the inborn tyranny of years?
Broken and trembling to the yoke she bore,
Till by the voice of him and his compeers
Roused up too much wrath which follows o'er-
    grown fears?

82

They made themselves a fearful monument!   770
The wreck of old opinions—things which grew,
Breathed from the birth of time: the veil they
    rent,
And what behind it lay, all earth shall view.
But good with ill they also overthrew,
Leaving but ruins, wherewith to rebuild
Upon the same foundations, and renew
Dungeons and thrones, which the same hour
    refilled,
As heretofore, because ambition was self-willed.

83

But this will not endure, nor be endured!
Mankind have felt their strength, and made it
    felt.   780
They might have used it better, but allured
By their new vigor, sternly have they dealt
On one another; pity ceased to melt
With her once natural charities. But they,
Who in oppression's darkness caved had dwelt,
They were not eagles, nourished with the day;
What marvel then, at times, if they mistook their
    prey?

84

What deep wounds ever closed without a scar?
The heart's bleed longest, and but heal to wear
That which disfigures it; and they who war   790
With their own hopes, and have been van-
    quished, bear
Silence, but not submission: in his lair
Fixed Passion holds his breath, until the hour
Which shall atone for years; none need despair:
It came, it cometh, and will come,—the power
To punish or forgive—in *one* we shall be slower.

85

Clear, placid Leman! thy contrasted lake,
With the wild world I dwelt in, is a thing
Which warns me with its stillness to forsake
Earth's troubled waters for a purer spring.   800
This quiet sail is as a noiseless wing
To waft me from distraction; once I loved
Torn ocean's roar, but thy soft murmuring
Sounds sweet as if a Sister's voice reproved,
That I with stern delights should e'er have been so
    moved.

86

It is the hush of night, and all between
Thy margin and the mountains, dusk, yet clear,
Mellow'd and mingling, yet distinctly seen,
Save darken'd Jura, whose capt heights appear
Precipitously steep; and drawing near,   810
There breathes a living fragrance from the shore,
Of flowers yet fresh with childhood; on the ear
Drops the light drip of the suspended oar,
Or chirps the grasshopper one good-night carol
    more;—

87

He is an evening reveller, who makes
His life an infancy, and sings his fill;—
At intervals, some bird from out the brakes
Starts into voice a moment, then is still.
There seems a floating whisper on the hill,
But that is fancy, for the starlight dews   820
All silently their tears of love instil,
Weeping themselves away, till they infuse
Deep into Nature's breast the spirit of her hues.

88

Ye stars, which are the poetry of heaven!
If in your bright leaves we would read the fate
Of men and empires,—'tis to be forgiven,
That in our aspirations to be great,
Our destinies o'erleap their mortal state,
And claim a kindred with you; for ye are
A beauty and a mystery, and create   830
In us such love and reverence from afar
That fortune, fame, power, life, have named them-
    selves a star.

89

All heaven and earth are still—though not in
    sleep,
But breathless, as we grow when feeling most;
And silent, as we stand in thoughts too deep:—
All heaven and earth are still. From the high host
Of stars to the lull'd lake and mountain-coast,
All is concentrated in a life intense,
Where not a beam nor air nor leaf is lost,
But hath a part of being, and a sense   840
Of that which is of all Creator and defence.

90

Then stirs the feeling infinite, so felt
In solitude where we are *least* alone;
A truth, which through our being then doth melt
And purifies from self: it is a tone,
The soul and source of music, which makes
    known
Eternal harmony, and sheds a charm,
Like to the fabled Cytherea's zone,
Binding all things with beauty;—'twould disarm
The spectre Death, had he substantial power to
    harm.   850

91

Not vainly did the early Persian make
His altar the high places and the peak
Of earth-o'ergazing mountains, and thus take
A fit and unwall'd temple, there to seek
The Spirit, in whose honour shrines are weak
Uprear'd of human hands. Come, and compare
Columns and idol-dwellings, Goth or Greek,
With Nature's realms of worship, earth and air,
Nor fix on fond abodes to circumscribe thy pray'r!

92

The sky is changed!—and such a change! Oh
    night,   860
And storm, and darkness, ye are wondrous
    strong,
Yet lovely in your strength, as is the light
Of a dark eye in woman! Far along,

848. Cytherea's zone: the famed Girdle of Venus, which gave the wearer the special power to inspire love.

From peak to peak the rattling crags among,
Leaps the live thunder! Not from one lone
    cloud,
But every mountain now hath found a tongue,
And Jura answers, through her misty shroud,
Back to the joyous Alps who call to her aloud!

93

And this is in the night:—Most glorious night!
Thou wert not sent for slumber! let me be   870
A sharer in thy fierce and far delight,
A portion of the tempest and of thee!
How the lit lake shines, a phosphoric sea,
And the big rain comes dancing to the earth!
And now again 'tis black,—and now, the glee
Of the loud hills shakes with its mountain-mirth,
As if they did rejoice o'er a young earthquake's
    birth.

94

Now, where the swift Rhone cleaves his way
    between
Heights which appear as lovers who have parted
In hate, whose mining depths so intervene   880
That they can meet no more, though broken-
    hearted!
Though in their souls, which thus each other
    thwarted,
Love was the very root of the fond rage
Which blighted their life's bloom and then
    departed—
Itself expired, but leaving them an age
Of years all winters, war within themselves to
    wage:—

95

Now, where the quick Rhone thus hath cleft his
    way,
The mightiest of the storms hath ta'en his stand:
For here, not one, but many, make their play,
And fling their thunder-bolts from hand to
    hand,   890
Flashing and cast around. Of all the band,
The brightest through these parted hills hath
    fork'd
His lightnings, as if he did understand,
That in such gaps as desolation work'd,

There the hot shaft should blast whatever therein
    lurk'd.

96

Sky, mountains, river, winds, lake, lightnings! ye,
With night, and clouds, and thunder, and a soul
To make these felt and feeling, well may be
Things that have made me watchful; the far roll
Of your departing voices, is the knoll   900
Of what in me is sleepless,—if I rest.
But where of ye, oh tempests, is the goal?
Are ye like those within the human breast,
Or do ye find at length, like eagles, some high nest?

97

Could I embody and unbosom now
That which is most within me,—could I wreak
My thoughts upon expression, and thus throw
Soul, heart, mind, passions, feelings, strong or
    weak,
All that I would have sought, and all I seek,
Bear, know, feel and yet breathe—into *one*
    word,   910
And that one word were Lightning, I would
    speak;
But as it is, I live and die unheard,
With a most voiceless thought, sheathing it as a
    sword.

98

The morn is up again, the dewy morn,
With breath all incense and with cheek all
    bloom,
Laughing the clouds away with playful scorn,
And living as if earth contain'd no tomb,—
And glowing into day. We may resume
The march of our existence; and thus I,
Still on thy shores, fair Leman! may find
    room   920
And food for meditation, nor pass by
Much that may give us pause if ponder'd fittingly.

99

Clarens, sweet Clarens, birthplace of deep Love!
Thine air is the young breath of passionate
    thought,

900. knoll: knell. 923. Clarens: village on Lake Geneva.

Thy trees take root in Love; the snows above,
The very Glaciers have his colours caught,
And sunset into rose-hues sees them wrought
By rays which sleep there lovingly: the rocks,
The permanent crags, tell here of Love, who
    sought
In them a refuge from the worldly shocks,   930
Which stir and sting the soul with hope that woos,
    then mocks.

100

Clarens! by heavenly feet thy paths are trod,—
Undying Love's, who here ascends a throne
To which the steps are mountains; where the god
Is a pervading life and light,—so shone
Not on those summits solely, nor alone
In the still cave and forest; o'er the flower
His eye is sparkling and his breath hath blown,
His soft and summer breath, whose tender power
Passes the strength of storms in their most desolate
    hour.   940

101

All things are here of *him;* from the black pines
Which are his shade on high, and the loud roar
Of torrents where he listeneth, to the vines
Which slope his greet path downward to the
    shore,
Where the bow'd waters meet him, and adore,
Kissing his feet with murmurs; and the wood,
The covert of old trees with trunks all hoar,
But light leaves, young as joy, stands where it
    stood,
Offering to him and his a populous solitude,—

102

A populous solitude of bees and birds,   950
And fairy-form'd and many-colour'd things,
Who worship him with notes more sweet than
    words,
And innocently open their glad wings,
Fearless and full of life: the gush of springs,
And fall of lofty fountains, and the bend
Of stirring branches, and the bud which brings
The swiftest thought of beauty, here extend,
Mingling, and made by Love, unto one mighty end.

103

He who hath loved not, here would learn that
    lore,
And make his heart a spirit; he who knows   960
That tender mystery, will love the more,
For this is Love's recess, where vain men's woes
And the world's waste have driven him far from
    those,
For 'tis his nature to advance or die;
He stands not still, but or decays or grows
Into a boundless blessing, which may vie
With the immortal lights in its eternity!

104

'Twas not for fiction chose Rousseau this spot,
Peopling it with affections; but he found
It was the scene which passion must allot   970
To the mind's purified beings; 'twas the ground
Where early Love his Psyche's zone unbound,
And hallow'd it with loveliness. 'Tis lone,
And wonderful, and deep, and hath a sound,
And sense, and sight of sweetness; here the
    Rhone
Hath spread himself a couch, the Alps have rear'd
    a throne.

105

Lausanne and Ferney, ye have been the abodes
Of names which unto you bequeath'd a name;
Mortals, who sought and found, by dangerous
    roads,
A path to perpetuity of fame: 980
They were gigantic minds, and their steep aim
Was, Titan-like, on daring doubts to pile
Thoughts which should call down thunder and
    the flame
Of Heaven, again assail'd, if Heaven the while
On man and man's research could deign do more
    than smile.

977. **Lausanne and Ferney:** two famous sites in Switzerland. In Lausanne Edward Gibbon (1737–1794) completed his great *Decline and Fall of the Roman Empire.* Voltaire (1694–1778) lived at Ferney for nine years before his death. Stanza 106 is devoted to Voltaire, 107 to Gibbon.

106

The one was fire and fickleness, a child,
Most mutable in wishes, but in mind
A wit as various,—gay, grave, sage, or wild,—
Historian, bard, philosopher, combined.
He multiplied himself among mankind,   990
The Proteus of their talents; but his own
Breathed most in ridicule,—which, as the wind,
Blew where it listed, laying all things prone,—
Now to o'erthrow a fool, and now to shake a
        throne.

107

The other, deep and slow, exhausting thought,
And hiving wisdom with each studious year,
In meditation dwelt, with learning wrought,
And shaped his weapon with an edge severe,
Sapping a solemn creed with solemn sneer;
The lord of irony,—that master-spell,   1000
Which stung his foes to wrath which grew from
        fear,
And doom'd him to the zealot's ready Hell,
Which answers to all doubts so eloquently well.

108

Yet, peace be with their ashes for by them,
If merited, the penalty is paid;
It is not ours to judge, far less condemn;
The hour must come when such things shall be
        made
Known unto all,—or hope and dread allay'd
By slumber, on one pillow,—in the dust,
Which, thus much we are sure, must lie
        decay'd;   1010
And when it shall revive, as is our trust,
'Twill be to be forgiven, or suffer what is just.

109

But let me quit man's works again to read
His Maker's, spread around me, and suspend
This page, which from my reveries I feed
Until it seems prolonging without end.
The clouds above me to the white Alps tend,
And I must pierce them, and survey whate'er
May be permitted, as my steps I bend

To their most great and growing region,
        where   1020
The earth to her embrace compels the powers of
air

110

Italia! too, Italia! looking on thee,
Full flashes on the soul the light of ages,
Since the fierce Carthaginian almost won thee,
To the last halo of the chiefs and sages
Who glorify thy consecrated pages;
Thou wert the throne and grave of empires; still
The fount, at which the panting mind assuages
Her thirst of knowledge, quaffing there her fill,
Flows from the eternal source of Rome's imperial
        hill.   1030

111

Thus far have I proceeded in a theme
Renew'd with no kind auspices:—to feel
We are not what we have been, and to deem
We are not what we should be, and to steel
The heart against itself; and to conceal,
With a proud caution, love, or hate, or aught,—
Passion or feeling, purpose, grief, or zeal,—
Which is the tyrant spirit of our thought,
Is a stern task of soul;—no matter—it is taught.

112

And for these words, thus woven into
        song,   1040
It may be that they are a harmless wile,—
The colouring of the scenes which fleet along,
Which I would seize, in passing, to beguile
My breast, or that of others, for a while.
Fame is the thirst of youth,—but I am not
So young as to regard men's frown or smile
As loss of guerdon of a glorious lot;
I stood and stand alone,—remember'd or forgot.

113

I have not loved the world, nor the world me;
I have not flattered its rank breath, nor
        bowed   1050

1024. Carthaginian: Hannibal.

To its idolatries a patient knee,
Nor coined my cheek to smiles, nor cried aloud
In worship of an echo; in the crowd
They could not deem me one of such; I stood
Amongst them, but not of them; in a shroud
Of thoughts which were not their thoughts, and
    still could,
Had I not filed my mind, which thus itself
    subdued.

114

I have not loved the world, nor the world me,—
But let us part fair foes; I do believe,
Though I have found them not, that there may
    be   1060
Words which are things, hopes which will not
    deceive,
And virtues which are merciful, nor weave
Snares for the failing; I would also deem
O'er others' griefs that some sincerely grieve;
That two, or one, are almost what they seem,
That goodness is no name, and happiness no dream.

115

My daughter! with thy name this song begun;
My daughter! with thy name thus much shall end;
I see thee not, I hear thee not, but none
Can be so wrapt in thee; thou art the
    friend   1070
To whom the shadows of far years extend:
Albeit my brow thou never shouldst behold,
My voice shall with thy future visions blend,
And reach into thy heart, when mine is cold,
A token and a tone, even from thy father's mould.

116

To aid thy mind's development, to watch
Thy dawn of little joys, to sit and see
Almost thy very growth, to view thee catch
Knowledge of objects,—wonders yet to thee!
To hold thee lightly on a gentle knee,   1080
And print on thy soft cheek a parent's kiss,—
This, it should seem, was not reserved for me;
Yet this was in my nature: as it is,
I know not what is there, yet something like to this.

1057. filed: defiled.

117

Yet, though dull hate as duty should be taught,
I know that thou wilt love me; though my name
Should be shut from thee, as a spell still fraught
With desolation, and a broken claim:
Though the grave closed between us,—'twere the
    same,
I know that thou wilt love me; though to
    drain   1090
My blood from out thy being were an aim,
And an attainment,—all would be in vain,—
Still thou wouldst love me, still that more than life
    retain.

118

The child of love, though born in bitterness,
And nurtured in convulsion,—of thy sire
These were the elements, and thine no less.
As yet such are around thee, but thy fire
Shall be more tempered, and thy hope far higher.
Sweet be thy cradled slumbers! O'er the sea
And from the mountains where I now
    respire,   1100
Fain would I waft such blessing upon thee,
As, with a sign, I deem thou might'st have been to
    me.

from CANTO IV

1

I stood in Venice, on the "Bridge of Sighs";
A palace and a prison on each hand:
I saw from out the wave her structures rise
As from the stroke of the enchanter's wand:
A thousand years their cloudy wings expand
Around me, and a dying Glory smiles
O'er the far times, when many a subject land
Looked to the wingèd Lion's marble piles,
Where Venice sate in state, throned on her hundred
    isles!

2

She looks a sea Cybele, fresh from ocean,   10
Rising with her tiara of proud towers

CANTO IV. 1. "Bridge of Sighs": the renowned covered
bridge over which prisoners were taken from the Doge's
Palace to San Marco Prison. 8. wingèd Lion: emblem
of St. Mark, patron saint of Venice. 10. Cybele: in
Greek mythology, mother of the gods.

At airy distance, with majestic motion,
A ruler of the waters and their powers:
And such she was;   her daughters had their
    dowers
From spoils of nations, and the exhaustless East
Poured in her lap all gems in sparkling showers.
In purple was she robed, and of her feast
Monarchs partook, and deemed their dignity
    increased.

3

In Venice Tasso's echoes are no more,
And silent rows the songless gondolier;   20
Her palaces are crumbling to the shore,
And music meets not always now the ear:
Those days are gone—but Beauty still is here.
States fall, arts fade—but Nature doth not die,
Nor yet forget how Venice once was dear,
The pleasant place of all festivity,
The revel of the earth, the masque of Italy!

4

But unto us she hath a spell beyond
Her name in story, and her long array
Of mighty shadows, whose dim forms
    despond   30
Above the dogeless city's vanished sway;
Ours is a trophy which will not decay
With the Rialto; Shylock and the Moor,
And Pierre, cannot be swept or worn away—
The keystones of the arch! though all were o'er,
For us repeopled were the solitary shore.

5

The beings of the mind are not of clay;
Essentially immortal, they create
And multiply in us a brighter ray
And more beloved existence: that which
    Fate   40
Prohibits to dull life, in this our state
Of mortal bondage, by these spirits supplied,
First exiles, then replaces what we hate;

31. dogeless: Napoleon had deposed the last doge (a
duke) of Venice in 1797. 33. Rialto: center of business
in Venice.

Watering the heart whose early flowers have
    died,
And with a fresher growth replenishing the void.

6

Such is the refuge of our youth and age,
The first from Hope, the last from Vacancy;
And this worn feeling peoples many a page,
And, may be, that which grows beneath mine
    eye.
Yet there are things whose strong reality   50
Outshines our fairy-land; in shape and hues
More beautiful than our fantastic sky,
And the strange constellations which the Muse
O'er her wild universe is skilful to diffuse:

7

I saw or dream'd of such,—but let them go,—
They came like truth, and disappear'd like
    dreams;
And whatsoe'er they were—are now but so.
I could replace them if I would; still teems
My mind with many a form which aptly seems
Such as I sought for, and at moments
    found: 60
Let these too go, for waking Reason deems
Such over-weening phantasies unsound,
And other voices speak and other sights surround.

8

I've taught me other tongues, and in strange eyes
Have made me not a stranger—to the mind
Which is itself, no changes bring surprise;
Nor is it harsh to make, nor hard to find
A country with—ay, or without mankind;
Yet was I born where men are proud to be,
Not without cause; and should I leave
    behind   70
The inviolate island of the sage and free,
And seek me out a home by a remoter sea,

9

Perhaps I loved it well; and should I lay
My ashes in a soil which is not mine,
My spirit shall resume it—if we may
Unbodied choose a sanctuary. I twine

My hopes of being remember'd in my line
With my land's language: if too fond and far
These aspirations in their scope incline,—
If my fame should be, as my fortunes are,   80
Of hasty growth and blight, and dull Oblivion bar

10

My name from out the temple where the dead
Are honour'd by the nations—let it be,
And light the laurels on a loftier head!
And be the Spartan's epitaph on me,
"Sparta hath many a worthier son than he."
Meantime I seek no sympathies, nor need;
The thorns which I have reap'd are of the tree
I planted,—they have torn me—and I bleed:
I should have known what fruit would spring from
    such a seed.   90

11

The spouseless Adriatic mourns her lord;
And annual marriage now no more renew'd,
The Bucentaur lies rotting unrestored,
Neglected garment of her widowhood!
St. Mark yet sees his lion where he stood
Stand, but in mockery of his wither'd power,
Over the proud Place where an Emperor sued,
And monarchs gazed and envied in the hour
When Venice was a queen with an unequall'd
    dower.

12

The Suabian sued, and now the Austrian
    reigns—   100
An Emperor tramples where an Emperor knelt;
Kingdoms are shrunk to provinces, and chains
Clank over sceptred cities; nations melt
From power's high pinnacle, when they have felt
The sunshine for a while, and downward go
Like lauwine loosen'd from the mountain's
    belt;—

85. "Sparta . . . he": reply of the mother of Brasidas, a Spartan general killed in battle in 422 B.C., when strangers praised his feats.

Oh, for one hour of blind old Dandolo,
Th' octogenarian chief, Byzantium's conquering foe!

13

Before St. Mark still glow his steeds of brass,
Their gilded collars glittering in the sun;   110
But is not Doria's menace come to pass?
Are they not *bridled?*—Venice, lost and won,
Her thirteen hundred years of freedom done,
Sinks, like a seaweed, into whence she rose!
Better be whelmed beneath the waves, and shun,
Even in destruction's depth, her foreign foes,
From whom submission wrings an infamous repose.

14

In youth she was all glory,—a new Tyre;
Her very by-word sprung from victory,
The "Planter of the Lion," which through
    fire   120
And blood she bore o'er subject earth and sea;
Though making many slaves, herself still free,
And Europe's bulwark 'gainst the Ottomite;
Witness Troy's rival, Candia! Vouch it, ye
Immortal waves that saw Lepanto's fight!
For ye are names no time nor tyranny can blight.

15

Statues of glass—all shivered— the long file
Of her dead Doges are declined to dust;
But where they dwelt, the vast and sumptuous
    pile
Bespeaks the pageant of their splendid
    trust;   130
Their sceptre broken, and their sword in rust,
Have yielded to the stranger: empty halls,
Thin streets, and foreign aspects, such as must
Too oft remind her who and what enthrals,
Have flung a desolate cloud o'er Venice' lovely
    walls.

109–11. steeds . . . menace: Doria, the Genoese leader, had pledged in 1379 to bridle the bronze horses in front of St. Mark's Church. 124. Candia: in Crete, defended for twenty-four years against the Turks. 125 Lepanto's fight: the great naval victory of the Venetians over the Turks in 1571.

16

When Athens' armies fell at Syracuse,
And fettered thousands bore the yoke of war,
Redemption rose up in the Attic muse,
Her voice their only ransom from afar:
See! as they chant the tragic hymn, the car   140
Of the o'ermastered victor stops, the reins
Fall from his hands, his idle scimitar
Starts from its belt—he rends his captive's chains,
And bids him thank the bard for freedom and his
    strains.

17

Thus, Venice, if no stronger claim were thine,
Were all thy proud historic deeds forgot,
Thy choral memory of the bard divine,
Thy love of Tasso, should have cut the knot
Which ties thee to thy tyrants; and thy lot
Is shameful to the nations,—most of all,   150
Albion! to thee: the ocean queen should not
Abandon ocean's children; in the fall
Of Venice, think of thine, despite thy watery wall.

18

I loved her from my boyhood; she to me
Was as a fairy city of the heart,
Rising like water-columns from the sea,
Of joy the sojourn, and of wealth the mart;
And Otway, Radcliffe, Schiller, Shakspeare's art,
Had stamped her image in me, and even so,
Although I found her thus, we did not
    part;   160
Perchance even dearer in her day of woe,
Than when she was a boast, a marvel, and a show.

19

I can repeople with the past—and of
The present there is still for eye and thought,
And meditation chastened down, enough;

136–39. **Syracuse . . . ransom:** The historian Plutarch records that when the Athenians were captured at Syracuse in 413 B.C., some gained freedom by reciting passages from the plays of Euripides.

And more, it may be, than I hoped or sought;
And of the happiest moments which were
    wrought
Within the web of my existence, some
From thee, fair Venice! have their colors caught:
There are some feelings time cannot
    benumb   170
Nor torture shake, or mine would now be cold and
    dumb.

20

But from their nature will the tannen grow
Loftiest on loftiest and least shelter'd rocks,
Rooted in barrenness, where nought below
Of soil supports them 'gainst the Alpine shocks
Of eddying storms; yet springs the trunk, and
    mocks
The howling tempest, till its height and frame
Are worthy of the mountains from whose blocks
Of bleak, gray granite into life it came,
And grew a giant tree;—the mind may grow the
    same.   180

21

Existence may be borne, and the deep root
Of life and sufferance make its firm abode
In bare and desolated bosoms: mute
The camel labours with the heaviest load,
And the wolf dies in silence,—not bestow'd
In vain should such example be; if they,
Things of ignoble or of savage mood,
Endure and shrink not, we of nobler clay
May temper it to bear,—it is but for a day.

22

All suffering doth destroy, or is destroy'd   190
Even by the sufferer; and, in each event,
Ends:—Some, with hope replenish'd and
    rebuoy'd,
Return to whence they came—with like intent,
And weave their web again; some, bow'd and
    bent,
Wax gray and ghastly, withering ere their time,
And perish with the reed on which they leant;

172. **tannen:** fir trees.

Some seek devotion, toil, war, good or crime,
According as their souls were form'd to sink or
    climb.

23

But ever and anon of griefs subdued
There comes a token like a scorpion's
    sting,   200
Scarce seen, but with fresh bitterness imbued;
And slight withal may be the things which bring
Back on the heart the weight which it would
    fling
Aside for ever: it may be a sound,—
A tone of music, summer's eve, or spring,
A flower, the wind, the ocean,—which shall
    wound,
Striking the electric chain wherewith we are darkly
    bound;

24

And how and why we know not, nor can trace
Home to its cloud this lightning of the mind,
But feel the shock renew'd, nor can efface   210
The blight and blackening which it leaves
    behind.
Which out of things familiar, undesign'd,
When least we deem of such, calls up to view
The spectres whom no exorcism can bind,
The cold—the changed—perchance the dead—
    anew,
The mourn'd, the loved, the lost—too many!—yet
    how few!

25

But my soul wanders; I demand it back
To meditate amongst decay, and stand
A ruin amidst ruins; there to track
Fall'n states and buried greatness, o'er a
    land   220
Which *was* the mightiest in its old command,
And *is* the loveliest, and must ever be
The master-mould of Nature's heavenly hand,
Wherein were cast the heroic and the free,
The beautiful, the brave—the lords of earth and
    sea,

26

The commonwealth of kings, the men of Rome!
And even since, and now, fair Italy,
Thou art the garden of the world, the home
Of all Art yields, and Nature can decree;
Even in thy desert, what is like to thee?   230
Thy very weeds are beautiful, thy waste
More rich than other climes' fertility;
Thy wreck a glory, and thy ruin graced
With an immaculate charm which cannot be
    defaced.

27

The moon is up, and yet it is not night—
Sunset divides the sky with her, a sea
Of glory streams along the Alpine height
Of blue Friuli's mountains; Heaven is free
From clouds, but of all colours seems to be
Melted to one vast Iris of the West,   240
Where the Day joins the past Eternity;
While, on the other hand, meek Dian's crest
Floats through the azure air, an island of the blest!

28

A single star is at her side, and reigns
With her o'er half the lovely heaven; but still
Yon sunny sea heaves brightly, and remains
Roll'd o'er the peak of the far Rhætian hill,
As Day and Night contending were, until
Nature reclaim'd her order: gently flows
The deep-dyed Brenta, where their hues
    instil   250
The odorous purple of a new-born rose,
Which streams upon her stream, and glass'd within
    it glows,

29

Fill'd with the face of heaven, which from afar
Comes down upon the waters; all its hues,
From the rich sunset to the rising star,
Their magical variety diffuse.
And now they change; a paler shadow strews
Its mantle o'er the mountains; parting day

247. **Rhætian hill:** Rhætia was an ancient province in northern Italy. **250. Brenta:** river flowing into the Gulf of Venice.

Dies like the dolphin, whom each pang imbues
With a new colour as it gasps away,   260
The last still loveliest, till—'tis gone—and all is
    gray.

30

There is a tomb in Arqua;—rear'd in air,
Pillar'd in their sarcophagus, repose
The bones of Laura's lover: here repair
Many familiar with his well-sung woes,
The pilgrims of his genius. He arose
To raise a language, and his land reclaim
From the dull yoke of her barbaric foes;
Watering the tree which bears his lady's name
With his melodious tears, he gave himself to
    fame.   270

31

They keep his dust in Arqua where he died,
The mountain-village where his latter days
Went down the vale of years; and 'tis their
    pride—
An honest pride, and let it be their praise—
To offer to the passing stranger's gaze
His mansion and his sepulchre; both plain
And venerably simple, such as raise
A feeling more accordant with his strain
Than if a pyramid form'd his monumental fane.

32

And the soft quiet hamlet where he dwelt   280
Is one of that complexion which seems made
For those who their mortality have felt,
And sought a refuge from their hopes decay'd
In the deep umbrage of a green hill's shade,
Which shows a distant prospect far away
Of busy cities, now in vain display'd
For they can lure no further; and the ray
Of a bright sun can make sufficient holiday,

33

Developing the mountains, leaves, and flowers,
And shining in the brawling brook,
    where-by,   290

262. **Arqua:** in central Italy. Petrarch spent his last
years here. 264. **Laura's lover:** Petrarch.

Clear as its current, glide the sauntering hours
With a calm languor, which, though to the eye
Idlesse it seem, hath its morality.
If from society we learn to live,
'Tis solitude should teach us how to die;
It hath no flatterers; vanity can give
No hollow aid; alone—man with his God must
    strive:

34

Or, it may be, with demons, who impair
The strength of better thoughts, and seek their
    prey
In melancholy bosoms, such as were   300
Of moody texture from their earliest day
And loved to dwell in darkness and dismay,
Deeming themselves predestined to a doom
Which is not of the pangs that pass away;
Making the sun like blood, the earth a tomb,
The tomb a hell, and hell itself a murkier gloom.

35

Ferrara, in thy wide and grass-grown streets,
Whose symmetry was not for solitude,
There seems as 'twere a curse upon the seats
Of former sovereigns, and the antique
    brood   310
Of Este, which for many an age made good
Its strength within thy walls, and was of yore
Patron or tyrant, as the changing mood
Of petty power impell'd, of those who wore
The wreath which Dante's brow alone had worn
    before.

36

And Tasso is their glory and their shame:
Hark to his strain and then survey his cell!
And see how dearly earn'd Torquato's fame,
And where Alfonso bade his poet dwell.
The miserable despot could not quell   320
The insulted mind he sought to quench, and
    blend

307. **Ferrara:** seat of the House of Este. 316. **Tasso:**
The stanza recounts the story that Torquato Tasso, the
great Italian poet, was imprisoned as a madman by
Alfonso II because of Tasso's love for the Duke's sister.

With the surrounding maniacs, in the hell
Where he had plunged it. Glory without end
Scatter'd the clouds away, and on that name attend

37

The tears and praises of all time; while thine
Would rot in its oblivion—in the sink
Of worthless dust which from thy boasted line
Is shaken into nothing—but the link
Thou formest in his fortunes bids us think
Of thy poor malice, naming thee with
    scorn.   330
Alfonso! how thy ducal pageants shrink
From thee! if in another station born,
Scarce fit to be the slave of him thou madest to
    mourn:—

38

Thou! form'd to eat, and be despised, and die,
Even as the beasts that perish, save that thou
Hadst a more splendid trough and wider sty;
He! with a glory round his furrow'd brow,
Which emanated then, and dazzles now,
In face of all his foes, the Cruscan quire,
And Boileau, whose rash envy could allow   340
No strain which shamed his country's creaking
    lyre,
That whetstone of the teeth—monotony in wire!

39

Peace to Torquato's injured shade! 'twas his
In life and death to be the mark where Wrong
Aim'd with her poison'd arrows, but to miss.
Oh, victor unsurpass'd in modern song!
Each year brings forth its millions; but how long
The tide of generations shall roll on,
And not the whole combined and countless
    throng
Compose a mind like thine? Though all in
    one   350
Condensed their scatter'd rays, they would not form
    a sun.

339–40. Cruscan . . . Boileau: Tasso's works were severely criticized by the Florentine Accademia della Crusca and by the eminent French critic Nicolas Boileau.

40

Great as thou art, yet parallel'd by those,
Thy countrymen, before thee born to shine,
The Bards of Hell and Chivalry: first rose
The Tuscan father's comedy divine;
Then, not unequal to the Florentine
The southern Scott, the minstrel who call'd forth
A new creation with his magic line,
And, like the Ariosto of the North,
Sang ladye-love and war, romance and knightly
    worth   360

41

The lightning rent from Ariosto's bust
The iron crown of laurel's mimic'd leaves;
Nor was the ominous element unjust,
For the true laurel-wreath which Glory weaves
Is of the tree no bolt of thunder cleaves,
And the false semblance but disgraced his brow;
Yet still, if fondly Superstition grieves,
Know, that the lightning sanctifies below
Whate'er it strikes;—yon head is doubly sacred
    now.

42

Italia! oh, Italia! thou who hast   370
The fatal gift of beauty, which became
A funeral dower of present woes and past,
On thy sweet brow is sorrow plough'd by
    shame,
And annals graved in characters of flame.
Oh, God! that thou wert in thy nakedness
Less lovely or more powerful, and couldst claim
Thy right, and awe the robbers back, who press
To shed thy blood and drink the tears of thy
    distress;

43

Then mightst thou more appal; or, less desired,
Be homely and be peaceful, undeplored   380
For thy destructive charms; then, still untired,
Would not be seen the armèd torrents pour'd
Down the deep Alps; nor would the hostile horde
Of many-nation'd spoilers from the Po

354. Bards: a reference to Dante and Ariosto.

Quaff blood and water; nor the stranger's sword
Be thy sad weapon of defence, and so,
Victor or vanquish'd, thou the slave of friend or foe.

44

Wandering in youth, I traced the path of him,
The Roman friend of Rome's least-mortal mind,
The friend of Tully. As my bark did skim   390
The bright blue waters with a fanning wind,
Came Megara before me, and behind
Ægina lay, Piræus on the right,
And Corinth on the left; I lay reclined
Along the prow, and saw all these unite
In ruin, even as he had seen the desolate sight;—

45

For Time hath not rebuilt them, but up-rear'd
Barbaric dwellings on their shatter'd site,
Which only make more mourn'd and more
        endear'd
The few last rays of their far-scatter'd light   400
And the crush'd relics of their vanish'd might.
The Roman saw these tombs in his own age,
These sepulchres of cities which excite
Sad wonder, and his yet surviving page
The moral lesson bears, drawn from such
        pilgrimage.

46

That page is now before me, and on mine
His country's ruin added to the mass
Of perish'd states he mourn'd in their decline,
And I in desolation. All that *was*
Of then destruction *is;* and now, alas!   410
Rome—Rome imperial, bows her to the storm,
In the same dust and blackness, and we pass
The skeleton of her Titanic form,
Wrecks of another world whose ashes still are
        warm.

47

Yet, Italy! through every other land
Thy wrongs should ring, and shall, from side to
        side;

389. Roman friend: Servius Sulpicius. **390. Tully:** Marcus Tullius Cicero (106–43 B.C.), the great Roman statesman and orator.

Mother of Arts, as once of arms; thy hand
Was then our guardian, and is still our guide;
Parent of our Religion, whom the wide
Nations have knelt to for the keys of
        heaven!   420
Europe, repentant of her parricide,
Shall yet redeem thee, and, all backward driven,
Roll the barbarian tide, and sue to be forgiven.

48

But Arno wins us to the fair white walls,
Where the Etrurian Athens claims and keeps
A softer feeling for her fairy halls.
Girt by her theatre of hills, she reaps
Her corn and wine and oil, and Plenty leaps
To laughing life with her redundant horn.
Along the banks where smiling Arno
        sweeps   430
Was modern Luxury of Commerce born,
And buried Learning rose, redeem'd to a new
        morn.

49

There, too, the Goddess loves in stone, and fills
The air around with beauty. We inhale
The ambrosial aspect, which, beheld, instils
Part of its immortality; the veil
Of heaven is half undrawn; within the pale
We stand, and in that form and face behold
What mind can make when Nature's self would
        fail;
And to the fond idolaters of old   440
Envy the innate flash which such a soul could
        mould.

50

We gaze and turn away, and know not where,
Dazzled and drunk with beauty, till the heart
Reels with its fulness; there—for ever there—
Chain'd to the chariot of triumphal Art,
We stand as captives and would not depart.
Away!—there need no words nor terms precise,
The paltry jargon of the marble mart
Where Pedantry gulls Folly—we have eyes:
Blood, pulse, and breast confirm the Dardan
        Shepherd's prize.   450

51

Appear'dst thou not to Paris in this guise?
Or to more deeply blest Anchises? or,
In all thy perfect goddess-ship, when lies
Before thee thy own vanquish'd Lord of War?
And gazing in thy face as toward a star,
Laid on thy lap, his eyes to thee upturn,
Feeding on thy sweet cheek; while thy lips are
With lava kisses melting while they burn,
Shower'd on his eyelids, brow, and mouth, as from
    an urn!

52

Glowing and circumfused in speechless
    love,   460
Their full divinity inadequate
That feeling to express or to improve,
The gods become as mortals, and man's fate
Has moments like their brightest; but the weight
Of earth recoils upon us;—let it go!
We can recall such visions, and create,
From what has been or might be, things which
    grow
Into thy statue's form and look like gods below.

53

I leave to learnèd fingers and wise hands,
The artist and his ape, to teach and tell   470
How well his connoisseurship understands
The graceful bend and the voluptuous swell:
Let these describe the undescribable;
I would not their vile breath should crisp the
    stream
Wherein that image shall for ever dwell,
The unruffled mirror of the loveliest dream
That ever left the sky on the deep soul to beam.

54

In Santa Croce's holy precincts lie
Ashes which make it holier, dust which is
Even in itself an immortality,   480
Though there were nothing save the past, and
    this,

453. goddess: Venus de Medici.

The particle of those sublimities
Which have relapsed to chaos: here repose
Angelo's, Alfieri's bones, and his,
The starry Galileo, with his woes;
Here Machiavelli's earth return'd to whence it rose.

55

These are four minds, which, like the elements,
Might furnish forth creation. Italy!
Time, which hath wrong'd thee with ten
    thousand rents
Of thine imperial garment, shall deny,   490
And hath denied, to every other sky
Spirits which soar from ruin:—thy decay
Is still impregnate with divinity,
Which gilds it with revivifying ray;
Such as the great of yore, Canova is today.

56

But where repose the all Etruscan three—
Dante, and Petrarch, and, scarce less than they,
The Bard of Prose, creative spirit, he
Of the Hundred Tales of love—where did they
    lay
Their bones, distinguish'd from our common
    clay   500
In death as life? Are they resolved to dust,
And have their country's marbles nought to say?
Could not her quarries furnish forth one bust?
Did they not to her breast their filial earth intrust?

57

Ungrateful Florence! Dante sleeps afar,
Like Scipio, buried by the upbraiding shore;
Thy factions, in their worse than civil war,
Proscribed the bard whose name for evermore
Their children's children would in vain adore
With the remorse of ages; and the crown   510
Which Petrarch's laureate brow supremely wore,
Upon a far and foreign soil had grown,
His life, his fame, his grave, though rifled—not
    thine own.

495. Canova: the Italian sculptor Antonio Canova
(1757–1822).

58

Boccaccio to his parent earth bequeath'd
His dust; and lies it not her Great among,
With many a sweet and solemn requiem breathed
O'er him who form'd the Tuscan's siren tongue?
That music in itself, whose sounds are song,
The poetry of speech? No;—even his tomb
Uptorn must bear the hyæna bigot's
     wrong,   520
No more amidst the meaner dead find room,
Nor claim a passing sigh, because it told for *whom!*

59

And Santa Croce wants their mighty dust,—
Yet for this want more noted, as of yore
The Cæsar's pageant, shorn of Brutus' bust,
Did but of Rome's best Son remind her more.
Happier Ravenna! on thy hoary shore,
Fortress of falling empire, honour'd sleeps
The immortal exile; Arqua, too, her store
Of tuneful relics proudly claims and keeps,   530
While Florence vainly begs her banish'd dead, and
    weeps.

60

What is her pyramid of precious stones,
Of porphyry, jasper, agate, and all hues
Of gem and marble, to encrust the bones
Of merchant-dukes? The momentary dews
Which, sparkling to the twilight stars, infuse
Freshness in the green turf that wraps the dead,
Whose names are mausoleums of the Muse,
Are gently prest with far more reverent tread
Than ever paced the slab which paves the princely
    head.   540

. . .

95

I speak not of men's creeds—they rest between
Man and his Maker—but of things allow'd,

525. **Brutus' bust**: The busts of Brutus and Cassius were not carried in the funeral procession of Junia, sister of Brutus and wife of Cassius.

Averr'd, and known—and daily, hourly seen—
The yoke that is upon us doubly bow'd   850
And the intent of tyranny avow'd,
The edict of Earth's rulers, who are grown
The apes of him who humbled once the proud
And shook them from their slumbers on the
    throne;
Too glorious, were this all his mighty arm had done.

96

Can tyrants but by tyrants conquer'd be,
And Freedom find no champion and no child
Such as Columbia saw arise when she
Sprung forth a Pallas, arm'd and undefiled?
Or must such minds be nourish'd in the
    wild,   860
Deep in the unpruned forest, 'midst the roar
Of cataracts, where nursing Nature smiled
On infant Washington? Has Earth no more
Such seeds within her breast, or Europe no such
    shore?

97

But France got drunk with blood to vomit crime,
And fatal have her Saturnalia been
To Freedom's cause, in every age and clime;
Because the deadly days which we have seen,
And vile Ambition, that built up between
Man and his hopes an adamantine wall,   870
And the base pageant last upon the scene,
Are grown the pretext for the eternal thrall
Which nips life's tree, and dooms man's worst—his
    second fall.

98

Yet, Freedom, yet thy banner, torn but flying,
Streams like the thunder-storm *against* the wind;
Thy trumpet voice, though broken now and
    dying,

858. **Columbia**: America. 859. **Pallas**: Pallas Athene, goddess of wisdom, fabled to have sprung full grown from the head of Zeus, her father. 865. **France**: This stanza recounts Byron's attitude toward the perversions (Saturnalia) of the French Revolution—the Reign of Terror, the imperialistic ambitions, the reactionary settlements of Vienna and Paris.

The loudest still the tempest leaves behind:
Thy tree hath lost its blossoms, and the rind,
Chopp'd by the axe, looks rough and little worth,
But the sap lasts,—and still the seed we
    find   880
Sown deep, even in the bosom of the North;
So shall a better spring less bitter fruit bring forth.

99

There is a stern round tower of other days,
Firm as a fortress, with its fence of stone,
Such as an army's baffled strength delays,
Standing with half its battlements alone,
And with two thousand years of ivy grown,
The garland of eternity, where wave
The green leaves over all by time o'er-thrown;—
What was this tower of strength? within its
    cave   890
What treasure lay so lock'd, so hid? A woman's
    grave.

100

But who was she, the lady of the dead,
Tomb'd in a palace? Was she chaste and fair?
Worthy a king's—or more—a Roman's bed?
What race of chiefs and heroes did she bear?
What daughter of her beauties was the heir?
How lived, how loved, how died she? Was she
    not
So honour'd—and conspicuously there,
Where meaner relics must not dare to rot,
Placed to commemorate a more than mortal
    lot?   900

101

Was she as those who love their lords, or they
Who love the lords of others?—such have been
Even in the olden time, Rome's annals say.
Was she a matron of Cornelia's mien,
Or the light air of Egypt's graceful queen,
Profuse of joy—or 'gainst it did she war,
Inveterate in virtue? Did she lean
To the soft side of the heart, or wisely bar
Love from amongst her griefs?—for such the
    affections are.

102

Perchance she died in youth: it may be,
    bow'd   910
With woes far heavier than the ponderous tomb
That weigh'd upon her gentle dust, a cloud
Might gather o'er her beauty, and a gloom
In her dark eye, prophetic of the doom
Heaven gives its favourites—early death; yet
    shed
A sunset charm around her, and illume
With hectic light, the Hesperus of the dead,
Of her consuming cheek the autumnal leaf-like red.

103

Perchance she died in age—surviving all,
Charms, kindred, children—with the silver
    gray   920
On her long tresses, which might yet recall,
It may be, still a something of the day
When they were braided, and her proud array
And lovely form were envied, praised, and eyed
By Rome.—But whither would Conjecture stray?
Thus much alone we know—Metella died,
The wealthiest Roman's wife. Behold his love or
    pride!

104

I know not why, but standing thus by thee,
It seems as if I had thine inmate known,
Thou tomb! and other days come back on
    me   930
With recollected music, though the tone
Is changed and solemn, like the cloudy groan
Of dying thunder on the distant wind;
Yet could I seat me by this ivied stone
Till I had bodied forth the heated mind
Forms from the floating wreck which Ruin leaves
    behind;

105

And from the planks, far shatter'd o'er the rocks,
Built me a little bark of hope, once more
To battle with the ocean and the shocks
Of the loud breakers, and the ceaseless roar   940
Which rushes on the solitary shore

Where all lies founder'd that was ever dear.
But could I gather from the wave-worn store
Enough for my rude boat, where should I steer?
There woos no home, nor hope, nor life, save what
    is here.

106

Then let the winds howl on! their harmony
Shall henceforth be my music, and the night
The sound shall temper with the owlets' cry,
As I now hear them, in the fading light
Dim o'er the bird of darkness' native site,   950
Answering each other on the Palatine,
With their large eyes all glistening gray and
    bright,
And sailing pinions. Upon such a shrine
What are our petty griefs?—let me not number
    mine.

107

Cypress and ivy, weed and wallflower grown
Matted and mass'd together, hillocks heap'd
On what were chambers, arch crush'd, column
    strown
In fragments, choked up vaults, and frescos
    steep'd
In subterranean damps where the owl peep'd,
Deeming it midnight:—Temples, baths, or
    halls?   960
Pronounce who can; for all that Learning reap'd
From her research hath been, that these are
    walls—
Behold the Imperial Mount! 'tis thus the mighty
    falls.

. . .

130

Oh, Time! the beautifier of the dead,
Adorner of the ruin, comforter
And only healer when the heart hath bled—
Time! the corrector where our judgments err,
The test of truth, love,—sole philosopher,
For all besides are sophists, from thy thrift

951. **Palatine:** the Imperial Mount, chief of Rome's
seven hills.

Which never loses though it doth defer—
Time, the avenger! unto thee I lift
My hands and eyes and heart, and crave of thee
    a gift: 1170

131

Amidst this wreck, where thou hast made a
    shrine
And temple more divinely desolate,
Among thy mightier offerings here are mine,
Ruins of years—though few, yet full of fate:—
If thou hast ever seen me too elate,
Hear me not; but if calmly I have borne
Good, and reserved my pride against the hate
Which shall not whelm me, let me not have worn
This iron in my soul in vain—shall *they* not mourn?

132

And thou, who never yet of human
    wrong   1180
Left the unbalanced scale, great Nemesis!
Here, where the ancient paid thee homage
    long—
Thou, who didst call the Furies from the abyss,
And round Orestes bade them howl and hiss
For that unnatural retribution—just,
Had it but been from hands less near—in this
Thy former realm, I call thee from the dust!
Dost thou not hear my heart?—Awake! thou shalt,
    and must.

133

It is not that I may not have incurr'd
For my ancestral faults or mine the
    wound   1190
I bleed withal, and, had it been conferr'd
With a just weapon, it had flow'd unbound;
But now my blood shall not sink in the ground;
To thee I do devote it—*thou* shalt take
The vengeance, which shall yet be sought and
    found,
Which if *I* have not taken for the sake—
But let that pass—I sleep, but thou shalt yet awake.

1181. **Nemesis:** Greek goddess of retribution.

134

And if my voice break forth, 'tis not that now
I shrink from what is suffer'd; let him speak
Who hath beheld decline upon my brow,   1200
Or seen my mind's convulsion leave it weak:
But in this page a record will I seek.
Not in the air shall these my words disperse,
Though I be ashes; a far hour shall wreak
The deep prophetic fulness of this verse,
And pile on human heads the mountain of my
    curse!

135

That curse shall be Forgiveness. Have I not—
Hear me, my mother Earth! behold it, Heaven!—
Have I not had to wrestle with my lot?
Have I not suffer'd things to be forgiven?   1210
Have I not had my brain sear'd, my heart riven,
Hopes sapp'd, name blighted, Life's life lied
    away?
And only not to desperation driven,
Because not altogether of such clay
As rots into the souls of those whom I survey.

136

From mighty wrongs to petty perfidy
Have I not seen what human things could do?
From the loud roar of foaming calumny
To the small whisper of the as paltry few,
And subtler venom of the reptile crew,   1220
The Janus glance of whose significant eye,
Learning to lie with silence, would *seem* true,
And without utterance, save the shrug or sigh,
Deal round to happy fools its speechless obloquy.

137

But I have lived, and have not lived in vain:
My mind may lose its force, my blood its fire,
And my frame perish even in conquering pain;
But there is that within me which shall tire
Torture and Time, and breathe when I expire;

1221. Janus: the two-faced Roman god.

Something unearthly which they deem not
    of,   1230
Like the remember'd tone of a mute lyre,
Shall on their soften'd spirits sink, and move
In hearts all rocky now the late remorse of love.

138

The seal is set.—Now welcome, thou dread
    power!
Nameless, yet thus omnipotent, which here
Walk'st in the shadow of the midnight hour
With a deep awe, yet all distinct from fear;
Thy haunts are ever where the dead walls rear
Their ivy mantles, and the solemn scene
Derives from thee a sense so deep and
    clear   1240
That we become a part of what has been,
And grow unto the spot, all-seeing but unseen.

139

And here the buzz of eager nations ran,
In murmur'd pity or loud-roar'd applause,
As man was slaughter'd by his fellow man.
And wherefore slaughter'd? wherefore, but
    because
Such were the bloody Circus' genial laws,
And the imperial pleasure.—Wherefore not?
What matters where we fall to fill the maws
Of worms—on battle-plains or listed spot?   1250
Both are but theatres where the chief actors rot.

140

I see before me the Gladiator lie:
He leans upon his hand—his manly brow
Consents to death, but conquers agony,
And his droop'd head sinks gradually low—
And through his side the last drops, ebbing slow
From the red gash, fall heavy, one by one,
Like the first of a thunder-shower; and now
The arena swims around him—he is gone,
Ere ceased the inhuman shout which hail'd the
    wretch who won.   1260

1250. listed spot: the arena. 1252. Gladiator: Byron's
picture was inspired by the famous statue of the Dying
Gaul.

141

He heard it, but he heeded not—his eyes
Were with his heart and that was far away;
He reck'd not of the life he lost nor prize,
But where his rude hut by the Danube lay,
There were his young barbarians all at play,
There was their Dacian mother—he, their sire,
Butcher'd to make a Roman holiday—
All this rush'd with his blood.—Shall he expire
And unavenged?—Arise! ye Goths, and glut your
  ire!

142

But here, where Murder breathed her bloody
  steam;   1270
And here, where buzzing nations choked the
  ways,
And roar'd or murmur'd like a mountain stream
Dashing or winding as its torrent strays;
Here, where the Roman millions' blame or praise
Was death or life, the playthings of a crowd,
My voice sounds much, and fall the stars' faint
  rays
On the arena void—seats crush'd—walls
  bow'd—
And galleries, where my steps seem echoes
  strangely loud.

143

A ruin—yet what ruin! From its mass
Walls, palaces, half-cities, have been
  rear'd;   1280
Yet oft the enormous skeleton ye pass,
And marvel where the spoil could have appear'd.
Hath it indeed been plunder'd, or but clear'd?
Alas! developed, opens the decay,
When the colossal fabric's form is near'd:
It will not bear the brightness of the day,
Which streams too much on all years, man, have
  reft away.

1267. **Roman holiday:** The Emperor Trajan brought
back to Rome 10,000 captured Dacians to serve as
gladiators to entertain the citizenry.

144

But when the rising moon begins to climb
Its topmost arch and gently pauses there;
When the stars twinkle through the loops of
  time,   1290
And the low night-breeze waves along the air
The garland forest, which the gray walls wear
Like laurels on the bald first Cæsar's head;
When the light shines serene but doth not glare,
Then in this magic circle raise the dead:
Heroes have trod this spot—'tis on their dust ye
  tread.

145

"While stands the Coliseum, Rome shall stand;
When falls the Coliseum, Rome shall fall;
And when Rome falls—the World." From our
  own land
Thus spake the pilgrims o'er this mighty
  wall   1300
In Saxon times, which we are wont to call
Ancient; and these three mortal things are still
On their foundations, and unalter'd all;
Rome and her Ruin past Redemption's skill,
The World, the same wide den—of thieves, or
  what ye will.

146

Simple, erect, severe, austere, sublime—
Shrine of all saints and temple of all gods,
From Jove to Jesus—spared and blest by time;
Looking tranquillity, while falls or nods
Arch, empire, each thing round thee, and man
  plods   1310
His way through thorns to ashes—glorious dome!
Shalt thou not last? Time's scythe and tyrants'
  rods
Shiver upon thee—sanctuary and home
Of art and piety—Pantheon!—pride of Rome!

147

Relic of nobler days and noblest arts!
Despoil'd, yet perfect, with thy circle spreads
A holiness appealing to all hearts—
To art a model; and to him who treads

Rome for the sake of ages, Glory sheds
Her light through thy sole aperture; to
    those   1320
Who worship, here are altars for their beads;
And they who feel for genius may repose
Their eyes on honour'd forms whose busts around
    them close.

148

There is a dungeon, in whose dim drear light
What do I gaze on? Nothing: Look again!
Two forms are slowly shadow'd on my sight—
Two insulated phantoms of the brain:
It is not so; I see them full and plain—
An old man, and a female young and fair,
Fresh as a nursing mother, in whose vein   1330
The blood is nectar;—but what doth she there,
With her unmantled neck, and bosom white and
    bare?

149

Full swells the deep pure fountain of young life,
Where *on* the heart and *from* the heart we took
Our first and sweetest nurture, when the wife,
Blest into mother, in the innocent look
Or even the piping cry of lips that brook
No pain and small suspense, a joy perceives
Man knows not, when from out its cradled nook
She sees her little bud put forth its
    leaves—   1340
What may the fruit be yet?—I know not, Cain was
    Eve's.

150

But here youth offers to old age the food,
The milk of his own gift:—it is her sire
To whom she renders back the debt of blood
Born with her birth. No; he shall not expire
While in those warm and lovely veins the fire
Of health and holy feeling can provide
Great Nature's Nile, whose deep stream rises
    higher
Than Egypt's river:—from that gentle side
Drink, drink and live, old man! Heaven's realm
    holds no such tide.   1350

151

The starry fable of the milky way
Has not thy story's purity; it is
A constellation of a sweeter ray,
And sacred Nature triumphs more in this
Reverse of her decree than in the abyss
Where sparkle distant worlds. Oh, holiest nurse!
No drop of that clear stream its way shall miss
To thy sire's heart, replenishing its source
With life, as our freed souls rejoin the universe.

152

Turn to the Mole which Hadrian rear'd on
    high,   1360
Imperial mimic of old Egypt's piles,
Colossal copyist of deformity,
Whose travell'd phantasy from the far Nile's
Enormous model doom'd the artist's toils
To build for giants, and for his vain earth,
His shrunken ashes, raise this dome. How smiles
The gazer's eye with philosophic mirth,
To view the huge design which sprung from such
    a birth!

153

But lo, the dome, the vast and wondrous dome
To which Diana's marvel was a cell,   1370
Christ's mighty shrine above his martyr's tomb!
I have beheld the Ephesian's miracle—
Its columns strew the wilderness, and dwell
The hyæna and the jackal in their shade;
I have beheld Sophia's bright roofs swell
Their glittering mass i' the sun, and have survey'd
Its sanctuary the while the usurping Moslem pray'd;

154

But thou, of temples old or altars new,
Standest alone, with nothing like to thee—
Worthiest of God, the holy and the true.   1380
Since Zion's desolation, when that He

1369. the dome: Church of St. Peter. 1370. Diana's
marvel: second temple of Diana at Ephesus. 1375. Sophia's bright roofs: Church of St. Sophia in Constan-
tinople (Istanbul).

Forsook his former city, what could be,
Of earthly structures, in his honour piled
Of a sublimer aspect? Majesty,
Power, Glory, Strength, and Beauty, all are aisled
In this eternal ark of worship undefiled.

155

Enter: its grandeur overwhelms thee not;
And why? it is not lessen'd; but thy mind,
Expanded by the genius of the spot,
Has grown colossal, and can only find   1390
A fit abode wherein appear enshrined
Thy hopes of immortality; and thou
Shalt one day, if found worthy, so defined,
See thy God face to face as thou dost now
His Holy of Holies, nor be blasted by his brow.

156

Thou movest—but increasing with the advance,
Like climbing some great Alp, which still doth
          rise,
Deceived by its gigantic elegance;
Vastness which grows, but grows to harmonise—
All musical in its immensities;   1400
Rich marble, richer painting, shrines where
          flame
The lamps of gold, and haughty dome which
          vies
In air with Earth's chief structures, though their
          frame
Sits on the firm-set ground—and this the clouds
          must claim.

157

Thou seest not all; but piecemeal thou must
          break
To separate contemplation the great whole;
And as the ocean many bays will make,
That ask the eye—so here condense thy soul
To more immediate objects, and control
Thy thoughts until thy mind hath got by
          heart   1410
Its eloquent proportions, and unroll
In mighty graduations, part by part,
The glory which at once upon thee did not dart,

158

Not by its fault—but thine. Our outward sense
Is but of gradual grasp: and as it is
That what we have of feeling most intense
Outstrips our faint expression; even so this
Outshining and o'erwhelming edifice
Fools our fond gaze, and greatest of the great
Defies at first our Nature's littleness,   1420
Till, growing with its growth, we thus dilate
Our spirits to the size of that they contemplate.

159

Then pause, and be enlighten'd; there is more
In such a survey than the sating gaze
Of wonder pleased, or awe which would adore
The worship of the place, or the mere praise
Of art and its great masters, who could raise
What former time, nor skill, nor thought could
          plan;
The fountain of sublimity displays
Its depth, and thence may draw the mind of
          man   1430
Its golden sands, and learn what great conceptions
          can.

160

Or, turning to the Vatican, go see
Laocoön's torture dignifying pain—
A father's love and mortal's agony
With an immortal's patience blending. Vain
The struggle; vain, against the coiling strain
And gripe and deepening of the dragon's grasp,
The old man's clench; the long envenom'd chain
Rivets the living links, the enormous asp
Enforces pang on pang, and stifles gasp on
          gasp.   1440

161

Or view the Lord of the unerring bow,
The God of life and poesy and light,—
The Sun in human limbs array'd, and brow
All radiant from his triumph in the fight;
The shaft hath just been shot—the arrow bright
With an immortal's vengeance; in his eye

1441. Lord: the Apollo Belvedere.

And nostril beautiful disdain and might
And majesty flash their full lightnings by,
Developing in that one glance the Deity.

162

But in his delicate form—a dream of
    Love,   1450
Shaped by some solitary nymph whose breast
Long'd for a deathless lover from above
And madden'd in that vision—are exprest
All that ideal beauty ever bless'd
The mind with in its most unearthly mood,
When each conception was a heavenly guest—
A ray of immortality—and stood,
Starlike, around, until they gather'd to a god!

163

And if it be Prometheus stole from Heaven
The fire which we endure, it was repaid   1460
By him to whom the energy was given
Which this poetic marble hath array'd
With an eternal glory—which, if made
By human hands, is not of human thought;
And Time himself hath hallow'd it, nor laid
One ringlet in the dust; nor hath it caught
A tinge of years, but breathes the flame with which
    'twas wrought.

164

But where is he, the Pilgrim of my song,
The being who upheld it through the past?
Methinks he cometh late and tarries long,   1470
He is no more—these breathings are his last;
His wanderings done, his visions ebbing fast,
And he himself as nothing:—if he was
Aught but a phantasy, and could be class'd
With forms which live and suffer—let that
    pass—
His shadow fades away into Destruction's mass,

165

Which gathers shadow, substance, life, and all
That we inherit in its mortal shroud,
And spreads the dim and universal pall
Through which all things grow phantoms and the
    cloud   1480

Between us sinks and all which ever glow'd,
Till Glory's self is twilight, and displays
A melancholy halo scarce allow'd
To hover on the verge of darkness;—rays
Sadder than saddest night, for they distract the
    gaze,

166

And send us prying into the abyss,
To gather what we shall be when the frame
Shall be resolved to something less than this
Its wretched essence; and to dream of fame,
And wipe the dust from off the idle name   1490
We never more shall hear,—but never more,
Oh, happier thought! can we be made the same:
It is enough in sooth that *once* we bore
These fardels of the heart—the heart whose sweat
    was gore.

167

Hark! forth from the abyss a voice proceeds,
A long low distant murmur of dread sound,
Such as arises when a nation bleeds
With some deep and immedicable wound;
Through storm and darkness yawns the rending
    ground;
The gulf is thick with phantoms, but the
    chief   1500
Seems royal still, though with her head
    discrown'd;
And pale, but lovely, with maternal grief
She clasps a babe to whom her breast yields no
    relief.

168

Scion of chiefs and monarchs, where art thou?
Fond hope of many nations, art thou dead?
Could not the grave forget thee, and lay low
Some less majestic, less beloved head?
In the sad midnight, while thy heart still bled,
The mother of a moment, o'er thy boy,
Death hush'd that pang for ever; with thee
    fled   1510
The present happiness and promised joy
Which fill'd the imperial isles so full it seem'd to
    cloy.

1494. fardels: burdens.

169

Peasants bring forth in safety.   Can it be,
Oh thou that wert so happy, so adored!
Those who weep not for kings shall weep for
    thee,
And Freedom's heart, grown heavy, cease to
    hoard
Her many griefs for ONE; for she had pour'd
Her orisons for thee, and o'er thy head
Beheld her Iris.—Thou, too, lonely lord,
And desolate consort—vainly wert thou
    wed!   1500
The husband of a year! the father of the dead!

170

Of sackcloth was thy wedding garment made;
Thy bridal's fruit is ashes; in the dust
The fair-hair'd Daughter of the Isles is laid,
The love of millions! How we did intrust
Futurity to her! and, though it must
Darken above our bones, yet fondly deem'd
Our children should obey her child, and bless'd
Her and her hoped-for seed, whose promise
    seem'd
Like stars to shepherds' eyes:—'twas but a meteor
    beam'd.   1530

171

Woe unto us, not her; for she sleeps well:
The fickle reek of popular breath, the tongue
Of hollow counsel, the false oracle,
Which from the birth of monarchy hath rung
Its knell in princely ears till the o'erstung
Nations have arm'd in madness, the strange fate
Which tumbles mightiest sovereigns, and hath
    flung
Against their blind omnipotence a weight
Within the opposing scale which crushes soon or
    late,—

172

These might have been her destiny; but
    no,   1540
Our hearts deny it: and so young, so fair,
Good without effort, great without a foe:

But now a bride and mother—and now *there!*
How many ties did that stern moment tear!
From thy Sire's to his humblest subject's breast
Is link'd the electric chain of that despair,
Whose shock was as an earthquake's, and
    opprest
The land which loved thee so that none could
    love thee best.

173

Lo, Nemi! navell'd in the woody hills
So far, that the uprooting wind which
    tears   1550
The oak from his foundation, and which spills
The ocean o'er its boundary, and bears
Its foam against the skies, reluctant spares
The oval mirror of thy glassy lake;—
And, calm as cherish'd hate, its surface wears
A deep cold settled aspect nought can shake,
All coil'd into itself and round, as sleeps the snake.

174

And near Albano's scarce divided waves
Shine from a sister valley; and afar
The Tiber winds, and the broad ocean
    laves   1560
The Latian coast where sprung the Epic war,
"Arms and the Man," whose re-ascending star
Rose o'er an empire: but beneath thy right
Tully reposed from Rome; and where yon bar
Of girdling mountains intercepts the sight
The Sabine farm was till'd, the weary bard's delight.

175

But I forget.—My Pilgrim's shrine is won,
And he and I must part—so let it be:
His task and mine alike are nearly done;
Yet once more let us look upon the sea;   1570
The midland ocean breaks on him and me,
And from the Alban Mount we now behold
Our friend of youth, that ocean, which when we
Beheld it last by Calpe's rock unfold
Those waves, we follow'd on till the dark Euxine
    roll'd

1574. **Calpe's rock:** Gibraltar. 1575. **Euxine:** Black Sea.

176

Upon the blue Symplegades. Long years—
Long, though not very many—since have done
Their work on both; some suffering and some
    tears
Have left us nearly where we had begun:
Yet not in vain our mortal race hath run;　1580
We have had our reward, and it is here,—
That we can yet feel gladden'd by the sun,
And reap from earth, sea, joy almost as dear
As if there were no man to trouble what is clear.

177

Oh that the Desert were my dwelling-place,
With one fair Spirit for my minister,
That I might all forget the human race,
And, hating no one, love but only her!
Ye Elements, in whose ennobling stir
I feel myself exalted, can ye not　1590
Accord me such a being? Do I err
In deeming such inhabit many a spot,
Though with them to converse can rarely be our
    lot?

178

There is a pleasure in the pathless woods,
There is a rapture on the lonely shore,
There is society where none intrudes,
By the deep Sea, and music in its roar:
I love not Man the less, but Nature more,
From these our interviews, in which I steal
From all I may be or have been before,　1600
To mingle with the Universe, and feel
What I can ne'er express, yet can not all conceal.

179

Roll on, thou deep and dark blue Ocean, roll!
Ten thousand fleets sweep over thee in vain;
Man marks the earth with ruin, his control
Stops with the shore; upon the watery plain
The wrecks are all thy deed, nor doth remain
A shadow of man's ravage, save his own,
When, for a moment, like a drop of rain,

He sinks into thy depths with bubbling
    groan,　1610
Without a grave, unknell'd, uncoffin'd, and
    unknown.

180

His steps are not upon thy paths, thy fields
Are not a spoil for him,—thou dost arise
And shake him from thee; the vile strength he
    wields
For earth's destruction thou dost all despise,
Spurning him from thy bosom to the skies,
And send'st him, shivering in thy playful spray
And howling, to his Gods, where haply lies
His petty hope in some near port or bay,
And dashest him again to earth:—there let him
    lay.　1620

181

The armaments which thunderstrike the walls
Of rock-built cities, bidding nations quake
And monarchs tremble in their capitals,
The oak leviathans, whose huge ribs make
Their clay creator the vain title take
Of lord of thee and arbiter of war,—
These are thy toys, and, as the snowy flake,
They melt into thy yeast of waves, which mar
Alike the Armada's pride or spoils of Trafalgar.

182

Thy shores are empires, changed in all save
    thee—　1630
Assyria, Greece, Rome, Carthage, what are they?
Thy waters wash'd them power while they were
    free,
And many a tyrant since; their shores obey
The stranger, slave, or savage; their decay
Has dried up realms to deserts:—not so thou,
Unchangeable save to thy wild waves' play;
Time writes no wrinkle on thine azure brow;
Such as creation's dawn beheld, thou rollest now.

1576. **Symplegades:** two islands between the Black Sea
and the Bosporus.

1629. **Armada's . . . Trafalgar:** A large part of the Spanish Armada was lost in storms in 1588. Storms also took
many of the French ships captured by Lord Nelson at
Trafalgar in 1805.

183

Thou glorious mirror, where the Almighty's form
Glasses itself in tempests; in all time,   1640
Calm or convulsed—in breeze, or gale, or storm,
Icing the pole, or in the torrid clime
Dark-heaving;—boundless, endless, and
    sublime—
The image of Eternity—the throne
Of the Invisible; even from out thy slime
The monsters of the deep are made; each zone
Obeys thee; thou goest forth, dread, fathomless,
    alone.

184

And I have loved thee, Ocean! and my joy
Of youthful sports was on thy breast to be
Borne, like thy bubbles, onward. From a
    boy   1650
I wanton'd with thy breakers—they to me
Were a delight; and if the freshening sea
Made them a terror—'twas a pleasing fear,
For I was as it were a child of thee,
And trusted to thy billows far and near,
And laid my hand upon thy mane—as I do here.

185

My task is done—my song hath ceased—my
    theme
Has died into an echo; it is fit
The spell should break of this protracted dream.
The torch shall be extinguish'd which hath
    lit   1660
My midnight lamp—and what is writ, is writ,—
Would it were worthier! but I am not now
That which I have been—and my visions flit
Less palpably before me—and the glow
Which in my spirit dwelt is fluttering, faint, and low.

186

Farewell! a word that must be, and hath been—
A sound which makes us linger;—yet—farewell!
Ye, who have traced the Pilgrim to the scene
Which is his last, if in your memories dwell
A thought which once was his, if on ye
    swell   1670

A single recollection, not in vain
He wore his sandal-shoon and scallop-shell;
Farewell! with *him* alone may rest the pain,
If such there were—with *you*, the moral of his
    strain!

1817   1818

MANFRED

A DRAMATIC POEM

"There are more things in heaven and earth,
*   Horatio,*
Than are dreamt of in your philosophy." *

DRAMATIS PERSONÆ

MANFRED	WITCH OF THE ALPS
CHAMOIS HUNTER	ARIMANES
ABBOT OF ST. MAURICE	NEMESIS
MANUEL	THE DESTINIES
HERMAN	SPIRITS, &C.

The SCENE of the Drama is amongst the Higher
Alps—partly in the Castle of Manfred, and partly
in the Mountains.

ACT I

SCENE I

MANFRED *alone.—Scene, a Gothic Gallery.*
Time, Midnight.

MANFRED.   The lamp must be replenished, but
    even then
It will not burn so long as I must watch:
My slumbers—if I slumber—are not sleep,
But a continuance of enduring thought,

1672. sandal-shoon and scallop-shell: symbols of the
pilgrim, the former suggesting his travels by land; the
latter, worn in his hat, suggesting his travels by sea.

---

* *Hamlet,* I, v, 166–67.

Which then I can resist not: in my heart
There is a vigil, and these eyes but close
To look within; and yet I live, and bear
The aspect and the form of breathing men.
But grief should be the instructor of the wise;
Sorrow is knowledge: they who know the most   10
Must mourn the deepest o'er the fatal truth,
The tree of knowledge is not that of life.
Philosophy and science, and the springs
Of wonder, and the wisdom of the world,
I have essayed, and in my mind there is
A power to make these subject to itself—
But they avail not: I have done men good,
And I have met with good even among men—
But this availed not: I have had my foes,
And none have baffled, many fallen before
    me—   20
But this availed not:—Good, or evil, life,
Powers, passions, all I see in other beings,
Have been to me as rain unto the sands,
Since that all-nameless hour. I have no dread,
And feel the curse to have no natural fear,
Nor fluttering throb, that beats with hopes or
    wishes,
Or lurking love of something on the earth.
Now to my task.—
              Mysterious agency!
Ye spirits of the unbounded universe!
Whom I have sought in darkness and in
    light—   30
Ye, who do compass earth about, and dwell
In subtler essence—ye, to whom the tops
Of mountains inaccessible are haunts,
And earth's and ocean's caves familiar things—
I call upon ye by the written charm
Which gives me power upon you—Rise! Appear!
           [A pause.]
They come not yet.—Now by the voice of him
Who is the first among you—by this sign,
Which makes you tremble—by the claims of him
Who is undying,—Rise! Appear——Appear!   40
           [A pause.]
If it be so—Spirits of earth and air,
Ye shall not thus elude me: by a power,
Deeper than all yet urged, a tyrant-spell,
Which had its birthplace in a star condemned,
The burning wreck of a demolished world,
A wandering hell in the eternal space
By the strong curse which is upon my soul,

The thought which is within me and around me,
I do compel ye to my will—Appear!

*[A star is seen at the darker end of the gallery:
it is stationary; and a voice is heard singing.]*

FIRST SPIRIT

Mortal! to thy bidding bowed,   50
From my mansion in the cloud,
Which the breath of twilight builds
And the summer's sunset gilds
With the azure and vermilion,
Which is mixed for my pavilion;
Though thy quest may be forbidden,
On a star-beam I have ridden:
To thine adjuration bowed,
Mortal—be thy wish avowed!

VOICE OF THE SECOND SPIRIT

Mont Blanc is the monarch of mountains;   60
    They crowned him long ago
On a throne of rocks, in a robe of clouds,
    With a diadem of snow.
Around his waist are forests braced,
    The avalanche in his hand;
But ere it fall, that thundering ball
    Must pause for my command.
The glacier's cold and restless mass
    Moves onward day by day;
But I am he who bids it pass,   70
    Or with its ice delay.
I am the spirit of the place,
    Could make the mountain bow
And quiver to his caverned base—
    And what with me would *thou?*

VOICE OF THE THIRD SPIRIT

In the blue depth of the waters,
    Where the wave hath no strife,
Where the wind is a stranger,
    And the sea-snake hath life,
Where the mermaid is decking   80
    Her green hair with shells,
Like the storm on the surface
    Came the sound of thy spells;
O'er my calm Hall of Coral
    The deep echo rolled—
To the Spirit of Ocean
    Thy wishes unfold!

FOURTH SPIRIT

Where the slumbering earthquake
  Lies pillowed on fire,
And the lakes of bitumen   90
  Rise boilingly higher;
Where the roots of the Andes
  Strike deep in the earth,
As their summits to heaven
  Shoot soaringly forth;
I have quitted my birthplace
  Thy bidding to bide—
Thy spell hath subdued me,
  Thy will be my guide!

FIFTH SPIRIT

I am the rider of the wind   100
  The stirrer of the storm;
The hurricane I left behind
  Is yet with lightning warm;
To speed to thee, o'er shore and sea
  I swept upon the blast:
The fleet I met sailed well, and yet
  'Twill sink ere night be past.

SIXTH SPIRIT

My dwelling is the shadow of the night,
Why doth thy magic torture me with light?

SEVENTH SPIRIT

The star which rules thy destiny   110
Was ruled, ere earth began, by me:
It was a world as fresh and fair
As e'er revolved round sun in air;
Its course was free and regular,
Space bosomed not a lovelier star.
The hour arrived—and it became
A wandering mass of shapeless flame,
A pathless comet, and a curse,
The menace of the universe;
Still rolling on with innate force,   120
Without a sphere, without a course,
A bright deformity on high,
The monster of the upper sky!
And thou! beneath its influence born—
Thou worm! whom I obey and scorn—
Forced by a power (which is not thine,
And lent thee but to make thee mine)
For this brief moment to descend,

Where these weak spirits round thee bend
And parley with a thing like thee——   130
What wouldst thou, child of clay! with me?

THE SEVEN SPIRITS

Earth, ocean, air, night, mountains, winds, thy star,
  Are at thy beck and bidding, child of clay!
Before thee at thy quest their spirits are—
  What wouldst thou with us, son of mortals—say?
MAN.   Forgetfulness—
FIRST SPIRIT.   Of what—of whom—and why?
MAN.   Of that which is within me; read it there—
Ye know it, and I cannot utter it.
  SPIRIT.   We can but give thee that which we
    possess: 140
Ask of us subjects, sovereignty, the power
O'er earth—the whole, or portion—or a sign
Which shall control the elements, whereof
We are dominators,—each and all,
These shall be thine.
  MAN.   Oblivion, self-oblivion.
Can ye not wring from out the hidden realms
Ye offer so profusely what I ask?
  SPIRIT.   It is not in our essence, in our skill;
But—thou may'st die.
  MAN.   Will death bestow it on me?
  SPIRIT.   We are immortal, and do not
    forget;   150
We are eternal; and to us the past
Is, as the future, present. Art thou answered?
  MAN.   Ye mock me—but the power which
    brought ye here
Hath made you mine. Slaves, scoff not at my will!
The mind, the spirit, the Promethean spark,
The lightning of my being, is as bright,
Pervading, and far darting as your own,
And shall not yield to yours, though cooped in clay!
Answer, or I will teach you what I am.
  SPIRIT.   We answer as we answered; our
    reply   160
Is even in thine own words.
  MAN.   Why say ye so?
  SPIRIT.   If, as thou say'st, thine essence be as
    ours,
We have replied in telling thee, the thing
Mortals call death hath naught to do with us.
  MAN.   I then have called ye from your realms in
    vain;
Ye cannot, or ye will not, aid me.

SPIRIT.   Say,
What we possess we offer; it is thine:
Bethink ere thou dismiss us; ask again—
Kingdom, and sway, and strength, and length of
    days—
  MAN.   Accursed! what have I to do with
    days?   170
They are too long already.—Hence—begone!
  SPIRIT.   Yet pause: being here, our will would
    do thee service;
Bethink thee, is there then no other gift
Which we can make not worthless in thine eyes?
  MAN.   No, none: yet stay—one moment, ere we
    part,
I would behold ye face to face. I hear
Your voices, sweet and melancholy sounds,
As music on the waters; and I see
The steady aspect of a clear large star;
But nothing more. Approach me as ye are,   180
Or one, or all, in your accustomed forms.
  SPIRIT.   We have no forms, beyond the elements
Of which we are the mind and principle:
But choose a form—in that we will appear.
  MAN.   I have no choice; there is no form on
    earth
Hideous or beautiful to me. Let him,
Who is most powerful of ye, take such aspect
As unto him may seem most fitting—Come!
  SEVENTH SPIRIT (*appearing in the shape of a*
    beautiful female figure). Behold!
  MAN.   Oh God! if it be thus, and *thou*
Art not a madness and a mockery,   190
I yet might be most happy, I will clasp thee,
And we again will be—
        [*The figure vanishes.*]
           My heart is crushed!
    [MANFRED *falls senseless.*]

(*A voice is heard in the Incantation which follows.*)

When the moon is on the wave,
  And the glow-worm in the grass,
And the meteor on the grave,
  And the wisp on the morass;
When the falling stars are shooting,
And the answered owls are hooting,
And the silent leaves are still
In the shadow of the hill,   200
Shall my soul be upon thine,
With a power and with a sign.

Though thy slumber may be deep,
Yet thy spirit shall not sleep;
There are shades that will not vanish,
There are thoughts thou canst not banish;
By a power to thee unknown,
Thou canst never be alone;
Thou art wrapt as with a shroud,
Thou art gathered in a cloud;   210
And forever shalt thou dwell
In the spirit of this spell.

Though thou seest me not pass by,
Thou shalt feel me with thine eye
As a thing that, though unseen,
Must be near thee, and hath been;
And when in that secret dread
Thou hast turned around thy head,
Thou shalt marvel I am not
As thy shadow on the spot,   220
And the power which thou dost feel
Shall be what thou must conceal.

And a magic voice and verse
Hath baptized thee with a curse;
And a spirit of the air
Hath begirt thee with a snare;
In the wind there is a voice
Shall forbid thee to rejoice;
And to thee shall night deny
All the quiet of her sky;   230
And the day shall have a sun,
Which shall make thee wish it done.

From thy false tears I did distil
An essence which hath strength to kill;
From thy own heart I then did wring
The black blood in its blackest spring;
From thy own smile I snatched the snake,
For there it coiled as in a brake;
From thy own lip I drew the charm
Which gave all these their chiefest harm;   240
In proving every poison known,
I found the strongest was thine own.

By thy cold breast and serpent smile,
By thy unfathomed gulfs of guile,
By that most seeming virtuous eye,
By thy shut soul's hypocrisy;
By the perfection of thine art
Which passed for human thine own heart;

ACT I. Sc. i. 238. brake: thicket.

By thy delight in others' pain,
And by thy brotherhood of Cain,   250
I call upon thee! and compel
Thyself to be thy proper hell!

And on thy head I pour the vial
Which doth devote thee to this trial;
Nor to slumber, nor to die,
Shall be in thy destiny;
Though thy death shall still seem near
To thy wish, but as a fear;
Lo! the spell now works around thee,
And the clankless chain hath bound thee;   260
O'er thy heart and brain together
Hath the word been passed—now wither!

SCENE II

The Mountain of the Jungfrau.—Time, Morning.—

MANFRED *alone upon the Cliffs.*

MAN. The spirits I have raised abandon me,
The spells which I have studied baffle me,
The remedy I recked of tortured me;
I lean no more on superhuman aid;
It hath no power upon the past, and for
The future, till the past be gulfed in darkness,
It is not of my search.—My mother earth!
And thou fresh breaking day, and you, ye
         mountains,
Why are ye beautiful? I cannot love ye.
And thou, the bright eye of the universe,   10
That openest over all, and unto all
Art a delight—thou shin'st not on my heart.
And you, ye crags, upon whose extreme edge
I stand, and on the torrent's brink beneath
Behold the tall pines dwindled as to shrubs
In dizziness of distance; when a leap,
A stir, a motion, even a breath, would bring
My breast upon its rocky bosom's bed
To rest forever—wherefore do I pause?
I feel the impulse—yet I do not plunge;   20
I see the peril—yet do not recede;
And my brain reels—and yet my foot is firm:
There is a power upon me which withholds,
And makes it my fatality to live;
If it be life to wear within myself
This barrenness of spirit, and to be
My own soul's sepulchre, for I have ceased

To justify my deeds unto myself—
The last infirmity of evil. Ay,
Thou winged and cloud-cleaving minister,   30
         [*An eagle passes.*]
Whose happy flight is highest into heaven,
Well may'st thou swoop so near to me—I should be
Thy prey, and gorge thine eaglets; thou art gone
Where the eye cannot follow thee; but thine
Yet pierces downward, onward, or above,
With a pervading vision.—Beautiful!
How beautiful is all this visible world!
How glorious in its action and itself!
But we, who name ourselves its sovereigns, we,
Half dust, half deity, alike unfit   40
To sink or soar, with our mixed essence make
A conflict of its elements, and breathe
The breath of degradation and of pride,
Contending with low wants and lofty will,
Till our mortality predominates,
And men are—what they name not to themselves,
And trust not to each other. Hark! the note,
     [*The Shepherd's pipe in the distance is heard.*]
The natural music of the mountain reed—
For here the patriarchal days are not
A pastoral fable—pipes in the liberal air,   50
Mixed with the sweet bells of the sauntering herd;
My soul would drink these echoes. Oh, that I were
The viewless spirit of a lovely sound,
A living voice, a breathing harmony,
A bodiless enjoyment—born and dying
With the blest tone which made me!

     Enter from below a CHAMOIS° HUNTER.
     CHAMOIS HUNTER.   Even so
This way the chamois leapt: her nimble feet
Have baffled me; my gains today will scarce
Repay my break-neck travail.—What is here?
Who seems not of my trade, and yet hath
         reached   60
A height which none even of our mountaineers,
Save our best hunters, may attain: his garb
Is goodly, his mien manly, and his air
Proud as a free-born peasant's, at this distance:
I will approach him nearer.
     MAN. (*not perceiving the other*). To be thus—
Gray-haired with anguish, like these blasted pines,
Wrecks of a single winter, barkless, branchless,
A blighted trunk upon a cursed root,

° **chamois:** a wild mountain sheep.

Which but supplies a feeling to decay—
And to be thus, eternally but thus,   70
Having been otherwise! Now furrowed o'er
With wrinkles, ploughed by moments,—not by
     years,—
And hours, all tortured into ages—hours
Which I outlive!—Ye toppling crags of ice!
Ye avalanches, whom a breath draws down
In mountainous o'erwhelming, come and crush me!
I hear ye momently above, beneath,
Crash with a frequent conflict; but ye pass,
And only fall on things that still would live;
On the young flourishing forest, or the hut   80
And hamlet of the harmless villager.

    c. hun. The mists begin to rise from up the
     valley;
I'll warn him to descend, or he may chance
To lose at once his way and life together.

    man. The mists boil up around the glaciers;
     clouds
Rise curling fast beneath me, white and sulphury,
Like foam from the roused ocean of deep hell,
Whose every wave breaks on a living shore,
Heaped with the damned like pebbles.—I am
     giddy.

    c. hun. I must approach him cautiously; if near,
A sudden step will startle him, and he   91
Seems tottering already.

    man.   Mountains have fallen,
Leaving a gap in the clouds, and with the shock
Rocking their Alpine brethren; filling up
The ripe green valleys with destruction's splinters;
Damming the rivers with a sudden dash,
Which crushed the waters into mist and made
Their fountains find another channel—thus,
Thus, in its old age, did Mount Rosenberg—
Why stood I not beneath it?   100

    c. hun.   Friend! have a care,
Your next step may be fatal!—for the love
Of him who made you, stand not on that brink!

    man. (*not hearing him*). Such would have been
     for me a fitting tomb;
My bones had then been quiet in their depth;
They had not then been strewn upon the rocks
For the wind's pastime—as thus—thus they shall
     be—
In this one plunge.—Farewell, ye opening heavens!

Sc. ii. 99. **Mount Rosenberg**: Mount Rossberg in Switzerland, site of a great landslide in 1806.

Look not upon me thus reproachfully—
Ye were not meant for me—Earth! take these
     atoms!

[*As* manfred *is in act to spring from the cliff, the*
    chamois hunter *seizes and retains him with a*
     sudden grasp.]

    c. hun. Hold, madman!—though aweary of thy
     life,   110
Stain not our pure vales with thy guilty blood:
Away with me—I will not quit my hold.

    man. I am most sick at heart—nay, grasp me
     not—
I am all feebleness—the mountains whirl
Spinning around me—I grow blind—

                        What art thou?

    c. hun. I'll answer that anon. Away with me!
The clouds grow thicker—there—now lean on
     me—
Place your foot here—here, take this staff, and
     cling
A moment to that shrub—now give me your hand,
And hold fast by my girdle—softly—well—   120
The Chalet will be gained within an hour:
Come on, we'll quickly find a surer footing,
And something like a pathway, which the torrent
Hath washed since winter.—Come, 'tis bravely
     done—
You should have been a hunter.—Follow me.

[*As they descend the rocks with difficulty, the*
    scene closes.]

ACT II

SCENE I

A Cottage amongst the Bernese Alps.

manfred *and the* chamois hunter.

    c. hun. No, no—yet pause—thou must not yet
     go forth:
Thy mind and body are alike unfit
To trust each other, for some hours, at least;
When thou art better, I will be thy guide—
But whither?

    man.   It imports not: I do know
My route full well, and need no further guidance.

C. HUN. Thy garb and gait bespeak thee of high
    lineage—
One of the many chiefs, whose castled crags
Look o'er the lower valleys—which of these
May call thee lord? I only know their portals;   10
My way of life leads me but rarely down
To bask by the huge hearths of those old halls,
Carousing with the vassals; but the paths,
Which step from out our mountains to their doors,
I know from childhood—which of these is thine?
    MAN. No matter.
    C. HUN.   Well, sir, pardon me the question,
And be of better cheer. Come, taste my wine;
'Tis of an ancient vintage; many a day
'T has thawed my veins among our glaciers, now
Let it do thus for thine. Come, pledge me
    fairly.   20
    MAN. Away, away! there's blood upon the brim!
Will it then never—never sink in the earth?
    C. HUN. What dost thou mean? thy senses
    wander from thee.
    MAN. I say 'tis blood—my blood! the pure warm
    stream
Which ran in the veins of my fathers, and in ours
When we were in our youth, and had one heart,
And loved each other as we should not love,
And this was shed: but still it rises up,
Coloring the clouds, that shut me out from heaven,
Where thou art not—and I shall never be.   30
    C. HUN. Man of strange words, and some half-
    maddening sin,
Which makes thee people vacancy, whate'er
Thy dread and sufferance be, there's comfort yet—
The aid of holy men, and heavenly patience—
    MAN. Patience and patience! Hence—that word
    was made
For brutes of burthen, not for birds of prey;
Preach it to mortals of a dust like thine,—
I am not of thine order.
    C. HUN.   Thanks to heaven!
I would not be of thine for the free fame
Of William Tell; but whatsoe'er thine ill,   40
It must be borne, and these wild starts are useless.
    MAN. Do I not bear it?—Look on me—I live.
    C. HUN. This is convulsion, and no healthful life.
    MAN. I tell thee, man! I have lived many years,
Many long years, but they are nothing now
To those which I must number: ages—ages—
Space and eternity—and consciousness,
With the fierce thirst of death—and still unslaked!

C. HUN. Why, on thy brow the seal of middle
    age
Hath scarce been set; I am thine elder far.   50
    MAN. Think'st thou existence doth depend on
    time?
It doth; but actions are our epochs: mine
Have made my days and nights imperishable,
Endless, and all alike, as sands on the shore,
Innumerable atoms; and one desert,
Barren and cold, on which the wild waves break,
But nothing rests, save carcasses and wrecks,
Rocks, and the salt-surf weeds of bitterness.
    C. HUN. Alas! he's mad—but yet I must not leave
    him.
    MAN. I would I were—for then the things I
    see   60
Would be but a distempered dream.
    C. HUN.   What is it
That thou dost see, or think thou look'st upon?
    MAN. Myself, and thee—a peasant of the Alps—
Thy humble virtues, hospitable home,
And spirit patient, pious, proud, and free;
Thy self-respect, grafted on innocent thoughts;
Thy days of health, and nights of sleep; thy toils,
By danger dignified, yet guiltless; hopes
Of cheerful old age and a quiet grave,
With cross and garland over its green turf,   70
And thy grandchildren's love for epitaph;
This do I see—and then I look within—
It matters not—my soul was scorched already!
    C. HUN. And wouldst thou then exchange thy lot
    for mine?
    MAN. No, friend! I would not wrong thee, nor
    exchange
My lot with living being: I can bear—
However wretchedly, 'tis still to bear—
In life what others could not brook to dream,
But perish in their slumber.
    C. HUN.   And with this—
This cautious feeling for another's pain,   80
Canst thou be black with evil?—say not so.
Can one of gentle thoughts have wreaked revenge
Upon his enemies?
    MAN.   Oh! no, no, no!
My injuries came down on those who loved me—
On those whom I best loved: I never quelled
An enemy, save in my just defence—
But my embrace was fatal.

ACT II. Sc. i. 85. quelled: killed.

C. HUN.   Heaven give thee rest!
And penitence restore thee to thyself;
My prayers shall be for thee.
    MAN.   I need them not—
But can endure thy pity. I depart—   90
'Tis time—farewell!—Here's gold, and thanks for
    thee;
No words—it is thy due. Follow me not—
I know my path—the mountain peril's past:
And once again I charge thee, follow not!
                    [*Exit* MANFRED.]

            SCENE II

A lower Valley in the Alps.—A Cataract.

            Enter MANFRED.
    MAN.   It is not noon—the sunbow's rays still
        arch
The torrent with the many hues of heaven,
And roll the sheeted silver's waving column
O'er the crag's headlong perpendicular,
And fling its lines of foaming light along
And to and fro, like the pale courser's tail,
The giant steed, to be bestrode by death,
As told in the Apocalypse. No eyes
But mine now drink this sight of loveliness;
I should be sole in this sweet solitude,   10
And with the Spirit of the place divide
The homage of these waters.—I will call her.
    [MANFRED *takes some of the water into the
    palm of his hand, and flings it into the air
    muttering the adjuration. After a pause, the*
    WITCH OF THE ALPS *rises beneath the arch of
    the sunbow of the torrent.*]
Beautiful spirit! with thy hair of light,
And dazzling eyes of glory, in whose form
The charms of earth's least mortal daughters grow
To an unearthly stature, in an essence
Of purer elements; while the hue of youth,—
Carnationed like a sleeping infant's cheek,
Rocked by the beating of her mother's heart,
Or the rose tints, which summer's twilight
    leaves   20
Upon the lofty glacier's virgin snow,
The blush of earth embracing with her heaven,—
Tinge thy celestial aspect, and make tame
The beauties of the sunbow which bends o'er thee.
Beautiful Spirit! in thy calm clear brow,

Wherein is glassed serenity of soul,
Which of itself shows immortality,
I read that thou wilt pardon to a son
Of Earth, whom the abstruser powers permit
At times to commune with them—if that he   30
Avail him of his spells—to call thee thus,
And gaze on thee a moment.
    WITCH OF THE ALPS.   Son of Earth!
I know thee, and the powers which give thee
    power;
I know thee for a man of many thoughts,
And deeds of good and ill, extreme in both,
Fatal and fated in thy sufferings.
I have expected this—what wouldst thou with me?
    MAN.   To look upon thy beauty—nothing
        further.
The face of the earth hath maddened me, and I
Take refuge in her mysteries, and pierce   40
To the abodes of those who govern her—
But they can nothing aid me. I have sought
From them what they could not bestow, and now
I search no further.
    WITCH.   What could be the quest
Which is not in the power of the most powerful,
The rulers of the invisible?
    MAN.   A boon;
But why should I repeat it? 'twere in vain.
    WITCH.   I know not that; let thy lips utter it.
    MAN.   Well, though it torture me, 'tis but the
        same;
My pangs shall find a voice. From my youth
    upwards   50
My spirit walked not with the souls of men,
Nor looked upon the earth with human eyes;
The thirst of their ambition was not mine,
The aim of their existence was not mine;
My joys, my griefs, my passions, and my powers,
Made me a stranger; though I wore the form
I had no sympathy with breathing flesh,
Nor midst the creatures of clay that girded me
Was there but one who—but of her anon.
I said with men, and with the thoughts of
    men,   60
I held but slight communion; but instead,
My joy was in the wilderness,—to breathe
The difficult air of the iced mountain's top,
Where the birds dare not build, nor insect's wing
Flit o'er the herbless granite; or to plunge
Into the torrent, and to roll along
On the swift whirl of the new breaking wave

Of river-stream, or ocean, in their flow.
In these my early strength exulted; or
To follow through the night the moving moon,   70
The stars and their development; or catch
The dazzling lightnings till my eyes grew dim;
Or to look, list'ning, on the scattered leaves,
While autumn winds were at their evening song.
These were my pastimes, and to be alone;
For if the beings, of whom I was one,—
Hating to be so,—crossed me in my path,
I felt myself degraded back to them,
And was all clay again. And then I dived,
In my lone wanderings, to the caves of death,   80
Searching its cause in its effect; and drew
From withered bones, and skulls, and heaped up
        dust,
Conclusions most forbidden. Then I passed
The nights of years in sciences untaught,
Save in the old time; and with time and toil,
And terrible ordeal, and such penance
As in itself hath power upon the air,
And spirits that do compass air and earth,
Space, and the people infinite, I made
Mine eyes familiar with Eternity,   90
Such as, before me, did the Magi, and
He who from their fountain dwellings raised
Eros and Anteros, at Gadara,
As I do thee;—and with my knowledge grew
The thirst of knowledge, and the power and joy
Of this most bright intelligence, until—
    WITCH.   Proceed.
    MAN.   Oh! I but thus prolonged my words,
Boasting these idle attributes, because
As I approach the core of my heart's grief—   100
But to my task. I have not named to thee
Father, or mother, mistress, friend, or being,
With whom I wore the chain of human ties;
If I had such, they seemed not such to me;
Yet there was one—
    WITCH.   Spare not thyself—proceed.
    MAN.   She was like me in lineaments; her eyes,
Her hair, her features, all, to the very tone
Even of her voice, they said were like to mine;
But softened all, and tempered into beauty:

Sc. ii. 92–93. He . . . Gadara: a reference to Iamblichus,
a fourth-century philosopher, who supposedly called up
Eros, the god of love, and Anteros, the god who
avenged disappointed love, from the springs in Gadara,
Syria, which bore their names.

She had the same lone thoughts and
        wanderings,   110
The quest of hidden knowledge, and a mind
To comprehend the universe; nor these
Alone, but with them gentler powers than mine,
Pity, and smiles, and tears—which I had not;
And tenderness—but that I had for her;
Humility—and that I never had.
Her faults were mine—her virtues were her own—
I loved her, and destroyed her!
    WITCH.   With thy hand?
    MAN.   Not with my hand, but heart—which
        broke her heart;
It gazed on mine, and withered. I have shed   120
Blood, but not hers—and yet her blood was shed;
I saw—and could not stanch it.
    WITCH.   And for this—
A being of the race thou dost despise,
The order, which thine own would rise above,
Mingling with us and ours,—thou dost forego
The gifts of our great knowledge, and shrink'st back
In recreant mortality—Away!
    MAN.   Daughter of air! I tell thee, since that
        hour—
But words are breath—look on me in my sleep,
Or watch my watchings—Come and sit by
        me!   130
My solitude is solitude no more,
But peopled with the furies;—I have gnashed
My teeth in darkness till returning morn,
Then cursed myself till sunset;—I have prayed
For madness as a blessing—'tis denied me.
I have affronted death—but in the war
Of elements the waters shrunk from me,
And fatal things passed harmless; the cold hand
Of an all-pitiless demon held me back,
Back by a single hair, which would not break.   140
In fantasy, imagination, all
The affluence of my soul—which one day was
A Crœsus in creation—I plunged deep,
But, like an ebbing wave, it dashed me back
Into the gulf of my unfathomed thought.
I plunged amidst mankind—Forgetfulness
I sought in all, save where 'tis to be found,
And that I have to learn; my sciences,
My long-pursued and superhuman art,
Is mortal here: I dwell in my despair—   150
And live—and live forever.
    WITCH.   It may be
That I can aid thee.

MAN.   To do this thy power
Must wake the dead, or lay me low with them.
Do so—in any shape—in any hour—
With any torture—so it be the last.
   WITCH.   That is not in my province; but if thou
Wilt swear obedience to my will, and do
My bidding, it may help thee to thy wishes.
   MAN.   I will not swear—Obey! and whom? the
     spirits
Whose presence I command, and be the slave   160
Of those who served me—Never!
   WITCH.   Is this all?
Hast thou no gentler answer?—Yet bethink thee,
And pause ere thou rejectest.
   MAN.   I have said it.
   WITCH.   Enough! I may retire then—say!
   MAN.   Retire!

[*The* WITCH *disappears.*]

MAN. (*alone*).   We are the fools of time and
    terror. Days
Steal on us, and steal from us; yet we live,
Loathing our life, and dreading still to die.
In all the days of this detested yoke—
This vital weight upon the struggling heart,
Which sinks with sorrow, or beats quick with pain,
Or joy that ends in agony or faintness—   171
In all the days of past and future, for
In life there is no present, we can number
How few—how less than few—wherein the soul
Forbears to pant for death, and yet draws back
As from a stream in winter, though the chill
Be but a moment's. I have one resource
Still in my science—I can call the dead,
And ask them what it is we dread to be:
The sternest answer can but be the grave,   180
And this is nothing. If they answer not—
The buried prophet answered to the Hag
Of Endor; and the Spartan Monarch drew
From the Byzantine maid's unsleeping spirit
An answer and his destiny—he slew
That which he loved, unknowing what he slew,

182–83. buried . . . Endor: In I Samuel 28, Samuel's
spirit, raised by the witch of Endor, foretells that King
Saul will be killed in battle. 183–91. Spartan . . . vengeance: Pausanius mistakenly killed his mistress. When
he remorsefully asked the priests to summon up her
spirit so that she might forgive him, the spirit foretold
that he would soon be free. He died shortly thereafter.

And died unpardoned—though he called in aid
The Phyxian Jove, and in Phigalia roused
The Arcadian Evocators to compel
The indignant shadow to depose her wrath,   190
Or fix her term of vengeance—she replied
In words of dubious import, but fulfilled.
If I had never lived, that which I love
Had still been living; had I never loved,
That which I love would still be beautiful,
Happy and giving happiness. What is she?
What is she now?—a sufferer for my sins—
A thing I dare not think upon—or nothing.
Within few hours I shall not call in vain—
Yet in this hour I dread the thing I dare: 200
Until this hour I never shrunk to gaze
On spirit, good or evil—now I tremble,
And feel a strange cold thaw upon my heart.
But I can act even what I most abhor,
And champion human fears.—The night
    approaches.

[*Exit.*]

SCENE III

The Summit of the Jungfrau Mountain.

Enter FIRST DESTINY.

FIRST DESTINY.   The moon is rising broad, and
    round, and bright;
And here on snows, where never human foot
Of common mortal trod, we nightly tread,
And leave no traces: o'er the savage sea,
The glassy ocean of the mountain ice,
We skim its rugged breakers, which put on
The aspect of a tumbling tempest's foam,
Frozen in a moment—a dead whirlpool's image:
And this most steep fantastic pinnacle,
The fretwork of some earthquake—where the
    clouds   10
Pause to repose themselves in passing by—
Is sacred to our revels, or our vigils;
Here do I wait my sisters, on our way
To the Hall of Arimanes, for tonight
Is our great festival—'tis strange they come not.

Sc. iii. 14. Hall of Arimanes: Ahriman is the name of
the principle of evil in the ancient Persian religion of
Zoroaster. He controls the physical universe and inflicts
upon mankind the evils of tyranny and natural catastrophe.

A VOICE *without, singing*

The captive usurper,
    Hurled down from the throne,
Lay buried in torpor,
    Forgotten and lone;
I broke through his slumbers,   20
    I shivered his chain,
I leagued him with numbers—
    He's tyrant again!
With the blood of a million he'll answer my care,
With a nation's destruction—his flight and despair.

SECOND VOICE, *without*

The ship sailed on, the ship sailed fast,
But I left not a sail, and I left not a mast;
There is not a plank of the hull or the deck,
And there is not a wretch to lament o'er his wreck;
Save one, whom I held, as he swam, by the
        hair,   30
And he was a subject, well worthy my care;
A traitor on land, and a pirate at sea—
But I saved him to wreak further havoc for me!

FIRST DESTINY, *answering*

The city lies sleeping;
    The morn, to deplore it,
May dawn on it weeping:
    Sullenly, slowly,
The black plague flew o'er it—
    Thousands lie lowly;
Tens of thousands shall perish;   40
    The living shall fly from
The sick they should cherish;
    But nothing can vanquish
The touch that they die from.
    Sorrow and anguish,
And evil and dread,
    Envelop a nation;
The blest are the dead,
    Who see not the sight
Of their own desolation;   50
    This work of a night—
This wreck of a realm—this deed of my doing—
For ages I've done, and shall still be renewing!

Enter the SECOND *and* THIRD DESTINIES.

THE THREE

Our hands contain the hearts of men,
    Our footsteps are their graves;

We only give to take again
    The spirits of our slaves!

FIRST DESTINY   Welcome!—Where's Nemesis?
SECOND DESTINY.   At some great work;
But what I know not, for my hands were full.
    THIRD DESTINY.   Behold she cometh.   60

Enter NEMESIS.

FIRST DES.   Say, where hast thou been?
My sisters and thyself are slow tonight.
    NEMESIS.   I was detained repairing shattered
        thrones,
Marrying fools, restoring dynasties,
Avenging men upon their enemies,
And making them repent their own revenge;
Goading the wise to madness; from the dull
Shaping our oracles to rule the world
Afresh, for they were waxing out of date,
And mortals dared to ponder for themselves,   70
To weigh kings in the balance, and to speak
Of freedom, the forbidden fruit.—Away!
We have outstayed the hour—mount we our clouds.

[*Exeunt.*]

SCENE IV

The Hall of ARIMANES. ARIMANES *on his Throne, a
Globe of Fire, surrounded by the* SPIRITS.

Hymn of the SPIRITS

Hail to our Master!—Prince of earth and air!
    Who walks the clouds and waters—in his hand
The sceptre of the elements, which tear
    Themselves to chaos at his high command!
He breatheth—and a tempest shakes the sea;
    He speaketh—and the clouds reply in thunder;
He gazeth—from his glance the sunbeams flee;
    He moveth—earthquakes rend the world asunder.
Beneath his footsteps the volcanoes rise;
    His shadow is the pestilence; his path   10
The comets herald through the crackling skies;
    And planets turn to ashes at his wrath.
To him war offers daily sacrifice;
    To him death pays his tribute; life is his,
With all its infinite of agonies—
    And his the spirit of whatever is!

Enter the DESTINIES *and* NEMESIS.

FIRST DES.   Glory to Arimanes! on the earth
His power increaseth—both my sisters did
His bidding, nor did I neglect my duty!
　　SECOND DES.   Glory to Arimanes! we who bow 20
The necks of men, bow down before his throne!
　　THIRD DES.   Glory to Arimanes! we await His
　　nod!
　　NEM.   Sovereign of sovereigns! we are thine,
And all that liveth, more or less, is ours,
And most things wholly so; still to increase
Our power, increasing thine, demands our care,
And we are vigilant. Thy late commands
Have been fulfilled to the utmost.

Enter MANFRED.

　　A SPIRIT   What is here?
A mortal!—Thou most rash and fatal wretch,
Bow down and worship!   30
　　SECOND SPIRIT   I do know the man—
A Magian of great power, and fearful skill!
　　THIRD SPIRIT.   Bow down and worship, slave!—
　　What, know'st thou not
Thine and our sovereign?—Tremble, and obey!
　　ALL THE SPIRITS.   Prostrate thyself, and thy con-
　　demned clay,
Child of the earth! or dread the worst.
　　MAN.   I know it;
And yet ye see I kneel not.
　　FOURTH SPIRIT.   'Twill be taught thee.
　　MAN.   'Tis taught already;—many a night on the
　　earth,
On the bare ground, have I bowed down my face,
And strewed my head with ashes; I have known 40
The fullness of humiliation, for
I sunk before my vain despair, and knelt
To my own desolation.
　　FIFTH SPIRIT.   Dost thou dare
Refuse to Arimanes on his throne
What the whole earth accords, beholding not
The terror of his glory?—Crouch, I say.
　　MAN.   Bid *him* bow down to that which is above
　　him,
The overruling Infinite—the Maker
Who made him not for worship—let him kneel,
And we will kneel together.
　　THE SPIRITS.   Crush the worm! 50
Tear him to pieces!—

　　FIRST DES.   Hence! avaunt!—he's mine.
Prince of the powers invisible! This man
Is of no common order, as his port
And presence here denote; his sufferings
Have been of an immortal nature, like
Our own; his knowledge, and his powers and will,
As far as is compatible with clay,
Which clogs the ethereal essence, have been such
As clay hath seldom borne; his aspirations
Have been beyond the dwellers of the earth,   60
And they have only taught him what we know—
That knowledge is not happiness, and science
But an exchange of ignorance for that
Which is another kind of ignorance.
This is not all—the passions, attributes
Of earth and heaven, from which no power, nor
　　being,
Nor breath from the worm upwards is exempt,
Have pierced his heart, and in their consequence
Made him a thing which I, who pity not,
Yet pardon those who pity. He is mine,   70
And thine, it may be; be it so, or not,
No other spirit in this region hath
A soul like his—or power upon his soul.
　　NEM.   What doth he here then?
　　FIRST DES.   Let him answer that.
　　MAN.   Ye know what I have known; and with-
　　out power
I could not be amongst ye: but there are
Powers deeper still beyond—I come in quest
Of such, to answer unto what I seek.
　　NEM.   What wouldst thou?
　　MAN.   Thou canst not reply to me.
Call up the dead—my question is for them.   80
　　NEM.   Great Arimanes, doth thy will avouch
The wishes of this mortal?
　　ARIMANES.   Yea.
　　NEM.   Whom wouldst thou
Uncharnel?
　　MAN.   One without a tomb—call up
Astarte.

NEMESIS

Shadow! or spirit!
　　Whatever thou art,
Which still doth inherit
　　The whole or a part
Of the form of thy birth,
　　Of the mould of thy clay,   90
Which returned to the earth,—
　　Reappear to the day!

Bear what thou borest,
       The heart and the form,
And the aspect thou worest
       Redeem from the worm
Appear!—Appear!—Appear!
Who sent thee there requires thee here!

[*The* PHANTOM OF ASTARTE *rises and stands
       in the midst.*]

MAN.   Can this be death? there's bloom upon her
       cheek;
But now I see it is no living hue,   100
But a strange hectic—like the unnatural red
Which autumn plants upon the perished leaf.
It is the same! Oh, God! that I should dread
To look upon the same—Astarte!—No,
I cannot speak to her—but bid her speak—
Forgive me or condemn me.

NEMESIS

By the power which hath broken
       The grave which enthralled thee,
Speak to him who hath spoken,
       Or those who have called thee!
MAN.   She is silent,   110
And in that silence I am more than answered.
   NEM.   My power extends no further. Prince of
       Air!
It rests with thee alone—command her voice.
   ARI.   Spirit—obey this sceptre!
   NEM.   Silent still!
She is not of our order, but belongs
To the other powers. Mortal! thy quest is vain,
And we are baffled also.
   MAN.   Hear me, hear me—
Astarte! my beloved! speak to me:
I have so much endured—so much endure—
Look on me! the grave hath not changed thee
       more   120
Than I am changed for thee. Thou lovedst me
Too much, as I loved thee: we were not made
To torture thus each other, though it were
The deadliest sin to love as we have loved.
Say that thou loath'st me not—that I do bear
This punishment for both—that thou wilt be
One of the blessed—and that I shall die;
For hitherto all hateful things conspire
To bind me in existence—in a life
Which makes me shrink from immortality—   130

A future like the past. I cannot rest.
I know not what I ask, nor what I seek:
I feel but what thou art, and what I am;
And I would hear yet once before I perish
The voice which was my music—Speak to me!
For I have called on thee in the still night,
Startled the slumbering birds from the hushed
       boughs,
And woke the mountain wolves, and made the
       caves
Acquainted with thy vainly echoed name,
Which answered me—many things answered
       me—   140
Spirits and men—but thou wert silent all.
Yet speak to me! I have outwatched the stars,
And gazed o'er heaven in vain in search of thee.
Speak to me! I have wandered o'er the earth,
And never found thy likeness—Speak to me!
Look on the fiends around—they feel for me:
I fear them not, and feel for thee alone—
Speak to me! though it be in wrath;—but say—
I reck not what—but let me hear thee once—
This once—once more!
       PHANTOM OF ASTARTE.   Manfred!
   MAN.   Say on, say on—   150
I live but in the sound—it is thy voice!
   PHAN.   Manfred! Tomorrow ends thine earthly
       ills.
Farewell!
   MAN.   Yet one word more—am I forgiven?
   PHAN.   Farewell!
   MAN.   Say, shall we meet again?
   PHAN.   Farewell!
   MAN.   One word for mercy!
Say, thou lovest me.
   PHAN.   Manfred!

[*The* SPIRIT OF ASTARTE *disappears.*]

   NEM.   She's gone, and will not be recalled;
Her words will be fulfilled. Return to the earth.
   A SPIRIT.   He is convulsed.—This is to be a
       mortal
And seek the things beyond mortality.   160
   ANOTHER SPIRIT.   Yet, see, he mastereth himself,
       and makes
His torture tributary to his will.
Had he been one of us, he would have made
An awful spirit.
   NEM.   Hast thou further question

Of our great sovereign, or his worshippers?

MAN.   None.

NEM.   Then for a time farewell.

MAN.   We meet then! Where? On the earth?—
Even as thou wilt: and for the grace accorded
I now depart a debtor. Fare ye well!

[*Exit* MANFRED.]

(*Scene closes.*)

ACT III

SCENE I

A Hall in the Castle of MANFRED.

MANFRED *and* HERMAN.

MAN.   What is the hour?

HERMAN.   It wants but one till sunset,
And promises a lovely twilight.

MAN.   Say,
Are all things so disposed of in the tower
As I directed?

HER.   All, my lord, are ready:
Here is the key and casket.

MAN.   It is well:
Thou may'st retire.

[*Exit* HERMAN.]

MAN. (*alone*).   There is a calm upon me—
Inexplicable stillness! which till now,
Did not belong to what I knew of life.
If that I did not know philosophy
To be of all our vanities the motliest,   10
The merest word that ever fooled the ear
From out the schoolman's jargon, I should deem
The golden secret, the sought "Kalon," found,
And seated in my soul. It will not last,
But it is well to have known it, though but once:
It hath enlarged my thoughts with a new sense,
And I within my tablets would note down
That there is such a feeling. Who is there?

Re-enter HERMAN.

HER.   My lord, the abbot of St. Maurice craves
To greet your presence.

ACT III. Sc. i. 13. "Kalon": the supreme good.

Enter the ABBOT OF ST. MAURICE.

ABBOT.   Peace be with Count Manfred!   20

MAN.   Thanks, holy father! welcome to these
walls;
Thy presence honors them, and blesseth those
Who dwell within them.

ABBOT.   Would it were so, Count!—
But I would fain confer with thee alone.

MAN.   Herman, retire—What would my reverend
guest?

ABBOT.   Thus, without prelude:—Age and zeal,
my office,
And good intent, must plead my privilege;
Our near, though not acquainted neighborhood,
May also be my herald. Rumors strange,
And of unholy nature, are abroad,   30
And busy with thy name; a noble name
For centuries: may he who bears it now
Transmit it unimpaired!

MAN.   Proceed,—I listen.

ABBOT.   'Tis said thou holdest converse with the
things
Which are forbidden to the search of man;
That with the dwellers of the dark abodes,
The many evil and unheavenly spirits
Which walk the valley of the shade of death,
Thou communest. I know that with mankind,
Thy fellows in creation, thou dost rarely   40
Exchange thy thoughts, and that thy solitude
Is as an anchorite's, were it but holy.

MAN.   And what are they who do avouch these
things?

ABBOT.   My pious brethren—the sacred peas-
antry—
Even thy own vassals—who do look on thee
With most unquiet eyes. Thy life's in peril.

MAN.   Take it.

ABBOT.   I come to save, and not destroy:
I would not pry into thy secret soul;
But if these things be sooth, there still is time
For penitence and pity: reconcile thee   50
With the true church, and through the church to
heaven.

MAN.   I hear thee. This is my reply: whate'er
I may have been, or am, doth rest between
Heaven and myself. I shall not choose a mortal
To be my mediator. Have I sinned
Against your ordinances? prove and punish!

ABBOT.   My son! I did not speak of punishment,
But penitence and pardon;—with thyself

The choice of such remains—and for the last,
Our institutions and our strong belief   60
Have given me power to smooth the path from sin
To higher hope and better thoughts; the first
I leave to heaven,—"Vengeance is mine alone!"
So saith the Lord, and with all humbleness
His servant echoes back the awful word.

    MAN.   Old man! there is no power in holy men,
Nor charm in prayer, nor purifying form
Of penitence, nor outward look, nor fast,
Nor agony—nor, greater than all these,
The innate tortures of that deep despair,   70
Which is remorse without the fear of hell,
But all in all sufficient to itself
Would make a hell of heaven—can exorcise
From out the unbounded spirit the quick sense
Of its own sins, wrongs, sufferance, and revenge
Upon itself; there is no future pang
Can deal that justice on the self-condemned
He deals on his own soul.

    ABBOT.   All this is well;
For this will pass away, and be succeeded
By an auspicious hope, which shall look up   80
With calm assurance to that blessed place,
Which all who seek may win, whatever be
Their earthly errors, so they be atoned:
And the commencement of atonement is
The sense of its necessity. Say on—
And all our church can teach thee shall be taught;
And all we can absolve thee shall be pardoned.

    MAN.   When Rome's sixth emperor was near his
       last,
The victim of a self-inflicted wound,
To shun the torments of a public death   90
From senates once his slaves, a certain soldier,
With show of loyal pity, would have stanched
The gushing throat with his officious robe;
The dying Roman thrust him back, and said—
Some empire still in his expiring glance—
"It is too late—is this fidelity?"

    ABBOT.   And what of this?

    MAN.   I answer with the Roman—
"It is too late!"

    ABBOT.   It never can be so,
To reconcile thyself with thy own soul,
And thy own soul with heaven. Hast thou no
       hope?   100
'Tis strange—even those who do despair above,

88. **Rome's sixth emperor**: Nero.

Yet shape themselves some fantasy on earth,
To which frail twig they cling, like drowning men.

    MAN.   Ay—father! I have had those earthly
       visions,
And noble aspirations in my youth,
To make my own the mind of other men,
The enlightener of nations; and to rise
I knew not whither—it might be to fall;
But fall, even as the mountain-cataract,
Which, having leapt from its more dazzling
       height,   110
Even in the foaming strength of its abyss
(Which casts up misty columns that become
Clouds raining from the re-ascended skies),
Lies low but mighty still.—But this is past,
My thoughts mistook themselves.

    ABBOT.   And wherefore so?

    MAN.   I could not tame my nature down; for he
Must serve who fain would sway; and soothe, and
       sue,
And watch all time, and pry into all place,
And be a living lie, who would become
A mighty thing amongst the mean, and such   120
The mass are; I disdained to mingle with
A herd, though to be leader—and of wolves.
The lion is alone, and so am I.

    ABBOT.   And why not live and act with other
      men?

    MAN.   Because my nature was averse from life;
And yet not cruel; for I would not make,
But find a desolation. Like the wind,
The red-hot breath of the most lone Simoom,
Which dwells but in the desert, and sweeps o'er
The barren sands which bear no shrubs to
       blast,   130
And revels o'er their wild and arid waves,
And seeketh not, so that it is not sought,
But being met is deadly,—such hath been
The course of my existence; but there came
Things in my path which are no more.

    ABBOT.   Alas!
I 'gin to fear that thou art past all aid
From me and from my calling; yet so young,
I still would—

    MAN.   Look on me! there is an order
Of mortals on the earth, who do become
Old in their youth, and die ere middle age,   140
Without the violence of warlike death;
Some perishing of pleasure, some of study,
Some worn with toil, some of mere weariness,

Some of disease, and some insanity,
And some of withered or of broken hearts;
For this last is a malady which slays
More than are numbered in the lists of fate,
Taking all shapes, and bearing many names.
Look upon me! for even of all these things
Have I partaken; and of all these things,   150
One were enough; then wonder not that I
Am what I am, but that I ever was
Or having been, that I am still on earth.
   ABBOT.   Yet, hear me still—
   MAN.   Old man! I do respect
Thine order, and revere thine years; I deem
Thy purpose pious, but it is in vain:
Think me not churlish; I would spare thyself,
Far more than me, in shunning at this time
All further colloquy; and so—farewell.
        [*Exit* MANFRED.]

   ABBOT.   This should have been a noble creature:
   he   160
Hath all the energy which would have made
A goodly frame of glorious elements,
Had they been wisely mingled; as it is,
It is an awful chaos—light and darkness,
And mind and dust, and passions and pure thoughts
Mixed, and contending without end or order,—
All dormant or destructive; he will perish,
And yet he must not; I will try once more.
For such are worth redemption; and my duty
Is to dare all things for a righteous end.   170
I'll follow him—but cautiously, though surely.
        [*Exit* ABBOT.]

SCENE II

Another Chamber.

MANFRED *and* HERMAN.

   HER.   My lord, you bade me wait on you at
   sunset:
He sinks behind the mountain.
   MAN.   Doth he so?
I will look on him.
   [MANFRED *advances to the Window of the Hall.*]
           Glorious orb! the idol
Of early nature, and the vigorous race
Of undiseased mankind, the giant sons

Of the embrace of angels, with a sex
More beautiful than they, which did draw down
The erring spirits who can ne'er return.—
Most glorious orb! that wert a worship, ere
The mystery of thy making was revealed!   10
Thou earliest minister of the Almighty,
Which gladdened, on their mountain tops, the
   hearts
Of the Chaldean shepherds, till they poured
Themselves in orisons! Thou material God!
And representative of the unknown—
Who chose thee for his shadow! Thou chief star!
Center of many stars! which mak'st our earth
Endurable, and temperest the hues
And hearts of all who walk within thy rays!
Sire of the seasons! Monarch of the climes,   20
And those who dwell in them! for near or far,
Our inborn spirits have a tint of thee
Even as our outward aspects;—thou dost rise,
And shine, and set in glory. Fare thee well!
I ne'er shall see thee more. As my first glance
Of love and wonder was for thee, then take
My latest look; thou wilt not beam on one
To whom the gifts of life and warmth have been
Of a more fatal nature. He is gone:
I follow.   30
        [*Exit* MANFRED.]

SCENE III

The Mountains—The Castle of MANFRED *at some
distance—A Terrace before a Tower.—Time, Twilight.*

HERMAN, MANUEL, *and other Dependants of*
MANFRED.

   HER.   'Tis strange enough; night after night, for
   years,
He hath pursued long vigils in this tower,
Without a witness. I have been within it,—
So have we all been ofttimes; but from it,
Or its contents, it were impossible
To draw conclusions absolute, of aught
His studies tend to. To be sure, there is
One chamber where none enter: I would give
The fee of what I have to come these three years,

Sc. iii. 9. **fee of:** possession of.

To pore upon its mysteries.

MANUEL.   'Twere dangerous: 10
Content thyself with what thou know'st already.

HER.   Ah! Manuel! thou art elderly and wise,
And couldst say much; thou hast dwelt within the
        castle—
How many years is't?

MANUEL.   Ere Count Manfred's birth,
I served his father, whom he nought resembles.

HER.   There be more sons in like predicament.
But wherein do they differ?

MANUEL.   I speak not
Of features or of form, but mind and habits;
Count Sigismund was proud, but gay and free,—
A warrior and a reveller; he dwelt not   20
With books and solitude, nor made the night
A gloomy vigil, but a festal time,
Merrier than day; he did not walk the rocks
And forests like a wolf, nor turn aside
From men and their delights.

HER.   Beshrew the hour,
But those were jocund times! I would that such
Would visit the old walls again; they look
As if they had forgotten them.

MANUEL.   These walls
Must change their chieftain first. Oh! I have seen
Some strange things in them, Herman.

HER.   Come, be friendly,   30
Relate me some to while away our watch:
I've heard thee darkly speak of an event
Which happened hereabouts, by this same tower.

MANUEL.   That was a night indeed! I do remem-
        ber
'Twas twilight, as it may be now, and such
Another evening;—yon red cloud, which rests
On Eigher's pinnacle, so rested then,—
So like that it might be the same; the wind
Was faint and gusty, and the mountain snows
Began to glitter with the climbing moon;   40
Count Manfred was, as now, within his tower,—
How occupied, we knew not, but with him
The sole companion of his wanderings
And watchings—her, whom of all earthly things
That lived, the only thing he seemed to love,—
As he, indeed, by blood was bound to do,
The lady Astarte, his—

                    Hush! who comes here?

37. **Eigher's pinnacle:** a mountain east of the famed
Jungfrau.

Enter the ABBOT.

ABBOT.   Where is your master?

HER.   Yonder in the tower.

ABBOT.   I must speak with him.

MANUEL.   'Tis impossible;
He is most private, and must not be thus   50
Intruded on.

ABBOT.   Upon myself I take
The forfeit of my fault, if fault there be—
But I must see him.

HER.   Thou hast seen him once
This eve already.

ABBOT.   Herman! I command thee,
Knock, and apprize the Count of my approach.

HER.   We dare not.

ABBOT.   Then it seems I must be herald
Of my own purpose.

MANUEL.   Reverend father stop—
I pray you pause.

ABBOT.   Why so?

MANUEL.   But step this way,
And I will tell you further.

                    [*Exeunt.*]

SCENE IV

Interior of the Tower.

MANFRED *alone.*

MAN.   The stars are forth, the moon above the
        tops
Of the snow-shining mountains.—Beautiful !
I linger yet with nature, for the night
Hath been to me a more familiar face
Than that of man; and in her starry shade
Of dim and solitary loveliness,
I learned the language of another world.
I do remember me, that in my youth,
When I was wandering,—upon such a night
I stood within the Coliseum's wall,   10
'Midst the chief relics of almighty Rome;
The trees which grew along the broken arches
Waved dark in the blue midnight, and the stars
Shone through the rents of ruin; from afar
The watch-dog bayed beyond the Tiber; and
More near from out the Cæsar's palace came
The owl's long cry, and, interruptedly,
Of distant sentinels the fitful song

Begun and died upon the gentle wind.
Some cypresses beyond the time-worn breach   20
Appeared to skirt the horizon, yet they stood
Within a bowshot. Where the Cæsars dwelt,
And dwell the tuneless birds of night, amidst
A grove which springs through levelled battlements,
And twines its roots with the imperial hearths,
Ivy usurps the laurel's place of growth;
But the gladiator's bloody Circus stands,
A noble wreck in ruinous perfection,
While Cæsar's chambers, and the Augustan halls,
Grovel on earth in indistinct decay.   30
And thou didst shine, thou rolling moon, upon
All this, and cast a wide and tender light,
Which softened down the hoar austerity
Of rugged desolation, and filled up,
As 'twere anew, the gaps of centuries;
Leaving that beautiful which still was so,
And making that which was not, till the place
Became religion, and the heart ran o'er
With silent worship of the great of old,—
The dead but sceptred sovereigns, who still
    rule   40
Our spirits from their urns.
                    'Twas such a night!
'Tis strange that I recall it at this time;
But I have found our thoughts take wildest flight
Even at the moment when they should array
Themselves in pensive order.

Enter the ABBOT

ABBOT.   My good lord!
I crave a second grace for this approach;
But yet let not my humble zeal offend
By its abruptness—all it hath of ill
Recoils on me; its good in the effect
May light upon your head—could I say
    heart—   50
Could I touch *that*, with words or prayers, I should
Recall a noble spirit which hath wandered;
But is not yet all lost.
MAN.   Thou know'st me not;
My days are numbered, and my deeds recorded;
Retire, or 'twill be dangerous—Away!
    ABBOT.   Thou dost not mean to menace me?
MAN.   Not I;
I simply tell thee peril is at hand,
And would preserve thee.
    ABBOT.   What dost thou mean?

MAN.   Look there!
What dost thou see?
    ABBOT.   Nothing.
MAN.   Look there, I say,
And steadfastly;—now tell me what thou
    seest.   60
    ABBOT.   That which should shake me, but I fear
    it not:
I see a dusk and awful figure rise,
Like an infernal god, from out the earth;
His face wrapt in a mantle, and his form
Robed as with angry clouds: he stands between
Thyself and me—but I do fear him not.
    MAN.   Thou has no cause; he shall not harm
    thee, but
His sight may shock thine old limbs into palsy.
I say to thee—Retire!
    ABBOT.   And I reply—
Never—till I have battled with this fiend:—   70
What doth he here?
    MAN.   Why—ay—what doth he here?
I did not send for him,—he is unbidden.
    ABBOT.   Alas! lost mortal! what with guests like
    these
Hast thou to do? I tremble for thy sake:
Why doth he gaze on thee, and thou on him?
Ah! he unveils his aspect: on his brow
The thunder-scars are graven: from his eye
Glares forth the immortality of hell—
Avaunt!—
    MAN.   Pronounce—what is thy mission?
    SPIRIT.   Come!
    ABBOT.   What art thou, unknown being? answer!
    —speak!   80
    SPIRIT.   The genius of this mortal.—Come! 'tis
    time.
    MAN.   I am prepared for all things, but deny
The power which summons me. Who sent thee
    here?
    SPIRIT.   Thou'lt know anon—Come! come!
    MAN.   I have commanded
Things of an essence greater far than thine,
And striven with thy masters. Get hee hence!
    SPIRIT.   Mortal! thine hour is come—Away!
    I say.
    MAN.   I knew, and know my hour is come, but
    not
To render up my soul to such as thee:

Away! I'll die as I have lived—alone.   90
   SPIRIT.   Then I must summon up my brethren.
   —Rise!

[Other SPIRITS *rise up]*

   ABBOT.   Avaunt! ye evil ones!—Avaunt! I say;
Ye have no power where piety hath power,
And I do charge ye in the name—
   SPIRIT.   Old man!
We know ourselves, our mission, and thine order;
Waste not thy holy words on idle uses,
It were in vain: this man is forfeited.
Once more I summon him—Away! Away!
   MAN.   I do defy ye,—though I feel my soul
Is ebbing from me, yet I do defy ye;   100
Nor will I hence, while I have earthly breath
To breathe my scorn upon ye—earthly strength
To wrestle, though with spirits; what ye take
Shall be ta'en limb by limb.
   SPIRIT.   Reluctant mortal!
Is this the Magian who would so pervade
The world invisible, and make himself
Almost our equal? Can it be that thou
Art thus in love with life? the very life
Which made thee wretched!
   MAN.   Thou false fiend, thou liest!
My life is in its last hour,—*that* I know,   110
Nor would redeem a moment of that hour;
I do not combat against death, but thee
And thy surrounding angels; my past power,
Was purchased by no compact with thy crew,
But by superior science—penance, daring,
And length of watching, strength of mind, and skill
In knowledge of our fathers—when the earth
Saw men and spirits walking side by side,
And gave ye no supremacy: I stand
Upon my strength—I do defy—deny—   120
Spurn back, and scorn ye!—
   SPIRIT.   But thy many crimes
Have made thee—
   MAN.   What are they to such as thee?
Must crimes be punished but by other crimes,
And greater criminals?—Back to thy hell!
Thou hast no power upon me, *that* I feel;
Thou never shalt possess me, *that* I know:
What I have done is done; I bear within
A torture which could nothing gain from thine:
The mind which is immortal makes itself
Requital for its good or evil thoughts,—   130

Is its own origin of ill and end
And its own place and time; its innate sense,
When stripped of this mortality, derives
No color from the fleeing things without,
But is absorbed in sufferance or in joy,
Born from the knowledge of its own desert.
Thou didst not tempt me, and thou couldst not
   tempt me;
I have not been thy dupe, nor am thy prey—
But was my own destroyer, and will be
My own hereafter.—Back, ye baffled
   fiends!—   140
The hand of death is on me—but not yours.

[The DEMONS *disappear.]*

   ABBOT.   Alas! how pale thou art—thy lips are
   white—
And thy breast heaves—and in thy gasping throat
The accents rattle: Give thy prayers to heaven—
Pray—albeit but in thought,—but die not thus.
   MAN.   'Tis over—my dull eyes can fix thee not;
But all things swim around me, and the earth
Heaves as it were beneath me. Fare thee well!
Give me thy hand.
   ABBOT.   Cold—cold—even to the heart—
But yet one prayer—Alas! how fares it with
   thee?   150
   MAN.   Old man! 'tis not so difficult to die.
            *[*MANFRED *expires.]*

   ABBOT.   He's gone—his soul hath ta'en its
   earthless flight;
Whither? I dread to think—but he is gone.
1816–17   *1817*

FROM
Don Juan

Difficile est proprie communia dicere.*—HORACE

*"Dost thou think, because thou art virtuous, there
shall be no more cakes and ale?—Yes, by Saint
Anne, and ginger shall be hot i' the mouth, too!"*
   —SHAKESPEARE, *Twelfth Night, or What You Will.*

---

* "It is difficult to write about common things." (*Art of
Poetry*, ii, 3, 128.)

FRAGMENT

On the back of the Poet's MS. of Canto I.

I would to heaven that I were so much clay,
  As I am blood, bone, marrow, passion, feeling—
Because at least the past were pass'd away—
  And for the future—(but I write this reeling,
Having got drunk exceedingly to-day,
  So that I seem to stand upon the ceiling)
I say—the future is a serious matter—
And so—for God's sake—hock and soda-water!

DEDICATION

1

Bob Southey! You're a poet—Poet-laureate,
  And representative of all the race;
Although 'tis true that you turned out a Tory at
  Last,—yours has lately been a common case;
And now, my Epic Renegade! what are ye at?
  With all the Lakers, in and out of place?
A nest of tuneful persons, to my eye
Like "four and twenty Blackbirds in a pye;

2

"Which pye being opened they began to sing"
  (This old song and new simile holds good),   10
"A dainty dish to set before the King,"
  Or Regent, who admires such kind of food;—
And Coleridge, too, has lately taken wing,
  But like a hawk encumbered with his hood,—
Explaining metaphysics to the nation—
I wish he would explain his Explanation.

3

You, Bob! are rather insolent, you know,
  At being disappointed in your wish
To supersede all warblers here below,
  And be the only Blackbird in the dish;   20

DON JUAN. FRAGMENT. **8. hock:** a German wine frequently taken with water to relieve a hangover.
DEDICATION. **6. Lakers:** the Lake Poets, chiefly Wordsworth, Coleridge, and Southey, all of whom had been staunch liberals, but who became staunch conservatives after the excesses of the French Revolution. **8. pye:** a pun on the lacklustre Henry Pye, poet laureate preceding Southey. **12. Regent:** Prince of Wales, later King George IV.

And then you overstrain yourself, or so,
  And tumble downward like the flying fish
Gasping on deck, because you soar too high, Bob,
And fall, for lack of moisture quite a-dry, Bob!

4

And Wordsworth, in a rather long "Excursion"
  (I think the quarto holds five hundred pages),
Has given a sample from the vasty version
  Of his new system to perplex the sages;
'Tis poetry—at least by his assertion,
  And may appear so when the dog-star
    rages—   30
And he who understands it would be able
To add a story to the Tower of Babel.

5

You—Gentlemen! by dint of long seclusion
  From better company, have kept your own
At Keswick, and, through still continued fusion
  Of one another's minds, at last have grown
To deem as a most logical conclusion,
  That Poesy has wreaths for you alone:
There is a narrowness in such a notion,
Which makes me wish you'd change your lakes for
    ocean.   40

6

I would not imitate the petty thought,
  Nor coin my self-love to so base a vice,
For all the glory your conversion brought,
  Since gold alone should not have been its price.
You have your salary: was 't for that you wrought?
  And Wordsworth has his place in the Excise.
You're shabby fellows—true—but poets still,
And duly seated on the immortal hill.

7

Your bays may hide the baldness of your brows—
  Perhaps some virtuous blushes;—let them
    go—   50
To you I envy neither fruit nor boughs—
  And for the fame you would engross below,

46. Excise: To the dismay of Byron and other radicals, the young Wordsworth, so given to republican sympathies, accepted a government position as Distributor of Stamps for Westmorland.

The field is universal, and allows
  Scope to all such as feel the inherent glow;
Scott, Rogers, Campbell, Moore, and Crabbe, will
    try
'Gainst you the question with posterity.

8

For me, who, wandering with pedestrian Muses,
  Contend not with you on the winged steed,
I wish your fate may yield ye, when she chooses,
  The fame you envy, and the skill you need;   60
And recollect a poet nothing loses
  In giving to his brethren their full meed
Of merit, and complaint of present days
Is not the certain path to future praise.

9

He that reserves his laurels for posterity
  (Who does not often claim the bright reversion)
Has generally no great crop to spare it, he
  Being only injured by his own assertion;
And although here and there some glorious rarity
  Arise like Titan from the sea's immersion,   70
The major part of such appellants go
To—God knows where—for no one else can know.

10

If, fallen in evil days on evil tongues,
  Milton appealed to the Avenger, Time,
If Time, the Avenger, execrates his wrongs,
  And makes the word "Miltonic" mean "*sublime*,"
He deigned not to belie his soul in songs,
  Nor turn his very talent to a crime;
He did not loathe the Sire to laud the Son,
But closed the tyrant-hater he begun.   80

11

Think'st thou, could he—the blind Old Man—arise,
  Like Samuel from the grave, to freeze once more
The blood of monarchs with his prophecies,
  Or be alive again—again all hoar
With time and trials, and those helpless eyes,
  And heartless daughters—worn—and pale—and
    poor;

Would *he* adore a sultan? *he* obey
The intellectual eunuch Castlereagh?

12

Cold-blooded, smooth-faced, placid miscreant!
  Dabbling its sleek young hands in Erin's
    gore,   90
And thus for wider carnage taught to pant,
  Transferred to gorge upon a sister shore,
The vulgarest tool that Tyranny could want,
  With just enough of talent, and no more,
To lengthen letters by another fixed,
And offer poison long already mixed.

13

An orator of such set trash of phrase
  Ineffably—legitimately vile,
That even its grossest flatterers dare not praise,
  Nor foes—all nations—condescend to
    smile;   100
Not even a sprightly blunder's spark can blaze
  From that Ixion grindstone's ceaseless toil,
That turns and turns to give the world a notion
Of endless torments and perpetual motion.

14

A bungler even in its disgusting trade,
  And botching, patching, leaving still behind
Something of which its masters are afraid,
  States to be curbed, and thoughts to be confined,
Conspiracy or Congress to be made—
  Cobbling at manacles for all mankind—   110
A tinkering slave-maker, who mends old chains,
With God and man's abhorrence for its gains.

15

If we may judge of matter by the mind,
  Emasculated to the marrow *It*
Hath but two objects, how to serve, and bind,
  Deeming the chain it wears even men may fit,

88. **Castlereagh:** Robert Stewart, Viscount Castlereagh (1769–1822), leading Tory statesman between 1812 and 1822, and a force for repression in Ireland and England. **102. Ixion:** In Greek mythology, Ixion was bound to an ever-moving wheel.

Entropius of its many masters,—blind
   To worth as freedom, wisdom as to wit,
Fearless—because *no* feeling dwells in ice,
Its very courage stagnates to a vice.   120

16

Where shall I turn me not to *view* its bonds,
   For I will never *feel* them;—Italy!
Thy late reviving Roman soul desponds
   Beneath the lie this State-thing breathed o'er
         thee—
Thy clanking chain, and Erin's yet green wounds,
   Have voices—tongues to cry aloud for me.
Europe has slaves, allies, kings, armies still,
And Southey lives to sing them very ill.

17

Meantime, Sir Laureate, I proceed to dedicate,
   In honest simple verse, this song to you.   130
And, if in flattering strains I do not predicate,
   'Tis that I will retain my "buff and blue";
My politics as yet are all to educate:
   Apostasy's so fashionable, too,
To keep *one* creed's a task grown quite Herculean:
Is it not so, my Tory, Ultra-Julian?
                              Venice, September 16, 1818

CANTO THE FIRST

1

I want a hero: an uncommon want,
   When every year and month sends forth a new
         one,
Till, after cloying the gazettes with cant,
   The age discovers he is not the true one:
Of such as these I should not care to vaunt,
   I'll therefore take our ancient friend Don Juan—
We all have seen him, in the pantomime,
Sent to the devil somewhat ere his time.

117. **Entropius:** a eunuch who was minister of the Roman emperor Arcadius. 132. **"buff and blue":** colors of
the Whig party. 136. **Ultra-Julian:** a reference to Julian
the Apostate.

2

Vernon, the butcher Cumberland, Wolfe, Hawke,
   Prince Ferdinand, Granby, Burgoyne, Keppel,
         Howe,   10
Evil and good, have had their tithe of talk,
   And filled their sign-posts then, like Wellesley
         now;
Each in their turn like Banquo's monarchs stalk,
   Followers of fame, "nine farrow" of that sow:
France, too, had Buonaparté and Dumourier
Recorded in the Moniteur and Courier.

3

Barnave, Brissot, Condorcet, Mirabeau,
   Pétion, Clootz, Danton, Marat, La Fayette,
Were French, and famous people, as we know;
   And there were others, scarce forgotten yet,   20
Joubert, Hoche, Marceau, Lannes, Desaix, Moreau,
   With many of the military set,
Exceedingly remarkable at times,
But not at all adapted to my rhymes.

4

Nelson was once Britannia's god of war,
   And still should be so, but the tide is turned;
There's no more to be said of Trafalgar,
   'Tis with our hero quietly inurned;
Because the army's grown more popular,
   At which the naval people are concerned,   30
Besides, the prince is all for the land-service,
Forgetting Duncan, Nelson, Howe, and Jervis.

5

Brave men were living before Agamemnon
   And since, exceeding valorous and sage,

CANTO I. **9–10. Vernon . . . Howe:** a list of famous or infamous eighteenth-century generals and admirals. **12.
Wellesley:** Duke of Wellington. **16. Moniteur and
Courier:** French newspapers. **17–18. Barnave . . . La
Fayette:** a catalogue of French philosophers and politicians, most of whom were active in the Revolution.
21. Joubert . . . Moreau: French generals during the
revolutionary and Napoleonic wars. **27. Trafalgar:** Nelson was killed at the Battle of Trafalgar, October 21,
1805. **32. Duncan . . . Jervis:** British admirals.

A good deal like him too, though quite the same
    none;
But then they shone not on the poet's page,
And so have been forgotten:—I condemn none,
    But can't find any in the present age
Fit for my poem (that is, for my new one);
So, as I said, I'll take my friend Don Juan.   40

6

Most epic poets plunge "in medias res"
    (Horace makes this the heroic turnpike road),
And then your hero tells, when'er you please,
    What went before—by way of episode,
While seated after dinner at his ease,
    Beside his mistress in some soft abode,
Palace, or garden, paradise, or cavern,
Which serves the happy couple for a tavern.

7

That is the usual method, but not mine—
    My way is to begin with the beginning;   50
The regularity of my design
    Forbids all wanderings as the worst of sinning,
And therefore I shall open with a line
    (Although it cost me half an hour in spinning)
    Narrating somewhat of Don Juan's father,
And also of his mother, if you'd rather.

8

In Seville was he born, a pleasant city,
    Famous for oranges and women—he
Who has not seen it will be much to pity,
    So says the proverb—and I quite agree;   60
Of all the Spanish towns is none more pretty,
    Cadiz, perhaps—but that you soon may see:—
Don Juan's parents lived beside the river,
A noble stream, and called the Guadalquivir.

9

His father's name was Jóse—*Don,* of course,
    A true Hidalgo, free from every stain
Of Moor or Hebrew blood, he traced his source
    Through the most Gothic gentlemen of Spain;

66. **Hidalgo:** a member of the lower Spanish nobility.

A better cavalier ne'er mounted horse,
    Or, being mounted, e'er got down again,   70
Than Jóse, who begot our hero, who
Begot—but that's to come—Well, to renew:

10

His mother was a learned lady, famed
    For every branch of every science known—
In every Christian language ever named,
    With virtues equalled by her wit alone:
She made the cleverest people quite ashamed,
    And even the good with inward envy groan,
Finding themselves so very much exceeded
In their own way by all the things that she did.   80

11

Her memory was a mine: she knew by heart
    All Calderon and greater part of Lopé,
So that if any actor missed his part
    She could have served him for the prompter's
        copy;
For her Feinagle's were an useless art,
    And he himself obliged to shut up shop—he
Could never make a memory so fine as
That which adorned the brain of Donna Inez.

12

Her favorite science was the mathematical,
    Her noblest virtue was her magnanimity;   90
Her wit (she sometimes tried at wit) was Attic all,
    Her serious sayings darkened to sublimity;
In short, in all things she was fairly what I call
    A prodigy—her morning dress was dimity,
Her evening silk, or, in the summer, muslin,
And other stuffs, with which I won't stay puzzling.

13

She knew the Latin—that is, "the Lord's prayer,"
    And Greek—the alphabet—I'm nearly sure;

82. **Calderon . . . Lopé:** the great Spanish dramatists
Calderon (1600–1681) and Lopé de Vega (1562–
1635). 85. **Feinagle:** Gregor von Feinagle, inventor of
a memory-training theory.

She read some French romances here and there,
　　Although her mode of speaking was not
　　　　pure;   100
For native Spanish she had no great care,
　　At least her conversation was obscure;
Her thoughts were theorems, her words a problem,
As if she deemed that mystery would ennoble 'em.

14

She liked the English and the Hebrew tongue,
　　And said there was analogy between 'em;
She proved it somehow out of sacred song,
　　But I must leave the proofs to those who've seen
　　　　'em,
But this I heard her say, and can't be wrong,
　　And all may think which way their judgments
　　　　lean 'em,   110
" 'Tis strange—the Hebrew noun which means 'I
　　am,'
The English always use to govern d—n."

15

Some women use their tongues—she *looked* a
　　lecture,
　　Each eye a sermon, and her brow a homily,
An all-in-all sufficient self-director,
　　Like the lamented late Sir Samuel Romilly,
The Law's expounder, and the State's corrector,
　　Whose suicide was almost an anomaly—
One sad example more, that "All is vanity,"—
(The jury brought their verdict in "Insanity.")   120

16

In short, she was a walking calculation,
　　Miss Edgeworth's novels stepping from their
　　　　covers,
Or Mrs. Trimmer's books on education,
　　Or "Cœlebs' Wife" set out in quest of lovers,

116. Sir Samuel Romilly: Lady Byron's lawyer. He
committed suicide after the death of his wife. 122-24.
Miss Edgeworth's ... "Cœlebs' Wife": Maria Edgeworth (1767–1849), author of *Castle Rackrent*; Sarah
Trimmer (1741–1810), author of children's books and
didactic tales; *Cœlebs in Search of a Wife* was a
preachy novel by Hannah More (1745–1833). The
general reference is to pretentious and pedestrian
women writers.

Morality's prim personification,
　　In which not Envy's self a flaw discovers;
To others' share let "female errors fall,"
For she had not even one—the worst of all.

17

Oh! she was perfect past all parallel—
　　Of any modern female saint's comparison;   130
So far above the cunning powers of hell,
　　Her guardian angel had given up his garrison;
Even her minutest motions went as well
　　As those of the best time-piece made by Harrison:
In virtues nothing earthly could surpass her,
Save thine "incomparable oil," Macassar!

18

Perfect she was, but as perfection is
　　Insipid in this naughty world of ours,
Where our first parents never learned to kiss
　　Till they were exiled from their earlier
　　　　bowers,   140
Where all was peace, and innocence, and bliss
　　(I wonder how they got through the twelve
　　　　hours),
Don Jóse, like a lineal son of Eve,
Went plucking various fruit without her leave.

19

He was a mortal of the careless kind,
　　With no great love for learning, or the learned,
Who chose to go where'er he had a mind,
　　And never dreamed his lady was concerned;
The world, as usual, wickedly inclined
　　To see a kingdom or a house o'erturned,   150
Whispered he had a mistress, some said *two*,
But for domestic quarrels *one* will do.

20

Now Donna Inez had, with all her merit,
　　A great opinion of her own good qualities;

134. Harrison: John Harrison (1693–1776), a great
watchmaker. 136. Macassar: a popular hair-oil from
the island of Macassar.

Neglect, indeed, requires a saint to bear it,
    And such, indeed, she was in her moralities;
But then she had a devil of a spirit,
    And sometimes mixed up fancies with realities,
And let few opportunities escape
Of getting her liege lord into a scrape.   160

21

This was an easy matter with a man
    Oft in the wrong, and never on his guard;
And even the wisest, do the best they can,
    Have moments, hours, and days, so unprepared,
That you might "brain them with their lady's fan";
    And sometimes ladies hit exceeding hard,
And fans turn into falchions in fair hands,
And why and wherefore no one understands.

22

'Tis pity learned virgins ever wed
    With persons of no sort of education,   170
Or gentlemen, who, though well born and bred,
    Grow tired of scientific conversation;
I don't choose to say much upon this head,
    I'm a plain man, and in a single station,
But—Oh! ye lords of ladies intellectual,
Inform us truly, have they not hen-pecked you all?

23

Don Jóse and his lady quarrelled—why,
    Not any of the many could divine,
Though several thousand people chose to try,
    'Twas surely no concern of theirs nor mine;   180
I loathe that low vice—curiosity;
    But if there's anything in which I shine,
'Tis in arranging all my friends' affairs,
Not having, of my own, domestic cares.

24

And so I interfered, and with the best
    Intentions, but their treatment was not kind;
I think the foolish people were possessed,
    For neither of them could I ever find,
Although their porter afterwards confessed—
    But that's no matter, and the worst's
        behind,   190
For little Juan o'er me threw, down stairs,
A pail of housemaid's water unawares.

25

A little curly-headed, good-for-nothing,
    And mischief-making monkey from his birth,
His parents ne'er agreed except in doting
    Upon the most unquiet imp on earth;
Instead of quarrelling, had they been but both in
    Their senses, they'd have sent young master forth
To school, or had him soundly whipped at home,
To teach him manners for the time to come.   200

26

Don Jóse and the Donna Inez led
    For some time an unhappy sort of life,
Wishing each other, not divorced, but dead;
    They lived respectably as man and wife,
Their conduct was exceedingly well-bred,
    And gave no outward signs of inward strife,
Until at length the smothered fire broke out,
And put the business past all kind of doubt.

27

For Inez called some druggists and physicians,
    And tried to prove her loving lord was
        mad,   210
But as he had some lucid intermissions,
    She next decided he was only *bad;*
Yet when they asked her for her depositions,
    No sort of explanation could be had,
Save that her duty both to man and God
Required this conduct—which seemed very odd.

28

She kept a journal, where his faults were noted,
    And opened certain trunks of books and letters,
All which might, if occasion served, be quoted;
    And then she had all Seville for abettors,   220
Besides her good old grandmother (who doted);
    The hearers of her case became repeaters,
Then advocates, inquisitors, and judges,
Some for amusement, others for old grudges.

29

And then this best and meekest woman bore
    With such serenity her husband's woes,

Just as the Spartan ladies did of yore,
　　Who saw their spouses killed, and nobly chose
Never to say a word about them more—
　　Calmly she heard each calumny that rose,　230
And saw *his* agonies with such sublimity,
That all the world exclaimed, "What magnanimity!"

30

No doubt this patience, when the world is damning
　　us,
　　Is philosophic in our former friends;
'Tis also pleasant to be deemed magnaminous,
　　The more so in obtaining our own ends;
And what the lawyers call a "*malus animus*"
　　Conduct like this by no means comprehends:
Revenge in person's certainly no virtue,
But then 'tis not *my* fault, if *others* hurt you.　240

31

And if our quarrels should rip up old stories,
　　And help them with a lie or two additional,
I'm not to blame, as you well know—no more is
　　Any one else—they were become traditional;
Besides, their resurrection aids our glories
　　By contrast, which is what we just were wishing
　　all:
And science profits by this resurrection—
Dead scandals form good subjects for dissection.

32

Their friends had tried at reconciliation,
　　Then their relations, who made matters
　　　worse,　　250
('Twere hard to tell upon a like occasion
　　To whom it may be best to have recourse—
I can't say much for friend or yet relation):
　　The lawyers did their utmost for divorce,
But scarce a fee was paid on either side
Before, unluckily, Don Jóse died.

33

He died: and most unluckily, because,
　　According to all hints I could collect

237. "*malus animus*": malice aforethought.

From counsel learned in those kinds of laws
　　(Although their talk's obscure and circum-
　　　spect),　　260
His death contrived to spoil a charming cause;
　　A thousand pities also with respect
To public feeling, which on this occasion
Was manifested in a great sensation.

34

But ah! he died; and buried with him lay
　　The public feeling and the lawyers' fees:
His house was sold, his servants sent away,
　　A Jew took one of his two mistresses,
A priest the other—at least so they say:
　　I asked the doctors after his disease—　270
He died of the slow fever called the tertian,
And left his widow to her own aversion.

35

Yet Jóse was an honorable man,
　　That I must say, who knew him very well;
Therefore his frailties I'll no further scan,
　　Indeed there were not many more to tell:
And if his passions now and then outran
　　Discretion, and were not so peaceable
As Numa's (who was also named Pompilius),
He had been ill brought up, and was born
　　bilious.　　280

36

Whate'er might be his worthlessness or worth,
　　Poor fellow! he had many things to wound him,
Let's own—since it can do no good on earth—
　　It was a trying moment that which found him
Standing alone beside his desolate hearth,
　　Where all his household gods lay shivered round
　　him:
No choice was left his feelings or his pride,
Save death or Doctors' Commons—so he died.

37

Dying intestate, Juan was sole heir
　　To a chancery suit, and messuages and
　　　lands,　　290

279. Numa: second King of Rome, who ruled through
forty years of peace. 288. Doctors' Commons: divorce
courts. 290. messuages: houses with adjacent buildings
and lands.

Which, with a long minority and care,
　Promised to turn out well in proper hands:
Inez became sole guardian, which was fair,
　And answered but to nature's just demands;
An only son left with an only mother
Is brought up much more wisely than another.

38

Sagest of women, even of widows, she
　Resolved that Juan should be quite a paragon,
And worthy of the noblest pedigree:
　(His sire was of Castile, his dam from
　　Aragon).   300
Then for accomplishments of chivalry,
　In case our lord the king should go to war again,
He learned the arts of riding, fencing, gunnery,
And how to scale a fortress—or a nunnery.

39

But that which Donna Inez most desired,
　And saw into herself each day before all
The learned tutors whom for him she hired,
　Was, that his breeding should be strictly moral:
Much into all his studies she inquired,
　And so they were submitted first to her, all,   310
Arts, sciences, no branch was made a mystery
To Juan's eyes, excepting natural history.

40

The languages, especially the dead,
　The sciences, and most of all the abstruse,
The arts, at least all such as could be said
　To be the most remote from common use,
In all these he was much and deeply read:
　But not a page of anything that's loose,
Or hints continuation of the species,
　Was ever suffered, lest he should grow
　　vicious.   320

41

His classic studies made a little puzzle,
　Because of filthy loves of gods and goddesses,
Who in the earlier ages raised a bustle,
　But never put on pantaloons or bodices;

His reverend tutors had at times a tussle,
　And for their Æneids, Iliads, and Odysseys,
Were forced to make an odd sort of apology,
For Donna Inez dreaded the Mythology.

42

Ovid's a rake, as half his verses show him,
　Anacreon's morals are a still worse sample,   330
Catullus scarcely has a decent poem,
　I don't think Sappho's Ode a good example,
Although Longinus tells us there is no hymn
　Where the sublime soars forth on wings more
　　ample;
But Virgil's songs are pure, except that horrid one
Beginning with "Formosum Pastor Corydon."

43

Lucretius' irreligion is too strong
　For early stomachs, to prove wholesome food;
I can't help thinking Juvenal was wrong,
　Although no doubt his real intent was
　　good,   340
For speaking out so plainly in his song,
　So much indeed as to be downright rude;
And then what proper person can be partial
To all those nauseous epigrams of Martial?

44

Juan was taught from out the best edition,
　Expurgated by learned men, who place,
Judiciously, from out the schoolboy's vision,
　The grosser parts; but, fearful to deface
Too much their modest bard by this omission,
　And pitying sore this mutilated case,   350
They only add them all in an appendix,
Which saves, in fact, the trouble of an index;

329–31. **Ovid . . . Catullus:** Ovid, Anacreon, and Catullus were classical poets famed for their realistic love poetry. **332. Sappho's Ode:** *Ode to Aphrodite* by the renowned Greek woman poet of Lesbos. **336. "Formosum Pastor Corydon":** a reference to Eclogue II of Virgil's *Bucolics*, which recounts the love of the shepherd Corydon for the beautiful boy Alexis. **337–39. Lucretius' . . . Juvenal:** Lucretius wrote the classic *De Rerum Natura*, a poem advancing a totally materialistic theory of creation. Juvenal was the great and vivid satirist of the vices of first-century Rome.

45

For there we have them all "at one fell swoop,"
  Instead of being scattered through the pages;
They stand forth marshalled in a handsome troop,
  To meet the ingenuous youth of future ages,
Till some less rigid editor shall stoop
  To call them back into their separate cages,
Instead of standing staring all together,
Like garden gods—and not so decent either.   360

46

The Missal too (it was the family Missal)
  Was ornamented in a sort of way
Which ancient mass-books often are, and this all
  Kinds of grotesques illumined; and how they,
Who saw those figures on the margin kiss all,
  Could turn their optics to the text and pray,
Is more than I know—But Don Juan's mother
Kept this herself, and gave her son another.

47

Sermons he read, and lectures he endured,
  And homilies, and lives of all the saints;   370
To Jerome and to Chrysostom inured,
  He did not take such studies for restraints;
But how faith is acquired, and then insured,
  So well not one of the aforesaid paints
As Saint Augustine in his fine Confessions,
Which make the reader envy his transgressions.

48

This, too, was a sealed book to little Juan—
  I can't but say that his mamma was right,
If such an education was the true one.
  She scarcely trusted him from out her
      sight;   380
Her maids were old, and if she took a new one,
  You might be sure she was a perfect fright,
She did this during even her husband's life—
I recommend as much to every wife.

49

Young Juan waxed in godliness and grace;
  At six a charming child and at eleven

With all the promise of as fine a face
  As e'er to man's maturer growth was given.
He studied steadily and grew apace,
  And seemed, at least, in the right road to
      heaven,   390
For half his days were passed at church, the other
Between his tutors, confessor, and mother.

50

At six, I said, he was a charming child,
  At twelve he was a fine, but quiet boy;
Although in infancy a little wild,
  They tamed him down amongst them: to destroy
His natural spirit not in vain they toiled,
  At least it seemed so; and his mother's joy
Was to declare how sage, and still, and steady,
Her young philosopher was grown already.   400

51

I had my doubts, perhaps I have them still,
  But what I say is neither here nor there:
I knew his father well, and have some skill
  In character—but it would not be fair
From sire to son to augur good or ill:
  He and his wife were an ill sorted pair—
But scandal's my aversion—I protest
Against all evil speaking, even in jest.

52

For my part I say nothing—nothing—but
  This I will say—my reasons are my own—   410
That if I had an only son to put
  To school (as God be praised that I have none),
'Tis not with Donna Inez I would shut
  Him up to learn his catechism alone,
No—no—I'd send him out betimes to college,
For there it was I picked up my own knowledge.

53

For there one learns—'tis not for me to boast,
  Though I acquired—but I pass over *that*,
As well as all the Greek I since have lost:
  I say that there's the place—but "*Verbum
      sat*,"   420

420. "*Verbum sat*": A word to the wise is sufficient.

I think I picked up too, as well as most,
    Knowledge of matters—but no matter *what*—
I never married—but, I think, I know
That sons should not be educated so.

54

Young Juan now was sixteen years of age,
    Tall, handsome, slender, but well knit: he seemed
Active, though not so sprightly, as a page;
    And everybody but his mother deemed
Him almost man; but she flew in a rage
    And bit her lips (for else she might have
      screamed)   430
If any said so, for to be precocious
Was in her eyes a thing the most atrocious.

55

Amongst her numerous acquaintance, all
    Selected for discretion and devotion,
There was the Donna Julia, whom to call
    Pretty were but to give a feeble notion
Of many charms in her as natural
    As sweetness to the flower, or salt to ocean,
Her zone to Venus, or his bow to Cupid,
(But this last simile is trite and stupid).   440

56

The darkness of her Oriental eye
    Accorded with her Moorish origin;
(Her blood was not all Spanish, by the by;
    In Spain, you know, this is a sort of sin).
When proud Granada fell, and, forced to fly,
    Boabdil wept, of Donna Julia's kin
Some went to Africa, some stayed in Spain,
Her great great grandmamma chose to remain.

57

She married (I forget the pedigree)
    With an Hidalgo, who transmitted down   450
His blood less noble than such blood should be;
    At such alliances his sires would frown,

446. **Boabdil:** the last Moorish king of Granada, he surrendered to the Spaniards in 1492.

In that point so precise in each degree
    That they bred *in and in,* as might be shown,
Marrying their cousins—nay, their aunts, and
    nieces,
Which always spoils the breed, if it increases.

58

This heathenish cross restored the breed again,
    Ruined its blood, but much improved its flesh;
For from a root the ugliest in old Spain
    Sprung up a branch as beautiful as fresh;   460
The sons no more were short, the daughters plain:
    But there's a rumor which I fain would hush,
'Tis said that Donna Julia's grandmamma
Produced her Don more heirs at love than law.

59

However this might be, the race went on
    Improving still through every generation,
Until it centered in an only son,
    Who left an only daughter: my narration
May have suggested that this single one
    Could be but Julia (whom on this occasion   470
I shall have much to speak about), and she
Was married, charming, chaste, and twenty-three.

60

Her eye (I'm very fond of handsome eyes)
    Was large and dark, suppressing half its fire
Until she spoke, then through its soft disguise
    Flashed an expression more of pride than ire,
And love than either; and there would arise
    A something in them which was not desire,
But would have been, perhaps, but for the soul
Which struggled through and chastened down the
    whole.   480

61

Her glossy hair was clustered o'er a brow
    Bright with intelligence, and fair, and smooth;
Her eyebrow's shape was like the aërial bow,
    Her cheek all purple with the beam of youth,
Mounting, at times, to a transparent glow,
    As if her veins ran lightning; she, in sooth,
Possessed an air and grace by no means common:
Her stature tall—I hate a dumpy woman.

62

Wedded she was some years, and to a man
   Of fifty, and such husbands are in plenty;   490
And yet, I think, instead of such a ONE
   'Twere better to have TWO of five-and-twenty,
Especially in countries near the sun:
   And now I think on 't, "mi vien in mente,"
Ladies even of the most uneasy virtue
Prefer a spouse whose age is short of thirty.

63

'Tis a sad thing, I cannot choose but say,
   And all the fault of that indecent sun,
Who cannot leave alone our helpless clay,
   But will keep baking, broiling, burning on,   500
That howsoever people fast and pray,
   The flesh is frail, and so the soul undone:
What men call gallantry, and gods adultery,
Is much more common where the climate's sultry.

64

Happy the nations of the moral North!
   Where all is virtue, and the winter season
Sends sin, without a rag on, shivering forth
   ('Twas snow that brought St. Anthony to
      reason):
Where juries cast up what a wife is worth,
   By laying whate'er sum, in mulct, they please
      on   510
The lover, who must pay a handsome price,
Because it is a marketable vice.

65

Alfonso was the name of Julia's lord,
   A man well looking for his years, and who
Was neither much beloved nor yet abhorred:
   They lived together as most people do,
Suffering each others' foibles by accord,
   And not exactly either *one* or *two*;
Yet he was jealous, though he did not show it,
For jealousy dislikes the world to know it.   520

494. "mi vien in mente": It comes to mind. **508. St.
Anthony:** should be St. Francis of Assisi, as Byron noted
on his proof-sheets. **510. mulct:** penalty.

66

Julia was—yet I never could see why—
   With Donna Inez quite a favorite friend;
Between their tastes there was small sympathy,
   For not a line had Julia ever penned:
Some people whisper (but, no doubt, they lie,
   For malice still imputes some private end)
That Inez had, ere Don Alfonso's marriage,
Forgot with him her very prudent carriage;

67

And that still keeping up the old connexion,
   Which time had lately rendered much more
      chaste,   530
She took his lady also in affection,
   And certainly this course was much the best:
She flattered Julia with her sage protection,
   And complimented Don Alfonso's taste;
And if she could not (who can?) silence scandal,
At least she left it a more slender handle.

68

I can't tell whether Julia saw the affair
   With other people's eyes, or if her own
Discoveries made, but none could be aware
   Of this, at least no symptom e'er was shown;   540
Perhaps she did not know, or did not care,
   Indifferent from the first, or callous grown:
I'm really puzzled what to think or say,
She kept her her counsel in so close a way.

69

Juan she saw, and, as a pretty child,
   Caressed him often—such a thing might be
Quite innocently done, and harmless styled,
   When she had twenty years, and thirteen he;
But I am not so sure I should have smiled
   When he was sixteen, Julia twenty-three;   550
These few short years make wondrous alterations,
Particularly amongst sun-burnt nations.

70

Whate'er the cause might be, they had become
   Changed; for the dame grew distant, the youth
      shy,

Their looks cast down, their greetings almost dumb,
   And much embarrassment in either eye;
There surely will be little doubt with some
   That Donna Julia knew the reason why,
But as for Juan, he had no more notion
Than he who never saw the sea of ocean.   560

71

Yet Julia's very coldness still was kind,
   And tremulously gentle her small hand
Withdrew itself from his, but left behind
   A little pressure, thrilling, and so bland
And slight, so very slight, that to the mind
   'Twas but a doubt; but ne'er magician's wand
Wrought change with all Armida's fairy art
Like what this light touch left on Juan's heart.

72

And if she met him, though she smiled no more,
   She looked a sadness sweeter than her
      smile,   570
As if her heart had deeper thoughts in store
   She must not own, but cherished more the while
For that compression in its burning core;
   Even innocence itself has many a wile,
And will not dare to trust itself with truth,
And love is taught hypocrisy from youth.

73

But passion most dissembles, yet betrays
   Even by its darkness; as the blackest sky
Foretells the heaviest tempest, it displays
   Its workings through the vainly guarded
      eye,   580
And in whatever aspect it arrays
   Itself, 'tis still the same hypocrisy:
Coldness or anger, even disdain or hate,
Are masks it often wears, and still too late.

74

Then there were sighs, the deeper for suppression,
   And stolen glances, sweeter for the theft,
And burning blushes, though for no transgression,
   Tremblings when met, and restlessness when left;

All these are little preludes to possession,
   Of which young passion cannot be bereft,   590
And merely tend to show how greatly love is
Embarrassed at first starting with a novice.

75

Poor Julia's heart was in an awkward state;
   She felt it going, and resolved to make
The noblest efforts for herself and mate,
   For honor's, pride's, religion's, virtue's sake.
Her resolutions were most truly great,
   And almost might have made a Tarquin quake:
She prayed the Virgin Mary for her grace,
As being the best judge of a lady's case.   600

76

She vowed she never would see Juan more,
   And next day paid a visit to his mother,
And looked extremely at the opening door,
   Which, by the Virgin's grace, let in another;
Grateful she was, and yet a little sore—
   Again it opens, it can be no other,
'Tis surely Juan now—No! I'm afraid
That night the Virgin was no further prayed.

77

She now determined that a virtuous woman
   Should rather face and overcome tempta-
      tion,   610
That flight was base and dastardly, and no man
   Should ever give her heart the least sensation;
That is to say, a thought beyond the common
   Preference, that we must feel upon occasion,
For people who are pleasanter than others,
But then they only seem so many brothers.

78

And even if by chance—and who can tell?
   The devil's so very sly—she should discover
That all within was not so very well,
   And, if still free, that such or such a lover   620

---

598. Tarquin: legendary Roman family noted for its proud, cruel kings.

Might please perhaps, a virtuous wife can quell
  Such thoughts, and be the better when they're
    over;
And if the man should ask, 'tis but denial:
I recommend young ladies to make trial.

79

And then there are such things as love divine,
  Bright and immaculate, unmixed and pure,
Such as the angels think so very fine,
  And matrons, who would be no less secure,
Platonic, perfect, "just such love as mine":
  Thus Julia said—and thought so, to be sure;   630
And so I'd have her think, were I the man
On whom her reveries celestial ran.

80

Such love is innocent, and may exist
  Between young persons without any danger:
A hand may first, and then a lip be kist;
  For my part, to such doings I'm a stranger,
But *hear* these freedoms form the utmost list
  Of all o'er which such love may be a ranger:
If people go beyond, 'tis quite a crime,
But not my fault—I tell them all in time.   640

81

Love, then, but love within its proper limits
  Was Julia's innocent determination
In young Don Juan's favor, and to him its
  Exertion might be useful on occasion;
And, lighted at too pure a shrine to dim its
  Ethereal lustre, with what sweet persuasion
He might be taught, by love and her together—
I really don't know what, nor Julia either.

82

Fraught with this fine intention, and well fenced
  In mail of proof—her purity of soul,   650
She, for the future of her strength convinced,
  And that her honor was a rock, or mole,
Exceeding sagely from that hour dispensed
  With any kind of troublesome control;
But whether Julia to the task was equal
Is that which must be mentioned in the sequel.

83

Her plan she deemed both innocent and feasible,
  And, surely, with a stripling of sixteen
Not scandal's fangs could fix on much that's
    seizable,
  Or if they did so, satisfied to mean   660
Nothing but what was good, her breast was peace-
    able:
  A quiet conscience makes one so serene!
Christians have burnt each other, quite persuaded
That all the Apostles would have done as they did.

84

And if in the mean time her husband died,
  But Heaven forbid that such a thought should
    cross
Her brain, though in a dream! (and then she
    sighed)
  Never could she survive that common loss;
But just suppose that moment should betide,
  I only say suppose it—*inter nos.*   670
(This should be *entre nous*, for Julia thought
In French, but then the rhyme would go for nought.)

85

I only say, suppose this supposition:
  Juan being then grown up to man's estate
Would fully suit a widow of condition,
  Even seven years hence it would not be too late;
And in the interim (to pursue this vision)
  The mischief, after all, could not be great,
For he would learn the rudiments of love,
I mean the seraph way of those above.   680

86

So much for Julia. Now we'll turn to Juan.
  Poor little fellow! he had no idea
Of his own case, and never hit the true one;
  In feelings quick as Ovid's Miss Medea,
He puzzled over what he found a new one,
  But not as yet imagined it could be a

684. Medea: a reference to Medea's sudden falling in
love with Jason (Ovid, *Metamorphoses*, VII, 10–12)

Thing quite in course, and not at all alarming,
Which, with a little patience, might grow charming.

87

Silent and pensive, idle, restless, slow,
   His home deserted for the lonely wood,   690
Tormented with a wound he could not know,
   His, like all deep grief, plunged in solitude:
I'm fond myself of solitude or so,
   But then, I beg it may be understood,
By solitude I mean a Sultan's, not
A hermit's, with a haram for a grot.

88

"Oh Love! in such a wilderness as this,
   Where transport and security entwine,
Here is the empire of thy perfect bliss,
   And here thou art a god indeed divine."   700
The bard I quote from does not sing amiss,
   With the exception of the second line,
For that same twining "transport and security"
Are twisted to a phrase of some obscurity.

89

The poet meant, no doubt, and thus appeals
   To the good sense and senses of mankind,
The very thing which everybody feels,
   As all have found on trial, or may find,
That no one likes to be disturbed at meals
   Or love.—I won't say more about
      "entwined"   710
Or "transport," as we knew all that before,
But beg "Security" will bolt the door.

90

Young Juan wandered by the glassy brooks,
   Thinking unutterable things; he threw
Himself at length within the leafy nooks
   Where the wild branch of the cork forest grew;
There poets find materials for their books,
   And every now and then we read them through,
So that their plan and prosody are eligible,

697–700. "Oh . . . divine": lines from Thomas Campbell's poem *Gertrude of Wyoming*.

Unless, like Wordsworth, they prove
   unintelligible.   720

91

He, Juan (and not Wordsworth), so pursued
   His self-communion with his own high soul,
Until his mighty heart, in its great mood,
   Had mitigated part, though not the whole
Of its disease; he did the best he could
   With things not very subject to control,
And turned, without perceiving his condition,
Like Coleridge, into a metaphysician.

92

He thought about himself, and the whole earth,
   Of man the wonderful, and of the stars,   730
And how the deuce they ever could have birth;
   And then he thought of earthquakes, and of wars,
How many miles the moon might have in girth,
   Of air-balloons, and of the many bars
To perfect knowledge of the boundless skies;—
And then he thought of Donna Julia's eyes.

93

In thoughts like these true wisdom may discern
   Longings sublime, and aspirations high,
Which some are born with, but the most part learn
   To plague themselves withal, they know not
      why: 740
'Twas strange that one so young should thus concern
   His brain about the action of the sky;
If *you* think 'twas philosophy that this did,
I can't help thinking puberty assisted.

94

He pored upon the leaves, and on the flowers,
   And heard a voice in all the winds; and then
He thought of wood-nymphs and immortal bowers,
   And how the goddesses came down to men:
He missed the pathway, he forgot the hours,
   And when he looked upon his watch again,   750
He found how much old Time had been a winner—
He also found that he had lost his dinner.

95

Sometimes he turned to gaze upon his book,
  Boscan, or Garcilasso;—by the wind
Even as the page is rustled while we look,
  So by the poesy of his own mind
Over the mystic leaf his soul was shook,
  As if 'twere one whereon magicians bind
Their spells, and give them to the passing gale
According to some good old woman's tale.   760

96

Thus would he while his lonely hours away
  Dissatisfied, nor knowing what he wanted;
Nor glowing reverie, nor poet's lay,
  Could yield his spirit that for which it panted,
A bosom whereon he his head might lay,
  And hear the heart beat with the love it granted,
With—several other things which I forget,
Or which, at least, I need not mention yet.

97

Those lonely walks, and lengthening reveries,
  Could not escape the gentle Julia's eyes;   770
She saw that Juan was not at his ease;
  But that which chiefly may, and must surprise,
Is, that the Donna Inez did not tease
  Her only son with question or surmise;
Whether it was she did not see, or would not,
Or, like all very clever people, could not.

98

This may seem strange, but yet 'tis very common;
  For instance—gentlemen, whose ladies take
Leave to o'erstep the written rights of woman,
  And break the—Which commandment is 't they
    break?   780
(I have forgot the number, and think no man
  Should rashly quote, for fear of a mistake.)
I say, when these same gentlemen are jealous,
They make some blunder, which their ladies tell us.

754. **Boscan, or Garcilasso:** Juan Boscan (1500–1544)
and Garcilaso de la Vega (1503–1536) were Spanish
poets.

99

A real husband always is suspicious,
  But still no less suspects in the wrong place,
Jealous of some one who had no such wishes,
  Or pandering blindly to his own disgrace,
By harboring some dear friend extremely vicious;
  The last indeed's infallibly the case: 790
And when the spouse and friend are gone off wholly,
He wonders at their vice, and not his folly.

100

Thus parents also are at times short-sighted;
  Though watchful as the lynx, they ne'er discover,
The while the wicked world beholds delighted,
  Young Hopeful's mistress, or Miss Fanny's lover,
Till some confounded escapade has blighted
  The plan of twenty years, and all is over;
And then the mother cries, the father swears,
And wonders why the devil he got heirs.   800

101

But Inez was so anxious, and so clear
  Of sight, that I must think, on this occasion,
She had some other motive much more near
  For leaving Juan to this new temptation,
But what that motive was, I shan't say here;
  Perhaps to finish Juan's education,
Perhaps to open Don Alfonso's eyes,
In case he thought his wife too great a prize.

102

It was upon a day, a summer's day;—
  Summer's indeed a very dangerous season,   810
And so is spring about the end of May;
  The sun, no doubt, is the prevailing reason;
But whatsoe'er the cause is, one may say,
  And stand convicted of more truth than treason,
That there are months which nature grows more
    merry in,—
March has its hares, and May must have its heroine.

103

'Twas on a summer's day—the sixth of June:—
  I like to be particular in dates,

Not only of the age, and year, but moon;
   They are a sort of post-house, where the
      Fates   820
Change horses, making history change its tune,
   Then spur away o'er empires and o'er states,
Leaving at last not much besides chronology,
Excepting the post-obits of theology.

104

'Twas on the sixth of June, about the hour
   Of half-past six—perhaps still nearer seven—
When Julia sate within as pretty a bower
   As e'er held houri in that heathenish heaven
Described by Mahomet, and Anacreon Moore,
   To whom the lyre and laurels have been
      given,   830
With all the trophies of triumphant song—
He won them well, and may he wear them long!

105

She sate, but not alone; I know not well
   How this same interview had taken place,
And even if I knew, I should not tell—
   People should hold their tongues in any case;
No matter how or why the thing befell,
   But there were she and Juan, face to face—
When two such faces are so, 'twould be wise,
But very difficult, to shut their eyes.   840

106

How beautiful she looked! her conscious heart
   Glowed in her cheek, and yet she felt no wrong.
Oh Love! how perfect is thy mystic art,
   Strengthening the weak, and trampling on the
      strong!
How self-deceitful is the sagest part
   Of mortals whom thy lure hath led along!—
The precipice she stood on was immense,
So was her creed in her own innocence.

824. post-obits: in a legal sense, bonds that mature after death. Byron here is probably applying the terminology to the churches' promises of a life after death. **829. Anacreon Moore:** a name given to the poet Thomas Moore, who began his career by publishing a translation of Anacreon's odes.

107

She thought of her own strength, and Juan's youth,
   And of the folly of all prudish fears,   850
Victorious virtue, and domestic truth,
   And then of Don Alfonso's fifty years:
I wish these last had not occurred, in sooth,
   Because that number rarely much endears,
And through all climes, the snowy and the sunny,
Sounds ill in love, whate'er it may in money.

108

When people say, "I've told you *fifty* times,"
   They mean to scold, and very often do;
When poets say, "I've written *fifty* rhymes,"
   They make you dread that they'll recite them
      too;   860
In gangs of *fifty*, thieves commit their crimes;
   At *fifty* love for love is rare, 'tis true,
But then, no doubt, it equally as true is,
A good deal may be bought for *fifty* Louis.

109

Julia had honor, virtue, truth, and love
   For Don Alfonso; and she inly swore,
By all the vows below to powers above,
   She never would disgrace the ring she wore,
Nor leave a wish which wisdom might reprove;
   And while she pondered this, besides much
      more,   870
One hand on Juan's carelessly was thrown,
Quite by mistake—she thought it was her own;

110

Unconsciously she leaned upon the other,
   Which played within the tangles of her hair;
And to contend with thoughts she could not smother
   She seemed, by the distraction of her air,
'Twas surely very wrong in Juan's mother
   To leave together this imprudent pair,
She who for many years had watched her son so—
I'm very certain *mine* would not have done so.   880

111

The hand which still held Juan's, by degrees
   Gently, but palpably confirmed its grasp,

As if it said, "Detain me, if you please";
    Yet there's no doubt she only meant to clasp
His fingers with a pure Platonic squeeze;
    She would have shrunk as from a toad or asp,
Had she imagined such a thing could rouse
A feeling dangerous to a prudent spouse.

112

I cannot know what Juan thought of this,
    But what he did, is much what you would
        do;   890
His young lip thanked it with a grateful kiss,
    And then, abashed at its own joy, withdrew
In deep despair, lest he had done amiss,—
    Love is so very timid when 'tis new:
She blushed, and frowned not, but she strove to
        speak,
And held her tongue, her voice was grown so weak.

113

The sun set, and up rose the yellow moon;
    The devil's in the moon for mischief; they
Who called her CHASTE, methinks, began too soon
    Their nomenclature; there is not a day,   900
The longest, not the twenty-first of June,
    Sees half the business in a wicked way,
On which three single hours of moonshine smile—
And then she looks so modest all the while.

114

There is a dangerous silence in that hour,
    A stillness, which leaves room for the full soul
To open all itself, without the power
    Of calling wholly back its self-control;
The silver light which, hallowing tree and tower,
    Sheds beauty and deep softness o'er the
        whole,   910
Breathes also to the heart, and o'er it throws
A loving languor, which is not repose.

115

And Julia sate with Juan, half embraced
    And half retiring from the glowing arm,
Which trembled like the bosom where 'twas placed;
    Yet still she must have thought there was no harm,

Or else 'twere easy to withdraw her waist;
    But then the situation had its charm,
And then——God knows what next—I can't go on;
I'm almost sorry that I e'er begun.   920

116

Oh Plato! Plato! you have paved the way,
    With your confounded phantasies, to more
Immoral conduct by the fancied sway
    Your system feigns o'er the controlless core
Of human hearts, than all the long array
    Of poets and romancers:—You're a bore,
A charlatan, a coxcomb—and have been,
At best, no better than a go-between.

117

And Julia's voice was lost, except in sighs,
    Until too late for useful conversation;   930
The tears were gushing from her gentle eyes,
    I wish, indeed, they had not had occasion;
But who, alas! can love, and then be wise?
    Not that remorse did not oppose temptation;
A little still she strove, and much repented,
And whispering "I will ne'er consent"—consented.

118

'Tis said that Xerxes offered a reward
    To those who could invent him a new pleasure:
Methinks the requisition's rather hard,
    And must have cost his majesty a treasure;   940
For my part, I'm a moderate-minded bard,
    Fond of a little love (which I call leisure);
I care not for new pleasures, as the old
Are quite enough for me, so they but hold.

119

Oh Pleasure! you're indeed a pleasant thing,
    Although one must be damned for you, no doubt:
I make a resolution every spring
    Of reformation, ere the year run out,
But somehow, this my vestal vow takes wing,
    Yet still, I trust, it may be kept throughout; 950
I'm very sorry, very much ashamed,
And mean, next winter, to be quite reclaimed.

120

Here my chaste Muse a liberty must take—
    Start not; still chaster reader—she'll be nice
      hence-
Forward, and there is no great cause to quake;
    This liberty is a poetic licence,
Which some irregularity may make
    In the design, and as I have a high sense
Of Aristotle and the Rules, 'tis fit
To beg his pardon when I err a bit.   960

121

This licence is to hope the reader will
    Suppose from June the sixth (the fatal day
Without whose epoch my poetic skill
    For want of facts would all be thrown away),
But keeping Julia and Don Juan still
    In sight, that several months have passed; we'll
      say
'Twas in November, but I'm not so sure
About the day—the era's more obscure.

122

We'll talk of that anon.—'Tis sweet to hear
    At midnight on the blue and moonlit deep   970
The song and oar of Adria's gondolier,
    By distance mellowed, o'er the waters sweet;
'Tis sweet to see the evening star appear;
    'Tis sweet to listen as the night-winds creep
From leaf to leaf; 'tis sweet to view on high
The rainbow, based on ocean, span the sky.

123

'Tis sweet to hear the watch-dog's honest bark
    Bay deep-mouthed welcome as we draw near
      home;
'Tis sweet to know there is an eye will mark
    Our coming, and look brighter when we
      come;   980
'Tis sweet to be awakened by the lark,
    Or lulled by falling waters; sweet the hum

Of bees, the voice of girls, the song of birds,
The lisp of children, and their earliest words.

124

Sweet is the vintage, when the showering grapes
    In Bacchanal profusion reel to earth,
Purple and gushing; sweet are our escapes
    From civic revelry to rural mirth;
Sweet to the miser are his glittering heaps,
    Sweet to the father is his first-born's birth,   990
Sweet is revenge—especially to women,
Pillage to soldiers, prize-money to seamen.

125

Sweet is a legacy, and passing sweet
    The unexpected death of some old lady
Or gentleman of seventy years complete,
    Who've made "us youth" wait too—too long
      already
For an estate, or cash, or country seat,
    Still breaking, but with stamina so steady
That all the Israelites are fit to mob its
Next owner for their double-damned post-
      obits.   1000

126

'Tis sweet to win, no matter how, one's laurels,
    By blood or ink; 'tis sweet to put an end
To strife; 'tis sometimes sweet to have our quarrels,
    Particularly with a tiresome friend:
Sweet is old wine in bottles, ale in barrels;
    Dear is the helpless creature we defend
Against the world; and dear the schoolboy spot
We ne'er forget, though there we are forgot.

127

But sweeter still than this, than these, than all,
    Is first and passionate love—it stands alone,   1010
Like Adam's recollection of his fall;
    The tree of knowledge has been plucked—all's
      known—

---

971. **Adria:** the Adriatic sea. The specific reference is
to the singing gondoliers of Venice.

996. **"us youth":** The aging Falstaff complains, "They
hate us youth" in I *Henry IV*, II, ii, 93.

And life yields nothing further to recall
  Worthy of this ambrosial sin, so shown,
No doubt in fable, as the unforgiven
Fire which Prometheus filched for us from heaven.

128

Man's a strange animal, and makes strange use
  Of his own nature, and the various arts,
And likes particularly to produce
  Some new experiment to show his parts;   1020
This is the age of oddities let loose,
  Where different talents find their different marts;
You'd best begin with truth, and when you've lost
      your
Labor, there's a sure market for imposture.

129

What opposite discoveries we have seen!
  (Signs of true genius, and of empty pockets.)
One makes new noses, one a guillotine,
  One breaks your bones, one sets them in their
      sockets;
But vaccination certainly has been
  A kind antithesis to Congreve's rockets,   1030
With which the Doctor paid off an old pox,
By borrowing a new one from an ox.

130

Bread has been made (indifferent) from potatoes;
  And galvanism has set some corpses grinning,
But has not answered like the apparatus
  Of the Humane Society's beginning,
By which men are unsuffocated gratis:
  What wondrous new machines have late been
      spinning!
I said the small pox has gone out of late;
Perhaps it may be followed by the great.   1040

1030. **Congreve's rockets:** Sir William Congreve (1772–1828) had invented a rocket used at the battle of Leipzig (1813). 1031. **Doctor:** Edward Jenner (1749–1823) made the first vaccine against smallpox in 1796. 1034. **galvanism:** Luigi Galvani (1737–1798), who gave his name to the process of galvanism by experiments in creating muscular movement by sending electric currents through a corpse. 1036–37: **Humane . . . gratis:** a reference to the Royal Humane Society, founded in 1774 to revive drowning persons. 1040. **great [pox]:** syphilis.

131

'Tis said the great came from America;
  Perhaps it may set out on its return,—
The population there so spreads, they say
  'Tis grown high time to thin it in its turn,
With war, or plague, or famine, any way,
  So that civilisation they may learn;
And which in ravage the more loathsome evil is—
Their real lues, or our pseudo-syphilis?

132

This is the patent age of new inventions
  For killing bodies, and for saving souls,   1050
All propagated with the best intentions;
  Sir Humphrey Davy's lantern, by which coals
Are safely mined for in the mode he mentions,
  Tombuctoo travels, voyages to the Poles,
Are ways to benefit mankind, as true
Perhaps, as shooting them at Waterloo.

133

Man's a phenomenon, one knows not what,
  And wonderful beyond all wondrous measure;
'Tis pity though, in this sublime world, that
  Pleasure's a sin, and sometimes sin's a
      pleasure;   1060
Few mortals know what end they would be at,
  But whether glory, power, or love, or treasure,
The path is through perplexing ways, and when
The goal is gained, we die, you know—and then—

134

What then?—I do not know, no more do you—
  And so good night.—Return we to our story:
'Twas in November, when fine days are few,
  And the far mountains wax a little hoary,
And clap a white cape on their mantles blue;
  And the sea dashes round the promontory,   1070
And the loud breaker boils against the rock,
And sober suns must set at five o'clock.

1052. **lantern:** Sir Humphrey Davy invented a safety lamp for coal miners. 1054. **Tombuctoo . . . Poles:** a reference to contemporary travel books.

135

'Twas, as the watchmen say, a cloudy night;
   No moon, no stars, the wind was low or loud
By gusts, and many a sparkling hearth was bright
   With the piled wood, round which the family
      crowd;
There's something cheerful in that sort of light,
   Even as a summer sky's without a cloud;
I'm fond of fire, and crickets, and all that,
A lobster salad, and champagne, and chat.   1080

136

'Twas midnight—Donna Julia was in bed,
   Sleeping, most probably,—when at her door
Arose a clatter might awake the dead,
   If they had never been awoke before,
And that they have been so we all have read,
   And are to be so, at the least, once more;—
The door was fastened, but with voice and fist
First knocks were heard, then "Madam—Madam—
      hist!

137

"For God's sake, Madam—Madam—here's my
      master,
   With more than half the city at his back—   1090
Was ever heard of such a curst disaster!
   'Tis not my fault—I kept good watch—Alack!
Do pray undo the bolt a little faster—
   They're on the stair just now, and in a crack
Will all be here; perhaps he yet may fly—
Surely the window's not so *very* high!"

138

By this time Don Alfonso was arrived,
   With torches, friends, and servants in great
      number;
The major part of them had long been wived,
   And therefore paused not to disturb the
      slumber   1100
Of any wicked woman, who contrived
   By stealth her husband's temples to encumber:
Examples of this kind are so contagious,
Were *one* not punished, *all* would be outrageous.

139

I can't tell how, or why, or what suspicion
   Could enter into Don Alfonso's head;
But for a cavalier of his condition
   It surely was exceedingly ill-bred,
Without a word of previous admonition,
   To hold a levee round his lady's bed,   1110
And summon lackeys, armed with fire and sword,
To prove himself the thing he most abhorred.

140

Poor Donna Julia! starting as from sleep
   (Mind—that I do not say—she had not slept),
Began at once to scream, and yawn, and weep;
   Her maid, Antonia, who was an adept,
Contrived to fling the bed-clothes in a heap,
   As if she had just now from out them crept:
I can't tell why she should take all this trouble
To prove her mistress had been sleeping
      double.   1120

141

But Julia mistress, and Antonia maid,
   Appeared like two poor harmless women, who
Of goblins, but still more of men afraid,
   Had thought one man might be deterred by two,
And therefore side by side were gently laid,
   Until the hours of absence should run through,
And truant husband should return, and say,
"My dear, I was the first who came away."

142

Now Julia found at length a voice, and cried,
   "In heaven's name, Don Alfonso, what d' ye
      mean?   1130
Has madness seized you? would that I had died
   Ere such a monster's victim I had been!
What may this midnight violence betide,
   A sudden fit of drunkenness or spleen?
Dare you suspect me, whom the thought would
      kill?
Search, then, the room!"—Alfonso said, "I will."

143

He searched, *they* searched, and rummaged every-
    where,
  Closet and clothes-press, chest and window-seat.
And found much linen, lace, and several pair
  Of stockings, slippers, brushes, combs,
    complete,   1140
With other articles of ladies fair,
  To keep them beautiful, or leave them neat:
Arras they pricked and curtains with their swords,
And wounded several shutters, and some boards.

144

Under the bed they searched, and there they
    found—
  No matter what—it was not that they sought;
They opened windows, gazing if the ground
  Had signs of footmarks, but the earth said
    nought;
And then they stared each other's faces round:
  'Tis odd, not one of all these seekers
    thought,   1150
And seems to me almost a sort of blunder,
Of looking *in* the bed as well as under.

145

During this inquisition Julia's tongue
  Was not asleep—"Yes, search and search," she
    cried,
"Insult on insult heap, and wrong on wrong!
  It was for this that I became a bride!
For this in silence I have suffered long
  A husband like Alfonso at my side;
But now I'll bear no more, nor here remain,
If there be law or lawyers in all Spain.   1160

146

"Yes, Don Alfonso! husband now no more.
  If ever you indeed deserved the name,
Is't worthy of your years?—you have three-score—
  Fifty, or sixty, it is all the same—
Is't wise or fitting, causeless to explore
  For facts against a virtuous woman's fame?
Ungrateful, perjured, barbarous Don Alfonso,
How dare you think your lady would go on so?

147

"Is it for this I have disdained to hold
  The common privileges of my sex?   1170
That I have chosen a confessor so old
  And deaf, that any other it would vex,
And never once he has had cause to scold,
  But found my very innocence perplex
So much, he always doubted I was married—
How sorry you will be when I've miscarried!

148

"Was it for this that no Cortejo e'er
  I yet have chosen from out the youth of Seville?
Is it for this I scarce went anywhere,
  Except to bull-fights, mass, play, rout, and
    revel?   1180
Is it for this, whate'er my suitors were,
  I favored none—nay, was almost uncivil?
Is it for this that General Count O'Reilly,
Who took Algiers, declares I used him vilely?

149

"Did not the Italian Musico Cazzani
  Sing at my heart six months at least in vain?
Did not his countryman, Count Corniani,
  Call me the only virtuous wife in Spain?
Were there not also Russians, English, many?
  The Count Strongstroganoff I put in pain,   1190
And Lord Mount Coffeehouse, the Irish peer,
Who killed himself for love (with wine) last year.

150

"Have I not had two bishops at my feet?
  The Duke of Ichar, and Don Fernan Nunez?
And is it thus a faithful wife you treat?
  I wonder in what quarter now the moon is:
I praise your vast forbearance not to beat
  Me also, since the time so opportune is—

1177. Cortejo: "The Spanish 'Cortejo' is much the same
as the Italian 'Cavalier Servente'" (Byron's note).
1183. O'Reilly: "Donna Julia here made a mistake.
Count O'Reilly did not take Algiers but Algiers very
nearly took him; he and his army retreated with great
loss, and not much credit, from before that city in the
year 1775" (Byron's note).

Oh, valiant man! with sword drawn and cocked
    trigger,
Now, tell me, don't you cut a pretty figure?   1200

151

"Was it for this you took your sudden journey,
    Under pretence of business indispensable,
With that sublime of rascals your attorney,
    Whom I see standing there, and looking sensible
Of having played the fool? though both I spurn, he
    Deserves the worst, his conduct's less defensible,
Because, no doubt, 'twas for his dirty fee,
And not from any love to you nor me.

152

"If he comes here to take a deposition,
    By all means let the gentleman proceed;   1210
You've made the apartment in a fit condition:—
    There's pen and ink for you, sir, when you
      need—
Let everything be noted with precision,
    I would not you for nothing should be fee'd—
But as my maid's undrest, pray turn your spies out."
"Oh!" sobbed Antonia, "I could tear their eyes out."

153

"There is the closet, there the toilet, there
    The antechamber—search them under, over;
There is the sofa, there the great arm-chair,
    The chimney—which would really hold a
      lover.
I wish to sleep, and beg you will take care   1220
    And make no further noise, till you discover
The secret cavern of this lurking treasure—
And when 'tis found, let me, too, have that pleasure.

154

"And now, Hidalgo! now that you have thrown
    Doubt upon me, confusion over all,
Pray have the courtesy to make it known
    Who is the man you search for? how d'ye call
Him? what's his lineage? let him but be shown—
    I hope he's young and handsome—is he
      tall?   1230

Tell me— and be assured, that since you stain
Mine honor thus, it shall not be in vain.

155

"At least, perhaps, he has not sixty years,
    At that age he would be too old for slaughter,
Or for so young a husband's jealous fears—
    (Antonia! let me have a glass of water.)
I am ashamed of having shed these tears,
    They are unworthy of my father's daughter;
My mother dreamed not in my natal hour,
That I should fall into a monster's power.   1240

156

"Perhaps 'tis of Antonia you are jealous,
    You saw that she was sleeping by my side,
When you broke in upon us with your fellows;
    Look where you please—we've nothing, sir, to
      hide;
Only another time, I trust, you'll tell us,
    Or for the sake of decency abide
A moment at the door, that we may be
Dressed to receive so much good company.

157

"And now, sir, I have done, and say no more;
    The little I have said may serve to show   1250
The guileless heart in silence may grieve o'er
    The wrongs to whose exposure it is slow:—
I leave you to your conscience as before,
    'Twill one day ask you, *why* you used me so?
God grant you feel not then the bitterest grief!
Antonia! where's my pocket-handkerchief?"

158

She ceased, and turned upon her pillow; pale
    She lay, her dark eyes flashing through their
      tears,
Like skies that rain and lighten; as a veil,
    Waved and o'ershading her wan cheek,
      appears   1260
Her streaming hair; the black curls strive, but fail,
    To hide the glossy shoulder, which uprears
Its snow through all;—her soft lips lie apart,
And louder than her breathing beats her heart.

159

The Senhor Don Alfonso stood confused;
   Antonia bustled round the ransacked room,
And, turning up her nose, with looks abused
   Her master, and his myrmidons, of whom
Not one, except the attorney, was amused;
   He, like Achates, faithful to the tomb,   1270
So there were quarrels, cared not for the cause,
Knowing they must be settled by the laws.

160

With prying snub-nose, and small eyes, he stood,
   Following Antonia's motions here and there,
With much suspicion in his attitude;
   For reputations he had little care;
So that a suit or action were made good,
   Small pity had he for the young and fair,
And ne'er believed in negatives, till these
Were proved by competent false witnesses.   1280

161

But Don Alfonso stood with downcast looks,
   And, truth to say, he made a foolish figure;
When, after searching in five hundred nooks,
   And treating a young wife with so much rigor,
He gained no point, except some self-rebukes,
   Added to those his lady with such vigor
Had poured upon him for the last half hour,
Quick, thick, and heavy—as a thunder-shower.

162

At first he tried to hammer an excuse,
   To which the sole reply was tears and
      sobs,   1290
And indications of hysterics, whose
   Prologue is always certain throes, and throbs,
Gasps, and whatever else the owners choose:
   Alfonso saw his wife, and thought of Job's;
He saw too, in perspective, her relations,
And then he tried to muster all his patience.

163

He stood in act to speak, or rather stammer,
   But sage Antonia cut him short before
The anvil of his speech received the hammer,
   With "Pray, sir, leave the room and say no
      more,   1300
Or madam dies."—Alfonso muttered, "D—n her."
   But nothing else, the time of words was o'er;
He cast a rueful look or two, and did,
He knew not wherefore, that which he was bid.

164

With him retired his *"posse comitatus,"*
   The attorney last, who lingered near the door
Reluctantly, still tarrying there as late as
   Antonia let him—not a little sore
At this most strange and unexplained *"hiatus"*
   In Don Alfonso's facts, which just now
      wore   1310
An awkward look; as he revolved the case,
The door was fastened in his legal face.

165

No sooner was it bolted, than—Oh shame!
   Oh sin! Oh sorrow! and Oh womankind!
How can you do such things and keep your fame,
   Unless this world, and t' other too, be blind?
Nothing so dear as an unfilched good name!
   But to proceed—for there is more behind:
With much heartfelt reluctance be it said,
Young Juan slipped, half-smothered, from the
      bed.   1320

166

He had been hid—I don't pretend to say
   How, nor can I indeed describe the where—
Young, slender, and packed easily, he lay,
   No doubt, in little compass, round or square;
But pity him I neither must nor may
   His suffocation by that pretty pair;

1270. **Achates:** the loyal friend of Aeneas in Virgil's
Aeneid.

1305. *"posse comitatus":* a body of citizens summoned
to keep order.

'Twere better, sure, to die so, than be shut
With maudlin Clarence in his Malmsey butt.

167

And, secondly, I pity not, because
   He had no business to commit a sin,   1330
Forbid by heavenly, fined by human laws,
   At least 'twas rather early to begin;
But at sixteen the conscience rarely gnaws
   So much as when we call our old debts in
At sixty years, and draw the accompts of evil,
And find a deuced balance with the devil.

168

Of his position I can give no notion:
   'Tis written in the Hebrew Chronicle,
How the physicians, leaving pill and potion,
   Prescribed, by way of blister, a young
     belle,   1340
When old King David's blood grew dull in motion,
   And that the medicine answered very well;
Perhaps 'twas in a different way applied,
For David lived, but Juan nearly died.

169

What's to be done? Alfonso will be back
   The moment he has sent his fools away.
Antonia's skill was put upon the rack,
   But no device could be brought into play—
And how to parry the renewed attack?
   Besides, it wanted but few hours of day: 1350
Antonia puzzled; Julia did not speak,
But pressed her bloodless lip to Juan's cheek.

170

He turned his lip to hers, and with his hand
   Called back the tangles of her wandering hair;
Even then their love they could not all command,
   And half forgot their danger and despair:
Antonia's patience now was at a stand—
   "Come, come, 'tis no time now for fooling there,"

1328. **Clarence:** See *Richard III*, I, iv, 276. The Duke
of Clarence was drowned in a barrel of Malmsey wine.
1338. **Hebrew Chronicle:** See *I Kings,* 1:1–3.

She whispered in great wrath—"I must deposit
This pretty gentleman within the closet: 1360

171

"Pray, keep your nonsense for some luckier night—
   Who can have put my master in this mood?
What will become on't—I'm in such a fright,
   The devil's in the urchin, and no good—
Is this a time for giggling? this a plight?
   Why, don't you know that it may end in blood?
You'll lose your life, and I shall lose my place,
My mistress all, for that half-girlish face.

172

"Had it but been for a stout cavalier
   Of twenty-five or thirty—(come, make
     haste)   1370
But for a child, what piece of work is here!
   I really, madam, wonder at your taste—
(Come, sir, get in)—my master must be near:
   There, for the present, at the least, he's fast,
And if we can but till the morning keep
Our counsel—(Juan, mind, you must not sleep)."

173

Now, Don Alfonso entering, but alone,
   Closed the oration of the trusty maid:
She loitered, and he told her to be gone,
   An order somewhat sullenly obeyed;   1380
However, present remedy was none,
   And no great good seemed answered if she staid;
Regarding both with slow and sidelong view,
She snuffed the candle, curtsied, and withdrew.

174

Alfonso paused a minute—then begun
   Some strange excuses for his late proceeding:
He would not justify what he had done,
   To say the best, it was extreme ill-breeding;
But there were ample reasons for it, none
   Of which he specified in this his pleading: 1390
His speech was a fine sample, on the whole,
Of rhetoric, which the learned call "*rigmarole.*"

175

Julia said nought; though all the while there rose
　　A ready answer, which at once enables
A matron, who her husband's foible knows,
　　By a few timely words to turn the tables,
Which, if it does not silence, still must pose,—
　　Even if it should comprise a pack of fables;
'Tis to retort with firmness, and when he
Suspects with *one,* do you reproach with
　　　　three.   1400

176

Julia, in fact, had tolerable grounds,—
　　Alfonso's loves with Inez were well known;
But whether 'twas that one's own guilt confounds—
　　But that can't be, as has been often shown,
A lady with apologies abounds;—
　　It might be that her silence sprang alone
From delicacy to Don Juan's ear,
To whom she knew his mother's fame was dear.

177

There might be one more motive, which makes two,
　　Alfonso ne'er to Juan had alluded,—   1410
Mentioned his jealousy, but never who
　　Had been the happy lover, he concluded,
Concealed amongst his premises; 'tis true,
　　His mind the more o'er this its mystery brooded;
To speak of Inez now were, one may say,
Like throwing Juan in Alfonso's way.

178

A hint, in tender cases, is enough;
　　Silence is best: besides there is a *tact*—
(That modern phrase appears to me sad stuff,
　　But it will serve to keep my verse com-
　　　　pact)—   1420
Which keeps, when pushed by questions rather
　　　　rough,
　　A lady always distant from the fact:
The charming creatures lie with such a grace,
There's nothing so becoming to the face.

179

They blush, and we believe them, at least I
　　Have always done so; 'tis of no great use,

In any case, attempting a reply,
　　For then their eloquence grows quite profuse;
And when at length they're out of breath, they sigh,
　　And cast their languid eyes down, and let
　　　　loose   1430
A tear or two, and then we make it up;
And then— and then—and then—sit down and
　　　　sup.

180

Alfonso closed his speech, and begged her pardon,
　　Which Julia half withheld, and then half granted,
And laid conditions, he thought very hard, on,
　　Denying several little things he wanted:
He stood like Adam lingering near his garden,
　　With useless penitence perplexed and haunted,
Beseeching she no further would refuse,
When, lo! he stumbled o'er a pair of shoes.   1440

181

A pair of shoes!—what then? not much, if they
　　Are such as fit with ladies' feet, but these
(No one can tell how much I grieve to say)
　　Were masculine; to see them, and to seize,
Was but a moment's act.—Ah! well-a-day!
　　My teeth begin to chatter, my veins freeze—
Alfonso first examined well their fashion,
And then flew out into another passion.

182

He left the room for his relinquished sword,
　　And Julia instant to the closet flew.   1450
"Fly, Juan, fly; for heaven's sake—not a word—
　　The door is open—you may yet slip through
The passage you so often have explored—
　　Here is the garden-key—Fly—fly—Adieu!
Haste—haste! I hear Alfonso's hurrying feet—
Day has not broke—there's no one in the street."

183

None can say that this was not good advice,
　　The only mischief was, it came too late;
Of all experience 'tis the usual price,
　　A sort of income-tax laid on by fate: 1460
Juan had reached the room-door in a trice,
　　And might have done so by the garden-gate,

But met Alfonso in his dressing-gown,
Who threatened death—so Juan knocked him
    down.

184

Dire was the scuffle, and out went the light;
    Antonia cried out "Rape!" and Julia "Fire!"
But not a servant stirred to aid the fight.
    Alfonso, pommelled to his heart's desire,
Swore lustily he'd be revenged this night;
    And Juan, too, blasphemed an octave
        higher;   1470
His blood was up: though young, he was a Tartar,
And not at all disposed to prove a martyr.

185

Alfonso's sword had dropped ere he could draw it,
    And they continued battling hand to hand,
For Juan very luckily ne'er saw it;
    His temper not being under great command,
If at that moment he had chanced to claw it,
    Alfonso's days had not been in the land
Much longer.—Think of husbands', lovers' lives!
And how ye may be doubly widows—wives!   1480

186

Alfonso grappled to detain the foe,
    And Juan throttled him to get away,
And blood ('twas from the nose) began to flow;
    At last, as they more faintly wrestling lay,
Juan contrived to give an awkward blow,
    And then his only garment quite gave way;
He fled, like Joseph, leaving it; but there,
I doubt, all likeness ends between the pair.

187

Lights came at length, and men, and maids, who
        found
    An awkward spectacle their eyes before;   1490
Antonia in hysterics, Julia swooned,
    Alfonso leaning, breathless, by the door;
Some half-torn drapery scattered on the ground,
    Some blood, and several footsteps, but no more:

1487. **Joseph:** a reference to the story of Joseph, who
resisted the advances of King Potiphar's wife (*Genesis*
39:7–18).

Juan the gate gained, turned the key about,
And liking not the inside, locked the out.

188

Here ends this canto.—Need I sing, or say,
    How Juan, naked, favored by the night,
Who favors what she should not, found his way,
    And reached his home in an unseemly
        plight?   1500
The pleasant scandal which arose next day,
    The nine days' wonder which was brought to
        light,
And how Alfonso sued for a divorce,
Were in the English newspapers, of course.

189

If you would like to see the whole proceedings,
    The depositions and the cause at full,
The names of all the witnesses, the pleadings
    Of counsel to nonsuit, or to annul,
There's more than one edition, and the readings
    Are various, but they none of them are
        dull;   1510
The best is that in short-hand ta'en by Gurney,
Who to Madrid on purpose made a journey.

190

But Donna Inez, to divert the train
    Of one of the most circulating scandals
That had for centuries been known in Spain,
    At least since the retirement of the Vandals,
First vowed (and never had she vowed in vain)
    To Virgin Mary several pounds of candles;
And then, by the advice of some old ladies,
She sent her son to be shipped off from
        Cadiz.   1520

191

She had resolved that he should travel through
    All European climes, by land or sea,
To mend his former morals, and get new,
    Especially in France and Italy

1511. **Gurney:** William Gurney (1777–1855), famous
shorthand specialist, reported many of the most celebrated trials.

(At least this is the thing most people do).
   Julia was sent into a convent: she
Grieved, but, perhaps, her feelings may be better
Shown in the following copy of her Letter:—

192

"They tell me 'tis decided you depart:
   'Tis wise—'tis well, but not the less a
      pain;   1530
I have no further claim on your young heart,
   Mine is the victim, and would be again:
To love too much has been the only art
   I used;—I write in haste, and if a stain
Be on this sheet, 'tis not what it appears;
My eyeballs burn and throb, but have no tears.

193

"I loved, I love you, for this love have lost
   State, station, heaven, mankind's, my own
      esteem,
And yet cannot regret what it hath cost,
   So dear is still the memory of that dream;   1540
Yet, if I name my guilt, 'tis not to boast,
   None can deem harshlier of me than I deem.
I trace this scrawl because I cannot rest—
I've nothing to reproach or to request.

194

"Man's love is of man's life a thing apart,
   'Tis woman's whole existence; man may range
The court, camp, church, the vessel, and the mart;
   Sword, gown, gain, glory, offer in exchange
Pride, fame, ambition, to fill up his heart,
   And few there are whom these cannot
      estrange;   1550
Men have all these resources, we but one,
To love again, and be again undone.

195

"You will proceed in pleasure, and in pride,
   Beloved and loving many; all is o'er
For me on earth, except some years to hide
   My shame and sorrow deep in my heart's core:
These I could bear, but cannot cast aside
   The passion which still rages as before,—

And so farewell—forgive me, love me—No,
That word is idle now—but let it go.   1560

196

"My breast has been all weakness, is so yet;
   But still I think I can collect my mind;
My blood still rushes where my spirit's set,
   As roll the waves before the settled wind;
My heart is feminine, nor can forget—
   To all, except one image, madly blind;
So shakes the needle, and so stands the pole,
As vibrates my fond heart to my fixed soul.

197

"I have no more to say, but linger still,
   And dare not set my seal upon this sheet,   1570
And yet I may as well the task fulfil,
   My misery can scarce be more complete:
I had not lived till now, could sorrow kill;
   Death shuns the wretch who fain the blow would
      meet,
And I must even survive this last adieu,
And bear with life to love and pray for you!"

198

This note was written upon gilt-edged paper
   With a neat little crow-quill, slight and new;
Her small white hand could hardly reach the taper,
   It trembled as magnetic needles do,   1580
And yet she did not let one tear escape her:
   The seal a sun-flower; *Elle vous suit partout,*"
The motto, cut upon a white cornelian;
The wax was superfine, its hue vermilion.

199

This was Don Juan's earliest scrape; but whether
   I shall proceed with his adventures is
Dependent on the public altogether;
   We'll see, however, what they say to this,
Their favor in an author's cap's a feather,
   And no great mischief's done by their
      caprice;   1590

1582. *"Elle vous suit partout"*: "She follows you every-where." **1583. cornelian:** stone of translucent quartz.

And if their approbation we experience,
Perhaps they'll have some more about a year hence.

200

My poem's epic, and is meant to be
    Divided in twelve books; each book containing,
With love, and war, a heavy gale at sea,
    A list of ships, and captains, and kings reigning,
New characters; the episodes are three:
    A panoramic view of hell's in training
After the style of Virgil and of Homer,
So that my name of Epic's no misnomer.   1600

201

All these things will be specified in time,
    With strict regard to Aristotle's rules,
The *Vade Mecum* of the true sublime,
    Which makes so many poets, and some fools:
Prose poets like blank-verse, I'm fond of rhyme,
    Good workmen never quarrel with their tools;
I've got new mythological machinery,
And very handsome supernatural scenery.

202

There's only one slight difference between
    Me and my epic brethren gone before,   1610
And here the advantage is my own, I ween
    (Not that I have not several merits more,
But this will more peculiarly be seen);
    They so embellish, that 'tis quite a bore
Their labyrinth of fables to thread through,
Whereas this story's actually true.

203

If any person doubt it, I appeal
    To history, tradition, and to facts,
To newspapers, whose truth all know and feel,
    To plays in five, and operas in three acts: 1620
All these confirm my statement a good deal,
    But that which more completely faith exacts
Is, that myself, and several now in Seville,
Saw Juan's last elopement with the devil.

1603. *Vade Mecum*: a guide or handbook (lit. "Go with me").

204

If ever I should condescend to prose,
    I'll write poetical commandments, which
Shall supersede beyond all doubt all those
    That went before; in these I shall enrich
My text with many things that no one knows,
    And carry precept to the highest pitch: 1630
I'll call the work "Longinus o'er a Bottle,
Or, Every Poet his *own* Aristotle."

205

Thou shalt believe in Milton, Dryden, Pope;
    Thou shalt not set up Wordsworth, Coleridge,
        Southey;
Because the first is crazed beyond all hope,
    The second drunk, the third so quaint and
        mouthy:
With Crabbe it may be difficult to cope,
    And Campbell's Hippocrene is somewhat
        drouthy:
Thou shalt not steal from Samuel Rogers, nor
Commit—flirtation with the muse of Moore.   1640

206

Thou shalt not covet Mr. Sotheby's Muse,
    His Pegasus, nor anything that's his;
Thou shalt not bear false witness like "the Blues"—
    (There's one, at least, is very fond of this);
Thou shalt not write, in short, but what I choose:
    This is true criticism, and you may kiss—
Exactly as you please, or not,—the rod;
And if you don't, I'll lay it on, by G—d!

207

If any person should presume to assert
    This story is not moral, first, I pray,   1650
That they will not cry out before they're hurt,
    Then that they'll read it o'er again, and say.

1638. **Hippocrene**: fountain on Mount Helicon. In Greek myth the poet who drank from it was inspired. 1641. **Mr. Sotheby**: William Sotheby (1757–1833), a translator. 1643. **"the Blues"**: a reference to the Blue-stockings, pretentious women interested in politics and literature.

(But, doubtless, nobody will be so pert),
  That this is not a moral tale, though gay;
Besides, in Canto Twelfth, I mean to show,
The very place where wicked people go.

208

If, after all, there should be some so blind
  To their own good this warning to despise,
Led by some tortuosity of mind,
  Not to believe my verse and their own
    eyes,   1660
And cry that they "the moral cannot find,"
  I tell him, if a clergyman, he lies;
Should captains the remark, or critics, make,
They also lie too—under a mistake.

209

The public approbation I expect,
  And beg they'll take my word about the moral,
Which I with their amusement will connect
  (So children cutting teeth receive a coral);
Meantime they'll doubtless please to recollect
  My epical pretensions to the laurel: 1670
For fear some prudish readers should grow skittish,
I've bribed my grandmother's review—the British.

210

I sent it in a letter to the Editor,
  Who thanked me duly by return of post—
I'm for a handsome article his creditor;
  Yet, if my gentle Muse he please to roast,
And break a promise after having made it her,
  Denying the receipt of what it cost,
And smear his page with gall instead of honey,
All I can say is—that he had the money.   1680

211

I think that with this holy new alliance
  I may ensure the public, and defy
All other magazines of art or science,
  Daily, or monthly, or three monthly; I
Have not essayed to multiply their clients,
  Because they tell me 'twere in vain to try,
And that the Edinburgh Review and Quarterly
Treat a dissenting author very martyrly.

212

"*Non ego hoc ferrem calida juventâ*
  Consule Planco," Horace said, and so   1690
Say I: by which quotation there is meant a
  Hint that some six or seven good years ago
(Long ere I dreamt of dating from the Brenta)
  I was most ready to return a blow,
And would not brook at all this sort of thing
In my hot youth—when George the Third was
  King.

213

But now at thirty years my hair is gray—
  (I wonder what it will be like at forty?
I thought of a peruke the other day—)
  My heart is not much greener; and, in
    short, I   1700
Have squandered my whole summer while 'twas
  May,
  And feel no more the spirit to retort; I
Have spent my life, both interest and principal,
And deem not, what I deemed, my soul invincible.

214

No more—no more—Oh! never more on me
  The freshness of the heart can fall like dew,
Which out of all the lovely things we see
  Extracts emotions beautiful and new,
Hived in our bosoms like the bag o' the bee.
  Think'st thou the honey with those objects
    grew?   1710
Alas! 'twas not in them, but in thy power
To double even the sweetness of a flower.

215

No more—no more—Oh! never more, my heart,
  Canst thou be my sole world, my universe!

1689–90. "*Non . . . Planco*": "I should not have endured this in the heat of youth when Plancus was consul." Horace, *Odes,* III, xiv, 27–28. **1693. Brenta:** a river near Venice.

Once all in all, but now a thing apart,
　　Thou canst not be my blessing or my curse:
The illusion's gone for ever, and thou art
　　Insensible, I trust, but none the worse,
And in thy stead I've got a deal of judgment
　　Though heaven knows how it ever found a
　　　　lodgment.　　　　　　　　　　　1720

216

My days of love are over; me no more
　　The charms of maid, wife, and still less of widow,
Can make the fool of which they made before,—
　　In short, I must not lead the life I did do;
The credulous hope of mutual minds is o'er,
　　The copious use of claret is forbid too,
So for a good old-gentlemanly vice,
I think I must take up with avarice.

217

Ambition was my idol, which was broken
　　Before the shrines of Sorrow, and of
　　　　Pleasure;　　　　　　　　　　　1730
And the two last have left me many a token
　　O'er which reflection may be made at leisure;
Now, like Friar Bacon's brazen head, I've spoken
　　"Time is, Time was, Time's past";—a chymic
　　　　treasure
Is glittering youth, which I have spent betimes—
My heart in passion, and my head on rhymes.

218

What is the end of fame? 'tis but to fill
　　A certain portion of uncertain paper:
Some liken it to climbing up a hill,
　　Whose summit, like all hills, is lost in
　　　　vapor;　　　　　　　　　　　　1740
For this men write, speak, preach, and heroes kill,
　　And bards burn what they call their "midnight
　　　　taper,"
To have, when the original is dust,
A name, a wretched picture, and worse bust.

1733. Bacon's ... head: See Robert Greene's play *Friar Bacon and Friar Bungay*, scene xi, ll. 59 ff. **1734: chymic:** counterfeit.

219

What are the hopes of man? Old Egypt's King
　　Cheops erected the first pyramid
And largest, thinking it was just the thing
　　To keep his memory whole, and mummy hid:
But somebody or other rummaging,
　　Burglariously broke his coffin's lid:　　1750
Let not a monument give you or me hopes,
Since not a pinch of dust remains of Cheops.

220

But I, being fond of true philosophy,
　　Say very often to myself, "Alas!
All things that have been born were born to die,
　　And flesh (which Death mows down to hay) is
　　　　grass;
You've passed your youth not so unpleasantly,
　　And if you had it o'er again—'twould pass—
So thank your stars that matters are no worse,
And read your Bible, sir, and mind your
　　　　purse."　　　　　　　　　　　1760

221

But for the present, gentle reader! and
　　Still gentler purchaser! the bard—that 's I—
Must, with permission, shake you by the hand,
　　And so your humble servant, and good-bye!
We meet again, if we should understand
　　Each other; and if not, I shall not try
Your patience further than by this short sample—
'Twere well if others followed my example.

222

"Go, little book, from this my solitude!
　　I cast thee on the waters—go thy ways!　　1770
And if, as I believe, thy vein be good,
　　The world will find thee after many days."
When Southey's read, and Wordsworth understood,
　　I can't help putting in my claim to praise—
The four first rhymes are Southey's, every line:
For God's sake, reader! take them not for mine!
　1818　　　　　　　　　　　　　　　1819

1769–72. "Go ... days": from Robert Southey's *Epilogue to the Lay of the Laureate.*

From CANTO THE SECOND

1

Oh ye! who teach the ingenuous youth of nations,
    Holland, France, England, Germany, or Spain,
I pray ye flog them upon all occasions—
    It mends their morals, never mind the pain:
The best of mothers and of educations
    In Juan's case were but employed in vain.
Since, in a way that's rather of the oddest, he
Became divested of his native modesty.

2

Had he but been placed at a public school,
    In the third form, or even in the fourth,   10
His daily task had kept his fancy cool,
    At least, had he been nurtured in the North:
Spain may prove an exception to the rule,
    But then exceptions always prove its worth—
A lad of sixteen causing a divorce
Puzzled his tutors very much, of course.

3

I can't say that it puzzles me at all,
    If all things be considered: first, there was
His lady-mother, mathematical,
    A—never mind;—his tutor, an old ass;   20
A pretty woman—(that's quite natural,
    Or else the thing had hardly come to pass)
A husband rather old, not much in unity
With his young wife—a time, and opportunity.

4

Well—well; the World must turn upon its axis,
    And all Mankind turn with it, heads or tails,
And live and die, make love and pay our taxes,
    And as the veering wind shifts, shift our sails;
The King commands us, and the Doctor quacks us,
    The Priest instructs, and so our life exhales,   30
A little breath, love, wine, ambition, fame,
Fighting, devotion, dust,—perhaps a name.

5

I said that Juan had been sent to Cadiz—
    A pretty town, I recollect it well—

'Tis there the mart of the colonial trade is,
    (Or was, before Peru learned to rebel),
And such sweet girls!—I mean, such graceful ladies,
    Their very walk would make your bosom swell;
I can't describe it, though so much it strike,
Nor liken it—I never saw the like: 40

6

An Arab horse, a stately stag, a barb
    New broke, a camelopard, a gazelle,
No—none of these will do;—and then their garb,
    Their veil and petticoat—Alas! to dwell
Upon such things would very near absorb
    A canto—then their feet and ankles,—well,
Thank Heaven I've got no metaphor quite ready,
(And so, my sober Muse—come, let's be steady—

7

Chaste Muse!—well,—if you must, you must)—
        the veil
    Thrown back a moment with the glancing
        hand,   50
While the o'erpowering eye, that turns you pale,
    Flashes into the heart:—All sunny land
Of Love! when I forget you, may I fail
    To say my prayers—but never was there planned
A dress through which the eyes give such a volley,
Excepting the Venetian Fazzioli.

8

But to our tale: the Donna Inez sent
    Her son to Cadiz only to embark;
To stay there had not answered her intent,
    But why?—we leave the reader in the
        dark—   60
'Twas for a voyage the young man was meant,
    As if a Spanish ship were Noah's ark,
To wean him from the wickedness of earth,
And send him like a Dove of Promise forth.

9

Don Juan bade his valet pack his things
    According to directions, then received

CANTO II. **56. Fazzioli:** kerchiefs or veils worn by members of lower religious orders.

A lecture and some money: for four springs
   He was to travel; and though Inez grieved
(As every kind of parting has its stings),
   She hoped he would improve—perhaps
      believed: 70
A letter, too, she gave (he never read it)
Of good advice—and two or three of credit.

10

In the mean time, to pass her hours away,
   Brave Inez now set up a Sunday school
For naughty children, who would rather play
   (Like truant rogues) the devil, or the fool;
Infants of three years old were taught that day,
   Dunces were whipped, or set upon a stool:
The great success of Juan's education
Spurred her to teach another generation.   80

11

Juan embarked—the ship got under way,
   The wind was fair, the water passing rough;
A devil of a sea rolls in that bay,
   As I, who've crossed it oft, know well enough;
And, standing on the deck, the dashing spray
   Flies in one's face, and makes it weather-tough:
And there he stood to take, and take again,
His first—perhaps his last—farewell of Spain.

12

I can't but say it is an awkward sight
   To see one's native land receding through   90
The growing waters; it unmans one quite,
   Especially when life is rather new:
I recollect Great Britain's coast looks white,
   But almost every other country's blue,
When gazing on them, mystified by distance,
We enter on our nautical existence.

13

So Juan stood, bewildered on the deck:
   The wind sung, cordage strained, and sailors
      swore,
And the ship creaked, the town became a speck,
   From which away so fair and fast they bore.   100
The best of remedies is a beef-steak

Against sea-sickness; try it, Sir, before
You sneer, and I assure you this is true,
For I have found it answer—so may you.

14

Don Juan stood, and, gazing from the stern
   Beheld his native Spain receding far:
First partings form a lesson hard to learn,
   Even nations feel this when they go to war;
There is a sort of unexpressed concern,
   A kind of shock that sets one's heart ajar,   110
At leaving even the most unpleasant people
And places—one keeps looking at the steeple.

15

But Juan had got many things to leave,
   His mother, and a mistress, and no wife,
So that he had much better cause to grieve
   Than many persons more advanced in life:
And if we now and then a sigh must heave
   At quitting even those we quit in strife,
No doubt we weep for those the heart endears—
That is, till deeper griefs congeal our tears.   120

16

So Juan wept, as wept the captive Jews
   By Babel's waters, still remembering Sion:
I'd weep,—but mine is not a weeping Muse,
   And such light griefs are not a thing to die on:
Young men should travel, if but to amuse
   Themselves: and the next time their servants tie
      on
Behind their carriages their new portmanteau,
Perhaps it may be lined with this my canto.

17

And Juan wept, and much he sighed and thought,
   While his salt tears dropped into the salt
      sea,   130
"Sweets to the sweet"; (I like so much to quote;
   You must excuse this extract,—'tis where she,

131. **"Sweets to the sweets"**: *Hamlet*, V, i, 265.

The Queen of Denmark, for Ophelia brought
   Flowers to the grave;) and, sobbing often, he
Reflected on his present situation,
And seriously resolved on reformation.

18

"Farewell, my Spain! a long farewell!" he cried,
   "Perhaps I may revisit thee no more,
But die, as many exiled heart hath died,
   Of its own thirst to see again thy shore: 140
Farewell, where Guadalquivir's waters glide!
   Farewell, my mother! and, since all is o'er
Farewell, too, dearest Julia!—(here he drew
Her letter out again, and read it through.)

19

"And oh! if e'er I should forget, I swear—
   But that's impossible, and cannot be—
Sooner shall this blue Ocean melt to air,
   Sooner shall Earth resolve itself to sea,
Than I resign thine image, oh, my fair!
   Or think of anything, excepting thee;   150
A mind diseased no remedy can physic—
(Here the ship gave a lurch, and he grew sea-sick.)

20

"Sooner shall Heaven kiss earth—(here he fell
     sicker)
   Oh Julia! what is every other woe?—
(For God's sake let me have a glass of liquor;
   Pedro, Battista, help me down below.)
Julia, my love!—(you rascal, Pedro, quicker)—
   Oh, Julia!—(this curst vessel pitches so)—
Belovèd Julia, hear me still beseeching!"
(Here he grew inarticulate with retching.)   160

21

He felt that chilling heaviness of heart,
   Or rather stomach, which, alas! attends,
Beyond the best apothecary's art,
   The loss of Love, the treachery of friends,
Or death of those we dote on, when a part
   Of us dies with them as each fond hope ends:
No doubt he would have been much more pathetic,
But the sea acted as a strong emetic.

22

Love's a capricious power: I've known it hold
   Out through a fever caused by its own
     heat,   170
But be much puzzled by a cough and cold,
   And find a quinsy very hard to treat:
Against all noble maladies he's bold,
   But vulgar illnesses don't like to meet,
Nor that a sneeze should interrupt his sigh,
Nor inflammation redden his blind eye.

23

But worst of all is nausea, or a pain
   About the lower region of the bowels;
Love, who heroically breathes a vein,
   Shrinks from the application of hot towels,   180
And purgatives are dangerous to his reign,
   Sea-sickness death: his love was perfect, how else
Could Juan's passion, while the billows roar,
Resist his stomach, ne'er at sea before?

24

The ship, called the most holy "Trinidada,"
   Was steering duly for the port Leghorn;
For there the Spanish family Moncada
   Were settled long ere Juan's sire was born:
They were relations, and for them he had a
   Letter of introduction, which the morn   190
Of his departure had been sent him by
His Spanish friends for those in Italy.

25

His suite consisted of three servants and
   A tutor, the licentiate Pedrillo,
Who several languages did understand,
   But now lay sick and speechless on his pillow,
And, rocking in his hammock, longed for land,
   His headache being increased by every billow;
And the waves oozing through the port-hole made
His berth a little damp, and him afraid.   200

---

172. quinsy: sore throat. **179. breathes a vein:** draws blood. **194. licentiate:** having a university degree, licensed to teach.

26

'Twas not without some reason, for the wind
   Increased at night, until it blew a gale;
And though 'twas not much to a naval mind,
   Some landsmen would have looked a little pale,
For sailors are, in fact, a different kind:
   At sunset they began to take in sail,
For the sky showed it would come on to blow,
And carry away, perhaps, a mast or so.

27

At one o'clock the wind with sudden shift
   Threw the ship right into the trough of the
      sea,   210
Which struck her aft, and made an awkward rift,
   Started the stern-post, also shattered the
Whole of her stern-frame, and, ere she could lift
   Herself from out her present jeopardy,
The rudder tore away: 'twas time to sound
The pumps, and there were four feet water found.

28

One gang of people instantly was put
   Upon the pumps, and the remainder set
To get up part of the cargo, and what not;
   But they could not come at the leak as yet;   220
At last they did get at it really, but
   Still their salvation was an even bet:
The water rushed through in a way quite puzzling,
While they thrust sheets, shirts, jackets, bales of
      muslin,

29

Into the opening; but all such ingredients
   Would have been vain, and they must have gone
      down,
Despite of all their efforts and expedients,
   But for the pumps: I'm glad to make them
      known
To all the brother tars who may have need hence,
   For fifty tons of water were upthrown   230
By them per hour, and they had all been undone,
But for the maker, Mr. Mann, of London.

30

As day advanced the weather seemed to abate,
   And then the leak they reckoned to reduce,
And keep the ship afloat, though three feet yet
   Kept two hand—and one chain-pump still in use.
The wind blew fresh again: as it grew late
   A squall came on, and while some guns broke
      loose,
A gust—which all descriptive power transcends—
Laid with one blast the ship on her beam
      ends.   240

31

There she lay, motionless, and seemed upset;
   The water left the hold, and washed the decks,
And made a scene men do not soon forget;
   For they remember battles, fires, and wrecks,
Or any other thing that brings regret,
   Or breaks their hopes, or hearts, or heads, or
      necks:
Thus drownings are much talked of by the divers,
And swimmers, who may chance to be survivors.

32

Immediately the masts were cut away,
   Both main and mizen; first the mizen went,   250
The main-mast followed: but the ship still lay
   Like a mere log, and baffled our intent.
Foremast and bowsprit were cut down, and they
   Eased her at last (although we never meant
To part with all till every hope was blighted),
And then with violence the old ship righted.

33

It may be easily supposed, while this
   Was going on, some people were unquiet,
That passengers would find it much amiss
   To lose their lives, as well as spoil their
      diet;   260
That even the able seaman, deeming his
   Days nearly o'er, might be disposed to riot,
As upon such occasions tars will ask
For grog, and sometimes drink rum from the cask.

34

There's nought, no doubt; so much the spirit calms
　As rum and true religion: thus it was,
Some plundered, some drank spirits, some sung
　　psalms,
　The high wind made the treble, and as bass
The hoarse harsh waves kept time; fright cured the
　　qualms
　Of all the luckless landsmen's sea-sick
　　maws:　　　　　　　　　　　　　　　270
Strange sounds of wailing, blasphemy, devotion,
Clamoured in chorus to the roaring Ocean.

35

Perhaps more mischief had been done, but for
　Our Juan, who, with sense beyond his years,
Got to the spirit-room, and stood before
　It with a pair of pistols; and their fears,
As if Death were more dreadful by his door
　Of fire than water, spite of oaths and tears,
Kept still aloof the crew, who, ere they sunk;
Thought it would be becoming to die drunk.　280

36

"Give us more grog," they cried, "for it will be
　All one an hour hence." Juan answered, "No!
'Tis true that Death awaits both you and me,
　But let us die like men, not sink below
Like brutes":—and thus his dangerous post kept he,
　And none liked to anticipate the blow;
And even Pedrillo, his most reverend tutor,
Was for some rum a disappointed suitor.

37

The good old gentleman was quite aghast,
　And made a loud and pious lamentation;　290
Repented all his sins, and made a last
　Irrevocable vow of reformation;
Nothing should tempt him more (this peril past)
　To quit his academic occupation,
In cloisters of the classic Salamanca,
To follow Juan's wake, like Sancho Panca.

38

But now there came a flash of hope once more;
　Day broke, and the wind lulled: the masts were
　　gone,
The leak increased; shoals round her, but no shore,
　The vessel swam, yet still she held her own.　300
They tried the pumps again, and though, before,
　Their desperate efforts seemed all useless grown,
A glimpse of sunshine set some hands to bale—
The stronger pumped, the weaker thrummed a sail.

39

Under the vessel's keel the sail was passed,
　And for the moment it had some effect;
But with a leak, and not a stick of mast,
　Nor rag of canvas, what could they expect?
But still 'tis best to struggle to the last,
　'Tis never too late to be wholly wrecked:　310
And though 'tis true that man can only die once,
'Tis not so pleasant in the Gulf of Lyons.

40

There winds and waves had hurled them, and from
　　thence,
　Without their will, they carried them away;
For they were forced with steering to dispense,
　And never had as yet a quiet day
On which they might repose, or even commence
　A jurymast or rudder, or could say
The ship would swim an hour, which, by good luck,
Still swam—though not exactly like a duck.　320

41

The wind, in fact, perhaps, was rather less,
　But the ship laboured so, they scarce could hope
To weather out much longer; the distress
　Was also great with which they had to cope
For want of water, and their solid mess
　Was scant enough: in vain the telescope
Was used—nor sail nor shore appeared in sight,
Nought but the heavy sea, and coming night.

42

Again the weather threatened,—again blew
  A gale, and in the fore and after-hold 330
Water appeared; yet though the people knew
  All this, the most were patient, and some bold,
Until the chains and leathers were worn through
  Of all our pumps:—a wreck complete she rolled,
At mercy of the waves, whose mercies are
Like human beings during civil war.

43

Then came the carpenter, at last, with tears
  In his rough eyes, and told the captain, he
Could do no more: he was a man in years,
  And long had voyaged through many a stormy
    sea, 340
And if he wept at length they were not fears
  That made his eyelids as a woman's be,
But he, poor fellow, had a wife and children,—
Two things for dying people quite bewildering.

44

The ship was evidently settling now
  Fast by the head; and, all distinction gone,
Some went to prayers again, and made a vow
  Of candles to their saints—but there were none
To pay them with; and some looked o'er the bow;
  Some hoisted out the boats; and there was
    one 350
That begged Pedrillo for an absolution,
Who told him to be dammed—in his confusion.

45

Some lashed them in their hammocks; some put on
  Their best clothes, as if going to a fair;
Some cursed the day on which they saw the Sun,
  And gnashed their teeth, and, howling, tore their
    hair;
And others went on as they had begun,
  Getting the boats out, being well aware
That a tight boat will live in a rough sea,
Unless with breakers close beneath her lee. 360

46

The worst of all was, that in their condition,
  Having been several days in great distress,
'Twas difficult to get out such provision
  As now might render their long suffering less:
Men, even when dying, dislike inanition;
  Their stock was damaged by the weather's stress:
Two casks of biscuit, and a keg of butter,
Were all that could be thrown into the cutter.

47

But in the long-boat they contrived to stow
  Some pounds of bread, though injured by the
    wet; 370
Water, a twenty-gallon cask or so;
  Six flasks of wine; and they contrived to get
A portion of their beef up from below,
  And with a piece of pork, moreover, met,
But scarce enough to serve them for a luncheon—
Then there was rum, eight gallons in a puncheon.

48

The other boats, the yawl and pinnace, had
  Been stove in the beginning of the gale;
And the long-boat's condition was but bad,
  As there were but two blankets for a sail, 380
And one oar for a mast, which a young lad
  Threw in by good luck over the ship's rail;
And two boats could not hold, far less be stored,
To save one half the people then on board.

49

'Twas twilight, and the sunless day went down
  Over the waste of waters; like a veil,
Which, if withdrawn, would but disclose the frown
  Of one whose hate is masked but to assail.
Thus to their hopeless eyes the night was shown,
  And grimly darkled o'er the faces pale, 390
And the dim desolate deep: twelve days had Fear
Been their familiar, and now Death was here.

376. **puncheon**: large cask.

50

Some trial had been making at a raft,
  With little hope in such a rolling sea,
A sort of thing at which one would have laughed,
  If any laughter at such times could be,
Unless with people who too much have quaffed,
  And have a kind of wild and horrid glee,
Half epileptical, and half hysterical:—
  Their preservation would have been a
    miracle.   400

51

At half-past eight o'clock, booms, hencoops, spars,
  And all things, for a chance, had been cast loose,
That still could keep afloat the struggling tars,
  For yet they strove, although of no great use:
There was no light in heaven but a few stars,
  The boats put off o'ercrowded with their crews;
She gave a heel, and then a lurch to port,
And, going down head foremost—sunk, in short.

52

Then rose from sea to sky the wild farewell—
  Then shrieked the timid, and stood still the
    brave,—   410
Then some leaped overboard with dreadful yell,
  As eager to anticipate their grave;
And the sea yawned around her like a hell,
  And down she sucked with her the whirling
    wave,
Like one who grapples with his enemy,
And strives to strangle him before he die.

53

And first one universal shriek there rushed,
  Louder than the loud Ocean, like a crash
Of echoing thunder; and then all was hushed,
  Save the wild wind and the remorseless
    dash   420
Of billows; but at intervals there gushed,
  Accompanied by a convulsive splash,
A solitary shriek, the bubbling cry
Of some strong swimmer in his agony.

54

The boats, as stated, had got off before,
  And in them crowded several of the crew;
And yet their present hope was hardly more
  Than what it had been, for so strong it blew
There was slight chance of reaching any shore;
  And then they were too many, though so
    few—   430
Nine in the cutter, thirty in the boat,
Were counted in them when they got afloat.

55

All the rest perished; near two hundred souls
  Had left their bodies; and what's worse, alas!
When over Catholics the Ocean rolls,
  They must wait several weeks before a mass
Takes off one peak of purgatorial coals,
  Because, till people know what's come to pass,
They won't lay out their money on the dead—
It costs three francs for every mass that's
    said.   440

56

Juan got into the long-boat, and there
  Contrived to help Pedrillo to a place;
It seemed as if they had exchanged their care,
  For Juan wore the magisterial face
Which courage gives, while poor Pedrillo's pair
  Of eyes were crying for their owner's case:
Battista, though, (a name called shortly Tita),
Was lost by getting at some aqua-vita.

57

Pedro, his valet, too, he tried to save,
  But the same cause, conductive to his loss,   450
Left him so drunk, he jumped into the wave,
  As o'er the cutter's edge he tried to cross,
And so he found a wine-and-watery grave;
  They could not rescue him although so close,
Because the sea ran higher every minute,
And for the boat—the crew kept crowding in it.

442. Pedrillo: Don Juan's tutor.

58

A small old spaniel,—which had been Don Jóse's,
  His father's, whom he loved, as ye may think,
For on such things the memory reposes
  With tenderness—stood howling on the
    brink,   460
Knowing, (dogs have such intellectual noses!)
  No doubt, the vessel was about to sink;
And Juan caught him up, and ere he stepped
Off threw him in, then after him he leaped.

59

He also stuffed his money where he could
  About his person, and Pedrillo's too,
Who let him do, in fact, whate'er he would,
  Not knowing what himself to say, or do,
As every rising wave his dread renewed;
  But Juan, trusting they might still get
    through,   470
And deeming there were remedies for any ill,
Thus re-embarked his tutor and his spaniel.

60

'Twas a rough night, and blew so stiffly yet,
  That the sail was becalmed between the seas,
Though on the wave's high top too much to set,
  They dared not take it in for all the breeze:
Each sea curled o'er the stern, and kept them wet,
  And made them bale without a moment's ease,
So that themselves as well as hopes were damped,
And the poor little cutter quickly swamped.   480

61

Nine souls more went in her: the long-boat still
  Kept above water, with an oar for mast,
Two blankets stitched together, answering ill
  Instead of sail, were to the oar made fast;
Though every wave rolled menacing to fill,
  And present peril all before surpassed,
They grieved for those who perished with the
    cutter,
And also for the biscuit-casks and butter.

62

The sun rose red and fiery, a sure sign
  Of the continuance of the gale: to run   490
Before the sea until it should grow fine,
  ˉ Was all that for the present could be done:
A few tea-spoonfuls of their rum and wine
  Were served out to the people, who begun
To faint, and damaged bread wet through the bags,
And most of them had little clothes but rags.

63

They counted thirty, crowded in a space
  Which left scarce room for motion or exertion;
They did their best to modify their case,
  One half sate up, though numbed with the
    immersion,   500
While t' other half were laid down in their place,
  At watch and watch; thus, shivering like the
    tertian
Ague in its cold fit, they filled their boat,
With nothing but the sky for a great coat.

64

'Tis very certain the desire of life
  Prolongs it: this is obvious to physicians,
When patients, neither plagued with friends nor
    wife,
  Survive through very desperate conditions,
Because they still can hope, nor shines the knife
  Nor shears of Atropos before their visions: 510
Despair of all recovery spoils longevity,
And makes men's misery of alarming brevity.

65

'Tis said that persons living on annuities
  Are longer lived than others,—God knows why,
Unless to plague the grantors,—yet so true it is,
  That some, I really think, *do* never die:
Of any creditors the worst a Jew it is,
  And *that* 's their mode of furnishing supply:
In my young days they lent me cash that way,
Which I found very troublesome to pay.   520

510. **Atropos:** In Greek myth, the one among the three
Fates who cut the thread of life.

66

'Tis thus with people in an open boat,
   They live upon the love of Life, and bear
More than can be believed, or even thought,
   And stand like rocks the tempest's wear and
      tear;
And hardship still has been the sailor's lot,
   Since Noah's ark went cruising here and there;
She had a curious crew as well as cargo,
Like the first old Greek privateer, the Argo.

67

But man is a carnivorous production,
   And must have meals, at least one meal a
      day;   530
He cannot live, like woodcocks, upon suction,
   But, like the shark and tiger, must have prey;
Although his anatomical construction
   Bears vegetables, in a grumbling way,
Your labouring people think, beyond all question,
Beef, veal, and mutton, better for digestion.

68

And thus it was with this our hapless crew;
   For on the third day there came on a calm,
And though at first their strength it might renew,
   And lying on their weariness like balm,   540
Lulled them like turtles sleeping on the blue
   Of Ocean, when they woke they felt a qualm,
And fell all ravenously on their provision,
Instead of hoarding it with due precision.

69

The consequence was easily foreseen—
   They ate up all they had, and drank their wine,
In spite of all remonstrances, and then
   On what, in fact, next day were they to dine?
They hoped the wind would rise, these foolish men!
   And carry them to shore; these hopes were
      fine,
                         550
But as they had but one oar, and that brittle,
It would have been more wise to save their victual.

528. Argo: In the Jason-Medea story of Greek myth,
the Argo was the ship in which Jason went in search of
the Golden Fleece.

70

The fourth day came, but not a breath of air,
   And Ocean slumbered like an unweaned child:
The fifth day, and their boat lay floating there,
   The sea and sky were blue, and clear, and mild—
With their one oar (I wish they had had a pair)
   What could they do? and Hunger's rage grew
      wild:
So Juan's spaniel, spite of his entreating,
Was killed, and portioned out for present
      eating.   560

71

On the sixth day they fed upon his hide,
   And Juan, who had still refused, because
The creature was his father's dog that died,
   Now feeling all the vulture in his jaws,
With some remorse received (though first denied)
   As a great favour one of the fore-paws,
Which he divided with Pedrillo, who
Devoured it, longing for the other too.

72

The seventh day, and no wind—the burning sun
   Blistered and scorched, and, stagnant on the
      sea,   570
They lay like carcasses; and hope was none,
   Save in the breeze that came not: savagely
They glared upon each other—all was done,
   Water, and wine, and food,—and you might see
The longings of the cannibal arise
(Although they spoke not) in their wolfish eyes.

73

At length one whispered his companion, who
   Whispered another, and thus it went round,
And then into a hoarser murmur grew,
   An ominous, and wild, and desperate
      sound;   580
And when his comrade's thought each sufferer
      knew,
   'Twas but his own, suppressed till now, he found;
And out they spoke of lots for flesh and blood,
And who should die to be his fellow's food.

74

But ere they came to this, they that day shared
  Some leathorn caps, and what remained of shoes;
And then they looked around them, and despaired,
  And none to be the sacrifice would choose;
At length the lots were torn up, and prepared,
  But of materials that must shock the
    Muse—   590
Having no paper, for the want of better,
They took by force from Juan Julia's letter.

75

The lots were made, and marked, and mixed, and
    handed,
  In silent horror, and their distribution
Lulled even the savage hunger which demanded,
  Like the Promethean vulture, this pollution;
None in particular had sought or planned it,
  'Twas Nature gnawed them to this resolution,
By which none were permitted to be neuter—
And the lot fell on Juan's luckless tutor.   600

76

He but requested to be bled to death:
  The surgeon had his instruments, and bled
Pedrillo, and so gently ebbed his breath,
  You hardly could perceive when he was dead.
He died as born, a Catholic in faith,
  Like most in the belief in which they 're bred,
And first a little crucifix he kissed,
And then held out his jugular and wrist.

77

The surgeon, as there was no other fee,
  Had his first choice of morsels for his
    pains;   610
But being thirstiest at the moment, he
  Preferred a draught from the fast-flowing veins;
Part was divided, part thrown in the sea,
  And such things as the entrails and the brains
Regaled two sharks, who followed o'er the billow—
The sailors ate the rest of poor Pedrillo.

78

The sailors ate him, all save three or four,
  Who were not quite so fond of animal food;

To these was added Juan, who, before
  Refusing his own spaniel, hardly could   620
Feel now his appetite increased much more;
  'Twas not to be expected that he should,
Even in extremity of their disaster,
Dine with them on his pastor and his master.

79

'Twas better that he did not; for, in fact,
  The consequence was awful in the extreme;
For they, who were most ravenous in the act,
  Went raging mad—Lord! how they did
    blaspheme!
And foam, and roll, with strange convulsions
    racked,
  Drinking salt-water like a mountain-
    stream,   630
Tearing, and grinning, howling, screeching,
    swearing,
And, with hyæna-laughter, died despairing.

80

Their numbers were much thinned by this infliction,
  And all the rest were thin enough, Heaven
    knows;
And some of them had lost their recollection,
  Happier than they who still perceived their woes;
But other pondered on a new dissection,
  As if not warned sufficiently by those
Who had already perished, suffering madly,
For having used their appetites so sadly.   640

81

And next they thought upon the master's mate,
  As fattest; but he saved himself, because,
Besides being much averse from such a fate,
  There were some other reasons: the first was,
He had been rather indisposed of late;
  And—that which chiefly proved his saving
    clause—
Was a small present made to him at Cadiz,
By general subscription of the ladies.

82

Of poor Pedrillo something still remained,
  But was used sparingly,—some were
    afraid,   650

And others still their appetites constrained,
   Or but at times a little supper made;
All except Juan, who throughout abstained,
   Chewing a piece of bamboo, and some lead:
At length they caught two Boobies, and a Noddy,
And then they left off eating the dead body.

83

And if Pedrillo's fate should shocking be,
   Remember Ugolino condescends
To eat the head of his arch-enemy
   The moment after he politely ends   660
His tale: if foes be food in Hell, at sea
   'Tis surely fair to dine upon our friends,
When Shipwreck's short allowance grows too
     scanty,
Without being much more terrible than Dante.

84

And the same night there fell a shower of rain,
   For which their mouths gaped, like the cracks of
     earth
When dried to summer dust; till taught by pain,
   Men really know not what good water's worth;
If you had been in Turkey or in Spain,
   Or with a famished boat's-crew had your
     berth,   670
Or in the desert heard the camel's bell,
You'd wish yourself where Truth is—in a well.

85

It poured down torrents, but they were no richer
   Until they found a ragged piece of sheet,
Which served them as a sort of spongy pitcher,
   And when they deemed its moisture was
     complete,
They wrung it out, and though a thirsty ditcher
   Might not have thought the scanty draught so
     sweet
As a full pot of porter, to their thinking
They ne'er till now had known the joys of
     drinking.   680

655. Boobies . . . Noddy: sea birds. **658. Ugolino:** See
Dante's *Inferno*, XXXIII, 76–78.

86

And their baked lips, with many a bloody crack,
   Sucked in the moisture, which like nectar
     streamed;
Their throats were ovens, their swollen tongues
     were black,
   As the rich man's in Hell, who vainly screamed
To beg the beggar, who could not rain back
   A drop of dew, when every drop had seemed
To taste of Heaven—If this be true, indeed,
Some Christians have a comfortable creed.

87

There were two fathers in this ghastly crew,
   And with them their two sons, of whom the
     one   690
Was more robust and hardy to the view,
   But he died early; and when he was gone,
His nearest messmate told his sire, who threw
   One glance at him, and said, "Heaven's will be
     done!
I can do nothing," and he saw him thrown
Into the deep without a tear or groan.

88

The other father had a weaklier child,
   Of a soft cheek, and aspect delicate;
But the boy bore up long, and with a mild
   And patient spirit held aloof his fate;   700
Little he said, and now and then he smiled,
   As if to win a part from off the weight
He saw increasing on his father's heart,
With the deep deadly thought, that they must part.

89

And o'er him bent his sire, and never raised
   His eyes from off his face, but wiped the foam
From his pale lips, and ever on him gazed,
   And when the wished-for shower at length was
     come,
And the boy's eyes, which the dull film half glazed,
   Brightened, and for a moment seemed to
     roam,   710
He squeezed from out a rag some drops of rain
Into his dying child's mouth—but in vain.

90

The boy expired—the father held the clay,
  And looked upon it long, and when at last
Death left no doubt, and the dead burthen lay
  Stiff on his heart, and pulse and hope were past,
He watched it wistfully, until away
  'Twas borne by the rude wave wherein 'twas
    cast;
Then he himself sunk down all dumb and shivering,
And gave no sign of life, save his limbs
    quivering.   720

91

Now overhead a rainbow, bursting through
  The scattering clouds, shone, spanning the dark
    sea,
Resting its bright base on the quivering blue;
  And all within its arch appeared to be
Clearer than that without, and its wide hue
  Waxed broad and waving, like a banner free,
Then changed like to a bow that's bent, and then
Forsook the dim eyes of these shipwrecked men.

92

It changed, of course; a heavenly Chameleon,
  The airy child of vapour and the sun,   730
Brought forth in purple, cradled in vermilion,
  Baptized in molten gold, and swathed in dun,
Glittering like crescents o'er a Turk's pavilion,
  And blending every colour into one,
Just like a black eye in a recent scuffle
(For sometimes we must box without the muffle).

93

Our shipwrecked seamen thought it a good omen—
  It is as well to think so, now and then;
'Twas an old custom of the Greek and Roman,
  And may become of great advantage when   740
Folks are discouraged; and most surely no men
  Had greater need to nerve themselves again
Than these, and so this rainbow looked like Hope—
Quite a celestial Kaleidoscope.

94

About this time a beautiful white bird,
  Webfooted, not unlike a dove in size

And plumage (probably it might have erred
  Upon its course), passed oft before their eyes,
And tried to perch, although it saw and heard
  The men within the boat, and in this guise   750
It came and went, and fluttered round them till
Night fell:—this seemed a better omen still.

95

But in this case I also must remark,
  'Twas well this bird of promise did not perch,
Because the tackle of our shattered bark
  Was not so safe for roosting as a church;
And had it been the dove from Noah's ark,
  Returning there from her successful search,
Which in their way that moment chanced to fall
They would have eat her, olive-branch and
    all.   760

96

With twilight it again come on to blow,
  But now with violence; the stars shone out,
The boat made way; yet now they were so low,
  They knew not where or what they were about;
Some fancied they saw land, and some said "No!"
  The frequent fog-banks gave them cause to
    doubt—
Some swore that they heard breakers, others guns,
And all mistook about the latter once.

97

As morning broke, the light wind died away,
  When he who had the watch sung out and
    swore,   770
If 'twas not land that rose with the Sun's ray,
  He wished that land he never might see more;
And the rest rubbed their eyes and saw a bay,
  Or thought they saw, and shaped their course
    for shore;
For shore it was, and gradually grew
Distinct, and high, and palpable to view.

98

And then of these some part burst into tears,
  And others, looking with a stupid stare,
Could not yet separate their hopes from fears,
  And seemed as if they had no further
    care;   780

While a few prayed—(the first time for some
          years)—
And at the bottom of the boat three were
Asleep: they shook them by the hand and head,
And tried to awaken them, but found them dead.

99

The day before, fast sleeping on the water,
     They found a turtle of the hawk's-bill kind,
And by good fortune, gliding softly, caught her,
     Which yielded a day's life, and to their mind
Proved even still a more nutritious matter,
     Because it left encouragement behind: 790
They thought that in such perils, more than chance
Had sent them this for their deliverance.

100

The land appeared a high and rocky coast,
     And higher grew the mountains as they drew,
Set by a current, toward it; they were lost
     In various conjectures, for none knew
To what part of earth they had been tost,
     So changeable had been the winds that blew;
Some thought it was Mount Ætna, some the
          highlands
Of Candia, Cyprus, Rhodes, or other islands.   800

101

Meantime the current, with a rising gale,
     Still set them onwards to the welcome shore,
Like Charon's bark of spectres, dull and pale;
     Their living freight was now reduced to four,
And three dead, whom their strength could not
          avail
     To heave into the deep with those before,
Though the two sharks still followed them, and
          dashed
The spray into their faces as they splashed.

102

Famine—despair—cold thirst and heat, had done
     Their work on them by turns, and thinned
          them to   810

Such things a mother had not known her son
     Amidst the skeletons of that gaunt crew;
By night chilled, by day scorched, thus one by one
     They perished, until withered to these few,
But chiefly by a species of self-slaughter,
In washing down Pedrillo with salt water.

103

As they drew nigh the land, which now was seen
     Unequal in its aspect here and there,
They felt the freshness of its growing green,
     That waved in forest-tops, and smoothed the
          air,   820
And fell upon their glazed eyes like a screen
     From glistening waves, and skies so hot and
          bare—
Lovely seemed any object that should sweep
Away the vast—salt—dread—eternal Deep.

104

The shore looked wild, without a trace of man,
     And girt by formidable waves; but they
Were mad for land, and thus their course they ran,
     Though right ahead the roaring breakers lay:
A reef between them also now began
     To show its boiling surf and bounding
          spray,   830
But finding no place for their landing better,
They ran the boat for shore,—and overset her.

105

But in his native stream, the Guadalquivir,
     Juan to lave his youthful limbs was wont;
And having learnt to swim in that sweet river,
     Had often turned the art to some account:
A better swimmer you could scarce see ever,
     He could, perhaps, have passed the Hellespont,
As once (a feat on which ourselves we prided)
Leander, Mr. Ekenhead, and I did.   840

106

So here, though faint, emaciated, and stark,
     He buoyed his boyish limbs, and strove to ply

800. **Candia**: Crete. 803. **Charon's bark**: In Greek myth,
Charon ferried the souls of the dead over the river Styx
to Hades.

840. **Mr. Ekenhead**: Lieutenant Ekenhead swam the
Hellespont with Byron.

With the quick wave, and gain, ere it was dark,
  The beach which lay before him, high and dry:
The greatest danger here was from a shark,
  That carried off his neighbour by the thigh;
As for the other two, they could not swim,
So nobody arrived on shore but him.

107

Nor yet had he arrived but for the oar,
  Which, providentially for him, was washed   850
Just as his feeble arms could strike no more,
  And the hard wave o'erwhelmed him as 'twas
        dashed
Within his grasp; he clung to it, and sore
  The waters beat while he thereto was lashed;
At last, with swimming, wading, scrambling, he
Rolled on the beach, half-senseless, from the sea:

108

There, breathless, with his digging nails he clung
  Fast to the sand, lest the returning wave,
From whose reluctant roar his life he wrung,
  Should suck him back to her insatiate
        grave: 860
And there he lay, full length, where he was flung,
  Before the entrance of a cliff-worn cave,
With just enough of life to feel its pain,
And deem that it was saved, perhaps in vain.

109

With slow and staggering effort he arose,
  But sunk again upon his bleeding knee
And quivering hand; and then he looked for those
  Who long had been his mates upon the sea;
But none of them appeared to share his woes,
  Save one, a corpse, from out the famished
        three,   870
Who died two days before, and now had found
An unknown barren beach for burial-ground.

110

And as he gazed, his dizzy brain spun fast,
  And down he sunk; and as he sunk, the sand
Swam round and round, and all his senses passed:
  He fell upon his side, and his stretched hand

Drooped dripping on the oar (their jury-mast),
  And, like a withered lily, on the land
His slender frame and pallid aspect lay,
  As fair a thing as e'er was formed of clay.   880

111

How long in his damp trance young Juan lay
  He knew not, for the earth was gone for him,
And time had nothing more of night nor day
  For his congealing blood, and senses dim;
And how this heavy faintness passed away
  He knew not, till each painful pulse and limb,
And tingling vein, seemed throbbing back to life,
For Death, though vanquished, still retired with
        strife.

112

His eyes he opened, shut, again unclosed,
  For all was doubt and dizziness; he
        thought   890
He still was in the boat, and had but dozed,
  And felt again with his despair o'erwrought,
And wished it death in which he had reposed,
  And then once more his feelings back were
        brought,
And slowly by his swimming eyes was seen
A lovely female face of seventeen.

113

'Twas bending close o'er his, and the small mouth
  Seemed almost prying into his for breath;
And chafing him, the soft warm hand of youth
  Recalled his answering spirits back from
        death;   900
And, bathing his chill temples, tried to soothe
  Each pulse to animation, till beneath
Its gentle touch and trembling care, a sigh
To these kind efforts made a low reply.

114

Then was the cordial poured, and mantle flung
  Around his scarce-clad limbs; and the fair arm
Raised higher the faint head which o'er it hung;
  And her transparent cheek, all pure and warm,

Pillowed his death-like forehead; then she wrung
　　His dewy curls, long drenched by every
　　　　storm;   910
And watched with eagerness each throb that drew
A sigh from his heaved bosom—and hers, too.

115

And lifting him with care into the cave,
　　The gentle girl, and her attendant,—one
Young, yet her elder, and of brow less grave,
　　And more robust of figure—then begun
To kindle fire, and as the new flames gave
　　Light to the rocks that roofed them, which the
　　　　sun
Had never seen, the maid, or whatsoe'er
She was, appeared distinct, and tall, and fair.   920

116

Her brow was overhung with coins of gold,
　　That sparkled o'er the auburn of her hair,
Her clustering hair, whose longer locks were rolled
　　In braids behind; and though her stature were
Even of the highest for a female mold,
　　They nearly reached her heel; and in her air
There was a something which bespoke command,
As one who was a lady in the land.

117

Her hair, I said, was auburn; but her eyes
　　Were black as death, their lashes the same
　　　　hue,   930
Of downcast length, in whose silk shadow lies
　　Deepest attraction; for when to the view
Forth from its raven fringe the full glance flies,
　　Ne'er with such force the swiftest arrow flew;
'Tis as the snake late coiled, who pours his length,
And hurls at once his venom and his strength.

118

Her brow was white and low, her cheek's pure dye
　　Like twilight rosy still with the set sun;
Short upper lip—sweet lips! that make us sigh
　　Ever to have seen such; for she was one   940
Fit for the model of a statuary
　　(A race of mere impostors, when all's done—

I've seen much finer women, ripe and real,
Than all the nonsense of their stone ideal).

119

I'll tell you why I say so, for 'tis just
　　One should not rail without a decent cause:
There was an Irish lady, to whose bust
　　I ne'er saw justice done, and yet she was
A frequent model; and if e'er she must
　　Yield to stern Time and Nature's wrinkling
　　　　laws,   950
They will destroy a face which mortal thought
Ne'er compass'd, nor less mortal chisel wrought.

120

And such was she, the lady of the cave:
　　Her dress was very different from the Spanish,
Simpler, and yet of colours not so grave;
　　For, as you know, the Spanish women banish
Bright hues when out of doors, and yet, while wave
　　Around them (what I hope will never vanish)
The basquina and the mantilla, they
Seem at the same time mystical and gay.   960

121

But with our damsel this was not the case:
　　Her dress was many-colour'd, finely spun;
Her locks curl'd negligently round her face,
　　But through them gold and gems profusely
　　　　shown:
Her girdle sparkled, and the richest lace
　　Flow'd in her veil, and many a precious stone
Flash'd on her little hand; but, what was shocking,
Her small snow feet had slippers, but no stocking.

122

The other female's dress was not unlike,
　　But of inferior materials: she   970
Had not so many ornaments to strike,
　　Her hair had silver only, bound to be
Her dowry; and her veil, in form alike,
　　Was coarser; and her air, though firm, less free;

959. basquina: a rich, outer petticoat. The **mantilla** is a veil that covers head and shoulders.

Her hair was thicker, but less long; her eyes
As black, but quicker, and of smaller size.

Full many a morsel for that Turkish trade,
By which, no doubt, a good deal may be made.

123

And these two tended him, and cheer'd him both
    With food and raiment, and those soft attentions,
Which are—(as I must own)—of female growth,
    And have ten thousand delicate inventions: 980
They made a most superior mess of broth,
    A thing which poesy but seldom mentions,
But the best dish that e'er was cook'd since Homer's
Achilles order'd dinner for new comers.

124

I'll tell you who they were, this female pair,
    Lest they should seem princesses in disguise;
Besides, I hate all mystery, and that air
    Of clap-trap, which your recent poets prize;
And so, in short, the girls they really were
    They shall appear before your curious eyes,   990
Mistress and maid; the first was only daughter
Of an old man, who lived upon the water.

125

A fisherman he had been in his youth,
    And still a sort of fisherman was he;
But other speculations were, in sooth,
    Added to his connexion with the sea,
Perhaps not so respectable, in truth:
    A little smuggling, and some piracy,
Left him, at last, the sole of many masters
Of an ill-gotten million of piastres.   1000

126

A fisher, therefore, was he,—though of men,
    Like Peter the Apostle,—and he fish'd
For wandering merchant vessels, now and then,
    And sometimes caught as many as he wish'd;
The cargoes he confiscated, and gain
    He sought in the slave-market too, and dish'd

127

He was a Greek, and on his isle had built
    (One of the wild and smaller Cyclades)   1010
A very handsome house from out his guilt,
    And there he lived exceedingly at ease;
Heavens knows what cash he got or blood he spilt,
    A sad old fellow was he, if you please;
But this I know, it was a spacious building,
Full of barbaric carving, paint, and gilding.

128

He had an only daughter, call'd Haidée,
    The greatest heiress of the Eastern Isles;
Besides, so very beautiful was she,
    Her dowry was as nothing to her smiles: 1020
Still in her teens, and like a lovely tree
    She grew to womanhood, and between whiles
Rejected several suitors, just to learn
How to accept a better in his turn.

129

And walking out upon the beach, below
    The cliff, towards sunset, on that day she found,
Insensible,—not dead, but nearly so,—
    Don Juan, almost famish'd, and half drown'd;
But being naked, she was shock'd, you know,
    Yet deem'd herself in common pity
        bound,   1030
As far as in her lay, "to take him in,
A stranger" dying, with so white a skin.

130

But taking him into her father's house
    Was not exactly the best way to save,
But like conveying to the cat the mouse,
    Or people in a trance into their grave;
Because the good old man had so much "*νους*,"
    Unlike the honest Arab thieves so brave,
He would have hospitality cured the stranger,
And sold him instantly when out of danger.   1040

983–84. **dish . . . comers**: a reference to the feast prepared by Achilles for Ajax, Ulysses, and Phoenix when the trio came to persuade the great hero to return to the war against Troy. **1000. piastres**: Turkish coins.

1037. "*νους*": the Greek word for "mind."

131

And therefore, with her maid, she thought it best
  (A virgin always on her maid relies)
To place him in the cave for present rest:
  And when, at last, he open'd his black eyes,
Their charity increased about their guest;
  And their compassion grew to such a size,
It open'd half the turnpike gates to heaven—
(St. Paul says, 'tis the toll which must be given).

132

They made a fire,—but such a fire as they
  Upon the moment could contrive with
    such   1050
Materials as were cast up round the bay,—
  Some broken planks, and oars,that to the touch
Were nearly tinder, since, so long they lay
  A mast was almost crumbled to a crutch;
But, by God's grace, here wrecks were in such
    plenty,
That there was fuel to have furnish'd twenty.

133

He had a bed of furs, and a pelisse,
  For Haidée stripp'd her sables off to make
His couch; and, that he might be more at ease,
  And warm, in case by chance he should
    awake,   1060
They also gave a petticoat apiece,
  She and her maid,—and promised by daybreak
To pay him a fresh visit, with a dish
For breakfast, of eggs, coffee, bread, and fish.

134

And thus they left him to his lone repose:
  Juan slept like a top, or like the dead,
Who sleep at last, perhaps (God only knows),
  Just for the present; and in his lull'd head
Not even a vision of his former woes
  Throbb'd in accursed dreams, which sometimes
    spread   1070
Unwelcome visions of our former years,
Till the eye, cheated, opens thick with tears.

. . .

1057. **pelisse:** a long fur coat.

173

It was such a pleasure to behold him, such
  Enlargement of existence to partake
Nature with him, to thrill beneath his touch,
  To watch him slumbering, and to see him
    wake: 1380
To live with him for ever were too much;
  But then the thought of parting made her quake:
He was her own, her ocean-treasure, cast
Like a rich wreck—her first love, and her last.

174

And thus a moon roll'd on, and fair Haidée
  Paid daily visits to her boy, and took
Such plentiful precautions, that still he
  Remain'd unknown within his craggy nook;
At last her father's prows put out to sea,
  For certain merchantmen upon the look,   1390
Not as of yore to carry off an Io,
But three Ragusan vessels bound for Scio.

175

Then came her freedom, for she had no mother,
  So that, her father being at sea, she was
Free as a married woman, or such other
  Female, as where she likes may freely pass,
Without even the encumbrance of a brother,
  The freest she that ever gazed on glass:
I speak of Christian lands in this comparison,
Where wives, at least, are seldom kept in
    garrison.   1400

176

Now see prolong'd her visits and her talk
  (For they must talk), and he had learnt to say
So much as to propose to take a walk,—
  For little had he wander'd since the day
On which, like a young flower snapp'd from the
    stalk,
  Drooping and dewy on the beach he lay,—
And thus they walk'd out in the afternoon,
And saw the sun set opposite the moon.

1391. **Io:** Io, the beautiful daughter of the King of
Argos, was carried off by Phoenician merchants.

177

It was a wild and breaker-beaten coast,
 With cliffs above, and a broad sandy
  shore,   1410
Guarded by shoals and rocks as by an host,
 With here and there a creek, whose aspect wore
A better welcome to the tempest-tost;
 And rarely ceased the haughty billow's roar,
Save on the dead long summer days, which make
The outstretch'd ocean glitter like a lake.

178

And the small ripple spilt upon the beach
 Scarcely o'erpass'd the cream of your champagne,
When o'er the brim the sparkling bumpers reach,
 That spring-dew of the spirit! the heart's
  rain!   1420
Few things surpass old wine; and they may preach
 Who please,—the more because they preach in
  vain,—
Let us have wine and woman, mirth and laughter,
Sermons and soda-water the day after.

179

Man, being reasonable, must get drunk;
 The best of life is but intoxication:
Glory, the grape, love, gold, in these are sunk
 The hopes of all men, and of every nation;
Without their sap, how branchless were the trunk
 Of life's strange tree, so fruitful on
  occasion: 1430
But to return,—Get very drunk; and when
You wake with headache, you shall see what then.

180

Ring for your valet—bid him quickly bring
 Some hock and soda-water, then you'll know
A pleasure worthy Xerxes the great king;
 For not the blest sherbet, sublimed with snow,
Nor the first sparkle of the desert-spring,
 Nor Burgundy in all its sunset glow,
After long travel, ennui, love, or slaughter,
Vie with that draught of hock and soda-
  water.   1440

181

The coast—I think it was the coast that I
 Was just describing—Yes, it *was* the coast—
Lay at this period quiet as the sky,
 The sands untumbled, the blue waves untost,
And all was stillness, save the sea-bird's cry,
 And dolphin's leap, and little billow crost
By some low rock or shelve, that made it fret
Against the boundary it scarcely wet.

182

And forth they wander'd, her sire being gone,
 As I have said, upon an expedition; 1450
And mother, brother, guardian, she had none,
 Save Zoe, who, although with due precision
She waited on her lady with the sun,
 Thought daily service was her only mission,
Bringing warm water, wreathing her long tresses,
And asking now and then for cast-off dresses.

183

It was the cooling hour, just when the rounded
 Red sun sinks down behind the azure hill,
Which then seems as if the whole earth it bounded,
 Circling all nature, hush'd, and dim, and
  still,   1460
With the far mountain-crescent half surrounded
 On one side, and the deep sea calm and chill
Upon the other, and the rosy sky,
With one star sparkling through it like an eye.

184

And thus they wander'd forth, and hand in hand,
 Over the shining pebbles and the shells,
Glided along the smooth and harden'd sand,
 And in the worn and wild receptacles
Work'd by the storms, yet work'd as it were
  plann'd,
 In hollow halls, with sparry roofs and
  cells,   1470
They turn'd to rest; and each clasp'd by an arm,
Yielded to the deep twilight's purple charm.

185

They look'd up to the sky, whose floating glow
 Spread like a rosy ocean, vast and bright;

They gazed upon the glittering sea below,
  Whence the broad moon rose circling into sight;
They heard the waves splash, and the wind so low,
  And saw each other's dark eyes darting light
Into each other—and, beholding this,
Their lips drew near, and clung into a kiss;   1480

186

A long, long kiss, a kiss of youth, and love,
  And beauty, all concentrating like rays
Into one focus, kindled from above;
  Such kisses as belong to early days,
Where heart, and soul, and sense, in concert move,
  And the blood's lava, and the pulse a blaze,
Each kiss a heart-quake,—for a kiss's strength,
I think, it must be reckon'd by its length.

187

By length I mean duration; theirs endured
  Heaven knows how long—no doubt they never
     reckon'd;   1490
And if they had, they could not have secured
  The sum of their sensations to a second:
They had not spoken; but they felt allured,
  As if their souls and lips each other beckon'd,
Which, being join'd, like swarming bees they
     clung—
Their hearts the flowers from whence the honey
     sprung.

188

They were alone, but not alone as they
  Who shut in chambers think it loneliness;
The silent ocean, and the starlight bay,
  The twilight glow, which momently grew
     less,   1500
The voiceless sands, and dropping caves, that lay
  Around them, made them to each other press,
As if there were no life beneath the sky
Save theirs, and that their life could never die.

189

They fear'd no eyes nor ears on that lone beach,
  They felt no terrors from the night, they were

All in all to each other: though their speech
  Was broken words, they *thought* a language
     there,—
And all the burning tongues the passions teach
  Found in one sigh the best interpreter   1510
Of nature's oracle—first love,—that all
Which Eve has left her daughters since her fall.

190

Haidée spoke not of scruples, ask'd no vows,
  Nor offer'd any; she had never heard
Of plight and promises to be a spouse,
  Or perils by a loving maid incurr'd;
She was all which pure ignorance allows,
  And flew to her young mate like a young bird;
And never having dreamt of falsehood, she
Had not one word to say of constancy.   1520

191

She loved, and was beloved—she adored,
  And she was worshipp'd; after nature's fashion,
Their intense souls, into each other pour'd,
  If souls could die, had perish'd in that passion,—
But by degrees their senses were restored,
  Again to be o'ercome, again to dash on;
And, beating 'gainst *his* bosom, Haidée's heart
Felt as if never more to beat apart.

192

Alas! they were so young, so beautiful,
  So lonely, loving, helpless, and the hour   1530
Was that in which the heart is always full,
  And, having o'er itself no further power,
Prompts deeds eternity cannot annul,
  But pays off moments in an endless shower
Of hell-fire—all prepared for people giving
Pleasure or pain to one another living.

193

Alas! for Juan and Haidée! they were
  So loving and so lovely—till then never,
Excepting our first parents, such a pair
  Had run the risk of being damn'd for
     ever;   1540

And Haidée, being devout as well as fair,
    Had, doubtless, heard about the Stygian river,
And hell and purgatory—but forgot
Just in the very crisis she should not.

194

They look upon each other, and their eyes
    Gleam in the moonlight; and her white arm
      clasps
Round Juan's head, and his around her lies
    Half buried in the tresses which it grasps;
She sits upon his knee, and drinks his sighs,
    He hers, until they end in broken gasps;   1550
And thus they form a group that's quite antique,
Half naked, loving, natural, and Greek.

195

And when those deep and burning moments pass'd,
    And Juan sunk to sleep within her arms,
She slept not, but all tenderly, though fast,
    Sustain'd his head upon her bosom's charms;
And now and then her eye to heaven is cast,
    And then on the pale cheek her breast now
      warms,
Pillow'd on her o'erflowing heart, which pants
With all it granted, and with all it grants.   1560

196

An infant when it gazes on a light,
    A child the moment when it drains the breast,
A devotee when soars the Host in sight,
    An Arab with a stranger for a guest,
A sailor when the prize has struck in fight,
    A miser filling his most hoarded chest,
Feel rapture; but not such true joy are reaping
As they who watch o'er what they love while
    sleeping.

197

For there it lies so tranquil, so beloved,
    All that it hath of life with us is living;   1570
So gentle, stirless, helpless, and unmoved,
    And all unconscious of the joy 'tis giving;

1542. **Stygian:** pertaining to the river Styx in Hades.

All it hath felt, inflicted, pass'd, and proved,
    Hush'd into depths beyond the watcher's diving;
There lies the thing we love with all its errors
And all its charms, like death without its terrors.

198

The lady watch'd her lover—and that hour
    Of Love's, and Night's, and Ocean's solitude,
O'erflow'd her soul with their united power;
    Amidst the barren sand and rocks so rude   1580
She and her wave-worn love had made their bower,
    Where nought upon their passion could intrude,
And all the stars that crowded the blue space
Saw nothing happier than her glowing face.

199

Alas! the love of women! it is known
    To be a lovely and a fearful thing;
For all of theirs upon that die is thrown,
    And if 'tis lost, life hath no more to bring
To them but mockeries of the past alone,
    And their revenge is as the tiger's spring,   1590
Deadly, and quick, and crushing; yet, as real
Torture is theirs, what they inflict they feel.

200

They are right; for man, to man so oft unjust,
    Is always so to women; one sole bond
Awaits them, treachery is all their trust;
    Taught to conceal, their bursting hearts despond
Over their idol, till some wealthier lust
    Buys them in marriage—and what rests beyond?
A thankless husband, next a faithless lover,
Then dressing, nursing, praying, and all's
    over.   1600

201

Some take a lover, some take drams or prayers,
    Some mind their household, others dissipation,
Some run away, and but exchange their cares,
    Losing the advantage of a virtuous station;
Few changes e'er can better their affairs,
    Theirs being an unnatural situation,
From the dull palace to the dirty hovel:
Some play the devil, and then write a novel.

202

Haidée was Nature's bride, and knew not this;
　　Haidée was Passion's child, born where the
　　　　sun　　　　　　　　　　　　　　　　　　1610
Showers triple light, and scorches even the kiss
　　Of his gazelle-eyed daughters; she was one
Made but to love, to feel that she was his
　　Who was her chosen: what was said or done
Elsewhere was nothing. She had nought to fear,
Hope, care, nor love beyond, her heart beat *here*.
1819　　　　　　　　　　　　　　　　　　*1819*

From CANTO THE THIRD

1

Hail, Muse! *et cætera*.—We left Juan sleeping,
　　Pillow'd upon a fair and happy breast,
And watch'd by eyes that never yet knew weeping,
　　And loved by a young heart, too deeply blest
To feel the poison through her spirit creeping,
　　Or know who rested there, a foe to rest,
Had soil'd the current of her sinless years,
And turn'd her pure heart's purest blood to tears!

2

Oh, Love! what is it in this world of ours
　　Which makes it fatal to be loved? Ah why　　10
With cypress branches hast thou wreathed thy
　　　　bowers,
　　And made thy best interpreter a sigh?
As those who dote on odours pluck the flowers,
　　And place them on their breast—but place to
　　　　die—
Thus the frail beings we would fondly cherish
Are laid within our bosoms but to perish.

3

In her first passion woman loves her lover,
　　In all the others all she loves is love,
Which grows a habit she can ne'er get over,
　　And fits her loosely—like an easy glove,　　20
As you may find, whene'er you like to prove her:
　　One man alone at first her heart can move;

She then prefers him in the plural number,
Not finding that the additions much encumber.

4

I know not if the fault be men's or theirs;
　　But one thing's pretty sure; a woman planted
(Unless at once she plunge for life in prayers)
　　After a decent time must be gallanted;
Although, no doubt, her first of love affairs
　　Is that to which her heart is wholly granted;　　30
Yet there are some, they say, who have had *none*,
But those who have ne'er end with only *one*.

5

'Tis melancholy, and a fearful sign
　　Of human frailty, folly, also crime,
That love and marriage rarely can combine,
　　Although they both are born in the same clime;
Marriage from love, like vinegar from wine—
　　A sad, sour, sober beverage—by time
Is sharpen'd from its high celestial flavour,
Down to a very homely household savour.　　40

6

There's something of antipathy, as 'twere,
　　Between their present and their future state;
A kind of flattery that's hardly fair
　　Is used until the truth arrives too late—
Yet what can people do, except despair?
　　The same things change their names at such a
　　　　rate;
For instance—passion in a lover's glorious,
But in a husband is pronounced uxorious.

7

Men grow ashamed of being so very fond;
　　They sometimes also get a little tired　　50
(But that, of course, is rare), and then despond:
　　The same things cannot always be admired,
Yet 'tis "so nominated in the bond,"
　　That both are tied till one shall have expired.
Sad thought! to lose the spouse that was adorning
Our days, and put one's servants into mourning.

CANTO III. **26. planted**: abandoned.

8

There's doubtless something in domestic doings
    Which forms, in fact, true love's antithesis;
Romances paint at full length people's wooings,
    But only give a bust of marriages;   60
For no one cares for matrimonial cooings,
    There's nothing wrong in a connubial kiss:
Think you, if Laura had been Petrarch's wife,
He would have written sonnets all his life?

9

All tragedies are finish'd by a death,
    All comedies are ended by a marriage;
The future states of both are left to faith,
    For authors fear description might disparage
The worlds to come of both, or fall beneath,
    And then both worlds would punish their
        miscarriage;   70
So leaving each their priest and prayer-book ready,
They say no more of Death or of the Lady.

10

The only two that in my recollection
    Have sung of heaven and hell, or marriage, are
Dante and Milton, and of both the affection
    Was hapless in their nuptials, for some bar
Of fault or temper ruin'd the connexion
    (Such things, in fact, it don't ask much to mar);
But Dante's Beatrice and Milton's Eve
Were not drawn from their spouses, you
        conceive.   80

11

Some persons say that Dante meant theology
    By Beatrice, and not a mistress—I,
Although my opinion may require apology,
    Deem this a commentator's phantasy,
Unless indeed it was from his own knowledge he
    Decided thus, and show'd good reason why;
I think that Dante's more abstruse ecstatics
Meant to personify the mathematics.

72. **Death . . . Lady:** A popular and tragic eighteenth-
century ballad was called "Death and the Lady."

12

Haidée and Juan were not married, but
    The fault was theirs, not mine: it is not fair,   90
Chaste reader, then, in any way to put
    The blame on me, unless you wish they were;
Then if you'd have them wedded, please to shut
    The book which treats of this erroneous pair,
Before the consequences grow too awful;
'Tis dangerous to read of loves unlawful.

13

Yet they were happy,—happy in the illicit
    Indulgence of their innocent desires;
But more imprudent grown with every visit,
    Haidée forgot the island was her sire's;   100
When we have what we like, 'tis hard to miss it,
    At least in the beginning, ere one tires;
Thus she came often, not a moment losing,
Whilst her piratical papa was cruising.

14

Let not his mode of raising cash seem strange,
    Although he fleeced the flags of every nation,
For into a prime minister but change
    His title, and 'tis nothing but taxation;
But he, more modest, took an humbler range
    Of life, and in an honester vocation   110
Pursued o'er the high seas his watery journey,
And merely practised as a sea-attorney.

15

The good old gentleman had been detain'd
    By winds and waves, and some important
        captures;
And, in the hope of more, at sea remain'd,
    Although a squall or two had damp'd his
        raptures,
By swamping one of the prizes; he had chain'd
    His prisoners, dividing them like chapters
In number'd lots; they all had cuffs and collars,
And averaged each from ten to a hundred
        dollars.   120

. . .

26

Lambro, our sea-solicitor, who had   201
    Much less experience of dry land than ocean,
On seeing his own chimney-smoke, felt glad;
    But not knowing metaphysics, had no notion
Of the true reason of his not being sad,
    Or that of any other strong emotion;
He loved his child, and would have wept the loss of
    her,
But knew the cause no more than a philosopher.

27

He saw his white walls shining in the sun,
    His garden trees all shadowy and green;   210
He heard his rivulet's light bubbling run,
    The distant dog-bark; and perceived between
The umbrage of the wood so cool and dun,
    The moving figures, and the sparkling sheen
Of arms (in the East all arm)—and various dyes
Of colour'd garbs, as bright as butterflies.

28

And as the spot where they appear he nears,
    Surprised at these unwonted signs of idling,
He hears—alas! no music of the spheres,
    But an unhallow'd, earthly sound of
        fiddling!   220
A melody which made him doubt his ears,
    The cause being past his guessing or unriddling;
A pipe, too, and a drum, and shortly after,
A most unoriental roar of laughter.

. . .

61

Old Lambro pass'd unseen a private gate,
    And stood within his hall at eventide;
Meantime the lady and her lover sate
    At wassail in their beauty and their pride:
An ivory inlaid table spread with state
    Before them, and fair slaves on every side;
Gems, gold, and silver, form'd the service mostly,
Mother of pearl and coral the less costly.

62

The dinner made about a hundred dishes;
    Lamb and pistachio nuts—in short, all
        meats,   490
And saffron soups, and sweetbreads; and the fishes
    Were of the finest that e'er flounced in nets,
Drest to a Sybarite's most pamper'd wishes;
    The beverage was various sherbets
Of raisin, orange, and pomegranate juice,
Squeezed through the rind, which makes it best for
    use.

63

These were ranged round, each in its crystal ewer,
    And fruits, and date-bread loaves closed the
        repast,
And Mocha's berry, from Arabia pure,
    In small fine China cups, came in at last;   500
Gold cups of filigree made to secure
    The hand from burning underneath them placed,
Cloves, cinnamon, and saffron too were boil'd
Up with the coffee, which (I think) they spoil'd.

64

The hangings of the room were tapestry, made
    Of velvet panels, each of different hue,
And thick with damask flowers of silk inlaid;
    And round them ran a yellow border too;
The upper border, richly wrought, display'd,
    Embroider'd delicately o'er with blue,   510
Soft Persian sentences, in lilac letters,
From poets, or the moralists their betters.

65

These Oriental writings on the wall,
    Quite common in those countries, are a kind
Of monitors adapted to recall,
    Like skulls at Memphian banquets, to the mind
The words which shook Belshazzar in his hall,
    And took his kingdom from him: You will find,
Though sages may pour out their wisdom's treasure,
There is no sterner moralist than Pleasure.   520

493. **Sybarite:** The dwellers of ancient Sybaris were renowned for their love of luxury and pleasure.

66

A beauty at the season's close grown hectic,
    A genius who has drunk himself to death,
A rake turn'd methodistic, or Eclectic
    (For that's the name they like to pray beneath)—
But most, an alderman struck apoplectic,
    Are things that really take away the breath,—
And show that late hours, wine, and love are able
To do not much less damage than the table.

67

Haidée and Juan carpeted their feet
    On crimson satin, border'd with pale
        blue;   530
Their sofa occupied three parts complete
    Of the apartment—and appear'd quite new;
The velvet cushions (for a throne more meet)
    Were scarlet, from whose glowing centre grew
A sun emboss'd in gold, whose rays of tissue,
Meridian-like, were seen all light to issue.

.   .   .

78

And now they were diverted by their suite,
    Dwarfs, dancing girls, black eunuchs, and a poet,
Which made their new establishment complete;
    The last was of great fame, and liked to show
        it: 620
His verses rarely wanted their due feet;
    And for his theme—he seldom sung below it,
He being paid to satirize or flatter,
As the psalm says, "inditing a good matter."

79

He praised the present, and abused the past,
    Reversing the good custom of old days,
An Eastern anti-jacobin at last
    He turn'd, preferring pudding to *no* praise—
For some few years his lot had been o'ercast
    By his seeming independent in his lays,   630
But now he sung the Sultan and the Pacha
With truth like Southey, and with verse like
        Crashaw.

523. **Eclectic:** The *Eclectic Review* was extremely critical of Byron and his works.

80

He was a man who had seen many changes,
    And always changed as true as any needle;
His polar star being one which rather ranges,
    And not the fix'd—he knew the way to wheedle:
So vile he 'scaped the doom which oft avenges;
    And being fluent (save indeed when fee'd ill),
He lied with such a fervour of intention—
There was no doubt he earn'd his laureate
        pension.   640

81

But he had genius,—when a turncoat has it,
    The "Vates irritabilis" takes care
That without notice few full moons shall pass it;
    Even good men like to make the public stare:—
But to my subject—let me see—what was it?—
    Oh!—the third canto—and the pretty pair—
Their loves, and feasts, and house, and dress, and
        mode
Of living in their insular abode.

82

Their poet, a sad trimmer, but no less
    In company a very pleasant fellow,   650
Had been the favourite of full many a mess
    Of men, and made them speeches when half
        mellow;
And though his meaning they could rarely guess,
    Yet still they deign'd to hiccup or to bellow
The glorious meed of popular applause,
Of which the first ne'er knows the second cause.

83

But now being lifted into high society,
    And having pick'd up several odds and ends
Of free thoughts in his travels, for variety,
    He deem'd, being in a lone isle, among
        friends,   660
That without any danger of a riot, he
    Might for long lying make himself amends;
And singing as he sung in his warm youth,
Agree to a short armistice with truth.

642. **"Vates irritabilis":** irritable prophet or poet.

84

He had travell'd 'mongst the Arabs, Turks, and
    Franks,
  And knew the self-loves of the different nations;
And having lived with people of all ranks,
  Had something ready upon most occasions—
Which got him a few presents and some thanks.
  He varied with some skill his adulations;   670
To "do at Rome as Romans do," a piece
Of conduct was which he observed in Greece.

85

Thus, usually, when he was asked to sing,
  He gave the different nations something national;
'Twas all the same to him—"God save the king,"
  Or "Ça ira," according to the fashion all:
His muse made increment of anything,
  From the high lyric down to the low rational:
If Pindar sang horse-races, what should hinder
Himself from being as pliable as Pindar?   680

86

In France, for instance, he would write a chanson;
  In England a six canto quarto tale;
In Spain he'd make a ballad or romance on
  The last war—much the same in Portugal;
In Germany, the Pegasus he'd prance on
  Would be old Goethe's—(see what says
    De Staël);
In Italy he'd ape the "Trecentisti";
In Greece, he'd sing some sort of hymn like this t'
    ye:

I

The isles of Greece, the isles of Greece!
  Where burning Sappho loved and sung.   690
Where grew the arts of war and peace,
  Where Delos rose, and Phœbus sprung!
Eternal summer gilds them yet,
But all, except their sun, is set.

II

The Scian and the Teian muse,
  The hero's harp, the lover's lute,
Have found the fame your shores refuse;
  Their place of birth alone is mute
To sound which echo further west
Than your sires' "Islands of the Blest."   700

III

The mountains look on Marathon—
  And Marathon looks on the sea;
And musing there an hour alone,
  I dream'd that Greece might still be free;
For standing on the Persians' grave,
I could not deem myself a slave.

IV

A king sate on the rocky brow
  Which looks o'er sea-born Salamis;
And ships, by thousands, lay below,
  And men in nations;—all were his!   710
He counted them at break of day—
And when the sun set where were they?

V

And where are they? and where art thou,
  My country? On thy voiceless shore
The heroic lay is tuneless now—
  The heroic bosom beats no more!
And must thy lyre, so long divine,
Degenerate into hands like mine?

VI

'Tis something, in the dearth of fame,
  Though link'd among a fetter'd race,   720
To feel at least a patriot's shame,
  Even as I sing, suffuse my face;
For what is left the poet here?
For Greeks a blush—for Greece a tear.

676. "Ça ira": "It will succeed," a song of the French revolutionists. 687. "Trecentisti": Italian writers of the fourteenth century. 692. Delos . . . Phœbus: the island of Delos, birthplace of Phœbus Apollo, was supposed to have arisen from the Aegean Sea.

695. Scian . . . Teian: Homer was supposedly born on the island of Scio; Anacreon on Teos. 700. "Islands of the Blest": the Cape Verde Islands or the Canaries. 707. king: Xerxes, king of Persia, watched the famed Battle of Salamis from Mt. Aegaleos.

VII

Must *we* but weep o'er days more blest?
　Must *we* but blush?—Our fathers bled.
Earth! render back from out thy breast
　A remnant of our Spartan dead!
Of the three hundred grant but three,
To make a new Thermopylæ!　　　730

VIII

What, silent still? and silent all?
　Ah! no;—the voices of the dead
Sound like a distant torrent's fall,
　And answer, "Let one living head,
But one arise,—we come, we come!"
'Tis but the living who are dumb.

IX

In vain—in vain: strike other chords;
　Fill high the cup with Samian wine!
Leave battles to the Turkish hordes,
　And shed the blood of Scio's vine!　　740
Hark! rising to the ignoble call—
How answer each bold Bacchanal!

X

You have the Pyrrhic dance as yet,
　Where is the Pyrrhic phalanx gone?
Of two such lessons, why forget
　The nobler and the manlier one?
You have the letters Cadmus gave—
Think ye he meant them for a slave?

XI

Fill high the bowl with Samian wine!
　We will not think of themes like these!　750
It made Anacreon's song divine:
　He served—but served Polycrates—

A tyrant; but our masters then
Were still, at least, our countrymen.

XII

The tyrant of the Chersonese
　Was freedom's best and bravest friend;
That tyrant was Miltiades!
　Oh! that the present hour would lend
Another despot of the kind!
Such claims as his were sure to bind.　　760

XIII

Fill high the bowl with Samian wine!
　On Suli's rock, and Parga's shore,
Exists the remnant of a line
　Such as the Doric mothers bore;
And there, perhaps, some seed is sown,
The Heracleidan blood might own.

XIV

Trust not for freedom to the Franks—
　They have a king who buys and sells;
In native swords, and native ranks,
　The only hope of courage dwells:　　770
But Turkish force, and Latin fraud,
Would break your shield, however broad.

XV

Fill high the bowl with Samian wine!
　Our virgins dance beneath the shade—
I see their glorious black eyes shine;
　But gazing on each glowing maid,
My own the burning tear-drop laves,
To think such breasts must suckle slaves.

XVI

Place me on Sunium's marbled steep,
　Where nothing, save the waves and I,　780
May hear our mutual murmurs sweep;
　There, swan-like, let me sing and die:

730. Thermopylæ: One of the celebrated feats of Greek military history occurred at the narrow pass of Thermopylæ, where three hundred Spartans under Leonidas held off the Persian hordes of Xerxes for three days (480 B.C.). **747. Cadmus:** legendary founder of Thebes, who supposedly introduced the alphabet into Greece.

755–57. Chersonese . . . Miltiades: Miltiades led the Greeks at Marathon. **762. Suli . . . Parga:** towns in Albania. **779. Sunium:** hill overlooking the sea at the southeastern tip of Greece.

A land of slaves shall ne'er be mine—
Dash down yon cup of Samian wine!

87

Thus sung, or would, or could, or should have sung,
    The modern Greek, in tolerable verse;
If not like Orpheus quite, when Greece was young,
    Yet in these times he might have done much
        worse:
His strain display'd some feeling—right or wrong;
    And feeling, in a poet, is the source   790
Of others' feelings; but they are such liars,
And take all colours—like the hands of dyers.

88

But words are things, and a small drop of ink,
    Falling like dew, upon a thought, produces
That which makes thousands, perhaps millions,
        think;
    'Tis strange, the shortest letter which man uses
Instead of speech, may form a lasting link
    Of ages; to what straits old Time reduces
Frail man when paper—even a rag like this,
Survives himself, his tomb, and all that's his!   800

. . .

110

But I'm digressing; what on earth has Nero,
    Or any such like sovereign buffoons,   970
To do with the transactions of my hero,
    More than such madmen's fellow man—the
        moon's?
Sure my invention must be down at zero,
    And I grown one of many "wooden spoons"
Of verse (the name with which we Cantabs please
To dub the last of honours in degrees).

111

I feel this tediousness will never do—
    'Tis being *too* epic, and I must cut down
(In copying) this long canto into two;
    They'll never find it out, unless I own   980
The fact, excepting some experienced few;
    And then as an improvement 'twill be shown:

I'll prove that such the opinion of the critic is
From Aristotle *passim.* See Ποιητικης.
1819–20   *1821*

[The return of Lambro, Haidée's father and a cruel
pirate, marks the end of the romance, the death of
Haidée, and the beginning of another phase of Juan's
wanderings.]

From CANTO THE ELEVENTH *

39

Don Juan was presented, and his dress   305
    And mien excited general admiration—
I don't know which was more admired or less:
    One monstrous diamond drew much observation,
Which Catherine in a moment of "ivresse"
    (In love or brandy's fervent fermentation)   310
Bestow'd upon him, as the public learn'd;
And, to say truth, it had been fairly earn'd.

40

Besides the ministers and underlings,
    Who must be courteous to the accredited
Diplomatists of rather wavering kings,
    Until their royal riddle's fully read,
The very clerks,—those somewhat dirty springs
    Of office, or the house of office, fed
By foul corruption into streams,—even they
Were hardly rude enough to earn their pay: 320

41

And insolence no doubt is what they are
    Employ'd for, since it is their daily labour,
In the dear offices of peace or war;
    And should you doubt, pray ask of your next
        neighbour,

---

984. Ποιητικης: Aristotle's *Poetics.*

* [Juan, after many wanderings over Europe and Asia
Minor, is now back in London as a representative of
Queen Catherine the Great of Russia. Canto XI is a
marvelous portrait of society at the time and especially
of the Bluestockings.]

CANTO XI. 309. "ivresse": intoxication.

When for a passport, or some other bar
　　To freedom, he applied (a grief and a bore),
If he found not his spawn of taxborn riches,
Like lap-dogs, the least civil sons of b——s.

42

But Juan was received with much "empresse-
　　ment:"—
　　These phrases of refinement I must borrow　330
From our next neighbours' land, where, like a
　　chessman,
　　There is a move set down for joy or sorrow
Not only in mere talking, but the press. Man
　　In islands is, it seems, downright and thorough,
More than on continents—as if the sea
(See Billingsgate) made even the tongue more
　　free.

43

And yet the British "Damme"'s rather Attic:
　　Your continental oaths are but incontinent,
And turn on things which no aristocratic
　　Spirit would name, and therefore even I won't
　　anent　340
This subject quote; as it would be schismatic
　　In politesse, and have a sound affronting in 't:—
But "Damme"'s quite ethereal, though too daring—
Platonic blasphemy, the soul of swearing.

44

For downright rudeness, ye may stay at home;
　　For true or false politeness (and scarce *that*
　　Now) you may cross the blue deep and white
　　foam—
　　The first the emblem (rarely though) of what
You leave behind, the next of much you come
　　To meet. However, 'tis no time to chat　350
On general topics: poems must confine
Themselves to unity, like this of mine.

45

In the great world,—which, being interpreted,
　　Meaneth the west or worst end of a city,
And about twice two thousand people bred
　　By no means to be very wise or witty,

336. **Billingsgate:** fish-market district near London Bridge. This reference is to the foul language spoken there. 340. **anent:** concerning.

But to sit up while others lie in bed,
　　And look down on the universe with pity,—
Juan, as an inveterate patrician,
Was well received by persons of condition.　360

46

He was a bachelor, which is a matter
　　Of import both to virgin and to bride,
The former's hymeneal hopes to flatter;
　　And (should she not hold fast by love or pride)
'Tis also of some moment to the latter:
　　A rib's a thorn in a wed gallant's side,
Requires decorum, and is apt to double
The horrid sin—and what's still worse, the trouble.

47

But Juan was a bachelor—of arts,
　　And parts, and hearts: he danced and sung, and
　　had　370
An air as sentimental as Mozart's
　　Softest of melodies; and could be sad
Or cheerful, without any "flaws or starts,"
　　Just at the proper time; and though a lad,
Had seen the world—which is a curious sight,
And very much unlike what people write.

48

Fair virgins blush'd upon him; wedded dames
　　Bloom'd also in less transitory hues;
For both commodities dwell by the Thames,
　　The painting and the painted; youth,
　　ceruse,　380
Against his heart preferr'd their usual claims,
　　Such as no gentleman can quite refuse:
Daughters admired his dress, and pious mothers
Inquired his income, and if he had brothers.

49

The milliners who furnish "drapery Misses"
　　Throughout the season, upon speculation

363. **hymeneal:** wedding. 385. **milliners:** High-born, fashionable females were provided by milliners with a wardrobe on credit; after the marriage, the young women would have their husbands make payment.

Of payment ere the honey-moon's last kisses
   Have waned into a crescent's coruscation,
Thought such an opportunity as this is,
   Of a rich foreigner's initiation,   390
Not to be overlook'd—and gave such credit,
That future bridegrooms swore, and sigh'd, and
      paid it.

50

The Blues, that tender tribe who sigh o'er sonnets,
   And with the pages of the last Review
Line the interior of their heads or bonnets,
   Advanced in all their azure's highest hue:
They talk'd bad French or Spanish, and upon its
   Late authors ask'd him for a hint or two;
And which was softest, Russian or Castilian?
And whether in his travels he saw Ilion?   400

51

Juan, who was a little superficial,
   And not in literature a great Drawcansir,
Examined by this learned and especial
   Jury of matrons, scarce knew what to answer:
His duties warlike, loving or official,
   His steady application as a dancer,
Had kept him from the brink of Hippocrene,
Which now he found was blue instead of green.

52

However, he replied at hazard, with
   A modest confidence and calm assurance,   410
Which lent his learned lucubrations pith,
   And pass'd for arguments of good endurance.
That prodigy, Miss Araminta Smith
   (Who at sixteen translated "Hercules Furens"
Into as furious English), with her best look,
Set down his sayings in her common-place book.

53

Juan knew several languages—as well
   He might—and brought them up with skill, in
      time

To save his fame with each accomplish'd belle,
   Who still regretted that he did not rhyme.   420
There wanted but this requisite to swell
   His qualities (with them) into sublime:
Lady Fitz-Frisky, and Miss Mævia Mannish,
Both long'd extremely to be sung in Spanish.

54

However, he did pretty well, and was
   Admitted as an aspirant to all
The coteries, and, as in Banquo's glass,
   At great assemblies or in parties small,
He saw ten thousand living authors pass,
   That being about their average numeral;   430
Also the eighty "greatest living poets,"
As every paltry magazine can show *its*.

· · ·

86

But how shall I relate in other cantos
   Of what befell our hero in the land,
Which 'tis the common cry and lie to vaunt as
   A moral country? But I hold my hand—
For I disdain to write an Atalantis;
   But 'tis as well at once to understand,
You are *not* a moral people, and you know it
Without the aid of too sincere a poet.

87

What Juan saw and underwent shall be
   My topic, with of course the due restriction   690
Which is required by proper courtesy;
   And recollect the work is only fiction,
And that I sing of neither mine nor me,
   Though every scribe, in some slight turn of
      diction,
Will hint allusions never *meant*. Ne'er doubt
This—when I speak, I *don't hint*, but *speak out*.

88

Whether he married with the third or fourth
   Offspring of some sage husband-hunting countess,

402. Drawcansir: a loud, boastful man in George Villiers' play *The Rehearsal* (1671). **414. "Hercules Furens":** a play by Seneca.

685. Atalantis: Mrs. Manley's *Secret Memoirs and Manners from the New Atalantis* (1709), a book filled with gossipy scandals involving prominent people of the day.

Or whether with some virgin of more worth
   (I mean in Fortune's matrimonial bounties)   700
He took to regularly peopling Earth,
   Of which your lawful awful wedlock fount is,—
Or whether he was taken in for damages,
For being too excursive in his homages,—

89

Is yet within the unread events of time.
   Thus far, go forth, thou lay, which I will back
Against the same given quantity of rhyme,
   For being as much the subject of attack
As ever yet was any work sublime,
   By those who love to say that white is black.   710
So much the better!—I may stand alone,
But would not change my free thoughts for a
   throne.

1822   *1823*

From CANTO THE FOURTEENTH*

1

If from great nature's or our own abyss
   Of thought we could but snatch a certainty,
Perhaps mankind might find the path they miss—
   But then 't would spoil much good philosophy.
One system eats another up, and this
   Much as old Saturn ate his progeny;
For when his pious consort gave him stones
In lieu of sons, of these he made no bones.

2

But System doth reverse the Titan's breakfast,
   And eats her parents, albeit the digestion   10
Is difficult. Pray tell me, can you make fast,
   After due search, your faith to any question?
Look back o'er ages, ere unto the stake fast
   You bind yourself, and call some mode the best
     one.
Nothing more true than *not* to trust your senses;
And yet what are your other evidences?

---

* [Juan, still in England, displays considerable upward
mobility. A member of high society, he lives at the
country estate of Lord Henry Amundeville and his wife,
Lady Adeline.]

3

For me, I know nought; nothing I deny,
   Admit, reject, contemn; and what know *you*,
Except perhaps that you were born to die?
   And both may after all turn out untrue.   20
An age may come, Font of Eternity,
   When nothing shall be either old or new.
Death, so call'd, is a thing which makes men weep,
And yet a third of life is pass'd in sleep.

4

A sleep without dreams, after a rough day
   Of toil, is what we covet most; and yet
How clay shrinks back from more quiescent clay!
   The very Suicide that pays his debt
At once without instalments (an old way
   Of paying debts, which creditors regret)   30
Lets out impatiently his rushing breath,
Less from disgust of life than dread of death.

5

'Tis round him, near him, here, there, every where;
   And there's a courage which grows out of fear,
Perhaps of all most desperate, which will dare
   The worst to *know* it:—when the mountains rear
Their peaks beneath your human foot, and there
   You look down o'er the precipice, and drear
The gulf of rock yawns,—you can't gaze a minute
Without an awful wish to plunge within it.   40

6

'Tis true, you don't—but, pale and struck with
   terror,
   Retire: but look into your past impression!
And you will find, though shuddering at the mirror
   Of your own thoughts, in all their self-confession,
The lurking bias, be it truth or error,
   To the *unknown*; a secret prepossession,
To plunge with all your fears—but where? You
   know not,
And that's the reason why you do—or do not.

7

But what's this to the purpose? you will say.
   Gent. reader, nothing; a mere speculation,   50

For which my sole excuse is—'tis my way;
 Sometimes *with* and sometimes without occasion
I write what's uppermost, without delay:
 This narrative is not meant for narration,
But a mere airy and fantastic basis,
To build up common things with common places.

8

You know, or don't know, that great Bacon saith,
 "Fling up a straw, 't will show the way the wind
  blows";
And such a straw, borne on by human breath,
 Is poesy, according as the mind glows; 60
A paper kite which flies 'twixt life and death,
 A shadow which the onward soul behind throws:
And mine's a bubble, not blown up for praise,
But just to play with, as an infant plays.

9

The world is all before me—or behind;
 For I have seen a portion of that same,
And quite enough for me to keep in mind;—
 Of passions, too, I have proved enough to blame,
To the great pleasure of our friends, mankind,
 Who like to mix some slight alloy with fame; 70
For I was rather famous in my time,
Until I fairly knock'd it up with rhyme.

10

I have brought this world about my ears, and eke
 The other; that's to say, the clergy, who
Upon my head have bid their thunders break
 In pious libels by no means a few.
And yet I can't help scribbling once a week,
 Tiring old readers, nor discovering new.
In youth I wrote because my mind was full,
And now because I feel it growing dull. 80

11

But "why then publish?"—There are no rewards
 Of fame or profit when the world grows weary.
I ask in turn,—Why do you play at cards?
 Why drink? Why read?—To make some hour
  less dreary.

It occupies me to turn back regards
 On what I've seen or ponder'd, sad or cheery;
And what I write I cast upon the stream,
To swim or sink—I have had at least my dream.

12

I think that were I *certain* of success,
 I hardly could compose another line: 90
So long I've battled either more or less,
 That no defeat can drive me from the Nine.
This feeling 'tis not easy to express,
 And yet 'tis not affected, I opine.
In play, there are two pleasures for your choosing—
The one is winning, and the other losing.

13

Besides, my Muse by no means deals in fiction:
 She gathers a repertory of facts,
Of course with some reserve and slight restriction,
 But mostly sings of human things and
  acts— 100
And that's one cause she meets with contradiction;
 For too much truth, at first sight, ne'er attracts;
And were her object only what's call'd glory,
With more ease too she'd tell a different story.

14

Love, war, a tempest—surely there's variety;
 Also a seasoning slight of lucubration;
A bird's-eye view, too, of that wild, Society;
 A slight glance thrown on men of every station.
If you have nought else, here's at least satiety
 Both in performance and in preparation; 110
And though these lines should only line portman-
 teaus,
Trade will be all the better for these Cantos.

15

The portion of this world which I at present
 Have taken up to fill the following sermon,
Is one of which there's no description recent.
 The reason why is easy to determine:
Although it seems both prominent and pleasant,
 There is a sameness in its gems and ermine,
A dull and family likeness through all ages,
Of no great promise for poetic pages. 120

16

With much to excite, there's little to exalt;
  Nothing that speaks to all men and all times;
A sort of varnish over every fault;
  A kind of common-place, even in their crimes;
Factitious passions, wit without much salt,
  A want of that true nature which sublimes
Whate'er it shows with truth; a smooth monotony
Of character, in those at least who have got any.

17

Sometimes, indeed, like soldiers off parade,
  They break their ranks and gladly leave the
    drill;   130
But then the roll-call draws them back afraid,
  And they must be or seem what they were: still
Doubtless it is a brilliant masquerade;
  But when of the first sight you have had your fill,
It palls—at least it did so upon me,
This paradise of pleasure and ennui.

18

When we have made our love, and gamed our
    gaming,
  Drest, voted, shone, and, may be, something
    more;
With dandies dined; heard senators declaiming;
  Seen beauties brought to market by the
    score,   140
Sad rakes to sadder husbands chastely taming;
  There's little left but to be bored or bore.
Witness those *"ci-devant jeunes hommes"* who stem
The stream, nor leave the world which leaveth
    them.

19

'Tis said—indeed a general complaint—
  That no one has succeeded in describing
The monde, exactly as they ought to paint:
  Some say, that authors only snatch, by bribing
The porter, some slight scandals strange and
    quaint,
  To furnish matter for their moral gibing;   150

And that their books have but one style in com-
    mon—
My lady's prattle, filter'd through her woman.

20

But this can't well be true, just now; for writers
  Are grown of the beau monde a part potential:
I've seen them balance even the scale with fighters,
  Especially when young, for that's essential.
Why do their sketches fail them as inditers
  Of what they deem themselves most consequen-
    tial,
The *real* portrait of the highest tribe?
'Tis that, in fact, there's little to describe.   160

.   .   .

31

Juan—in this respect, at least, like saints—   241
  Was all things unto people of all sorts,
And lived contentedly, without complaints,
  In camps, in ships, in cottages, or courts—
Born with that happy soul which seldom faints,
  And mingling modestly in toils or sports.
He likewise could be most things to all women,
Without the coxcombry of certain *she* men.

32

A fox-hunt to a foreigner is strange;
  'Tis also subject to the double danger   250
Of tumbling first, and having in exchange
  Some pleasant jesting at the awkward stranger:
But Juan had been early taught to range
  The wilds, as doth an Arab turn'd avenger,
So that his horse, or charger, hunter, hack,
Knew that he had a rider on his back.

33

And now in this new field, with some applause,
  He clear'd hedge, ditch, and double post, and
    rail,
And never *craned,* and made but few *"faux pas,"*
  And only fretted when the scent 'gan fail.   260
He broke, 'tis true, some statutes of the laws
  Of hunting—for the sagest youth is frail;

Rode o'er the hounds, it may be, now and then,
And once o'er several country gentlemen.

34

But on the whole, to general admiration
   He acquitted both himself and horse: the squires
Marvell'd at merit of another nation;
   The boors cried "Dang it! who'd have thought
      it?"—Sires,
The Nestors of the sporting generation,
   Swore praises, and recall'd their former
      fires;   270
The huntsman's self relented to a grin,
And rated him almost a whipper-in.

35

Such were his trophies—not of spear and shield,
   But leaps, and bursts, and sometimes foxes'
      brushes;
Yet I must own,—although in this I yield
   To patriot sympathy a Briton's blushes,—
He thought at heart like courtly Chesterfield,
   Who, after a long chase o'er hills, dales, bushes,
And what not, though he rode beyond all price,
Ask'd next day, "If men ever hunted *twice?*" 280

36

He also had a quality uncommon
   To early risers after a long chase,
Who wake in winter ere the cock can summon
   December's drowsy day to his dull race,—
A quality agreeable to woman,
   When her soft, liquid words run on apace,
Who likes a listener, whether saint or sinner,—
He did not fall asleep just after dinner;

37

But, light and airy, stood on the alert,
   And shone in the best part of dialogue, 290

By humouring always what they might assert,
   And listening to the topics most in vogue;
Now grave, now gay, but never dull or pert;
   And smiling but in secret—cunning rogue!
He ne'er presumed to make an error clearer;—
In short, there never was a better hearer.

38

And then he danced;—all foreigners excel
   The serious Angles in the eloquence
Of pantomine;—he danced, I say, right well,
   With emphasis, and also with good sense— 300
A thing in footing indispensable;
   He danced without theatrical pretence,
Not like a ballet-master in the van
Of his drill'd nymphs, but like a gentleman.

39

Chaste were his steps, each kept within due bound,
   And elegance was sprinkled o'er his figure;
Like swift Camilla, he scarce skimm'd the ground,
   And rather held in than put forth his vigour;
And then he had an ear for music's sound,
   Which might defy a crotchet critic's rigour. 310
Such classic pas—sans flaws—set off our hero,
He glanced like a personified Bolero;

40

Or, like a flying Hour before Aurora,
   In Guido's famous fresco which alone
Is worth a tour to Rome, although no more a
   Remnant were there of the old world's sole
      throne.
The *"tout ensemble"* of his movements wore a
   Grace of the soft ideal, seldom shown,
And ne'er to be described; for to the dolour
Of bards and prosers, words are void of
      colour.   320

41

No marvel then he was a favourite;
   A full-grown Cupid, very much admired;

CANTO XIV. **269. Nestors:** wise men. In Greek legend Nestor was the wise old counsellor who fought with the Greeks at Troy. **277. Chesterfield:** Philip Dormer Stanhope, fourth Earl of Chesterfield (1694–1773), English statesman, orator, and writer.

307. Camilla: a legendary Volscian queen. Virgil says she was so swift that she could run over a field of corn without bending a single blade.

A little spoilt, but by no means so quite;
  At least he kept his vanity retired.
Such was his tact, he could alike delight
  The chaste, and those who are not so much
    inspired.
The Duchess of Fitz-Fulke, who loved *"tracasserie,"*
Began to treat him with some small *"agacerie."*

42

She was a fine and somewhat full-blown blonde,
  Desirable, distinguish'd, celebrated   330
For several winters in the grand, *grand monde.*
  I'd rather not say what might be related
Of her exploits, for this were ticklish ground;
  Besides there might be falsehood in what's
    stated:
Her late performance had been a dead set
At Lord Augustus Fitz-Plantagenet.

43

This noble personage began to look
  A little black upon this new flirtation;
But such small licences must lovers brook,
  Mere freedoms of the female corporation.   340
Woe to the man who ventures a rebuke!
  'Twill but precipitate a situation
Extremely disagreeable, but common
To calculators when they count on woman.

44

The circle smiled, then whisper'd, and then sneer'd;
  The Misses bridled, and the matrons frown'd;
Some hoped things might not turn out as they
    fear'd;
  Some would not deem such women could be
    found;
Some ne'er believed one half of what they heard;
  Some look'd perplex'd, and others look'd pro-
    found;   350
And several pitied with sincere regret
Poor Lord Augustus Fitz-Plantagenet.

327. *"tracasserie"*: mischief. 328. *"agacerie"*: flirtatious-
ness.

45

But what is odd, none ever named the duke,
  Who, one might think, was something in the
    affair:
True, he was absent, and, 't was rumour'd, took
  But small concern about the when, or where,
Or what his consort did: if he could brook
  Her gaieties, none had a right to stare:
Theirs was that best of unions, past all doubt,
Which never meets, and therefore can't fall
    out.   360

46

But, oh! that I should ever pen so sad a line!
  Fired with an abstract love of virtue, she,
My Dian of the Ephesians, Lady Adeline,
  Began to think the duchess' conduct free;
Regretting much that she had chosen so bad a line,
  And waxing chiller in her courtesy,
Look'd grave and pale to see her friend's fragility,
For which most friends reserve their sensibility.

47

There's nought in this bad world like sympathy:
  'Tis so becoming to the soul and face,   370
Sets to soft music the harmonious sigh,
  And robes sweet friendship in a Brussels lace.
Without a friend, what were humanity,
  To hunt our errors up with a good grace?
Consoling us with—"Would you had thought twice!
Ah, if you had but follow'd my advice!"

48

O Job! you had two friends: one's quite enough,
  Especially when we are ill at ease;
They are but bad pilots when the weather's rough,
  Doctors less famous for their cures than
    fees.   380
Let no man grumble when his friends fall off,
  As they will do like leaves at the first breeze:
When your affairs come round, one way or t'other,
Go to the coffee-house, and take another.

363. Dian: Diana, goddess of Ephesus.

49

But this is not my maxim: had it been,
    Some heart-aches had been spared me: yet I care
        not—
I would not be a tortoise in his screen
    Of stubborn shell, which waves and weather
        wear not.
'Tis better on the whole to have felt and seen
    That which humanity may bear, or bear
        not: 390
'Twill teach discernment to the sensitive,
And not to pour their ocean in a sieve.

50

Of all the horrid, hideous notes of woe,
    Sadder than owl-songs or the midnight blast,
Is that portentous phrase, "I told you so,"
    Utter'd by friends, those prophets of the past,
Who, 'stead of saying what you now should do,
    Own they foresaw that you would fall at last,
And solace your slight lapse 'gainst "*bonos
        mores,*"
With a long memorandum of old stories.   400

51

The Lady Adeline's serene severity
    Was not confined to feeling for her friend,
Whose fame she rather doubted with posterity,
    Unless her habits should begin to mend:
But Juan also shared in her austerity,
    But mix'd with pity, pure as e'er was penn'd:
His inexperience moved her gentle ruth,
And (as her junior by six weeks) his youth.

52

These forty days' advantage of her years—
    And hers were those which can face calcula-
        tion,   410
Boldly referring to the list of peers
    And noble births, nor dread the enumeration—
Gave her a right to have maternal fears
    For a young gentleman's fit education,
Though she was far from that leap year, whose
        leap,
In female dates, strikes Time all of a heap.

53

This may be fix'd at somewhere before thirty—
    Say seven-and-twenty; for I never knew
The strictest in chronology and virtue
    Advance beyond, while they could pass for
        new.   420
O Time! why dost not pause? Thy scythe, so dirty
    With rust, should surely cease to hack and hew.
Reset it; shave more smoothly, also slower,
If but to keep thy credit as a mower.

54

But Adeline was far from that ripe age,
    Whose ripeness is but bitter at the best:
'Twas rather her experience made her sage,
    For she had seen the world and stood its test,
As I have said in—I forget what page;
    My Muse despises reference, as you have
        guess'd   430
By this time;—but strike six from seven-and-
        twenty,
And you will find her sum of years in plenty.

55

At sixteen she came out; presented, vaunted,
    She put all coronets into commotion:
At seventeen, too, the world was still enchanted
    With the new Venus of their brilliant ocean:
At eighteen, though below her feet still panted
    A hecatomb of suitors with devotion,
She had consented to create again
That Adam, call'd "The happiest of men."   440

56

Since then she had sparkled through three glowing
        winters,
    Admired, adored; but also so correct,
That she had puzzled all the acutest hinters,
    Without the apparel of being circumspect:
They could not even glean the slightest splinters
    From off the marble, which had no defect.
She had also snatch'd a moment since her marriage
To bear a son and heir—and one miscarriage.

57

Fondly the wheeling fire-flies flew around her,
  Those little glitterers of the London night;   450
But none of these possess'd a sting to wound her—
  She was a pitch beyond a coxcomb's flight.
Perhaps she wish'd an aspirant profounder;
  But whatsoe'er she wish'd, she acted right;
And whether coldness, pride, or virtue dignify
A woman, so she's good, what does it signify?

58

I hate a motive, like a lingering bottle
  Which with the landlord makes too long a stand,
Leaving all-claretless the unmoisten'd throttle,
  Especially with politics on hand;   460
I hate it, as I hate a drove of cattle,
  Who whirl the dust as simooms whirl the sand;
I hate it, as I hate an argument,
A laureate's ode, or servile peer's "content."

59

'Tis sad to hack into the roots of things,
  They are so much intertwisted with the earth;
So that the branch a goodly verdure flings,
  I reck not if an acorn gave it birth.
To trace all actions to their secret springs
  Would make indeed some melancholy
    mirth;   470
But this is not at present my concern,
And I refer you to wise Oxenstiern.

60

With the kind view of saving an éclat,
  Both to the duchess and diplomatist,
The Lady Adeline, as soon's she saw
  That Juan was unlikely to resist
(For foreigners don't know that a faux pas
  In England ranks quite on a different list
From those of other lands unblest with juries,
Whose verdict for such sin a certain cure
    is);—   480

61

The Lady Adeline resolved to take
  Such measures as she thought might best impede
The farther progress of this sad mistake.
  She thought with some simplicity indeed;
But innocence is bold even at the stake,
  And simple in the world, and doth not need
Nor use those palisades by dames erected,
Whose virtue lies in never being detected.

62

It was not that she fear'd the very worst:
  His Grace was an enduring, married man,   490
And was not likely all at once to burst
  Into a scene, and swell the clients' clan
Of Doctors' Commons: but she dreaded first
  The magic of her Grace's talisman,
And next a quarrel (as he seem'd to fret)
With Lord Augustus Fitz-Plantagenet.

63

Her Grace, too, pass'd for being an intrigante,
  And somewhat méchante in her amorous sphere;
One of those pretty, precious plagues, which haunt
  A lover with caprices soft and dear,   500
That like to make a quarrel, when they can't
  Find one, each day of the delightful year;
Bewitching, torturing, as they freeze or glow,
And—what is worst of all—won't let you go:

64

The sort of thing to turn a young man's head,
  Or make a Werter of him in the end.
No wonder then a purer soul should dread
  This sort of chaste liaison for a friend;
It were much better to be wed or dead,
  Than wear a heart a woman loves to rend.   510
'Tis best to pause, and think, ere you rush on,
If that a "bonne fortune" be really "bonne."

462. simooms: hot, violent, sand-laden winds. 472.
Oxenstiern: the famous Chancellor Oxenstiern (1583–
1654).

506. Werter: a reference to the young hero who committed suicide in Goethe's The Sufferings of Young
Werther.

65

And first, in the o'erflowing of her heart,
   Which really knew or thought it knew no guile,
She call'd her husband now and then apart,
   And bade him counsel Juan. With a smile
Lord Henry heard her plans of artless art
   To wean Don Juan from the siren's wile;
And answer'd, like a statesman or a prophet,
In such guise that she could make nothing of
     it.   520

. . .

85

Our gentle Adeline had one defect—
   Her heart was vacant, though a splendid mansion;
Her conduct had been perfectly correct,
   As she had seen nought claiming its expansion.
A wavering spirit may be easier wreck'd,
   Because 'tis frailer, doubtless, than a stanch one;
But when the latter works its own undoing,
Its inner crash is like an earthquake's ruin.   680

86

She loved her lord, or thought so; but *that* love
   Cost her an effort, which is a sad toil,
The stone of Sisyphus, if once we move
   Our feelings 'gainst the nature of the soil.
She had nothing to complain of, or reprove,
   No bickerings, no connubial turmoil:
Their union was a model to behold,
Serene and noble,—conjugal, but cold.

87

There was no great disparity of years,
   Though much in temper; but they never
     clash'd: 690
They moved like stars united in their spheres,
   Or like the Rhone by Leman's waters wash'd,

683. **Sisyphus:** In the Greek myth, Sisyphus was condemned to forever roll a great rock up a hill; after he reached the top, the stone rolled back.

Where mingled and yet separate appears
   The river from the lake, all bluely dash'd
Through the serene and placid glassy deep,
Which fain would lull its river-child to sleep.

88

Now when she once had ta'en an interest
   In any thing, however she might flatter
Herself that her intentions were the best,
   Intense intentions are a dangerous matter: 700
Impressions were much stronger than she guess'd,
   And gather'd as they run like growing water
Upon her mind; the more so, as her breast
Was not at first too readily impress'd.

89

But when it was, she had that lurking demon
   Of double nature, and thus doubly named—
Firmness yclept in heroes, kings, and seamen,
   That is, when they succeed; but greatly blamed
As *obstinacy*, both in men and women,
   Whene'er their triumph pales, or star is
     tamed:—   710
And 't will perplex the casuist in morality
To fix the due bounds of this dangerous quality.

90

Had Buonaparte won at Waterloo,
   It had been firmness; now 'tis pertinacity:
Must the event decide between the two?
   I leave it to your people of sagacity
To draw the line between the false and true,
   If such can e'er be drawn by man's capacity:
My business is with Lady Adeline,
Who in her way too was a heroine.   720

91

She knew not her own heart; then how should I?
   I think not she was *then* in love with Juan:
If so, she would have had the strength to fly
   The wild sensation, unto her a new one:
She merely felt a common sympathy
   (I will not say it was a false or true one)
In him, because she thought he was in danger,—
Her husband's friend, her own, young, and a
     stranger,

92

She was, or thought she was, his friend—and this
　Without the farce of friendship, or romance   730
Of Platonism, which leads so oft amiss
　Ladies who have studied friendship but in
　　France,
Or Germany, where people *purely* kiss.
　To thus much Adeline would not advance;
But of such friendship as man's may to man be
She was as capable as woman can be.

93

No doubt the secret influence of the sex
　Will there, as also in the ties of blood,
An innocent predominance annex,
　And tune the concord to a finer mood.   740
If free from passion, which all friendship checks,
　And your true feelings fully understood,
No friend like to a woman earth discovers,
So that you have not been nor will be lovers.

94

Love bears within its breast the very germ
　Of change; and how should this be otherwise?
That violent things more quickly find a term
　Is shown through nature's whole analogies;
And how should the most fierce of all be firm?
　Would you have endless lightning in the
　　skies?   750
Methinks Love's very title says enough:
How should "the tender passion" e'er be *tough?*

95

Alas! by all experience, seldom yet
　(I merely quote what I have heard from many)
Had lovers not some reason to regret
　The passion which made Solomon a zany.
I've also seen some wives (not to forget
　The marriage state, the best or worst of any)
Who were the very paragons of wives,
Yet made the misery of at least two lives.   760

96

I've also seen some female *friends* ('tis odd,
　But true—as, if expedient, I could prove)
That faithful were through thick and thin, abroad,
　At home, far more than ever yet was Love—
Who did not quit me when Oppression trod
　Upon me; whom no scandal could remove;
Who fought, and fight, in absence, too, my battles,
Despite the snake Society's loud rattles.

97

Whether Don Juan and chaste Adeline
　Grew friends in this or any other sense,   770
Will be discuss'd hereafter, I opine:
　At present I am glad of a pretence
To leave them hovering, as the effect is fine,
　And keeps the atrocious reader in *suspense;*
The surest way for ladies and for books
To bait their tender, or their tenter, hooks.

98

Whether they rode, or walk'd, or studied Spanish
　To read Don Quixote in the original,
A pleasure before which all others vanish;
　Whether their talk was of the kind call'd
　　"small,"   780
Or serious, are the topics I must banish
　To the next Canto; where perhaps I shall
Say something to the purpose, and display
Considerable talent in my way.

99

Above all, I beg all men to forbear
　Anticipating aught about the matter:
They'll only make mistakes about the fair,
　And Juan too, especially the latter.
And I shall take a much more serious air
　Than I have yet done, in this epic satire.   790
It is not clear that Adeline and Juan
Will fall; but if they do, 'twill be their ruin.

100

But great things spring from little:—Would you
　think,

That in our youth, as dangerous a passion
  As e'er brought man and woman to the brink
    Of ruin, rose from such a slight occasion,
  As few would ever dream could form the link
    Of such a sentimental situation?
You'll never guess, I'll bet you millions, milliards—
It all sprung from a harmless game at bil-
      liards.   800

101

'Tis strange,—but true; for truth is always strange;
  Stranger than fiction; if it could be told,
How much would novels gain by the exchange!
  How differently the world would men behold!
How oft would vice and virtue places change!
  The new world would be nothing to the old,
If some Columbus of the moral seas
Would show mankind their souls' antipodes.

102

What "antres vast and deserts idle" then
  Would be discover'd in the human soul!   810
What icebergs in the hearts of mighty men,
  With self-love in the centre as their pole!
What Anthropophagi are nine of ten
  Of those who hold the kingdoms in control!
Were things but only call'd by their right name,
Cæsar himself would be ashamed of fame.
1823   *1823*

From CANTO THE FIFTEENTH

1

Ah!—What should follow slips from my reflection;
  Whatever follows ne'ertheless may be
As à-propos of hope or retrospection,
  As though the lurking thought had follow'd free.
All present life is but an interjection,
  An "Oh!" or "Ah!" of joy or misery,
Or a "Ha! ha!" or "Bah!"—a yawn, or "Pooh!"
Of which perhaps the latter is most true.

809. "antres...idle": See *Othello*, I, iii, 140. 813.
Anthropophagi: cannibals.

2

But, more or less, the whole's a syncopé
  Or a singultus—emblems of emotion,   10
The grand antithesis to great ennui,
  Wherewith we break our bubbles on the
      ocean,—
That watery outline of eternity,
  Or miniature at least, as is my notion,
Which ministers unto the soul's delight,
In seeing matters which are out of sight.

3

But all are better than the sigh supprest,
  Corroding in the cavern of the heart,
Making the countenance a masque of rest,
  And turning human nature to an art.   20
Few men dare show their thoughts of worst or
      best;
  Dissimulation always sets apart
A corner for herself; and therefore fiction
Is that which passes with least contradiction.

4

Ah! who can tell? Or rather, who can not
  Remember, without telling, passion's errors?
The drainer of oblivion, even the sot,
  Hath got blue devils for his morning mirrors:
What though on Lethe's stream he seem to float,
  He cannot sink his tremors or his terrors;   30
The ruby glass that shakes within his hand
Leaves a sad sediment of Time's worst sand.

5

And as for love—O love!—We will proceed.
  The Lady Adeline Amundeville,
A pretty name as one would wish to read,
  Must perch harmonious on my tuneful quill.
There's music in the sighing of a reed;
  There's music in the gushing of a rill;
There's music in all things, if men had ears:
Their earth is but an echo of the spheres.   40

CANTO XV. **9. syncopé**: fainting. **10. singultus**: hiccups.

6

The Lady Adeline, right honourable,
    And honour'd, ran a risk of growing less so;
For few of the soft sex are very stable
    In their resolves—alas! that I should say so!
They differ as wine differs from its label,
    When once decanted;—I presume to guess so,
But will not swear: yet both upon occasion,
Till old, may undergo adulteration.

7

But Adeline was of the purest vintage,
    The unmingled essence of the grape; and
        yet   50
Bright as a new Napoleon from its mintage,
    Or glorious as a diamond richly set;
A page where Time should hesitate to print age,
    And for which Nature might forego her debt—
Sole creditor whose process doth involve in't
The luck of finding every body solvent.

8

O Death! thou dunnest of all duns! thou daily
    Knockest at doors, at first with modest tap,
Like a meek tradesman when, approaching palely,
    Some splendid debtor he would take by sap: 60
But oft denied, as patience 'gins to fail, he
    Advances with exasperated rap,
And (if let in) insists, in terms unhandsome,
On ready money, or "a draft on Ransom."

9

Whate'er thou takest, spare a while poor Beauty!
    She is so rare, and thou hast so much prey.
What though she now and then may slip from duty,
    The more 's the reason why you ought to stay.
Gaunt Gourmand! with whole nations for your
        booty,
    You should be civil in a modest way: 70
Suppress, then, some slight feminine diseases,
And take as many heroes as Heaven pleases.

10

Fair Adeline, the more ingenuous
    Where she was interested (as was said),

Because she was not apt, like some of us,
    To like too readily, or too high bred
To show it (points we need not now discuss)—
    Would give up artlessly both heart and head
Unto such feelings as seem'd innocent,
For objects worthy of the sentiment.   80

11

Some parts of Juan's history, which Rumour,
    That live gazette, had scatter'd to disfigure,
She had heard; but women hear with more good
        humour
    Such aberrations than we men of rigour:
Besides, his conduct, since in England, grew more
    Strict, and his mind assumed a manlier vigour;
Because he had, like Alcibiades,
The art of living in all climes with ease.

12

His manner was perhaps the more seductive,
    Because he ne'er seem'd anxious to seduce;   90
Nothing affected, studied, or constructive
    Of coxcombry or conquest: no abuse
Of his attractions marr'd the fair perspective,
    To indicate a Cupidon broke loose,
And seem to say, "Resist us if you can"—
Which makes a dandy while it spoils a man.

13

They are wrong—that's not the way to set about it;
    As, if they told the truth, could well be shown.
But, right or wrong, Don Juan was without it;
    In fact, his manner was his own alone;   100
Sincere he was—at least you could not doubt it,
    In listening merely to his voice's tone.
The devil hath not in all his quiver's choice
An arrow for the heart like a sweet voice.

14

By nature soft, his whole address held off
    Suspicion: though not timid, his regard

87. **Alcibiades:** Athenian politician and general (450?-404 B.C.). 94. **Cupidon:** a beau or cupid.

Was such as rather seem'd to keep aloof,
　　To shield himself than put you on your guard:
Perhaps 'twas hardly quite assured enough,
　　But modesty 's at times its own reward,　　110
Like virtue; and the absence of pretension
Will go much farther than there's need to mention.

15

Serene, accomplish'd, cheerful but not loud;
　　Insinuating without insinuation;
Observant of the foibles of the crowd,
　　Yet ne'er betraying this in conversation;
Proud with the proud, yet courteously proud,
　　So as to make them feel he knew his station
And theirs:—without a struggle for priority,
He neither brook'd nor claim'd superiority.　　120

16

That is, with men: with women he was what
　　They pleased to make or take him for; and their
Imagination 's quite enough for that:
　　So that the outline 's tolerably fair,
They fill the canvass up—and "verbum sat."
　　If once their phantasies be brought to bear
Upon an object, whether sad or playful,
They can transfigure brighter than a Raphael.

17

Adeline, no deep judge of character,
　　Was apt to add a colouring from her own:　　130
'Tis thus the good will amiably err,
　　And eke the wise, as has been often shown.
Experience is the chief philosopher,
　　But saddest when his science is well known:
And persecuted sages teach the schools
Their folly in forgetting there are fools.

.　.　.

27

We'll do our best to make the best on 't:—March!
　　March, my Muse! If you cannot fly, yet
　　　　flutter;　　210
And when you may not be sublime, be arch,
　　Or starch, as are the edicts statesmen utter.
We surely may find something worth research:
　　Columbus found a new world in a cutter,
Or brigantine, or pink, of no great tonnage,
While yet America was in her non-age.

28

When Adeline, in all her growing sense
　　Of Juan's merits and his situation,
Felt on the whole an interest intense,—
　　Partly perhaps because a fresh sensation,　　220
Or that he had an air of innocence,
　　Which is for innocence a sad temptation,—
As women hate half measures, on the whole,
She 'gan to ponder how to save his soul.

29

She had a good opinion of advice,
　　Like all who give and eke receive it gratis,
For which small thanks are still the market price,
　　Even where the article at highest rate is:
She thought upon the subject twice or thrice,
　　And morally decided, the best state is　　230
For morals, marriage; and this question carried,
She seriously advised him to get married.

30

Juan replied, with all becoming deference,
　　He had a predilection for that tie;
But that, at present, with immediate reference
　　To his own circumstances, there might lie
Some difficulties, as in his own preference,
　　Or that of her to whom he might apply:
That still he'd wed with such or such a lady,
If that they were not married all already.　　240

31

Next to the making matches for herself,
　　And daughters, brothers, sisters, kith or kin,
Arranging them like books on the same shelf,
　　There's nothing women love to dabble in
More (like a stock-holder in growing pelf)
　　Than match-making in general: 'tis no sin
Certes, but a preventative, and therefore
That is, no doubt, the only reason wherefore.

32

But never yet (except of course a miss
    Unwed, or mistress never to be wed,   250
Or wed already, who object to this)
    Was there chaste dame who had not in her head
Some drama of the marriage unities,
    Observed as strictly both at board and bed
As those of Aristotle, though sometimes
They turn out melodrames or pantomimes.

33

They generally have some only son,
    Some heir to a large property, some friend
Of an old family, some gay Sir John,
    Or grave Lord George, with whom perhaps
        might end   260
A line, and leave posterity undone,
    Unless a marriage was applied to mend
The prospect and their morals: and besides,
They have at hand a blooming glut of brides.

34

From these they will be careful to select,
    For this an heiress, and for that a beauty;
For one a songstress who hath no defect,
    For t'other one who promises much duty;
For this a lady no one can reject,
    Whose sole accomplishments were quite a
        booty;   270
A second for her excellent connections;
A third, because there can be no objections.

35

When Rapp the Harmonist embargo'd marriage
    In his harmonious settlement (which flourishes
Strangely enough as yet without miscarriage,
    Because it breeds no more mouths than it
        nourishes,
Without those sad expenses which disparage
    What Nature naturally most encourages)—

273. Rapp the Harmonist: a reference to the Harmonists, a German colony in America that restricted births. They were a peaceful and flourishing people.

Why call'd he "Harmony" a state sans wedlock?
Now here I've got the preacher at a dead
    lock,   280

36

Because he either meant to sneer at harmony
    Or marriage, by divorcing them thus oddly.
But whether reverend Rapp learn'd this in Germany
    Or no, 'tis said his sect is rich and godly,
Pious and pure, beyond what I can term any
    Of ours, although they propagate more broadly
My objection 's to his title, not his ritual,
Although I wonder how it grew habitual.

37

But Rapp is the reverse of zealous matrons,
    Who favour, malgré Malthus, generation—   290
Professors of that genial art, and patrons
    Of all the modest part of propagation;
Which after all at such a desperate rate runs,
    That half its produce tends to emigration,
That sad result of passions and potatoes—
Two weeds which pose our economic Catos.

38

Had Adeline read Malthus? I can't tell;
    I wish she had: his book's the eleventh com-
        mandment,
Which says, "Thou shall not marry," unless *well*:
    This he (as far as I can understand)
        meant.   300
'Tis not my purpose on his views to dwell
    Nor canvass what so "eminent a hand" meant;
But certes it conducts to lives ascetic,
Or turning marriage into arithmetic.

39

But Adeline, who probably presumed
    That Juan had enough of maintenance,
Or *separate* maintenance, in case 't was doom'd—
    As on the whole it is an even chance
That bridegrooms, after they are fairly *groom'd*,
    May retrograde a little in the dance   310
Of marriage (which might form a painter's fame,

Like Holbein's "Dance of Death"—but 'tis the
   same);—

40

But Adeline determined Juan's wedding
   In her own mind, and that's enough for woman:
But then, with whom? There was the sage Miss
   Reading,
   Miss Raw, Miss Flaw, Miss Showman, and Miss
   Knowman,
And the two fair co-heiresses Giltbedding.
   She deem'd his merits something more than com-
   mon:
All these were unobjectionable matches,
And might go on, if well wound up, like
   watches.   320

41

There was Miss Millpond, smooth as summer's sea,
   That usual paragon, an only daughter,
Who seem'd the cream of equanimity
   Till skimm'd—and then there was some milk and
   water,
With a slight shade of blue too, it might be,
   Beneath the surface; but what did it matter?
Love's riotous, but marriage should have quiet,
And being consumptive, live on a milk diet.

42

And then there was the Miss Audacia Shoestring,
   A dashing demoiselle of good estate,   330
Whose heart was fix'd upon a star or blue string;
   But whether English dukes grew rare of late,
Or that she had not harp'd upon the true string,
   By which such sirens can attract our great,
She took up with some foreign younger brother,
A Russ or Turk—the one 's as good as t'other.

43

And then there was—but why should I go on,
   Unless the ladies should go off?—there was

321. **Miss Millpond:** still another disparaging reference
to Byron's wife, Annabella Milbanke.

Indeed a certain fair and fairy one,
   Of the best class, and better than her
   class,—   340
Aurora Raby, a young star who shone
   O'er life, too sweet an image for such glass,
A lovely being, scarcely form'd or moulded,
A rose with all its sweetest leaves yet folded;

44

Rich, noble, but an orphan; left an only
   Child to the care of guardians good and kind;
But still her aspect had an air so lonely!
   Blood is not water; and where shall we find
Feelings of youth like those which overthrown lie
   By death, when we are left, alas! behind,   350
To feel, in friendless palaces, a home
Is wanting, and our best ties in the tomb?

45

Early in years, and yet more infantine
   In figure, she had something of sublime
In eyes which sadly shone, as seraphs' shine.
   All youth—but with an aspect beyond time;
Radiant and grave—as pitying man's decline;
   Mournful—but mournful of another's crime,
She look'd as if she sat by Eden's door.
And grieved for those who could return no
   more.   360

46

She was a Catholic, too, sincere, austere,
   As far as her own gentle heart allow'd,
And deem'd that fallen worship far more dear
   Perhaps because 'twas fallen: her sires were
   proud
Of deeds and days when they had fill'd the ear
   Of nations, and had never bent or bow'd
To novel power; and as she was the last,
She held their old faith and old feelings fast.

47

She gazed upon a world she scarcely knew,
   As seeking not to know it; silent, lone,   370
As grows a flower, thus quietly she grew,
   And kept her heart serene within its zone.

There was awe in the homage which she drew;
  Her spirit seem'd as seated on a throne
Apart from the surrounding world, and strong
In its own strength—most strange in one so young!

Whereas insisting in or out of season
  Convinces all men, even a politician;
Or—what is just the same—it wearies out.
So the end's gain'd, what signifies the route?

48

Now it so happen'd, in the catalogue
  Of Adeline, Aurora was omitted,
Although her birth and wealth had given her vogue
  Beyond the charmers we have already
    cited;   380
Her beauty also seem'd to form no clog
  Against her being mention'd as well fitted,
By many virtues, to be worth the trouble
Of single gentlemen who would be double.

52

Why Adeline had this slight prejudice—
  For prejudice it was—against a creature   410
As pure as sanctity itself from vice,
  With all the added charm of form and feature,
For me appears a question far too nice,
  Since Adeline was liberal by nature;
But nature's nature, and has more caprices
Than I have time, or will, to take to pieces.

49

And this omission, like that of the bust
  Of Brutus at the pageant of Tiberius,
Made Juan wonder, as no doubt he must.
  This he express'd half smiling and half serious;
When Adeline replied with some disgust,
  And with an air, to say the least, imperious,   390
She marvell'd "what he saw in such a baby
As that prim, silent, cold Aurora Raby?"

53

Perhaps she did not like the quiet way
  With which Aurora on those baubles look'd,
Which charm most people in their earlier day:
  For there are few things by mankind less
    brook'd,   420
And womankind too, if we so may say,
  Than finding thus their genius stand rebuked,
Like "Anthony's by Cæsar," by the few
Who look upon them as they ought to do.

50

Juan rejoin'd—"She was a Catholic,
  And therefore fittest, as of his persuasion;
Since he was sure his mother would fall sick,
  And the Pope thunder excommunication,
If—" But here Adeline, who seem'd to pique
  Herself extremely on the inoculation
Of others with her own opinions, stated—
As usual—the same reason which she late
    did.   400

54

It was not envy—Adeline had none;
  Her place was far beyond it, and her mind.
It was not scorn—which could not light on one
  Whose greatest *fault* was leaving few to find.
It was not jealousy, I think: but shun
  Following the "ignes fatui" of mankind.   430
It was not—but 'tis easier far, alas!
To say what it was not than what it was.

51

And wherefore not? A reasonable reason,
  If good, is none the worse for repetition;
If bad, the best way's certainly to tease on,
  And amplify: you lose much by concision,

55

Little Aurora deem'd she was the theme
  Of such discussion. She was there a guest;
A beauteous ripple of the brilliant stream
  Of rank and youth, though purer than the rest,
Which flow'd on for a moment in the beam
  Time sheds a moment o'er each sparkling crest.

385–86: bust ... Tiberius: Tiberius Caesar refused to
allow the bust of Brutus to be carried in the funeral
procession of Junia, Brutus' sister.

423. "Anthony's by Caesar": See *Macbeth*, III, i, 55–57.

Had she known this, she would have calmly
    smiled—
She had so much, or little, of the child.   440

56

The dashing and proud air of Adeline
Imposed not upon her: she saw her blaze
Much as she would have seen a glow-worm shine,
    Then turn'd unto the stars for loftier rays.
Juan was something she could not divine,
    Being no sibyl in the new world's ways;
Yet she was nothing dazzling by the meteor,
Because she did not pin her faith on feature.

57

His fame too,—for he had that kind of fame
    Which sometimes plays the deuce with
        womankind,   450
A heterogeneous mass of glorious blame,
    Half virtues and whole vices being combined;
Faults which attract because they are not tame;
    Follies trick'd out so brightly that they blind:—
These seals upon her wax made no impression,
Such was her coldness or her self-possession.

58

Juan knew nought of such a character—
    High, yet resembling not his lost Haidée;
Yet each was radiant in her proper sphere:
    The island girl, bred up by the lone sea,   460
More warm, as lovely, and not less sincere,
    Was Nature's all: Aurora could not be,
Nor would be thus:—the difference in them
Was such as lies between a flower and gem.

59

Having wound up with this sublime comparison,
    Methinks we may proceed upon our narrative,
And, as my friend Scott says, "I sound my
      warison";
    Scott, the superlative of my comparative—

467. "I . . . warison": See *The Lay of the Last Minstrel,*
IV, 24:17–20. **warison:** war cry.

Scott, who can paint your Christian knight or
    Saracen,
    Serf, lord, man, with such skill as none would
      share it, if   470
There had not been one Shakspeare and Voltaire,
Of one or both of whom he seems the heir.

60

I say, in my slight way I may proceed
    To play upon the surface of humanity.
I write the world, nor care if the world read,
    At least for this I cannot spare its vanity.
My Muse hath bred, and still perhaps may breed
    More foes by this same scroll: when I began it, I
Thought that it might turn out so—*now I know* it,
But still I am, or was, a pretty poet.   480

61

The conference or congress (for it ended
    As congresses of late do) of the Lady
Adeline and Don Juan rather blended
    Some acids with the sweets—for she was heady;
But, ere the matter could be marr'd or mended,
    The silvery bell rang, not for "dinner ready,"
But for that hour, call'd *half-hour,* given to dress,
Though ladies' robes seem scant enough for less.

. . .

74

Amidst this tumult of fish, flesh, and fowl,
    And vegetables, all in masquerade,
The guests were placed according to their roll,
    But various as the various meats display'd:
Don Juan sat next an "à l'Espagnole"—
    No damsel, but a dish, as hath been said;   590
But so far like a lady, that 'twas drest
Superbly, and contain'd a world of zest.

75

By some odd chance too, he was placed between
    Aurora and the Lady Adeline—
A situation difficult, I ween,
    For man therein, with eyes and heart, to dine.
Also the conference which we have seen
    Was not such as to encourage him to shine;

For Adeline, addressing few words to him,
With two transcendent eyes seem'd to look
  through him.   600

76

I sometimes almost think that eyes have ears:
 This much is sure, that, out of earshot, things
Are somehow echoed to the pretty dears,
 Of which I can't tell whence their knowledge
  springs.
Like that same mystic music of the spheres,
 Which no one hears, so loudly though it rings,
'Tis wonderful how oft the sex have heard
Long dialogues—which pass'd without a word!

77

Aurora sat with that indifference
 Which piques a preux chevalier—as it
  ought: 610
Of all offences that's the worst offence,
 Which seems to hint you are not worth a thought.
Now Juan, though no coxcomb in pretence,
 Was not exactly pleased to be so caught;
Like a good ship entangled among ice,
And after so much excellent advice.

78

To his gay nothings, nothing was replied,
 Or something which was nothing, as urbanity
Required. Aurora scarcely look'd aside,
 Nor even smiled enough for any vanity. 620
The devil was in the girl! Could it be pride?
 Or modesty, or absence, or inanity?
Heaven knows! But Adeline's malicious eyes
Sparkled with her successful prophecies,

79

And look'd as much as if to say, "I said it";
 A kind of triumph I'll not recommend,
Because it sometimes, as I have seen or read it,
 Both in the case of lover and of friend,
Will pique a gentleman, for his own credit,
 To bring what was a jest to a serious end: 630

610. preux chevalier: gallant knight.

For all men prophesy what *is* or *was*,
And hate those who won't let them come to pass.

80

Juan was drawn thus into some attentions,
 Slight but select, and just enough to express,
To females of perspicuous comprehensions,
 That he would rather make them more than less.
Aurora at the last (so history mentions,
 Though probably much less a fact than guess)
So far relax'd her thoughts from their sweet prison,
As once or twice to smile, if not to listen. 640

81

From answering she began to question; this
 With her was rare: and Adeline, who as yet
Thought her predictions went not much amiss,
 Began to dread she'd thaw to a coquette—
So very difficult, they say, it is
 To keep extremes from meeting, when once set
In motion; but she here too much refined—
Aurora's spirit was not of that kind.

82

But Juan had a sort of winning way,
 A proud humility, if such there be, 650
Which show'd such deference to what females say,
 As if each charming word were a decree.
His tact, too, temper'd him from grave to gay,
 And taught him when to be reserved or free:
He had the art of drawing people out,
Without their seeing what he was about.

83

Aurora, who in her indifference
 Confounded him in common with the crowd
Of flatterers, though she deem'd he had more sense
 Than whispering foplings, or than witlings
  loud—   660
Commenced (from such slight things will great
  commence)
 To feel that flattery which attracts the proud
Rather by deference than compliment,
And wins even by a delicate dissent.

84

And then he had good looks;—that point was
 carried
 Nem. con. amongst the women, which I grieve
To say leads oft to *crim. con.* with the married—
 A case which to the juries we may leave,
Since with digressions we too long have tarried.
 Now though we know of old that looks
  deceive,   670
And always have done, somehow these good looks
Make more impression than the best of books.

85

Aurora, who look'd more on books than faces,
 Was very young, although so very sage,
Admiring more Minerva than the Graces,
 Especially upon a printed page.
But Virtue's self, with all her tightest laces,
 Has not the natural stays of strict old age;
And Socrates, that model of all duty,
Own'd to a penchant, though discreet, for
 beauty.   680

86

And girls of sixteen are thus far Socratic,
 But innocently so, as Socrates;
And really, if the sage sublime and Attic
 At seventy years had phantasies like these,
Which Plato in his dialogues dramatic
 Has shown, I know not why they should
  displease
In virgins—always in a modest way,
Observe; for that with me 's a "sine qua."

87

Also observe, that, like the great Lord Coke
 (See Littleton), whene'er I have express'd 690
Opinions two, which at first sight may look
 Twin opposites, the second is the best.

---

666. *Nem. con.*: no one opposing; unanimously. 667.
crim. con.: criminal conversation; adultery. 689–90.
Coke . . . Littleton: a reference to Lord Coke's commentary on Littleton's *Institutes of the Laws of England.*

Perhaps I have a third, too, in a nook,
 Or none at all—which seems a sorry jest:
But if a writer should be quite consistent,
 How could he possibly show things existent?

88

If people contradict themselves, can I
 Help contradicting them, and every body,
Even my veracious self?—But that's a a lie:
 I never did so, never will—how should I? 700
He who doubts all things nothing can deny:
 Truth's fountains may be clear—her streams are
  muddy,
And cut through such canals of contradiction,
That she must often navigate o'er fiction.

89

Apologue, fable, poesy, and parable,
 Are false, but may be render'd also true,
By those who sow them in a land that's arable.
 'Tis wonderful what fable will not do!
'Tis said it makes reality more bearable:
 But what's reality? Who has its clue? 710
Philosophy? No: she too much rejects.
Religion? *Yes;* but which of all her sects?

90

Some millions must be wrong, that's pretty clear;
 Perhaps it may turn out that all were right.
God help us! Since we have need on our career
 To keep our holy beacons always bright,
'Tis time that some new prophet should appear,
 Or old indulge man with a second sight.
Opinions wear out in some thousand years,
Without a small refreshment from the
 spheres.   720

91

But here again, why will I thus entangle
 Myself with metaphysics? None can hate
So much as I do any kind of wrangle;
 And yet, such is my folly, or my fate,
I always knock my head against some angle
 About the present, past, or future state.

Yet I wish well to Trojan and to Tyrian,
For I was bred a moderate Presbyterian.

92

But though I am a temperate theologian,
  And also meek as a metaphysician,   730
Impartial between Tyrian and Trojan,
  As Eldon on a lunatic commission,—
In politics my duty is to show John
  Bull something of the lower world's condition.
It makes my blood boil like the springs of Hecla,
To see men let these scoundrel sovereigns break
      law.

93

But politics, and policy, and piety,
  Are topics which I sometimes introduce,
Not only for the sake of their variety,
  But as subservient to a moral use;   740
Because my business is to *dress* society,
  And stuff with *sage* that very verdant goose.
And now, that we may furnish with some matter all
Tastes, we are going to try the supernatural.

94

And now I will give up all argument;
  And positively henceforth no temptation
Shall "fool me to the top of my bent":—
  Yes, I'll begin a thorough reformation.
Indeed, I never knew what people meant
  By deeming that my Muse's conversation   750
Was dangerous;—I think she is as harmless
As some who labour more and yet may charm less.

95

Grim reader! did you ever see a ghost?
  No; but you have heard—I understand—be
      dumb!
And don't regret the time you may have lost,
  For you have got that pleasure still to come:

And do not think I mean to sneer at most
  Of these things, or by ridicule benumb
That source of the sublime and the mysterious:—
  For certain reasons my belief is serious.   760

96

Serious? You laugh;—you may: that will I not;
  My smiles must be sincere or not at all.
I say I do believe a haunted spot
  Exists—and where? That shall I not recall,
Because I'd rather it should be forgot,
  "Shadows the soul of Richard" may appal.
In short, upon that subject I've some qualms very
Like those of the philosopher of Malmsbury.

97

The night (I sing by night—sometimes an
      owl,   770
  And now and then a nightingale) is dim,
And the loud shriek of sage Minerva's fowl
  Rattles around me her discordant hymn:
Old portraits from old walls upon me scowl—
  I wish to heaven they would not look so grim;
The dying embers dwindle in the grate—
I think too that I have sate up too late:

98

And therefore, though 'tis by no means my way
  To rhyme at noon—when I have other things
To think of, if I ever think—I say
  I feel some chilly midnight shudderings,   780
And prudently postpone, until mid-day,
  Treating a topic which, alas! but brings
Shadows;—but you must be in my condition
Before you learn to call this superstition.

99

Between two worlds life hovers like a star,
  'Twixt night and morn, upon the horizon's verge.
How little do we know that which we are!
  How less what we may be! The eternal surge

732. Eldon: John Scott, Earl of Eldon, as Lord Chancellor sat in 1822–23 on a case involving the sanity of Lord Portsmouth. **735. Hecla**: volcano in Iceland. **747. "fool . . . bent"**: See *Hamlet*, III, ii, 408.

766. "Shadows . . . Richard": See *Richard III*, V, iii, 217–20. **768. philosopher of Malmsbury**: Thomas Hobbes, who, according to Byron, was afraid of ghosts.

Of time and tide rolls on, and bears afar
   Our bubbles; as the old burst, new emerge,   790
Lash'd from the foam of ages; while the graves
Of empires heave but like some passing waves.
1823   *1824*

From CANTO THE SIXTEENTH

8

The dinner and the soirée too were done,
   The supper too discuss'd, the dames admired,
The banqueteers had dropp'd off one by one—
   The song was silent, and the dance expired: 60
The last thin petticoats were vanish'd, gone
   Like fleecy clouds into the sky retired,
And nothing brighter gleam'd through the saloon
Than dying tapers—and the peeping moon.

9

The evaporation of a joyous day
   Is like the last glass of champagne, without
The foam which made its virgin bumper gay;
   Or like a system coupled with a doubt;
Or like a soda bottle when its spray
   Has sparkled and let half its spirit out;   70
Or like a billow left by storms behind,
Without the animation of the wind;

10

Or like an opiate, which brings troubled rest,
   Or none; or like—like nothing that I know
Except itself;—such is the human breast;
   A thing, of which similitudes can show
No real likeness,—like the old Tyrian vest
   Dyed purple, none at present can tell how,
If from a shell-fish or from cochineal.
So perish every tyrant's robe piece-meal!   80

11

But next to dressing for a rout or ball,
   Undressing is a woe; our robe de chambre

CANTO XVI. **79. cochineal:** an insect from which purple
dye is made.

May sit like that of Nessus, and recall
   Thoughts quite as yellow, but less clear than
     amber.
Titus exclaim'd, "I've lost a day!" Of all
   The nights and days most people can remember,
(I have had of both, some not to be disdain'd,)
I wish they'd state how many they have gain'd.

12

And Juan, on retiring for the night,
   Felt restless, and perplex'd, and
     compromised: 90
He thought Aurora Raby's eyes more bright
   Than Adeline (such is advice) advised;
If he had known exactly his own plight,
   He probably would have philosophised;
A great resource to all, and ne'er denied
Till wanted; therefore Juan only sigh'd.

13

He sigh'd;—the next resource is the full moon,
   Where all sighs are deposited; and now
It happen'd luckily, the chaste orb shone
   As clear as such a climate will allow;   100
And Juan's mind was in the proper tone
   To hail her with the apostrophe—"O thou!"
Of amatory egotism the *Tuism*,
Which further to explain would be a truism.

14

But lover, poet, or astronomer,
   Shepherd, or swain, whoever may behold,
Feel some abstraction when they gaze on her:
   Great thoughts we catch from thence (besides a
     cold
Sometimes, unless my feelings rather err);
   Deep secrets to her rolling light are told;   110

83. Nessus: another reference to the legend of Hercules'
being killed by wearing the poisoned cloak of the cen-
taur Nessus. **85. Titus . . . day:** The Roman emperor Titus, who tried to act on every petition, supposedly made
the quoted exclamation if a day went by without his
answering a request. **103. Tuism:** a manufactured word.
Based on the Latin "tu" (you), it suggests the opposite
of egoism.

The ocean's tides and mortals' brains she sways,
And also hearts, if there be truth in lays.

15

Juan felt somewhat pensive, and disposed
   For contemplation rather than his pillow:
The Gothic chamber, where he was enclosed,
   Let in the rippling sound of the lake's billow,
With all the mystery by midnight caused:
   Below his window waved (of course) a willow;
And he stood gazing out on the cascade
That flash'd and after darken'd in the shade.   120

16

Upon his table or his toilet,—*which*
   Of these is not exactly ascertain'd—
(I state this, for I am cautious to a pitch
   Of nicety, where a fact is to be gain'd,)
A lamp burn'd high, while he leant from a niche,
   Where many a Gothic ornament remain'd,
In chisell'd stone and painted glass, and all
That time has left our fathers of their hall.

17

Then, as the night was clear though cold, he threw
   His chamber door wide open—and went
     forth   130
Into a gallery, of a sombre hue,
   Long, furnish'd with old pictures of great worth,
Of knights and dames heroic and chaste too,
   As doubtless should be people of high birth.
But by dim lights the portraits of the dead
Have something ghastly, desolate, and dread.

18

The forms of the grim knight and pictured saint
   Look living in the moon; and as you turn
Backward and forward to the echoes faint
   Of your own footsteps—voices from the
     urn   140
Appear to wake, and shadows wild and quaint
   Start from the frames which fence their aspects
     stern,
As if to ask how you can dare to keep
A vigil there, where all but death should sleep.

19

And the pale smile of beauties in the grave,
   The charms of other days, in starlight gleams,
Glimmer on high; their buried locks still wave
   Along the canvas; their eyes glance like dreams
On ours, or spars within some dusky cave,
   But death is imaged in their shadowy
     beams.   150
A picture is the past; even ere its frame
Be gilt, who sate hath ceased to be the same.

20

As Juan mused on mutability,
   Or on his mistress—terms synonymous—
No sound except the echo of his sigh
   Or step ran sadly through that antique house;
When suddenly he heard, or thought so, nigh,
   A supernatural agent—or a mouse,
Whose little nibbling rustle will embarrass
Most people as it plays along the arras.   160

21

It was no mouse, but lo! a monk, array'd
   In cowl and beads, and dusky garb, appear'd,
Now in the moonlight, and now lapsed in shade,
   With steps that trod as heavy, yet unheard;
His garments only a slight murmur made;
   He moved as shadowy as the Sisters weird,
But slowly; and as he passed Juan by,
Glanced, without pausing, on him a bright eye.

22

Juan was petrified; he had heard a hint
   Of such a spirit in these halls of old,   170
But thought, like most men, there was nothing in 't
   Beyond the rumour which such spots unfold,
Coin'd from surviving superstition's mint,
   Which passes ghosts in currency like gold,
But rarely seen, like gold compared with paper.
And did he see this? or was it a vapour?

23

Once, twice, thrice pass'd, repass'd—the thing of
   air,

Or earth beneath, or heaven, or t'other place:
And Juan gazed upon it with a stare,
 Yet could not speak or move; but, on its
  base   180
As stands a statue, stood: he felt his hair
 Twine like a knot of snakes around his face;
He tax'd his tongue for words, which were not
  granted,
To ask the reverend person what he wanted.

24

The third time, after a still longer pause,
 The shadow pass'd away—but where? the hall
Was long, and thus far there was no great cause
 To think his vanishing unnatural:
Doors there were many, through which, by the laws
 Of physics, bodies whether short or tall 190
Might come or go; but Juan could not state
Through which the spectre seem'd to evaporate.

25

He stood—how long he knew not, but it seem'd
 An age—expectant, powerless, with his eyes
Strain'd on the spot where first the figure gleam'd;
 Then by degrees recall'd his energies,
And would have pass'd the whole off as a dream,
 But could not wake; he was, he did surmise,
Waking already, and return'd at length
Back to his chamber, shorn of half his
  strength.   200

26

All there was as he left it: still his taper
 Burnt, and not *blue*, as modest tapers use,
Receiving sprites with sympathetic vapour;
 He rubb'd his eyes, and they did not refuse
Their office; he took up an old newspaper;
 The paper was right easy to peruse;
He read an article the king attacking,
And a long eulogy of "patent blacking."

27

This savour'd of this world; but his hand shook—
 He shut his door, and after having read 210

208. "patent blacking": advertisements for shoe blacking, often written in doggerel.

A paragraph, I think about Horne Tooke,
 Undrest, and rather slowly went to bed.
There, couch'd all snugly on his pillow's nook,
 With what he had seen his phantasy he fed;
And though it was no opiate, slumber crept
Upon him by degrees, and so he slept.

28

He woke betimes; and, as may be supposed,
 Ponder'd upon his visitant or vision,
And whether it ought not to be disclosed,
 At risk of being quizz'd for superstition. 220
The more he thought, the more his mind was posed;
 In the mean time, his valet, whose precision
Was great, because his master brook'd no less,
Knock'd to inform him it was time to dress.

29

He dress'd; and like young people he was wont
 To take some trouble with his toilet, but
This morning rather spent less time upon 't;
 Aside his very mirror soon was put;
His curls fell negligently o'er his front,
 His clothes were not curb'd to their usual
  cut,   230
His very neckcloth's Gordian knot was tied
Almost an hair's breadth too much on one side.

30

And when he walk'd down into the saloon,
 He sate him pensive o'er a dish of tea,
Which he perhaps had not discover'd soon,
 Had it not happen'd scalding hot to be,
Which made him have recourse unto his spoon;
 So much distrait he was, that all could see
That something was the matter—Adeline
The first—but *what* she could not well divine. 240

31

She look'd, and saw him pale, and turn'd as pale
 Herself; then hastily look'd down, and mutter'd

211. **Horne Tooke:** a philologist and political reformer
(1736–1812).

Something, but what's not stated in my tale.
  Lord Henry said, his muffin was ill-butter'd;
The Duchess of Fitz-Fulke play'd with her veil,
  And look'd at Juan hard, but nothing utter'd.
Aurora Raby with her large dark eyes
Survey'd him with a kind of calm surprise.

32

But seeing him all cold and silent still,
  And everybody wondering more or less,   250
Fair Adeline enquired "If he were ill?"
  He started, and said, "Yes—no—rather—yes."
The family physician had great skill,
  And being present, now began to express
His readiness to feel his pulse and tell
The cause, but Juan said, "He was quite well."

33

"Quite well; yes,—no."—These answers were mysterious,
  And yet his looks appear'd to sanction both,
However they might savour of delirious;
  Something like illness of a sudden growth   260
Weigh'd on his spirit, though by no means serious:
  But for the rest, as he himself seem'd loth
To state the case, it might be ta'en for granted
It was not the physician that he wanted.

34

Lord Henry, who had now discuss'd his chocolate,
  Also the muffin whereof he complain'd,
Said, Juan had not got his usual look elate,
  At which he marvell'd, since it had not rain'd;
Then ask'd her Grace what news were of the duke
    of late?
  Her Grace replied, his Grace was rather
    pain'd   270
With some slight, light, hereditary twinges
Of gout, which rusts aristocratic hinges.

35

Then Henry turn'd to Juan, and address'd
  A few words of condolence on his state:

"You look," quote he, "as if you had had your rest
  Broke in upon by the Black Friar of late."
"What Friar?" said Juan; and he did his best
  To put the question with an air sedate,
Or careless; but the effort was not valid
To hinder him from growing still more pallid.   280

36

"Oh! have you never heard of the Black Friar?
  The spirit of these walls?"—"In truth not I."
"Why Fame—but Fame you know's sometimes a
    liar—
  Tells an odd story, of which by and by:
Whether with time the spectre has grown shyer,
  Or that our sires had a more gifted eye
For such sights, though the tale is half believed,
The Friar of late has not been oft perceived.

37

"The last time was——"—"I pray," said Adeline—
  (Who watch'd the changes of Don Juan's
    brow,   290
And from its context thought she could divine
  Connexions stronger than he chose to avow
With this same legend)—"if you but design
  To jest, you'll choose some other theme just now,
Because the present tale has oft been told,
And is not much improved by growing old."

38

"Jest!" quoth Milor; "why, Adeline, you know
  That we ourselves—'twas in the honeymoon—
Saw——"—"Well, no matter, 'twas so long ago;
  But, come, I'll set your story to a tune."   300
Graceful as Dian, when she draws her bow,
  She seiz'd her harp, whose strings were kindled
    soon
As touch'd, and plaintively began to play
The air of "'Twas a Friar of Orders Gray."

39

"But add the words," cried Henry, "which you
    made;

276. **Black Friar:** Byron believed the legend that a Black Friar's ghost haunted his ancestral home, Newstead Abbey.

For Adeline is half a poetess,"
Turning round to the rest, he smiling said.
  Of course the others could not but express
In courtesy their wish to see display'd
  By one *three* talents, for there were no
      less—   310
The voice, the words, the harper's skill, at once
Could hardly be united by a dunce.

40

After some fascinating hesitation,—
  The charming of these charmers, who seem
      bound,
I can't tell why, to this dissimulation,—
  Fair Adeline, with eyes fix'd on the ground
At first, then kindling into animation,
  Added her sweet voice to the lyric sound,
And sang with much simplicity,—a merit
Not the less precious, that we seldom hear it.   320

I

Beware! beware! of the Black Friar,
  Who sitteth by Norman stone,
For he mutters his prayer in the midnight air,
  And his mass of the days that are gone.
When the Lord of the Hill, Amundeville,
  Made Norman Church his prey,
And expell'd the friars, one friar still
  Would not be driven away.

II

Though he came in his might, with King
      Henry's right,
  To turn church lands to lay,   330
With sword in hand, and torch to light
  Their walls, if they said nay;
A monk remain'd, unchased, unchain'd,
  And he did not seem form'd of clay,
For he's seen in the porch, and he's seen in the
      church,
  Though he is not seen by day.

III

And whether for good, or whether for ill,
  It is not mine to say;

But still with the house of Amundeville
  He abideth night and day.   340
By the marriage-bed of their lords, 'tis said,
  He flits on the bridal eve;
And 'tis held as faith, to their bed of death
  He comes—but not to grieve.

IV

When an heir is born, he's heard to mourn,
  And when aught is to befall
That ancient line, in the pale moonshine
  He walks from hall to hall.
His form you may trace, but not his face,
  'Tis shadow'd by his cowl;   350
But his eyes may be seen from the folds be-
      tween,
  And they seem of a parted soul.

V

But beware! beware! of the Black Friar,
  He still retains his sway,
For he is yet the church's heir
  Whoever may be the lay.
Amundeville is lord by day,
  But the monk is lord by night;
Nor wine nor wassail could raise a vassal
  To question that friar's right.   360

VI

Say nought to him as he walks the hall,
  And he'll say nought to you;
He sweeps along in his dusky pall,
  As o'er the grass the dew.
Then grammercy! for the Black Friar;
  Heaven sain him! fair or foul,
And whatsoe'er may be his prayer,
  Let ours be for his soul.

41

The lady's voice ceased, and the thrilling wires
  Died from the touch that kindled them to
      sound;   370
And the pause follow'd, which when song expires
  Pervades a moment those who listen round;

And then of course the circle much admires,
   Nor less applauds, as in politeness bound,
The tones, the feelings, and the execution,
To the performer's diffident confusion.

42

Fair Adeline, though in a careless way,
   As if she rated such accomplishment
As the mere pastime of an idle day,
   Pursued an instant for her own content,   380
Would now and then, as 'twere *without* display,
   Yet *with* display in fact, at times relent
To such performances with haughty smile,
To show she *could,* if it were worth her while.

43

Now this (but we will whisper it aside)
   Was—pardon the pedantic illustration—
Trampling on Plato's pride with greater pride,
   As did the Cynic on some like occasion:
Deeming the sage would be much mortified,
   Or thrown into a philosophic passion,   390
For a spoilt carpet—but the "Attic bee"
Was much consoled by his own repartee.

44

Thus Adeline would throw into the shade
   (By doing easily, whene'er she chose,
What dilettanti do with vast parade)
   Their sort of *half profession;* for it grows
To something like this when too oft display'd;
   And that it is so, everybody knows,
Who have heard Miss That or This, or Lady
     T'other,
Show off—to please their company or
     mother.   400

387–92. Trampling . . . repartee: Diogenes, the great cynic, trod on the carpet of Plato's house. In a bit of repartee, Diogenes says that he is trampling on the pride of Plato. Plato, however, tells Diogenes that his trampling is another kind of pride. "Attic Bee" was a name given to Plato because, according to legend, bees had settled on his lips when he was a baby—a symbol of the sweetness of his words to come.

45

Oh! the long evenings of duets and trios!
   The admirations and the speculations;
The "Mamma Mia's!" and the "Amor Mio's!"
   The "Tanti palpiti's" on such occasions:
The "Lasciami's," and quavering "Addio's!"
   Amongst our own most musical of nations;
With "Tu mi chamas's" from Portingale,
To soothe our ears, lest Italy should fail.

46

In Babylon's bravuras—as the Home-
   Heart-ballads of Green Erin or Gray High-
     lands,   410
That bring Lochaber back to eyes that roam
   O'er far Atlantic continents or islands,
The calentures of music which o'ercome
   All mountaineers with dreams that they are nigh
     lands,
No more to be beheld but in such visions—
Was Adeline well versed, as compositions.

47

She also had a twilight tinge of *"Blue,"*
   Could write rhymes, and compose more than she
     wrote,
Made epigrams occasionally too
   Upon her friends, as everybody ought.   420
But still from that sublimer azure hue,
   So much the present dye, she was remote;
Was weak enough to deem Pope a great poet,
And what was worse, was not ashamed to show it.

48

Aurora—since we are touching upon taste,
   Which now-a-days is the thermometer
By whose degrees all characters are class'd—
   Was more Shakespearian, if I do not err.
The worlds beyond this world's perplexing waste
   Had more of her existence, for in her   430

404. "Tanti palpiti's": "heart throbs." **405. "Lasciami's . . . Addio's":** "allow me's" and "farewells." **410. Heart-ballads . . . Highlands:** the ballads of Thomas Moore and Sir Walter Scott.

There was a depth of feeling to embrace
Thoughts, boundless, deep, but silent too as Space.

49

Not so her gracious, graceful, graceless Grace,
  The full-grown Hebe of Fitz-Fulke, whose mind,
If she had any, was upon her face,
  And that was of a fascinating kind.
A little turn for mischief you might trace
  Also thereon,—but that's not much, we find
Few females without some such gentle leaven,
For fear we should suppose us quite in
    heaven.   440

50

I have not heard she was at all poetic,
  Though once she was seen reading the "Bath
    Guide,"
And "Hayley's Triumphs," which she deem'd
    pathetic,
  Because she said *her temper* had been tried
So much, the bard had really been prophetic
  Of what she had gone through with—since a
    bride.
But of all verse, what most insured her praise
Were sonnets to herself, or "bouts rimés.'

51

'Twere difficult to say what was the object
  Of Adeline, in bringing this same lay   450
To bear on what appear'd to her the subject
  Of Juan's nervous feelings on that day.
Perhaps she merely had the simple project
  To laugh him out of his supposed dismay;
Perhaps she might wish to confirm him in it,
Though why I cannot say—at least this minute.

52

But so far the immediate effect
  Was to restore him to his self-propriety,

434. **Hebe:** goddess of youth. 442. **"Bath Guide":** the famous *New Bath Guide* of Christopher Anstey. 443. **"Haley's Triumphs":** William Hayley's poems *The Triumph of Temper* and *The Triumph of Music*. 448. **"bouts rimés":** the last words or rhymes of verses given to a poet to be filled up.

A thing quite necessary to the elect,
  Who wish to take the tone of their society: 460
In which you cannot be too circumspect,
  Whether the mode be persiflage or piety,
But wear the newest mantle of hypocrisy,
Of pain of much displeasing the gynocracy.

53

And therefore Juan now began to rally
  His spirits, and without more explanation
To jest upon such themes in many a sally.
  Her Grace, too, also seized the same occasion,
With various similar remarks to tally,
  But wish'd for a still more detail'd narration   470
Of this same mystic friar's curious doings,
About the present family's death and wooings.

54

Of these few could say more than has been said;
  They pass'd as such things do, for superstition
With some, while others, who had more in dread
  The theme, half credited the strange tradition;
And much was talk'd on all sides on that head:
  But Juan, when cross-question'd on the vision,
Which some supposed (though he had not avow'd
    it)
Had stirr'd him, answer'd in a way to cloud it.   480

55

And then, the mid-day having worn to one,
  The company prepared to separate;
Some to their several pastimes, or to none,
  Some wondering 'twas so early, some so late.
There was a goodly match too, to be run
  Between some greyhounds on my lord's estate,
And a young race-horse of old pedigree,
Match'd for the spring, whom several went to see.

56

There was a picture-dealer who had brought
  A special Titian, warranted original,   490
So precious that it was not to be bought,
  Though princes the possessor were besieging all.

464. **gynocracy:** rule by women.

The king himself had cheapen'd it, but thought
   The civil list he deigns to accept (obliging all
His subjects by his gracious acceptation)—
Too scanty, in those times of low taxation—

57

But as Lord Henry was a connoisseur,—
   The friend of artists, if not arts,—the owner,
With motives the most classical and pure,
   So that he would have been the very donor,   500
Rather than seller, had his wants been fewer,
   So much he deem'd his patronage an honour,
Had brought the capo d'opera, not for sale,
But for his judgment—never known to fail.

58

There was a modern Goth, I mean a Gothic
   Bricklayer of Babel, call'd an architect,
Brought to survey these grey walls, which though
     so thick,
   Might have from time acquired some slight
     defect;
Who, after rummaging the Abbey through thick
   And thin, produced a plan whereby to erect   510
New buildings of correctest conformation,
And throw down old, which he call'd *restoration*.

59

The cost would be a trifle—an "old song,"
   Set to some thousands ('tis the usual burden
Of that same tune, when people hum it long)—
   The price would speedily repay its worth in
An edifice no less sublime than strong,
   By which Lord Henry's good taste would go
     forth in
Its glory, through all ages shining sunny,
For Gothic daring shown in English money.   520

60

There were two lawyers busy on a mortgage
   Lord Henry wish'd to raise for a new purchase;

503. **capo d'opera**: masterpiece.

Also a lawsuit upon tenures burgage,
   And one on tithes, which sure are Discord's
     torches,
Kindling Religion till she throws down her gage,
   "Untying" squires "to fight against the churches;"
There was a prize ox, a prize pig, and ploughman,
For Henry was a sort of Sabine showman.

61

There were two poachers caught in a steel trap,
   Ready for gaol, their place of convales-
     cence;   530
There was a country girl in a close cap
   And scarlet cloak (I hate the sight to see, since—
Since—since—in youth, I had the sad mishap—
   But luckily I have paid few parish fees since):
That scarlet cloak, alas! unclosed with rigour,
Presents the problem of a double figure.

62

A reel within a bottle is a mystery,
   One can't tell how it e'er got in or out;
Therefore the present piece of natural history
   I leave to those who are fond of solving
     doubt;   540
And merely state, though not for the consistory,
   Lord Henry was a justice, and that Scout
The constable, beneath a warrant's banner,
Had bagg'd this poacher upon Nature's manor.

63

Now justices of peace must judge all pieces
   Of mischief of all kinds, and keep the game
And morals of the country from caprices
   Of those who have not a licence for the same;
And of all things, excepting tithes and leases,
   Perhaps these are most difficult to tame: 550
Preserving partridges and pretty wenches
Are puzzles to the most precautious benches.

523. **tenures burgage**: property for which rent was paid
to the lord of the borough. 526. **"Untying . . . churches"**:
See *Macbeth*, IV, i, 50–53. 528. **Sabine showman**: gentleman farmer.

64

The present culprit was extremely pale,
    Pale as if painted so; her cheek being red
By nature, as in higher dames less hale
    'Tis white, at least when they just rise from bed.
Perhaps she was ashamed of seeming frail,
    Poor soul! for she was country born and bred,
And knew no better in her immorality
Than to wax white—for blushes are for
        quality.   560

65

Her black, bright, downcast, yet espiègle eye,
    Had gather'd a large tear into its corner,
Which the poor thing at times essay'd to dry,
    For she was not a sentimental mourner
Parading all her sensibility,
    Nor insolent enough to scorn the scorner,
But stood in trembling, patient tribulation,
To be call'd up for her examination.

66

Of course these groups were scatter'd here and
        there,
    Not nigh the gay saloon of ladies gent.   570
The lawyers in the study; and in air
    The prize pig, ploughman, poachers; the men
        sent
From town, viz. architect and dealer, were
    Both busy (as a general in his tent
Writing despatches) in their several stations,
Exulting in their brilliant lucubrations.

67

But this poor girl was left in the great hall,
    While Scout, the parish guardian of the frail,
Discuss'd (he hated beer yclept the "small")
    A mighty mug of moral double ale.   580
She waited until Justice could recall
    Its kind attentions to their proper pale,
To name a thing in nomenclature rather
Perplexing for most virgins—a child's father.

561. espiègle: coy.

68

You see here was enough of occupation
    For the Lord Henry, link'd with dogs and horses.
There was much bustle too, and preparation
    Below stairs on the score of second courses;
Because, as suits their rank and situation,
    Those who in counties have great land
        resources   590
Have "public days," when all men may carouse,
Though not exactly what's call'd "open house."

69

But once a week or fortnight, uninvited
    (Thus we translate a general invitation),
All country gentlemen, esquired or knighted,
    May drop in without cards, and take their station
At the full board, and sit alike delighted
    With fashionable wines and conversation;
And, as the isthmus of the grand connexion,
Talk o'er themselves the past and next elec-
        tion.   600

. . .

86

But "en avant!" The light loves languish o'er
    Long banquets and too many guests,
        although   730
A slight repast makes people love much more,
    Bacchus and Ceres being, as we know,
Even from our grammar upwards, friends of yore
    With vivifying Venus, who doth owe
To these the invention of champagne and truffles:
Temperance delights her, but long fasting ruffles.

87

Dully pass'd o'er the dinner of the day;
    And Juan took his place, he knew not where,
Confused, in the confusion, and distrait,
    And sitting as if nail'd upon his chair: 740
Though knives and forks clang'd round as in a fray,
    He seem'd unconscious of all passing there,
Till some one, with a groan, exprest a wish
(Unheeded twice) to have a fin or fish.

88

On which, at the *third* asking of the bans,
  He started; and perceiving smiles around
Broadening to grins, he colour'd more than once,
  And hastily—as nothing can confound
A wise man more than laughter from a dunce—
  Inflicted on the dish a deadly wound,   750
And with such hurry, that, ere he could curb it,
He had paid his neighbour's prayer with half a
    turbot.

89

This was no bad mistake, as it occurr'd,
  The supplicator being an amateur;
But others, who were left with scarce a third,
  Were angry—as they well might, to be sure.
They wonder'd how a young man so absurd
  Lord Henry at his table should endure;
And this, and his not knowing how much oats
Had fall'n last market, cost his host three
    votes.   760

90

They little knew, or might have sympathised,
  That he the night before had seen a ghost,
A prologue which but slightly harmonised
  With the substantial company engross'd
By matter, and so much materialised,
  That one scarce knew at what to marvel most
Of two things—how (the question rather odd is)
Such bodies could have souls, or souls such bodies.

91

But what confused him more than smile or stare,
  From all the 'squires and 'squiresses
    around,   770
Who wonder'd at the abstraction of his air,
  Especially as he had been renown'd
For some vivacity among the fair,
  Even in the country circle's narrow bound—
(For little things upon my lord's estate
Were good small talk for others still less great)—

92

Was, that he caught Aurora's eye on his,
  And something like a smile upon her cheek.

Now this he really rather took amiss:
  In those who rarely smile, their smile be-
    speaks   780
A strong external motive; and in this
  Smile of Aurora's there was nought to pique
Or hope, or love, with any of the wiles
Which some pretend to trace in ladies' smiles.

93

'Twas a mere quiet smile of contemplation,
  Indicative of some surprise and pity;
And Juan grew carnation with vexation,
  Which was not very wise, and still less witty,
Since he had gain'd at least her observation,
  A most important outwork of the city—   790
As Juan should have known, had not his senses
By last night's ghost been driven from their
    defences.

94

But what was bad, she did not blush in turn,
  Nor seem embarrass'd—quite the contrary;
Her aspect was as usual, still—*not* stern—
  And she withdrew, but cast not down, her eye,
Yet grew a little pale—with what? concern?
  I know not; but her colour ne'er was high—
Though sometimes faintly flush'd—and always
    clear,
As deep seas in a sunny atmosphere.   800

95

But Adeline was occupied by fame
  This day; and watching, witching, condescending
To the consumers of fish, fowl, and game,
  And dignity with courtesy so blending,
As all must blend whose part it is to aim
  (Especially as the sixth year is ending)
At their lord's, son's, or similar connexion's
Safe conduct through the rocks of reëlections.

96

Though this was most expedient on the whole,
  And usual—Juan, when he cast a glance   810
On Adeline while playing her grand rôle,
  Which she went through as though it were a
    dance,

Betraying only now and then her soul
  By a look scarce perceptibly askance
(Of weariness or scorn), began to feel
Some doubt how much of Adeline was *real;*

97

So well she acted all and every part
  By turns—with that vivacious versatility,
Which many people take for want of heart.
  They err—'tis merely what is call'd mobil-
    ity,   820
A thing of temperament and not of art,
  Though seeming so, from its supposed facility;
And false—though true; for surely they're sincerest
Who are strongly acted on by what is nearest.

98

This makes your actors, artists, and romancers,
  Heroes sometimes, though seldom—sages never;
But speakers, bards, diplomatists, and dancers,
  Little that's great, but much of what is clever;
Most orators, but very few financiers,
  Though all Exchequer chancellors en-
    deavour,   830
Of late years, to dispense with Cocker's rigours,
And grow quite figurative with their figures.

99

The poets of arithmetic are they
  Who, though they prove not two and two to be
Five, as they might do in a modest way,
  Have plainly made it out that four are three,
  Judging by what they take, and what they pay.
  The Sinking Fund's unfathomable sea,
That most unliquidating liquid, leaves
The debt unsunk, yet sinks all it receives.   840

100

While Adeline dispensed her airs and graces,
  The fair Fitz-Fulke seem'd very much at ease;

831. **Cocker's rigours:** a reference to Cocker's *Arithmetic,* a book still in use despite its publication date of
1677. 838. **Sinking Fund:** a plan devised by Prime Minister Walpole in 1717–18 in order to reduce the national
debt. It proved to be a disastrous scheme and was
abolished in 1823.

Though too well bred to quiz men to their faces,
  Her laughing blue eyes with a glance could seize
The ridicules of people in all places—
  That honey of your fashionable bees—
And store it up for mischievous enjoyment;
And this at present was her kind employment.

101

However, the day closed, as days must close;
  The evening also waned—and coffee came.   850
Each carriage was announced, and ladies rose,
  And curtsying off, as curtsies country dame,
Retired: with most unfashionable bows
  Their docile esquires also did the same,
Delighted with their dinner and their host,
But with the Lady Adeline the most.

102

Some praised her beauty: others her great grace;
  The warmth of her politeness, whose sincerity
Was obvious in each feature of her face,
  Whose traits were radiant with the rays of
    verity.   860
Yes: *she* was truly worthy *her* high place!
  No one could envy her deserved prosperity.
And then her dress—what beautiful simplicity
Draperied her form with curious felicity!

103

Meanwhile sweet Adeline deserved their praises,
  By an impartial indemnification
For all her past exertion and soft phrases,
  In a most edifying conversation,
Which turn'd upon their late guests' miens and
    faces,
  And families, even to the last relation;   870
Their hideous wives, their horrid selves and dresses,
And truculent distortion of their tresses.

104

True, *she* said little—'twas the rest that broke
  Forth into universal epigram;

But then 'twas to the purpose what she spoke:
  Like Addison's "faint praise," so wont to damn,
Her own but served to set off every joke,
  As music chimes in with a melodrame.
How sweet the task to shield an absent friend!
I ask but this of mine, to—*not* defend.   880

105

There were but two exceptions to this keen
  Skirmish of wits o'er the departed; one
Aurora, with her pure and placid mien;
  And Juan, too, in general behind none
In gay remark on what he had heard or seen,
  Sate silent now, his usual spirits gone:
In vain he heard the others rail or rally,
He would not join them in a single sally.

106

'Tis true he saw Aurora look as though
  She approved his silence; she perhaps mis-
    took   890
Its motive for that charity we owe
  But seldom pay the absent, nor would look
Farther; it might or it might not be so.
  But Juan, sitting silent in his nook,
Observing little in his reverie,
Yet saw this much, which he was glad to see.

107

The ghost at least had done him this much good,
  In making him as silent as a ghost,
If in the circumstances which ensued
  He gain'd esteem where it was worth the
    most.   900
And certainly Aurora had renew'd
  In him some feelings he had lately lost
Or harden'd; feelings which, perhaps ideal,
Are so divine, that I must deem them real:—

108

The love of higher things and better days;
  The unbounded hope, and heavenly ignorance

Of what is call'd the world, and the world's ways;
  The moments when we gather from a glance
More joy than from all future pride or praise,
  Which kindle manhood, but can ne'er en-
    trance   910
The heart in an existence of its own,
Of which another's bosom is the zone.

109

Who would not sigh Αἲ αἲ τὰν Κυθέρειαν
  That *hath* a memory, or that *had* a heart?
Alas! *her* star must fade like that of Dian:
  Ray fades on ray, as years on years depart.
Anacreon only had the soul to tie an
  Unwithering myrtle round the unblunted dart
Of Eros: but though thou hast play'd us many
    tricks,
Still we respect thee, "Alma Venus Genetrix!"   920

110

And full of sentiments, sublime as billows
  Heaving between this world and worlds beyond,
Don Juan, when the midnight hours of pillows
  Arrived, retired to his; but to despond
Rather than rest. Instead of poppies, willows
  Waved o'er his couch; he meditated, fond
Of those sweet bitter thoughts which banish sleep,
And make the worldling sneer, the youngling weep.

111

The night was as before: he was undrest,
  Saving his night-gown, which is an un-
    dress;   930
Completely "sans culotte," and without vest;
  In short, he hardly could be clothed with less:
But apprehensive of his spectral guest,
  He sate with feelings awkward to express
(By those who have not had such visitations),
Expectant of the ghost's fresh operations.

913. Αἲ αἲ τὰν Κυθέρειαν: The Greek words, "Woe, woe for Cytherea" are from Bion's beautiful *Elegy on Adonis*, l. 28. 920. "Alma . . . Genetrix": "Dear life-giving Mother," the stirring first line of Lucretius' *De Rerum Natura* where Venus is addressed as mother of Aeneas and of the Romans. 931. "sans culotte": without trousers.

112

And not in vain he listen'd;—Hush! what's that?
  I see—I see—Ah, no!—'tis not—yet 'tis—
Ye powers! it is the—the—the—Pooh! the cat!
  The devil may take that stealthy pace of
      his!   940
So like a spiritual pit-a-pat,
  Or tiptoe of an amatory Miss,
Gliding the first time to a rendezvous,
And dreading the chaste echoes of her shoe.

113

Again—what is 't? The wind? No, no,—this time
  It is the sable Friar as before,
With awful footsteps regular as rhyme,
  Or (as rhymes may be in these days) much more.
Again through shadows of the night sublime,
  When deep sleep fell on men, and the world
      wore   950
The starry darkness round her like a girdle
Spangled with gems—the monk made his blood
      curdle.

114

A noise like to wet fingers drawn on glass,
  Which sets the teeth on edge; and a slight clatter
Like showers which on the midnight gusts will pass,
  Sounding like very supernatural water,
Came over Juan's ear, which throbb'd, alas!
  For immaterialism's a serious matter;
So that even those whose faith is the most great
In souls immortal, shun them tête-à tête.   960

115

Were his eyes open?—Yes! and his mouth too.
  Surprise has this effect—to make one dumb,
Yet leave the gate which eloquence slips through
  As wide, as if a long speech were to come.
Nigh and more nigh the awful echoes drew,
  Tremendous to a mortal tympanum:
His eyes were open, and (as was before
Stated) his mouth. What open'd next?—the door.

116

It open'd with a most infernal creak,
  Like that of hell. "Lasciate ogni speranza   970
Voi ch' entrate!" The hinge seem'd to speak,
  Dreadful as Dante's *rima*, or this stanza;
Or—but all words upon such themes are weak:
  A single shade's sufficient to entrance a
Hero—for what is substance to a spirit?
Or how is 't *matter* trembles to come near it?

117

The door flew wide, not swiftly,—but, as fly
  The sea-gulls, with a steady, sober flight—
And then swung back; nor close—but stood awry,
  Half letting in long shadows on the light,   980
Which still in Juan's candlesticks burn'd high,
  For he had two, both tolerably bright,
And in the doorway, darkening darkness, stood
The sable Friar in his solemn hood.

118

Don Juan shook, as erst he had been shaken
  The night before; but being sick of shaking,
He first inclined to think he had been mistaken;
  And then to be ashamed of such mistaking;
His own internal ghost began to awaken
  Within him, and to quell his corporal quak-
      ing—   990
Hinting that soul and body on the whole
Were odds against a disembodied soul.

119

And then his dread grew wrath, and his wrath
      fierce,
  And he arose, advanced—the shade retreated;
But Juan, eager now the truth to pierce,
  Followed, his veins no longer cold, but heated,
Resolved to thrust the mystery carte and tierce,
  At whatsoever risk of being defeated:
The ghost stopp'd, menaced, then retired, until

970–71. "Lasciate . . . entrate": the famous words from
Dante's *Inferno*, III, 9, "Abandon hope, all you who
enter here." 997. carte and tierce: positions for thrusting in fencing.

He reach'd the ancient wall, then stood stone
   still.   1000

120

Juan put forth one arm—Eternal powers!
  It touch'd no soul, nor body, but the wall,
On which the moonbeams fell in silvery showers,
  Chequer'd with all the tracery of the hall;
He shudder'd, as no doubt the bravest cowers
  When he can't tell what 'tis that doth appal.
How odd, a single hobgoblin's nonentity
Should cause more fear than a whole host's identity!

121

But still the shade remain'd: the blue eyes glared,
  And rather variably for stony death;   1010
Yet one thing rather good the grave had spared,
  The ghost had a remarkably sweet breath.
A straggling curl show'd he had been fair-hair'd;
  A red lip, with two rows of pearls beneath,
Gleam'd forth, as through the casement's ivy shroud
The moon peep'd, just escaped from a grey cloud.

122

And Juan, puzzled, but still curious, thrust
  His other arm forth—Wonder upon wonder!
It press'd upon a hard but glowing bust,
  Which beat as if there was a warm heart
      under.   1020
He found, as people on most trials must,
  That he had made at first a silly blunder,
And that in his confusion he had caught
Only the wall, instead of what he sought.

123

The ghost, if ghost it were, seem'd a sweet soul
  As ever lurk'd beneath a holy hood:
A dimpled chin, a neck of ivory, stole
  Forth into something much like flesh and blood;
Back fell the sable frock and dreary cowl,
  And they reveal'd—alas! that e'er they
      should!   1030
In full, voluptuous, but *not o'er*grown bulk,
The phantom of her frolic Grace—Fitz-Fulke!

1823   1824

THE VISION
OF JUDGMENT

BY QUEVEDO REDIVIVUS*

SUGGESTED BY THE COMPOSITION SO
ENTITLED BY THE AUTHOR OF
"WAT TYLER" **

1

Saint Peter sat by the celestial gate:
  His keys were rusty, and the lock was dull,
So little trouble had been given of late;
  Not that the place by any means was full,
But since the Gallic era "eighty-eight"
  The devils had ta'en a longer, stronger pull,
And "a pull altogether," as they say
At sea—which drew most souls another way.

2

The angels all were singing out of tune,
  And hoarse with having little else to do,   10
Excepting to wind up the sun and moon,
  Or curb a runaway young star or two,
Or wild colt of a comet, which too soon
  Broke out of bounds o'er th' ethereal blue,
Splitting some planet with its playful tail,
As boats are sometimes by a wanton whale.

3

The guardian seraphs had retired on high,
  Finding their charges past all care below;
Terrestrial business fill'd nought in the sky
  Save the recording angel's black bureau;   20
Who found, indeed, the facts to multiply
  With such rapidity of vice and woe,

---

* *Quevedo Resurrected.* Francisco Gomez de Quevedo
y Villegas (1580–1635) was the author of a sequence
of visions.
** Robert Southey, author of *A Vision of Judgment*, a
bombastic tribute by a formal radical to George III.
Southey's radical drama *Wat Tyler* had, without his
knowledge, been published in 1817 to the great embarrassment of the now Conservative Laureate.
THE VISION OF JUDGMENT. 5. **"eighty-eight"**: the year
1788, the beginning of the events culminating in the
French Revolution.

That he had stripp'd off both his wings in quills,
And yet was in arrear of human ills.

4

His business so augmented of late years,
    That he was forced, against his will no doubt,
(Just like those cherubs, earthly ministers,)
    For some resource to turn himself about,
And claim the help of his celestial peers,
    To aid him ere he should be quite worn out   30
By the increased demand for his remarks;
Six angels and twelve saints were named his clerks.

5

This was a handsome board—at least for heaven;
    And yet they had even then enough to do,
So many conquerors' cars were daily driven,
    So many kingdoms fitted up anew;
Each day too slew its thousands six or seven,
    Till at the crowning carnage, Waterloo,
They threw their pens down in divine disgust—
The page was so besmear'd with blood and
        dust.   40

6

This by the way; 'tis not mine to record
    What angels shrink from: even the very devil
On this occasion his own work abhorr'd,
    So surfeited with the infernal revel:
Though he himself had sharpen'd every sword,
    It almost quench'd his innate thirst of evil.
(Here Satan's sole good work deserves insertion—
'Tis, that he has both generals in reversion.)

7

Let's skip a few short years of hollow peace,
    Which peopled earth no better, hell as wont,   50
And heaven none—they form the tyrant's lease,
    With nothing but new names subscribed upon 't;
'Twill one day finish: meantime they increase,
    "With seven heads and ten horns," and all in
        front,

47–48. Satan ... reversion: Satan had a claim on both
Wellington and Napoleon.

Like Saint John's foretold beast; but ours are born
Less formidable in the head than horn.

8

In the first year of freedom's second dawn
    Died George the Third; although no tyrant, one
Who shielded tyrants, till each sense withdrawn
    Left him nor mental nor external sun: 60
A better farmer ne'er brush'd dew from lawn,
    A worse king never left a realm undone!
He died—but left his subjects still behind,
One half as mad—and t'other no less blind.

9

He died! his death made no great stir on earth;
    His burial made some pomp; there was profusion
Of velvet, gilding, brass, and no great dearth
    Of aught but tears—save those shed by collusion.
For these things may be bought at their true worth;
    Of elegy there was the due infusion—   70
Bought also; and the torches, cloaks, and banners,
Heralds, and relics of old Gothic manners,

10

Form'd a sepulchral melodrame. Of all
    The fools who flock'd to swell or see the show,
Who cared about the corpse? The funeral
    Made the attraction, and the black the woe.
There throbb'd not there a thought which pierced
        the pall;
    And when the gorgeous coffin was laid low,
It seem'd the mockery of hell to fold
The rottenness of eighty years in gold.   80

11

So mix his body with the dust! It might
    Return to what it *must* far sooner, were
The natural compound left alone to fight
    Its way back into earth, and fire, and air;
But the unnatural balsams merely blight
    What nature made him at his birth, as bare

57. year: 1820, the beginnings of revolutionary rumblings in Italy.

As the mere million's base unmummied clay—
Yet all his spices but prolong decay.

12

He's dead—and upper earth with him has done;
   He's buried; save the undertaker's bill,   90
Or lapidary scrawl, the world is gone
   For him, unless he left a German will;
But where's the proctor who will ask his son?
   In whom his qualities are reigning still,
Except that household virtue, most uncommon,
Of constancy to a bad, ugly woman.

13

"God save the king!" It is a large economy
   In God to save the like; but if he will
Be saving, all the better; for not once am I
   Of those who think damnation better still: 100
I hardly know too if not quite alone am I
   In this small hope of bettering future ill
By circumscribing, with some slight restriction,
The eternity of hell's hot jurisdiction.

14

I know this is unpopular; I know
   'Tis blasphemous; I know one may be damn'd
For hoping no one else may e'er be so;
   I know my catechism; I know we're cramm'd
With the best doctrines till we quite o'erflow;
   I know that all save England's church have
      shamm'd,   110
And that the other twice two hundred churches
And synagogues have made a *damn'd* bad pur-
    chase.

15

God help us all! God help me too! I am,
   God knows, as helpless as the devil can wish,
And not a whit more difficult to damn,
   Than is to bring to land a late-hook'd fish,
Or to the butcher to purvey the lamb;
   Not that I'm fit for such a noble dish,

92. **German will**: the Georges were, of course, of the German House of Hanover.

As one day will be that immortal fry
Of almost everybody born to die.   120

16

Saint Peter sat by the celestial gate,
   And nodded o'er his keys; when, lo! there came
A wondrous noise he had not heard of late—
   A rushing sound of wind, and stream, and flame;
In short, a roar of things extremely great,
   Which would have made aught save a saint
      exclaim;
But he, with first a start and then a wink,
Said, "There's another star gone out, I think!"

17

But ere he could return to his repose,
   A cherub flapp'd his right wing o'er his
      eyes—   130
At which St. Peter yawn'd, and rubb'd his nose:
   "Saint porter," said the angel, "prithee rise!"
Waving a goodly wing, which glow'd, as glows
   An earthly peacock's tail, with heavenly dyes:
To which the saint replied, "Well, what's the mat-
    ter?
   "Is Lucifer come back with all this clatter?"

18

"No," quoth the cherub; "George the Third is dead."
   "And who *is* George the Third?" replied the
      apostle:
"*What George? what Third?*" "The king of En-
    gland," said
   The angel. "Well! he won't find kings to
      jostle   140
Him on his way; but does he wear his head;
   Because the last we saw here had a tustle,
And ne'er would have got into heaven's good
    graces,
Had he not flung his head in all our faces.

19

"He was, if I remember, king of France;
   That head of his, which could not keep a crown

141–42. **wear . . . last**: Louis XVI was beheaded in 1793.

On earth, yet ventured in my face to advance
   A claim to those of martyrs—like my own:
If I had had my sword, as I had once
   When I cut ears off, I had cut him down;   150
But having but my *keys,* and not my brand,
I only knock'd his head from out his hand.

20

"And then he set up such a headless howl,
   That all the saints came out and took him in;
And there he sits by St. Paul, cheek by jowl;
   That fellow Paul—the parvenù! The skin
Of St. Bartholomew, which makes his cowl
   In heaven, and upon earth redeem'd his sin
So as to make a martyr, never sped
Better than did this weak and wooden head.   160

21

"But had it come up here upon its shoulders,
   There would have been a different tale to tell:
The fellow-feeling in the saint's beholders
   Seems to have acted on them like a spell;
And so this very foolish head heaven solders
   Back on its trunk: it may be very well,
And seems the custom here to overthrow
Whatever has been wisely done below."

22

The angel answer'd, "Peter! do not pout:
   The king who comes has head and all
     entire,   170
And never knew much what it was about—
   He did as doth the puppet—by its wire,
And will be judged like all the rest, no doubt:
   My business and your own is not to inquire
Into such matters, but to mind our cue—
Which is to act as we are bid to do."

23

While thus they spake, the angelic caravan,
   Arriving like a rush of mighty wind,

---

156. **parvenu:** Johnny-come-lately. **156–57. skin . . .
Bartholomew:** St. Bartholomew was martyred by being
skinned alive.

Cleaving the fields of space, as doth the swan
   Some silver stream (say Ganges, Nile, or
     Inde,   180
Or Thames, or Tweed), and 'midst them an old man
   With an old soul, and both extremely blind,
Halted before the gate, and in his shroud
Seated their fellow-traveller on a cloud.

24

But bringing up the rear of this bright host
   A Spirit of a different aspect waved
His wings, like thunder-clouds above some coast
   Whose barren beach with frequent wrecks is
     paved;
His brow was like the deep when tempest-toss'd;
   Fierce and unfathomable thoughts en-
     graved   190
Eternal wrath on his immortal face,
And *where* he gazed a gloom pervaded space.

25

As he drew near, he gazed upon the gate
   Ne'er to be enter'd more by him or Sin,
With such a glance of supernatural hate,
   As made Saint Peter wish himself within;
He patter'd with his keys at a great rate,
   And sweated through his apostolic skin:
Of course his perspiration was but ichor,
Or some such other spiritual liquor.   200

26

The very cherubs huddled all together,
   Like birds when soars the falcon; and they felt
A tingling to the tip of every feather,
   And form'd a circle like Orion's belt
Around their poor old charge; who scarce knew
     whither
   His guards had led him, though they gently dealt
With royal manes (for by many stories,
And true, we learn the angels all are Tories).

27

As things were in this posture, the gate flew
   Asunder, and the flashing of its hinges   210

---

199. **ichor:** heavenly fluid.

Flung over space an universal hue
   Of many-colour'd flame, until its tinges
Reach'd even our speck of earth, and made a new
   Aurora borealis spread its fringes
O'er the North Pole; the same seen, when ice-
      bound,
By Captain Parry's crew, in "Melville's Sound."

28

And from the gate thrown open issued beaming
   A beautiful and mighty Thing of Light,
Radiant with glory, like a banner streaming
   Victorious from some world-o'erthrowing
      fight: 220
My poor comparisons must needs be teeming
   With earthly likenesses, for here the night
Of clay obscures our best conceptions, saving
Johanna Southcote, or Bob Southey raving.

29

'Twas the archangel Michael: all men know
   The make of angels and archangels, since
There's scarce a scribbler has not one to show,
   From the fiends' leader to the angels' prince.
There also are some altar-pieces, though
   I really can't say that they much evince   230
One's inner notions of immortal spirits;
But let the connoisseurs explain *their* merits.

30

Michael flew forth in glory and in good;
   A goodly work of him from whom all glory
And good arise; the portal past—he stood;
   Before him the young cherubs and saints hoary—
(I say *young*, begging to be understood
   By looks, not years; and should be very sorry
To state, they were not older than St. Peter,
But merely that they seem'd a little sweeter).   240

31

The cherubs and the saints bow'd down before
   That arch-angelic hierarch, the first
Of essences angelical, who wore
   The aspect of a god; but this ne'er nursed

216. Captain Parry: In 1819–20 Captain Edward Parry journeyed in search of a Northwest Passage. He and his crew wintered in Melville Sound, Greenland in 1819.

Pride in his heavenly bosom, in whose core
   No thought, save for his Master's service, durst
Intrude, however glorified and high;
He knew him but the viceroy of the sky.

32

He and the sombre silent Spirit met—
   They knew each other both for good and
      ill;   250
Such was their power, that neither could forget
   His former friend and future foe; but still
There was a high, immortal, proud regret
   In either's eye, as if 'twere less their will
Than destiny to make the eternal years
Their date of war, and their "champ clos" the
      spheres.

33

But here they were in neutral space: we know
   From Job, that Satan hath the power to pay
A heavenly visit thrice a year or so;
   And that the "sons of God," like those of
      clay,   260
Must keep him company; and we might show
   From the same book, in how polite a way
The dialogue is held between the Powers
Of Good and Evil—but 'twould take up hours.

34

And this is not a theologic tract,
   To prove with Hebrew and with Arabic
If Job be allegory or a fact,
   But a true narrative; and thus I pick
From out the whole but such and such an act
   As sets aside the slightest thought of trick.   270
'Tis every tittle true, beyond suspicion,
And accurate as any other vision.

35

The spirits were in neutral space, before
   The gate of heaven; like eastern thresholds is
The place where Death's grand cause is argued o'er,
   And souls despatch'd to that world or to this;

256. "champ clos": a field enclosed for a tournament.

And therefore Michael and the other wore
   A civil aspect: though they did not kiss,
Yet still between his Darkness and his Brightness
There pass'd a mutual glance of great polite-
     ness.   280

36

The Archangel bow'd, not like a modern beau,
   But with a graceful oriental bend,
Pressing one radiant arm just where below
   The heart in good men is supposed to tend.
He turn'd as to an equal, not too low,
   But kindly; Satan met his ancient friend
With more hauteur, as might an old Castilian
Poor noble meet a mushroom rich civilian.

37

He merely bent his diabolic brow
   An instant; and then raising it, he stood   290
In act to assert his right or wrong, and show
   Cause why King George by no means could or
     should
Make out a case to be exempt from woe
   Eternal, more than other kings, endued
With better sense and hearts, whom history
     mentions,
Who long have "paved hell with their good
     intentions."

38

Michael began: "What wouldst thou with this man,
   Now dead, and brought before the Lord? What
     ill
Hath he wrought since his mortal race began,
   That thou canst claim him? Speak! and do thy
     will,   300
If it be just: if in this earthly span
   He hath been greatly failing to fulfil
His duties as a king and mortal, say,
And he is thine; if not, let him have way."

39

"Michael!" replied the Prince of Air, "even here,
   Before the Gate of him thou servest, must
I claim my subject: and will make appear

That as he was my worshipper in dust,
So shall he be in spirit, although dear
   To thee and thine, because nor wine nor
     lust   310
Were of his weaknesses; yet on the throne
He reign'd o'er millions to serve me alone.

40

"Look to *our* earth, or rather *mine;* it was,
   Once, more thy master's: but I triumph not
In this poor planet's conquest; nor, alas!
   Need he thou servest envy me my lot:
With all the myriads of bright worlds which pass
   In worship round him, he may have forgot
Yon weak creation of such paltry things:
I think few worth damnation save their
     kings,—   320

41

"And these but as a kind of quit-rent, to
   Assert my right as lord: and even had
I such an inclination, 'twere (as you
   Well know) superfluous; they are grown so bad,
That hell has nothing better left to do
   Than leave them to themselves: so much more
     mad
And evil by their own internal curse,
Heaven cannot make them better, nor I worse.

42

"Look to the earth, I said, and say again:
   When this old, blind, mad, helpless, weak, poor
     worm   330
Began in youth's first bloom and flush to reign,
   The world and he both wore a different form,
And much of earth and all the watery plain
   Of ocean call'd him king: through many a storm
His isles had floated on the abyss of time;
For the rough virtues chose them for their clime.

43

"He came to his sceptre young; he leaves it old:
   Look to the state in which he found his realm,

And left it; and his annals too behold,
　　How to a minion first he gave the helm;   340
How grew upon his heart a thirst for gold,
　　The beggar's vice, which can but overwhelm
The meanest hearts; and for the rest, but glance
Thine eye along America and France.

44

" 'Tis true, he was a tool from first to last
　　(I have the workmen safe); but as a tool
So let him be consumed. From out the past
　　Of ages, since mankind have known the rule
Of monarchs—from the bloody rolls amass'd
　　Of sin and slaughter—from the Cæsar's
　　　　school,   350
Take the worst pupil; and produce a reign
More drench'd with gore, more cumber'd with the
　　slain.

45

"He ever warr'd with freedom and the free:
　　Nations as men, home subjects, foreign foes,
So that they utter'd the word 'Liberty!'
　　Found George the Third their first opponent.
　　　　Whose
History was ever stain'd as his will be
　　With national and individual woes?
I grant his household abstinence; I grant
His neutral virtues, which most monarchs
　　want;   360

46

"I know he was a constant consort; own
　　He was a decent sire, and middling lord.
All this is much, and most upon a throne;
　　As temperance, if at Apicius' board,
Is more than at an anchorite's supper shown.
　　I grant him all the kindest can accord;
And this was well for him, but not for those
Millions who found him what oppression chose.

47

"The New World shook him off; the Old yet groans
　　Beneath what he and his prepared, if not   370
Completed: he leaves heirs on many thrones
　　To all his vices, without what begot
Compassion for him—his tame virtues; drones
　　Who sleep, or despots who have now forgot
A lesson which shall be re-taught them, wake
Upon the thrones of earth; but let them quake!

48

"Five millions of the primitive, who hold
　　The faith which makes ye great on earth, im-
　　　　plored
A *part* of that vast *all* they held of old,—
　　Freedom to worship—not alone your Lord,   380
Michael, but you, and you, Saint Peter! Cold
　　Must be your souls, if you have not abhorr'd
The foe to Catholic participation
In all the license of a Christian nation.

49

"True! he allow'd them to pray God; but as
　　A consequence of prayer, refused the law
Which would have placed them upon the same base
　　With those who did not hold the saints in awe."
But here Saint Peter started from his place,
　　And cried, "You may the prisoner with-
　　　　draw: 390
Ere heaven shall ope her portals to this Guelph,
While I am guard, may I be damn'd myself!

50

"Sooner will I with Cerberus exchange
　　My office (and *his* is no sinecure)
Than see this royal Bedlam bigot range
　　The azure fields of heaven, of that be sure!"
"Saint!" replied Satan, "you do well to avenge
　　The wrongs he made your satellites endure;
And if to this exchange you should be given,
I'll try to coax *our* Cerberus up to heaven."   400

340. minion . . . helm: a reference to John Stuart, Earl of Bute, George III's former tutor, whom he made Prime Minister in 1762. 364. Apicius: a celebrated Roman epicure of the first century A.D.

391. Guelph: family name of the House of Hanover. 393. Cerberus: the three-headed dog which guarded the gates of Hades.

51

Here Michael interposed: "Good saint! and devil!
   Pray, not so fast; you both outrun discretion.
Saint Peter! you were wont to be more civil!
   Satan! excuse this warmth of his expression,
And condescension to the vulgar's level:
   Even saints sometimes forget themselves in
      session.
Have you got more to say?"—"No."—"If you
   please,
I'll trouble you to call your witnesses."

52

Then Satan turn'd and waved his swarthy hand,
   Which stirr'd with its electric qualities   410
Clouds farther off than we can understand,
   Although we find him sometimes in our skies;
Infernal thunder shook both sea and land
   In all the planets, and hell's batteries
Let off the artillery, which Milton mentions
As one of Satan's most sublime inventions.

53

This was a signal unto such damn'd souls
   As have the privilege of their damnation
Extended far beyond the mere controls
   Of worlds past, present, or to come; no
      station   420
Is theirs particularly in the rolls
   Of hell assign'd; but where their inclination
Or business carries them in search of game,
They may range freely—being damn'd the same.

54

They're proud of this—as very well they may,
   It being a sort of knighthood, or gilt key
Stuck in their loins; or like to an "entré"
   Up the back stairs, or such free-masonry.

426. **gilt key:** the insignia, worn at the belt, of the Lord
Chamberlain.

I borrow my comparisons from clay,
   Being clay myself. Let not those spirits be   430
Offended with such base low likenesses;
We know their posts are nobler far than these.

55

When the great signal ran from heaven to hell—
   About ten million times the distance reckon'd
From our sun to its earth, as we can tell
   How much time it takes up, even to a second,
For every ray that travels to dispel
   The fogs of London, through which, dimly
      beacon'd,
The weathercocks are gilt some thrice a year,
If that the *summer* is not too severe:—   440

56

I say that I can tell—'twas half a minute:
   I know the solar beams take up more time
Ere, packed up for their journey, they begin it;
   But then their telegraph is less sublime,
And if they ran a race, they would not win it
   'Gainst Satan's couriers bound for their own
      clime.
The sun takes up some years for every ray
To reach its goal—the devil not half a day.

57

Upon the verge of space, about the size
   Of half-a-crown, a little speck appear'd   450
(I've seen a something like it in the skies
   In the Ægean, ere a squall); it near'd,
And, growing bigger, took another guise;
   Like an aërial ship it tack'd and steer'd,
Or *was* steer'd (I am doubtful of the grammar
Of the last phrase, which makes the stanza stam-
     mer;—

58

But take your choice); and then it grew a cloud;
   And so it was—a cloud of witnesses.
But such a cloud! No land e'er saw a crowd
   Of locusts numerous as the heavens saw
     these;   460

They shadow'd with their myriads space; their loud
   And varied cries were like those of wild geese
(If nations may be liken'd to a goose),
And realised the phrase of "hell broke loose."

59

Here crash'd a sturdy oath of stout John Bull,
   Who damn'd away his eyes as heretofore:
There Paddy brogued "By Jasus!"—"What's your
     wull?"
   The temperate Scot exclaim'd: the French ghost
     swore
In certain terms I shan't translate in full,
   As the first coachman will; and 'midst the
     war,   470
The voice of Jonathan was heard to express,
"*Our* president is going to war, I guess."

60

Besides there were the Spaniard, Dutch, and Dane;
   In short, an universal shoal of shades,
From Otaheite's isle to Salisbury Plain,
   Of all climes and professions, years and trades,
Ready to swear against the good king's reign,
   Bitter as clubs in cards are against spades:
All summon'd by this grand "subpoena," to
Try if kings mayn't be damn'd like me or you.   480

61

When Michael saw this host, he first grew pale,
   As angels can; next, like Italian twilight,
He turn'd all colours—as a peacock's tail,
   Or sunset streaming through a Gothic skylight
In some old abbey, or a trout not stale,
   Or distant lightning on the horizon *by* night,
Or a fresh rainbow, or a grand review
Of thirty regiments in red, green, and blue.

62

Then he address'd himself to Satan: "Why—
   My good old friend, for such I deem you,
     though   490
Our different parties make us fight so shy,
   I ne'er mistake you for a *personal* foe;
Our difference is *political*, and I
   Trust that, whatever may occur below,
You know my great respect for you: and this
Makes me regret what'er you do amiss—

63

"Why, my dear Lucifer, would you abuse
   My call for witnesses? I did not mean
That you should half of earth and hell produce;
   'Tis even superfluous, since two honest,
     clean,   500
True testimonies are enough: we lose
   Our time, nay, our eternity, between
The accusation and defence: if we
Hear both, 'twill stretch our immortality."

64

Satan replied, "To me the matter is
   Indifferent, in a personal point of view:
I can have fifty better souls than this
   With far less trouble than we have gone through
Already; and I merely argued his
   Late majesty of Britain's case with you   510
Upon a point of form: you may dispose
Of him; I've kings enough below, God knows!"

65

Thus spoke the Demon (late call'd "multifaced"
   By multo-scribbling Southey). "Then we'll call
One or two persons of the myriads placed
   Around our congress, and dispense with all
The rest," quoth Michael: "Who may be so graced
   As to speak first? there's choice enough—who
     shall
It be?" Then Satan answer'd, "There are many;
But you may choose Jack Wilkes as well as
     any."   520

---

464. "hell broke loose": *Paradise Lost*, IV, 918. **475.**
Otaheite's isle: Tahiti.

520. Jack Wilkes: John Wilkes (1727–1797), a strong
opponent of George III. He became Lord Mayor of
London in 1774.

66

A merry, cock-eyed, curious-looking sprite
    Upon the instant started from the throng,
Dress'd in a fashion now forgotten quite;
    For all the fashions of the flesh stick long
By people in the next world; where unite
    All the costumes since Adam's, right or wrong,
From Eve's fig-leaf down to the petticoat,
Almost as scanty, of days less remote.

67

The spirit look'd around upon the crowds
    Assembled, and exclaim'd, "My friend of
        all   530
The spheres, we shall catch cold amongst these
        clouds;
    So let's to business: why this general call?
If those are freeholders I see in shrouds,
    And 'tis for an election that they bawl,
Behold a candidate with unturn'd coat!
Saint Peter, may I count upon your vote?"

68

"Sir," replied Michael, "you mistake; these things
    Are of a former life, and what we do
Above is more august; to judge of kings
    Is the tribunal met: so now you know."   540
"Then I presume those gentlemen with wings,"
    Said Wilkes, "are cherubs; and that soul below
Looks much like George the Third, but to my mind
A good deal older—Bless me! is he blind?"

69

"He is what you behold him, and his doom
    Depends upon his deeds," the Angel said.
"If you have aught to arraign in him, the tomb
    Gives license to the humblest beggar's head
To lift itself against the loftiest."—"Some,"
    Said Wilkes, "don't wait to see them laid in
        lead,   550
For such a liberty—and I, for one,
Have told them what I thought beneath the sun."

70

"Above the sun repeat, then, what thou hast
    To urge against him," said the Archangel. "Why,"
Replied the spirit, "since old scores are past,
    Must I turn evidence? In faith, not I.
Besides, I beat him hollow at the last,
    With all his Lords and Commons: in the sky
I don't like ripping up old stories, since
His conduct was but natural in a prince.   560

71

"Foolish, no doubt, and wicked, to oppress
    A poor unlucky devil without a shilling;
But then I blame the man himself much less
    Than Bute and Grafton, and shall be unwilling
To see him punish'd here for their excess,
    Since they were both damn'd long ago, and still
        in
Their place below: for me, I have forgiven,
And vote his 'habeas corpus' into heaven."

72

"Wilkes," said the Devil, "I understand all this;
    You turn'd to half a courtier ere you died,   570
And seem to think it would not be amiss
    To grow a whole one on the other side
Of Charon's ferry; you forget that his
    Reign is concluded; whatsoe'er betide,
He won't be sovereign more: you've lost your
        labour
For at the best he will but be your neighbour.

73

"However, I knew what to think of it,
    When I beheld you in your jesting way
Flitting and whispering round about the spit
    Where Belial, upon duty for the day,   580
With Fox's lard was basting William Pitt,
    His pupil; I know what to think, I say:

564. **Bute and Grafton:** Ministers of George III. **581.
Fox ... Pitt:** Charles James Fox (1749–1806), the famous Whig statesman, was a very fat man. William Pitt
(1759–1806) served as Prime Minister.

That fellow even in hell breeds farther ills;
I'll have him *gagg'd*—'twas one of his own bills.

74

"Call Junius!" From the crowd a shadow stalk'd,
    And at the name there was a general squeeze,
So that the very ghosts no longer walk'd
    In comfort, at their own aërial ease,
But were all ramm'd, and jamm'd (but to be balk'd,
    As we shall see), and jostled hands and
        knees,   590
Like wind compress'd and pent within a bladder,
Or like a human colic, which is sadder.

75

The shadow came—a tall, thin, grey-hair'd figure,
    That look'd as it had been a shade on earth;
Quick in its motions, with an air of vigour,
    But nought to mark its breeding or its birth:
Now it wax'd little, then again grew bigger,
    With now an air of gloom, or savage mirth;
But as you gazed upon its features, they
Changed every instant—to *what*, none could
        say.   600

76

The more intently the ghosts gazed, the less
    Could they distinguish whose the features were;
The Devil himself seem'd puzzled even to guess;
    They varied like a dream—now here, now there;
And several people swore from out the press,
    They knew him perfectly; and one could swear
He was his father: upon which another
Was sure he was his mother's cousin's brother:

77

Another, that he was a duke, or knight,
    An orator, a lawyer, or a priest,   610
A nabob, a man-midwife; but the wight
    Mysterious changed his countenance at least

585. **Junius:** pseudonym for a mystery figure in
eighteenth-century politics who wrote a series of letters
attacking George III and his government. Junius was
probably Sir Philip Francis (1740–1818).

As oft as they their minds: though in full sight
    He stood, the puzzle only was increased;
The man was a phantasmagoria in
    Himself—he was so volatile and thin.

78

The moment that you had pronounced him *one*,
    Presto! his face changed, and he was another;
And when that change was hardly well put on,
    It varied, till I don't think his own mother   620
(If that he had a mother) would her son
    Have known, he shifted so from one to t'other;
Till guessing from a pleasure grew a task,
At this epistolary "Iron Mask."

79

For sometimes he like Cerberus would seem—
    "Three gentlemen at once" (as sagely says
Good Mrs. Malaprop); then you might deem
    That he was not even *one*; now many rays
Were flashing round him; and now a thick steam
    Hid him from sight—like fogs on London
        days: 630
Now Burke, now Tooke, he grew to people's
        fancies,
And certes often like Sir Philip Francis.

80

I've an hypothesis—'tis quite my own;
    I never let it out till now, for fear
Of doing people harm about the throne,
    And injuring some minister or peer,
On whom the stigma might perhaps be blown;
    It is—my gentle public, lend thine ear!
'Tis, that what Junius we are wont to call
Was *really, truly*, nobody at all.   640

81

I don't see wherefore letters should not be
    Written without hands, since we daily view

624. "**Iron Mask**": the famous Man in the Iron Mask
was imprisoned in the Bastille by Louis XIV. **627. Mrs.
Malaprop:** a character in Sheridan's comedy *The Rivals*
famed for her misuse of the language—hence our word
"malapropism."

Them written without heads; and books, we see,
    Are fill'd as well without the latter too:
And really till we fix on somebody
    For certain sure to claim them as his due,
Their author, like the Niger's mouth, will bother
The world to say if *there* be mouth or author.

82

"And who and what art thou?" the Archangel said.
    "For *that* you may consult my title-page,"   650
Replied this mighty shadow of a shade:
    "If I have kept my secret half an age,
I scarce shall tell it now."—"Canst thou upbraid,"
    Continued Michael, "George Rex, or allege
Aught further?" Junius answer'd, "You had better
First ask him for *his* answer to my letter:

83

"My charges upon record will outlast
    The brass of both his epitaph and tomb."
"Repent'st thou not,' said Michael, "of some past
    Exaggeration? something which may doom   660
Thyself if false, as him if true? Thou wast
    Too bitter—is it not so?—in thy gloom
Of passion?"—"Passion!" cried the phantom dim,
"I loved my country, and I hated him.

84

"What I have written, I have written: let
    The rest be on his head or mine!" So spoke
Old "Nominis Umbra"; and while speaking yet,
    Away he melted in celestial smoke.
Then Satan said to Michael, "Don't forget
    To call George Washington, and John Horne
        Tooke,   670
And Franklin";—but at this time there was heard
A cry for room, though not a phantom stirr'd.

85

At length with jostling, elbowing, and the aid
    Of cherubim appointed to that post,
The devil Asmodeus to the circle made
    His way, and look'd as if his journey cost

667. **"Nominis Umbra":** shadow of a name.

Some trouble. When his burden down he laid,
    "What's this?" cried Michael; "why, 'tis not a
        ghost?"
"I know it," quoth the incubus; "but he
Shall be one, if you leave the affair to me.   680

86

"Confound the renegado! I have sprain'd
    My left wing, he's so heavy; one would think
Some of his works about his neck were chain'd.
    But to the point; while hovering o'er the brink
Of Skiddaw (where as usual it still rain'd),
    I saw a taper, far below me, wink,
And stooping, caught this fellow at a libel—
No less on history than the Holy Bible.

87

"The former is the devil's scripture, and
    The latter yours, good Michael: so the
        affair   690
Belongs to all of us, you understand.
    I snatch'd him up just as you see him there,
And brought him off for sentence out of hand:
    I've scarcely been ten minutes in the air—
At least a quarter it can hardly be:
I dare say that his wife is still at tea."

88

Here Satan said, "I know this man of old,
    And have expected him for some time here;
A sillier fellow you will scarce behold,
    Or more conceited in his petty sphere: 700
But surely it was not worth while to fold
    Such trash below your wing, Asmodeus dear:
We had the poor wretch safe (without being bored
With carriage) coming of his own accord.

89

"But since he's here, let's see what he has done."
    "Done!" cried Asmodeus, "he anticipates
The very business you are now upon,
    And scribbles as if head clerk to the Fates.

685. **Skiddaw:** mountain in the Lake District near
Southey's home.

Who knows to what his ribaldry may run,
   When such an ass as this, like Balaam's,
      prates?"   710
"Let's hear," quoth Michael, "what he has to say:
You know we're bound to that in every way."

90

Now the bard, glad to get an audience, which
   By no means often was his case below,
Began to cough, and hawk, and hem, and pitch
   His voice into that awful note of woe
To all unhappy hearers within reach
   Of poets when the tide of rhyme's in flow;
But stuck fast with his first hexameter,
Not one of all whose gouty feet would stir.   720

91

But ere the spavin'd dactyls could be spurr'd
   Into recitative, in great dismay
Both cherubim and seraphim were heard
   To murmur loudly through their long array;
And Michael rose ere he could get a word
   Of all his founder'd verses under way,
And cried, "For God's sake stop, my friend! 'twere
    best—
Non Di, non homines—you know the rest."

92

A general bustle spread throughout the throng,
   Which seem'd to hold all verse in detesta-
      tion;   730
The angels had of course enough of song
   When upon service; and the generation
Of ghosts had heard too much in life, not long
   Before, to profit by a new occasion.
The monarch, mute till then, exclaim'd "What!
   what!
Pye come again? No more—no more of that!"

93

The tumult grew; an universal cough
   Convulsed the skies, as during a debate,
When Castlereagh has been up long enough
   (Before he was first minister of state,   740
I mean—the *slaves hear now*); some cried "Off,
   off!"
   As at a farce; till, grown quite desperate,
The bard Saint Peter pray'd to interpose
(Himself an author) only for his prose.

94

The varlet was not an ill-favour'd knave;
   A good deal like a vulture in the face,
With a hook nose and a hawk's eye, which gave
   A smart and sharper-looking sort of grace
To his whole aspect, which, though rather grave,
   Was by no means so ugly as his case;   750
But that, indeed, was hopeless as can be,
Quite a poetic felony "*de se.*"

95

Then Michael blew his trump, and still'd the noise
   With one still greater, as is yet the mode
On earth besides; except some grumbling voice,
   Which now and then will make a slight inroad
Upon decorous silence, few will twice
   Lift up their lungs when fairly overcrow'd;
And now the bard could plead his own bad cause,
With all the attitudes of self-applause.   760

96

He said—(I only give the heads)—he said,
   He meant no harm in scribbling; 'twas his way
Upon all topics; 'twas, besides, his bread,
   Of which he butter'd both sides; 'twould delay
Too long the assembly (he was pleased to dread),
   And take up rather more time than a day,
To name his works—he would but cite a few—
"Wat Tyler"—"Rhymes on Blenheim"—"Waterloo."

710. Balaam's: See Numbers 22:28. **728. Non...
homines:** Horace's famous axiom in his *Art of Poetry,*
ll. 372–73: "Neither gods nor men will tolerate mediocre poets." **736. Pye:** Henry Pye, Laureate before
Southey and a bad poet.

752. felony "*de se*": suicide. **768. Wat...Waterloo:**
Southey's *Wat Tyler* (1794), *The Battle of Blenheim*
(1798), and *The Poet's Pilgrimage to Waterloo* (1816).

97

He had written praises of a regicide;
　He had written praises of all kings what
　　　ever;　　　　　　　　　　　　　　　　770
He had written for republics far and wide,
　And then against them bitterer than ever:
For pantisocracy he once had cried
　Aloud, a scheme less moral than 'twas clever;
Then grew a hearty anti-jacobin—
Had turn'd his coat—and would have turn'd his
　　　skin.

98

He had sung against all battles, and again
　In their high praise and glory; he had call'd
Reviewing "the ungentle craft," and then
　Become as base a critic as e'er crawl'd—　　780
Fed, paid, and pamper'd by the very men
　By whom his muse and morals had been maul'd:
He had written much blank verse, and blanker
　　　prose,
And more of both than anybody knows.

99

He had written Wesley's life:—here turning round
　To Satan, "Sir, I'm ready to write yours,
In two octavo volumes, nicely bound,
　With notes and preface, all that most allures
The pious purchaser; and there's no ground
　For fear, I can choose my own reviewers:　　790
So let me have the proper documents,
That I may add you to my other saints."

100

Satan bow'd, and was silent. "Well, if you,
　With amiable modesty, decline
My offer, what says Michael? There are few
　Whose memoirs could be render'd more divine.
Mine is a pen of all work; not so new
　As it was once, but I would make you shine
Like your own trumpet. By the way, my own
Has more of brass in it, and is as well blown.　　800

101

"But talking about trumpets, here's my Vision!
　Now you shall judge, all people; yes, you shall

Judge with my judgment, and by my decision
　Be guided who shall enter heaven or fall.
I settle all these things by intuition,
　Times present, past, to come, heaven, hell, and
　　　all,
Like King Alfonso. When I thus see double,
I save the Deity some worlds of trouble."

102

He ceased, and drew forth an MS.; and no
　Persuasion on the part of devils, saints,　　810
Or angels, now could stop the torrent; so
　He read the first three lines of the contents;
But at the fourth, the whole spiritual show
　Had vanish'd, with variety of scents,
Ambrosial and sulphureous, as they sprang,
Like lightning, off from his "melodious twang."

103

Those grand heroics acted as a spell:
　The angels stopp'd their ears and plied their
　　　pinions;
The devils ran howling, deafen'd, down to hell;
　The ghosts fled, gibbering, for their own domin-
　　　ions—　　　　　　　　　　　　　　　　820
(For 'tis not yet decided where they dwell,
　And I leave every man to his opinions);
Michael took refuge in his trump—but, lo!
His teeth were set on edge, he could not blow!

104

Saint Peter, who has hitherto been known
　For an impetuous saint, upraised his keys,
And at the fifth line knock'd the poet down;
　Who fell like Phaëton, but more at ease,
Into his lake, for there he did not drown;
　A different web being by the Destinies　　830
Woven for the Laureate's final wreath, whene'er
Reform shall happen either here or there.

807. King Alfonso: King of Castile. Byron speaks in a note of the king saying in regard to the Ptolomean system that "had he been consulted at the beginning of the world, he would have spared the Maker some absurdities." **828. Phaëton:** Apollo's son, who was killed by Zeus and hurled into a river when he tried to drive the chariot of the sun across the sky.

105

He first sank to the bottom—like his works,
    But soon rose to the surface—like himself;
For all corrupted things are buoy'd like corks,
    By their own rottenness, light as an elf,
Or wisp that flits o'er a morass: he lurks,
    It may be, still, like dull books on a shelf,
In his own den, to scrawl some "Life" or "Vision,"
As Welborn says—"the devil turn'd preci-
        sian."   840

106

As for the rest, to come to the conclusion
    Of this true dream, the telescope is gone
Which kept my optics free from all delusion,
    And show'd me what I in my turn have shown;
All I saw farther, in the last confusion,
    Was, that King George slipp'd into heaven for
        one;
And when the tumult dwindled to a calm,
I left him practising the hundredth psalm.

1821   *1822*

ON THIS DAY I COMPLETE
MY THIRTY-SIXTH YEAR

'Tis time this heart should be unmoved,
    Since others it hath ceased to move:
Yet, though I cannot be beloved,
        Still let me love!

840. **Welborn:** a character in Massinger's play *A New Way to Pay Old Debts* (1633). **precisian:** Puritan.

My days in the yellow leaf;
    The flowers and fruits of love are gone;
The worm, the canker, and the grief
        Are mine alone!

The fire that on my bosom preys
    Is lone as some volcanic isle;   10
No torch is kindled at its blaze—
        A funeral pile.

The hope, the fear, the jealous care,
    The exalted portion of the pain
And power of love, I cannot share,
        But wear the chain.

But 'tis not *thus*—and 'tis not *here*—
    Such thoughts should shake my soul, nor *now*,
Where glory decks the hero's bier,
        Or binds his brow.   20

The sword, the banner, and the field,
    Glory and Greece, around me see!
The Spartan, borne upon his shield,
        Was not more free.

Awake! (not Greece—she *is* awake!)
    Awake, my spirit! Think through *whom*
Thy life-blood tracks its parent lake,
        And then strike home!

Tread those reviving passions down,
    Unworthy manhood!—unto thee   30
Indifferent should the smile or frown
        Of beauty be.

If thou regrett'st thy youth, *why live?*
    The land of honorable death
Is here:—up to the field, and give
        Away thy breath!

Seek out—less often sought than found—
    A soldier's grave, for thee the best;
Then look around, and choose thy ground,
        And take thy rest.   40

1824   *1824*

Percy Bysshe Shelley

1792–1822

The student of Shelley is continually struck by the image of the young, earthbound mortal in search of an ideal realm of brightness, beauty, and love. The "power" of *Mont Blanc,* the "Spirit of Beauty" of the *Hymn to Intellectual Beauty,* the Skylark soaring higher and higher, the force of the West Wind—these, and so many others, are the gods he worships, the goals he pursues in his life and in his art. It is easy to say that they are elusive and ultimately unreachable, that language is inadequate to embody them; but they are no less real for the questing poet as he struggles with word and image to convey the vision of his dreams. How often his eloquent *A Defence of Poetry* serves as his manifesto; how many of his utterances in that document have become part of our way of thinking and talking about poets and poetry. "Poetry is the record of the best and happiest moments of the happiest and best minds." Or, "Poets are the unacknowledged legislators of the world." Or, the moving "Poetry thus makes immortal all that is best and most beautiful in the world; it arrests the vanishing apparitions which haunt the interlunations of life, and veiling them, or in language or in form, sends them forth among mankind, bearing sweet news of kindred joy to those with whom their sisters abide—abide, because there is no real portal of expression from the caverns of the spirit which they inhabit into the universe of things. Poetry redeems from decay the visitations of the divinity in man."

Shelley, like his fellow Romantics, was a child of the French Revolution; from his earliest days he was a rebellious spirit. Born on August 4, 1792, he was a joyous and buoyant youth, fascinated by the Gothic and the magical, intrigued by the romances of writers like Ann Radcliffe and Monk Lewis, and angered by all forms of tyranny, whether political or parental. His father, Timothy Shelley, a wealthy and successful country squire who was later to become a member of Parliament, a man uninterested in intellectual adventure or in great moral causes, epitomized everything that his son came to detest in society; and the gap between parent and child widened as the years passed. Shelley's rebellious temperament manifested itself early, as the ten-year-old schoolboy at Sion House Academy and the young man later at Eton was revolted by the cruelty of his schoolmasters and the mocking of his fellow students who referred to him as "Mad Shelley."

Shelley was never very devoted to formal curricula. His early love of science was fostered by his enthusiastic experiments in chemistry and astronomy; the scenery around Eton nourished his love of the beauties of nature. He read widely and eagerly in Lucretius, and later in Helvetius, Holbach, Locke, Voltaire, and Hume, to name some major writers, developing as he read the spirit of rationalistic materialism that characterized his early thought and underlay his hatred of all institutions and his gospel of philanthropy. Unquestionably the book that influenced him most was the *Political Justice* of William Godwin (who was later to be his father-in-law), a book which seemed to articulate, however simplistically, the new revolutionary faith. Shelley lasted less than a year at University College, Oxford; his radical pamphlet, *The Necessity of Atheism,* shocked the authorities, and he and his co-author, Thomas Jefferson Hogg, were expelled. Even worse, he was so adamant that he refused to provide the retraction and apology sought by his father, and was virtually disowned.

Now poor and an outcast, but still an ardent revolutionary, he eloped in 1811 with Harriet Westbrook, a fellow radical and soul-sister, but hardly a woman he loved, and the couple were married in Edinburgh. Meanwhile he had met his intellectual hero Godwin, and his desire for change and reform was stirred even more. He supported all kinds of causes, from Catholic emancipation in Ireland to a defense of Tom Paine's *Age of Reason* when a printer was prosecuted for publishing the document. His own great work of the period was the sprawling and exuberant *Queen Mab,* with its idyllic portrait of mankind as virtuous and peaceful, its attack on the evils of government, and its prophecy of an era of universal love and happiness.

In 1814 he met and fell in love with Mary Godwin, and, after his utopian suggestion that Harriet live with them as an intellectual companion failed, he eloped with Mary to the Continent in July, returning to England in September. Politics seemed to be less a concern from this point on. His major poem *Alastor* was written at this time, a quest romance presenting the tragedy of the idealist whose ideals are shattered by reality. The death of his grandfather, Sir Bysshe Shelley, brought a measure of financial security, although the demands of Godwin and Shelley's chronic inability to hold on to money always seemed to plague him.

Shelley and Mary left England for Switzerland in the summer of 1816, and there followed a period of great creativity. It seems that the grandeur of the Alps, the meeting with Byron, the reading of Wordsworth's poetry, and a new enthusiasm for idealistic philosophers like Plato, Berkeley, and Spinoza tempered his materialistic attitudes and his posture as an active radical. A new optimism is notable in his poetry. There are no more sweeping attacks on religion; indeed

Shelley is increasingly attracted to the idea of a Spirit of Nature. His "Hymn to Intellectual Beauty" expresses his yearning for such a Spirit, invisible and transcendent, to be sure, but revealed at times faintly even in this world of shadows:

> Thy light alone—like mist o'er mountains driven,
>   Or music by the night-wind sent
>   Through strings of some still instrument,
>   Or moonlight on a midnight stream,
> Gives grace and truth to life's unquiet dream.

"Mont Blanc," still in awe of the Divine Power, nevertheless questions its benevolence, wonders about its remoteness from human concerns:

>   Its home
> The voiceless lightning in these solitudes
> Keeps innocently, and like vapour broods
> Over the snow. The secret Strength of things
> Which governs thought, and to the infinite dome
> Of Heaven is as a law, inhabits thee!
> And what were thou, and earth, and stars, and sea,
> If to the human mind's imaginings
> Silence and solitude were vacancy?

A short return-visit to England in 1816 brought a darker vision. The suicide of Mary's half-sister and the probable suicide of Harriet, Shelley's feeling of responsibility for both, the court's denial of the custody of his children born of Harriet, poor health, the societal gossip about his lifestyle: all of these weighed heavily on him. He married Mary, and in March of 1818 he left for Italy, never to return.

The last five years of Shelley's life offer us everything that is distinctive in his work. Nature seems less governed by Necessity than by Love, and he develops more fully in his work the idea of a Transcendent Spirit revealing itself in natural beauty and human love. Indeed, there is an oracular note as he prophesies the emergence of Goodness and Truth in the world. The great lyrical drama, *Prometheus Unbound,* begun in 1818 and completed in 1820, ends with triumphal hymns of liberation as Prometheus and Asia, humankind and its ideal love, are reunited, and the tyranny of Jupiter is overthrown. These are also the years of great lyrics like "Ode to the West Wind," "To a Skylark," "The Cloud"; of longer narrative poems like *The Sensitive Plant* and *Epipsychidion;* of *Adonais,* the great pastoral elegy on the death of Keats, poems of quest, of confidence, of sensuous beauty. His optimism, never unqualified, is marred deeply by the tragic fragment, *The Triumph of Life,* written shortly before his death on July 8, 1822.

Shelley's poetry, although it has had its loyal supporters like Browning, Mill, Francis Thompson, Yeats, and others, has, until about thirty years ago, labored under the criticism of major figures like Matthew Arnold, F. R. Leavis, and the so-called New Critics. Arnold's oft-quoted portrait of the poet as a "beautiful but ineffectual angel, beating in the void his luminous wings in vain" bespeaks a strong Victorian and early twentieth-century attitude of a well-intentioned, idealistic artist, in love with abstract ideas and romantic dreams, whose works lack philosophical toughness and a realistic vision of the world and its possibilities. F. R. Leavis's celebrated essay provides an equally familiar twentieth-century approach. To read Shelley, he argues, one must switch off intelligence, must be prepared to follow the poet's cloudy imagery without question; must, as in the case of the "Ode to the West Wind," accept "a general tendency of the images to forget the status of the metaphor or simile that introduced them and to assume an autonomy and a right to propagate, so that we lose in confused generations and perspectives the perception or thought that was the ostensible *raison d'être* of imagery." Relatively recent criticism has seemed eager to reexamine the entire body of his poetry, its ideas and its expression, in an attempt to free it from preconceptions and prejudices and view it in a new light. Clearly the work of Carlos Baker, Harold Bloom, David Perkins, and Earl Wasserman is a significant part of this criticism.

It is interesting that Shelley himself can be seen as providing a useful critical introduction to his own poetry, that his *Defence of Poetry* can be extremely helpful in coming to terms with the wide range of his poetic effort, lyric, narrative, and dramatic. He is not, it would seem, a poet-critic who would mislead us into expecting of his poetry anything but what we find. The demands of his subject, rather than *a priori* theories, are an underlying concern, a concern that governs every aspect of rhythm, language, and imagery. Poets, he argues in the *Defence*, are not so much the servants of an established poetic language as they are "the authors of language and of music, of the dance, and architecture, and statuary and painting; they are the institutors of laws, and the founders of civil society, and the inventors of the arts of life, and the teachers, who draw into a certain propinquity with the beautiful and true, that partial apprehension of the agencies of the invisible world which is called religion." The poet, he further says, "participates in the eternal, the infinite, and the one; as far as relates to his conceptions, time and place and number are not." Language is more directly representative of the inner life with all of its complex shadings. It is "arbitrarily produced by the imagination, and has relation to thoughts alone." Hence, although he can at times be vivid and concrete in expression, one does not find in the poems a carefully reasoned series of arguments articulated with scientific precision, but rather a poetry of thought, of vision which struggles with the inadequacies of language to embody that thought or vision. The struggle does not end in despair, however, but in a poetry which expresses the artist's restlessness with a world failed or failing, a skepticism about human capabilities, and yet holds up a dream of the transcendent that can only be rendered by a style that glimpses or suggests, or by a barrage of images, no one of which can fully do justice to the poet's desires.

One searches in vain, then, for the sharp intellectual analogies of a Donne or the richly denotative diction of a Dryden or Pope in Shelley's poetry. This is not to suggest that one is better than the other, but rather that there are different kinds of excellence and that the critic's standard must be rooted not in one narrow criterion, but in a criterion of appropriateness, in the fitness of language to convey the vision of the poet.

The great quest of Shelley's poetry from the beginning is for a power which transcends the fickle, transitory shadows of mortal life. The searching tragic poet of *Alastor* is characterized thus:

> By solemn vision, and bright silver dream,
> His infancy was nurtured. Every sight
> And sound from the vast earth and ambient air,
> Sent to his heart its choicest impulses.

The dream is beyond language, and yet language, at times tortured and copious, is all there is to embody it. The brilliant "Mont Blanc" and "Hymn to Intellectual Beauty," beautifully crafted poems, venerate the transcendent power and suggest, as Shelley often does, the gap between permanence and flux, between unchanging beauty and an ever-changing world of illusion. Note the swift, spontaneous movement, achieved largely through the skillful use of short vowel sounds and a wonderfully varied iambic rhythm, as the following lines from "Mont Blanc" convey the flux of earthly things:

> The fields, the lakes, the forests, and the streams,
> Ocean, and all the living things that dwell
> Within the daedal earth; lightning and rain,
> Earthquake, and fiery flood, and hurricane,
> The torpor of the year when feeble dreams
> Visit the hidden buds, or dreamless sleep
> Holds every future leaf and flower;—the bound
> With which from that detested trance they leap;
> The works and ways of man, their death and birth,
> And that of him and all that his may be;
> All things that move and breathe with toil and sound
> Are born and die; revolve, subside, and swell.

Note also the slower movement, the sense of awe, achieved largely through a more regular rhythm and long vowel sounds, as Shelley tries to image the power in the loftiness and remoteness of the mountain:

> Mont Blanc yet gleams on high:—the power is there,
> The still and solemn power of many sights,
> And many sounds, and much of life and death.
> In the calm darkness of the moonless nights,
> In the lone glare of day, the snows descend
> Upon that Mountain.

The effect of the contrast is dramatic, even if not visually perfect; and when Shelley avoids the obscurity and self-indulgence that mars sections of his poetry, such a contrast comes close to his ideal.

The great celebration poems of 1818 to 1821 are wonderfully realized. Shelley's gifts always seem more suited to the lyric rather than the narrative or dramatic modes. The poet-speaker of "To a Skylark," with a joyous music and a rhythm that imitates the flight of the bird, marvels at the skylark's power:

> Higher still and higher
>   From the earth thou springest
> Like a cloud of fire;
>   The blue depth thou wingest
> And singing still dost soar, and soaring ever singest,

and then, in a series of apt and vivid similes, attempts to capture the perfection of this magical creature of the sky, closing with a mortal's prayer to "thou scorner of the ground!":

> Teach me half the gladness
>   That thy brain must know,
> Such harmonious madness
>   From my lips would flow
> The world should listen then—as I am listening now.

"Ode to the West Wind," in spite of "I fall upon the thorns of life! I bleed!," is a poem of hope after despondency. The sheer energy of the verse, the central image of divine inspiration bearing his message to a lost world as the West Wind drives "withered leaves to quicken a new birth!," are again climaxed by a prayer and hope, "O, Wind, / If Winter comes, can Spring be far behind?" The supreme irony of "The Cloud," with its rapidly shifting patterns suggesting the impermanence of life, is that what is seemingly most symbolic of change ultimately promises permanence. The militant voice of the cloud, "I change, but I cannot die," is followed by a thematically powerful and visually spectacular image, the kind of image that gives the lie to the objection that Shelley was incapable of the concrete:

> For after the rain when with never a stain
>   The pavilion of Heaven is bare,
> And the winds and sunbeams with their convex gleams
>   Build up the blue dome of air,
> I silently laugh at my own cenotaph,
>   And out of the caverns of rain,
> Like a child from the womb, like a ghost from the tomb,
>   I arise and unbuild it again.

Shelley's greatest achievements, although each in its own way flawed by his familiar digressiveness and self-concern, are the great pastoral elegy, *Adonais,* and the epic drama, *Prometheus Unbound.* Both, with a combination of philosophical strength and symbolic richness, preach a belief in the power of beauty and love and in their ultimate triumph. Adonais, the young John Keats dead before his time, becomes for Shelley symbolic of the slow decay of the creative imagination in an increasingly mechanized and materialistic world. Yet, as in

Milton's *Lycidas,* death gives way to life. The poet's light and spirit still are a source of inspiration, a hope that the things of the spirit will never perish. "The soul of Adonais, like a star, / Beacons from the abode where the Eternals are." Prometheus and Asia, mankind and the love it desperately needs and seeks, no longer separated but one, are the promise of a future of freedom and happiness as the ringing final lines of Demogorgon proclaim:

> To suffer woes which Hope thinks infinite;
> To forgive wrongs darker than death or night;
>   To defy Power, which seems omnipotent;
> To love, and bear; to hope till Hope creates
> From its own wreck the thing it contemplates;
>   Neither to change, nor falter, nor repent;
> This, like thy glory, Titan, is to be
> Good, great and joyous, beautiful and free;
> This is alone Life, Joy, Empire, and Victory.

Shelley, then, is a poet not easily reducible to categories. Of late, critics have done much to break down the image of a gentle, otherworldly dreamer whose work seems far removed from the needs of a doomed world. They have called attention to his skepticism, his urbanity, his modernity. We might perhaps, setting aside questions of personal attitudes toward the poet, call attention to the complexity of his work, to its deep awareness of human limitation and possibility. Shelley is, quite obviously, the poet of those who hope for a better world. He is the prophetic artist, convinced of his mission, stridently confident at times, in love with his dreams and searching for a language to dramatize them. The great words of Earth in *Prometheus Unbound* speak more forcefully than any commentary:

> Man, oh, not men! a chain of linked thought,
>   Of love and might to be divided not,
> Compelling the elements with adamantine stress;
>   As the sun rules, even with a tyrant's gaze,
>   The unquiet republic of the maze
> Of planets, struggling fierce towards heaven's free wilderness.

Suggestions for Further Reading

For many years Newman I. White's *Shelley* (1940) has been the standard biography, but, while still a very useful book, it must give way to Richard Holmes's *Shelley: The Pursuit* (1975), a comprehensive and penetrating study of the life and work. John Buxton's, *Byron and Shelley: The History of a Friendship* (1968) is an interesting discussion of the relationship of the two poets.

Useful studies of Shelley's thought are Carl Grabo, *The Magic Plant* (1936); Carlos Baker, *Shelley's Major Poetry: The Fabric of a Vision* (1948); James A. Notopoulos' massive and stimulating *The Platonism of Shelley* (1949); Kenneth N. Cameron, *Shelley: Genesis of a Radical* (1950).

Students interested in matters of method and technique will find the following works helpful: R. H. Fogle, *The Imagery of Keats and Shelley* (1949); the discussion of Shelley in David Perkins, *The Quest for Permanence* (1959); and Harold Bloom, *Shelley's Mythmaking* (1959). Earl Wasserman's *Shelley: A Critical Reading* (1971) is clearly the fullest and most insightful treatment of the poems, and should be in every student's library.

Shelley: A Collection of Critical Essays, ed. George M. Ridenour (1965), is a very useful collection of important statements by major critics of Shelley.

TO WORDSWORTH

Poet of Nature, thou hast wept to know
That things depart which never may return:
Childhood and youth, friendship and love's first
　　glow,
Have fled like sweet dreams, leaving thee to mourn.
These common woes I feel. One loss is mine
Which thou too feel'st, yet I alone deplore.
Thou wert as a lone star, whose light did shine
On some frail bark in winter's midnight roar:
Thou hast like to a rock-built refuge stood
Above the blind and battling multitude:　　　　　　10
In honoured poverty thy voice did weave
Songs consecrate to truth and liberty,—
Deserting these, thou leavest me to grieve,
Thus having been, that thou shouldst cease to be.

1815　　　　　　　　　　　　　　　　　*1816*

MUTABILITY

We are as clouds that veil the midnight moon;
　　How restlessly they speed, and gleam, and quiver,
Streaking the darkness radiantly!—yet soon
　　Night closes round, and they are lost for ever:

Or like forgotten lyres, whose dissonant strings
　　Give various response to each varying blast,
To whose frail frame no second motion brings
　　One mood or modulation like the last.

We rest—a dream has power to poison sleep;
　　We rise—one wandering thought pollutes the
　　　　day;　　　　　　　　　　　　　　　　　　10
We feel, conceive or reason, laugh or weep;
　　Embrace fond woe, or cast our cares away:

It is the same!—For, be it joy or sorrow,
　　The path of its departure still is free:
Man's yesterday may ne'er be like his morrow;
　　Nought may endure but Mutability.

1815　　　　　　　　　　　　　　　　　*1816*

ALASTOR

OR

THE SPIRIT OF SOLITUDE

*Nondum amabam, et amare amabam, quaerebam
　　quid amarem, amans amare.*°

Confess. St. August.

Preface

The poem entitled *Alastor* may be considered as allegorical of one of the most interesting situations of the human mind. It represents a youth of uncorrupted feelings and adventurous genius led forth by an imagination inflamed and purified through familiarity with all that is excellent and majestic to the contemplation of the universe. He drinks deep of the fountains of knowledge and is still insatiate. The magnificence and beauty of the external world sinks profoundly into the frame of his conceptions and affords to their modifications a variety not to be exhausted. So long as it is possible for his desires to point towards objects thus infinite and unmeasured, he is joyous and tranquil and self-possessed. But the period arrives when these objects cease to suffice. His mind is at length suddenly awakened and thirsts for intercourse with an intelligence similar to itself. He images to himself the Being whom he loves. Conversant with speculations of the sublimest and

---

° "I did not yet love, and I loved to love;
　　I searched for what I should love, loving to love."

most perfect natures, the vision in which he embodies his own imaginations unites all of wonderful or wise or beautiful, which the poet, the philosopher, or the lover could depicture. The intellectual faculties, the imagination, the functions of sense, have their respective requisitions on the sympathy of corresponding powers in other human beings. The Poet is represented as uniting these requisitions, and attaching them to a single image. He seeks in vain for a prototype of his conception. Blasted by his disappointment, he descends to an untimely grave.

The picture is not barren of instruction to actual men. The Poet's self-centered seclusion was avenged by the furies of an irresistible passion pursuing him to speedy ruin. But that Power, which strikes the luminaries of the world with sudden darkness and extinction by awakening them to too exquisite a perception of its influences, dooms to a slow and poisonous decay those meaner spirits that dare to abjure its dominion. Their destiny is more abject and inglorious as their delinquency is more contemptible and pernicious. They who, deluded by no generous error, instigated by no sacred thirst of doubtful knowledge, duped by no illustrious superstition, loving nothing on this earth, and cherishing no hopes beyond, yet keep aloof from sympathies with their kind, rejoicing neither in human joy nor mourning with human grief; these, and such as they, have their apportioned curse. They languish, because none feel with them their common nature. They are morally dead. They are neither friends, nor lovers, nor fathers, nor citizens of the world, nor benefactors of their country. Among those who attempt to exist without human sympathy, the pure and tenderhearted perish through the intensity and passion of their search after its communities, when the vacancy of their spirit suddenly makes itself felt. All else, selfish, blind, and torpid, are those unforeseeing multitudes who constitute, together with their own, the lasting misery and loneliness of the world. Those who love not their fellow-beings live unfruitful lives, and prepare for their old age a miserable grave.

> The good die first,
> And those whose hearts are dry as summer dust,
> Burn to the socket!°

                    [Shelley]
                    DECEMBER 14, 1815

Earth, ocean, air, belovèd brotherhood!
If our great Mother has imbued my soul
With aught of natural piety to feel
Your love, and recompense the boon with mine;
If dewy morn, and odorous noon, and even,

° Wordsworth, *The Excursion*, ll. 500–502.

With sunset and its gorgeous ministers,
And solemn midnight's tingling silentness;
If autumn's hollow sighs in the sere wood,
And winter robing with pure snow and crowns
Of starry ice the grey grass and bare boughs;   10
If spring's voluptuous pantings when she breathes
Her first sweet kisses, have been dear to me;
If no bright bird, insect, or gentle beast
I consciously have injured, but still loved
And cherished these my kindred; then forgive
This boast, belovèd brethren, and withdraw
No portion of your wonted favour now!

Mother of this unfathomable world!
Favour my solemn song, for I have loved
Thee ever, and thee only; I have watched   20
Thy shadow, and the darkness of thy steps,
And my heart ever gazes on the depth
Of thy deep mysteries. I have made my bed
In charnels and on coffins, where black death
Keeps record of the trophies won from thee,
Hoping to still these obstinate questionings
Of thee and thine, by forcing some lone ghost
Thy messenger, to render up the tale
Of what we are. In lone and silent hours,
When night makes a weird sound of its own
         stillness,   30
Like an inspired and desperate alchymist
Staking his very life on some dark hope,
Have I mixed awful talk and asking looks
With my most innocent love, until strange tears
Uniting with those breathless kisses, made
Such magic as compels the charmèd night
To render up thy charge: . . . and, though ne'er yet
Thou hast unveiled thy inmost sanctuary,
Enough from incommunicable dream,
And twilight phantasms, and deep noon-day
         thought,   40
Has shone within me, that serenely now
And moveless, as a long-forgotten lyre
Suspended in the solitary dome
Of some mysterious and deserted fane,
I wait thy breath, Great Parent, that my strain
May modulate with murmurs of the air,
And motions of the forests and the sea,
And voice of living beings, and woven hymns
Of night and day, and the deep heart of man.

There was a Poet whose untimely tomb   50
No human hands with pious reverence reared,
But the charmed eddies of autumnal winds

Built o'er his mouldering bones a pyramid
Of mouldering leaves in the waste wilderness:
A lovely youth,—no mourning maiden decked
With weeping flowers, or votive cypress wreath,
The lone couch of his everlasting sleep:
Gentle, and brave, and generous,—no lorn bard
Breathed o'er his dark fate one melodious sigh:
He lived, he died, he sung, in solitude.   60
Strangers have wept to hear his passionate notes,
And virgins, as unknown he passed, have pined
And wasted for fond love of his wild eyes.
The fire of those soft orbs has ceased to burn,
And Silence, too enamoured of that voice,
Locks its mute music in her rugged cell.

    By solemn vision, and bright silver dream,
His infancy was nurtured. Every sight
And sound from the vast earth and ambient air,
Sent to his heart its choicest impulses.   70
The fountains of divine philosophy
Fled not his thirsting lips, and all of great,
Or good, or lovely, which the sacred past
In truth or fable consecrates, he felt
And knew. When early youth had passed, he left
His cold fireside and alienated home
To seek strange truths in undiscovered lands.
Many a wide waste and tangled wilderness
Has lured his fearless steps; and he has bought
With his sweet voice and eyes, from savage
            men,   80
His rest and food. Nature's most secret steps
He like her shadow has pursued, where'er
The red volcano overcanopies
Its fields of snow and pinnacles of ice
With burning smoke, or where bitumen lakes
On black bare pointed islets ever beat
With sluggish surge, or where the secret caves
Rugged and dark, winding among the springs
Of fire and poison, inaccessible
To avarice or pride, their starry domes   90
Of diamond and of gold expand above
Numberless and immeasurable halls,
Frequent with crystal column, and clear shrines
Of pearl, and thrones radiant with chrysolite.
Nor had that scene of ampler majesty
Than gems or gold, the varying roof of heaven
And the green earth, lost in his heart its claims
To love and wonder; he would linger long
In lonesome vales, making the wild his home,
Until the doves and squirrels would partake   100

From his innocuous hand his bloodless food,
Lured by the gentle meaning of his looks,
And the wild antelope, that starts whene'er
The dry leaf rustles in the brake, suspend
Her timid steps to gaze upon a form
More graceful than her own.
                                His wandering step,
Obedient to high thoughts, has visited
The awful ruins of the days of old:
Athens, and Tyre, and Balbec, and the waste
Where stood Jerusalem, the fallen towers   110
Of Babylon, the eternal pyramids,
Memphis and Thebes, and whatsoe'er of strange
Sculptured on alabaster obelisk,
Or jasper tomb, or mutilated sphynx,
Dark Æthiopia in her desert hills
Conceals. Among the ruined temples there,
Stupendous columns, and wild images
Of more than man, where marble dæmons watch
The Zodiac's brazen mystery, and dead men
Hang their mute thoughts on the mute walls
            around,   120
He lingered, poring on memorials
Of the world's youth, through the long burning day
Gazed on those speechless shapes, nor, when the
            moon
Filled the mysterious halls with floating shades
Suspended he that task, but ever gazed
And gazed, till meaning on his vacant mind
Flashed like strong inspiration, and he saw
The thrilling secrets of the birth of time.

    Meanwhile an Arab maiden brought his food,
Her daily portion, from her father's tent,   130
And spread her matting for his couch, and stole
From duties and repose to tend his steps:—
Enamoured, yet not daring for deep awe
To speak her love:—and watched his nightly sleep,
Sleepless herself, to gaze upon his lips
Parted in slumber, whence the regular breath
Of innocent dreams arose: then, when red morn
Made paler the pale moon, to her cold home
Wildered, and wan, and panting, she returned.

    The Poet wandering on, through Arabie   140
And Persia, and the wild Carmanian waste,
And o'er the aërial mountains which pour down

ALASTOR. **109. Balbec:** a ruined city of Syria, near
Damascus. **141. Carmanian waste:** the desert of Ker-
man in southern Persia.

Indus and Oxus from their icy caves,
In joy and exultation held his way;
Till in the vale of Cashmire, far within
Its loneliest dell, where odorous plants entwine
Beneath the hollow rocks a natural bower,
Beside a sparkling rivulet he stretched
His languid limbs. A vision on his sleep
There came, a dream of hopes that never yet   150
Had flushed his cheek. He dreamed a veilèd maid
Sate near him, talking in low solemn tones.
Her voice was like the voice of his own soul
Heard in the calm of thought; its music long,
Like woven sounds of streams and breezes, held
His inmost sense suspended in its web
Of many-coloured woof and shifting hues.
Knowledge and truth and virtue were her theme,
And lofty hopes of divine liberty,
Thoughts the most dear to him, and poesy,   160
Herself a poet. Soon the solemn mood
Of her pure mind kindled through all her frame
A permeating fire: wild numbers then
She raised, with voice stifled in tremulous sobs,
Subdued by its own pathos: her fair hands
Were bare alone, sweeping from some strange harp
Strange symphony, and in their branching veins
The eloquent blood told an ineffable tale.
The beating of her heart was heard to fill
The pauses of her music, and her breath   170
Tumultuously accorded with those fits
Of intermitted song. Sudden she rose,
As if her heart impatiently endured
Its bursting burthen: at the sound he turned,
And saw by the warm light of their own life
Her glowing limbs beneath the sinuous veil
Of woven wind, her outspread arms now bare,
Her dark locks floating in the breath of night,
Her beamy bending eyes, her parted lips
Outstretched, and pale, and quivering eagerly.   180
His strong heart sunk and sickened with excess
Of love. He reared his shuddering limbs and quelled
His gasping breath, and spread his arms to meet
Her panting bosom:—she drew back a while,
Then, yielding to the irresistible joy,
With frantic gesture and short breathless cry
Folded his frame in her dissolving arms.
Now blackness veiled his dizzy eyes, and night
Involved and swallowed up the vision; sleep,

151. **veilèd maid:** Alastor.

Like a dark flood suspended in its course,   190
Rolled back its impulse on his vacant brain.

Roused by the shock he started from his trance—
The cold white light of morning, the blue moon
Low in the west, the clear and garish hills,
The distinct valley and the vacant woods,
Spread round him where he stood. Whither have
      fled
The hues of heaven that canopied his bower
Of yesternight? The sounds that soothed his sleep,
The mystery and the majesty of Earth,
The joy, the exultation? His wan eyes   200
Gaze on the empty scene as vacantly
As ocean's moon looks on the moon in heaven.
The spirit of sweet human love has sent
A vision to the sleep of him who spurned
Her choicest gifts. He eagerly pursues
Beyond the realms of dream that fleeting shade;
He overleaps the bounds. Alas! Alas!
Were limbs, and breath, and being intertwined
Thus treacherously? Lost, lost, for ever lost,
In the wide pathless desert of dim sleep,   210
That beautiful shape! Does the dark gate of death
Conduct to thy mysterious paradise,
O Sleep? Does the bright arch of rainbow clouds,
And pendent mountains seen in the calm lake,
Lead only to a black and watery depth,
While death's blue vault, with loathliest vapours
      hung,
Where every shade which the foul grave exhales
Hides its dead eye from the detested day,
Conducts, O Sleep, to thy delightful realms?
This doubt with sudden tide flowed on his
      heart,   220
The insatiate hope which it awakened, stung
His brain even like despair.
                              While daylight held
The sky, the Poet kept mute conference
With his still soul. At night the passion came,
Like the fierce fiend of a distempered dream,
And shook him from his rest, and led him forth
Into the darkness.—As an eagle grasped
In folds of the green serpent, feels her breast
Burn with the poison, and precipitates
Through night and day, tempest, and calm, and
      cloud,
Frantic with dizzying anguish, her blind flight   230
O'er the wide aëry wilderness: thus driven
By the bright shadow of that lovely dream,

Beneath the cold glare of the desolate night,
Through tangled swamps and deep precipitous dells,
Startling with careless step the moonlight snake,
He fled. Red morning dawned upon his flight,
Shedding the mockery of its vital hues
Upon his cheek of death. He wandered on
Till vast Aornos seen from Petra's steep   240
Hung o'er the low horizon like a cloud;
Through Balk, and where the desolated tombs
Of Parthian kings scatter to every wind
Their wasting dust, wildly he wandered on,
Day after day a weary waste of hours,
Bearing within his life the brooding care
That ever fed on its decaying flame.
And now his limbs were lean; his scattered hair
Sered by the autumn of strange suffering
Sung dirges in the wind; his listless hand   250
Hung like dead bone within its withered skin;
Life, and the lustre that consumed it, shone
As in a furnace burning secretly
From his dark eyes alone. The cottagers,
Who ministered with human charity
His human wants, beheld with wondering awe
Their fleeting visitant. The mountaineer,
Encountering on some dizzy precipice
That spectral form, deemed that the Spirit of wind
With lightning eyes, and eager breath, and
    feet   260
Disturbing not the drifted snow, had paused
In its career: the infant would conceal
His troubled visage in his mother's robe
In terror at the glare of those wild eyes,
To remember their strange light in many a dream
Of after-times; but youthful maidens, taught
By nature, would interpret half the woe
That wasted him, would call him with false names
Brother, and friend, would press his pallid hand
At parting, and watch, dim through tears, the
    path   270
Of his departure from their father's door.

    At length upon the lone Chorasmian shore
He paused, a wide and melancholy waste
Of putrid marshes. A strong impulse urged
His steps to the sea-shore. A swan was there,
Beside a sluggish stream among the reeds.

240. **Aornos . . . Petra:** Mt. Mahabunn and the Rock of
Sogdia in Afghanistan. 242. **Balk:** a province of Afghanistan. 272. **Chorasmian shore:** the Aral Sea.

It rose as he approached, and with strong wings
Scaling the upward sky, bent its bright course
High over the immeasurable main.
His eyes pursued its flight.—"Thou hast a
    home,   280
Beautiful bird; thou voyagest to thine home,
Where thy sweet mate will twine her downy neck
With thine, and welcome thy return with eyes
Bright in the lustre of their own fond joy
And what am I that I should linger here,
With voice far sweeter than thy dying notes,
Spirit more vast than thine, frame more attuned
To beauty, wasting these surpassing powers
In the deaf air, to the blind earth, and heaven
That echoes not my thoughts?" A gloomy
    smile   290
Of desperate hope wrinkled his quivering lips.
For sleep, he knew, kept most relentlessly
Its precious charge, and silent death exposed,
Faithless perhaps as sleep, a shadowy lure,
With doubtful smile mocking its own strange charms.

    Startled by his own thoughts he looked around.
There was no fair fiend near him, not a sight
Or sound of awe but in his own deep mind.
A little shallop floating near the shore
Caught the impatient wandering of his gaze.   300
It had been long abandoned, for its sides
Gaped wide with many a rift, and its frail joints
Swayed with the undulations of the tide.
A restless impulse urged him to embark
And meet lone Death on the drear ocean's waste;
For well he knew that mighty Shadow loves
The slimy caverns of the populous deep.

    The day was fair and sunny, sea and sky
Drank its inspiring radiance, and the wind
Swept strongly from the shore, blackening the
    waves.   310
Following his eager soul, the wanderer
Leaped in the boat, he spread his cloak aloft
On the bare mast, and took his lonely seat,
And felt the boat speed o'er the tranquil sea
Like a torn cloud before the hurricane.

    As one that in a silver vision floats
Obedient to the sweep of odorous winds
Upon resplendent clouds, so rapidly
Along the dark and ruffled waters fled
The straining boat.—A whirlwind swept it on,   320

With fierce gusts and precipitating force,
Through the white ridges of the chafèd sea.
The waves arose. Higher and higher still
Their fierce necks writhed beneath the tempest's
     scourge
Like serpents struggling in a vulture's grasp.
Calm and rejoicing in the fearful war
Of wave ruining on wave, and blast on blast
Descending, and black flood on whirlpool driven
With dark obliterating course, he sate:
As if their genii were ministers   330
Appointed to conduct him to the light
Of those belovèd eyes, the Poet sate
Holding the steady helm. Evening came on,
The beams of sunset hung their rainbow hues
High 'mid the shifting domes of sheeted spray
That canopied his path o'er the waste deep;
Twilight, ascending slowly from the east,
Entwined in duskier wreaths her braided locks
O'er the fair front and radiant eyes of day;
Night followed, clad with stars. On every side   340
More horribly the multitudinous streams
Of ocean's mountainous waste to mutual war
Rushed in dark tumult thundering, as to mock
The calm and spangled sky. The little boat
Still fled before the storm; still fled, like foam
Down the steep cataract of a wintry river;
Now pausing on the edge of the riven wave;
Now leaving far behind the bursting mass
That fell, convulsing ocean: safely fled—
As if that frail and wasted human form,   350
Had been an elemental god.

                    At midnight
The moon arose: and lo! the ethereal cliffs
Of Caucasus, whose icy summits shone
Among the stars like sunlight, and around
Whose caverned base the whirlpools and the waves
Bursting and eddying irresistibly
Rage and resound for ever.—Who shall save?—
The boat fled on,—the boiling torrent drove,—
The crags closed round with black and jagged arms,
The shattered mountain overhung the sea,   360
And faster still, beyond all human speed,
Suspended on the sweep of the smooth wave,
The little boat was driven. A cavern there
Yawned, and amid its slant and winding depths
Ingulfed the rushing sea. The boat fled on
With unrelaxing speed.—"Vision and Love!"
The Poet cried aloud, "I have beheld
The path of thy departure. Sleep and death

Shall not divide us long!"
                    The boat pursued
The windings of the cavern. Daylight shone   370
At length upon that gloomy river's flow,
Now, where the fiercest war among the waves
Is calm, on the unfathomable stream
The boat moved slowly. Where the mountain, riven,
Exposed those black depths to the azure sky,
Ere yet the flood's enormous volume fell
Even to the base of Caucasus, with sound
That shook the everlasting rocks, the mass
Filled with one whirlpool all that ample chasm;
Stair above stair the eddying waters rose,   380
Circling immeasurably fast, and laved
With alternating dash the gnarlèd roots
Of mighty trees, that stretched their giant arms
In darkness over it. I' the midst was left,
Reflecting, yet distorting every cloud,
A pool of treacherous and tremendous calm.
Seized by the sway of the ascending stream,
With dizzy swiftness, round, and round, and round,
Ridge after ridge the straining boat arose,
Till on the verge of the extremest curve,   390
Where, through an opening of the rocky bank,
The waters overflow, and a smooth spot
Of glassy quiet mid those battling tides
Is left, the boat paused shuddering.—Shall it sink
Down the abyss? Shall the reverting stress
Of that resistless gulf embosom it?
Now shall it fall?—A wandering stream of wind,
Breathed from the west, has caught the expanded
     sail,
And, lo! with gentle motion, between banks
Of mossy slope, and on a placid stream,   400
Beneath a woven grove it sails, and, hark!
The ghastly torrent mingles its far roar,
With the breeze murmuring in the musical woods.
Where the embowering trees recede, and leave
A little space of green expanse, the cove
Is closed by meeting banks, whose yellow flowers
For ever gaze on their own drooping eyes,
Reflected in the crystal calm. The wave
Of the boat's motion marred their pensive task,
Which nought but vagrant bird, or wanton
     wind,   410
Or falling spear-grass, or their own decay
Had e'er disturbed before. The Poet longed
To deck with their bright hues his withered hair,
But on his heart its solitude returned,
And he forbore. Not the strong impulse hid

In those flushed cheeks, bent eyes, and shadowy
    frame
Had yet performed its ministry: it hung
Upon his life, as lightning in a cloud
Gleams, hovering ere it vanish, ere the floods
Of night close over it.
                        The noonday sun   420
Now shone upon the forest, one vast mass
Of mingling shade, whose brown magnificence
A narrow vale embosoms. There, huge caves,
Scooped in the dark base of their aëry rocks
Mocking its moans, respond and roar for ever.
The meeting boughs and implicated leaves
Wove twilight o'er the Poet's path, as led
By love, or dream, or god, or mightier Death,
He sought in Nature's dearest haunt, some bank,
Her cradle, and his sepulchre. More dark   430
And dark the shades accumulate. The oak,
Expanding its immense and knotty arms,
Embraces the light beech. The pyramids
Of the tall cedar overarching, frame
Most solemn domes within, and far below,
Like clouds suspended in an emerald sky,
The ash and the acacia floating hang
Tremulous and pale. Like restless serpents, clothed
In rainbow and in fire, the parasites,
Starred with ten thousand blossoms, flow
    around   440
The grey trunks, and, as gamesome infants' eyes,
With gentle meanings, and most innocent wiles,
Fold their beams round the hearts of those that love,
These twine their tendrils with the wedded boughs
Uniting their close union; the woven leaves
Make net-work of the dark blue light of day,
And the night's noontide clearness, mutable
As shapes in the weird clouds. Soft mossy lawns
Beneath these canopies extend their swells,
Fragrant with perfumed herbs, and eyed with
    blooms   450
Minute yet beautiful. One darkest glen
Sends from its woods of musk-rose, twined with
    jasmine,
A soul-dissolving odour, to invite
To some more lovely mystery. Through the dell,
Silence and Twilight here, twin-sisters, keep
Their noonday watch, and sail among the shades,
Like vaporous shapes half seen; beyond, a well,
Dark, gleaming, and of most translucent wave,
Images all the woven boughs above,
And each depending leaf, and every speck   460

Of azure sky, darting between their chasms;
Nor aught else in the liquid mirror laves
Its portraiture, but some inconstant star
Between one foliaged lattice twinkling fair,
Or, painted bird, sleeping beneath the moon,
Or gorgeous insect floating motionless,
Unconscious of the day, ere yet his wings
Have spread their glories to the gaze of noon.

    Hither the Poet came. His eyes beheld
Their own wan light through the reflected
    lines   470
Of his thin hair, distinct in the dark depth
Of that still fountain; as the human heart,
Gazing in dreams over the gloomy grave,
Sees its own treacherous likeness there. He heard
The motion of the leaves, the grass that sprung
Startled and glanced and trembled even to feel
An unaccustomed presence, and the sound
Of the sweet brook that from the secret springs
Of that dark fountain rose. A Spirit seemed
To stand beside him—clothed in no bright
    robes   480
Of shadowy silver or enshrining light
Borrowed from aught the visible world affords
Of grace, or majesty, or mystery;—
But, undulating woods, and silent well,
And leaping rivulet, and evening gloom
Now deepening the dark shades, for speech assum-
    ing,
Held commune with him, as if he and it
Were all that was,—only . . . when his regard
Was raised by intense pensiveness, . . . two eyes,
Two starry eyes, hung in the gloom of
    thought,   490
And seemed with their serene and azure smiles
To beckon him.
                    Obedient to the light
That shone within his soul, he went, pursuing
The windings of the dell.—The rivulet
Wanton and wild, through many a green ravine
Beneath the forest flowed. Sometimes it fell
Among the moss with hollow harmony
Dark and profound. Now on the polished stones
It danced; like childhood laughing as it went:
Then, through the plain in tranquil wanderings
    crept,   500
Reflecting every herb and drooping bud
That overhung its quietness.—"O stream!
Whose source is inaccessibly profound,

Whither do thy mysterious waters tend?
Thou imagest my life. Thy darksome stillness,
Thy dazzling waves, thy loud and hollow gulfs,
Thy searchless fountain, and invisible course
Have each their type in me: and the wide sky,
And measureless ocean may declare as soon
What oozy cavern or what wandering cloud   510
Contains thy waters, as the universe
Tell where these living thoughts reside, when
    stretched
Upon thy flowers my bloodless limbs shall waste
I' the passing wind!"

              Beside the grassy shore
Of the small stream he went; he did impress
On the green moss his tremulous step, that caught
Strong shuddering from his burning limbs. As one
Roused by some joyous madness from the couch
Of fever, he did move; yet, not like him,
Forgetful of the grave, where, when the flame   520
Of his frail exultation shall be spent,
He must descend. With rapid steps he went
Beneath the shade of trees, beside the flow
Of the wild babbling rivulet; and now
The forest's solemn canopies were changed
For the uniform and lightsome evening sky.
Grey rocks did peep from the spare moss, and
    stemmed
The struggling brook: tall spires of windlestrae
Threw their thin shadows down the rugged slope,
And nought but gnarlèd trunks of ancient
    pines   530
Branchless and blasted, clenched with grasping
    roots
The unwilling soil. A gradual change was here,
Yet ghastly. For, as fast years flow away,
The smooth brow gathers, and the hair grows thin
And white, and where irradiate dewy eyes
Had shone, gleam stony orbs:—so from his steps
Bright flowers departed, and the beautiful shade
Of the green groves, with all their odorous winds
And musical motions. Calm, he still pursued
The stream, that with a larger volume now   540
Rolled through the labyrinthine dell; and there
Fretted a path through its descending curves
With its wintry speed. On every side now rose
Rocks, which, in unimaginable forms,
Lifted their black and barren pinnacles

528. windlestrae: a rough grass used in basket-making.

In the light of evening, and, its precipice
Obscuring the ravine, disclosed above,
Mid toppling stones, black gulfs and yawning caves,
Whose windings gave ten thousand various tongues
To the loud stream. Lo! where the pass
    expands   550
Its stony jaws, the abrupt mountain breaks,
And seems, with its accumulated crags,
To overhang the world: for wide expand
Beneath the wan stars and descending moon
Islanded seas, blue mountains, mighty streams,
Dim tracts and vast, robed in the lustrous gloom
Of leaden-coloured even, and fiery hills
Mingling their flames with twilight, on the verge
Of the remote horizon. The near scene,
In naked and severe simplicity,   560
Made contrast with the universe. A pine,
Rock-rooted, stretched athwart the vacancy
Its swinging boughs, to each inconstant blast
Yielding one only response, at each pause
In most familiar cadence, with the howl
The thunder and the hiss of homeless streams
Mingling its solemn song, whilst the broad river,
Foaming and hurrying o'er its rugged path,
Fell into that immeasurable void
Scattering its waters to the passing winds.   570

    Yet the grey precipice and solemn pine
And torrent, were not all;—one silent nook
Was there. Even on the edge of that vast mountain,
Upheld by knotty roots and fallen rocks,
It overlooked in its serenity
The dark earth, and the bending vault of stars.
It was a tranquil spot, that seemed to smile
Even in the lap of horror. Ivy clasped
The fissured stones with its entwining arms,
And did embower with leaves for ever green,   580
And berries dark, the smooth and even space
Of its inviolated floor, and here
The children of the autumnal whirlwind bore,
In wanton sport, those bright leaves, whose decay,
Red, yellow, or ethereally pale,
Rivals the pride of summer. 'Tis the haunt
Of every gentle wind, whose breath can teach
The wilds to love tranquillity. One step,
One human step alone, has ever broken
The stillness of its solitude:—one voice   590
Alone inspired its echoes;—even that voice
Which hither came, floating among the winds,
And led the loveliest among human forms

To make their wild haunts the depository
Of all the grace and beauty that endued
Its motions, render up its majesty,
Scatter its music on the unfeeling storm,
And to the damp leaves and blue cavern mould,
Nurses of rainbow flowers and branching moss,
Commit the colours of that varying cheek,   600
That snowy breast, those dark and drooping eyes.

The dim and hornèd moon hung low, and poured
A sea of lustre on the horizon's verge
That overflowed its mountains. Yellow mist
Filled the unbounded atmosphere, and drank
Wan moonlight even to fulness: not a star
Shone, not a sound was heard; the very winds,
Danger's grim playmates, on that precipice
Slept, clasped in his embrace.—O, storm of death!
Whose sightless speed divides this sullen
        night: 610
And thou, colossal Skeleton, that, still
Guiding its irresistible career
In thy devastating omnipotence,
Art king of this frail world, from the red field
Of slaughter, from the reeking hospital,
The patriot's sacred couch, the snowy bed
Of innocence, the scaffold and the throne,
A mighty voice invokes thee. Ruin calls
His brother Death. A rare and regal prey
He hath prepared, prowling around the
        world;   620
Glutted with which thou mayst repose, and men
Go to their graves like flowers or creeping worms,
Nor ever more offer at thy dark shrine
The unheeded tribute of a broken heart.

When on the threshold of the green recess
The wanderer's footsteps fell, he knew that death
Was on him. Yet a little, ere it fled,
Did he resign his high and holy soul
To images of the majestic past,
That paused within his passive being now,   630
Like winds that bear sweet music, when they
        breathe
Through some dim latticed chamber. He did place
His pale lean hand upon the rugged trunk
Of the old pine. Upon an ivied stone
Reclined his languid head, his limbs did rest,
Diffused and motionless, on the smooth brink
Of that obscurest chasm;—and thus he lay,
Surrendering to their final impulses
The hovering powers of life. Hope and despair,

The torturers, slept; no mortal pain or fear   640
Marred his repose, the influxes of sense,
And his own being unalloyed by pain,
Yet feebler and more feeble, calmly fed
The stream of thought, till he lay breathing there
At peace, and faintly smiling:—his last sight
Was the great moon, which o'er the western line
Of the wide world her mighty horn suspended,
With whose dun beams inwoven darkness seemed
To mingle. Now upon the jagged hills
It rests, and still as the divided frame   650
Of the vast meteor sunk, the Poet's blood,
That ever beat in mystic sympathy
With nature's ebb and flow, grew feebler still:
And when two lessening points of light alone
Gleamed through the darkness, the alternate gasp
Of his faint respiration scarce did stir
The stagnate night:—till the minutest ray
Was quenched, the pulse yet lingered in his heart.
It paused—it fluttered. But when heaven remained
Utterly black, the murky shades involved   660
An image, silent, cold, and motionless,
As their own voiceless earth and vacant air.
Even as a vapour fed with golden beams
That ministered on sunlight, ere the west
Eclipses it, was now that wondrous frame—
No sense, no motion, no divinity—
A fragile lute, on whose harmonious strings
The breath of heaven did wander—a bright stream
Once fed with many-voicèd waves—a dream
Of youth, which night and time have quenched for
        ever,   670
Still, dark, and dry, and unremembered now.

O, for Medea's wondrous alchemy,
Which wheresoe'er it fell made the earth gleam
With bright flowers, and the wintry boughs exhale
From vernal blooms fresh fragrance! O, that God,
Profuse of poisons, would concede the chalice
Which but one living man has drained, who now,
Vessel of deathless wrath, a slave that feels
No proud exemption in the blighting curse
He bears, over the world wanders for ever,   680
Lone as incarnate death! O, that the dream
Of dark magician in his visioned cave,
Raking the cinders of a crucible

677. **one living man:** the Wandering Jew, supposedly
condemned to roam the earth until the Second Coming
because he had refused Christ a resting-place on the
journey to Calvary.

For life and power, even when his feeble hand
Shakes in its last decay, were the true law
Of this so lovely world! But thou art fled
Like some frail exhalation; which the dawn
Robes in its golden beams,—ah! thou hast fled!
The brave, the gentle, and the beautiful,   689
The child of grace and genius. Heartless things
Are done and said i' the world, and many worms
And beasts and men live on, and mighty Earth
From sea and mountain, city and wilderness,
In vesper low or joyous orison,
Lifts still its solemn voice:—but thou art fled—
Thou canst no longer know or love the shapes
Of this phantasmal scene, who have to thee
Been purest ministers, who are, alas!
Now thou art not. Upon those pallid lips
So sweet even in their silence, on those eyes   700
That image sleep in death, upon that form
Yet safe from the worm's outrage, let no tear
Be shed—not even in thought. Nor, when those
        hues
Are gone, and those divinest lineaments,
Worn by the senseless wind, shall live alone
In the frail pauses of this simple strain,
Let not high verse, mourning the memory
Of that which is no more, or painting's woe
Or sculpture, speak in feeble imagery
Their own cold powers. Art and eloquence,   710
And all the shows o' the world are frail and vain
To weep a loss that turns their lights to shade.
It is a woe too "deep for tears," when all
Is reft at once, when some surpassing Spirit,
Whose light adorned the world around it, leaves
Those who remain behind, not sobs or groans,
The passionate tumult of a clinging hope;
But pale despair and cold tranquillity,
Nature's vast frame, the web of human things,
Birth and the grave, that are not as they were.   720
1815   *1816*

MONT BLANC

LINES WRITTEN IN THE VALE
OF CHAMOUNI

I

The everlasting universe of things
Flows through the mind, and rolls its rapid waves,
Now dark—now glittering—now reflecting gloom—
Now lending splendour, where from secret springs
The source of human thought its tribute brings
Of waters,—with a sound but half its own,
Such as a feeble brook will oft assume
In the wild woods, among the mountains lone,
Where waterfalls around it leap for ever,
Where woods and winds contend, and a vast
        river   10
Over its rocks ceaselessly bursts and raves.

II

Thus thou, Ravine of Arve—dark, deep Ravine—
Thou many-coloured, many-voiced vale,
Over whose pines, and crags, and caverns sail
Fast cloud-shadows and sunbeams: awful scene,
Where Power in likeness of the Arve comes down
From the ice-gulfs that gird his secret throne,
Bursting through these dark mountains like the
        flame
Of lightning through the tempest;—thou dost lie,
Thy giant brood of pines around thee clinging,   20
Children of elder time, in whose devotion
The chainless winds still come and ever came
To drink their odours, and their mighty swinging
To hear—an old and solemn harmony;
Thine earthly rainbows stretched across the sweep
Of the aethereal waterfall, whose veil
Robes some unsculptured image; the strange sleep
Which when the voices of the desert fail
Wraps all in its own deep eternity;—
Thy caverns echoing to the Arve's commotion,   30
A loud, lone sound no other sound can tame;
Thou art pervaded with that ceaseless motion,
Thou art the path of that unresting sound—
Dizzy Ravine! and when I gaze on thee
I seem as in a trance sublime and strange
To muse on my own separate fantasy,
My own, my human mind, which passively
Now renders and receives fast influencings,
Holding an unremitting interchange
With the clear universe of things around;   40
One legion of wild thoughts, whose wandering
        wings
Now float above thy darkness, and now rest
Where that or thou are no unbidden guest,
In the still cave of the witch Poesy,

MONT BLANC. **12. Arve:** The river Arve runs through
the Alpine valley of Chamouni in Southern France.

Seeking among the shadows that pass by,
Ghosts of all things that are, some shade of thee,
Some phantom, some faint image; till the breast
From which they fled recalls them, thou art there!

III

Some say that gleams of a remoter world
Visit the soul in sleep,—that death is slumber,   50
And that its shapes the busy thoughts outnumber
Of those who wake and live.—I look on high;
Has some unknown omnipotence unfurled
The veil of life and death? or do I lie
In dream, and does the mightier world of sleep
Spread far around and inaccessibly
Its circles? For the very spirit fails,
Driven like a homeless cloud from steep to steep
That vanishes among the viewless gales!
Far, far above, piercing the infinite sky,   60
Mont Blanc appears,—still, snowy, and serene—
Its subject mountains their unearthly forms
Pile around it, ice and rock; broad vales between
Of frozen floods, unfathomable deeps,
Blue as the overhanging heaven, that spread
And wind among the accumulated steeps;
A desert peopled by the storms alone,
Save when the eagle brings some hunter's bone,
And the wolf tracks her there—how hideously
Its shapes are heaped around! rude, bare, and
    high,   70
Ghastly, and scarred, and riven.—Is this the scene
Where the old Earthquake-daemon taught her
    young
Ruin? Were these their toys? or did a sea
Of fire envelop once this silent snow?
None can reply—all seems eternal now.
The wilderness has a mysterious tongue
Which teaches awful doubt, or faith so mild,
So solemn, so serene, that man may be,
But for such faith, with nature reconciled;
Thou hast a voice, great Mountain, to repeal   80
Large codes of fraud and woe; not understood
By all, but which the wise, and great, and good
Interpret, or make felt, or deeply feel.

IV

The fields, the lakes, the forests, and the streams,
Ocean, and all the living things that dwell

Within the daedal earth; lightning, and rain,
Earthquake, and fiery flood, and hurricane,
The torpor of the year when feeble dreams
Visit the hidden buds, or dreamless sleep
Holds every future leaf and flower;—the
    bound   90
With which from that detested trance they leap;
The works and ways of man, their death and birth,
And that of him and all that his may be;
All things that move and breathe with toil and
    sound
Are born and die; revolve, subside, and swell.
Power dwells apart in its tranquillity,
Remote, serene, and inaccessible:
And *this*, the naked countenance of earth,
On which I gaze, even these primaeval mountains
Teach the adverting mind. The glaciers creep   100
Like snakes that watch their prey, from their far
    fountains,
Slow rolling on; there, many a precipice,
Frost and the Sun in scorn of mortal power
Have piled: dome, pyramid, and pinnacle,
A city of death, distinct with many a tower
And wall impregnable of beaming ice.
Yet not a city, but a flood of ruin
Is there, that from the boundaries of the sky
Rolls its perpetual stream; vast pines are strewing
Its destined path, or in the mangled soil   110
Branchless and shattered stand; the rocks, drawn
    down
From yon remotest waste, have overthrown
The limits of the dead and living world,
Never to be reclaimed. The dwelling-place
Of insects, beasts, and birds, becomes its spoil;
Their food and their retreat for ever gone,
So much of life and joy is lost. The race
Of man flies far in dread; his work and dwelling
Vanish, like smoke before the tempest's stream,
And their place is not known. Below, vast
    caves   120
Shine in the rushing torrents' restless gleam,
Which from those secret chasms in tumult welling
Meet in the vale, and one majestic River,
The breath and blood of distant lands, for ever
Rolls its loud waters to the ocean-waves,
Breathes its swift vapours to the circling air.

86. daedal: intricately designed. Daedalus was the famous artist who designed the Labyrinth of Crete. **123. one . . . river:** a reference to the joining of the Arve and Rhone.

V

Mont Blanc yet gleams on high:—the power is
    there,
The still and solemn power of many sights,
And many sounds, and much of life and death.
In the calm darkness of the moonless nights,   130
In the lone glare of day, the snows descend
Upon that Mountain; none beholds them there,
Nor when the flakes burn in the sinking sun,
Or the star-beams dart through them:—Winds
    contend
Silently there, and heap the snow with breath
Rapid and strong, but silently! Its home
The voiceless lightning in these solitudes
Keeps innocently, and like vapour broods
Over the snow. The secret Strength of things
Which governs thought, and to the infinite
    dome   140
Of Heaven is as a law, inhabits thee!
And what were thou, and earth, and stars, and sea,
If to the human mind's imaginings
Silence and solitude were vacancy?

1816   *1817*

HYMN
TO INTELLECTUAL BEAUTY

I

The awful shadow of some unseen Power
  Floats though unseen among us,—visiting
  This various world with as inconstant wing
As summer winds that creep from flower to
    flower,—
Like moonbeams that behind some piny mountain
    shower,
  It visits with inconstant glance
  Each human heart and countenance;
Like hues and harmonies of evening,—
  Like clouds in starlight widely spread,—
  Like memory of music fled,—   10
  Like aught that for its grace may be
Dear, and yet dearer for its mystery.

II

Spirit of BEAUTY, that dost consecrate
  With thine own hues all thou dost shine upon
Of human thought or form,—where art thou
    gone?
Why dost thou pass away and leave our state,
This dim vast vale of tears, vacant and desolate?
  Ask why the sunlight not for ever
  Weaves rainbows o'er yon mountain-river,
Why aught should fail and fade that once is
    shown,   20
  Why fear and dream and death and birth
  Cast on the daylight of this earth
  Such gloom,—why man has such a scope
For love and hate, despondency and hope?

III

No voice from some sublimer world hath ever
  To sage or poet these responses given—
  Therefore the names of Demon, Ghost, and
    Heaven,
Remain the records of their vain endeavour,
Frail spells—whose uttered charm might not avail
    to sever
  From all we hear and all we see,   30
  Doubt, chance, and mutability.
Thy light alone—like mist o'er mountains driven,
  Or music by the night-wind sent
  Through strings of some still instrument,
  Or moonlight on a midnight stream,
Gives grace and truth to life's unquiet dream.

IV

Love, Hope, and Self-esteem, like clouds depart
  And come, for some uncertain moments lent.
  Man were immortal, and omnipotent,
Didst thou, unknown and awful as thou art,   40
Keep with thy glorious train firm state within his
    heart.
  Thou messenger of sympathies,
  That wax and wane in lovers' eyes—
Thou—that to human thought art nourishment,
  Like darkness to a dying flame!
  Depart not as thy shadow came,
  Depart not—lest the grave should be,
Like life and fear, a dark reality.

V

While yet a boy I sought for ghosts, and sped
  Through many a listening chamber, cave and
    ruin,   50

And starlight wood, with fearful steps pursuing
Hopes of high talk with the departed dead.
I called on poisonous names with which our youth
    is fed;
      I was not heard—I saw them not—
      When musing deeply on the lot
Of life, at that sweet time when winds are wooing
      All vital things that wake to bring
      News of birds and blossoming,—
      Sudden, thy shadow fell on me;
I shrieked, and clasped my hands in ecstasy!   60

VI

I vowed that I would dedicate my powers
    To thee and thine—have I not kept the vow?
    With beating heart and streaming eyes, even
      now
I call the phantoms of a thousand hours
Each from his voiceless grave: they have in visioned
    bowers
    Of studious zeal or love's delight
    Outwatched with me the envious night—
They know that never joy illumed my brow
    Unlinked with hope that thou wouldst free
    This world from its dark slavery,   70
    That thou—O awful LOVELINESS,
Wouldst give whate'er these words cannot express.

VII

The day becomes more solemn and serene
    When noon is past—there is a harmony
    In autumn, and a lustre in its sky,
Which through the summer is not heard or seen,
As if it could not be, as if it had not been!
    Thus let thy power, which like the truth
    Of nature on my passive youth
Descended, to my onward life supply   80
    Its calm—to one who worships thee,
    And every form containing thee,
    Whom, SPIRIT fair, thy spells did bind
To fear himself, and love all human kind.
1816   *1817*

OZYMANDIAS

I met a traveller from an antique land
Who said: Two vast and trunkless legs of stone

Stand in the desert . . . Near them, on the sand,
Half sunk, a shattered visage lies, whose frown,
And wrinkled lip, and sneer of cold command,
Tell that its sculptor well those passions read
Which yet survive, stamped on these lifeless things,
The hand that mocked them, and the heart that fed:
And on the pedestal these words appear:
"My name is Ozymandias, king of kings: 10
Look on my works, ye Mighty, and despair!"
Nothing beside remains. Round the decay
Of that colossal wreck, boundless and bare
The lone and level sands stretch far away.
1817   *1818*

STANZAS

WRITTEN IN DEJECTION, NEAR NAPLES

I

The sun is warm, the sky is clear,
    The waves are dancing fast and bright,
Blue isles and snowy mountains wear
    The purple noon's transparent might,
    The breath of the moist earth is light,
Around its unexpanded buds;
    Like many a voice of one delight,
The winds, the birds, the ocean floods,
The City's voice itself, is soft like Solitude's.

II

I see the Deep's untrampled floor   10
    With green and purple seaweeds strown;
I see the waves upon the shore,
    Like light dissolved in star-showers, thrown:
    I sit upon the sands alone,—
The lightning of the noontide ocean
    Is flashing round me, and a tone
Arises from its measured motion,
How sweet! did any heart now share in my emotion.

III

Alas! I have nor hope nor health,
    Nor peace within nor calm around,   20
Nor that content surpassing wealth
    The sage in meditation found,
    And walked with inward glory crowned—

Nor fame, nor power, nor love, nor leisure.
    Others I see whom these surround—
    Smiling they live, and call life pleasure;—
To me that cup has been dealt in another measure.

IV

Yet now despair itself is mild,
    Even as the winds and waters are;
I could lie down like a tired child,   30
    And weep away the life of care
    Which I have borne and yet must bear,
Till death like sleep might steal on me,
    And I might feel in the warm air
My cheek grow cold, and hear the sea
Breathe o'er my dying brain its last monotony.

V

Some might lament that I were cold,
    As I, when this sweet day is gone,
Which my lost heart, too soon grown old,
    Insults with this untimely moan;   40
    They might lament—for I am one
Whom men love not,—and yet regret;
    Unlike this day, which, when the sun
    Shall on its stainless glory set,
Will linger, though enjoyed, like joy in memory yet.
1818   *1824*

SONNET

LIFT NOT THE PAINTED VEIL

Lift not the painted veil which those who live
Call Life: though unreal shapes be pictured there,
And it but mimic all we would believe
With colours idly spread,—behind, lurk Fear
And Hope, twin Destinies; who ever weave
Their shadows, o'er the chasm, sightless and drear.
I knew one who had lifted it—he sought,
For his lost heart was tender, things to love,
But found them not, alas! nor was there aught
The world contains, the which he could
    approve.   10
Through the unheeding many he did move,
A splendour among shadows, a bright blot
Upon this gloomy scene, a Spirit that strove
For truth, and like the Preacher found it not.
1818   *1824*

PROMETHEUS UNBOUND

A LYRICAL DRAMA IN FOUR ACTS

Preface

The Greek tragic writers, in selecting as their subject any portion of their national history or mythology, employed in their treatment of it a certain arbitrary discretion. They by no means conceived themselves bound to adhere to the common interpretation or to imitate in story as in title their rivals and predecessors. Such a system would have amounted to a resignation of those claims to preference over their competitors which incited the composition. The Agamemnonian story was exhibited on the Athenian theatre with as many variations as dramas.

I have presumed to employ a similar licence. The *Prometheus Unbound* of Æschylus supposed the reconciliation of Jupiter with his victim as the price of the disclosure of the danger threatened to his empire by the consummation of his marriage with Thetis. Thetis, according to this view of the subject, was given in marriage to Peleus, and Prometheus, by the permission of Jupiter, delivered from his captivity by Hercules. Had I framed my story on this model, I should have done no more than have attempted to restore the lost drama of Æschylus; an ambition which, if my preference to this mode of treating the subject had incited me to cherish, the recollection of the high comparison such an attempt would challenge might well abate. But, in truth, I was averse from a catastrophe so feeble as that of reconciling the Champion with the Oppressor of mankind. The moral interest of the fable, which is so powerfully sustained by the sufferings and endurance of Prometheus, would be annihilated if we could conceive of him as unsaying his high language and quailing before his successful and perfidious adversary. The only imaginary being resembling in any degree Prometheus, is Satan; and Prometheus is, in my judgement, a more poetical character than Satan, because, in addition to courage, and majesty, and firm and patient opposition to omnipotent force, he is susceptible of being described as exempt from the taints of ambition, envy, revenge, and a desire for personal aggrandisement, which, in the Hero of *Paradise Lost*, interfere with the interest. The character of Satan engenders in the mind a pernicious casuistry which leads us to weigh his faults with his wrongs, and to excuse the former because the latter exceed all measure. In the minds of those who consider that magnificent fiction with a religious feeling it engenders something worse. But Prometheus is, as it were, the type of the highest perfection of moral and intellectual nature, impelled by the purest and the truest motives to the best and noblest ends.

This Poem was chiefly written upon the mountainous ruins of the Baths of Caracalla, among the flowery glades, and thickets of odoriferous blossoming trees, which are extended in ever winding labyrinths upon its immense platforms and dizzy arches suspended in the air. The bright blue sky of Rome, and the effect of the vigorous awakening spring in that divinest climate, and the new life with which it drenches the spirits even to intoxication, were the inspiration of this drama.

The imagery which I have employed will be found, in many instances, to have been drawn from the operations of the human mind, or from those external actions by which they are expressed. This is unusual in modern poetry, although Dante and Shakespeare are full of instances of the same kind: Dante indeed more than any other poet, and with greater success. But the Greek poets, as writers to whom no resource of awakening the sympathy of their contemporaries was unknown, were in the habitual use of this power; and it is the study of their works (since a higher merit would probably be denied me) to which I am willing that my readers should impute this singularity.

One word is due in candour to the degree in which the study of contemporary writings may have tinged my composition, for such has been a topic of censure with regard to poems far more popular, and indeed more deservedly popular, than mine. It is impossible that any one who inhabits the same age with such writers as those who stand in the foremost ranks of our own, can conscientiously assure himself that his language and tone of thought may not have been modified by the study of the productions of those extraordinary intellects. It is true, that, not the spirit of their genius, but the forms in which it has manifested itself, are due less to the peculiarities of their own minds than to the peculiarity of the moral and intellectual condition of the minds among which they have been produced. Thus a number of writers possess the form, whilst they want the spirit of those whom, it is alleged, they imitate; because the former is the endowment of the age in which they live, and the latter must be the uncommunicated lightning of their own mind.

The peculiar style of intense and comprehensive imagery which distinguishes the modern literature of England, has not been, as a general power, the product of the imitation of any particular writer. The mass of capabilities remains at every period materially the same; the circumstances which awaken it to action perpetually change. If England were divided into forty republics, each equal in population and extent to Athens, there is no reason to suppose but that, under institutions not more perfect than those of Athens, each would produce philosophers and poets equal to those who (if we except Shakespeare) have never been surpassed. We owe the great writers of the golden age of our literature to that fervid awakening of the public mind which shook to dust the oldest and most oppressive form of the Christian religion. We owe Milton to the progress and development of the same spirit; the sacred Milton was, let it ever be remembered, a republican, and a bold inquirer into morals and religion. The great writers of our own age are, we have reason to suppose, the companions and forerunners of some unimagined change in our social condition or the opinions which cement it. The cloud of mind is discharging its collected lightning, and the equilibrium between institutions and opinions is now restoring, or is about to be restored.

As to imitation, poetry is a mimetic art. It creates, but it creates by combination and representation. Poetical abstractions are beautiful and new, not because the portions of which they are composed had no previous existence in the mind of man or in nature, but because the whole produced by their combination has some intelligible and beautiful analogy with those sources of emotion and thought, and with the contemporary condition of them: one great poet is a masterpiece of nature which another not only ought to study but must study. He might as wisely and as easily determine that his mind should no longer be the mirror of all that is lovely in the visible universe, as exclude from his contemplation the beautiful which exists in the writings of a great contemporary. The pretence of doing it would be a presumption in any but the greatest; the effect, even in him, would be strained, unnatural, and ineffectual. A poet is the combined product of such internal powers as modify the nature of others; and of such external influences as excite and sustain these powers; he is not one, but both. Every man's mind is, in this respect, modified by all the objects of nature and art; by every word and every suggestion which he ever admitted to act upon his consciousness; it is the mirror upon which all forms are reflected, and in which they compose one form. Poets, not otherwise than philosophers, painters, sculptors, and musicians, are, in one sense, the creators, and, in another, the creations, of their age. From this subjection the loftiest do not escape. There is a similarity between Homer and Hesiod, between Æschylus and Euripides, between Virgil and Horace, between Dante and Petrarch, between Shakespeare and Fletcher, between Dryden and Pope; each has a generic resemblance under which their specific distinctions are arranged. If this similarity be the result of imitation, I am willing to confess that I have imitated.

Let this opportunity be conceded to me of acknowledging that I have, what a Scotch philosopher characteristically terms, "a passion for reforming the world": what passion incited him to write and publish his book, he omits to explain. For my part I had rather be damned with Plato and Lord Bacon, than go to Heaven with Paley and Malthus.* But it is a mistake to suppose that I dedicate my poetical compositions solely to the direct enforcement of reform, or that I consider them in any degree as containing a reasoned system on the theory of human life. Didactic poetry is my abhorrence; nothing can be equally well expressed in prose that is not tedious and supererogatory in verse. My purpose has hitherto been simply to familiarise the highly refined imagination of the more select classes of poetical readers with beautiful idealisms of moral excellence; aware that until the mind can love, and admire, and trust, and hope, and endure, reasoned principles of moral conduct are seeds cast upon the highway of life which the unconscious passenger tramples into dust, although they would bear the harvest of his happiness. Should I live to accomplish what I purpose, that is, produce a systematical history of what appear to me to be the genuine elements of human society, let not the advocates of injustice and superstition flatter themselves that I should take Æschylus rather than Plato as my model.

The having spoken of myself with unaffected freedom will need little apology with the candid; and let the uncandid consider that they injure me less than their own hearts and minds by misrepresentation. Whatever talents a person may possess to amuse and instruct others, be they ever so inconsiderable, he is yet bound to exert them: if his attempt be ineffectual, let the punishment of an unaccomplished purpose have been sufficient; let none trouble themselves to heap the dust of oblivion upon his efforts; the pile they raise will betray his grave which might otherwise have been unknown. [Shelley]

DRAMATIS PERSONÆ

PROMETHEUS

DEMOGORGON

JUPITER

THE EARTH

OCEAN

APOLLO

MERCURY

---

* **William Paley** (1743–1805), an English theologian and utilitarian philosopher, who argued that the existence of God could be demonstrated by reason. **Thomas Malthus** (1766–1834), an economist and political theorist famous for his theory that things like war and famine are necessary to control population.

ASIA	
PANTHEA	*Oceanides*
IONE	

HERCULES

THE PHANTASM OF JUPITER

THE SPIRIT OF THE EARTH

THE SPIRIT OF THE MOON

SPIRITS OF THE HOURS

SPIRITS, ECHOES, FAUNS, FURIES

ACT I

SCENE—*A Ravine of Icy Rocks in the Indian Caucasus.* PROMETHEUS *is discovered bound to the Precipice.* PANTHEA *and* IONE *are seated at his feet. Time, night. During the Scene, morning slowly breaks.*

PROMETHEUS.   Monarch of Gods and Dæmons,
        and all Spirits
But One, who throng those bright and rolling worlds
Which Thou and I alone of living things
Behold with sleepless eyes! regard this Earth
Made multitudinous with thy slaves, whom thou
Requitest for knee-worship, prayer, and praise,
And toil, and hecatombs of broken hearts,
With fear and self-contempt and barren hope.
Whilst me, who am thy foe, eyeless in hate,
Hast thou made reign and triumph, to thy scorn,   10
O'er mine own misery and thy vain revenge.
Three thousand years of sleep-unsheltered hours,
And moments aye divided by keen pangs
Till they seemed years, torture and solitude,
Scorn and despair,—these are mine empire:—
More glorious far than that which thou surveyest
From thine unenvied throne, O Mighty God!
Almighty, had I deigned to share the shame
Of thine ill tyranny, and hung not here
Nailed to this wall of eagle-baffling mountain,   20
Black, wintry, dead, unmeasured; without herb,
Insect, or beast, or shape or sound of life.
Ah me! alas, pain, pain ever, for ever!

No change, no pause, no hope! Yet I endure.
I ask the Earth, have not the mountains felt?
I ask yon Heaven, the all-beholding Sun,

PROMETHEUS UNBOUND. ACT I. **1. Monarch:** Jupiter. The two principal adversaries, Jupiter and Prometheus, are introduced immediately.

Has it not seen? The Sea, in storm or calm,
Heaven's ever-changing Shadow, spread below,
Have its deaf waves not heard my agony?
Ah me! alas, pain, pain ever, for ever!   30

The crawling glaciers pierce me with the spears
Of their moon-freezing crystals, the bright chains
Eat with their burning cold into my bones.
Heaven's winged hound, polluting from thy lips
His beak in poison not his own, tears up
My heart; and shapeless sights come wandering by,
The ghastly people of the realm of dream,
Mocking me: and the Earthquake-fiends are charged
To wrench the rivets from my quivering wounds
When the rocks split and close again behind: 40
While from their loud abysses howling throng
The genii of the storm, urging the rage
Of whirlwind, and afflict me with keen hail.
And yet to me welcome is day and night,
Whether one breaks the hoar frost of the morn,
Or starry, dim, and slow, the other climbs
The leaden-coloured east; for then they lead
The wingless, crawling hours, one among whom
—As some dark Priest hales the reluctant victim—
Shall drag thee, cruel King, to kiss the blood   50
From these pale feet, which then might trample thee
If they disdained not such a prostrate slave.
Disdain! Ah no! I pity thee. What ruin
Will hunt thee undefended through the wide
          Heaven!
How will thy soul, cloven to its depth with terror,
Gape like a hell within! I speak in grief,
Not exultation, for I hate no more,
As then ere misery made me wise. The curse
Once breathed on thee I would recall. Ye Mountains,
Whose many-voicèd Echoes, through the mist   60
Of cataracts, flung the thunder of that spell!
Ye icy Springs, stagnant with wrinkling frost,
Which vibrated to hear me, and then crept
Shuddering through India! Thou serenest Air,
Through which the Sun walks burning without
          beams!
And ye swift Whirlwinds, who on poised wings
Hung mute and moveless o'er yon hushed abyss,
As thunder, louder than your own, made rock
The orbèd world! If then my words had power,
Though I am changed so that aught evil wish   70
Is dead within; although no memory be

34–36. hound . . . heart: According to the Greek myth,
a vulture fed on his entrails daily.

Of what is hate, let them not lose it now!
What was that curse? for ye all heard me speak.

FIRST VOICE *(from the Mountains)*
Thrice three hundred thousand years
     O'er the Earthquake's couch we stood:
Oft, as men convulsed with fears,
     We trembled in our multitude.

SECOND VOICE *(from the Springs)*
Thunderbolts had parched our water,
     We had been stained with bitter blood,
And had run mute, 'mid shrieks of
          slaughter,   80
     Thro' a city and a solitude.

THIRD VOICE *(from the Air)*
I had clothed, since Earth uprose,
     Its wastes in colours not their own,
And oft had my serene repose
     Been cloven by many a rending groan.

FOURTH VOICE *(from the Whirlwinds)*
We had soared beneath these mountains
     Unresting ages; nor had thunder,
Nor yon volcano's flaming fountains,
     Nor any power above or under
Ever made us mute with wonder.   90

FIRST VOICE
But never bowed our snowy crest
As at the voice of thine unrest.

SECOND VOICE
Never such a sound before
To the Indian waves we bore.
A pilot asleep on the howling sea
Leaped up from the deck in agony,
And heard, and cried, "Ah, woe is me!"
And died as mad as the wild waves be.

THIRD VOICE
By such dread words from Earth to Heaven
My still realm was never riven: 100
When its wound was closed, there stood
Darkness o'er the day like blood.

FOURTH VOICE
And we shrank back: for dreams of ruin
To frozen caves our flight pursuing
Made us keep silence—thus—and thus—
Though silence is as hell to us.

THE EARTH.   The tongueless Caverns of the
     craggy hills
Cried, "Misery!" then; the hollow Heaven replied,
"Misery!" And the Ocean's purple waves,
Climbing the land, howling to the lashing
     winds,   110
And the pale nations heard it, "Misery!"
   PRO.   I heard a sound of voices: not the voice
Which I gave forth. Mother, thy sons and thou
Scorn him, without whose all-enduring will
Beneath the fierce omnipotence of Jove,
Both they and thou had vanished, like thin mist
Unrolled on the morning wind. Know ye not me,
The Titan? He who made his agony
The barrier to your else all-conquering foe?
Oh, rock-embosomed lawns, and snow-fed
     streams,   120
Now seen athwart frore vapours, deep below,
Through whose o'ershadowing woods I wandered
     once
With Asia, drinking life from her loved eyes;
Why scorns the spirit which informs ye, now
To commune with me? me alone, who checked,
As one who checks a fiend-drawn charioteer,
The falsehood and the force of him who reigns
Supreme, and with the groans of pining slaves
Fills your dim glens and liquid wildernesses:
Why answer ye not, still? Brethren!
    THE EARTH.   They dare not.   130
   PRO.   Who dares? for I would hear that curse
     again.
Ha, what an awful whisper rises up!
'Tis scarce like sound: it tingles through the frame
As lightning tingles, hovering ere it strike.
Speak, Spirit! from thine inorganic voice
I only know that thou art moving near
And love. How cursed I him?
    THE EARTH.   How canst thou hear
Who knowest not the language of the dead?
    PRO.   Thou art a living spirit; speak as they.
    THE EARTH.   I dare not speak like life, lest
     Heaven's fell King   140
Should hear, and link me to some wheel of pain
More torturing than the one whereon I roll.

---

121. frore: frozen. 123. Asia: one of the Oceanides and
wife of Prometheus. Mary Shelley's note is interesting:
"When the benefactor of mankind is liberated, Nature
resumes the beauty of her prime, and is united to her
husband, the emblem of the human race, in perfect and
happy union."

Subtle thou art and good, and though the Gods
Hear not this voice, yet thou art more than God,
Being wise and kind: earnestly hearken now.
    PRO.   Obscurely through my brain, like shadows
     dim,
Sweep awful thoughts, rapid and thick. I feel
Faint, like one mingled in entwining love;
Yet 'tis not pleasure.
    THE EARTH.   No, thou canst not hear:
Thou art immortal, and this tongue is known   150
Only to those who die.
    PRO.   And what art thou,
O, melancholy Voice?
    THE EARTH.   I am the Earth,
Thy mother; she within whose stony veins,
To the last fibre of the loftiest tree
Whose thin leaves trembled in the frozen air,
Joy ran, as blood within a living frame,
When thou didst from her bosom, like a cloud
Of glory, arise, a spirit of keen joy!
And at thy voice her pining sons uplifted
Their prostrate brows from the polluting dust,   160
And our almighty Tyrant with fierce dread
Grew pale, until his thunder chained thee here.
Then, see those million worlds which burn and roll
Around us: their inhabitants beheld
My sphered light wane in wide Heaven; the sea
Was lifted by strange tempest, and new fire
From earthquake-rifted mountains of bright snow
Shook its portentous hair beneath Heaven's frown;
Lightning and Inundation vexed the plains;
Blue thistles bloomed in cities; foodless toads   170
Within voluptuous chambers panting crawled:
When Plague had fallen on man, and beast, and
     worm,
And Famine; and black blight on herb and tree;
And in the corn, and vines, and meadow-grass,
Teemed ineradicable poisonous weeds
Draining their growth, for my wan breast was dry
With grief; and the thin air, my breath, was stained
With the contagion of a mother's hate
Breathed on her child's destroyer; ay, I heard
Thy curse, the which, if thou rememberest not,   180
Yet my innumerable seas and streams,
Mountains, and caves, and winds, and yon wide air,
And the inarticulate people of the dead,
Preserve, a treasured spell. We mediate
In secret joy and hope those dreadful words,
But dare not speak them.
    PRO.   Venerable mother!

All else who live and suffer take from thee
Some comfort; flowers, and fruits, and happy sounds,
And love, though fleeting; these may not be mine.
But mine own words, I pray, deny me not.   190
   THE EARTH.   They shall be told. Ere Babylon was
    dust,
The Magus Zoroaster, my dead child,
Met his own image walking in the garden.
That apparition, sole of men, he saw.
For know there are two worlds of life and death:
One that which thou beholdest; but the other
Is underneath the grave, where do inhabit
The shadows of all forms that think and live
Till death unite them and they part no more;
Dreams and the light imaginings of men,   200
And all that faith creates or love desires,
Terrible, strange, sublime and beauteous shapes.
There thou art, and dost hang, a writhing shade,
'Mid whirlwind-peopled mountains; all the gods
Are there, and all the powers of nameless worlds,
Vast, sceptred phantoms; heroes, men, and beasts;
And Demogorgon, a tremendous gloom;
And he, the supreme Tyrant, on his throne
Of burning gold. Son, one of these shall utter
The curse which all remember. Call at will   210
Thine own ghost, or the ghost of Jupiter,
Hades or Typhon, or what mightier Gods
From all-prolific Evil, since thy ruin
Have sprung, and trampled on my prostrate sons.
Ask, and they must reply: so the revenge
Of the Supreme may sweep through vacant shades,
As rainy wind through the abandoned gate
Of a fallen palace.
   PRO.   Mother, let not aught
Of that which may be evil, pass again
My lips, or those of aught resembling me.   220
Phantasm of Jupiter, arise, appear!

IONE

My wings are folded o'er mine ears:
   My wings are crossèd o'er mine eyes:
Yet through their silver shade appears,
   And through their lulling plumes arise,

192. **Magus Zoroaster:** founder of the ancient Persian
religion (Zoroastrianism) which taught that the powers
of light and darkness are locked in a struggle that will
end with the triumph of light. 212. **Hades or Typhon:**
Pluto is god of Hades; Typhon is the son of the Earth,
associated with great natural disturbances.

A Shape, a throng of sounds;
   May it be no ill to thee
O thou of many wounds!
Near whom, for our sweet sister's sake,
Ever thus we watch and wake.   230

PANTHEA

The sound is of whirlwind underground,
   Earthquake, and fire, and mountains cloven;
The shape is awful like the sound,
   Clothed in dark purple, star-inwoven.
A sceptre of pale gold
   To stay steps proud, o'er the slow cloud
His veinèd hand doth hold.
Cruel he looks, but calm and strong,
Like one who does, not suffers wrong.

   PHANTASM OF JUPITER.   Why have the secret
   powers of this strange world   240
Driven me, a frail and empty phantom, hither
On direst storms? What unaccustomed sounds
Are hovering on my lips, unlike the voice
With which our pallid race hold ghastly talk
In darkness? And, proud sufferer, who art thou?
   PRO.   Tremendous Image, as thou art must be
He whom thou shadowest forth. I am his foe,
The Titan. Speak the words which I would hear,
Although no thought inform thine empty voice.
   THE EARTH.   Listen! And though your echoes
   must be mute,   250
Gray mountains, and old woods, and haunted
   springs,
Prophetic caves, and isle-surrounding streams,
Rejoice to hear what yet ye cannot speak.
   PHAN.   A spirit seizes me and speaks within:
It tears me as fire a thunder-cloud.
   PANTHEA.   See, how he lifts his mighty looks, the
   Heaven
Darkens above. He speaks!
   IONE.   O shelter me!
   PRO.   I see the curse on gestures proud and cold,
And looks of firm defiance, and calm hate,
And such despair as mocks itself with smiles,   260
Written as on a scroll: yet speak: Oh, speak!

PHANTASM

Fiend, I defy thee! with a calm, fixed mind,
   All that thou canst inflict I bid thee do;
Foul Tyrant both of Gods and Human-kind,
   One only being shalt thou not subdue.

Rain then thy plagues upon me here,
Ghastly disease, and frenzying fear;
And let alternate frost and fire
Eat into me, and be thine ire
Lightning, and cutting hail, and legioned
    forms   270
Of furies, driving by upon the wounding storms.

Ay, do thy worst. Thou art omnipotent.
    O'er all things but thyself I gave thee power,
And my own will. Be thy swift mischiefs sent
    To blast mankind, from yon ethereal tower.
Let thy malignant spirit move
In darkness over those I love:
On me and mine I imprecate
The utmost torture of thy hate;
And thus devote to sleepless agony,   280
This undeclining head while thou must reign on
    high.

But thou, who art the God and Lord: O, thou,
    Who fillest with thy soul this world of woe,
To whom all things of Earth and Heaven do bow
    In fear and worship: all-prevailing foe!
I curse thee! let a sufferer's curse
Clasp thee, his torturer, like remorse;
Till thine Infinity shall be
A robe of envenomed agony;
And thine Omnipotence a crown of pain,   290
To cling like burning gold round thy dissolving
    brain.

Heap on thy soul, by virtue of this Curse,
    Ill deeds, then be thou damned, beholding
      good;
Both infinite as is the universe,
    And thou, and thy self-torturing solitude.
An awful image of calm power
Though now thou sittest, let the hour
Come, when thou must appear to be
That which thou art internally;
And after many a false and fruitless crime   300
Scorn track thy lagging fall through boundless space
    and time.

PRO.   Were these my words, O Parent?
THE EARTH.   They were thine.
PRO.   It doth repent me: words are quick and
    vain:
Grief for awhile is blind, and so was mine.
I wish no living thing to suffer pain.

THE EARTH

Misery, Oh misery to me,
That Jove at length should vanquish thee.
Wail, howl aloud, Land and Sea,
The Earth's rent heart shall answer ye.
Howl, Spirits of the living and the dead,   310
Your refuge, your defence lies fallen and vanquishèd.

FIRST ECHO

Lies fallen and vanquishèd!

SECOND ECHO

Fallen and vanquishèd!

IONE

Fear not: 'tis but some passing spasm,
    The Titan is unvanquished still.
But see, where through the azure chasm
    Of yon forked and snowy hill
Trampling the slant winds on high
    With golden-sandalled feet, that glow
Under plumes of purple dye,   320
Like rose-ensanguined ivory,
    A Shape comes now,
Stretching on high from his right hand
A serpent-cinctured wand.

PANTHEA.   'Tis Jove's world-wandering herald,
Mercury.

IONE

And who are those with hydra tresses
    And iron wings that climb the wind,
Whom the frowning God represses
    Like vapours steaming up behind,
Clanging loud, an endless crowd—   330

PANTHEA

These are Jove's tempest-walking hounds,
Whom he gluts with groans and blood,
When charioted on sulphurous cloud
    He bursts Heaven's bounds.

IONE

Are they now led, from the thin dead
On new pangs to be fed?

324. serpent-cinctured wand: the caduceus, snake-entwined staff carried by Mercury. **326. hydra:** snake-like.

PANTHEA

The Titan looks as ever, firm, not proud.

FIRST FURY.   Ha! I scent life!

SECOND FURY.   Let me but look into his eyes!

THIRD FURY.   The hope of torturing him smells
    like a heap

Of corpses, to a death-bird after battle.   340

    FIRST FURY.   Darest thou delay, O Herald! take
    cheer, Hounds

Of Hell: what if the Son of Maia soon

Should make us food and sport—who can please
    long

The Omnipotent?

    MERCURY.   Back to your towers of iron,

And gnash, beside the streams of fire and wail,

Your foodless teeth. Geryon, arise! and Gorgon,

Chimæra, and thou Sphinx, subtlest of fiends

Who ministered to Thebes Heaven's poisoned wine,

Unnatural love, and more unnatural hate:

These shall perform your task.

    FIRST FURY.   Oh, mercy! mercy!   350

We die with our desire: drive us not back!

    MER.   Crouch then in silence.

                        Awful Sufferer!

To thee unwilling, most unwillingly

I come, by the great Father's will driven down,

To execute a doom of new revenge.

Alas! I pity thee, and hate myself

That I can do no more: aye from thy sight

Returning, for a season, Heaven seems Hell,

So thy worn form pursues me night and day,

Smiling reproach. Wise art thou, firm and
        good,   360

But vainly wouldst stand forth alone in strife

Against the Omnipotent; as yon clear lamps

That measure and divide the weary years

From which there is no refuge, long have taught

And long must teach. Even now thy Torturer arms

With the strange might of unimagined pains

The powers who scheme slow agonies in Hell,

And my commission is to lead them here,

Or what more subtle, foul, or savage fiends

People the abyss, and leave them to their task.   370

Be it not so! there is a secret known

To thee, and to none else of living things,

Which may transfer the sceptre of wide Heaven,

The fear of which perplexes the Supreme:

Clothe it in words, and bid it clasp his throne

In intercession; bend thy soul in prayer,

And like a suppliant in some gorgeous fane,

Let the will kneel within thy haughty heart:

For benefits and meek submission tame

The fiercest and the mightiest.

    PRO.   Evil minds   380

Change good to their own nature. I gave all

He has; and in return he chains me here

Years, ages, night and day: whether the Sun

Split my parched skin, or in the moony night

The crystal-wingèd snow cling round my hair:

Whilst my belovèd race is trampled down

By his thought-executing ministers.

Such is the tyrant's recompense: 'tis just:

He who is evil can receive no good;

And for a world bestowed, or a friend lost,   390

He can feel hate, fear, shame; not gratitude:

He but requites me for his own misdeed.

Kindness to such is keen reproach, which breaks

With bitter stings the light sleep of Revenge.

Submission, thou dost know I cannot try:

For what submission but that fatal word,

The death-seal of mankind's captivity,

Like the Sicilian's hair-suspended sword,

Which trembles o'er his crown, would he accept,

Or could I yield? Which yet I will not yield.   400

Let others flatter Crime, where it sits throned

In brief Omnipotence: secure are they:

For Justice, when triumphant, will weep down

Pity, not punishment, on her own wrongs,

Too much avenged by those who err. I wait,

Enduring thus, the retributive hour

Which since we spake is even nearer now.

But hark, the hell-hounds clamour: fear delay:

Behold! Heaven lowers under thy Father's frown.

    MER.   Oh, that we might be spared: I to
        inflict   410

And thou to suffer! Once more answer me:

Thou knowest not the period of Jove's power?

    PRO.   I know but this, that it must come.

    MER.   Alas!

Thou canst not count thy years to come of pain?

---

342. **Son of Maia:** Mercury. **346–49. Geryon . . . hate:**
Geryon, Gorgon, and Chimæra were fabled monsters
of Greek mythology. The Sphinx devoured all who
could not solve her mysterious riddle; it was at length
solved by Oedipus.

398. **Sicilian's . . . sword:** the fabled sword of Damocles.

PRO.   They last while Jove must reign: nor more,
    nor less
Do I desire or fear.
    MER.   Yet pause, and plunge
Into Eternity, where recorded time,
Even all that we imagine, age on age,
Seems but a point, and the reluctant mind
Flags wearily in its unending flight,   420
Till it sink, dizzy, blind, lost, shelterless;
Perchance it has not numbered the slow years
Which thou must spend in torture, unreprieved?
    PRO.   Perchance no thought can count them, yet
    they pass.
    MER.   If thou might'st dwell among the Gods the
    while
Lapped in voluptuous joy?
    PRO.   I would not quit
This bleak ravine, these unrepentant pains.
    MER.   Alas! I wonder at, yet pity thee.
    PRO.   Pity the self-despising slaves of Heaven,
Not me, within whose mind sits peace serene,   430
As light in the sun, throned: how vain is talk!
Call up the fiends.
    IONE.   O, sister, look! White fire
Has cloven to the roots yon huge snow-loaded
    cedar;
How fearfully God's thunder howls behind!
    MER.   I must obey his words and thine: alas!
Most heavily remorse hangs at my heart!
    PANTHEA.   See where the child of Heaven, with
    wingèd feet,
Runs down the slanted sunlight of the dawn.
    IONE.   Dear sister, close thy plumes over thine
    eyes
Lest thou behold and die: they come: they
    come   440
Blackening the birth of day with countless wings,
And hollow underneath, like death.
    FIRST FURY.   Prometheus!
    SECOND FURY.   Immortal Titan!
    THIRD FURY.   Champion of Heaven's slaves!
    PRO.   He whom some dreadful voice invokes is
    here,
Prometheus, the chained Titan. Horrible forms,
What and who are ye? Never yet there came
Phantasms so foul through monster-teeming Hell
From the all-miscreative brain of Jove;
Whilst I behold such execrable shapes,
Methinks I grow like what I contemplate,   450
And laugh and stare in loathsome sympathy.

    FIRST FURY.   We are the ministers of pain, and
    fear,
And disappointment, and mistrust, and hate,
And clinging crime, and as lean dogs pursue
Through wood and lake some struck and sobbing
    fawn,
We track all things that weep, and bleed, and live,
When the great King betrays them to our will.
    PRO.   Oh! many fearful natures in one name,
I know ye; and these lakes and echoes know
The darkness and the clangour of your wings.   460
But why more hideous than your loathèd selves
Gather ye up in legions from the deep?
    SECOND FURY.   We knew not that: Sisters, re-
    joice, rejoice!
    PRO.   Can aught exult in its deformity?
    SECOND FURY.   The beauty of delight makes
    lovers glad,
Gazing on one another: so are we.
As from the rose which the pale priestess kneels
To gather for her festal crown of flowers
The aërial crimson falls, flushing her cheek,
So from our victim's destined agony   470
The shade which is our form invests us round,
Else we are shapeless as our mother Night.
    PRO.   I laugh your power, and his who sent you
    here,
To lowest scorn. Pour forth the cup of pain.
    FIRST FURY.   Thou thinkest we will rend thee
    bone from bone,
And nerve from nerve, working like fire within?
    PRO.   Pain is my element, as hate is thine;
Ye rend me now: I care not.
    SECOND FURY.   Dost imagine
We will but laugh into thy lidless eyes?
    PRO.   I weigh not what ye do, but what ye
    suffer,   480
Being evil. Cruel was the power which called
You, or aught else so wretched, into light.
    THIRD FURY.   Thou think'st we will live through
    thee, one by one,
Like animal life, and though we can obscure not
The soul which burns within, that we will dwell
Beside it, like a vain loud multitude
Vexing the self-content of wisest men:
That we will be dread thought beneath thy brain,
And foul desire round thine astonished heart,
And blood within thy labyrinthine veins   490
Crawling like agony?
    PRO.   Why, ye are thus now;

Yet am I king over myself, and rule
The torturing and conflicting throngs within,
As Jove rules you when Hell grows mutinous.

CHORUS OF FURIES

From the ends of the earth, from the ends of the
    earth,
Where the night has its grave and the morning its
    birth,
        Come, come, come!
Oh, ye who shake hills with the scream of your
    mirth,
When cities sink howling in ruin; and ye
Who with wingless footsteps trample the sea,   500
And close upon Shipwreck and Famine's track,
Sit chattering with joy on the foodless wreck;
        Come, come, come!
    Leave the bed, low, cold, and red,
    Strewed beneath a nation dead;
    Leave the hatred, as in ashes
      Fire is left for future burning:
    It will burst in bloodier flashes
      When ye stir it, soon returning:
    Leave the self-contempt implanted   510
    In young spirits, sense-enchanted,
      Misery's yet unkindled fuel:
    Leave Hell's secrets half unchanted
      To the maniac dreamer; cruel
    More than ye can be with hate
      Is he with fear.
        Come, come, come!
We are steaming up from Hell's wide gate
And we burthen the blast of the atmosphere,
But vainly we toil till ye come here.   520

IONE.   Sister, I hear the thunder of new wings.
PANTHEA.   These solid mountains quiver with
    the sound
Even as the tremulous air: their shadows make
The space within my plumes more black than night.

FIRST FURY

Your call was a wingèd car
Driven on whirlwinds fast and far;
It rapt us from red gulfs of war.

SECOND FURY

From wide cities, famine-wasted;

THIRD FURY

Groans half heard, and blood untasted;

FOURTH FURY

Kingly conclaves stern and cold,   530
Where blood with gold is bought and sold;

FIFTH FURY

From the furnace, white and hot,
In which—

A FURY

    Speak not: whisper not:
I know all that ye would tell,
But to speak might break the spell
Which must bend the Invincible,
    The stern of thought;
He yet defies the deepest power of Hell.

A FURY

Tear the veil!

ANOTHER FURY

    It is torn.

CHORUS

        The pale stars of the morn
Shine on a misery, dire to be borne.   540
Dost thou faint, mighty Titan? We laugh to scorn.
Dost thou boast the clear knowledge thou waken'dst
    for man?
Then was kindled within him a thirst which outran
Those perishing waters; a thirst of fierce fever,
Hope, love, doubt, desire, which consume him for
    ever.
    One came forth of gentle worth
    Smiling on the sanguine earth;
    His words outlived him, like swift poison
      Withering up truth, peace, and pity.
    Look! where round the wide horizon   550
      Many a million-peopled city
    Vomits smoke in the bright air.
    Hark that outcry of despair!
    'Tis his mild and gentle ghost
      Wailing for the faith he kindled:
    Look again, the flames almost
      To a glow-worm's lamp have dwindled:

527. rapt: forcefully carried away.

546. One: Christ.

The survivors round the embers
    Gather in dread.
                   Joy, joy, joy!   560
Past ages crowd on thee, but each one remembers,
And the future is dark, and the present is spread
Like a pillow of thorns for thy slumberless head.

SEMICHORUS I

Drops of bloody agony flow
From his white and quivering brow.
Grant a little respite now:
See a disenchanted nation
Springs like day from desolation;
To Truth its state is dedicate,
And Freedom leads it forth, her
    mate;   570
A legioned band of linkèd brothers
Whom Love calls children—

SEMICHORUS II

                          'Tis another's:
See how kindred murder kin:
'Tis the vintage-time for death and sin:
Blood, like new wine, bubbles within:
    Till Despair smothers
The struggling world, which slaves and tyrants win.
    [*All the* FURIES *vanish, except one.*]
    IONE.   Hark, sister! what a low yet dreadful
    groan
Quite unsuppressed is tearing up the heart
Of the good Titan, as storms tear the deep,   580
And beasts hear the sea moan in inland caves.
Darest thou observe how the fiends torture him?
    PANTHEA.   Alas! I looked forth twice, but will no
    more.
    IONE.   What didst thou see?
    PANTHEA.   A woeful sight: a youth
With patient looks nailed to a crucifix.
    IONE.   What next?
    PANTHEA.   The heaven around, the earth below
Was peopled with thick shapes of human death,
All horrible, and wrought by human hands,
And some appeared the work of human hearts,
For men were slowly killed by frowns and
    smiles: 590
And other sights too foul to speak and live
Were wandering by. Let us not tempt worse fear
By looking forth: those groans are grief enough.
    FURY.   Behold an emblem: those who do endure

Deep wrongs for man, and scorn, and chains, but
    heap
Thousandfold torment on themselves and him.
    PRO.   Remit the anguish of that lighted stare;
Close those wan lips; let that thorn-wounded brow
Stream not with blood; it mingles with thy tears!
Fix, fix those tortured orbs in peace and
    death,   600
So thy sick throes shake not that crucifix,
So those pale fingers play not with thy gore.
O, horrible! Thy name I will not speak,
It hath become a curse. I see, I see
The wise, the mild, the lofty, and the just,
Whom thy slaves hate for being like to thee,
Some hunted by foul lies from their heart's home,
An early-chosen, late-lamented home;
As hooded ounces cling to the driven hind;
Some linked to corpses in unwholesome cells: 610
Some—Hear I not the multitude laugh loud?—
Impaled in lingering fire: and mighty realms
Float by my feet, like sea-uprooted isles,
Whose sons are kneaded down in common blood
By the red light of their own burning homes.
    FURY.   Blood thou canst see, and fire; and canst
    hear groans;
Worse things, unheard, unseen, remain behind.
    PRO.   Worse?
    FURY.   In each human heart terror survives
The ravin it has gorged: the loftiest fear
All that they would disdain to think were
    true: 620
Hypocrisy and custom make their minds
The fanes of many a worship, now outworn.
They dare not devise good for man's estate,
And yet they know not that they do not dare.
The good want power, but to weep barren tears.
The powerful goodness want: worse need for them.
The wise want love; and those who love want wis-
    dom;
And all best things are thus confused to ill.
Many are strong and rich, and would be just,
But live among their suffering fellow-men   630
As if none felt: they know not what they do.
    PRO.   Thy words are like a cloud of wingèd
    snakes;
And yet I pity those they torture not.

---

609. hooded ounces: leopards used in India for hunting
deer. They are kept hooded until their prey is in sight.

FURY.   Thou pitiest them? I speak no more!
[*Vanishes.*]

PRO.   Ah woe!
Ah woe! Alas! pain, pain ever, for ever!
I close my tearless eyes, but see more clear
Thy works within my woe-illumèd mind,
Thou subtle tyrant! Peace is in the grave.
The grave hides all things beautiful and good:
I am a God and cannot find it there,   640
Nor would I seek it: for, though dread revenge,
This is defeat, fierce king, not victory.
The sights with which thou torturest gird my soul
With new endurance, till the hour arrives
When they shall be no types of things which are.
    PANTHEA.   Alas! what sawest thou?
    PRO.   There are two woes:
To speak, and to behold; thou spare me one.
Names are there, Nature's sacred watchwords, they
Were borne aloft in bright emblazonry;
The nations thronged around, and cried
        aloud,   650
As with one voice, Truth, liberty, and love!
Suddenly fierce confusion fell from heaven
Among them: there was strife, deceit, and fear:
Tyrants rushed in, and did divide the spoil.
This was the shadow of the truth I saw.
    THE EARTH.   I felt thy torture, son; with such
        mixed joy
As pain and virtue give. To cheer thy state
I bid ascend those subtle and fair spirits,
Whose homes are the dim caves of human thought,
And who inhabit, as birds wing the wind,   660
Its world-surrounding aether: they behold
Beyond that twilight realm, as in a glass,
The future: may they speak comfort to thee!
    PANTHEA.   Look, sister, where a troop of spirits
        gather,
Like flocks of clouds in spring's delightful weather,
Thronging in the blue air!
    IONE.   And see! more come,
Like fountain-vapours when the winds are dumb,
That climb up the ravine in scattered lines.
And, hark! is it the music of the pines?
Is it the lake? Is it the waterfall?   670
    PANTHEA.   'Tis something sadder, sweeter far
        than all.

CHORUS OF SPIRITS

From unremembered ages we
Gentle guides and guardians be

Of heaven-oppressed mortality;
And we breathe, and sicken not,
The atmosphere of human thought:
Be it dim, and dank, and gray,
Like a storm-extinguished day,
Travelled o'er by dying gleams;
    Be it bright as all between   680
Cloudless skies and windless streams,
    Silent, liquid, and serene;
As the birds within the wind,
    As the fish within the wave,
As the thoughts of man's own mind
    Float through all above the grave;
We make there our liquid lair,
Voyaging cloudlike and unpent
Through the boundless element:
Thence we bear the prophecy   690
Which begins and ends in thee!

IONE.   More yet come, one by one: the air around
    them
Looks radiant as the air around a star.

FIRST SPIRIT

On a battle-trumpet's blast
I fled hither, fast, fast, fast,
'Mid the darkness upward cast.
From the dust of creeds outworn,
From the tyrant's banner torn,
Gathering 'round me, onward borne,
There was mingled many a cry—   700
Freedom! Hope! Death! Victory!
Till they faded through the sky;
And one sound, above, around,
One sound beneath, around, above,
Was moving; 'twas the soul of Love;
'Twas the hope, the prophecy,
Which begins and ends in thee.

SECOND SPIRIT

A rainbow's arch stood on the sea,
Which rocked beneath, immovably;
And the triumphant storm did flee,   710
Like a conqueror, swift and proud,
Between, with many a captive cloud,
A shapeless, dark and rapid crowd,
Each by lightning riven in half:
I heard the thunder hoarsely laugh:
Mighty fleets were strewn like chaff
And spread beneath, a hell of death,

O'er the white waters. I alit
On a great ship lightning-split,
And speeded hither on the sigh   720
Of one who gave an enemy
His plank, then plunged aside to die.

THIRD SPIRIT

I sate beside a sage's bed,
And the lamp was burning red
Near the book where he had fed,
When a Dream with plumes of flame,
To his pillow hovering came,
And I knew it was the same
Which had kindled long ago
Pity, eloquence, and woe;   730
And the world awhile below
Wore the shade its lustre made.
It has borne me here as fleet
As Desire's lightning feet:
I must ride it back ere morrow,
Or the sage will wake in sorrow.

FOURTH SPIRIT

On a poet's lips I slept
Dreaming like a love-adept
In the sound his breathing kept;
Nor seeks nor finds he mortal blisses,   740
But feeds on the aëreal kisses
Of shapes that haunt thought's
    wildernesses.
He will watch from dawn to gloom
The lake-reflected sun illume
The yellow bees in the ivy-bloom,
Nor heed nor see, what things they
    be;
But from these create he can
Forms more real than living man,
Nurslings of immortality!
One of these awakened me,   750
And I sped to succour thee.

IONE

Behold'st thou two shapes from the east and west
Come, as two doves to one belovèd nest,
Twin nurslings of the all-sustaining air
On swift still wings glide down the atmosphere?
And, hark! their sweet, sad voices! 'tis despair
Mingled with love and then dissolved in sound.

PANTHEA.   Canst thou speak, sister? all my words
    are drowned.

IONE.   Their beauty gives me voice. See how they
    float
On their sustaining wings of skiey grain,   760
Orange and azure deepening into gold:
Their soft smiles light the air like a star's fire.

CHORUS OF SPIRITS

Hast thou beheld the form of Love?

FIFTH SPIRIT

                    As over wide dominions
I sped, like some swift cloud that wings the wide
    air's wildernesses,
That planet-crested shape swept by on lightning-
    braided pinions,
Scattering the liquid joy of life from his ambrosial
    tresses:
His footsteps paved the world with light; but as I
    passed 'twas fading,
And hollow Ruin yawned behind: great sages
    bound in madness,
And headless patriots, and pale youth who perished,
    unupbraiding,
Gleamed in the night. I wandered o'er, till thou, O
    King of sadness,   770
Turned by thy smile the worst I saw to recollected
    gladness.

SIXTH SPIRIT

Ah, sister! Desolation is a delicate thing:
    It walks not on the earth, it floats not on the air,
But treads with lulling footstep, and fans with silent
    wing
    The tender hopes which in their hearts the best
        and gentlest bear;
Who, soothed to false repose by the fanning plumes
    above
    And the music-stirring motion of its soft and busy
        feet,
Dream visions of aëreal joy, and call the monster,
    Love,
    And wake, and find the shadow Pain, as he whom
        now we greet.

CHORUS

Though Ruin now Love's shadow be,   780
Following him, destroyingly,
    On Death's white and wingèd steed,
Which the fleetest cannot flee,
    Trampling down both flower and weed,

Man and beast, and foul and fair,
Like a tempest through the air;
Thou shalt quell this horseman grim,
Woundless though in heart or limb.

PRO.   Spirits! how know ye this shall be?

CHORUS

In the atmosphere we breathe,   790
As buds grow red when the snow-storms flee,
    From Spring gathering up beneath,
Whose mild winds shake the elder brake,
And the wandering herdsmen know
That the white-thorn soon will blow:
Wisdom, Justice, Love, and Peace,
When they struggle to increase,
    Are to us as soft winds be
    To shepherd boys, the prophecy
    Which begins and ends in thee.   800
IONE.   Where are the Spirits fled?
PANTHEA.   Only a sense
Remains of them, like the omnipotence
Of music, when the inspired voice and lute
Languish, ere yet the responses are mute,
Which through the deep and labyrinthine soul,
Like echoes through long caverns, wind and roll.
    PRO.   How fair these airborn shapes! and yet I
        feel
Most vain all hope but love; and thou art far,
Asia! who, when my being overflowed,
Wert like a golden chalice to bright wine   810
Which else had sunk into the thirsty dust.
All things are still: alas! how heavily
This quiet morning weighs upon my heart;
Though I should dream I could even sleep with
        grief
If slumber were denied not. I would fain
Be what it is my destiny to be,
The saviour and the strength of suffering man,
Or sink into the original gulf of things:
There is no agony, and no solace left;
Earth can console, Heaven can torment no
        more.   820
    PANTHEA.   Hast thou forgotten one who watches
        thee
The cold dark night, and never sleeps but when
The shadow of thy spirit falls on her?
    PRO.   I said all hope was vain but love: thou
        lovest.

787. quell: kill.

PANTHEA.   Deeply in truth; but the eastern star
        looks white,
And Asia waits in that far Indian vale,
The scene of her sad exile; rugged once
And desolate and frozen, like this ravine;
But now invested with fair flowers and herbs,
And haunted by sweet airs and sounds, which
        flow   830
Among the woods and waters, from the aether
Of her transforming presence, which would fade
If it were mingled not with thine. Farewell!

END OF THE FIRST ACT

ACT II

SCENE I—*Morning. A lovely Vale in the Indian
        Caucasus.* ASIA *alone.*

ASIA.   From all the blasts of heaven thou hast
        descended:
Yes, like a spirit, like a thought, which makes
Unwonted tears throng to the horny eyes,
And beatings haunt the desolated heart,
Which should have learnt repose: thou hast
        descended
Cradled in tempests; thou dost wake, O Spring!
O child of many winds! As suddenly
Thou comest as the memory of a dream,
Which now is sad because it hath been sweet;
Like genius, or like joy which riseth up   10
As from the earth, clothing with golden clouds
The desert of our life.
This is the season, this the day, the hour;
At sunrise thou shouldst come, sweet sister mine,
Too long desired, too long delaying, come!
How like death-worms the wingless moments crawl!
The point of one white star is quivering still
Deep in the orange light of widening morn
Beyond the purple mountains: through a chasm
Of wind-divided mist the darker lake   20
Reflects it: now it wanes: it gleams again
As the waves fade, and as the burning threads
Of woven cloud unravel in pale air:
'Tis lost! and through yon peaks of cloud-like snow
The roseate sunlight quivers: hear I not
The Æolian music of her sea-green plumes
Winnowing the crimson dawn?
                                    [PANTHEA *enters.*]
                                    I feel, I see

Those eyes which burn through smiles that fade in
    tears,
Like stars half quenched in mists of silver dew.
Belovèd and most beautiful, who wearest   30
The shadow of that soul by which I live,
How late thou art! the spherèd sun had climbed
The sea; my heart was sick with hope, before
The printless air felt thy belated plumes.
    PANTHEA.   Pardon, great Sister! but my wings
      were faint
With the delight of a remembered dream,
As are the noontide plumes of summer winds
Satiate with sweet flowers. I was wont to sleep
Peacefully, and awake refreshed and calm
Before the sacred Titan's fall, and thy   40
Unhappy love, had made, through use and pity,
Both love and woe familiar to my heart
As they had grown to thine: erewhile I slept
Under the glaucous caverns of old Ocean
Within dim bowers of green and purple moss,
Our young Ione's soft and milky arms
Locked then, as now, behind my dark, moist hair,
While my shut eyes and cheek were pressed within
The folded depth of her life-breathing bosom:
But not as now, since I am made the wind   50
Which fails beneath the music that I bear
Of thy most wordless converse; since dissolved
Into the sense with which love talks, my rest
Was troubled and yet sweet; my waking hours
Too full of care and pain.
    ASIA.   Lift up thine eyes,
And let me read thy dream.
    PANTHEA.   As I have said
With our sea-sister at his feet I slept.
The mountain mists, condensing at our voice
Under the moon, had spread their snowy flakes,
From the keen ice shielding our linked sleep.   60
Then two dreams came. One, I remember not.
But in the other his pale wound-worn limbs
Fell from Prometheus, and the azure night
Grew radiant with the glory of that form
Which lives unchanged within, and his voice fell
Like music which makes giddy the dim brain,
Faint with intoxication of keen joy:
"Sister of her whose footsteps pave the world
With loveliness—more fair than aught but her,
Whose shadow thou art—lift thine eyes on me."   70

ACT II. SCENE I. **44. glaucous:** greenish blue. Glaucus
was a sea-god.

I lifted them: the overpowering light
Of that immortal shape was shadowed o'er
By love; which, from his soft and flowing limbs,
And passion-parted lips, and keen, faint eyes,
Steamed forth like vaporous fire; an atmosphere
Which wrapped me in its all-dissolving power,
As the warm aether of the morning sun
Wraps ere it drinks some cloud of wandering dew.
I saw not, heard not, move not, only felt
His presence flow and mingle through my blood   80
Till it became his life, and his grew mine,
And I was thus absorbed, until it passed,
And like the vapours when the sun sinks down,
Gathering again in drops upon the pines,
And tremulous as they, in the deep night
My being was condensed; and as the rays
Of thought were slowly gathered, I could hear
His voice, whose accents lingered ere they died
Like footsteps of far melody: thy name
Among the many sounds alone I heard   90
Of what might be articulate; though still
I listened through the night when sound was none.
Ione wakened then, and said to me:
"Canst thou divine what troubles me to-night?
I always knew what I desired before,
Nor ever found delight to wish in vain.
But now I cannot tell thee what I seek;
I know not; something sweet, since it is sweet
Even to desire; it is thy sport, false sister;
Thou hast discovered some enchantment old,   100
Whose spells have stolen my spirit as I slept
And mingled it with thine: for when just now
We kissed, I felt within thy parted lips
The sweet air that sustained me, and the warmth
Of the life-blood, for loss of which I faint,
Quivered between our intertwining arms."
I answered not, for the Eastern star grew pale,
But fled to thee.
    ASIA.   Thou speakest, but thy words
Are as the air: I feel them not: Oh, lift
Thine eyes, that I may read his written soul!   110
    PANTHEA.   I lift them though they droop beneath
      the load
Of that they would express: what canst thou see
But thine own fairest shadow imaged there?
    ASIA.   Thine eyes are like the deep, blue,
      boundless heaven
Contracted to two circles underneath
Their long, fine lashes; dark, far, measureless,
Orb within orb, and line through line inwoven.

PANTHEA.   Why lookest thou as if a spirit passed?
ASIA.   There is a change: beyond their inmost
    depth
I see a shade, a shape: 'tis He, arrayed   120
In the soft light of his own smiles, which spread
Like radiance from the cloud-surrounded moon.
Prometheus, it is thine! depart not yet!
Say not those smiles that we shall meet again
Within that bright pavilion which their beams
Shall build o'er the waste world? The dream is told.
What shape is that between us? Its rude hair
Roughens the wind that lifts it, its regard
Is wild and quick, yet 'tis a thing of air,
For through its gray robe gleams the golden
    dew   130
Whose stars the noon has quenchèd not.
    DREAM.   Follow! Follow!
    PANTHEA.   It is mine other dream.
    ASIA.   It disappears.
    PANTHEA.   It passes now into my mind.
    Methought
As we sate here, the flower-infolding buds
Burst on yon lightning-blasted almond-tree,
When swift from the white Scythian wilderness
A wind swept forth wrinkling the Earth with frost:
I looked, and all the blossoms were blown down;
But on each leaf was stamped, as the blue bells
Of Hyacinth tell Apollo's written grief,   140
O, FOLLOW, FOLLOW!
    ASIA.   As you speak, your words
Fill, pause by pause, my own forgotten sleep
With shapes. Methought among these lawns
    together
We wandered, underneath the young gray dawn,
And multitudes of dense white fleecy clouds
Were wandering in thick flocks along the mountains
Shepherded by the slow, unwilling wind;
And the white dew on the new-bladed grass,
Just piercing the dark earth, hung silently;
And there was more which I remember not: 150
But on the shadows of the morning clouds,
Athwart the purple mountain slope, was written
FOLLOW, O, FOLLOW! as they vanished by;
And on each herb, from which Heaven's dew had
    fallen,

---

128. regard: face. 140. Hyacinth . . . grief: When Apollo
accidentally killed young Hyacinthus, a flower sprang
from his blood; its petals were marked with the mournful expression AI, AI ("Alas" in Greek).

The like was stamped, as with a withering fire;
A wind arose among the pines; it shook
The clinging music from their boughs, and then
Low, sweet, faint sounds, like the farewell of ghosts,
Were heard: O, FOLLOW, FOLLOW, FOLLOW ME!
And then I said: "Panthea, look on me."   160
But in the depth of those belovèd eyes
Still I saw, FOLLOW, FOLLOW!
    ECHO.   Follow, follow!
    PANTHEA.   The crags, this clear spring morning,
    mock our voices
As they were spirit-tongued.
    ASIA.   It is some being
Around the crags. What fine clear sounds! O, list!

    ECHOES (*unseen*)

Echoes we: listen!
    We cannot stay:
As dew-stars glisten
    Then fade away—
        Child of Ocean!   170
    ASIA.   Hark! Spirits speak. The liquid responses
Of their aëreal tongues yet sound.
    PANTHEA.   I hear.

    ECHOES

O, follow, follow,
    As our voice recedeth
Through the caverns hollow,
    Where the forest spreadeth;
        (*More distant.*)
    O, follow, follow!
    Through the cavern hollow,
As the song floats thou pursue,
Where the wild bee never flew,   180
Through the noontide darkness deep,
By the odour-breathing sleep
Of faint night flowers, and the waves
At the fountain-lighted caves,
While our music, wild and sweet,
Mocks thy gently falling feet,
        Child of Ocean!
    ASIA.   Shall we pursue the sound? It grows more
    faint
And distant.
    PANTHEA.   List! the strain floats nearer now.

    ECHOES

In the world unknown   190
    Sleeps a voice unspoken;

By thy step alone
  Can its rest be broken;
    Child of Ocean!

ASIA.   How the notes sink upon the ebbing wind!

ECHOES

  O, follow, follow!
   Through the caverns hollow,
As the song floats thou pursue,
By the woodland noontide dew;
By the forest, lakes, and fountains,   200
Through the many-folded mountains;
To the rents, and gulfs, and chasms,
Where the Earth reposed from spasms,
On the day when He and thou
Parted, to commingle now;
      Child of Ocean!

ASIA.   Come, sweet Panthea, link thy hand in
  mine,
And follow, ere the voices fade away.

SCENE II—*A Forest, intermingled with Rocks and
Caverns.* ASIA *and* PANTHEA *pass into it. Two
young* FAUNS *are sitting on a Rock listening.*

SEMICHORUS I OF SPIRITS

The path through which that lovely twain
  Have passed, by cedar, pine, and yew,
  And each dark tree that ever grew,
  Is curtained out from Heaven's wide blue;
Nor sun, nor moon, nor wind, nor rain,
    Can pierce its interwoven bowers,
  Nor aught, save where some cloud of dew,
Drifted along the earth-creeping breeze,
Between the trunks of the hoar trees,
    Hangs each a pearl in the pale flowers   10
  Of the green laurel, blown anew;
And bends, and then fades silently,
One frail and fair anemone:
Or when some star of many a one
That climbs and wanders through steep night,
Has found the cleft through which alone
Beams fall from high those depths upon
Ere it is borne away, away,
By the swift Heavens that cannot stay,
It scatters drops of golden light,   20
Like lines of rain that ne'er unite;

And the gloom divine is all around,
And underneath is the mossy ground.

SEMICHORUS II

There the voluptuous nightingales,
  Are awake through all the broad noonday.
When one with bliss or sadness fails,
    And through the windless ivy-boughs,
  Sick with sweet love, droops dying away
On its mate's music-panting bosom;
Another from the swinging blossom,   30
    Watching to catch the languid close
  Of the last strain, then lifts on high
  The wings of the weak melody,
'Till some new strain of feeling bear
  The song, and all the woods are mute;
When there is heard through the dim air
The rush of wings, and rising there
  Like many a lake-surrounded flute,
Sounds overflow the listener's brain
So sweet, that joy is almost pain.   40

SEMICHORUS I

There those enchanted eddies play
  Of echoes, music-tongued, which draw,
  By Demogorgon's mighty law,
  With melting rapture, or sweet awe,
All spirits on that secret way;
  As inland boats are driven to Ocean
Down streams made strong with mountain-thaw:
    And first there comes a gentle sound
    To those in talk or slumber bound,
  And wakes the destined soft emotion,—   50
Attracts, impels them; those who saw
  Say from the breathing earth behind
  There steams a plume-uplifting wind
Which drives them on their path, while they
  Believe their own swift wings and feet
The sweet desires within obey:
And so they float upon their way,
Until, still sweet, but loud and strong,
The storm of sound is driven along,
    Sucked up and hurrying: as they fleet   60
    Behind, its gathering billows meet
And to the fatal mountain bear
Like clouds amid the yielding air.

ACT II. SCENE II. **62. fatal mountain:** of Demogorgon, a
mysterious Power, perhaps of Necessity.

FIRST FAUN.   Canst thou imagine where those
    spirits live
Which make such delicate music in the woods?
We haunt within the least frequented caves
And closest coverts, and we know these wilds,
Yet never meet them, though we hear them oft:
Where may they hide themselves?
    SECOND FAUN.   'Tis hard to tell:
I have heard those more skilled in spirits say,   70
The bubbles, which the enchantment of the sun
Sucks from the pale faint water-flowers that pave
The oozy bottom of clear lakes and pools,
Are the pavilions where such dwell and float
Under the green and golden atmosphere
Which noontide kindles through the woven leaves;
And when these burst, and the thin fiery air,
The which they breathed within those lucent domes,
Ascends to flow like meteors through the night,
They ride on them, and rein their headlong
    speed,   80
And bow their burning crests, and glide in fire
Under the waters of the earth again.
    FIRST FAUN.   If such live thus, have others other
    lives,
Under pink blossoms or within the bells
Of meadow flowers, or folded violets deep,
Or on their dying odours, when they die,
Or in the sunlight of the spherèd dew?
    SECOND FAUN.   Ay, many more which we may
    well divine.
But, should we stay to speak, noontide would come,
And thwart Silenus find his goats undrawn,   90
And grudge to sing those wise and lovely songs
Of Fate, and Chance, and God, and Chaos old,
And Love, and the chained Titan's woful doom,
And how he shall be loosed, and make the earth
One brotherhood: delightful strains which cheer
Our solitary twilights, and which charm
To silence the unenvying nightingales.

SCENE III—*A Pinnacle of Rock among Moun-
    tains.* ASIA *and* PANTHEA.

PANTHEA.   Hither the sound has borne us—to
    the realm
Of Demogorgon, and the mighty portal,
Like a volcano's meteor-breathing chasm,

90. thwart: angry.

Whence the oracular vapour is hurled up
Which lonely men drink wandering in their youth,
And call truth, virtue, love, genius, or joy,
That maddening wine of life, whose dregs they
    drain
To deep intoxication; and uplift,
Like Mænads who cry loud, Evoe! Evoe!
The voice which is contagion to the world.   10
    ASIA.   Fit throne for such a Power! Magnificent!
How glorious art thou, Earth! And if thou be
The shadow of some spirit lovelier still,
Though evil stain its work, and it should be
Like its creation, weak yet beautiful,
I could fall down and worship that and thee.
Even now my heart adoreth: Wonderful!
Look, sister, ere the vapour dim thy brain:
Beneath is a wide plain of billowy mist,
As a lake, paving in the morning sky,   20
With azure waves which burst in silver light,
Some Indian vale. Behold it, rolling on
Under the curdling winds, and islanding
The peak whereon we stand—midway, around,
Encinctured by the dark and blooming forests,
Dim twilight lawns, and stream-illumèd caves,
And wind-enchanted shapes of wandering mist;
And far on high the keen sky-cleaving mountains
From icy spires of sun-like radiance fling
The dawn, as lifted Ocean's dazzling spray,   30
From some Atlantic islet scattered up,
Spangles the wind with lamp-like water-drops.
The vale is girdled with their walls, a howl
Of cataracts from their thaw-cloven ravines,
Satiates the listening wind, continuous, vast,
Awful as silence. Hark! the rushing snow!
The sun-awakened avalanche! whose mass,
Thrice sifted by the storm, had gathered there
Flake after flake, in heaven-defying minds
As thought by thought is piled, till some great
    truth   40
Is loosened, and the nations echo round,
Shaken to their roots, as do the mountains now.
    PANTHEA.   Look how the gusty sea of mist is
    breaking
In crimson foam, even at our feet! it rises
As Ocean at the enchantment of the moon
Round foodless men wrecked on some oozy isle.
    ASIA.   The fragments of the cloud are scattered
    up;

ACT II. SCENE III. 9. Mænads: ferocious female attendants of Bacchus.

The wind that lifts them disentwines my hair;
Its billows now sweep o'er mine eyes; my brain
Grows dizzy; see'st thou shapes within the
    mist?   50
    PANTHEA.   A countenance with beckoning
    smiles: there burns
An azure fire within its golden locks!
Another and another: hark! they speak!

SONG OF SPIRITS

To the deep, to the deep,
        Down, down!
Through the shade of sleep,
Through the cloudy strife
Of Death and of Life;
Through the veil and the bar
Of things which seem and are   60
Even to the steps of the remotest throne,
        Down, down!

While the sound whirls around,
        Down, down!
As the fawn draws the hound,
As the lightning the vapour,
As a weak moth the taper;
Death, despair; love, sorrow;
Time both; to-day, to-morrow;
As steel obeys the spirit of the stone,   70
        Down, down!

Through the gray, void abysm,
        Down, down!
Where the air is no prism,
And the moon and stars are not,
And the cavern-crags wear not
The radiance of Heaven,
Nor the gloom to Earth given,
Where there is One pervading, One alone,
        Down, down!   80
In the depth of the deep,
        Down, down!
Like veiled lightning asleep,
Like the spark nursed in embers,
The last look Love remembers,
Like a diamond, which shines
On the dark wealth of mines,
A spell is treasured but for thee alone.
        Down, down!

We have bound thee, we guide thee;   90
        Down, down!

With the bright form beside thee;
Resist not the weakness,
Such strength is in meekness
That the Eternal, the Immortal,
Must unloose through life's portal
The snake-like Doom coiled underneath his throne
        By that alone.

SCENE IV—*The Cave of* DEMOGORGON.
    ASIA *and* PANTHEA.

    PANTHEA.   What veilèd form sits on that ebon
    throne?
    ASIA.   The veil has fallen.
    PANTHEA.   I see a mighty darkness
Filling the seat of power, and rays of gloom
Dart round, as light from the meridian sun,
Ungazed upon and shapeless; neither limb,
Nor form, nor outline; yet we feel it is
A living Spirit.
    DEMOGORGON.   Ask what thou wouldst know.
    ASIA.   What canst thou tell?
    DEM.   All things thou dar'st demand.
    ASIA.   Who made the living world?
    DEM.   God.
    ASIA.   Who made all
That it contains? thought, passion, reason, will,   10
Imagination?
    DEM.   God: Almighty God.
    ASIA.   Who made that sense which, when the
    winds of Spring
In rarest visitation, or the voice
Of one belovèd heard in youth alone,
Fills the faint eyes with falling tears which dim
The radiant looks of unbewailing flowers,
And leaves this peopled earth a solitude
When it return no more?
    DEM.   Merciful God.
    ASIA.   And who made terror, madness, crime,
    remorse,
Which from the links of the great chain of
    things,   20
To every thought within the mind of man
Sway and drag heavily, and each one reels
Under the load towards the pit of death;
Abandoned hope, and love that turns to hate;
And self-contempt, bitterer to drink than blood;
Pain, whose unheeded and familiar speech
Is howling, and keen shrieks, day after day;
And Hell, or the sharp fear of Hell?

DEM.   He reigns.
ASIA.   Utter his name: a world pining in pain
Asks but his name; curses shall drag him down.   30
DEM.   He reigns.
ASIA.   I feel, I know it: who?
DEM.   He reigns.
ASIA.   Who reigns? There was the Heaven and
    Earth at first,
And Light and Love; then Saturn, from whose
    throne
Time fell, an envious shadow: such the state
Of the earth's primal spirits beneath his sway,
As the calm joy of flowers and living leaves
Before the wind or sun has withered them
And semivital worms; but he refused
The birthright of their being, knowledge, power,
The skill which wields the elements, the
    thought   40
Which pierces this dim universe like light,
Self-empire, and the majesty of love;
For thirst of which they fainted. Then Prometheus
Gave wisdom, which is strength, to Jupiter,
And with this law alone, "Let man be free,"
Clothed him with the dominion of wide Heaven.
To know nor faith, nor love, nor law; to be
Omnipotent but friendless is to reign;
And Jove now reigned; for on the race of man
First famine, and then toil, and then disease,   50
Strife, wounds, and ghastly death unseen before,
Fell; and the unseasonable seasons drove
With alternating shafts of frost and fire,
Their shelterless, pale tribes to mountain caves:
And in their desert hearts fierce wants he sent,
And mad disquietudes, and shadows idle
Of unreal good, which levied mutual war,
So ruining the lair wherein they raged.
Prometheus saw, and waked the legioned hopes
Which sleep within folded Elysian flowers,   60
Nepenthe, Moly, Amaranth, fadeless blooms,
That they might hide with thin and rainbow wings
The shape of Death; and Love he sent to bind
The disunited tendrils of that vine
Which bears the wine of life, the human heart;
And he tamed fire which, like some beast of prey,
Most terrible, but lovely, played beneath
The frown of man; and tortured to his will

ACT II. SCENE IV. **33. Saturn:** leader of the Titans, who
ruled before the Olympian gods. **61. Nepenthe...
Amaranth:** a catalogue of magic flowers.

Iron and gold, the slaves and signs of power,
And gems and poisons, and all subtlest forms   70
Hidden beneath the mountains and the waves.
He gave man speech, and speech created thought,
Which is the measure of the universe;
And Science struck the thrones of earth and heaven,
Which shook, but fell not; and the harmonious mind
Poured itself forth in all-prophetic song;
And music lifted up the listening spirit
Until it walked, exempt from mortal care,
Godlike, o'er the clear billows of sweet sound;
And human hands first mimicked and then
    mocked,   80
With moulded limbs more lovely than its own,
The human form, till marble grew divine;
And mothers, gazing, drank the love men see
Reflected in their race, behold, and perish.
He told the hidden power of herbs and springs,
And Disease drank and slept. Death grew like sleep.
He taught the implicated orbits woven
Of the wide-wandering stars; and how the sun
Changes his lair, and by what secret spell
The pale moon is transformed, when her broad
    eye   90
Gazes not on the interlunar sea:
He taught to rule, as life directs the limbs,
The tempest-wingèd chariots of the Ocean,
And the Celt knew the Indian. Cities then
Were built, and through their snow-like columns
    flowed
The warm winds, and the azure aether shone,
And the blue sea and shadowy hills were seen.
Such, the alleviations of his state,
Prometheus gave to man, for which he hangs
Withering in destined pain: but who rains
    down   100
Evil, the immedicable plague, which, while
Man looks on his creation like a God
And sees that it is glorious, drives him on,
The wreck of his own will, the scorn of earth,
The outcast, the abandoned, the alone?
Not Jove: while yet his frown shook Heaven, ay,
    when
His adversary from adamantine chains
Cursed him, he trembled like a slave. Declare
Who is his master? Is he too a slave?
DEM.   All spirits are enslaved which serve things
    evil: 110
Thou knowest if Jupiter be such or no.
ASIA.   Whom calledst thou God?

DEM.   I spoke but as ye speak,
For Jove is the supreme of living things.
   ASIA.   Who is the master of the slave?
   DEM   If the abysm
Could vomit forth its secrets.—But a voice
Is wanting, the deep truth is imageless;
For what would it avail to bid thee gaze
On the revolving world? What to bid speak
Fate, Time, Occasion, Chance, and Change? To
   these
All things are subject but eternal Love.   120
   ASIA.   So much I asked before, and my heart
   gave
The response thou hast given; and of such truths
Each to itself must be the oracle.
One more demand; and do thou answer me
As mine own soul would answer, did it know
That which I ask. Prometheus shall arise
Henceforth the sun of this rejoicing world:
When shall the destined hour arrive?
   DEM.   Behold!
   ASIA.   The rocks are cloven, and through the
   purple night
I see cars drawn by rainbow-wingèd steeds   130
Which trample the dim winds: in each there stands
A wild-eyed charioteer urging their flight.
Some look behind, as fiends pursued them there,
And yet I see no shapes but the keen stars:
Others, with burning eyes, lean forth, and drink
With eager lips the wind of their own speed,
As if the thing they loved fled on before,
And now, even now, they clasped it. Their bright
   locks
Stream like a comet's flashing hair: they all
Sweep onward.
   DEM.   These are the immortal Hours,   140
Of whom thou didst demand. One waits for thee.
   ASIA.   A spirit with a dreadful countenance
Checks its dark chariot by the craggy gulf.
Unlike thy brethren, ghastly charioteer,
Who art thou? Whither wouldst thou bear me?
   Speak!
   SPIRIT.   I am the shadow of a destiny
More dread than is my aspect: ere yon planet
Has set, the darkness which ascends with me
Shall wrap in lasting night heaven's kingless throne.
   ASIA.   What meanest thou?
   PANTHEA.   That terrible shadow floats   150
Up from its throne, as may the lurid smoke
Of earthquake-ruined cities o'er the sea.

Lo! it ascends the car; the coursers fly
Terrified: watch its path among the stars
Blackening the night!
   ASIA.   Thus I am answered: strange!
   PANTHEA.   See, near the verge, another chariot
   stays;
An ivory shell inlaid with crimson fire,
Which comes and goes within its sculptured rim
Of delicate strange tracery; the young spirit
That guides it has the dove-like eyes of hope;   160
How its soft smiles attract the soul! as light
Lures wingèd insects through the lampless air.

SPIRIT

My coursers are fed with the lightning,
   They drink of the whirlwind's stream,
And when the red morning is bright'ning
   They bathe in the fresh sunbeam;
   They have strength for their swiftness I deem,
Then ascend with me, daughter of Ocean.

I desire: and their speed makes night kindle;
   I fear they outstrip the Typhoon;   170
Ere the cloud piled on Atlas can dwindle
   We encircle the earth and the moon:
   We shall rest from long labours at noon:
Then ascend with me, daughter of Ocean.

SCENE V—The Car pauses within a Cloud on the top of a snowy Mountain. ASIA, PANTHEA, and the SPIRIT OF THE HOUR.

SPIRIT

On the brink of the night and the morning
   My courses are wont to respire;
But the Earth has just whispered a warning
   That their flight must be swifter than fire;
   They shall drink the hot speed of desire!

   ASIA.   Thou breathest on their nostrils, but my
   breath
Would give them swifter speed.
   SPIRIT.   Alas! it could not.
   PANTHEA.   Oh Spirit! pause, and tell whence is
   the light
Which fills this cloud? the sun is yet unrisen.
   SPIRIT.   The sun will rise not until noon.
   Apollo   10
Is held in heaven by wonder; and the light
Which fills this vapour, as the aëreal hue

Of fountain-gazing roses fills the water,
Flows from thy mighty sister.
    PANTHEA.   Yes, I feel—
    ASIA.   What is it with thee, sister? Thou art pale.
    PANTHEA.   How thou art changed! I dare not
      look on thee;
I feel but see thee not. I scarce endure
The radiance of thy beauty. Some good change
Is working in the elements, which suffer
Thy presence thus unveiled. The Nereids tell   20
That on the day when the clear hyaline
Was cloven at thine uprise, and thou didst stand
Within a veinèd shell, which floated on
Over the calm floor of the crystal sea,
Among the Ægean isles, and by the shores
Which bear thy name; love, like the atmosphere
Of the sun's fire filling the living world,
Burst from thee, and illumined earth and heaven
And the deep ocean and the sunless caves
And all that dwells within them; till grief cast   30
Eclipse upon the soul from which it came:
Such art thou now; nor is it I alone,
Thy sister, thy companion, thine own chosen one,
But the whole world which seeks thy sympathy.
Hearest thou not sounds i' the air which speak the
    love
Of all articulate beings? Feelest thou not
The inanimate winds enamoured of thee? List!

[*Music.*]

    ASIA.   Thy words are sweeter than aught else but
    his
Whose echoes they are: yet all love is sweet,
Given or returned. Common as light is love,   40
And its familiar voice wearies not ever.
Like the wide heaven, the all-sustaining air,
It makes the reptile equal to the God:
They who inspire it most are fortunate,
As I am now; but those who feel it most
Are happier still, after long sufferings,
As I shall soon become.
    PANTHEA.   List! Spirits speak.

VOICE IN THE AIR, *singing*

Life of Life! thy lips enkindle
    With their love the breath between them;
And thy smiles before they dwindle   50
    Make the cold air fire; then screen them

ACT II. SCENE V. **21. hyaline**: ocean.

In those looks, where whoso gazes
Faints, entangled in their mazes.

Child of Light! thy limbs are burning
    Through the vest which seems to hide them;
As the radiant lines of morning
    Through the clouds ere they divide them;
And this atmosphere divinest
Shrouds thee wheresoe'er thou shinest.

Fair are others; none beholds thee,   60
    But thy voice sounds low and tender
Like the fairest, for it folds thee
    From the sight, that liquid splendour,
And all feel, yet see thee never,
As I feel now, lost for ever!

Lamp of Earth! where'er thou movest
    Its dim shapes are clad with brightness,
And the souls of whom thou lovest
Walk upon the winds with lightness,
Till they fail, as I am failing,   70
Dizzy, lost, yet unbewailing!

ASIA

My soul is an enchanted boat,
    Which, like a sleeping swan, doth float
Upon the silver waves of thy sweet singing;
    And thine doth like an angel sit
    Beside a helm conducting it,
Whilst all the winds with melody are ringing.
    It seems to float ever, for ever,
    Upon that many-winding river,
    Between mountains, woods, abysses,   80
    A paradise of wildernesses!
Till, like one in slumber bound,
Borne to the ocean, I float down, around,
Into a sea profound, of ever-spreading sound:

    Meanwhile thy spirit lifts its pinions
    In music's most serene dominions;
Catching the winds that fan that happy heaven.
    And we sail on, away, afar,
    Without a course, without a star,
But, by the instinct of sweet music driven;   90
    Till through Elysian garden islets
    By thee, most beautiful of pilots,
    Where never mortal pinnace glided,
    The boat of my desire is guided;
Realms where the air we breathe is love,
Which in the winds and on the waves doth move,
Harmonizing this earth with what we feel above.

We have passed Age's icy caves,
  And Manhood's dark and tossing waves,
And Youth's smooth ocean, smiling to betray: 100
  Beyond the glassy gulfs we flee
  Of shadow-peopled Infancy,
Through Death and Birth, to a diviner day;
  A paradise of vaulted bowers,
  Lit by downward-gazing flowers,
  And watery paths that wind between
  Wildernesses calm and green,
Peopled by shapes too bright to see,
And rest, having beheld; somewhat like thee;
Which walk upon the sea, and chant
   melodiously!   110

END OF THE SECOND ACT

ACT III

SCENE I—*Heaven.* JUPITER *on his Throne;*
THETIS *and the other* DEITIES *assembled.*

JUPITER.   Ye congregated powers of heaven,
   who share
The glory and the strength of him ye serve,
Rejoice, henceforth I am omnipotent.
All else had been subdued to me; alone
The soul of man, like unextinguished fire,
Yet burns towards heaven with fierce reproach, and
   doubt,
And lamentation, and reluctant prayer,
Hurling up insurrection, which might make
Our antique empire insecure, though built
On eldest faith, and hell's coeval, fear;   10
And though my curses through the pendulous air,
Like snow on herbless peaks, fall flake by flake,
And cling to it; though under my wrath's night
It climbs the crags of life, step after step,
Which wound it, as ice wounds unsandalled feet,
It yet remains supreme o'er misery,
Aspiring, unrepressed, yet soon to fall:
Even now have I begotten a strange wonder,
That fatal child, the terror of the earth,
Who waits but till the destined hour arrive,   20
Bearing from Demogorgon's vacant throne
The dreadful might of ever-living limbs
Which clothed that awful spirit unbeheld,

To redescend, and trample out the spark.
Pour forth heaven's wine, Idæan Ganymede,
And let it fill the Dædal cups like fire,
And from the flower-inwoven soil divine
Ye all-triumphant harmonies arise,
As dew from earth under the twilight stars:
Drink! be the nectar circling through your veins   30
The soul of joy, ye ever-living Gods,
Till exultation burst in one wide voice
Like music from Elysian winds.
                    And thou
Ascend beside me, veilèd in the light
Of the desire which makes thee one with me,
Thetis, bright image of eternity!
When thou didst cry, "Insufferable might!
God! Spare me! I sustain not the quick flames,
The penetrating presence; all my being,
Like him whom the Numidian seps did thaw   40
Into a dew with poison, is dissolved,
Sinking through its foundations:" even then
Two mighty spirits, mingling, made a third
Mightier than either, which, unbodied now,
Between us floats, felt, although unbeheld,
Waiting the incarnation, which ascends,
(Hear ye the thunder of the fiery wheels
Griding the winds?) from Demogorgon's throne.
Victory! victory! Feel'st thou not, O world,
The earthquake of his chariot thundering up   50
Olympus?

[*The Car of the* HOUR *arrives.* DEMOGORGON
descends, and moves towards the Throne of
JUPITER.]

         Awful shape, what art thou? Speak!
   DEM.   Eternity. Demand no direr name.
Descend, and follow me down the abyss.
I am thy child, as thou wert Saturn's child;
Mightier than thee: and we must dwell together
Henceforth in darkness. Lift thy lightnings not.
The tyranny of heaven none may retain,
Or reassume, or hold, succeeding thee:
Yet if thou wilt, as 'tis the destiny
Of trodden worms to writhe till they are dead,   60
Put forth thy might.
   JUPITER.   Detested prodigy!

ACT III. SCENE I. **19. fatal child:** Jupiter's son by Thetis
who will eventually conquer Demogorgon.

25. Idæan Ganymede: cupbearer of the gods on Mt.
Ida. **40. him:** Sabellus, a Roman soldier. **seps:** a poisonous serpent. **48. Griding:** penetrating.

Even thus beneath the deep Titanian prisons
I trample thee! thou lingerest?

              Mercy! mercy!
No pity, no release, no respite! Oh,
That thou wouldst make mine enemy my judge,
Even where he hangs, seared by my long revenge,
On Caucasus! he would not doom me thus.
Gentle, and just, and dreadless, is he not
The monarch of the world? What then art thou?
No refuge! no appeal!

            Sink with me then,   70
We two will sink on the wide waves of ruin,
Even as a vulture and a snake outspent
Drop, twisted in inextricable fight,
Into a shoreless sea. Let hell unlock
Its moulded oceans of tempestuous fire,
And whelm on them into the bottomless void
This desolated world, and thee, and me,
The conqueror and the conquered, and the wreck
Of that for which they combated.
                  Ai! Ai!
The elements obey me not. I sink   80
Dizzily down, ever, for ever, down.
And, like a cloud, mine enemy above
Darkens my fall with victory! Ai, Ai!

SCENE II—*The Mouth of a great River in the
Island Atlantis.* OCEAN *is discovered reclining
near the Shore;* APOLLO *stands beside him.*

OCEAN.   He fell, thou sayest, beneath his
    conqueror's frown?
APOLLO.   Ay, when the strife was ended which
    made dim
The orb I rule, and shook the solid stars,
The terrors of his eye illumined heaven
With sanguine light, through the thick ragged skirts
Of the victorious darkness, as he fell:
Like the last glare of day's red agony,
Which, from a rent among the fiery clouds,
Burns far along the tempest-wrinkled deep.
   OCEAN.   He sunk to the abyss? To the dark
    void?
                                10
   APOLLO.   An eagle so caught in some bursting
    cloud
On Caucasus, his thunder-baffled wings

79. Ai: Greek for "woe," "alas."

Entangled in the whirlwind, and his eyes
Which gazed on the undazzling sun, now blinded
By the white lightning, while the ponderous hail
Beats on his struggling form, which sinks at length
Prone, and the aëreal ice clings over it.
   OCEAN.   Henceforth the fields of heaven-
    reflecting sea
Which are my realm, will heave, unstained with
    blood,
Beneath the uplifting winds, like plains of corn   20
Swayed by the summer air; my streams will flow
Round many-peopled continents, and round
Fortunate isles; and from their glassy thrones
Blue Proteus and his humid nymphs shall mark
The shadow of fair ships, as mortals see
The floating bark of the light-laden moon
With that white star, its sightless pilot's crest,
Borne down the rapid sunset's ebbing sea;
Tracking their path no more by blood and groans,
And desolation, and the mingled voice   30
Of slavery and command; but by the light
Of wave-reflected flowers, and floating odours,
And music soft, and mild, free, gentle voices,
And sweetest music, such as spirits love.
   APOLLO.   And I shall gaze not on the deeds
    which make
My mind obscure with sorrow, as eclipse
Darkens the sphere I guide; but list, I hear
The small, clear, silver lute of the young Spirit
That sits i' the morning star.
   OCEAN.   Thou must away;
Thy steeds will pause at even, till when
    farewell: 40
The loud deep calls me home even now to feed it
With azure calm out of the emerald urns
Which stand for ever full beside my throne.
Behold the Nereids under the green sea,
Their wavering limbs borne on the wind-like stream,
Their white arms lifted o'er their streaming hair
With garlands pied and starry sea-flower crowns,
Hastening to grace their mighty sister's joy.
             [*A sound of waves is heard.*]
It is the unpastured sea hungering for calm.
Peace, monster; I come now. Farewell.
   APOLLO.   Farewell.   50

SCENE III—*Caucasus.* PROMETHEUS, HERCU-
LES, IONE, *the* EARTH, SPIRITS, ASIA, *and* PAN-

THEA, *borne in the Car with the* SPIRIT OF THE HOUR. HERCULES *unbinds* PROMETHEUS, *who descends.*

HERCULES.   Most glorious among Spirits, thus
    doth strength
To wisdom, courage, and long-suffering love,
And thee, who art the form they animate,
Minister like a slave.
    PRO.   Thy gentle words
Are sweeter even than freedom long desired
And long delayed.
             Asia, thou light of life,
Shadow of beauty unbeheld: and ye,
Fair sister nymphs, who made long years of pain
Sweet to remember, through your love and care:
Henceforth we will not part. There is a cave,   10
All overgrown with trailing odorous plants,
Which curtain out the day with leaves and flowers,
And paved with veinèd emerald, and a fountain
Leaps in the midst with an awakening sound.
From its curved roof the mountain's frozen tears
Like snow, or silver, or long diamond spires,
Hang downward, raining forth a doubtful light:
And there is heard the ever-moving air,
Whispering without from tree to tree, and birds,
And bees; and all around are mossy seats,   20
And the rough walls are clothed with long soft grass;
A simple dwelling, which shall be our own;
Where we will sit and talk of time and change,
As the world ebbs and flows, ourselves unchanged.
What can hide man from mutability?
And if ye sigh, then I will smile; and thou,
Ione, shalt chant fragments of sea-music,
Until I weep, when ye shall smile away
The tears she brought, which yet were sweet to shed.
We will entangle buds and flowers and beams   30
Which twinkle on the fountain's brim, and make
Strange combinations out of common things,
Like human babes in their brief innocence;
And we will search, with looks and words of love,
For hidden thoughts, each lovelier than the last,
Our unexhausted spirits; and like lutes
Touched by the skill of the enamoured wind,
Weave harmonies divine, yet ever new,
From difference sweet where discord cannot be;
And hither come, sped on the charmèd winds,   40
Which meet from all the points of heaven, as bees
From every flower aëreal Enna feeds,

At their known island-homes in Himera,
The echoes of the human world, which tell
Of the low voice of love, almost unheard,
And dove-eyed pity's murmured pain, and music,
Itself the echo of the heart, and all
That tempers or improves man's life, now free;
And lovely apparitions,—dim at first,
Then radiant, as the mind, arising bright   50
From the embrace of beauty (whence the forms
Of which these are the phantoms), casts on them
The gathered rays which are reality—
Shall visit us, the progeny immortal
Of Paintings, Sculpture, and rapt Poesy,
And arts, though unimagined, yet to be.
The wandering voices and the shadows these
Of all that man becomes, the mediators
Of that best worship, love, by him and us
Given and returned; swift shapes and sounds,
    which grow   60
More fair and soft as man grows wise and kind,
And, veil by veil, evil and error fall:
Such virtue has the cave and place around.
       [*Turning to the* SPIRIT OF THE HOUR.]
For thee, fair Spirit, one toil remains. Ione,
Give her that curvèd shell, which Proteus old
Made Asia's nuptial boon, breathing within it
A voice to be accomplished, and which thou
Didst hide in grass under the hollow rock.
    IONE.   Thou most desired Hour, more loved and
    lovely
Than all thy sisters, this is the mystic shell;   70
See the pale azure fading into silver
Lining it with a soft yet glowing light:
Looks it not like lulled music sleeping there?
    SPIRIT.   It seems in truth the fairest shell of
    Ocean:
Its sound must be at once both sweet and strange.
    PRO.   Go, borne over the cities of mankind
On whirlwind-footed coursers: once again
Outspeed the sun around the orbèd world;
And as thy chariot cleaves the kindling air,
Thou breathe into the many-folded shell,   80
Loosening its mighty music; it shall be
As thunder mingled with clear echoes: then
Return; and thou shalt dwell beside our cave.

ACT III. SCENE III. **42. Enna:** ancient Sicilian town. **43. Himera:** district on the north coast of Sicily.

And thou, O, Mother Earth!—

THE EARTH.   I hear, I feel;
Thy lips are on me, and their touch runs down
Even to the adamantine central gloom
Along these marble nerves; 'tis life, 'tis joy,
And through my withered, old, and icy frame
The warmth of an immortal youth shoots down
Circling. Henceforth the many children fair   90
Folded in my sustaining arms; all plants,
And creeping forms, and insects rainbow-winged,
And birds, and beasts, and fish, and human shapes,
Which drew disease and pain from my wan bosom,
Draining the poison of despair, shall take
And interchange sweet nutriment; to me
Shall they become like sister-antelopes
By one fair dam, snow-white and swift as wind,
Nursed among lilies near a brimming stream.
The dew-mists of my sunless sleep shall float   100
Under the stars like balm: night-folded flowers
Shall suck unwithering hues in their repose:
And men and beasts in happy dreams shall gather
Strength for the coming day, and all its joy:
And death shall be the last embrace of her
Who takes the life she gave, even as a mother
Folding her child, says, "Leave me not again."

ASIA.   Oh, mother! wherefore speak the name of
      death?
Cease they to love, and move, and breathe, and
      speak,
Who die?

THE EARTH.   It would avail not to reply: 110
Thou art immortal, and this tongue is known
But to the uncommunicating dead.
Death is the veil which those who live call life:
They sleep, and it is lifted: and meanwhile
In mild variety the seasons mild
With rainbow-skirted showers, and odorous winds,
And long blue meteors cleansing the dull night,
And the life-kindling shafts of the keen sun's
All-piercing bow, and the dew-mingled rain
Of the calm moonbeams, a soft influence mild,   120
Shall clothe the forests and the fields, ay, even
The crag-built deserts of the barren deep,
With ever-living leaves, and fruits, and flowers.
And thou! There is a cavern where my spirit
Was panted forth in anguish whilst thy pain
Made my heart mad, and those who did inhale it
Became mad too, and built a temple there,
And spoke, and were oracular, and lured
The erring nations round to mutual war,

And faithless faith, such as Jove kept with
      thee;   130
Which breath now rises, as amongst tall weeds
A violet's exhalation, and it fills
With a serener light and crimson air
Intense, yet soft, the rocks and woods around;
It feeds the quick growth of the serpent vine,
And the dark linked ivy tangling wild,
And budding, blown, or odour-faded blooms
Which star the winds with points of coloured light,
As they rain through them, and bright golden globes
Of fruit, suspended in their own green heaven,   140
And through their veinèd leaves and amber stems
The flowers whose purple and translucid bowls
Stand ever mantling with aëreal dew,
The drink of spirits: and it circles round,
Like the soft waving wings of noonday dreams,
Inspiring calm and happy thoughts, like mine,
Now thou art thus restored. This cave is thine.
Arise! Appear!
[A SPIRIT *rises in the likeness of a winged child.*]
                  This is my torch-bearer;
Who let his lamp out in old time with gazing
On eyes from which he kindled it anew   150
With love, which is as fire, sweet daughter mine,
For such is that within thine own. Run, wayward,
And guide this company beyond the peak
Of Bacchic Nysa, Mænad-haunted mountain,
And beyond Indus and its tribute rivers,
Trampling the torrent streams and glassy lakes
With feet unwet, unwearied, undelaying,
And up the green ravine, across the vale,
Beside the windless and crystalline pool,
Where ever lies, on unerasing waves,   160
The image of a temple, built above,
Distinct with column, arch, and architrave,
And palm-like capital, and over-wrought,
And populous with most living imagery,
Praxitelean shapes, whose marble smiles
Fill the hushed air with everlasting love.
It is deserted now, but once it bore
Thy name, Prometheus; there the emulous youths
Bore to thy honour through the divine gloom
The lamp which was thine emblem: even as
      those   170
Who bear the untransmitted torch of hope
Into the grave, across the night of life,

---

154. Nysa: mountain where Bacchus was nursed by the
Mænads.

As thou hast borne it most triumphantly
To this far goal of Time. Depart, farewell.
Beside that temple is the destined cave.

SCENE IV—*A Forest. In the Background a
Cave.* PROMETHEUS, ASIA, PANTHEA, IONE, *and
the* SPIRIT OF THE EARTH.

IONE.   Sister, it is not earthly: how it glides
Under the leaves! how on its head there burns
A light, like a green star, whose emerald beams
Are twined with its fair hair! how, as it moves,
The splendour drops in flakes upon the grass!
Knowest thou it?
PANTHEA.   It is the delicate spirit
That guides the earth through heaven. From afar
The populous constellations call that light
The loveliest of the planets; and sometimes
It floats along the spray of the salt sea,   10
Or makes its chariot of a foggy cloud,
Or walks through fields or cities while men sleep,
Or o'er the mountain tops, or down the rivers,
Or through the green waste wilderness, as now,
Wondering at all it sees. Before Jove reigned
It loved our sister Asia, and it came
Each leisure hour to drink the liquid light
Out of her eyes, for which it said it thirsted
As one bit by a dipsas, and with her
It made its childish confidence, and told her   20
All it had known or seen, for it saw much,
Yet idly reasoned what it saw; and called her—
For whence it sprung it knew not, nor do I—
Mother, dear mother.
THE SPIRIT OF THE EARTH (*running to* ASIA).
            Mother, dearest mother;
May I then talk with thee as I was wont?
May I then hide my eyes in thy soft arms,
After thy looks have made them tired of joy?
May I then play beside thee long noons,
When work is none in the bright silent air?
ASIA.   I love thee, gentlest being, and
    henceforth   30
Can cherish thee unenvied: speak, I pray:
Thy simple talk once solaced, now delights.
SPIRIT OF THE EARTH.   Mother, I am grown
    wiser, though a child
Cannot be wise like thee, within this day;

ACT III. SCENE IV. **19. dipsas:** serpent whose bite caused
unbearable thirst.

And happier too; happier and wiser both.
Thou knowest that toads, and snakes, and loathly
    worms,
And venomous and malicious beasts, and boughs
That bore ill berries in the woods, were ever
An hindrance to my walks o'er the green world:
And that, among the haunts of humankind,   40
Hard-featured men, or with proud, angry looks,
Or cold, staid gait, or false and hollow smiles,
Or the dull sneer of self-loved ignorance,
Or other such foul masks, with which ill thoughts
Hide that fair being whom we spirits call man;
And women too, ugliest of all things evil,
(Though fair, even in a world where thou art fair,
When good and kind, free and sincere like thee),
When false or frowning, made me sick at heart
To pass them, though they slept, and I unseen.   50
Well, my path lately lay through a great city
Into the woody hills surrounding it:
A sentinel was sleeping at the gate:
When there was heard a sound, so loud, it shook
The towers amid the moonlight, yet more sweet
Than any voice but thine, sweetest of all;
A long, long sound, as it would never end:
And all the inhabitants leaped suddenly
Out of their rest, and gathered in the streets,
Looking in wonder up to Heaven, while yet   60
The music pealed along. I hid myself
Within a fountain in the public square,
Where I lay like the reflex of the moon
Seen in a wave under green leaves; and soon
Those ugly human shapes and visages
Of which I spoke as having wrought me pain,
Passed floating through the air, and fading still
Into the winds that scattered them; and those
From whom they passed seemed mild and lovely
    forms
After some foul disguise had fallen, and all   70
Were somewhat changed, and after brief surprise
And greetings of delighted wonder, all
Went to their sleep again: and when the dawn
Came, wouldst thou think that toads, and snakes,
    and efts,
Could e'er be beautiful? yet so they were,
And that with little change of shape or hue:
All things had put their evil nature off:
I cannot tell my joy, when o'er a lake
Upon a drooping bough with nightshade twined,
I saw two azure halcyons clinging downward   80
And thinning one bright bunch of amber berries,

With quick long beaks, and in the deep there lay
Those lovely forms imaged as in a sky;
So, with my thoughts full of these happy changes,
We meet again, the happiest change of all.
    ASIA.   And never will we part, till thy chaste
        sister
Who guides the frozen and inconstant moon
Will look on thy more warm and equal light
Till her heart thaw like flakes of April snow
And love thee.
    SPIRIT OF THE EARTH.   What; as Asia loves Pro-
        metheus?   90
    ASIA.   Peace, wanton, thou art yet not old
        enough.
Think ye by gazing on each other's eyes
To multiply your lovely selves, and fill
With spherèd fires the interlunar air?
    SPIRIT OF THE EARTH.   Nay, mother, while my
        sister trims her lamp
'Tis hard I should go darkling.
    ASIA.   Listen; look!

[The SPIRIT OF THE HOUR *enters.]*

    PRO.   We feel what thou hast heard and seen:
        yet speak.
    SPIRIT OF THE HOUR.   Soon as the sound had
        ceased whose thunder filled
The abysses of the sky and the wide earth,
There was a change: the impalpable thin air   100
And the all-circling sunlight were transformed,
As if the sense of love dissolved in them
Had folded itself round the spherèd world.
My vision then grew clear, and I could see
Into the mysteries of the universe:
Dizzy as with delight I floated down,
Winnowing the lightsome air with languid plumes,
My coursers sought their birthplace in the sun,
Where they henceforth will live exempt from toil,
Pasturing flowers of vegetable fire;   110
And where my moonlike car will stand within
A temple, gazed upon by Phidian forms
Of thee, and Asia, and the Earth, and me,
And you fair nymphs looking the love we feel,—
In memory of the tidings it has borne,—
Beneath a dome fretted with graven flowers,
Poised on twelve columns of resplendent stone,
And open to the bright and liquid sky.

86. **chaste sister:** Diana, the moon-goddess.

Yoked to it by an amphisbænic snake
The likeness of those wingèd steeds will mock   120
The flight from which they find repose. Alas,
Whither has wandered now my partial tongue
When all remains untold which ye would hear?
As I have said, I floated to the earth:
It was, as it is still, the pain of bliss
To move, to breathe, to be; I wandering went
Among the haunts and dwellings of mankind,
And first was disappointed not to see
Such mighty change as I had felt within
Expressed in outward things; but soon I
    looked,   130
And behold, thrones were kingless, and men walked
One with the other even as spirits do,
None fawned, none trampled; hate, disdain, or fear,
Self-love or self-contempt, on human brows
No more inscribed, as o'er the gate of hell,
"All hope abandon ye who enter here";
None frowned, none trembled, none with eager fear
Gazed on another's eye of cold command,
Until the subject of a tyrant's will
Became, worse fate, the abject of his own,   140
Which spurred him, like an outspent horse, to death.
None wrought his lips in truth-entangling lines
Which smiled the lie his tongue disdained to speak;
None, with firm sneer, trod out in his own heart
The sparks of love and hope till there remained
Those bitter ashes, a soul self-consumed,
And the wretch crept a vampire among men,
Infecting all with his own hideous ill;
None talked that common, false, cold, hollow talk
Which makes the heart deny the *yes* it
    breathes,   150
Yet question that unmeant hypocrisy
With such a self-mistrust as has no name.
And women, too, frank, beautiful, and kind
As the free heaven which rains fresh light and dew
On the wide earth, past; gentle radiant forms,
From custom's evil taint exempt and pure;
Speaking the wisdom once they could not think,
Looking emotions once they feared to feel,
And changed to all which once they dared not be,
Yet being now, made earth like heaven; nor
    pride,   160
Nor jealousy, nor envy, nor ill shame,

119. **amphisbænic snake:** mythical serpent with a head
at each end, and capable of moving in either direction.
136. **"All . . . here":** the famous warning inscribed over
the entrance to Hell in Dante's *Inferno.*

The bitterest of those drops of treasured gall,
Spoilt the sweet taste of the nepenthe, love.

Thrones, altars, judgment-seats, and prisons—
    wherein,
And beside which, by wretched men were borne
Sceptres, tiaras, swords, and chains, and tomes
Of reasoned wrong, glozed on by ignorance,
Were like those monstrous and barbaric shapes,
The ghosts of a no-more-remembered fame,
Which, from their unworn obelisks, look forth   170
In triumph o'er the palaces and tombs
Of those who were their conquerors, mouldering
    round.
These imaged, to the pride of kings and priests,
A dark yet mighty faith, a power as wide
As is the world it wasted, and are now
But an astonishment; even so the tools
And emblems of its last captivity,
Amid the dwellings of the peopled earth,
Stand, not o'erthrown, but unregarded now.
And those foul shapes, abhorred by god and
    man,—   180
Which, under many a name and many a form
Strange, savage, ghastly, dark and execrable,
Were Jupiter, the tyrant of the world;
And which the nations, panic-stricken, served
With blood, and hearts broken by long hope, and
    love
Dragged to his altars soiled and garlandless,
And slain amid men's unreclaiming tears,
Flattering the thing they feared, which fear was
    hate,—
Frown, mouldering fast, o'er their abandoned
    shrines:
The painted veil, by those who were, called
    life,   190
Which mimicked, as with colours idly spread,
All men believed or hoped, is torn aside;
The loathsome mask has fallen, the man remains
Sceptreless, free, uncircumscribed, but man
Equal, unclassed, tribeless, and nationless,
Exempt from awe, worship, degree, the king
Over himself; just, gentle, wise: but man
Passionless?—no, yet free from guilt or pain,
Which were, for his will made or suffered them,
Nor yet exempt, though ruling them like
    slaves,   200
From chance, and death, and mutability,

167. glozed on: explained, glossed.

The clogs of that which else might oversoar
The loftiest star of unascended heaven,
Pinnacled dim in the intense inane.

END OF THE THIRD ACT

ACT IV

SCENE—*A Part of the Forest near the Cave of*
PROMETHEUS. PANTHEA *and* IONE *are sleeping:*
they awaken gradually during the first Song.

VOICE OF UNSEEN SPIRITS

The pale stars are gone!
  For the sun, their swift shepherd,
  To their folds them compelling,
    In the depths of the dawn,
Hastes, in the meteor-eclipsing array, and they flee
  Beyond his blue dwelling,
    As fawns flee the leopard.
      But where are ye?

A Train of dark FORMS *and* SHADOWS *passes*
    by confusedly, singing.

    Here, oh, here:
    We bear the bier   10
Of the Father of many a cancelled year.
    Spectres we
    Of the dead Hours be,
We bear Time to his tomb in eternity.

    Strew, oh, strew
    Hair, not yew!
Wet the dusty pall with tears, not dew!
    Be the faded flowers
    Of Death's bare bowers
Spread on the corpse of the King of Hours!   20

    Haste, oh, haste!
    As shades are chased,
Trembling, by day, from heaven's blue waste.
    We melt away,
    Like dissolving spray,
From the children of a diviner day,
    With the lullaby
    Of winds that die
On the bosom of their own harmony!

IONE

What dark forms were they?   30

PANTHEA

The past Hours weak and gray,
With the spoil which their toil
  Raked together
From the conquest but One could foil.

IONE

Have they passed?

PANTHEA

            They have passed;
They outspeeded the blast,
While 'tis said, they are fled—

IONE

Whither, oh, whither?

PANTHEA

To the dark, to the past, to the dead.

VOICE OF UNSEEN SPIRITS

Bright clouds float in heaven,   40
Dew-stars gleam on earth,
Waves assemble on ocean,
They are gathered and driven
By the storm of delight, by the panic of glee!
They shake with emotion,
They dance in their mirth.
      But where are ye?

The pine boughs are singing
Old songs with new gladness,
The billows and fountains   50
Fresh music are flinging,
Like the notes of a spirit from land and from sea;
The storms mock the mountains
With the thunder of gladness.
      But where are ye?

IONE.   What charioteers are these?
PANTHEA.   Where are their chariots?

SEMICHORUS OF HOURS

The voice of the Spirits of Air and of Earth
  Have drawn back the figured curtain of sleep
Which covered our being and darkened our birth
  In the deep.

A VOICE

In the deep?

SEMICHORUS II

Oh, below the deep.   60

SEMICHORUS I

An hundred ages we had been kept
  Cradled in visions of hate and care,
And each one who waked as his brother slept,
  Found the truth—

SEMICHORUS II

  Worse than his visions were!

SEMICHORUS I

We have heard the lute of Hope in sleep;
  We have known the voice of Love in dreams;
We have felt the wand of Power, and leap—

SEMICHORUS II

  As the billows leap in the morning beams!

CHORUS

Weave the dance on the floor of the breeze,
  Pierce with song heaven's silent light,   70
Enchant the day that too swiftly flees,
  To check its flight ere the cave of Night.

Once the hungry Hours were hounds
  Which chased the day like a bleeding deer,
And it limped and stumbled with many wounds
  Through the nightly dells of the desert year.

But now, oh weave the mystic measure
  Of music, and dance, and shapes of light,
Let the Hours, and the spirits of might and pleasure,
  Like the clouds and sunbeams, unite.

A VOICE

                        Unite!   80

PANTHEA.   See, where the Spirits of the human
      mind
Wrapped in sweet sounds, as in bright veils,
      approach.

CHORUS OF SPIRITS

We join the throng
  Of the dance and the song,
By the whirlwind of gladness borne along;
  As the flying-fish leap
  From the Indian deep,
And mix with the sea-birds, half asleep.

CHORUS OF HOURS

Whence come ye, so wild and so fleet,
For sandals of lightning are on your feet,   90
And your wings are soft and swift as thought,
And your eyes are as love which is veilèd not?

CHORUS OF SPIRITS

We come from the mind
Of human kind
Which was late so dusk, and obscene, and blind;
Now 'tis an ocean
Of clear emotion,
A heaven of serene and mighty motion.

From that deep abyss
Of wonder and bliss,   100
Whose caverns are crystal palaces;
From those skiey towers
Where Thought's crowned powers
Sit watching your dance, ye happy Hours!

From the dim recesses
Of woven caresses,
Where lovers catch ye by your loose tresses;
From the azure isles,
Where sweet Wisdom smiles,
Delaying your ships with her siren wiles.   110

From the temples high
Of Man's ear and eye,
Roofed over Sculpture and Poesy;
From the murmurings
Of the unsealed springs
Where Science bedews her Dædal wings.

Years after years,
Through blood, and tears,
And a thick hell of hatreds, and hopes, and fears,
We waded and flew,   120
And the islets were few
Where the bud-blighted flowers of happiness grew.

Our feet now, every palm,
Are sandalled with calm,
And the dew of our winds is a rain of balm;
And beyond our eyes
The human love lies
Which makes all it gazes on Paradise.

CHORUS OF SPIRITS AND HOURS

Then weave the web of the mystic measure;
From the depths of the sky and the ends of the
    earth,   130

Come, swift Spirits of might and of pleasure,
Fill the dance and the music of mirth,
As the waves of a thousand streams rush by
To an ocean of splendour and harmony!

CHORUS OF SPIRITS

Our spoil is won,
Our task is done,
We are free to dive, or soar, or run;
Beyond and around,
Or within the bound
Which clips the world with darkness round   140

We'll pass the eyes
Of the starry skies
Into the hoar deep to colonize:
Death, Chaos, and Night,
From the sound of our flight,
Shall flee, like mist from a tempest's might.

And Earth, Air, and Light,
And the Spirit of Might,
Which drives round the stars in their fiery flight;
And Love, Thought, and Breath,   150
The powers that quell Death,
Wherever we soar shall assemble beneath.

And our singing shall build
In the void's loose field
A world for the Spirit of Wisdom to wield;
We will take our plan
From the new world of man,
And our work shall be called the Promethean.

CHORUS OF HOURS

Break the dance, and scatter the song:
Let some depart, and some remain.   160

SEMICHORUS I

We, beyond heaven, are driven along:

SEMICHORUS II

Us the enchantments of earth retain:

SEMICHORUS I

Ceaseless, and rapid, and fierce, and free,
With the Spirits which build a new earth and sea,
And a heaven where yet heaven could never be.

SEMICHORUS II

Solemn, and slow, and serene, and bright,
Leading the Day and outspeeding the Night,
With the powers of a world of perfect light.

SEMICHORUS I

We whirl, singing loud, round the gathering sphere,
Till the trees, and the beasts, and the clouds
    appear   170
From its chaos made calm by love, not fear.

SEMICHORUS II

We encircle the ocean and mountains of earth,
And the happy forms of its death and birth
Change to the music of our sweet mirth.

CHORUS OF HOURS AND SPIRITS

Break the dance, and scatter the song,
    Let some depart, and some remain,
Wherever we fly we lead along
In leashes, like starbeams, soft yet strong,
    The clouds that are heavy with love's sweet rain.

PANTHEA.   Ha! they are gone!
    IONE.   Yet feel you no delight   180
From the past sweetness?
    PANTHEA.   As the bare green hill
When some soft cloud vanishes into rain,
Laughs with a thousand drops of sunny water
To the unpavilioned sky!
    IONE.   Even whilst we speak
New notes arise. What is that awful sound?
    PANTHEA.   'Tis the deep music of the rolling
        world
Kindling within the strings of the waved air
Æolian modulations.
    IONE.   Listen too,
How every pause is filled with under-notes,
Clear, silver, icy, keen, awakening tones,   190
Which pierce the sense, and live within the soul,
As the sharp stars pierce winter's crystal air
And gaze upon themselves within the sea.
    PANTHEA.   But see where through two openings
        in the forest
Which hanging branches overcanopy,
And where two runnels of a rivulet,
Between the close moss violet-inwoven,
Have made their path of melody, like sisters
Who part with sighs that they may meet in smiles
Turning their dear disunion to an isle   200
Of lovely grief, a wood of sweet sad thoughts;
Two visions of strange radiance float upon
The ocean-like enchantment of strong sound,
Which flows intenser, keener, deeper yet
Under the ground and through the windless air.

IONE.   I see a chariot like that thinnest boat,
In which the Mother of the Months is borne
By ebbing light into her western cave,
When she upsprings from interlunar dreams;
O'er which is curved an orblike canopy   210
Of gentle darkness, and the hills and woods,
Distinctly seen through that dusk aery veil,
Regard like shapes in an enchanter's glass;
Its wheels are solid clouds, azure and gold,
Such as the genii of the thunderstorm
Pile on the floor of the illumined sea
When the sun rushes under it; they roll
And move and grow as with an inward wind;
Within it sits a wingèd infant, white
Its countenance, like the whiteness of bright
    snow,   220
Its plumes are as feathers of sunny frost,
Its limbs gleam white, through the wind-flowing
    folds
Of its white robe, woof of ethereal pearl.
Its hair is white, the brightness of white light
Scattered in strings; yet its two eyes are heavens
Of liquid darkness, which the Deity
Within seems pouring, as a storm is poured
From jagged clouds, out of their arrowy lashes,
Tempering the cold and radiant air around,
With fire that is not brightness; in its hand   230
It sways a quivering moonbeam, from whose point
A guiding power directs the chariot's prow
Over its wheelèd clouds, which as they roll
Over the grass, and flowers, and waves, wake
    sounds,
Sweet as a singing rain of silver dew.
    PANTHEA.   And from the other opening in the
        wood
Rushes, with loud and whirlwind harmony,
A sphere, which is as many thousand spheres,
Solid as crystal, yet through all its mass
Flow, as through empty space, music and
    light: 240
Ten thousand orbs involving and involved,
Purple and azure, white, and green, and golden,
Sphere within sphere; and every space between
Peopled with unimaginable shapes,
Such as ghosts dream dwell in the lampless deep,
Yet each inter-transpicuous, and they whirl
Over each other with a thousand motions,

ACT IV. **207. Mother of the Months:** Diana. **213. Regard:**
appear. **246. inter-transpicuous:** inter-transparent.

Upon a thousand sightless axles spinning,
And with the force of self-destroying swiftness,
Intensely, slowly, solemnly roll on,   250
Kindling with mingled sounds, and many tones,
Intelligible words and music wild.
With mighty whirl the multitudinous orb
Grinds the bright brook into an azure mist
Of elemental subtlety, like light;
And the wild odour of the forest flowers,
The music of the living grass and air,
The emerald light of leaf-entangled beams
Round its intense yet self-conflicting speed,
Seem kneaded into one aëreal mass   260
Which drowns the sense. Within the orb itself,
Pillowed upon its alabaster arms,
Like to a child o'erwearied with sweet toil,
On its own folded wings, and wavy hair,
The Spirit of the Earth is laid asleep,
And you can see its little lips are moving,
Amid the changing light of their own smiles,
Like one who talks of what he loves in dream.
    IONE.   'Tis only mocking the orb's harmony.
    PANTHEA.   And from a star upon its forehead,
       shoot,   270
Like swords of azure fire, or golden spears
With tyrant-quelling myrtle overtwined,
Embleming heaven and earth united now,
Vast beams like spokes of some invisible wheel
Which whirl as the orb whirls, swifter than thought,
Filling the abyss with sun-like lightenings,
And perpendicular now, and now transverse,
Pierce the dark soil, and as they pierce and pass,
Make bare the secrets of the earth's deep heart;
Infinite mines of adamant and gold,   280
Valueless stones, and unimagined gems,
And caverns on crystalline columns poised
With vegetable silver overspread;
Wells of unfathomed fire, and water springs
Whence the great sea, even as a child, is fed,
Whose vapours clothe earth's monarch mountain-
    tops
With kingly, ermine snow. The beams flash on
And make appear the melancholy ruins
Of cancelled cycles: anchors, beaks of ships;
Planks turned to marble; quivers, helms, and
    spears,   290

And gorgon-headed targes, and the wheels
Of scythèd chariots, and the emblazonry
Of trophies, standards, and armorial beasts,
Round which death laughed, sepulchred emblems
Of dead destruction, ruin within ruin!
The wrecks beside of many a city vast,
Whose population which the earth grew over
Was mortal, but not human; see, they lie,
Their monstrous works, and uncouth skeletons,
Their statues, homes and fanes; prodigious
    shapes   300
Huddled in gray annihilation, split,
Jammed in the hard, black deep; and over these,
The anatomies of unknown wingèd things,
And fishes which were isles of living scale,
And serpents, bony chains, twisted around
The iron crags, or within heaps of dust
To which the tortuous strength of their last pangs
Had crushed the iron crags; and over these
The jagged alligator, and the might
Of earth-convulsing behemoth, which once   310
Were monarch beasts, and on the slimy shores,
And weed-overgrown continents of earth,
Increased and multiplied like summer worms
On an abandoned corpse, till the blue globe
Wrapped deluge round it like a cloak, and they
Yelled, gasped, and were abolished; or some God
Whose throne was in a comet, passed, and cried,
"Be not!" And like my words they were no more.

THE EARTH

The joy, the triumph, the delight, the madness!
The boundless, overflowing, bursting glad-
    ness,   320
The vaporous exultation not to be confined!
  Ha! ha! the animation of delight
  Which wraps me, like an atmosphere of light,
And bears me as a cloud is borne by its own wind.

THE MOON

Brother mine, calm wanderer,
  Happy globe of land and air,
Some Spirit is darted like a beam from thee,
  Which penetrates my frozen frame,
  And passes with the warmth of flame,

272. **tyrant-quelling myrtle:** The slayers of the Athenian tyrant Hipparchus concealed their swords under branches of myrtle (symbolic of love). 281. **Valueless:** priceless.

291. **gorgon-headed targes:** shields decorated with the head of the mythical Medusa, the Gorgon. Those who looked on Medusa were turned to stone. 310. **behemoth:** the huge animal described in the Book of Job.

With love, and odour, and deep melody   330
    Through me, through me!

THE EARTH

Ha! ha! the caverns of my hollow mountains,
My cloven fire-crags, sound-exulting fountains
Laugh with a vast and inextinguishable laughter.
    The oceans, and the deserts, and the abysses,
    And the deep air's unmeasured wildernesses,
Answer from all their clouds and billows, echoing
    after.

They cry aloud as I do. Sceptred curse,
    Who all our green and azure universe
Threatenedst to muffle round with black destruc-
    tion, sending   340
    A solid cloud to rain hot thunderstones,
    And splinter and knead down my children's
    bones,
All I bring forth, to one void mass battering and
    blending,—

Until each crag-like tower, and storied column,
    Palace, and obelisk, and temple solemn,
My imperial mountains crowned with cloud, and
    snow, and fire;
    My sea-like forests, every blade and blossom
    Which finds a grave or cradle in my bosom,
Were stamped by thy strong hate into a lifeless
    mire:

How art thou sunk, withdrawn, covered, drunk
    up   350
    By thirsty nothing, as the brackish cup
Drained by a desert-troop, a little drop for all;
    And from beneath, around, within, above,
    Filling thy void annihilation, love
Bursts in like light on caves cloven by the thunder-
    ball.

THE MOON

The snow upon my lifeless mountains
Is loosened into living fountains,
My solid oceans flow, and sing, and shine:
    A spirit from my heart bursts forth,
    It clothes with unexpected birth   360
My cold bare bosom: Oh! it must be thine
    On mine, on mine!

Gazing on thee I feel, I know
Green stalks burst forth, and bright flowers grow,

And living shapes upon my bosom move:
    Music is in the sea and air,
    Wingèd clouds soar here and there,
Dark with the rain new buds are dreaming of:
    'Tis love, all love!

THE EARTH

It interpenetrates my granite mass,   370
    Through tangled roots and trodden clay doth pass
Into the utmost leaves and delicatest flowers;
    Upon the winds, among the clouds 'tis spread,
    It wakes a life in the forgotten dead,
They breathe a spirit up from their obscurest
    bowers.

And like a storm bursting its cloudy prison
    With thunder, and with whirlwind, has arisen
Out of the lampless caves of unimagined being:
    With earthquake shock and swiftness making
    shiver
    Thought's stagnant chaos, unremoved for
    ever,   380
Till hate, and fear, and pain, light-vanquished
    shadows, fleeing,

Leave Man, who was a many-sided mirror
    Which could distort to many a shape of error
This true fair world of things, a sea reflecting love;
    Which over all his kind, as the sun's heaven
    Gliding o'er ocean, smooth, serene, and even,
Darting from starry depths radiance and life, doth
    move:

Leave Man, even as a leprous child is left,
    Who follows a sick beast to some warm cleft
Of rocks, through which the might of healing
    springs is poured;   390
    Then when it wanders home with rosy smile,
    Unconscious, and its mother fears awhile
It is a spirit, then, weeps on her child restored.

Man, oh, not men! a chain of linkèd thought,
    Of love and might to be divided not,
Compelling the elements with adamantine stress;
    As the sun rules, even with a tyrant's gaze,
    The unquiet republic of the maze
Of planets, struggling fierce towards heaven's free
    wilderness.

Man, one harmonious soul of many a soul,   400
    Whose nature is its own divine control,

Where all things flow to all, as rivers to the sea;
  Familiar acts are beautiful through love;
  Labour, and pain, and grief, in life's green grove
Sport like tame beasts, none know how gentle they
      could be!

  His will, with all mean passions, bad delights,
  And selfish cares, its trembling satellites,
A spirit ill to guide, but mighty to obey,
  Is as a tempest-wingèd ship, whose helm
  Love rules, through waves which dare not over-
      whelm,   410
Forcing life's wildest shores to own its sovereign
    sway

  All things confess his strength. Through the cold
    mass
  Of marble and of colour his dreams pass;
Bright threads whence mothers weave the robes
    their children wear;
  Language is a perpetual Orphic song,
  Which rules with Dædal harmony a throng
Of thoughts and forms, which else senseless and
    shapeless were.

  The lightning is his slave; heaven's utmost deep
  Gives up her stars, and like a flock of sheep
They pass before his eye, are numbered, and roll
    on!   420
  The tempest is his steed, he strides the air;
  And the abyss shouts from her depth laid bare,
Heaven, hast thou secrets? Man unveils me; I have
    none.

THE MOON

  The shadow of white death has passed
  From my path in heaven at last,
A clinging shroud of solid frost and sleep;
  And through my newly-woven bowers,
  Wander happy paramours,
Less mighty, but as mild as those who keep
      Thy vales more deep.   430

THE EARTH

  As the dissolving warmth of dawn may fold
  A half unfrozen dew-globe, green, and gold,
And crystalline, till it becomes a wingèd mist,
  And wanders up the vault of the blue day,
  Outlives the noon, and on the sun's last ray
Hangs o'er the sea, a fleece of fire and amethyst.

THE MOON

  Thou art folded, thou art lying
  In the light which is undying
Of thine own joy, and heaven's smile divine;
  All suns and constellations shower   440
  On thee a light, a life, a power
Which doth array thy sphere; thou pourest thine
      On mine, on mine!

THE EARTH

  I spin beneath my pyramid of night,
  Which points into the heavens dreaming delight,
Murmuring victorious joy in my enchanted sleep;
  As a youth lulled in love-dreams faintly sighing,
  Under the shadow of his beauty lying,
Which round his rest a watch of light and warmth
    doth keep.

THE MOON

  As in the soft and sweet eclipse,   450
  When soul meets soul on lovers' lips,
High hearts are calm, and brightest eyes are dull;
  So when thy shadow falls on me,
  Then am I mute and still, by thee
Covered; of thy love, Orb most beautiful,
      Full, oh, too full!

  Thou art speeding round the sun
  Brightest world of many a one;
  Green and azure sphere which shinest
  With a light which is divinest   460
  Among all the lamps of Heaven
  To whom life and light is given;
  I, thy crystal paramour
  Borne beside thee by a power
  Like the polar Paradise
  Magnet-like of lovers' eyes;
  I, a most enamoured maiden
  Whose weak brain is overladen
  With the pleasure of her love,
  Maniac-like around thee move   470
  Gazing, an insatiate bride,
  On thy form from every side
  Like a Mænad, round the cup
  Which Agave lifted up
  In the weird Cadmæan forest.
  Brother, wheresoe'er thou soarest

474. **Agave**: daughter of Cadmus, King of Thebes. She
participated in the Bacchic orgies.

I must hurry, whirl and follow
Through the heavens wide and hollow,
Sheltered by the warm embrace
Of thy soul from hungry space,   480
Drinking from thy sense and sight
Beauty, majesty, and might,
As a lover or a chameleon
Grows like what it looks upon,
As a violet's gentle eye
Gazes on the azure sky
Until its hue grows like what it beholds,
As a gray and watery mist
Glows like solid amethyst
Athwart the western mountain it enfolds,   490
When the sunset sleeps
        Upon its snow—

THE EARTH

And the weak day weeps
        That it should be so.
Oh, gentle Moon, the voice of thy delight
Falls on me like thy clear and tender light
Soothing the seaman, borne the summer night,
        Through isles for ever calm;
Oh, gentle Moon, thy crystal accents pierce
The caverns of my pride's deep universe,   500
Charming the tiger joy, whose tramplings fierce
        Made wounds which need thy balm.
    PANTHEA.   I rise as from a bath of sparkling
        water,
A bath of azure light, among dark rocks,
Out of the stream of sound.
    IONE.   Ah me! sweet sister,
The stream of sound has ebbed away from us,
And you pretend to rise out of its wave,
Because your words fall like the clear, soft dew
Shaken from a bathing wood-nymph's limbs and
        hair.
    PANTHEA.   Peace! peace! A mighty Power, which
        is as darkness,   510
Is rising out of Earth, and from the sky
Is showered like night, and from within the air
Bursts, like eclipse which had been gathered up
Into the pores of sunlight: the bright visions,
Wherein the singing spirits rode and shone,
Gleam like pale meteors through a watery night.
    IONE.   There is a sense of words upon mine ear.
    PANTHEA.   An universal sound like words: Oh,
        list!

DEMOGORGON

Thou, Earth, calm empire of a happy soul,
    Sphere of divinest shapes and harmonies,   520
Beautiful orb! gathering as thou dost roll
    The love which paves thy path along the skies:

THE EARTH

I hear: I am as a drop of dew that dies.

DEMOGORGON

Thou, Moon, which gazest on the nightly Earth
    With wonder, as it gazes upon thee;
Whilst each to men, and beasts, and the swift birth
    Of birds, is beauty, love, calm, harmony:

THE MOON

I hear: I am a leaf shaken by thee!

DEMOGORGON

Ye Kings of suns and stars, Dæmons and Gods,
    Aetherial Dominations, who possess   530
Elysian, windless, fortunate abodes
    Beyond Heaven's constellated wilderness:

A VOICE *from above*

Our great Republic hears, we are blest, and bless.

DEMOGORGON

Ye happy Dead, whom beams of brightest verse
    Are clouds to hide, not colours to portray,
Whether your nature is that universe
    Which once ye saw and suffered—

A VOICE *from beneath*

                            Or as they
Whom we have left, we change and pass away.

DEMOGORGON

Ye elemental Genii, who have homes
    From man's high mind even to the central
        stone   540
Of sullen lead; from heaven's star-fretted domes
    To the dull weed some sea-worm battens on:

A CONFUSED VOICE

We hear: thy words waken Oblivion.

DEMOGORGON

Spirits, whose homes are flesh: ye beasts and birds,
  Ye worms, and fish; ye living leaves and buds;
Lightning and wind; and ye untameable herds,
  Meteors and mists, which throng air's soli-
    tudes:—

A VOICE

Thy voice to us is wind among still woods.

DEMOGORGON

Man, who wert once a despot and a slave;
  A dupe and a deceiver; a decay;   550
A traveller from the cradle to the grave
  Through the dim night of this immortal day:

ALL

Speak: thy strong words may never pass away.

DEMOGORGON

This is the day, which down the void abysm
At the Earth-born's spell yawns for Heaven's
    despotism,
  And Conquest is dragged captive through the
    deep:
Love, from its awful throne of patient power
In the wise heart, from the last giddy hour
  Of dread endurance, from the slippery, steep,
And narrow verge of crag-like agony, springs   560
And folds over the world its healing wings.

Gentleness, Virtue, Wisdom, and Endurance,
These are the seals of that most firm assurance
  Which bars the pit over Destruction's strength;
And if, with infirm hand, Eternity,
Mother of many acts and hours, should free
  The serpent that would clasp her with his length;
These are the spells by which to reassume
An empire o'er the disentangled doom.

To suffer woes which Hope thinks infinite;   570
To forgive wrongs darker than death or night;
  To defy Power, which seems omnipotent;
To love, and bear; to hope till Hope creates
From its own wreck the thing it contemplates;
  Neither to change, nor falter, nor repent;
This, like thy glory, Titan, is to be
Good, great and joyous, beautiful and free;
This is alone Life, Joy, Empire, and Victory.

1818–19   .   *1820*

SONNET: ENGLAND IN 1819

An old, mad, blind, despised, and dying king,—
Princes, the dregs of their dull race, who flow
Through public scorn,—mud from a muddy
    spring,—
Rulers who neither see, nor feel, nor know,
But leech-like to their fainting country cling,
Till they drop, blind in blood, without a blow,—
A people starved and stabbed in the untilled
    field,—
An army, which liberticide and prey
Makes as a two-edged sword to all who wield,—
Golden and sanguine laws which tempt and
    slay;   10
Religion Christless, Godless—a book sealed;
A Senate,—Time's worst statute unrepealed,—
Are graves, from which a glorious Phantom may
Burst, to illumine our tempestuous day.

1819   *1839*

SONG TO THE MEN OF ENGLAND

I

Men of England, wherefore plough
For the lords who lay ye low?
Wherefore weave with toil and care
The rich robes your tyrants wear?

II

Wherefore feed, and clothe, and save,
From the cradle to the grave,
Those ungrateful drones who would
Drain your sweat—nay, drink your blood?

III

Wherefore, Bees of England, forge
Many a weapon, chain, and scourge,   10
That these stingless drones may spoil
The forced produce of your toil?

SONNET: ENGLAND IN 1819. **1. king:** George III. **12.
Time's worst statute:** laws excluding Dissenters and
Roman Catholics from holding public office.

IV

Have ye leisure, comfort, calm,
Shelter, food, love's gentle balm?
Or what is it ye buy so dear
With your pain and with your fear?

V

The seed ye sow, another reaps;
The wealth ye find, another keeps;
The robes ye weave, another wears;
The arms ye forge, another bears.   20

VI

Sow seed,—but let no tyrant reap;
Find wealth,—let no impostor heap;
Weave robes,—let not the idle wear;
Forge arms,—in your defence to bear.

VII

Shrink to your cellars, holes, and cells;
In halls ye deck another dwells.
Why shake the chains ye wrought? Ye see
The steel ye tempered glance on ye.

VIII

With plough and spade, and hoe and loom,
Trace your grave, and build your tomb,   30
And weave your winding-sheet, till fair
England be your sepulchre.

1819   *1839*

ODE TO THE WEST WIND

This poem was conceived and chiefly written in a
wood that skirts the Arno, near Florence, and on a
day when that tempestuous wind, whose tempera-
ture is at once mild and animating, was collecting
the vapours which pour down the autumnal rains.
They began, as I foresaw, at sunset with a violent
tempest of hail and rain, attended by that magnificent thunder and lightning peculiar to the Cisal-
pine regions.

The phenomenon alluded to at the conclusion
of the third stanza is well known to naturalists. The
vegetation at the bottom of the sea, of rivers, and
of lakes, sympathizes with that of the land in the
change of seasons, and is consequently influenced
by the winds which announce it.   [Shelley]

I

O wild West Wind, thou breath of Autumn's being,
Thou, from whose unseen presence the leaves dead
Are driven, like ghosts from an enchanter fleeing,

Yellow, and black, and pale, and hectic red,
Pestilence-stricken multitudes: O thou,
Who chariotest to their dark wintry bed

The wingèd seeds, where they lie cold and low,
Each like a corpse within its grave, until
Thine azure sister of the Spring shall blow

Her clarion o'er the dreaming earth, and fill   10
(Driving sweet buds like flocks to feed in air)
With living hues and odours plain and hill:

Wild Spirit, which art moving everywhere;
Destroyer and preserver; hear, oh, hear!

II

Thou on whose stream, mid the steep sky's com-
            motion,
Loose clouds like earth's decaying leaves are shed,
Shook from the tangled boughs of Heaven and
            Ocean,

Angels of rain and lightning: there are spread
On the blue surface of thine aëry surge,
Like the bright hair uplifted from the head   20

Of some fierce Mænad, even from the dim verge
Of the horizon to the zenith's height,
The locks of the approaching storm. Thou dirge

Of the dying year, to which this closing night
Will be the dome of a vast sepulchre,
Vaulted with all thy congregated might

Of vapours, from whose solid atmosphere
Black rain, and fire, and hail will burst: oh, hear!

III

Thou who didst waken from his summer dreams
The blue Mediterranean, where he lay,   30
Lulled by the coil of his crystalline streams,

Beside a pumice isle in Baiæ's bay,
And saw in sleep old palaces and towers
Quivering within the wave's intenser day,

All overgrown with azure moss and flowers
So sweet, the sense faints picturing them! Thou
For whose path the Atlantic's level powers

Cleave themselves into chasms, while far below
The sea-blooms and the oozy woods which wear
The sapless foliage of the ocean, know   40

Thy voice, and suddenly grow gray with fear,
And tremble and despoil themselves: oh, hear!

IV

If I were a dead leaf thou mightest bear;
If I were a swift cloud to fly with thee;
A wave to pant beneath thy power, and share

The impulse of thy strength, only less free
Than thou, O uncontrollable! If even
I were as in my boyhood, and could be

The comrade of thy wanderings over Heaven,
As then, when to outstrip thy skiey speed   50
Scarce seemed a vision; I would ne'er have striven

As thus with thee in prayer in my sore need.
Oh, lift me as a wave, a leaf, a cloud!
I fall upon the thorns of life! I bleed!

A heavy weight of hours has chained and bowed
One too like thee: tameless, and swift, and proud.

V

Make me thy lyre, even as the forest is:
What if my leaves are falling like its own!
The tumult of thy mighty harmonies

ODE TO THE WEST WIND. **32. pumice:** a light volcanic lava. **Baiæ:** ancient Roman resort whose submerged ruins can be seen north of Naples.

Will take from both a deep, autumnal tone,   60
Sweet though in sadness. Be thou, Spirit fierce,
My spirit! Be thou me, impetuous one!

Drive my dead thoughts over the universe
Like withered leaves to quicken a new birth!
And, by the incantation of this verse,

Scatter, as from an unextinguished hearth
Ashes and sparks, my words among mankind!
Be through my lips to unawakened earth

The trumpet of a prophecy! O, Wind,
If Winter comes, can Spring be far behind?   70
1819   1820

THE SENSITIVE PLANT

PART FIRST

A Sensitive Plant in a garden grew,
And the young winds fed it with silver dew,
And it opened its fan-like leaves to the light,
And closed them beneath the kisses of Night.

And the Spring arose on the garden fair,
Like the Spirit of Love felt everywhere;
And each flower and herb on Earth's dark breast
Rose from the dreams of its wintry rest.

But none ever trembled and panted with bliss
In the garden, the field, or the wilderness,   10
Like a doe in the noontide with love's sweet want,
As the companionless Sensitive Plant.

The snowdrop, and then the violet,
Arose from the ground with warm rain wet,
And their breath was mixed with fresh odour, sent
From the turf, like the voice and the instrument.

Then the pied wind-flowers and the tulip tall,
And narcissi, the fairest among them all,
Who gaze on their eyes in the stream's recess,
Till they die of their own dear loveliness;   20

And the Naiad-like lily of the vale,
Whom youth makes so fair and passion so pale
That the light of its tremulous bells is seen
Through their pavilions of tender green;

And the hyacinth purple, and white, and blue,
Which flung from its bells a sweet peal anew
Of music so delicate, soft, and intense,
It was felt like an odour within the sense;

And the rose like a nymph to the bath addressed,
Which unveiled the depth of her glowing
    breast,   30
Till, fold after fold, to the fainting air
The soul of her beauty and love lay bare:

And the wand-like lily, which lifted up,
As a Mænad, its moonlight-coloured cup,
Till the fiery star, which is its eye,
Gazed through clear dew on the tender sky;

And the jessamine faint, and the sweet tuberose,
The sweetest flower for scent that blows;
And all rare blossoms from every clime
Grew in that garden in perfect prime.   40

And on the stream whose inconstant bosom
Was pranked, under boughs of embowering blos-
    som,
With golden and green light, slanting through
Their heaven of many a tangled hue,

Broad water-lilies lay tremulously,
And starry river-buds glimmered by,
And around them the soft stream did glide and
    dance
With a motion of sweet sound and radiance.

And the sinuous paths of lawn and moss,
Which led through the garden along and
    across,   50
Some open at once to the sun and the breeze,
Some lost among bowers of blossoming trees,

Were all paved with daisies and delicate bells
As fair as the fabulous asphodels,
And flow'rets which, drooping as day drooped too,
Fell into pavilions, white, purple, and blue,
To roof the glow-worm from the evening dew.

And from this undefiled Paradise
The flowers (as an infant's awakening eyes
Smile on its mother, whose singing sweet   60
Can first lull, and at last must awaken it),

When Heaven's blithe winds had unfolded them,
As mine-lamps enkindle a hidden gem,
Shone smiling to Heaven, and every one
Shared joy in the light of the gentle sun;

For each one was interpenetrated
With the light and the odour its neighbour shed,
Like young lovers whom youth and love make dear
Wrapped and filled by their mutual atmosphere.

But the Sensitive Plant which could give small
    fruit   70
Of the love which it felt from the leaf to the root,
Received more than all, it loved more than ever,
Where none wanted but it, could belong to the
    giver,—

For the Sensitive Plant has no bright flower;
Radiance and odour are not its dower;
It loves, even like Love, its deep heart is full,
It desires what it has not, the Beautiful!

The light winds which from unsustaining wings
Shed the music of many murmurings;
The beams which dart from many a star   80
Of the flowers whose hues they bear afar;

The plumèd insects swift and free,
Like golden boats on a sunny sea,
Laden with light and odour, which pass
Over the gleam of the living grass;

The unseen clouds of the dew, which lie
Like fire in the flowers till the sun rides high,
Then wander like spirits among the spheres,
Each cloud faint with the fragrance it bears;

The quivering vapours of dim noontide,   90
Which like a sea o'er the warm earth glide,
In which every sound, and odour, and beam,
Move, as reeds in a single stream;

Each and all like ministering angels were
For the Sensitive Plant sweet joy to bear,
Whilst the lagging hours of the day went by
Like windless clouds o'er a tender sky.

And when evening descended from Heaven above,
And the Earth was all rest, and the air was all love,
And delight, though less bright, was far more
    deep,   100
And the day's veil fell from the world of sleep,

And the beasts, and the birds, and the insects were
    drowned
In an ocean of dreams without a sound;
Whose waves never mark, though they ever impress
The light sand which paves it, consciousness;

(Only overhead the sweet nightingale
Ever sang more sweet as the day might fail,
And snatches of its Elysian chant
Were mixed with the dreams of the Sensitive
    Plant);—

The Sensitive Plant was the earliest   110
Upgathered into the bosom of rest;
A sweet child weary of its delight,
The feeblest and yet the favourite,
Cradled within the embrace of Night.

PART SECOND

There was a Power in this sweet place,
An Eve in this Eden; a ruling Grace
Which to the flowers, did they waken or dream,
Was as God is to the starry scheme.

A Lady, the wonder of her kind,
Whose form was upborne by a lovely mind
Which, dilating, had moulded her mien and mo-
　　tion
Like a sea-flower unfolded beneath the ocean,

Tended the garden from morn to even:
And the meteors of that sublunar Heaven,   10
Like the lamps of the air when Night walks forth,
Laughed round her footsteps up from the Earth!

She had no companion of mortal race,
But her tremulous breath and her flushing face
Told, whilst the morn kissed the sleep from her
　　eyes,
That her dreams were less slumber than Paradise:

As if some bright Spirit for her sweet sake
Had deserted Heaven while the stars were awake,
As if yet around her he lingering were,
Though the veil of daylight concealed him from
　　her.   20

Her step seemed to pity the grass it pressed;
You might hear by the heaving of her breast,
That the coming and going of the wind
Brought pleasure there and left passion behind.

And wherever her aëry footstep trod,
Her trailing hair from the grassy sod
Erased its light vestige, with shadowy sweep,
Like a sunny storm o'er the dark green deep.

I doubt not the flowers of that garden sweet
Rejoiced in the sound of her gentle feet;   30
I doubt not they felt the spirit that came
From her glowing fingers through all their frame.

She sprinkled bright water from the stream
On those that were faint with the sunny beam;

And out of the cups of the heavy flowers
She emptied the rain of the thunder-showers.

She lifted their heads with her tender hands,
And sustained them with rods and osier-bands;
If the flowers had been her own infants, she
Could never have nursed them more tenderly.   40

And all killing insects and gnawing worms,
And things of obscene and unlovely forms,
She bore, in a basket of Indian woof,
Into the rough woods far aloof,—

In a basket, of grasses and wild-flowers full,
The freshest her gentle hands could pull
For the poor banished insects, whose intent,
Although they did ill, was innocent.

But the bee and the beamlike ephemeris
Whose path is the lightning's, and soft moths that
　　kiss   50
The sweet lips of the flowers, and harm not, did she
Make her attendant angels be.

And many an antenatal tomb,
Where butterflies dream of the life to come,
She left clinging round the smooth and dark
Edge of the odorous cedar bark.

This fairest creature from earliest Spring
Thus moved through the garden ministering
All the sweet season of Summertide,
And ere the first leaf looked brown—she died!   60

PART THIRD

Three days the flowers of the garden fair,
Like stars when the moon is awakened, were,
Or the waves of Baiæ, ere luminous
She floats up through the smoke of Vesuvius.

And on the fourth, the Sensitive Plant
Felt the sound of the funeral chant,
And the steps of the bearers, heavy and slow,
And the sobs of the mourners, deep and low;

The weary sound and the heavy breath,
And the silent motions of passing death,   10
And the smell, cold, oppressive, and dank,
Sent through the pores of the coffin-plank;

THE SENSITIVE PLANT. PART THIRD. 3. **Baiæ**: ancient
Roman resort near Naples.

The dark grass, and the flowers among the grass,
Were bright with tears as the crowd did pass;
From their sighs the wind caught a mournful tone,
And sate in the pines, and gave groan for groan.

The garden, once fair, became cold and foul,
Like the corpse of her who had been its soul,
Which at first was lovely as if in sleep,
Then slowly changed, till it grew a heap   20
To make men tremble who never weep.

Swift Summer into the Autumn flowed,
And frost in the midst of the morning rode,
Though the noonday sun looked clear and bright,
Mocking the spoil of the secret night.

The rose-leaves, like flakes of crimson snow,
Paved the turf and the moss below.
The lilies were drooping, and white, and wan,
Like the head and the skin of a dying man.

And Indian plants, of scent and hue   30
The sweetest that ever were fed on dew,
Leaf by leaf, day after day,
Were massed into the common clay.

And the leaves, brown, yellow, and gray, and red,
And white with the whiteness of what is dead,
Like troops of ghosts on the dry wind passed;
Their whistling noise made the birds aghast.

And the gusty winds waked the wingèd seeds,
Out of their birthplace of ugly weeds,
Till they clung round many a sweet flower's
    stem,   40
Which rotted into the earth with them.

The water-blooms under the rivulet
Fell from the stalks on which they were set;
And the eddies drove them here and there,
As the winds did those of the upper air.

Then the rain came down, and the broken stalks
Were bent and tangled across the walks;
And the leafless network of parasite bowers
Massed into ruin; and all sweet flowers.

Between the time of the wind and the snow   50
All loathliest weeds began to grow,
Whose coarse leaves were splashed with many a
    speck,
Like the water-snake's belly and the toad's back.

And thistles, and nettles, and darnels rank,
And the dock, and henbane, and hemlock dank,
Stretched out its long and hollow shank,
And stifled the air till the dead wind stank.

And plants, at whose names the verse feels loath,
Filled the place with a monstrous undergrowth,
Prickly, and pulpous, and blistering, and blue,   60
Livid, and starred with a lurid dew.

And agarics, and fungi, with mildew and mould
Started like mist from the wet ground cold;
Pale, fleshy, as if the decaying dead
With a spirit of growth had been animated!

Spawn, weeds, and filth, a leprous scum,
Made the running rivulet thick and dumb,
And at its outlet flags huge as stakes
Damned it up with roots knotted like water-snakes.

And hour by hour, when the air was still,   70
The vapours arose which have strength to kill;
At morn they were seen, at noon they were felt,
At night they were darkness no star could melt.

And unctuous meteors from spray to spray
Crept and flitted in broad noonday
Unseen; every branch on which they alit
By a venomous blight was burned and bit.

The Sensitive Plant, like one forbid,
Wept, and the tears within each lid
Of its folded leaves, which together grew,   80
Were changed to a blight of frozen glue.

For the leaves soon fell, and the branches soon
By the heavy axe of the blast were hewn;
The sap shrank to the root through every pore
As blood to a heart that will beat no more.

For Winter came: the wind was his whip:
One choppy finger was on his lip:
He had torn the cataracts from the hills
And they clanked at his girdle like manacles;

His breath was a chain which without a sound   90
The earth, and the air, and the water bound;
He came, fiercely driven, in his chariot-throne
By the tenfold blasts of the Arctic zone.

Then the weeds which were forms of living death
Fled from the frost to the earth beneath.

62. agarics: a type of fungus.

Their decay and sudden flight from frost
Was but like the vanishing of a ghost!

And under the roots of the Sensitive Plant
The moles and the dormice died for want:
The birds dropped stiff from the frozen air   100
And were caught in the branches naked and bare.

First there came down a thawing rain
And its dull drops froze on the boughs again;
Then there steamed up a freezing dew
Which to the drops of the thaw-rain grew;

And a northern whirlwind, wandering about
Like a wolf that had smelt a dead child out,
Shook the boughs thus laden, and heavy, and stiff,
And snapped them off with his rigid griff.

When Winter had gone and Spring came back   110
The Sensitive Plant was a leafless wreck;
But the mandrakes, and toadstools, and docks, and
        darnels,
Rose like the dead from their ruined charnels.

CONCLUSION

Whether the Sensitive Plant, or that
Which within its boughs like a Spirit sat,
Ere its outward form had known decay,
Now felt this change, I cannot say.

Whether that Lady's gentle mind,
No longer with the form combined
Which scattered love, as stars do light,   120
Found sadness, where it left delight,

I dare not guess; but in this life
Of error, ignorance, and strife,
Where nothing is, but all things seem,
And we the shadows of the dream,

It is a modest creed, and yet
Pleasant if one considers it,
To own that death itself must be,
Like all the rest, a mockery.

That garden sweet, that lady fair,   130
And all sweet shapes and odours there,
In truth have never passed away:
'Tis we, 'tis ours, are changed; not they.

109. griff: grip.

For love, and beauty, and delight,
There is no death nor change: their might
Exceeds our organs, which endure
No light, being themselves obscure.
1820   *1820*

THE CLOUD

I bring fresh showers for the thirsting flowers,
        From the seas and the streams;
I bear light shade for the leaves when laid
        In their noonday dreams.
From my wings are shaken the dews that waken
        The sweet buds every one,
When rocked to rest on their mother's breast,
        As she dances about the sun.
I wield the flail of the lashing hail,
        And whiten the green plains under,   10
And then again I dissolve it in rain,
        And laugh as I pass in thunder.

I sift the snow on the mountains below,
        And their great pines groan aghast;
And all the night 'tis my pillow white,
        While I sleep in the arms of the blast.
Sublime on the towers of my skiey bowers,
        Lightning my pilot sits;
In a cavern under is fettered the thunder,
        It struggles and howls at fits;   20
Over earth and ocean, with gentle motion,
        This pilot is guiding me,
Lured by the love of the genii that move
        In the depths of the purple sea;
Over the rills, and the crags, and the hills,
        Over the lakes and the plains,
Wherever he dream, under mountain or stream,
        The Spirit he loves remains;
And I all the while bask in Heaven's blue smile,
        Whilst he is dissolving in rains.   30

The sanguine Sunrise, with his meteor eyes,
        And his burning plumes outspread,
Leaps on the back of my sailing rack,
        When the morning star shines dead;
As on the jag of a mountain crag,
        Which an earthquake rocks and swings,
An eagle alit one moment may sit
        In the light of its golden wings.

And when Sunset may breathe, from the lit sea
    beneath,
    Its ardours of rest and of love,   40
And the crimson pall of eve may fall
    From the depth of Heaven above,
With wings folded I rest, on mine aëry nest,
    As still as a brooding dove.

That orbèd maiden with white fire laden,
    Whom mortals call the Moon,
Glides glimmering o'er my fleece-like floor,
    By the midnight breezes strewn;
And wherever the beat of her unseen feet,
    Which only the angels hear,   50
May have broken the woof of my tent's thin roof,
    The stars peep behind her and peer;
And I laugh to see them whirl and flee,
    Like a swarm of golden bees,
When I widen the rent in my wind-built tent,
    Till the calm rivers, lakes, and seas,
Like strips of the sky fallen through me on high,
    Are each paved with the moon and these.

I bind the Sun's throne with a burning zone,
    And the Moon's with a girdle of pearl;   60
The volcanoes are dim, and the stars reel and swim,
    When the whirlwinds my banner unfurl.
From cape to cape, with a bridge-like shape,
    Over a torrent sea,
Sunbeam-proof, I hang like a roof,—
    The mountains its columns be.
The triumphal arch through which I march
    With hurricane, fire, and snow,
When the Powers of the air are chained to my chair,
    Is the million-coloured bow;   70
The sphere-fire above its soft colours wove,
    While the moist Earth was laughing below.

I am the daughter of Earth and Water,
    And the nursling of the Sky;
I pass through the pores of the ocean and shores;
    I change, but I cannot die.
For after the rain when with never a stain
    The pavilion of Heaven is bare,
And the winds and sunbeams with their convex
    gleams
    Build up the blue dome of air,   80

THE CLOUD. 81. cenotaph: a monument or empty tomb
honoring someone whose body is elsewhere.

I silently laugh at my own cenotaph,
    And out of the caverns of rain,
Like a child from the womb, like a ghost from the
    tomb,
    I arise and unbuild it again.
1820   *1820*

TO A SKYLARK

Hail to thee, blithe Spirit!
    Bird thou never wert,
That from Heaven, or near it,
    Pourest thy full heart
In profuse strains of unpremeditated art.

Higher still and higher
    From the earth thou springest
Like a cloud of fire;
    The blue deep thou wingest,
And singing still dost soar, and soaring ever singest.

In the golden lightning   11
    Of the sunken sun,
O'er which clouds are bright'ning,
    Thou dost float and run;
Like an unbodied joy whose race is just begun.

The pale purple even
    Melts around thy flight;
Like a star of Heaven,
    In the broad daylight
Thou art unseen, but yet I hear thy shrill
    delight,   20

Keen as are the arrows
    Of that silver sphere,
Whose intense lamp narrows
    In the white dawn clear
Until we hardly see—we feel that it is there.

All the earth and air
    With thy voice is loud,
As, when night is bare,
    From one lonely cloud
The moon rains out her beams, and Heaven is over-
    flowed.   30

What thou art we know not;
    What is most like thee?
From rainbow clouds there flow not

Drops so bright to see
As from thy presence showers a rain of melody.

Like a Poet hidden
 In the light of thought,
Singing hymns unbidden,
 Till the world is wrought
To sympathy with hopes and fears it heeded
 not: 40

Like a high-born maiden
 In a palace-tower,
Soothing her love-laden
 Soul in secret hour
With music sweet as love, which overflows her
 bower:

Like a glow-worm golden
 In a dell of dew,
Scattering unbeholden
 Its aëreal hue
Among the flowers and grass, which screen it from
 the view!   50

Like a rose embowered
 In its own green leaves,
By warm winds deflowered,
 Till the scent it gives
Makes faint with too much sweet those heavy-
 wingèd thieves:

Sound of vernal showers
 On the twinkling grass,
Rain-awakened flowers,
 All that ever was
Joyous, and clear, and fresh, thy music doth
 surpass: 60

Teach us, Sprite or Bird,
 What sweet thoughts are thine:
I have never heard
 Praise of love or wine
That panted forth a flood of rapture so divine.

Chorus Hymeneal,
 Or triumphal chant,
Matched with thine would be all
 But an empty vaunt,

A thing wherein we feel there is some hidden
 want.   70

What objects are the fountains
 Of thy happy strain?
What fields, or waves, or mountains?
 What shapes of sky or plain?
What love of thine own kind? what ignorance of
 pain?

With thy clear keen joyance
 Languor cannot be:
Shadow of annoyance
 Never came near thee:
Thou lovest—but ne'er knew love's sad satiety.   80

Waking or asleep,
 Thou of death must deem
Things more true and deep
 Than we mortals dream,
Or how could thy notes flow in such a crystal
 stream?

We look before and after,
 And pine for what is not:
Our sincerest laughter
 With some pain is fraught;
Our sweetest songs are those that tell of saddest
 thought.   90

Yet if we could scorn
 Hate, and pride, and fear;
If we were things born
 Not to shed a tear,
I know not how thy joy we ever should come near.

Better than all measures
 Of delightful sound,
Better than all treasures
 That in books are found,
Thy skill to poet were, thou scorner of the ground!

Teach me half the gladness   101
 That thy brain must know,
Such harmonious madness
 From my lips would flow
The world should listen then—as I am listening
 now.

TO A SKYLARK. **66. Hymeneal:** pertaining to a wedding
or marriage.

1820   *1820*

EPIPSYCHIDION*

VERSES ADDRESSED TO THE NOBLE
AND UNFORTUNATE LADY, EMILIA V——,
NOW IMPRISONED IN THE CONVENT OF——

L'anima amante si slancia fuori del creato, e si
crea nell' infinito un Mondo tutto per essa, diverso
assai da questo oscuro e pauroso baratro.

Her Own Words

ADVERTISEMENT

The Writer of the following lines died at Florence, as he was preparing for a voyage to one of the wildest of the Sporades,[1] which he had bought, and where he had fitted up the ruins of an old building, and where it was his hope to have realised a scheme of life, suited perhaps to that happier and better world of which he is now an inhabitant, but hardly practicable in this. His life was singular; less on account of the romantic vicissitudes which diversified it, than the ideal tinge which it received from his own character and feelings. The present Poem, like the *Vita Nuova* of Dante, is sufficiently intelligible to a certain class of readers without a matter-of-fact history of the circumstances to which it relates; and to a certain other class it must ever remain incomprehensible, from a defect of a common organ of perception for the ideas of which it treats. Not but that *gran vergogna sarebbe a colui, che rimasse cosa sotto veste di figura, o di colore rettorico: e domandato non sapesse denudare le sue parole da cotal veste, in guisa che avessero verace intendimento.*[2]

The present poem appears to have been intended by the Writer as the dedication to some longer one. The stanza on the opposite page [below] is almost a literal translation from Dante's famous Canzone

* The title is best translated as "soul out of my soul." The noble and unfortunate lady is Emilia Viviani, whom Shelley met in 1820 and who had been placed in a convent by her father, a Pisan nobleman. Her own words can be translated: "The loving soul projects itself beyond the creation and creates in the infinite a world of its own, very different from this dark and fearful cavern."

EPIPSYCHIDION. ADVERTISEMENT. **1. Sporades:** islands in the Aegean sea. **2. gran...intendimento:** D. G. Rossetti's translation: "It were a shameful thing if one should rhyme under the semblance of metaphor or rhetorical similitude and afterwards being questioned thereof, should be unable to rid his words of such semblance into such guise as could be truly understood."

Voi, ch' intendendo, il terzo ciel movete,[3] *etc.*

The presumptuous application of the concluding lines to his own composition will raise a smile at the expense of my unfortunate friend: be it a smile not of contempt, but pity.   S.

My Song, I fear that thou wilt find but few
Who fitly shall conceive thy reasoning,
Of such hard matter dost thou entertain;
Whence, if by misadventure, chance should bring
Thee to base company (as chance may do),
Quite unaware of what thou dost contain,
I prithee, comfort thy sweet self again,
My last delight! tell them that they are dull,
And bid them own that thou art beautiful.

EPIPSYCHIDION

Sweet Spirit! Sister of that orphan one,
Whose empire is the name thou weepest on,
In my heart's temple I suspend to thee
These votive wreaths of withered memory.

Poor captive bird! who, from thy narrow cage,
Pourest such music, that I might assuage
The rugged hearts of those who prisoned thee,
Were they not deaf to all sweet melody;
This song shall be thy rose: its petals pale
Are dead, indeed, my adored Nightingale!   10
But soft and fragrant is the faded blossom,
And it has no thorn left to wound thy bosom.

High, spirit-wingèd Heart! who dost for ever
Beat thine unfeeling bars with vain endeavour,
Till those bright plumes of thought, in which
     arrayed
It over-soared this low and worldly shade,
Lie shattered; and thy panting, wounded breast
Stains with dear blood its unmaternal nest!
I weep vain tears: blood would less bitter be,
Yet poured forth gladlier, could it profit thee.   20

Seraph of Heaven! too gentle to be human,
Veiling beneath that radiant form of Woman
All that is insupportable in thee
Of light, and love, and immortality!
Sweet Benediction in the eternal Curse!
Veiled Glory of this lampless Universe!
Thou Moon beyond the clouds! Thou living Form
Among the Dead! Thou Star above the Storm!

3. Voi...movete: "You who, all-knowing, move the Third Heaven."

EPIPSYCHIDION. **1. Sweet Spirit:** Emilia. **orphan one:** Mary Shelley. **2. the name:** Shelley himself.

Thou Wonder, and thou Beauty, and thou Terror!
Thou Harmony of Nature's art! Thou Mirror   30
In whom, as in the splendour of the Sun,
All shapes look glorious which thou gazest on!
Ay, even the dim words which obscure thee now
Flash, lightning-like, with unaccustomed glow;
I pray thee that thou blot from this sad song
All of its much mortality and wrong,
With those clear drops, which start like sacred dew
From the twin lights thy sweet soul darkens
    through,
Weeping, till sorrow becomes ecstasy:
Then smile on it, that it may not die.   40

  I never thought before my death to see
Youth's vision thus made perfect. Emily,
I love thee; though the world by no thin name
Will hide that love from its unvalued shame.
Would we two had been twins of the same mother!
Or, that the name my heart lent to another
Could be a sister's bond for her and thee,
Blending two beams of one eternity!
Yet were one lawful and the other true,
These names, though dear, could paint not, as is
    due,   50
How beyond refuge I am thine. Ah me!
I am not thine: I am a part of *thee*.

  Sweet Lamp! my moth-like Muse has burned its
    wings
Or, like a dying swan who soars and sings,
Young Love should teach Time, in his own gray
    style,
All that thou art. Art thou not void of guile,
A lovely soul formed to be blessed and bless?
A well of sealed and secret happiness,
Whose waters like blithe light and music are,
Vanquishing dissonance and gloom? A Star   60
Which moves not in the moving heavens, alone?
A Smile amid dark frowns? a gentle tone
Amid rude voices? a belovèd light?
A Solitude, a Refuge, a Delight?
A Lute, which those whom Love has taught to play
Make music on, to soothe the roughest day
And lull fond Grief asleep? a buried treasure?
A cradle of young thoughts of wingless pleasure?
A violet-shrouded grave of Woe?—I measure
The world of fancies, seeking one like thee,   70
And find—alas! mine own infirmity.

She met me, Stranger, upon life's rough way,
And lured me towards sweet Death; as Night by
    Day,
Winter by Spring, or Sorrow by swift Hope,
Led into light, life, peace. An antelope,
In the suspended impulse of its lightness,
Were less aethereally light: the brightness
Of her divinest presence trembles through
Her limbs, as underneath a cloud of dew
Embodied in the windless heaven of June   80
Amid the splendour-wingèd stars, the Moon
Burns, inextinguishably beautiful:
And from her lips, as from a hyacinth full
Of honey dew, a liquid murmur drops,
Killing the sense with passion; sweet as stops
Of planetary music heard in trance.
In her mild lights the starry spirits dance,
The sunbeams of those wells which ever leap
Under the lightnings of the soul—too deep
For the brief fathom-line of thought or sense.   90
The glory of her being, issuing thence,
Stains the dead, blank, cold air with a warm shade
Of unentangled intermixture, made
By Love, of light and motion: one intense
Diffusion, one serene Omnipresence,
Whose flowing outlines mingle in their flowing,
Around her cheeks and utmost fingers glowing
With the unintermitted blood, which there
Quivers, (as in a fleece of snow-like air
The crimson pulse of living morning quiver,)   100
Continuously prolonged, and ending never,
Till they are lost, and in that Beauty furled
Which penetrates and clasps and fills the world;
Scarce visible from extreme loveliness.
Warm fragrance seems to fall from her light dress
And her loose hair; and where some heavy tress
The air of her own speed has disentwined,
The sweetness seems to satiate the faint wind;
And in the soul a wild odour is felt,
Beyond the sense, like fiery dews that melt   110
Into the bosom of a frozen bud.—
See where she stands! a moral shape indued
With love and life and light and deity,
And motion which may change but cannot die;
An image of some bright Eternity;
A shadow of some golden dream; a Splendour
Leaving the third sphere pilotless; a tender

50. These names: sister and wife.

72. She: the ideal of Beauty. 117. third sphere: that of
Venus, goddess of love.

Reflection of the eternal Moon of Love
Under whose motions life's dull billows move;
A Metaphor of Spring and Youth and Morn-
        ing;   120
A Vision like incarnate April, warning,
With smiles and tears, Frost the Anatomy
Into his summer grave.
                        Ah, woe is me!
What have I dared? where am I lifted? how
Shall I descend, and perish not? I know
That Love makes all things equal: I have heard
By mine own heart this joyous truth averred:
The spirit of the worm beneath the sod
In love and worship, blends itself with God.

    Spouse! Sister! Angel! Pilot of the Fate   130
Whose course has been so starless! O too late
Beloved! O too soon adored, by me!
For in the fields of Immortality
My spirit should at first have worshipped thine,
A divine presence in a place divine;
Or should have moved beside it on this earth,
A shadow of that substance, from its birth;
But not as now:—I love thee; yes, I feel
That on the fountain of my heart a seal
Is set, to keep its waters pure and bright   140
For thee, since in those *tears* thou hast delight.
We—are we not formed, as notes of music are,
For one another, though dissimilar;
Such difference without discord, as can make
Those sweetest sounds, in which all spirits shake
As trembling leaves in a continuous air?

    Thy wisdom speaks in me, and bids me dare
Beacon the rocks on which high hearts are wrecked.
I never was attached to that great sect,
Whose doctrine is, that each one should
        select   150
Out of the crowd a mistress or a friend,
And all the rest, though fair and wise, commend
To cold oblivion, though it is in the code
Of modern morals, and the beaten road
Which those poor slaves with weary footsteps tread,
Who travel to their home among the dead
By the broad highway of the world, and so
With one chained friend, perhaps a jealous foe,
The dreariest and the longest journey go.

    True Love in this differs from gold and
        clay,   160
That to divide is not to take away.

Love is like understanding, that grows bright,
Gazing on many truths; 'tis like thy light,
Imagination! which from earth and sky,
And from the depths of human fantasy,
As from a thousand prisms and mirrors, fills
The Universe with glorious beams, and kills
Error, the worm, with many a sun-like arrow
Of its reverberated lightning. Narrow
The heart that loves, the brain that contem-
        plates,   170
The life that wears, the spirit that creates
One object, and one form, and builds thereby
A sepulchre for its eternity.

    Mind from its object differs most in this:
Evil from good; misery from happiness;
The baser from the nobler; the impure
And frail, from what is clear and must endure.
If you divide suffering and dross, you may
Diminish till it is consumed away;
If you divide pleasure and love and thought,   180
Each part exceeds the whole; and we know not
How much, while any yet remains unshared,
Of pleasure may be gained, of sorrow spared:
This truth is that deep well, whence sages draw
The unenvied light of hope; the eternal law
By which those live, to whom this world of life
Is as a garden ravaged, and whose strife
Tills for the promise of a later birth
The wilderness of this Elysian earth.

    There was a Being whom my spirit oft   190
Met on its visioned wanderings, far aloft,
In the clear golden prime of my youth's dawn,
Upon the fairy isles of sunny lawn,
Amid the enchanted mountains, and the caves
Of divine sleep, and on the air-like waves
Of wonder-level dream, whose tremulous floor
Paved her light steps;—on an imagined shore,
Under the gray beak of some promontory
She met me, robed in such exceeding glory,
That I beheld her not. In solitudes   200
Her voice came to me through the whispering
        woods,
And from the fountains, and the odours deep
Of flowers, which, like lips murmuring in their sleep
Of the sweet kisses which had lulled them there,
Breathed but of *her* to the enamoured air;

190. **Being:** Agnes, the Ideal Beauty envisioned in his
youth and still the object of his quest.

And from the breezes whether low or loud,
And from the rain of every passing cloud,
And from the singing of the summer-birds,
And from all sounds, all silence. In the words
Of antique verse and high romance,—in
    form,   210
Sound, colour—in whatever checks that Storm
Which with the shattered present chokes the past;
And in that best philosophy, whose taste
Makes this cold common hell, our life, a doom
As glorious as a fiery martyrdom;
Her Spirit was the harmony of truth.—

Then, from the caverns of my dreamy youth
I sprang, as one sandalled with plumes of fire,
And towards the lodestar of my one desire,
I flitted, like a dizzy moth, whose flight   220
Is as a dead leaf's in the owlet light,
When it would seek in Hesper's setting sphere
A radiant death, a fiery sepulchre,
As if it were a lamp of earthly flame.—
But She, whom prayers or tears then could not
    tame,
Passed, like a God throned on a wingèd planet,
Whose burning plumes to tenfold swiftness fan it,
Into the dreary cone of our life's shade;
And as a man with mighty loss dismayed,
I would have followed, though the grave be-
    tween   230
Yawned like a gulf whose spectres are unseen:
When a voice said:—"O thou of hearts the weakest,
The phantom is beside thee whom thou seekest."
Then I—"Where?"—the world's echo answered
    "where?"
And in that silence, and in my despair,
I questioned every tongueless wind that flew
Over my tower of mourning, if it knew
Whither 'twas fled, this soul out of my soul;
And murmured names and spells which have
    control
Over the sightless tyrants of our fate;   240
But neither prayer nor verse could dissipate
The night which closed on her; nor uncreate
That world within this Chaos, mine and me,
Of which she was the veiled Divinity,
The world I say of thoughts that worshipped her:
And therefore I went forth, with hope and fear
And every gentle passion sick to death,
Feeding my course with expectation's breath,

221. **owlet**: dim, dusky. 222. **Hesper**: the evening star.

Into the wintry forest of our life;
And struggling through its error with vain
    strife,   250
And stumbling in my weakness and my haste,
And half bewildered by new forms, I passed,
Seeking among those untaught foresters
If I could find one form resembling hers,
In which she might have masked herself from me.
There,—One, whose voice was venomed melody
Sate by a well, under blue nightshade bowers;
The breath of her false mouth was like faint flowers,
Her touch was as electric poison,—flame
Out of her looks into my vitals came,   260
And from her living cheeks and bosom flew
A killing air, which pierced like honey-dew
Into the core of my green heart, and lay
Upon its leaves; until, as hair grown gray
O'er a young brow, they hid its unblown prime
With ruins of unseasonable time.

In many mortal forms I rashly sought
The shadow of that idol of my thought.
And some were fair—but beauty dies away:
Others were wise—but honeyed words
    betray: 270
And One was true—oh! why not true to me?
Then, as a hunted deer that could not flee,
I turned upon my thoughts, and stood at bay,
Wounded and weak and panting; the cold day
Trembled, for pity of my strife and pain.
When, like a noonday dawn, there shone again
Deliverance. One stood on my path who seemed
As like the glorious shape which I had dreamed
As is the Moon, whose changes ever run
Into themselves, to the eternal Sun;   280
The cold chaste Moon, the Queen of Heaven's
    bright isles,
Who makes all beautiful on which she smiles,
That wandering shrine of soft yet icy flame
Which ever is transformed, yet still the same,
And warms not but illumines. Young and fair
As the descended Spirit of that sphere,
She hid me, as the Moon may hide the night
From its own darkness, until all was bright
Between the Heaven and Earth of my calm mind,
And, as a cloud charioted by the wind,   290
She led me to a cave in that wild place,
And sate beside me, with her downward face
Illumining my slumbers, like the Moon
Waxing and waning o'er Endymion.
And I was laid asleep, spirit and limb,

And all my being became bright or dim
As the Moon's image in a summer sea,
According as she smiled or frowned on me;
And there I lay, within a chaste cold bed:
Alas, I then was nor alive nor dead:—   300
For at her silver voice came Death and Life,
Unmindful each of their accustomed strife,
Masked like twin babes, a sister and a brother,
The wandering hopes of one abandoned mother,
And through the cavern without wings they flew,
And cried "Away, he is not of our crew."
I wept, and though it be a dream, I weep.

What storms then shook the ocean of my sleep,
Blotting that Moon, whose pale and waning lips
Then shrank as in the sickness of eclipse;—   310
And how my soul was as a lampless sea,
And who was then its Tempest; and when She,
The Planet of that hour, was quenched, what frost
Crept o'er those waters, till from coast to coast
The moving billows of my being fell
Into a death of ice, immovable;—
And then—what earthquakes made it gape and
          split,
The white Moon smiling all the while on it,
These words conceal:—If not, each word would be
The key of staunchless tears. Weep not for
          me!   320

At length, into the obscure Forest came
The Vision I had sought through grief and shame.
Athwart that wintry wilderness of thorns
Flashed from her motion splendour like the Morn's,
And from her presence life was radiated
Through the gray earth and branches bare and
          dead;
So that her way was paved, and roofed above
With flowers as soft as thoughts of budding love;
And music from her respiration spread
Like light,—all other sounds were penetrated   330
By the small, still, sweet spirit of that sound,
So that the savage winds hung mute around;
And odours warm and fresh fell from her hair
Dissolving the dull cold in the frore air:
Soft as an Incarnation of the Sun,
When light is changed to love, this glorious One
Floated into the cavern where I lay,
And called my Spirit, and the dreaming clay
Was lifted by the thing that dreamed below
As smoke by fire, and in her beauty's glow   340

334. frore: frosty.

I stood, and felt the dawn of my long night
Was penetrating me with living light:
I knew it was the Vision veiled from me
So many years—that it was Emily.

Twin Spheres of light who rule this passive
          Earth,
This world of love, this *me;* and into birth
Awaken all its fruits and flowers, and dart
Magnetic might into its central heart;
And lift its billows and its mists, and guide
By everlasting laws, each wind and tide   350
To its fit cloud, and its appointed cave;
And lull its storms, each in the craggy grave
Which was its cradle, luring to faint bowers
The armies of the rainbow-wingèd showers;
And, as those married lights, which from the towers
Of Heaven look forth and fold the wandering globe
In liquid sleep and splendour, as a robe;
And all their many-mingled influence blend,
If equal, yet unlike, to one sweet end;—
So ye, bright regents, with alternate sway   360
Govern my sphere of being, night and day!
Thou, not disdaining even a borrowed might;
Thou, not eclipsing a remoter light;
And, through the shadow of the seasons three,
From Spring to Autumn's sere maturity,
Light it into the Winter of the tomb,
Where it may ripen to a brighter bloom.
Thou too, O Comet beautiful and fierce,
Who drew the heart of this frail Universe
Towards thine own; till, wrecked in that con-
          vulsion,   370
Alternating attraction and repulsion,
Thine went astray and that was rent in twain;
Oh, float into our azure heaven again!
Be there Love's folding-star at thy return;
The living Sun will feed thee from its urn
Of golden fire; the Moon will veil her horn
In thy last smiles; adoring Even and Morn
Will worship thee with incense of calm breath
And lights and shadows; as the star of Death
And Birth is worshipped by those sisters wild   380
Called Hope and Fear—upon the heart are piled
Their offerings,—of this sacrifice divine
A World shall be the altar.
                    Lady mine,
Scorn not these flowers of thought, the fading birth

374. folding-star: the evening star, which rises as the
sheep are being gathered into the fold.

Which from its heart of hearts that plant puts forth
Whose fruit, made perfect by the sunny eyes,
Will be as of the trees of Paradise.

The day is come, and thou wilt fly with me.
To whatsoe'er of dull mortality
Is mine, remain a vestal sister still;   390
To the intense, the deep, the imperishable.
Not mine but me, henceforth be thou united
Even as a bride, delighting and delighted.
The hour is come:—the destined Star has risen
Which shall descend upon a vacant prison.
The walls are high, the gates are strong, thick set
The sentinels—but true Love never yet
Was thus constrained: it overleaps all fence:
Like lightning, with invisible violence
Piercing its continents; like Heaven's free
    breath,   400
Which he who grasps can hold not; liker Death,
Who rides upon a thought, and makes his way
Through temple, tower, and palace, and the array
Of arms: more strength has Love than he or they;
For it can burst his charnel, and make free
The limbs in chains, the heart in agony,
The soul in dust and chaos.
                        Emily,
A ship is floating in the harbour now,
A wind is hovering o'er the mountain's brow;
There is a path on the sea's azure floor,   410
No keel has ever ploughed that path before;
The halcyons brood around the foamless isles;
The treacherous Ocean has forsworn its wiles;
The merry mariners are bold and free:
Say, my heart's sister, wilt thou sail with me?
Our bark is as an albatross, whose nest
Is a far Eden of the purple East;
And we between her wings will sit, while Night,
And Day, and Storm, and Calm, pursue their flight,
Our ministers, along the boundless Sea,   420
Treading each other's heels, unheededly.
It is an isle under Ionian skies,
Beautiful as a wreck of Paradise,
And, for the harbours are not safe and good,
This land would have remained a solitude
But for some pastoral people native there,
Who from the Elysian, clear, and golden air
Draw the last spirit of the age of gold,
Simple and spirited; innocent and bold.
The blue Aegean girds this chosen home,   430
With ever-changing sound and light and foam,
Kissing the sifted sands, and caverns hoar;

And all the winds wandering along the shore
Undulate with the undulating tide:
There are thick woods where sylvan forms abide;
And many a fountain, rivulet, and pond,
As clear as elemental diamond,
Or serene morning air; and far beyond,
The mossy tracks made by the goats and deer
(Which the rough shepherd treads but once a
    year)   440
Pierce into glades, caverns, and bowers, and halls
Built round with ivy, which the waterfalls
Illumining, with sound that never fails
Accompany the noonday nightingales;
And all the place is peopled with sweet airs;
The light clear element which the isle wears
Is heavy with the scent of lemon-flowers,
Which floats like mist laden with unseen showers,
And falls upon the eyelids like faint sleep;
And from the moss violets and jonquils peep,   450
And dart their arrowy odour through the brain
Till you might faint with that delicious pain.
And every motion, odour, beam, and tone,
With that deep music is in unison:
Which is a soul within the soul—they seem
Like echoes of an antenatal dream.—
It is an isle 'twixt Heaven, Air, Earth, and Sea,
Cradled, and hung in clear tranquillity;
Bright as that wandering Eden Lucifer,
Washed by the soft blue Oceans of young air.   460
It is a favoured place. Famine or Blight,
Pestilence, War and Earthquake, never light
Upon its mountain-peaks; blind vultures, they
Sail onward far upon their fatal way:
The wingèd storms, chanting their thunder-psalm
To other lands, leave azure chasms of calm
Over this isle, or weep themselves in dew,
From which its fields and woods ever renew
Their green and golden immortality.
And from the sea there rise, and from the sky   470
There fall, clear exhalations, soft and bright,
Veil after veil, each hiding some delight,
Which Sun or Moon or zephyr draw aside,
Till the isle's beauty, like a naked bride
Glowing at once with love and loveliness,
Blushes and trembles at its own excess:
Yet, like a buried lamp, a Soul no less
Burns in the heart of this delicious isle,
An atom of th' Eternal, whose own smile

---

459. Lucifer: light-bearer, the morning star.

Unfolds itself, and may be felt, not seen   480
O'er the gray rocks, blue waves, and forests green,
Filling their bare and void interstices.—
But the chief marvel of the wilderness
Is a lone dwelling, built by whom or how
None of the rustic island-people know:
'Tis not a tower of strength, though with its height
It overtops the woods; but, for delight,
Some wise and tender Ocean-King, ere crime
Had been invented, in the world's young prime,
Reared it, a wonder of that simple time,   490
An envy of the isles, a pleasure-house
Made sacred to his sister and his spouse.
It scarce seems now a wreck of human art,
But, as it were Titanic; in the heart
Of Earth having assumed its form, then grown
Out of the mountains, from the living stone,
Lifting itself in caverns light and high:
For all the antique and learnèd imagery
Has been erased, and in the place of it
The ivy and the wild-vine interknit   500
The volumes of their many-twining stems;
Parasite flowers illume with dewy gems
The lampless halls, and when they fade, the sky
Peeps through their winter-woof of tracery
With moonlight patches, or star atoms keen,
Or fragments of the day's intense serene;—
Working mosaic on their Parian floors.
And, day and night, aloof, from the high towers
And terraces, the Earth and Ocean seem
To sleep in one another's arms, and dream   510
Of waves, flowers, clouds, woods, rocks, and all that
          we
Read in their smiles, and call reality.

This isle and house are mine, and I have vowed
Thee to be lady of the solitude.—
And I have fitted up some chambers there
Looking towards the golden Eastern air,
And level with the living winds, which flow
Like waves above the living waves below.—
I have sent books and music there, and all
Those instruments with which high Spirits
          call   520
The future from its cradle, and the past
Out of its grave, and make the present last
In thoughts and joys which sleep, but cannot die,
Folded within their own eternity.

507. Parian: marble gathered from the fabled isle of
Paros.

Our simple life wants little, and true taste
Hires not the pale drudge Luxury, to waste
The scene it would adorn, and therefore still,
Nature with all her children haunts the hill.
The ring-dove, in the embowering ivy, yet
Keeps up her love-lament, and the owls flit   530
Round the evening tower, and the young stars
          glance
Between the quick bats in their twilight dance;
The spotted deer bask in the fresh moonlight
Before our gate, and the slow, silent night
Is measured by the pants of their calm sleep.
Be this our home in life, and when years heap
Their withered hours, like leaves, on our decay,
Let us become the overhanging day,
The living soul of this Elysian isle,
Conscious, inseparable, one. Meanwhile   540
We two will rise, and sit, and walk together
Under the roof of blue Ionian weather
And wander in the meadows, or ascend
The mossy mountains, where the blue heavens bend
With lightest winds, to touch their paramour;
Or linger, where the pebble-paven shore,
Under the quick, faint kisses of the sea
Trembles and sparkles as with ecstasy,—
Possessing and possessed by all that is
Within that calm circumference of bliss,   550
And by each other, till to love and live
Be one:—or, at the noontide hour, arrive
Where some old cavern hoar seems yet to keep
The moonlight of the expired night asleep,
Through which the awakened day can never peep;
A veil for our seclusion, close as night's,
Where secure sleep may kill thine innocent lights;
Sleep, the fresh dew of languid love, the rain
Whose drops quench kisses till they burn again.
And we will talk, until thought's melody   560
Become too sweet for utterance, and it die
In words, to live again in looks, which dart
With thrilling tone into the voiceless heart,
Harmonizing silence without a sound.
Our breath shall intermix, our bosoms bound,
And our veins beat together; and our lips
With other eloquence than words, eclipse
The soul that burns between them, and the wells
Which boil under our being's inmost cells,
The fountains of our deepest life, shall be   570
Confused in Passion's golden purity,
As mountain-springs under the morning sun.
We shall become the same, we shall be one

Spirit within two frames, oh! wherefore two?
One passion in twin-hearts, which grows and grew,
Till like two meteors of expanding flame,
Those spheres instinct with it become the same,
Touch, mingle, are transfigured; ever still
Burning, yet ever inconsumable:
In one another's substance finding food,   580
Like flames too pure and light and unimbued
To nourish their bright lives with baser prey,
Which point to Heaven and cannot pass away:
One hope within two wills, one will beneath
Two overshadowing minds, one life, one death,
One Heaven, one Hell, one immortality,
And one annihilation. Woe is me!
The wingèd words on which my soul would pierce
Into the height of Love's rare Universe,
Are chains of lead around its flight of fire—   590
I pant, I sink, I tremble, I expire!

Weak Verses, go, kneel at your Sovereign's feet,
And say:—"We are the masters of thy slave;
What wouldest thou with us and ours and thine?"
Then call your sisters from Oblivion's cave,
All singing loud: "Love's very pain is sweet,
But its reward is in the world divine
Which, if not here, it builds beyond the grave."
So shall ye live when I am here. Then haste
Over the hearts of men, until ye meet   800
Marina, Vanna, Primus, and the rest,
And bid them love each other and be blessed:
And leave the troop which errs, and which reproves,
And come and be my guest,—for I am Love's.

1821   *1821*

ADONAIS

AN ELEGY ON THE DEATH OF JOHN KEATS

Preface

It is my intention to subjoin to the London edition
of this poem a criticism upon the claims of its lamented object to be classed among the writers of
the highest genius ·who have adorned our age. My
known repugnance to the narrow principles of taste
on which several of his earlier compositions were

601. Marina, Vanna, Primus: Mary Shelley, Jane and
Edward Williams.

modelled proves, at least, that I am an impartial
judge. I consider the fragment of Hyperion as second to nothing that was ever produced by a writer
of the same years.

John Keats died at Rome of a consumption, in
his twenty-fourth year, on the [23rd] of [Feb.]
1821; and was buried in the romantic and lonely
cemetery of the Protestants in that city, under the
pyramid which is the tomb of Cestius and the
massy walls and towers, now mouldering and desolate, which formed the circuit of ancient Rome. The
cemetery is an open space among the ruins, covered
in winter with violets and daisies. It might make
one in love with death to think that one should be
buried in so sweet a place.

The genius of the lamented person to whose
memory I have dedicated these unworthy verses
was not less delicate and fragile than it was beautiful; and where cankerworms abound what wonder
if its young flower was blighted in the bud? The
savage criticism on his *Endymion*, which appeared
in the *Quarterly Review*, produced the most violent
effect on his susceptible mind; the agitation thus
originated ended in the rupture of a blood-vessel
in the lungs; a rapid consumption ensued, and the
succeeding acknowledgments from more candid
critics of the true greatness of his powers were ineffectual to heal the wound thus wantonly inflicted.

It may be well said that these wretched men
know not what they do. They scatter their insults
and their slanders without heed as to whether the
poisoned shaft lights on a heart made callous by
many blows, or one like Keats's composed of more
penetrable stuff. One of their associates is, to my
knowledge, a most base and unprincipled calumnia-
tor. As to *Endymion*, was it a poem, whatever
might be its defects, to be treated contemptuously
by those who had celebrated with various degrees
of complacency and panegyric *Paris* and *Woman*
and a *Syrian Tale*, and Mrs. Lefanu and Mr. Barrett
and Mr. Howard Payne and a long list of the illustrious obscure? Are these the men who in their
venal good nature presumed to draw a parallel
between the Rev. Mr. Milman and Lord Byron?
What gnat did they strain at here after having
swallowed all those camels? Against what woman
taken in adultery dares the foremost of these literary prostitutes to cast his opprobrious stone? Miserable man! you, one of the meanest, have wantonly
defaced one of the noblest specimens of the workmanship of God. Nor shall it be your excuse that,
murderer as you are, you have spoken daggers but
used none.

The circumstances of the closing scene of poor
Keats's life were not made known to me until the
Elegy was ready for the press. I am given to understand that the wound which his sensitive spirit had
received from the criticism of *Endymion* was exas-
perated by the bitter sense of unrequited benefits;
the poor fellow seems to have been hooted from the
stage of life no less by those on whom he had

wasted the promise of his genius than those on whom he had lavished his fortune and his care. He was accompanied to Rome and attended in his last illness by Mr. Severn, a young artist of the highest promise, who, I have been informed, "almost risked his own life, and sacrificed every prospect to un-wearied attendance upon his dying friend." Had I known these circumstances before the completion of my poem, I should have been tempted to add my feeble tribute of applause to the more solid recompense which the virtuous man finds in the recollection of his own motives. Mr. Severn can dispense with a reward from "such stuff as dreams are made of." His conduct is a golden augury of the success of his future career—may the unex-tinguished Spirit of his illustrious friend animate the creations of his pencil, and plead against Obliv-ion for his name! [Shelley]

’Αστὴρ πρὶν μὲν ἔλαμπες ἐνὶ ζωοῖσιν Ἐῶος.
νῦν δὲ θανὼν λάμπεις Ἕσπερος ἐν φθιμένοις.—

Plato°

1

I weep for Adonais—he is dead!
O, weep for Adonais! though our tears
Thaw not the frost which binds so dear a head!
And thou, sad Hour, selected from all years
To mourn our loss, rouse thy obscure compeers,
And teach them thine own sorrow, say: "With me
Died Adonais; till the Future dares
Forget the Past, his fate and fame shall be
An echo and a light unto eternity!"

2

Where wert thou, mighty Mother, when he lay,   10
When thy Son lay, pierced by the shaft which flies
In darkness? where was lorn Urania
When Adonais died? With veilèd eyes,

° Thou wert the morning star among the living,
  Ere thy fair light had fled;—
Now, having died, thou art, as Hesperus, giving
  New splendour to the dead.

(Shelley's translation)

ADONAIS. **1. Adonais:** a variant of Adonis, the beautiful youth loved by Aphrodite and slain by a wild boar. **12. Urania:** Muse of astronomy, inspirer of poetry.

'Mid listening Echoes, in her Paradise
She sate, while one, with soft enamoured breath,
Rekindled all the fading melodies,
With which, like flowers that mock the corse beneath,
He had adorned and hid the coming bulk of Death.

3

Oh, weep for Adonais—he is dead!
Wake, melancholy Mother, wake and weep!   20
Yet wherefore? Quench within their burning bed
Thy fiery tears, and let thy loud heart keep
Like his, a mute and uncomplaining sleep;
For he is gone, where all things wise and fair
Descend;—oh, dream not that the amorous Deep
Will yet restore him to the vital air;
Death feeds on his mute voice, and laughs at our despair.

4

Most musical of mourners, weep again!
Lament anew, Urania!—He died,
Who was the Sire of an immortal strain,   30
Blind, old, and lonely, when his country's pride,
The priest, the slave, and the liberticide,
Trampled and mocked with many a loathèd rite
Of lust and blood; he went, unterrified,
Into the gulf of death; but his clear Sprite
Yet reigns o'er earth; the third among the sons of light.

5

Most musical of mourners, weep anew!
Not all to that bright station dared to climb;
And happier they their happiness who knew,
Whose tapers yet burn through that night of time   40
In which suns perished; others more sublime,
Struck by the envious wrath of man or god,
Have sunk, extinct in their refulgent prime;
And some yet live, treading the thorny road,
Which leads, through toil and hate, to Fame's serene abode.

---

29. He: Milton. **36. third:** Homer and Dante are the other epic poets.

6

But now, thy youngest, dearest one, has
    perished—
The nursling of thy widowhood, who grew,
Like a pale flower by some sad maiden cherished,
And fed with true-love tears, instead of dew;
Most musical of mourners, weep anew!   50
Thy extreme hope, the loveliest and the last,
The bloom, whose petals, nipped before they
    blew,
Died on the promise of the fruit, is waste;
The broken lily lies—the storm is overpast.

7

To that high Capital, where kingly Death
Keeps his pale court in beauty and decay,
He came; and bought, with price of purest
    breath,
A grave among the eternal.—Come away!
Haste, while the vault of blue Italian day
Is yet his fitting charnel-roof! while still   60
He lies, as if in dewy sleep he lay;
Awake him not! surely he takes his fill
Of deep and liquid rest, forgetful of all ill.

8

He will awake no more, oh, never more!—
Within the twilight chamber spreads apace
The shadow of white Death, and at the door
Invisible Corruption waits to trace
His extreme way to her dim dwelling-place;
The eternal Hunger sits, but pity and awe
Soothe her pale rage, nor dares she to
    deface   70
So fair a prey, till darkness, and the law
Of change, shall o'er his sleep the mortal curtain
    draw.

9

Oh, weep for Adonais!—The quick Dreams,
The passion-wingèd Ministers of thought,
Who were his flocks, whom near the living
    streams

Of his young spirit he fed, and whom he taught
The love which was its music, wander not,—
Wander no more, from kindling brain to brain,
But droop there, whence they sprung; and mourn
    their lot
Round the cold heart, where, after their sweet
    pain,   80
They ne'er will gather strength, or find a home
    again.

10

And one with trembling hands clasps his cold
    head,
And fans him with her moonlight wings, and
    cries;
"Our love, our hope, our sorrow, is not dead;
See, on the silken fringe of his faint eyes,
Like dew upon a sleeping flower, there lies
A tear some Dream has loosened from his brain."
Lost Angel of a ruined Paradise!
She knew not 'twas her own; as with no stain
She faded, like a cloud which had outwept its
    rain.   90

11

One from a lucid urn of starry dew
Washed his light limbs as if embalming them;
Another clipped her profuse locks, and threw
The wreath upon him, like an anadem,
Which frozen tears instead of pearls begem;
Another in her wilful grief would break
Her bow and wingèd reeds, as if to stem
A greater loss with one which was more weak;
And dull the barbèd fire against his frozen cheek.

12

Another Splendour on his mouth alit,   100
That mouth, whence it was wont to draw the
    breath
Which gave it strength to pierce the guarded
    wit
And pass into the panting heart beneath
With lightning and with music: the damp death
Quenched its caress upon his icy lips;
And, as a dying meteor stains a wreath

55. Capital: Rome.

94. anadem: garland.

Of moonlight vapour, which the cold night clips,
It flushed through his pale limbs, and passed to its
    eclipse.

13

And others came . . . Desires and Adorations,
Wingèd Persuasions and veiled Destinies,   110
Splendours, and Glooms, and glimmering Incar-
    nations
Of hopes and fears, and twilight Phantasies;
And Sorrow, with her family of Sighs,
And Pleasure, blind with tears, led by the gleam
Of her own dying smile instead of eyes,
Came in slow pomp,—the moving pomp might
    seem
Like pageantry of mist on an autumnal stream.

14

All he had loved, and moulded into thought,
From shape, and hue, and odour, and sweet
    sound,
Lamented Adonais. Morning sought   120
Her eastern watch-tower, and her hair unbound,
Wet with the tears which should adorn the
    ground,
Dimmed the aëreal eyes that kindle day;
Afar the melancholy thunder moaned,
Pale Ocean in unquiet slumber lay,
And the wild Winds flew round, sobbing in their
    dismay.

15

Lost Echo sits amid the voiceless mountains,
And feeds her grief with his remembered lay,
And will no more reply to winds or fountains,
Or amorous birds perched on the young green
    spray,   130
Or herdsman's horn, or bell at closing day;
Since she can mimic not his lips, more dear
Than those for whose disdain she pined away
Into a shadow of all sounds:—a drear
Murmur, between their songs, is all the woodmen
    hear.

16

Grief made the young Spring wild, and she threw
    down
Her kindling buds, as if she Autumn were,
Or they dead leaves; since her delight is flown,
For whom should she have waked the sullen
    year?
To Phoebus was not Hyacinth so dear   140
Nor to himself Narcissus, as to both
Thou, Adonais: wan they stand and sere
Amid the faint companions of their youth,
With dew all turned to tears; odour, to sighing ruth.

17

Thy spirit's sister, the lorn nightingale,
Mourns not her mate with such melodious pain;
Not so the eagle, who like thee could scale
Heaven, and could nourish in the sun's domain
Her mighty youth with morning, doth complain,
Soaring and screaming round her empty
    nest,   150
As Albion wails for thee: the curse of Cain
Light on his head who pierced thy innocent
    breast,
And scared the angel soul that was its earthly guest!

18

Ah, woe is me! Winter is come and gone,
But grief returns with the revolving year;
The airs and streams renew their joyous tone;
The ants, the bees, the swallows reappear;
Fresh leaves and flowers deck the dead Seasons'
    bier;
The amorous birds now pair in every brake,
And build their mossy homes in field and
    brere;   160
And the green lizard, and the golden snake,
Like unimprisoned flames, out of their trance
    awake.

19

Through wood and stream and field and hill and
    Ocean

---

107. clips: embraces. 133–34. those . . . sounds: a reference to Echo, whose unrequited love for Narcissus
caused her to fade away until only her voice remained.

140. Phoebus . . . Hyacinth: Phoebus (Apollo) accidentally slew his beloved Hyacinth. 141. Narcissus: youth
who fell in love with his own reflection in a pool. 160.
brere: briar.

A quickening life from the Earth's heart has burst
As it has ever done, with change and motion,
From the great morning of the world when first
God dawned on Chaos; in its stream immersed,
The lamps of Heaven flash with a softer light;
All baser things pant with life's sacred thirst;
Diffuse themselves; and spend in love's de-
    light,   170
The beauty and the joy of their renewèd might.

20

The leprous corpse, touched by this spirit tender,
Exhales itself in flowers of gentle breath;
Like incarnations of the stars, when splendour
Is changed to fragrance, they illumine death
And mock the merry worm that wakes beneath;
Nought we know, dies. Shall that alone which
    knows
Be as a sword consumed before the sheath
By sightless lightning?—the intense atom glows
A moment, then is quenched in a most cold repose.

21

Alas! that all we loved of him should be,   181
But for our grief, as if it had not been,
And grief itself be mortal! Woe is me!
Whence are we, and why are we? of what scene
The actors or spectators? Great and mean
Meet massed in death, who lends what life must
    borrow.
As long as skies are blue, and fields are green,
Evening must usher night, night urge the
    morrow,
Month follow month with woe, and year wake year
    to sorrow.

22

He will awake no more, oh, never more!   190
"Wake thou," cried Misery, "childless Mother,
    rise
Out of thy sleep, and slake, in thy heart's core,
A wound more fierce than his, with tears and
    sighs."
And all the Dreams that watched Urania's eyes,
And all the Echoes whom their sister's song
Had held in holy silence, cried: "Arise!"
Swift as a Thought by the snake Memory stung,
From her ambrosial rest the fading Splendour
    sprung.

23

She rose like an autumnal Night, that springs
Out of the East, and follows wild and drear   200
The golden Day, which, on eternal wings,
Even as a ghost abandoning a bier,
Had left the Earth a corpse. Sorrow and fear
So struck, so roused, so rapt Urania;
So saddened round her like an atmosphere
Of stormy mist; so swept her on her way
Even to the mournful place where Adonais lay.

24

Out of her secret Paradise she sped,
Through camps and cities rough with stone, and
    steel,
And human hearts, which to her aery tread   210
Yielding not, wounded the invisible
Palms of her tender feet where'er they fell:
And barbèd tongues, and thoughts more sharp
    than they,
Rent the soft Form they never could repel,
Whose sacred blood, like the young tears of May,
Paved with eternal flowers that undeserving way.

25

In the death-chamber for a moment Death,
Shamed by the presence of that living Might,
Blushed to annihilation, and the breath
Revisited those lips, and Life's pale light   220
Flashed through those limbs, so late her dear de-
    light.
"Leave me not wild and drear and comfortless,
As silent lightning leaves the starless night!
Leave me not!" cried Urania: her distress
Roused Death: Death rose and smiled, and met her
    vain caress.

26

"Stay yet awhile! speak to me once again;
Kiss me, so long but as a kiss may live;
And in my heartless breast and burning brain

That word, that kiss, shall all thoughts else
   survive,
With food of saddest memory kept alive,   230
Now thou art dead, as if it were a part
Of thee, my Adonais! I would give
All that I am to be as thou now art!
But I am chained to Time, and cannot thence de-
   part!

27

"O gentle child, beautiful as thou wert,
Why didst thou leave the trodden path of men
Too soon, and with weak hands though mighty
   heart
Dare the unpastured dragon in his den?
Defenceless as thou wert, oh, where was then
Wisdom the mirrored shield, or scorn the
   spear?   240
Or hadst thou waited the full cycle, when
Thy spirit should have filled its crescent sphere,
The monsters of life's waste had fled from thee like
   deer.

28

"The herded wolves, bold only to pursue;
The obscene ravens, clamorous o'er the dead;
The vultures to the conqueror's banner true
Who feed where Desolation first has fed,
And whose wings rain contagion;—how they
   fled,
When, like Apollo, from his golden bow
The Pythian of the age one arrow sped   250
And smiled!—The spoilers tempt no second blow,
They fawn on the proud feet that spurn them lying
   low.

29

"The sun comes forth, and many reptiles spawn;
He sets, and each ephemeral insect then
Is gathered into death without a dawn,

And the immortal stars awake again;
So is it in the world of living men:
A godlike mind soars forth, in its delight
Making earth bare and veiling heaven, and when
It sinks, the swarms that dimmed or shared its
   light   260
Leave to its kindred lamps the spirit's awful
   night."

30

Thus ceased she: and the mountain shepherds
   came,
Their garlands sere, their magic mantles rent;
The Pilgrim of Eternity, whose fame
Over his living head like Heaven is bent,
An early but enduring monument,
Came, veiling all the lightnings of his song
In sorrow; from her wilds Ierne sent
The sweetest lyrist of her saddest wrong,
And Love taught Grief to fall like music from his
   tongue.   270

31

Midst others of less note, came one frail Form,
A phantom among men; companionless
As the last cloud of an expiring storm
Whose thunder is its knell; he, as I guess,
Had gazed on Nature's naked loveliness,
Actaeon-like, and now he fled astray
With feeble steps o'er the world's wilderness,
And his own thoughts, along that rugged way,
Pursued, like raging hounds, their father and their
   prey.

32

A pardlike Spirit beautiful and swift—   280
A Love in desolation masked;—a Power
Girt round with weakness;—it can scarce uplift
The weight of the superincumbent hour;
It is a dying lamp, a falling shower,
A breaking billow;—even whilst we speak
Is it not broken? On the withering flower

238–40. **dragon . . . spear:** Perseus was able to slay Medusa, whose gaze turned the beholder to stone, by looking at her reflection in his shield. 244–46. **wolves . . . vultures:** a reference to the critics whose harsh reviews were believed to have killed Keats. 250. **Pythian of the age:** Byron, whose *English Bards and Scotch Reviewers* savagely satirized the critics. Like Apollo, he slew the serpent Python.

264. **Pilgrim of Eternity:** the wandering Byron. 268–69. **Ierne . . . lyrist:** Thomas Moore, the great lyric poet of Ireland (Ierne). 271. **frail Form:** a self-portrait of Shelley. 276. **Actaeon-like:** Actaeon, having seen Diana bathing, was transformed by the goddess into a stag and killed by his own dogs. 280. **pardlike:** like a leopard.

The killing sun smiles brightly; on a cheek
The life can burn in blood, even while the heart
    may break.

33

His head was bound with pansies overblown,
And faded violets, white, and pied, and
    blue;   290
And a light spear topped with a cypress cone,
Round whose rude shaft dark ivy-tresses grew
Yet dripping with the forest's noonday dew,
Vibrated, as the ever-beating heart
Shook the weak hand that grasped it; of that
    crew
He came the last, neglected and apart;
A herd-abandoned deer struck by the hunter's dart.

34

All stood aloof, and at his partial moan
Smiled through their tears; well knew that gentle
    band
Who in another's fate now wept his own,   300
As in the accents of an unknown land
He sung new sorrow; sad Urania scanned
The Stranger's mien, and murmured: "Who art
    thou?"
He answered not, but with a sudden hand
Made bare his branded and ensanguined brow,
Which was like Cain's or Christ's—oh! that it should
    be so!

35

What softer voice is hushed over the dead?
Athwart what brow is that dark mantle thrown?
What form leans sadly o'er the white death-bed,
In mockery of monumental stone,   310
The heavy heart heaving without a moan?
If it be He, who, gentlest of the wise,
Taught, soothed, loved, honoured the departed
    one,
Let me not vex, with inharmonious sighs,
The silence of that heart's accepted sacrifice.

310. **mockery:** imitation. 312. **gentlest . . . wise:** a reference to Leigh Hunt, who had supported Keats.

36

Our Adonais has drunk poison—oh!
What deaf and viperous murderer could crown
Life's early cup with such a draught of woe?
The nameless worm would now itself disown:
It felt, yet could escape, the magic tone   320
Whose prelude held all envy, hate, and wrong,
But what was howling in one breast alone,
Silent with expectation of the song,
Whose master's hand is cold, whose silver lyre
    unstrung.

37

Live thou, whose infamy is not thy fame!
Live! fear no heavier chastisement from me,
Thou noteless blot on a remembered name!
But be thyself, and know thyself to be!
And ever at thy season be thou free
To spill the venom when thy fangs o'erflow;   330
Remorse and Self-contempt shall cling to thee;
Hot Shame shall burn upon thy secret brow,
And like a beaten hound tremble thou shalt—as
    now.

38

Nor let us weep that our delight is fled
Far from these carrion kites that scream below;
He wakes or sleeps with the enduring dead;
Thou canst not soar where he is sitting now.—
Dust to the dust! but the pure spirit shall flow
Back to the burning fountain whence it came,
A portion of the Eternal, which must glow   340
Through time and change, unquenchably the
    same,
Whilst thy cold embers choke the sordid hearth of
    shame.

39

Peace, peace! he is not dead, he doth not sleep—
He hath awakened from the dream of life—
'Tis we, who lost in stormy visions, keep
With phantoms an unprofitable strife,

319. **nameless worm:** the anonymous reviewers who
attacked Keats in the *Quarterly* and *Blackwood's.*

And in mad trance, strike with our spirit's knife
Invulnerable nothings.—*We* decay
Like corpses in a charnel; fear and grief
Convulse us and consume us day by day,   350
And cold hopes swarm like worms within our living
    clay.

40

He has outsoared the shadow of our night;
Envy and calumny and hate and pain,
And that unrest which men miscall delight,
Can touch him not and torture not again;
From the contagion of the world's slow stain
He is secure, and now can never mourn
A heart grown cold, a head grown gray in vain;
Nor, when the spirit's self has ceased to burn,
With sparkless ashes load an unlamented urn.   360

41

He lives, he wakes—'tis Death is dead, not he;
Mourn not for Adonais.—Thou young Dawn,
Turn all thy dew to splendour, for from thee
The spirit thou lamentest is not gone;
Ye caverns and ye forests, cease to moan!
Cease, ye faint flowers and fountains, and thou
    Air,
Which like a mourning veil thy scarf hadst
    thrown
O'er the abandoned Earth, now leave it bare
Even to the joyous stars which smile on its despair!

42

He is made one with Nature: there is
    heard   370
His voice in all her music, from the moan
Of thunder, to the song of night's sweet bird;
He is a presence to be felt and known
In darkness and in light, from herb and stone,
Spreading itself where'er that Power may move
Which has withdrawn his being to its own;
Which wields the world with never-wearied love,
Sustains it from beneath, and kindles it above.

43

He is a portion of the loveliness
Which once he made more lovely: he doth bear

His part, while the one Spirit's plastic stress   381
Sweeps through the dull dense world, compel-
    ling there,
All new successions to the forms they wear;
Torturing th' unwilling dross that checks its flight
To its own likeness, as each mass may bear;
And bursting in its beauty and its might
From trees and beasts and men into the Heaven's
    light.

44

The splendours of the firmament of time
May be eclipsed, but are extinguished not;
Like stars to their appointed height they
    climb,   390
And death is a low mist which cannot blot
The brightness it may veil. When lofty thought
Lifts a young heart above its mortal lair,
And love and life contend in it, for what
Shall be its earthly doom, the dead live there
And move like winds of light on dark and stormy
    air.

45

The inheritors of unfulfilled renown
Rose from their thrones, built beyond mortal
    thought,
Far in the Unapparent. Chatterton
Rose pale,—his solemn agony had not   400
Yet faded from him; Sidney, as he fought
And as he fell and as he lived and loved
Sublimely mild, a Spirit without spot,
Arose; and Lucan, by his death approved:
Oblivion as they rose shrank like a thing reproved.

46

And many more, whose names on Earth are dark,
But whose transmitted effluence cannot die
So long as fire outlives the parent spark.
Rose, robed in dazzling immortality.
"Thou art become as one of us," they cry,   410
"It was for thee yon kingless sphere has long
Swung blind in unascended majesty,

381. plastic: shaping. **399–404. Chatterton . . . approved:**
young men of promise who died before they had gained
complete fulfillment.

Silent alone amid an Heaven of Song.
Assume thy wingèd throne, thou Vesper of our
    throng!"

47

Who mourns for Adonais? Oh, come forth,
Fond wretch! and know thyself and him aright.
Clasp with thy panting soul the pendulous Earth;
As from a centre, dart thy spirit's light
Beyond all worlds, until its spacious might
Satiate the void circumference: then shrink   420
Even to a point within our day and night;
And keep thy heart light lest it make thee sink
When hope has kindled hope, and lured thee to the
    brink.

48

Or go to Rome, which is the sepulchre,
Oh, not of him, but of our joy: 'tis nought
That ages, empires, and religions there
Lie buried in the ravage they have wrought:
For such as he can lend,—they borrow not
Glory from those who made the world their prey;
And he is gathered to the kings of thought   430
Who waged contention with their time's decay,
And of the past are all that cannot pass away.

49

Go thou to Rome,—at once the Paradise,
The grave, the city, and the wilderness;
And where its wrecks like shattered mountains
    rise,
And flowering weeds, and fragrant copses dress
The bones of Desolation's nakedness
Pass, till the spirit of the spot shall lead
Thy footsteps to a slope of green access
Where, like an infant's smile, over the dead   440
A light of laughing flowers along the grass is
    spread;

50

And gray walls moulder round, on which dull
    Time
Feeds, like slow fire upon a hoary brand;

And one keen pyramid with wedge sublime,
Pavilioning the dust of him who planned
This refuge for his memory, doth stand
Like flame transformed to marble; and beneath,
A field is spread, on which a newer band
Have pitched in Heaven's smile their camp of
    death,
Welcoming him we lose with scarce extinguished
    breath.   450

51

Here pause: these graves are all too young as yet
To have outgrown the sorrow which consigned
Its charge to each; and if the seal is set,
Here, on one fountain of a mourning mind,
Break it not thou! too surely shalt thou find
Thine own well full, if thou returnest home,
Of tears and gall. From the world's bitter wind
Seek shelter in the shadow of the tomb.
What Adonais is, why fear we to become?

52

The One remains, the many change and
    pass;   460
Heaven's light forever shines, Earth's shadows
    fly;
Life, like a dome of many-coloured glass,
Stains the white radiance of Eternity,
Until Death tramples it to fragments.—Die,
If thou wouldst be with that which thou dost
    seek!
Follow where all is fled!—Rome's azure sky,
Flowers, ruins, statues, music, words, are weak
The glory they transfuse with fitting truth to speak.

53

Why linger, why turn back, why shrink, my
    Heart?
Thy hopes are gone before: from all things
    here   470
They have departed; thou shouldst now depart!
A light is passed from the revolving year,
And man, and woman; and what still is dear
Attracts to crush, repels to make thee wither.

---

424. Rome: Keats was buried in the Protestant cemetery in Rome.

444. one keen pyramid: the tomb of Gaius Cestius, a
Roman tribune.

The soft sky smiles,—the low wind whispers
  near:
'Tis Adonais calls! oh, hasten thither,
No more let Life divide what Death can join together.

54

That Light whose smile kindles the Universe,
That Beauty in which all things work and move,
That Benediction which the eclipsing
  Curse   480
Of birth can quench not, that sustaining Love
Which through the web of being blindly wove
By man and beast and earth and air and sea,
Burns bright or dim, as each are mirrors of
The fire for which all thirst; now beams on me,
Consuming the last clouds of cold mortality.

55

The breath whose might I have invoked in song
Descends on me; my spirit's bark is driven,
Far from the shore, far from the trembling
  throng
Whose sails were never to the tempest
  given;   490
The massy earth and spherèd skies are riven!
I am borne darkly, fearfully, afar;
Whilst, burning through the inmost veil of
  Heaven,
The soul of Adonais, like a star,
Beacons from the abode where the Eternal are.

1821   *1821*

THE TRIUMPH OF LIFE

Swift as a spirit hastening to his task
Of glory and of good, the Sun sprang forth
Rejoicing in his splendour, and the mask

Of darkness fell from the awakened Earth—
The smokeless altars of the mountain snows
Flamed above crimson clouds, and at the birth

Of light, the Ocean's orison arose,
To which the birds tempered their matin lay.
All flowers in field or forest which unclose

Their trembling eyelids to the kiss of day,   10
Swinging their censers in the element,
With orient incense lit by the new ray

Burned slow and inconsumably, and sent
Their odorous sighs up to the smiling air;
And, in succession due, did continent,

Isle, ocean, and all things that in them wear
The form and character of mortal mould,
Rise as the Sun their father rose, to bear

Their portion of the toil, which he of old
Took as his own, and then imposed on them: 20
But I, whom thoughts which must remain untold

Had kept as wakeful as the stars that gem
The cone of night, now they were laid asleep
Stretched my faint limbs beneath the hoary stem

Which an old chestnut flung athwart the steep
Of a green Apennine: before me fled
The night; behind me rose the day; the deep

Was at my feet, and Heaven above my head,—
When a strange trance over my fancy grew
Which was not slumber, for the shade it spread   30

Was so transparent, that the scene came through
As clear as when a veil of light is drawn
O'er evening hills, they glimmer; and I knew

That I had felt the freshness of that dawn
Bathe in the same cold dew my brow and hair,
And sate as thus upon that slope of lawn

Under the self-same bough, and heard as there
The birds, the fountains and the ocean hold
Sweet talk in music through the enamoured air,
And then a vision on my brain was rolled.   40

As in that trance of wondrous thought I lay,
This was the tenour of my waking dream:—
Methought I sate beside a public way

Thick strewn with summer dust, and a great stream
Of people there was hurrying to and fro,
Numerous as gnats upon the evening gleam,

All hastening onward, yet none seemed to know
Whither he went, or whence he came, or why
He made one of the multitude, and so

Was borne amid the crowd, as through the sky   50
One of the million leaves of summer's bier;
Old age and youth, manhood and infancy,

Mixed in one mighty torrent did appear,
Some flying from the thing they feared, and some
Seeking the object of another's fear;

And others, as with steps towards the tomb,
Pored on the trodden worms that crawled beneath,
And others mournfully within the gloom

Of their own shadow walked, and called it death;
And some fled from it as it were a ghost,   60
Half fainting in the affliction of vain breath:

But more, with motions which each other crossed,
Pursued or shunned the shadows the clouds threw,
Or birds within the noonday aether lost,

Upon that path where flowers never grew,—
And, weary with vain toil and faint for thirst,
Heard not the fountains, whose melodious dew

Out of their mossy cells forever burst;
Nor felt the breeze which from the forest told
Of grassy paths and wood-lawns interspersed   70

With overarching elms and caverns cold,
And violet banks where sweet dreams brood, but
        they
Pursued their serious folly as of old.

And as I gazed, methought that in the way
The throng grew wilder, as the woods of June
When the south wind shakes the extinguished day,

And a cold glare, intenser than the noon,
But icy cold, obscured with blinding light
The sun, as he the stars. Like the young moon—

When on the sunlit limits of the night   80
Her white shell trembles amid crimson air,
And whilst the sleeping tempest gathers might—

Doth, as the herald of its coming, bear
The ghost of its dead mother, whose dim form
Bends in dark aether from her infant's chair,—

So came a chariot on the silent storm
Of its own rushing splendour, and a Shape
So sate within, as one whom years deform,

Beneath a dusky hood and double cape,
Crouching within the shadow of a tomb;   90
And o'er what seemed the head a cloud-like crape

Was bent, a dun and faint aethereal gloom
Tempering the light. Upon the chariot-beam
A Janus-visaged Shadow did assume

The guidance of that wonder-wingèd team;
The shapes which drew it in thick lightenings
Were lost:—I heard alone on the air's soft stream

The music of their ever-moving wings.
All the four faces of that Charioteer
Had their eyes banded; little profit brings   100

Speed in the van and blindness in the rear,
Nor then avail the beams that quench the sun,—
Or that with banded eyes could pierce the sphere

Of all that is, has been or will be done;
So ill was the car guided—but it passed
With solemn speed majestically on.

The crowd gave way, and I arose aghast,
Or seemed to rise, so mighty was the trance,
And saw, like clouds upon the thunder-blast,

The million with fierce song and maniac
        dance   110
Raging around—such seemed the jubilee
As when to greet some conqueror's advance

Imperial Rome poured forth her living sea
From senate-house, and forum, and theatre,
When   upon the free

Had bound a yoke, which soon they stooped to
        bear.
Nor wanted here the just similitude
Of a triumphal pageant, for where'er

The chariot rolled, a captive multitude
Was driven;—all those who had grown old in power
Or misery,—all who had their age subdued   121

By action or by suffering, and whose hour
Was drained to its last sand in weal or woe,
So that the trunk survived both fruit and flower;—

All those whose fame or infamy must grow
Till the great winter lay the form and name
Of this green earth with them for ever low;—

All but the sacred few who could not tame
Their spirits to the conqueror—but as soon
As they had touched the world with living
        flame,   130

Fled back like eagles to their native noon,
Or those who put aside the diadem
Of earthly thrones or gems . . .

Were there, of Athens or Jerusalem,
Were neither mid the mighty captives seen,
Nor mid the ribald crowd that followed them,

Nor those who went before fierce and obscene.
The wild dance maddens in the van, and those
Who lead it—fleet as shadows on the green,

Outspeed the chariot, and without repose   140
Mix with each other in tempestuous measure
To savage music, wilder as it grows,

They, tortured by their agonizing pleasure,
Convulsed and on the rapid whirlwinds spun
Of that fierce Spirit, whose unholy leisure

Was soothed by mischief since the world begun,
Throw back their heads and loose their streaming
      hair;
And in their dance round her who dims the sun,

Maidens and youths fling their wild arms in air
As their feet twinkle; they recede, and now   150
Bending with each other's atmosphere,

Kindle invisibly—and as they glow,
Like moths by light attracted and repelled,
Oft to their bright destruction come and go,

Till like two clouds into one vale impelled,
That shake the mountains when their lightnings
      mingle
And die in rain—the fiery band which held

Their natures, snaps—while the shock still may
      tingle;
One falls and then another in the path
Senseless—nor is the desolation single,   160

Yet ere I can say *where*—the chariot hath
Passed over them—nor other trace I find
But as of foam after the ocean's wrath

Is spent upon the desert shore;—behind,
Old men and women foully disarrayed,
Shake their gray hairs in the insulting wind,

And follow in the dance, with limbs decayed,
Seeking to reach the light which leaves them still
Farther behind and deeper in the shade.

But not the less with impotence of will   170
They wheel, though ghastly shadows interpose
Round them and round each other, and fulfil

Their work, and in the dust from whence they rose
Sink, and corruption veils them as they lie,
And past in these performs what   in those.

Struck to the heart by this sad pageantry,
Half to myself I said—"And what is this?
Whose shape is that within the car? And why—"

I would have added—"is all here amiss?—"
But a voice answered—"Life!"—I turned, and knew
(O Heaven, have mercy on such wretched-
      ness!)   181

That what I thought was an old root which grew
To strange distortion out of the hill side,
Was indeed one of those deluded crew,

And that the grass, which methought hung so wide
And white, was but his thin discoloured hair,
And that the holes it vainly sought to hide,

Were or had been eyes:—"If thou canst, forbear
To join the dance, which I had well forborne!"
Said the grim Feature (of my thought
      aware).   190

"I will unfold that which to this deep scorn
Led me and my companions, and relate
The progress of the pageant since the morn;

"If thirst of knowledge shall not then abate,
Follow it thou even to the night, but I
Am weary."—Then like one who with the weight

Of his own words is staggered, wearily
He paused; and ere he could resume, I cried:
"First, who art thou?"—"Before thy memory,

"I feared, loved, hated, suffered, did and
      died,   200
And if the spark with which Heaven lit my spirit
Had been with purer nutriment supplied,

"Corruption would not now thus much inherit
Of what was once Rousseau,—nor this disguise
Stain that which ought to have disdained to wear it;

"If I have been extinguished, yet there rise
A thousand beacons from the spark I bore"—
"And who are those chained to the car?"—"The
      wise,

"The great, the unforgotten,—they who wore
Mitres and helms and crowns, or wreaths of
      light,   210
Signs of thought's empire over thought—their lore

"Taught them not this, to know themselves; their
    might
Could not repress the mystery within,
And for the morn of truth they feigned, deep night

"Caught them ere evening."—"Who is he with chin
Upon his breast, and hands crossed on his chain?"—
"The child of a fierce hour; he sought to win

"The world, and lost all that it did contain
Of greatness, in its hope destroyed; and more
Of fame and peace than virtue's self can gain   220

"Without the opportunity which bore
Him on its eagle pinions to the peak
From which a thousand climbers have before

"Fallen, as Napoleon fell."—I felt my cheek
Alter, to see the shadow pass away,
Whose grasp had left the giant world so weak

That every pigmy kicked it as it lay;
And much I grieved to think how power and will
In opposition rule our mortal day,

And why God made irreconcilable   230
Good and the means of good; and for despair
I half disdained mine eyes' desire to fill

With the spent vision of the times that were
And scarce have ceased to be.—"Dost thou be-
    hold,"
Said my guide, "those spoilers spoiled, Voltaire,

"Frederick, and Paul, Catherine, and Leopold,
And hoary anarchs, demagogues, and sage
    names which the world thinks always old,

"For in the battle Life and they did wage,
She remained conqueror. I was overcome   240
By my own heart alone, which neither age,

"Nor tears, nor infamy, nor now the tomb
Could temper to its object."   "Let them pass,"
I cried, "the world and its mysterious doom

"Is not so much more glorious than it was,
That I desire to worship those who drew
New figures on its false and fragile glass

"As the old faded."—"Figures ever new
Rise on the bubble, paint them as you may;
We have but thrown, as those before us
    threw,   250

"Our shadows on it as it passed away.
But mark now chained to the triumphal chair
The mighty phantoms of an elder day;

"All that is mortal of great Plato there
Expiates the joy and woe his master knew not;
The star that ruled his doom was far too fair,

"And life, where long that flower of Heaven grew
    not,
Conquered that heart by love, which gold, or pain,
Or age, or sloth, or slavery could subdue not.

"And near him walk the   twain,   260
The tutor and his pupil, whom Dominion
Followed as tame as vulture in a chain.

"The world was darkened beneath either pinion
Of him whom from the flock of conquerors
Fame singled out for her thunder-bearing minion;

"The other long outlived both woes and wars,
Throned in the thoughts of men, and still had kept
The jealous key of Truth's eternal doors,

"If Bacon's eagle spirit had not lept
Like lightning out of darkness—he compelled   270
The Proteus shape of Nature, as it slept

"To wake, and lead him to the caves that held
The treasure of the secrets of its reign.
See the great bards of elder time, who quelled

"The passions which they sung, as by their strain
May well be known: their living melody
Tempers its own contagion to the vein

"Of these who are infected with it—I
Have suffered what I wrote, or viler pain!
And so my words have seeds of misery   280

"Even as the deeds of others, not as theirs."
And then he pointed to a company,

'Midst whom I quickly recognized the heirs
Of Caesar's crime, from him to Constantine;
The anarch chiefs, whose force and murderous
    snares

THE TRIUMPH OF LIFE. 236. Frederick . . . Leopold:
Frederick the Great of Prussia; Czar Paul of Russia;
Catherine the Great. Leopold II of the Holy Roman
Empire.

261. tutor . . . pupil: Aristotle and Alexander the Great.

Had founded many a sceptre-bearing line,
And spread the plague of gold and blood abroad:
And Gregory and John, and men divine,

Who rose like shadows between man and God;
Till that eclipse, still hanging over heaven,   290
Was worshipped by the world o'er which they
          strode,

For the true sun it quenched—"The power was
          given
But to destroy," replied the leader:—"I
Am one of those who have created, even

"If it be but a world of agony."—
"Whence camest thou? and whither goest thou?
How did thy course begin?" I said, "and why?

"Mine eyes are sick of this perpetual flow
Of people, and my heart sick of one sad thought—
Speak!"—"Whence I am, I partly seem to
          know,   300

"And how and by what paths I have been brought
To this dread pass, methinks even thou mayest
          guess;—
Why this should be, my mind can compass not;

"Whither the conqueror hurries me, still less;—
But follow thou, and from spectator turn
Actor or victim in this wretchedness,

"And what thou wouldst be taught I then may learn
From thee. Now listen:—In the April prime,
When all the forest-tips began to burn

"With kindling green, touched by the azure clime
Of the young season, I was laid asleep   311
Under a mountain, which from unknown time

"Had yawned into a cavern, high and deep;
And from it came a gentle rivulet,
Whose water, like clear air, in its calm sweep

"Bent the soft grass, and kept for ever wet
The stems of the sweet flowers, and filled the grove
With sounds, which whoso hears must needs forget

"All pleasure and all pain, all hate and love,
Which they had known before that hour of
          rest;   320
A sleeping mother then would dream not of

"Her only child who died upon the breast
At eventide—a king would mourn no more
The crown of which his brows were dispossessed

"When the sun lingered o'er his ocean floor
To gild his rival's new prosperity.
Thou wouldst forget thus vainly to deplore

"Ills, which if ills can find no cure from thee,
The thought of which no other sleep will quell,
Nor other music blot from memory,   330

"So sweet and deep is the oblivious spell;
And whether life had been before that sleep
The Heaven which I imagine, or a Hell

"Like this harsh world in which I wake to weep,
I know not. I arose, and for a space
The scene of woods and waters seemed to keep,

"Though it was now broad day, a gentle trace
Of light diviner than the common sun
Sheds on the common earth, and all the place

"Was filled with magic sounds woven into
          one   340
Oblivious melody, confusing sense
Amid the gliding waves and shadows dun;

"And, as I looked, the bright omnipresence
Of morning through the orient cavern flowed,
And the sun's image radiantly intense

"Burned on the waters of the well that glowed
Like gold, and threaded all the forest's maze
With winding paths of emerald fire; there stood

"Amid the sun, as he amid the blaze
Of his own glory, on the vibrating   350
Floor of the fountain, paved with flashing rays,

"A Shape all light, which with one hand did fling
Dew on the earth, as if she were the dawn,
And the invisible rain did ever sing

"A silver music on the mossy lawn;
And still before me on the dusky grass,
Iris her many-coloured scarf had drawn:

"In her right hand she bore a crystal glass,
Mantling with bright Nepenthe; the fierce splendour
Fell from her as she moved under the mass   360

288. **Gregory . . . John:** Pope Gregory the Great and possibly St. John.

357. **Iris:** the rainbow. 359. **Nepenthe:** a drug bringing forgetfulness.

"Of the deep cavern, and with palms so tender,
Their tread broke not the mirror of its billow,
Glided along the river, and did bend her

"Head under the dark boughs, till like a willow
Her fair hair swept the bosom of the stream
That whispered with delight to be its pillow.

"As one enamoured is upborne in dream
O'er lily-paven lakes, mid silver mist,
To wondrous music, so this shape might seem

"Partly to tread the waves with feet which
          kissed   370
The dancing foam; partly to glide along
The air which roughened the moist amethyst,

"Or the faint morning beams that fell among
The trees, or the soft shadows of the trees;
And her feet, ever to the ceaseless song

"Of leaves, and winds, and waves, and birds, and
          bees,
And falling drops, moved in a measure new
Yet sweet, as on the summer evening breeze,

"Up from the lake a shape of golden dew
Between two rocks, athwart the rising moon,   380
Dances i' the wind, where never eagle flew;

"And still her feet, no less than the sweet tune
To which they moved, seemed as they moved to
          blot
The thoughts of him who gazed on them; and soon

"All that was, seemed as if it had been not;
And all the gazer's mind was strewn beneath
Her feet like embers; and she, thought by thought,

"Trampled its sparks into the dust of death;
As day upon the threshold of the east
Treads out the lamps of night, until the
          breath   390

"Of darkness re-illumine even the least
Of heaven's living eyes—like day she came,
Making the night a dream; and ere she ceased

"To move, as one between desire and shame
Suspended, I said—'If, as it doth seem,
Thou comest from the realm without a name

"Into this valley of perpetual dream,
Show whence I came, and where I am, and why—
Pass not away upon the passing stream.'

" 'Arise and quench thy thirst,' was her reply.   400
And as a shut lily stricken by the wand
Of dewy morning's vital alchemy,

"I rose; and, bending at her sweet command,
Touched with faint lips the   cup she raised,
And suddenly my brain became as sand

"Where the first wave had more than half erased
The track of deer on desert Labrador;
Whilst the fierce wolf from which they fled amazed,

"Leaves his stamp visibly upon the shore,
Until the second bursts;—so on my sight   410
Burst a new vision, never seen before,

"And the fair shape waned in the coming light,
As veil by veil the silent splendour drops
From Lucifer, amid the chrysolite

"Of sunrise, ere it tinge the mountain-tops;
And as the presence of that fairest planet,
Although unseen, is felt by one who hopes

"That his day's path may end as he began it,
In that star's smile, whose light is like the scent
Of a jonquil when evening breezes fan it,   420

"Or the soft note in which his dear lament
The Brescian shepherd breathes, or the caress
That turned his weary slumber to content;

"So knew I in that light's severe excess
The presence of that Shape which on the stream
Moved, as I moved along the wilderness,

"More dimly than a day-appearing dream,
The ghost of a forgotten form of sleep;
A light of heaven, whose half-extinguished beam

"Through the sick day in which we wake to
          weep   430
Glimmers, for ever sought, for ever lost;
So did that shape its obscure tenour keep

"Beside my path, as silent as a ghost;
But the new Vision, and the cold bright car,
With solemn speed and stunning music, crossed

"The forest, and as if from some dread war
Triumphantly returning, the loud million
Fiercely extolled the fortune of her star.

414. chrysolite: a yellow-green gem.

"A moving arch of victory, the vermilion
And green and azure plumes of Iris had   440
Built high over her wind-winged pavilion,

"And underneath aethereal glory clad
The wilderness, and far before her flew
The tempest of the splendour, which forbade

"Shadow to fall from leaf and stone; the crew
Seemed in that light, like atomies to dance
Within a sunbeam;—some upon the new

"Embroidery of flowers, that did enhance
The grassy vesture of the desert, played,
Forgetful of the chariot's swift advance;   450

"Others stood gazing, till within the shade
Of the great mountain its light left them dim;
Others outspeeded it; and others made

"Circles around it, like the clouds that swim
Round the high moon in a bright sea of air;
And more did follow, with exulting hymn,

"The chariot and the captives fettered there:—
But all like bubbles on an eddying flood
Fell into the same track at last, and were

"Borne onward.—I among the multitude   460
Was swept—me, sweetest flowers delayed not long;
Me, not the shadow nor the solitude;

"Me, not that falling stream's Lethean song;
Me, not the phantom of that early Form
Which moved upon its motion—but among

"The thickest billows of that living storm
I plunged, and bared my bosom to the clime
Of that cold light, whose airs too soon deform.

"Before the chariot had begun to climb
The opposing steep of that mysterious dell,   470
Behold a wonder worthy of the rhyme

"Of him who from the lowest depths of hell,
Through every paradise and through all glory,
Love led serene, and who returned to tell

"The words of hate and awe; the wondrous story
How all things are transfigured except Love;
For deaf as is a sea, which makes hoary,

472. him: Dante.

"The world can hear not the sweet notes that move
The sphere whose light is melody to lovers—
A wonder worthy of his rhyme.—The grove   480

"Grew dense with shadows to its inmost covers,
The earth was gray with phantoms, and the air
Was peopled with dim forms, as when there hovers

"A flock of vampire-bats before the glare
Of the tropic sun, bringing, ere evening,
Strange night upon some Indian isle;—thus were

"Phantoms diffused around; and some did fling
Shadows of shadows, yet unlike themselves,
Behind them; some like eaglets on the wing

"Were lost in the white day; others like elves   490
Danced in a thousand unimagined shapes
Upon the sunny streams and grassy shelves;

"And others sate chattering like restless apes
On vulgar hands, . . .
Some made a cradle of the ermined capes

"Of kingly mantles; some across the tiar
Of pontiffs sate like vultures; others played
Under the crown which girt with empire

"A baby's or an idiot's brow, and made
Their nests in it. The old anatomies   500
Sate hatching their bare broods under the shade

"Of daemon wings, and laughed from their dead
          eyes
To reassume the delegated power,
Arrayed in which those worms did monarchize,

"Who made this earth their charnel. Others more
Humble, like falcons, sate upon the fist
Of common men, and round their heads did soar;

"Or like small gnats and flies, as thick as mist
On evening marshes, thronged about the brow
Of lawyers, statesmen, priest and theorist;—   510

"And others, like discoloured flakes of snow
On fairest bosoms and the sunniest hair,
Fell, and were melted by the youthful glow

"Which they extinguished; and, like tears, they were
A veil to those from whose faint lids they rained
In drops of sorrow. I became aware

"Of whence those forms proceeded which thus
    stained
The track in which we moved. After brief space,
From every form the beauty slowly waned;

"From every firmest limb and fairest face   520
The strength and freshness fell like dust, and left
The action and the shape without the grace

"Of life. The marble brow of youth was cleft
With care; and in those eyes where once hope
    shone,
Desire, like a lioness bereft

"Of her last cub, glared ere it died; each one
Of that great crowd sent forth incessantly
These shadows, numerous as the dead leaves blown

"In autumn evening from a poplar tree.
Each like himself and like each other were   530
At first; but some distorted seemed to be

"Obscure clouds, moulded by the casual air;
And of this stuff the car's creative ray
Wrought all the busy phantoms that were there,

"As the sun shapes the clouds: thus on the way
Mask after mask fell from the countenance
And form of all; and long before the day

"Was old, the joy which waked like heaven's glance
The sleepers in the oblivious valley, died;
And some grew weary of the ghastly dance,   540

"And fell, as I have fallen, by the wayside;—
Those soonest from whom forms most shadows
    passed,
And least of strength and beauty did abide."

"Then, what is life?" I cried—The cripple cast
His eye upon that car, which now had rolled
Onward, as if that look must be the last,

And answered, "Happy those for whom the gold
Of . . ."

1822   1824

[As mentioned in the Introduction, Shelley never completed *The Triumph of Life*. Hence, the reader will note
gaps in the text and the absence of a conclusion.]

A DEFENCE OF POETRY*

According to one mode of regarding those two
classes of mental action, which are called reason
and imagination, the former may be considered as
mind contemplating the relations borne by one
thought to another, however produced; and the
latter, as mind acting upon those thoughts so as to
colour them with its own light, and composing from
them, as from elements, other thoughts, each containing within itself the principle of its own in-
tegrity. The one is the $\tau\grave{o}$ $\pi o\iota\epsilon\tilde{\iota}\nu$, or the principle of
synthesis, and has for its object those forms which
are common to universal nature and existence itself;
the other is the $\tau\grave{o}$ $\lambda o\gamma\acute{\iota}\zeta\epsilon\iota\nu$, or principle of analysis,
and its action regards the relations of things, simply
as relations; considering thoughts, not in their integral unity, but as the algebraical representations
which conduct to certain general results. Reason is
the enumeration of quantities already known; imagination is the perception of the value of those
quantities, both separately and as a whole. Reason
respects the differences, and imagination the similitudes of things. Reason is to imagination as the
instrument to the agent, as the body to the spirit,
as the shadow to the substance.

Poetry, in a general sense, may be defined to be
"the expression of the imagination": and poetry is
connate with the origin of man. Man is an instrument over which a series of external and internal
impressions are driven, like the alternations of an
ever-changing wind over an Æolian lyre, which
move it by their motion to ever-changing melody.
But there is a principle within the human being,
and perhaps within all sentient beings, which acts
otherwise than in the lyre, and produces not melody, alone, but harmony, by an internal adjustment
of the sounds or motions thus excited to the impressions which excite them. It is as if the lyre
could accommodate its chords to the motions of

---

* *A Defence* was composed in 1821 as a reply to
Thomas Love Peacock's *The Four Ages of Poetry*,
which argued that poetry was in its last stages of decline. Shelley's document is an eloquent account of the
experience of poetic creation and of the moral and
social power of poetry.

that which strikes them, in a determined proportion of sound; even as the musician can accommodate his voice to the sound of the lyre. A child at play by itself will express its delight by its voice and motions; and every inflection of tone and every gesture will bear exact relation to a corresponding antitype in the pleasurable impressions which awakened it; it will be the reflected image of that impression; and as the lyre trembles and sounds after the wind has died away, so the child seeks, by prolonging in its voice and motions the duration of the effect, to prolong also a consciousness of the cause. In relation to the objects which delight a child, these expressions are what poetry is to higher objects. The savage (for the savage is to ages what the child is to years) expresses the emotions produced in him by surrounding objects in a similar manner; and language and gesture together with plastic or pictorial imitation, become the image of the combined effect of those objects and of his apprehension of them. Man in society, with all his passions and his pleasures, next becomes the object of the passions and pleasures of man; an additional class of emotions produces an augmented treasure of expressions; and language, gesture, and the imitative arts become at once the representation and the medium, the pencil and the picture, the chisel and the statue, the chord and the harmony. The social sympathies, or those laws from which, as from its elements, society results, begin to develop themselves from the moment that two human beings co-exist; the future is contained within the present as the plant within the seed; and equality, diversity, unity, contrast, mutual dependence, become the principles alone capable of affording the motives according to which the will of a social being is determined to action, inasmuch as he is social; and constitute pleasure in sensation, virtue in sentiment, beauty in art, truth in reasoning, and love in the intercourse of kind. Hence men, even in the infancy of society, observe a certain order in their words and actions, distinct from that of the objects and the impressions represented by them, all expression being subject to the laws of that from which it proceeds. But let us dismiss those more general considerations which might involve an inquiry into the principles of society itself, and restrict our view to the manner in which the imagination is expressed upon its forms.

In the youth of the world, men dance and sing and imitate natural objects, observing in these actions, as in all others, a certain rhythm or order. And, although all men observe a similar, they observe not the same order in the motions of the dance, in the melody of the song, in the combinations of language, in the series of their imitations of natural objects. For there is a certain order or rhythm belonging to each of these classes of mimetic representation, from which the hearer and the spectator receive an intenser and purer pleasure than from any other: the sense of an approximation to this order has been called taste by modern writers. Every man in the infancy of art, observes an order which approximates more or less closely to that from which this highest delight results: but the diversity is not sufficiently marked, as that its gradations should be sensible, except in those instances where the predominance of this faculty of approximation to the beautiful (for so we may be permitted to name the relation between this highest pleasure and its cause) is very great. Those in whom it exists in excess are poets, in the most universal sense of the word; and the pleasure resulting from the manner in which they express the influence of society or nature upon their own minds, communicates itself to others, and gathers a sort of reduplication from that community. Their language is vitally metaphorical; that is, it marks the before unapprehended relations of things and perpetuates their apprehension, until the words which represent them become, through time, signs for portions or classes of thought instead of pictures of integral thoughts; and then, if no new poets should arise to create afresh the associations which have been thus disorganized, language will be dead to all the nobler purposes of human intercourse. These similitudes or relations are finely said by Lord Bacon to be "the same footsteps of nature impressed upon the various subjects of the world"—and he considers the faculty which perceives them as the storehouse of axioms common to all knowledge. In the infancy of society every author is necessarily a poet, because language itself is poetry; and to be a poet is to apprehend the true and the beautiful, in a word, the good which exists in the relation subsisting, first between existence and perception, and secondly between perception and expression. Every original language near to its source is in itself the chaos of a cyclic poem: the copiousness of lexicography and the distinctions of grammar are the works of a later age, and are merely the catalogue and the form of the creations of poetry.

But poets, or those who imagine and express this indestructible order, are not only the authors of language and of music, of the dance, and architecture, and statuary, and painting; they are the institutors of laws, and the founders of civil society, and the inventors of the arts of life, and the teachers, who draw into a certain propinquity with the beautiful and the true, that partial apprehension of the agencies of the invisible world which is called religion. Hence all original religions are allegorical, or susceptible of allegory, and, like Janus, have a double face of false and true. Poets, according to the circumstances of the age and nation in which they appeared, were called, in the earlier epochs of the world, legislators or prophets; a poet essentially comprises and unites both these characters. For he not only beholds intensely the present as it is, and discovers those laws according to which present things ought to be ordered, but he beholds the future in the present, and his thoughts are the germs of the flower and the fruit of latest time. Not that I assert poets to be prophets in the gross sense of the word, or that they can foretell the form as surely as they foreknow the spirit of events: such is the pretence of superstition, which would make poetry an attribute of prophecy, rather than prophecy an attribute of poetry. A poet participates in the eternal, the infinite, and the one; as far as relates to his conceptions, time and place and number are not. The grammatical forms which express the moods of time, and the difference of persons, and the distinction of place, are convertible with respect to the highest poetry without injuring it as poetry; and the choruses of Æschylus, and the *Book of Job*, and Dante's *Paradise*, would afford, more than any other writings, examples of this fact, if the limits of this essay did not forbid citation. The creations of sculpture, painting, and music are illustrations still more decisive.

Language, colour, form, and religious and civil habits of action, are all the instruments and materials of poetry; they may be called poetry by that figure of speech which considers the effect as a synonym of the cause. But poetry in a more restricted sense expresses those arrangements of language, and especially metrical language, which are created by that imperial faculty, whose throne is curtained within the invisible nature of man. And this springs from the nature itself of language, which is a more direct representation of the actions and passions of our internal being, and is susceptible of more various and delicate combinations, than colour, form, or motion, and is more plastic and obedient to the control of that faculty of which it is a creation. For language is arbitrarily produced by the imagination, and has relation to thoughts alone; but all other materials, instruments, and conditions of art, have relations among each other, which limit and interpose between conception and expression. The former is as a mirror which reflects, the latter as a cloud which enfeebles, the light of which both are mediums of communication. Hence the fame of sculptors, painters, and musicians, although the intrinsic powers of the great masters of these arts may yield in no degree to that of those who have employed language as the hieroglyphic of their thoughts, has never equalled that of poets in the restricted sense of the term; as two performers of equal skill will produce unequal effects from a guitar and a harp. The fame of legislators and founders of religions, so long as their institutions last, alone seems to exceed that of poets in the restricted sense; but it can scarcely be a question, whether, if we deduct the celebrity which their flattery of the gross opinions of the vulgar usually conciliates, together with that which belonged to them in their higher character of poets, any excess will remain.

We have thus circumscribed the word poetry within the limits of that art which is the most familiar and the most perfect expression of the faculty itself. It is necessary, however, to make the circle still narrower, and to determine the distinction between measured and unmeasured language; for the popular division into prose and verse is inadmissible in accurate philosophy.

Sounds as well as thoughts have relation both between each other and towards that which they represent, and a perception of the order of those relations has always been found connected with the perception of the order of the relations of thoughts. Hence the language of poets has ever affected a certain uniform and harmonious recurrence of sound, without which it were not poetry, and which is scarcely less indispensable to the communication of its influence, than the words themselves without reference to that peculiar order. Hence the vanity of translation; it were as wise to cast a violet into a crucible that you might discover the formal principle of its colour and odour, as to seek to transfuse from one language into another the creations of a poet. The plant must spring again from its seed, or it will bear no flower—and this is the burthen of the curse of Babel.

An observation of the regular mode of the recurrence of harmony in the language of poetical minds, together with its relation to music, produced metre, or a certain system of traditional forms of harmony of language. Yet it is by no means essential that a poet should accommodate his language to this traditional form, so that the harmony, which is its spirit, be observed. The practice is indeed convenient and popular, and to be preferred, especially in such composition as includes much action: but every great poet must inevitably innovate upon the example of his predecessors in the exact structure of his peculiar versification. The distinction between poets and prose writers is a vulgar error. The distinction between philosophers and poets has been anticipated. Plato was essentially a poet—the truth and splendour of his imagery, and the melody of his language, are the most intense that it is possible to conceive. He rejected the measure of the epic, dramatic, and lyrical forms, because he sought to kindle a harmony in thoughts divested of shape and action, and he forebore to invent any regular plan of rhythm which would include, under determinate forms, the varied pauses of his style. Cicero sought to imitate the cadence of his periods, but with little success. Lord Bacon was a poet. His language has a sweet and majestic rhythm, which satisfies the sense, no less than the almost superhuman wisdom of his philosophy satisfies the intellect; it is a strain which distends, and then bursts the circumference of the reader's mind, and pours itself forth together with it into the universal element with which it has perpetual sympathy. All the authors of revolutions in opinion are not only necessarily poets as they are inventors, nor even as their words unveil the permanent analogy of things by images which participate in the life of truth; but as their periods are harmonious and rhythmical, and contain in themselves the elements of verse; being the echo of the eternal music. Nor are those supreme poets, who have employed traditional forms of rhythm on account of the form and action of their subjects, less capable of perceiving and teaching the truth of things, than those who have omitted that form. Shakespeare, Dante, and Milton (to confine ourselves to modern writers) are philosophers of the very loftiest power.

A poem is the very image of life expressed in its eternal truth. There is this difference between a story and a poem, that a story is a catalogue of detached facts, which have no other connection than time, place, circumstance, cause and effect; the other is the creation of actions according to the unchangeable forms of human nature, as existing in the mind of the creator, which is itself the image of all other minds. The one is partial, and applies only to a definite period of time, and a certain combination of events which can never again recur; the other is universal, and contains within itself the germ of a relation to whatever motives or actions have place in the possible varieties of human nature. Time, which destroys the beauty and the use of the story of particular facts, stripped of the poetry which should invest them, augments that of poetry, and for ever develops new and wonderful applications of the eternal truth which it contains. Hence epitomes have been called the moths of just history; they eat out the poetry of it. A story of particular facts is as a mirror which obscures and distorts that which should be beautiful: poetry is a mirror which makes beautiful that which is distorted.

The parts of a composition may be poetical, without the composition as a whole being a poem. A single sentence may be considered as a whole, though it may be found in the midst of a series of unassimilated portions; a single word even may be a spark of inextinguishable thought. And thus all the great historians, Herodotus, Plutarch, Livy, were poets; and although the plan of these writers, especially that of Livy, restrained them from developing this faculty in its highest degree, they made copious and ample amends for their subjection, by filling all the interstices of their subjects with living images.

Having determined what is poetry, and who are poets, let us proceed to estimate its effects upon society.

Poetry is ever accompanied with pleasure: all spirits on which it falls open themselves to receive the wisdom which is mingled with its delight. In the infancy of the world, neither poets themselves nor their auditors are fully aware of the excellence of poetry, for it acts in a divine and unapprehended manner, beyond and above consciousness; and it is reserved for future generations to contemplate and measure the mighty cause and effect in all the strength and splendour of their union. Even in modern times, no living poet ever arrived at the fulness of his fame; the jury which sits in judgment upon a poet, belonging as he does to all time, must be composed of his peers; it must be impanelled by Time from the selectest of the wise of many generations. A poet is a nightingale, who sits in darkness and sings to cheer its own solitude with sweet sounds; his auditors are as men entranced by the melody of an unseen musician, who feel that they are moved and softened, yet know not whence or why. The poems of Homer and his contemporaries were the delight of infant Greece; they were the elements of that social system which is the column upon which all succeeding civilization has reposed. Homer embodied the ideal perfection of his age in human character; nor can we doubt that those who read his verses were awakened to an ambition of becoming like to Achilles, Hector, and Ulysses; the truth and beauty of friendship, patriotism, and persevering devotion to an object, were unveiled to their depths in these immortal creations; the sentiments of the auditors must have been refined and enlarged by a sympathy with such great and lovely impersonations, until from admiring they imitated, and from imitation they identified themselves with the objects of their admiration. Nor let it be objected that these characters are remote from moral perfection, and that they are by no means to be considered as edifying patterns for general imitation. Every epoch, under names more or less specious, has deified its peculiar errors; Revenge is the naked idol of the worship of a semi-barbarous age; and Self-deceit is the veiled image of unknown evil, before which luxury and satiety lie prostrate. But a poet considers the vices of his contemporaries as a temporary dress in which his creations must be arrayed, and which cover without concealing the eternal proportions of their beauty. An epic or dramatic personage is understood to wear them around his soul, as he may the ancient armour or the modern uniform around his body; whilst it is easy to conceive a dress more graceful than either. The beauty of the internal nature cannot be so far concealed by its accidental vesture, but that the spirit of its form shall communicate itself to the very disguise, and indicate the shape it hides from the manner in which it is worn. A majestic form and graceful motions will express themselves through the most barbarous and tasteless costume. Few poets of the highest class have chosen to exhibit the beauty of their conceptions in its naked truth and splendour; and it is doubtful whether the alloy of costume, habit, etc., be not necessary to temper this planetary music for mortal ears.

The whole objection, however, of the immorality of poetry rests upon a misconception of the manner in which poetry acts to produce the moral improvement of man. Ethical science arranges the elements which poetry has created, and propounds schemes and proposes examples of civil and domestic life: nor is it for want of admirable doctrines that men hate, and despise, and censure, and deceive, and subjugate one another. But poetry acts in another and diviner manner. It awakens and enlarges the mind itself by rendering it the receptacle of a thousand unapprehended combinations of thought. Poetry lifts the veil from the hidden beauty of the world, and makes familiar objects be as if they were not familiar; it reproduces all that it represents, and the impersonations clothed in its Elysian light stand thenceforward in the minds of those who have once contemplated them, as memorials of that gentle and exalted content which extends itself over all thoughts and actions with which it co-exists. The great secret of morals is love; or a going out of our own nature, and an identification of ourselves with the beautiful which exists in thought, action, or person, not our own. A man, to be greatly good, must imagine intensely and comprehensively; he must put himself in the place of another and of many others; the pains and pleasures of his species must become his own. The great instrument of moral good is the imagination; and poetry administers to the effect by acting upon the cause. Poetry enlarges the circumference of the imagination by replenishing it with thoughts of ever new delight, which have the power of attracting and assimilating to their own nature all other thoughts, and which form new intervals and interstices whose void forever craves fresh food. Poetry strengthens the faculty which is the organ of the moral nature of man, in the same manner as exercise strengthens a limb. A poet therefore would do ill to embody his own conceptions of right and wrong, which are usually those of his place and time, in his poetical creations, which participate in neither. By this assumption of the inferior office of interpreting the effect, in which perhaps after all he might acquit himself but imperfectly, he would resign a glory in the participation of the cause. There was little danger that Homer, or any of the eternal poets, should have so far misunderstood themselves as to have abdicated this throne of their widest dominion. Those in whom the poetical faculty, though great, is less intense, as Euripides, Lucan, Tasso, Spenser, have frequently affected a moral aim, and the effect of their poetry is diminished in exact proportion to the degree in which they compel us to advert to this purpose.

Homer and the cyclic poets were followed at a certain interval by the dramatic and lyrical poets of Athens, who flourished contemporaneously with all that is most perfect in the kindred expressions of the poetical faculty; architecture, painting, music, the dance, sculpture, philosophy, and, we may add, the forms of civil life. For although the scheme of Athenian society was deformed by many imperfections which the poetry existing in chivalry and Christianity has erased from the habits and institutions of modern Europe; yet never at any other period has so much energy, beauty, and virtue, been developed; never was blind strength and stubborn form so disciplined and rendered subject to the will of man, or that will less repugnant to the dictates of the beautiful and the true, as during the century which preceded the death of Socrates. Of no other epoch in the history of our species have we records and fragments stamped so visibly with the image of the divinity in man. But it is poetry alone, in form, in action, or in language, which has rendered this epoch memorable above all others, and the storehouse of examples to everlasting time. For written poetry existed at that epoch simultaneously with the other arts, and it is an idle inquiry to demand which gave and which received the light, which all, as from a common focus, have scattered over the darkest periods of succeeding time. We know no more of cause and effect than a constant conjunction of events: poetry is ever found to co-exist with whatever other arts contribute to the happiness and perfection of man. I appeal to what has already been established to distinguish between the cause and the effect.

It was at the period here adverted to, that the drama had its birth; and however a succeeding writer may have equalled or surpassed those few great specimens of the Athenian drama which have been preserved to us, it is indisputable that the art itself never was understood or practised according to the true philosophy of it, as at Athens. For the Athenians employed language, action, music, painting, the dance, and religious institutions, to produce a common effect in the representation of the highest idealisms of passion and of power; each division in the art was made perfect in its kind by artists of the most consummate skill, and was disciplined into a beautiful proportion and unity one towards the other. On the modern stage a few only of the elements capable of expressing the image of the poet's conception are employed at once. We have tragedy without music and dancing; and music and dancing without the highest impersonations of which they are the fit accompaniment, and both without religion and solemnity. Religious institution has indeed been usually banished from the stage. Our system of divesting the actor's face of a mask, on which the many expressions appropriated to his dramatic character might be molded into one permanent and unchanging expression, is favorable only to a partial and inharmonious effect; it is fit for nothing but a monologue, where all the attention may be directed to some great master of ideal mimicry. The modern practice of blending comedy with tragedy, though liable to great abuse in point of practice, is undoubtedly an extension of the dramatic circle; but the comedy should be as in *King Lear*, universal, ideal, and sublime. It is perhaps the intervention of this principle which determines the balance in favor of *King Lear* against the *Oedipus Tyrannus* or the *Agamemnon*, or, if you will, the trilogies with which they are connected; unless the intense power of the choral poetry, especially that of the latter, should be considered as restoring the equilibrium. *King Lear*, if it can sustain this comparison, may be judged to be the most perfect specimen of the dramatic art existing in the world; in spite of the narrow conditions to which the poet was subjected by the ignorance of the philosophy of the drama which has prevailed in modern Europe. Calderon, in his religious *Autos*, has attempted to fulfil some of the high conditions of dramatic representation neglected by Shakespeare; such as the establishing a relation between the drama and religion, and the accommodating them to music and dancing; but he omits the observation of conditions still more important, and more is lost than gained by a substitution of the rigidly defined and ever-repeated idealisms of a distorted superstition for the living impersonations of the truth of human passion.

But I digress.—The connexion of scenic exhibitions with the improvement or corruption of the manners of men, has been universally recognized: in other words, the presence or absence of poetry in its most perfect and universal form, has been found to be connected with good and evil in conduct or habit. The corruption which has been imputed to the drama as an effect, begins, when the poetry employed in its constitution ends: I appeal to the history of manners whether the periods of the growth of the one and the decline of the other have not corresponded with an exactness equal to any example of moral cause and effect.

The drama at Athens, or wheresoever else it may have approached to its perfection, ever co-existed with the moral and intellectual greatness of the age. The tragedies of the Athenian poets are as mirrors in which the spectator beholds himself, under a thin disguise of circumstance, stripped of all but that ideal perfection and energy which every one feels to be the internal type of all that he loves, admires, and would become. The imagination is enlarged by a sympathy with pains and passions so mighty, that they distend in their conception the capacity of that by which they are conceived; the good affections are strengthened by pity, indignation, terror, and sorrow; and an exalted calm is prolonged from the satiety of this high exercise of them into the tumult of familiar life: even crime is disarmed of half its horror and all its contagion by being represented as the fatal consequence of the unfathomable agencies of nature; error is thus divested of its wilfulness; men can no longer cherish it as the creation of their choice. In a drama of the highest order there is little food for censure or hatred; it teaches rather self-knowledge and self-respect. Neither the eye nor the mind can see itself, unless reflected upon that which it resembles. The drama, so long as it continues to express poetry, is a prismatic and many-sided mirror, which collects the brightest rays of human nature and divides and reproduces them from the simplicity of these elementary forms,

and touches them with majesty and beauty, and multiplies all that it reflects, and endows it with the power of propagating its like wherever it may fall.

But in periods of the decay of social life, the drama sympathizes with that decay. Tragedy becomes a cold imitation of the form of the great masterpieces of antiquity, divested of all harmonious accompaniment of the kindred arts; and often the very form misunderstood, or a weak attempt to teach certain doctrines, which the writer considers as moral truths; and which are usually no more than specious flatteries of some gross vice or weakness, with which the author, in common with his auditors, are infected. Hence what has been called the classical and domestic drama. Addison's *Cato* is a specimen of the one; and would it were not superfluous to cite examples of the other! To such purposes poetry cannot be made subservient! Poetry is a sword of lightning, ever unsheathed, which consumes the scabbard that would contain it. And thus we observe that all dramatic writings of this nature are unimaginative in a singular degree; they affect sentiment and passion, which, divested of imagination, are other names for caprice and appetite. The period in our own history of the grossest degradation of the drama is the reign of Charles II, when all forms in which poetry had been accustomed to be expressed became hymns to the triumph of kingly power over liberty and virtue. Milton stood alone illuminating an age unworthy of him. At such periods the calculating principle pervades all the forms of dramatic exhibition, and poetry ceases to be expressed upon them. Comedy loses its ideal universality: wit succeeds to humor; we laugh from self-complacency and triumph, instead of pleasure; malignity, sarcasm, and contempt, succeed to sympathetic merriment; we hardly laugh, but we smile. Obscenity, which is ever blasphemy against the divine beauty in life, becomes, from the very veil which it assumes, more active if less disgusting: it is a monster for which the corruption of society for ever brings forth new food, which it devours in secret.

The drama being that form under which a greater number of modes of expression of poetry are susceptible of being combined than any other, the connexion of poetry and social good is more observable in the drama than in whatever other form.

And it is indisputable that the highest perfection of human society has ever corresponded with the highest dramatic excellence; and that the corruption or the extinction of the drama in a nation where it has once flourished, is a mark of a corruption of manners, and an extinction of the energies which sustain the soul of social life. But, as Machiavelli says of political institutions, that life may be preserved and renewed, if men should arise capable of bringing back the drama to its principles. And this is true with respect to poetry in its most extended sense: all language, institution and form, require not only to be produced but to be sustained: the office and character of a poet participates in the divine nature as regards providence, no less than as regards creation.

Civil war, the spoils of Asia, and the fatal predominance first of the Macedonian, and then of the Roman arms, were so many symbols of the extinction or suspension of the creative faculty in Greece. The bucolic writers,[1] who found patronage under the lettered tyrants of Sicily and Egypt, were the latest representatives of its most glorious reign. Their poetry is intensely melodious; like the odor of the tuberose, it overcomes and sickens the spirit with excess of sweetness; whilst the poetry of the preceding age was as a meadow-gale of June, which mingles the fragrance of all the flowers of the field, and adds a quickening and harmonizing spirit of its own, which endows the sense with a power of sustaining its extreme delight. The bucolic and erotic delicacy in written poetry is correlative with that softness in statuary, music, and the kindred arts, and even in manners and institutions, which distinguished the epoch to which I now refer. Nor is it the poetical faculty itself, or any misapplication of it, to which this want of harmony is to be imputed. An equal sensibility to the influence of the senses and the affections is to be found in the writings of Homer and Sophocles: the former, especially, has clothed sensual and pathetic images with irresistible attraction. Their superiority over these succeeding writers consists in the presence of those thoughts which belong to the inner faculties of our nature, not in the absence of those which are connected with the external: their incomparable perfection consists in a harmony of the union of all. It is not what the erotic poets have, but what they have not, in which their imperfection consists. It

is not inasmuch as they were poets, but inasmuch as they were not poets, that they can be considered with any plausibility as connected with the corruption of their age. Had that corruption availed so as to extinguish in them the sensibility to pleasure, passion, and natural scenery, which is imputed to them as an imperfection, the last triumph of evil would have been achieved. For the end of social corruption is to destroy all sensibility to pleasure; and, therefore, it is corruption. It begins at the imagination and the intellect as at the core, and distributes itself thence as a paralysing venom, through the affections into the very appetites, until all become a torpid mass in which hardly sense survives. At the approach of such a period, poetry ever addresses itself to those faculties which are the last to be destroyed, and its voice is heard, like the footsteps of Astræa,[2] departing from the world. Poetry ever communicates all the pleasure which men are capable of receiving: it is ever still the light of life; the source of whatever of beautiful or generous or true can have place in an evil time. It will readily be confessed that those among the luxurious citizens of Syracuse and Alexandria, who were delighted with the poems of Theocritus, were less cold, cruel, and sensual than the remnant of their tribe. But corruption must utterly have destroyed the fabric of human society before poetry can ever cease. The sacred links of that chain have never been entirely disjoined, which descending through the minds of many men is attached to those great minds, whence as from a magnet the invisible effluence is sent forth, which at once connects, animates, and sustains the life of all. It is the faculty which contains within itself the seeds at once of its own and of social renovation. And let us not circumscribe the effects of the bucolic and erotic poetry within the limits of the sensibility of those to whom it was addressed. They may have perceived the beauty of those immortal compositions, simply as fragments and isolated portions: those who are more finely organized, or born in a happier age, may recognize them as episodes to that great poem, which all poets, like the co-operating thoughts of one great mind, have built up since the beginning of the world.

The same revolutions within a narrower sphere had place in ancient Rome; but the actions and forms of its social life never seem to have been

A DEFENCE OF POETRY. **1. bucolic writers:** pastoral poets.

2. Astræa: goddess of Justice.

perfectly saturated with the poetical elements. The Romans appear to have considered the Greeks as the selectest treasuries of the selectest forms of manners and of nature, and to have abstained from creating in measured language, sculpture, music, or architecture, anything which might bear a particular relation to their own condition, whilst it should bear a general one to the universal constitution of the world. But we judge from partial evidence, and we judge perhaps partially. Ennius, Varro, Pacuvius, and Accius, all great poets, have been lost. Lucretius is in the highest, and Virgil in a very high sense, a creator. The chosen delicacy of the expressions of the latter, are as a mist of light which conceal from us the intense and exceeding truth of his conceptions of nature. Livy is instinct with poetry. Yet Horace, Catullus, Ovid, and generally the other great writers of the Virgilian age, saw man and nature in the mirror of Greece. The institutions also, and the religion of Rome were less poetical than those of Greece, as the shadow is less vivid than the substance. Hence poetry in Rome, seemed to follow, rather than accompany, the perfection of political and domestic society. The true poetry of Rome lived in its institutions; for whatever of beautiful, true, and majestic, they contained, could have sprung only from the faculty which creates the order in which they consist. The life of Camillus, the death of Regulus; the expectation of the senators, in their godlike state, of the victorious Gauls: the refusal of the republic to make peace with Hannibal, after the battle of Cannæ, were not the consequences of a refined calculation of the probable personal advantage to result from such a rhythm and order in the shows of life, to those who were at once the poets and the actors of these immortal dramas. The imagination beholding the beauty of this order, created it out of itself according to its own idea; the consequence was empire, and the reward everliving fame. These things are not the less poetry *quia carent vate sacro*.[3] They are the episodes of that cyclic poem written by Time upon the memories of men. The Past, like an inspired rhapsodist, fills the theatre of everlasting generations with their harmony.

At length the ancient system of religion and manners had fulfilled the circle of its revolutions. And the world would have fallen into utter anarchy and darkness, but that there were found poets among the authors of the Christian and chivalric systems of manners and religion, who created forms of opinion and action never before conceived; which, copied into the imaginations of men, became as generals to the bewildered armies of their thoughts. It is foreign to the present purpose to touch upon the evil produced by these systems: except that we protest, on the ground of the principles already established, that no portion of it can be attributed to the poetry they contain.

It is probable that the poetry of Moses, Job, David, Solomon, and Isaiah, had produced a great effect upon the mind of Jesus and his disciples. The scattered fragments preserved to us by the biographers of this extraordinary person, are all instinct with the most vivid poetry. But his doctrines seem to have been quickly distorted. At a certain period after the prevalence of a system of opinions founded upon those promulgated by him, the three forms into which Plato had distributed the faculties of mind underwent a sort of apotheosis, and became the object of the worship of the civilized world. Here it is to be confessed that "Light seems to thicken," and

The crow makes wing to the rooky wood,
Good things of day begin to droop and drowse,
And night's black agents to their preys do rouse.[4]

But mark how beautiful an order has sprung from the dust and blood of this fierce chaos! how the world, as from a resurrection, balancing itself on the golden wings of knowledge and of hope, has reassumed its yet unwearied flight into the heaven of time. Listen to the music, unheard by outward ears, which is as a ceaseless and invisible wind, nourishing its everlasting course with strength and swiftness.

The poetry in the doctrines of Jesus Christ, and the mythology and institutions of the Celtic conquerors of the Roman empire, outlived the darkness and the convulsions connected with their growth and victory, and blended themselves into a new fabric of manners and opinion. It is an error to impute the ignorance of the dark ages to the Christian doctrines or the predominance of the Celtic nations. Whatever of evil their agencies may have

---

3. quia . . . sacro: "because they do not have an inspired prophet" (Horace, *Odes*, IV. ix. 28).

4. The . . . rouse: *Macbeth*, III, ii, 50–53.

contained sprang from the extinction of the poetical principle, connected with the progress of despotism and superstition. Men, from causes too intricate to be here discussed, had become insensible and selfish: their own will had become feeble, and yet they were its slaves, and thence the slaves of the will of others: lust, fear, avarice, cruelty, and fraud, characterized a race amongst whom no one was to be found capable of *creating* in form, language, or institution. The moral anomalies of such a state of society are not justly to be charged upon any class of events immediately connected with them, and those events are most entitled to our approbation which could dissolve it most expeditiously. It is unfortunate for those who cannot distinguish words from thoughts, that many of these anomalies have been incorporated into our popular religion.

It was not until the eleventh century that the effects of the poetry of the Christian and chivalric systems began to manifest themselves. The principle of equality had been discovered and applied by Plato in his *Republic,* as the theoretical rule of the mode in which the materials of pleasure and of power, produced by the common skill and labour of human beings, ought to be distributed among them. The limitations of this rule were asserted by him to be determined only by the sensibility of each, or the utility to result to all. Plato, following the doctrines of Timaeus and Pythagoras, taught also a moral and intellectual system of doctrine, comprehending at once the past, present, and the future condition of man. Jesus Christ divulged the sacred and eternal truths contained in these views to mankind, and Christianity, in its abstract purity, became the exoteric expression of the esoteric doctrines of the poetry and wisdom of antiquity. The incorporation of the Celtic nations with the exhausted population of the south, impressed upon it the figure of the poetry existing in their mythology and institutions. The result was a sum of the action and reaction of all the causes included in it; for it may be assumed as a maxim that no nation or religion can supersede any other without incorporating into itself a portion of that which it supersedes. The abolition of personal and domestic slavery, and the emancipation of women from a great part of the degrading restraints of antiquity, were among the consequences of these events.

The abolition of personal slavery is the basis of the highest political hope that it can enter into the mind of man to conceive. The freedom of women produced the poetry of sexual love. Love became a religion, the idols of whose worship were ever present. It was as if the statues of Apollo and the Muses had been endowed with life and motion, and had walked forth among their worshippers; so that earth became peopled by the inhabitants of a diviner world. The familiar appearance and proceedings of life became wonderful and heavenly, and a paradise was created as out of the wrecks of Eden. And as this creation itself is poetry, so its creators were poets; and language was the instrument of their art: "Galeotto fù il libro, e chi lo scrisse." [5] The Provençal Trouveurs,[6] or inventors, preceded Petrarch, whose verses are as spells, which unseal the inmost enchanted fountains of the delight which is in the grief of love. It is impossible to feel them without becoming a portion of that beauty which we contemplate: it were superfluous to explain how the gentleness and the elevation of mind connected with these sacred emotions can render men more amiable, more generous and wise, and lift them out of the dull vapours of the little world of self. Dante understood the secret things of love even more than Petrarch. His *Vita Nuova* is an inexhaustible fountain of purity of sentiment and language: it is the idealized history of that period, and those intervals of his life which were dedicated to love. His apotheosis of Beatrice in Paradise, and the gradations of his own love and her loveliness, by which as by steps he feigns himself to have ascended to the throne of the Supreme Cause, is the most glorious imagination of modern poetry. The acutest critics have justly reversed the judgment of the vulgar, and the order of the great acts of the "Divine Drama," in the measure of the admiration which they accord to the Hell, Purgatory, and Paradise. The latter is a perpetual hymn of everlasting love. Love, which found a worthy poet in Plato alone of all the ancients, has been celebrated by a chorus of the greatest writers of the renovated world; and the music has penetrated the caverns of society, and its echoes still drown the dissonance of arms and superstition. At successive intervals, Ariosto, Tasso, Shakespeare, Spenser, Calderon, Rousseau, and the great writers of our own age,

5. **Galeotto . . . scrisse:** "Galeotto was the book and he who wrote it" (Dante, *Inferno,* V. 137). 6. **Trouveurs:** troubadours.

have celebrated the dominion of love, planting as it were trophies in the human mind of that sublimest victory over sensuality and force. The true relation borne to each other by the sexes into which human kind is distributed, has become less misunderstood; and if the error which confounded diversity with inequality of the powers of the two sexes has been partially recognized in the opinions and institutions of modern Europe, we owe this great benefit to the worship of which chivalry was the law, and poets the prophets.

The poetry of Dante may be considered as the bridge thrown over the stream of time, which unites the modern and ancient world. The distorted notions of invisible things which Dante and his rival Milton have idealized, are merely the mask and the mantle in which these great poets walk through eternity enveloped and disguised. It is a difficult question to determine how far they were conscious of the distinction which must have subsisted in their minds between their own creeds and that of the people. Dante at least appears to wish to mark the full extent of it by placing Riphaeus, whom Virgil calls *justissimus unus*,[7] in Paradise, and observing a most heretical caprice in his distribution of rewards and punishments. And Milton's poem contains within itself a philosophical refutation of that system, of which, by a strange and natural antithesis, it has been a chief popular support. Nothing can exceed the energy and magnificence of the character of Satan as expressed in *Paradise Lost*. It is a mistake to suppose that he could ever have been intended for the popular personification of evil. Implacable hate, patient cunning, and a sleepless refinement of device to inflict the extremest anguish on an enemy, these things are evil; and, although venial in a slave, are not to be forgiven in a tyrant; although redeemed by much that ennobles his defeat in one subdued, are marked by all that dishonours his conquest in the victor. Milton's Devil as a moral being is as far superior to his God, as one who perseveres in some purpose which he has conceived to be excellent in spite of adversity and torture, is to one who in the cold security of undoubted triumph inflicts the most horrible revenge upon his enemy, not from any mistaken notion of inducing him to repent of a perseverance in enmity, but with the alleged design

of exasperating him to deserve new torments. Milton has so far violated the popular creed (if this shall be judged to be a violation) as to have alleged no superiority of moral virtue to his God over his Devil. And this bold neglect of a direct moral purpose is the most decisive proof of the supremacy of Milton's genius. He mingled as it were the elements of human nature as colours upon a single pallet, and arranged them in the composition of his great picture according to the laws of epic truth; that is, according to the laws of that principle by which a series of actions of the external universe and of intelligent and ethical beings is calculated to excite the sympathy of succeeding generations of mankind. The *Divina Commedia* and *Paradise Lost* have conferred upon modern mythology a systematic form; and when change and time shall have added one more superstition to the mass of those which have arisen and decayed upon the earth, commentators will be learnedly employed in elucidating the religion of ancestral Europe, only not utterly forgotten because it will have been stamped with the eternity of genius.

Homer was the first and Dante the second epic poet: that is, the second poet, the series of whose creations bore a defined and intelligible relation to the knowledge and sentiment and religion and political conditions of the age in which he lived, and of the ages which followed it: developing itself in correspondence with their development. For Lucretius had limed the wings of his swift spirit in the dregs of the sensible world;[8] and Virgil, with a modesty that ill became his genius, had affected the fame of an imitator, even whilst he created anew all that he copied; and none among the flock of mock-birds, though their notes were sweet, Apollonius Rhodius, Quintus Calaber, Nonnus, Lucan, Statius, or Claudian,[9] have sought even to fulfil a single condition of epic truth. Milton was the third epic poet.[10] For if the title of epic in its highest sense be refused to the *Aeneid*, still less can it be conceded to the *Orlando Furioso*, the *Gerusalemme Liberata*, the *Lusiad*, or the *Fairy Queen*.[11]

Dante and Milton were both deeply penetrated

7. *justissimus unus:* "the most just."

8. Lucretius ... world: a reference to the Roman philosopher of materialism and author of *De Rerum Natura*. 9. Apollonius ... Claudian: Greek and Roman poets. 10. third epic poet: after Homer and Dante. 11. Orlando ... Queen: chief works of Ariosto, Tasso, Camoëns, and Spenser.

with the ancient religion of the civilized world; and its spirit exists in their poetry probably in the same proportion as its forms survived in the unreformed worship of modern Europe. The one preceded and the other followed the Reformation at almost equal intervals. Dante was the first religious reformer, and Luther surpassed him rather in the rudeness and acrimony, than in the boldness of his censures of papal usurpation. Dante was the first awakener of entranced Europe; he created a language, in itself music and persuasion, out of a chaos of inharmonious barbarism. He was the congregator of those great spirits who presided over the resurrection of learning; the Lucifer of that starry flock which in the thirteenth century shone forth from republican Italy, as from a heaven, into the darkness of the benighted world. His very words are instinct with spirit; each is as a spark, a burning atom of inextinguishable thought; and many yet lie covered in the ashes of their birth, and pregnant with a lightning which has yet found no conductor. All high poetry is infinite; it is as the first acorn, which contained all oaks potentially. Veil after veil may be undrawn, and the inmost naked beauty of the meaning never exposed. A great poem is a fountain for ever overflowing with the waters of wisdom and delight; and after one person and one age has exhausted all its divine effluence which their peculiar relations enable them to share, another and yet another succeeds, and new relations are ever developed, the source of an unforeseen and an unconceived delight.

The age immediately succeeding to that of Dante, Petrarch, and Boccaccio, was characterized by a revival of painting, sculpture, music, and architecture. Chaucer caught the sacred inspiration, and the superstructure of English literature is based upon the materials of Italian invention.

But let us not be betrayed from a defence into a critical history of poetry and its influence on society. Be it enough to have pointed out the effects of poets, in the large and true sense of the word, upon their own and all succeeding times.

But poets have been challenged to resign the civic crown to reasoners and mechanists on another plea. It is admitted that the exercise of the imagination is most delightful, but it is alleged, that that of reason is more useful. Let us examine as the grounds of this distinction, what is here meant by utility. Pleasure or good, in a general sense, is that which the consciousness of a sensitive and intelligent being seeks, and in which, when found, it acquiesces. There are two kinds of pleasure, one durable, universal and permanent; the other transitory and particular. Utility may either express the means of producing the former or the latter. In the former sense, whatever strengthens and purifies the affections, enlarges the imagination, and adds spirit to sense, is useful. But a narrower meaning may be assigned to the word utility, confining it to express that which banishes the importunity of the wants of our animal nature, the surrounding men with security of life, the dispersing the grosser delusions of superstition, and the conciliating such a degree of mutual forbearance among men as may consist with the motives of personal advantage.

Undoubtedly the promoters of utility, in this limited sense, have their appointed office in society. They follow the footsteps of poets, and copy the sketches of their creations into the book of common life. They make space, and give time. Their exertions are of the highest value, so long as they confine their administration of the concerns of the inferior powers of our nature within the limits due to the superior ones. But whilst the sceptic destroys gross superstitions, let him spare to deface, as some of the French writers have defaced, the eternal truths charactered upon the imaginations of men. Whilst the mechanist abridges, and the political economist combines labour, let them beware that their speculations, for want of correspondence with those first principles which belong to the imagination, do not tend, as they have in modern England, to exasperate at once the extremes of luxury and want. They have exemplified the saying, "To him that hath, more shall be given; and from him that hath not, the little that he hath shall be taken away." [12] The rich have become richer, and the poor have become poorer; and the vessel of the state is driven between the Scylla and Charybdis of anarchy and depotism. Such are the effects which must ever flow from an unmitigated exercise of the calculating faculty.

It is difficult to define pleasure in its highest sense; the definition involving a number of apparent paradoxes. For, from an inexplicable defect of harmony in the constitution of human nature, the pain of the inferior is frequently connected with the plea-

12. "To . . . away": Matthew 25:29; Mark 4:25.

sures of the superior portions of our being. Sorrow, terror, anguish, despair itself, are often the chosen expressions of an approximation to the highest good. Our sympathy in tragic fiction depends on this principle; tragedy delights by affording a shadow of the pleasure which exists in pain. This is the source also of the melancholy which is inseparable from the sweetest melody. The pleasure that is in sorrow is sweeter than the pleasure of pleasure itself. And hence the saying, "It is better to go to the house of mourning, than to the house of mirth." [13] Not that this highest species of pleasure is necessarily linked with pain. The delight of love and friendship, the ecstasy of the admiration of nature, the joy of the perception and still more of the creation of poetry, is often wholly unalloyed.

The production and assurance of pleasure in this highest sense is true utility. Those who produce and preserve this pleasure are poets or poetical philosophers.

The exertions of Locke, Hume, Gibbon, Voltaire, Rousseau, and their disciples, in favour of oppressed and deluded humanity, are entitled to the gratitude of mankind. Yet it is easy to calculate the degree of moral and intellectual improvement which the world would have exhibited, had they never lived. A little more nonsense would have been talked for a century or two; and perhaps a few more men, women, and children, burnt as heretics. We might not at this moment have been congratulating each other on the abolition of the Inquisition in Spain. But it exceeds all imagination to conceive what would have been the moral condition of the world if neither Dante, Petrarch, Boccaccio, Chaucer, Shakespeare, Calderon, Lord Bacon, nor Milton, had ever existed; if Raphael and Michael Angelo had never been born; if the Hebrew poetry had never been translated; if a revival of the study of Greek literature had never taken place; if no monuments of ancient sculpture had been handed down to us; and if the poetry of the religion of the ancient world had been extinguished together with its belief. The human mind could never, except by the intervention of these excitements, have been awakened to the invention of the grosser sciences, and that application of analytical reasoning to the aberrations of society, which it is now attempted to exalt over the direct expression of the inventive and creative faculty itself.

We have more moral, political and historical wisdom, than we know how to reduce into practice; we have more scientific and economical knowledge than can be accommodated to the just distribution of the produce which it multiplies. The poetry in these systems of thought, is concealed by the accumulation of facts and calculating processes. There is no want of knowledge respecting what is wisest and best in morals, government, and political economy, or at least, what is wiser and better than what men now practise and endure. But we let "*I dare not* wait upon *I would*, like the poor cat in the adage." [14] We want the creative faculty to imagine that which we know; we want the generous impulse to act that which we imagine; we want the poetry of life: our calculations have outrun conception; we have eaten more than we can digest. The cultivation of those sciences which have enlarged the limits of the empire of man over the external world, has, for want of the poetical faculty, proportionally circumscribed those of the internal world; and man, having enslaved the elements, remains himself a slave. To what but a cultivation of the mechanical arts in a degree disproportioned to the presence of the creative faculty, which is the basis of all knowledge, is to be attributed the abuse of all invention for abridging and combining labour, to the exasperation of the inequality of mankind? From what other cause has it arisen that the discoveries which should have lightened, have added a weight to the curse imposed on Adam? Poetry, and the principle of Self, of which money is the visible incarnation, are the God and Mammon of the world.

The functions of the poetical faculty are twofold; by one it creates new materials of knowledge and power and pleasure; by the other it engenders in the mind a desire to reproduce and arrange them according to a certain rhythm and order which may be called the beautiful and the good. The cultivation of poetry is never more to be desired than at periods when, from an excess of the selfish and calculating principle, the accumulation of the materials of external life exceed the quantity of the power of assimilating them to the internal laws of human nature. The body has then become too unwieldy for that which animates it.

13. "It ... mirth": Ecclesiastes 7:2.

14. "I ... adage": See *Macbeth*, I, vii, 44–45.

Poetry is indeed something divine. It is at once the center and circumference of knowledge; it is that which comprehends all science, and that to which all science must be referred. It is at the same time the root and blossom of all other systems of thought; it is that from which all spring, and that which adorns all; and that which, if blighted, denies the fruit and the seed, and withholds from the barren world the nourishment and the succession of the scions of the tree of life. It is the perfect and consummate surface and bloom of things; it is as the odour and the colour of the rose to the texture of the elements which compose it, as the form and splendour of unfaded beauty to the secrets of anatomy and corruption. What were virtue, love, patriotism, friendship—what were the scenery of this beautiful universe which we inhabit; what were our consolations on this side of the grave—and what were our aspirations beyond it, if poetry did not ascend to bring light and fire from those eternal regions where the owl-winged faculty of calculation dare not ever soar? Poetry is not like reasoning, a power to be exerted according to the determination of the will. A man cannot say, "I will compose poetry." The greatest poet even cannot say it; for the mind in creation is as a fading coal, which some invisible influence, like an inconstant wind, awakens to transitory brightness; this power arises from within, like the colour of a flower which fades and changes as it is developed, and the conscious portions of our natures are unprophetic either of its approach or its departure. Could this influence be durable in its original purity and force, it is impossible to predict the greatness of the results; but when composition begins, inspiration is already on the decline, and the most glorious poetry that has ever been communicated to the world is probably a feeble shadow of the original conceptions of the poet. I appeal to the greatest poets of the present day, whether it be not an error to assert that the finest passages of poetry are produced by labour and study. The toil and the delay recommended by critics can be justly interpreted to mean no more than a careful observation of the inspired moments, and an artificial connexion of the spaces between their suggestions by the intertexture of conventional expressions; a necessity only imposed by the limitedness of the poetical faculty itself; for Milton conceived the *Paradise Lost* as a whole before he executed it in portions. We have his own authority

also for the muse having "dictated" to him the "unpremeditated song." [15] And let this be an answer to those who would allege the fifty-six various readings of the first line of the *Orlando Furioso*. Compositions so produced are to poetry what mosaic is to painting. The instinct and intuition of the poetical faculty is still more observable in the plastic and pictorial arts; a great statue or picture grows under the power of the artist as a child in the mother's womb; and the very mind which directs the hands in formation is incapable of accounting to itself for the origin, the gradations, or the media of the process.

Poetry is the record of the best and happiest moments of the happiest and best minds. We are aware of evanescent visitations of thought and feeling sometimes associated with place or person, sometimes regarding our own mind alone, and always arising unforeseen and departing unbidden, but elevating and delightful beyond all expression: so that even in the desire and the regret they leave, there cannot but be pleasure, participating as it does in the nature of its object. It is as it were the interpenetration of a diviner nature through our own; but its footsteps are like those of a wind over the sea, which the morning calm erases, and whose traces remain only, as on the wrinkled sand which paves it. These and corresponding conditions of being are experienced principally by those of the most delicate sensibility and the most enlarged imagination; and the state of mind produced by them is at war with every base desire. The enthusiasm of virtue, love, patriotism, and friendship, is essentially linked with such emotions; and whilst they last, self appears as what it is, an atom to a universe. Poets are not only subject to these experiences as spirits of the most refined organization, but they can colour all that they combine with the evanescent hues of this ethereal world; a word, a trait in the representation of a scene or a passion, will touch the enchanted chord, and reanimate, in those who have ever experienced these emotions, the sleeping, the cold, the buried image of the past. Poetry thus makes immortal all that is best and most beautiful in the world; it arrests the vanishing apparitions which haunt the interlunations of life, and veiling them, or in language or in form, sends them forth among mankind, bearing sweet news of

15. muse ... song: *Paradise Lost*, IX, 23–24.

kindred joy to those with whom their sisters abide—abide, because there is no portal of expression from the caverns of the spirit which they inhabit into the universe of things. Poetry redeems from decay the visitations of the divinity in man.

Poetry turns all things to loveliness; it exalts the beauty of that which is most beautiful, and it adds beauty to that which is most deformed; it marries exultation and horror, grief and pleasure, eternity and change; it subdues to union under its light yoke, all irreconcilable things. It transmutes all that it touches, and every form moving within the radiance of its presence is changed by wondrous sympathy to an incarnation of the spirit which it breathes; its secret alchemy turns to potable gold the poisonous waters which flow from death through life; it strips the veil of familiarity from the world, and lays bare the naked and sleeping beauty, which is the spirit of its forms.

All things exist as they are perceived; at least in relation to the percipient. "The mind is its own place, and of itself can make a heaven of hell, a hell of heaven." [16] But poetry defeats the curse which binds us to be subjected to the accident of surrounding impressions. And whether it spreads its own figured curtain, or withdraws life's dark veil from before the scene of things, it equally creates for us a being within our being. It makes us the inhabitants of a world to which the familiar world is a chaos. It reproduces the common universe of which we are portions and percipients, and it purges from our inward sight the film of familiarity which obscures from us the wonder of our being. It compels us to feel that which we perceive, and to imagine that which we know. It creates anew the universe, after it has been annihilated in our minds by the recurrence of impressions blunted by reiteration. It justifies the bold and true words of Tasso: *Non merita nome di creatore, se non Iddio ed il Poeta.*[17]

A poet, as he is the author to others of the highest wisdom, pleasure, virtue and glory, so he ought personally to be the happiest, the best, the wisest, and the most illustrious of men. As to his glory, let time be challenged to declare whether the fame of any other institutor of human life be comparable to that of a poet. That he is the wisest, the happiest,

and the best, inasmuch as he is a poet, is equally incontrovertible; the greatest poets have been men of the most spotless virtue, of the most consummate prudence, and, if we would look into the interior of their lives, the most fortunate of men: and the exceptions, as they regard those who possessed the poetic faculty in a high yet inferior degree, will be found on consideration to confirm rather than destroy the rule. Let us for a moment stoop to the arbitration of popular breath, and usurping and uniting in our own persons the incompatible characters of accuser, witness, judge, and executioner, let us decide without trial, testimony, or form, that certain motives of those who are "there sitting where we dare not soar," [18] are reprehensible. Let us assume that Homer was a drunkard, that Virgil was a flatterer, that Horace was a coward, that Tasso was a madman, that Lord Bacon was a peculator, that Raphael was a libertine, that Spenser was a poet laureate. It is inconsistent with this division of our subject to cite living poets, but posterity has done ample justice to the great names now referred to. Their errors have been weighed and found to have been dust in the balance; if their sins were as scarlet, they are now white as snow: they have been washed in the blood of the mediator and redeemer, Time. Observe in what a ludicrous chaos the imputations of real or fictitious crime have been confused in the contemporary calumnies against poetry and poets; consider how little is as it appears—or appears as it is; look to your own motives, and judge not, lest ye be judged.

Poetry, as has been said, differs in this respect from logic, that it is not subject to the control of the active powers of the mind, and that its birth and recurrence have no necessary connexion with consciousness or will. It is presumptuous to determine that these are the necessary conditions of all mental causation, when mental effects are experienced unsusceptible of being referred to them. The frequent recurrence of the poetical power, it is obvious to suppose, may produce in the mind a habit of order and harmony correlative with its own nature and with its effects upon other minds. But in the intervals of inspiration, and they may be frequent without being durable, a poet becomes a man, and is abandoned to the sudden reflux of the influences under which others habitually live. But as he is

16. "The ... heaven": *Paradise Lost,* I, 254–55. 17. Non ... Poeta: "No one deserves the name of creator except God and the Poet."

18. "there ... soar": *Paradise Lost,* IV, 829.

more delicately organized than other men, and sensible to pain and pleasure, both his own and that of others, in a degree unknown to them, he will avoid the one and pursue the other with an ardour proportioned to this difference. And he renders himself obnoxious to calumny, when he neglects to observe the circumstances under which these objects of universal pursuit and flight have disguised themselves in one another's garments.

But there is nothing necessarily evil in this error, and thus cruelty, envy, revenge, avarice, and the passions purely evil, have never formed any portion of the popular imputations on the lives of poets.

I have thought it most favorable to the cause of truth to set down these remarks according to the order in which they were suggested to my mind, by a consideration of the subject itself, instead of observing the formality of a polemical reply; but if the view which they contain be just, they will be found to involve a refutation of the arguers against poetry, so far at least as regards the first division of the subject. I can readily conjecture what should have moved the gall of some learned and intelligent writers who quarrel with certain versifiers; I confess myself like them, unwilling to be stunned by the Theseids of the hoarse Codri[19] of the day. Bavius and Mævius[20] undoubtedly are, as they ever were, insufferable persons. But it belongs to a philosophical critic to distinguish rather than confound.

The first of these remarks has related to poetry in its elements and principles; and it has been shown, as well as the narrow limits assigned them would permit, that what is called poetry, in a restricted sense, has a common source with all other forms of order and of beauty, according to which the materials of human life are susceptible of being arranged, and which is poetry in a universal sense.

The second part will have for its object an application of these principles to the present state of the cultivation of poetry, and a defence of the at-

tempt to idealize the modern forms of manners and opinions, and compel them into a subordination to the imaginative and creative faculty. For the literature of England, an energetic development of which has ever preceded or accompanied a great and free development of the national will, has arisen as it were from a new birth. In spite of the low-thoughted envy which would undervalue contemporary merit, our own will be a memorable age in intellectual achievements, and we live among such philosophers and poets as surpass beyond comparison any who have appeared since the last national struggle for civil and religious liberty. The most unfailing herald, companion, and follower of the awakening of a great people to work a beneficial change in opinion or institution, is poetry. At such periods there is an accumulation of the power of communicating and receiving intense and impassioned conceptions respecting man and nature. The persons in whom this power resides may often, as far as regards many portions of their nature, have little apparent correspondence with that spirit of good of which they are the ministers. But even whilst they deny and abjure, they are yet compelled to serve the power which is seated on the throne of their own soul. It is impossible to read the compositions of the most celebrated writers of the present day without being startled with the electric life which burns within their words. They measure the circumference and sound the depths of human nature with a comprehensive and all-penetrating spirit, and they are themselves perhaps the most sincerely astonished at its manifestations; for it is less their spirit than the spirit of the age. Poets are the hierophants[21] of an unapprehended inspiration; the mirrors of the gigantic shadows which futurity casts upon the present; the words which express what they understand not; the trumpets which sing to battle, and feel not what they inspire; the influence which is moved not, but moves. Poets are the unacknowledged legislators of the world.

1821   *1840*

---

19. **Codri:** a type name for bad poets. Codrus supposedly wrote a dreadful tragedy about Theseus. **20. Bavius and Mævius:** mediocre Roman poets (see Virgil's *Eclogues*).

21. **hierophants:** priests.

William Hazlitt

1778–1830

It is only in recent years, and largely due to the writings of W. J. Bate, that William Hazlitt has emerged as a major figure in English Romanticism, a philosopher, an aesthetician, and a practical critic whose ideals of gusto, sympathy, and imagination, whose judgments on Chaucer, Spenser, Shakespeare, Milton, and his own contemporaries stand as major contributions to an understanding of the spirit of the age. An unpleasant character at best, he possessed few of those winning personal qualities that would draw the modern student to him. An awkward and consistently hostile man, an unregenerate political liberal, a harried and prolific journalist, a person of stormy love affairs and tempestuous marriages, he nevertheless managed to produce a psychologically-oriented criticism that not only bespeaks the new concerns of his contemporaries, but anticipates a great many concerns of later nineteenth- and twentieth-century criticism. He is truly a paradoxical figure; on the one hand, self-centered, boisterous, and contemptuous of adversaries; on the other, preoccupied with the notion of the natural disinterestedness of the human mind and with the kind of art that sets personality in the background and conveys a rich sense of reality, a firm grasp of the object or character being represented. Indeed, it is fair to say that Hazlitt's earlier reputation as a great familiar essayist, the author of "On Reading Old Books," "The Fight," "My First Acquaintance with Poets," and others, must give way to his increasing importance as a spokesman for the Romantic spirit in the arts.

Hazlitt's background goes a long way toward helping us to understand his strong self-image as the underdog, as the dissenter against the political, religious, and literary establishment. He was born on April 10, 1778 in Maidstone, Kent, the son of a courageous and outspoken Unitarian minister who supported strongly the American and French struggles for freedom. Never a preacher eager to concern himself with the sensitivities of his congregations, he moved frequently, preaching his radical Christianity in Ireland and in New York, Philadelphia, and the environs of Boston in America. The family settled in America in 1783, when William was five, and remained there, none too happily, until 1787, when the father brought them home and settled at Wem in Shropshire where he held a pulpit.

William attended the Unitarian College in Hackney from 1793–95 in preparation for a career in ministry. It was there that he fell under the spell of his tutor, Joseph Priestley, the great scientist, critic, and philosophical and political radical, and quickly ended any thoughts of life as a clergyman. Freed of any sense of obligation to follow a church career, he now began to read widely and to follow up a growing interest in painting under the tutelage of his brother in London. He met both Wordsworth and Coleridge in 1798, and was obviously impressed and influenced by both men.

From 1805 forward Hazlitt committed himself totally to writing. His first important effort was the philosophical *Essay on the Principles of Human Action,* the treatise in which he first expounded his ideas on disinterestedness and sympathy. Journalism was to preoccupy him for the rest of his career, however, as he devoted himself more and more to the craft of reviewer and critic, with the *Morning Chronicle* in 1813, the *Edinburgh Review* and Leigh Hunt's *Examiner* in 1814, the *Times* in 1817. In quick succession he produced his *Lectures on the English Poets* and *View of the English Stage* in 1818; *Lectures on the English Comic Writers* in 1819; *Lectures on the Dramatic Literature of the Age of Elizabeth* in 1820; and the famous *Table Talk, or, Original Essays* in 1821.

Meanwhile Hazlitt's personal life was disastrous. His marriage to Sarah Stoddart, a continuing warfare, ended in 1822; his hopes to marry the fickle Sarah Walker were shattered; and still a second marriage to Isabella Bridgewater ended when she abandoned him because of constant conflict between her and the son of his first marriage. His last years were somewhat more tranquil although he continued to write feverishly, producing in 1825 his great masterpiece *The Spirit of the Age: or Contemporary Portraits,* a vivid series of biographical and historical sketches that capture the flavor of the people, books, and events of the turbulent and exciting years through which he lived. Hazlitt died on September 18, 1830.

Hazlitt's literary theory can perhaps best be understood in the light of his recurring praise of emotional strength as the central excellence of a work of art. Before he proceeds to any consideration of form or technique, he must be satisfied that this criterion is fulfilled. "Poetry is the language of the imagination and the passions," he writes in his essay *On Poetry in General.* "It relates to whatever comes home to the bosoms and businesses of men; for nothing but what so comes home to them in the most general and intelligible shape, can be a subject for poetry." Poetry, he contends, "is only the highest eloquence of passion, the most vivid form of expression that can be given to our conception of anything, whether pleasurable or painful, mean or dignified, delightful or distressing." "Gusto," Hazlitt's famous synonym for emotional excitement, "is power or passion defining any object." In the coloring of a Titian, whose "heads seem to think" and whose "bodies seem to feel"; in Michael Angelo's forms which "everywhere obtrude the sense of power upon the eye" and in his limbs which convey "an idea of muscular strength, of moral grandeur, and even of intellectual dignity"; in the vital "tangible character" of Rembrandt's portraits; in the Greek statues whose "beauty is power"; in Shakespeare, Milton, Pope's compliments, Dryden's satires, and Gay's *Beggar's Opera*—in all of these and many others, Hazlitt finds that unique power.

At the same time that Hazlitt singled out emotion as the dominant source of aesthetic pleasure, he was quick to separate it from a mere outpouring of personal feeling, from mere egocentricity and self-expression. From the time of his earliest writings he had seen man's emotional nature as central but as potentially dangerous. Moderation was the great ideal; strong emotion must be rooted in the larger reality of persons and things beyond the self, must be proportionate to that which evokes it. As in moral action, so also in art; true greatness involves losing the sense of personal identity in something grander and dearer than our own petty concerns. Shakespeare is, in this connection, always Hazlitt's greatest hero. In the famous essay *On Shakespeare and Milton,* he argues that Shakespeare "had only to think of anything in order to become that thing, with all the circumstances belonging to it." No critic pays a higher tribute to the great dramatist:

> The striking peculiarity of Shakespeare's mind was its generic quality, its power of communication with all other minds—so that it contained a universe of thought and feeling within itself, and had no one peculiar bias, or exclusive excellence more than another. He was just like any other man, but that he was like all other men. He was the least of an egotist that it was possible to be. He was nothing in himself; but he was all that others were, or that they could become.

True emotional immediacy, then, is a vigorous and absorbing quality, turned not simply inward upon the self, but outward toward the world. Hence Hazlitt is quick to call attention to the egotism of his contemporaries, to the self-centeredness of a Rousseau or a Wordsworth. In his judgment the only quality which Rousseau possessed to a noteworthy degree was "extreme sensibility or an acute and even morbid feeling of all that related to his own impressions, to the objects and events of his life. He had the most intense consciousness of his own existence. ... His craving after excitement was an appetite and a disease." Wordsworth and Rousseau were alike; in Rousseau's rhapsodical outburst on discovering periwinkles and Wordsworth's exhilaration at finding the linnet's nest with five blue eggs, "both create an interest out of nothing, or rather out of their own feelings. ... Rousseau, in a word, interests you in certain objects by interesting you in himself; Mr. Wordsworth would persuade you that the most insignificant objects are interesting in themselves, because he is interested in them."

On the contrary, Shakespeare and Milton did not "surround the meanest objects with the morbid feelings and devouring egotism of the writers' own minds." These great writers "owe their power over the human mind to their having had a deeper sense than others of what was grand in the objects of nature or affecting in the events of human life." Hazlitt stresses consistently the need for the artist's intense understanding of and sympathy with that which is beyond the merely subjective, for a firm grasp of reality that involves mind, imagination, and passion. Hence his concept of imitation is distinctive; it is the product of genius, an essentially imaginative activity, stirring the faculty to make comparisons, to realize things more vividly. Imitation, he suggests in his essay on the subject, interests and gives pleasure "by exciting a more intense perception of truth, and calling out the powers of observation and comparison." True imitation shakes our stereotypes, gives the lie to our ideologies, undercuts our prejudices. It can even "render an object, displeasing in itself, a source of pleasure, not by repetition of the same idea, but by suggesting new ideas, directing new properties, and endless shades of difference, just as a close and continued contemplation of an object itself would do." Imagination gathers a strength from nature which no other source can provide.

A corollary of this need for art to stay in close touch with the real is Hazlitt's notion, one that had great appeal for young Keats, of the sympathetic quality of the imagination and the great dependence of art upon it. The imagination can go beyond the self, can identify with its object, and thereby achieve a wondrous objectivity and concreteness, a rich sense of the mysterious depths of human experience. Hence gusto, as Bate so brilliantly describes it in his essay on Hazlitt in *Criticism: The Major Texts,* is "a strong excitement of the imagination by which geared to its highest activity, it seizes and drains out the dynamic and living character of its object into telling expression." Such a power, Hazlitt claims, is not gained through centuries of improvement in the arts; indeed, the arts, as he argues in his famous essay, are not progressive. Great genius can flourish at any time, often in the dawn of a culture. "Those arts," he contends, "which depend on individual genius and incommunicable power, have always leaped at once from infancy to manhood, from the first dawn of invention to their meridian height and dazzling lustre, and have in general declined ever after."

Hazlitt stands then, along with Wordsworth and Coleridge, as a major Romantic critical theorist. At his best his work has a modern ring, especially his discussions of genius, sympathy, and impersonality in art. What stands out most sharply is his persistent quest for justification of emotional power as the keystone of great art and his plea for an understanding of this power in more objective ways as an escape from maudlin feeling, participation in the living reality of nature, and an expression of this participation with vividness and intensity.

Suggestions For Further Readings

Herschel Baker's *William Hazlitt* (1962) is clearly the definitive biography, a masterpiece of comprehensiveness and of deep sensitivity to the mind of Hazlitt and to the many facets of his career. Ralph Wardle's recent biography *Hazlitt* (1971) is also helpful, providing a detailed treatment of Hazlitt's complex life.

W. J. Bate's seminal essay on Hazlitt, which forms the introduction to the selections in his anthology, *Criticism: The Major Texts* (1952), remains the most penetrating study of Hazlitt's contributions as a critic and should be required reading for any student beginning a study of the subject. Also recommended are Elizabeth Schneider, *The Aesthetics of William Hazlitt* (1933); W. P. Albrecht, *Hazlitt and the Creative Imagination* (1965); and Roy Park's *Hazlitt and the Spirit of the Age* (1971).

OBSERVATIONS ON MR. WORDSWORTH'S POEM THE EXCURSION

The poem of *The Excursion* resembles that part of the country in which the scene is laid. It has the same vastness and magnificence, with the same nakedness and confusion. It has the same overwhelming, oppressive power. It excites or recalls the same sensations which those who have traversed that wonderful scenery must have felt. We are surrounded with the constant sense and superstitious awe of the collective power of matter, of the gigantic and eternal forms of nature, on which, from the beginning of time, the hand of man has made no impression. Here are no dotted lines, no hedge-row beauties, no box-tree borders, no gravel walks, no square mechanic inclosures; all is left loose and irregular in the rude chaos of aboriginal nature. The boundaries of hill and valley are the poet's only geography, where we wander with him incessantly over deep beds of moss and waving fern, amidst the troops of red-deer and wild animals. Such is the severe simplicity of Mr. Wordsworth's taste, that we doubt whether he would not reject a druidical temple, or time-hallowed ruin as too modern and artificial for his purpose. He only familiarises himself or his readers with a stone, covered with lichens, which has slept in the same spot of ground from the creation of the world, or with the rocky fissure between two mountains caused by thunder, or with a cavern scooped out by the sea. His mind is, as it were, coëval with the primary forms of things; his imagination holds immediately from nature, and "owes no allegiance" but "to the elements."

The *Excursion* may be considered as a philosophical pastoral poem,—as a scholastic romance. It is less a poem on the country, than on the love of the country. It is not so much a description of natural objects, as of the feelings associated with them; not an account of the manners of rural life, but the result of the poet's reflections on it. He does not present the reader with a lively succession of images or incidents, but paints the outgoings of his own heart, the shapings of his own fancy. He may be said to create his own materials; his thoughts are his real subject. His understanding broods over that which is "without form and void," and "makes it pregnant." He sees all things in himself. He hardly ever avails himself of remarkable objects or situations, but, in general, rejects them as interfering with the workings of his own mind, as disturbing the smooth, deep, majestic current of his own feelings. Thus his descriptions of natural scenery are not brought home distinctly to the naked eye by forms and circumstances, but every object is seen through the medium of innumerable recollections, is clothed with the haze of imagination like a glittering vapour, is obscured with the excess of glory, has the shadowy brightness of a waking dream. The image is lost in the sentiment, as sound in the multiplication of echoes.

And visions, as prophetic eye avow,
Hang on each leaf, and cling to every bough.

In describing human nature, Mr. Wordsworth equally shuns the common 'vantage-grounds of popular story, of striking incidents, or fatal catastrophe, as cheap and vulgar modes of producing an effect. He scans the human race as the naturalist measures the earth's zone, without attending to the picturesque points of view, the abrupt inequalities of surface. He contemplates the passions and habits of men, not in their extremes, but in their first elements; their follies and vices, not at their height, with all their embossed evils upon their heads, but as lurking in embryo,—the seeds of the disorder inwoven with our very constitution. He only sympathises with those simple forms of feeling, which mingle at once with his own identity, or with the stream of general humanity. To him the great and the small are the same; the near and the remote; what appears, and what only is. The general and the permanent, like the Platonic ideas, are his only realities. All accidental varieties and individual contrasts are lost in an endless continuity of feeling, like drops of water in the ocean-stream! An intense intellectual egotism swallows up every thing. Even the dialogues introduced in the present volume are soliloquies of the same character, taking different views of the subject. The recluse, the pastor, and the pedlar, are three persons in one poet. We ourselves disapprove of these "interlocutions between Lucius and Caius" as impertinent babbling, where there is no dramatic distinction of character. But the evident scope and tendency of Mr. Wordsworth's mind is the reverse of dramatic. It resists all change of character, all variety of scenery, all the bustle, machinery, and pantomime of the stage, or of real life,—whatever might relieve, or relax, or change the direction of its own activity, jealous of all competition. The power of his mind preys upon itself. It is as if there were nothing but himself and the universe. He lives in the busy solitude of his own heart; in the deep silence of thought. His imagination lends life and feeling only to "the bare trees and mountains bare"; peoples the viewless tracts of air, and converses with the silent clouds!

We could have wished that our author had given to his work the form of a didactic poem altogether, with only occasional digressions or allusions to particular instances. But he has chosen to encumber himself with a load of narrative and description, which sometimes hinders the progress and effect of the general reasoning, and which, instead of being inwoven with the text, would have come in better in plain prose as notes at the end of the volume. Mr. Wordsworth, indeed, says finely, and perhaps as truly as finely:

> Exchange the shepherd's frock of native grey
> For robes with regal purple tinged; convert
> The crook into a sceptre; give the pomp
> Of circumstance; and here the tragic Muse
> Shall find apt subjects for her highest art.
> Amid the groves, beneath the shadowy hills,
> The generations are prepared; the pangs,
> The internal pangs, are ready; the dread strife
> Of poor humanity's afflicted will
> Struggling in vain with ruthless destiny.

But he immediately declines availing himself of these resources of the rustic moralist: for the priest,

who officiates as "the sad historian of the pensive plain" says in reply:

> "Our system is not fashioned to preclude
> That sympathy which you for others ask:
> And I could tell, not travelling for my theme
> Beyond the limits of these humble graves,
> Of strange disasters; but I pass them by,
> Loth to disturb what Heaven hath hushed to
>   peace."

There is, in fact, in Mr. Wordsworth's mind an evident repugnance to admit anything that tells for itself, without the interpretation of the poet,—a fastidious antipathy to immediate effect,—a systematic unwillingness to share the palm with his subject. Where, however, he has a subject presented to him, "such as the meeting soul may pierce," and to which he does not grudge to lend the aid of his fine genius, his powers of description and fancy seem to be little inferior to those of his classical predecessor, Akenside. Among several others which we might select we give the following passage, describing the religion of ancient Greece:

> In that fair clime, the lonely herdsman,
>   stretch'd
> On the soft grass through half a summer's day,
> With music lulled his indolent repose:
> And in some fit of weariness, if he,
> When his own breath was silent, chanced to
>   hear
> A distant strain, far sweeter than the sounds
> Which his poor skill could make, his fancy
>   fetch'd,
> Even from the blazing chariot of the sun,
> A beardless youth, who touched a golden lute,
> And filled the illumined groves with
>   ravishment.
> The nightly hunter, lifting up his eyes
> Towards the crescent moon, with grateful
>   heart
> Called on the lovely wanderer, who bestowed
> That timely light, to share his joyous sport:
> And hence, a beaming Goddess with her
>   Nymphs
> Across the lawn and through the darksome
>   grove,
> (Nor unaccompanied with tuneful notes
> By echo multiplied from rock or cave),
> Swept in the storm of chase, as moon and stars
> Glance rapidly along the clouded heavens,
> When winds are blowing strong. The traveller
>   slaked
> His thirst from rill, or gushing fount, and
>   thanked
> The Naiad. Sun beams, upon distant hills
> Gliding apace, with shadows in their train,

Might, with small help from fancy, be
    transformed
Into fleet Oreads, sporting visibly.
The zephyrs fanning as they passed their wings
Lacked not for love fair objects, whom they
    wooed
With gentle whisper. Withered boughs
    grotesque,
Stripped of their leaves and twigs by hoary
    age,
From depth of shaggy covert peeping forth
In the low vale, or on steep mountain side:
And sometimes intermixed with stirring horns
Of the live deer, or goat's depending beard;
These were the lurking satyrs, a wild brood
Of gamesome Deities! or Pan himself,
The simple shepherd's awe-inspiring God.

The foregoing is one of a succession of splendid passages equally enriched with philosophy and poetry, tracing the fictions of Eastern mythology to the immediate intercourse of the imagination with Nature, and to the habitual propensity of the human mind to endow the outward forms of being with life and conscious motion. With this expansive and animating principle, Mr. Wordsworth has forcibly, but somewhat severely, contrasted the cold, narrow, lifeless spirit of modern philosophy:

How, shall our great discoverers obtain
From sense and reason less than these
    obtained,
Though far misled? Shall men for whom our
    age
Unbaffled powers of vision hath perpared,
To explore the world without and world
    within,
Be joyless as the blind? Ambitious souls—
Whom earth at this late season hath produced
To regulate the moving sphere, and weigh
The planets in the hollow of their hand;
And they who rather dive than soar, whose
    pains
Have solved the elements, or analysed
The thinking principle—shall they in fact
Prove a degraded race? And what avails
Renown, if their presumption make them such?
Inquire of ancient wisdom; go, demand
Of mighty nature, if 'twas ever meant
That we should pry far off, yet be unraised;
That we should pore, and dwindle as we pore,
Viewing all objects unremittingly
In disconnection dead and spiritless;
And still dividing and dividing still
Break down all grandeur, still unsatisfied
With the perverse attempt, while littleness
May yet become more little; waging thus
An impious warfare with the very life
Of our own souls! And if indeed there be

An all-pervading spirit, upon whom
Our dark foundations rest, could he design,
That this magnificent effect of power,
The earth we tread, the sky which we behold
By day, and all the pomp which night reveals,
That these—and that superior mystery,
Our vital frame, so fearfully devised,
And the dread soul within it—should exist
Only to be examined, pondered, searched,
Probed, vexed, and criticised—to be prized
No more than as a mirror that reflects
To proud Self-love her own intelligence?

From the chemists and metaphysicians our author turns to the laughing sage of France, Voltaire. "Poor gentleman, it fares no better with him, for he's a wit." We cannot, however, agree with Mr. Wordsworth that *Candide* is *dull*. It is, if our author pleases, "the production of a scoffer's pen," or it is any thing but dull. It may not be proper in a grave, discreet, orthodox, promising young divine, who studies his opinions in the contraction or distension of his patron's brow, to allow any merit to a work like *Candide;* but we conceive that it would have been more manly in Mr. Wordsworth, nor do we think it would have hurt the cause he espouses, if he had blotted out the epithet, after it had peevishly escaped him. Whatsoever savours of a little, narrow, inquisitorial spirit, does not sit well on a poet and a man of genius. The prejudices of a philosopher are not natural. There is a frankness and sincerity of opinion, which is a paramount obligation in all questions of intellect, though it may not govern the decisions of the spiritual courts, who may, however, be safely left to take care of their own interests. There is a plain directness and simplicity of understanding, which is the only security against the evils of levity, on the one hand, or of hypocrisy on the other. A speculative bigot is a solecism in the intellectual world. We can assure Mr. Wordsworth, that we should not have bestowed so much serious consideration on a single voluntary perversion of language, but that our respect for his character makes us jealous of his smallest faults!

With regard to his great philippic against the contractedness and egotism of philosophical pursuits, we only object to its not being carried further. We shall not affirm with Rousseau (his authority would perhaps have little weight with Mr. Wordsworth)—"*Tout homme réfléchi est méchant*"; but we conceive that the same reasoning which Mr. Wordsworth applies so eloquently and justly to the natural philosopher and metaphysician may be extended to the moralist, the divine, the politician, the orator, the artist, and even the poet. And why so? Because wherever an intense activity is given to any one faculty, it necessarily prevents the due and natural exercise of others. Hence all those professions or pursuits, where the mind is exclusively occupied with the ideas of things as they exist in the imagination or understanding, as they call for the exercise of intellectual activity, and not as they are connected with practical good or evil, must check the genial expansion of the moral sentiments and social affections; must lead to a cold and dry abstraction, as they are found to suspend the animal functions, and relax the bodily frame. Hence the complaint of the want of natural sensibility and constitutional warmth of attachment in those persons who have been devoted to the pursuit of any art or science,—of their restless morbidity of temperament, and indifference to every thing that does not furnish an occasion for the display of the mental superiority and the gratification of their vanity. The philosophical poet himself, perhaps, owes some of his love of nature to the opportunity it affords him of analyzing his own feelings, and contemplating his own powers,—of making every object about him a whole length mirror to reflect his favourite thoughts, and of looking down on the frailties of others in undisturbed leisure, and from a more dignified height.

One of the most interesting parts of this work is that in which the author treats of the French Revolution, and of the feelings connected with it, in ingenuous minds, in its commencement and its progress. The *solitary*, who, by domestic calamities and disappointments, had been cut off from society, and almost from himself, gives the following account of the manner in which he was roused from his melancholy:

> From that abstraction I was roused—and how?
> Even as a thoughtful shepherd by a flash
> Of lightning, startled in a gloomy cave
> Of these wild hills. For, lo! the dread Bastile,
> With all the chambers in its horrid towers,
> Fell to the ground: by violence o'erthrown
> Of indignation; and with shouts that drowned
> The crash it made in falling! From the wreck
> A golden palace rose, or seemed to rise,
> The appointed seat of equitable law
> And mild paternal sway. The potent shock
> I felt; the transformation I perceived,
> As marvellously seized as in that moment,
> When, from the blind mist issuing, I beheld

> Glory—beyond all glory ever seen,
> Dazzling the soul! Meanwhile prophetic harps
> In every grove were ringing, "War shall cease:
> Did ye not hear that conquest is abjured?
> Bring garlands, bring forth choicest flowers to
>   deck
> The tree of liberty!"—My heart rebounded:
> My melancholy voice the chorus joined.
> Thus was I reconverted to the world;
> Society became my glittering bride,
> And airy hopes my children. From the depths
> Of natural passion seemingly escaped,
> My soul diffused itself in wide embrace
> Of institutions and the forms of things.
>   ——If with noise
> And acclamation, crowds in open air
> Expressed the tumult of their minds, my voice
> There mingled, heard or not. And in still
>   groves,
> Where wild enthusiasts tuned a pensive lay
> Of thanks and expectation, in accord
> With their belief, I sang Saturnian rule
> Returned—a progeny of golden years
> Permitted to descend, and bless mankind.

>   .   .   .

> Scorn and contempt forbid me to proceed!
> But history, time's slavish scribe, will tell
> How rapidly the zealots of the cause
> Disbanded—or in hostile ranks appeared:
> Some, tired of honest service; these outdone,
> Disgusted, therefore, or appalled by aims
> Of fiercer zealots. So confusion reigned,
> And the more faithful were compelled to
>   exclaim,
> As Brutus did to virtue, "Liberty,
> I worshipped thee, and find thee but a shade!"
> SUCH RECANTATION HAD FOR ME NO CHARM,
> NOR WOULD I BEND TO IT.

The subject is afterwards resumed, with the same magnanimity and philosophical firmness:

>   ——For that other loss,
> The loss of confidence in social man,
> By the unexpected transports of our age
> Carried so high, that every thought which
>   looked
> Beyond the temporal destiny of the kind—
> To many seemed superfluous; as no cause
> For such exalted confidence could e'er
> Exist; so, none is now for such despair.
> The two extremes are equally remote
> From truth and reason; do not, then, confound
> One with the other, but reject them both;
> And choose the middle point, whereon to build
> Sound expectations. This doth he advise
> Who shared at first the illusion. At this day,
> When a Tartarian darkness overspreads
> The groaning nations; when the impious rule,
> By will or by established ordinance,

Their own dire agents, and constrain the good
To acts which they abhor; though I bewail
This triumph, yet the pity of my heart
Prevents me not from owning that the law,
By which mankind now suffers, is most just.
For by superior energies; more strict
Affiance in each other; faith more firm
In their unhallowed principles, the bad
Have fairly earned a victory o'er the weak,
The vacillating, inconsistent good.

In the application of these memorable lines, we should, perhaps, differ a little from Mr. Wordsworth; nor can we indulge with him in the fond conclusion afterwards hinted at, that one day *our* triumph, the triumph of humanity and liberty, may be complete. For this purpose, we think several things necessary which are impossible. It is a consummation which cannot happen till the nature of things is changed, till the many become as united as the *one*, till romantic generosity shall be as common as gross selfishness, till reason shall have acquired the obstinate blindness of prejudice, till the love of power and of change shall no longer goad man on to restless action, till passion and will, hope and fear, love and hatred, and the objects proper to excite them, that is, alternate good and evil, shall no longer sway the bosoms and businesses of men. All things move, not in progress, but in a ceaseless round; our strength lies in our weakness; our virtues are built on our vices; our faculties are as limited as our being; nor can we lift man above his nature more than above the earth he treads. But though we cannot weave over again the airy, unsubstantial dream, which reason and experience have dispelled,

What though the radiance, which was once so
    bright,
Be now for ever taken from our sight,
Though nothing can bring back the hour
Of glory in the grass, of splendour in the
    flower:—

yet we will never cease, nor be prevented from returning on the wings of imagination to that bright dream of our youth; that glad dawn of the day-star of liberty; that spring-time of the world, in which the hopes and expectations of the human race seemed opening in the same gay career with our own; when France called her children to partake her equal blessings beneath her laughing skies; when the stranger was met in all her villages with dance and festive songs, in celebration of a new and golden era; and when, to the retired and contemplative student, the prospects of human happiness and glory were seen ascending like the steps of Jacob's ladder, in bright and never-ending succession. The dawn of that day was suddenly overcast; that season of hope is past; it is fled with the other dreams of our youth, which we cannot recal, but has left behind it traces, which are not to be effaced by Birth-day and Thanks-giving odes, or the chaunting of *Te Deums* in all the churches of Christendom. To those hopes eternal regrets are due; to those who maliciously and wilfully blasted them, in the fear that they might be accomplished, we feel no less what we owe—hatred and scorn as lasting!

THE SAME SUBJECT CONTINUED

Mr. Wordsworth's writings exhibit all the internal power, without the external form of poetry. He has scarcely any of the pomp and decoration and scenic effect of poetry: no gorgeous palaces nor solemn temples awe the imagination; no cities rise "with glistering spires and pinnacles adorned" [1]; we meet with no knights pricked forth on airy steeds; no hair-breadth 'scapes and perilous accidents by flood or field. Either from the predominant habit of his mind not requiring the stimulus of outward impressions, or from the want of an imagination teeming with various forms, he takes the common every-day events and objects of nature, or rather seeks those that are the most simple and barren of effect; but he adds to them a weight of interest from the resources of his own mind, which makes the most insignificant things serious and even formidable. All other interests are absorbed in the deeper interest of his own thoughts, and find the same level. His mind magnifies the littleness of his subject, and raises its meanness; lends it his strength, and clothes it with borrowed grandeur. With him, a molehill, covered with wild thyme, assumes the importance of "the great vision of the guarded mount" [2]: a puddle is filled with preternatural faces, and agitated with the fiercest storms of passion.

The extreme simplicity which some persons have

THE SAME SUBJECT CONTINUED. 1. Milton, *Paradise Lost*, III, 550. 2. Milton, *Lycidus*, l. 161.

objected to in Mr. Wordsworth's poetry, is to be found only in the subject and the style: the sentiments are subtle and profound. In the latter respect, his poetry is as much above the common standard or capacity, as in the other it is below it. His poems bear a distant resemblance to some of Rembrandt's landscapes, who, more than any other painter, created the medium through which he saw nature, and out of the stump of an old tree, a break in the sky, and a bit of water, could produce an effect almost miraculous.

Mr. Wordsworth's poems in general are the history of a refined and contemplative mind, conversant only with itself and nature. An intense feeling of the associations of this kind is the peculiar and characteristic feature of all his productions. He has described the love of nature better than any other poet. This sentiment, inly felt in all its force, and sometimes carried to an excess, is the source both of his strength and of his weakness. However we may sympathise with Mr. Wordsworth in his attachment to groves and fields, we cannot extend the same admiration to their inhabitants, or to the manners of country life in general. We go along with him, while he is the subject of his own narrative, but we take leave of him when he makes pedlars and ploughmen his heroes and the interpreters of his sentiments. It is, we think, getting into low company, and company, besides, that we do not like. We take Mr. Wordsworth himself for a great poet, a fine moralist, and a deep philosopher; but if he insists on introducing us to a friend of his, a parish clerk, or the barber of the village, who is as wise as himself, we must be excused if we draw back with some little want of cordial faith. We are satisfied with the friendship which subsisted between *Parson Adams* and *Joseph Andrews*. The author himself lets out occasional hints that all is not as it should be amongst these northern Arcadians. Though, in general, he professes to soften the harsher features of rustic vice, he has given us one picture of depraved and inveterate selfishness, which we apprehend could only be found among the inhabitants of these boasted mountain districts. The account of one of his heroines concludes as follows:

A sudden illness seiz'd her in the strength
Of life's autumnal season. Shall I tell
How on her bed of death the matron lay,
To Providence submissive, so she thought;
But fretted, vexed, and wrought upon—almost
To anger, by the malady that gripped
Her prostrate frame with unrelaxing power,
As the fierce eagle fastens on the lamb.
She prayed, she moaned—her husband's sister
    watched
Her dreary pillow, waited on her needs;
And yet the very sound of that kind foot
Was anguish to her ears! "And must she rule
Sole mistress of this house when I am gone?
Sit by my fire—possess what I possessed—
Tend what I tended—calling it her own!"
Enough;—I fear too much. Of nobler feeling
Take this example:—One autumnal evening,
While she was yet in prime of health and
    strength,
I well remember, while I passed her door,
Musing with loitering step, and upward eye
Turned tow'rds the planet Jupiter, that hung
Above the centre of the vale, a voice
Roused me, her voice;—it said, "That glorious
    star
In its untroubled element will shine
As now it shines, when we are laid in earth,
And safe from all our sorrows." She is safe,
And her uncharitable acts, I trust,
And harsh unkindnesses, are all forgiven;
Though, in this vale, remembered with deep
    awe!

We think it is pushing our love of the admiration of natural objects a good deal too far, to make it a set-off against a story like the preceding.

All country people hate each other. They have so little comfort that they envy their neighbours the smallest pleasure or advantage, and nearly grudge themselves the necessaries of life. From not being accustomed to enjoyment, they become hardened and averse to it—stupid, for want of thought—selfish, for want of society. There is nothing good to be had in the country, or, if there is, they will not let you have it. They had rather injure themselves than oblige any one else. Their common mode of life is a system of wretchedness and self-denial, like what we read of among barbarous tribes. You live out of the world. You cannot get your tea and sugar without sending to the next town for it: you pay double, and have it of the worst quality. The small-beer is sure to be sour—the milk skimmed—the meat bad, or spoiled in the cooking. You cannot do a single thing you like; you cannot walk out or sit at home, or write or read, or think or look as if you did, without being subject to impertinent curiosity. The apothecary annoys you with his complaisance; the parson with his superciliousness. If you are poor, you are despised; if you are rich, you are feared and hated. If you do any one a favour, the whole neighbourhood is up in arms; the clamour is like that of a rookery; and the person himself, it is ten to one, laughs at you for your pains, and takes the first opportunity of shewing you that he labours under no uneasy sense of obligation. There is a perpetual round of mischief-making and backbiting for want of any better amusement. There are no shops, no taverns, no theatres, no opera, no concerts, no pictures, no public-buildings, no crowded streets, no noise of coaches, or of courts of law,—neither courtiers nor courtesans, no literary parties, no fashionable routs, no society, no books, or knowledge of books. Vanity and luxury are the civilisers of the world, and sweeteners of human life. Without objects either of pleasure or action, it grows harsh and crabbed: the mind becomes stagnant, the affections callous, and the eye dull. Man left to himself soon degenerates into a very disagreeable person. Ignorance is always bad enough; but rustic ignorance is intolerable. Aristotle has observed, that tragedy purifies the affections by terror and pity. If so, a company of tragedians should be established at the public expence, in every village or hundred, as a better mode of education than either Bell's or Lancaster's.[3] The benefits of knowledge are never so well understood as from seeing the effects of ignorance, in their naked, undisguised state, upon the common country people. Their selfishness and insensibility are perhaps less owing to the hardships and privations, which make them, like people out at sea in a boat, ready to devour one another, than to their having no idea of anything beyond themselves and their immediate sphere of action. They have no knowledge of, and consequently can take no interest in, anything which is not an object of their senses, and of their daily pursuits. They hate all strangers, and have generally a nick-name for the inhabitants of the next village. The two young noblemen in Guzman d'Alfarache,[4] who went to visit their mistresses only a league out of Madrid, were set upon by the peasants, who came round them calling out, "A wolf." Those who have no enlarged or liberal ideas, can have no disinterested or generous sentiments. Persons who are in the habit of reading novels and romances, are com-

3. Andrew Bell and Joseph Lancaster were contemporary educational theorists and reformers. 4. A novel by Mateo Aleman.

pelled to take a deep interest in, and to have their affections strongly excited by, fictitious characters and imaginary situations; their thoughts and feelings are constantly carried out of themselves, to persons they never saw, and things that never existed: history enlarges the mind, by familiarising us with the great vicissitudes of human affairs, and the catastrophes of states and kingdoms; the study of morals accustoms us to refer our actions to a general standard of right and wrong; and abstract reasoning, in general, strengthens the love of truth, and produces an inflexibility of principle which cannot stoop to low trick and cunning. Books, in Lord Bacon's phrase, are "a discipline of humanity." Country people have none of these advantages, nor any others to supply the place of them. Having no circulating libraries to exhaust their love of the marvellous, they amuse themselves with fancying the disasters and disgraces of their particular acquaintance. Having no hump-backed *Richard* to excite their wonder and abhorrence, they make themselves a bug-bear of their own, out of the first obnoxious person they can lay their hands on. Not having the fictitious distresses and gigantic crimes of poetry to stimulate their imagination and their passions, they vent their whole stock of spleen, malice, and invention, on their friends and next-door neighbours. They get up a little pastoral drama at home, with fancied events, but real characters. All their spare time is spent in manufacturing and propagating the lie for the day, which does its office, and expires. The next day is spent in the same manner. It is thus that they embellish the simplicity of rural life! The common people in civilised countries are a kind of domesticated savages. They have not the wild imagination, the passions, the fierce energies, or dreadful vicissitudes of the savage tribes, nor have they the leisure, the indolent enjoyments and romantic superstitions, which belonged to the pastoral life in milder climates, and more remote periods of society. They are taken out of a state of nature, without being put in possession of the refinements of art. The customs and institutions of society cramp their imaginations without giving them knowledge. If the inhabitants of the mountainous districts described by Mr. Wordsworth are less gross and sensual than others, they are more selfish. Their egotism becomes more concentrated, as they are more insulated, and their purposes more inveterate, as they have less competition to struggle with. The weight of matter which surrounds them, crushes the finer sympathies. Their minds become hard and cold, like the rocks which they cultivate. The immensity of their mountains makes the human form appear little and insignificant. Men are seen crawling between Heaven and earth, like insects to their graves. Nor do they regard one another more than flies on a wall. Their physiognomy expresses the materialism of their character, which has only one principle—rigid self-will. They move on with their eyes and foreheads fixed, looking neither to the right nor to the left, with a heavy slouch in their gait, and seeming as if nothing would divert them from their path. We do not admire this plodding pertinacity, always directed to the main chance. There is nothing which excites so little sympathy in our minds, as exclusive selfishness. If our theory is wrong, at least it is taken from pretty close observation, and is, we think, confirmed by Mr. Wordsworth's own account.

Of the stories contained in the latter part of the volume, we like that of the Whig and Jacobite friends, and of the good knight, Sir Alfred Irthing, the best. The last reminded us of a fine sketch of a similar character in the beautiful poem of *Hart Leap Well*. To conclude,—if the skill with which the poet had chosen his materials had been equal to the power which he has undeniably exerted over them, if the objects (whether persons or things) which he makes use of as the vehicle of his sentiments, had been such as to convey them in all their depth and force, then the production before us might indeed "have proved a monument," as he himself wishes it, worthy of the author, and of his country. Whether, as it is, this very original and powerful performance may not rather remain like one of those stupendous but half-finished structures, which have been suffered to moulder into decay, because the cost and labour attending them exceeded their use or beauty, we feel that it would be presumptuous in us to determine.

1814   *1814*

WHY THE ARTS ARE NOT PROGRESSIVE

It is often made a subject of complaint and surprise, that the arts in this country, and in modern times, have not kept pace with the general progress of society and civilisation in other respects, and it has been proposed to remedy the deficiency by more carefully availing ourselves of the advantages which time and circumstances have placed within our reach, but which we have hitherto neglected, the study of the antique, the formation of academies, and the distribution of prizes.

First, the complaint itself, that the arts do not attain that progressive degree of perfection which might reasonably be expected from them, proceeds on a false notion, for the analogy appealed to in support of the regular advances of art to higher degrees of excellence, totally fails; it applies to science, not to art. Secondly, the expedients proposed to remedy the evil by adventitious means are only calculated to confirm it. The arts hold immediate communication with nature, and are only derived from that source. When the inspiration of genius is fled, all the attempts to recall it are no better than the tricks of galvanism to restore the dead to life. The arts may be said to resemble Antaeus in his struggle with Hercules, who was strangled when he was raised above the ground, and only revived and recovered his strength when he touched his mother earth.

Nothing is more contrary to the fact than the supposition that in what we understand by the *fine arts,* as painting and poetry, relative perfection is only the result of repeated efforts, and that what has been once well done constantly leads to something better. What is mechanical, reducible to rule, or capable of demonstration, is progressive, and admits of gradual improvement: what is not mechanical or definite, but depends on genius, taste, and feeling, very soon becomes stationary or retrograde, and loses more than it gains by transfusion. The contrary opinion is, indeed, a common error, which has grown up, like many others, from transferring an analogy of one kind to something quite distinct, without thinking of the difference in the nature of the things, or attending to the difference of the results. For most persons, finding what wonderful advances have been made in biblical criticism, in chemistry, in mechanics, in geometry, astronomy, etc.—*i.e.*, in things depending on mere inquiry and experiment, or on absolute demonstration, have been led hastily to conclude, that there was a general tendency in the efforts of the human intellect to improve by repetition, and in all other arts and institutions to grow perfect and mature by time. We look back upon the theological creed of our ancestors, and their discoveries in natural philosophy, with a smile of pity; science, and the arts connected with it, have all had their infancy, their youth, and manhood, and seem to have in them no principle of limitation or decay; and, inquiring no farther about the matter, we infer, in the height of our self-congratulation, and in the intoxication of our pride, that the same progress has been, and will continue to be, made in all other things which are the work of man. The fact, however, stares us so plainly in the face, that one would think the smallest reflection must suggest the truth, and overturn our sanguine theories. The greatest poets, the ablest orators, the best painters, and the finest sculptors that the world ever saw, appeared soon after the birth of these arts, and lived in a state of society which was, in other respects, comparatively barbarous. Those arts, which depend on individual genius and incommunicable power, have always leaped at once from infancy to manhood, from the first rude dawn of invention to their meridian height and dazzling lustre, and have in general declined ever after. This is the peculiar distinction and privilege of each, of science and of art; of the one, never to attain its utmost summit of perfection, and of the other, to arrive at it almost at once. Homer, Chaucer, Spenser, Shakspeare, Dante, and Ariosto (Milton alone was of a later age, and not the worse for it), Raphael, Titian, Michael Angelo, Correggio, Cervantes, and Boccaccio—all lived near the beginning of their arts—perfected, and all but created them. These giant sons of genius stand, indeed, upon the earth, but they tower above their fellows, and the long line of their successors does not interpose anything to obstruct their view, or lessen their brightness. In strength and stature they are unrivalled, in grace and beauty they have never been surpassed. In after-ages, and more refined periods (as they are called), great men have arisen one by one, as it were by throes and at intervals: though in general the best of these cultivated and artificial minds were of an inferior order, as Tasso and Pope among poets, Guido and Vandyke among painters. But in the earliest stages of the arts, when the first mechanical difficulties had been got over, and the language as it were acquired, they rose by clusters and in constellations, never to rise again.

The arts of painting and poetry are conversant with the world of thought within us, and with the world of sense without us—with what we know, and see, and feel intimately. They flow from the sacred shrine of our own breasts, and are kindled at the living lamp of nature. The pulse of the passions assuredly beat as high, the depths and soundings of the human heart were as well understood three thousand years ago, as they are at present; the face of nature and "the human face divine," shone as bright then as they have ever done. It is this light, reflected by true genius on art, that marks out its path before it, and sheds a glory round the Muses' feet, like that which "circled Una's angel face,

And made a sunshine in the shady place." [1]

Nature is the soul of art. There is a strength in the imagination that reposes entirely on nature, which nothing else can supply. There is in the old poets and painters a vigour and grasp of mind, a full possession of their subject, a confidence and firm faith, a sublime simplicity, an elevation of thought, proportioned to their depth of feeling, an increasing force and impetus, which moves, penetrates, and kindles all that comes in contact with it, which seems, not theirs, but given to them. It is this reliance on the power of nature which has produced those masterpieces by the Prince of Painters, in which expression is all in all, where one spirit, that of truth, pervades every part, brings down heaven to earth, mingles cardinals and popes with angels and apostles, and yet blends and harmonises the whole by the true touches and intense feeling of what is beautiful and grand in nature. It was the same trust in nature that enabled Chaucer to describe the patient sorrow of Griselda; or the delight of that young beauty in the Flower and the Leaf, shrouded in her bower, and listening, in the morning of the year, to the singing of the nightingale, while her joy rises with the rising song, and gushes out afresh at every pause, and is borne along with the full tide of pleasure, and still increases and repeats and prolongs itself, and knows no ebb. It is thus that Boccaccio, in the divine story of the Hawk, has represented Frederigo Alberigi steadily contemplating his favourite Falcon (the wreck and remnant of his fortune), and glad to see how fat and fair a bird she is, thinking what a dainty repast

WHY THE ARTS ARE NOT PROGRESSIVE. 1. *Faerie Queene*, I, iii, 4.

she would make for his Mistress, who had deigned to visit him in his low cell. So Isabella mourns over her pot of Basile, and never asks for any thing but that. So Lear calls out for his poor fool, and invokes the heavens, for they are old like him. So Titian impressed on the countenance of that young Neapolitan nobleman in the Louvre, a look that never passed away. So Nicolas Poussin describes some shepherds wandering out in the morning of the spring, and coming to a tomb with this inscription, "I ALSO WAS AN ARCADIAN."

In general, it must happen in the first stages of the Arts, that as none but those who had a natural genius for them would attempt to practise them, so none but those who had a natural taste for them would pretend to judge of or criticise them. This must be an incalculable advantage to the man of true genius, for it is no other than the privilege of being tried by his peers. In an age when connoisseurship had not become a fashion; when religion, war, and intrigue, occupied the time and thoughts of the great, only those minds of superior refinement would be led to notice the works of art, who had a real sense of their excellence; and in giving way to the powerful bent of his own genius, the painter was most likely to consult the taste of his judges. He had not to deal with pretenders to taste, through vanity, affectation, and idleness. He had to appeal to the higher faculties of the soul; to that deep and innate sensibility to truth and beauty, which required only a proper object to have its enthusiasm excited; and to that independent strength of mind, which, in the midst of ignorance and barbarism, hailed and fostered genius, wherever it met with it. Titian was patronised by Charles V, Count Castiglione was the friend of Raphael. These were true patrons, and true critics; and as there were no others, (for the world, in general, merely looked on and wondered), there can be little doubt, that such a period of dearth of factitious patronage would be the most favourable to the full development of the greatest talents, and the attainment of the highest excellence.

The diffusion of taste is not the same thing as the improvement of taste; but it is only the former of these objects that is promoted by public institutions and other artificial means. The number of candidates for fame, and of pretenders to criticism, is thus increased beyond all proportion, while the quantity of genius and feeling remains the same; with this difference, that the man of genius is lost in the crowd of competitors, who would never have become such but from encouragement and example; and that the opinion of those few persons whom nature intended for judges, is drowned in the noisy suffrages of shallow smatterers in taste. The principle of universal suffrage, however applicable to matters of government, which concern the common feelings and common interests of society is by no means applicable to matters of taste, which can only be decided upon by the most refined understandings. The highest efforts of genius, in every walk of art can never be properly understood by the generality of mankind: There are numberless beauties and truths which lie far beyond their comprehension. It is only as refinement and sublimity are blended with other qualities of a more obvious and grosser nature, that they pass current with the world. Taste is the highest degree of sensibility, or the impression made on the most cultivated and sensible of minds, as genius is the result of the highest powers both of feeling and invention. It may be objected, that the public taste is capable of gradual improvement, because, in the end, the public do justice to works of the greatest merit. This is a mistake. The reputation ultimately, and often slowly affixed to works of genius is stamped upon them by authority, not by popular consent or the common sense of the world. We imagine that the admiration of the works of celebrated men has become common, because the admiration of their names has become so. But does not every ignorant connoisseur pretend the same veneration, and talk with the same vapid assurance of Michael Angelo, though he has never seen even a copy of any of his pictures, as if he had studied them accurately,— merely because Sir Joshua Reynolds has praised him? Is Milton more popular now than when the *Paradise Lost* was first published? Or does he not rather owe his reputation to the judgment of a few persons in every successive period, accumulating in his favour, and over-powering by its weight the public indifference? Why is Shakspeare popular? Not from his refinement of character or sentiment, so much as from his power of telling a story, the variety and invention, the tragic catastrophe and broad farce of his plays. Spenser is not yet understood. Does not Boccaccio pass to this day for a writer of ribaldry, because his jests and lascivious tales were all that caught the vulgar ear, while the story of the Falcon is forgotten!

1814

1814

ON IMITATION

Objects in themselves disagreeable or indifferent, often please in the imitation. A brick-floor, a pewter-table, an ugly cur barking, a Dutch boor smoking or playing at skittles, the inside of a shambles, a fishmonger's or a greengrocer's stall, have been made very interesting as pictures by the fidelity, skill, and spirit, with which they have been copied. One source of the pleasure thus received is undoubtedly the surprise or feeling of admiration, occasioned by the unexpected coincidence between the imitation and the object. The deception, however, not only pleases at first sight, or from mere novelty; but it continues to please upon farther acquaintance, and in proportion to the insight we acquire into the distinctions of nature and of art. By far the most numerous class of connoisseurs are the admirers of pictures of *still life*, which have nothing but the elaborateness of the execution to recommend them. One chief reason, it should seem then, why imitation pleases, is, because, by exciting curiosity, and inviting a comparison between the object and the representation, it opens a new field of inquiry, and leads the attention to a variety of details and distinctions not perceived before. This latter source of the pleasure derived from imitation has never been properly insisted on.

The anatomist is delighted with a coloured plate, conveying the exact appearance of the progress of certain diseases, or of the internal parts and dissections of the human body. We have known a Jennerian Professor as much enraptured with a delineation of the different stages of vaccination, as a florist with a bed of tulips, or an auctioneer with a collection of Indian shells. But in this case, we find that not only the imitation pleases,— the objects themselves give as much pleasure to the professional inquirer, as they would pain to the uninitiated. The learned amateur is struck with the beauty of the coats of the stomach laid bare, or contemplates with eager curiosity the transverse section of the brain, divided on the new Spurzheim[1] principles. It is here, then, the number of the parts, their distinctions, connections, structure, uses; in short, an entire new set of ideas, which occupies the mind of the student, and overcomes

the sense of pain and repugnance, which is the only feeling that the sight of a dead and mangled body presents to ordinary men. It is the same in art as in science. The painter of still life, as it is called, takes the same pleasure in the object as the spectator does in the imitation; because by habit he is led to perceive all those distinctions in nature, to which other persons never pay any attention till they are pointed out to them in the picture. The vulgar only see nature as it is reflected to them from art; the painter sees the picture in nature, before he transfers it to the canvass. He refines, he analyses, he remarks fifty things, which escape common eyes; and this affords a distinct source of reflection and amusement to him, independently of the beauty or grandeur of the objects themselves, or of their connection with other impressions besides those of sight. The charm of the Fine Arts, then, does not consist in any thing peculiar to imitation, even where only imitation is concerned, since *there*, where art exists in the highest perfection, namely, in the mind of the artist, the object excites the same or greater pleasure, before the imitation exists. Imitation renders an object, displeasing in itself, a source of pleasure, not by repetition of the same idea, but by suggesting new ideas, by detecting new properties, and endless shades of difference, just as a close and continued contemplation of the object itself would do. Art shows us nature, divested of the medium of our prejudices. It divides and decompounds objects into a thousand curious parts, which may be full of variety, beauty, and delicacy in themselves, though the object to which they belong may be disagreeable in its general appearance, or by association with other ideas. A painted marigold is inferior to a painted rose only in form and colour: it loses nothing in point of smell. Yellow hair is perfectly beautiful in a picture. To a person lying with his face close to the ground in a summer's day, the blades of spear-grass will appear like tall forest trees, shooting up into the sky; as an insect seen through a microscope is magnified into an elephant. Art is the microscope of the mind, which sharpens the wit as the other does the sight; and converts every object into a little universe in itself. Art may be said to draw aside the veil from nature. To those who are perfectly unskilled in the practice, unimbued with the principles of art, most objects present Raphael's Galatea; in the dark shadows of Rembrandt as well as in the splendid colours of Rubens; in an angel's

ON IMITATION. 1. J. S. Spurzheim (1776–1832) was a phrenologist.

or in a butterfly's wings. They see with different eyes from the multitude. But true genius, though it has new sources of pleasure opened to it, does not lose its sympathy with humanity. It combines truth of imitation with effect, the parts with the whole, the means with the end. The mechanic artist sees only that which nobody else sees, and is conversant only with the technical language and difficulties of his art. A painter, if shewn a picture, will generally dwell upon the academic skill displayed in it, and the knowledge of the received rules of composition. A musician, if asked to play a tune, will select that which is the most difficult and the least intelligible. The poet will be struck with the harmony of versification, or the elaborateness of the arrangement in a composition. The conceits in Shakspeare were his greatest delight; and improving upon this perverse method of judging, the German writers, Goethe and Schiller, look upon Werter and The Robbers as the worst of all their works, because they are the most popular. Some artists among ourselves have carried the same principle to a singular excess.° If professors themselves are liable to this kind of pedantry, connoisseurs and dilettanti, who have less sensibility and more affectation, are almost wholly swayed by it. They see nothing in a picture but the execution. They are proud of their knowledge in proportion as it is a secret. The worst judges of pictures in the United Kingdom are, first, picture-dealers; next, perhaps, the Directors of the British Institution; and after them, in all probability, the Members of the Royal Academy.

1816   *1816*

° "We here allude particularly to Turner, the ablest landscape painter now living, whose pictures are, however, too much abstractions of aerial perspective, and representations not so properly of the objects of nature as of the medium through which they are seen. They are the triumph of the knowledge of the artist, and of the power of the pencil over the barrenness of the subject. They are pictures of the elements of air, earth, and water. The artist delights to go back to the first chaos of the world, or to that state of things when the waters were separated from the dry land, and light from darkness, but as yet no living thing nor tree bearing fruit was seen upon the face of the earth. All is "without form and void." Some one said of his landscapes that they were *pictures of nothing, and very like.*" [Hazlitt's note.]

From ON THE CHARACTER OF ROUSSEAU

Madame de Stael, in her Letters on the Writings and Character of Rousseau, gives it as her opinion, "that the imagination was the first faculty of his mind, and that this faculty even absorbed all the others." And she farther adds, "Rousseau had great strength of reason on abstract questions, or with respect to objects, which have no reality but in the mind." Both these opinions are radically wrong. Neither imagination nor reason can properly be said to have been the original predominant faculties of his mind. The strength both of imagination and reason, which he possessed, was borrowed from the excess of another faculty; and the weakness and poverty of reason and imagination, which are to be found in his works, may be traced to the same source, namely, that these faculties in him were artificial, secondary, and dependant, operating by a power not theirs, but lent to them. The only quality which he possessed in an eminent degree, which alone raised him above ordinary men, and which gave to his writings and opinions an influence greater, perhaps, than has been exerted by any individual in modern times, was extreme sensibility, or an acute and even morbid feeling of all that related to his own impressions, to the objects and events of his life. He had the most intense consciousness of his own existence. No object that had once made an impression on him was ever after effaced. Every feeling in his mind became a passion. His craving after excitement was an appetite and a disease. His interest in his own thoughts and feelings was always wound up to the highest pitch; and hence the enthusiasm which he excited in others. He owed the power which he exercised over the opinions of all Europe, by which he created numberless disciples, and overturned established systems, to the tyranny which his feelings, in the first instance, exercised over himself. The dazzling blaze of his reputation was kindled by the same fire that fed upon his vitals. His ideas differed from those of other men only in their force and intensity. His genius was the effect of his temperament. He created nothing, he demonstrated nothing, by a pure effort of the understanding. His fictitious characters are modifications of his own being, reflections and shadows of himself. His speculations are the obvious exaggerations of a mind, giving a loose to its habitual impulses, and moulding all nature to its own purposes. Hence his enthusiasm and his eloquence, bearing down all opposition. Hence the warmth and the luxuriance, as well as the sameness of his descriptions. Hence the frequent verboseness of his style; for passion lends force and reality to language, and makes words supply the place of imagination. Hence the tenaciousness of his logic, the acuteness of his observations, the refinement and the inconsistency of his reasoning. Hence his keen penetration, and his strange want of comprehension of mind: for the same intense feeling which enabled him to discern the first principles of things, and seize some one view of a subject in all its ramifications, prevented him from admitting the operation of other causes which interfered with his favourite purpose, and involved him in endless wilful contradictions. Hence his excessive egotism, which filled all objects with himself, and would have occupied the universe with his smallest interest. Hence his jealousy and suspicion of others; for no attention, no respect or sympathy, could come up to the extravagant claims of his self-love. Hence his dissatisfaction with himself and with all around him; for nothing could satisfy his ardent longings after good, his restless appetite of being. Hence his feelings, overstrained and exhausted, recoiled upon themselves, and produced his love of silence and repose, his feverish aspirations after the quiet and solitude of nature. Hence in part also his quarrel with the artificial institutions and distinctions of society, which opposed so many barriers to the unrestrained indulgence of his will, and allured his imagination to scenes of pastoral simplicity or of savage life, where the passions were either not excited or left to follow their own impulse,—where the petty vexations and irritating disappointments of common life had no place,—and where the tormenting pursuits of arts and sciences were lost in pure animal enjoyment, or indolent repose. Thus he describes the first savage wandering for ever under the shade of magnificent forests, or by the side of mighty rivers, smit with the unquenchable love of nature!

The best of all his works is the *Confessions*, though it is that which has been least read, because it contains the fewest set paradoxes or general opinions. It relates entirely to himself; and no one was ever so much at home on this subject as he was.

From the strong hold which they had taken of his mind, he makes us enter into his feelings as if they had been our own, and we seem to remember every incident and circumstance of his life as if it had happened to ourselves. . . .

Rousseau, in all his writings, never once lost sight of himself. He was the same individual from first to last. The spring that moved his passions never went down, the pulse that agitated his heart never ceased to beat. It was this strong feeling of interest, accumulating in his mind, which overpowers and absorbs the feelings of his readers. He owed all his power to sentiment. The writer who most nearly resembles him in our own times is the author of the *Lyrical Ballads*. We see no other difference between them, than that the one wrote in prose and the other in poetry; and that prose is perhaps better adapted to express those local and personal feelings, which are inveterate habits in the mind, than poetry, which embodies its imaginary creations. We conceive that Rousseau's exclamation, "*Ah, voilà de la pervenche*," [1] comes more home to mind than Mr. Wordsworth's discovery of the linnet's nest "with five blue eggs," or than his address to the cuckoo, beautiful as we think it is; and we will confidently match the Citizen of Geneva's adventures on the Lake of Bienne against the Cumberland Poet's floating dreams on the Lake of Grasmere. Both create an interest out of nothing, or rather out of their own feelings; both weave numberless recollections into one sentiment; both wind their own being round whatever object occurs to them. But Rousseau, as a prose-writer, gives only the habitual and personal impression. Mr. Wordsworth, as a poet, is forced to lend the colours of imagination to impressions which owe all their force to their identity with themselves, and tries to paint what is only to be felt. Rousseau, in a word, interests you in certain objects by interesting you in himself: Mr. Wordsworth would persuade you that the most insignificant objects are interesting in themselves, because he is interested in them. If he had met with Rousseau's favourite periwinkle, he would have *translated* it into the most beautiful of flowers. This is not imagination, but want of sense. If his jealousy of the sympathy of others makes him avoid what is beautiful and grand in nature, why does he under-

on the character of rousseau. 1. "Ah! there are periwinkles." (*Confessions*, I, 6.)

take elaborately to describe other objects? *His* nature is a mere Dulcinea del Toboso, and he would make a Vashti of her. Rubens appears to have been as extravagantly attached to his three wives, as Raphael was to his Fornarina; but their faces were not so classical. The three greatest egotists that we know of, that is, the three writers who felt their own being most powerfully and exclusively, are Rousseau, Wordsworth, and Benvenuto Cellini. As Swift somewhere says, we defy the world to furnish out a fourth.

1816   *1816*

ON GUSTO

Gusto in art is power or passion defining any object. It is not so difficult to explain this term in what relates to expression (of which it may be said to be the highest degree) as in what relates to things without expression, to the natural appearances of objects, as mere colour or form. In one sense, however, there is hardly any object entirely devoid of expression, without some character of power belonging to it, some precise association with pleasure or pain: and it is in giving this truth of character from the truth of feeling, whether in the highest or the lowest degree, but always in the highest degree of which the subject is capable, that gusto consists.

There is a gusto in the colouring of Titian. Not only do his heads seem to think—his bodies seem to feel. This is what the Italians mean by the *morbidezza* of his flesh-colour. It seems sensitive and alive all over; not merely to have the look and texture of flesh, but the feeling in itself. For example, the limbs of his female figures have a luxurious softness and delicacy, which appears conscious of the pleasure of the beholder. As the objects themselves in nature would produce an impression on the sense, distinct from every other object, and having something divine in it, which the heart owns and the imagination consecrates, the objects in the picture preserve the same impression, absolute, unimpaired, stamped with all the truth of passion, the pride of the eye, and the charm of beauty. Rubens makes his flesh-colour like flowers; Albano's is like ivory; Titian's is like flesh, and like nothing else. It is as different from that of other painters, as the skin is from a piece of white or red drapery thrown over it. The blood circulates here and there, the blue veins just appear, the rest is distinguished throughout only by that sort of tingling sensation to the eye, which the body feels within itself. This is gusto. Vandyke's flesh-colour, though it has great truth and purity, wants gusto. It has not the internal character, the living principle in it. It is a smooth surface, not a warm, moving mass. It is painted without passion, with indifference. The hand only had been concerned. The impression slides off from the eye, and does not, like the tones of Titian's pencil, leave a sting behind it in the mind of the spectator. The eye does not acquire a taste or appetite for what it sees. In a word, gusto in painting is where the impression made on one sense excites by affinity those of another.

Michael Angelo's forms are full of gusto. They everywhere obtrude the sense of power upon the eye. His limbs convey an idea of muscular strength, of moral grandeur, and even of intellectual dignity: they are firm, commanding, broad, and massy, capable of executing with ease the determined purposes of the will. His faces have no other expression than his figures, conscious power and capacity. They appear only to think what they shall do, and to know that they can do it. This is what is meant by saying that his style is hard and masculine. It is the reverse of Correggio's, which is effeminate. That is, the gusto of Michael Angelo consists in expressing energy of will without proportionable sensibility, Correggio's in expressing exquisite sensibility without energy of will. In Correggio's faces as well as figures we see neither bones nor muscles, but then what a soul is there, full of sweetness and of grace—pure, playful, soft, angelical! There is sentiment enough in a hand painted by Correggio to set up a school of history painters. Whenever we look at the hands of Correggio's women or of Raphael's, we always wish to touch them.

Again, Titian's landscapes have a prodigious gusto, both in the colouring and forms. We shall never forget one that we saw many years ago in the Orleans Gallery of Acteon hunting. It had a brown, mellow, autumnal look. The sky was of the colour of stone. The winds seemed to sing through the rustling branches of the trees, and already you might hear the twanging of bows resound through the tangled mazes of the wood. Mr. West,[1] we understand, has this landscape. He will know if this description of it is just. The landscape background of the St. Peter Martyr is another well known instance of the power of this great painter to give a romantic interest and an appropriate character to the objects of his pencil, where every circumstance adds to the effect of the scene,—the bold trunks of the tall forest trees, the trailing ground plants, with that tall convent spire rising in the distance, amidst the blue sapphire mountains and the golden sky.

Rubens has a great deal of gusto in his Fauns and Satyrs, and in all that expresses motion, but in nothing else. Rembrandt has it in everything: everything in his pictures has a tangible character. If he puts a diamond in the ear of a burgomaster's wife, it is of the first water; and his furs and stuffs are proof against a Russian winter. Raphael's gusto was only in expression; he had no idea of the character of anything but the human form. The dryness and poverty of his style in other respects is a phenomenon in the art. His trees are like sprigs of grass stuck in a book of botanical specimens. Was it that Raphael never had time to go beyond the walls of Rome? That he was always in the streets, at church, or in the bath? He was not one of the Society of Arcadians.[2]

Claude's landscapes, perfect as they are, want gusto. This is not easy to explain. They are perfect abstractions of the visible images of things; they speak the visible language of nature truly. They resemble a mirror or a microscope. To the eye only they are more perfect than any other landscapes that ever were or will be painted; they give more of nature, as cognisable by one sense alone; but they lay an equal stress on all visible impressions. They do not interpret one sense by another; they do not distinguish the character of different objects as we are taught, and can only be taught, to distinguish them by their effect on the different senses. That is, his eye wanted imagination: it did not strongly sympathise with his other faculties. He saw the atmosphere, but he did not feel it. He painted the trunk of a tree or a rock in the fore-

ground as smooth—with as complete an abstraction of the gross, tangible impression, as any other part of the picture. His trees are perfectly beautiful, but quite immovable; they have a look of enchantment. In short, his landscapes are unequalled imitations of nature, released from its subjection to the elements, as if all objects were become a delightful fairy vision, and the eye had rarefied and refined away the other senses.

The gusto in the Greek statues is of a very singular kind. The sense of perfect form nearly occupies the whole mind, and hardly suffers it to dwell on any other feeling. It seems enough for them *to be*, without acting or suffering. Their forms are ideal, spiritual. Their beauty is power. By their beauty they are raised above the frailties of pain or passion; by their beauty they are deified.

The infinite quantity of dramatic invention in Shakspeare takes from his gusto. The power he delights to show is not intense, but discursive. He never insists on anything as much as he might, except a quibble. Milton has great gusto. He repeats his blows twice; grapples with and exhausts his subject. His imagination has a double relish of its objects, an inveterate attachment to the things he describes, and to the words describing them.

> —Or where Chinese drive
> With sails and wind their *cany* waggons *light*.
>
> Wild above rule or art, *enormous* bliss.[3]

There is a gusto in Pope's compliments, in Dryden's satires, and Prior's tales; and among prose writers Boccaccio and Rabelais had the most of it. We will only mention one other work which appears to us to be full of gusto, and that is the *Beggar's Opera*. If it is not, we are altogether mistaken in our notions on this delicate subject.

1816   *1816*

ON GENIUS AND COMMON SENSE

We hear it maintained by people of more gravity than understanding, that genius and taste are strictly reducible to rules, and that there is a rule for every thing. So far is it from being true that the finest breath of fancy is a definable thing, that

ON GUSTO. 1. Benjamin West (1738–1820), painter and president of the Royal Academy. 2. "Raphael not only could not paint a landscape; he could not paint people in a landscape. . . . He has nothing romantic about him." (Hazlitt).

3. *Paradise Lost*, III, 438–39; V, 297.

the plainest common sense is only what Mr. Locke would have called a *mixed mode*, subject to a particular sort of acquired and undefinable tact. It is asked, "If you do not know the rule by which a thing is done, how can you be sure of doing it a second time?" And the answer is, "If you do not know the muscles by the help of which you walk, how is it you do not fall down at every step you take?" In art, in taste, in life, in speech, you decide from feeling, and not from reason; that is, from the impression of a number of things on the mind, which impression is true and well-founded, though you may not be able to analyse or account for it in the several particulars. In a gesture you use, in a look you see, in a tone you hear, you judge of the expression, propriety, and meaning from habit, not from reason or rules; that is to say, from innumerable instances of like gestures, looks, and tones, in innumerable other circumstances. variously modified, which are too many and too refined to be all distinctly recollected, but which do not therefore operate the less powerfully upon the mind and eye of taste. Shall we say that these impressions (the immediate stamp of nature) do not operate in a given manner till they are classified and reduced to rules, or is not the rule itself grounded upon the truth and certainty of that natural operation? How then can the distinction of the understanding as to the manner in which they operate be necessary to their producing their due and uniform effect upon the mind? If certain effects did not regularly arise out of certain causes in mind as well as matter, there could be no rule given for them: nature does not follow the rule, but suggests it. Reason is the interpreter and critic of nature and genius, not their lawgiver and judge. He must be a poor creature indeed whose practical convictions do not in- almost all cases outrun his deliberate understanding, or who does not feel and know much more than he can give a reason for.—Hence the distinction between eloquence and wisdom, between ingenuity and common sense. A man may be dextrous and able in explaining the grounds of his opinions, and yet may be a mere sophist, because he only sees one half of a subject. Another may feel the whole weight of a question, nothing relating to it may be lost upon him, and yet he may be able to give no account of the manner in which it affects him, or to drag his reasons from their silent lurking-places. This last will be a wise man, though neither a logician nor rhetorician. Goldsmith was a fool to Dr. Johnson in argument; that is, in assigning the specific grounds of his opinions: Dr. Johnson was a fool to Goldsmith in the fine tact, the airy, intuitive faculty with which he skimmed the surfaces of things, and unconsciously formed his opinions. Common sense is the just result of the sum-total of such unconscious impressions in the ordinary occurrences of life, as they are treasured up in the memory, and called out by the occasion. Genius and taste depend much upon the same principle exercised on loftier ground and in more unusual combinations.

I am glad to shelter myself from the charge of affection or singularity in this view of an often debated but ill-understood point, by quoting a passage from Sir Joshua Reynolds's Discourses, which is full, and, I think, conclusive to the purpose. He says:

> I observe, as a fundamental ground common to all the Arts with which we have any concern in this Discourse, that they address themselves only to two faculties of the mind, its imagination and its sensibility.
>
> All theories which attempt to direct or to control the Art, upon any principles falsely called rational, which we form to ourselves upon a supposition of what ought in reason to be the end or means of Art, independent of the known first effect produced by objects on the imagination, must be false and delusive. For though it may appear bold to say it, the imagination is here the residence of truth. If the imagination be affected, the conclusion is fairly drawn; if it be not affected, the reasoning is erroneous, because the end is not obtained; the effect itself being the test, and the only test, of the truth and efficacy of the means.
>
> There is in the commerce of life, as in Art, a sagacity which is far from being contradictory to right reason, and is superior to any occasional exercise of that faculty; which supersedes it; and does not wait for the slow progress of deduction, but goes at once, by what appears a kind of intuition, to the conclusion. A man endowed with this faculty feels and acknowledges the truth, though it is not always in his power, perhaps, to give a reason for it; because he cannot recollect and bring before him all the materials that gave birth to his opinion; for very many and very intricate considerations may unite to form the principle, even of small and minute parts, involved in, or dependent on, a great system of things:—though these in process of time are

forgotten, the right impression still remains fixed in his mind.

This impression is the result of the accumulated experience of our whole life, and has been collected, we do not always know how, or when. But this mass of collective observation, however acquired, ought to prevail over that reason, which, however powerfully exerted on any particular occasion, will probably comprehend but a partial view of the subject; and our conduct in life, as well as in the arts, is or ought to be generally governed by this habitual reason: it is our happiness that we are enabled to draw on such funds. If we were obliged to enter into a theoretical deliberation on every occasion before we act, life would be at a stand, and Art would be impracticable.

It appears to me therefore [continues Sir Joshua] that our first thoughts, that is, the effect which any thing produces on our minds, on its first appearance, is never to be forgotten; and it demands for that reason, because it is the first, to be laid up with care. If this be not done, the artist may happen to impose on himself by partial reasoning; by a cold consideration of those animated thoughts which proceed, not perhaps from caprice or rashness (as he may afterwards conceit), but from the fulness of his mind, enriched with the copious stores of all the various inventions which he had ever seen, or had ever passed in his mind. These ideas are infused into his design, without any conscious effort; but if he be not on his guard, he may reconsider and correct them, till the whole matter is reduced to a common-place invention.

This is sometimes the effect of what I mean to caution you against; that is to say, an unfounded distrust of the imagination and feeling, in favour of narrow, partial, confined, argumentative theories, and of principles that seem to apply to the design in hand; without considering those general impressions on the fancy in which real principles of *sound reason*, and of much more weight and importance, are involved, and, as it were, lie hid under the appearance of a sort of vulgar sentiment. Reason, without doubt, must ultimately determine every thing; at this minute it is required to inform us when that very reason is to give way to feeling.[1]

Mr. Burke, by whom the foregoing train of thinking was probably suggested, has insisted on the same thing, and made rather a perverse use of it in several parts of his Reflections on the French Revolution; and Windham in one of his Speeches has clenched it into an aphorism—"There is nothing so true as habit." Once more I would say, common sense is tacit reason. Conscience is the same tacit sense of right and wrong, or the impression of our moral experience and moral apprehensions on the mind which, because it works unseen, yet certainly, we suppose to be an instinct, implanted in the mind; as we sometimes attribute the violent operations of our passions, of which we can neither trace the source nor assign the reason, to the instigation of the Devil!

I shall here try to go more at large into this subject, and to give such instances and illustrations of it as occur to me.

One of the persons who had rendered themselves obnoxious to Government, and been included in a charge for high treason in the year 1794, had retired soon after into Wales to write an epic poem and enjoy the luxuries of a rural life. In his peregrinations through that beautiful scenery, he had arrived one fine morning at the inn at Llangollen, in the romantic valley of that name. He had ordered his breakfast, and was sitting at the window in all the dalliance of expectation, when a face passed of which he took no notice at the instant—but when his breakfast was brought in presently after, he found his appetite for it gone, the day had lost its freshness in his eye, he was uneasy and spiritless; and without any cause that he could discover, a total change had taken place in his feelings. While he was trying to account for this odd circumstance, the same face passed again—it was the face of Taylor the spy; and he was no longer at a loss to explain the difficulty. He had before caught only a transient glimpse, a passing side-view of the face; but though this was not sufficient to awaken a distinct idea in his memory, his feelings, quicker and surer, had taken the alarm; a string had been touched that gave a jar to his whole frame, and would not let him rest, though he could not at all tell what was the matter with him. To the flitting, shadowy, half-distinguished profile that had glided by his window was linked unconsciously and mysteriously, but inseparably, the impression of the trains that had been laid for him by this person;— in this brief moment, in this dim, illegible shorthand of the mind he had just escaped the speeches of the Attorney and Solicitor-General over again; the gaunt figure of Mr. Pitt glared by him; the

ON GENIUS AND COMMON SENSE. 1. *Discourse*, XIII, vol. ii, pp. 113–17. [Hazlitt]

walls of a prison enclosed him; and he felt the hands of the executioner near him, without knowing it till the tremor and disorder of his nerves gave information to his reasoning faculties that all was not well within. That is, the same state of mind was recalled by one circumstance in the series of association that had been produced by the whole set of circumstances at the time, though the manner in which this was done was not immediately perceptible. In other words, the feeling of pleasure or pain, of good or evil, is revived, and acts instantaneously upon the mind, before we have time to recollect the precise objects which have originally given birth to it. The incident here mentioned was merely, then, one case of what the learned understand by the *association of ideas:* but all that is meant by feeling or common sense is nothing but the different cases of the association of ideas, more or less true to the impression of the original circumstances, as reason begins with the more formal developement of those circumstances, or pretends to account for the different cases of the association of ideas. But it does not follow that the dumb and silent pleading of the former (though sometimes, nay often mistaken) is less true than that of its babbling interpreter, or that we are never to trust its dictates without consulting the express authority of reason. Both are imperfect, both are useful in their way, and therefore both are best together, to correct or to confirm one another. It does not appear that in the singular instance above mentioned, the sudden impression on the mind was superstition or fancy, though it might have been thought so, had it not been proved by the event to have a real physical and moral cause. Had not the same face returned again, the doubt would never have been properly cleared up, but would have remained a puzzle ever after, or perhaps have been soon forgot.—By the law of association, as laid down by physiologists, any impression in a series can recal any other impression in that series without going through the whole in order: so that the mind drops the intermediate links, and passes on rapidly and by stealth to the more striking effects of pleasure or pain which have naturally taken the strongest hold on it. By doing this habitually and skilfully with respect to the various impressions and circumstances with which our experience makes us acquainted, it forms a series of unpremeditated conclusions on almost all sub-

jects that can be brought before it, as just as they are of ready application to human life; and common sense is the name of this body of unassuming but practical wisdom. Common sense, however, is an impartial, instinctive result of truth and nature, and will therefore bear the test and abide the scrutiny of the most severe and patient reasoning. It is indeed incomplete without it. By ingrafting reason on feeling, we "make assurance double sure."

'Tis the last key-stone that makes up the
  arch—
Then stands it a triumphal mark! Then men
Observe the strength, the height, the why and
  when
It was erected: and still walking under,
Meet some new matter to look up, and
  wonder.

But reason, not employed to interpret nature, and to improve and perfect common sense and experience, is, for the most part, a building without a foundation.—The criticism exercised by reason then on common sense may be as severe as it pleases, but it must be as patient as it is severe. Hasty, dogmatical, self-satisfied reason is worse than idle fancy, or bigotted prejudices. It is systematic, ostentatious in error, closes up the avenues of knowledge, and "shuts the gates of wisdom on mankind." It is not enough to shew that there is no reason for a thing, that we do not see the reason of it: if the common feeling, if the involuntary prejudice sets in strong in favour of it, if, in spite of all we can do, there is a lurking suspicion on the side of our first impressions, we must try again, and believe that truth is mightier than we. So, in offering a definition of any subject, if we feel a misgiving that there is any fact or circumstance omitted, but of which we have only a vague apprehension, like a name we cannot recollect, we must ask for more time, and not cut the matter short by an arrogant assumption of the point in dispute. Common sense thus acts as a check-weight on sophistry, and suspends our rash and superficial judgments. On the other hand, if not only no reason can be given for a thing, but every reason is clear against it, and we can account from ignorance, from authority, from interest, from different causes, for the prevalence of an opinion or sentiment, then we have a right to conclude that we have mistaken a prejudice for an instinct, or have confounded a false and partial impression with the fair and unavoidable inference from general observation. Mr. Burke said that we ought not to reject every prejudice, but should separate the husk of prejudice from the truth it encloses, and so try to get at the kernel within; and thus far he was right.[2] But he was wrong in insisting that we are to cherish our prejudices, "because they are prejudices": for if they are all well-founded, there is no occasion to inquire into their origin or use; and he who sets out to philosophise upon them, or make the separation Mr. Burke talks of in this spirit and with this previous determination, will be very likely to mistake a maggot or a rotten canker for the precious kernel of truth, as was indeed the case with our political sophist.

There is nothing more distinct than common sense and vulgar opinion. Common sense is only a judge of things that fall under common observation, or immediately come home to the business and bosoms of men. This is of the very essence of its principle, the basis of its pretensions. It rests upon the simple process of feeling, it anchors in experience. It is not, nor it cannot be, the test of abstract, speculative opinions. But half the opinions and prejudices of mankind, those which they hold in the most unqualified approbation and which have been instilled into them under the strongest sanctions, are of this latter kind, that is, opinions, not which they have ever thought, known, or felt one tittle about, but which they have taken up on trust from others, which have been palmed on their understandings by fraud or force, and which they continue to hold at the peril of life, limb, property, and character, with as little warrant from common sense in the first instance as appeal to reason in the last. The *ultima ratio regum* proceeds upon a very different plea. Common sense is neither priestcraft nor state-policy. Yet "there's the rub that makes absurdity of so long life"; and, at the same time, gives the sceptical philosophers the advantage over us. Till nature has fair play allowed it, and is not adulterated by political and polemical quacks (as it so often has been), it is impossible to appeal to it as a defence against the errors and extravagances of mere reason. If we talk of common sense, we are twitted

2. In *Reflections on the Revolution in France.*

with vulgar prejudices, and asked how we distinguish the one from the other: but common and received opinion is indeed "a compost heap" of crude notions, got together by the pride and passions of individuals, and reason is itself the thrall or manumitted slave of the same lordly and besotted masters, dragging its servile chain, or committing all sorts of Saturnalian licences, the moment it feels itself freed from it.—If ten millions of Englishmen are furious in thinking themselves right in making war upon thirty millions of Frenchmen, and if the last are equally bent upon thinking the others always in the wrong, though it is a common and national prejudice, both opinions cannot be the dictate of good sense: but it may be the infatuated policy of one or both governments to keep their subjects always at variance. If a few centuries ago all Europe believed in the infallibility of the Pope, this was not an opinion derived from the proper exercise or erroneous direction of the common sense of the people: common sense had nothing to do with it—they believed whatever their priests told them. England at present is divided into Whigs and Tories, Churchmen and Dissenters: both parties have numbers on their side; but common sense and party-spirit are two different things. Sects and heresies are upheld partly by sympathy, and partly by the love of contradiction: if there was nobody of a different way of thinking, they would fall to pieces of themselves. If a whole court say the same thing, this is no proof that they think it, but that the individual at the head of the court has said it: if a mob agree for a while in shouting the same watch-word, this is not to me an example of the *sensus communis;* they only repeat what they have heard repeated by others. If indeed a large proportion of the people are in want of food, of clothing, of shelter, if they are sick, miserable, scorned, oppressed, and if each feeling it in himself, they all say so with one voice and one heart, and lift up their hands to second their appeal, this I should say was but the dictate of common sense, the cry of nature. But to waive this part of the argument, which it is needless to push farther, I believe that the best way to instruct mankind is not by pointing out to them their mutual errors, but by teaching them to think rightly on indifferent matters, where they will listen with patience in order to be amused, and where they do not con sider a definition or a syllogism as the greatest injury you can offer them.

There is no rule for expression. It is got at solely by *feeling*, that is, on the principle of the association of ideas, and by transferring what has been found to hold good in one case (with the necessary modifications) to others. A certain look has been remarked strongly indicative of a certain passion or trait of character, and we attach the same meaning to it or are affected in the same pleasurable or painful manner by it, where it exists in a less degree, though we can define neither the look itself nor the modification of it. Having got the general clue, the exact result may be left to the imagination to vary, to extenuate or aggravate it according to circumstances. In the admirable profile of Oliver Cromwell after ——, the drooping eye-lids, as if drawing a veil over the fixed, penetrating glance, the nostrils somewhat distended, and lips compressed so as hardly to let the breath escape him, denote the character of the man for high-reaching policy and deep designs as plainly as they can be written. How is it that we decipher this expression in the face? First, by feeling it: and how is it that we feel it? Not by pre-established rules, but by the instinct of analogy, by the principle of association, which is subtle and sure in proportion as it is variable and indefinite. A circumstance, apparently of no value, shall alter the whole interpretation to be put upon an expression or action; and it shall alter it thus powerfully because in proportion to its very insignificance it shews a strong general principle at work that extends in its ramifications to the smallest things. This in fact will make all the difference between minuteness and subtlety or refinement; for a small or trivial effect may in given circumstances imply the operation of a great power. Stillness may be the result of a blow too powerful to be resisted; silence may be imposed by feelings too agonising for utterance. The minute, the trifling and insipid, is that which is little in itself, in its causes and its consequences: the subtle and refined is that which is slight and evanescent at first sight, but which mounts up to a mighty sum in the end, which is an essential part of an important whole, which has consequences greater than itself, and where more is meant than meets the eye or ear. We complain sometimes of littleness in a Dutch picture, where there are a vast number of distinct parts and objects, each small in itself, and leading to nothing else. A sky of Claude's cannot fall under this censure, where one imperceptible gradation is as it were the scale to another, where the broad arch of heaven is piled up of endlessly intermediate gold and azure tints, and where an infinite number of minute, scarce noticed particulars blend and melt into universal harmony. The subtlety in Shakespear, of which there is an immense deal every where scattered up and down, is always the instrument of passion, the vehicle of character. The action of a man pulling his hat over his forehead is indifferent enough in itself, and, generally speaking, may mean any thing or nothing: but in the circumstances in which Macduff is placed, it is neither insignificant nor equivocal.

> What! man, ne'er pull your hat upon your
>   brows, &c.[3]

It admits but of one interpretation or inference, that which follows it:—

> Give sorrow words: the grief that does not
>   speak,
> Whispers the o'er-fraught heart, and bids it
>   break.

The passage in the same play, in which Duncan and his attendants are introduced commenting on the beauty and situation of Macbeth's castle, though familiar in itself, has been often praised for the striking contrast it presents to the scenes which follow.—The same look in different circumstances may convey a totally different expression. Thus the eye turned round to look at you without turning the head indicates generally slyness or suspicion: but if this is combined with large expanded eye-lids or fixed eye-brows, as we see it in Titian's pictures, it will denote calm contemplation or piercing sagacity, without any thing of meanness or fear of being observed. In other cases, it may imply merely indolent enticing voluptuousness, as in Lely's portraits of women. The languor or weakness of the eye-lids gives the amorous turn to the expression. How should there be a rule for all this beforehand, seeing it depends on circumstances ever varying, and scarce discernible but by their effect on the mind? Rules are applicable to abstractions, but expression is concrete and individual. We know the meaning of certain looks, and

---

3. *Macbeth*, IV, 3.

we feel how they modify one another in conjunction. But we cannot have a separate rule to judge of all their combinations in different degrees and circumstances, without foreseeing all those combinations, which is impossible: or, if we did foresee them, we should only be where we are, that is, we could only make the rule as we now judge without it, from imagination and the feeling of the moment. The absurdity of reducing expression to a preconcerted system was perhaps never more evidently shewn than in a picture of the Judgment of Solomon by so great a man as N. Poussin, which I once heard admired for the skill and discrimination of the artist in making all the women, who are ranged on one side, in the greatest alarm at the sentence of the judge, while all the men on the opposite side see through the design of it. Nature does not go to work or cast things in a regular mould in this sort of way. I once heard a person remark of another—"He has an eye like a vicious horse." This was a fair analogy. We all, I believe, have noticed the look of an horse's eye, just before he is going to bite or kick. But will any one, therefore, describe to me exactly what that look is? It was the same acute observer that said of a self-sufficient prating music-master—"He talks on all subjects *at sight*"—which expressed the man at once by an allusion to his profession. The coincidence was indeed perfect. Nothing else could compare to the easy assurance with which this gentleman would volunteer an explanation of things of which he was most ignorant; but the *nonchalance* with which a musician sits down to a harpsichord to play a piece he has never seen before. My physiognomical friend would not have hit on this mode of illustration without knowing the profession of the subject of his criticism; but having this hint given him, it instantly suggested itself to his "sure trailing." The manner of the speaker was evident; and the association of the music-master sitting down to play at sight, lurking in his mind, was immediately called out by the strength of his impression of the character. The feeling of character, and the felicity of invention in explaining it, were nearly allied to each other. The first was so wrought up and running over, that the transition to the last was easy and unavoidable. When Mr. Kean was so much praised for the action of Richard in his last struggle with his triumphant antagonist, where he stands, after his sword is wrested from him, with his hands stretched out, "as if his will could not be disarmed, and the very phantoms of his despair had a withering power," he said that he borrowed it from seeing the last efforts of Painter in his fight with Oliver. This assuredly did not lessen the merit of it. Thus it ever is with the man of real genius. He has the feeling of truth already shrined in his own breast, and his eye is still bent on nature to see how she expresses herself. When we thoroughly understand the subject, it is easy to translate from one language into another. Raphael, in muffling up the figure of Elymas the Sorcerer in his garments, appears to have extended the idea of blindness even to his clothes. Was this design? Probably not; but merely the feeling of analogy thoughtlessly suggesting this device, which being so suggested was retained and carried on, because it flattered or fell in with the original feeling. The tide of passion, when strong, overflows and gradually insinuates itself into all nooks and corners of the mind. Invention (of the best kind) I therefore do not think so distinct a thing from feeling, as some are apt to imagine. The springs of pure feeling will rise and fill the moulds of fancy that are fit to receive it. There are some striking coincidences of colour in well-composed pictures, as in a straggling weed in the foreground streaked with blue or red to answer to a blue or red drapery, to the tone of the flesh or an opening in the sky:—not that this was intended, or done by rule (for then it would presently become affected and ridiculous), but the eye being imbued with a certain colour, repeats and varies it from a natural sense of harmony, a secret craving and appetite for beauty, which in the same manner soothes and gratifies the eye of taste, though the cause is not understood. *Tact, finesse,* is nothing but the being completely aware of the feeling belonging to certain situations, passions, &c. and the being consequently sensible to their slightest indications or movements in others. One of the most remarkable instances of this sort of faculty is the following story, told of Lord Shaftesbury, the grandfather of the author of the Characteristics. He had been to dine with Lady Clarendon and her daughter, who was at that time privately married to the Duke of York (afterwards James II.) and as he returned home with another nobleman who had accompanied him, he suddenly turned to him, and

said, "Depend upon it, the Duke has married
Hyde's daughter." His companion could not comprehend what he meant; but on explaining himself,
he said, "Her mother behaved to her with an attention and a marked respect that it is impossible
to account for in any other way; and I am sure of
it." His conjecture shortly afterwards proved to be
the truth. This was carrying the prophetic spirit of
common sense as far as it could go.—

1821   *1821*

FROM

Lectures on the English Poets

ON SHAKESPEARE AND MILTON

The striking peculiarity of Shakespeare's mind was
its generic quality, its power of communication
with all other minds—so that it contained a universe of thought and feeling within itself, and had
no one peculiar bias, or exclusive excellence more
than another. He was just like any other man, but
that he was like all other men. He was the least of
an egotist that it was possible to be. He was nothing in himself; but he was all that others were, or
that they could become. He not only had in himself
the germs of every faculty and feeling, but he
could follow them by anticipation, intuitively, into
all their conceivable ramifications, through every
change of fortune or conflict of passion, or turn of
thought. He had "a mind reflecting ages past,"
and present:—all the people that ever lived are
there. There was no respect of persons with him.
His genius shone equally on the evil and on the
good, on the wise and the foolish, the monarch
and the beggar: "All corners of the earth, kings,
queens, and states, maids, matrons, nay, the secrets of the grave," are hardly hid from his searching glance. He was like the genius of humanity,
changing places with all of us at pleasure, and
playing with our purposes as with his own. He
turned the globe round for his amusement, and
surveyed the generations of men, and the individuals as they passed, with their different concerns,
passions, follies, vices, virtues, actions, and motives—as well those that they knew, as those which
they did not know, or acknowledge to themselves.
The dreams of childhood, the ravings of despair,
were the toys of his fancy. Airy beings waited at
his call, and came at his bidding. Harmless fairies
"nodded to him, and did him curtesies": and the
night-hag bestrode the blast at the command of
"his so potent art." The world of spirits lay open
to him, like the world of real men and women:
and there is the same truth in his delineations of
the one as of the other; for if the preternatural
characters he describes could be supposed to exist,
they would speak, and feel, and act, as he makes
them. He had only to think of anything in order
to become that thing, with all the circumstances
belonging to it. When he conceived of a character,
whether real or imaginary, he not only entered into
all its thoughts and feelings, but seemed instantly,
and as if by touching a secret spring, to be surrounded with all the same objects, "subject to the
same skyey influences," the same local, outward,
and unforeseen accidents which would occur in
reality. Thus the character of Caliban not only
stands before us with a language and manners of
its own, but the scenery and situation of the enchanted island he inhabits, the traditions of the
place, its strange noises, its hidden recesses, "his
frequent haunts and ancient neighbourhood," are
given with a miraculous truth of nature, and with
all the familiarity of an old recollection. The whole
"coheres semblably together" in time, place, and
circumstance. In reading this author, you do not
merely learn what his characters say,—you see
their persons. By something expressed or understood, you are at no loss to decipher their peculiar
physiognomy, the meaning of a look, the grouping,
the by-play, as we might see it on stage. A word, an
epithet paints a whole scene, or throws us back
whole years in the history of the person represented. So (as it has been ingeniously remarked)
when Prospero describes himself as left alone in
the boat with his daughter, the epithet which he
applies to her, "Me and thy *crying* self," flings
the imagination instantly back from the grown
woman to the helpless condition of infancy, and
places the first and most trying scene of his misfortunes before us, with all that he must have
suffered in the interval. How well the silent anguish of Macduff is conveyed to the reader, by

the friendly expostulation of Malcolm—"What! man, ne'er pull your hat upon your brows!" Again, Hamlet, in the scene with Rosencrans and Guildenstern, somewhat abruptly concludes his fine soliloquy on life by saying, "Man delights not me, nor woman neither, though by your smiling you seem to say so." Which is explained by their answer—"My lord, we had no such stuff in our thoughts. But we smiled to think, if you delight not in man, what lenten entertainment the players shall receive from you, whom we met on the way":—as if while Hamlet was making this speech, his two old schoolfellows from Wittenberg had been really standing by, and he had seen them smiling by stealth, at the idea of the players crossing their minds. It is not "a combination and a form" of words, a set speech or two, a preconcerted theory of a character, that will do this: but all the persons concerned must have been present in the poet's imagination, as at a kind of rehearsal; and whatever would have passed through their minds on the occasion, and have been observed by others, passed through his, and is made known to the reader.... The account of Ophelia's death begins thus:

There is a willow hanging o'er a brook,
That shows its hoary leaves in the glassy
    stream.—

Now this is an instance of the same unconscious power of mind which is as true to nature as itself. The leaves of the willow are, in fact, white underneath, and it is this part of them which would appear "hoary" in the reflection in the brook. The same sort of intuitive power, the same faculty of bringing every object in nature, whether present or absent, before the mind's eye, is observable in the speech of Cleopatra, when conjecturing what were the employments of Anthony in his absence:—"He's speaking now, or murmuring, where's my serpent of old Nile?" How fine to make Cleopatra have this consciousness of her own character, and to make her feel that it is this for which Antony is in love with her! She says, after the battle of Actium, when Antony has resolved to risk another fight, "It is my birthday; I had thought to have held it poor: but since my lord is Antony again, I will be Cleopatra." What other poet would have thought of such a casual resource of the imagination, or would have dared to avail himself of it?

The thing happens in the play as it might have happened in fact.—That which, perhaps, more than anything else distinguishes the dramatic productions of Shakespeare from all others, is this wonderful truth and individuality of conception. Each of his characters is as much itself, and as absolutely independent of the rest, as well as of the author, as if they were living persons, not fictions of the mind. The poet may be said, for the time, to identify himself with the character he wishes to represent, and to pass from one to another, like the same soul successively animating different bodies. By an art like that of the ventriloquist, he throws his imagination out of himself, and makes every word appear to proceed from the mouth of the person in whose name it is given. His plays alone are properly expressions of the passions, not descriptions of them. His characters are real beings of flesh and blood; they speak like men, not like authors. One might suppose that he had stood by at the time, and overheard what passed. As in our dreams we hold conversations with ourselves, make remarks, or communicate intelligence, and have no idea of the answer which we shall receive, and which we ourselves make, till we hear it: so the dialogues in Shakespeare are carried on without any consciousness of what is to follow, without any appearance of preparation or premeditation. The gusts of passion come and go like sounds of music borne on the wind. Nothing is made out by formal inference and analogy, by climax and antithesis: all comes, or seems to come, immediately from nature. Each object and circumstance exists in his mind, as it would have existed in reality: each several train of thought and feeling goes on of itself, without confusion or effort. In the world of his imagination, everything has a life, a place, and being of its own!

Chaucer's characters are sufficiently distinct from one another, but they are too little varied in themselves, too much like identical propositions. They are consistent, but uniform; we get no new idea of them from first to last; they are not placed in different lights, nor are their subordinate *traits* brought out in new situations; they are like portraits or physiognomical studies, with the distinguishing features marked with inconceivable truth and precision, but that preserve the same unaltered air and attitude. Shakespeare's are historical figures, equally true and correct, but put into action, where every nerve and muscle is displayed in the struggle with others, with all the effect of collision and contrast, with every variety of light and shade. Chaucer's characters are narrative, Shakespeare's dramatic, Milton's epic. That is, Chaucer told only as much of his story as he pleased, as was required for a particular purpose. He answered for his characters himself. In Shakespeare they are introduced upon the stage, are liable to be asked all sorts of questions, and are forced to answer for themselves. In Chaucer we perceive a fixed essence of character. In Shakespeare there is a continual composition and decomposition of its elements, a fermentation of every particle in the whole mass, by its alternate affinity or antipathy to other principles which are brought in contact with it. Till the experiment is tried, we do not know the result, the turn which the character will take in its new circumstances. Milton took only a few simple principles of character, and raised them to the utmost conceivable grandeur, and refined them from every base alloy. His imagination, "nigh sphered in Heaven," claimed kindred only with what he saw from that height, and could raise to the same elevation with itself. He sat retired and kept his state alone, "playing with wisdom"; while Shakespeare mingled with the crowd, and played the host, "to make society the sweeter welcome."

The passion in Shakespeare is of the same nature as his delineation of character. It is not some one habitual feeling or sentiment preying upon itself, growing out of itself, and moulding everything to itself; it is passion modified by passion, by all the other feelings to which the individual is liable, and to which others are liable with him; subject to all the fluctuations of caprice and accident; calling into play all the resources of the understanding and all the energies of the will; irritated by obstacles or yielding to them; rising from small beginnings to its utmost height; now drunk with hope, now stung to madness, now sunk in despair, now blown to air with a breath, now raging like a torrent. The human soul is made the sport of fortune, the prey of adversity: it is stretched on the wheel of destiny, in restless ecstasy. The passions are in a state of projection. Years are melted down to moments, and every instant teems with fate. We know the results, we see the process. Thus after Iago has been boasting to himself of the effect of his poisonous suggestions on the mind of Othello, "which, with a little act upon the blood, will work like mines of sulphur," he adds—

Look where he comes! not poppy, nor mandragora,
Nor all the drowsy syrups of the East,
Shall ever medicine thee to that sweet sleep
Which thou ow'dst yesterday.—

And he enters at this moment, like the crested serpent, crowned with his wrongs and raging for revenge! The whole depends upon the turn of a thought. A word, a look, blows the spark of jealousy into a flame; and the explosion is immediate and terrible as a volcano. The dialogues in *Lear*, in *Macbeth*, that between Brutus and Cassius, and nearly all those in Shakespeare, where the interest is wrought up to its highest pitch, afford examples of this dramatic fluctuation of passion. The interest in Chaucer is quite different; it is like the course of a river, strong, and full, and increasing. In Shakespeare, on the contrary, it is like the sea, agitated this way and that, and loud-lashed by furious storms; while in the still pauses of the blast, we distinguish only the cries of despair, or the silence of death! Milton, on the other hand, takes the imaginative part of passion—that which remains after the event, which the mind reposes on when all is over, which looks upon circumstances from the remotest elevation of thought and fancy, and abstracts them from the world of action to that of contemplation. The objects of dramatic poetry affect us by sympathy, by their nearness to ourselves, as they take us by surprise, or force us upon action, "while rage with rage doth sympathize": the objects of epic poetry affect us through the medium of the imagination, by magnitude and distance, by their permanence and universality. The one fills us with terror and pity, the other with admiration and delight. There are certain objects that strike the imagination, and inspire awe in the very idea of them, independently of any dramatic interest, that is, of any connexion with the vicissitudes of human life. For instance, we cannot think of the pyramids of Egypt, of a Gothic ruin, or an old Roman encampment, without a certain emotion, a sense of power and sublimity coming over the mind. The heavenly bodies that hang over our heads wherever we go, and "in their untroubled element shall shine when we are laid in dust, and all our cares forgotten," affect us in the same way. Thus Satan's address to the Sun[1] has an epic, not a dramatic interest; for though the second person in the dialogue makes no answer and feels no concern, yet the eye of that vast luminary is upon him, like the eye of heaven, and seems conscious of what he says, like a universal presence. Dramatic poetry and epic, in their perfection, indeed, approximate to and strengthen one another. Dramatic poetry borrows aid from the dignity of persons and things, as the heroic does from human passion, but in theory they are distinct.—When Richard II calls for the looking-glass to contemplate his faded majesty in it, and bursts into that affecting exclamation: "Oh, that I were a mockery-king of snow, to melt away before the sun of Bolingbroke," we have here the utmost force of human passion, combined with the ideas of regal splendour and fallen power. When Milton says of Satan:

> ———His form had not yet lost
> All her original brightness, nor appear'd
> Less than archangel ruin'd, and th' excess
> Of glory obscur'd;——[2]

the mixture of beauty, or grandeur, and pathos, from the sense of irreparable loss, of never-ending, unavailing regret, is perfect.

The great fault of a modern school of poetry is, that it is an experiment to reduce poetry to a mere effusion of natural sensibility; or what is worse, to divest it both of imaginary splendour and human passion, to surround the meanest objects with the morbid feelings and devouring egotism of the writers' own minds. Milton and Shakespeare did not so understand poetry. They gave a more liberal interpretation both to nature and art. They did not do all they could to get rid of the one and the other, to fill up the dreary void with the Moods of their own Minds. They owe their power over the human mind to their having had a deeper sense than others of what was grand in the objects of nature, or affecting in the events of human life. But to the men I speak of there is nothing interesting, nothing heroical, but themselves. To them the fall

of gods or of great men is the same. They do not enter into the feeling. They cannot understand the terms. They are even debarred from the last poor, paltry consolation of an unmanly triumph over fallen greatness; for their minds reject, with a convulsive effort and intolerable loathing, the very idea that there ever was, or was thought to be, anything superior to themselves. All that has ever excited the attention or admiration of the world, they look upon with the most perfect indifference; and they are surprised to find that the world repays their indifference with scorn. "With what measure they mete, it has been meted to them again."—

Shakespeare's imagination is of the same plastic kind as his conception of character or passion. "It glances from heaven to earth, from earth to heaven." Its movement is rapid and devious. It unites the most opposite extremes; or, as Puck says, in boasting of his own feats, "puts a girdle round about the earth in forty minutes." He seems always hurrying from his subject, even while describing it; but the stroke, like the lightning's, is sure as it is sudden. He takes the widest possible range, but from that very range he has his choice of the greatest variety and aptitude of materials. He brings together images the most alike, but placed at the greatest distance from each other; that is, found in circumstances of the greatest dissimilitude. From the remoteness of his combinations, and the celerity with which they are effected, they coalesce the more indissolubly together. The more the thoughts are strangers to each other, and the longer they have been kept asunder, the more intimate does their union seem to become. . . .

It remains to speak of the faults of Shakespeare. They are not so many or so great as they have been represented; what there are, are chiefly owing to the following causes:—The universality of his genius was, perhaps, a disadvantage to his single works; the variety of his resources, sometimes diverting him from applying them to the most effectual purposes. He might be said to combine the powers of Aeschylus and Aristophanes, of Dante and Rabelais, in his own mind. If he had been only half what he was, he would perhaps have appeared greater. The natural ease and indifference of his temper made him sometimes less scrupulous than he might have been. He is relaxed and careless in critical places; he is in earnest

LECTURES. ON SHAKESPEARE AND MILTON. 1. *Paradise Lost*, IV, 31 ff. 2. *Ibid.*, I, 591–94.

throughout only in *Timon, Macbeth,* and *Lear.* Again, he had no models of acknowledged excellence constantly in view to stimulate his efforts, and by all that appears, no love of fame. He wrote for the "great vulgar and the small," in his time, not for posterity. If Queen Elizabeth and the maids of honour laughed heartily at his worst jokes, and the catcalls in the gallery were silent at his best passages, he went home satisfied, and slept the next night well. He did not trouble himself about Voltaire's criticisms. He was willing to take advantage of the ignorance of the age in many things; and if his plays pleased others, not to quarrel with them himself. His very facility of production would make him set less value on his own excellences, and not care to distinguish nicely between what he did well or ill. His blunders in chronology and geography do not amount to above half a dozen, and they are offences against chronology and geography, not against poetry. As to the unities, he was right in setting them at defiance. He was fonder of puns than became so great a man. His barbarisms were those of his age. His genius was his own. He had no objection to float down with the stream of common taste and opinion: he rose above it by his own buoyancy, and an impulse which he could not keep under, in spite of himself or others, and "his delights did show most dolphinlike." . . .

Shakespeare discovers in his writings little religious enthusiasm, and an indifference to personal reputation; he had none of the bigotry of his age, and his political prejudices were not very strong. In these respects, as well as in every other, he formed a direct contrast to Milton. Milton's works are a perpetual invocation to the Muses; a hymn to Fame. He had his thoughts constantly fixed on the contemplation of the Hebrew theocracy, and of a perfect commonwealth; and he seized the pen with a hand just warm from the touch of the ark of faith. His religious zeal infused its character into his imagination; so that he devotes himself with the same sense of duty to the cultivation of his genius, as he did to the exercise of virtue, or the good of his country. The spirit of the poet, the patriot, and the prophet, vied with each other in his breast. His mind appears to have held equal communion with the inspired writers, and with the bards and sages of ancient Greece and Rome;—

Blind Thamyris, and blind Maconides,
And Tiresias, and Phineus, prophets old.

He had a high standard, with which he was always comparing himself, nothing short of which could satisfy his jealous ambition. He thought of nobler forms and nobler things than those he found about him. He lived apart, in the solitude of his own thoughts, carefully excluding from his mind whatever might distract its purposes or alloy its purity, or damp its zeal. "With darkness and with dangers compassed round," he had the mighty models of antiquity always present to his thoughts, and determined to raise a monument of equal height and glory, "piling up every stone of lustre from the brook," for the delight and wonder of posterity. He had girded himself up, and as it were, sanctified his genius to this service from his youth. . . .

Milton, therefore, did not write from casual impulse, but after a severe examination of his own strength, and with a resolution to leave nothing undone which it was in his power to do. He always labours, and almost always succeeds. He strives hard to say the finest things in the world, and he does say them. He adorns and dignifies his subject to the utmost: he surrounds it with every possible association of beauty or grandeur, whether moral, intellectual, or physical. He refines on his descriptions of beauty; loading sweets on sweets, till the sense aches at them; and raises his images of terror to a gigantic elevation, that "makes Ossa like a wart." In Milton, there is always an appearance of effort: in Shakespeare, scarcely any.

Milton has borrowed more than any other writer, and exhausted every source of imitation, sacred or profane; yet he is perfectly distinct from every other writer. He is a writer of centos, and yet in originality scarcely inferior to Homer. The power of his mind is stamped on every line. The fervour of his imagination melts down and renders malleable, as in a furnace, the most contradictory materials. In reading his works, we feel ourselves under the influence of a mighty intellect, that the nearer it approaches to others, becomes more distinct from them. The quantity of art in him shows the strength of his genius: the weight of his intellectual obligations would have oppressed any other writer. Milton's learning has the effect of intuition. He describes objects, of which he could only have read in books, with the vividness of actual observation. His imagination has the force of nature. . . .

We might be tempted to suppose that the vividness with which he describes visible objects, was owing to their having acquired an unusual degree of strength in his mind, after the privation of his sight; but we find the same palpableness and truth in the descriptions which occur in his early poems. In *Lycidas* he speaks of "the great vision of the guarded mount," with that preternatural weight of impression with which it would present itself suddenly to "the pilot of some small night-foundered skiff." ... There is also the same depth of impression in his descriptions of the objects of all the different senses, whether colours, or sounds, or smells—the same absorption of his mind in whatever engaged his attention at the time. It has been indeed objected to Milton, by a common perversity of criticism, that his ideas were musical rather than picturesque, as if because they were in the highest degree musical, they must be (to keep the sage critical balance even, and to allow no one man to possess two qualities at the same time) proportionably deficient in other respects. But Milton's poetry is not cast in any such narrow, common-place mould; it is not so barren of resources. His worship of the Muse was not so simple or confined. A sound arises "like a steam of rich distilled perfumes"; we hear the pealing organ, but the incense on the altars is also there, and the statues of the gods are ranged around! The ear indeed predominates over the eye, because it is more immediately affected, and because the language of music blends more immediately with, and forms a more natural accompaniment to, the variable and indefinite associations of ideas conveyed by words. But where the associations of the imagination are not the principal thing, the individual object is given by Milton with equal force and beauty. The strongest and best proof of this, as a characteristic power of his mind, is, that the persons of Adam and Eve, of Satan, &c. are always accompanied, in our imagination, with the grandeur of the naked figure; they convey to us the ideas of sculpture. ...

Again, nothing can be more magnificent than the portrait of Beelzebub:

> With Atlantean shoulders fit to bear
> The weight of mightiest monarchies:

Or the comparison of Satan, as he "lay floating many a rood," to "that sea beast,"

> Leviathan, which God of all his works
> Created hugest that swim the ocean-stream!

What a force of imagination is there in this last expression! What an idea it conveys of the size of that hugest of created beings, as if it shrunk up the ocean to a stream, and took up the sea in its nostrils as a very little thing! Force of style is one of Milton's greatest excellences. Hence, perhaps, he stimulates us more in the reading, and less afterwards. The way to defend Milton against all impugners, is to take down the book and read it. ...
1818   *1818*

FROM

The Spirit of the Age

LORD BYRON

Lord Byron and Sir Walter Scott are among writers now living the two, who would carry away a majority of suffrages as the greatest geniuses of the age. The former would, perhaps, obtain the preference with the fine gentlemen and ladies (squeamishness apart)—the latter with the critics and the vulgar. We shall treat of them in the same connection, partly on account of their distinguished pre-eminence, and partly because they afford a complete contrast to each other. In their poetry, in their prose, in their politics, and in their tempers, no two men can be more unlike.

If Sir Walter Scott may be thought by some to have been

> Born universal heir to all humanity,

it is plain Lord Byron can set up no such pretension. He is, in a striking degree, the creature of his own will. He holds no communion with his kind; but stands alone, without mate or fellow—

> As if a man were author of himself,
> And owned no other kin.[1]

He is like a solitary peak, all access to which is cut off not more by elevation than distance. He is

THE SPIRIT OF THE AGE. LORD BYRON. 1. "As ... kin": *Coriolanus*, V, iii, 36–37.

seated on a lofty eminence, "cloud-capt," or reflecting the last rays of setting suns; and in his poetical moods, reminds us of the fabled Titans, retired to a ridgy steep, playing on their Pan's-pipes, and taking up ordinary men and things in their hands with haughty indifference. He raises his subject to himself, or tramples on it; he neither stoops to, nor loses himself in it. He exists not by sympathy, but by antipathy. He scorns all things, even himself. Nature must come to him to sit for her picture—he does not go to her. She must consult his time, his convenience, and his humour; and wear a *sombre* or a fantastic garb, or his Lordship turns his back upon her. There is no ease, no unaffected simplicity of manner, no "golden mean." All is strained, or petulant in the extreme. His thoughts are sphered and crystalline; his style "prouder than when blue Iris bends"; his spirit fiery, impatient, wayward, indefatigable. Instead of taking his impressions from without, in entire and almost unimpaired masses, he moulds them according to his own temperament, and heats the materials of his imagination in the furnace of his passions.—Lord Byron's verse glows like a flame, consuming every thing in its way; Sir Walter Scott's glides like a river, clear, gentle, harmless. The poetry of the first scorches, that of the last scarcely warms. The light of the one proceeds from an internal source, ensanguined, sullen, fixed; the other reflects the hues of Heaven, or the face of nature, glancing vivid and various. The productions of the Northern Bard have the rust and the freshness of antiquity about them; those of the Noble Poet cease to startle from their extreme ambition of novelty, both in style and matter. Sir Walter's rhymes are "silly sooth"—

And dally with the innocent of thought,
Like the old age—[2]

his Lordship's Muse spurns *the olden time,* and affects all the supercilious airs of a modern fine lady and an upstart. The object of the one writer is to restore us to truth and nature: the other chiefly thinks how he shall display his own power, or vent his spleen, or astonish the reader either by starting new subjects and trains of speculation, or by expressing old ones in a more striking and emphatic manner than they have been expressed before. He cares little what it is he says, so that he can say it

differently from others. This may account for the charges of plagiarism which have been repeatedly brought against the Noble Poet—if he can borrow an image or sentiment from another, and heighten it by an epithet or an allusion of greater force and beauty than is to be found in the original passage, he thinks he shows his superiority of execution in this in a more marked manner than if the first suggestion had been his own. It is not the value of the observation itself he is solicitous about; but he wishes to shine by contrast—even nature only serves as a foil to set off his style. He therefore takes the thoughts of others (whether contemporaries or not) out of their mouths, and is content to make them his own, to set his stamp upon them, by imparting to them a more meretricious gloss, a higher relief, a greater loftiness of tone, and a characteristic inveteracy of purpose. Even in those collateral ornaments of modern style, slovenliness, abruptness, and eccentricity (as well as in terseness and significance), Lord Byron, when he pleases, defies competition and surpasses all his contemporaries. Whatever he does, he must do in a more decided and daring manner than any one else—he lounges with extravagance, and yawns so as to alarm the reader! Self-will, passion, the love of singularity, a disdain of himself and of others (with a conscious sense that this is among the ways and means of procuring admiration) are the proper categories of his mind: he is a lordly writer, is above his own reputation, and condescends to the Muses with a scornful grace!

Lord Byron, who in his politics is a *liberal,* in his genius is haughty and aristocratic: Walter Scott, who is an aristocrat in principle, is popular in his writings, and is (as it were) equally *servile* to nature and to opinion. The genius of Sir Walter is essentially imitative, or "denotes a foregone conclusion"[3]: that of Lord Byron is self-dependent; or at least requires no aid, is governed by no law, but the impulses of its own will. We confess, however much we may admire independence of feeling and erectness of spirit in general or practical questions, yet in works of genius we prefer him who bows to the authority of nature, who appeals to actual objects, to mouldering superstitions, to history, observation, and tradition, before him who only consults the pragmatical and restless workings

2. "And . . . age": *Twelfth Night,* II, iv, 47–49.

3. "denotes . . . conclusion": *Othello,* III, iii, 428.

of his own breast, and gives them out as oracles to the world. We like a writer (whether poet or prose-writer) who takes in (or is willing to take in) the range of half the universe in feeling, character, description, much better than we do one who obstinately and invariably shuts himself up in the Bastile of his own ruling passions. In short, we had rather be Sir Walter Scott (meaning thereby the Author of Waverley) than Lord Byron, a hundred times over. And for the reason just given, namely, that he casts his descriptions in the mould of nature, ever-varying, never tiresome, always interesting and always instructive, instead of casting them constantly in the mould of his own individual impressions. He gives us man as he is, or as he was, in almost every variety of situation, action, and feeling. Lord Byron makes man after his own image, woman after his own heart; the one is a capricious tyrant, the other a yielding slave; he gives us the misanthrope and the voluptuary by turns; and with these two characters, burning or melting in their own fires, he makes out everlasting centos of himself. He hangs the cloud, the film of his existence over all outward things—sits in the centre of his thoughts, and enjoys dark nights, bright day, the glitter and the gloom "in cell monastic"—we see the mournfall pall, the crucifix, the death's heads, the faded chaplet of flowers, the gleaming tapers, the agonized growl of genius, the wasted form of beauty—but we are still imprisoned in a dungeon, a curtain intercepts our view, we do not breathe freely the air of nature or of our own thoughts—the other admired author draws aside the curtain, and the veil of egotism is rent, and he shows us the crowd of living men and women, the endless groups, the landscape back-ground, the cloud and the rainbow, and enriches our imaginations and relieves one passion by another, and expands and lightens reflection, and takes away that tightness at the breast which arises from thinking or wishing to think that there is nothing in the world out of a man's self!—In this point of view, the Author of Waverley is one of the greatest teachers of morality that ever lived, by emancipating the mind from petty, narrow, and bigotted prejudices: Lord Byron is the greatest pamperer of those prejudices, by seeming to think there is nothing else worth encouraging but the seeds or the full luxuriant growth of dogmatism and self-conceit. In reading the *Scotch Novels,* we never think about the author,

except from a feeling of curiosity respecting our unknown benefactor: in reading Lord Byron's works, he himself is never absent from our minds. The colouring of Lord Byron's style, however rich and dipped in Tyrian dyes, is nevertheless opaque, is in itself an object of delight and wonder: Sir Walter Scott's is perfectly transparent. In studying the one, you seem to gaze at the figures cut in stained glass, which exclude the view beyond, and where the pure light of Heaven is only a means of setting off the gorgeousness of art: in reading the other, you look through a noble window at the clear and varied landscape without. Or to sum up the distinction in one word, Sir Walter Scott is the most *dramatic* writer now living; and Lord Byron is the least so. It would be difficult to imagine that the Author of Waverley is in the smallest degree a pedant; as it would be hard to persuade ourselves that the author of Childe Harold and Don Juan is not a coxcomb, though a provoking and sublime one. In this decided preference given to Sir Walter Scott over Lord Byron, we distinctly include the prose-works of the former; for we do not think his poetry alone by any means entitles him to that precedence. Sir Walter in his poetry, though pleasing and natural, is a comparative trifler: it is in his anonymous productions that he has shown himself for what he is!—

Intensity is the great and prominent distinction of Lord Byron's writings. He seldom gets beyond force of style, nor has he produced any regular work or masterly whole. He does not prepare any plan before-hand, nor revise and retouch what he has written with polished accuracy. His only object seems to be to stimulate himself and his readers for the moment—to keep both alive, to drive away *ennui*, to substitute a feverish and irritable state of excitement for listless indolence or even calm enjoyment. For this purpose he pitches on any subject at random without much thought or delicacy—he is only impatient to begin—and takes care to adorn and enrich it as he proceeds with "thoughts that breathe and words that burn." [4] He composes (as he himself has said) whether he is in the bath, in his study, or on horseback—he writes as habitually as others talk or think—and whether we have the inspiration of the Muse or not, we always find the spirit of the man of genius breathing from his

4. "thoughts . . . burn": Gray's "Progress of Poesy."

verse. He grapples with his subject, and moves, penetrates, and animates it by the electric force of his own feelings. He is often monotonous, extravagant, offensive; but he is never dull, or tedious, but when he writes prose. Lord Byron does not exhibit a new view of nature, or raise insignificant objects into importance by the romantic associations with which he surrounds them; but generally (at least) takes common-place thoughts and events, and endeavours to express them in stronger and statelier language than others. His poetry stands like a Martello tower by the side of his subject. He does not, like Mr. Wordsworth, lift poetry from the ground, or create a sentiment out of nothing. He does not describe a daisy or a periwinkle, but the cedar or the cypress: not "poor men's cottages, but princes' palaces." [5] His *Childe Harold* contains a lofty and impassioned review of the great events of history, of the mighty objects left as wrecks of time, but he dwells chiefly on what is familiar to the mind of every schoolboy; has brought out few new traits of feeling or thought; and has done no more than justice to the reader's preconceptions by the sustained force and brilliancy of his style and imagery.

Lord Byron's earlier productions, *Lara,* the *Corsair,* &c. were wild and gloomy romances, put into rapid and shining verse. They discover the madness of poetry, together with the inspiration: sullen, moody, capricious, fierce, inexorable, gloating on beauty, thirsting for revenge, hurrying from the extremes of pleasure to pain, but with nothing permanent, nothing healthy or natural. The gaudy decorations and the morbid sentiments remind one of flowers strewed over the face of death! In his *Childe Harold* (as has been just observed) he assumes a lofty and philosophic tone, and "reasons high of providence, fore-knowledge, will, and fate." [6] He takes the highest points in the history of the world, and comments on them from a more commanding eminence: he shows us the crumbling monuments of time, he invokes the great names, the mighty spirit of antiquity. The universe is changed into a stately mausoleum:—in solemn measures he chaunts a hymn to fame. Lord Byron has strength and elevation enough to fill up the moulds of our classical and time-hallowed recollec-

tions, and to rekindle the earliest aspirations of the mind after greatness and true glory with a pen of fire. The names of Tasso, of Ariosto, of Dante, of Cincinnatus, of Cæsar, of Scipio, lose nothing of their pomp or their lustre in his hands, and when he begins and continues a strain of panegyric on such subjects, we indeed sit down with him to a banquet of rich praise, brooding over imperishable glories,

Till Contemplation has her fill. [7]

Lord Byron seems to cast himself indignantly from "this bank and shoal of time," or the frail tottering bark that bears up modern reputation, into the huge sea of ancient renown, and to revel there with untired, outspread plume. Even this in him is spleen—his contempt of his contemporaries makes him turn back to the lustrous past, or project himself forward to the dim future!—Lord Byron's tragedies, Faliero, Sardanapalus, &c. are not equal to his other works. They want the essence of the drama. They abound in speeches and descriptions, such as he himself might make either to himself or others, lolling on his couch of a morning, but do not carry the reader out of the poet's mind to the scenes and events recorded. They have neither action, character, nor interest, but are a sort of *gossamer* tragedies, spun out, and glittering, and spreading a flimsy veil over the face of nature. Yet he spins them on. Of all that he has done in this way the *Heaven and Earth* (the same subject as Mr. Moore's *Loves of the Angels*) is the best. We prefer it even to *Manfred. Manfred* is merely himself, with a fancy-drapery on: but in the dramatic fragment published in the *Liberal,* [8] the space between Heaven and Earth, the stage on which his characters have to pass to and fro, seems to fill his Lordship's imagination; and the Deluge, which he has so finely described, may be said to have drowned all his own idle humours.

We must say we think little of our author's turn for satire. His "English Bards and Scotch Reviewers" is dogmatical and insolent, but without refinement or point. He calls people names, and tries to transfix a character with an epithet, which does not stick, because it has no other foundation than

---

5. "poor . . . palaces": *The Merchant of Venice,* I, ii, 14.
6. "reasons . . . fate": *Paradise Lost,* II, 558.

7. "Till . . . fill": John Dyer's "Grongar Hill," l. 26. 8. Liberal: the radical periodical published by Leigh Hunt.

his own petulance and spite; or he endeavours to degrade by alluding to some circumstance of external situation. He says of Mr. Wordsworth's poetry, that "it is his aversion." That may be: but whose fault is it? This is the satire of a lord, who is accustomed to have all his whims or dislikes taken for gospel, and who cannot be at the pains to do more than signify his contempt or displeasure. If a great man meets with a rebuff which he does not like, he turns on his heel, and this passes for a repartee. The Noble Author says of a celebrated barrister and critic, that he was "born in a garret sixteen stories high." The insinuation is not true; or if it were, it is low. The allusion degrades the person who makes, not him to whom it is applied. This is also the satire of a person of birth and quality, who measures all merit by external rank, that is, by his own standard. So his Lordship, in a "Letter to the Editor of My Grandmother's Review," addresses him fifty times as *"my dear Robarts"*; nor is there any other wit in the article. This is surely a mere assumption of superiority from his Lordship's rank, and is the sort of *quizzing* he might use to a person who came to hire himself as a valet to him at *Long's*[9]—the waiters might laugh, the public will not. In like manner, in the controversy about Pope, he claps Mr. Bowles on the back with a coarse facetious familiarity, as if he were his chaplain whom he had invited to dine with him, or was about to present to a benefice. The reverend divine might submit to the obligation, but he has no occasion to subscribe to the jest. If it is a jest that Mr. Bowles should be a parson, and Lord Byron a peer, the world knew this before; there was no need to write a pamphlet to prove it.

The *Don Juan* indeed has great power; but its power is owing to the force of the serious writing, and to the oddity of the contrast between that and the flashy passages with which it is interlarded. From the sublime to the ridiculous there is but one step. You laugh and are surprised that any one should turn round and *travestie* himself: the drollery is in the utter discontinuity of ideas and feelings. He makes virtue serve as a foil to vice; *dandyism* is (for want of any other) a variety of genius. A classical intoxication is followed by the splashing of soda-water, by frothy effusions of ordinary bile. After the lightning and the hurricane,

we are introduced to the interior of the cabin and the contents of wash-hand basins. The solemn hero of tragedy plays *Scrub* in the farce. This is "very tolerable and not to be endured."[10] The Noble Lord is almost the only writer who has prostituted his talents in this way. He hallows in order to desecrate; takes a pleasure in defacing the images of beauty his hands have wrought; and raises our hopes and our belief in goodness to Heaven only to dash them to the earth again, and break them in pieces the more effectually from the very height they have fallen. Our enthusiasm for genius or virtue is thus turned into a jest by the very person who has kindled it, and who thus fatally quenches the sparks of both. It is not that Lord Byron is sometimes serious and sometimes trifling, sometimes profligate, and sometimes moral—but when he is most serious and most moral, he is only preparing to mortify the unsuspecting reader by putting a pitiful *hoax* upon him. This is a most unaccountable anomaly. It is as if the eagle were to build its eyry in a common sewer, or the owl were seen soaring to the mid-day sun. Such a sight might make one laugh, but one would not wish or expect it to occur more than once.

In fact, Lord Byron is the spoiled child of fame as well as fortune. He has taken a surfeit of popularity, and is not contented to delight, unless he can shock the public. He would force them to admire in spite of decency and common sense—he would have them read what they would read in no one but himself, or he would not give a rush for their applause. He is to be "a chartered libertine,"[11] from whom insults are favours, whose contempt is to be a new incentive to admiration. His Lordship is hard to please: he is equally averse to notice or neglect, enraged at censure and scorning praise. He tries the patience of the town to the very utmost, and when they show signs of weariness or disgust, threatens to *discard* them. He says he will write on, whether he is read or not. He would never write another page, if it were not to court popular applause, or to affect a superiority over it. In this respect also, Lord Byron presents a striking contrast to Sir Walter Scott. The latter takes what part of the public favour falls to his share, without grumbling (to be sure he has no

10. "very . . . endured": *Much Ado About Nothing*, III, iii, 35–36. 11. "a . . . libertine": *Henry V*, I, i, 48.

reason to complain); the former is always quarrelling with the world about his *modicum* of applause, the *spolia opima* of vanity, and ungraciously throwing the offerings of incense heaped on his shrine back in the faces of his admirers. Again, there is no taint in the writings of the Author of Waverley, all is fair and natural and *above-board:* he never outrages the public mind. He introduces no anomalous character: broaches no staggering opinion. If he goes back to old prejudices and superstitions as a relief to the modern reader, while Lord Byron floats on swelling paradoxes—

Like proud seas under him;[12]

if the one defers too much to the spirit of antiquity, the other panders to the spirit of the age, goes to the very edge of extreme and licentious speculation, and breaks his neck over it. Grossness and levity are the playthings of his pen. It is a ludicrous circumstance that he should have dedicated his *Cain* to the worthy Baronet! Did the latter ever acknowledge the obligation? We are not nice, not very nice; but we do not particularly approve those subjects that shine chiefly from their rottenness: nor do we wish to see the Muses drest out in the flounces of a false or questionable philosophy, like *Portia* and *Nerissa* in the garb of Doctors of Law. We like metaphysics as well as Lord Byron; but not to see them making flowery speeches, nor dancing a measure in the fetters of verse. We have as good as hinted, that his Lordship's poetry consists mostly of a tissue of superb common-places; even his paradoxes are *common-place.* They are familiar in the schools: they are only new and striking in his dramas and stanzas, by being out of place. In a word, we think that poetry moves best within the circle of nature and received opinion: speculative theory and subtle casuistry are forbidden ground to it. But Lord Byron often wanders into this ground wantonly, wilfully, and unwarrantably. The only apology we can conceive for the spirit of some of Lord Byron's writings, is the spirit of some of those opposed to him. They would provoke a man to write anything. "Farthest from them is best." [13] The extravagance and license of the one seems a proper antidote to the bigotry and narrowness of the other. The first *Vision of Judgment* was a set-off to the second, though

None but itself could be its parallel.[14]

Perhaps the chief cause of most of Lord Byron's errors is, that he is that anomaly in letters and in society, a Noble Poet. It is a double privilege, almost too much for humanity. He has all the pride of birth and genius. The strength of his imagination leads him to indulge in fantastic opinions; the elevation of his rank sets censure at defiance. He becomes a pampered egotist. He has a seat in the House of Lords, a niche in the Temple of Fame. Every-day mortals, opinions, things are not good enough for him to touch or think of. A mere nobleman is, in his estimation, but "the tenth transmitter of a foolish face" [15]: a mere man of genius is no better than a worm. His Muse is also a lady of quality. The people are not polite enough for him: the Court not sufficiently intellectual. He hates the one and despises the other. By hating and despising others, he does not learn to be satisfied with himself. A fastidious man soon grows querulous and splenetic. If there is nobody but ourselves to come up to our idea of fancied perfection, we easily get tired of our idol. When a man is tired of what he is, by a natural perversity he sets up for what he is not. If he is a poet, he pretends to be a metaphysician: if he is a patrician in rank and feeling, he would fain be one of the people. His ruling motive is not the love of the people, but of distinction; not of truth, but of singularity. He patronizes men of letters out of vanity, and deserts them from caprice, or from the advice of friends. He embarks in an obnoxious publication to provoke censure, and leaves it to shift for itself for fear of scandal. We do not like Sir Walter's gratuitous servility: we like Lord Byron's preposterous *liberalism* little better. He may affect the principles of equality, but he resumes his privilege of peerage, upon occasion. His Lordship has made great offers of service to the Greeks—money and horses. He is at present in Cephalonia, waiting the event!

We had written thus far when news came of the death of Lord Byron, and put an end at once to a

12. "Like . . . him": John Fletcher's *Two Noble Kinsmen*, II, ii, 23. 13. "Farthest . . . best": *Paradise Lost*, I, 247.

14. "None . . . parallel": the line is ultimately from Lewis Theobald's play *The Double Falsehood* (1727). 15. "the . . . face": from Richard Savage's *The Bastard* (1728).

strain of somewhat peevish invective, which was intended to meet his eye, not to insult his memory. Had we known that we were writing his epitaph, we must have done it with a different feeling. As it is, we think it better and more like himself, to let what we had written stand, than to take up our leaden shafts, and try to melt them into "tears of sensibility," or mould them into dull praise, and an affected show of candour. We were not silent during the author's life-time, either for his reproof or encouragement (such as we could give, and *he* did not disdain to accept) nor can we now turn undertakers' men to fix the glittering plate upon his coffin, or fall into the procession of popular woe.— Death cancels every thing but truth; and strips a man of every thing but genius and virtue. It is a sort of natural canonization. It makes the meanest of us sacred—it installs the poet in his immortality, and lifts him to the skies. Death is the great assayer of the sterling ore of talent. At his touch the drossy particles fall off, the irritable, the personal, the gross, and mingle with the dust—the finer and more ethereal part mounts with the winged spirit to watch over our latest memory, and protect our bones from insult. We consign the least worthy qualities to oblivion, and cherish the nobler and imperishable nature with double pride and fondness. Nothing could show the real superiority of genius in a more striking point of view than the idle contests and the public indifference about the place of Lord Byron's interment, whether in Westminster Abbey or his own family-vault. A king must have a coronation—a nobleman a funeral-procession.—The man is nothing without the pageant. The poet's cemetery is the human mind, in which he sows the seeds of never-ending thought— his monument is to be found in his works:

> Nothing can cover his high fame but Heaven;
> No pyramids set off his memory,
> But the eternal substance of his greatness.[16]

Lord Byron is dead: he also died a martyr to his zeal in the cause of freedom, for the last, best hopes of man. Let that be his excuse and his epitaph!

1824   *1825*

16. "Nothing . . . greatness": Beaumont and Fletcher's *The False One* (1647), II, i.

John Keats

1795-1821

John Keats is certainly a poet of inauspicious beginnings. The son of a livery-stable keeper at a London inn, he was sent to Enfield School at the age of eight. Here he had the good fortune of being tutored by Charles Cowden Clarke, son of the headmaster; and out of this relationship came his early love of literature, especially of writers like Homer and Spenser. Both of his parents died before he was fifteen, and he was taken out of school without ever receiving the kind of formal training and guidance needed by a young man with such zest for beauty and art. After the death of their parents, the Keats children, John, Tom, George, and Fanny, were placed under the none-too-affectionate guardianship of a niggardly and insensitive man named Richard Abbey, a person with little understanding of or sympathy for John's growing commitment to the calling of poetry. Abbey apprenticed him to a surgeon, and he was licensed as an apothecary in 1816, but, disenchanted with his craft, he soon abandoned it to devote himself to writing.

The young Keats was relentless in his dedication. He read widely not only in poetry, but in history and in the literature of travel and adventure. He absorbed great encyclopedic books like Lemprière's *Classical Dictionary*, Tooke's *Pantheon*, and Spence's *Polymetis*. Spenser, with his great gifts for the pictorial and musical; Milton, with his sense of epic scope and largeness of vision; Shakespeare, with his remarkable gift of sympathy that enabled him to become a hundred different characters—these were his greatest artistic heroes. Keats was also fortunate in his friends, a group that included the already mentioned Clarke; Leigh Hunt, the liberal editor of *The Examiner*; Benjamin Haydon, Joseph Severn, Richard

Woodhouse, and others, all of whom were attracted by the grace and charm of the young man and by the promise of his first efforts in poetry.

The first efforts, however, including his first volume, *Poems* of 1817, reveal the pains of apprenticeship. Although there are flashes of what is to come—the vivid and sensuous imagery, the sharpness of conception, the firm grasp of the subject— too often the good qualities are buried in laxity of structure and lushness and slovenliness of expression that mar the overall effect. Poems like the "Imitation of Spenser," "I Stood Tiptoe," and "Sleep and Poetry" are cases in point. Lines like "sweet buds which with a modest pride / Pull droopingly, in a slanting curve aside, / Their scantily leaved, and finely tapering stems"; "and with a chasten'd light / Hid in the fringes of your eyelids white"; the expansiveness of the question, "What is more gentle than a wind in summer?"

> More healthful than the leafiness of dales?
> More secret than a nest of nightingales?
> More serene than Cordelia's countenance?
> More full of visions than a high romance?
> What but thee, Sleep? Soft closer of our eyes!
> Low murmurer of tender lullabies!
> Light hoverer around our happy pillows!
> Wreather of poppy buds, and weeping willows!
> Silent entangler of a beauty's tresses!

—these and so many other examples reveal a sentimentality and flaccidity that undercut the enthusiasm and joy of the young poet. His long poem, *Endymion* (1817), although admirable for its epic aspirations and its use of the Endymion-Diana myth to express the hero's quest for ideal beauty, nevertheless fails as a poem. The often-remembered brilliance of the opening, "A Thing of beauty is a joy forever: / Its loveliness increases; it will never / Pass into nothingness," of the mellifluous rhythm, of the rich pictorialism, is again marred by the sheer length of the poem, by its digressiveness, by its self-indulgent emotionalism. The poem was savagely treated by critics in *Blackwood's Magazine* and the *Quarterly Review*. *Blackwood's* inaugurated the "Cockney school" label to describe the poetry, with the infamous John Wilson Croker defining Cockneyism as "the most incongruous ideas in the most uncouth language."

Yet in spite of the intensity of the attack on his early work, Keats's modesty enabled him to benefit from the criticism. First, it pointed up, however cruelly, what he had already recognized as thematic and stylistic problems. His preface to *Endymion* had spoken of "great inexperience, immaturity, and every error denoting a feverish attempt, rather than a deed accomplished." He goes on to say that "the foundations are too sandy. It is just that this youngster should die away: a sad thought for me, if I had not some hope that while it is dwindling I may be plotting, and fitting myself for some verses fit to live." Second, it confirmed him in his resolution, so eloquently expressed in the letters, to widen his awareness of the world outside himself, to grow in self-discipline, to develop what he described as "negative capability," the power to minimize the demands of the ego and to lose one's identity in the pursuit of the concrete reality of nature. It is this marvelous capacity for self-criticism that gives the lie to the legend of Keats as the delicate, neurotic aesthetic wounded by the slings and arrows of outrageous critics.

Keats's last four years produced the body of great poetry on which his reputation chiefly rests. In the odes a growing tightness of form, economy of expression, and concreteness of diction and imagery are notable. His third volume, *Lamia, Isabella, The Eve of St. Agnes, and Other Poems* (1820) was well received by critics and general readers; but the worsening of his tubercular condition and the realization that he could never marry his beloved Fanny Brawne dulled his sense of success. In September of 1820 he sailed for Italy in hopes that the warm climate would be a restorative, but his health continued to decline. He died in Rome on February 23, 1821, and was buried in the Protestant cemetery there.

In his poetry and in his remarkable letters on life and literature, Keats consistently adhered to the idea that art is not mere self-expression, but a vision and revelation of truth deeply felt and assimilated by the artist. The poet, at least the true poet, is not a dreamer isolated from humankind, but a person in close sympathy with the joy and sorrow of experience. In an October 27, 1818 letter to Richard Woodhouse, he writes:

> As to the poetical Character itself (I mean that sort of which, if I am anything, I am a Member; that sort distinguished from the wordsworthian or egotistical sublime; which is a thing per se and stands alone) it is not itself—it has no self—it is everything and nothing—It has no character—it enjoys light and shade; it lives in gusto, be it foul or fair, high or low, rich or poor, mean or elevated—It has as much delight in conceiving an Iago as an Imogen.

Like Shelley and Byron, he was deeply distressed by the human condition. The opening of "Ode to a Nightingale" captures this sadness in richly sensuous language:

> My heart aches, and a drowsy numbness pains
> My sense as though of hemlock I had drunk,
> Or emptied some dull opiate to the drains
> One minute past, and Lethe-wards had sunk.

There is also the vivid picture of the transitoriness of earthly pleasures, of:

> The weariness, the fever, and the fret
> Here, where men sit and hear each other groan;
> Where palsy shakes a few, sad, last gray hairs,
> Where youth grows pale, and spectre-thin, and dies;
> Where but to think is to be but full of sorrow
> And leaden-eyed despairs,
> Where beauty cannot keep her lustrous eyes,
> Or new love pine at them beyond to morrow.

Yet, in spite of all this, Keats was deeply committed to the belief that happiness and fulfillment can be achieved on earth. "What the imagination seizes as beauty must be truth," he writes to Benjamin Bailey on November 22, 1817; and, later, in the same letter, he speaks of "another favorite Speculation of mine, that we shall enjoy ourselves here after by having what we call happiness on Earth repeated in a finer tone and so repeated."

The great odes, as well as narrative poems like "La Belle Dame Sans Merci" and *Lamia*, convey a powerful sense of the inseparability of joy and sadness in life, and also of how art, by confronting the complexity of experience, can bring us a richer sense of beauty and ultimately the highest kind of wisdom. These poems are preoccupied with the human yearnings for immortal bliss, for some union with the eternal. In the song of the nightingale, in the Grecian urn, humankind, if it has eyes to see and ears to hear, can find a bridge to what we will know hereafter. In autumn, one finds not an early ending, but a beginning, a sense of ripeness and maturity that has a beauty to rival the vitality and brilliance of spring. "Hedge-crickets sing; and now with treble soft / The red-breast whistles from a garden-croft; / And gathering swallows twitter in the skies." Life is not to be escaped; it is to be savored not as the "vale of tears," but as "The vale of Soul-making," a place, in Keats's words, "to school an Intelligence and make it a soul. A place where the heart must feel and suffer in a thousand diverse ways!"

The poet of *The Fall of Hyperion* (1819) stands as an ideal. Having passed from a garden of sensuous delight to a temple of knowledge, he finally reaches the altar where he learns the true meaning of art, its ultimate connection with life, its selflessness and total dedication to beauty. It is this wisdom, previously alien to the dreaming poet, that wins the reward of seeing Hyperion, a god of brute strength, overthrown by Apollo, a god of beauty and enlightenment who achieved divinity by sympathy with the joys and sorrows of humanity. The poem's relaxed and flowing rhythms, the firm and richly concrete language and imagery reveal a poet who has mastered a vision and found a form in which to embody and express it. *The Fall of Hyperion* is a testament to Keats's own development as man and artist.

Suggestions For Further Reading

The definitive biography is W. J. Bate, *John Keats* (1963), that rare example of a biography which blends the poet's life and work without doing a disservice to either. Other valuable biographical studies are Aileen Ward, *John Keats: The Making of a Poet* (1963); Robert Gittings, *John Keats* (1968); and Douglas Bush, *John Keats* (1966), a superb introduction to the life and works that should prove especially helpful to the students just beginning Keats studies.

Most valuable for the study of Keats's poems are Richard Harter Fogle, *The Imagery of Keats and Shelley* (1949); Earl Wasserman, *The Finer Tone* (1953), a brilliant reading of some of the major poems; David Perkins's essay on Keats in *The Quest for Permanence* (1959); and Stuart Sperry's recent *Keats the Poet* (1973).

TO BYRON

Byron! how sweetly sad thy melody!
  Attuning still the soul to tenderness,
  As if soft Pity, with unusual stress,
Had touch'd her plaintive lute, and thou, being by,
Hadst caught the tones, nor suffer'd them to die.
  O'ershading sorrow doth not make thee less
  Delightful: thou thy griefs dost dress
With a bright halo, shining beamily,
As when a cloud the golden moon doth veil,
  Its sides are ting'd with a resplendent glow,   10
Through the dark robe oft amber rays prevail,
  And like fair veins in sable marble flow;
Still warble, dying swan! still tell the tale,
  The enchanting tale, the tale of pleasing woe.

1814   1848

TO ONE WHO HAS
BEEN LONG IN CITY PENT

To one who has been long in city pent,
  'Tis very sweet to look into the fair
  And open face of heaven,—to breathe a prayer
Full in the smile of the blue firmament.
Who is more happy, when, with heart's content,
  Fatigued he sinks into some pleasant lair
  Of wavy grass, and reads a debonair
And gentle tale of love and languishment?
Returning home at evening, with an ear
  Catching the notes of Philomel,—an eye   10
Watching the sailing cloudlet's bright career,
  He mourns that day so soon has glided by:
E'en like the passage of an angel's tear
  That falls through the clear ether silently.

1816   1817

TO ONE WHO HAS BEEN LONG IN CITY PENT. **10. Philo-**
mel: the nightingale.

TO
CHARLES COWDEN CLARKE*

Oft have you seen a swan superbly frowning,
And with proud breast his own white shadow
            crowning;
He slants his neck beneath the waters bright
So silently, it seems a beam of light
Come from the galaxy: anon he sports,—
With outspread wings the Naiad Zephyr courts,
Or ruffles all the surface of the lake
In striving from its crystal face to take
Some diamond water drops, and them to treasure
In milky nest, and sip them off at leisure.   10
But not a moment can he there insure them,
Nor to such downy rest can he allure them;
For down they rush as though they would be free,
And drop like hours into eternity.
Just like that bird am I in loss of time,
Whene'er I venture on the stream of rhyme;
With shatter'd boat, oar snapt, and canvas rent
I slowly sail, scarce knowing my intent;
Still scooping up the water with my fingers,
In which a trembling diamond never lingers.   20
By this, friend Charles, you may full plainly see
Why I have never penn'd a line to thee:
Because my thoughts were never free, and clear,
And little fit to please a classic ear;
Because my wine was of too poor a savour
For one whose palate gladdens in the flavour
Of sparkling Helicon:—small good it were
To take him to a desert rude, and bare,
Who had on Baiæ's shore reclin'd at ease,
While Tasso's page was floating in a breeze   30
That gave soft music from Armida's bowers,
Mingled with fragrance from her rarest flowers:
Small good to one who had by Mulla's stream

---

* The son of Keats's headmaster at Enfield school. The
young Clarke introduced Keats to the delights of poetry.

TO CHARLES COWDEN CLARKE. **27. Helicon:** the fountain
of the Muses is on Mount Helicon. **29. Baiæ's shore:** a
vacation spot near Naples. **31. Armida:** a mysterious
charmer in Tasso's great epic *Jerusalem Delivered*. **33.
Mulla's stream:** an Irish river near Edmund Spenser's
home. Belphœbe, Una, and Archimago, the names in
the lines that follow, are characters in Spenser's *Faerie
Queene*.

Fondled the maidens with the breasts of cream;
Who had beheld Belphœbe in a brook,
And lovely Una in a leafy nook,
And Archimago leaning o'er his book:
Who had of all that's sweet tasted, and seen,
From silv'ry ripple, up to beauty's queen;
From the sequester'd haunts of gay Titania,   40
To the blue dwelling of divine Urania:
One, who, of late, had ta'en sweet forest walks
With him who elegantly chats, and talks—
The wrong'd Libertas,—who has told you stories
Of laurel chaplets, and Apollo's glories;
Of troops chivalrous prancing through a city,
And tearful ladies made for love, and pity:
With many else which I have never known.
Thus have I thought; and days on days have flown
Slowly, or rapidly—unwilling still   50
For you to try my dull, unlearnèd quill.
Nor should I now, but that I've known you long;
That you first taught me all the sweets of song:
The grand, the sweet, the terse, the free, the fine;
What swell'd with pathos, and what right divine:
Spenserian vowels that elope with ease,
And float along like birds o'er summer seas;
Miltonian storms, and more, Miltonian tenderness;
Michael in arms, and more, meek Eve's fair
    slenderness,
Who read for me the sonnet swelling loudly   60
Up to its climax and then dying proudly?
Who found for me the grandeur of the ode,
Growing, like Atlas, stronger from its load?
Who let me taste that more than cordial dram,
The sharp, the rapier-pointed epigram?
Show'd me that epic was of all the king,
Round, vast, and spanning all like Saturn's ring?
You too upheld the veil from Clio's beauty,
And pointed out the patriot's stern duty;
The might of Alfred, and the shaft of Tell;   70
The hand of Brutus, that so grandly fell
Upon a tyrant's head. Ah! had I never seen,
Or known your kindness, what might I have been?
What my enjoyments in my youthful years,
Bereft of all that now my life endears?
And can I e'er these benefits forget?

And can I e'er repay the friendly debt?
No, doubly no;—yet should these rhymings please,
I shall roll on the grass with two-fold ease:
For I have long time been my fancy feeding   80
With hopes that you would one day think the
    reading
Of my rough verses not an hour misspent;
Should it e'er be so, what a rich content!
Some weeks have pass'd since last I saw the spires
In lucent Thames reflected:—warm desires
To see the sun o'erpeep the eastern dimness,
And morning shadows, streaking into slimness
Across the lawny fields, and pebbly water;
To mark the time as they grow broad, and shorter;
To feel the air that plays about the hills,   90
And sips its freshness from the little rills;
To see high, golden corn wave in the light
When Cynthia smiles upon a summer's night,
And peers among the cloudless jet and white,
As though she were reclining in a bed
Of bean blossoms, in heaven freshly shed.
No sooner had I stepp'd into these pleasures
Than I began to think of rhymes and measures:
The air that floated by me seem'd to say
"Write! thou wilt never have a better day."   100
And so I did. When many lines I'd written,
Though with their grace I was not oversmitten,
Yet, as my hand was warm, I thought I'd better
Trust to my feelings, and write you a letter.
Such an attempt required an inspiration
Of a peculiar sort,—a consummation;—
Which, had I felt, these scribblings might have
    been
Verses from which the soul would never wean:
But many days have passed since last my heart
Was warm'd luxuriously by divine Mozart;   110
By Arne delighted, or by Handel madden'd;
Or by the song of Erin pierc'd and sadden'd:
What time you were before the music sitting,
And the rich notes to each sensation fitting.
Since I have walk'd with you through shady lanes
That freshly terminate in open plains,
And revel'd in a chat that ceased not
When at night-fall among your books we got:
No, nor when supper came, nor after that,—

41. **Urania:** Muse of astronomy, inspirer of great poetry.
44. **Libertas:** Leigh Hunt, friend of Keats, and the publisher of the radical magazine *The Examiner*. 68. **Clio:** Muse of history.

111. **Arne:** Thomas Arne (1710–1778), celebrated English composer. 112. **song of Erin:** a reference to Thomas Moore's *Irish Melodies*.

Nor when reluctantly I took my hat;   120
No, nor till cordially you shook my hand
Mid-way between our homes:—your accents bland
Still sounded in my ears, when I no more
Could hear your footsteps touch the grav'ly floor.
Sometimes I lost them, and then found again;
You chang'd the footpath for the grassy plain.
In those still moments I have wish'd you joys
That well you know to honour:—"Life's very toys
With him," said I, "will take a pleasant charm;
It cannot be that aught will work him
    harm."   130
These thoughts now come o'er me with all their
    might.—
Again I shake your hand,—friend Charles, good
    night.

September 1816   1817

ON FIRST LOOKING INTO CHAPMAN'S HOMER°

Much have I travell'd in the realms of gold,
    And many goodly states and kingdoms seen;
    Round many western islands have I been
Which bards in fealty to Apollo hold.
Oft of one wide expanse had I been told
    That deep-brow'd Homer ruled as his demesne;
    Yet did I never breathe its pure serene
Till I heard Chapman speak out loud and bold:
Then felt I like some watcher of the skies
    When a new planet swims into his ken;   10
Or like stout Cortez when with eagle eyes
    He star'd at the Pacific—and all his men
Look'd at each other with a wild surmise—
    Silent, upon a peak in Darien.

1816   1817

° The sonnet records Keats's great enthusiasm on reading, with his friend Charles Cowden Clarke, George
Chapman's great Elizabethan translation of Homer.

SLEEP AND POETRY

As I lay in my bed slepe full unmete
Was unto me, but why that I ne might
Rest I ne wist, for there n'as erthly wight
[As I suppose] had more of hertis ese
Than I, for I n'ad sicknesse nor disese.

CHAUCER

What is more gentle than a wind in summer?
What is more soothing than the pretty hummer
That stays one moment in an open flower,
And buzzes cheerily from bower to bower?
What is more tranquil than a musk-rose blowing
In a green island, far from all men's knowing?
More healthful than the leafiness of dales?
More secret than a nest of nightingales?
More serene than Cordelia's countenance?
More full of visions than a high romance?   10
What, but thee Sleep? Soft closer of our eyes!
Low murmurer of tender lullabies!
Light hoverer around our happy pillows!
Wreather of poppy buds, and weeping willows!
Silent entangler of a beauty's tresses!
Most happy listener! when the morning blesses
Thee for enlivening all the cheerful eyes
That glance so brightly at the new sun-rise.

But what is higher beyond thought than thee?
Fresher than berries of a mountain tree?   20
More strange, more beautiful, more smooth, more
    regal,
Than wings of swans, than doves, than dim-seen
    eagle?
What is it? And to what shall I compare it?
It has a glory, and nought else can share it:
The thought thereof is awful, sweet, and holy,
Chasing away all worldliness and folly;
Coming sometimes like fearful claps of thunder,
Or the low rumblings earth's regions under;
And sometimes like a gentle whispering
Of all the secrets of some wond'rous thing   30
That breathes about us in the vacant air;
So that we look around with prying stare,
Perhaps to see shapes of light, aerial lymning,
And catch soft floatings from a faint heard hymning;
To see the laurel wreath, on high suspended,

That is to crown our name when life is ended.
Sometimes it gives a glory to the voice,
And from the heart up-springs, rejoice! rejoice!
Sounds which will reach the Framer of all things,
And die away in ardent mutterings.   40

No one who once the glorious sun has seen,
And all the clouds, and felt his bosom clean
For his great Maker's presence, but must know
What 'tis I mean, and feel his being glow:
Therefore no insult will I give his spirit,
By telling what he sees from native merit.

O Poesy! for thee I hold my pen
That am not yet a glorious denizen
Of thy wide heaven—Should I rather kneel
Upon some mountain-top until I feel   50
A glowing splendour round about me hung,
And echo back the voice of thine own tongue?
O Poesy! for thee I grasp my pen
That am not yet a glorious denizen
Of thy wide heaven; yet, to my ardent prayer,
Yield from thy sanctuary some clear air,
Smoothed from intoxication by the breath
Of flowering bays, that I may die a death
Of luxury, and my young spirit follow
The morning sun-beams to the great Apollo   60
Like a fresh sacrifice; or, if I can bear
The o'erwhelming sweets, 'twill bring to me the fair
Visions of all places: a bowery nook
Will be elysium—an eternal book
Whence I may copy many a lovely saying
About the leaves, and flowers—about the playing
Of nymphs in woods, and fountains; and the shade
Keeping a silence round a sleeping maid;
And many a verse from so strange influence
That we must ever wonder how, and whence   70
It came. Also imaginings will hover
Round my fire-side, and haply there discover
Vistas of solemn beauty, where I'd wander
In happy silence, like the clear Meander
Through its lone vales; and where I found a spot
Of awfuller shade, or an enchanted grot,
Or a green hill o'erspread with chequered dress
Of flowers, and fearful from its loveliness,
Write on my tablets all that was permitted,
All that was for our human senses fitted.   80

Then the events of this wide world I'd seize
Like a strong giant, and my spirit teaze
Till at its shoulders it should proudly see
Wings to find out an immortality.

Stop and consider! life is but a day;
A fragile dew-drop on its perilous way
From a tree's summit; a poor Indian's sleep
While his boat hastens to the monstrous steep
Of Montmorenci. Why so sad a moan?
Life is the rose's hope while yet unblown;   90
The reading of an ever-changing tale;
The light uplifting of a maiden's veil;
A pigeon tumbling in clear summer air;
A laughing school-boy, without grief or care,
Riding the springy branches of an elm.

O for ten years, that I may overwhelm
Myself in poesy; so I may do the deed
That my own soul has to itself decreed.
Then will I pass the countries that I see
In long perspective, and continually   100
Taste their pure fountains. First the realm I'll pass
Of Flora, and old Pan: sleep in the grass,
Feed upon apples red, and strawberries,
And choose each pleasure that my fancy sees;
Catch the white-handed nymphs in shady places,
To woo sweet kisses from averted faces,—
Play with their fingers, touch their shoulders white
Into a pretty shrinking with a bite
As hard as lips can make it: till agreed,
A lovely tale of human life we'll read.   110
And one will teach a tame dove how it best
May fan the cool air gently o'er my rest;
Another, bending o'er her nimble tread,
Will set a green robe floating round her head,
And still will dance with ever varied ease,
Smiling upon the flowers and the trees:
Another will entice me on, and on
Through almond blossoms and rich cinnamon;
Till in the bosom of a leafy world
We rest in silence, like two gems upcurl'd   120
In the recesses of a pearly shell.

And can I ever bid these joys farewell?
Yes, I must pass them for a nobler life,
Where I may find the agonies, the strife
Of human hearts: for lo! I see afar,
O'ersailing the blue cragginess, a car

SLEEP AND POETRY. **74. Meander:** the river in Asia
Minor known for its remarkably winding course. The
word has passed into our vocabulary.

89. Montmorenci: a river in Quebec with swift-moving
rapids and waterfalls.

And steeds with streamy manes—the charioteer
Looks out upon the winds with glorious fear:
And now the numerous tramplings quiver lightly
Along a huge cloud's ridge; and now with sprightly
Wheel downward come they into fresher
     skies,   131
Tipt round with silver from the sun's bright eyes.
Still downward with capacious whirl they glide;
And now I see them on the green-hill's side
In breezy rest among the nodding stalks.
The charioteer with wond'rous gesture talks
To the trees and mountains; and there soon appear
Shapes of delight, of mystery, and fear,
Passing along before a dusky space
Made by some mighty oaks: as they would
     chase   140
Some ever-fleeting music on they sweep.
Lo! how they murmur, laugh, and smile, and weep:
Some with upholden hand and mouth severe;
Some with their faces muffled to the ear
Between their arms; some, clear in youthful bloom,
Go glad and smilingly athwart the gloom;
Some looking back, and some with upward gaze;
Yes, thousands in a thousand different ways
Flit onward—now a lovely wreath of girls
Dancing their sleek hair into tangled curls;   150
And now broad wings. Most awfully intent
The driver of those steeds is forward bent,
And seems to listen: O that I might know
All that he writes with such a hurrying glow.

The visions all are fled—the car is fled
Into the light of heaven, and in their stead
A sense of real things comes doubly strong,
And, like a muddy stream, would bear along
My soul to nothingness: but I will strive
Against all doubtings, and will keep alive   160
The thought of that same chariot, and the strange
Journey it went.

        Is there so small a range
In the present strength of manhood, that the high
Imagination cannot freely fly
As she was wont of old? prepare her steeds,
Paw up against the light, and do strange deeds
Upon the clouds? Has she not shown us all?
From the clear space of ether, to the small
Breath of new buds unfolding? From the meaning
Of Jove's large eye-brow, to the tender
     greening   170
Of April meadows? Here her altar shone,

E'en in this isle; and who could paragon
The fervid choir that lifted up a noise
Of harmony, to where it aye will poise
Its mighty self of convoluting sound,
Huge as a planet, and like that roll round,
Eternally around a dizzy void?
Ay, in those days the Muses were nigh cloy'd
With honors; nor had any other care
Than to sing out and sooth their wavy hair.   180

Could all this be forgotten? Yes, a schism
Nurtured by foppery and barbarism,
Made great Apollo blush for this his land.
Men were thought wise who could not understand
His glories: with a puling infant's force
They sway'd about upon a rocking horse,
And thought it Pegasus. Ah dismal soul'd!
The winds of heaven blew, the ocean roll'd
Its gathering waves—ye felt it not. The blue
Bared its eternal bosom, and the dew   190
Of summer nights collected still to make
The morning precious: beauty was awake!
Why were ye not awake? But ye were dead
To things ye knew not of,—were closely wed
To musty laws lined out with wretched rule
And compass vile: so that ye taught a school
Of dolts to smooth, inlay, and clip, and fit,
Till, like the certain wands of Jacob's wit,
Their verses tallied. Easy was the task:
A thousand handicraftsmen wore the mask   200
Of Poesy. Ill-fated, impious race!
That blasphemed the bright Lyrist to his face,
And did not know it,—no, they went about,
Holding a poor, decrepid standard out
Mark'd with most flimsy mottos, and in large
The name of one Boileau!

              O ye whose charge
It is to hover round our pleasant hills!
Whose congregated majesty so fills
My boundly reverence, that I cannot trace
Your hallowed names, in this unholy place,   210

---

173. **fervid choir**: Elizabethan poets. **181–206**: the famous negative critique of Augustan poetry for its excessively regular iambic pentameter couplets, its neglect of the concrete beauties of nature, etc. **198. Jacob's wit**: a reference to the stratagem of Jacob (*Genesis*, 30) in placing a variety of rods in front of his cattle in order to strengthen their offspring. **206. Boileau**: French poet and critic (1636–1711), whose *Art poétique* set forth French neoclassic ideals of art.

So near those common folk; did not their shames
Affright you? Did our old lamenting Thames
Delight you? Did ye never cluster round
Delicious Avon, with a mournful sound,
And weep? Or did ye wholly bid adieu
To regions where no more the laurel grew?
Or did ye stay to give a welcoming
To some lone spirits who could proudly sing
Their youth away, and die? 'Twas even so:
But let me think away those times of woe: 220
Now 'tis a fairer season; ye have breathed
Rich benedictions o'er us; ye have wreathed
Fresh garlands: for sweet music has been heard
In many places;—some has been upstirr'd
From out its crystal dwelling in a lake,
By a swan's ebon bill; from a thick brake,
Nested and quiet in a valley mild,
Bubbles a pipe; fine sounds are floating wild
About the earth: happy are ye and glad.
These things are doubtless: yet in truth we've
      had   230
Strange thunders from the potency of song;
Mingled indeed with what is sweet and strong,
From majesty: but in clear truth the themes
Are ugly clubs, the Poets Polyphemes
Disturbing the grand sea. A drainless shower
Of light is poesy; 'tis the supreme of power;
'Tis might half slumb'ring on its own right arm.
The very archings of her eye-lids charm
A thousand willing agents to obey,
And still she governs with the mildest sway: 240
But strength alone though of the Muses born
Is like a fallen angel: trees uptorn,
Darkness, and worms, and shrouds, and sepulchres
Delight it; for it feeds upon the burrs,
And thorns of life; forgetting the great end
Of poesy, that it should be a friend
To sooth the cares, and lift the thoughts of man.

    Yet I rejoice: a myrtle fairer than
E'er grew in Paphos, from the bitter weeds
Lifts its sweet head into the air, and feeds   250

A silent space with ever sprouting green.
All tenderest birds there find a pleasant screen,
Creep through the shade with jaunty fluttering,
Nibble the little cupped flowers and sing.
Then let us clear away the choking thorns
From round its gentle stem; let the young fawns,
Yeaned in after times, when we are flown,
Find a fresh sward beneath it, overgrown
With simple flowers: let there nothing be
More boisterous than a lover's bended knee;   260
Nought more ungentle than the placid look
Of one who leans upon a closed book;
Nought more untranquil than the grassy slopes
Between two hills. All hail delightful hopes!
As she was wont, th' imagination
Into most lovely labyrinths will be gone,
And they shall be accounted poet kings
Who simply tell the most heart-easing things.
O may these joys be ripe before I die.

Will not some say that I presumptuously   270
Have spoken? that from hastening disgrace
'Twere better far to hide my foolish face?
That whining boyhood should with reverence bow
Ere the dread thunderbolt could reach? How!
If I do hide myself, it sure shall be
In the very fane, the light of Poesy:
If I do fall, at least I will be laid
Beneath the silence of a poplar shade;
And over me the grass shall be smooth shaven;
And there shall be a kind memorial graven.   280
But off Despondence! miserable bane!
They should not know thee, who athirst to gain
A noble end, are thirsty every hour.
What though I am not wealthy in the dower
Of spanning wisdom; though I do not know
The shiftings of the mighty winds that blow
Hither and thither all the changing thoughts
Of man: though no great minist'ring reason sorts
Out the dark mysteries of human souls
To clear conceiving: yet there ever rolls   290
A vast idea before me, and I glean
Therefrom my liberty; thence too I've seen
The end and aim of Poesy. 'Tis clear
As anything most true; as that the year
Is made of the four seasons—manifest
As a large cross, some old cathedral's crest,
Lifted to the white clouds. Therefore should I
Be but the essence of deformity,

218–19. lone . . . die: a reference to Thomas Chatterton
(1752–1770), who committed suicide at age seventeen.
224–25. some . . . lake: probably contemporary poets
such as Wordsworth and Coleridge. 226–28. from . . .
pipe: probably a reference to Leigh Hunt, a poet who
greatly influenced Keats's early work. 230–35. yet . . .
sea: probably a reference to Lord Byron and the rabble-
rousing power of his poetry. Polyphemes are the one-
eyed giants in Homer's *Odyssey*.

257. Yeaned: born.

A coward, did my very eye-lids wink
At speaking out what I have dared to think.   300
Ah! rather let me like a madman run
Over some precipice; let the hot sun
Melt my Dedalian wings, and drive me down
Convuls'd and headlong! Stay! an inward frown
Of conscience bids me be more calm awhile.
An ocean dim, sprinkled with many an isle,
Spreads awfully before me. How much toil!
How many days! what desperate turmoil!
Ere I can have explored its widenesses.
Ah, what a task! upon my bended knees,   310
I could unsay those—no, impossible!
Impossible!

      For sweet relief I'll dwell
On humbler thoughts, and let this strange assay
Begun in gentleness die so away.
E'en now all tumult from my bosom fades:
I turn full hearted to the friendly aids
That smooth the path of honour; brotherhood,
And friendliness the nurse of mutual good.
The hearty grasp that sends a pleasant sonnet
Into the brain ere one can think upon it;   320
The silence when some rhymes are coming out;
And when they're come, the very pleasant rout:
The message certain to be done to-morrow.
'Tis perhaps as well that it should be to borrow
Some precious book from out its snug retreat,
To cluster round it when we next shall meet.
Scarce can I scribble on; for lovely airs
Are fluttering round the room like doves in pairs;
Many delights of that glad day recalling,
When first my senses caught their tender
    falling.   330
And with these airs come forms of elegance
Stooping their shoulders o'er a horse's prance.
Careless, and grand—fingers soft and round
Parting luxuriant curls;—and the swift bound
Of Bacchus from his chariot, when his eye
Made Ariadne's cheek look blushingly.
Thus I remember all the pleasant flow
Of words at opening a portfolio.

Things such as these are ever harbingers
To trains of peaceful images: the stirs   340

303. Dedalian wings: daring, venturesome. In Greek
mythology Dedalus, in spite of his father's advice to
the contrary, flew so close to the sun that the wax wings
invented by his father melted, and he crashed into the
sea.

Of a swan's neck unseen among the rushes:
A linnet starting all about the bushes:
A butterfly, with golden wings broad parted,
Nestling a rose, convuls'd as though it smarted
With over pleasure—many, many more,
Might I indulge at large in all my store
Of luxuries: yet I must not forget
Sleep, quiet with his poppy coronet:
For what there may be worthy in these rhymes
I partly owe to him: and thus, the chimes   350
Of friendly voices had just given place
To as sweet a silence, when I 'gan retrace
The pleasant day, upon a couch at ease.
It was a poet's house who keeps the keys
Of pleasure's temple. Round about were hung
The glorious features of the bards who sung
In other ages—cold and sacred busts
Smiled at each other. Happy he who trusts
To clear Futurity his darling fame!
Then there were fauns and satyrs taking aim   360
At swelling apples with a frisky leap
And reaching fingers, 'mid a luscious heap
Of vine-leaves. Then there rose to view a fane
Of liny marble, and thereto a train
Of nymphs approaching fairly o'er the sward:
One, loveliest, holding her white hand toward
The dazzling sun-rise: two sisters sweet
Bending their graceful figures till they meet
Over the trippings of a little child:
And some are hearing, eagerly, the wild   370
Thrilling liquidity of dewy piping.
See, in another picture, nymphs are wiping
Cherishingly Diana's timorous limbs;—
A fold of lawny mantle dabbling swims
At the bath's edge, and keeps a gentle motion
With the subsiding crystal: as when ocean
Heaves calmly its broad swelling smoothness o'er
Its rocky marge, and balances once more
The patient weeds; that now unshent by foam
Feel all about their undulating home.   380

Sappho's meek head was there half smiling down
At nothing; just as though the earnest frown
Of over thinking had that moment gone
From off her brow, and left her all alone.

Great Alfred's too, with anxious pitying eyes,
As if he always listened to the sighs

354. a poet's house: Leigh Hunt's cottage, often a
source of inspiration for Keats. **379. unshent:** unharmed.

Of the goaded world; and Kosciusko's worn
By horrid suffrance—mightily forlorn.

Petrarch, outstepping from the shady green,
Starts at the sight of Laura; nor can wean   390
His eyes from her sweet face. Most happy they!
For over them was seen a free display
Of out-spread wings, and from between them shone
The face of Poesy: from off her throne
She overlook'd things that I scarce could tell.
The very sense of where I was might well
Keep Sleep aloof: but more than that there came
Thought after thought to nourish up the flame
Within my breast; so that the morning light
Surprised me even from a sleepless night;   400
And up I rose refresh'd, and glad, and gay,
Resolving to begin that very day
These lines; and howsoever they be done,
I leave them as a father does his son.
1816   *1817*

ON SEEING THE ELGIN
MARBLES *

My spirit is too weak—mortality
    Weighs heavily on me like unwilling sleep,
    And each imagin'd pinnacle and steep
Of godlike hardship, tells me I must die
Like a sick Eagle looking at the sky.
    Yet 'tis a gentle luxury to weep
    That I have not the cloudy winds to keep,
Fresh for the opening of the morning's eye.
Such dim-conceivèd glories of the brain
    Bring round the heart an undescribable
        feud;   10
So do these wonders a most dizzy pain,
    That mingles Grecian grandeur with the rude
Wasting of old Time—with a billowy main—
    A sun—a shadow of a magnitude.
1817   *1817*

---

* These marbles, figures from the Parthenon, were secured and sold to the British Museum by Lord Elgin
in 1816. For Keats, they were a continuing source of
delight and fascination.

387. Kosciusko: Thaddeus Kosciusko (1746–1817),
Polish patriot who fought on the colonists' side in the
American Revolution.

ON SITTING DOWN TO READ
KING LEAR ONCE AGAIN

O golden-tongued Romance, with serene lute!
    Fair plumèd Syren, Queen of far-away!
    Leave melodizing on this wintry day,
Shut up thine olden pages, and be mute:
Adieu! for once again the fierce dispute,
    Betwixt damnation and impassion'd clay
    Must I burn through; once more humbly assay
The bitter-sweet of this Shakespearian fruit.
Chief Poet! and ye clouds of Albion,
    Begetters of our deep eternal theme,   10
When through the old oak forest I am gone,
    Let me not wander in a barren dream,
But when I am consumèd in the fire,
Give me new Phœnix wings to fly at my desire.
1818   *1838*

WHEN I HAVE FEARS

When I have fears that I may cease to be
    Before my pen has glean'd my teeming brain,
Before high-pilèd books, in charactery,
    Hold like rich garners the full-ripen'd grain;
When I behold, upon the night's starr'd face,
    Huge cloudy symbols of a high romance,
And think that I may never live to trace
    Their shadows, with the magic hand of chance;
And when I feel, fair creature of an hour,
    That I shall never look upon thee more,   10
Never have relish in the faery power
    Of unreflecting love;—then on the shore
Of the wide world I stand alone, and think
Till love and fame to nothingness do sink.
1818   *1848*

TO HOMER

Standing aloof in giant ignorance,
    Of thee I hear and of the Cyclades,
As one who sits ashore and longs perchance
    To visit dolphin-coral in deep seas.

ON SITTING DOWN TO READ KING LEAR ONCE AGAIN. **14.
Phœnix:** the legendary bird which continually arose to
new life out of the ashes of its previous life.

So thou wast blind;—but then the veil was rent;
   For Jove uncurtain'd Heaven to let thee live,
And Neptune made for thee a spumy tent,
   And Pan made sing for thee his forest-hive;
Aye, on the shores of darkness there is light,
   And precipices show untrodden green；   10
There is a budding morrow in midnight,—
   There is a triple sight in blindness keen;
Such seeing hadst thou, as it once befel
To Dian, Queen of Earth, and Heaven, and Hell.

1818   *1848*

HYPERION°

BOOK ONE

Deep in the shady sadness of a vale
Far sunken from the healthy breath of morn,
Far from the fiery noon, and eve's one star,
Sat gray-hair'd Saturn, quiet as a stone,
Still as the silence round about his lair;
Forest on forest hung about his head
Like cloud on cloud. No stir of air was there,
Not so much life as on a summer's day
Robs not one light seed from the feather'd grass,
But where the dead leaf fell, there did it rest.   10
A stream went voiceless by, still deadened more
By reason of his fallen divinity
Spreading a shade: the Naiad 'mid her reeds
Press'd her cold finger closer to her lips.

Along the margin-sand large foot marks went,
No further than to where his feet had stray'd,
And slept there since. Upon the sodden ground
His old right hand lay nerveless, listless, dead,
Unsceptred; and his realmless eyes were closed;
While his bow'd head seem'd list'ning to the
      Earth,   20
His ancient mother, for some comfort yet.

It seem'd no force could wake him from his place;
But there came one, who with a kindred hand
Touch'd his wide shoulders, after bending low

With reverence, though to one who knew it not.
She was a Goddess of the infant world;
By her in stature the tall Amazon
Had stood a pigmy's height: she would have ta'en
Achilles by the hair and bent his neck;
Or with a finger stay'd Ixion's wheel.   30
Her face was large as that of Memphian sphinx,
Pedestal'd haply in a palace court,
When sages look'd to Egypt for their lore.
But oh! how unlike marble was that face:
How beautiful, if sorrow had not made
Sorrow more beautiful than Beauty's self.
There was a listening fear in her regard,
As if calamity had but begun;
As if the vanward clouds of evil days
Had spent their malice, and the sullen rear   40
Was with its stored thunder labouring up.
One hand she press'd upon that aching spot
Where beats the human heart, as if just there,
Though an immortal, she felt cruel pain:
The other upon Saturn's bended neck
She laid, and to the level of his ear
Leaning with parted lips, some words she spake
In solemn tenour and deep organ tone:
Some mourning words, which in our feeble tongue
Would come in these like accents; O how frail   50
To that large utterance of the early Gods!
"Saturn, look up!—though wherefore, poor old
      King?
I have no comfort for thee, no not one:
I cannot say, 'O wherefore sleepest thou?'
For heaven is parted from thee, and the earth
Knows thee not, thus afflicted, for a God;
And ocean too, with all its solemn noise,
Has from thy sceptre pass'd; and all the air
Is emptied of thine hoary majesty.
Thy thunder, conscious of the new command,   60
Rumbles reluctant o'er our fallen house;
And thy sharp lightning in unpractised hands
Scorches and burns our once serene domain.
O aching time! O moments big as years!
All as ye pass swell out the monstrous truth,
And press it so upon our weary griefs
That unbelief has not a space to breathe.
Saturn, sleep on:—O thoughtless, why did I

° Hyperion was the blazing sun-god of the fallen Titans.
Keats was fascinated by the Hyperion myth, and dealt
with it in both of his poetic fragments—*Hyperion* and
The Fall of Hyperion.

HYPERION. BOOK ONE. **23. one:** Thea, wife and sister of
Hyperion.

30. Ixion: legendary king who dared to love Juno, and
was condemned by Jupiter to the never-ending punishment of being bound to a revolving wheel of fire in the
infernal regions.

Thus violate thy slumbrous solitude?
Why should I ope thy melancholy eyes?   70
Saturn, sleep on! while at thy feet I weep."

As when, upon a trancèd summer-night,
Those green-rob'd senators of mighty woods,
Tall oaks, branch-charmèd by the earnest stars,
Dream, and so dream all night without a stir,
Save from one gradual solitary gust
Which comes upon the silence, and dies off
As if the ebbing air had but one wave;
So came these words and went; the while in tears
She touch'd her fair large forehead to the
          ground,   80
Just where her falling hair might be outspread
A soft and silken mat for Saturn's feet.
One moon, with alteration slow, had shed
Her silver seasons four upon the night,
And still these two were postured motionless,
Like natural sculpture in cathedral cavern;
The frozen God still couchant on the earth,
And the sad Goddess weeping at his feet:
Until at length old Saturn lifted up
His faded eyes, and saw his kingdom gone,   90
And all the gloom and sorrow of the place,
And that fair kneeling Goddess; and then spake,
As with a palsied tongue, and while his beard
Shook horrid with such aspen-malady:
"O tender spouse of gold Hyperion,
Thea, I feel thee ere I see thy face;
Look up, and let me see our doom in it;
Look up, and tell me if this feeble shape
Is Saturn's, tell me, if thou hear'st the voice
Of Saturn; tell me, if this wrinkling brow,   100
Naked and bare of its great diadem,
Peers like the front of Saturn. Who had power
To make me desolate? whence came the strength?
How was it nurtur'd to such bursting forth,
While Fate seem'd strangled in my nervous grasp?
But it is so; and I am smother'd up,
And buried from all godlike exercise
Of influence benign on planets pale,
Of admonitions to the winds and seas,
Of peaceful sway above man's harvesting,   110
And all those acts which Deity supreme
Doth ease its heart of love in.—I am gone
Away from my own bosom: I have left
My strong identity, my real self,
Somewhere between the throne, and where I sit
Here on this spot of earth. Search, Thea, search!

Open thine eyes eterne, and sphere them round
Upon all space: space starr'd, and lorn of light;
Space region'd with life-air; and barren void;
Spaces of fire, and all the yawn of hell.—   120
Search, Thea, search! and tell me, if thou seest
A certain shape or shadow, making way
With wings or chariot fierce to repossess
A heaven he lost erewhile: it must—it must
Be of ripe progress—Saturn must be King.
Yes, there must be a golden victory;
There must be Gods thrown down, and trumpets
          blown
Of triumph calm, and hymns of festival
Upon the gold clouds metropolitan,
Voices of soft proclaim, and silver stir   130
Of strings in hollow shells: and there shall be
Beautiful things made new, for the surprise
Of the sky-children; I will give command:
Thea! Thea! Thea! where is Saturn?"

This passion lifted him upon his feet,
And made his hands to struggle in the air,
His Druid locks to shake and ooze with sweat,
His eyes to fever out, his voice to cease.
He stood, and heard not Thea's sobbing deep;
A little time, and then again he snatch'd   140
Utterance thus.—"But cannot I create?
Cannot I form? Cannot I fashion forth
Another world, another universe,
To overbear and crumble this to naught?
Where is another chaos? Where?"—That word
Found way unto Olympus, and made quake
The rebel three.—Thea was startled up,
And in her bearing was a sort of hope,
As thus she quick-voic'd spake, yet full of awe.
"This cheers our fallen house: come to our
          friends,   150
O Saturn! come away, and give them heart;
I know the covert, for thence came I hither."
Thus brief; then with beseeching eyes she went
With backward footing through the shade a space:
He follow'd, and she turn'd to lead the way
Through agèd boughs, that yielded like the mist
Which eagles cleave upmounting from their nest.

Meanwhile in other realms big tears were shed,
More sorrow like to this, and such like woe,
Too huge for mortal tongue or pen of scribe: 160
The Titans fierce, self-hid, or prison-bound,

147. **rebel three:** Jupiter, Neptune, and Pluto.

Groan'd for the old allegiance once more,
And listen'd in sharp pain for Saturn's voice.
But one of the whole mammoth-brood still kept
His sov'reignty, and rule, and majesty;—
Blazing Hyperion on his orbèd fire
Still sat, still snuff'd the incense, teeming up
From man to the sun's God; yet unsecure:
For as among us mortals omens drear
Fright and perplex, so also shuddered he— 170
Not at dog's howl, or gloom-bird's hated screech,
Or the familiar visiting of one
Upon the first toll of his passing-bell,
Or prophesyings of the midnight lamp;
But horrors, portion'd to a giant nerve,
Oft made Hyperion ache. His palace bright
Bastion'd with pyramids of glowing gold,
And touch'd with shade of bronzèd obelisks,
Glar'd a blood-red through all its thousand courts,
Arches, and domes, and fiery galleries; 180
And all its curtains of Aurorian clouds
Flush'd angerly: while sometimes eagle's wings,
Unseen before by Gods or wondering men,
Darken'd the place; and neighing steeds were heard,
Not heard before by Gods or wondering men.
Also, when he would taste the spicy wreaths
Of incense, breath'd aloft from sacred hills,
Instead of sweets, his ample palate took
Savour of poisonous brass and metal sick:
And so, when harbour'd in the sleepy west, 190
After the full completion of fair day,—
For rest divine upon exalted couch
And slumber in the arms of melody,
He pac'd away the pleasant hours of ease
With stride colossal, on from hall to hall;
While far within each aisle and deep recess,
His wingèd minions in close clusters stood,
Amaz'd and full of fear; like anxious men
Who on wide plains gather in panting troops,
When earthquakes jar their battlements and
    towers. 200
Even now, while Saturn, rous'd from icy trance,
Went step for step with Thea through the woods,
Hyperion, leaving twilight in the rear,
Came slope upon the threshold of the west:
Then, as was wont, his palace-door flew ope
In smoothest silence, save what solemn tubes,
Blown by the serious Zephyrs, gave of sweet
And wandering sounds, slow-breathèd melodies;
And like a rose in vermeil tint and shape,
In fragrance soft, and coolness to the eye, 210

That inlet to severe magnificence
Stood full blown, for the God to enter in.

He enter'd, but he enter'd full of wrath;
His flaming robes stream'd out beyond his heels,
And gave a roar, as if of earthly fire,
That scar'd away the meek ethereal Hours
And made their dove-wings tremble. On he flared,
From stately nave to nave, from vault to vault,
Through bowers of fragrant and enwreathèd light,
And diamond-paved lustrous long arcades, 220
Until he reach'd the great main cupola;
There standing fierce beneath, he stamped his foot,
And from the basements deep to the high towers
Jarr'd his own golden region; and before
The quavering thunder thereupon had ceas'd,
His voice leapt out, despite of godlike curb,
To this result: "O dreams of day and night!
O monstrous forms! O effigies of pain!
O spectres busy in a cold, cold gloom!
O lank-ear'd Phantoms of black-weeded pools! 230
Why do I know ye? why have I seen ye? why
Is my eternal essence thus distraught
To see and to behold these horrors new?
Saturn is fallen, am I too to fall?
Am I to leave this haven of my rest,
This cradle of my glory, this soft clime,
This calm luxuriance of blissful light,
These crystalline pavilions, and pure fanes,
Of all my lucent empire? It is left
Deserted, void, nor any haunt of mine. 240
The blaze, the splendour, and the symmetry,
I cannot see—but darkness, death and darkness.
Even here, into my centre of repose,
The shady visions come to domineer,
Insult, and blind, and stifle up my pomp.—
Fall!—No, by Tellus and her briny robes!
Over the fiery frontier of my realms
I will advance a terrible right arm
Shall scare that infant thunderer, rebel Jove,
And bid old Saturn take his throne again."— 250
He spake, and ceas'd, the while a heavier threat
Held struggle with his throat but came not forth;
For as in theatres of crowded men
Hubbub increases more they call out "Hush!"
So at Hyperion's words the Phantoms pale
Bestirr'd themselves, thrice horrible and cold;
And from the mirror'd level where he stood

246. **Tellus:** goddess of the Earth.

A mist arose, as from a scummy marsh.
At this, through all his bulk an agony
Crept gradual, from the feet unto the crown,   260
Like a lithe serpent vast and muscular
Making slow way, with head and neck convuls'd
From over-strainèd might. Releas'd, he fled
To the eastern gates, and full six dewy hours
Before the dawn in season due should blush,
He breath'd fierce breath against the sleepy portals,
Clear'd them of heavy vapours, burst them wide
Suddenly on the ocean's chilly streams.
The planet orb of fire, whereon he rode
Each day from east to west the heavens
        through,   270
Spun round in sable curtaining of clouds;
Not therefore veiled quite, blindfold, and hid,
But ever and anon the glancing spheres,
Circles, and arcs, and broad-belting colure,
Glow'd through, and wrought upon the muffling
        dark
Sweet-shaped lightnings from the nadir deep
Up to the zenith,—hieroglyphics old
Which sages and keen-eyed astrologers
Then living on the earth, with labouring thought
Won from the gaze of many centuries: 280
Now lost, save what we find on remnants huge
Of stone, or marble swart; their import gone,
Their wisdom long since fled.—Two wings this orb
Possess'd for glory, two fair argent wings,
Ever exalted at the God's approach:
And now, from forth the gloom their plumes
        immense
Rose, one by one, till all outspreaded were;
While still the dazzling globe maintain'd eclipse,
Awaiting for Hyperion's command.
Fain would he have commanded, fain took
        throne   290
And bid the day begin, if but for change.
He might not:—No, though a primeval God:
The sacred seasons might not be disturb'd.
Therefore the operations of the dawn
Stay'd in their birth, even as here 'tis told.
Those silver wings expanded sisterly,
Eager to sail their orb; the porches wide
Open'd upon the dusk demesnes of night;
And the bright Titan, phrenzied with new woes,

Unus'd to bend, by hard compulsion bent   300
His spirit to the sorrow of the time;
And all along a dismal rack of clouds,
Upon the boundaries of day and night,
He stretch'd himself in grief and radiance faint.
There as he lay, the Heaven with its stars
Look'd down on him with pity, and the voice
Of Cœlus, from the universal space,
Thus whisper'd low and solemn in his ear.
"O brightest of my children dear, earth-born
And sky-engendered, Son of Mysteries   310
All unrevealèd even to the powers
Which met at thy creating; at whose joys
And palpitations sweet, and pleasures soft,
I, Cœlus, wonder, how they came and whence;
And at the fruits thereof what shapes they be,
Distinct, and visible; symbols divine,
Manifestations of that beauteous life
Diffus'd unseen throughout eternal space;
Of these new-form'd art thou, oh brightest child!
Of these, thy brethren and the Goddesses!   320
There is sad feud among ye, and rebellion
Of son against his sire. I saw him fall,
I saw my first-born tumbled from his throne!
To me his arms were spread, to me his voice
Found way from forth the thunders round his
        head!
Pale wox I, and in vapours hid my face.
Art thou, too, near such doom? vague fear there is:
For I have seen my sons most unlike Gods.
Divine ye were created, and divine
In sad demeanour, solemn, undisturb'd,   330
Unruffled, like high Gods, ye liv'd and ruled:
Now I behold in you fear, hope, and wrath;
Actions of rage and passion; even as
I see them, on the mortal world beneath,
In men who die.—This is the grief, O Son!
Sad sign of ruin, sudden dismay, and fall!
Yet do thou strive; as thou art capable,
As thou canst move about, an evident God;
And canst oppose to each malignant hour
Ethereal presence:—I am but a voice;   340
My life is but the life of winds and tides,
No more than winds and tides can I avail:—
But thou canst.—Be thou therefore in the van
Of circumstance; yea, seize the arrow's barb
Before the tense string murmur.—To the earth!
For there thou wilt find Saturn, and his woes.

274. **colure:** either of two imaginary circles of the celestial sphere intersecting each other at right angles at the poles.

307. **Cœlus:** god of the sky. 323. **first-born:** Saturn.

Meantime I will keep watch on thy bright sun,
And of thy seasons be a careful nurse."—
Ere half this region-whisper had come down,
Hyperion arose, and on the stars   350
Lifted his curvèd lids, and kept them wide
Until it ceas'd; and still he kept them wide:
And still they were the same bright, patient stars.
Then with a slow incline of his broad breast,
Like to a diver in the pearly seas,
Forward he stoop'd over the airy shore,
And plung'd all noiseless into the deep night.

BOOK TWO

Just at the self-same beat of Time's wide wings
Hyperion slid into the rustled air,
And Saturn gain'd with Thea that sad place
Where Cybele and the bruised Titans mourn'd.
It was a den where no insulting light
Could glimmer on their tears; where their own
        groans
They felt, but heard not, for the solid roar
Of thunderous waterfalls and torrents hoarse,
Pouring a constant bulk, uncertain where.
Crag jutting forth to crag, and rocks that
        seem'd   10
Ever as if just rising from a sleep,
Forehead to forehead held their monstrous horns;
And thus in thousand hugest phantasies
Made a fit roofing to this nest of woe.
Instead of thrones, hard flint they sat upon,
Couches of rugged stone, and slaty ridge
Stubborn'd with iron. All were not assembled:
Some chain'd in torture, and some wandering.
Cœus, and Gyges, and Briareüs,
Typhon, and Dolor, and Porphyrion,   20
With many more, the brawniest in assault,
Were pent in regions of laborious breath;
Dungeon'd in opaque element, to keep
Their clenchèd teeth still clench'd, and all their
        limbs
Lock'd up like veins of metal, crampt and screw'd;
Without a motion, save of their big hearts
Heaving in pain, and horribly convuls'd
With sanguine feverous boiling gurge of pulse.

Mnemosyne was straying in the world;
Far from her moon had Phœbe wandered;   30
And many else were free to roam abroad,
But for the main, here found they covert drear.
Scarce images of life, one here, one there,
Lay vast and edgeways; like a dismal cirque
Of Druid stones, upon a forlorn moor,
When the chill rain begins at shut of eve,
In dull November, and their chancel vault,
The Heaven itself, is blinded throughout night.
Each one kept shroud, nor to his neighbour gave
Or word, or look, or action of despair.   40
Creüs was one; his ponderous iron mace
Lay by him, and a shatter'd rib of rock
Told of his rage, ere he thus sank and pined.
Iäpetus another; in his grasp,
A serpent's plashy neck; its barbèd tongue
Squeez'd from the gorge, and all its uncurl'd length
Dead; and because the creature could not spit
Its poison in the eyes of conquering Jove.
Next Cottus: prone he lay, chin uppermost,
As though in pain; for still upon the flint   50
He ground severe his skull, with open mouth
And eyes at horrid working. Nearest him
Asia, born of most enormous Caf,
Who cost her mother Tellus keener pangs,
Though feminine, than any of her sons:
More thought than woe was in her dusky face,
For she was prophesying of her glory;
And in her wide imagination stood
Palm-shaded temples, and high rival fanes,
By Oxus or in Ganges' sacred isles.   60
Even as Hope upon her anchor leans,
So leant she, not so fair, upon a tusk
Shed from the broadest of her elephants.
Above her, on a crag's uneasy shelve,
Upon his elbow rais'd, all prostrate else,
Shadow'd Enceladus; once tame and mild
As grazing ox unworried in the meads;
Now tiger-passion'd, lion-thoughted, wroth,
He meditated, plotted, and even now
Was hurling mountains in that second war,   70
Not long delay'd, that scar'd the younger Gods

HYPERION. BOOK TWO. 4. **Cybele:** wife of Saturn, mother
of the Olympian gods. 19–20. **Cœus . . . Porphyrion:** the
names of several Titans.

29. Mnemosyne: goddess of Memory, mother of the
Muses. **41. Creüs:** a Titan god of the sea. **44. Iäpetus:**
another Titan, father of Prometheus. **49. Cottus:** a
hundred-handed giant. **53. Asia:** daughter of Oceanus
and Tethys. **Caf:** in Mohammedan mythology, a mountain that surrounded the earth. **66. Enceladus:** a hun-
dred-armed giant.

To hide themselves in forms of beast and bird.
Not far hence Atlas; and beside him prone
Phorcus, the sire of Gorgons. Neighbour'd close
Oceanus, and Tethys, in whose lap
Sobb'd Clymene among her tangled hair.
In midst of all lay Themis, at the feet
Of Ops the queen all clouded round from sight;
No shape distinguishable, more than when
Thick night confounds the pine-tops with the
    clouds: 80
And many else whose names may not be told.
For when the Muse's wings are air-ward spread,
Who shall delay her flight? And she must chaunt
Of Saturn, and his guide, who now had climb'd
With damp and slippery footing from a depth
More horrid still. Above a sombre cliff
Their heads appear'd, and up their stature grew
Till on the level height their steps found ease:
Then Thea spread abroad her trembling arms
Upon the precincts of this nest of pain,   90
And sidelong fix'd her eye on Saturn's face:
There saw she direst strife; the supreme God
At war with all the frailty of grief,
Of rage, of fear, anxiety, revenge,
Remorse, spleen, hope, but most of all despair.
Against these plagues he strove in vain; for Fate
Had pour'd a mortal oil upon his head,
A disanointing poison: so that Thea,
Affrighted, kept her still, and let him pass
First onwards in, among the fallen tribe.   100

As with us mortal men, the laden heart
Is persecuted more, and fever'd more,
When it is nighing to the mournful house
Where other hearts are sick of the same bruise;
So Saturn, as he walk'd into the midst,
Felt faint, and would have sunk among the rest,
But that he met Enceladus's eye,
Whose mightiness, and awe of him, at once
Came like an inspiration; and he shouted,
"Titans, behold your God!" at which some
    groan'd;   110
Some started on their feet; some also shouted;
Some wept, some wail'd, all bow'd with reverence;
And Ops, uplifting her black folded veil,
Show'd her pale cheeks, and all her forehead wan,
Her eye-brows thin and jet, and hollow eyes.

76. Clymene: daughter of Oceanus and wife of Iäpetus.
77. Themis: daughter of Saturn and Ops. **78. Ops:**
Cybele.

There is a roaring in the bleak-grown pines
When Winter lifts his voice; there is a noise
Among immortals when a God gives sign,
With hushing finger, how he means to load
His tongue with the full weight of utterless
    thought,   120
With thunder, and with music, and with pomp:
Such noise is like the roar of bleak-grown pines:
Which, when it ceases in this mountain'd world,
No other sound succeeds; but ceasing here,
Among these fallen, Saturn's voice therefrom
Grew up like organ, that begins anew
Its strain, when other harmonies, stopt short,
Leave the dinn'd air vibrating silverly.
Thus grew it up—"Not in my own sad breast,
Which is its own great judge and searcher out,   130
Can I find reason why ye should be thus:
Not in the legends of the first of days,
Studied from that old spirit-leaved book
Which starry Uranus with finger bright
Sav'd from the shores of darkness, when the waves
Low-ebb'd still hid it up in shallow gloom;—
And the which book ye know I ever kept
For my firm-based footstool:—Ah, infirm!
Not there, nor in sign, symbol, or portent
Of element, earth, water, air, and fire,—   140
At war, at peace, or inter-quarreling
One against one, or two, or three, or all
Each several one against the other three,
As fire with air loud warring when rain-floods
Drown both, and press them both against earth's
    face,
Where, finding sulphur, a quadruple wrath
Unhinges the poor world;—not in that strife,
Wherefrom I take strange lore, and read it deep,
Can I find reason why ye should be thus:
No, no-where can unriddle, though I search,   150
And pore on Nature's universal scroll
Even to swooning, why ye, Divinities,
The first-born of all shap'd and palpable Gods,
Should cower beneath what, in comparison,
Is untremendous might. Yet ye are here,
O'erwhelm'd, and spurn'd, and batter'd, ye are
    here!
O Titans, shall I say, 'Arise!'—Ye groan:
Shall I say 'Crouch!'—Ye groan. What can I then?
O Heaven wide! O unseen parent dear!
What can I? Tell me, all ye brethren Gods,   160
How we can war, how engine our great wrath!

161. engine: carry out.

O speak your counsel now, for Saturn's ear
Is all a-hunger'd. Thou, Oceanus,
Ponderest high and deep; and in thy face
I see, astonied, that severe content
Which comes of thought and musing: give us
  help!"

So ended Saturn; and the God of the Sea,
Sophist and sage, from no Athenian grove,
But cogitation in his watery shades,
Arose, with locks not oozy, and began,   170
In murmurs, which his first-endeavouring tongue
Caught infant-like from the far-foamed sands.
"O ye, whom wrath consumes! who, passion stung,
Writhe at defeat, and nurse your agonies!
Shut up your senses, stifle up your ears,
My voice is not a bellows unto ire.
Yet listen, ye who will, whilst I bring proof
How ye, perforce, must be content to stoop:
And in the proof much comfort will I give,
If ye will take that comfort in its truth.   180
We fall by course of Nature's law, not force
Of thunder, or of Jove. Great Saturn, thou
Hast sifted well the atom-universe;
But for this reason, that thou art the King,
And only blind from sheer supremacy,
One avenue was shaded from thine eyes,
Through which I wandered to eternal truth.
And first, as thou wast not the first of powers,
So art thou not the last; it cannot be:
Thou art not the beginning nor the end.   190
From chaos and parental darkness came
Light, the first fruits of that intestine broil,
That sullen ferment, which for wondrous ends
Was ripening in itself. The ripe hour came,
And with it light, and light, engendering
Upon its own producer, forthwith touch'd
The whole enormous matter into life.
Upon that very hour, our parentage,
The Heavens and the Earth, were manifest:
Then thou first-born, and we the giant-race,   200
Found ourselves ruling new and beauteous realms.
Now comes the pain of truth, to whom 'tis pain;
O folly! for to bear all naked truths,
And to envisage circumstance, all calm,
That is the top of sovereignty. Mark well!
As Heaven and Earth are fairer, fairer far
Than Chaos and blank Darkness, though once
  chiefs;
And as we show beyond that Heaven and Earth

In form and shape compact and beautiful,
In will, in action free, companionship,   210
And thousand other signs of purer life;
So on our heels a fresh perfection treads,
A power more strong in beauty, born of us
And fated to excel us, as we pass
In glory that old Darkness: nor are we
Thereby more conquer'd, than by us the rule
Of shapeless Chaos. Say, doth the dull soil
Quarrel with the proud forests it hath fed,
And feedeth still, more comely than itself?
Can it deny the chiefdom of green groves?   220
Or shall the tree be envious of the dove
Because it cooeth, and hath snowy wings
To wander wherewithal and find its joys?
We are such forest-trees, and our fair boughs
Have bred forth, not pale solitary doves,
But eagles golden-feather'd, who do tower
Above us in their beauty, and must reign
In right thereof; for 'tis the eternal law
That first in beauty should be first in might:
Yea, by that law, another race may drive   230
Our conquerors to mourn as we do now.
Have ye beheld the young God of the Seas,
My dispossessor? Have ye seen his face?
Have ye beheld his chariot, foam'd along
By noble wingèd creatures he hath made?
I saw him on the calmed waters scud,
With such a glow of beauty in his eyes,
That it enforc'd me to bid sad farewell
To all my empire: farewell sad I took,
And hither came, to see how dolorous fate   240
Had wrought upon ye; and how I might best
Give consolation in this woe extreme.
Receive the truth, and let it be your balm."

Whether through poz'd conviction, or disdain,
They guarded silence, when Oceanus
Left murmuring, what deepest thought can tell?
But so it was, none answer'd for a space,
Save one whom none regarded, Clymene;
And yet she answer'd not, only complain'd,
With hectic lips, and eyes up-looking mild,   250
Thus wording timidly among the fierce:
"O father, I am here the simplest voice,
And all my knowledge is that joy is gone,
And this thing woe crept in among our hearts,

---

232. young . . . Seas: a reference to Neptune. **244. poz'd:**
confused, puzzled.

There to remain for ever, as I fear:
I would not bode of evil, if I thought
So weak a creature could turn off the help
Which by just right should come of mighty Gods;
Yet let me tell my sorrow, let me tell
Of what I heard, and how it made me weep,   260
And know that we had parted from all hope.
I stood upon a shore, a pleasant shore,
Where a sweet clime was breathed from a land
Of fragrance, quietness, and trees, and flowers.
Full of calm joy it was, as I of grief;
Too full of joy and soft delicious warmth;
So that I felt a movement in my heart
To chide, and to reproach that solitude
With songs of misery, music of our woes;
And sat me down, and took a mouthèd shell   270
And murmur'd into it, and made melody—
O melody no more! for while I sang,
And with poor skill let pass into the breeze
The dull shell's echo, from a bowery strand
Just opposite, an island of the sea,
There came enchantment with the shifting wind,
That did both drown and keep alive my ears.
I threw my shell away upon the sand,
And a wave fill'd it, as my sense was fill'd
With that new blissful golden melody.   280
A living death was in each gush of sounds,
Each family of rapturous hurried notes,
That fell, one after one, yet all at once,
Like pearl beads dropping sudden from their string:
And then another, then another strain,
Each like a dove leaving its olive perch,
With music wing'd instead of silent plumes,
To hover round my head, and make me sick
Of joy and grief at once. Grief overcame,
And I was stopping up my frantic ears,   290
When, past all hindrance of my trembling hands,
A voice came sweeter, sweeter than all tune,
And still it cried, 'Apollo! young Apollo!
'The morning-bright Apollo! young Apollo!'
I fled, it follow'd me, and cried 'Apollo!'
O Father, and O Brethren, had ye felt
Those pains of mine; O Saturn, hadst thou felt,
Ye would not call this too indulgèd tongue
Presumptuous, in thus venturing to be heard."

So far her voice flow'd on, like timorous brook   300
That, lingering along a pebbled coast,
Doth fear to meet the sea: but sea it met,
And shudder'd; for the overwhelming voice

Of huge Enceladus swallow'd it in wrath:
The ponderous syllables, like sullen waves
In the half-glutted hollows of reef-rocks,
Came booming thus, while still upon his arm
He lean'd; not rising, from supreme contempt.
"Or shall we listen to the over-wise,
Or to the over-foolish, Giant-Gods?   310
Not thunderbolt on thunderbolt, till all
That rebel Jove's whole armoury were spent,
Not world on world upon these shoulders piled,
Could agonize me more than baby-words
In midst of this dethronement horrible.
Speak! roar! shout! yell! ye sleepy Titans all.
Do ye forget the blows, the buffets vile?
Are ye not smitten by a youngling arm?
Dost thou forget, sham Monarch of the Waves,
Thy scalding in the seas? What, have I rous'd   320
Your spleens with so few simple words as these?
O joy! for now I see ye are not lost:
O joy! for now I see a thousand eyes
Wide-glaring for revenge!"—As this he said,
He lifted up his stature vast, and stood,
Still without intermission speaking thus:
"Now ye are flames, I'll tell you how to burn,
And purge the ether of our enemies;
How to feed fierce the crooked stings of fire,
And singe away the swollen clouds of Jove,   330
Stifling that puny essence in its tent.
O let him feel the evil he hath done;
For though I scorn Oceanus's lore,
Much pain have I for more than loss of realms:
The days of peace and slumberous calm are fled;
Those days, all innocent of scathing war,
When all the fair Existences of heaven
Came open-eyed to guess what we would speak:—
That was before our brows were taught to frown,
Before our lips knew else but solemn sounds;   340
That was before we knew the wingèd thing,
Victory, might be lost, or might be won.
And be ye mindful that Hyperion,
Our brightest brother, still is undisgraced—
Hyperion, lo! his radiance is here!"

All eyes were on Enceladus's face,
And they beheld, while still Hyperion's name
Flew from his lips up to the vaulted rocks,
A pallid gleam across his features stern:
Not savage, for he saw full many a God   350
Wroth as himself. He look'd upon them all,
And in each face he saw a gleam of light,

But splendider in Saturn's, whose hoar locks
Shone like the bubbling foam about a keel
When the prow sweeps into a midnight cove.
In pale and silver silence they remain'd,
'Till suddenly a splendour, like the morn,
Pervaded all the beetling gloomy steeps,
All the sad spaces of oblivion,
And every gulf, and every chasm old,   360
And every height, and every sullen depth,
Voiceless, or hoarse with loud tormented streams:
And all the everlasting cataracts,
And all the headlong torrents far and near,
Mantled before in darkness and huge shade,
Now saw the light and made it terrible.
It was Hyperion:—a granite peak
His bright feet touch'd, and there he stay'd to view
The misery his brilliance had betray'd
To the most hateful seeing of itself.   370
Golden his hair of short Numidian curl,
Regal his shape majestic, a vast shade
In midst of his own brightness, like the bulk
Of Memnon's image at the set of sun
To one who travels from the dusking East:
Sighs, too, as mournful as that Memnon's harp
He utter'd, while his hands contemplative
He press'd together, and in silence stood.
Despondence seiz'd again the fallen Gods
At sight of the dejected King of Day,   380
And many hid their faces from the light:
But fierce Enceladus sent forth his eyes
Among the brotherhood; and, at their glare,
Uprose Iäpetus, and Creüs too,
And Phorcus, sea-born, and together strode
To where he towered on his eminence.
There those four shouted forth old Saturn's name;
Hyperion from the peak loud answered, "Saturn!"
Saturn sat near the Mother of the Gods,
In whose face was no joy, though all the Gods   390
Gave from their hollow throats the name of
    "Saturn!"

BOOK THREE

Thus in alternate uproar and sad peace,
Amazèd were those Titans utterly.

374–76. **Memnon's . . . harp:** The huge statue of the
Egyptian Memnon near the Valley of the Kings supposedly gave forth musical sounds when struck by the
rays of the sun. 389. **Mother of the Gods:** Cybele.

O leave them, Muse! O leave them to their woes;
For thou art weak to sing such tumults dire:
A solitary sorrow best befits
Thy lips, and antheming a lonely grief.
Leave them, O Muse! for thou anon wilt find
Many a fallen old Divinity
Wandering in vain about bewildered shores.
Meantime touch piously the Delphic harp,   10
And not a wind of heaven but will breathe
In aid soft warble from the Dorian flute;
For lo! 'tis for the Father of all verse.
Flush every thing that hath a vermeil hue,
Let the rose glow intense and warm the air,
And let the clouds of even and of morn
Float in voluptuous fleeces o'er the hills;
Let the red wine within the goblet boil,
Cold as a bubbling well; let faint-lipp'd shells,
On sands, or in great deeps, vermilion turn   20
Through all their labyrinths; and let the maid
Blush keenly, as with some warm kiss surpris'd.
Chief isle of the embowered Cyclades,
Rejoice, O Delos, with thine olives green,
And poplars, and lawn-shading palms, and beech,
In which the Zephyr breathes the loudest song,
And hazels thick, dark-stemm'd beneath the shade:
Apollo is once more the golden theme!
Where was he, when the Giant of the Sun
Stood bright, amid the sorrow of his peers?   30
Together had he left his mother fair
And his twin-sister sleeping in their bower,
And in the morning twilight wandered forth
Beside the osiers of a rivulet,
Full ankle-deep in lilies of the vale.
The nightingale had ceas'd, and a few stars
Were lingering in the heavens, while the thrush
Began calm-throated. Throughout all the isle
There was no covert, no retired cave
Unhaunted by the murmurous noise of waves,   40
Though scarcely heard in many a green recess.
He listen'd, and he wept, and his bright tears
Went trickling down the golden bow he held
Thus with half-shut suffusèd eyes he stood,
While from beneath some cumbrous boughs hard
    by
With solemn step an awful Goddess came,
And there was purport in her looks for him,
Which he with eager guess began to read

HYPERION. BOOK THREE. 13. **Father of all verse:** Apollo.
34. **osiers:** willows.

Perplex'd, the while melodiously he said:
"How cam'st thou over the unfooted sea?   50
Or hath that antique mien and robed form
Mov'd in these vales invisible till now?
Sure I have heard those vestments sweeping o'er
The fallen leaves, when I have sat alone
In cool mid-forest. Surely I have traced
The rustle of those ample skirts about
These grassy solitudes, and seen the flowers
Lift up their heads, as still the whisper pass'd.
Goddess! I have beheld those eyes before,
And their eternal calm, and all that face,   60
Or I have dream'd."—"Yes," said the supreme
         shape,
"Thou hast dream'd of me; and awaking up
Didst find a lyre all golden by thy side,
Whose strings touch'd by thy fingers, all the vast
Unwearied ear of the whole universe
Listen'd in pain and pleasure at the birth
Of such new tuneful wonder. Is't not strange
That thou shouldst weep, so gifted? Tell me, youth,
What sorrow thou canst feel; for I am sad
When thou dost shed a tear: explain thy griefs   70
To one who in this lonely isle hath been
The watcher of thy sleep and hours of life,
From the young day when first thy infant hand
Pluck'd witless the weak flowers, till thine arm
Could bend that bow heroic to all times.
Show thy heart's secret to an ancient Power
Who hath forsaken old and sacred thrones
For prophecies of thee, and for the sake
Of loveliness new born."—Apollo then,
With sudden scrutiny and gloomless eyes,   80
Thus answer'd, while his white melodious throat
Throbb'd with the syllables.—"Mnemosyne!
Thy name is on my tongue, I know not how;
Why should I tell thee what thou so well seest?
Why should I strive to show what from thy lips
Would come no mystery? For me, dark, dark,
And painful vile oblivion seals my eyes:
I strive to search wherefore I am so sad,
Until a melancholy numbs my limbs;
And then upon the grass I sit, and moan,   90
Like one who once had wings.—O why should I
Feel curs'd and thwarted, when the liegeless air
Yields to my step aspirant? why should I
Spurn the green turf as hateful to my feet?
Goddess benign, point forth some unknown thing:
Are there not other regions than this isle?

What are the stars? There is the sun, the sun!
And the most patient brilliance of the moon!
And stars by thousands! Point me out the way
To any one particular beauteous star,   100
And I will flit into it with my lyre,
And make its silvery splendour pant with bliss.
I have heard the cloudy thunder: Where is power?
Whose hand, whose essence, what divinity
Makes this alarum in the elements,
While I here idle listen on the shores
In fearless yet in aching ignorance?
O tell me, lonely Goddess, by thy harp,
That waileth every morn and eventide,
Tell me why thus I rave, about these groves!   110
Mute thou remainest—mute! yet I can read
A wondrous lesson in thy silent face:
Knowledge enormous makes a God of me.
Names, deeds, grey legends, dire events, rebellions,
Majesties, sovran voices, agonies,
Creations and destroyings, all at once
Pour into the wide hollows of my brain,
And deify me, as if some blithe wine
Or bright elixir peerless I had drunk,
And so become immortal."—Thus the God,   120
While his enkindled eyes, with level glance
Beneath his white soft temples, stedfast kept
Trembling with light upon Mnemosyne.
Soon wild commotions shook him, and made flush
All the immortal fairness of his limbs;
Most like the struggle at the gate of death;
Or liker still to one who should take leave
Of pale immortal death, and with a pang
As hot as death's is chill, with fierce convulse
Die into life: so young Apollo anguish'd: 130
His very hair, his golden tresses famed
Kept undulation round his eager neck.
During the pain Mnemosyne upheld
Her arms as one who prophesied.—At length
Apollo shriek'd;—and lo! from all his limbs
Celestial   *   *   *   *   *   *   *

1818–19   1820

THE EVE OF ST. AGNES *

1

St. Agnes' Eve—Ah, bitter chill it was!
The owl, for all his feathers, was a-cold;
The hare limp'd trembling through the frozen
  grass,
And silent was the flock in woolly fold:
Numb were the Beadsman's fingers, while he told
His rosary, and while his frosted breath,
Like pious incense from a censer old,
Seem'd taking flight for heaven, without a death,
Past the sweet Virgin's picture, while his prayer he
  saith.

2

His prayer he saith, this patient, holy man;   10
Then takes his lamp, and riseth from his knees,
And back returneth, meagre, barefoot, wan,
Along the chapel aisle by slow degrees:
The sculptur'd dead, on each side, seem to freeze,
Emprison'd in black, purgatorial rails:
Knights, ladies, praying in dumb orat'ries,
He passeth by; and his weak spirit fails
To think how they may ache in icy hoods and
  mails.

3

Northward he turneth through a little door,
And scarce three steps, ere Music's golden
  tongue   20
Flatter'd to tears this agèd man and poor;
But no—already had his deathbell rung:
The joys of all his life were said and sung:
His was harsh penance on St. Agnes' Eve:
Another way he went, and soon among
Rough ashes sat he for his soul's reprieve,
And all night kept awake, for sinner's sake to
  grieve.

4

That ancient Beadsman heard the prelude soft;
And so it chanc'd, for many a door was wide,

---

* January 20. St. Agnes was a Roman virgin who was
martyred during the reign of Diocletian.

From hurry to and fro. Soon, up aloft,   30
The silver, snarling trumpets 'gan to chide:
The level chambers, ready with their pride,
Were glowing to receive a thousand guests:
The carved angels, ever eager-eyed,
Star'd, where upon their heads the cornice rests,
With hair blown back, and wings put cross-wise
  on their breasts.

5

At length burst in the argent revelry,
With plume, tiara, and all rich array,
Numerous as shadows haunting fairily
The brain, new stuff'd, in youth, with triumphs
  gay   40
Of old romance. These let us wish away,
And turn, sole-thoughted, to one Lady there,
Whose heart had brooded, all that wintry day,
On love, and wing'd St. Agnes' saintly care,
As she had heard old dames full many times
  declare.

6

They told her how, upon St. Agnes' Eve,
Young virgins might have visions of delight,
And soft adorings from their loves receive
Upon the honey'd middle of the night,
If ceremonies due they did aright;   50
As, supperless to bed they must retire,
And couch supine their beauties, lilly white;
Nor look behind, nor sideways, but require
Of Heaven with upward eyes for all that they
  desire.

7

Full of this whim was thoughtful Madeline:
The music, yearning like a God in pain,
She scarcely heard: her maiden eyes divine,
Fix'd on the floor, saw many a sweeping train
Pass by—she heeded not at all: in vain
Came many a tiptoe, amorous cavalier,   60
And back retir'd; not cool'd by high disdain,
But she saw not: her heart was otherwhere:
She sigh'd for Agnes' dreams, the sweetest of the
  year.

8

She danc'd along with vague, regardless eyes,
Anxious her lips, her breathing quick and short:
The hallow'd hour was near at hand: she sighs
Amid the timbrels, and the throng'd resort
Of whisperers in anger, or in sport;
'Mid looks of love, defiance, hate, and scorn,
Hoodwink'd with faery fancy; all amort,   70
Save to St. Agnes and her lambs unshorn,
And all the bliss to be before to-morrow morn.

9

So, purposing each moment to retire,
She linger'd still. Meantime, across the moors,
Had come young Porphyro, with heart on fire
For Madeline. Beside the portal doors,
Buttress'd from moonlight, stands he, and implores
All saints to give him sight of Madeline,
But for one moment in the tedious hours,
That he might gaze and worship all unseen;   80
Perchance speak, kneel, touch, kiss—in sooth such
        things have been.

10

He ventures in: let no buzz'd whisper tell:
All eyes be muffled, or a hundred swords
Will storm his heart, Love's fev'rous citadel:
For him, those chambers held barbarian hordes,
Hyena foemen, and hot-blooded lords,
Whose very dogs would execrations howl
Against his lineage: not one breast affords
Him any mercy, in that mansion foul,
Save one old beldame, weak in body and in
        soul.   90

11

Ah, happy chance! the agèd creature came,
Shuffling along with ivory-headed wand,
To where he stood, hid from the torch's flame,
Behind a broad hall-pillar, far beyond
The sound of merriment and chorus bland:

THE EVE OF ST. AGNES. **70. all amort:** apparently dead.
71. St. Agnes . . . lambs: On the feast of St. Agnes two
lambs were sacrificed during the celebration of Holy
Mass. The wool was later used by the nuns.

He startled her; but soon she knew his face,
And grasp'd his fingers in her palsied hand,
Saying, "Mercy, Porphyro! hie thee from this place;
They are all here to-night, the whole blood-thirsty
        race!

12

Get hence! get hence! there's dwarfish Hilde-
        brand;   100
He had a fever late, and in the fit
He cursèd thee and thine, both house and land:
Then there's that old Lord Maurice, not a whit
More tame for his gray hairs—Alas me! flit!
Flit like a ghost away."—"Ah, Gossip dear,
We're safe enough; here in this arm-chair sit,
And tell me how"—"Good Saints! not here, not
        here;
Follow me, child, or else these stones will be thy
        bier."

13

He follow'd through a lowly archèd way,
Brushing the cobwebs with his lofty plume,   110
And as she mutter'd "Well-a—well-a-day!"
He found him in a little moonlight room,
Pale, lattic'd, chill, and silent as a tomb.
"Now tell me where is Madeline," said he,
"O tell me, Angela, by the holy loom
Which none but secret sisterhood may see,
When they St. Agnes' wool are weaving piously."

14

"St. Agnes! Ah! it is St. Agnes' Eve—
Yet men will murder upon holy days:
Thou must hold water in a witch's sieve.   120
And be liege lord of all the Elves and Fays,
To venture so: it fills me with amaze
To see thee, Porphyro!—St. Agnes' Eve!
God's help! my lady fair the conjuror plays
This very night: good angels her deceive!
But let me laugh awhile, I've mickle time to
        grieve."

105. Gossip: godmother. The word has since acquired
negative connotations. **126. mickle:** much.

15

Feebly she laugheth in the languid moon,
While Porphyro upon her face doth look,
Like puzzled urchin on an agèd crone
Who keepeth clos'd a wond'rous riddle-book,   130
As spectacled she sits in chimney nook.
But soon his eyes grew brilliant, when she told
His lady's purpose; and he scarce could brook
Tears, at the thought of those enchantments cold,
And Madeline asleep in lap of legends old.

16

Sudden a thought came like a full-blown rose,
Flushing his brow, and in his painèd heart
Made purple riot: then doth he propose
A stratagem, that makes the beldame start:
"A cruel man and impious thou art: 140
Sweet lady, let her pray, and sleep, and dream
Alone with her good angels, far apart
From wicked men like thee. Go, go!—I deem
Thou canst not surely be the same that thou didst
      seem."

17

"I will not harm her, by all saints I swear,"
Quoth Porphyro: "O may I ne'er find grace
When my weak voice shall whisper its last prayer,
If one of her soft ringlets I displace,
Or look with ruffian passion in her face:
Good Angela, believe me by these tears;   150
Or I will, even in a moment's space,
Awake, with horrid shout, my foemen's ears,
And beard them, though they be more fang'd than
      wolves and bears."

18

"Ah! why wilt thou affright a feeble soul?
A poor, weak, palsy-stricken, churchyard thing,
Whose passing-bell may ere the midnight toll;
Whose prayers for thee, each morn and evening,
Were never miss'd."—Thus plaining, doth she bring
A gentler speech from burning Porphyro;
So woful, and of such deep sorrowing,   160
That Angela gives promise she will do
Whatever he shall wish, betide her weal or woe.

19

Which was, to lead him, in close secrecy,
Even to Madeline's chamber, and there hide
Him in a closet, of such privacy
That he might see her beauty unespied,
And win perhaps that night a peerless bride,
While legion'd faeries pac'd the coverlet,
And pale enchantment held her sleepy-eyed.
Never on such a night have lovers met.   170
Since Merlin paid his Demon all the monstrous
      debt.

20

"It shall be as thou wishest," said the Dame:
All cates and dainties shall be storèd there
Quickly on this feast-night: by the tambour frame
Her own lute thou wilt see: no time to spare,
For I am slow and feeble, and scarce dare
On such a catering trust my dizzy head.
Wait here, my child, with patience; kneel in prayer
The while: Ah! thou must needs the lady wed,
Or may I never leave my grave among the
      dead."   180

21

So saying, she hobbled off with busy fear.
The lover's endless minutes slowly pass'd:
The dame return'd, and whisper'd in his ear
To follow her; with agèd eyes aghast
From fright of dim espial. Safe at last,
Through many a dusky gallery, they gain
The maiden's chamber, silken, hush'd, and chaste;
Where Porphyro took covert, pleas'd amain.
His poor guide hurried back with agues in her
      brain.

22

Her falt'ring hand upon the balustrade,   190
Old Angela was feeling for the stair,
When Madeline, St. Agnes' charmèd maid,
Rose, like a mission'd spirit, unaware:

171. **Merlin . . . debt:** In Arthurian legend Merlin, the
son of a demon, disappeared in a storm triggered by his
own magic power. **173. cates:** delicacies. **174. tambour
frame:** embroidery frame shaped like a drum.

With silver taper's light, and pious care,
She turn'd, and down the agèd gossip led
To a safe level matting. Now prepare,
Young Porphyro, for gazing on that bed;
She comes, she comes again, like ring-dove fray'd
    and fled.

23

Out went the taper as she hurried in;
Its little smoke, in pallid moonshine, died: 200
She clos'd the door, she panted, all akin
To spirits of the air, and visions wide:
No uttered syllable, or, woe betide!
But to her heart, her heart was voluble,
Paining with eloquence her balmy side;
As though a tongueless nightingale should swell
Her throat in vain, and die, heart-stifled, in her
    dell.

24

A casement high and triple-arch'd there was,
All garlanded with carven imag'ries
Of fruits, and flowers, and bunches of knot-
    grass,   210
And diamonded with panes of quaint device,
Innumerable of stains and splendid dyes,
As are the tiger-moth's deep-damask'd wings;
And in the midst, 'mong thousand heraldries,
And twilight saints, and dim emblazonings,
A shielded scutcheon blush'd with blood of queens
    and kings.

25

Full on this casement shone the wintry moon,
And threw warm gules on Madeline's fair breast,
As down she knelt for heaven's grace and boon;
Rose-bloom fell on her hands, together prest,   220
And on her silver cross soft amethyst,
And on her hair a glory, like a saint:
She seem'd a splendid angel, newly drest,
Save wings, for heaven:—Porphyro grew faint:
She knelt, so pure a thing, so free from mortal
    taint.

218. gules: the heraldic color red.

26

Anon his heart revives: her vespers done,
Of all its wreathèd pearls her hair she frees;
Unclasps her warmèd jewels one by one;
Loosens her fragrant boddice; by degrees
Her rich attire creeps rustling to her knees: 230
Half-hidden, like a mermaid in sea-weed,
Pensive awhile she dreams awake, and sees,
In fancy, fair St. Agnes in her bed,
But dares not look behind, or all the charm is fled.

27

Soon, trembling in her soft and chilly nest,
In sort of wakeful swoon, perplex'd she lay,
Until the poppied warmth of sleep oppress'd
Her soothèd limbs, and soul fatigued away;
Flown, like a thought, until the morrow-day;
Blissfully haven'd both from joy and pain;   240
Clasp'd like a missal where swart Paynims pray;
Blinded alike from sunshine and from rain,
As though a rose should shut, and be a bud again.

28

Stol'n to this paradise, and so entranced,
Porphyro gazed upon her empty dress,
And listen'd to her breathing, if it chanced
To wake into a slumberous tenderness;
Which when he heard, that minute did he bless,
And breath'd himself: then from the closet crept,
Noiseless as fear in a wide wilderness,   250
And over the hush'd carpet, silent, stept,
An 'tween the curtains peep'd, where, lo!—how fast
    she slept.

29

Then by the bed-side, where the faded moon
Made a dim, silver twilight, soft he set
A table, and, half anguish'd, threw thereon
A cloth of woven crimson, gold, and jet:—
O for some drowsy Morphean amulet!
The boisterous, midnight, festive clarion,

241. swart Paynims: black pagans. **257. Morphean amulet:** a sleep-inducing charm. Morpheus is the god of sleep.

The kettle-drum, and far-heard clarinet,
Affray his ears, though but in dying tone:— 260
The hall door shuts again, and all the noise is gone.

30

And still she slept an azure-lidded sleep,
In blanchèd linen, smooth, and lavender'd,
While he from forth the closet brought a heap
Of candied apple, quince, and plum, and gourd;
With jellies soother than the creamy curd,
And lucent syrops, tinct with cinnamon;
Manna and dates, in argosy transferr'd
From Fez; and spicèd dainties, every one,
From silken Samarcand to cedar'd Lebanon.   270

31

These delicates he heap'd with glowing hand
On golden dishes and in baskets bright
Of wreathèd silver: sumptuous they stand
In the retired quiet of the night,
Filling the chilly room with perfume light.—
"And now, my love, my seraph fair, awake!
Thou art my heaven, and I thine eremite:
Open thine eyes, for meek St. Agnes' sake,
Or I shall drowse beside thee, so my soul doth
        ache."

32

Thus whispering, his warm, unnervèd arm   280
Sank in her pillow. Shaded was her dream
By the dusk curtains:—'twas a midnight charm
Impossible to melt as icèd stream:
The lustrous salvers in the moonlight gleam;
Broad golden fringe upon the carpet lies:
It seem'd he never, never could redeem
From such a stedfast spell his lady's eyes;
So mus'd awhile, entoil'd in woofèd phantasies.

33

Awakening up, he took her hollow lute,—
Tumultuous,—and, in chords that tenderest
        be,   290
He play'd an ancient ditty, long since mute,

In Provence call'd, "La belle dame sans mercy":
Close to her ear touching the melody;—
Wherewith disturb'd, she utter'd a soft moan:
He ceased—she panted quick—and suddenly
Her blue affrayèd eyes wide open shone:
Upon his knees he sank, pale as smooth-sculptured
        stone.

34

Her eyes were open, but she still beheld,
Now wide awake, the vision of her sleep:
There was a painful change, that night
        expell'd   300
The blisses of her dream so pure and deep
At which fair Madeline began to weep,
And moan forth witless words with many a sigh;
While still her gaze on Porphyro would keep;
Who knelt, with joinèd hands and piteous eye,
Fearing to move or speak, she look'd so dreamingly.

35

"Ah, Porphyro!" said she, "but even now
Thy voice was at sweet tremble in mine ear,
Made tuneable with every sweetest vow;
And those sad eyes were spiritual and clear: 310
How chang'd thou art! how pallid, chill, and drear!
Give me that voice again, my Porphyro,
Those looks immortal, those complainings dear!
Oh leave me not in this eternal woe,
For if thou diest, my Love, I know not where to
        go."

36

Beyond a mortal man impassion'd far
At these voluptuous accents, he arose,
Ethereal, flush'd, and like a throbbing star
Seen mid the sapphire heaven's deep repose,
Into her dream he melted, as the rose   320
Blendeth its odour with the violet,—
Solution sweet: meantime the frost-wind blows
Like Love's alarum pattering the sharp sleet
Against the window-panes; St. Agnes' moon hath
        set.

292. **La belle dame sans mercy**: title of a poem by
Alain Chartier, fifteenth-century French poet.

37

'Tis dark: quick pattereth the flaw-blown sleet:
"This is no dream, my bride, my Madeline!"
'Tis dark: the icèd gusts still rave and beat:
"No dream, alas! alas! and woe is mine!
Porphyro will leave me here to fade and pine.—
Cruel! what traitor could thee hither bring?   330
I curse not, for my heart is lost in thine,
Though thou forsakest a deceivèd thing;—
A dove forlorn and lost with sick unprunèd wing."

38

"My Madeline! sweet dreamer! lovely bride!
Say, may I be for aye thy vassal blest?
Thy beauty's shield, heart-shap'd and vermeil
        dyed?
Ah, silver shrine, here will I take my rest
After so many hours of toil and quest,
A famish'd pilgrim,—sav'd by miracle.
Though I have found, I will not rob thy nest   340
Saving of thy sweet self; if thou think'st well
To trust, fair Madeline, to no rude infidel.

39

"Hark! 'tis an elfin-storm from faery land,
Of haggard seeming, but a boon indeed:
Arise—arise! the morning is at hand;—
The bloated wassaillers will never heed:—
Let us away, my love, with happy speed;
There are nb ears to hear, or eyes to see,—
Drown'd all in Rhenish and the sleepy mead:
Awake! arise! my love, and fearless be,   350
For o'er the southern moors I have a home for
        thee."

40

She hurried at his words, beset with fears,
For there were sleeping dragons all around,
At glaring watch, perhaps, with ready spears—
Down the wide stairs a darkling way they found.—
In all the house was heard no human sound.
A chain-droop'd lamp was flickering by each door;
The arras, rich with horseman, hawk, and hound,

325. flaw-blown: wind-blown. 358. arras: tapestry.

Flutter'd in the besieging wind's uproar;
And the long carpets rose along the gusty
        floor.   360

41

They glide, like phantoms, into the wide hall;
Like phantoms, to the iron porch, they glide;
Where lay the Porter, in uneasy sprawl,
With a huge empty flaggon by his side:
The wakeful bloodhound rose, and shook his hide,
But his sagacious eye an inmate owns:
By one, and one, the bolts full easy slide:—
The chains lie silent on the footworn stones;—
The key turns, and the door upon its hinges groans.

42

And they are gone: aye, ages long ago   370
These lovers fled away into the storm.
That night the Baron dreamt of many a woe,
And all his warrior-guests, with shade and form
Of witch, and demon, and large coffin-worm,
Were long be-nightmar'd. Angela the old
Died palsy-twitch'd, with meagre face deform;
The Beadsman, after thousand aves told,
For aye unsought for slept among his ashes cold.

1819   *1820*

WHY DID I LAUGH

Why did I laugh to-night? No voice will tell:
    No God, no Demon of severe response,
Deigns to reply from heaven or from Hell.
    Then to my human heart I turn at once.
Heart! Thou and I are here sad and alone;
    Say, wherefore did I laugh? O mortal pain!
O Darkness! Darkness! ever must I moan,
    To question Heaven and Hell and Heart in vain.
Why did I laugh? I know this Being's lease,
    My fancy to its utmost blisses spreads;   10
Yet would I on this very midnight cease,
    And the world's gaudy ensigns see in shreds;
Verse, Fame, and Beauty are intense indeed,
But Death intenser—Death is Life's high meed.

1819   *1848*

LA BELLE DAME SANS MERCI*

O, what can ail thee, knight-at-arms,
    Alone and palely loitering?
The sedge has wither'd from the lake,
    And no birds sing.

O, what can ail thee, knight-at-arms,
    So haggard and so woe-begone?
The squirrel's granary is full,
    And the harvest's done.

I see a lilly on thy brow,
    With anguish moist and fever dew,   10
And on thy cheeks a fading rose
    Fast withereth too.

I met a lady in the meads,
    Full beautiful—a faery's child,
Her hair was long, her foot was light,
    And her eyes were wild.

I made a garland for her head,
    And bracelets too, and fragrant zone;
She look'd at me as she did love,
    And made sweet moan.   20

I set her on my pacing steed,
    And nothing else saw all day long,
For sidelong would she bend and sing
    A faery's song.

She found me roots of relish sweet,
    And honey wild, and manna dew,
And sure in language strange she said
    "I love thee true."

She took me to her elfin grot,
    And there she wept and sigh'd full sore,   30
And there I shut her wild wild eyes
    With kisses four.

And there she lull'd me asleep,
    And there I dream'd—Ah! woe betide!
The latest dream I ever dream'd
    On the cold hill side.

I saw pale kings and princes too,
    Pale warriors, death-pale were they all;

They cried, "La Belle Dame sans Merci
    Hath thee in thrall!"   40

I saw their starved lips in the gloam,
    With horrid warning gapèd wide,
And I awoke, and found me here,
    On the cold hill's side.

And this is why I sojourn here,
    Alone and palely loitering,
Though the sedge is wither'd from the lake,
    And no birds sing.

1819   1820

TO SLEEP

O soft embalmer of the still midnight,
    Shutting, with careful fingers and benign,
Our gloom-pleas'd eyes, embower'd from the light,
    Enshaded in forgetfulness divine;
O soothest Sleep! if so it please thee, close
    In midst of this thine hymn, my willing eyes,
Or wait the Amen, ere thy poppy throws
    Around my bed its lulling charities;
Then save me, or the passèd day will shine
Upon my pillow, breeding many woes;   10
    Save me from curious conscience, that still lords
Its strength for darkness, burrowing like a mole;
    Turn the key deftly in the oilèd wards,
And seal the hushèd Casket of my soul.

1819   1838

ODE TO PSYCHE

O Goddess! hear these tuneless numbers, wrung
    By sweet enforcement and remembrance dear,
And pardon that thy secrets should be sung
    Even into thine own soft-conchèd ear:
Surely I dreamt to-day, or did I see
    The wingèd Psyche with awaken'd eyes?

---

* There is a later and, in the opinion of most critics, a poorer version of the poem.

ODE TO PSYCHE. **1. Goddess:** Psyche, in classical mythology, is the soul. Cupid, the son of Venus, falls in love with a mortal Psyche in the version of Apuleius, a Latin writer of the second century. A jealous Venus punishes her, but Jupiter renders her immortal so that the lovers may live happily forever. Keats's treatment of the myth is distinctive, and has been read by critics in remarkably differing ways. **4. soft-conchèd:** shell-shaped.

I wander'd in a forest thoughtlessly,
   And, on the sudden, fainting with surprise,
Saw two fair creatures, couchèd side by side
   In deepest grass, beneath the whisp'ring
      roof   10
   Of leaves and trembled blossoms, where there
      ran
      A brooklet, scarce espied:

'Mid hush'd, cool-rooted flowers, fragrant-eyed,
   Blue, silver-white, and budded Tyrian,
They lay calm-breathing on the bedded grass;
   Their arms embracèd, and their pinions too;
   Their lips touch'd not, but had not bade adieu,
As if disjoinèd by soft-handed slumber,
And ready still past kisses to outnumber
   At tender eye-dawn of aurorean love: 20
      The wingèd boy I knew;
   But who wast thou, O happy, happy dove?
      His Psyche true!

O latest born and loveliest vision far
   Of all Olympus' faded hierarchy!
Fairer than Phœbe's sapphire-region'd star,
   Or Vesper, amorous glow-worm of the sky;
Fairer than these, though temple thou hast none,
      Nor altar heap'd with flowers;
Nor virgin-choir to make delicious moan   30
      Upon the midnight hours;
No voice, no lute, no pipe, in incense sweet
   From chain-swung censer teeming;
No shrine, no grove, no oracle, no heat
   Of pale-mouth'd prophet dreaming.

O brightest! though too late for antique vows,
   Too, too late for the fond believing lyre,
When holy were the haunted forest boughs,
   Holy the air, the water, and the fire;
Yet even in these days so far retir'd   40
   From happy pieties, thy lucent fans,
   Fluttering among the faint Olympians,
I see, and sing, by my own eyes inspir'd.
So let me be thy choir, and make a moan
      Upon the midnight hours;
Thy voice, thy lute, thy pipe, thy incense sweet
   From swingèd censer teeming;

Thy shrine, thy grove, thy oracle, thy heat
   Of pale-mouth'd prophet dreaming.

Yes, I will be thy priest, and build a fane   50
   In some untrodden region of my mind,
Where branchèd thoughts, new grown with
      pleasant pain,
   Instead of pines shall murmur in the wind:
Far, far around shall those dark-cluster'd trees
   Fledge the wild-ridgèd mountains steep by steep;
And there by zephyrs, streams, and birds, and bees,
   The moss-lain Dryads shall be lull'd to sleep;
And in the midst of this wide quietness
A rosy sanctuary will I dress
With the wreath'd trellis of a working brain,   60
   With buds, and bells, and stars without a name,
With all the gardener Fancy e'er could feign,
   Who breeding flowers, will never breed the same:
And there shall be for thee all soft delight
   That shadowy thought can win,
A bright torch, and a casement ope at night,
   To let the warm Love in!

1819   1820

ODE TO A NIGHTINGALE

I

My heart aches, and a drowsy numbness pains
   My sense, as though of hemlock I had drunk,
Or emptied some dull opiate to the drains
   One minute past, and Lethe-wards had sunk:
'Tis not through envy of thy happy lot,
   But being too happy in thine happiness,—
      That thou, light-wingèd Dryad of the trees,
      In some melodious plot
Of beechen green, and shadows numberless,
   Singest of summer in full-throated ease.   10

II

O, for a draught of vintage! that hath been
   Cool'd a long age in the deep-delvèd earth,
Tasting of Flora and the country green,
   Dance, and Provençal song, and sunburnt mirth!

---

14. Tyrian: purple. 26. Phœbe's . . . star: the moon was
protected by Phœbe, her goddess. 27. Vesper: the evening star. 41. fans: wings.

50. fane: temple.

Their pleasures in a long immortal dream.
One warm, flush'd moment, hovering, it might seem
Dash'd by the wood-nymph's beauty, so he
    burn'd,   130
Then, lighting on the printless verdure, turn'd
To the swoon'd serpent, and with languid arm,
Delicate, put to proof the lythe Caducean charm.
So done, upon the nymph his eyes he bent
Full of adoring tears and blandishment,
And towards her stept: she, like a moon in wane,
Faded before him, cower'd, nor could restrain
Her fearful sobs, self-folding like a flower
That faints into itself at evening hour:
But the God fostering her chillèd hand,   140
She felt the warmth, her eyelids open'd bland,
And, like new flowers at morning song of bees
Bloom'd, and gave up her honey to the lees.
Into the green-recessed woods they flew;
Nor grew they pale, as mortal lovers do.

Left to herself, the serpent now began
To change; her elfin blood in madness ran,
Her mouth foam'd, and the grass, therewith
    besprent,
Wither'd at dew so sweet and virulent;
Her eyes in torture fix'd, and anguish drear,   150
Hot, glaz'd, and wide, with lid-lashes all sear,
Flash'd phosphor and sharp sparks, without one
    cooling tear.
The colours all inflam'd throughout her train,
She writh'd about, convuls'd with scarlet pain:
A deep volcanian yellow took the place
Of all her milder-moonèd body's grace;
And, as the lava ravishes the mead,
Spoilt all her silver mail, and golden brede;
Made gloom of all her frecklings, streaks and bars,
Eclips'd her crescents, and lick'd up her stars: 160
So that, in moments few, she was undrest
Of all her sapphires, greens, and amethyst,
And rubious-argent: of all these bereft,
Nothing but pain and ugliness were left.
Still shone her crown; that vanish'd, also she
Melted and disappear'd as suddenly;
And in the air, her new voice luting soft,
Cried, "Lycius! gentle Lycius!"—Borne aloft
With the bright mists about the mountains hoar
These words dissolv'd: Crete's forests heard no
    more.   170

133. **put . . . charm:** touched her with the Caduceus, a
magical serpent-entwined staff.

Whither fled Lamia, now a lady bright,
A full-born beauty new and exquisite?
She fled into that valley they pass o'er
Who go to Corinth from Cenchreas' shore;
And rested at the foot of those wild hills,
The rugged founts of the Peræan rills,
And of that other ridge whose barren back
Stretches, with all its mist and cloudy rack,
South-westward to Cleone. There she stood
About a young bird's flutter from a wood,   180
Fair, on a sloping green of mossy tread,
By a clear pool, wherein she passionèd
To see herself escap'd from so sore ills,
While her robes flaunted with the daffodils.

Ah, happy Lycius!—for she was a maid
More beautiful than ever twisted braid,
Or sigh'd, or blush'd, or on spring-flowered lea
Spread a green kirtle to the minstrelsy:
A virgin purest lipp'd, yet in the lore
Of love deep learnèd to the red heart's core: 190
Not one hour old, yet of sciential brain
To unperplex bliss from its neighbour pain;
Define their pettish limits, and estrange
Their points of contact, and swift counterchange;
Intrigue with the specious chaos, and dispart
Its most ambiguous atoms with sure art;
As though in Cupid's college she had spent
Sweet days a lovely graduate, still unshent,
And kept his rosy terms in idle languishment.

Why this fair creature chose so faerily   200
By the wayside to linger, we shall see;
But first 'tis fit to tell how she could muse
And dream, when in the serpent prison-house,
Of all she list, strange or magnificent:
How, ever, where she will'd, her spirit went;
Whether to faint Elysium, or where
Down through tress-lifting waves the Nereids fair
Wind into Thetis' bower by many a pearly stair;
Or where God Bacchus drains his cups divine,
Stretch'd out, at ease, beneath a glutinous
    pine;   210
Or where in Pluto's gardens palatine
Mulciber's columns gleam in far piazzian line.
And sometimes into cities she would send
Her dream, with feast and rioting to blend;

174. **Cenchreas' shore:** on the eastern harbor of Corinth.
198. **unshent:** unspoiled, innocent. 212. **Mulciber:** another name for Vulcan, god of fire.

And once, while among mortals dreaming thus,
She saw the young Corinthian Lycius
Charioting foremost in the envious race,
Like a young Jove with calm uneager face,
And fell into a swooning love of him.
Now on the moth-time of that evening dim   220
He would return that way, as well she knew,
To Corinth from the shore; for freshly blew
The eastern soft wind, and his galley now
Grated the quaystones with her brazen prow
In port Cenchreas, from Egina isle
Fresh anchor'd; whither he had been awhile
To sacrifice to Jove, whose temple there
Waits with high marble doors for blood and incense
     rare.
Jove heard his vows, and better'd his desire;
For by some freakful chance he made retire   230
From his companions, and set forth to walk,
Perhaps grown wearied of their Corinth talk:
Over the solitary hills he fared,
Thoughtless at first, but ere eve's star appeared
His phantasy was lost, where reason fades,
In the calm'd twilight of Platonic shades.
Lamia beheld him coming, near, more near—
Close to her passing, in indifference drear,
His silent sandals swept the mossy green;
So neighbour'd to him, and yet so unseen   240
She stood: he pass'd, shut up in mysteries,
His mind wrapp'd like his mantle, while her eyes
Follow'd his steps, and her neck regal white
Turn'd—syllabling thus, "Ah, Lycius bright,
And will you leave me on the hills alone?
Lycius, look back! and be some pity shown."
He did; not with cold wonder fearingly,
But Orpheus-like at an Eurydice;
For so delicious were the words she sung,
It seem'd he had lov'd them a whole summer
     long: 250
And soon his eyes had drunk her beauty up,
Leaving no drop in the bewildering cup,
And still the cup was full,—while he, afraid
Lest she should vanish ere his lip had paid
Due adoration, thus began to adore;
Her soft look growing coy, she saw his chain so
     sure:
"Leave thee alone! Look back! Ah, Goddess, see

Whether my eyes can ever turn from thee!
For pity do not this sad heart belie—
Even as thou vanishest so shall I die.   260
Stay! though a Naiad of the rivers, stay!
To thy far wishes will thy streams obey:
Stay! though the greenest woods be thy domain,
Alone they can drink up the morning rain:
Though a descended Pleiad, will not one
Of thine harmonious sisters keep in tune
Thy spheres, and as thy silver proxy shine?
So sweetly to these ravish'd ears of mine
Came thy sweet greeting, that if thou shouldst fade
Thy memory will waste me to a shade:—   270
For pity do not melt!"—"If I should stay,"
Said Lamia, "here, upon this floor of clay,
And pain my steps upon these flowers too rough,
What canst thou say or do of charm enough
To dull the nice remembrance of my home?
Thou canst not ask me with thee here to roam
Over these hills and vales, where no joy is,—
Empty of immortality and bliss!
Thou art a scholar, Lycius, and must know
That finer spirits cannot breathe below   280
In human climes, and live: Alas! poor youth,
What taste of purer air hast thou to soothe
My essence? What serener palaces,
Where I may all my many senses please,
And by mysterious sleights a hundred thirsts
     appease?
It cannot be—Adieu!" So said, she rose
Tiptoe with white arms spread. He, sick to lose
The amorous promise of her lone complain,
Swoon'd, murmuring of love, and pale with pain.
The cruel lady, without any show   290
Of sorrow for her tender favourite's woe,
But rather, if her eyes could brighter be,
With brighter eyes and slow amenity,
Put her new lips to his, and gave afresh
The life she had so tangled in her mesh:
And as he from one trance was wakening
Into another, she began to sing,
Happy in beauty, life, and love, and every thing,
A song of love, too sweet for earthly lyres,
While, like held breath, the stars drew in their
     panting fires.   300
And then she whisper'd in such trembling tone,

248. Orpheus-like: a reference to the famous story of Orpheus, allowed by Pluto to lead his wife Eurydice back from the underworld on condition that he not look back at her. Orpheus did look back and lost her forever.

265. Pleiad: one of seven daughters of Atlas, the Pleiades. They were transformed into a heavenly constellation.

As those who, safe together met alone
For the first time through many anguish'd days,
Use other speech than looks; bidding him raise
His drooping head, and clear his soul of doubt,
For that she was a woman, and without
Any more subtle fluid in her veins
Than throbbing blood, and that the self-same
    pains
Inhabited her frail-strung heart as his.
And next she wonder'd how his eyes could
    miss   310
Her face so long in Corinth, where, she said,
She dwelt but half retir'd, and there had led
Days happy as the gold coin could invent
Without the aid of love; yet in content
Till she saw him, as once she pass'd him by,
Where 'gainst a column he leant thoughtfully
At Venus' temple porch, 'mid baskets heap'd
Of amorous herbs and flowers, newly reap'd
Late on that eve, as 'twas the night before
The Adonian feast; whereof she saw no more, 320
But wept alone those days, for why should she
    adore?
Lycius from death awoke into amaze,
To see her still, and singing so sweet lays;
Then from amaze into delight he fell
To hear her whisper woman's lore so well;
And every word she spake entic'd him on
To unperplex'd delight and pleasure known.
Let the mad poets say whate'er they please
Of the sweets of Faeries, Peris, Goddesses,
There is not such a treat among them all.   330
Haunters of cavern, lake, and waterfall,
As a real woman, lineal indeed
From Pyrrha's pebbles or old Adam's seed.
Thus gentle Lamia judg'd, and judg'd aright,
That Lycius could not love in half a fright,
So threw the goddess off, and won his heart
More pleasantly by playing woman's part,
With no more awe than what her beauty gave,
That, while it smote, still guaranteed to save.
Lycius to all made eloquent reply,   340
Marrying to every word a twinborn sigh;
And last, pointing to Corinth, ask'd her sweet,
If 'twas too far that night for her soft feet.
The way was short, for Lamia's eagerness

333. **Pyrrha's pebbles:** According to legend, after the Great Flood Deucalion and Pyrrha repopulated the barren earth by throwing pebbles that turned into human beings.

Made, by a spell, the triple league decrease
To a few paces; not at all surmised
By blinded Lycius, so in her comprized.
They pass'd the city gates, he knew not how
So noiseless, and he never thought to know.

As men talk in a dream, so Corinth all,   350
Throughout her palaces imperial,
And all her populous streets and temples lewd,
Mutter'd, like tempest in the distance brew'd,
To the wide-spreaded night above her towers.
Men, women, rich and poor, in the cool hours,
Shuffled their sandals o'er the pavement white,
Companion'd or alone; while many a light
Flared, here and there, from wealthy festivals,
And threw their moving shadows on the walls,
Or found them cluster'd in the corniced shade 360
Of some arch'd temple door, or dusky colonnade.

Muffling his face, of greeting friends in fear,
Her fingers he press'd hard, as one came near
With curl'd gray beard, sharp eyes, and smooth
    bald crown.
Slow-stepp'd, and robed in philosophic gown:
Lycius shrank closer, as they met and past,
Into his mantle, adding wings to haste,
While huried Lamia trembled: "Ah," said he,
"Why do you shudder, love, so ruefully?
Why does your tender palm dissolve in
    dew?"—   370
"I'm wearied," said fair Lamia: "tell me who
Is that old man? I cannot bring to mind
His features:—Lycius! wherefore did you blind
Yourself from his quick eyes?" Lycius replied,
" 'Tis Apollonius sage, my trusty guide
And good instructor; but to-night he seems
The ghost of folly haunting my sweet dreams."

While yet he spake they had arrived before
A pillar'd porch, with lofty portal door,
Where hung a silver lamp, whose phosphor
    glow   380
Reflected in the slabbèd steps below,
Mild as a star in water; for so new,
And so unsullied was the marble hue,
So through the crystal polish, liquid fine,
Ran the dark veins, that none but feet divine
Could e'er have touch'd there. Sounds Æolian
Breath'd from the hinges, as the ample span
Of the wide doors disclos'd a place unknown
Some time to any, but those two alone,

And a few Persian mutes, who that same year   390
Were seen about the markets: none knew where
They could inhabit; the most curious
Were foil'd, who watch'd to trace them to their
  house:
And but the flitter-wingèd verse must tell,
For truth's sake, what woe afterwards befel,
'Twould humour many a heart to leave them thus,
Shut from the busy world of more incredulous.

PART II

Love in a hut, with water and a crust,
Is—Love, forgive us!—cinders, ashes, dust;
Love in a palace is perhaps at last
More grievous torment than a hermit's fast:—
That is a doubtful tale from faery land,
Hard for the non-elect to understand.
Had Lycius liv'd to hand his story down,
He might have given the moral a fresh frown,
Or clench'd it quite: but too short was their bliss
To breed distrust and hate, that make the soft voice
  hiss. 10
Beside, there, nightly, with terrific glare,
Love, jealous grown of so complete a pair,
Hover'd and buzz'd his wings, with fearful roar,
Above the lintel of their chamber door,
And down the passage cast a glow upon the floor.

For all this came a ruin: side by side
They were enthroned, in the even tide,
Upon a couch, near to a curtaining
Whose airy texture, from a golden string,
Floated into the room, and let appear 20
Unveil'd the summer heaven, blue and clear,
Betwixt two marble shafts:—there they reposed,
Where use had made it sweet, with eyelids closed,
Saving a tythe which love still open kept,
That they might see each other while they almost
  slept;
When from the slope side of a suburb hill,
Deafening the swallow's twitter, came a thrill
Of trumpets—Lycius started—the sounds fled,
But left a thought, a buzzing in his head.
For the first time, since first he harbour'd in 30
That purple-linèd palace of sweet sin,
His spirit pass'd beyond its golden bourn
Into the noisy world almost forsworn.
The lady, ever watchful, penetrant,
Saw this with pain, so arguing a want
Of something more, more than her empery

Of joys; and she began to moan and sigh
Because he mused beyond her, knowing well
That but a moment's thought is passion's passing
  bell.
"Why do you sigh, fair creature?" whisper'd
  he: 40
"Why do you think?" return'd she tenderly:
"You have deserted me;—where am I now?
Not in your heart while care weighs on your brow:
No, no, you have dismiss'd me; and I go
From your breast houseless: ay, it must be so."
He answer'd, bending to her open eyes,
Where he was mirror'd small in paradise,
"My silver planet, both of eve and morn!
Why will you plead yourself so sad forlorn,
While I am striving how to fill my heart 50
With deeper crimson, and a double smart?
How to entangle, trammel up and snare
Your soul in mine, and labyrinth you there
Like the hid scent in an unbudded rose?
Ay, a sweet kiss—you see your mighty woes.
My thoughts! shall I unveil them? Listen then!
What mortal hath a prize, that other men
May be confounded and abash'd withal,
But lets it sometimes pace abroad majestical,
And triumph, as in thee I should rejoice 60
Amid the hoarse alarm of Corinth's voice.
Let my foes choke, and my friends shout afar,
While through the throngèd streets your bridal car
Wheels round its dazzling spokes."—The lady's
  cheek
Trembled; she nothing said, but, pale and meek,
Arose and knelt before him, wept a rain
Of sorrows at his words; at last with pain
Beseeching him, the while his hand she wrung,
To change his purpose. He thereat was stung,
Perverse, with stronger fancy to reclaim 70
Her wild and timid nature to his aim:
Besides, for all his love, in self despite,
Against his better self, he took delight
Luxurious in her sorrows, soft and new,
His passion, cruel grown, took on a hue
Fierce and sanguineous as 'twas possible
In one whose brow had no dark veins to swell.
Fine was the mitigated fury, like
Apollo's presence when in act to strike
The serpent—Ha, the serpent! certes, she 80
Was none. She burnt, she lov'd the tyranny,
And, all subdued, consented to the hour
When to the bridal he should lead his paramour.

Whispering in midnight silence, said the youth,
"Sure some sweet name thou hast, though, by my
    truth,
I have not ask'd it, ever thinking thee
Not mortal, but of heavenly progeny,
As still I do. Hast any mortal name,
Fit appellation for this dazzling frame?
Or friends or kinsfolk on the citied earth,   90
To share our marriage feast and nuptial mirth?"
"I have no friends," said Lamia, "no, not one;
My presence in wide Corinth hardly known:
My parents' bones are in their dusty urns
Sepulchred, where no kindled incense burns,
Seeing all their luckless race are dead, save me,
And I neglect the holy rite for thee.
Even as you list invite your many guests;
But if, as now it seems, your vision rests
With any pleasure on me, do not bid   100
Old Apollonius—from him keep me hid."
Lycius, perplex'd at words so blind and blank,
Made close inquiry; from whose touch she shrank,
Feigning a sleep; and he to the dull shade
Of deep sleep in a moment was betray'd.

It was the custom then to bring away
The bride from home at blushing shut of day,
Veil'd, in a chariot, heralded along
By strewn flowers, torches, and a marriage song,
With other pageants: but this fair unknown   110
Had not a friend. So being left alone,
(Lycius was gone to summon all his kin)
And knowing surely she could never win
His foolish heart from its mad pompousness,
She set herself, high-thoughted, how to dress
The misery in fit magnificence.
She did so, but 'tis doubtful how and whence
Came, and who were her subtle servitors.
About the halls, and to and from the doors,
There was a noise of wings, till in short space   120
The glowing banquet-room shone with wide-arched
    grace.
A haunting music, sole perhaps and lone
Supportress of the faery-roof, made moan
Throughout, as fearful the whole charm might
    fade.
Fresh carvèd cedar, mimicking a glade
Of palm and plantain, met from either side,
High in the midst, in honour of the bride:
Two palms and then two plantains, and so on,
From either side their stems branch'd one to one

All down the aislèd place; and beneath all   130
There ran a stream of lamps straight on from wall
    to wall.
So canopied, lay an untasted feast
Teeming with odours. Lamia, regal drest,
Silently paced about, and as she went,
In pale contented sort of discontent,
Mission'd her viewless servants to enrich
The fretted splendour of each nook and niche.
Between the tree-stems, marbled plain at first,
Came jasper pannels; then, anon, there burst
Forth creeping imagery of slighter trees,   140
And with the larger wove in small intricacies.
Approving all, she faded at self-will,
And shut the chamber up, close, hush'd and still,
Complete and ready for the revels rude,
When dreadful guests would come to spoil her
    solitude.

The day appear'd, and all the gossip rout.
O senseless Lycius! Madman! wherefore flout
The silent-blessing fate, warm cloister'd hours,
And show to common eyes these secret bowers?
The herd approach'd; each guest, with busy
    brain,   150
Arriving at the portal, gaz'd amain,
And enter'd marveling: for they knew the street,
Remember'd it from childhood all complete
Without a gap, yet ne'er before had seen
That royal porch, that high-built fair demesne;
So in they hurried, all, maz'd, curious and keen:
Save one, who look'd thereon with eye severe,
And with calm-planted steps walk'd in austere;
'Twas Apollonius: something too he laugh'd,
As though some knotty problem, that had
    daft   160
His patient thought, had now begun to thaw,
And solve and melt:—'twas just as he foresaw.

He met within the murmurous vestibule
His young disciple. " 'Tis no common rule,
Lycius," said he, "for uninvited guest
To force himself upon you, and infest
With an unbidden presence the bright throng
Of younger friends; yet must I do this wrong,
And you forgive me." Lycius blush'd, and led
The old man through the inner doors broad-
    spread;   170
With reconciling words and courteous mien
Turning into sweet milk the sophist's spleen.

Of wealthy lustre was the banquet-room,

Fill'd with pervading brilliance and perfume:
Before each lucid pannel fuming stood
A censer fed with myrrh and spicèd wood,
Each by a sacred tripod held aloft,
Whose slender feet wide-swerv'd upon the soft
Wool-woofèd carpets: fifty wreaths of smoke
From fifty censers their light voyage took   180
To the high roof, still mimick'd as they rose
Along the mirror'd walls by twin-clouds odorous.
Twelve spherèd tables, by silk seats insphered,
High as the level of a man's breast rear'd
On libbard's paws, upheld the heavy gold
Of cups and goblets, and the store thrice told
Of Ceres' horn, and, in huge vessels, wine
Come from the gloomy tun with merry shine.
Thus loaded with a feast the tables stood,
Each shrining in the midst the image of a God.   190

When in an antichamber every guest
Had felt the cold sponge to pleasure press'd,
By minist'ring slaves, upon his hands and feet,
And fragrant oils with ceremony meet
Pour'd on his hair, they all mov'd to the feast
In white robes, and themselves in order placed
Around the silken couches, wondering
    Whence all this mighty cost and blaze of wealth
        could spring.

Soft went the music the soft air along,
While fluent Greek a vowel'd undersong   200
Kept up among the guests, discoursing low
At first, for scarcely was the wine at flow;
But when the happy vintage touch'd their brains,
Louder they talk, and louder come the strains
Of powerful instruments:—the gorgeous dyes,
The space, the splendour of the draperies,
The roof of awful richness, nectarous cheer,
Beautiful slaves, and Lamia's self, appear,
Now, when the wine has done its rosy deed,
And every soul from human trammels freed,   210
No more so strange; for merry wine, sweet wine,
Will make Elysian shades not too fair, too divine.
Soon was God Bacchus at meridian height;
Flush'd were their cheeks, and bright eyes double
        bright:
Garlands of every green, and every scent
From vales deflower'd, or forest-trees branch-rent,
In baskets of bright osier'd gold were brought
High as the handles heap'd, to suit the thought
Of every guest; that each, as he did please,

Might fancy-fit his brows, silk-pillow'd at his
        ease.   220
What wreath for Lamia? What for Lycius?
What for the sage, old Apollonius?
Upon her aching forehead be there hung
The leaves of willow and of adder's tongue;
And for the youth, quick, let us strip for him
The thyrsus, that his watching eyes may swim
Into forgetfulness; and, for the sage,
Let spear-grass and the spiteful thistle wage
War on his temples. Do not all charms fly
At the mere touch of cold philosophy?   230
There was an awful rainbow once in heaven:
We know her woof, her texture; she is given
In the dull catalogue of common things.
Philosophy will clip an Angel's wings,
Conquer all mysteries by rule and line,
Empty the haunted air, and gnomèd mine—
Unweave a rainbow, as it erewhile made
The tender-person'd Lamia melt into a shade.

By her glad Lycius sitting, in chief place,
Scarce saw in all the room another face,   240
Till, checking his love trance, a cup he took
Full brimm'd, and opposite sent forth a look
'Cross the broad table, to beseech a glance
From his old teacher's winkled countenance,
And pledge him. The bald-head philosopher
Had fix'd his eye, without a twinkle or stir
Full on the alarmèd beauty of the bride,
Brow-beating her fair form, and troubling her sweet
        pride.
Lycius then press'd her hand, with devout touch,
As pale it lay upon the rosy couch: 250
'Twas icy, and the cold ran through his veins;
Then sudden it grew hot, and all the pains
Of an unnatural heat shot to his heart.
"Lamia, what means this? Wherefore dost thou
        start?
Know'st thou that man?" Poor Lamia answer'd not.
He gaz'd into her eyes, and not a jot
Own'd they the lovelorn piteous appeal:
More, more he gaz'd: his human senses reel:
Some hungry spell that loveliness absorbs;
There was no recognition in those orbs.   260
"Lamia!" he cried—and no soft-toned reply.
The many heard, and the loud revelry
Grew hush; the stately music no more breathes;
The myrtle sicken'd in a thousand wreaths.

LAMIA. PART II. **185. libbard's:** leopard's. **187. Ceres'**
horn: a bounteous, harvest horn.

226. thyrsus: staff of Bacchus covered with grapevine
and ivy.

By faint degrees, voice, lute, and pleasure ceased;
A deadly silence step by step increased,
Until it seem'd a horrid presence there,
And not a man but felt the terror in his hair.
"Lamia!" he shriek'd; and nothing but the shriek
With its sad echo did the silence break.   270
"Begone, foul dream!" he cried, gazing again
In the bride's face, where now no azure vein
Wander'd on fair-spaced temples; no soft bloom
Misted the cheek; no passion to illume
The deep-recessèd vision:—all was blight;
Lamia, no longer fair, there sat a deadly white.
"Shut, shut those juggling eyes, thou ruthless man!
Turn them aside, wretch! or the righteous ban
Of all the Gods, whose dreadful images
Here represent their shadowy presences,   280
May pierce them on the sudden with the thorn
Of painful blindness; leaving thee forlorn,
In trembling dotage to the feeblest fright
Of conscience, for their long offended might,
For all thine impious proud-heart sophistries,
Unlawful magic, and enticing lies.
Corinthians! look upon that grey-beard wretch!
Mark how, possess'd, his lashless eyelids stretch
Around his demon eyes; Corinthians, see!
My sweet bride withers at their potency."   290
"Fool!" said the sophist, in an under tone
Gruff with contempt; which a death-nighing moan
From Lycius answer'd, as heart-struck and lost,
He sank supine beside the aching ghost.
"Fool! Fool!" repeated he, while his eyes still
Relented not, nor mov'd; "from every ill
Of life have I preserv'd thee to this day,
And shall I see thee made a serpent's prey?"
Then Lamia breath'd death breath; the sophist's
          eye,
Like a sharp spear, went through her utterly,   300
Keen, cruel, perceant, stinging: she, as well
As her weak hand could any meaning tell,
Motion'd him to be silent; vainly so,
He look'd and look'd again a level—No!
"A serpent!" echoed he; no sooner said,
Than with a frightful scream she vanishèd:
And Lycius' arms were empty of delight,
As were his limbs of life, from that same night.
On the high couch he lay!—his friends came
          round—
Supported him—no pulse, or breath they
          found,   310
And, in its marriage robe, the heavy body wound.

1819   *1820*

THE FALL OF HYPERION
A DREAM

CANTO ONE

Fanatics have their dreams, wherewith they weave
A paradise for a sect; the savage too
From forth the loftiest fashion of his sleep
Guesses at Heaven; pity these have not
Trac'd upon vellum or wild Indian leaf
The shadows of melodious utterance.
But bare of laurel they live, dream, and die;
For Poesy alone can tell her dreams,—
With the fine spell of words alone can save
Imagination from the sable chain   10
And dumb enchantment—Who alive can say,
"Thou art no Poet—may'st not tell thy dreams?"
Since every man whose soul is not a clod
Hath visions, and would speak, if he had lov'd,
And been well nurtured in his mother tongue.
Whether the dream now purpos'd to rehearse
Be poet's or fanatic's will be known
When this warm scribe, my hand, is in the grave.

Methought I stood where trees of every clime,
Palm, myrtle, oak, and sycamore, and beech,   20
With plantane, and spice-blossoms, made a screen,
In neighbourhood of fountains by the noise
Soft-showering in mine ears and by the touch
Of scent, not far from roses. Turning round
I saw an arbour with a drooping roof
Of trellis vines, and bells, and larger blooms,
Like floral censers, swinging light in air;
Before its wreathèd doorway, on a mound
Of moss, was spread a feast of summer fruits,
Which, nearer seen, seem'd refuse of a meal   30
By angel tasted or our Mother Eve;
For empty shells were scatter'd on the grass,
And grape-stalks but half bare, and remnants more,
Sweet-smelling, whose pure kinds I could not know.
Still was more plenty than the fabled horn
Thrice emptied could pour forth, at banqueting
For Proserpine return'd to her own fields,
Where the white heifers low. And appetite,
More yearning than on earth I ever felt,
Growing within, I ate deliciously;   40
And, after not long, thirsted; for thereby

THE FALL OF HYPERION. CANTO ONE. **37. Proserpine:** the
mortal woman who had been made queen of the underworld was allowed to return to earth each year for six
months. Her coming marked the beginning of spring.

Stood a cool vessel of transparent juice,
Sipp'd by the wander'd bee, the which I took,
And, pledging all the mortals of the world,
And all the dead whose names are in our lips,
Drank. That full draught is parent of my theme.
No Asian poppy nor elixir fine
Of the soon-fading, jealous Caliphat,
No poison gender'd in close monkish cell,
To thin the scarlet conclave of old men,   50
Could so have rapt unwilling life away.
Among the fragrant husks and berries crush'd
Upon the grass, I struggled hard against
The domineering potion, but in vain.
The cloudy swoon came on, and down I sunk,
Like a Silenus on an antique vase.
How long I slumber'd 'tis a chance to guess.
When sense of life return'd, I started up
As if with wings, but the fair trees were gone,
The mossy mound and arbour were no more: 60
I look'd around upon the carvèd sides
Of an old sanctuary with roof august,
Builded so high, it seem'd that filmèd clouds
Might spread beneath, as o'er the stars of heaven.
So old the place was, I remember'd none
The like upon the earth: what I had seen
Of gray cathedrals, buttress'd walls, rent towers,
The superannuations of sunk realms,
Or Nature's rocks toil'd hard in waves and winds,
Seem'd but the faulture of decrepit things   70
To that eternal domèd monument.
Upon the marble at my feet there lay
Store of strange vessels, and large draperies,
Which needs had been of dyed asbestos wove,
Or in that place the moth could not corrupt,
So white the linen, so, in some, distinct
Ran imageries from a sombre loom.
All in a mingled heap confus'd there lay
Robes, golden tongs, censer and chafing-dish,
Girdles, and chains, and holy jewelries.   80

Turning from these with awe, once more I rais'd
My eyes to fathom the space every way;
The embossèd roof, the silent massy range
Of columns north and south, ending in mist
Of nothing; then to eastward, where black gates
Were shut against the sunrise evermore.
Then to the west I look'd, and saw far off
An image, huge of feature as a cloud,

48. **Caliphat:** caliphs were regarded as great leaders or sultans, the successors of Mohammed.

At level of whose feet an altar slept,
To be approach'd on either side by steps   90
And marble balustrade, and patient travail
To count with toil the innumerable degrees.
Towards the altar sober-pac'd I went,
Repressing haste, as too unholy there;
And, coming nearer, saw beside the shrine
One minist'ring; and there arose a flame.
When in mid-day the sickening east-wind
Shifts sudden to the south, the small warm rain
Melts out the frozen incense from all flowers,
And fills the air with so much pleasant health   100
That even the dying man forgets his shroud;—
Even so that lofty sacrificial fire,
Sending forth Maian incense, spread around
Forgetfulness of everything but bliss,
And clouded all the altar with soft smoke;
From whose white fragrant curtains thus I heard
Language pronounc'd: "If thou canst not ascend
These steps, die on that marble where thou art.
Thy flesh, near cousin to the common dust,
Will parch for lack of nutriment,—thy bones   110
Will wither in few years, and vanish so
That not the quickest eye could find a grain
Of what thou now art on that pavement cold.
The sands of thy short life are spent this hour,
And no hand in the universe can turn
Thy hourglass, if these gummèd leaves be burnt
Ere thou canst mount up these immortal steps."
I heard, I look'd: two senses both at once,
So fine, so subtle, felt the tyranny
Of that fierce threat and the hard task
          proposed.   120
Prodigious seem'd the toil; the leaves were yet
Burning,—when suddenly a palsied chill
Struck from the pavèd level up my limbs,
And was ascending quick to put cold grasp
Upon those streams that pulse beside the throat!
I shriek'd, and the sharp anguish of my shriek
Stung my own ears—I strove hard to escape
The numbness, strove to gain the lowest step.
Slow, heavy, deadly was my pace: the cold
Grew stifling, suffocating, at the heart;   130
And when I clasp'd my hands I felt them not.
One minute before death, my icèd foot touch'd
The lowest stair; and, as it touch'd, life seem'd

96. **One minist'ring:** a reference to Moneta, Roman goddess of memory, who is to be the teacher and guide of the poet. 103. **Maian:** Maia was one of the daughters of Atlas.

To pour in at the toes: I mounted up,
As once fair angels on a ladder flew
From the green turf to heaven. "Holy Power,"
Cried I, approaching near the hornèd shrine,
"What am I that should so be saved from death?
What am I that another death come not
To choke my utterance, sacrilegious, here?"   140
Then said the veilèd Shadow: "Thou hast felt
What 'tis to die and live again before
Thy fated hour; that thou hadst power to do so
Is thy own safety; thou hast dated on
Thy doom." "High Prophetess," said I, "purge off,
Benign, if so it please thee, my mind's film."
"None can usurp this height," returned that shade,
"But those to whom the miseries of the world
Are misery, and will not let them rest.
All else who find a haven in the world,   150
Where they may thoughtless sleep away their days,
If by a chance into this fane they come,
Rot on the pavement where thou rotted'st half."
"Are there not thousands in the world," said I,
Encourag'd by the sooth voice of the shade,
"Who love their fellows even to the death;
Who feel the giant agony of the world;
And more, like slaves to poor humanity,
Labour for mortal good? I sure should see
Other men here, but I am here alone."   160
"Those whom thou spak'st of are no visionaries,"
Rejoin'd that voice,—"they are no dreamers weak;
They seek no wonder but the human face,
No music but a happy-noted voice—
They come not here, they have no thought to
          come—
And thou art here, for thou art less than they.
What benefit canst thou do, or all thy tribe,
To the great world? Thou art a dreaming thing,
A fever of thy self—think of the earth;
What bliss, even in hope, is there for thee?   170
What haven? every creature hath its home;
Every sole man hath days of joy and pain,
Whether his labours be sublime or low—
The pain alone, the joy alone, distinct:
Only the dreamer venoms all his days,
Bearing more woe than all his sins deserve.
Therefore, that happiness be somewhat shar'd,
Such things as thou art are admitted oft
Into like gardens thou didst pass erewhile,
And suffer'd in these temples: for that cause   180
Thou standest safe beneath this statue's knees."
"That I am favour'd for unworthiness,

By such propitious parley medicin'd
In sickness not ignoble, I rejoice,
Aye, and could weep for love of such award."
So answer'd I, continuing, "If it please,
Majestic shadow, tell me: sure not all
Those melodies sung into the world's ear
Are useless: sure a poet is a sage;
A humanist, physician to all men.   190
That I am none I feel, as vultures feel
They are no birds when eagles are abroad.
What am I then: thou spakest of my tribe:
What tribe?" The tall shade veil'd in drooping
          white
Then spake, so much more earnest, that the breath
Moved the thin linen folds that drooping hung
About a golden censer from the hand
Pendent—"Art thou not of the dreamer tribe?
The poet and the dreamer are distinct,
Diverse, sheer opposite, antipodes.   200
The one pours out a balm upon the world,
The other vexes it." Then shouted I
Spite of myself, and with a Pythia's spleen,
"Apollo! faded! O far-flown Apollo!
Where is thy misty pestilence to creep
Into the dwellings, through the door crannies
Of all mock lyricists, large self-worshippers
And careless Hectorers in proud bad verse?
Though I breathe death with them it will be life
To see them sprawl before me into graves.   210
Majestic shadow, tell me where I am,
Whose altar this, for whom this incense curls;
What image this whose face I cannot see
For the broad marble knees; and who thou art,
Of accent feminine so courteous?"

Then the tall shade, in drooping linens veil'd,
Spake out, so much more earnest, that her breath
Stirr'd the thin folds of gauze that drooping hung
About a golden censer, from her hand
Pendent; and by her voice I knew she shed   220
Long-treasured tears. "This temple, sad and lone
Is all spar'd from the thunder of a war
Foughten long since by giant Hierarchy
Against rebellion: this old Image here,
Whose carvèd features wrinkled as he fell,
Is Saturn's; I, Moneta, left supreme,
Sole priestess of his desolation."—
I had no words to answer, for my tongue,
Useless, could find about its roofèd home

203. Pythia: priestess of the oracle of Apollo at Delphi.

No syllable of a fit majesty   230
To make rejoinder to Moneta's mourn:
There was a silence, while the altar's blaze
Was fainting for sweet food. I look'd thereon,
And on the pavèd floor, where nigh were piled
Faggots of cinnamon, and many heaps
Of other crispèd spicewood: then again
I look'd upon the altar, and its horns
Whiten'd with ashes, and its lang'rous flame,
And then upon the offerings again;
And so by turns—till sad Moneta cried: 240
"The sacrifice is done, but not the less
Will I be kind to thee for thy good will.
My power, which to me is still a curse,
Shall be to thee a wonder; for the scenes
Still swooning vivid through my globèd brain,
With an electral changing misery,
Thou shalt with these dull mortal eyes behold
Free from all pain, if wonder pain thee not."
As near as an immortal's spherèd words
Could to a mother's soften, were these last: 250
And yet I had a terror of her robes,
And chiefly of the veils, that from her brow
Hung pale, and curtain'd her in mysteries,
That made my heart too small to hold its blood.
This saw that Goddess, and with sacred hand
Parted the veils. Then saw I a wan face,
Not pined by human sorrows, but bright-blanch'd
By an immortal sickness which kills not;
It works a constant change, which happy death
Can put no end to; deathwards progressing   260
To no death was that visage; it had pass'd
The lily and the snow; and beyond these
I must not think now, though I saw that face.
But for her eyes I should have fled away.
They held me back with a benignant light,
Soft mitigated by divinest lids
Half closed, and visionless entire they seem'd
Of all external things—they saw me not,
But, in blank splendour, beam'd like the mild moon,
Who comforts those she sees not, who knows
        not   270
What eyes are upward cast. As I had found
A grain of gold upon a mountain's side,
And, twing'd with avarice, strain'd out my eyes
To search its sullen entrails rich with ore,
So, at the view of sad Moneta's brow,
I ached to see what things the hollow brow
Behind enwombed: what high tragedy
In the dark secret Chambers of her skull
Was acting, that could give so dread a stress

To her cold lips, and fill with such a light   280
Her planetary eyes, and touch her voice
With such a sorrow.—"Shade of Memory!"
Cried I, with act adorant at her feet,
"By all the gloom hung round thy fallen house,
By this last temple, by the golden age,
By great Apollo, thy dear foster-child,
And by thyself, forlorn divinity,
The pale Omega of a wither'd race,
Let me behold, according as thou saidst,
What in thy brain so ferments to and fro.—"   290
No sooner had this conjuration pass'd
My devout lips, than side by side we stood
(Like a stunt bramble by a solemn Pine)
Deep in the shady sadness of a vale
Far sunken from the healthy breath of morn,
Far from the fiery noon and eve's one star.
Onward I look'd beneath the gloomy boughs,
And saw what first I thought an Image huge,
Like to the Image pedestall'd so high
In Saturn's Temple; then Moneta's voice   300
Came brief upon mine ear,—"So Saturn sat
When he had lost his realms—" whereon there
        grew
A power within me of enormous ken,
To see as a god sees, and take the depth
Of things as nimbly as the outward eye
Can size and shape pervade. The lofty theme
Of those few words hung vast before my mind
With half-unravell'd web. I sat myself
Upon an eagle's watch, that I might see,
And seeing ne'er forget. No stir of life   310
Was in this shrouded vale, not so much air
As in the zoning of a summer's day
Robs not one light seed from the feather'd grass;
But where the dead leaf fell, there did it rest:
A stream went voiceless by, still deaden'd more
By reason of the fallen Divinity
Spreading more shade; the Naiad 'mid her reeds
Press'd her cold finger closer to her lips.

Along the margin sand large footmarks went
No farther than to where old Saturn's feet   320
Had rested, and there slept, how long a sleep!
Degraded, cold, upon the sodden ground
His old right hand lay nerveless, listless, dead,
Unsceptred, and his realmless eyes were clos'd;
While his bow'd head seem'd listening to the Earth,
His ancient mother, for some comfort yet.

It seem'd no force could wake him from his place;
But there came one who, with a kindred hand,

Touch'd his wide shoulders, after bending low
With reverence, though to one who knew it
    not.   330
Then came the griev'd voice of Mnemosyne,
And griev'd I hearken'd. "That divinity
Whom thou saw'st step from yon forlornest wood,
And with slow pace approach our fallen king,
Is Thea, softest-natur'd of our brood."
I mark'd the Goddess, in fair statuary
Surpassing wan Moneta by the head,
And in her sorrow nearer woman's tears.
There was a list'ning fear in her regard,
As if calamity had but begun;   340
As if the vanward clouds of evil days
Had spent their malice, and the sullen rear
Was with its storèd thunder labouring up.
One hand she press'd upon that aching spot
Where beats the human heart; as if just there,
Though an immortal, she felt cruel pain;
The other upon Saturn's bended neck
She laid, and to the level of his ear
Leaning with parted lips, some words she spoke
In solemn tenour and deep organ tone;   350
Some mourning words, which in our feeble tongue
Would come in this like accenting; how frail
To that large utterance of the early Gods!

"Saturn, look up! and for what, poor lost king?
I have no comfort for thee; no—not one;
I cannot cry, *Wherefore thus sleepest thou?*
For Heaven is parted from thee, and the Earth
Knows thee not, so afflicted, for a God.
The Ocean, too, with all its solemn noise,
Has from thy sceptre pass'd; and all the air   360
Is emptied of thy hoary Majesty.
Thy thunder, captious at the new command,
Rumbles reluctant o'er our fallen house;
And thy sharp lightning in unpractised hands
Scorches and burns our once serene domain.
With such remorseless speed still come new woes,
That unbelief has not a space to breathe.
Saturn! sleep on:—me thoughtless, why should I
Thus violate thy slumbrous solitude?
Why should I ope thy melancholy eyes?   370
Saturn! sleep on, while at thy feet I weep."

As when upon a trancèd summer night
Forests, branch-charmèd by the earnest stars,
Dream, and so dream all night, without a noise,
Save from one gradual solitary gust

331. **Mnemosyne**: the Greek name for Moneta.

Swelling upon the silence; dying off;
As if the ebbing air had but one wave,
So came those words and went; the while in tears
She press'd her fair large forehead to the earth,
Just where her fallen hair might spread in
    curls,   380
A soft and silken mat for Saturn's feet.
Long, long these two were postured motionless,
Like sculpture builded up upon the grave
Of their own power. A long awful time
I look'd upon them: still they were the same;
The frozen God still bending to the Earth,
And the sad Goddess weeping at his feet.
Moneta silent. Without stay or prop,
But my own weak mortality, I bore
The load of this eternal quietude,   390
The unchanging gloom and the three fixèd shapes
Ponderous upon my senses, a whole moon;
For by my burning brain I measured sure
Her silver seasons shedded on the night,
And every day by day methought I grew
More gaunt and ghostly. Oftentimes I pray'd
Intense, that Death would take me from the vale
And all its burthens—Gasping with despair
Of change, hour after hour I curs'd myself;
Until old Saturn rais'd his faded eyes,   400
And look'd around, and saw his kingdom gone,
And all the gloom and sorrow of the place,
And that fair kneeling Goddess at his feet.
As the moist scent of flowers, and grass, and leaves
Fills forest-dells with a pervading air,
Known to the woodland nostril, so the words
Of Saturn fill'd the mossy glooms around,
Even to the hollows of time-eaten oaks,
And to the windings in the foxes' holes,
With sad, low tones, while thus he spake, and
    sent   410
Strange musings to the solitary Pan.
"Moan, brethren, moan; for we are swallow'd up
And buried from all godlike exercise
Of influence benign on planets pale,
And peaceful sway above man's harvesting,
And all those acts which Deity supreme
Doth ease its heart of love in. Moan and wail.
Moan, brethren, moan; for lo! the rebel spheres
Spin round, the stars their antient courses keep,
Clouds still with shadowy moisture haunt the
    earth,   420
Still suck their fill of light from sun and moon,
Still buds the tree, and still the sea-shores murmur.
There is no death in all the universe,

No smell of Death—there shall be death—moan,
    moan;
Moan, Cybele, moan, for thy pernicious babes
Have changed a god into a shaking Palsy.
Moan, brethren, moan, for I have no strength left;
Weak as the reed—weak—feeble as my voice—
O, O, the pain, the pain of feebleness.
Moan, moan, for still I thaw—or give me
    help: 430
Throw down those Imps, and give me victory.
Let me hear other groans; and trumpets blown
Of triumph calm, and hymns of festival,
From the gold peaks of heaven's high pilèd clouds;
Voices of soft proclaim, and silver stir
Of strings in hollow shells; and let there be
Beautiful things made new, for the surprise
Of the sky-children—" So he feebly ceas'd,
With such a poor and sickly-sounding pause,
Methought I heard some old man of the
    earth   440
Bewailing earthly loss; nor could my eyes
And ears act with that pleasant unison of sense
Which marries sweet sound with the grace of form,
And dolourous accent from a tragic harp
With large-limb'd visions. More I scrutinized.
Still fix'd he sat beneath the sable trees,
Whose arms spread straggling in wild serpent
    forms,
With leaves all hush'd; his awful presence there
(Now all was silent) gave a deadly lie
To what I erewhile heard: only his lips   450
Trembled amid the white curls of his beard.
They told the truth, though, round, the snowy locks
Hung nobly, as upon the face of heaven
A mid day fleece of clouds. Thea arose,
And stretch'd her white arm through the hollow
    dark,
Pointing some whither: whereat he too rose
Like a vast giant seen by men at sea
To grow pale from the waves at dull midnight.
They melted from my sight into the woods:
Ere I could turn, Moneta cried, "These twain   460
Are speeding to the families of grief,
Where, roof'd in by black rocks, they waste in
    pain
And darkness for no hope."—And she spake on,
As ye may read who can unwearied pass
Onward from the Antechamber of this dream,
Where even at the open doors awhile
I must delay, and glean my memory
Of her high phrase:—perhaps no further dare.

CANTO TWO

"Mortal, that thou mayst understand aright,
I humanize my sayings to thine ear,
Making comparisons of earthly things;
Or thou might'st better listen to the wind,
Whose language is to thee a barren noise,
Though it blows legend-laden through the trees—
In melancholy realms big tears are shed,
More sorrow like to this, and such like woe,
Too huge for mortal tongue, or pen of scribe.
The Titans fierce, self-hid or prison-bound,   10
Groan for the old allegiance once more,
Listening in their doom for Saturn's voice.
But one of the whole eagle-brood still keeps
His sov'reignty, and rule, and majesty;
Blazing Hyperion on his orbèd fire
Still sits, still snuffs the incense teeming up
From man to the Sun's God—yet unsecure,
For as upon the Earth dire prodigies
Fright and perplex, so also shudders he;
Not at dog's howl, or gloom-bird's Even
    screech,   20
Or the familiar visitings of one
Upon the first toll of his passing bell:
But horrors, portion'd to a giant nerve,
Make great Hyperion ache. His palace bright,
Bastion'd with pyramids of glowing gold,
And touched with shade of bronzèd obelisks,
Glares a blood-red through all the thousand Courts,
Arches, and domes, and fiery galleries;
And all its curtains of Aurorian clouds
Flush angerly; when he would taste the
    wreaths   30
Of incense breath'd aloft from sacred hills,
Instead of sweets, his ample palate takes
Savour of poisonous brass and metals sick.
Wherefore when harbour'd in the sleepy West,
After the full completion of fair day,
For rest divine upon exalted couch
And slumber in the arms of melody,
He paces through the pleasant hours of ease,
With strides colossal, on from Hall to Hall,
While, far within each aisle and deep recess,   40
His wingèd minions in close clusters stand
Amaz'd, and full of fear; like anxious men,
Who on a wide plain gather in sad troops,
When earthquakes jar their battlements and towers.
Even now while Saturn, roused from icy trance,
Goes, step for step, with Thea from yon woods,

Hyperion, leaving twilight in the rear,
Is sloping to the threshold of the West.—
Thither we tend." Now in clear light I stood,
Relieved from the dusk vale. Mnemosyne   50
Was sitting on a square-edg'd polish'd stone,
That in its lucid depth reflected pure
Her priestess-garments. My quick eyes ran on
From stately nave to nave, from vault to vault,
Through bowers of fragrant and enwreathèd light,
And diamond-pavèd lustrous long arcades.
Anon rush'd by the bright Hyperion;
His flaming robes stream'd out beyond his heels,
And gave a roar, as if of earthly fire,
That scared away the meek ethereal hours,   60
And made their dove-wings tremble. On he flared.

* * * * * * * * * * * * * * *

1819   *1856*

TO AUTUMN

I

Season of mists and mellow fruitfulness,
    Close bosom-friend of the maturing sun;
Conspiring with him how to load and bless
    With fruit the vines that round the thatch-eves
        run;
To bend with apples the moss'd cottage-trees,
    And fill all fruit with ripeness to the core;
        To swell the gourd, and plump the hazel shells
    With a sweet kernel; to set budding more,
And still more, later flowers for the bees,
Until they think warm days will never cease,   10
        For Summer has o'er-brimm'd their clammy
            cells.

II

Who hath not seen thee oft amid thy store?
    Sometimes whoever seeks abroad may find
Thee sitting careless on a granary floor,
    Thy hair soft-lifted by the winnowing wind;
Or on a half-reap'd furrow sound asleep,
    Drows'd with the fume of poppies, while thy
        hook
        Spares the next swath and all its twinèd
            flowers:
And sometimes like a gleaner thou dost keep
    Steady thy laden head across a brook;   20

Or by a cyder-press, with patient look,
    Thou watchest the last oozings hours by hours.

III

Where are the songs of Spring? Ay, where are they?
    Think not of them, thou hast thy music too,—
While barrèd clouds bloom the soft-dying day,
    And touch the stubble-plains with rosy hue;
Then in a wailful choir the small gnats mourn
    Among the river sallows, borne aloft
        Or sinking as the light wind lives or dies;
And full-grown lambs loud bleat from hilly
        bourn;   30
    Hedge-crickets sing; and now with treble soft
    The red-breast whistles from a garden-croft;
        And gathering swallows twitter in the skies.

1819   *1820*

BRIGHT STAR

Bright star, would I were stedfast as thou art—
    Not in lone splendour hung aloft the night
And watching, with eternal lids apart,
    Like nature's patient, sleepless Eremite,
The moving waters at their priestlike task
    Of pure ablution round earth's human shores,
Or gazing on the new soft fallen mask
    Of snow upon the mountains and the moors—
No—yet still stedfast, still unchangeable,
    Pillow'd upon my fair love's ripening breast,   10
To feel for ever its soft fall and swell,
    Awake for ever in a sweet unrest,
Still, still to hear her tender-taken breath,
And so live ever—or else swoon to death.

1819   *1838*

LETTERS

I. TO BENJAMIN BAILEY

[NOVEMBER 22, 1817]

Hampstead

My dear Bailey,
    I will get over the first part of this (*unsaid*)
Letter as soon as possible for it relates to the affair

TO AUTUMN. **28.** sallows: willows. **30.** bourn: area, region.

of poor Crips—To a Man of your nature, such a Letter as Haydon's must have been extremely cutting—What occasions the greater part of the World's Quarrels? simply this, two Minds meet and do not understand each other time enough to p[r]aevent any shock or surprise at the conduct of either party—As soon as I had known Haydon three days I had got enough of his character not to have been surp[r]ised at such a Letter as he has hurt you with. Nor when I knew it was it a principle with me to drop his acquaintance although with you it would have been an imperious feeling. I wish you knew all that I think about Genius and the Heart—and yet I think you are thoroughly acquainted with my innermost breast in that respect or you could not have known me even thus long and still hold me worthy to be your dear friend. In passing however I must say of one thing that has pressed upon me lately and encreased my Humility and capability of submission and that is this truth —Men of Genius are great as certain ethereal Chemicals operating on the Mass of neutral intellect—but they have not any individuality, any determined Character. I would call the top and head of those who have a proper self Men of Power—

But I am running my head into a Subject which I am certain I could not do justice to under five years s[t]udy and 3 vols octavo—and moreover long to be talking about the Imagination—so my dear Bailey do not think of this unpleasant affair if possible—do not—I defy any ha[r]m to come of it—I defy—I'll shall write to Crips this Week and reque[s]t him to tell me all his goings on from time to time by Letter wherever I may be—it will all go on well—so dont because you have suddenly discover'd a Coldness in Haydon suffer yourself to be teased. Do not my dear fellow. O I wish I was as certain of the end of all your troubles as that of your momentary start about the authenticity of the Imagination. I am certain of nothing but of the holiness of the Heart's affections and the truth of Imagination—What the imagination seizes as Beauty must be truth—whether it existed before or not—for I have the same Idea of all our Passions as of Love they are all in their sublime, creative of essential Beauty—In a Word, you may know my favorite Speculation by my first Book and the little song I sent in my last—which is a representation from the fancy of the probable mode of operating in these Matters—The Imagination may be compared to

Adam's dream[1]—he awoke and found it truth. I am the more zealous in this affair, because I have never yet been able to perceive how any thing can be known for truth by consequitive reasoning— and yet it must be—Can it be that even the greatest Philosopher ever (~~when~~) arrived at his goal without putting aside numerous objections—However it may be, O for a Life of Sensations rather than of Thoughts. It is "a Vision of the form of Youth" a Shadow of reality to come—and this consideration had further conv[i]nced me for it has come as auxiliary to another favorite Speculation of mine, that we shall enjoy ourselves here after by having what we called happiness on Earth repeated in a finer tone and so repeated—And yet such a fate can only befall those who delight in sensation rather than hunger as you do after Truth—Adam's dream will do here and seems to be a conviction that Imagination and its empyreal reflection is the same as human Life and its spiritual repetition. But as I was saying—the simple imaginative Mind may have its rewards in the repeti[ti]on of its own silent Working coming continually on the spirit with a fine suddenness—to compare great things with small —have you never by being surprised with an old Melody—in a delicious place—by a delicious voice, fe[l]t over again your very speculations and surmises at the time it first operated on your soul—do you not remember forming to yourself the singer's face more beautiful than it was possible and yet with the elevation of the Moment you did not think so—even then you were mounted on the Wings of Imagination so high—that the Prototype must be here after—that delicious face you will see—What a time! I am continually running away from the subject—sure this cannot be exactly the case with a complex Mind—one that is imaginative and at the same time careful of its fruits—who would exist partly on sensation partly on thought—to whom it is necessary that years should bring the philosophic Mind—such an one I consider your's and therefore it is necessary to your eternal Happiness that you not only drink this old Wine of Heaven which I shall call the redigestion of our most ethereal Musings on Earth; but also increase in knowledge and know all things. I am glad to hear you are in a fair Way for Easter—you will soon get through your unpleasant reading and then!

1. *Paradise Lost*, VIII, 452–90.

—but the world is full of troubles and I have not much reason to think myself pesterd with many—I think Jane or Marianne[2] has a better opinion of me than I deserve—for really and truly I do not think my Brothers illness connected with mine—you know more of the real Cause than they do—nor have I any chance of being rack'd as you have been —you perhaps at one time thought there was such a thing as Worldly Happiness to be arrived at, at certain periods of time marked out—you have of necessity from your disposition been thus led away —I scarcely remember counting upon any Happiness—I look not for it if it be not in the present hour—nothing startles me beyond the Moment. The setting sun will always set me to rights—or if a Sparrow come before my Window I take part in its existince and pick about the Gravel. . . .

Your affectionate friend
JOHN KEATS—

II. TO GEORGE AND THOMAS KEATS

[DECEMBER 21, 1817]
Hampstead Sunday

My dear Brothers,

I must crave your pardon for not having written ere this.°°° I saw Kean[3] return to the public in Richard III, & finely he did it, & at the request of Reynolds I went to criticise his Luke in Riches— the critique is in todays champion, which I send you with the Examiner in which you will find very proper lamentation on the obsoletion of christmas Gambols & pastimes: but it was mixed up with so much egotism of that drivelling nature that pleasure is entirely lost. Hone the publisher's trial, you must find very amusing; & as Englishmen very ~~amusing~~ encouraging—his *Not Guilty* is a thing, which not to have been, would have dulled still more Liberty's Emblazoning—Lord Ellenborough has been paid in his own coin—Wooler & Hone[4] have done us an essential service—I have had two very pleasant evenings with Dilke[5] yesterday & today; & am at this moment just come from him & feel in the humour to go on with this, began in the morning, & from which he came to fetch me. I spent Friday evening with Wells & went the next morning to see *Death on the Pale horse*. It is a wonderful picture, when West's[6] age is considered; But there is nothing to be intense upon; no women one feels mad to kiss; no face swelling into reality. the excellence of every Art is its intensity, capable of making all disagreeables evaporate, from their being in close relationship with Beauty & Truth— Examine King Lear & you will find this examplified throughout; but in this picture we have unpleasantness without any momentous depth of speculation excited, in which to bury its repulsiveness—The picture is larger than Christ rejected—I dined with Haydon the sunday after you left, & had a very pleasant day, I dined too (for I have been out too much lately) with Horace Smith & met his two Brothers with Hill & Kingston & one Du Bois,[7] they only served to convince me, how superior humour is to wit in respect to enjoyment—These men say things which make one start, without making one feel, they are all alike; their manners are alike; they all know fashionables; they have a mannerism in their very eating & drinking, in their mere handling a Decanter—They talked of Kean & his low company—Would I were with that company instead of yours said I to myself! I know such like acquaintance will never do for me & yet I am going to Reynolds, on wednesday—Brown & Dilke walked with me & back from the Christmas pantomime. I had not a dispute but a disquisition with Dilke, on various subjects; several things dovetailed in my mind, & at once it struck me, what quality went to form a Man of Achievement especially in Literature & which Shakespeare posessed so enormously—I mean *Negative Capability*, that is when man is capable of being in uncertainties, Mysteries, doubts, without any irritable reaching after fact & reason— Coleridge, for instance, would let go by a fine isolated verisimilitude caught from the Penetralium of mystery, from being incapable of remaining con-

---

2. **Jane . . . Marianne:** sisters of John Hamilton Reynolds. 3. **Kean:** Edmund Kean (1787–1833), the famous Shakesperean actor. 4. **Wooler & Hone:** two liberals recently acquitted on a charge of libel. Lord Ellenborough was an eminent conservative judge.

5. **Dilke:** Charles Dilke (1789–1864), friend of Keats, a writer for several journals, and for a time editor of *The Athenaeum.* 6. **West:** Benjamin West (1738–1820), painter and for a time president of the Royal Academy. 7. **Horace Smith . . . Du Bois:** a group of literary men of the day.

tent with half knowledge. This pursued through Volumes would perhaps take us no further than this, that with a great poet the sense of Beauty overcomes every other consideration, or rather obliterates all consideration.

Shelley's poem[8] is out, & there are words about its being objected too, as much as Queen Mab was. Poor Shelley I think he has his Quota of good qualities, in sooth la!! Write soon to your most sincere friend & affectionate Brother.

JOHN

III. TO J. H. REYNOLDS

[FEBRUARY 3, 1818]

Hampstead Tuesday

My dear Reynolds,

I thank you for your dish of Filberts—Would I could get a basket of them by way of desert every day for the sum of two pence—[9] Would we were a sort of ethereal Pigs, & turn'd loose to feed upon spiritual Mast & Acorns—which would be merely being a squirrel & feed upon filberts. for what is a squirrel but an airy pig, or a filbert but a sort of archangelical acorn. About the nuts being worth cracking, all I can say is that there are a throng of delightful Images ready drawn simplicity is the only thing. the first is the best on account of the first line, and the "arrow—foil'd of its antler'd food" —and moreover (and this is the only word or two I find fault with, the more because I have had so much reason to shun it as a quicksand) the last has "tender and true"—We must cut this, and not be rattlesnaked into any more of the like—It may be said that we ought to read our Contemporaries. that Wordsworth &c should have their due from us. but for the sake of a few fine imaginative or domestic passages, are we to be bullied into a certain Philosophy engendered in the whims of an Egotist— Every man has his speculations, but every man does not brood and peacock over them till he makes a false coinage and deceives himself—Many a man can travel to the very bourne of Heaven, and yet want confidence to put down his halfseeing. Sancho will invent a Journey heavenward as well as any

body. We hate poetry that has a palpable design upon us—and if we do not agree seems to put its hand in its breeches pocket. Poetry should be great & unobtrusive, a thing which enters into one's soul, and does not startle it or amaze it with itself but with its subject.—How beautiful are the retired flowers! how would they lose their beauty were they to throng into the highway crying out, "admire me I am a violet! dote upon me I am a primrose!" Modern poets differ from the Elizabethans in this. Each of the moderns like an Elector of Hanover governs his petty state, & knows how many straws are swept daily from the Causeways in all his dominions & has a continual itching that all the Housewives should have their coppers well scoured: the antients were Emperors of vast Provinces, they had only heard of the remote ones and scarcely cared to visit them.—I will cut all this—I will have no more of Wordsworth or Hunt in particular— Why should we be of the tribe of Manasseh, when we can wander with Esau? why should we kick against the Pricks, when we can walk on Roses? Why should we be owls, when we can be Eagles? Why be teased with "nice Eyed wagtails," [10] when we have in sight "the Cherub Contemplation"? [11] —Why with Wordsworth "Matthew with a bough of wilding in his hand" when we can have Jacques "under an oak" &c[12]—The secret of the Bough of Wilding will run through your head faster than I can write it—Old Matthew spoke to him some years ago on some nothing, & because he happens in an Evening Walk to imagine the figure of the old man —he must stamp it down in black & white, and it is henceforth sacred—I don't mean to deny Wordsworth's grandeur & Hunt's merit, but I mean to say we need not be teazed with grandeur & merit— when we can have them uncontaminated & unobtrusive. Let us have the old Poets, & Robin Hood Your letter and its sonnets gave me more pleasure than will the 4th Book of Childe Harold & the whole of any body's life & opinions. . . .

Yr sincere friend and Coscribbler

JOHN KEATS—

---

8. **Shelley's poem:** *Laon and Cythna,* later converted into *The Revolt of Islam.* 9. a reference to two sonnets on Robin Hood by Reynolds.

10. "nice . . . wagtails": a quotation from Leigh Hunt, poet and friend of Keats. 11. "**the Cherub Contemplation**": Milton, *Il Penseroso,* l. 54. 12. "**under an oak**": Shakespeare, *As You Like It,* II, i, 31.

IV. TO J. H. REYNOLDS

[MAY 3, 1818]

Teignmouth

My dear Reynolds,

... Have you not seen a Gull, an orc, a sea Mew, or any thing to bring this Line to a proper length, and also fill up this clear part; that like the Gull I may *dip*—I hope, not out of sight—and also, like a Gull, I hope to be lucky in a good sized fish— This crossing a letter is not without its association —for chequer work leads us naturally to a Milk-maid, a Milkmaid to Hogarth Hogarth to Shake-speare Shakespear to Hazlitt—Hazlitt to Shake-speare and thus by merely pulling an apron string we set a pretty peal of Chimes at work—Let them chime on while, with your patience,—I will return to Wordsworth—whether or no he has an extended vision or a circumscribed grandeur—whether he is an eagle in his nest, or on the wing—And to be more explicit and to show you how tall I stand by the giant, I will put down a simile of human life as far as I now perceive it; that is, to the point to which I say we both have arrived—Well—I com-pare human life to a large Mansion of Many Apart-ments, two of which I can only describe, the doors of the rest being as yet shut upon me—The first we step into we call the infant or thoughtless Chamber, in which we remain as long as we do not think—We remain there a long while, and notwith-standing the doors of the second Chamber remain wide open, showing a bright appearance, we care not to hasten to it; but are at length imperceptibly impelled by the awakening of the thinking principle —within us—we no sooner get into the second Chamber, which I shall call the Chamber of Maiden-Thought, than we become intoxicated with the light and the atmosphere, we see nothing but pleasant wonders, and think of delaying there for ever in delight: However among the effects this breathing is father of is that tremendous one of sharpening one's vision into the heart and nature of Man—of convincing ones nerves that the World is full of Misery and Heartbreak, Pain, Sickness and oppression—whereby This Chamber of Maiden Thought becomes gradually darken'd and at the same time on all sides of it many doors are set open —but all dark—all leading to dark passages—We see not the ballance of good and evil. We are in a Mist—*We* are now in that state—We feel the "bur-den of the Mystery," To this point was Wordsworth come, as far as I can conceive when he wrote "Tintern Abbey" and it seems to me that his Genius is explorative of those dark Passages. Now if we live, and go on thinking, we too shall explore them. he is a Genius and superior [to] us, in so far as he can, more than we, make discoveries, and shed a light in them—Here I must think Wordsworth is deeper than Milton—though I think it has de-pended more upon the general and gregarious advance of intellect, than individual greatness of Mind—From the Paradise Lost and the other Works of Milton, I hope it is not too presuming, even between ourselves to say, his Philosophy, human and divine, may be tolerably understood by one not much advanced in years, In his time en-glishmen were just emancipated from a great super-stition—and Men had got hold of certain points and resting places in reasoning which were too newly born to be doubted, and too much opposed by the Mass of Europe not to be thought etherial and authentically divine—who could gainsay his ideas on virtue, vice, and Chastity in Comus, just at the time of the dismissal of Cod-pieces and a hundred other disgraces? who would not rest satis-fied with his hintings at good and evil in the Paradise Lost, when just free from the inquisition and burrning in Smithfield? The Reformation pro-duced such immediate and great benefits, that Protestantism was considered under the immediate eye of heaven, and its own remaining Dogmas and superstitions, then, as it were, regenerated, consti-tuted those resting places and seeming sure points of Reasoning—from that I have mentioned, Milton, whatever he may have thought in the sequel, ap-pears to have been content with these by his writings—He did not think into the human heart, as Wordsworth has done—Yet Milton as a Philos-op[h]er, had sure as great powers as Wordsworth —What is then to be inferr'd? O many things—It proves there is really a grand march of intellect—, It proves that a mighty providence subdues the mightiest Minds to the service of the time being, whether it be in human Knowledge or Religion—I have often pitied a Tutor who has to hear "Nom^e: Musa" [13]—so often dinn'd into his ears—I hope you

13. "Nom^e: Musa": the familiar beginning of the first declension in Latin grammar: "Nominative Case: Musa."

may not have the same pain in this scribbling—I may have read these things before, but I never had even a thus dim perception of them; and moreover I like to say my lesson to one who will endure my tediousness for my own sake—After all there is certainly something real in the World—Moore's present to Hazlitt is real—I like that Moore, and am glad [that] I saw him at the Theatre just before I left Town. Tom[14] has spit a leetle blood this afternoon, and that is rather a damper—but I know—the truth is there is something real in the World Your third Chamber of Life shall be a lucky and a gentle one—stored with the wine of love—and the Bread of Friendship—When you see George if he should not have recēd a letter from me tell him he will find one at home most likely—tell Bailey I hope soon to see him—Remember me to all The leaves have been out here, for MONY a day—I have written to George for the first stanzas of my Isabel—I shall have them soon and will copy the whole out for you.

Your affectionate friend
JOHN KEATS—

V. TO J. A. HESSEY

[OCTOBER 8, 1818]

My dear Hessey,

You are very good in sending me the letter from the Chronicle—and I am very bad in not acknowledging such a kindness sooner.—pray forgive me.—It has so chanced that I have had that paper every day—I have seen today's. I cannot but feel indebted to those Gentlemen who have taken my part—As for the rest, I begin to get a little acquainted with my own strength and weakness.—Praise or blame has but a momentary effect on the man whose love of beauty in the abstract makes him a severe critic of his own Works. My own domestic criticism has given me pain without comparison beyond what Blackwood or the Quarterly could possibly inflict. and also when I feel I am right, no external praise can give me such a glow as my own solitary reperception & ratification of what is fine. J. S.[15] is perfectly right in regard to

the slip-shod Endymion. That it is so is no fault of mine.—No!—though it may sound a little paradoxical. It is as good as I had power to make it—by myself—Had I been nervous about its being a perfect piece, & with that view asked advice, & trembled over every page, it would not have been written; for it is not in my nature to fumble—I will write independently.—I have written independently *without Judgment*.—I may write independently & *with judgment* hereafter.—The Genius of Poetry must work out its own salvation in a man: It cannot be matured by law & precept, but by sensation & watchfulness in itself—That which is creative must create itself—In Endymion, I leaped headlong into the Sea, and thereby have become better acquainted with the Soundings, the quicksands, & the rocks, than if I had stayed upon the green shore, and piped a silly pipe, and took tea & comfortable advice.—I was never afraid of failure; for I would sooner fail than not be among the greatest—But I am nigh getting into a rant. So, with remembrances to Taylor and Woodhouse[16] &c I am

Yrs very sincerely
JOHN KEATS—

VI. TO RICHARD WOODHOUSE

[OCTOBER 27, 1818]

My dear Woodhouse,

Your Letter gave me a great satisfaction; more on account of its friendliness, than any relish of that matter in it which is accounted so acceptable in the 'genus irritabile' [17] The best answer I can give you is in a clerklike manner to make some observations on two principle points, which seem to point like indices into the midst of the whole pro and con, about genius, and views and atchievements and ambition and coetera. 1st As to the poetical Character itself, (I mean that sort of which, if I am any thing, I am a Member; that sort distinguished from the wordsworthian or egotistical sublime; which is a thing per se and stands alone) it is not itself—it has no self—it is every thing and nothing—It has no character—it enjoys light and shade; it lives in

---

14. **Tom:** Keats's brother. 15. **J.S.:** Other critics have speculated that J.S. is John Scott, a critic of Keats's early work.

16. **Woodhouse:** Richard Woodhouse (1788–1834), friend of Keats, admirer of his poetry, lawyer and editor for Taylor and Hessey, Keats's publishers. 17. *'genus irritabile'*: a reference to poets as the "irritable race." (See Horace, *Epistles,* II, ii, 102.)

gusto, be it foul or fair, high or low, rich or poor, mean or elevated—It has as much delight in conceiving an Iago as an Imogen. What shocks the virtuous philosop[h]er, delights the camelion Poet. It does no harm from its relish of the dark side of things any more than from its taste for the bright one; because they both end in speculation. A Poet is the most unpoetical of any thing in existence; because he has no Identity—he is continually in for—and filling some other Body—The Sun, the Moon, the Sea and Men and Women who are creatures of impulse are poetical and have about them an unchangeable attribute—the poet has none; no identity—he is certainly the most unpoetical of all God's Creatures. If then he has no self, and if I am a Poet, where is the Wonder that I should say I would write no more? Might I not at that very instant [have] been cogitating on the Characters of Saturn and Ops? It is a wretched thing to confess; but is a very fact that not one word I ever utter can be taken for granted as an opinion growing out of my identical nature—how can it, when I have no nature? When I am in a room with People if I ever am free from speculating on creations of my own brain, then not myself goes home to myself: but the identity of every one in the room begins to press upon me that, I am in a very little time anhilated—not only among Men; it would be the same in a Nursery of children: I know not whether I make myself wholly understood: I hope enough so to let you see that no dependence is to be placed on what I said that day.

In the second place I will speak of my views, and of the life I purpose to myself—I am ambitious of doing the world some good: if I should be spared that may be the work of maturer years—in the interval I will assay to reach to as high a summit in Poetry as the nerve bestowed upon me will suffer. The faint conceptions I have of Poems to come brings the blood frequently into my forehead—All I hope is that I may not lose all interest in human affairs—that the solitary indifference I feel for applause even from the finest Spirits, will not blunt any acuteness of vision I may have. I do not think it will—I feel assured I should write from the mere yearning and fondness I have for the Beautiful even if my night's labours should be burnt every morning and no eye ever shine upon them. But even now I am perhaps not speaking from myself; but from some character in whose soul I now live.

I am sure however that this next sentence is from myself. I feel your anxiety, good opinion and friendliness in the highest degree, and am

Your's most sincerely
JOHN KEATS—

VII. TO GEORGE AND GEORGIANA KEATS

[APRIL 21, 1819]

My dear Brother & Sister,

... The common cognomen of this world among the misguided and superstitious is "a vale of tears" from which we are to be redeemed by a certain arbitra[r]y interposition of God and taken to Heaven—What a little circumscribed straightene[d] notion! Call the world if you Please "The vale of Soul-making." Then you will find out the use of the world (I am speaking now in the highest terms for human nature, admitting it to be immortal, which I will here take for granted for the purpose of showing a thought which has struck me concerning it) I say "*Soul-making*" Soul as distinguished from an Intelligence—There may be intelligences or sparks of the divinity in millions—but they are not Souls till they acquire identities, till each one is personally itself. Intelligences are atoms of perception—they know and they see and they are pure, in short they are God—how then are Souls to be made? How then are these sparks which are God to have identity given them—so as ever to possess a bliss peculiar to each one's individual existence? How, but by the medium of a world like this? This point I sincerely wish to consider because I think it a grander system of salvation than the Christian religion—or rather it is a system of Spirit-creation—This is effected by three grand materials acting the one upon the other for a series of years—These three Materials are the *Intelligence*—the *human heart* (as distinguished from intelligence or Mind) and the *World* or *Elemental space* suited for the proper action of *Mind and Heart* on each other for the purpose of forming the *Soul* or *Intelligence destined to possess the sense of Identity*. I can scarcely express what I but dimly perceive—and yet I think I perceive it—that you may judge the more clearly I will put it in the most homely form possible—I will call the *world* a School instituted for the purpose of teaching little children to read—I will call the *human heart* the *horn Book* used in that School—and I will call the *Child able to read, the Soul* made from that *school* and its *hornbook.* Do you not see how necessary a World of Pains and troubles is to school an Intelligence and make it a soul? A Place where the heart must feel and suffer in a thousand diverse ways! Not merely is the Heart a Hornbook, It is the Mind's Bible, it is the Mind's experience, it is the teat from which the Mind or intelligence sucks its identity—As various as the Lives of Men are—so various become their souls, and thus does God make individual beings, Souls, Identical Souls of the sparks of his own essence—This appears to me a faint sketch of a system of Salvation which does not affront our reason and humanity—I am convinced that many difficulties which Christians labor under would vanish before it—There is one which even now Strikes me—the Salvation of Children— In them the Spark or intelligence returns to God without any identity—it having had no time to learn of, and be altered by, the heart—or seat of the human Passions—It is pretty generally suspected that the Christian scheme has been copied from the ancient Persian and Greek Philosophers. Why may they not have made this simple thing even more simple for common apprehension by introducing Mediators and Personages in the same manner as in the heathen mythology abstractions are personified—Seriously I think it probable that this System of Soul-making—may have been the Parent of all the more palpable and personal Schemes of Redemption, among the Zoroastrians the Christians and the Hindoos. For as one part of the human species must have their carved Jupiter; so another part must have the palpable and named Mediatior and savior, their Christ their Oromanes and their Vishnu—If what I have said should not be plain enough, as I fear it may not be, I will put you in the place where I began in this series of thoughts—I mean, I began by seeing how man was formed by circumstances—and what are circumstances but touchstones of his heart? and what are touchstones but provings of his heart? and what are provings of his heart but fortifiers or alterers of his nature? and what is his altered nature but his Soul?—and what was his Soul before it came into the world and had these provings and alterations and perfectionings?—An intelligence without Identity—and how is this Identity to be made? Through

the medium of the Heart? And how is the heart to become this Medium but in a world of Circumstances?—There now I think what with Poetry and Theology you may thank your Stars that my pen is not very long-winded—Yesterday I received two Letters from your Mother and Henry which I shall send by young Birkbeck with this . . .

> Your ever Affectionate Brother
> JOHN KEATS—

VIII. TO PERCY BYSSHE SHELLEY

[AUGUST 16, 1820]

Hampstead

My dear Shelley,

I am very much gratified that you, in a foreign country, and with a mind almost over occupied, should write to me in the strain of the Letter beside me. If I do not take advantage of your invitation it will be prevented by a circumstance I have very much at heart to prophesy—There is no doubt that an english winter would put an end to me, and do so in a lingering hateful manner, therefore I must either voyage or journey to Italy as a soldier marches up to a battery. My nerves at present are the worst part of me, yet they feel soothed when I think that come what extreme may, I shall not be destined to remain in one spot long enough to take a hatred of any four particular bed-posts. I am glad you take any pleasure in my poor Poem;—which I would willingly take the trouble to unwrite, if possible, did I care so much as I have done about Reputation. I received a copy of the Cenci, as from yourself from Hunt. There is only one part of it I am judge of; the Poetry, and dramatic effect, which by many spirits now a days is considered the mammon. A modern work it is said must have a purpose, which may be the God—*an artist* must serve Mammon—he must have "self concentration" selfishness perhaps. You I am sure will forgive me for sincerely remarking that you might curb your magnanimity and be more of an artist, and 'load every rift' of your subject with ore. The thought of such discipline must fall like cold chains upon you, who perhaps never sat with your wings furl'd for six Months together. And is not this extraordina[r]y talk for the writer of Endymion? whose mind was like a pack of scattered cards—I am pick'd up and sorted to a pip. My Imagination is a Monastry and

I am its Monk—you must explain my metap^cs [18] to yourself. I am in expectation of Prometheus every day. Could I have my own wish for its interest effected you would have it still in manuscript —or be but now putting an end to the second act. I remember you advising me not to publish my first-blights, on Hampstead heath—I am returning advice upon your hands. Most of the Poems in the volume I send you have been written above two years, and would never have been publish'd but from a hope of gain; so you see I am inclined enough to take your advice now. I must exp[r]ess once more my deep sense of your kindness, adding my sincere thanks and respects for Mrs Shelley. In the hope of soon seeing you [I] remain

most sincerely [yours,]
JOHN KEATS—

18. metap^cs: metaphysics.

Selected Modern Critical Essays

◆————————

Alfred North Whitehead

THE ROMANTIC REACTION*

My last lecture described the influence upon the eighteenth century of the narrow and efficient scheme of scientific concepts which it had inherited from its predecessor. That scheme was the product of a mentality which found the Augustinian theology extremely congenial. The Protestant Calvinism and the Catholic Jansenism exhibited man as helpless to co-operate with Irresistible Grace: the contemporary scheme of science exhibited man as helpless to co-operate with the irresistible mechanism of nature. The mechanism of God and the mechanism of matter were the monstrous issues of limited metaphysics and clear logical intellect. Also the seventeenth century had genius, and cleared the world of muddled thought. The eighteenth century

continued the work of clearance, with ruthless efficiency. The scientific scheme has lasted longer than the theological scheme. Mankind soon lost interest in Irresistible Grace; but it quickly appreciated the competent engineering which was due to science. Also in the first quarter of the eighteenth century, George Berkeley launched his philosophical criticism against the whole basis of the system. He failed to disturb the dominant current of thought. In my last lecture I developed a parallel line of argument, which would lead to a system of thought basing nature upon the concept of organism, and not upon the concept of matter. In the present lecture, I propose in the first place to consider how the concrete educated thought of men has viewed this opposition of mechanism and organism. It is in literature that the concrete outlook of humanity receives its expression. Accordingly it is to literature that we must look, particularly in its more concrete forms, namely in poetry and in drama, if we hope to discover the inward thoughts of a generation.

We quickly find that the Western peoples exhibit on a colossal scale a peculiarity which is popularly supposed to be more especially characteristic of the Chinese. Surprise is often expressed that a Chinaman can be of two religions, a Confucian for some occasions and a Buddhist for other occasions. Whether this is true of China I do not know; nor do I know whether, if true, these two attitudes are really inconsistent. But there can be no doubt that an analogous fact is true of the West, and that the two attitudes involved are inconsistent. A scientific realism, based on mechanism, is conjoined with an unwavering belief in the world of men and of the higher animals as being composed of self-determining organisms. This radical inconsistency at the basis of modern thought accounts for much that is half-hearted and wavering in our civilisation. It would be going too far to say that it distracts thought. It enfeebles it, by reason of the inconsistency lurking in the background. After all, the men of the Middle Ages were in pursuit of an excellency of which we have nearly forgotten the existence. They set before themselves the ideal of the attainment of a harmony of the understanding. We are content with superficial orderings from diverse arbitrary starting points. For instance, the enterprises produced by the individualistic energy of the European peoples presuppose physical actions directed to final causes. But the science which is employed in their development is based on a philosophy which asserts that physical causation is supreme, and which disjoins the physical cause from the final end. It is not popular to dwell on the absolute contradiction here involved. It is the fact, however you gloze it over with phrases. Of course, we find in the eighteenth century Paley's famous argument, that mechanism presupposes a God who is the author of nature. But even before Paley put the argument into its final form, Hume had written the retort, that the God whom you will find will be the sort of God who makes that mechanism. In other words, that mechanism can, at most, presuppose a mechanic, and not merely *a* mechanic but *its* mechanic. The only way of mitigating mechanism is by the discovery that it is not mechanism.

When we leave apologetic theology, and come to ordinary literature, we find, as we might expect, that the scientific outlook is in general simply ignored. So far as the mass of literature is concerned, science might never have been heard of. Until recently nearly all writers have been soaked in classical and renaissance literature. For the most part, neither philosophy nor science interested them, and their minds were trained to ignore them.

There are exceptions to this sweeping statement; and, even if we confine ourselves to English literature, they concern some of the greatest names; also the indirect influence of science has been considerable.

A sidelight on this distracting inconsistency in modern thought is obtained by examining some of those great serious poems in English literature, whose general scale gives them a didactic character. The relevant poems are Milton's *Paradise Lost*, Pope's *Essay on Man*. Wordsworth's *Excursion*, Tennyson's *In Memoriam*. Milton, though he is writing after the Restoration, voices the theological aspect of the earlier portion of his century, untouched by the influence of the scientific materialism. Pope's poem represents the effect on popular thought of the intervening sixty years which includes the first period of assured triumph for the scientific movement. Wordsworth in his whole being expresses a conscious reaction against the mentality of the eighteenth century. This mentality means nothing else than the acceptance of the scientific ideas at their full face value. Wordsworth was not bothered by any intellectual antagonism. What moved him was a moral repulsion. He felt that something had been left out, and that what had been left out comprised everything that was most important. Tennyson is the mouthpiece of the attempts of the waning romantic movement in the second quarter of the nineteenth century to come to terms with science. By this time the two elements in modern thought had disclosed their fundamental divergence by their jarring interpretations of the course of nature and the life of man. Tennyson stands in this poem as the perfect example of the distraction which I have already mentioned. There are opposing visions of the world, and both of them command his assent by appeals to ultimate intuitions from which there seems no escape. Tennyson goes to the heart of the difficulty. It is the problem of mechanism which appalls him,

" 'The stars,' she whispers, 'blindly run.' "

This line states starkly the whole philosophic problem implicit in the poem. Each molecule blindly runs. The human body is a collection of molecules.

Therefore, the human body blindly runs, and therefore there can be no individual responsibility for the actions of the body. If you once accept that the molecule is definitely determined to be what it is, independently of any determination by reason of the total organism of the body, and if you further admit that the blind run is settled by the general mechanical laws, there can be no escape from this conclusion. But mental experiences are derivative from the actions of the body, including of course its internal behaviour. Accordingly, the sole function of the mind is to have at least some of its experiences settled for it, and to add such others as may be open to it independently of the body's motions, internal and external.

There are then two possible theories as to the mind. You can either deny that it can supply for itself any experiences other than those provided for it by the body, or you can admit them.

If you refuse to admit the additional experiences, then all individual moral responsibility is swept away. If you do admit them, then a human being may be responsible for the state of his mind though he has no responsibility for the actions of his body. The enfeeblement of thought in the modern world is illustrated by the way in which this plain issue is avoided in Tennyson's poem. There is something kept in the background, a skeleton in the cupboard. He touches on almost every religious and scientific problem, but carefully avoids more than a passing allusion to this one.

This very problem was in full debate at the date of the poem. John Stuart Mill was maintaining his doctrine of determinism. In this doctrine volitions are determined by motives, and motives are expressible in terms of antecedent conditions including states of mind as well as states of the body.

It is obvious that this doctrine affords no escape from the dilemma presented by a thoroughgoing mechanism. For if the volition affects the state of the body, then the molecules in the body do not blindly run. If the volition does not affect the state of the body, the mind is still left in its uncomfortable position.

Mill's doctrine is generally accepted, especially among scientists, as though in some way it allowed you to accept the extreme doctrine of materialistic mechanism, and yet mitigated its unbelievable consequences. It does nothing of the sort. Either the bodily molecules blindly run, or they do not. If they do blindly run, the mental states are irrelevant in discussing the bodily actions.

I have stated the arguments concisely, because in truth the issue is a very simple one. Prolonged discussion is merely a source of confusion. The question as to the metaphysical status of molecules does not come in. The statement that they are mere formulae has no bearing on the argument. For presumably the formulae mean something. If they mean nothing, the whole mechanical doctrine is likewise without meaning, and the question drops. But if the formulae mean anything, the argument applies to exactly what they do mean. The traditional way of evading the difficulty—other than the simple way of ignoring it—is to have recourse to some form of what is now termed "vitalism." This doctrine is really a compromise. It allows a free run to mechanism throughout the whole of inanimate nature, and holds that the mechanism is partially mitigated within living bodies. I feel that this theory is an unsatisfactory compromise. The gap between living and dead matter is too vague and problematical to bear the weight of such an arbitrary assumption, which involves an essential dualism somewhere.

The doctrine which I am maintaining is that the whole concept of materialism only applies to very abstract entities, the products of logical discernment. The concrete enduring entities are organisms, so that the plan of the *whole* influences the very characters of the various subordinate organisms which enter into it. In the case of an animal, the mental states enter into the plan of the total organism and thus modify the plans of the successive subordinate organisms until the ultimate smallest organisms, such as electrons, are reached. Thus an electron within a living body is different from an electron outside it, by reason of the plan of the body. The electron blindly runs either within or without the body; but it runs within the body in accordance with its character within the body; that is to say, in accordance with the general plan of the body, and this plan includes the mental state. But the principle of modification is perfectly general throughout nature, and represents no property peculiar to living bodies. In subsequent lectures it will be explained that this doctrine involves the abandonment of the traditional scientific materialism, and the substitution of an alternative doctrine of organism.

I shall not discuss Mill's determinism, as it lies outside the scheme of these lectures. The foregoing discussion has been directed to secure that either determinism or free will shall have some relevance, unhampered by the difficulties introduced by materialistic mechanism, or by the compromise of vitalism. I would term the doctrine of these lectures, the theory of *organic mechanism*. In this theory, the molecules may blindly run in accordance with the general laws, but the molecules differ in their intrinsic characters according to the general organic plans of the situations in which they find themselves.

The discrepancy between the materialistic mechanism of science and the moral intuitions, which are presupposed in the concrete affairs of life, only gradually assumed its true importance as the centuries advanced. The different tones of the successive epochs to which the poems, already mentioned, belong are curiously reflected in their opening passages. Milton ends his introduction with the prayer,

"That to the height of this great argument
I may assert eternal Providence
And justify the ways of God to men."

To judge from many modern writers on Milton, we might imagine that the *Paradise Lost* and the *Paradise Regained* were written as a series of experiments in blank verse. This was certainly not Milton's view of his work. To "justify the ways of God to men" was very much his main object. He recurs to the same idea in the *Samson Agonistes*.

"Just are the ways of God
And justifiable to men."

We note the assured volume of confidence, untroubled by the coming scientific avalanche. The actual date of the publication of the *Paradise Lost* lies just beyond the epoch to which it belongs. It is the swan-song of a passing world of untroubled certitude.

A comparison between Pope's *Essay on Man* and the *Paradise Lost* exhibits the change of tone in English thought in the fifty or sixty years which separate the age of Milton from the age of Pope. Milton addresses his poem to God, Pope's poem is addressed to Lord Bolingbroke,

"Awake, my St. John! leave all meaner things
To low ambition and the pride of kings.
Let us (since life can little more supply

Than just to look about us and to die)
Expatiate free o'er all this scene of man;
A mighty maze! but not without a plan."

Compare the jaunty assurance of Pope,

"A mighty maze! but not without a plan."

with Milton's

"Just are the ways of God
And justifiable to men."

But the real point to notice is that Pope as well as Milton was untroubled by the great perplexity which haunts the modern world. The clue which Milton followed was to dwell on the ways of God in dealings with man. Two generations later we find Pope equally confident that the enlightened methods of modern science provided a plan adequate as a map of the "mighty maze."

Wordsworth's *Excursion* is the next English poem on the same subject. A prose preface tells us that it is a fragment of a larger projected work described as "A philosophical poem containing views of Man, Nature, and Society."

Very characteristically the poem begins with the line,

" 'Twas summer, and the sun had mounted high."

Thus the romantic reaction started neither with God nor with Lord Bolingbroke, but with nature. We are here witnessing a conscious reaction against the whole tone of the eighteenth century. That century approached nature with the abstract analysis of science, whereas Wordsworth opposes to the scientific abstractions his full concrete experience.

A generation of religious revival and of scientific advance lies between the *Excursion* and Tennyson's *In Memoriam*. The earlier poets had solved the perplexity by ignoring it. That course was not open to Tennyson. Accordingly his poem begins thus:

"Strong Son of God, immortal Love,
Whom, we, that have not seen Thy face,
By faith, and faith alone, embrace,
Believing where we cannot prove."

The note of perplexity is struck at once. The nineteenth century has been a perplexed century, in a sense which is not true of any of its predecessors of the modern period. In the earlier times there were opposing camps, bitterly at variance on questions which they deemed fundamental. But, except for a few stragglers, either camp was whole-hearted. The importance of Tennyson's poem lies in the fact that it exactly expressed the character of its period. Each individual was divided against himself. In the earlier times, the deep thinkers were the clear thinkers,—Descartes, Spinoza, Locke, Leibniz. They knew exactly what they meant and said it. In the nineteenth century, some of the deeper thinkers among theologians and philosophers were muddled thinkers. Their assent was claimed by incompatible doctrines; and their efforts at reconciliation produced inevitable confusion.

Matthew Arnold, even more than Tennyson, was the poet who expressed this mood of individual distraction which was so characteristic of this century. Compare with *In Memoriam* the closing lines of Arnold's *Dover Beach:*

"And we are here as on a darkling plain
Swept with confused alarms of struggle and
    flight,
Where ignorant armies clash by night."

Cardinal Newman in his *Apologia pro Vita Sua* mentions it as a peculiarity of Pusey, the great Anglican ecclesiastic, "He was haunted by no intellectual perplexities." In this respect Pusey recalls Milton, Pope, Wordsworth, as in contrast with Tennyson, Clough, Matthew Arnold, and Newman himself.

So far as concerns English literature we find, as might be anticipated, the most interesting criticism of the thoughts of science among the leaders of the romantic reaction which accompanied and succeeded the epoch of the French Revolution. In English literature, the deepest thinkers of this school were Coleridge, Wordsworth, and Shelley. Keats is an example of literature untouched by science. We may neglect Coleridge's attempt at an explicit philosophical formulation. It was influential in his own generation; but in these lectures it is my object only to mention those elements of the thought of the past which stand for all time. Even with this limitation, only a selection is possible. For our purposes Coleridge is only important by his influence on Wordsworth. Thus Wordsworth and Shelley remain.

Wordsworth was passionately absorbed in nature. It has been said of Spinoza, that he was drunk with God. It is equally true that Wordsworth was drunk with nature. But he was a thoughtful, well-read man, with philosophical interests, and sane even to the point of prosiness. In addition, he was a genius. He weakens his evidence by his dislike of science. We all remember his scorn of the poor man whom he somewhat hastily accuses of peeping and botanising on his mother's grave. Passage after passage could be quoted from him, expressing this repulsion. In this respect, his characteristic thought can be summed up in his phrase, "We murder to dissect."

In this latter passage, he discloses the intellectual basis of his criticism of science. He alleges against science its absorption in abstractions. His consistent theme is that the important facts of nature elude the scientific method. It is important therefore to ask, what Wordsworth found in nature that failed to receive expression in science. I ask this question in the interest of science itself; for one main position in these lectures is a protest against the idea that the abstractions of science are irreformable and unalterable. Now it is emphatically not the case that Wordsworth hands over inorganic matter to the mercy of science, and concentrates on the faith that in the living organism there is some element that science cannot analyse. Of course he recognises, what no one doubts, that in some sense living things are different from lifeless things. But that is not his main point. It is the brooding presence of the hills which haunts him. His theme is nature *insolido*, that is to say, he dwells on that mysterious presence of surrounding things, which imposes itself on any separate element that we set up as an individual for its own sake. He always grasps the whole of nature as involved in the tonality of the particular instance. That is why he laughs with the daffodils, and finds in the primrose thoughts "too deep for tears."

Wordsworth's greatest poem is, by far, the first book of *The Prelude*. It is pervaded by this sense of the haunting presences of nature. A series of magnificent passages, too long for quotation, express this idea. Of course, Wordsworth is a poet writing a poem, and is not concerned with dry philosophical statements. But it would hardly be possible to express more clearly a feeling for nature, as exhibiting entwined prehensive unities, each suffused with modal presences of others:

"Ye Presences of Nature in the sky
And on the earth! Ye Visions of the hills!
And Souls of lonely places! can I think

A vulgar hope was yours when ye employed
Such ministry, when ye through many a year
Haunting me thus among my boyish sports,
On caves and trees, upon the woods and hills,
Impressed upon all forms the characters
Of danger or desire; and thus did make
The surface of the universal earth,
With triumph and delight, with hope and fear,
Work like a sea? . . ."

In thus citing Wordsworth, the point which I wish to make is that we forget how strained and paradoxical is the view of nature which modern science imposes on our thoughts. Wordsworth, to the height of genius, expresses the concrete facts of our apprehension, facts which are distorted in the scientific analysis. Is it not possible that the standardised concepts of science are only valid within narrow limitations, perhaps too narrow for science itself?

Shelley's attitude to science was at the opposite pole to that of Wordsworth. He loved it, and is never tired of expressing in poetry the thoughts which it suggests. It symbolises to him joy, and peace, and illumination. What the hills were to the youth of Wordsworth, a chemical laboratory was to Shelley. It is unfortunate that Shelley's literary critics have, in this respect, so little of Shelley in their own mentality. They tend to treat as a casual oddity of Shelley's nature what was, in fact, part of the main structure of his mind, permeating his poetry through and through. If Shelley had been born a hundred years later, the twentieth century would have seen a Newton among chemists.

For the sake of estimating the value of Shelley's evidence it is important to realise this absorption of his mind in scientific ideas. It can be illustrated by lyric after lyric. I will choose one poem only, the fourth act of his *Prometheus Unbound*. The Earth and the Moon converse together in the language of accurate science. Physical experiments guide his imagery. For example, the Earth's exclamation,

"The vaporous exultation not to be confined!"

is the poetic transcript of "the expansive force of gases," as it is termed in books on science. Again, take the Earth's stanza,

"I spin beneath my pyramid of night,
Which points into the heavens—dreaming delight,
Murmuring victorious joy in my enchanted sleep;

As a youth lulled in love-dreams faintly sighing,
Under the shadow of his beauty lying,
Which round his rest a watch of light and warmth doth keep."

This stanza could only have been written by someone with a definite geometrical diagram before his inward eye—a diagram which it has often been my business to demonstrate to mathematical classes. As evidence, note especially the last line which gives poetical imagery to the light surrounding night's pyramid. This idea could not occur to anyone without the diagram. But the whole poem and other poems are permeated with touches of this kind.

Now the poet, so sympathetic with science, so absorbed in its ideas, can simply make nothing of the doctrine of secondary qualities which is fundamental to its concepts. For Shelley nature retains its beauty and its colour. Shelley's nature is in its essence a nature of organisms, functioning with the full content of our perceptual experience. We are so used to ignoring the implication of orthodox scientific doctrine, that it is difficult to make evident the criticism upon it which is thereby implied. If anybody could have treated it seriously, Shelley would have done so.

Furthermore Shelley is entirely at one with Wordsworth as to the interfusing of the Presence in nature. Here is the opening stanza of his poem entitled *Mont Blanc*:

"The everlasting universe of Things
Flows through the Mind, and rolls its rapid waves,
Now dark—now glittering—now reflecting gloom—
Now lending splendour, where from secret springs
The source of human thought its tribute brings
Of waters,—with a sound but half its own,
Such as a feeble brook will oft assume
In the wild woods, among the Mountains lone,
Where waterfalls around it leap for ever,
Where woods and winds contend, and a vast river
Over its rocks ceaselessly bursts and raves."

Shelley has written these lines with explicit reference to some form of idealism, Kantian or Berkeleyan or Platonic. But however you construe him, he is here an emphatic witness to a prehensive unification as constituting the very being of nature.

Berkeley, Wordsworth, Shelley are representative of the intuitive refusal seriously to accept the abstract materialism of science.

There is an interesting difference in the treatment of nature by Wordsworth and by Shelley, which brings forward the exact questions we have got to think about. Shelley thinks of nature as changing, dissolving, transforming as it were at a fairy's touch. The leaves fly before the West Wind

"Like ghosts from an enchanter fleeing."

In his poem *The Cloud* it is the transformations of water which excite his imagination. The subject of the poem is the endless, eternal, elusive change of things:

"I change but I cannot die."

This is one aspect of nature, its elusive change: a change not merely to be expressed by locomotion, but a change of inward character. This is where Shelley places his emphasis, on the change of what cannot die.

Wordsworth was born among hills; hills mostly barren of trees, and thus showing the minimum of change with the seasons. He was haunted by the enormous permanences of nature. For him change is an incident which shoots across a background of endurance,

"Breaking the silence of the seas
Among the farthest Hebrides."

Every scheme for the analysis of nature has to face these two facts, *change* and *endurance*. There is yet a third fact to be placed by it, *eternality*, I will call it. The mountain endures. But when after ages it has been worn away, it has gone. If a replica arises, it is yet a new mountain. A colour is eternal. It haunts time like a spirit. It comes and it goes. But where it comes, it is the same colour. It neither survives nor does it live. It appears when it is wanted. The mountain has to time and space a different relation from that which colour has. In the previous lecture, I was chiefly considering the relation to space-time of things which, in my sense of the term, are eternal. It was necessary to do so before we can pass to the consideration of the things which endure.

Also we must recollect the basis of our procedure. I hold that philosophy is the critic of abstractions. Its function is the double one, first of harmonising them by assigning to them their right relative

status as abstractions, and secondly of completing them by direct comparison with more concrete intuitions of the universe, and thereby promoting the formation of more complete schemes of thought. It is in respect to this comparison that the testimony of great poets is of such importance. Their survival is evidence that they express deep intuitions of mankind penetrating into what is universal in concrete fact. Philosophy is not one among the sciences with its own little scheme of abstractions which it works away at perfecting and improving. It is the survey of sciences, with the special objects of their harmony, and of their completion. It brings to this task, not only the evidence of the separate sciences, but also its own appeal to concrete experience. It confronts the sciences with concrete fact.

The literature of the nineteenth century, especially its English poetic literature, is a witness to the discord between the aesthetic intuitions of mankind and the mechanism of science. Shelley brings vividly before us the elusiveness of the eternal objects of sense as they haunt the change which infects underlying organisms. Wordsworth is the poet of nature as being the field of enduring permanences carrying within themselves a message of tremendous significance. The eternal objects are also there for him,

"The light that never was, on sea or land."

Both Shelley and Wordsworth emphatically bear witness that nature cannot be divorced from its aesthetic values, and that these values arise from the cumulation, in some sense, of the brooding presence of the whole on to its various parts. Thus we gain from the poets the doctrine that a philosophy of nature must concern itself at least with these six notions: change, value, eternal objects, endurance, organism, interfusion.

We see that the literary romantic movement at the beginning of the nineteenth century, just as much as Berkeley's philosophical idealistic movement a hundred years earlier, refused to be confined within the materialistic concepts of the orthodox scientific theory. We know also that when in these lectures we come to the twentieth century, we shall find a movement in science itself to reorganise its concepts, driven thereto by its own intrinsic development.

It is, however, impossible to proceed until we have settled whether this refashioning of ideas is to be carried out on an objectivist basis or on a subjectivist basis. By a subjectivist basis I mean the belief that the nature of our immediate experience is the outcome of the perceptive peculiarities of the subject enjoying the experience. In other words, I mean that for this theory what is perceived is not a partial vision of a complex of things generally independent of that act of cognition; but that it merely is the expression of the individual peculiarities of the cognitive act. Accordingly what is common to the multiplicity of cognitive acts is the ratiocination connected with them. Thus, though there is a common world of thought associated with our sense-perceptions, there is no common world to think about. What we do think about is a common conceptual world applying indifferently to our individual experiences which are strictly personal to ourselves. Such a conceptual world will ultimately find its complete expression in the equations of applied mathematics. This is the extreme subjectivist position. There is of course the half-way house of those who believe that our perceptual experience does tell us of a common objective world; but that the things perceived are merely the outcome for us of this world, and are not *in themselves* elements in the common world itself.

Also there is the objectivist position. This creed is that the actual elements perceived by our senses are *in themselves* the elements of a common world; and that this world is a complex of things, including indeed our acts of cognition, but transcending them. According to this point of view the things experienced are to be distinguished from our knowledge of them. So far as there is dependence, the *things* pave the way for the *cognition,* rather than *vice versa.* But the point is that the actual things experienced enter into a common world which transcends knowledge, though it includes knowledge. The intermediate subjectivists would hold that the things experienced only indirectly enter into the common world by reason of their dependence on the subject who is cognising. The objectivist holds that the things experienced and the cognisant subject enter into the common world on equal terms. In these lectures I am giving the outline of what I consider to be the essentials of an objectivist philosophy adapted to the requirement of science and to the concrete experience of mankind. Apart from the detailed criticism of the difficulties raised by subjectivism in any form, my broad reasons for dis-

trusting it are three in number. One reason arises from the direct interrogation of our perceptive experience. It appears from this interrogation that we are *within* a world of colours, sounds, and other sense-objects, related in space and time to enduring objects such as stones, trees, and human bodies. We seem to be ourselves elements of this world in the same sense as are the other things which we perceive. But the subjectivist, even the moderate intermediate subjectivist, makes this world, as thus described, depend on us, in a way which directly traverses our naïve experience. I hold that the ultimate appeal is to naïve experience and that is why I lay such stress on the evidence of poetry. My point is, that in our sense-experience we know away from and beyond our own personality; whereas the subjectivist holds that in such experience we merely know about our own personality. Even the intermediate subjectivist places our personality between the world we know of and the common world which he admits. The world we know of is for him the internal strain of our personality under the stress of the common world which lies behind.

My second reason for distrusting subjectivism is based on the particular content of experience. Our historical knowledge tells us of ages in the past when, so far as we can see, no living being existed on earth. Again it also tells us of countless starsystems, whose detailed history remains beyond our ken. Consider even the moon and the earth. What is going on within the interior of the earth, and on the far side of the moon! Our perceptions lead us to infer that there is something happening in the stars, something happening within the earth, and something happening on the far side of the moon. Also they tell us that in remote ages there were things happening. But all these things which it appears certainly happened, are either unknown in detail, or else are reconstructed by inferential evidence. In the face of this content of our personal experience, it is difficult to believe that the experienced world is an attribute of our own personality. My third reason is based upon the instinct for action. Just as sense-perception seems to give knowledge of what lies beyond individuality, so action seems to issue in an instinct for self-transcendence. The activity passes beyond self into the known transcendent world. It is here that final ends are of importance. For it is not activity urged from behind, which passes out into the veiled world of the intermediate subjectivist. It is activity directed to determinate ends in the known world; and yet it is activity transcending self and it is activity within the known world. It follows therefore that the world, as known, transcends the subject which is cognisant of it.

The subjectivist position has been popular among those who have been engaged in giving a philosophical interpretation to the recent theories of relativity in physical science. The dependence of the world of sense on the individual percipient seems an easy mode of expressing the means involved. Of course, with the exception of those who are content with themselves as forming the entire universe, solitary amid nothing, everyone wants to struggle back to some sort of objectivist position. I do not understand how a common world of thought can be established in the absence of a common world of sense. I will not argue this point in detail; but in the absence of a transcendence of thought, or a transcendence of the world of sense, it is difficult to see how the subjectivist is to divest himself of his solitariness. Nor does the intermediate subjectivist appear to get any help from his unknown world in the background.

The distinction between realism and idealism does not coincide with that between objectivism and subjectivism. Both realists and idealists can start from an objective standpoint. They may both agree that the world disclosed in sense-perception is a common world, transcending the individual recipient. But the objective idealist, when he comes to analyse what the reality of this world involves, finds that cognitive mentality is in some way inextricably concerned in every detail. This position the realist denies. Accordingly these two classes of objectivists do not part company till they have arrived at the ultimate problem of metaphysics. There is a great deal which they share in common. This is why, in my last lecture, I said that I adopted a position of provisional realism.

In the past, the objectivist position has been distorted by the supposed necessity of accepting the classical scientific materialism, with its doctrine of simple location. This has necessitated the doctrine of secondary and primary qualities. Thus the secondary qualities, such as the sense-objects, are dealt with on subjectivist principles. This is a half-hearted position which falls an easy prey to subjectivist criticism.

If we are to include the secondary qualities in the common world, a very drastic reorganisation of our fundamental concept is necessary. It is an evident fact of experience that our apprehensions of the external world depend absolutely on the occurrences within the human body. By playing appropriate tricks on the body a man can be got to perceive, or not to perceive, almost anything. Some people express themselves as though bodies, brains, and nerves were the only real things in an entirely imaginary world. In other words, they treat bodies on objectivist principles, and the rest of the world on subjectivist principles. This will not do; especially, when we remember that it is the experimenter's perception of another person's body which is in question as evidence.

But we have to admit that the body is the organism whose states regulate our cognisance of the world. The unity of the perceptual field therefore must be a unity of bodily experience. In being aware of the bodily experience, we must thereby be aware of aspects of the whole spatio-temporal world as mirrored within the bodily life.

This is the solution of the problem which I gave in my last lecture. I will not repeat myself now, except to remind you that my theory involves the entire abandonment of the notion that simple location is the primary way in which things are involved in space-time. In a certain sense, everything is everywhere at all times. For every location involves an aspect of itself in every other location. Thus every spatio-temporal standpoint mirrors the world.

If you try to imagine this doctrine in terms of our conventional views of space and time, which presuppose simple location, it is a great paradox. But if you think of it in terms of our naïve experience, it is a mere transcript of the obvious facts. You are in a certain place perceiving things. Your perception takes place where you are, and is entirely dependent on how your body is functioning. But this functioning of the body in one place, exhibits for your cognisance an aspect of the distant environment, fading away into the general knowledge that there are things beyond. If this cognisance conveys knowledge of a transcendent world, it must be because the event which is the bodily life unifies in itself aspects of the universe.

This is a doctrine extremely consonant with the vivid expression of personal experience which we find in the nature-poetry of imaginative writers such as Wordsworth or Shelley. The brooding, immediate presences of things are an obsession to Wordsworth. What the theory does do is to edge cognitive mentality away from being the necessary substratum of the unity of experience. That unity is now placed in the unity of an event. Accompanying this unity, there may or there may not be cognition.

At this point we come back to the great question which was posed before us by our examination of the evidence afforded by the poetic insight of Wordsworth and Shelley. This single question has expanded into a group of questions. What are enduring things, as distinguished from the eternal objects, such as colour and shape? How are they possible? What is their status and meaning in the universe? It comes to this: What is the status of the enduring stability of the order of nature? There is the summary answer, which refers nature to some greater reality standing behind it. This reality occurs in the history of thought under many names, The Absolute, Brahma, The Order of Heaven, God. The delineation of final metaphysical truth is no part of this lecture. My point is that any summary conclusion jumping from our conviction of the existence of such an order of nature to the easy assumption that there is an ultimate reality which, in some unexplained way, is to be appealed to for the removal of perplexity, constitutes the great refusal of rationality to assert its rights. We have to search whether nature does not in its very being show itself as self-explanatory. By this I mean, that the sheer statement, of what things are, may contain elements explanatory of why things are. Such elements may be expected to refer to depths beyond anything which we can grasp with a clear apprehension. In a sense, all explanation must end in an ultimate arbitrariness. My demand is, that the ultimate arbitrariness of matter of fact from which our formulation starts should disclose the same general principles of reality, which we dimly discern as stretching away into regions beyond our explicit powers of discernment. Nature exhibits itself as exemplifying a philsophy of the evolution of organisms subject to determinate conditions. Examples of such conditions are the dimensions of space, the laws of nature, the determinate enduring entities, such as atoms and electrons, which exemplify these laws. But the very nature of these entities, the very nature of their spatiality and temporality, should exhibit the arbitrariness of these conditions as the outcome of a wider evolution beyond nature itself, and within which nature is but a limited mode.

One all-pervasive fact, inherent in the very character of what is real is the transition of things, the passage one to another. This passage is not a mere linear procession of discrete entities. However we fix a determinate entity, there is always a narrower determination of something which is presupposed in our first choice. Also there is always a wider determination into which our first choice fades by transition beyond itself. The general aspect of nature is that of evolutionary expansiveness. These unities, which I call events, are the emergence into actuality of something. How are we to characterise the something which thus emerges? The name *"event"* given to such a unity, draws attention to the inherent transitoriness, combined with the actual unity. But this abstract word cannot be sufficient to characterise what the fact of the reality of an event is in itself. A moment's thought shows us that no one idea can in itself be sufficient. For every idea which finds its significance in each event must represent something which contributes to what realisation is in itself. Thus no one word can be adequate. But conversely, nothing must be left out. Remembering the poetic rendering of our concrete experience, we see at once that the element of value, of being valuable, of having value, of being an end in itself, of being something which is for its own sake, must not be omitted in any account of an event as the most concrete actual something. "Value" is the word I use for the intrinsic reality of an event. Value is an element which permeates through and through the poetic view of nature. We have only to transfer to the very texture of realisation in itself that value which we recognise so readily in terms of human life. This is the secret of Wordsworth's worship of nature. Realisation therefore is in itself the attainment of value. But there is no such thing as mere value. Value is the outcome of limitation. The definite finite entity is the selected mode which is the shaping of attainment; apart from such shaping into individual matter of fact there is no attainment. The mere fusion of all that there is would be the nonentity of indefiniteness. The salvation of reality is its obstinate, irreducible, matter-of-fact entities, which are limited to be no other than themselves. Neither science, nor art, nor creative action can tear itself away from obstinate, irreducible, limited facts. The endurance of things has its significance in the self-retention of that which imposes itself as a definite attainment for its own sake. That which endures is limited, obstructive, intolerant, infecting its environment with its own aspects. But it is not self-sufficient. The aspects of all things enter into its very nature. It is only itself as drawing together into its own limitation the larger whole in which it finds itself. Conversely it is only itself by lending its aspects to this same environment in which it finds itself. The problem of evolution is the development of enduring harmonies of enduring shapes of value, which merge into higher attainments of things beyond themselves. Aesthetic attainment is interwoven in the texture of realisation. The endurance of an entity represents the attainment of a limited aesthetic success, though if we look beyond it to its external effects, it may represent an aesthetic failure. Even within itself, it may represent the conflict between a lower success and a higher failure. The conflict is the presage of disruption.

The further discussion of the nature of enduring objects and of the conditions they require will be relevant to the consideration of the doctrine of evolution which dominated the latter half of the nineteenth century. The point which in this lecture I have endeavoured to make clear is that the nature-poetry of the romantic revival was a protest on behalf of the organic view of nature, and also a protest against the exclusion of value from the essence of matter of fact. In this aspect of it, the romantic movement may be conceived as a revival of Berkeley's protest which had been launched a hundred years earlier. The romantic reaction was a protest on behalf of value.

M. H. Abrams

STRUCTURE AND STYLE
IN THE GREATER ROMANTIC LYRIC*

There is no accepted name for the kind of poem I want to talk about, even though it was a distinctive and widely practiced variety of the longer Romantic lyric and includes some of the greatest Romantic achievements in any form. Coleridge's "Eolian Harp," "Frost at Midnight," "Fears in Solitude," and "Dejection: An Ode" exemplify the type, as does Wordsworth's "Tintern Abbey," his "Ode: Intimations of Immortality," and (with a change in initial reference from scene to painting) his "Elegiac Stanzas Suggested by a Picture of Peele Castle in a Storm." Shelley's "Stanzas Written in Dejection" follows the formula exactly, and his "Ode to the West Wind" is a variant on it. Of Keats's odes, that to a Nightingale is the one which approximates the pattern most closely. Only Byron, among the major poets, did not write in this mode at all.

These instances yield a paradigm for the type. Some of the poems are called odes, while the others approach the ode in having lyric magnitude and a serious subject, feelingfully meditated. They present a determinate speaker in a particularized, and usually a localized, outdoor setting, whom we overhear as he carries on, in a fluent vernacular which rises easily to a more formal speech, a sustained colloquy, sometimes with himself or with the outer scene, but more frequently with a silent human auditor, present or absent. The speaker begins with a description of the landscape; an aspect or change of aspect in the landscape evokes a varied but integral process of memory, thought, anticipation, and feeling which remains closely intervolved with the outer scene. In the course of this meditation the lyric speaker achieves an insight, faces up to a tragic loss, comes to a moral decision, or resolves an emotional problem. Often the poem rounds upon itself to end where it began, at the outer scene, but with an altered mood and deepened understanding which is the result of the intervening meditation.

* From *From Sensibility to Romanticism: Essays Presented to Frederick A. Pottle* edited by Frederick W Hilles and Harold Bloom. Copyright © 1965 by Oxford University Press, Inc. Reprinted by permission.

What shall we call this Romantic genre? To label these poems simply nature lyrics is not only inadequate, but radically misleading. We have not yet entirely recovered from the earlier critical stress on Wordsworth's statement that "I have at all times endeavoured to look steadily at my subject," to the neglect of his repeated warnings that accurate natural description, though a necessary, is an inadequate condition for poetry. Like Blake and Coleridge, Wordsworth manifested wariness, almost terror, at the threat of the corporeal eye and material object to tyrannize over the mind and imagination, in opposition to that normative experience in which

The mind is lord and master—outward sense
The obedient servant of her will.[1]

In the extended lyrics we are considering, the visual report is invariably the occasion for a meditation which turns out to constitute the *raison d'être* of the poem. Romantic writers, though nature poets, were humanists above all, for they dealt with the non-human only insofar as it is the occasion for the activity which defines man: thought, the process of intellection.

"The descriptive-meditative poem" is a possible, but a clumsy term. *Faute de mieux,* I shall call this poetic type "the greater Romantic lyric," intending to suggest, not that it is a higher achievement than other Romantic lyrics, but that it displaced what neo-classical critics had called "the greater ode"—the elevated Pindaric, in distinction to "the lesser ode" modeled chiefly on Horace—as the favored form for the long lyric poem.

The repeated out-in-out process, in which mind confronts nature and their interplay constitutes the poem, is a remarkable phenomenon in literary history. If we don't find it strange, it is because our responses have been dulled by long familiarity with such a procedure not only in the Romantic poets, but in their many successors who played variations on the mode, from Matthew Arnold and Walt Whitman—both "Dover Beach" and "Crossing Brooklyn Ferry," for example, closely follow the pattern of the greater Romantic lyric—to Wallace Stevens and W. H. Auden. But at the beginning of the nineteenth century this procedure in the lyric was part of a new and exciting poetic strategy, no less epidemic than Donne's in his day, or T. S. Eliot's in the period after the first World War. For several decades poets did not often talk about the great

issues of life, death, love, joy, dejection, or God without talking at the same time about the landscape. Wordsworth's narrative of Michael emerges from a description of the scene around "the tumultuous brook of Green-head Ghyll," to which in the end it returns:

and the remains
Of the unfinished Sheep-fold may be seen
Beside the boisterous brook of Green-head
Ghyll.

Coleridge's great, neglected love-poem, "Recollections of Love," opens with a Quantock scene revisited after eight years have passed, and adverts suddenly to the River Greta at the close:

But when those meek eyes first did seem
To tell me, Love within you wrought—
O Greta, dear domestic stream!

Has not, since then, Love's prompture deep,
Has not Love's whisper evermore
Been ceaseless, as thy gentle roar?
Sole voice, when other voices sleep,
Dear under-song in clamor's hour.

Keats's first long poem of consequence, though it is his introduction to an *ars poetica,* represents what he saw, then what he thought, while he "stood tiptoe upon a little hill." Shelley treats the theme of permanence in change by describing the mutations of a cloud, defines the pure Idea of joy in a meditation on the flight and song of a skylark, and presents his ultimate concept of the secret and impersonal power behind all process in a description of Mont Blanc and the Vale of Chamouni. Wordsworth's *Prelude* can be viewed as an epic expansion of the mode of "Tintern Abbey," both in overall design and local tactics. It begins with the description of a landscape visited in maturity, evokes the entire life of the poet as a protracted meditation on things past, and presents the growth of the poet's mind as an interaction with the natural milieu by which it is fostered, from which it is tragically alienated, and to which in the resolution it is restored, with a difference attributable to the intervening experiences; the poem ends at the time of its beginning.

What I have called "the greater lyric," then, is only a special instance of a very widespread manner of proceeding in Romantic poetry; but it is of great interest because it was the earliest Romantic formal invention, which at once demonstrated the stability of organization and the capacity to engender successors which define a distinct lyric species. New lyric forms are not as plenty as blackberries, and when one turns up, it is worth critical attention. Suppose, therefore, that we ask some questions about this one: about its genesis, its nearest literary antecedents, and the reasons why this way of proceeding, out of the alternatives in common lyric practice, should have appealed so powerfully to the Romantic sensibility. Inquiry into some probable causes of the structure and style of the greater lyric will take us not only to the evolution of certain descriptive genres in the seventeenth and eighteenth centuries, but also to contemporary developments in philosophy and in theology, and to the spiritual posture in which many poets, as well as philosophers, found themselves at the end of the Enlightenment.

COLERIDGE AND WORDSWORTH

In this investigation Coleridge must be our central reference, not only because he had the most to say about these matters in prose, but because it was he, not Wordsworth, who inaugurated the greater Romantic lyric, firmly established its pattern, and wrote the largest number of instances. Wordsworth's first trial in the extended lyric was "Tintern Abbey," which he composed in July 1798. Up to that time his only efforts in the long descriptive and reflective mode were the schoolboy effort, "The Vale of Esthwaite," and the two tour-poems of 1793, "An Evening Walk" and "Descriptive Sketches." The first of these was written in octosyllabic and the latter two in heroic couplets, and all differ in little but merit and the detail of single passages from hundreds of eighteenth-century predecessors.[2] Coleridge, however, as early as 20 August, 1795, composed a short first version of "The Eolian Harp," and in 1796—two years before "Tintern Abbey"—expanded it to fifty-six lines which established, in epitome, the ordonnance, materials, and style of the greater lyric.[3] It is in the dramatic mode of intimate talk to an unanswering auditor in easy blank verse paragraphs. It begins with a description of the peaceful outer scene; this, in parallel with the vagrant sounds evoked from a wind-harp, calls forth a recollection in tranquillity of earlier experiences in the same setting and leads to a sequence of reflections which are suggested by, and also incorporate, perceptual qualities of the scene. The poem closes with a summary reprise of the opening description of "PEACE, and this COT, and THEE, heart-honour'd Maid!"

Between the autumn of 1796 and the spring of 1798 Coleridge composed a number of variations on this lyric type including "Reflections on Having Left a Place of Retirement," "This Lime-tree Bower," "Fears in Solitude," and "The Nightingale." To these writings Professor G. M. Harper applied the term which Coleridge himself used for "The Nightingale," "conversation poems"; very aptly, because they are written (though some of them only intermittently) in a blank verse which at its best captures remarkably the qualities of the intimate speaking voice, yet remains capable of adapting without strain to the varying levels of the subject-matter and feeling. And within this period, in February of 1798, Coleridge produced one of the masterpieces of the greater lyric, perfectly modulated and proportioned, but so successful in the quiet way that it hides its art that it has only recently attracted its meed of critical admiration. The poem is "Frost at Midnight," and it follows, but greatly enlarges and subtilizes the pattern of "The Eolian Harp." What seems at first impression to be the free association of its central meditation turns out to have been called forth, qualified, and controlled by the opening description, which evokes the strangeness in the familiar surroundings of the solitary and wakeful speaker: the "secret ministry" of the frost, the "strange and extreme silentness" of "sea, and hill, and wood," the life of the sleeping village "inaudible as dreams," and the film that flutters on the grate "the sole unquiet thing." In consonance with these elements, and directed especially by the rhythm of the seemingly unnoticed breathing of a sleeping infant, the meditative mind disengages itself from the physical locale, moves back in time to the speaker's childhood, still farther back, to his own infancy, then forward to express, in the intonation of a blessing, the hope that his son shall have the life in nature that his father lacked; until, in anticipating the future, it incorporates both the present scene and the results of the remembered past in the enchanting close—

> Whether the eave-drops fall
> Heard only in the trances of the blast,
> Or if the secret ministry of frost
> Shall hang them up in silent icicles,
> Quietly shining to the quiet Moon.

In the original version this concluding sentence trailed off in six more verse-lines, which Coleridge, in order to emphasize the lyric rondure, later excised. Plainly, Coleridge worked out the lyric device of the return-upon-itself—which he used in "Reflections on Having Left a Place of Retirement" and "Fears in Solitude," as well as in "The Eolian Harp" and "Frost at Midnight"—in a deliberate endeavor to transform a segment of experience broken out of time into a sufficient aesthetic whole. "The common end of all *narrative*, nay, of *all*, Poems," he wrote to Joseph Cottle in 1815, "is to convert a *series* into a *Whole:* to make those events, which in real or imagined History move on in a *strait* Line, assume to our Understandings a *circular* motion—the snake with its Tail in its Mouth." [4] From the time of the early Greek philosophers, the circle had been the shape of perfection; and in occult philosophy the *ouroboros*, the tail-eating snake, had become the symbol for eternity and for the divine process of creation, since it is complete, self-sufficient, and endless. For Coleridge the perfect shape for the descriptive-meditative-descriptive poem was precisely the one described and exemplified in T. S. Eliot's "East Coker," which begins: "In my beginning is my end," and ends: "In my end is my beginning"; another modern writer who knew esoteric lore designed *Finnegans Wake* so that the headless sentence which begins the book completes the tailless sentence with which it ends.

Five months after the composition of "Frost at Midnight," Wordsworth set out on a walking tour with his sister. Reposing on a high bank of the River Wye, he remembered this among others of Coleridge's conversation poems—the dramatic mode of address to an unanswering listener in flexible blank verse; the opening description which evolves into a sustained meditation assimilating perceptual, personal, and philosophical elements; the free movement of thought from the present scene to recollection in tranquillity, to prayer-like prediction, and back to the scene; even some of Coleridge's specific concepts and phrases—and in the next four or five days' walk, worked out "Lines Composed a Few Miles above Tintern Abbey" and appended it forthwith to *Lyrical Ballads*, which was already in press.

To claim that it was Coleridge who deflected Wordsworth's poetry into a channel so entirely con-genial to him is in no way to derogate Wordsworth's achievement, nor his powers of invention. "Tintern Abbey" has greater dimension and intricacy and a more various verbal orchestration than "Frost at Midnight." In its conclusion Wordsworth managed Coleridge's specialty, the return-upon-itself, with a mastery of involuted reference without match in the poems of its begetter. "Tintern Abbey" also inaugurated the wonderfully functional device Wordsworth later called the "two consciousnesses": a scene is revisited, and the remembered landscape ("the picture of the mind") is superimposed on the picture before the eye; the two landscapes fail to match, and so set a problem ("a sad perplexity") which compels the meditation. Wordsworth played variations on this stratagem in all his later trials in the greater lyric, and in *The Prelude* he expanded it into a persisting double awareness of things as they are and as they were, and so anticipated the structural principle of the most influential masterpiece of our own century, Proust's *À la recherche du temps perdu*.

NOTES

1. *The Prelude* (1850), XII, 222–3. Even Keats, though he sometimes longed for a life of sensations rather than of thought, objected to the poems of John Clare that too often "the Description overlaid and stifled that which ought to be the prevailing Idea." (Letter to John Clare from John Taylor, 27 September 1820, quoted by Edmund Blunden, *Keats' Publisher* [London, 1936], p. 80).

2. *Descriptive Sketches* (1793) drew from a contemporary reviewer the cry: "More descriptive poetry! Have we not yet enough? . . . Yes; more, and yet more: so it is decreed." *The Monthly Review*, 2d series, XII (1793), 216–17; cited by Robert A. Aubin, *Topographical Poetry in XVIII-Century England* (New York, 1936), p. 255; see also pp. 217–19.

3. Perhaps that is the reason for Coleridge's later judgment that "The Eolian Harp" was "the most perfect poem I ever wrote." (Quoted by J. D. Campbell, ed., *The Poetical Works of S. T. Cole-*

ridge, London, 1893, p. 578). The first version of the poem and a manuscript version of 1797 (Coleridge then entitled it "Effusion") are reproduced in *The Complete Poetical Works*, ed. E. H. Coleridge (2 vols.; Oxford, 1912), II, 1021-3. For an account of the revisions of the poem, see H. J. W. Milley, "Some Notes on Coleridge's 'Eolian Harp,'" *Modern Philology*, XXXVI (1938-39), 359-75

4. *Collected Letters*, ed. Earl Leslie Griggs (Oxford, 1956–   ), IV, 545.

S. Foster Damon

WILLIAM BLAKE: HIS PHILOSOPHY AND SYMBOLS*

His spirit recovered its pristine liberty and saw the mud walls of flesh and blood. Being alive, he was in the spirit all his days. While his body therefore was inclosed in this world, his soul was in the temple of Eternity, and clearly beheld the infinite life and omnipresence of God: having conversation with invisible, spiritual, and immaterial things, which were its companions, itself being invisible, spiritual, and immaterial. Kingdoms and Ages did surround him, as clearly as the hills and mountains: and therefore the Kingdom of God was ever round about him. Everything was one way or other his sovereign delight and transcendant pleasure, as in Heaven everything will be every one's peculiar treasure.

THOMAS TRAHERNE: *Centuries of Meditations*, iii, 95.

The key to everything Blake ever wrote or painted lies in his mysticism. We must understand this thoroughly before we can pass to a consideration of his works.

The Mystic is one of the eternal Types of Humanity. Rare though he be, he has left such deep impresses upon history, that the modern psychologists have been particularly interested in the workings of his mind; especially since all mystics have a surprising sameness, no matter from what culture or creed they may have sprung.

The test by which the Mystic is positively recognized is the "ecstasy." During such moments, he enters a peculiar state of mental illumination, in which he is exalted above the world as we know it, into a supersensuous state, where he is violently united with Ultimate Truth. This "Truth" he may call "God," "Beauty," "Law," or any other name; but it is always One and always Truth. This Union with the One combines pain and pleasure, emotion and knowledge, nature and supernature, body and soul, man and God. Those who have experienced it can imagine no higher state of existence; and generally their whole lives thereafter are devoted to revealing on earth this ineffable secret.

Blake was subject to these ecstasies, and he never seems to have emerged from one without wresting some great Truth from the Eternity which he had entered; for he was not of that type which is content to let slip what it has learned. The strange poem in the letter to his friend Butts (Oct. 2, 1800) describes such a vision: how by the sea one day his eyes expanded "into regions of fire remote from desire"; how everything in the world appeared as "men seen afar"; and how eventually they were all combined into "One Man," the Christ, on whose bosom Blake reposed. His epic, *Milton*, is the record of one instant of such vision. His *Invention of Job* shows the Just Man saved from his own justice by such a vision. Are all these literary fantasies?

If we choose to think so, we can still turn to Blake's copy of Swedenborg's *Wisdom of the Angels concerning Divine Love and Wisdom*, in which he made curious notes. On page 33 (¶ 40), the text reads: "The human Mind . . . cannot investigate it, *without keeping the Understanding some time in spiritual light*"; Blake underlined the italicized words and added: "this, Man can do while in the body." On page 200 (¶ 241), the text reads: "Every one who consults his Reason, *whilst it is in the Light . . .*"; and Blake again underlined the words here italicized. Yet once more, on page 220 (¶ 257) Blake marked a phrase of Swedenborg's as of great importance: "But still Man, in whom the spiritual Degree is open, comes into that Wisdom when he dies, and *may also come into it by laying aside the Sensations of the Body, and by Influx from above at the same Time into the Spirituals of his Mind.*" Opposite these words Blake jotted two notes: "this is while in the Body"; and "This is to be understood as unusual in our time but common in ancient."

The intensity of such an experience is extraordinary. A flash—a second—fills even the most ardent persecutor (such as Paul) with the conviction of truth, and backs this conviction with immense strength to further the very religion which till then he has hated with his whole soul.

The experience is always the same, no matter in what land or level of civilization it occurs. It is above all creeds, for experience must have authority over theory. More than that, Mysticism is the source itself of every creed; all the founders of the great religions were mystics; and their religions are at heart attempts to bring the beatific state to every man. Mysticism explains all religions, all antique mysteries, and perhaps even such exotic sects as those of the Alchemists and the Rosicrucians. Many parallels of theirs with Blake's ideas will be pointed out later; since mystics, in telling of their experience, "speak the same language," even to using the same symbols.

The principal thing of which they are all convinced is that, whatever this material world may be, there is another, so much more real and more ecstatic, that words can only stammer about it. Heaven is not a comforting hypothesis nor an exterior reward for the unrewarded: it is an actual state within us. The mystics have been there, and they know. Naturally they try to show others the way, and they have left many fascinating maps.

Miss Evelyn Underhill [1] divides the Way into five stages: (1) the awakening to a sense of divine reality; (2) the consequent purgation of the Self, when it realizes its own imperfections; (3) an enhanced return of the sense of the divine order, after the Self has achieved its detachment from the world; (4) the "Dark Night of the Soul," or the crucifixion of the Self in the absence of the divine;

(5) and the complete union with Truth, the attainment of that which the third state had perceived as a possibility.

Blake passed through these identical five states. His complete works, which are an accurate record of his life, fall into these same divisions. The first three states are named by him "Innocence," "Experience," and "Revolution." The fourth state was passed in silence; while the fifth state was a return to "Innocence" with the added wisdom of "Experience."

Blake had not yet reached the first state when he wrote the *Poetical Sketches*, which were finished when he was twenty. They reveal practically no sense of the transcendent. One poem, *The Couch of Death*, which contains a vision of Heaven, sounds like a literary exercise; and *Fresh from the dewy hill* describes only an earthly passion, however much it suggests Neoplatonic adoration. Neither does Blake's next work, the unfinished *Island in the Moon* (1786–1789) show any sign of illumination. But the *Songs of Innocence* (1789) are entirely inspired by mystical perception; therefore between the last page of *An Island in the Moon* (after Feb. 1787) and 1789, the first illumination must have taken place.

Blake left no record of this first great moment; but we can conjecture what happened, from what we know of this part of his life.

He was thirty, married, and thoroughly dissatisfied with himself. His only worldly recognition had come from a small circle of Blue-Stockings hunting culture and literary lions. Through them he had printed his first book, a small volume with which he was disgusted, for he could only see how derivative his verses were, and how much better they should have been. Naturally he could not envisage our historical perspective, by which we place that volume as one of the great milestones in the progress of English poetry.

He felt that he had not justified his existence. He had not yet found his predestined way of expressing himself. Such a moment occurs in the life of every author, and it is always abysmally melancholy.

Blake's discontent took the form of a satire against his friends the Blue-Stockings, whose superficiality he could not help despising. He burlesqued their conversations, their intellectual pretensions, and their literary tastes. Into their mouths he put song after absurd song.

But these songs turned into poetry, for all his intentions. From satire they became the real thing; and Blake began to see that he might yet do something, that his gift for poetry was not a mere ferment of adolescence.

Then a very heavy blow fell. In February 1787 his beloved younger brother, Robert, whom he was teaching to draw and paint, died. Blake expended every possible effort to save him, watching day and night by his bedside. But he was useless. And at the end he suddenly saw his brother's soul ascending, "clapping its hands for joy" at the great release.

"Fear and Hope are—Vision," Blake wrote later, under a picture of just such a death-bed.[2] At this moment, the conviction that there is a World of Eternity rolled irresistibly over his exhausted mind. His brother could not be dead; he had only passed into a higher, happier life. Religion had been teaching this for centuries; and now Blake himself had *seen*. Whereupon, absolutely worn out, he went to bed and slept for three days and nights.

And now his latent gift for poetry sprang of itself into expression. What he wrote he still added to *An Island in the Moon*; but that satire had become inadequate and silly. He knew that his lyrics deserved better presentation than any ordinary printed book could give them, that they called for some unusual and beautiful setting. The problem challenged him; and like all such problems, it remained working in his subconscious mind.

Can we wonder, then, that Robert, closer to Blake in death even than in life, should have come to him "in a vision of the night," bringing the solution of the problem?[3] Blake was instructed to etch the text and its decoration on a copper-plate, take impresses in coloured ink, and finally paint each page by hand.

As was his custom, Blake recorded this process in *An Island in the Moon*; then, fired with his new idea, he abandoned the satire forever, for his new work. It was called *Songs of Innocence,* and has since taken its place among the most beautiful books of the world.

The Mystical Path always begins in the Garden of Eden. Shafts of transcendental light pour down and apotheosize visibly the entire world. "When I went in the morning into the fields to work," wrote another mystic after his conversion,[4] "the glory of God appeared in all his visible creation. I well remember we reaped oats, and how every straw and head of the oats seemed, as it were, arrayed in a kind of rainbow glory, or to glow, if I may so express it, in the glory of God." This same light saturates the *Songs of Innocence* and *The Book of Thel*. No mundane landscape ever glittered with such strange, ecstatic iridescences; no actual children ever lived such heightened, untroubled existences. And "Innocence"—sacramental perception—became for Blake one of the permanent "states" through which souls pass. The effect of this illumination never left him.

Many poets, among them Shelley, Wordsworth, and Walt Whitman, often attain to a mild sense of this splendour and unity of the universe. They seldom go farther; Blake passed them all, exploring the whole extent of the Mystic Way.

Another fact about Illumination is important. It is more than a state of emotion; it is a state of knowledge as well. A new truth is perceived. Most mystics are unable to express, or even to remember, what they have learned. Blake always wrested from his visions some transcendental theory which he recorded in his work.

This time he discovered that the Mystical Paradise is the same as that in which children dwell. Heaven *literally* "lies about us in our infancy."[5] This was the very Eden from which Adam, and all men, fell. "That is heaven," Blake said once, leading a friend to a window, and pointing to a group of children at play.[6] No doubt he remembered that his own "visions" began at the age of four.[7] Of course, he admitted, "Some Children are Fools, and so are some old Men. But there is a vast Majority on the side of Imagination or Spiritual Sensation"; therefore it is not surprising that Blake wrote of his books, "Particularly they have been Elucidated by Children."[8]

Such seems to have been Blake's first illumination.

But after mystical joy follows reaction, the purgation. "The world is evil," says the mystic; "why?" And Blake, in a new book, remorselessly wrote against each of the best *Songs of Innocence* a *Song of Experience*. He substituted *The Tyger* of wrath for *The Lamb* of love; *Infant Sorrow* for *Infant Joy*; and so on. This state of cynicism he called "Experience." *Tiriel*, his first Prophetic Book, is of this period, preoccupied with the error of the world's way. *The Gates of Paradise* must also have been conceived about this time. Looking back upon the state, he wrote:[9]

. . . Terrors appear in the Heaven above,
And in Hell beneath, and a mighty and awful
    change threatened the Earth.

The change came, but it was for the good. The American and French Revolutions promised a better world; and stirred Blake to a new enthusiasm, from which he deducted the theory that apparent Evil, such as War, is only Energy working against established order. This was a new perception of Truth; all his problems seemed solved by it; and he hailed the light triumphantly in another book, *The Marriage of Heaven and Hell* (1793). "A new heaven is begun . . ."; and the third state of the Path was reached: the return of the sense of the transcendent. In the same year, urged perhaps by the expectation of death,[10] he began the series of Prophetic Books engraved at Lambeth ("Lambeth! The Bride, the Lamb's Wife, loveth thee: Thou are one with her & knowest not of self in thy supreme joy," he fondly wrote later[11]); and before the series was ended in 1795, two years later, the "supreme joy" of creation produced seven books of strange poetry and matchless decoration.

This period of inspiration meant a great deal to him. In *Milton*, he described this descent of the Poetic Spirit, Los; and added a full-page illustration of the moment, a picture vibrating with metallic flames. The appearance of Los seems more than a figure of speech. Blake's words are filled with the physical sensation of actual presence:

And Los behind me stood: a terrible flaming
    Sun: just close
Behind my back: I turned round in terror, and
    behold,
Los stood in that fierce-glowing fire. . . .

Los then enters into Blake, who at once beholds the eternal functioning of the Imagination throughout the Universe.

The tremendous creative energy which produced the Lambeth books is one of the three characteristics of the new illumination.[12] Of the other two, the first, the "joyous apprehension of the absolute," is undoubtedly signified by the many paintings of sunrises which Blake did at this period,[13] and his faith in the transcendental effects of Revolution;[14] while the second characteristic, the "cleansing of the doors of perception," has itself been made famous by Blake's quatrain:

To see a World in a grain of sand,
And a Heaven in a wild flower,

Hold Infinity in the palm of your hand,
And Eternity in an hour.

But perhaps this is too "poetical" to be trusted; let us turn to a letter of the same period.[15]

I know This World is a World of Imagination and Vision. I see Everything I paint in This World, but Every body does not see alike. To the Eyes of a Miser, a Guinea is more beautiful than the Sun, and a bag worn with the use of Money has more beautiful proportions than a Vine filled with Grapes. The tree which moves some to tears of joy is in the Eyes of others only a Green thing which stands in the way. Some see Nature all Ridicule and Deformity, and by these I shall not regulate my proportions; and some scarce see Nature at all. But to the Eyes of the Man of Imagination, Nature is Imagination itself. As a Man is, so he sees.

But the Lambeth books show an increasing pessimism. This is the familiar reaction. From the exultation of *America*, through the ominous vortices of *Europe*, to the terrible nadir of *Urizen* and the two books of *Los*, there is a direct descent, which ends with the wail of *Ahania*. To the blackness of Blake's thought was added presently the bitterness of artistic sterility, and the fourth stage, the "Dark Night of the Soul," passed in silence.

Before this Night set in completely, there was an illusory increase of light. In 1800 Blake moved to Felpham, to a cottage near the poet Hayley's "Hermitage." The change from city to seashore, the relief from monetary anxiety (for Hayley was giving him a lot of engraving to do), and the promise of a sympathetic friend, all conspired to make Blake believe that his mundane troubles were over. His poem *To Mrs. Flaxman* breathes with supernatural light. In a letter to her husband, Blake wrote: "Heaven opens here on all sides her golden gates; her windows are not obstructed by vapours; voices of celestial inhabitants are most distinctly heard, and their forms more distinctly seen; and my cottage is also a shadow of their houses. . . . And now begins a new life. . . . " To Thomas Butts a few days later, Blake wrote of his "first vision of light," the ecstasy which came over him on the beach.

But all this, as has been hinted, was illusory. Hayley was a gentleman, but also a fool, who kept Blake either busy engraving ("a work of magnitude," said Blake), or miniature-painting—of all things! What wonder that all Blake's inspiration for his own painting or poetry stopped completely!

One of his worst troubles at this time was the fear of poverty, by which Hayley seems to have held his nose to the grindstone. Blake could not make much money by his own poems and paintings, neither could he give up these "treasures in heaven" just to make money by the nerve-racking work of engraving plates for others, work which often offended his deepest principles. But the greatest suffering he underwent came from the final conviction that the world was deaf to his messages. Even Hayley, the outward friend, despised them. But Blake *knew* his own worth; and it was characteristic of him that he directed his appeal to the "Young Men of a New Age," rather than change his chosen mode of expression one jot.[16]

He complained to one friend only, Thomas Butts. Their letters during this period show only too clearly how Blake was tortured by the galling patronage of Hayley, the "best-seller" in verse. Blake realized that Hayley was kind, that he was trying to help him along by giving him profitable work; but "Corporeal friends are spiritual enemies," and finally Blake wrote Butts his sincere opinion of Hayley, adding: "Indeed, by my late firmness I have brought down his affected loftiness, and he begins to think I have some genius," and ends this sentence with an outburst of contempt: "as if genius and assurance were the same thing!"

This "late firmness" was a burst of wrath which began a series of events in Blake's spiritual life so far-reaching in results, that he recorded them in a fifty-page poem, the Prophetic Book *Milton*. The poem is entirely personal throughout; it is one of the most important documents of mystical psychology in existence.

It describes Blake's return to mental illumination and his final awakening to the "Unitive Life," the last stage of the Mystic Way. Blake begins with an account of the "firmness," told as a spiritual act in Eternity; Hayley (or rather, Hayley's type) being completely disguised, as Blake thought, under the name of Satan! After various difficulties, Blake recognizes his spiritual enemy, and casts off all the intolerable obligations.

At last he is prepared for the final communion with the unseen world. His first vision is pictured on page 36, and labelled, to prevent any doubt, "Blake's Cottage at Felpham." He is walking in the garden, and the angelic visitor, Ololon, descends. Other spirits follow, each apparition preceding a sudden understanding of some truth. Faster and faster the states of vision and of knowledge alternate, until at the last, Unity is achieved: a unity which is "One Man, Jesus the Saviour, wonderful!"

How "real" was this? What did Blake actually see? He told Crabb Robinson that he saw it "in imagination"; and Blake generally was careful to describe all his visions as such; but this cannot satisfy us. It was unmistakably a mystical vision; what is a mystical vision?

In anticipation of a future chapter, it should be explained that Blake never was known to show the slightest belief in the *objective* reality of any vision. *"Where did you see all that, Mr. Blake?"* *"In here"* (pointing to his forehead) is a formula recurring again and again under various guises, in his poems as well as in his biographies.

And yet the violent reality of this vision is underscored. "I turn'd round in terror . . . sudden I beheld . . . words distinct . . . more distinct than any earthly . . . trumpets innumerable sounding articulate" are a few of the phrases, showing his intimate participation in the visionary action. And finally, in a column of fire and a roaring of trumpets, the vision ends.

> Terror-struck in the Vale I stood, at that immortal sound.
> My bones trembled. I fell outstretch'd upon the path
> A moment; & my Soul return'd into its mortal state. . . .
> And my sweet Shadow of Delight[17] stood trembling by my side.
> Immediately the Lark mounted with a loud trill from Felpham's Vales.

Such was the experience which abruptly swung Blake from the "Dark Night" into the raptures of the Unitive Life. It was marked outwardly by a farewell to Hayley and a return to London. He called it a "Last Judgment," a casting-out of error; which explains his fondness for that particular subject.[18] In October 1804, he was even reconciled to the "spiritual enemy" Hayley, and wrote him:

> O lovely Felpham, parent of immortal friendships, to thee I am eternally indebted for my three years' rest from perturbation and the strength I now enjoy. Suddenly, on the day after visiting the Truchsessian Gallery of pictures, I was again enlightened with the light I enjoyed in my youth, and which has for exactly twenty years[19] been closed from me as by a door and by window-shutters. . . . Dear

Sir, excuse my enthusiasm, or rather madness, for I am really drunk with intellectual vision whenever I take a pencil or graver into my hand, even as I used to be in my youth, and as I have not been for twenty dark, but very profitable years.

So at last Blake reached the Unitive Life, the ultimate stage of the Mystic Way. What he had suffered, we can hardly guess. One picture is surely a record: the Crucifixion in the *Jerusalem*, a Crucifixion which, for its feeling, ranks among the greatest ever executed. The night is completely black, in spite of a faint thread of light on the horizon. Hardly more than apprehended is the upturned face of Man gazing upon his tortured God. But the worshipper's faith is unshaken.

And now this was passed. Blake's faith was justified, his inspiration had returned. His state may be verified by a comparison with Miss Underhill's analysis of the ultimate stage.

There are three characteristics. The first is a complete absorption in the interests of the Infinite. Blake devoted the rest of his life to interpreting it by pen and graver. The second is the consciousness of strength, of acting by Divine authority, with an invulnerable serenity. This might well serve as an appreciation of Blake alone! The third is the expression of that strength in some kind of worldly activity. Paul established Christianity; Jeanne d'Arc drove the English from France; Catherine of Siena dominated Italian politics; St. Teresa reformed her order; Blake produced a series of books which reveal the incessant flow of inspiration.

It is profitless to search here for facts about his subsequent spiritual life. One or two facts show that even he could still be reached by circumstance. There is on the tenth page of the *MS. Book* a note: "Tuesday Jan. 20, 1807, between Two and Seven in the Evening—Despair." There was anger over two outrageous attacks in Leigh Hunt's *Examiner*. On the other hand, the *MS. Book* contains a mysterious note dated May 23, 1810: "Found the Word Golden," which has been conjectured to mean "Found the Bible inspired," though that was an already old doctrine with him. Beyond these few items there seem to be no indications of mental turmoil or change of attitude towards the world temporal or spiritual.

As he lived, so he died, singing triumphantly upon his death-bed the hymns which soared upward from his subconscious mind, confident that at last he was passing directly to that Union which he had already known in the flesh.[20]

Thus the five States of the Mystic Way were manifested in Blake's life and works. Naturally he tended to see everything in the same divisions. All history fell into this order: first there was the "Innocence" of unfallen Eternity; then the "Experience" of the Fall; next the appearance of the spiritual Revolutionist, Jesus; whose doctrines were misinterpreted during the "Dark Night" of the following eighteen centuries; which was, however, about to end in the new revelation of Truth and the redemption of Mankind.

One of Blake's most cryptic poems, *The Mental Traveller*, resolves into an analysis of the five States. In accordance with Blake's customary arrangement of composition, it does not begin with the first State, Innocence, because that is not self-conscious. Only in Experience does man begin to feel his separate selfhood. The recognition of errors and sufferings, whether interior or exterior, brings about an immediate reaction. This newborn reaction is "The Babe," who in the Prophetic Books is named Orc. The Babe is crucified by the Old Woman, Custom; but this crucifixion, far from killing the boy, matures him. At last he breaks loose; and the third State, Revolution, is reached. The Old Woman becomes the youthful bride of Orc; Nature is subjected to the creative instinct. He establishes the Truth for which he has suffered; his hearth welcomes all the outcast. But the fourth State is at hand. From his Truth springs Dogma ("the Female Babe") who becomes so sacred that none dare touch her. Blake elsewhere named her Rahab. She sets up her tyranny, indulging her chance favourites, but driving out the very Truth from which she sprang. This is the Dark Night of the Soul. Orc, now aged, wanders through the desert of error, seeking for a new ideal, which is Freedom (Jerusalem). In his pursuit of her, he grows younger and younger again, until the last State is reached, the ultimate Union. Blake, believing that the States move in an eternal cycle, identifies the last and first. Man is now a Babe again in the delights of the first State of ecstasy. In the arms of Freedom he has re-entered Innocence. But it cannot last; Freedom becomes aged into Custom; the Babe again is crucified; and the poem ends while the cycle continues.

This detailed emphasis upon Blake's mystical life is important. Many have ignored, and some few have even denied,[21] Blake's mysticism; while those who mention it speak vaguely, as without knowledge of the matter. Mysticism was *always* the inner impulse of everything Blake wrote or painted, from the *Songs of Innocence* to his last works; if we do not recognize this, we only wonder and aimlessly admire. It is the source of all his doctrines, for it was an actual experience which took precedence of the established faiths and theories. We become ridiculous in protesting against the authority which visions have over seers. Their answer is simply: "I have seen"; and they will not argue as theory what they have known as fact.

But to us who are not seers, visions cannot be authoritative. Blake realized that; and he expended his energy, not in apologizing for his visions, but in teaching the truths they revealed. These truths he intended to be self-justified; they are propped by no appeals to supernaturalism.

The central task he set himself was:

To open the Eternal Worlds, to open the Immortal Eyes
Of Man inwards into the Worlds of Thought: into Eternity;
Ever expanding in the Bosom of God, the Human Imagination;[22]

or, in other words, to teach all mankind how to reach the Paradise of Mysticism, the Garden planted in the brain.

Many other mystics have tried to tell the Ineffable Secret; it is their great tragedy that they all have failed. Mystics, like poets, are born to their inheritance, and words of light mean nothing to the blind.

Among the great poets, only one other—Dante—has described the Mystical Path. Did he succeed? It is hard to say. Dante limited himself for the most part to simple psychology described in terms of the established symbols. Yet even so, when he begins penetrating the abstraction of his Paradise, our interest rapidly vanishes. We are fitter to understand Hell. What we really enjoy in Dante is the poetry, not the fundamental ideas. Probably only one in a thousand understands Dante's Paradise; the rest see nothing but the outward aspects of the images, never suspecting that they are only symbols of something very different, something esoteric.

Therefore Dante, for all his success as a poet, had no success in bringing his mystical message to any but the elect. Blake fails—and succeeds—in precisely the same way.

But Blake falls far below Dante in the literary presentation of the Mystic Way. Dante's lines always remain poetry, however occult his ideas; Blake's do not always. And the contrast is made stronger by the fact that with Blake the general reader *knows* he does not understand, while with Dante he guesses vaguely at meanings, and puts the vital phrases aside as "mere poetry."

There is one more important aspect of Blake as a mystic. In him we find no rejections, no disgusting temptations, terrible starvings or lashings of mind or flesh, no cult of filth; nothing morbid or ascetic whatsoever, not even a disposition towards solemnity or pitiful self-accusations. The normal life, *heightened*, was his idea. He never lost his grip on this world. Even his ecstasies came uninvoked. He left no systems of meditation or magical ceremonies to invoke deity; prayer was his sole method. And at the highest moments of the ecstasy, he puzzles in the back of his mind: "How can I make other men see this?"

It is the purpose of this book to uncover these mysteries of which he wrote. They are not morbid, unbalanced ravings; they contain definite ideas expressed as Blake thought best. There is no need of any spiritual Illumination to comprehend these ideas, for they are self-explanatory, even to the nonmystical.

But is any one entirely non-mystical? Blake, with his amazing psychological insight, decided not.[23] **Indeed, how else can we account for such things as** the wide response to the quatrain already quoted:

To see a World in a Grain of Sand?

Judged from the purely rational point of view, this is nothing but nonsense.

There has been tremendous response to all Blake's work, both poetry and painting, in the past few years. To those who have known Blake's works intimately, they already have meant much, even with their principal messages undelivered. Is it not likely, then, that what remains may be equally human, equally worth hearing?

NOTES

1. *Mysticism: A Study in the Nature and Development of Man's Spiritual Consciousness,* by Evelyn Underhill (4th ed. N.Y., 1912), p. 205.

2. *Gates of Paradise,* plate 13, the turning point of the series. Cf. also *Job,* plate 13.

3. Gilchrist, ch. ix. J. T. Smith (*Nollekens and his Times*) simply says "in one of his visionary imaginings." Allan Cunningham (*Life of Blake*) is the most dramatic; he says that Blake "was made aware that the spirit of his favourite brother Robert was in the room, and to this celestial vistor he applied for counsel." It is noteworthy that Blake's imaginings were especially apt to be active at night.

4. Quoted by W. James (*Varieties of Religious Experience*) from Leuba. His two chapters on Conversion, as well as Miss Underhill's (*Mysticism,* Pt. II. ch. 2), are filled with case after case, all reporting this intense and very real sense of a new light. I must ask the reader to remember that I am not trying to prove any transcendental theories myself. I am only trying to show how Blake underwent certain definite psychological experiences recognized by science: and that these experiences were the inspiration of his work.

5. The "hysterical rapture" which Wordsworth's poem caused to Blake in his last years is recorded in H. C. R., Feb. 27, 1852.

6. Palmer's letter in Gilchrist, ch. xxxiii.

7. However, these were only the imaginings likely to occur to any sensitive child brought up in a religious household.

8. Letter to Trusler, Aug. 23, 1799.

9. Letter to Flaxman, Sept. 12, 1800.

10. "I say I shant live five years. And if I live one it will be a Wonder. June 1793."—*MS. Book.*

11. *Jerusalem,* 12:41–42.

12. Underhill, pp. 288–289.

13. *Marriage,* plates 11, 21; *Visions, Argument; America,* plates 2, 6, 7.

14. See the last line of *America.*

15. Letter to Trusler, Aug. 23, 1799.

16. See the letter to Butts, July 6, 1803; also the Preface to *Milton.*

17. Blake's wife.

18. There is a picture in Blair's *Grave;* one in *Job;* a water-colour done for the Countess of Egremont; a fresco (since lost); an ink drawing owned by Mr. W. A. White; plate 7 of *America;* besides various sketches. The *MS. Book* contains a famous literary description, with which should be mentioned the letter to Ozias Humphrey (1808) and the climax of all three epics.

19. "Exactly twenty years" is a misstatement of enthusiasm. In 1784 the *Poetical Sketches* had been printed for a year, and the *Songs of Innocence* had not even been thought of. Judging by Blake's own works, the terrible period of sterility had lasted only nine years, beginning in 1795, after *Ahania* was engraved.

20. The three designs ending the three epics symbolize the moment of death as the mystical ecstasy. In each the soul is represented as a woman, since it is in the presence of God. The last sketch for *The Four Zoas* represents this soul leaping enraptured from the earth, which has become a tiny globe beneath its feet. The last plate of *Milton* represents the soul in adoration between two seraphim. But the last plate of *Jerusalem* is Blake's finest depiction of the ultimate union. God holds the soul tightly clasped; and together they soar upwards in a region of pure fire.

21. Theodore Maynard in *The Poetry Review,* 1916, vol. vii, p. 317. Irving Babbitt: *Rousseau and Romanticism,* 1919, p. 152. Professor Babbitt's contention that either Blake or Buddha could not be a mystic, because their doctrines differ, is as absurd as claiming that, of two men, one cannot be intoxicated because one goes to sleep while the other breaks windows open.

22. *Jerusalem,* 5:18–20. See also *Milton,* 3:7–8.

23. H. C. R., Dec. 17, 1825. See also W. R. Inge's *Philosophy of Plotinus,* ii, 144.

Northrop Frye

THE RISING GOD*

Samuel Johnson attempted to refute Berkeley by kicking a stone: in doing so he merely transferred his perception of the stone to another sense, but his feeling that the stone existed independently of his foot would possibly have survived even a mention of that fact. Berkeley's argument was that there is a reality about things apart from our perception of them, and, as all reality is mental, this reality must be an idea in the mind of God. Now God and man are different things to Berkeley, and this sudden switch from one to the other leaves a gap in the middle of his thought. Blake, by postulating a world of imagination higher than that of sense, indicates a way of closing the gap which is completed by identifying God with human imagination:

> Man is All Imagination. God is Man & exists in us & we in him.

> The Eternal Body of Man is The Imagination, that is, God himself. . . . It manifests itself in his Works of Art (In Eternity All is Vision).[1]

Man in his creative acts and perceptions is God, and God is Man. God is the eternal Self, and the worship of God is self-development. This disentangles the idea raised in the preceding chapter of the two worlds of perception. This world is one of perceiver and perceived, of subject and objects; the world of imagination is one of creators and creatures. In his creative activity the artist expresses the creative activity of God; and as all men are contained in Man or God, so all creators are contained in the Creator.

This doctrine of God further explains how a visionary can be said to be normal rather than ab-

normal, even though his appearance may be rare. The sane man is normal not because he is just like everyone else but because he is superior to the lunatic; the healthy man is normal because he is superior to the cripple. That is, they are most truly themselves. The visionary is supreme normality because most of his contemporaries are privative just as cripples and lunatics are. Whatever he is from their point of view, he is more of a man than they, and it is his successes that make him truly "human," not his failures or weaknesses, as they are apt to say. Hence the visionary expresses something latent in all men; and just as it is only in themselves that the latter find God, so it is only in the visionary that they can see him found. As imagination *is* life, no one is born without any imagination except the stillborn, but those who cut their imagination down as far as they can, deny, as far as they can, their own manhood and their divinity which is that manhood. They will therefore turn their backs on the genius who greatly acts and greatly perceives; but they retain the power to enter into kinship with him:

> The worship of God is: Honouring his gifts in other men, each according to his genius, and loving the greatest men best: those who envy or calumniate great men hate God; for there is no other God.[2]

The identity of God and man is qualified by the presence in man of the tendency to deny God by self-restriction. Thus, though God is the perfection of man, man is not wholly God: otherwise there would be no point in bringing in the idea of God at all. On the other hand, the infinite variety of men is no argument against the unity of God. Such ideas as "mankind" and "humanity" are only generalized; but the fact that an acorn produces only an oak indicates the fact of species or class as clearly as it indicates the fallacy of a generalized

---

* From *Fearful Symmetry: A Study of William Blake*, (copyright 1947 © 1969 by Princeton University Press; Princeton Paperback, 1969) pp. 30–54. Reprinted by permission of Princeton University Press.

tree. Blake's word "form" always includes this unity of species: he says, for instance:

> The Oak is cut down by the Ax, the Lamb falls
>   by the Knife,
> But their Forms Eternal Exist For-ever.[3]

Similarly, God is not only the genius but the genus of man, the "Essence" from which proceed the individuals or "Identities" mentioned in Blake's note on Swedenborg:

> Essence is not Identity, but from Essence proceeds Identity & from one Essence may proceed many Identities. . . .

> If the Essence was the same as the Identity, there could be but one Identity, which is false. Heaven would upon this plan be but a Clock. . . .[4]

(Blake is attacking what seems to him a tendency to pantheism in Swedenborg.) Just as the perceived object derives its reality from being not only perceived but related to a unified imagination, so the perceiver must derive his from being related to the universal perception of God. If God is the only Creator, he is the only Perceiver as well. In every creative act or perception, then, the act or perception is universal and the perceived object particular. And we have already met the converse of this principle, that when the perception is egocentric the perceived object is general. There are thus two modes of existence. The ego plays with shadows like the men in Plato's cave; to perceive the particular and imagine the real is to perceive and imagine as part of a Divine Body. A hand or eye is individual because it is an organ of a body: separated from the body it loses all individuality beyond what is dead and useless. That is why the imagination is constructive and communicable and why the "memory" is circular and sterile. The universal perception of the particular is the "divine image" of the *Songs of Innocence*; the egocentric perception of the general is the "human abstract" of the *Songs of Experience*. This is the basis of Blake's theory of good and evil which we shall meet in the next chapter.

There are two corollaries of this. One is that we perceive *as* God: we do not perceive God. "No man hath seen God at any time," because true perception is creation, and God cannot be created. We may see the divine aspect of great men, but when we do the divine in us recognizes itself. The other

is, that, as we cannot perceive anything higher than a man, nothing higher than Man can exist. The artist proves this by the fact that he can paint God only as a man, though if he is reproducing senile and epicene ideas of God he will paint an enfeebled old man out of compliment to them. But there is no form of life superior to our own; and the acceptance of Jesus, as the fullness of both God and Man entails the rejection of all attributes of divinity which are not human:

> Man can have no idea of any thing greater than Man, as a cup cannot contain more than its capaciousness. But God is a man, not because he is so perceiv'd by man, but because he is the creator of man.[5]

Naturally those brought up on abstract ideas will begin by denying both of these postulates, so let us see what success they have with their theology.

2

We have quoted Blake as saying that the idea of "proportion" means nothing except in relation to a concrete thing which possesses it. The proportions of a real thing are part of its "living form." We can only detach the idea of proportion from reality through what he calls "mathematic form"; generalized symmetry without reference to perceived objects. Now this idea of "mathematic form" has always had a peculiar importance for abstract reasoners, who try to comprehend God's creative power through the abstract idea of creation, or "design."

Hence there is a recurrent desire to believe that some simpler pattern, expressible perhaps in some mathematical formula, underlies the complications of our universe. I say complications, for this line of thought takes the world as complicated rather than complex. Pythagoras began with the patterns of simple arithmetic and the cardinal numbers; the *Timaeus* attempted to work out the geometrical shapes considered most fitting (this word will meet us again) from which to deduce all phenomena; and with the elaboration of the Ptolemaic universe the tendency spread in all directions. Many of its manifestations, particularly those that still survive, are occult, or at least highly speculative. But actually the whole tendency to symmetrical pattern-making in thought is very inadequately described as occultism, which is only a specialized department of it. Pattern-making extends over philosophy from Pythagoras to the Renaissance as a kind of intermediate stage between magic and science.

These latter two are psychologically very similar, we are told; both attempt to manipulate the laws of nature for man's purposes. And if this tendency to explain the world as a complication of simple mathematical formulae is, as we suggest, intermediate between magic and science and psychologically allied to both, we should expect Blake's attitude to it to be much the same as his attitude to science. Briefly, it may be said that the whole Pythagorean tradition in thought, from the *Timaeus* to our own day, has nothing to do with Blake and appears in him only in the form of parody. He simply did not believe in "the mystical Mathematicks of the City of Heaven." "The Gods of Greece & Egypt were Mathematical Diagrams—See Plato's Works," [6] he says. It sounds flippant, but it was the most serious criticism he had to offer.

It is worth insisting on this, because occultists are frequently attracted to Blake, and the above statement may well surprise anyone who has noticed the role that recurring cardinal numbers and even diagrams play in the later prophecies. But real things have mathematical principles inherent in them, and a work of art, which is a synthesis of real things, has mathematical principles inherent in its unity. Blake distinguishes between the art of "mathematic form," like Greek architecture, which displays a tendency to generalized symmetry, and the art of "living form," like Gothic architecture, which has kept that symmetry properly subordinated.[7] But the Gothic arch and spire would soon collapse without mathematical principles. The Apocalypse in the Bible is an imaginative and visionary work of art, but it is not the less so for making a symbolic use of the number seven. The recurrence of this number is part of its unity as a poem, not an attempt to indicate a sevenfold aspect of things in general. Similarly in Blake all recurrent numbers and diagrams must be explained in terms of their context and their relation to the poems, not as indicating in Blake any affinity with mathematical mysticism.

3

The poetic basis of symmetrical thought is now fairly clear to us since the Copernican universe replaced the Ptolemaic one. But the later system has developed new methods of conceiving an impersonal and abstract God which are equally antithetical to Blake, and these, being more contemporary, bear the main brunt of his attack, and form the basis for his treatment of Newton. The vast size of the Copernican universe has encouraged many timid souls to feel that the creation of it must be ascribed to an impersonal Power, whose nature can be understood only through our ideas of mechanical force. Hence the true followers of such a God are "men of destiny"; men of force or cunning rather than intelligence or imagination, and those unfortunate enough to possess the latter would do well to avoid him, or rather it. It is true that the more striking manifestations of this religion are later than Blake: when to the ice-cold and ether-breathing deity of the Copernican system was added the immense stretch of geological time, in which nothing particularly cheerful seems to have occurred, gods like the "immanent Will" of Hardy's *Dynasts* were developed of a ferocity unknown to Blake's age. Blake, however, in his depiction of the chilling terror of his character Urizen, the god of empty space and blind will, shows a remarkably prophetic insight into these dinosaur-haunted theologies.

He himself regards the "immanent Will" account of God as superstitious. Not, of course, because he has any more faith in the benevolent avuncular God who explains away all suffering and injustice at the Last Judgment and proves himself to have had the best intentions all along. Nor does he agree with those who accept it negatively and feel that its "right worship is defiance." [8] He disagrees with it on the same ground that he disagrees with Locke's account of abstract ideas. Locke extends involuntary and automatic reflexes to include the passive reception of sense impressions, which to Blake should be the products of an active consciousness. Similarly, the worshiper of "immanent Will" is extending the subconscious activity of the heartbeat from sense experience to the whole universe. And he does it by exactly the same process of trying to find a least common denominator for his general principles. A man, a dog and a tree are all alive; therefore life must be inherently and really some kind of "life force" common to them which can only be identified with the lowest possible limit of life—protoplasm, perhaps. But as the boundary between living things and moving things is difficult

to trace, the "immanent Will" is bound to sink below "life force" to take in all other forms of motion
in a more inclusive generalization still.

It is much better, as in the previous case, to go
to work the other way. A man, a dog and a tree are
all alive; but the man is the most alive; and it is
in man that we should look for the image, or form,
of universal life. There can be no "life force" apart
from things possessing it: universal life is the totality of living things, and God has intelligence, judgment, purpose and desire because we are alive and
possess these things.

The Darwinian universe merely adds the tyranny
of time and will to the tyranny of space and reason
with which Blake was already acquainted, and suggests a generalized energy abstracted from form
supplementing the generalized form abstracted
from energy which we find in Locke's conception
of substance. "No Omnipotence can act against
order," Blake says.[9] If Blake had lived a century
later he would undoubtedly have taken sides at
once with Butler and Shaw and claimed that alterations in an organism are produced by the development of the organism's "imagination"; and the doctrine of environmental stimulus in time would have
fitted into the same plane in his thought as Locke's
doctrine of involuntary sense perception in space.

As a matter of fact Blake does use the persistence
of life as an argument that the hold of life on the
world is not precarious. Lightning may kill a man,
but it cannot beget him: life can come only from
life, and must go straight back to the creation at
least, which implies the primacy of creative over
destructive energy. Worshipers of the "immanent
Will" see its most striking effects in the latter, and
in the irony and tragedy it suggests, but this must
be subordinate to the power of incubation. We have
already noticed that Blake's words "form" and "image" mean a species persisting through time: "The
Oak dies as well as the Lettuce, but Its Eternal
Image & Individuality never dies, but renews by
its seed." [10] Further, when Blake says: "Each thing
is its own cause and its own effect," [11] he means
that life is not itself caused by anything external to
it, and there is no causality which is not part of an
organic process. Accidents happen, but when they
do they are not part of a larger superhuman
scheme; they are part of the breakdown of human
schemes, and their "meaning" depends on what
the human mind does with them.

Blake was familiar enough with the earlier manifestations of life-force worship in eighteenth century primitivism. That postulated a "nature" as the
body of life from which man has sprung, and that
too attempted to cut parts away from human imagination by asserting that the latter was diseased
and adulterated insofar as it had developed away
from nature. Blake had no use for the noble savage
or for the cult of the natural man; he disliked
Rousseau enough to give an attack on him a prominent place in *Jerusalem*. Civilization is in more
than one sense supernatural: it is something which
man's superiority over nature has evolved, and the
central symbol of the imagination in all Blake's
work is the city. "Where man is not, nature is
barren," [12] he says. Of all animals, man is the most
hopelessly maladjusted to nature: that is why he
outdistances the animals, the supreme triumph of
the imagination which has developed and conquered rather than survived and "fitted."

4

Thus we find ourselves unable to conceive of anything superhuman in the direction of either design
or power. The same thing happens when we try
to conceive a "perfect" God. Perfection, when it
means anything, means the full development of all
one's imagination. This is what Jesus meant when
he said "Be ye therefore perfect." But many timid
abstract thinkers feel that this is irreverent, and
that perfection lies in the completeness with which
a quality is abstracted from a real thing. God is thus
thought to be "pure" goodness. Such a God could
never have created Falstaff, to whom he would be
vastly inferior. If this idea of "pure" perfection is
pressed a little further it dissolves in negatives, as
all abstract ideas do. God is infinite, inscrutable,
incomprehensible—all negative words, and a negative communion with some undefined ineffability
is its highest development. What Blake thinks of
this he has put into one of his most brilliant epigrams:

> God Appears & God is Light
> To those poor Souls who dwell in Night,
> But does a Human Form Display
> To those who Dwell in Realms of day.[13]

It is an old quibble that God cannot move because
to move is to alter and to alter would be to lessen

his perfection. As long as this means abstract perfection, the argument is unanswerable: a negatively perfect God is not a Creator.

In the first chapter of Genesis we read of a God, or Gods, called Elohim, who can be reconciled with a philosophical First Cause. So completely is he a God of unconscious and automatic order that he created the sun, moon and stars chiefly to provide a calendar for Jewish ritual, and rested on the Sabbath to institute a ceremonial law. In the next chapter we come across a folklore God named Jehovah, a fussy, scolding, bad-tempered but kindly deity who orders his disobedient children out of his garden after making clothes for them, who drowns the world in a fit of anger and repeoples it in a fit of remorse. Such a God has much to learn, but he come far closer to what Jesus meant by a Father than the other, and gets a correspondingly higher place in Blake's symbolism.[14]

Even when we try to think of the superhuman in terms of intelligence and imagination we run into difficulties. To be is to be perceived, and we perceive nothing higher than man. The one certain inference from this is that we cannot conceive an essentially superhuman imagination, and when we try to imagine above human nature we always imagine below it. It has been said that grasshoppers are like gods in that they are without blood or feeling. Such gods are therefore as much inferior to man as grasshoppers are, or would be if they could exist. We can imagine men who can do things we cannot; who can fly, who perspire instead of excreting food, who converse by intuition instead of words. But these are differences in attributes, not in substance: the latter we cannot imagine. In Blake there are no characters who represent anything qualitatively superior to man in the way that a man is superior to a fish. There is no "chain of being" in Blake and no trace of any of the creatures invented by those who believe in a chain of being: no gods, no eons, no emanations (in the Gnostic sense: Blake's use of this term is different), no world-soul, no angelic intelligences bound on the spindle of necessity. If they had any intelligence they would get off it, as man got off the spindle of nature.

This is important as throwing some light on Blake's ideas of inspiration. It is true that Blake often makes remarks implying an external spiritual agency. He speaks, for instance, of his poems as "dictated," and of himself as their "secretary." [15] But usually the term "angel" or "spirit' in Blake, when not used in an ironic sense, means the imagination functioning as inspiration, and the fact that inspiration often takes on a purpose of its own which appears to be independent of the will is familiar to every creative artist. Blake says, for instance: "Every man's leading propensity ought to be call'd his leading Virtue & his good Angel." [16] It is the same with the "dictation" of his poetry:

> When this Verse was first dictated to me, I consider'd a Monotonous Cadence . . . to be a necessary and indispensible part of Verse. But I soon found . . .

If the inspiration were anything external to Blake he would have had no choice in the matter. "Spirits are organized men," he says, and he would agree with Paul that "the spirits of the prophets are subject to the prophets." [17]

The spirit which is the organized man may also be, however, the imagination which has got itself disentangled from its present world through the process we call death. The imagination cannot exist except as a bodily form, but the body is only what others on the same plane of existence see of the soul or mind. Hence when the imagination changes its world it can change its bodily form as completely as the lepidoptera which have suggested most of the images of immortality. Christianity has always insisted on the resurrection of the body, though the two facts that the risen body is spiritual and that it is a body are hard to keep both in mind at once. All belief in ghosts or shades or in any form of spirit conceived as less than bodily is superstitious: there is no *animula vagula blandula* in Blake.

5

There is no divinity in sky, nature or thought superior to our selves. Hence there is in Blake no acceptance of the *données* of existence as such, no Leibnitzian idea of the perfection of *established* order. Nor is there any idea of finding in nature external hints or suggestions of God; all such intuitions are implanted by the mind on nature. Nature is there for us to transform; it is neither a separate creation of God nor an objective counterpart of ourselves. Blake criticized Wordsworth sharply for ascribing to nature what he should have ascribed to his own mind and for believing in the correspondence of human and natural orders:

How exquisitely the individual Mind
(And the progressive powers perhaps no less
Of the whole species) to the external World
Is fitted:—and how exquisitely, too—
Theme this but little heard of among men—
The external World is fitted to the Mind.

"You shall not bring me down to believe such fitting & fitted," is Blake's comment on this passage.[18]

We arrive at the emotions of acceptance and obedience only at the price of stifling part of our imaginations. In terms of man's desires, we see nothing outside man worthy of respect. Nature is miserably cruel, wasteful, purposeless, chaotic and half dead. It has no intelligence, no kindness, no love and no innocence. Man under natural law is more pitiful than Diogenes' plucked cock. In a state of nature man must surrender intelligence for ferocity and cunning, kindness and pity for a relentless fight to survive, love for the reproductive instinct, innocence for obedience to humiliating laws.

When we look up from the earth to the whizzing balls of ice and fire in the sky we see there merely an extension of nature. It is instinctive with the ignorant to worship the sun as the giver of life, and superstition of this sort is described by Blake as ignorant honesty, beloved of God and man.[19] The advance of knowledge in revealing the deadness and remoteness of the sun should not destroy this instinct for worship, but it should eliminate the sun as a possible object of it. Unthinkable distances and endless resources for killing anyone who might conceivably approach them is all the response the heavens afford to the exploring imagination. They therefore cannot be connected with any feeling of love, reverence, loyalty or anything else we associate with a personal God. And an impersonal God can be worshiped only by the servile, the self-hypnotized, the hypocritical, or at most the resigned.

However, it is all very well to abuse nature, but the divinity in us which Blake postulates is hardly more reassuring. We are capable of depths of cruelty and folly that sink below anything in nature. Yet is not the source of evil the natural weakness of man's body, the form his mind takes in the physical World? Our sight is feeble compared to the lynx; our movements stumbling and foolish compared to a bird; our strength and beauty grotesque compared to the tiger. Once we begin to think in terms of wish and desire, we find ourselves beating prison bars. Our desire to see goes far beyond any telescope. We are ashamed of our bodies, and though the shame itself is shameful, particularly when we realize that they are the forms of our souls, it is there, and it is hard to love a Creator who could, for instance, make our "places of joy & love excrementitious." [20] We are fearfully and wonderfully made, but in terms of what our imaginations suggest we could be, we are a hideous botch. The man who does not use his imagination is the natural man, and the natural man, according to all versions of Christianity except Deism, can do nothing good; yet what does the imagination do except reveal to us our own impotence?

The realization that the world we desire and create with our imaginations is both better and more real than the world we see leads us to regard the latter world as "fallen." It is a cheap print or reproduction of what was once the vision of the unbounded creative power of God, and all great visions in art lead up to visions of the unfallen world, called Paradise in the Bible and the Golden Age in the Classics. "The Nature of my Work is Visionary or Imaginative," said Blake; "it is an Endeavour to Restore what the Ancients call'd the Golden Age." [21] In Christian terms, this means that the end of art is the recovery of Paradise. The Bible tells us that in Paradise man was integrated with God: nature to him was not ocean and wilderness but his own property, symbolized by a garden or park which is what the word "Paradise" means; animals were neither ferocious nor terrified, and life had no pain or death.

In Blake there are certain modifications of the orthodox account of the Fall. One is that as all reality is mental, the fall of man's mind involved a corresponding fall of the physical world. Another is, that as God is Man, Blake follows some of the Gnostics and Boehme in believing that the fall of man involved a fall in part of the divine nature. Not all, for then there would be no imagination left to this one; but part, because it is impossible to derive a bad world from a good God, without a great deal of unconvincing special pleading and an implicit denial of the central fact of Christianity, the identity of God and Man. The conclusion for Blake, and the key to much of his symbolism, is that the fall of man and the creation of the physical world were the same event.

All works of civilization, all the improvements

and modifications of the state of nature that man has made, prove that man's creative power is literally supernatural. It is precisely because man is superior to nature that he is so miserable in a state of nature. Now in a state of nature, in which we use as little imagination as possible, our minds exist in the form only of our dirty, fragile, confined bodies, and from that point of view man is a speck of life precariously perched on a larger speck in a corner of a huge, mysterious, indifferent, lifeless cosmos. When the subject exists in a cramped distortion the object will necessarily exist in a monstrous distortion. The visionary insists that everything in the physical world which we call real is a matter of perspective and associations:

> How do you know but ev'ry Bird that cuts the
>   airy way,
> Is an immense world of delight, clos'd by your
>   senses five? [22]

There is nothing particularly lovable about a wolf or a fox, but there may be about a dog. Man has caught and trained the dog; he has developed the dog's intelligence and has projected his own imagination on him. He loves the dog more than the wolf because there is more of man in the dog. We get out of nature what we put into it, and the training of a dog is an imaginative victory over nature. So an artist catches and trains the objects of his vision; he can put human imagination into them, make them intelligible and responsive. In a picture every detail is significant and relevant to the whole design. That is an image of the world the visionary wants to live in; a world so fully possessed by the human imagination that its very rocks and clouds are more alive and more responsive than the dogs in this world are. Up to a point we can talk to a dog and make him talk back; we cannot make a tree talk back, but in a higher world we could create the tree as completely as we create sons and daughters in this world. The Classical dryad represents a partial attempt to transform an object of perception into a creature:

> ... the forms of all things are derived from
>   their Genius, which by the Ancients was call'd
>   an Angel & Spirit & Demon. [23]

The *Metamorphoses* of Ovid record the converse process, of humanized creatures dwindling into objects of perception, which implies that they are images of the fall of man. As our imaginations expand the world takes on a growing humanity, for to see things as created by God and in God is the same as seeing things as created by Man and in Man:

> ... Each grain of Sand,
> Every Stone of the Land,
> Each rock & each hill,
> Each fountain & rill,
> Each herb & each tree,
> Mountain, hill, earth & sea,
> Cloud, Meteor & Star,
> Are Men seen Afar. [24]

The fallen world is the world of the *Songs of Experience*: the unfallen world is the world of the *Songs of Innocence*. Naturally those who live most easily in the latter are apt to be, from the point of view of those absorbed wholly in the former, somewhat naïve and childlike. In fact most of them are actually children. Children live in a protected world which has something, in epitome, of the intelligibility of the state of innocence, and they have an imaginative recklessness which derives from that. The child who cries to have the moon as a plaything, who slaps a table for hurting him when he bumps his head, who can transform the most unpromising toy into a congenial companion, has something which the adult can never wholly abandon without collapsing into mediocrity.

The paradisal Eden of the Bible is described in terms of a pastoral placidity which may suggest to an unsympathetic reader that Adam fell because he outgrew it: the suggestion is much stronger in *Paradise Lost*. Yet this association of innocence with naïveté is by no means adequate. An unfallen world completely vitalized by the imagination suggests human beings of gigantic strength and power inhabiting it, such as we find hinted at in the various Titanic myths. The vision of such beings would be able to penetrate all the mysteries of the world, searching into mountains or stars with equal ease, as in this description of the bound Titan Orc:

> His eyes, the lights of his large soul, contract
>   or else expand;
> Contracted they behold the secrets of the infi-
>   nite mountains,
> The veins of gold & silver & the hidden things
>   of Vala,
> Whatever grows from its pure bud or breathes
>   a fragrant soul;
> Expanded they behold the terrors of the Sun &
>   Moon,
> The Elemental Planets & the Orbs of eccentric
>   fire. [25]

Even in those moments when most "we feel that we are greater than we know," this feeling is not so much one of individuality as of integration into a higher unit or body of life. This body, of course, is ultimately God, the totality of all imagination. But even men who cannot reach the idea of God believe in the reality of larger human bodies, such as nations, cities or races, and even speak of them as fathers or mothers. It takes a genuine faith to see a nation or race as a larger human being, or form of human existence, and a good deal of such faith is undoubtedly idolatry. Still, there is a partial idea of God in it, and in a Utopia or millennium it would become direct knowledge or vision, such as Milton suggests when he says that "a Commonwealth ought to be but as one huge Christian personage, one mighty growth, and stature of an honest man." [26] Hence these gigantic forms which inhabit the unfallen world are, on nearer view, human aggregates of the kind which inspire loyalty even in this world:

> . . . these various States I have seen in my Imagination; when distant they appear as One Man, but as you approach they appear multitudes of Nations.[27]

This exactly fits what we have just said, that the fall of man involved a fall in part but not all of the divine nature. The particular "Giant form" or "Eternal" to which we belong has fallen, the aggregate of spirits we call mankind or humanity and Blake calls Albion (Adam in Blake has his regular place as the symbol of the physical body or the natural man). When Albion or mankind fell, the unity of man fell too, and although our imagination tells us we belong to some larger organism even if we cannot see it as God, in the meantime we are locked up in separated opaque scattered bodies. If the whole of mankind were once more integrated in a single spiritual body the universe as we see it would burst.

Theology distinguishes between "natural" and "revealed" religion, the former being the vision of God which man develops with his fallen reason and the latter the vision communicated to him by inspired prophets. To Blake "There Is No Natural Religion." The only reason that people believe in it is that they are unwilling to believe in the identity of God and Man. If there is evil in nature, it must be our fault and not God's; therefore God created the world good, the extent to which man's fall altered that goodness being a disputed point. But if we stop trying to rescue the credit of an abstract and pure goodness, we can easily see that all religion is revealed. The Greek word for revelation is "apocalypse," and the climax of Christain teaching is in the "Revelation" or Apocalypse at the end of the Bible which tells us that there is an end to time as well as a beginning and a middle, a resurrection as well as a birth and a death; and that in this final revelation of the unfallen world all mystery will vanish: John's symbol is the burning of the Great Whore who is called Mystery. Such a revelation involves the destruction of the present world, when the sun will be turned into darkness and the moon into blood and the stars will fall from heaven like ripe figs. It moves on to a new heaven and earth (*i.e.,* an earth renewed or revealed in the form of heaven), in which the chaos of nature becomes our own garden, as in Paradise, a world no longer continuously perceived but continually created:

> In futurity
> I prophetic see
> That the earth from sleep
> (Grave the sentence deep)
> Shall arise and seek
> For her maker meek;
> And the desert wild
> Become a garden mild.[28]

Now when something is revealed to us we see it, and the response to this revelation is not faith in the unseen or hope in divine promises but vision, seeing face to face after we have been seeing through a glass darkly. Vision is the end of religion, and the destruction of the physical universe is the clearing of our own eyesight. Art, because it affords a systematic training in this kind of vision, is the medium through which religion is revealed. The Bible is the vehicle of revealed religion because it is a unified vision of human life and therefore, as Blake says, "the Great Code of Art." [29] And if all art is visionary, it must be apocalyptic and revelatory too: the artist does not wait to die before he lives in the spiritual world into which John was caught up. To quote Wordsworth again in a passage which explains why Blake admired as well as criticized him:

> . . . The unfettered clouds and region of the
>   Heavens,
> Tumult and peace, the darkness and the
>   light—

Were all like workings of one mind, the
    features
Of the same face, blossoms upon one tree;
Characters of the great Apocalypse,
The types and symbols of Eternity [30]

According to Wordsworth the perceived forms of
the eternal world are those which are constantly perceived in this one, and it is not in the grandiose or
exceptional experience that "the types and symbols
of Eternity" are to be found. Blake is merely extending this principle when he says in "Auguries of
Innocence":

> To see a World in a Grain of Sand
> And a Heaven in a Wild Flower,
> Hold Infinity in the palm of your hand
> And Eternity in an hour. [31]

Such perception, as the title of the poem makes
clear, is an "augury" of the paradisal unfallen state.
The last two lines bring us to the next step in the
argument.

Those who, like Locke, attempt to separate existence from perception are also separating time from
space, as we exist in time and perceive in space.
Those who, like the artists, accept the mental nature
of reality, know that we perceive a thing at a definite moment, and that there is thus a quality of
time inherent in all perception; and, on the other
hand, that existence is in a body, which has a spatial
extension. We are back again to Blake's doctrine
that "Reason is the bound or outward circumference of Energy," that energy and form, existence
and perception, are the same thing. Consequently
every act of the imagination, every such union of
existence and perception, is a time-space complex,
not time plus space, but time *times* space, so to
speak, in which time and space as we know them
disappear, as hydrogen and oxygen disappear when
they become water.

This is what the words "eternal" and "infinite"
mean in Blake. Eternity is not endless time, nor
infinity endless space: they are the entirely different
mental categories through which we perceive the
unfallen world. A spiritual world which is visualized
as a world of unchanging order, symbolized by the
invariable interrelations of mathematics, is not an
eternal world but a spatial one, from which time
has simply been eliminated. And, to complete the
antithesis, a spiritual world visualized as one of
unchanging duration is a world of abstract time,

from which the "bounding outline" or spatial limits
of existence have been eliminated. The Lockian can
conceive of eternity and infinity only in either or
both of these ways: that is why he uses two words,
one suggesting time and the other space, for the
same thing. But his two categories have nothing to
do with real infinity and eternity; nor, in fact, has
he two of them: all he has in each case is the indefinite, which is the opposite of the infinite or eternal,
and one of the most sinister words in Blake's symbolism.

Clock time is a mental nightmare like all other
abstract ideas. An impalpable present vanishing between an irrevocable past and an unknown future,
it is the source of all our ideas of fate and causality.
It suggests an inexorable march of inevitably succeeding events in which everything is a necessary
consequence of causes stretching back to an unknown God as a First Cause and stretching on into
a future which would be completely predictable if
it were not too complicated. Its only possible symbol not only for Blake but even for those who believe in it is the chain, which is also a symbol of
slavery. At best time is "the mercy of Eternity" [32];
its swiftness makes more tolerable the conditions of
our fallen state.

To the imaginative eye there is a more definite
shape to time. In most religious allegories, including
Blake's, this is indicated by the boundaries ascribed
to it, a beginning at the creation or fall and an end
at the apocalypse. This is a convenient way of expressing the fact that the fallen world is temporal
and the unfallen eternal, but it is not essential, and
is even misleading when carried too far. "In the
beginning God created the heaven and earth": if
we try to visualize what happened *before* that, we
get an impression of extraordinary bleakness. This
is because we cannot think of eternity except by
extending time indefinitely, when we think of it as
a continuation of this world:

> Many suppose that before the Creation All was
> Solitude & Chaos. This is the most pernicious
> Idea that can enter the Mind. . . . Eternity
> Exists, and All things in Eternity, Independent
> of Creation which was an act of Mercy. [33]

Orthodox ideas of the joys of heaven and the torments of hell also deal with the indefinite rather
than the eternal.

The religious idea of "salvation" depends on
transcending this view of time. The man survives

the death of the natural part of him as the total form of his imaginative acts, as the human creation out of nature which he has made. When Blake says, "Eternity is in love with the productions of time," [34] he means in part that every imaginative victory won on this earth, whether by the artist, the prophet, the martyr, or by those who achieve triumphs of self-sacrifice, kindliness and endurance, is a permanent reality, while the triumphs of the unimaginative are lost. Existence and perception being the same thing, man exists eternally by virtue of, and to the extent of, his perception of eternity. Any doctrine of personal immortality which conceives of it either as the survival of the individual or of the disappearance of the individual into some objective form of generalized being, such as matter or force or the collective memory of posterity, is again thinking of the eternal as the indefinite.

The same principles apply to space. The universe stretches out to indefiniteness in all directions, and to the fallen eye it is without any kind of limit or outline. All that this suggests to the imagination is the latter's own insignificance and helplessness. Yet somehow we manage to shrug it off and go on with our own concerns. By doing so we indicate that as far as our lives go there is something about time and space that is not real, and something about us that is. However man may have tumbled into this world of indefinite space, he does not belong to it at all. Real space for him is the eternal here; where we are is always the center of the universe, and the circumference of our affairs is the circumference of the universe, just as real time is the "eternal Now" [35] of our personal experience. The ordinary man assumes, as a working hypothesis, that all the universe outside his range is not worth bothering one's head about unduly. The visionary sees, as the final revelation of the Word which God speaks to his mind, that the whole "outside" universe is a shadow of an eclipsed Man.

6

According to Locke ideas come from space into the mind; according to Blake space is a state of mind. But, as fallen man sees around him only the ruins of a fallen world which his own fall produced, space is a low state of mind. In higher states, where the world we live in is not objective but created, space is no longer an indefinite extent but the form of what we create. This portion of Blake's argument

comes, *mutatis mutandis,* from Swedenborg.[36] Let us now return to that crucial passage about the two suns discussed in the last chapter and give it again in its proper context:

> Error is Created. Truth is Eternal. Error, or Creation, will be Burned up, & then, & not till Then, Truth or Eternity will appear. It is Burnt up the Moment Men cease to behold it. I assert for My Self that I do not behold the outward Creation & that to me it is hindrance & not Action; it is as the dirt upon my feet, No part of Me. "What," it will be Question'd, "When the Sun rises, do you not see a round disk of fire somewhat like a Guinea?" O no, no, I see an Innumerable company of the Heavenly host crying, "Holy, Holy, Holy is the Lord God Almighty." I Question not my Corporeal or Vegetative Eye any more than I would Question a Window concerning a Sight. I look thro' it & not with it.

We have said that there are at least three levels of imagination. The lowest is that of the isolated individual reflecting on his memories of perception and evolving generalizations and abstract ideas. This world is single, for the distinction of subject and object is lost and we have only a brooding subject left. Blake calls this world Ulro; it is his hell, and his symbols for it are symbols of sterility, chiefly rocks and sand. Above it is the ordinary world we live in, a double world of subject and object, of organism and environment, which Blake calls Generation. No living thing is completely adjusted to this world except the plants, hence Blake usually speaks of it as vegetable. Above it is the imaginative world, and Blake divides this into an upper and a lower part, so that the three worlds expand into four.

Imagination very often begins with a vision of wonderful and unearthly beauty. The writings of many visionaries are full of a childlike delight in a paradisal world which is the same world that other people see, but seen differently. Traherne's *Centuries of Meditations* is a typical book of this kind: the feeling that with the purging of vision one is enabled to possess the entire universe is particularly strong there. Sexual love dwells in the same paradisal state, and from such a love we may proceed up a ladder of love to an imaginative awakening, as in the traditional philosophy of love derived from the *Symposium*.

Love and wonder, then, are stages in an imaginative expansion: they establish a permanent unity of subject and object, and they lift us from a world of subject and object to a world of lover and beloved. Yet they afford us only a lower Paradise after all. Wonder would doubtless have been defined by Blake differently from Johnson's "effect of novelty upon ignorance," [37] but perhaps he would only have substituted "innocence" for the last word. Ultimately, our attitude to what we see is one of mental conquest springing from active energy. Love and wonder are relaxations from this state: they do not produce the visions of art but an imaginative receptivity. The "Renaissance of Wonder" to Blake could be nothing more than a preliminary imaginative revolt from the fallen world. The imaginative intensity which finds delight and beauty in considering the lilies may remain suffusing us with a vague and unlocalized joy, and with this we may well be content. But the impulse to make some kind of creation out of it is still there, and poetry and painting are the result of the perseverance of vision in conquest. The highest possible state, therefore, is not the union of lover and beloved, but of creator and creature, of energy and form. This latter is the state for which Blake reserves the name Eden. The lower Paradise he calls Beulah, a term derived from Isaiah which means "married," and is used to describe the relation of a land to its people.[38] Eden in Blake's symbolism is a fiery city of the spiritual sun; Beulah is the garden of Genesis in which the gods walk in the cool of the day.

As Ulro is a single and Generation a double world, so Beulah is triple, the world of lover, beloved and mutual creation; the father, the mother and the child. In Eden these three are contained in the unified imagination symbolized in the Bible by the four "Zoas" or living creatures around the throne or chariot of God, described by Ezekiel and John.[39] This world therefore is fourfold, expanding to infinity like the four points of the compass which in this world point to the indefinite. To recapitulate:

> Now I a fourfold vision see,
> And a fourfold vision is given to me;
> 'Tis fourfold in my supreme delight
> And threefold in soft Beulah's night
> And twofold Always. May God us keep
> From Single vision & Newton's sleep! [40]

(The twofold vision here, however, is not that of Generation, but the ability to see an unfallen world as well as a fallen one.)

7

We began this chapter by showing that for Blake there can be no question of finding God through either the understanding or the will. That is because the distinction between them, which it is necessary to make first in order to get rid of one of them later, is a distinction based on the "Two Horn'd Reasoning, Cloven Fiction" of the Lockian universe. Those for whom subject and object, existence and perception, activity and thought, are all parts of a gigantic antithesis, will naturally conceive of man as split between an egocentric will and a reason which establishes contact with the nonego. Believers in the cloven fiction tend to come to rest finally in either a will-philosophy or a reason-philosophy, trying in each case to minimize the importance of the one they reject, because they are seeking to unify their ideas by reducing the problem from the double world of Generation to the single world of Ulro. One group assumes that will and energy exist by themselves *in vacuo*, and the other makes similar assumptions about necessity and established order.

We saw in the last chapter that for Blake the subjective navel-gazer and the objective atomist make the identical blunder of chopping the world in two, and differ only about which piece of it they are to seize. Those who seek understanding and power form a similar, or rather part of the same, false contrast. One group pursues God into an indefinite omnipotence, the other into an indefinite omniscience, and both lose sight of his humanity and personality. We may put the same point in another way. The will and the reason may be good or bad: if they are to be good, they must meet the standards or conditions of goodness. The will has to meet the standards ordinarily called justice and morality; the reason has to meet the standard of truth. Now these forms of the "good" as we should expect, have in common the impersonal and general quality of law. That two and two make four is equally true for everyone; that a murderer shall be hanged applies to all members of the state which adopts such a law. Here again, the "subject" with which we start seems to get lost in both directions, and to disappear into the uniformity of guinea-sun perceivers.

Hence the "good" is traditionally threefold in division, and includes a middle term of "beauty" which, unlike the other two, seems to have a per-

sonal and human reference, and, though it undoubtedly possesses laws, they are laws of a much more
flexible kind, which are able to allow for the differences that actually do exist among human beings.
Now it is clear that Blake's dislike of antithetical
modes of thought will not be appeased by adding a
middle term, even one regarded as a *tertium quid*.
"Beauty" to Blake is not a third form of the good,
but good itself, the union in which the reality of the
other two consists; it is pursued not by feeling or
emotion or any part of the personality, but by the
imagination which is "the Real Man." [41] The product of "beauty" is art; art is civilization; and it is
only civilization that can give any value or any
meaning to those impersonalizing tendencies of the
mind which build up the imaginative forms of science and morality. Thus Blake's identification of
religion with art is utterly different from the Romantic identification of the religious and aesthetic
experiences. There is no place in his thought for
aesthetics, or general theories of abstract beauty.

8

If the highest state of man is fourfold in Blake's
symbolism, we should expect him to reject the doctrine of a threefold God. Here Blake follows his
master Swedenborg, who attacked the orthodox
Trinity as tritheistic. In *Paradise Lost*, Blake complains, "the Father is Destiny, the Son a Ratio of
the five senses, and the Holy Ghost Vacuum." [42]
In theology something is usually done with the
conceptions of power and wisdom, but the middle
term, as in the ethical diagram, is apt to prove
embarrassing and be tacitly dropped. Yet the conception of God as a Holy Spirit, the giver and in-
cubator of life, the indwelling person of God, the
eternal Self, is, once again, the unity in which the
reality of the other two consists. It was the Holy
Spirit that spoke by the prophets, which means that
it continues to speak by the artists who have prophetic imaginations. The "inspiration" which artists
have is therefore the breath or spirit of God which
dwells in the artist and is the artist. Such inspiration is the only proof we have of the existence of a
spiritual power greater than ourselves. Art, then,
is "the gift of God, the Holy Ghost." [43]

What did the Holy Spirit that spoke by the
prophets speak about? It prophesied the Messiah;
that is, it saw God as man and understood that

"God becomes as we are, that we may be as he
is." [44] In Milton this Messiah is a ratio of the five
senses because he created the fallen world with its
guinea-sun. Such a creative principle is a Nous, a
reason or mathematical order, the automatism by
which nature maintains enough permanence to
keep from dissolving into nonexistence. This Nous
is to be visualized as a Father rather than a Son,
a hoary "Ancient of Days" such as stretches out his
compasses (notice the mathematical symbol) in the
frontispiece to *Europe*.[45] Jesus is not a Nous but a
Logos, a compelling Word who continually recreates an unconscious floundering universe into something with beauty and intelligence. The Son and
the Holy Spirit are therefore the same thing. And
this Son or Spirit is also the universal Man who is
the unified form of our scattered imaginations, and
which we visualize as a Father. The three persons
of the Trinity are to be connected by ors rather
than ands, and the real God is fourfold, power,
love and wisdom contained within the unity of
civilized human imagination. This God is a God-
Man, the Jesus in whose eternal and infinite risen
body we find our own being after we have outgrown the imaginative infancy which the orthodox
conception of the Fatherhood of God implies for
us. The final revelation of Christianity is, therefore,
not that Jesus is God, but that "God is Jesus." [46]

The life of man is polarized between the Creator
and the Creation, more abundant life in the larger
human mind and body of God and acceptance of
the minimum life of nature and reason. Any real
religion contains much to encourage the imagination, but it is likely also to try to give some divine
sanction to the fallen world. Hence when its followers come to the place where they should make the
supreme effort to become part of a universal human
and divine creator (this place in Blake is the upper
limit of Beulah), they find nature and reason block-
ing the way in a divine disguise. Here they must
choose between the Word and the World, and if
their choice is wrong they will be like Goethe's
Faust, who, unable to grasp the meaning of "*das
Wort*," translates it as "*die Tat*," the thing made
as opposed to its Maker, and falls into the power of
a devil.

A certain amount of natural religion exists in all
Christian Churches, but it is only in Blake's own
time that the cult of reason and nature has been
precipitated from Christianity and made into a

dogmatic system with all loopholes for the imagination sealed off. This system is Deism, a term Blake associates, not only with both Voltaire and Rousseau, but with the whole culture of the Age of Reason and the return to nature. For Deism, God is a hypothesis necessary to account for the beginning of the chain of causality; otherwise human life should be confined to nature and reason. That is, its Father is destiny, its Logos the ratio of the five senses, and its Spirit of love and beauty a vacuum—the faults of Milton's thinking unified into a single systematic falsehood. Locke was responsible for Deism, whether he was a Deist himself or not; for his cloven fiction is the source of its separation of the divine and the human. This cleavage in religion produces an antithesis of idolaters: one the egocentric contemplative who broods over his soul, the other the antinomian who pursues a life of selfish expediency. Now while one may find handsome crops of both kinds of tares in all religions, it is only in Deism, which plants no wheat, that they cease to become hypocrites.

We shall never understand why Blake so hated Deism unless we understand not only what it was to him, but what he saw that it would soon become. That is, we must accept in Blake a certain amount of prophecy in the literal sense of anticipating the probable future, and must see in his conception of Deism a mental attitude which is still with us, the monstrous hydra which is the perverted vision of human society as an atomic aggregate of egos instead of as a larger human body. The closer man comes to the state of nature, the more he clings to the "reason" which enables him to deal with nature on its own terms. The natural society, whether we see it in primitive tribes or in exhausted civilizations, is a complicated mechanism of prescribed acts which always have a rational explanation, but make no sense whatever in terms of passion, energy, insight or wisdom. The natural man is not the solitary majestic lion that he would like to be: he is a buzzing and spineless insect, a flying head cut off at the neck, like the cherubs in Reynolds, equipped with a venomous sting and a stupefied sense of duty. So at least he appears in Blake, both as the Deist of Blake's time and as the "Druid" which Blake predicted he would soon become.

An apocalyptic mind, however, is apt to feel that his own time is the darkest hour before the dawn, and to Blake the appearance of this consolidated system of error suggested that it might well be followed by some prophet who, by refuting it, might be the herald of a genuine apocalypse. Swedenborg had said that the Last Judgment took place in the spiritual world in 1757. This did not impress Blake unduly, but neither did he forget altogether that he had been born in that year.[47]

NOTES

All references to Blake's own works are accompanied by the page reference to *The Writings of William Blake*, ed. Geoffrey Keynes, 3 vols., London, 1925. These page references are preceded by the letter "K" and the number of the volume.

The Arabic numeral following a reference to an engraved poem is the number of the plate; following a reference to *The French Revolution* or *Tiriel*, it is the number of the line as given in *The Poetical Works of William Blake*, ed. Sampson, Oxford U.P., 1905; following a reference to *A Descriptive Catalogue*, it is the number of the page in the original edition; following a reference to *Public Address* or *A Vision of the Last Judgment*, it is the number of the page of the Rossetti MS; following a reference to marginalia, it is the number of the page in the copy annotated by Blake. References to *The Four Zoas* are accompanied in parentheses by the line number as given in *The Prophetic Writings of William Blake*, ed. Sloss and Wallis, 2 vols., Oxford U.P., 1926. This variety of reference is confusing, but not easily avoidable.

The following abbreviations for Blake's works have been employed:

A.R.O.	*All Religions Are One*
B.A.	*The Book of Ahania*
B.L.	*The Book of Los*
B.T.	*The Book of Thel*
B.U.	*The Book of Urizen*
D.C.	*A Descriptive Catalogue*
E.G.	*The Everlasting Gospel*
F.R.	*The French Revolution*
F.Z.	*The Four Zoas*
G.P.	*The Gates of Paradise*
I.M.	*An Island in the Moon*
J.	*Jerusalem*
M.	*Milton*
M.H.H.	*The Marriage of Heaven and Hell*
N.N.R.	*There Is No Natural Religion*

P.A.   *Public Address* (Rossetti MS)
P.S.   *Poetical Sketches*
S.E.   *Songs of Experience*
S.I.   *Songs of Innocence*
S.L.   *The Song of Los*
S.Lib.   *A Song of Liberty*
V.D.A.   *Visions of the Daughters of Albion*
V.L.J.   *A Vision of the Last Judgment* (Rossetti MS)

1. Marg. to Berkeley, 219: K3, 356; Laocoön Aphorisms: K3, 358.

2. M.H.H. 23: K1, 194.

3. M. 35: K2, 356.

4. Marg. to Swedenborg's *Divine Love and Divine Wisdom*, 24: K1, 120–21.

5. Marg. to Swedenborg, 11: K1, 119.

6. Laocoön Aphorisms: K3, 358. The preceding phrase is from Browne, *The Gardens of Cyrus.*

7. *On Virgil*: K3, 362.

8. *Moby Dick,* ch. cxix.

9. Marg. to Lavater, 426: K1, 102.

10. V.L.J. 68–69: K3, 146.

11. Marg. to Lavater (conclusion): K1, 117.

12. M.H.H. 10: K1, 186.

13. "Auguries of Innocence": K2, 235.

14. See below, ch. 5; and cf. H. Crabb Robinson, *Reminiscences of Blake,* s. 1826 (*Selections,* ed. Morley, 23).

15. Letter to Butts, July 6, 1803: K2, 246.

16. Marg. to Lavater (conclusion): K1, 117; cf. J. 3: K3, 167.

17. D.C. 38: K3, 108, cf. I Cor. xiv, 32.

18. Marg. to Wordsworth's *Recluse*: K3, 379.

19. Marg. to Lavater, 342: K1, 98.

20. J. 88: K3, 305.

21. V.L.J. 71–72: K3, 146.

22. M.H.H. 7: K1, 184.

23. A.R.O. 1: K1, 131. For Ovid cf. V.L.J. 79: K3, 148.

24. Poem in Letter to Butts, Oct. 2, 1800: K2, 190.

25. F.Z. v (121–26): K2, 58–59.

26. Milton, *Of Reformation Touching Church Discipline in England,* Book ii, Introduction.

27. V.L.J. 76–77: K3, 149.

28. S.I., "A Little Girl Lost": K1, 150–151.

29. Laocoön Aphorisms: K3, 359.

30. Wordsworth, *The Prelude,* vi, 634–39.

31. "Auguries of Innocence": K2, 232.

32. M. 26: K2, 341.

33. V.L.J. 91–92: K3, 158.

34. M.H.H. 7: K1, 184.

35. Marg. to Lavater, 407: K1, 101.

36. See especially *Divine Love and Divine Wisdom,* i, 40–82. Cf. M. O. Percival, *William Blake's Circle of Destiny,* Columbia U.P., 1938, 83 f.

37. *Lives of the Poets:* "Yalden."

38. Isa. lxii, 4.

39. Ezek. i; Rev. iv.

40. Poem in Letter to Butts, Nov. 22, 1802: K2, 209.

41. Marg. to Berkeley, 241: K3, 356.

42. M.H.H. 6: K1, 183.

43. D.C. 46: K3, 112.

44. N.N.R. II, Application: K1, 131.

45. See Illustration 1, and note, p. 433.

46. Laocoön Aphorisms: K3, 359. Cf. *Faust,* I, 1224–37.

47. Swedenborg, *True Christian Religion,* 115. Cf. M.H.H. 3: K1, 182.

David Perkins

WORDSWORTH:
THE LINKING OF MAN AND NATURE*

Nothing is more widespread in contemporary criticism than our sense that the total work of an important writer embodies what Virginia Woolf once called a "private harmony." Here, of course, we differ from Renaissance and eighteenth-century critics, who frequently assumed that Homer, or some other poet, holds a mirror up to "nature" in all its fluid variety and scope. We are much more likely to think that any man has only a limited set of ideas or attitudes which are clarified and harmonized through a lifetime of effort, and hence to speak of the "universe" of some particular writer, or even of the "universe" of some major work. The word implies that the poetry consists of definite materials selected from a vaster potentiality, from what William James called the "blooming welter" of life, and ordered into a pattern. Hence one begins to define a writer's arrangement or vision of life when one considers not only what it includes, but also what has been left out. Wordsworth, Shelley, and Keats might all be described as "nature" poets. That is, they are "nature" poets if we mean that they closely observed natural phenomena, and that they expressed themselves largely through imagery and symbols drawn from nature. Yet despite their close observation, each of these poets focused primarily on particular aspects of nature to the exclusion of others, though what they focused on differed in each case.

Wordsworth was "haunted," as Whitehead said, "by the enormous permanences of nature." More or less ignoring the swift change and transformation that obsessed Shelley, he tended to notice "rocks/

Immutable, and everflowing streams." To a "mind intoxicate" with "the busy dance/ Of things that pass away," nature presents "a temperate show/ Of objects that endure." Even the images by which another poet might especially have depicted flux are often used by Wordsworth to express its opposite. In Shelley, for example, rivers and streams become metaphors of constant, sinuously rippled alteration; but in Wordsworth's poetry streams flow "in lasting current" and suggest the permanent qualities of nature—"Still glides the stream, and shall for ever glide." Here, of course, the double meaning of "still" puts exactly the qualities Wordsworth found in nature. Again Shelley might see a waterfall as an emblem of the turbulence and shifting variety of concrete life. Wordsworth, however, stands at a distance, and views even waterfalls as "stationary blasts." [1] Where Wordsworth does describe change and process in the natural world, it is slowed down until it scarcely intrudes upon the sense of permanence. Both Wordsworth and Shelley possessed, at times, a cosmic sweep; their imaginations extended to take in geological and astronomical mutations. But in Shelley these large scale transformations are speeded up until they become symbolic of the rapid flux he saw everywhere. In Wordsworth these planetary processes are retarded, and he dwells more on the unchanging continuity than on the dissolution of planets and stars.

Often in Wordsworth's poetry the permanence of nature is felt most strongly by contrast with the brevity of human life. If, for the sake of condensing a potentially tedious exposition, we confine ourselves to the stream imagery already mentioned, we find that the "flowing stream" habitually gives rise to a "thought . . . Of Life continuous, Being unimpaired;/ That hath been, is, and . . . shall endure." This "thought" at once generates its antithesis, "the blind walk of mortal accident" where

* Reprinted by permission of the authors and publishers from *The Quest for Permanence: The Symbolism of Wordsworth, Shelley, and Keats* by David Perkins, Cambridge, Mass.: Harvard University Press, Copyright © 1959 by the President and Fellows of Harvard College.

man grows old, and dwindles, and decays;
And countless generations of mankind
Depart, and leave no vestige where they trod.[2]

Usually this contrast is put more concretely, as in "The Fountain," where old Matthew, resting by a spring, reflects that it will "murmur on a thousand years,/ And flow as now it flows." At once he "cannot choose but think" of his own mortality. But the remorseless encroachments of time are not felt only in terms of individual life. In a situation frequent in Wordsworth's poetry, the stream flows by an architectural relic representing an enormous, vanished past. The men who built it are gone, and often the structure itself is falling into ruin under the "unimaginable touch of Time," but the stream is unchanged. Flowing forever with "unaltered face," it forms the stable background to the human shows passing on its banks.[3]

2

Wordsworth's treatment of man's impermanence thus seems to involve a good deal more than the matter of personal mortality. In fact, we begin to suspect that individual death itself becomes almost a symbol of something more troublesome. For one thing, as we have seen, the notion of impermanence —as contrasted with the unchanging presence of nature—extends beyond the mere individual to include whatever is characteristically associated with human nature or produced by it. There is, in Wordsworth, a comparative absence of the mixed pain and hope with which romantic and contemporary poets have tended to regard creative achievements. They have tended, that is, to see in the edifices of human thought, usually symbolized in architectural structures or some form of sculpture —Keats's Grecian urn, Yeats's bird of "hammered gold" or "moonlit dome"—a form of immortality which stands in sharp, often ironic contrast to flesh and blood. This is seldom the case in Wordsworth. Instead he insists that even the "consecrated works of Bard and Sage," what seem to be "adamantine holds of truth," will vanish. The creations of the "sovereign Intellect" may seem to "aspire to unconquerable life";

And yet we feel—we cannot choose but feel—
That they must perish.[4]

Only the "living Presence" of nature can be regarded as permanent and undying. Hence when Wordsworth insists on the mortality of man and his works, it should, perhaps, be construed as only a final instance of the chasm separating man from nature. Death itself is not an obsession with Wordsworth, nor does his quest primarily involve an attempt to find some reconciliation to the fact of death (as does that of Shelley, Keats, Yeats, or, for that matter, the Shakespeare of the sonnets). The great lines in the closing sonnet of *The River Duddon*—"We Men, who in our morn of youth defied/ The elements, must vanish;—be it so!"—are not bravado. They are a real acceptance, even though the acceptance is not placid or joyous. But what is not accepted, and is a constant "trouble" to his "dreams," is man's isolation from nature while he lives. The quest for permanence, in so far as Wordsworth is concerned, should be regarded rather as a quest for a certain kind of stability and reassurance while we are alive. For it was the clamorous bustle of desire, and all that it creates, that Wordsworth especially hoped to escape. The primary need, in other words, is that man should "forget his feeling" in so far as it is turbulent and "unmanageable," should "mitigate the fever of his heart"; and the hope is that he can do this by dwelling upon whatever, not "touched by welterings of passion," seems to contain and infuse "Transcendent peace/ And silence."[5]

In the *Prelude* Wordsworth describes a dream which seems to suggest two ways in which man may hope to "manage" his feeling and escape from the stormy cavern of his own mind. He had been reading in a rocky cave and, laying aside the book, began to muse

On poetry and geometric truth,
And their high privilege of lasting life,
From all internal injury exempt.   (V, 65–67)

Falling asleep, he dreamt that he was alone in a "wilderness." It was "black and void" (we remember that the mind can be a "dark pit" or "blank abyss"); and, as he looked about, "distress and fear/ Came creeping" over him (V, 72–74). At this point the usual wanderer figure appeared, this time in the guise of an Arab.[6] In his dream Wordsworth felt that the Arab wanderer was a "guide . . . who with unerring skill" would "lead" him "through the desert." "Underneath one arm" the Arab carried a stone, and "in the opposite hand a shell." The stone, he told Wordsworth, represents "Euclid's Elements"

—geometry or, more generally, abstract thought. The shell "is something of more worth," and it turns out to be a symbol of poetry or imagination in general (V, 72–89). Abstract thought and imagination, then, are both avenues by which man can ease or escape the burden of his feelings. The latter is "of more worth," but the tendency to view abstract speculation as an escape from the turbulence of personal feeling is still strong in Wordsworth, reminding us of Yeats in the Byzantium poems or of Johnson who, according to Mrs. Thrale, would turn to mathematics when he thought his fancy disordered.

When we speak of Wordsworth's attraction to abstract thought, and to geometry as a symbol of it, we do not picture him hurrying to purchase a copy of Euclid. We are dealing with a symbolic gesture which, of course, can become symbolic because it has some correspondence with literal human experience. At the same time, in view of Wordsworth's frequent attacks on mathematical logic and scientific abstraction elsewhere in his poetry, and his own aversion to studying mathematics at college, one may be surprised that he can discover any appeal in it, even as a symbol. The fact that he does so indicates how strongly he felt the need for a refuge, and it also suggests what he hoped to escape. The appeal of mathematics seems to be twofold. In the first place, through it one enters "an independent world"—a world "of permanent and universal sway" remote from "the disturbances of space and time." In the second place, geometry and abstract science are "created out of pure intelligence." By "pure" Wordsworth seems to mean not "touched by welterings of passion." Thus he speaks of Archimedes as a "pure abstracted soul,"[7] and the French Revolution was a time when there were many "speculative schemes"

> That promised to abstract the hopes of Man
> Out of his feelings, to be fixed thenceforth
> For ever in a purer element.   (XI, 225–227)

The hope, then, is that by the study of geometry man can center himself in a pure, unchanging, and independent world where he will escape from his own passions. Thus Wordsworth instances a person who was shipwrecked "upon a desert coast" (*Prelude*, VI, 144 ff.). He happened to have with him "A treatise of Geometry," and often he would "part from company and take this book . . . To spots re-

mote." There he would draw "diagrams" upon the sand,

> and thus
> Did oft beguile his sorrow, and almost
> Forget his feeling.   (VI, 152–154)

Generalizing upon this incident, Wordsworth remarks that although his own outward circumstances are very different, his needs are the same:

> So was it then with me, and so will be
> With Poets ever. Mighty is the charm
> Of those abstractions to a mind beset
> With images, and haunted by herself.
> (VI, 157–160)

But the effort to compose or suppress feeling through turning to abstraction is seldom finally successful. In the more or less autobiographical history related in the *Excursion*, Wordsworth tells how before the Boy's "eighteenth year . . . Accumulated feelings pressed his heart." He was "subdued" by the "turbulence . . . of his own mind" (I, 280–284). In this situation, he turned to the intellect, and "from the stillness of abstracted thought/ He asked repose" (I, 291–293):

> But vainly thus,
> And vainly by all other means, he strove
> To mitigate the fever of his heart.
> (I, 298–300)

Wordsworth, then, had little confidence in the "stone" of geometrical science as a resolution of the human dilemma. For abstract science works merely to suppress feeling. In fact, the "charm severe" of geometry—"the purer elements of truth involved/ In lines and numbers"—is

> Especially perceived where nature droops
> And feeling is suppressed.   (I, 253–256)

Hence any consolation geometry may offer is precariously liable to disintegrate. "That genuine knowledge, fraught with peace" (*Prelude*, XI, 354), can only grow from whatever composes and so changes the character of human passion at the same time that it draws it forth.

The gestures toward abstract speculation are important mainly in illustrating how strong the need for stability is. Of course, Wordsworth urges that a union with nature is what frees the mind from the stir and thrust of its own dark emotions. But his poetry records a vast number of personal instances when the tranquillity seems to have been achieved in a different way. In these instances, one can see a number of psychological processes at work, all of which have as their result a tamping down and minimizing of immediate emotional concern. Feeling, in other words, is not shunted aside in these responses. On the contrary, it is actively present, but pitched in a diminished and manageable way. This, of course, suggests how these responses fulfilled a genuine need. If allowed to roam at large, the native passions of an anxious or restless heart will prey on the economy of personal life. At the same time, they cannot be successfully caged, but must be gentled and domesticated while they are released. For Wordsworth, such a domestication could take place when the call to feeling is placed at a distance in space or time, weakened, so to speak, by the length of its journey. Or it could occur when what draws and focuses emotion is overwhelmed and almost lost in surrounding vastness. In either case, the result is that pressing human concerns are reduced in importance, and the heart is eased of their pull. In pursuing this subject, we shall have to consider the significance to Wordsworth of memory, history, the immensity of nature as contrasted with the human life it envelops, and a few other things. We shall be dealing, in other words, with reactions—both those which immediately involve nature and those which do not—which seem to have been sources of tranquillity and composure, but which Wordsworth did not usually recognize as such; for he almost invariably attributed the "calm existence that is mine when I/ Am worthy of myself" (*Prelude*, I, 349–350), to the union of the mind with nature.

3

The great enemy of human tranquillity, for Wordsworth, is

> passion over-near ourselves,
> Reality too close and too intense.
> (*Prelude*, XI, 57–58)

The desired attitude would be what he felt in the early days of the French Revolution:

> I looked upon these things
> As from a distance; heard, and saw, and felt,
> Was touched, but with no intimate concern.
> (*Prelude*, VI, 767–769)

As we have noticed, the various wanderers that people so much of Wordsworth's poetry seem placed in an attitude in which the totality of what they observe is seen as a single vista, in which, being reduced in scale, it becomes manageable. Even the city, the specific haunt of human stress and passion, can be contemplated with tranquil serenity from the vantage point of Westminster Bridge, particularly since, with its "smokeless air" it has not yet awakened and become a city. So, in the *Prelude*, as one leaves the city, its smoke, "by distance ruralized," is seen merely as a "curling cloud" (I, 88–89), as a part of the "face" of nature, instead of an indication of the presence of man. Wordsworth recollects such glimpses so frequently in his poetry because they were deeply satisfying to him. Viewed at a distance and amid the tranquillity of nature, man, with his desires and fears, can scarcely arouse strong feeling in the onlooker. Instead, he can be contemplated with a steady and detached calm. Furthermore, from a distance humanity, particularly rustic humanity, is seen together with clouds, hills, and trees virtually as part of a natural scene. No more a stranger, the human being seems reconciled and "fitted" to the surrounding universe.

But it is not only in a long spatial perspective that things can be viewed in this way. Through retrospection, events can also be contemplated "as from a distance" in time, and in the process even the most distressing occasions lose much of their power to obtrude and unsettle the mind's composure. Memory, then, provides another means through which human feeling, without being entirely shunned or suppressed, can be quieted and digested without any loss of personal tranquillity. By holding things at a distance, recollection enables the poet, like Emily returning to Rylstone, to receive

> the memory of old loves,
> Undisturbed and undistrest.
> (lines 1754–1755)

In this connection it is important to note that the bulk of Wordsworth's poetry is retrospective. Indeed, his well-known formulation of the source of poetry—"emotion recollected in tranquillity"—exactly defines the desired state of mind and the role of memory in helping to achieve it. He wants the emotion, but he does not want it to be immediate and pressing. He goes on to say that in the "mood" in which "successful composition generally begins," the "emotion is contemplated till . . . the tranquillity gradually disappears, and an emotion, kindred to that which was before the subject of contemplation, is gradually produced." But he at once adds that the "emotion, of whatever kind, and in whatever degree . . . is qualified . . . so that in describing any passions whatsoever, which are voluntarily described, the mind will, upon the whole, be in a state of enjoyment." In other words, emotions "of whatever kind," even the more "painful" ones, are not to be allowed to intrude so far as to spoil the mind's "overbalance of pleasure." [8] Wordsworth is remarkably vague in explaining why or how the emotion is "qualified" so that the mind can retain its "state of enjoyment." The reader can only suppose that it is because the emotion is "contemplated" rather than immediately felt. The poet may vividly recollect the original powerful feelings, but he does so from such a distance that the recollected emotion cannot be oppressive and disturbing, but can only rouse and excite the mind to a pleasurable activity. The desired state, even if in recalling powerful feelings the "tranquillity gradually disappears," still remains, perhaps, to be "touched, but with no intimate concern."

In addition to an unusually firm and active memory, Wordsworth possessed a powerful historical imagination, capable of vividly reconstructing the past and bringing it to his eye. In fact, his sense of history was so strong that sometimes, he says, it literally overwhelmed and obliterated his consciousness of the present. For example, once in his childhood as he "ranged at will" on "Sarum's Plain," "Time with his retinue of ages fled/ Backwards," and, becoming almost unaware of his present surroundings, he saw "Our dim ancestral Past in vision clear." He goes on, in the *Prelude* (XIII, 315–322) to describe the vision in detail—the "multitudes of men," the "single Briton clothed in wolfskin vest," and the like. Similarly, on his first entry into London, while sitting on the top of a coach, he saw

> vulgar men about me, trivial forms
> Of houses, pavements, streets, of men and
> 　　　things,—
> Mean shapes on every side.

But when he passed the "threshold" of the city "A weight of ages did at once descend/ Upon" his "heart," and the vivid sense of the enormous, van-

ished past momentarily usurped and virtually wiped out his consciousness of the "trivial" present (VIII, 544–552).

But we have been citing unusually intense and visionary experiences. Wordsworth's sense of history seems usually not to have blotted out the present but rather to have minimized its urgent stress and intrusion. Through the historical imagination, he was sometimes able to see the present, with all its restless concerns and demands, against so wide a background that it was reduced in importance and lost some of its power to agitate and alarm. When he was in France, "the experience of past ages" which he "carried about" with him prevented him from being "pressed upon" by "objects over near." In other words, Wordsworth was not at first passionately committed to the revolutionary cause, or, as he put it, "dipped/ Into the turmoil." Similarly, at Cambridge he saw the present life of the college through a veil of history, and therefore became more reconciled to it:

> 　　　here the vulgar light
> Of present, actual, superficial life,
> Gleaming through colouring of other times,
> Old usages and local privilege,
> Was welcome, softened, if not solemnised.

Even the "din" and confusion of London was "softened" and made less oppressive by his vivid

> 　　　　　　sense
> Of what in the Great City had been done
> And suffered, and was doing, suffering, still;

for his immediate consciousness of the "vulgar" and "trivial" life of the city was swallowed up in his imaginative "sense" of the "abyss of ages past." At such moments the city became less a present reality than a token or symbol of human destiny. As such, it could "support the test of thought," and Wordsworth's "young imagination" could sometimes find in it "no uncongenial element." [9]

4

In particular, the unsettling tug of immediate human concerns seems often to have been lessened, for Wordsworth, by his perception of an immense natural world surrounding and engulfing these concerns. Seen against the large, tranquil and impending forms of nature, human life itself becomes reduced in importance and human passions are felt

to be less urgent and compulsive. Indeed, one sometimes has an impression in reading Wordsworth—
an impression so contrary to his overt intentions
and obiter dicta and so significant for later poetry—
that man is a brief appearance on the surface, a
kind of fungus momentarily clinging to the bleak,
immutable rocks. For Wordsworth, the immediate
result of this kind of contrast was, of course, that
it tended to encourage a composed state of mind.
We have already mentioned the incident in the
Prelude (V, 435–455), where Wordsworth saw the
body of a drowned man raised from a lake, but
it is particularly relevant at this point. The episode
occurred in Wordsworth's childhood. He crossed
at twilight a peninsula on "Esthwaite's Lake," and
saw on the "opposite shore/ A heap of garments."
He watched them for a while, but no one came to
claim them.

> Meanwhile the calm lake
> Grew dark with all the shadows on its breast,
> And, now and then, a fish up-leaping snapped
> The breathless stillness.   (lines 439–442)

Next day, suspecting that someone had drowned,
men sounded with poles for the body.

> At last, the dead man, mid that beauteous
>   scene
> Of trees and hills and water, bolt upright
> Rose, with his ghastly face, a spectre shape
> Of terror.   (lines 448–451)

Wordsworth, however, was not frightened, for, as
he explains, he "had seen/ Such sights before" in
"faery land." In this characteristic incident, the
drowned man, a "shape/ Of terror," guiltily trans-
gressing on the breathless stillness, is an image of
humanity. Set against the enormous backdrop of
lake and hills, he can make little impression. Even
at the moment when he breaks the surface, Wordsworth notices the surrounding "beauteous scene."
The fear inspired by the drowned man and the
guilt he symbolizes have been swallowed in the
immensity of nature. A similar episode is Wordsworth's account of the death of a woodman in the
forest (*Prelude*, VIII, 437–450). The man is "withering by slow degrees," dying in other words, but
his death takes place

> 'mid gentle airs,
> Birds, running streams, and hills so beautiful
> On golden evenings, while the charcoal pile
> Breathed up its smoke.   (lines 446–449)

The charcoal pile breathing up its smoke may be an
implicit metaphor of the man breathing up his soul.
As such, it would help to define the tone of the
verse, which, in any case, converts the death to
something as natural and painless as the sunset
which envelops it. Here again human suffering has
been submerged in the tranquillity of nature, and
the poet's feelings are not called upon. This type
of response might seem of dubious moral worth;
but it at least helped Wordsworth to reach and
maintain the serene calm he sought.

One can even go further and suggest that the
contrast of human life with the immensity of nature
not only allowed Wordsworth to view human concerns with a detached composure, but that it also
permitted, and at times even stimulated, feelings of
tender benevolence directed to human life as a
whole—feelings which he earnestly desired to cultivate, and which stand in marked contrast to the
uneasy and frightened distress often provoked in
him by the contemplation of specifically human
life. One example is the description of a sunrise
in the *Prelude*:

> Magnificent
> The morning rose, in memorable pomp,
> Glorious as e'er I had beheld—in front,
> The sea lay laughing at a distance; near,
> The solid mountains shone, bright as the
>   clouds,
> Grain-tinctured, drenched in empyrean light;
> And in the meadows and the lower grounds
> Was all the sweetness of a common dawn—
> Dews, vapours, and the melody of birds,
> And labourers going forth to till the fields.
>   (IV, 323–332)

Wordsworth goes on to describe how deeply he was
moved by the spectacle. Like many of Wordsworth's most successful passages, this experience,
so powerfully felt and so majestically conveyed,
seems charged with some half-understood meaning
working below the surface description. Wordsworth
himself recognizes as much when, at the conclusion
of the vision, he says "On I walked/ In thankful
blessedness, which yet survives" (IV, 337–338). As
in many such passages, the symbolic suggestion is
obscure, and one can scarcely be explicit about it.
But the significance of these lines rests in the contrast between the "common dawn" with its rustic
chores, and what towers above it. The "solid mountains . . . drenched in empyrean light" are images or
sudden revelations of natural glory and spiritual

force resident in the cosmos. They are seen simultaneously with the common dawn, and the momentary vision is multidimensional and religious, discovering the numinous latent behind the concrete. At the same time the dawn draws its felt "sweetness" from the fact that it is "common," familiar, in contrast to the austere, unfamiliar glory of the mountain peaks. The laborers share in this "sweetness." In fact they are merely part of the landscape, and in such a setting can only be viewed with a tranquil eye of love.

A similar vision, less imaginatively intense, is that of the country people gathered for a fair upon the side of Mount Helvellyn. Dwarfed by the mountain which broods above them, they seem small, innocent, and helpless, and release a gush of sentiment. The *Prelude* describes Wordsworth's reaction quite explicitly:

> Immense
> Is the recess, the circumambient world
> Magnificent, by which they are embraced;
> They move about upon the soft green turf:
> How little they, they and their doings, seem,
> And all that they can further or obstruct!
> Through utter weakness pitiably dear,
> As tender infants are.   (VIII, 55–62)

The comparison to infants should be noticed, for to Wordsworth the embraced infant almost always symbolizes man at home in the universe. It is, however, the contrast between the human beings and the immense natural surroundings which permits him to view the rustics as "pitiably dear."

Finally, it should be noticed that Wordsworth seems often to have been aided in "managing" his feelings by a kind of schizoid retreat, by a partial tendency to deny the reality of a present situation. That is, when immediately confronted with a circumstance which might be expected to arouse a distressing concern and to prey upon tranquillity, Wordsworth frequently reacts by viewing the circumstance almost as make-believe or dream. For example, he deals with the dying woodman partly by weaving an imaginary tale about him. He fancies "pangs of disappointed love,/ And all the sad etcetera of the wrong" as the cause of his death (VIII, 441–442). Hence he can react to the death as though the woodman were a character in a story. In the same way, Wordsworth remarks that when the body of the drowned man rose from the lake, "no soul-debasing fear ... Possessed me." He

himself proceeds to account for this by saying that his

> inner eye had seen
> Such sights before, among the shining streams
> Of faery land, the forest of romance.
>   (V, 453–455)

He responded to the sight of the drowned man by almost denying its actual existence, seeing it instead as an episode in a romance; and the spirit of romance "hallowed the sad spectacle/ With decoration of ideal grace." Wordsworth also attributed this type of reaction to his friend, Beaupuy, who represents something of an ideal, and is praised for maintaining his serenity throughout the bloodletting of the French Revolution:

> He through the events
> Of that great change wandered in perfect
>   faith,
> As through a book, an old romance, or tale
> Of Fairy, or some dream of actions wrought
> Behind the summer clouds.
>   (*Prelude*, IX, 298–302)

In this connection we may also note Wordsworth's discussion of meter in the Preface to the *Lyrical Ballads,* a discussion, one may think, which throws at least as much light on Wordsworth's own general attitudes as it does on the effect of metrical arrangement in poetry. He remarks, of course, that the "end of Poetry is to produce excitement in co-existence with an overbalance of pleasure." "Excitement" is desired, that is, as long as it does not become "unmanageable" and intrusive. But it may get out of hand: "excitement is an unusual and irregular state of the mind" and "may be carried beyond its proper bounds." The use of meter, therefore, is in "tempering and restraining the passion" so that it is not allowed to interfere with a composed and "pleasurable" state of mind. Wordsworth's discussion, as he himself recognizes, is quite unsystematic. In general, however, he seems to advance two main explanations of the means or processes by which meter can restrain feeling. In the first place, by association the presence of meter wakens in the mind a remembrance of all the other feelings with which metrical language has been "connected." In Wordsworth's terms, "the mind has been accustomed" to meter "in various moods and in a less excited state." Hence, meter arouses "an intertexture of ordinary feeling, and of feeling not strictly and necessarily connected with the passion" immediately present in the poem. This large background of "ordinary" and even irrelevant feelings tends to minimize and dissipate the excitement aroused by a particular metrical arrangement or poem. The principle involved probably differs only slightly from the tempering of excitement derived from a sense of history; for in both cases the immediate occasion is held against a backdrop of past associations and loses much of its power to provoke strong feeling. Even more characteristic is what seems to be Wordsworth's alternative explanation of the efficacy of meter in restraining passion. The attraction of meter, as he speaks of it, is that it tends "to divest language . . . of its reality, and thus to throw a sort of half-consciousness of unsubstantial existence over the whole composition." [10]

5

The habits of mind we have been considering—a denial that can at times seem almost schizoid, the retreat to memory, the sense of history and of the tranquil sweep of nature—are only some of the modes of response which helped Wordsworth to achieve the serenity he so earnestly sought. Wordsworth himself, of course, felt that whatever abiding composure the mind attained was the result of its being linked, intertwined, or united with external nature. The ideal is an imaginative union so intimate and complete that the mind, instead of being imprisoned and engulfed in its distinctive human qualities, can virtually absorb the tone and characteristics of nature. Probably this linking is the principal theme of his poetry, not only in the *Prelude* and the *Excursion*—though there it is most obviously foremost—but also in shorter lyrics which frequently take up some limited aspect of the larger concern and become fully meaningful only in the light of Wordsworth's general preoccupations. It is significant that in a passage which concludes the first book of the *Recluse*—a poem conceived on an overwhelming scale as the grand repository of his opinions and his major achievement—Wordsworth, in a mood of Miltonic self-dedication, announces his "high argument" to be how the mind of man can be "wedded" to the "goodly universe":

—I, long before the blissful hour arrives,
Would chant, in lonely peace, the spousal
    verse
Of this great consummation.[11]

There can be no doubt that Wordsworth occasionally felt what seemed to be moments of oneness with external nature, and that he believed his mind to have been composed and to some extent permanently formed by such experiences. With a desperate, baffled honesty he repeatedly tries, throughout his poetry, to present these experiences as they had actually occurred; and he also tries to understand and explain the psychological processes involved—processes that established the union and permitted the composure. Wordsworth himself particularly stressed the role of either empathy or sympathetic identification in these moments of "linking."

From Hazlitt to the present day critics have tended to deny that Wordsworth possessed much sympathetic receptivity to the life around him. If it existed at all, it was certainly selective in accordance with his own intense preoccupations, directed only to some things, and specifically to nonhuman identities. In any personal instance recreated in the poetry, there is always a question whether we are dealing with the psychology of sympathetic participation, or rather with an outright imposition of his own feelings upon nature in a way too subjective to be thought of as sympathetic. The forms of nature, and particularly those which Wordsworth focused upon, are so passive, so obviously open to interpretation and manipulation, so lacking in specific identity or character, that it is a question whether they can permit much sympathetic response. But then, if we fall back upon a psychology of simple projection, we must at once add that a particular natural scene was not so blank and featureless that it allowed any or all feelings to be projected. It acted rather as a filter, permitting and intensifying some kinds of emotional response and inhibiting others. What is certain, however, is that Wordsworth tended to construe his responses as either sympathetic or empathic. As one quick example, we might cite his remark that "my favorite grove,/ Tossing in sunshine its dark boughs aloft . . . Wakes in me agitations like its own." (*Prelude*, VII, 44–47). The point is that the psychology of sympathy has a central place in his theoretical discourse. It is usually conceived in terms of its salutary effect in drawing man toward the forms of nature. What is more important is that it provided a way of accounting for the formative control which nature is felt to exert as it stamps its own tone and spirit upon the mind.

It is perhaps significant that when Wordsworth is meditating a particular moment or instance in his own life, complexities and cross-lights come to the fore to tangle and confuse his account of the psychology involved. It is mainly when he resorts to theoretical and general discourse, or when he constructs a narrative dealing with persons other than himself, that an empathic psychology is advanced in a clear-cut and single-minded way. For example, in "Ruth," where Wordsworth tells the story, which he so often repeats in various forms, of a maiden deserted by her lover, the wayward behavior of the lover is partially explained by the influence of his early natural surroundings (lines 121–136). He had been reared in Georgia, amid a climate and flora Wordsworth conceived as tropical. "The wind, the tempest," and the "tumult of a tropic sky" may have been "dangerous food," encouraging or reinforcing the originally "impetuous blood" of the youth. Similarly, the "fair trees and gorgeous flowers" may have "wrought" upon him by feeding "voluptuous thought." In short,

> Whatever in those climes he found
> Irregular in sight or sound
> Did to his mind impart
> A kindred impulse.   (lines 127–130)

In accord with the impetuous and irregular character bred or at least intensified by his early environment, he deserted his bride. This example is unusual in that nature's influence is not altogether beneficent. Of course, Wordsworth's habitual view was quite the reverse, and he stresses the moral elevation and discipline derived from intercourse with nature. Obviously nature's formative control operates most powerfully when the mind is pervious and openly receptive. From this consideration derives, in part, the ethical justification of the "wise passiveness" Wordsworth urges. Only when the mind is undistracted by the pull of human concerns can it receive the stamp and tone of nature.

NOTES

1. *Prelude*, VIII, 170–171; XIII, 29–32; VI, 675; *The River Duddon*, "After-Thought," line 5; *Prelude*, VI, 626.

2. *Excursion*, IV, 754–762.

3. *Ecclesiastical Sonnets*, "Mutability," line 14; "Yarrow Revisited," lines 105, 35.

4. *Prelude*, V, 15–42, *passim*.

5. *Prelude*, VI, 154; *Excursion*, I, 300; *Prelude*, VI, 138–140.

6. Cf. W. H. Auden's remarks on this passage, *The Enchafèd Flood* (New York, 1950), pp. 3–6.

7. *Prelude*, VI, 166, 131; XI, 330; VI, 167, 138; XI, 435.

8. Preface to the *Lyrical Ballads*, p. 940.

9. *Prelude*, IX, 331–337; VIII, 505–509; 625–627; XII, 63; VIII, 628, 639–640.

10. Preface to the *Lyrical Ballads*, p. 940.

11. Published as the "Prospectus" of the *Excursion*, lines 56–71.

Douglas Bush

WORDSWORTH:
A MINORITY REPORT*

When I received the pleasant invitation to participate in the centenary celebrations for Wordsworth,

I felt even more than the usual need of weighing my capacities. I remembered the shock I long ago gave a fellow graduate student when he discovered that I did not know the color of daffodils; it had been vain to declare that I had a quite satisfactory vision of flowers dancing in the wind, without any color at all. The invitation from Princeton came to

* Excerpts from Douglas Bush "A Minority Report," in *Wordsworth: Centenary Studies Presented at Cornell and Princeton Universities* (ed. Gilbert T. Dunklin): pp. 8–22. Reprinted by permission of Princeton University Press.

me during my first summer on a farm in Vermont, and I hoped that the Green Mountains might bring about the redemption of Peter Bell. However, though there were plenty of old gray stones on which to dream the time away, I sat on a stepladder with a can of paint; I could not reap the harvest of a quiet eye because my eyes were swollen with hay fever; I could not slake my thirst at every rill because our two springs had been condemned by the state laboratory; instead of cuckoos and skylarks singing outside, we had bees and hornets buzzing in the kitchen; instead of

The silence that is in the starry sky,
The sleep that is among the lonely hills,

we were kept awake through the night by a neighbor's horses trampling and snorting under our window. Little I saw in nature that was mine. And I thought of the devout Matthew Arnold's admission that Wordsworth's eyes avert their ken from half of human fate. These remarks are not wholly frivolous.

Everyone knows Benjamin Haydon's account of the immortal dinner at which he had among his guests Wordsworth, Keats, and Lamb, and also an unfortunate Comptroller of Stamps who had craved an introduction to Wordsworth. The worthy official, trying to keep his end up, confounded the company by asking Wordsworth "Don't you think, sir, Milton was a great genius?" whereupon the tipsy Lamb took up a candle and wanted to examine the gentleman's phrenological development. It is fairly obvious that Wordsworth was a great genius, that, historically, he ranks among the first five or six English poets. But after a hundred years one may perhaps venture the question, "Is he still, for us, a great poet?" It may be blasphemy or impudence even to put such a query into words, and many of my hearers, in a state of exemplary sobriety, may wish to examine my bumps. But the question cannot damage Wordsworth, and we may see where it leads us.

Mr. Garrod, I think, once remarked that Wordsworth was Coleridge's greatest work and, like Coleridge's other works, left unfinished. But probably neither Mr. Garrod nor anyone else would deny that, in poetry, Wordsworth was the most germinal force among the romantic poets. It was his share in the *Lyrical Ballads* that inaugurated a poetical and spiritual revolution (*The Ancient Mar-*

iner, though it rose far above most of Wordsworth's contributions, was unique and altogether inimitable). It was Wordsworth who, in that and later volumes, showed that poetry could be written in simple language about ordinary humble life. It was Wordsworth who set forth the romantic religion of nature that was to fill a growing spiritual vacuum; who upheld, against the claims of scientific and logical reason, the higher validity of imagination and intuition; who proclaimed the native grandeur of the human soul, and the soul's affinity with the creative spirit that rolls through all things, who maintained that man may be delivered from the bondage of actuality because he has free access to outward and inward sources of enduring beauty and joy and wisdom. All this and much more was Wordsworth's earnest message to mankind, the illumination that he himself—with the aid of his sister and Coleridge—had won from suffering and disillusionment. And while he was, and considered himself, a teacher, he was also a great artist in words, a poet who, at his best, has a purity of style that achieves the most difficult of artistic ends, such perfect communication of the experience that the verbal medium is almost forgotten. If romanticism was a great rebirth of the human spirit, and if Wordsworth was the root and center of English romanticism, an inspirer of multitudes of readers and of poets as diverse as Keats and Arnold, how can one raise any question of his greatness?

But in trying to estimate the present worth of any poet who has long enjoyed the status of a classic, we need at times to distinguish between historical and actual greatness. Historical greatness grows like a snowball, through its own momentum. Once an author is established as a quarry for scholarly research, all his major and minor writings, all major and minor problems, are accepted as of almost equal importance; the quest of truth commonly pushes aside questions of value. It is right that Wordsworthian specialists should try to ascertain, for instance, the nature of the poet's reaction to Godwinism in *The Borderers;* but the much larger body of non-specialists are still more right in regarding *The Borderers* as unreadable. I am not disparaging scholarship; I am merely remarking that scholarly activity is no criterion of a poet's actual value.

One might add that it is hard to say how much

equipment is needed by the reader of poetry in general and of Wordsworth in particular. For example, there is the little poem that contains one of Wordsworth's best-known utterances:

> One impulse from a vernal wood
> May teach you more of man,
> Of moral evil and of good,
> Than all the sages can.

When we read the simple poem as we happen to come on it, it may appeal to us over intellectual city-dwellers as a refreshing statement of what we have often felt in escaping from books of philosophy to the unperplexed beauties of nature. That is the obvious and unhistorical response, and it may be enough. But there was much more in Wordsworth's mind when, with playful exaggeration but fundamental seriousness, he rejected the age-old attempts of ethical philosophy to plumb the nature of man and good and evil and turned for true light to external nature. If we wish to understand him, we must know the development in the seventeenth and eighteenth centuries of scientific rationalism and the "enthusiastic" and "sentimental" reaction against it; we must know Wordsworth's own evolution, his early life among the northern hills, the growth of his passion for nature and of his faith in the common man and in the French Revolution, his loss of faith in the Revolution and his need of something to believe in, his ardent espousal of rationalistic thought, then his strong revulsion from all kinds of doctrinaire intellectualism, and his return to belief in the saving power of nature and man's emotional and imaginative intuition. The more we know of all those things, the better we can understand Wordsworth. At the same time, it must be granted that, in the way of historical and philosophical equipment, Wordsworth demands a good deal less from the reader than do most great poets. If it is axiomatic that the final arbiters of any poet's real value are the body of cultivated readers (from which scholars are not to be excluded), the axiom would seem to be especially true for Wordsworth.

It might be further assumed that literary critics, as the best-informed and most perceptive of general readers, are the natural interpreters of poetry, the natural guides for the public at large. In the nineteenth century the critics were as a rule in more or less accord with their readers and not too far ahead of them to be accepted as guides. During that century Wordsworth was pretty thoroughly assessed by many critics, beginning with Coleridge, and, though some did him no service by making him the builder of a philosophical system, on the whole the estimate was judicious. But for a later and very different age no such estimate remains altogether valid. And while modern scholarship has greatly enlarged and enriched our understanding of Wordsworth, modern criticism does not seem to have been greatly interested or very helpful in the process of revaluation. A few critics, far from exalting Wordsworth into a philosopher, have seen him chiefly as the lover of Annette Vallon; we need not linger with that view. Far more important has been the strong modernist hostility toward romantic poetry and the whole post-romantic tradition. Since romantic poetry was inspired by idealistic faith in man, it has been obnoxious to the age of anxiety; and since it was seldom a texture of intellectual wit and paradox, of ironic and oblique complexity, it has been obnoxious to those critics who identify poetry with the "metaphysical" sensibility and technique. This anti-romantic movement has embraced most of the literary intellectuals in the United States and England. Like earlier reactions, such as that of Wordsworth and Coleridge against the eighteenth century, our reaction has sprung from various causes, but in part—like that of Wordsworth and Coleridge—it has been a defense of the new kind of poetry born of our age. The poets of the nineteenth century, with a few exceptions, have been more or less submerged in the anti-romantic wave. As for Wordsworth, one has the impression that he has suffered less from critical hostility than from critical neglect, and neglect implies that a writer seems to be irrelevant, to lack significance for our time. It does not follow, of course, that Wordsworth is dead because he does not fit the rather narrow critical dogmatism that has been prevalent of late; he may be bigger than the fashionable dogmas. Or, if he does lack significance for us, it may be for different reasons.

We come back then to the general body of readers—never in any age a large body—who take poetry seriously, who read it with their whole being and not merely with detached historical or aesthetic intelligence, who think of it as the record of man's moments of vision, as the distillation of his highest and deepest experience. Without slighting the importance of either knowledge or technical analysis, such readers must ask themselves: "What does Wordsworth now actually mean to me? Do I find myself going back to him continually because he gives the kind of profound stimulus and satisfaction that I want?" This may sound naïve, but it seems to me the prime question that confronts each one of us. And it is not an easy question to answer, not merely because one does not know how other persons feel but because one is not quite sure how one feels one's self. Especially in our profession we grow so used to speaking with catholic authority on any author that it may be hard to distinguish between our public and our private sentiments, or even to be certain that we still have the capacity for private sentiments. Besides, in trying to answer the question for one's self, one cannot get rid of blind spots: I have a suspicion of writers who draw a main part of their spiritual sustenance from nature—a prejudice which in this case may be a quite fatal disqualification.

Wordsworth identified himself, and has always been identified by his readers, with a special message concerning nature's relation to man and man's relation to nature. While his mature experience was a natural sequel to that of his childhood and youth, it was not simply a spontaneous growth; it was a strong and conscious revolt against the scientific view of the world and man. To such temperaments as Wordsworth and Coleridge, it seemed that both the outer and the inner world had been thoroughly mechanized by scientists and psychologists; the physical universe and the soul of man were alike governed by mechanical laws and subject to rationalistic analysis. Wordsworth and Coleridge saw the universe and man as enveloped and interpenetrated by mystery and by the all-comprehending unity of spirit:

> Our destiny, our being's heart and home,
> Is with infinitude, and only there.

And one might add the still more familiar lines of *Tintern Abbey*:

> And I have felt
> A presence that disturbs me with the joy
> Of elevated thoughts; a sense sublime
> Of something far more deeply interfused,
> Whose dwelling is the light of setting suns,
> And the round ocean and the living air,
> And the blue sky, and in the mind of man:
> A motion and a spirit, that impels

> All thinking things, all objects of all thought,
> And rolls through all things.

Such opposed doctrines were not of course essentially new. In the seventeenth century the mechanistic thought of Descartes and Hobbes had aroused the Cambridge Platonists to assert the active reality and unity of spirit. And by the end of the eighteenth century Newtonian science, which at first had been welcomed by poets, and sensationalist psychology, which at first was welcomed by Coleridge and Wordsworth, had come to seem like mechanistic strait jackets imposed upon the universe and the human soul. In the century or more since Wordsworth and Coleridge died, science has gone infinitely farther than they could have anticipated in mechanizing civilization and the heart of man, and a good deal of modern poetry has carried on a new "romantic revolt" against the claims and the desiccating effects of scientific rationalism. All this being so, it might be supposed that Wordsworth would be the inspiration and tutelary genius of the modern movement, whereas it is clear that he is not, that he has meant very little to most modern poets. And what of the common reader, who nowadays is more conscious than ever before of the antagonism between science and any kind of religious or semi-religious idealism? He would be glad to have Wordsworth as a great ally, but does he turn to Wordsworth's faith in the spiritual power of nature and the deep illumination and joy that it offers to man? I do not think he does.

No one has ever revered Wordsworth more than Arnold (who, it has been said, had a tendency to regard himself as Wordsworth's widow), and no one wrote more earnestly of the poet's "healing power":

> He too upon a wintry clime
> Had fallen—on this iron time
> Of doubts, disputes, distractions, fears.
> He found us when the age had bound
> Our souls in its benumbing round;
> He spoke, and loos'd our heart in tears.
> He laid us as we lay at birth
> On the cool flowery lap of earth;
> Smiles broke from us and we had ease.
> The hills were round us, and the breeze
> Went o'er the sun-lit fields again:
> Our foreheads felt the wind and rain.
> Our youth return'd: for there was shed
> On spirits that had long been dead,
> Spirits dried up and closely-furl'd,
> The freshness of the early world.[1]

These lines, written in April 1850, express what Arnold felt that he and his age owed to Wordsworth. Almost thirty years later, in the essay that prefaced his anthology, Arnold delivered the verdict that Wordsworth was, and would remain, the greatest English poet after Shakespeare and Milton, and that he was superior to all modern continental poets, because the ample body of his poems, especially the many good short ones, were "superior in power, in interest, in the qualities which give enduring freshness, to that which any one of the others has left." But we may think that Arnold the semi-official critic was farther removed from his own deepest experience and convictions, and from ours, than Arnold the poet had been. Arnold's poetry in general is a troubled testimony that Wordsworth's healing power was not enough. Empedocles, the despairing representative of the restless and ruthless modern intellect, looked back with longing, as Arnold looked back to Wordsworth, upon that time when

> we receiv'd the shock of mighty thoughts
> On simple minds with a pure natural joy,

but he could only think of it as gone forever. Empedocles, or Arnold, saw no hope of man's regaining the capacity for simple, natural feeling that belonged to the youth of the race and the youth of the individual. Even the memorial tribute I quoted is a tacit admission that the poet of nature did not meet but withdrew from the problems of the modern mind. And, not to cite further evidence, Arnold made the plain statement with which we began, that

> Wordsworth's eyes avert their ken
> From half of human fate.

In other words, the poet's trust in nature, his trust in feeling, his hopefulness and joy, grew out of a temperament and out of circumstances which slighted the darker and grimmer elements in life, the miseries that flesh and mind are heir to, the high proportion of unhappiness in human existence. If in the middle of the nineteenth century the

> priest to us all
> Of the wonder and bloom of the world

could no longer relieve the spiritual distresses of the modern mind (not to mention other kinds of trouble), what can be said in the middle of the twentieth, when the world and man have gone so much farther into the sandy desert that Arnold so clearly saw, when science has become the dominant religion, when naturalistic and positivistic philosophy has made the general mind distrustful of everything except the empirical fact? Even if we grant that Wordsworth's rejection of rigorously mechanistic thought was essentially right (though it took science a long time to reorientate itself), it might still be said that his peculiar faith in nature evaded rather than transcended scientific rationalism. It could not and did not survive among his immediate poetic disciples, or indeed for himself.

At this point it might be well to anticipate one possible objection by recalling the famous passage on science in the Preface to the second edition of *Lyrical Ballads*:

"Poetry is the first and last of all knowledge—it is as immortal as the heart of man. If the labours of Men of science should ever create any material revolution, direct or indirect, in our condition, and in the impressions which we habitually receive, the Poet will sleep then no more than at present; he will be ready to follow the steps of the Man of science, not only in those general indirect effects, but he will be at his side, carrying sensation into the midst of the objects of the science itself. The remotest discoveries of the Chemist, the Botanist, or Mineralogist, will be as proper objects of the Poet's art as any upon which it can be employed, if the time should ever come when these things shall be familiar to us, and the relations under which they are contemplated by the followers of these respective sciences shall be manifestly and palpably material to us as enjoying and suffering beings. If the time should ever come when what is now called science, thus familiarised to men, shall be ready to put on, as it were, a form of flesh and blood, the Poet will lend his divine spirit to aid the transfiguration, and will welcome the Being thus produced, as a dear and genuine inmate of the household of man."

Wordsworth's prophecy sounds brave and reassuring, but it was to prove no more accurate than prophecies generally do.[2] His conception of nature, the main basis of his faith and his poetry, was hardly compatible with biology and the struggle for existence. Moreover, he could not foresee what a multiplied menace even machinery and gadgets were to become—the change, to go no further, from the surrey with the fringe on top to the sound of horns and motors in the spring. Wordsworth did see the rapacious commercialism and the spiritual debasement that accompanied the Industrial Revolution, but he could not foresee that science was to alter the whole tempo and quality of human life and thought and feeling, that it was to change not only the face but the soul of civilization and even threaten its survival. In a word, he dreamed of the humanizing of what was to grow more and more inhuman. That is not, certainly, a charge against Wordsworth in himself and in his own time, but it does have some bearing on Wordsworth in 1950. Since he, so to speak, offered a reply and an antidote to science, it is surely permissible to consider if the antidote was adequate. I do not of course mean to imply that a poet may not hold a belief or idea unless it is sanctioned by science, which operates on another level and has often been dogmatically wrong anyhow, but only that there are some hard facts which imaginative intuition cannot override or ignore.

In answer to these various large questions, many things might be said: that Arnold was only a single disconsolate voice, not an oracle for his own age or ours; that Wordsworth was not a primitivistic escapist and did not avert his eyes from human suffering, but fully recognized the common lot; that he remains a light and a stay for a multitude of modern readers; that, even if he does not, the fault is much less in him than in the temper of an especially troubled age; that science and positivistic thought, however dominant and arrogant, have not extinguished and cannot extinguish the life of the spirit, the human affections, the admiration, hope, and love by which we live; and that in any case the power of great poetry does not depend on the validity of the beliefs and ideas expressed by the poet (who is not a philosopher), but on the total experience we receive from reading him.

Most of these questions and answers are endlessly debatable, and I can only offer some highly debatable comments. Whether or not Wordsworth is actively cherished by a large number of modern readers I do not know, since one cannot sit down at the telephone and inquire, "Have you a book? What poet are you now reading?" So that question must be passed by. In regard to the validity and importance of a poet's philosophy, some readers and critics would deplore any emphasis on what a poet believes and says, and would insist that Wordsworth is entitled to the diplomatic immunity we freely grant to other and older poets who are still alive for us—the Greeks and Romans, Dante and the Christian poets of the English Renaissance from Chaucer to Milton. Well, granted that poetry is an aesthetic experience, it seems to me that unless it ministers, in more than aesthetic ways, to what used to be called our souls, there is not much reason for its being read or written. And I do not think that we common readers are able, even if we wish, to maintain an equal degree of receptivity, or an equally willing suspension of disbelief, toward all kinds of creeds; our knowledge and experience and individual temperaments make some congenial and some not. When we read the Greeks and Romans we may be conscious of being in a pagan and alien world, but we are also conscious of universal human values and, in some poets, of a view of life that is religious by any standard. As for the Christian poets, from Dante to Milton, we may or may not share the chief articles of their religious creed, but—to put the matter in its lowest terms—that creed is at least in our bones. It has the traditional dignity and authority of the greatest of historic religions, and—what is more important—it remains the highest inspiration and criterion of our own religious and ethical gropings because its recognition of what is evil and what is good, of the conflict between the natural and the supra-natural, between pride and humility, remains, even for many non-believers, the most penetrating revelation or insight that man has attained concerning his own nature. But I think that some basic beliefs of Wordsworth, whether we call them pantheism or primitivism, a private myth or auto-intoxication, or whether we use more laudatory names, are more alien to us, less realistic and less satisfying, than those of the pagan or the Christian poets.

In Wordsworth's gospel of nature and man the dualism of both classical and Christian ethics was pretty much dissolved. That fact might validate it for our naturalistic age, but naturalistic thinkers would probably boggle at Wordsworth's faith in the instinctive goodness of man and the inspiring goodness of nature. That Wordsworth's optimistic and humanitarian faith in man has a foundation of doubtful solidity and breadth I think is true. If recent poets and writers in general have been too much inclined to despair, Wordsworth can be charged with a partial view of the opposite kind. In saying that—not that it is a novel opinion—one may of course be an unwitting victim of the partial view characteristic of our melancholy time. But a similar conclusion might emerge from a comparison of Wordsworth with those poets who have most nearly arrived at a comprehensive view of human nature and experience. It would be unfair to Wordsworth, as it would be to most poets, to appeal to the greatest Greeks, or to Lucretius and Virgil, or to Dante and Shakespeare; but no one could object to a comparison with Spenser and Milton or the lesser Chapman and Greville, and I would submit that these and other classical-Christian poets of the Renaissance—whatever their varying poetic power —share a larger, more central, more realistic, and more permanently valid comprehension of the facts of human nature and human life. Wordsworth, like the other romantic poets, stood more or less outside Christianity and had to find a religion for himself; also, he inherited the sentimentalism of the eighteenth century. Though he gave it his own elevated complications and refinements, there was not much room in that doctrine for the sobering conception of man as fallen. If anyone asks, in astonishment, "Why should there be?" it might be said that a conviction of sin is likely to be more conducive to spiritual health than impulses from a vernal wood. One of the chief penalties that attend Wordsworth's kind of thought and feeling—as we see also in Emerson and others—is the loss or attenuation of the sense of evil, the tragic sense. What Wordsworth mourned in *Tintern Abbey* and *Intimations of Immortality* was, to be sure, the loss of what he had lived by, but that was the capacity for sensuous and emotional response to nature.

I am not forgetting that he wrote, with moving power and beauty, of

> the heavy and the weary weight
> Of all this unintelligible world,

though I cannot remember many great poems in which these words find a substantial "objective correlative." I am not forgetting, either, the painful reality of the struggles through which Wordsworth arrived at his belief in nature's beneficent ministry to man. I am only asking if we, who are more concerned with his poetry than his biography, can find there, not merely solace, but a realistic and sustaining consciousness of what we may call the human predicament, or, if you like, original sin. *Intimations of Immortality*, beautiful as it is, records a very individual kind of depression and a very individual solution. The loss that Wordsworth felt so intensely is not one that many people can share, nor is the positive gain in which he rejoiced—since our primal sympathy with man is rarely a compensation for our failing responsiveness to nature. And the passage on the six-year-old child as "Mighty Prophet! Seer blest!" is so unreal a fantasy that it may almost vitiate the whole. When we think of Henry Vaughan's *The Retreat*, we must—even if we say Vaughan's Christian faith was no more "authentic" than Wordsworth's pseudo-Platonism —we must admit that Vaughan's celebration of childish innocence, his grief for sin, and his longing for the pure light of heaven have a more than private validity. If these few remarks are distressingly flat-footed and blind, I can only say that I am not unaware of several recent, sympathetic, and admirable expositions of the ode, Mr. Trilling's among them.[3] And I might add that I would not go nearly so far as Mr. Fairchild in his formidable arraignment of the romantic poets.[4]

As Wordsworth's mythical or mystical view of nature was largely the creation of his own mind, so in a considerable degree his view of man was a mental abstraction or idealization rather imposed upon than drawn from flesh-and-blood humanity. He has a fair amount of poetry or verse about deserted mothers and their offspring, but that theme is not quite a major segment of normal experience. Nor is Wordsworth's abstract vision of life greatly broadened or deepened in other "objective" poems from *Guilt and Sorrow* to *Michael*; with all its beauty and pathos *Michael* is a simple pastoral. How often, we might ask, does Wordsworth make us feel "the fierce dispute Betwixt damnation and impassion'd clay?" To quote Keats is to recall the famous letter in which he said, among other things, that Milton's "Philosophy, human and divine, may be tolerably understood by one not much advanced in years," and that Wordsworth had penetrated more deeply into the human heart.[5] The latter opinion may be true, but Keats shows no sign of having understood *Paradise Lost* apart from its aesthetic qualities, and Milton's central consciousness of the war between good and evil in the world and in the soul of man seems to me to leave Wordsworth nowhere—unless we take in *The Excursion*, and most people do not regard it as an active part of the canon. In short, the ethical Wordsworth tends to see man with the somewhat blurred or far-sighted eyes of the mystical Wordsworth. The world of reflection and intuition in which he lives does not except at moments coalesce with our world. To our questionings about man in the universe, man in society, or even man in solitude, Wordsworth does not give much help toward an answer, or toward a realization of the problems.

It may be said, with indignation, that we have no right to expect such help from a poet. But as long as poets speak, and use words that have a meaning, I think we may ask what they mean and where their meaning stands in our scale of values—always remembering, as I hope I am, that we are not judges interpreting a fixed constitution, but that we read poetry because it purifies and enriches our values. It is obvious that Wordsworth's insights came rather from observation of his conscious and unconscious self than from observation of people, that a very high proportion of his writing was a record of his own inner history, his own feelings. He did not, like Chaucer or Shakespeare or Milton, lead the life of a man among men; he was for the most part a brooding recluse, wholly devoted to poetry. And it does not appear that he was actually very intimate with the kind of rural folk he some-times wrote about, or a very close observer of nature. He was an intensely subjective and intro-spective poet who had received an illumination that he had to express; but, as I have said, it was a very individual and peculiar illumination, which few can share except in its elementary phases, and which, for Wordsworth himself, excluded large areas of life. He thought of his main theme as "man, the heart of man, and human life," and doubtless many readers would warmly endorse that claim; and some would say, in the up-to-date language of psychology, that the poet created authentic myths and dealt with important states of mind. It seems to me that his main theme of contemplation was not so much man and nature but himself contemplating man and nature. That was not an unimportant subject, but has it a breadth and depth and concreteness that we in our altered world can recognize and respond to? Is Wordsworth's presentation of his experience of reality and man confined in general too closely to the terms of his personal creed to transcend it, to carry those larger implications that make poetry universal? Although Wordsworth's personal beliefs may be less

remote from ours than Mr. Eliot's, are we moved by most of his poetry as we are by *Four Quartets?*

So far we have been concerned with the Wordsworth of the great decade, who has always been *the* Wordsworth. But if it is improper to question the ethical value of impulses from a vernal wood, it would be still worse not to remember that the poet himself, through much of that decade, was led to increasing questioning of spontaneous impulse and to increasing acceptance of inward discipline and order, to a new vision of reality. One early product of such a mood was *Resolution and Independence.* Two years later came the very explicit *Ode to Duty,* in which, with a nostalgic tribute to those whose spontaneous love and joy are an unerring light, Wordsworth recognizes his need of a stronger control than blind trust in feeling. And then, in the *Character of the Happy Warrior* and *Elegiac Stanzas,* his embracing of the law of reason and conscience was emotionally strengthened by grief for the death of his brother—"A deep distress hath humanised my soul." The word "humanised" seems to imply an admission that there had been something inhuman in his detached serenity, and that the religion of nature was no very sure support against the real sorrows of mankind. We cannot pursue Wordsworth's ethical development through further poems, including *The Excursion,* and can only say that his half-Stoic, half-Christian appeal to self-discipline was the transitional stage between his earlier trust in pure feeling and his later more or less orthodox Christianity. But there is again the fact that "the poetry of Wordsworth" means, with a few exceptions, the poetry of his happy faith in nature and man; and some readers, even devout admirers, so dislike the *Ode to Duty, Laodamia,* and similar poems that they would say Wordsworth had only put off the old man to put on the old woman. Whatever his poetical fate, it does not seem necessary to conclude, for poets in general, that the attainment of moral wisdom means the end of poetry. As regards Wordsworth himself, the poetry of his great decade might have been greater if more of it had been born of conflict between the ideals of "unchartered freedom" and order. As it was, much of the poetry we have cherished was the outpouring of a too simple harmony of soul.

If Wordsworth is not an active force in our time (and the mainly negative evidence suggests that he is not), we have looked at some of the possible reasons, especially what may be thought the nebulous quality of his mysticism and of his sentimental ethics, and the really very limited range of experience that he explores. Most or all of what I have said may be quite wrong-headed—though I did not fully realize when I began to take stock of my opinions that I was cast for the sour role of devil's advocate or counsel for the prosecution. However, Wordsworth is not likely to be injured, and mine may be a *felix culpa* if it arouses ardent opposition. I shall gladly be a martyr in so good a cause— provided that those who kindle the fire will take oath that the poetry of Wordsworth is one of their most frequent and precious companions. In going further than I expected to in discussing possible barriers between Wordsworth and us, I have not, I may say, given an altogether fair account of even my own reactions, and the balance cannot be redressed in a limited space. But I should like to make a beginning.

If we common readers were compiling our own Wordsworth anthology, it would probably be a much smaller selection than Arnold made or than textbooks offer. There are many short poems, such as those addressed to flowers and birds, which make pleasant reading but which I at least could spare. We must have a few of the narrative and reflective poems, and of course *Tintern Abbey* and *Intimations of Immortality*. We probably read *The Prelude* more as a document than as a poem, and the choice of passages would have to be left to individual discretion; but one might venture to ask if more than fractions of the work can be called great poetry. *The Excursion*—which, I may remark, I have gone through much oftener than Francis Jeffrey and most modern readers—yields a few fine bits, such as that on the Greek religion of nature and some on reason and discipline. And the shorter poems on this last theme, which were referred to before, I should keep, not without misgivings as to whether Wordsworth's "new light" is always carried alive into the heart by passion.

For the rest, the poetry that seems to me the finest, that speaks to us most directly, is mainly of two kinds. One kind or group comprises some short poems in which nature is subordinated to humanity and in which there is little or no philosophizing. Of these *The Solitary Reaper* might stand as a perfect example. Here the slightest of rural incidents, which could have occurred in any country in any age, is not artificially heightened but simply realized, with a power of verbal and rhythmical suggestion that is at once homely and rich, concrete and magical. And to that may be added some other pieces of similar timeless and "commonplace" universality, such as the best of the Lucy poems.

The other group embraces a good many of the sonnets, those on Milton, on British ideals of the past and sins of the present, on Toussaint L'Ouverture, and kindred subjects, and some on various themes, from the sight of London at sunrise to mutability. In the public sonnets Wordsworth speaks, not with the voice of a bird-watcher, but in the ringing tones of a man among men, a man whose magnanimous idealism and profound anxiety entitle him to deal with nations and great events. Whatever the poet's debt to Milton, this poetry springs from real conflict and has massive strength. In these heroic sonnets, and in others of quieter nobility, Wordsworth is in line with the great poets back through Milton to the ancients. Because he has here a sober consciousness of the facts of human nature and life, he earns the right to celebrate man's unconquerable mind; he does make us feel that we are greater than we know. And perhaps our small anthology holds enough to carry Wordsworth through another hundred years.

NOTES

1. *Memorial Verses*, 42–57.

2. Parts of this paragraph are borrowed from *Science and English Poetry*, by Douglas Bush, New York, 1950.

3. *The Liberal Imagination*, New York, 1950, 129–59.

4. *Religious Trends in English Poetry, Volume III: 1780–1830*, New York, 1949.

5. Letter to John Hamilton Reynolds, May 3, 1818.

Willard Sperry

WORDSWORTH'S DECLINE*

Matthew Arnold is to be credited with the now familiar phrase about Wordsworth's "golden decade," those years from 1798 to 1808[1] in which "almost all his really first-rate work was done." The present critical fashion shortens this period by about two years and brings it to an end with the *Ode: Intimations of Immortality,* which was finished in 1806.

Like all dogmas, the theory that during his sixty years of literary life Wordsworth wrote first-rate poems for eight or ten years and third-rate verse for fifty years is over-simple. There are fine passages in *The Excursion* (1814), which may not be overlooked. There are noble lines, like those at the end of *Duddon Sonnets* (1820), as authentic as any Wordsworth ever wrote. *The Memorials of a Tour in Italy* (1837) reaffirms, at times, his earlier power over words. As late as 1842 *To the Clouds* recovers something of the imperious mood of the great decade. Yet Wordsworth could not be relied upon, after about 1806, to write poetry which bore upon its face the credentials of its greatness, and, failing inspiration, he manufactured verses. In general, therefore, there is warrant for Professor Garrod's statement that the last forty years of Wordsworth's life are "the most dismal anti-climax of which the history of literature holds record."

This anti-climax, which was Wordsworth's point of poetic arrival, has become our point of critical departure. We see the end from the beginning and read the early work in the light of the later. Much as we might like to isolate the poems of the golden decade and rid ourselves of the embarrassment of the subsequent work, we cannot in good conscience do so. There must have been some initial defect which brought on untimely, and hastened unduly, the processes of Wordsworth's poetic decline. Hence we seek the sources of the last sterility in the nature of the first fruitfulness.

The fading of splendid visions is a commonplace of human experience. In the terms of his history as a poet Wordsworth brooded much over the riddle. His verse concedes that the glories which come to us in early life are a mystery in their advent and a reproach in their loss. He never ceases to ask why they are given only to be withdrawn, whether memory can recover them and imagination recreate them to give them a permanent life in the mind. He confined himself mainly to the literary problem, but was not able to rid himself of the suspicion that the technical perplexity had a deeper significance.

Perhaps the supposed problem of Wordsworth's decline is insoluble, simply because it is not a problem at all. Bad verse is not a riddle; any journeyman can write it. The riddle is good poetry. Where does it come from, how is it written, what conscious part has the author in its making? Are we not reversing the issues when we ask why Wordsworth wrote mediocre poems for forty years? The real question is, How was Wordsworth able to write good poems for eight or ten years?

Poets have usually said that their best work is the product of inspiration. They are from time to time visited by some creative power, not themselves, which fulfils their talent as genius. In this experience poets are like prophets, saints, mystics; and poetry is akin to religion. Indeed, for Wordsworth poetry and religion were so nearly identical as to be indistinguishable.[2] Whether the faith common to artists and mystics is warranted, because grounded in the total reality of things, we do not know. We can only say that the persons concerned have never been satisfied with naturalistic accounts of the sources of their inspiration.

* Reprinted by permission of the publishers from *Wordsworth's Anti-Climax* by Willard L. Sperry, Cambridge, Mass.: Harvard University Press, Copyright © 1935 by the President and Fellows of Harvard College, © renewed 1963 by Muriel Bennett Sperry.

Wordsworth believed that he was a dedicated poet. He was rather too solemn in speaking of his dedication, and he is generally charged with undue egotism in the matter, but it is hard to see how he could have given the world a faithful record of his inner history and yet have escaped the charge. All men of genius have made the same claim and have invited the same criticism. There is no known circumlocution by which a saint or an artist can avoid the appearance of egotism. Infelicitous as Wordsworth may have been in references to his vocation, any periphrasis or false modesty would have been worse.

Meanwhile, no mystic has ever laid claim to constant inspiration. The experience is occasional and fugitive, and the classical literature of religious devotion is much concerned with the sorry anticlimaxes of the spiritual life. The periods of inspiration seem to be few and brief; the periods of dryness, bitterness, and of the dark night of the soul, many and interminable. Uninspired days and years stretch like a desert between rare oases of peace and power. If we allow Wordsworth eight or ten years of inspiration out of his sixty years of productive life, we can only say that, as these matters go, the ratio is in his favor. Most mystics have had to learn to be content with less. The real problem would seem to be, why and how Wordsworth maintained so high a level for so considerable a time as the golden decade.

Nevertheless, there is in the arts, as in religion, a regimen which makes inspiration more likely than otherwise it would be. "The poet, Wordsworth knew well," says Ernest de Selincourt, "was a craftsman who must toil with unremitting patience at every detail of his work, till it has gained a clearer outline, a fuller substance; not otherwise could it acquire that organic power which is the sure touchstone of art." Although Wordsworth urged upon others a wise passiveness, he was far from being a literary quietist. In his finished work the apparatus for making poetry is much in evidence. Only on the rarest occasions does he succeed in deleting from his verse all traces of the process of its composition. The *Tintern Abbey* lines are Wordsworth at a very high level, yet they are concerned with the manner of their own creation, and with the reassuring prospect of verses yet to come. There is something to be said for the theory that, working overmuch on the often motionless machinery of his genius, Words-

worth finally put it out of gear. I propose to return to this suggestion in a later chapter.

Within these general limits we have not merely a critical right, we have a critical duty, to try to understand the connection between the golden decade and the sterile years which followed. The inquiry now stands at the forefront of all criticism of Wordsworth, and every question which we ask about him turns out to be a facet of this major problem. If we could understand the causes and the nature of Wordsworth's anti-climax as a poet, we should be in a position to explain his worst verse, and, what is far more important, to understand his best verse.

The task should be undertaken with proper humility. We belong to a generation which prides itself on its critical acumen. We have no cause to preen ourselves because we see clearly the prosiness of Wordsworth's later work. The poet's more candid contemporaries were quite aware that there was a falling-off. The journals and letters of the time are filled with laments at the great man's inertia. There was *The Prelude* gathering dust in its pigeon-hole. Mrs. Wordsworth writes in wry humor from "Idle Mount which just now well supports that title."

By about 1820 Coleridge was calling attention to the declining excellence of Wordsworth's work. Crabb Robinson, than whom there was none more loyal, served notice on his friend that better things might be expected. "A poet who begins so early and so well as you did sets himself a severe task in the implied obligation to maintain his place." This was straight talk; we honor both its candor and its courage. He writes even more frankly to Dorothy and, having written, fears lest "the letter be thought impertinent"; yet he does not withdraw it,—he sends it, half-fearing and half-hoping that it may be passed on to the poet for his good. Plainly we have not allowed our genius for criticism to create at this late date an adventitious difficulty on which to show our skill. The dismal fact of the poet's waning powers was familiar to his immediate circle.

Perhaps the true pathos of Wordsworth's decline is this, that he could not disguise it from himself. The eleventh book of *The Prelude* gives us the first intimation of a fear, taking form in his mind, which was to mature in later years into a somber certainty:

the hiding-places of my power
Seem open; I approach, and then they close;
I see by glimpses now; when age comes on,
May scarcely see at all.

Thereafter this note was never wholly silenced, and at times it was the poet's dominant theme:

Dread Power! whom peace and calmness serve
No less than Nature's threatening voice,
If aught unworthy be my choice,
From THEE if I would swerve;
Oh, let Thy grace remind me of the light
Full early lost, and fruitlessly deplored;
Which, at this moment, on my waking sight
Appears to shine, by miracle restored;
My soul, though yet confined to earth,
Rejoices in a second birth!
—'Tis past, the visionary splendor fades;
And night approaches with her shades.

He was forty-eight when he wrote the above lines, and there were more than thirty years to run. Wordsworth, with such passages to his credit, cannot be accused of immoderate self-assurance. He felt in his members the intimate poignancy of that anti-climax which is for us merely a literary perplexity.

In dealing with the dogma of the decline, as with the fact, we must remember that Wordsworth's time-sheet of years was not that which we expect the artist to keep. The lives of most poets have been fierce and brief; they have been written out and often dead by middle age. The days of Wordsworth's years were, by reason of strength, four-score. Who knows what anti-climaxes we should have had to acknowledge and to regret had the productive lives of his contemporaries, Byron, Shelley, and Keats, reached to Wordsworth's great age? Death may well have been merciful to their literary names. They were all born after Wordsworth and died long before him. When we compare the shorter arc of their lives—Byron, 1788–1824; Shelley, 1792–1821; Keats, 1795–1821—with that of Wordsworth, 1770–1850, we can understand that we are dealing here with facts which are incommensurable. He was born eighteen years before the earliest of this trio and outlived the last of them by twenty-six years. As for Coleridge, who was critic as well as creator, his life, 1772–1834, fell eighteen years short of Wordsworth's.

Of the great poets who worked in maturity at large canvasses we may say, with some measure of fidelity to fact, that their best verse was finished, or at least conceived and well under way, before

they were fifty. Chaucer was forty-five when he finished *The Canterbury Tales*. Spenser published the first three books of *The Faerie Queen* in 1590, when he was thirty-eight. A second three followed in 1596. He was dead at forty-seven. Shakespeare's period of greatest productivity—the so-called "third period," which gave us *Hamlet, Othello, Macbeth*, and *Lear* among its ten or twelve plays—fell between the poet's thirty-sixth and forty-fifth years. Both Dante and Milton worked to the end, and *The Divine Comedy* and *Paradise Lost* carried them into their fifties, but Dante had begun the former in his forties and Milton had conceived the latter in his late thirties.

Of the moderns, Browning lived to something like Wordsworth's great age, but he wrote twenty years too long. The single volumes of Wordsworth and Browning, if printed in chronological order, divide at much the same place. We seldom go beyond *The Excursion* or *The Ring and the Book*, yet in each volume more than a third of the work is yet to come. The later Browning poems are marked by blemishes which even his greatest admirers cannot deny. But they cause us no resentment and create no literary problem; they are accepted as in the order of nature—the laborious work of an old man. If we judge Wordsworth otherwise, it is because we find in his earlier verse an austere excellence which Browning never achieved and to which, to do him justice, he never laid claim.

On any reasonable count, therefore, given the parallel of other literary lives, we may dismiss the last twenty, even the last thirty years, of Wordsworth's life as lying beyond the time when we have normal expectation of first-rate work from a poet. This takes us back to 1820. The period which compasses a culpable anti-climax is shortened to the ten or fifteen years which followed the golden decade. After 1820 on-coming age denied Wordsworth the power of sheer invention which is at its zenith in late youth and early manhood.[3]

Look at the other end of the calendar. Wordsworth was late in his authentic arrival. Our modern interest in the youthful Wordsworth concerns a time, when so far as his art was concerned the poet was still in embryo. The youthful Wordsworth was not writing poems; he was idling, traveling, thinking, and feeling. Two or three short poems follow his coming of age. In 1792–93 he wrote *Descriptive Sketches*. His two Godwinian ventures—*Guilt and*

Sorrow and *The Borderers*—fall between 1793 and 1796. *Descriptive Sketches,* for all its promise, was in the elder tradition; the Godwin poems were a passing phase and throw light on a particular period of the poet's history; neither belongs with his best work. Wordworth's characteristic poetry began with the *Lyrical Ballads*. The authentic poet, who is deplored as a lost leader in his later years, did not begin to write until he was nearly thirty.

We have, therefore, a Wordsworth finally embarked on his first productive period at a time of life when, with the average artist, the inventive power has begun to wane. The pent-up energy burst out like a flood through a broken dam. But in those first years of the golden decade Wordsworth was frankly experimenting both with his subjects and with his medium at an age when most poets have decided upon the one and have mastered the other. Although the initial energies of the artist may have begun to stale in him, Wordsworth was able in 1797–98 to compensate for the loss of early invention by his choice and treatment of subjects. He chose novel subjects, which made him at once an object of interest and controversy, and he treated them in such a manner as to win for himself a permanent place in English letters.

This delayed springtime might seem to have augured for Wordsworth an autumn harvest of better verse than is usually reaped by aging poets. Probably the exact reverse is the truth; for in matters of the mind, as in matters of the body, a skill that is mastered only in the late twenties or the early thirties never becomes second nature. Such techniques require conscious attention and lack the spontaneity of a habit formed at a time when body and mind are supple and yet in the making. The wonder is that at twenty-seven Wordsworth was able to do so well with a poetic method which he had only then defined to himself.

For all its essential nobility there is in much of Wordsworth's best verse a hint of mental rigidity, a felt want of flexibility. It lacks the unself-consciousness of youth. The noblest numbers achieve a mature majesty of which youth is incapable, but there is little of the margin of poetic high spirits which we find in the earliest and often the best verse of other poets. A certain stiffness to the point of rigidity suggests a man who had mastered his craft too late for his own good. Instead of promising a longer poetic life than normal for Wordsworth,

his late arrival must have prophesied a briefer life. The mature self-consciousness employed in the experimental *Lyrical Ballads,* so far from being the sign of genius gathering power, is the mark of an invention already beginning to decline. Thus, if we follow our first thought and say that Wordsworth ought to have written good verse ten years later than the average poet, because he started ten years after that poet, we are probably wrong. Our second thought satisfies us that his poetic life was shortened just because he was so slow in finding himself as a poet. Ideally, the *Lyrical Ballads* should have come a decade sooner.

Both Wordsworth and Dorothy gave to their contemporaries the strong suggestion of having grown old before their time.[4] In his gossip about the poets of the Lake School De Quincey tells us that at the time he knew them best both the poet and his sister seemed spent:

> Some people, it is notorious, live faster by much than others, the oil is burned out sooner in one constitution than in another; and the cause of this may be various; but in the Wordsworths one part of the cause is no doubt, a secret fire of temperament too fervid; the self-consuming energies of the brain that gnaw at the life strings forever.... There was in both such a premature expression of old age, that strangers invariably supposed them fifteen or twenty years older than they were.

De Quincey goes on to say that Wordsworth at thirty-eight was once mistaken for over sixty. Plainly there is in his decline a physiological factor to be reckoned with; less piquant perhaps than the emotional and the ethical factors, but none the less pertinent. The whole question of Wordsworth's dates is one which has been ignored and which ought to be reviewed. If De Quincey's testimony is to be trusted, and there is no reason to doubt it, we have a man who was nervously burnt out at forty. He had spent the bulk of his poetic patrimony. His best work had not been begun until he was twenty-seven or twenty-eight, and the fecundity of the next ten years proved costly to his energies. Wordsworth's anti-climax deserves diagnosis not merely at the hands of the psychiatrist and the casuist, but at the hands also of one initially wiser than both, the general medical practitioner! [5] The headaches, the exhaustion, the weariness of hand to the point of near-paralysis, are not to be ignored.

To turn, now, to another aspect of our riddle. It has been the fashion in recent years to attribute Wordsworth's poetic decline to his break with Coleridge. The inference is that, as their first friendship had flowered in verse of great beauty, an uninterrupted companionship would have continued to yield for many years profuse blossom of the same quality. As Coleridge had been the first cause, if not the actual author, of Wordsworth's best verse, so he might have continued in that office had the friendship remained inviolate. But after their parting—so runs the critical reflection—Wordsworth was helpless and relapsed into uninspired ventures which were an occasion for his talent but not for his genius.[6]

The open break came in 1810. Coleridge had gone to lodge with the Montagus, and for his friend's good as for their good, Wordsworth had warned them that, because of his habits, Coleridge might prove a difficult lodger. Montagu had found the warning warranted by the event, and in a moment of exasperation had repeated to Coleridge what he remembered Wordsworth to have said. When the first bitterness was past the moot point which remained was this,—had Wordsworth said that Coleridge "had rotted out his entrails" with drugs? Wordsworth denied the precise words, though admitting their substance. He did recall having said that, when Schiller's "body was opened up his entrails were, as it were, eaten up," and he suspected that this vigorous statement had been confused with his diagnosis of Coleridge.

As for Coleridge, he carried the scars of the hurt through all his latter years. If our common sense exonerates Wordsworth, our sympathies go out to Coleridge. His letters betray the depth of the wound:

> I must commence by telling you, great a weakness as it must appear, that so deep and so rankling is the wound, which Wordsworth has wantonly and without the slightest provocation inflicted in return for fifteen year's most enthusiastic self-despising and alas! self-injuring Friendship, (for as to his wretched agents, the Montagus, Carlisles, Knapps, etc., I despise them too much to be seriously hurt by anything, they for themselves can say or do) that I cannot return to Grasmere or its vicinity.
>
> (April, 1811)

> Meantime . . . what with the never-closing festering wound of Wordsworth and his family. . . . (October, 1811)

> The Grasmere business has kept me in a fever of agitation, and will end in complete alienation: I have refused to go over and Wordsworth has refused to apologize.
> (March, 1812)

> Had I been aware that Mr. Wordsworth's Poem had been announced publicly—for it is now many years since I have been in correspondence with him by letters. (April, 1819)

But Wordsworth had long foreseen the break. The unhappy incident of 1810 only gave semi-public acknowledgment to a fact which he had already accepted. As far as he was concerned the friendship had been imperiled for four or five years prior, because of Coleridge's inability or unwillingness to profit by the help which the poet and Dorothy tried to give him. They had loaned him money, which was never repaid; they had made plans for his good, which had gone astray from the start. The sources, whether journals, letters, or verse, all suggest that Coleridge had made it increasingly hard for Wordsworth and Dorothy to hold his confidence. Meanwhile it is clear that his wife's jealousy kept Coleridge more and more apart from the friends at Grasmere. His absences, growing longer as the years passed, must have been the price he paid for what little peace he had at home. Words in a letter to his wife suggest far more than they say, "Depend on it my dear Wife! that the more you sympathize with me in my kind manners and kind feelings to those at Grasmere the more I shall be likely to sympathize with you in your opinions respecting their faults and imperfections."

Yet as late as the spring of 1806 we find the Wordsworths unable to settle the matter of a new home until Coleridge, who was still included in their plans, returned from Malta. He reached England in August of that year, but lingered on in London before coming to Coleorton, whither the Wordsworths had moved. When he arrived "he was utterly changed. . . . He then scarcely ever spoke of anything that concerned him, or us, or our common friends."[7] He soon left them, apparently unable to endure the condemnation of his own conscience, which charged him in their society with his changed character. It must have been just after this parting that Wordsworth accepted and recorded the fact in verse. English poetry has no finer tribute to friendship achieved and no more tender elegy to friendship lost than is to be found in *A Complaint* (1806).

> There is a change—and I am poor;
> Your love hath been, nor long ago,
> A fountain at my fond heart's door,
> Whose only business was to flow;
> And flow it did: not taking heed
> Of its own bounty, or my need.
>
> What happy moments did I count!
> Blest was I then all bliss above!
> Now, for that consecrated fount
> Of murmuring, sparkling, living love,
> What have I? shall I dare to tell?
> A comfortless and hidden well.
>
> A well of love—it may be deep—
> I trust it is,—and never dry:
> What matter? if the waters sleep
> In silence and obscurity.
> —Such change, and at the very door
> Of my fond heart, hath made me poor.

Plainly Wordsworth felt bereft as a man and apprehensive as an artist. Without the troubling of the waters by his friend he feared lest the spring of verse in him might dry up. It is no accident that the *Complaint,* with its note of apprehension, was written in the year which saw also the great *Ode: Intimations of Immortality.* The period is that marking the end of the golden decade. Who knows whether the fear itself may not have had a stultifying effect on the poet's genius? In his poem he gave to later critics full warrant for finding in the break with Coleridge the major cause of his decline.

Meanwhile the trouble was of some years' standing. As early as 1803 the substance of the Alfoxden trinity—William, Dorothy, and Coleridge—was in process of being confounded and its persons put to confusion. On the 14th of August in that year the three started gaily on their Scotch tour, but within a fortnight Coleridge had left the other two. Dorothy is gentle in the *Recollections;* Coleridge was not well, could not stand the wet weather in an open carriage, and set off direct for Edinburgh. Nevertheless she and William kept crossing his path in the course of their wanderings, and it looks as though he had been more concerned to get away from them than to reach the city. Shortly after we find him complaining in letters to Poole that Words-

worth was indolent, mired in self-involution"; "benetted in hypochondriacal Fancies." "I now see very little of Wordsworth." That was toward the end of the year 1803. The unhappy misunderstanding over the "rotted entrails" seems to have been the climax of a considerable period of mutual distrust and criticism.

Let us examine the assumption that had this friendship continued uninterrupted over further years Wordsworth's genius would have had a longer life.

William Wordsworth is in many ways a baffling figure; he does not fit the common categories. He was strangely wanting in the power of abstract thought and curiously dependent upon others to supply him with the stuff of his speculations. He was accused in his lifetime of trafficking in systems and philosophies tricked out as poems, but these were seldom or never of his own devising. His systems were borrowed clothes and betray a foreign quality wherever they appear in his work.

On the other hand, Wordsworth seems not to have had initially the poet's power to see concrete facts, that is, to see them poetically. His youthful work abounds in faithful descriptions, but the insight which makes the later poems what they are is wanting in his early descriptive sketches; that work is description, not poetry. He was dependent upon some mind more philosophical than his own to point out to him the fact at which as a poet he should look. Once his gaze had been directed to it and fixed upon it, he could make it yield a poem. But apparently he had to wait for the speculative thinker to tell him what to look for in the world of concrete things.

The only one of Wordsworth's systems which has any interest today is that which deals with the origin of poems. Its theses were derived from the associationist psychology of the day and from the canons of the then dominant English "School of Taste." Wordsworth must have been familiar with both before he met Coleridge. Johnson's publishing house in London, which was one of his sanctuaries in 1793 and 1794, produced works in these fields. At a later time Coleridge's fiery transcendentalism was added to Wordsworth's speculative material, and the result was fused by interminable talk into a congruous whole. Having elaborated their system, the two friends immediately set to work to write poems in vindication of it. Their "experi-ments" were published as the *Lyrical Ballads*.

Thereafter the two men seem to part company mentally. Coleridge lacked the power of concen-trated and consecutive thought. He was versatile; he was always suggestive; he had in many ways far the more powerful mind; yet he was desultory. "The man rambled brilliantly," said Crabb Robin-son after hearing one of his public lectures, "he is absolutely incorrigible, but his *vitia* are indeed *splendid*." Wordsworth, on the contrary, was a man of dogged ways. His mind, once it had laid hold of an idea, could not release its hold until all the bearings of the idea had been explored and exhausted. Witness his conscientiousness in exam-ining thoroughly and then in finally discarding the superficial system of Godwin. That single intellec-tual adventure cost him three or four precious years, with little or no profit in the end. The sys-tem elaborated with Coleridge's aid had more sub-stance,—after a century it still remains one of the classic theories of poetry,—and to its vindication Wordsworth devoted the best years of his produc-tive life. If he wasted three years on Godwinism, he invested ten years to good purpose in his experi-ments with the theory of poetry which had been struck off in those interminable walks and talks around Racedown and Alfoxden. Indeed, to the very last, the theory remained the only one by which Wordsworth professed to write, and at the end of the golden decade it had assumed for him the dignity of an article of faith.

The traditional dogma suggests that Wordsworth would have continued to produce great poetry so long as his friendship with Coleridge lasted. The dogma demands a William Wordsworth who never existed. It requires of him a versatility which he wholly lacked. He did succeed in giving a local habitation and a name to the system which he professed and within which he labored. It took him years to do so, and while he was so employed he could not be diverted. Whatever other debt of gratitude we owe to Wordsworth, we owe him a debt beyond our power of payment for a brood-ing conscientiousness which yielded us noble poems in vindication of the joint theory of poetry. The theory may be declared false, but if so, not on the ground of interior inconsistencies. It can be de-clared false today only if the poems which were produced in accordance with it are declared fail-ures. Precisely because these poems, so far from being failures, are an indubitable success we are prohibited from dismissing the system as negligible. If then, as seems probable, we owe the final draft-ing of the system to Coleridge, we owe its demon-stration to Wordsworth.

Wordsworth's mind was not the sort required by the theory that he might have gone on writing good verse if the fountain of Coleridge's friend-ship had continued to flow freely at his door. We cannot imagine Wordsworth and Coleridge, let us say in 1806 or 1808, when the permutations and combinations of the theory of poetry elaborated in 1798 had been exhausted, joining forces for a sec-ond partnership in some volume of a quite different nature. Coleridge could have supplied the specu-lative half of such a second venture—"Oft, like a winged spider, I am entangled in a new spun web, but never fear for me, 'tis but the flutter of my wings, and I am off again!"—but it was not in Wordsworth's power to be thus versatile. On the contrary, the systematic webs which he spun for himself were so tough that he was more or less permanently entangled in them.

The truth is that by one of those happy accidents which from time to time occur Wordsworth and Coleridge met at a moment when each could do very much for the other.[8] The one needed further clarification of his thinking, the other needed the steadying influence of a character more stable than his own. Like all good things in life the fruits of that meeting rest in their own right. Conscious at-tempts to repeat the initial experience must have failed. In the mating and parting of these minds there was something akin to the instinctive proc-esses of nature. By the time they had left Somerset to go to Germany, Wordsworth and Coleridge had done, each for the other, all that was humanly pos-sible. Their separation soon after they reached Hamburg—Wordsworth to go on to Goslar and Coleridge to Ratzeburg—seems in retrospect a tacit admission which each made to himself, though not to the other, that the process of intellectual cross-fertilization had been completed, never to be resumed in its first passionateness. Intuitively they must have known that a second *Ancient Mariner* and a second *Tintern Abbey*, bound within the covers of another joint volume, were not in the order of nature.

It is true that in the tenth book of *The Prelude*

Wordsworth apostrophizes Coleridge warmly as "my own beloved Friend," and even says of the trip to Malta,

> To me the grief confined that Thou art gone.

But these generous protestations are tempered by a salutary reminder that all is not well with the exile:

> Thine be those motions strong and sanative,
> A ladder for thy Spirit to reascend
> To health and joy and pure contentedness.

The *Complaint*, which came two years later, was already in process.

Aside, then, from Wordsworth's own dread lest the loss of Coleridge's friendship might first still the surface waters and finally dry up the springs of his genius—and we have no way of knowing how far this insidious fear may have reacted upon his self-assurance—there is no reason to suppose that the break between the two friends, begun quite unconsciously at Hamburg and finally forced upon them both as a sorry reality in 1810, cost Wordsworth his productive power or in any way caused his poetic decline.

Common sense and conscience forbid us to take exception to Wordsworth's conduct. He was ready and anxious to help Coleridge as long as Coleridge was willing to be helped. It was Coleridge's misfortune—a sick man rather than a bad man—to become increasingly aware of his failings when in the company of the Wordsworths. On Wordsworth's side there never had been the self-abandonment in friendship which Coleridge had showed. Wordsworth was too cautious, too preoccupied, too self-centered to be capable of such generosity of mind and heart. His very correctness must have nettled the more sensitive Coleridge. We absolve William —and we doubly absolve Dorothy and Mary—of the least lack of considerate charity at any point between 1797 and 1810, yet had Wordsworth been a man of more impulsive nature, the difficulties might have been surmounted.

Crabb Robinson eventually effected a formal and public reconciliation, but the private wounds were never healed. To the last Wordsworth was careful to acknowledge his debt to his friend, but he was much too honest to pretend that personal relations had been restored in their prior intimacy. Our sympathies go out, rather, to Coleridge, who after all

the bitterness could still write (1828) with something of his first affection, "So only give my best love to Mr. and Mrs. Wordsworth, and Miss Wordsworth."

NOTES

1. A more meticulous chronology would date this decade 1797–1807, since *Lyrical Ballads* was in process a year before its printing.

2. See in his preface to the second edition of the *Lyrical Ballads* the passage beginning, "What is a poet?"

3. I was once in a dinner group which included John Sargent. After-dinner talk centered about the fact that most of the English poets writing at the beginning of the last century did their best work when they were very young men, and questions followed as to why this was so,—why, apparently, it was inevitable. Sargent said that he entirely understood it; that in his own case his inventive power was at its height when he was still a young man and had begun to decline even in his later twenties. One of the group said, "You don't mean that your best work is that of your early twenties?" "No," said Sargent, "I didn't say that. What I said was, my inventive power was at its height in my first years. As that waned I had to offset the loss of it by an increase of critical judgment in the selection and treatment of my subjects. On the whole I think that by so doing I more than compensated over the passing years for the loss of creative power, and that some of my latest works are also the best. But the process by which they were achieved was not that of sheer invention, for that faculty, with the artist, begins to flag very early."

4. Mrs. Threlkeld and her daughter, Elizabeth, give, in 1805, "a sad account of poor Dorothy, who is grown so thin and old that they should not have known her." She was, then, thirty-four.

5. Miss Edith Batho, in *The Later Wordsworth* (New York: Macmillan Company, 1933), pp. 318 ff., suggests that Wordsworth was from a very early time the victim of trachoma, and that this disease deprived him of sight for writing as well as for reading. This may have been so. But since Wordsworth often dictated his poems the brief is not convincing as an extenuation of his later work. Moreover, what of Milton in his blindness?

6. H. W. Garrod, *op. cit.*, p. 30: "If there was any medicine for the decline of power which stole over Wordsworth's poetry after 1807, it was perhaps to be sought from Coleridge. . . . It is hardly an accident that the period of the decline of power coincided with the period in which Wordsworth's gradual estrangement from Coleridge began."

7. D. W. to Mrs. Clarkson, November 6, 1806.

8. Cf. *The Quarterly Review*, LXV (1840), 234, "It is singular to observe in how many great revolutions, which have altered the course of human opinions and affairs, the impulse and direction has been given, not by one but by two minds, cooperating together, one representing the higher power of the intellect, and the other more feeling. Plato and Aristotle, Luther and Melancthon, Jerome and Augustine, Cranmer and Ridley were yoke fellows of this kind; so Wordsworth, the kind, gentle, affectionate Wordsworth, seems to have been almost paired with the acute, restless, deep-thinking Coleridge."

Robert Langbaum

THE EVOLUTION OF SOUL IN WORDSWORTH'S POETRY*

When Keats in a letter calls this world "The vale of Soul-making," he comes close to Wordsworth's way of thinking. For Keats says that we come into the world as pure potentiality or "Intelligence" and that we acquire a "Soul" or "sense of Identity" through "Circumstances." [1] And it is the main purport of Wordsworth's poetry to show the spiritual significance of this world, to show that we evolve a soul or identity through experience and that the very process of evolution is what we mean by *soul*.

To understand the implications of Wordsworth's view and why it is distinctively modern, we have to go back to the psychological assertions that Wordsworth was both absorbing and answering—we have to go back to Locke and Locke's disciple Hartley. The best analogy to the challenge raised by Locke is the challenge raised in our time by computers. For Lockean man is like a computer in that everything inside him comes from outside, through sensation; so that Lockean man gives back only what has been "programmed" into him. Even his choices are no evidence of free will; for once the idea of choice has entered his head, he must choose and he must choose between predetermined alternatives. "A man that is walking," says Locke, "to whom it is proposed to give off walking, is not at liberty, whether he will determine himself to walk, or give off walking or not: he must necessarily prefer one or the other of them; walking or not walking." [2] One would use the same line of reasoning to show that a computer, for all its ability to make choices, is not free.

Although Locke lays great emphasis on self-consciousness, in that he shows that the greatest part of mental life consists of reflections on our own ideas, his system does not, as Blake pointed out in "There is No Natural Religion," allow for anything new to come into the world, since Locke's "complex ideas" merely complicate a fixed number of sensations. Lockean self-consciousness is the sort we may well predict for the formidable computers of the future.

As computers become increasingly complex, as they become capable of making choices, learning and giving orders, we inevitably wonder at what point of complexity they can be considered human, as having a soul. Now in *The Prelude* Wordsworth was trying to answer some such ques-

° Reprinted by permission of the Modern Language Association of America from an essay reprinted from *PMLA*, 82 (1967), 265–72, and Robert Langbaum's *The Modern Spirit: Essays on the Continuity of Nineteenth and Twentieth Century Literature* (New York: Oxford University Press, 1970).

tion as this regarding Lockean man. If we consider that the human psyche is built up of sensations, then at what point do sensations add up to soul, or how do we jump from sensations to soul? We can understand Wordsworth's answer to Locke if we imagine him answering the question in regard to computers. His answer would be that computers will never be human until they are born and grow up.

If sensations turn into soul—into an ineffable quality that can never be accounted for by the sensations themselves—it is because the sensations reach an ever-changing mind that transforms them as a merely passive receiver, the sort of mind Locke likens to blank paper could not. No two succeeding sensations from the same object can be the same, because the later sensation reaches a mind already modified by the earlier sensation. Locke recognizes all this, but it remains for Wordsworth to draw the necessary conclusions in his poetry and for Coleridge to formulate them in his theory of the imagination. The necessary conclusions are summed up in the idea of interchange between man and nature—the idea that the mind modifies sensation as much as sensation modifies the mind.

It may be argued that computers, too, as they learn, offer a changing receiver to external data. This brings us to the second important point in Wordsworth's answer to Locke. Wordsworth portrays the mind as itself part of the nature it perceives; and it is this connection, sensed through what Wordsworth calls *joy*, that gives us confidence in the reality of ourselves and the external world. Dare one predict that no computer is likely to have this organic connection or to sense it through *joy*?

In *The Prelude*, Wordsworth tells us that his life began to the sound of the Derwent River that "loved / To blend his murmurs with my nurse's song" and "sent a voice / That flowed along my dreams," making

> ceaseless music that composed my thoughts
> To more than infant softness, giving me
> Amid the fretful dwellings of mankind
> A foretaste, a dim earnest, of the calm
> That Nature breathes among the hills and
>   groves.
>
> (1.270–281)[3]

There, in the best Lockean fashion, Wordsworth traces all his mature thoughts back to the sound of the river. But unlike Locke, Wordsworth presents the mind as an active principle. The nurse's song with which the river blends is a sign that the mind is analogous to the river; that is why the river's voice flows along the dreams of the growing Wordsworth. When we read that the river "loved / To blend," we understand that the baby did not merely receive but loved the river's sound, reached out to it as a flower reaches out to the sun and air and rain it has the potentiality to receive. The blending and interchange turn sensation into experience, an experience of joy that will in future years spread around the mature man's thoughts an affective tone—a tone objectified in "the calm / That Nature breathes." This tone, this atmosphere of the mind, sensed as at once inside and outside the mind, is what the mature man will call *soul*.

The river received on its "smooth breast the shadow of those towers" of Cockermouth Castle (1.283). The reflection of the towers was perceived, we gather, at a somewhat later age than the sound of the river. Visual sensations are in Wordsworth more intellectual than sensations of sound. The composite experience of river and towers—which might be understood as an experience of female and male principles—stands behind the experiences of beauty and fear described in the rest of Book 1, which are composite experiences of natural and moral power.

In Book II, the mature man's capacity for love is traced back to the contentment of the infant

>   who sinks to sleep
> Rocked on his Mother's breast; who with his
>   soul
> Drinks in the feelings of his Mother's eye!

Through his connection with his mother, he gains a sense of connection with nature, a connection portrayed through the imagery of flow and blending:

> No outcast he, bewildered and depressed;
> Along his infant veins are interfused
> The gravitation and the filial bond
> Of nature that connect him with the world.

The infant is from the start an active agent of perception who "drinks in" feelings. Because he inhabits the loving universe circumscribed for him by his mother's "Presence," he loves or reaches out to all that he beholds. That sense of "Presence," the baby's first apprehension of Deity, is produced by the sympathetic relation of mind to universe which is, says Wordsworth, the "Poetic spirit of our human life." The mind is portrayed as a relation and a process—a process *growing* from feeling through power, sense, thought, into the one great Mind and between subject and object, in such a way that the parts flow one into the other and can hardly be discriminated.

> For, feeling has to him imparted power
> That through the growing faculties of sense
> Doth like an agent of the one great Mind
> Create, creator and receiver both,
> Working but in alliance with the works
> Which it beholds.

This poetic spirit, says Wordsworth, is in most people "abated or suppressed" in later years. But in some few it remains "Pre-eminent till death," and those few are, we gather, poets (II. 235–265).

We have here an accounting for affect, for the value or "glory" we find in the world, which seems to contradict the accounting in the "Immortality Ode." The accounting in *The Prelude* is the authentically Wordsworthian one, because it is naturalistic, psychological, and sensationalist. The Platonic idea of preexistence is advanced in the "Ode" —Wordsworth tells us in the Fenwick note to that poem—as a figure of speech, as a fanciful and traditional way of generalizing the psychological phenomenon revealed to him by his own life— that "the Child is Father of the Man," that spirit is to be found in the primitive. "I took hold of the notion of pre-existence," says Wordsworth, "as having sufficient foundation in humanity for authorizing me to make for my purpose the best use of it I could as a Poet." The Platonic idea is used with fine artistry in the "Ode" as a counterpoint to the primitivist idea. It is the primitivist idea that takes over when in stanza ix Wordsworth gets down to the serious business of answering the question of the poem, the question posed by the adult's sense of loss. His answer is that nothing is lost. Even if we no longer experience the "glory" we experienced in childhood, "nature yet remembers." Our souls, he concludes in a strikingly primitivist image, can in a moment travel backward

> And see the Children sport upon the shore,
> And hear the mighty waters rolling evermore.

Yet the Platonic idea is not lost sight of even here. It is so blended with the primitivist idea that we can see that its function all along has been to ennoble and spiritualize the primitivist idea. Thus the sea is the physical sea where all life began; but the sea is also immortal, through its very age ageless and transcendent:

> Hence in a season of calm weather
> Though inland far we be,
> Our Souls have sight of that immortal sea
> Which brought us hither.

Growing-up has been mainly compared to a journey of the sun across the sky; now it is compared to a journey inland from the sea. Wordsworth explains the adult's sense of loss by telling us that we come down from the sky and up from the sea, and by blending the two directions to evoke an original spiritual source that is unlocatable.

The blending goes even farther in the imagery through which Wordsworth tells us that the adult responds to the objects before him because he sees them through the lens of his memory of childhood experiences. Those "first affections" and "shadowy recollections," he says,

> Are yet the fountain light of all our day,
> Are yet a master light of all our seeing.

There is an inextricable blending here of light and water, the ideal and the primitive, Platonic metaphysics and Lockean psychology.

We find the same blending in two adjacent passages of *The Prelude*, Book I. In the first, Wordsworth speaks of experiences that cannot be accounted for by the Lockean theory of memory and association he has been developing—experiences which would seem to require, to account for them, some Platonic theory of "first-born affinities" (I.555), of archetypes, of innate ideas. He had such an experience when gazing over an expanse of sea,

> Of shining water, gathering as it seem'd,
> Through every hair-breadth of that field of light,
> New pleasure—
>
> (I.578–580)

new, because not deriving from association with earlier pleasures. Wordsworth evokes the transcendent quality of the experience by turning shining *water* into a *field* of light, by dissolving both water and land into light. But in the next passage, he says that he loves to travel backward down through the corridors of memory, from forms down through sensations, to recover at the point where conscious memory fades out just such a vision of light:

Those recollected hours that have the charm
Of visionary things, those lovely forms
And sweet sensations that throw back our life,
And almost make remotest infancy
A visible scene, on which the sun is shining.
(1.631–635)

We have only to recall Locke's description of the mind as a dark closet penetrated by certain rays of light from the outside world,[4] we have only to recall this comparison, which is even more revealing of Locke's outlook than his better known comparison of the mind to white or blank paper, to understand the sense in which Wordsworth answers Locke. Yet it is Locke who supplies the concepts of memory and association through which Wordsworth can give psychological substantiation to his experience of his own mind as light or music. And it is important to note that the mind recognizes itself in an external sensation, that Wordsworth arrives at his concept of mind by tracing his life back to an original sensation—to "A visible scene, on which the sun is shining" or to the sound of the Derwent River.

Much ink has been spilled over the question whether Wordsworth believed that his apprehension of spirit came from outside or inside, whether he was a Lockean empiricist or a Platonic believer in innate ideas. The answer is that Wordsworth, when he is writing his best poetry, uses both doctrines as possibilities, blending them in such a way as to evoke the mystery he is talking about—the mystery of life, vitality, organic connection. The case should teach us something about the proper relation of ideas to poetry. And, indeed, Wordsworth himself pronounces on the subject in his first essay "Upon Epitaphs," where he speaks of the antithetical ideas of two Greek philosophers about the value of body in relation to soul. In spite of their opposite ideas, says Wordsworth, modulating from talk of thought to talk of feelings, "Each of these Sages was in sympathy with the best feelings of our Nature; feelings which, though they seem opposite to each other, have another and a finer connexion than that of contrast.—It is a connexion formed through the subtle progress by which, both in the natural and the moral world, qualities pass

insensibly into their contraries, and things revolve upon each other."[5]

The case also suggests why The Prelude, which Wordsworth wrote with his left hand or deepest artistic instinct while trying with his right hand or conscious will to write the long philosophical poem Coleridge had put him up to, why The Prelude is so much more successful than what we have of that long philosophical poem, The Recluse, of which The Excursion is Part Two. The Prelude is successful, and successful as an appropriately modern poem of ideas, just because Wordsworth did not consider that he was at that point writing a philosophical poem. In the passage I have quoted above, he is apologizing to Coleridge for not getting on with the philosophical poem but dwelling instead, out of "an infirmity of love" for them, on "days / Disowned by memory" (1.614–615)—by conscious memory, that is.

To understand what Wordsworth has achieved in The Prelude, we have only to read Coleridge's description, in his Table Talk for 21 July 1832, long after he himself had turned against Locke and Hartley, of the original plan of The Recluse.

The plan laid out, and, I believe, partly suggested by me, was, that Wordsworth should assume the station of a man in mental repose, one whose principles were made up, and so prepared to deliver upon authority a system of philosophy. He was to treat man as man,— a subject of eye, ear, touch, and taste, in contact with external nature, and informing the senses from the mind, and not compounding a mind out of the senses.

Aside from the fact that The Prelude portrays a mind in evolution not in repose, we precisely do not find there the doctrinaire anti-Lockean stand described by Coleridge.[6]

Wordsworth no sooner tells us in The Prelude, Book 1, how nature through "extrinsic passion" or association first peopled his "mind with forms sublime or fair," than he speaks of other pleasures

Which, if I err not, surely must belong
To those first-born affinities that fit
Our new existence to existing things,
And, in our dawn of being, constitute
The bond of union between life and joy.
(554–558)

Note the tentativeness of "if I err not," and how even innate affinities are traced back to a primitive origin which one may still understand to be natural. Such blending evokes "the bond of union between life and joy" that is Wordsworth's answer to the question at the heart of *The Prelude*, the question that no simply rational account of life can answer. I mean the question, why live at all, why bother to get up in the morning? As so often in Wordsworth's best lines, the answer is couched in words that are general, even vague. Yet the "Presence" evoked, to use that other vague but potent Wordsworthian word, is definite enough and the only answer to the question, "Why live?" We can infer that "the bond of union between life and joy" is the thing that will always distinguish human beings from computers. We can also infer that the philosopher's question, "Why live?" can only be answered by the poet. For the answer is that we take pleasure in the world we behold because we are one with it. And it is only the poet who can make pleasure and oneness real for us by just such blending as Wordsworth employs.

F. R. Leavis and Donald Davie have shown, through an analysis of Wordsworth's syntax, how he gives us poetry by blurring the thought.[7] One can say even more specifically that Wordsworth gives us poetry by being both Lockean and anti-Lockean at the same time. For Wordsworth answers Locke by using the Lockean concepts of memory and association. It is only through memory, says Locke, that the mind has any effectiveness, and he equates the self with the sum of conscious memory ("whatever has the consciousness of present and past actions, is the same person to whom they both belong"). But Locke does not speak of memory as modifying the actions remembered; these actions remain fixed, like the data "remembered" by a computer. It is in speaking of the accidental association of ideas that Locke recognizes a modifying and transforming process. Locke accounts for our irrational behavior and for affect—for what he calls our "sympathies and antipathies" —by the connection through "*chance* or *custom*" of ideas that have no correspondence in nature or logic. Through association, in other words, sensations and ideas are transformed into something other than they would be in themselves, with a value they would not have in themselves.

The difference between Locke and the romanticists is that Locke deplores the process of association as unamenable to reason;[8] whereas the roman-ticists glory in it because it shows the mind as creative and carries them over from sensation to value. It is significant that Wordsworth and Coleridge took their Locke by way of the eighteenth-century medical doctor, David Hartley, who builds his whole system on the theory of association that is in Locke only one proposition. From association, Hartley derives the affective responses of pleasure and pain which lead to Christian values and faith. Hartley must have seemed to Wordsworth and Coleridge to have transcendentalized Locke. In "Religious Musings," Coleridge hails Hartley as "of mortal kind / Wisest," because he is the first to establish value on a materialistic and therefore scientific basis—the "first who marked the ideal tribes / Up the fine fibres through the sentient brain" (368–370). Hartley comes close to calling this world a vale of soul-making when he says: "Some degree of spirituality is the necessary consequence of passing through life. The sensible pleasures and pains must be transferred by association more and more every day, upon things that afford neither sensible pleasure nor sensible pain in themselves, and so beget the intellectual pleasures and pains."[9] In other words, we grow spiritually by conferring spirituality upon the world. The issue between the Locke-Hartley doctrine and the Platonic doctrine of pre-existence is whether we gain or lose spirituality by living.

Nevertheless, Hartley's system remains mechanical because he does not recognize that the crucial element in Locke's theory of association is this— that only in speaking of association does Locke allow for any unconscious mental process. Wordsworth and Coleridge modify Hartley by dwelling on the unconscious aspects of the associative process. Thus Coleridge, in beginning to object to Hartley, says that "Association depends in a much greater degree on the recurrence of resembling states of feeling than on trains of ideas," and that "Ideas no more recall one another than the leaves in a tree, fluttering in the breeze, propagate their motion one to another."[10] Wordsworth says much the same thing when, in *The Prelude*, Book II, he describes the delayed effect of epiphanies:

> the soul,
> Remembering how she felt, but what she felt
> Remembering not, retains an obscure sense
> Of possible sublimity, whereto
> With growing faculties she doth aspire

With faculties still growing, feeling still
That whatsoever point they gain, they yet
Have something to pursue.

(315-322)

Association takes place not through the ideas or manifest content of an experience but through the affective tone, which can then be communicated to experiences with quite different manifest contents. Wordsworth makes clear what is implied in Coleridge's second statement—that this affective tone is a feeling of infinity which connects the individual mind with the Great Mind and cannot be entirely accounted for by the present, or even recollected, experience.

For Locke, we apprehend infinity as an idea of quantity—the result of our understanding that we can count indefinitely and can indefinitely add line segments to a given line segment. The idea is inapplicable, in the same way, to quality: "nobody ever thinks of infinite sweetness, or infinite whiteness." For Wordsworth, instead, we apprehend infinity as a feeling having to do with quality and organic wholeness—we cannot add to an organism as to a line segment. For Locke, the idea of infinity follows from our experience. For Wordsworth, we not only bring the feeling of infinity to later experiences through associated memory of earlier experiences, but the feeling somehow both rises out of and is anterior to even our primal experiences. The ambiguity is projected through the use of both memory and the fading-out of memory. Because the soul remembers not what but how she felt, we carry with us a feeling larger than anything we can remember of our primal experiences; and the soul grows, in this vale of soul making, toward a feeling of wholeness that seems recollected though we cannot say from where. Locke refutes the theory of pre-existence by saying that if a man has no memory at all of his previous existence, if he has "a consciousness that *cannot* reach beyond this new state," then he is not the same person who led the previous existence since "personal identity [reaches] no further than consciousness reaches." [11] Wordsworth's answer is to blur the line between remembering and forgetting, to introduce a notion of unconscious memory. By combining memory and association, Wordsworth sets the Lockean system in motion, infusing it with vitality, surrounding it with mystery, and carrying the mind back beyond conscious memory to the "dawn of

being" where it is undistinguishable from its first sensation.

Memory becomes in Wordsworth the instrument of the associative or transforming power. It is because we see with stereoscopic vision—as Roger Shattuck puts it in speaking, in *Proust's Binoculars*, of Proust's use of memory—it is because partly we see the tree before us and partly we see all the trees we have ever seen that we see from outside and inside and have not sensations but experiences.[12] That is the meaning of the crucial line in "Tintern Abbey": "The picture of the mind revives again." Wordsworth sees the present landscape through his mental picture of the landscape five years earlier. Because he discovers continuity in the disparate pictures through a principle of growth, he becomes aware of the pattern of his life—he binds his apparently disparate days together. He may be said to evolve his soul in becoming aware that his soul evolves. Included in the present experience is Wordsworth's sense that he will in future feed upon it, just as in the intervening five years he has fed on his last visit to this place. The experience includes, in other words, the consciousness of laying up treasure—not in heaven but in the memory. It is the point of "Tintern Abbey," "Immortality Ode," and *The Prelude* that this spiritual storehouse of memory *is* our soul.

In one of the earliest written passages of *The Prelude*, one of those passages that must have helped Wordsworth find his theme, the poet thanks nature, in a tone of religious solemnity, for having from his "first dawn / Of childhood" intertwined for him "The passions that build up our human soul" (1.405-407).[13] The whole poem traces this building-up process, but the words *soul* and *imagination* are used interchangeably and Wordsworth speaks more often of the building-up of imagination. That is because the poet or man of imagination is being used to epitomize a psychological process.

The poet, we are being told, is more spiritual than the rest of us because he *remembers* more than we do—though his remembering is often spoken of as a kind of forgetting: "By such forgetfulness the soul becomes, / Words cannot say how beautiful" (*Recluse* 1.297-298). The poet filters a present experience back through memory and the unconscious river in his veins—Wordsworth habitually speaks of thought as flowing in and out of the veins—to the external river that was his first sensation. That is why the poet can respond to the world and see it symbolically. That is why seeing is better than faith —it is revelation. "Nor did he believe,—he *saw*," says Wordsworth of the poetical Pedlar in *The Excursion* (1.232).

Wordsworth achieves his symbolic effects through a regression in the mind of the observer and in the object observed. He makes the human figure seem to evolve out of and pass back into the landscape —as in "The Thorn" and the Lucy poems, including "Lucy Gray." And he makes the landscape itself, in his most striking effects, seem to evolve out of water. In "Resolution and Independence," the old leech gatherer is seen by a pool. He is so old that he seems to hang on to life by a thread; and the observer understands this by carrying the old man's existence back to the line between the inanimate and the animate. The observer sees the old man as like a huge stone that seems almost alive because you cannot imagine how it got where it is, or as like a sea beast that at first seems part of the rock on which it lies. He is—if you assimilate this poem, as Geoffrey Hartman has so beautifully done, to the recurrent imagery of *The Prelude*—like something left behind by the inland sea that once covered the landscape.[14] Because the old man is seen through the eye of unconscious racial memory, he is transformed into an archetype of human endurance capable of alleviating the observer's distress.

In one of the epiphanies or "spots of time" of *The Prelude*, Book XII, Wordsworth recalls how as a boy he fled in terror from a low place, where a murderer had been hanged, to a hill where he saw a pool and a girl approaching it, bearing a pitcher on her head, her garments blowing in the wind. Through the conjunction with water and wind, the girl turns for the boy into an archetypal figure who transforms the unpleasant experience into a pleasant one; so that in later years, when Wordsworth was courting Mary Hutchinson, he often returned with her to this place, finding in "the naked pool and dreary crags" a "spirit of pleasure and youth's golden gleam" (264, 266). Here and elsewhere in Wordsworth—the same female figure with a basket on her head is remembered through water imagery in "The Two April Mornings"—water and memory, water as perhaps the counterpart of memory, turn

the individual event into an archetype; and it is through archetypalization that turbulence and pain are turned into spiritual treasure, into the recognition of that surrounding aura of pleasurable tranquillity which is soul. "How strange," says Wordsworth in speaking of soul-making,

> that all
> The terrors, pains, and early miseries,
> Regrets, vexations, lassitudes interfused
> Within my mind, should e'er have borne a part,
> And that a needful part in making up
> The calm existence that is mine when I
> Am worthy of myself!   (1.344–350)

The transformation of pain into pleasure is achieved through archetypalization and objectification. The terrifying boyhood experience of Book XII passes into the landscape, making it a pleasant and spiritually rewarding place to return to. Wordsworth says that "The sands of Westmoreland, the creeks and bays / Of Cumbria's rocky limits" can tell of his boyhood epiphanies; and that, conversely,

> The scenes which were a witness of that joy
> Remained in their substantial lineaments
> Depicted on the brain,   (1.567–568, 599–601)

that he remembered those early experiences as places.

The pleasurable tranquillity that is soul exists outside us as well as inside; it exists in those places hallowed by significant experiences. Place, in Wordsworth, is the spatial projection of psyche, because it is the repository of memory.[15] We can understand the relation in Wordsworth between mind and nature, once we understand that Wordsworth evolves his soul or sense of identity as he identifies more and more such hallowed places. We can understand the relation in Wordsworth between the themes of memory and growing up, once we understand that for Wordsworth you advance in life, by travelling back again to the beginning, by reassessing your life, by binding your days together anew.

In Coleridge's periodical *The Friend*, Wordsworth answers a conservative attack on the belief in progress, by saying that in the progress of the species and the individual mind we must often move backward in order to move forward. Progress

> neither is nor can be like that of a Roman road
> in a right line. It may be more justly compared
> to that of a river, which, both in its smaller

reaches and larger turnings, is frequently forced back towards its fountains by objects which can not otherwise be eluded or overcome; yet with an accompanying impulse that will insure its advancement hereafter, it is either gaining strength every hour, or conquering in secret some difficulty, by a labor that contributes as effectually to further it in its course, as when it moves forward uninterrupted in a line.

And Coleridge in *The Friend* uses "My Heart Leaps Up," the poem in which Wordsworth speaks of binding his days together, to support his idea that we must in growing up be able to correct the delusions of our childhood without repudiating the child who held them.

> If men laugh at the falsehoods that were imposed on themselves during their childhood, it is because they are not good and wise enough to contemplate the past in the present, and so to produce by a virtuous and thoughtful sensibility that continuity in their self-consciousness, which nature has made the law of their animal life. Ingratitude, sensuality, and hardness of heart, all flow from this source. Men are ungrateful to others only when they have ceased to look back on their former selves with joy and tenderness. They exist in fragments. Annihilated as to the past, they are dead to the future, or seek for the proofs of it everywhere, only not (where alone they can be found) in themselves.[16]

The old Pedlar of *The Excursion* shows that he has bound his days together; for age has

> not tamed his eye; that, under brows
> Shaggy and grey, had meanings which it
>   brought
> From years of youth; which, like a Being made
> Of many Beings, he had wondrous skill
> To blend with knowledge of the years to come,
> Human, or such as lie beyond the grave.
>   (1.428–433)

Because "like a Being made / Of many Beings," he possesses his past, he possesses the future too and seems to transcend time. The same is true of old Matthew in "The Two April Mornings," who, in the moment when he was able to immerse himself completely in the stream of time by remembering and reconciling himself to his daughter's death, became for the young narrator immortal:

> Matthew is in his grave, yet now,
> Methinks, I see him stand,

> As at that moment, with a bough
> Of wilding in his hand.

In *The Prelude*'s climactic "spot of time," the opiphany on Mt. Snowdon in Book XIV, the whole world seems under moonlight to be returned to water. The mist below is a silent sea, the hills around static billows; and this illusory sea stretches out into the real Atlantic. The optical illusion is substantiated when, through a rift in the mist, Wordsworth hears the roar of inland waters. The movement from sight to sound is always in Wordsworth a movement backward to the beginning of things, to sensation and the sentiment of Being; later, in Book XIV, Wordsworth says that he has in *The Prelude* traced the stream of imagination back from "light / And open day" to "the blind cavern whence is faintly heard / Its natal murmur" (195–197). Wordsworth understands, therefore, that he has had on Mt. Snowdon an epiphany of pure imagination or pure potentiality. He has beheld, in the moon over the waters, "the emblem of a mind" brooding over the abyss—waiting, like God in the opening passage of *Paradise Lost*, to bring forth the world. Wordsworth transcends even the beginning of things by moving back from sight to sound and then to an inextricable blending of sight and sound:

> the emblem of a mind
> That feeds upon infinity, that broods
> Over the dark abyss, intent to hear
> Its voices issuing forth to silent light
> In one continuous stream.   (70–74)

"This," says Wordsworth, "is the very spirit" with which "higher" or imaginative "minds" deal "With the whole compass of the universe" (90–93). Confronted with sensory experience, the poetical man travels back *that far* in order to perceive it imaginatively. He recreates the world in his imagination;[17] so that he can return to the scene before him, imposing upon it the picture in his mind and thus finding there the surrounding aura of calm that is his soul. Only by travelling back to the beginning can we achieve the "repose / In moral judgments," which is a sign that we have bound our ideas up with our primitive sensations. In borrowing, to describe the repose or calm, words of Holy Scripture, in describing it as "that peace Which passeth understanding" (126–128), Wordsworth shows that he considers his naturalistic revelation to be not only the equivalent of the Platonic idea, but this time the equivalent of Christian revelation itself.

UNIVERSITY OF VIRGINIA
Charlottesville

NOTES

1. To George and Georgiana Keats, 14 February–3 May 1819, *The Letters of John Keats*, ed. Hyder E. Rollins, 2 vols. (Cambridge, Mass., 1958), I, 102–104. Rollins thinks this passage may have been written when Keats was reading John Locke's *Essay Concerning Human Understanding*, especially Book II, Ch. xxvii, "Of Identity and Diversity."

2. *Essay*, collated and annotated by A. C. Fraser, 2 vols. (Oxford, 1894), Book II, Ch. xxi, Par. 24.

3. Ed. E. de Selincourt, 2nd ed. revised by H. Darbishire (Oxford, 1959). Other poems from *The Poetical Works of William Wordsworth*, ed. E. de Selincourt and H. Darbishire, 2nd ed., 5 vols. (Oxford, 1952–59).

4. Book II, Ch. xi, Par. 17.

5. *Wordsworth's Literary Criticism*, ed. Nowell C. Smith (London, 1905), p. 84.

6. Coleridge, too, shows an artistic instinct in advance of his theory. For though he asserts the superiority over *The Excursion* of Wordsworth's "thirteen books on the growth of an individual mind" (*The Prelude*), he concludes that Wordsworth possessed "the genius of a great philosophic poet" and "ought never to have abandoned the contemplative position . . . His proper title is *Spectator ab extra*." The virtue of *The Prelude*, however, is that its view is from *inside* life; it is concerned with the psychological process of evolving the principles on which an external stance might be taken.

7. *Revaluation* (London, 1936), Ch. v; *Articulate Energy: An Inquiry into the Syntax of English Poetry* (London, 1955), pp. 106–116. Colin Clarke, instead, finds the blurring precisely philosophical (*Romantic Paradox*, London, 1962). Leavis and Davie cite *Prelude* II. 233–254, about the infant at

his mother's breast—Leavis preferring the 1850, Davie the 1805, version. Leavis is right. The 1805 version is more abstract and lucid, but the 1850 is more poetical because more blended. After all, the "doctrinal passages of *The Excursion* . . . are," as Leavis observes, "plain enough."

8. Book II, Ch. xxvii, Par. 16; Ch. xxxiii.

9. *Observations on Man*, in Two Parts, 6th ed. corrected and revised (London, 1834), Prop. xiv, Cor. viii.

10. Quoted in N. P. Stalknecht, *Strange Seas of Thought*, 2nd ed. (Bloomington, 1962), p. 39.

11. Book II, Ch. xvii, Par. 6; Ch. xxvii, Par. 14.

12. New York, 1963, pp. 42–43. With the "impressions" before him, says Wordsworth in *The Excursion*,

would he still compare
All his remembrances, thoughts, shapes and
      forms;
And, being still unsatisfied with aught
Of dimmer character, he thence attained
An active power to fasten images
Upon his brain; and on their pictured lines
Intensely brooded, even till they acquired
The liveliness of dreams.   (1.141–148)

13. See *Excursion* IV.1264–66, written at about the same time:

—So build we up the Being that we are;
Thus deeply drinking-in the soul of things
We shall be wise perforce.

14. *The Unmediated Vision* (New Haven, 1954), pp. 33–34.

15. See Geoffrey Hartman's subtle analysis of Wordsworth's sense of place throughout *Wordsworth's Poetry 1787–1814* (New Haven and London, 1964).

16. S. T. Coleridge, *The Complete Works*, ed. W. G. T. Shedd, 7 vols. (New York, 1884), II. Wordsworth's "Reply to Mathetes" in Introduction, Second Section, p. 362 (see also p. 373): General Introduction, Essay v, p. 46.

17. "The primary IMAGINATION," says Coleridge, is "a repetition in the finite mind of the eternal act of creation" (*Biographia Literaria*, ed. J. Shawcross, Oxford, 1965, Ch. xiii, p. 202).

W. J. Bate

COLERIDGE: TRANSCENDENTALISM,
AND THE ORGANIC VIEW OF NATURE*

The character and value of Coleridge's writings are among the baffling problems in the history of literature. It is generally felt that he never fulfilled his promise, and there remains the debatable question of how much capacity he actually possessed. His own contemporaries felt the same admiration and misgivings that readers have since expressed. Men of talent spoke of Coleridge's genius and of the wonder with which people heard him. But his discourse became vaguer as the years passed; relatively little of what reached print was very coherent, and his admirers began to regard him with the same nostalgia with which his old school friend, Charles Lamb, viewed Coleridge's boyhood:

> Come back into memory, like as thou wert in the day-spring of thy fancies, with hope like a fiery column before thee—the dark pillar not yet turned—Samuel Taylor Coleridge—Logician, Metaphysician, Bard!—How have I seen the casual passer through the Cloisters, stand still, intranced with admiration (while he weighed the disproportion between the *speech* and the *garb* of the young Mirandula), to hear thee unfold . . . the mysteries of Jamblichus, or Plotinus (for even in those years thou waxedest not pale at such philosophic draughts), or reciting Homer in his Greek, or Pindar—while the walls of the old Grey Friars re-echoed to the accents of the *inspired charity-boy!*

Coleridge inspired the feeling, at first, that he was always on the point of doing something transcendent in metaphysics and esthetics; later, the feeling that he could have done so at one time. As the Victorian age got under way, he then passed into

the realm of legend. However, during the last half century the publication of long-forgotten works has at least tended to substantiate the range of his mind and the scattered brilliance of his insights. Closely as some of his works have been examined, his prose writings as a whole still constitute one of the most challenging unexplored territories in the history of critical thinking.

Yet to interpret Coleridge's criticism has been a scholarly pastime for over a century, and particularly within the last forty years or so. Certainly one of the reasons for his attractiveness is his attempt to combine so many different attitudes and to pursue so many problems. It is always possible, therefore, for one to find statements by Coleridge that are congenial with one's own personal beliefs. Because of the fragmentary and elusive quality of much of his writing, there is the constant temptation to abstract his statements from their context and develop them in whatever way one wishes, rather than to reconcile them with other attitudes of Coleridge and then try to discern a common basis and a common aim underlying all his critical attitudes. Another temptation—at least for scholars —has been to concentrate too exclusively on source-hunting. Certainly Coleridge's criticism provides a happy hunting ground for this purpose. In his early years he fell under the influence of David Hartley and the doctrine of the association of ideas, and later under the influence of Berkeley, Spinoza, the Neoplatonism of Plotinus and Jakob Boehme, and the German philosophy of his own day, especially that of Kant and Schelling. From these philosophers and from others Coleridge borrowed terms, phrases, and ideas with embarrassing freedom. But it would be a mistake to assume that if Coleridge took over a particular term or idea from Kant, for example, we have then only to turn to Kant for the explanation of what Coleridge was try-

*From *Criticism: The Major Texts* edited by Walter Jackson Bate, copyright 1952 by Harcourt Brace & Company and renewed 1980 by Walter Jackson Bate. Reprinted by permission of the publisher.

ing to say on this subject. Actually, he tended to take over terms or concepts from others because they seemed, for the time being, to help fill out or to fit in with more general ideas of his own—ideas that were quite different, in some cases, from those of the original writer. To take his borrowings as a starting point is not only futile but misleading. The student should refuse to be intimidated by the accretion of source studies that have barnacled over Coleridge's criticism, and should try to approach him as directly as possible.

II

Art, for Coleridge, is the "imitator" of nature; it tries to offer an "abridgement" of reality. In speaking of an imitation one cannot get very far without first understanding what it imitates. The interpretation of Coleridge's critical writing suggested here is that it comprises an attempt—a challenging but incomplete and uneven attempt—to combine the concreteness and the organic vitalism that the romantic movement prized, with the traditional values of classical rationalism and idealism; to support this union with a metaphysical basis; to outline a psychology appropriate to it; and then to apply it to the understanding and evaluating of art.

On the one hand, therefore, we have Coleridge emphasizing the natural, concrete world, not as a shadow of the ideal, still less as a subjective creation of one's own mind, but as an actual, vital, and organic unfolding of process. Accordingly, art—as the "mediator" between nature and man, as the explainer and transmitter of reality into terms of human feelings and reactions—must not lose its grasp of the concretely organic and become merely abstract. Much of Coleridge's preference for Shakespeare over the classical dramatists rests on this point. On the other hand, concrete life cannot exist apart from universal form. What makes a plant a plant, for example,—what distinguishes the plant from the soil, water, and sunlight of which it is composed—is the controlling *form* that funnels, unifies, and spins out these materials, so to speak, into a different thing, guiding and shaping them into a new individuality. And the finished, particular plant, therefore, is nothing except as it draws its character and existence from the form; it has no function apart from the form, the universal, any

more than the lungs can have a function or significance apart from the atmosphere they breathe.

The reality that we call "nature," in short, is neither to be found in the particular, the concrete, by itself, apart from the form, nor in the universal by itself. Instead, the reality of nature is to be found in a *process*, or *activity*, in which the universal and the particular fulfill each other. The universal gives to the particular its form, thus permitting it to flower into existence and become what it is. In a similar way, the universal must have the particular in order to fulfill *itself*. It cannot perform its function as a controlling form unless there is something being acted upon, something to *be* controlled and formed. In a sense, Coleridge's standpoint is very much like Aristotle's principle that form and matter exist only through each other. Yet Coleridge is always maintaining that he is a Platonist, not an Aristotelian. In fact, his basic aim seems to have been to try to reconcile the concrete, organic naturalism in which he believed with the Platonic doctrine that universal forms or "ideas" have an absolute existence of their own and can be known by man through reason. That is partly why he toyed with as many different philosophers as he did, hoping that each, in turn, might suggest how to reconcile these two convictions. The whole problem of Coleridge's Platonism leads to many complications. But we might loosely summarize his position as follows: universal forms or "ideas" do exist by themselves, as Plato said, and can be known by reason; but they become "real," they fulfill their potentiality and become truly themselves, only as they have something with and through which to work—only as they are functioning as creative and guiding principles. Unity, for example, exists as a universal form; but it cannot realize itself completely unless it is in the process of unifying opposition—of unifying what is diverse. Here Coleridge was much influenced by the Neoplatonism of Plotinus and Jakob Boehme.

III

Nature, then, should be regarded as concrete activity, organically evolving in accordance with universal forms. Hence Coleridge's emphasis on thinking in terms of "an *act*, instead of a *thing* or a *substance*." Art, therefore, as the "imitator" of nature, takes neither the form alone nor the concrete, individual thing alone as its model. It is directed to the focal point in which each substantiates and permits the other to realize itself. Art imitates a *process;* it tries to reveal the universal at work "within the thing, that which is active through form and figure"—to "interpret and understand the symbol, that the wings of the air-sylph are forming within the skin of the caterpillar." This is the central theme in Coleridge's Shakespearean criticism —that Shakespeare had "the *universal* which is potentially in each *particular,* opened out to him . . . not as an abstraction of observation of a variety of men, but as the substance capable of endless modifications." Shakespeare thus contrasts with Beaumont and Fletcher, whose dramatic characters are types pieced together from observing different men. It is as though one might "fit together a quarter of an orange, a quarter of an apple, and the like of a lemon and a pomegranate, and make it look like one round diverse colored fruit. But nature, who works *from within by evolution and assimilation* according to a law, cannot do it. Nor could Shakespeare, for he too worked in the spirit of nature, by *evolving the germ within* . . ."

Art, then, imitates the essential process of nature, the reconciliation of universal and particular. But it does not do so by directly "copying" its model, which would be an "idle rivalry" with nature. It does so by *translating* its insight into a given medium: into two-dimensional line and color in a painting, for example; into the unifying of sounds by rhythm and harmony in music; or, in a drama, into words, metaphors, verse-rhythms, and the interplay of characters and incidents, rounded and harmonized to an ordered end. In all such instances, art is characterized by a process of unified order emerging through what Coleridge calls "multëity" —a "fusion to force many into one." Therefore, in portraying its object, art does not offer a dead "copy"; but it duplicates the active principle of nature by presenting, within its *own* given medium, the same process of form organically controlling the diverse, concrete details. It is in this sense that Coleridge states that the symbols in art should be "living," that they should actively contain within themselves "the germinal causes in Nature," and that a true symbol "always partakes of the reality that it renders intelligible."

By thus translating and "abridging" reality into symbols that strike home to the human mind and heart, art serves as the "mediator" between nature and man. It achieves the "beautiful." Now beauty is not a mere subjective state of mind; this is the central point of the three essays, *On the Principles of Genial Criticism.* Rather, beauty arises only when what is being conceived is a universal form emerging through concrete diversity or "multëity." On the other hand, beauty is not truth, as it was for Keats. Beauty is a *way of approaching* the true and the good: it is a way of rendering truth *realizable* to the total mind, through the medium of humanly persuasive symbols. "Beauty is the shorthand hieroglyphic of Truth—the mediator between Truth and Feeling, the Head and the Heart." It is a means, in other words, rather than an ultimate end: "As light to the eye, even such is beauty to the mind . . . [a] *calling on* the soul."

IV

No aspect of Coleridge's criticism has so intrigued modern readers as his theory of the imagination. Discussion of it, however, has too often been confined merely to stating that the imagination, for Coleridge, "fuses" things together, and is "creative." The same remark could be made of any number of other critics. The important point is what it "fuses," and what—and how far—it "creates." Coleridge's actual remarks on the imagination, however, are surprisingly few, brief, and scattered. Perhaps the least satisfactory discussion is the one most frequently quoted: a page that concludes Chapter 13 of the *Biographia Litearia,* with its unclear distinction between "primary" and "secondary" imagination. He had considered publishing here, Coleridge tells us, a hundred-page discussion of the imagination, and it is led up to with much fanfare. But he decided to omit it because it would be "unintelligible" and printed only the conclusion. The reader may pardonably feel that this famous concluding passage is hardly more than an empty April-fool purse in his path. For it says very little indeed.

Coleridge's general theory of mind, in fact, should be approached, not as an independent subject by itself, but as a corollary to the more basic conceptions summarized in the last section above. In his psychology, the cornerstone—at least the premise that he continued to stress most strongly —is his distinction between "reason" and "understanding." The understanding is directed toward the concrete world—to the world we know through our senses. It classifies our sense impressions, and our associations and feeling drawn from these impressions; it abstracts and generalizes on the basis of them. Reason, on the other hand, is the direct insight into the universal. The distinction, as Coleridge says, is similar in a general way to that of the Platonic tradition, particularly common in the Renaissance, between "discursive" reason, which generalizes from sense-impressions, and "intuitive reason." [1]

Thus, in order to explain the means by which the mind conceives both the ultimate universal forms and at the same time the concrete, particular world, Coleridge postulated two different aspects of mind directed to each: reason, on the one hand, and the senses and understanding on the other. But thus to divide the mind into two separate capacities violated his own organic conception of nature. For nature is neither the universal nor the particular, but a process in which each declares and sustains the other. If the human mind were to realize this process, therefore, it could do so only through a "completing power," as he called it, which would join together what is grasped by the different aspects of the mind. This "completing power" of the mind he called the "imagination." In short, the material world has, in the human mind, a corresponding capacity in the senses and understanding. The universal has its counterpart in reason. And the creative activity of nature, which unites universal and particular, has *its* counterpart in the imagination, which "fuses" together the insights of reason with the impressions of the senses and the conceptions of the understanding. In order to stress this unique function of the imagination, Coleridge developed a distinction between "fancy" and "imagination," which was at one time mistakenly thought to have had a "German" source. But the distinction is of English origin, and had already become familiar in English critical terminology during the later eighteenth century. Its importance has probably been overrated; as Coleridge himself said, his "grievous fault" was that he was too much inclined to make and labor distinctions. What he was trying to do was to cut off the term "imagination" from its older meaning of an "image-making" faculty that simply reproduces and combines images derived from sense impressions.

In anchoring and "incorporating the reason in images of sense," and at the same time elevating and "organizing . . . the flux of the senses by the permanent and self-circling energies of the reason," the imagination creates a dynamic and emerging balance of "the general, with the concrete; the idea, with the image; the individual with the representative," and thus achieves a true insight that duplicates the reality to which it is turned. To this extent, the imagination is like the creative impulse of nature itself. Hence Coleridge's remark that the imagination is "a repetition in the finite mind of the eternal act of creation" (he does not mean that it spins something out of nothing); and to this extent the imagination serves as "the living Power and prime agent of all human Perception." But the imagination has another basic function. For this creative activity interpenetrates all forms of human response. It not only joins reason with the senses and understanding, but, in permeating the "whole man," it can transmute the realization it has attained into emotional persuasion and mold and develop human feeling accordingly. The imagination converts its awareness, in other words, into "beauty"—"the mediator between Truth and Feeling, the Head and the Heart," into a *calling on the soul*." This, in effect, is the ideal aim of art, as it draws upon the total function of the imagination: by employing "symbols" that convey truth to feeling, by infiltrating its insight into habitual motivations and harmonizing it "with that which is exclusively human," art can ideally serve as "the mediatress between, and reconciler of, nature and man." Art is ultimately to be valued, therefore, to the degree that it succeeds in attaining this end. Far from being an "expression of feeling," in the more extreme romantic sense, art seeks to inform, broaden, and develop feeling—to arouse "that sublime faculty by which a great mind becomes that on which it meditates." Indeed, feeling is nothing except as it is drawn outward into sympathetic participation, and takes on the character of what it conceives. It should be noted that the English romantic conception of the sympathetic imagination, to which Hazlitt gave the fullest expression, is a fundamental premise of Coleridge, particularly in his criticism of Shakespeare.

The scattered, critical fragments of this brilliant and often exasperating writer thus form a challenging pattern of thought that ultimately leads back to the greatest of classical premises: the conviction that truth is formative. "*The heart*," as Coleridge wrote in what is perhaps the most profoundly suggestive of his remarks "The *heart* should have *fed* upon the *truth*, as insects on a leaf, till it be tinged with the colour, and show its food in every . . . minutest fibre." Art, by infiltrating awareness into one's total response, by instilling a broadened realization into one's habitual ways of reacting and evaluating, thus "reconciles" man to reality, and by "assimilating him to Nature," is formative. It develops in man the imaginative capacity that serves as "the mediator between Truth and Feeling, the Head and the Heart," thus ministering to that end in which the "mind becomes that on which it meditates," and "truth . . . changes by domestication into power," into active fulfillment.

NOTES

1. This distinction is often considered to be the same as that made by Kant between *Vernunft* (reason) and *Verstand* (understanding). Kant's distinction had much to do with that of Coleridge. Coleridge's theory of "understanding," moreover, is very similar to Kant's. The difference comes in the conception of "reason." For Kant, the ultimate "ideas" by which reason arranges and synthesizes the judgments of understanding are merely necessary hypotheses rather than realities known to exist outside the mind; whereas, for Coleridge, they do so exist, and are actually known by reason. It was largely on this ground that Coleridge distinguished his own thought from most of the German philosophy of the period.

Robert Penn Warren

SIN AND REDEMPTION IN
THE ANCIENT MARINER*

In the preceding section I have tried to indicate some reasons inherent in Coleridge's aesthetic theory for believing that *The Ancient Mariner* is to be read at more than one level, that it has more than one "meaning." In this section, I shall look at the poem in terms of what I have called the primary perspective or primary theme—the theme which is the issue of the fable.

The fable, in broadest and simplest terms, is a story of crime and punishment and repentance and reconciliation (I have refrained from using the word *sin*, because one school of interpretation would scarcely accept the full burden of the implications of the word), an example, if we adopt for the moment Maud Bodkin's term, without necessarily adopting the full implications of her theory, of the archetypal story of Rebirth or the Night

* From *The Rime of the Ancient Mariner* by Samuel Taylor Coleridge, with a Commentary by Robert Penn Warren. Reprinted by permission of William Morris Agency, Inc. on behalf of Robert Penn Warren. Copyright © 1946 (renewed) by Robert Penn Warren.

Journey.[1] The Mariner shoots the bird; suffers various pains, the greatest of which is loneliness and spiritual anguish; upon recognizing the beauty of the foul sea snakes, experiences a gush of love for them and is able to pray; is returned miraculously to his home port, where he discovers the joy of human communion in God, and utters the moral, "He prayeth best who loveth best, etc." We arrive at the notion of a universal charity, which even Babbitt admits to be "unexceptionable"[2] in itself, the sense of the "One Life" in which all creation participates and which Coleridge perhaps derived from his neo-Platonic studies and which he had already celebrated, and was to celebrate, in other and more discursive poems.[3]

Such an account as the above, however, leaves certain questions unanswered, and perhaps the best way to get at those questions is to consider the nature of the Mariner's transgression. Many critics, even Lowes, for example,[4] dismiss the matter with such words as *wanton*, *trivial*, or *unthinking*. They are concerned with the act at the literal level only.

In substance, they ask: Did the Mariner as a man have a good practical reason for killing the bird? This literal-mindedness leads to the view that there is a monstrous and illogical discrepancy between the crime and the punishment, a view shared by persons as diverse in critical principles as Lowes with his aestheticism and Babbitt with his neo-humanistic moralism.[5] But we have to ask ourselves what is the symbolic reading of the act. And in asking ourselves this question, we have to remember that the symbol, in Coleridge's view, is not arbitrary, but *must contain in itself, literally considered, the seeds of the logic of its extension— that is, it must participate in the unity of which it is representative.*[6]

This question—what is the nature of the Mariner's act?—has received one answer in the theory advanced by Gingerich that the Mariner does not act but is constantly acted upon, that "he is pursued by a dark and sinister fate" after having done the deed "impulsively and wantonly" and presumably under necessity.[7] For Gingerich's theory is that the poem is a reflection of the doctrine of necessity which much occupied Coleridge's speculations during the years immediately leading up to the composition of *The Ancient Mariner.* "I am a complete necessitarian, and I understand the subject almost as well as Hartley himself, but I go farther than Hartley, and believe the corporeality of *thought,* namely that it is motion." [8] So the first problem we must consider is to what extent Coleridge was actually a necessitarian, at least in the poem.

It would seem that Gingerich has vastly oversimplified the whole matter, by choosing texts on one side of the question only, and sometimes by ignoring the context of a text chosen. He ignores, for example, the fact that even during the period when Coleridge professed devotion to Hartley he was under the powerful influence of his mystical studies (in Plato, Plotinus, Bruno, Boehme, etc.), and that looking back later[9] on his period of error he could say: "The writings of these mystics acted in no slight degree to prevent my mind from being imprisoned within the outline of any single dogmatic system. They contributed to keep alive the *heart* in the *head;* gave me an indistinct, yet stirring and working presentiment, that all the products of the mere *reflective* faculty partook of Death." [10] And in the sentence quoted by Gingerich in which Coleridge proclaims himself a complete

necessitarian, the context has been neglected: Coleridge proceeds to make a joke of the thrashing which "a certain uncouth automaton," Dr. Boyer, had visited upon one of his charges, a joke which indicates an awareness that the acceptance of the doctrine of necessity and materialism doesn't take the pain out of the offended buttocks. But to be more serious, it is possible to reach into another letter of the same general period and find Coleridge saying flatly, "I am a Berkleyan." [11] And this occurs in a long and passionate letter, really an essay, which is devoted to the attempt to convert John Thelwall to Christianity; and in the course of the letter there is a fervid discussion of sin and repentance,[12] concepts which Gingerich, extending certain texts from "Religious Musings" and other poems as a complete and tidy doctrine, denies to Coleridge.[13] Gingerich even goes so far in his ardor to support his cause as to say that in "The Eolian Harp" (1795) Coleridge "conceives universal life as automatous," [14] and proceeds to quote a few lines which in themselves might bear that interpretation.[15] But he simply ignores the rest of the poem. The concluding stanza, which I shall present, follows immediately upon his chosen passage:

> But thy more serious eye a mild reproof
> Darts, O beloved Woman! nor such thoughts
> Dim and unhallowed dost thou not reject,
> And biddest me walk humbly with my God.
> Meek daughter in the family of Christ!
> Well hast thou said and holily disprais'd
> These shapings of the unregenerate mind;
> Bubbles that glitter as they rise and break
> On vain Philosophy's aye-babbling spring.
> For never guiltless may I speak of him,
> The Incomprehensible! save when with awe
> I praise him, and with Faith that inly feels;
> Who with his saving mercies healed me,
> A sinful and most miserable man,
> Wilder'd and dark, and gave me to possess
> Peace, and this Cot, and thee, heart-honour'd
>   Maid!

And here the conclusion of the poem repudiates as "shapings of the unregenerate mind" the very statements by which Gingerich would argue for a relatively systematic necessitarianism. And we may note further in this passage that we find quite positively stated the idea of sin, a thing which, according to Gingerich, is not in the necessitarian system or in Coleridge's thought. But we can go to a direct, nonpoetic statement in the letters, made just after the completion of *The Ancient Mariner:* ". . . I believe most steadfastly in original sin; that from our mothers' wombs our understandings are darkened; and even where our understandings are in the light, that our organization is depraved and our volitions imperfect . . ." [16]

The point I wish to make is this: We cannot argue that Coleridge was a systematic necessitarian and that therefore the killing of the Albatross is merely the result of the necessary pattern of things and is not to be taken as sinful *per se* or in extension. The fact seems to be that Coleridge was early moving toward his later views, that he was not, as he says, committed to any dogmatic system, and that, as Shawcross points out,[17] the poems themselves "are sufficient to show us that his professed adherence to the necessitarian doctrines of his day was by no means the genuine conviction of his whole being." As early as 1794, he was, we may add, thinking of the mind as an active thing, the "shaping mind," [18] and claiming it for himself, and if we grant the power of mind in one sense we have broken the iron chain of necessity and the individual becomes a responsible agent[19] and not the patient which Babbitt and Gingerich assume the Mariner to be. What A. E. Powell says of Wordsworth, that he lived his philosophy long before he phrased it,[20] is equally true of Coleridge, and in addition to his living into a transcendental philosophy through the practice and love of poetry, he lived into the guilt of opium long before the Mariner shot the Albatross: he knew what guilt is, and if he longed for a view of the universe which would absolve him of responsibility and would comfort him with the thought of participation in the universal salvation promised by Hartley[21] and Priestley,[22] there was still the obdurate fact of his own experience. It seems that we have in these years a tortured churning around of the various interpretations of the fact, and the necessitarian philosophy is only one possible philosophy in suspension in that agitated brew. And we even have some evidence that in the period just before the composition of *The Ancient Mariner*—before he had struck upon that fable to embody his idea—the poet was meditating a long poem on the theme of the origin of evil. Early in 1797 Lamb wrote him: "I have a dim recollection that, when in town, you were talking of the Origin of Evil as a most prolific subject for a long poem." [23] As a matter of fact, Coleridge never did

"solve" his problem: he found peace simply by accepting the idea of Original Sin as a mystery.

In *Table Talk* he says: "A Fall of some sort or other—the creation, as it were, of the nonabsolute—is the fundamental postulate of the moral history of Man. Without this hypothesis, Man is unintelligible; with it every phenomenon is explicable. The mystery itself is too profound for human insight." [24]

In his more elaborate and systematic treatment of the subject Coleridge adds another point which is of significance for the poem. Original Sin is not hereditary sin; it is original with the sinner and is of his will. There is no previous determination of the will, for the will exists outside the chain of cause and effect, which is of Nature and not of Spirit. And as for the time of this act of sin, he says that the "subject stands in no relation to time, can neither be in time nor out of time." [25] The bolt whizzes from the crossbow and the bird falls and all comment that the Mariner has no proper dramatic motive or is the child of necessity or is innocent of everything except a little wantonness is completely irrelevant, for we are confronting the mystery of the corruption of the will, the mystery which is the beginning of the "moral history of Man." The fact that the act is unmotivated in any practical sense, that it appears merely perverse, has offended literalists and Aristotelians alike, and, for that matter, Wordsworth, who held that the Mariner had no "character" (and we may elaborate by saying that having no character he could exhibit no motive) and did not act but was acted upon.[26] The lack of motivation, the perversity, which flies in the face of the Aristotelian doctrine of *hamartia*, is exactly the significant thing about the Mariner's act. The act symbolizes the Fall, and the Fall has two qualities important here: it is a condition of will, as Coleridge says, "out of time," and it is the result of no single human motive.

One more comment, even though I have belabored this point. What is the nature of this sin, what is its content? Though the act which symbolizes the mystery of the Fall is appropriately without motive, the sin of the will must be the appropriate expression of the essence of the will. And we shall turn to a passage in *The Statesman's Manual*. Having just said that, in its "state of immanence or indwelling in reason and religion," the will appears indifferently as wisdom or love,

Coleridge proceeds: "But in its utmost abstraction and consequent state of reprobation, the will becomes Satanic pride and rebellious self-idolatry in the relations of the spirit to itself, and remorseless despotism relatively to others ... by the fearful resolve to find in itself alone the one absolute motive of action."[27] Then he sketches the portrait of the will in abstraction, concluding with the observation that "these are the marks, that have characterized the masters of mischief, the liberticides, the mighty hunters of mankind, from Nimrod to Bonaparte."[28]

We may observe a peculiar phrase, the "mighty hunters of mankind, from Nimrod to Bonaparte," and in this blending of the hunting of beasts and the hunting of man—for Nimrod was himself both the mighty hunter and the founder of the first military state—we have an identification that takes us straight to the crime of the Mariner. The Mariner did not kill a man but a bird, and the literal-minded readers have echoed Mrs. Barbauld and Leslie Stephen: what a lot of pother about a bird. But they forget that this bird is more than a bird. I do not intend, however, to rest my case on the phrase just quoted from *The Statesman's Manual*, for the phrase itself I take to be but an echo from the poem at the time when the author was revising and reliving his favorite poem. Let us go to the poem itself to learn the significance of the bird.

In the poem itself the same identification occurs: the hunting of the bird becomes the hunting of man. When the bird first appears,

> As if it had been a Christian soul,
> We hailed it in God's name.

It ate food "it ne'er had eat," and every day "came to the mariner's hollo," and then later perched on the mast or shroud for "vespers nine." It partakes of the human food and pleasure and devotions.[29] To make matters more explicit, Coleridge adds in the Gloss the statement that the bird was received with "hospitality" and adds, after the crime, that the Mariner "inhospitably killeth the pious bird of good omen." The crime is, symbolically, a murder, and a particularly heinous murder, for it involves the violation of hospitality and of gratitude (*pious* equals *faithful* and the bird is "of good omen") and of sanctity (the religious connotations of *pious*, etc.). This factor of betrayal in the crime is re-

emphasized in Part V when one of the Spirits says that the bird had "loved the man" who killed it.

But why did the poet not give us a literal murder in the first place? By way of answering this question, we must remember that the crime, to maintain its symbolic reference to the Fall, must be motiveless. But the motiveless murder of a man would truly raise the issue of probability. Furthermore, the literal shock of such an act, especially if perverse and unmotivated, would be so great that it would distract from the symbolic significance. The poet's problem, then, was to provide an act which, on one hand, would not accent the issue of probability or shockingly distract from the symbolic significance, but which, on the other hand, would be adequately criminal to justify the consequences. And the necessary criminality is established, we have seen, in two ways: (1) by making the gravity of the act depend on the state of the will which prompts it, and (2) by symbolically defining the bird as a "Christian soul," as "pious," etc.

There is, however, a third way in which the criminality is established. We can get at it by considering the observation that if a man had been killed, we could not have the "lesson of humanitarianism," which some critics, Henry Beers for instance, have taken to be the point of the poem. But we must remember that the humanitarianism itself is a superficial manifestation of a deeper concern, a sacramental conception of the universe, for the bird is hailed "in God's name," both literally and symbolically, and in the end we have, therefore, in the crime against Nature a crime against God. If a man had been killed, the secular nature of the crime—a crime then against man—would have overshadowed the ultimate religious significance involved. The idea of the crime against God rather than man is further emphasized by the fact that the cross is removed from the Mariner's neck to make place for the dead bird, and here we get a symbolic transference from Christ to the Albatross. Last, there is the crime against God.

It may be instructive to see how another writer has treated these questions in presenting a similar story of the crime against a brute. I refer to Poe's "The Black Cat." In this story precisely the same issues appear, but where Coleridge leaves the issues in fluid suspension and leaves the nature of the crime defined only in the general symbolic tissue of the poem, Poe gives an elaborate analysis of the motivation and meaning of the act:

> And then came, as if to my final and irrevocable overthrow, the spirit of Perverseness. Of this spirit philosophy takes no account. Yet I am not more sure that my soul lives, than I am that perverseness is one of the primitive impulses of the human heart—one of the indivisible primary faculties, or sentiments, which give direction to the character of man. Who has not, a hundred times, found himself committing a vile or a stupid action, for no other reason than because he knows he should *not*? Have we not a perpetual inclination, in the teeth of our best judgment, to violate that which is *Law*, merely because we understand it to be such? This spirit of perverseness, I say, came to my final overthrow. It was this unfathomable longing of the soul *to vex itself*—to offer violence to its own nature—to do wrong for the wrong's sake only— that urged me to continue and finally to consummate the injury I had inflicted upon the unoffending brute. One morning, in cold blood, I slipped a noose about its neck and hung it to the limb of a tree—hung it with the tears streaming from my eyes, and with the bitterest remorse at my heart—hung it *because* I knew that it had loved me, and *because* I felt it had given me no reason for offense—hung it *because* I knew that in so doing I was committing a sin—a deadly sin that would so jeopardize my immortal soul as to place it—if such a thing were possible—even beyond the reach of the infinite mercy of the Most Merciful and Most Terrible God.

All we have to do is read Original Sin for Perverseness; and Poe himself carries us from the psychological treatment under Perverseness to the theological treatment under Sin.

There is another interesting parallel of treatment, the identification, in the crime, of the brute with the human. In the poem the identification is achieved symbolically, as we have seen. But in the story we must have more than this: the police are to arrest the hero and they will not arrest him for killing a cat, even if the killing is symbolically and spiritually equivalent to a murder. But Poe makes the symbolic transference, too. There are two cats, the first is hanged outright. The second cat, which takes the place of the first to plague the conscience of the hero and to frighten him with the white gallows mark on the breast, trips the hero on the stair to the cellar. The man then aims a blow with an axe at this cat, but his wife stays his hand. The blow intended for the brute is then delivered on the woman. The symbolic transference is made but is made in terms of psychological treatment.[30]

To return to the problems raised by the poem: We have not yet done with the matter of crime and punishment. There is the question of the fellow mariners, who suffer death. Here we encounter not infrequently the objection that they do not merit their fate.[31] The tragic *hamartia*, we are told, is not adequate. The Gloss, however, flatly defines the nature of the crime of the fellow mariners: they have made themselves "accomplices." But apparently the Gloss needs a gloss. The fellow mariners have, in a kind of structural counterpoint (and such a counterpoint is, as we shall see, a characteristic of the poem), duplicated the Mariner's own crime of pride, of will in abstraction. That is, they make their desire the measure of the act: they first condemn the act, when they think the bird had brought the favorable breeze; then applaud the act when the fog clears and the breeze springs back up, now saying that the bird had brought the fog; then in the dead calm, again condemn the act. Their crime has another aspect: they have violated the sacramental conception of the universe, by making man's convenience the measure of an act, by isolating him from Nature and the "One Life." This point is picked up later in Part IV:

> The many men, so beautiful!
> And they all dead did lie:
> And a thousand thousand slimy things
> Lived on; and so did I.

The stanza seems important for the reading of the poem. The usual statement for the poem is that the Mariner moves from love of the sea snakes to a love of men (and in the broad sense this is true), but here we see that long before he blesses the snakes he is aware, in his guilt, of the beauty of the dead men, and protests against the fact that the slimy things should live while the beautiful men lie dead. In other words, we have here, even in his remorse, a repetition of the original crime against the sacramental view of the universe: man is still set over, in pride, against Nature. The Gloss points to the important thing here: "He despiseth the creatures of the calm."

There is one other aspect of the guilt of the

fellow mariners worthy of notice. They judge the moral content of an act by its consequence; in other words, they would make good disciples of Bishop Paley, who, according to Coleridge, was no moralist because he would judge the morality of an act by consequence and not "contemplate the same in its original spiritual source," [32] the state of the will. The will of the fellow mariners is corrupt. And this re-emphasizes the fact that what is at stake throughout is not the objective magnitude of the act performed—the bird is, literally, a trivial creature—but the spirit in which the act is performed, the condition of the will.

So much for the crime of the Mariner and the crime of his fellows. And we know the sequel, the regeneration of the Mariner.[33] He accepts, in the end, the sacramental view of the universe, and his will is released from its state of "utmost abstraction" and gains the state of "immanence" in wisdom and love. We shall observe the stages whereby this process is consummated—this primary theme of the "One Life" is developed—as we investigate the secondary theme, the theme of the imagination.

NOTES

1. Maud Bodkin, *Archetypal Patterns in Poetry* (Oxford, 1954), pp. 54–81.

2. Irving Babbitt, "Coleridge on Imagination," *On Being Creative* (Boston, 1932), pp. 115–126.

3. The theme of the sacramental vision appears in a very high percentage of Coleridge's poems. It is implied, of course, in some of the early poems, such as "To a Young Ass," but when it really takes hold on his mind, we have his first significant poetry in "Religious Musings" (1794) and "The Eolian Harp" (1795). The necessitarian ideas are sometimes associated with this theme, but there is no essential connection. The doctrine of necessity was simply one way of philosophizing the appetite for the Whole and the Vast, and the fact of the appetite is much more important than the doctrine which happened to be seized upon to justify it; the feeling preceded the idea.

4. *The Road to Xanadu* (Boston, 1927), pp. 298, 303.

5. "The fact is that it is impossible to extract any serious ethical purport from *The Ancient Mariner* —except perhaps a warning as to the fate of the innocent bystander; unless indeed one holds that it is fitting that, for having sympathized with the man who shot an albatross, 'four times fifty living men' should perish in torments unspeakable" (*op. cit.*, p. 119). This is the smug joke the literalists love, first perpetrated, I believe, by Leslie Stephen: "Indeed, the moral which would apparently be that people who sympathize with a man who shoots an albatross will die in prolonged torture of thirst, is open to obvious objections" ("Coleridge," *Hours in a Library* [New York, 1894], III, 359). This may also have been Mrs. Barbauld's objection, as suggested by Elizabeth Nitchie (*op. cit.*, p. 868). Lane Cooper continues the tradition: "Or what of the error committed by the two hundred fellows of the Ancient Mariner? For agreeing after the fact that it was good to slay the bird, they suffer excruciating tortures, and die in misery. Is their credulous mistake an adequate tragic *hamartia?*" ("Coleridge, Wordsworth, and Mr. Lowes," *PMLA*, XLIII, 583). It is not adequate, of course, if one insists on reading the act as mere act without considering the spiritual attitude of the fellow mariners which prompts their acceptance of the crime.

6. At some point the objection will undoubtedly be made that I am using statements made after the composition of *The Ancient Mariner* for the purpose of interpreting the poem. But I am not arguing, to take the present topic of symbolism, that because Coleridge held a certain doctrine of the symbol in 1817, the year of the *Biographia Literaria* and *The Statesman's Manual,* a poem written in 1797–1798 would necessarily embody the doctrine in practice. The later statements would only be relevant in so far as we can hold that those later statements represented a development of a position essentially held at the time of the composition of the poem itself. Now there is strong evidence that this is the case.

First, Coleridge says flatly that he had become aware of the special power of the imagination at an early date, his "twenty-fourth year." In the *Biographia Literaria* (I, 58–60) he describes the effect wrought upon him by the reading of a poem by Wordsworth, a poem which exhibited "the union of deep feeling with profound thought; the fine balance of truth in observing with the imaginative faculty in modifying the objects observed; and above all the original gift of spreading the tone, the *atmosphere,* and with it the depth and height of the ideal world around forms, incidents, and situations, of which, for the common view, custom had bedimmed all the lustre, had dried up the sparkle and the dew drops" (p. 59). Then a little later in discussing the concept of the imagination, he refers to the subject as one to which a poem of Wordsworth's had "first directed my attention" (p. 64). The whole discussion of the origin of the *Lyrical Ballads* makes it clear beyond doubt that the basic conception of the imagination had been arrived at early. We also have the evidence of *The Prelude,* which grew out of these discussions.

Second, we have the evidence in certain poems. The shaping power of the mind is referred to in early poems, such as the sonnet "To Richard Brinsley Sheridan, Esq." (1795) and "Lines on a Friend Who Died of a Frenzy Fever" (1794). Shawcross points out that even in "Religious Musings" (1794) there is a volitional effort on the part of the finite mind. (See Note 78.)

Third, though Coleridge wrote *The Ancient Mariner* in 1797–1798, he worked closely on it in the period just before the publication of *Sibylline Leaves* (1817), which belongs to the same period as the *Biographia Literaria* and *The Statesman's Manual.* In other words, his careful revision of the poem apparently indicates that it satisfactorily embodies his theories of composition as held in 1817. The fact that he continued to nurse the hope of completing *Christabel* indicates the same thing about that poem.

All in all, the evidence against this general view is based on the idea that the concept of the imagination was arrived at after the visit to Germany and the subsequent philosophical crisis. I do not deny that the crisis was real, but it seems to have resulted in a clarification of issues which had been brewing for a long time. Germany gave Coleridge form and authority, perhaps, but not the basic motivation for his final views. Yet even R. D. Havens (*The Mind of a Poet* [Baltimore, 1941]), immediately after remarking on the fact that a poem of Wordsworth had provoked Coleridge to speculation about the imagination, proceeds to say that "this revolutionary conception of the imagination" was "probably derived from Kant" (p. 206). For a discussion of the date of Coleridge's study of Kant, and of the needs which led him to accept Kant, see

Rene Wellek, *Kant in England* (Princeton, 1931), pp. 69–73.

7. S. F. Gingerich, "Coleridge," *Essays in the Romantic Poets* (New York, 1924), pp. 30–35. Wordsworth's famous comment on the poem in the note in the second edition of the *Lyrical Ballads* says that the poem has, among others, the defect that the hero "does not act, but is continually acted upon," a view persisting not only with Gingerich but with Cooper and Babbitt.

8. Letter to Southey, December 11, 1794, *Letters,* I, 113. There are other references in letters to the belief in necessitarianism, and a number of poems touch on the question in one way or another: "Religious Musings" (1794), "The Destiny of Nations" (1796), "Frost at Midnight" (1796), "The Nightingale" (1798), and Fears in Solitude" (1798). But the mere fact that the issue of necessity may be involved, directly or indirectly, in these poems does not prove the total acceptance of the doctrine.

9. *Biographia Literaria,* I, 74–107.

10. *Ibid.,* I, 98.

11. Letter to John Thelwall, December 17, 1796, *Letters,* I, 195. The context is interesting on the present and other counts. Thelwall has criticized the author's sonnet "Composed on a Journey Homeward; the Author having received Intelligence of the Birth of a Son, September 20, 1796," as being mystical because in the poem the father fears that the babe, being a spirit that has pre-existed in another sphere, may have been sent to earth merely as a temporary punishment for a "venial crime," and may be snatched back "to meet Heaven's quick reprieve." The letter: "Now that the thinking part of man, that is, the soul, existed previously to its appearance in its present body may be very wild philosophy, but it is very intelligible poetry; inasmuch as 'soul' is an orthodox word in all our poets, they meaning by 'soul' a being inhabiting our body, and playing upon it, like a musician enclosed in an organ whose keys are placed inwards. Now this opinion I do not hold; not that I am a materialist, but because I am a Berkleyan. Yet as you, who are not a Christian, wished you were, that we might meet in heaven, so I, who did not believe in this descending and incarcerated soul, yet said if my baby had died before I had seen him I should have struggled to believe it." Here we have in the background a fairly clear case of

the distinction between belief and pseudo belief, to adopt Richards' terms. Coleridge is using a fiction to express a state of feeling.

12. *Ibid.*, p. 201.

13. *Op. cit.*, pp. 18–40.

14. *Ibid.*, p. 25.

15. And what if all of animated nature,
Be but organic Harps diversely fram'd.
That tremble into thought, as o'er
    them sweeps
Plastic and vast, one intellectual
    breeze,
At once the Soul of each, and God of
    all?

16. Letter to George Coleridge, April, 1798, *Letters*, I, 241–242. We also find a text on the matter of sin and grace in "Sonnet on Receiving a Letter Informing me of the Birth of a Son." And if we look to the nightmare in Stanza VI of "Ode to the Departing Year," we find the same type of imagery which appears in the guilt dreams of "The Pains of Sleep," and which Mr. Abrams attributes to opium; the opium source of the imagery presumably means a guilt association.

Thus far I have tried to show, in attacking the notion that the Mariner is passive and that the killing of the Albatross can therefore have no moral content, that Coleridge was not committed to necessitarianism in any sense which would make it inevitable in the poem. But there is another line of approach to the question. If it be assumed that Coleridge did accept Hartley and Priestley, it still does not follow that the Mariner's act is without moral content, for we must do Coleridge the honor of supposing that he read the works of his masters a little more closely than some of the critics seem to have done. In Priestley's *Doctrine of Philosophical Necessity Illustrated* (Birmingham, 1782), pp. 142–164, there occurs a section entitled "Of the Nature of Remorse of Conscience, and of Praying for the Pardon of Sin, on the Doctrine of Necessity," which really develops Proposition XV of Chapter I of Part II of Hartley's *Observations on Man*. Priestley writes: "It is acknowledged that a necessarian, who, as such, believes that, strictly speaking, *nothing goes wrong*, but that everything is under the best direction possible . . . cannot accuse himself of having done wrong in the ultimate sense of the words. He has, therefore, in this strict

sense, nothing to do with repentance, confession, or pardon, which are all adapted to a different, imperfect, and fallacious view of things. . . . In the sublime, but accurate language of the apostle John, he will *dwell in love*, he will *dwell in God*, and *God in him;* so that, *not committing any sin*, he will have nothing to repent of. He will be *perfect, as his heavenly father is perfect*." But man does not live at that level of enlightenment and "because of influences to which we are all exposed" cannot constantly refer "everything to its primary cause." Therefore, he will "feel the sentiments of shame, remorse, and repentance, which arise mechanically from his referring actions to himself. And, oppressed with a sense of *guilt* he will have recourse to that *mercy* of which he will stand in need." Since no man, except for rare moments in the seasons of retirement and meditations, is ever more than an "imperfect necessitarian," all men have the experience of sin and remorse, and the sin, for mortal man who cannot see the complete pattern, has a content, and the content is the "almost irrevocable debasement of our minds by *looking off from God, living without him* . . . and *idolizing ourselves and the world;* considering other things as *proper agents* and *causes;* whereas, strictly speaking there is but *one cause,* but *one sole agent* in universal nature. Thus . . . all vice is reducible to idolatry. . . ." Thus at the level of mortal experience, the level at which the Mariner must live, his shooting of the Albatross would be an act of pride, of self-idolatry—the very word Coleridge uses later in describing Original Sin.

The point I am trying to make is, finally, this: Even on the view that Coleridge is influenced by the doctrines of the necessitarians, the killing of the Albatross still has, at the level of experience, a moral content and is not to be dismissed as merely a wanton or thoughtless act. It is an act for which, at the level of experience, man takes responsibility, for, as Priestley somewhat whimsically puts it, at the end of his chapter on guilt, "If . . . we cannot habitually ascribe *all* to God, but a part only, let it be (and so indeed it naturally will be) that which is *good;* and if we must ascribe anything to ourselves, let it be that which is *evil*."

There is, indeed, a shadowy relation between the vision of love to which the Mariner attains and the moments of vision which the necessitarians describe—the "self-annihilation" of Hartley—but the mystics had given Coleridge more rapturous descriptions of that state of bliss. Furthermore, the one thing that the poem does *not* establish is the notion that the crime and the subsequent horror are really part of a good; the Mariner never praises God for having given him the evil as a concealed good; instead, the horror of the crime and its consequences is never completely overpassed, and the agony of the Mariner continues to return at its uncertain hour. This is definitely not the way a poet of necessitarianism should end his tale.

17. J. Shawcross, *Biographia Literaria* (Oxford, 1907), I, iv.

18. "Lines on a Friend."

> To me hath Heaven with bounteous
> hand assign'd
> Energic Reason and a shaping mind.

Looking back in his later life, Coleridge placed the date of his release from the doctrine of necessitarianism very early: "Within twelve months after the writing of this poem ["Destiny of Nations," 1796] my bold Optimism, and Necessitarianism . . . gave way to the day-break of a more genial and less shallow system." Even if Coleridge was careless with dates, the evidence of this passage, taken in conjunction with other factors, is not to be ignored. In the first place, here Coleridge says "day-break," and so there is no necessary contradiction between this statement and the later date assigned elsewhere to the philosophical crisis which followed upon his German studies. There was a later crisis, but the dawn had come earlier in terms of his feelings, and he trusted the heart. We also know that he was so struck by a poem of Wordsworth's in 1797 that he recognized the active and creating mind which could be no part of the doctrine of necessitarianism taken strictly (*Biographia Literaria*, I, 58–60, 64). But Gingerich (*op. cit.*, p. 43) maintains that "Lines Written in the Hartz Forest" (1799) is the first poem to express the transcendental conception of the might of the mind.

19. Shawcross (*op cit.*, I, vii) points out that even in "Religious Musings," on which Gingerich leans so heavily for his necessitarian texts, the highest consciousness of God is "consequent upon an act, a volitional effort, in which the finite mind is brought into direct contact with an infinite whose essence, as Love, is itself activity."

20. *The Romantic Theory of Poetry* (London,

1926) p. 128. For further discussion of this point of the overemphasis of the Hartleyan influence, see H. N. Fairchild (*The Romantic Quest* [New York, 1931], pp. 106, 332, 341–342): "Transcendentalism was latent in Coleridge from his earliest reading of fairy tales. One can only say that it gradually develops until, stimulated by his experiences in Germany, it emerges from the eighteenth century ideas which have partly obscured it" (p. 342).

21. *Observations on Man*, Section V, "The Final Happiness of All Mankind in Some Distant State" (London, 1834), pp. 581–593.

22. *Op. cit.*, pp. 139–142. After saying that the necessitarian will "lean strongly to the belief of the everlasting happiness of all," Priestly simply quotes a long section from Section V of Hartley's work.

23. *Letters of Charles Lamb*, ed. E. V. Lucas (London, 1935), I, 95. R. C. Bald (*op. cit.*, p. 16) quotes from Lamb's letter and reports that Coleridge had already entered in his notebook (Gutch memorandum book, f. 21a) the topic for a projected poem: "The Origin of Evil, an Epic Poem." But Bald does not connect this with *The Ancient Mariner*. He says: "Some time in 1797, however, the subject changed; one of his other projects drew his attention to a more appropriate theme." But the case seems to be that Coleridge changed his subject, his fable, but not his theme.

There is also evidence of a more personal nature that Coleridge was obsessed by fear and guilt even before the full addiction to opium. For instance, there is his autobiographical note of January 11, 1805: "It is a most instructive part of my Life the fact, that I have been always preyed on by some Dread, and perhaps all my faulty actions have been the consequences of some Dread or other in my mind from fear of Pain, or Shame, not from prospect of Pleasure." And Coleridge lists the numerous dreads, from the boyhood horror of being detected with a sore head, through "a short-lived Fit of Fears from sex," to the "almost epileptic night-horrors in my sleep" (Bald, *op. cit.*, pp. 26–27).

Our knowledge of the poet's personal background helps us to define his dominant theme, but the critical argument can be rested on perfectly objective evidence in the poems themselves. Coleridge longed for the vision of universal love of "Religious Musings" or of the end of *The Ancient Mariner*, but we also have in "The Eolian Harp" the picture of the "sinful and most miserable man," who is "wilder'd and dark," and the nightmare in Section VI of the "Ode to the Departing Year," not to mention the later *Christabel,* "The Pains of Sleep," and *The Ancient Mariner* itself.

24. May 1, 1830.

25. *Aids to Reflection,* pp. 268–290; quotation on p. 287. Coleridge's emphasis later on the mystery of Original Sin may find a strange echo in the famous remark about *The Ancient Mariner* in *Table Talk,* to the effect that the poem, as a work of pure imagination, should have had no more moral than the tale in *The Arabian Nights* of the "merchant's sitting down to eat dates by the side of a well, and throwing the shells aside, and lo! a genie starts up and says he *must* kill the aforesaid merchant *because* one of the date shells had, it seems, put out the eye of the genie's son." But this account of the story of "The Genie and the Merchant," from the First Night, is not accurate. In fact, the careless date shell had killed the son of the genie. When the merchant begs for pity, the genie exclaims: "No mercy! Is it not just to kill him that has killed another?" And when the merchant then pleads his own lack of evil intention, the genie replies, "I must kill thee since thou hast killed my son." What is important here may be that the story referred to from *The Arabian Nights* is not merely a tale of the miraculous, but is one dealing with a random act and its apparently incommensurable punishment, much on the order of that in *The Ancient Mariner.* The mystery of sin and punishment is again before us. There is even a faint hint of a theological parallel with Christianity, the avenging Father and the Son who suffers at the hand of man. One can see why, perhaps, this particular story sprang to Coleridge's mind. But what did he mean by the statement about the moral and the use of this story as an example? He never said, we must remember, that his own poem should be meaningless or be without a "moral." He simply said that the moral should be less obtrusive. Then he offers an example of a story wherein a mysterious factor in life is caught up without any rationalization. It may be objected to all this that Coleridge, after all, didn't have the story straight, etc. The answer is that the error may well have been that of Henry Nelson Coleridge, who had the habit of putting down after reaching home the remarks of his distinguished kinsman (see Preface to *Table Talk*), and whose

memory of *The Arabian Nights* may well have been less perfect than that of Coleridge, to whom the book had been at one time almost a devotional work. Or Coleridge may simply have assumed full knowledge of the story on the part of his audience.

26. In connection with the note on the poem in the edition of the *Lyrical Ballads* of 1800, W. Hale White points out that Coleridge was, in a sense, party to the criticism; but he also says that Coleridge was always ready to depreciate his own poetry, and in any case it is certain that his pliable nature was dominated by Wordsworth's rugged assurance. And the fact remains that Coleridge, despite various revisions, did nothing to try to motivate the killing of the bird. (*A Description of the Wordsworth and Coleridge Manuscripts in the Possession of Mr. T. Norton Longman* [London, 1897], p. 25).

27. P. 458. If we transfer the terminology here to the pattern of *The Ancient Mariner,* we can describe the poem as the progression of the will from abstraction and self-idolatry to the state of immanence which expresses itself as wisdom or love—those being, as Coleridge says in the passage, two aspects of the same power, the "intelligential" and the "spiritual." We may observe that the punishment in the poem for the sin of self-idolatry and the resolve of the will to find in itself alone "one absolute motive," is fitted with Dantesque precision to the nature of the crime. It is, in fact, a mere extension of the crime. It is loneliness. And when the Mariner bites his own arm for the blood to drink instead of the healing universal rain, we have the last logical extension of "self-idolatry" converted to its own punishment.

28. *Ibid.,* p. 459.

29. Kenneth Burke, *The Philosophy of Literary Form* (Baton Rouge, 1941), pp. 28–29; treats the giving of food to the Albatross: "And since 'the very deep did rot' as a result of this murder, the Albatross should be expected also to contain, implicitly, by foreshadowing, the substance of the water snakes that grew in this rot. This may explain why the Mariner, who was to kill the Albatross, fed it 'biscuit worms' (in a later version this fatal incipience was obscured: 'It ate the things it ne'er had eat'). In totemic thought, as in the communion service, consubstantiality is got by eating food in common. 'Tell me what you eat, and I'll tell you what you are.'"

I am not much impressed by the argument here given for the incipience in the biscuit worms. The case is not helped, furthermore, by the fact that this was one of Wordsworth's suggestions. I am, however, inclined to follow the general idea of the taking of food with the crew as being a device for "humanizing" the Albatross.

30. The crime presented in *The Ancient Mariner*, the crime of self-assertion in the face of Law, was of peculiar appeal to the Romantics. "*Le sentiment presque ineffable, tant il est terrible, de la joie dans la damnation,*" says Baudelaire in his essay on *Richard Wagner et Tannhauser à Paris*. Shelley's interest in the crime of incest and his comments on the "poeticality" of the topic is an example of this. The crime against an animal is, of course, a special case of this self-assertion, the perversity of pride. Baudelaire, in his essay on Poe, quotes his own translation of the passage given above from "The Black Cat" (*Revue de Paris*, March and April, 1852). Flaubert's *Légende de saint Julien l'hospitalier* is another example of this twisted rendering of the Hymn of Saint Francis or the "jubilate Agno" of Christopher Smart.

31. See Note 7.

32. *Aids to Reflection*, p. 292. In various other places Coleridge also attacks this view of morality in terms of consequence.

W. J. Bate

CHRISTABEL AND KUBLA KHAN*

The realization in two or three months (January or February, 1798) that he was actually completing a work of this magnitude, and in a mode so unfamiliar to him, may have surprised Coleridge himself. Certainly it gave him a confidence he had never had before; and in the wake of the "Mariner" were written at least two, probably three, of the four finest poems he was yet to write—"Christabel"; the best of the conversation poems, "Frost at Midnight"; and, though the date is disputable, "Kubla Khan."

Yet he could never be of one mind about what he had done or was in the process of doing. As he passed the middle point of the "Ancient Mariner" and began to work toward its predetermined conclusion, qualifications and alternatives started to suggest themselves. Fortunately he was able to exclude them from the "Mariner" and divert them instead into the thought of other poems, particularly "Christabel," in which, as he said later in the *Biographia Literaria*, "I should have more nearly realized my ideal [had they been finished], than I had done in my first attempt." In other poems he would try something analogous but different, at once other and the same. With this thought he seems to have begun "Christabel" by December or January, a month or two before he finished the "Ancient Mariner." Characteristically he drew a new line of distinction in order to affirm his resolve and give himself fresh ground for proceeding. In place of the *supernatural* he would now concern himself more modestly with the *preternatural*—not what is necessarily *above* nature, in other words, but only what is outside the ordinary course of it or inexplicable by ordinary means. Warming to the thought of the distinction, he planned, or later said he planned, to write two essays that would clarify it further, though as was so often the case the essays were never written. The first of the two essays prefixed to the "Ancient Mariner" was to discuss "the uses of the Supernatural in poetry, and the principles which regulate its introduction," while the second, to serve as a preface to "Christabel," would deal with the uses of the "Preternatural."

He would now, he thought, be freer. For to begin with, the "supernatural" imposed a heavier burden of conscience, if not invention. It presupposed a frame of symbolic reference that would inevitably involve his own religious beliefs without his quite knowing yet where he really wanted to step or indeed felt at liberty to step. Moreover, there would be no need this time for "machinery." The obvious "moral," and with it the teasing provision of apparatus that encourages the reader to infer a one-for-one kind of allegory where "this" stands for "that," would be avoided. Instead the interplay—indeed interpenetration—of natural and "preternatural" would be complete. The result would then be of no more rational, of no more patently symbolic or allegorical significance than the tale from the *Arabian Nights* that Coleridge mentioned to Mrs. Barbauld. At the same time, as a beginning gesture of his confidence and his sense of doing something new, he selected a verse form quite different, yet in one important way analogous, to that of the "Mariner." Through it he would once again avoid the great but inhibition-inducing pentameter line that Shakespeare and Milton had so triumphantly used. But this time, instead of employing the ballad form as a basis, he would use a meter that disregarded metrical feet, and, whatever the number of syllables, contented itself simply with four accented beats in a line with a few variations and with interspersed use of rhyme. The concept behind it has interested poets from Scott and Byron to the present day, even inciting a few, especially Gerard Manley Hopkins, to emulate it in one way or another. It was perhaps the most successful part of the poem, as Coleridge himself gradually seems to have felt. There is a certain pathos in the fact that, as the years passed and the poem continued to remain unfinished, he tried increasingly to call attention to the novelty of its meter rather than to its other qualities. This is the aim of the self-defensive, attemptedly casual preface in 1816 that takes the place of the once-planned essay on the "preternatural."

With the escort of a different versification, and with his resolve heartened by a new definition of aim, Coleridge seems to have made rapid progress, possibly writing Part I within a month before he returned to the closing stages of the "Mariner." The setting for this adventure into the "preternatural" is medieval. A few words of summary, however unwelcome in the discussion of narrative generally, may be tolerated when we are confronted with only a fragment. The lady Christabel, living with her widowed father and betrothed to a knight who is far distant, leaves the castle at night to pray for her absent lover. This is the thoughtless courage of innocence, to which a forest at midnight is no more hazardous than the center of a castle. Meanwhile the poem repeatedly suggests that something dire awaits her. She proceeds, makes her prayer, and meets another woman ("Geraldine") who tells of her recent misfortunes (a story that would convince no one except an innocent and rather obtuse maid), implores pity and help, and is then protectively taken back to the castle by Christabel. Geraldine cannot by herself cross the threshold, which has been blessed against evil spirits. (The reader is thus alerted to the fact that she is an evil being.) Christabel, with whom Coleridge-as-habitual-usher is becoming rapidly identified, must lift her over it. But this once done, Christabel is no longer a free agent, and despite warnings to which she is impervious, leads Geraldine to her chamber. As Geraldine disrobes before entering Christabel's bed, she is forced to reveal something terrible to any eye not blinded by her spell: "her bosom, and half her side —A sight to dream of, not to tell." This is probably the withered, scaly bosom and side traditionally attributed to the sorceress.

The character of Geraldine coalesces several things, for the interest there is in the elusiveness and ambiguities of evil, its varied and quickly shifting nature, and above all its need for human welcome and embrace if it is to become completely alive and fulfill itself. In all of these respects the two principle prototypes of Geraldine's character supplement each other. To begin with, she is a sort of vampire—that is to say, a creature partly living through or by means of human beings, and to that extent dependent on them, like evil itself, for what she can be or do. At the same time she is a kind of "lamia," shifting between a mortal and immortal state; and with this is the implication that she *may* —just possibly—be a phantasm, existing immortally merely *in potentia*, able to attain concrete existence only through the mind of a human being. As compared with these more complex considerations, the sexual ambiguity that automatically leaps to the mind of the post-Freudian is perhaps relevant but by no means basic. If we use a little historical imagination, we quickly see that Coleridge's two other alternatives (that is, to make either Geraldine or Christabel a male) would have created impossible complications, and that, by contrast, the idea of Lesbianism—if admitted only by suggestion—was less likely to arouse in the reader a stock response. For a male vampire would not only have lost the mythical "lamia" properties that Geraldine can suggest, but, more important, would have put the poem too grossly on the level of the Gothic "shockers" of the day. Once the male vampire was admitted to Christabel's bedroom for the night (and how, given the whole conception of her character, was she to invite him into it?), there would not be much else to say. On the other hand, to have made Christabel herself a man, meekly succumbing to a female vampire, would have turned Coleridge's main character, already passive enough, into something so jelly-like as to be dangerously close to farce. In short, the practical inevitabilities of the poet in facing a situation should be kept in mind before we hasten to strain at them in other terms. Nor, in this case, does Coleridge make much capital anyway out of the inevitable. The real concern, to repeat, is the multi-sidedness of evil, its mercurial ability, when we think we have pinned it down or defined it, to take almost any shape, and share chameleon-like in any color, and, above all, to derive its strength, to fulfill itself, only through human cooperation. Finally, Geraldine is far from single-minded; she has moments of hesitation and self-misgiving. She is not, in fact, altogether free. As she approaches the maid's bed, "Ah! what a stricken look was hers." She seems to be trying to "lift some weight"; and she "seeks delay."

Implicit in the whole conception of the story, but far less developed, are also the ambiguities of virtue, presumably to be typified by Geraldine's counterpart, Christabel. Innocence, unless it is to be a mere accident within a vacuum, is forced to come close to evil in some way, though in the process it may be destroyed or altered. More specifically, open heartedness—that welcome and interest Coleridge felt himself to offer to all comers, all opinions —will inevitably expose itself and admit (precisely because it is so open) what could harm it.

The central thought, whatever else is involved, is plainly the open admission of evil by innocence. This does not mean we explain this puzzling fragment by relapsing into a reference to the Fall of Man. If Geraldine has some of the properties of the serpent, the castle is far from being an Eden, Christabel is no Eve, and there is no Adam at all.

But the idea of the Fall, as so frequently in Coleridge's more serious writing, does exist as a general backdrop. My own guess is that it was originally intended to be a little more than a backdrop, but that personal sympathies and projections, together with limitations of setting and above all the conceptions of the characters, began to conflict with themselves and with Coleridge's need to bring the story into a tolerable cleanliness of outline and get it to the press.

The principal embarrassments were those created by the character of Christabel herself. She was not emerging very clearly. Yet this was to be her story, not Geraldine's. With his usual vicariousness, Coleridge could do more than justice to the complex Geraldine. But his approach to his main character —like himself vulnerable and half-orphaned, benevolent, trustful, and misled—was hopelessly divided. She was to be at once a martyr[1] and at the same time an active participant. The first—the idea of martyrdom—tapped so forceful a well of identification in the writer that it took immediate precedence over the second interest, which was so much more necessary for the narrative. The betrayal of innocent trust and openheartedness was in effect what happened to the albatross, which had come so hospitably to the ship and was then slain. Similarly, this hospitality on the part of the "dove" Christabel is violated. In the second part of the poem, Christabel's father, Sir Leoline, welcomes the new guest, who imposes on his sympathies as she had on those of the daughter, this time by claiming to be the daughter of an old friend of his, Roland de Vaux of Tryermaine, with whom he had quarreled years ago. Here again the thought is that through our virtues—in the case of Christabel's father, the impulse for forgiveness—we become vulnerable.

The story, in short, was exploiting at far greater length one of the things that had personally most appealed to Coleridge when he had begun the "Mariner"—the betrayal of openheartedness. There the demands of the poem—the voyage, the theme of exploration, the need to concentrate on the Mariner himself, Wordsworth's suggestions for the plot, and the stark but helpful fact that even with so unusual a bird one could go only so far without becoming ridiculous—combined to modify this particular form of self-projection, turn it to profit, and hurry him on to other matters. Now, however, the identification with the martyred heart, unhindered from the beginning by external controls, had prematurely, almost self-defensively, solidified into a portrait of such simplicity of virtue, such purity of motive and thought, that he found himself limited to one of two choices, neither of them satisfactory. So passive and restricted a character could be allowed to suffer its martyrdom. But then, as when the albatross was shot, the action would all be one way, with Christabel on the receiving end; and the tale, unless it were to become tedious, would soon be over. The other alternative (unless he began all over again) was to admit into the character of this demure maiden, with her Christ-like name, something other than simple innocence, something that would actually take its own steps, make its own advances. Divided between these alternatives as he quickly wrote the first part of the poem, he moved within a middle ground, sometimes verging toward one side, and sometimes toward the other. He tries to suggest the confinement in which Christabel has lived, and underlines it when he begins the second part by stressing the death-mindedness of her father, who thinks back so obsessively to the loss of his wife when she had given birth to Christabel. There is more than a hint that Christabel, however docile, is naturally restive, understandably receptive to something different. It is presumably without her father's knowledge that she goes at night to the forest to pray. It is she who suggests that Geraldine share her chamber, and who says, even before they enter the castle, that they must move "as if in stealth." The "as if" is merely palliative to her own conscience. She is very much in earnest. The sight of her father's shield on the wall, after they enter, produces only one reaction: "O softly tread, said Christabel, / My father seldom sleepeth well"; and she takes off her shoes in order to move the more quietly.

The effect is not happy. We begin to have the impression of a person who, unless doomed from the start to the role of an automaton, is only too eager to skirt the borderline between security and risk, and, if in danger, is quite capable of subterfuge. This is not at all what was wanted, whatever direction the poem took. If the hope was to dramatize the subtleties of the human will, the inner debates, the tensions and self-betrayals of the open heart that he was trying to understand in himself, we have instead only the portrait of demureness

becoming sly—of the mouse softly advancing to the cheese. In short, the whole problem of finding motives and actions for Christabel (in other than her more spotless moments) had imposed an impossible psychological burden on Coleridge, forcing him as it did to re-examine and then drastically oversimplify his own. At the same time he further confronted the technical embarrassment that, with so simple and specialized a conception of virtue as Christabel typifies, any departure or change in her character will necessarily be a descent or falling off —a disintegration rather than a development. The eye, says Bacon, is more pleased by light emerging from a dark background than by darkness from a light ground ("Judge therefore of the pleasure of the heart by the pleasure of the eye"). And Coleridge, in the critical writing of the years ahead, was to be fond of saying much the same thing.

The whole concept of the poem, then, was too great for the vessel of this quasi-Gothic tale, with its admittedly suggestive atmosphere but with its small roster of characters, two of which—Christabel and her father—proved so limited for further development. That Coleridge could see this readily enough is shown by the extraordinary drop in his momentum when he began on the second part. Throughout the next three years, in fitful returns to the poem, he managed to write as much more as he had already written in a month. It is the piecemeal effect of Part II that makes "Christabel" seem to read, as Harold Bloom says, more like "a series of poems" than a single fragment. A final effort is made before the close to revert to the original theme and introduce more complexity into the character of Christabel. But Coleridge brakes his own effort, and the figure, though it rocks, does not otherwise move. He still cannot permit this simple innocence to depart from itself without the excuse of something like hypnosis. If she has so "drunken in" the look of the serpent-like eyes of Geraldine that her own features take on the same expression, it is still only "passively" that they "imitate / That look of dull and treacherous hate." "Her thoughts are gone." Helplessly a prey to inner conflict, she stands (it is twice repeated) "in dizzy trance." The fragment then stops except for a separate "Conclusion" that Coleridge, after still another year, tacked on to Part II: some lines, prompted by thoughts about his infant son Hartley, on the temptation of the parent, in the very excess of his love, to seek relief by rebuking the child with "words of unmeant bitterness" ("Perhaps 'tis pretty to force together / Thoughts so all unlike each other"). What Coleridge is here freer to express, because he is at last free of the story of Christabel herself and can now advance the suggestion in a gentler, more benevolent context, is the thought of the natural perversity, the uneasy and unpredictable contrasts within the human heart. In the excess of devotion we may begin to recoil, as if in some instinctive need for balance, and to rebuke, perhaps even to profane, what we most cherish. We are certainly expected to read the implication back into the whole fragment as one hint of what was afoot.

Admirers of Coleridge are forgivably unwilling to believe that anything but bad luck and acute personal problems prevented him from finishing "Christabel." But they forget Coleridge's immense fluency when he was confident of what he was doing. There was really nothing to prevent him during these three years (not to mention the next fifteen) from finishing the poem—except for the nature of the poem itself. The truth is that, by the close of the second part, the poem had almost completely disintegrated. Our love of Coleridge—and he was a lovable human being—and our admiration for the range of his genius should not prevent us from acknowledging as much. Naturally he talked about finishing the poem, as he often did about projects of which he was least confident (the "Mariner," he knew, could speak for itself). As with most of his unfinished prose works throughout the next thirty years, he tried to give the impression, to himself as much as to others, that the poem had simply been pushed to the back of the stove, and that, when the opportune moment arrived, more would appear than would ever have been expected. Teased to say how the poem would have ended (for he claimed to have it all in his head), he gave two versions that not only throw little light on the themes of the fragment thus far, but sharply conflict with other later remarks, especially the statement about the martyrdom of St. Teresa being present in his mind as he wrote the poem. Wordsworth, who knew the genesis and history of the poem so well, maintained that Coleridge never had any definite idea for the ending.

Meanwhile, Coleridge learned a great deal from "Christabel," more perhaps than from any other poem he ever wrote. It remained a thorn in his flesh, spurring him to consider and reconsider the dramatic development of character, and above all the need, in even the most vital sympathetic identification, for the poet first to "*eloign* himself" from his subject in order afterwards to return to it "with full effect."

The haunting "Kubla Khan," so unlike anything else in English, was also probably written during these months. Because the exact date is so uncertain, we discuss it last.[2] After it was written it was put aside with a reticence unusual in Coleridge, otherwise so ready to speak of his works. Even in his notebooks, intended for no eye but his own, he did not refer to it. Then, almost twenty years later (1816), when he was desperately trying to justify himself and was drawing on whatever capital he had, he printed it. By that time the habit of apology had become even stronger, and he prefixed to the poem an account stressing that it was being published only "as a psychological curiosity." The story, which may have been embellished for the occasion, has become part of the legendry of English literature:

> In the summer of the year 1797, the Author, then in ill health, had retired to a lonely farmhouse between Porlock and Linton, on the Exmoor confines of Somerset and Devonshire. In consequence of a slight indisposition, an anodyne had been prescribed, from the effects of which he fell asleep in his chair at the moment that he was reading the following sentence, or words of the same substance, in "Purchas's Pilgrimage": "Here the Khan Kubla commanded a palace to be built, and a stately garden thereunto. And thus ten miles of fertile ground were inclosed with a wall." The Author continued for about three hours in a profound sleep, at least of the external senses, during which time he has the most vivid confidence, that he could not have composed less than from two to three hundred lines.

Waking, he at once wrote down the present fifty-four lines of the poem but was suddenly interrupted by "a person on business from Porlock, and detained by him above an hour." When he returned to the poem, Coleridge found all memory of it fled except for the "general purport" and "eight or ten scattered lines and images."

The "general purport" was never divulged or even hinted at. It is more than possible that what we have is all there was to it. Certainly without

Coleridge's note, written so long afterwards, few readers would think "Kubla Khan" a fragment. In its self-sufficiency it differs from all of Coleridge's other poems that we actually know to be fragments. Moreover, how could Coleridge have been carrying with him, on his long walk from Nether Stowey, the huge folio of Purchas? He was certainly not likely to find it in the lonely farmhouse. More probably, he was simply remembering the words he mentions. He wanted the reader, however, to think that the subject had not been much in his mind (for the claim expressed in the poem violated almost every taboo he had about self-assertion) but only accidentally suggested by something he was reading. As for the man on business from Porlock: why should he be seeking out Coleridge, who had so few business dealings, and how, even so, would he have known that Coleridge, who had been seeking seclusion, was staying at this particular place? Indeed, there is no mention of either Purchas or the man from Porlock in the only earlier statement we have, attached to a holograph manuscript of the poem—a statement briefer but more circumstantial (from it we can also infer one of the two possible places where he wrote "Kubla Khan").[3] The poem, he says, was

> composed in a sort of Reverie brought on by two grains of Opium, taken to check a dysentery, at a Farm House between Porlock & Linton, a quarter of a mile from Culbone Church, in the fall of the year, 1797.

The "profound sleep" mentioned in the published account (as contrasted with this mere "Reverie," from a very light dose of opium) had two advantages. It would suggest that he was far from habituated to the drug, that a little of it would go a long way. Moreover, to admit that he was only in a sort of revery was also to admit that the conscious mind was working, that he was at least partly aware of what he was saying. This was not something he at all wished to do: this claim that he —Coleridge himself—might in poetry rival (might even have daydreamed of rivalling) the architectural splendor of an oriental monarch. Least of all could this be permitted to be his thought now, in 1816, after he had long abandoned poetry and was trying, from the wreckage of his life, to begin a very different career.

A note should also be added about the richness of Coleridge's reading distilled in the poem. As in

the "Ancient Mariner," and much of "Christabel," the gates of inhibition that Schiller said the self-conscious modern poet is forced to storm were lifted or bypassed. Lowes, in *The Road to Xanadu*, traces most of the relevant reading—Purchas, of course, James Bruce's *Travels to Discover the Source of the Nile*, Thomas Maurice's *History of Hindostan*, and William Bartram's *Travels through North & South Carolina*, together with Herodotus, Strabo, Seneca, *Paradise Lost*, and Burnet's *Sacred Theory of the Earth*. Since the pioneer work of Lowes, the list has been extended. But the pickings among possible verbal parallels tend now to be rather slight. In any case we are still left with the central problems of form and meaning, or, in Coleridgean terms, of form through meaning and meaning through form. Also of interest and stressed by Wylie Sypher is the landscape immediately above Culbone Church—probably the smallest parish church in England. Coming from the east, as Coleridge did from Nether Stowey, one suddenly encounters the long slope, some of it covered with cedar, that slants from a hill into a deep valley; and there are frequent glimpses of the sea. Descending from the area to Culbone Church is one of the steepest ravines in this part of England—heavily forested, rocky, and cavernous.

With none of Coleridge's major poems is less gained by avoiding the obvious. Even a surface interpretation of the "Ancient Mariner"—not to mention "Christabel"—faces difficulties. But in "Kubla Khan" the simplest and most direct interpretation is not only permitted but almost compelled by the poem. If we accept it, we find it immediately capable of further development. If we overlook or forget it, we are left with a more static conception of the poem. And it is very easy to overlook if we are too eager to elucidate some special part or aspect of the poem, or to apply something extraneous about Coleridge's medical or psychological history.

Whether the poem was really an introduction to something else or whether Coleridge had said about all he had to say, "Kubla Khan" falls into a simple, twofold division that was to prove congenial to the greater Romantic lyric, especially some of the odes of Shelley and Keats. To begin with, there is the "odal hymn," which postulates a challenge, ideal, or prototype that the poet hopes to reach or transcend. The second part, proceeding from that challenge, consists of one of those concluding "credos," those personal expressions of hope or ambition, that were to become more common in the later Romantic period (particularly associated with such poems as Shelley's "Ode to the West Wind" or Keats's "Ode to Psyche"). Here, in "Kubla Khan," the poet hopes to match in another way—even exceed, with something more lasting—what the princes of the earth have been able to perform.

The theme, in short, as so often in the Romantic lyrics that take this form, is the hope and precarious achievement of the human imagination itself. The universality of the poem evaporates if we concentrate too myopically on Kubla himself. He has been interpreted as everything from a remorseless Tartar despot (which may enter somewhat into the picture) to a symbol of God himself, whom the poet would hope to emulate in his own way. But Kubla, as Humphrey House said, is really "representative man." Moreover, whatever else can be said of him, this princely prototype of the human imagination is sharply dissociated from the religious and sacramental. Any association of the great religious domes of Christianity—of Byzantium and St. Peter's—is aesthetic, relevant only because of magnitude and splendor. (We need not linger with the more desperate equations of the dome with the maternal breast.) The religious censor in Coleridge, even at this stage of his life, is as strong as it was in Johnson. Harold Bloom rightly emphasizes that it encourages him to select a "remote dome in Xanadu," and thus avoid "the issue of the poet's relative sanctity against more than natural verities." A "religious" dome as an image of what the poet hopes to emulate or transcend would be out of the question: the claim is more modest. The need, in fact, is for what we now call "distance"—an image of power and magnificence sharply removed from the religious.[4] Moreover, whatever its splendor, and the apparent reconciliation of opposites that always intrigued Coleridge, precariousness is of the essence of this "sunny pleasure-dome with caves of ice."

Kubla, in other words, is man as he in general would be (including what we can only call the poet in man) placed in an enviable position of power in which he now seems able to gratify his vision—able imperially, if briefly, to "decree" a magnificence, a union or synthesis, to which the human heart aspires. The imagination hopes to keep its paradise secure, and Kubla "girdles" his around

with "walls and towers." The whole conception of Kubla is in the vein of those oriental allegories (themselves an elaboration of Ecclesiastes) in which the monarch is Everyman, but Everyman given what appears to be every opportunity to fulfill his dream. There is even something of a parallel (though in the "decree" of Kubla Khan the years have been melted down into moments) with Johnson's brooding passage in *Rasselas* on Cheops, the builder of the Great Pyramid, in which this "mighty structure"—the product of "that hunger of imagination which preys incessantly upon life"—is seen as a protest of will and hope against the "insufficiency of human enjoyments." A closer parallel is with Johnson's allegory of Seged, Emperor of Ethiopia (in the *Rambler*, Nos. 204 and 205). Seged ("the monarch of forty nations, the distributor of the waters of the Nile"), who has now ensured peace throughout his domain, resolves to retreat for ten short days to a place from which all trouble will be excluded. There, where "the sun played upon the water" and the grounds are interspersed with gardens, thick groves, and "bubbling fountains," Seged commands a great "house of pleasure, built in an island in the lake Dambea, to be prepared for his reception." But in this house of pleasure, where he hopes to be shut off from "tumult and care," his dreams are troubled by the thought of "deluge and invasion" in his dominions. So with Kubla, who has hoped to withdraw into a lasting present, from which both the ills of the past and the expectations for the future are excluded. But they cannot be excluded. They return in fact together—the past forecasting the future:

> And 'mid this tumult Kubla heard from far
> Ancestral voices prophesying war!

The point, of course, is that in the very commitment of the imagination to its dream, the closed paradise for which it has hoped proves incomplete and ultimately threatened—all the more since Kubla, like Lycius in Keats's "Lamia," seeks to impose his paradise directly into the midst of life and at the same time incorporate life within it. For this is no simple stream docile to the human will on the bank of which Kubla builds his "stately pleasure-dome" and which he boldly thinks to enclose within his grounds. Significantly there was no river in Purchas's account of Xanadu. This was Coleridge's own addition to the landscape of the poem. For at least a couple of years he had been thinking, indeed taking notes and "often moulding my thoughts into verse," of that long philosophical poem, "The Brook," in which he would treat the stream as an extended symbol of life "from its source in the hills" to its final disappearance into the sea. The association of river and life, which he felt no need to avoid as too conventional, had always attracted him.[5] But now, as contrasted with his earlier associations with the symbol, and this would include his prose account of "The Brook," the more placid ones, so congenial to his pliable nature, are condensed into the image of that short ten miles ("meandering in a mazy motion") in which, like Hogarth's famous serpentine or winding "line of beauty," the flow of the stream only appears to be amenable to human uses and aspirations. The real emphasis is on the mystery of the before and after of that deceptive ten miles—the "before" and "after" that Kubla had hoped to exclude: the creative violence of birth and creation, and the mystery of finality with which it sinks into a "sunless sea." Back in his poem "Religious Musings," he had spoken of "the immeasurable fount / Ebullient with creative deity." He had since been struck by a German poem, written by Count F. L. Stolberg, which he translated ("On a Cataract"). The cataract leaps, with "unperishing youth" from its chasms, "ceaseless renewing," "born in a *holy twilight,*" and then descends

> the cliff inaccessible;—
> Thou at once full-born
> Maddenest in thy joyance,
> Whirlest, shatter'st, splitt'st,
> Life invulnerable.

So, in "Kubla Khan," we have the "deep romantic chasm," at once "savage" and yet "holy" as are birth and creation themselves ("A savage place! as holy and enchanted / As e'er beneath a waning moon was haunted / By woman wailing for her demon lover"). From it emerge the "ceaseless" toil of the river, the fountains, the tossing fragments of rocks:

> And from this chasm, with ceaseless turmoil
>   seething,
> As if this earth in fast thick pants were
>   breathing,
> A mighty fountain momently was forced;
> Amid whose swift half-intermitted burst
> Huge fragments vaulted like rebounding hail,
> Or chaffy grain beneath the thresher's flail.

The end of the river, after the ten miles that Kubla tries to enclose, is equally mysterious as it reaches "caverns measureless to man" and then sinks "in tumult to a lifeless ocean." Despite his hope to control and "girdle round" even a part of this, Kubla hears simultaneously (a "mingled measure") the "tumult" of what came before and more ominously of what is to come. Meanwhile only "the *shadow* of the dome of pleasure" floats "midway on the waves" of the passing river. No other impression on the river, no other control of it, is achieved than the shadow cast by this dome, this "miracle of rare device."

The "credo" then follows. The principal interest is that it is so diffident. The *premise* is bold enough: the poet who will also "build that dome in air" will be like that other inspired orphan and singer, Amphion, who, abandoned as a child and left exposed with his brother on Mount Cithaeron, later proved able—as was no prince or architect—to build the great walls of Thebes with his music. He also echoes the Renaissance theme familiarly associated with Shakespeare's sonnets: "Not marble, nor the gilded monuments / Of princes shall outlive this powerful rhyme . . ." But Coleridge brings in his "credo" only vicariously, through the little five-line vignette of the Abyssinian maid:

> A damsel with a dulcimer
> In a vision once I saw:
> It was an Abyssinian maid,
> And on her dulcimer she played,
> Singing of Mount Abora.
> Could I revive within me
> Her symphony and song,
> To such a deep delight 'twould win me,
> That with music loud and long,
> I would build that dome in air . . .

We should resist the temptation to distract ourselves, at this point, by speculations of the crudely biographical sort at which Coleridge himself always laughed (e.g., the Abyssinian maid is Sara Hutchinson, Wordsworth's sister-in-law, while the "woman wailing for her demon lover" is Coleridge's wife). As Coleridge said of the word "stimulus" in medicine, this sort of speculation at most enables us to talk around a subject while giving us a delusive feeling that we are making some sort of headway. The real point of interest is the sudden modesty and indirectness of the Amphion-claim to build something more lasting though "in air." The music that will do so will come from him—if it comes at all—because he has heard the song of another ("in vision *once*"). And why an "Abyssinian maid"? Because, as the first version of the poem said, she was really singing of Mount *Amara*, which is actually in Abyssinia, that alternative seat of Paradise cited by Milton in Book IV of *Paradise Lost* ("Mount *Amara*, though this by some supposed / True Paradise under the Ethiop Line, / By Nilus head..."). Coleridge's own religious censor had naturally demanded that the song of paradise that he heard—the song the poet is inspired to emulate —should not be a song of the true Eden, just as it had demanded that Kubla's dome be secular, however splendid. But "Mount Amara," while resolving this difficulty, introduced another. To the devout it suggested a "*false* paradise," and however modestly he was hedging his credo, he was not saying that he wanted to draw his inspiration from an admittedly "false" paradise. Worse still, "Mount Amara" could suggest that the author was thinking of an "alternative" paradise, almost as good, perhaps better, at least for the purposes of art. The change to "Mount *Abora*" disposed of the problem.

What was Coleridge to do with this boastful assertion? For assertion it was, if not of deliberate intention, at least of unconscious desire. However muted and indirect the "credo," the self-involved challenge was there for himself and others to see (the poet reviving the "dome in air," while those that hear him close their eyes "in holy dread"). What greater contrast with the apologetic, deliberately relaxed mode of poetry in which he habitually walked? Here, in fact, the "Abyssinian maid," conceived as a vicarious, indirect contact with the source of inspiration, suddenly usurped his own habitual role. It was she who was serving as usher —and to the poet himself. One thinks ahead to the long-promised chapter in the *Biographia Literaria* (on the Imagination "or Esemplastic Power"), where he has been introducing himself in another way. Then, when the moment comes, he substitutes a long letter, ostensibly from another person, telling himself to wait: this is not the proper time.

The poem was put aside. It could so easily be misinterpreted as an expression of the writer's own hope. Of course it was not that! It was simply a fanciful embroidery of something he had read—in fact (as he implied in his account so many years later) a fanciful development of something he had been actually reading at that very moment—*Purchas his Pilgrimage* (that weighty folio which had somehow found its way to this lonely farmhouse). The years passed, including the terrible period from 1801 to 1816, until he was forty-four. Timidly, as he tried to get some practical use out of what he had written earlier, he escorted it, as he was to escort so much by that time, with a cloud of apology. He had been urged to publish it at the request "of a poet of great and deserved celebrity," Lord Byron, now at the height of his fame. Coleridge himself had finally agreed to publish it, but "rather as a psychological curiosity, than on the ground of any supposed *poetic* merits."

NOTES

1. "The story of the Christabel," he told James Gillman, "is partly founded on the notion, that the virtuous of this world save the wicked" (*Life of S. T. Coleridge*, [1838]. I, 283). The thought is extended in a remark to Thomas Allsop: Crashaw's lines on St. Teresa ("Since 'tis not to be had at home, / She'll travel to a martyrdome. / No home for her confesses she, / But where she may a martyr be") "were ever present to my mind whilst writing the second part of *Christabel;* if, indeed, by some subtle process of mind they did not suggest the first thought of the whole poem" (Allsop, *Letters, Conversations, and Recollections of S. T. Coleridge* [1836], II. 195–196).

2. Coleridge, in his preface, states it was written in the summer of 1797. An earlier, probably more accurate account gives the date as "the fall of the year," 1797. A third statement (not about the poem but about the retirement to the farmhouse near Linton) suggests May, 1798 (ably argued by Lawrence Hanson, *Coleridge: The Early Years* [1962], pp. 259–60). The date is exhaustively discussed by Elizabeth Schneider, *Coleridge, Opium, and Kubla Khan* (1953), pp. 153–237, and extended, not quite convincingly, to October, 1799, or the following spring.

3. One would be Ash Farm (still standing), exactly a quarter of a mile above Culbone Church. But about thirty years after the poem was written, Coleridge told his nephew he wrote it at a place he picturesquely remembered as "Brimstone Farm"

(actually "Broomstreet Farm," two miles from Culbone Church). The specific statement of the earlier account ("a quarter of a mile from Culbone Church") has more of a ring of probability. Names could more easily be confused by Coleridge, especially after several years. There is no reason why the simple "Ash Farm" should have remained permanently engraved on his memory, or even much noticed at the time, whereas the more unusual name of its neighbor, even if heard casually, could have caught his notice and as the years passed become associated with the incident.

4. If anything the dome partly represents those intermediate, less spiritualized attempts of the aspiring mind mentioned by Coleridge in "Religious Musings" (11. 201–210) to raise itself from the primitive through refinement and splendor—that

intermediate stage of development in which the imagination begins to "conjure up" a "host of new desires," leading to the arts of luxury ("the soft couch, and many-coloured robe, / The timbrel and *arched dome*"), but in the process stimulating "the inventive arts" that, by degrees, "unsensualized the mind."

5. So in the little poem, "Life," written when he was seventeen, the central image is his native river, the Otter ("May this . . . my course through Life portray"). Again, in the Latin ode he translated at Jesus College ("A Wish, Written in Jesus Wood"): he thinks of the course of his own "Life's little day" as he fancies this stream *meandering* round its native fields," through vales and "green retreats," until it finally "downward flowing with awaken'd speed / Embosoms in the Deep."

Leslie Marchand

BYRON IN THE TWENTIETH CENTURY*

Does Byron's poetry have any significant value for us today? The answer depends largely on the depth and catholicity of our concepts of poetry. Poetry can be many things. If we see value in only one kind (as critics have tended to do in every age), we will naturally denigrate all that does not conform to our current taste. If we demand "high seriousness" in poetry, which in Matthew Arnold's use of the term meant a particular moral slant, we will speak disparagingly of Dryden and Pope as poets of "an age of prose and reason"; we will find Chaucer and Burns "poetically unsound" because they lack "the accent of high seriousness." If we demand, as many twentieth century critics do, that poetry embody irony and ambiguity and paradox in a complex and intricate structure of words weighted with symbolic meaning, we shall give short shift to most other kinds of poetry, and particularly to the

work of those poets who, like Byron, seem, in T. S. Eliot's phrase, to have an "imperceptiveness" to words, to be making "sonorous affirmations of the commonplace." [1]

But if we start with a broad definition of poetry as a something plus, a heightened realization of some idea, mood, or meaningful moment, and not something concentrated and distilled according to a single formula, then Byron's best poetry, at least, has merits which can be appreciated by the most fastidious and sophisticated. Such an approach can clear the way for a better understanding and a fairer estimate of the work of a poet whose "sincerity and strength" have impressed critics from Goethe and Matthew Arnold to Eliot himself.

Among his merits are two which are particularly Byronic. By sheer genius he could make a statement of the commonplace ricochet past the platitude and lodge memorably in the mind, leaving reverberating harmonies of sound and sense. This is a virtue to be found in some stanzas of *Childe Harold* (Eliot notwithstanding) and in some of his tales and shorter lyrics, as well as in his satires. A second and greater

*From Chapter 1 of *Byron's Poetry: A Critical Introduction, Riverside Studies in Literature Edition,* by Leslie A. Marchand. Copyright © 1965 by Houghton Mifflin Company. Reprinted by permission.

merit is his facetious revelation of truths that are too threatening to the self-defensive ego to be presented without a comic mask. Byron was often most serious when he was most waggish. Mockery was the cover for intellectual and emotional honesty in a period solemnly tenacious of its own cant and complacent in its own certainties. When in his self-exile Byron achieved a kind of beyond-the-tomb freedom to speak his mind about all things, he found his true voice in *Don Juan*.

Byron had a sufficient contempt for "system," whether in criticism or poetry. After reading Leigh Hunt's manuscript of *Rimini*, he wrote Moore, "I told him that I deemed it good poetry at bottom, disfigured only by a strange style. His answer was, that his style was a system, or *upon system*, or some such cant; and, when a man talks of system, his case is hopeless." [2] Like most of the Romantics who indulged in the "spontaneous overflow of powerful feelings," Byron wrote many "unpremeditated" and uncorrected poems that cannot be defended. He apologized for them by saying: "I can never *recast* any thing. I am like the Tiger: if I miss the first spring, I go growling back to my jungle again; but if I do *hit*, it is crushing." [3]

For the most part one need not look for verbal subtleties in Byron. His irony is likely to be a brickbat, but hurled with such skill and force that when it does hit, it crushes. Writing to Murray after receiving a plea from his publisher to avoid "approximations to indelicacy" in *Don Juan*, Byron said: ". . . this reminds me of George Lamb's quarrel and Cambridge with Scrope Davies. 'Sir,' said George, 'he *hinted* at my *illegitimacy*.' 'Yes,' said Scrope, 'I called him a damned adulterous bastard'; the approximation and the hint are not unlike." [4]

One of the supposed weaknesses of Byron as a thinker which has lessened his stature among modern critics is his inability, or unwillingness, to adopt a fixed philosophy or permanent point of view. It is the same accusation that was made by Goethe and echoed by Arnold: "The moment he reflects, he is a child." But it may be that that very fact has given him a perennial freshness which makes him more congenial to the twentieth century than those of his contemporaries who adopted a "system" that can no longer answer the questions we perpetually ask about human life and destiny. If Coleridge may be thought a more profound philosopher, it is not because of the acceptance of absolutes and dogmas that made him an apologist for the contemporary orthodoxy in religion and politics. His reputation as a thinker rests rather on those "seminal" thoughts of his journals and conversations that penetrated to individual truths truths which might have been disquieting to the systems he supported had his rationalizations been less persuasive.

It is probable that the mind that inquires and questions has always expanded philosophic as well as scientific knowledge more than the mind that affirms and accepts. In an era when blood transfusion is as universal a remedy as blood-letting was when Byron died at Missolonghi, it is easy to sympathize with the instinctive skepticism which made him resist the application of leeches. The symbolic significance should not escape us when we consider his skepticism of no less tenaciously held beliefs in other spheres.

In any reassessment of Byron's value to us as a thinker we can do no better than to repeat Professor Fairchild's statement: ". . . one may justly be irritated by the common assumption that a man who refrains from believing in lofty and inspiring ideas for which there is no evidence whatever necessarily has an inferior mind. Although no one would undertake to prove that Byron was a profound thinker, he possessed a quality which many supposedly profound thinkers lack—a sense of the toughness of facts and an inability to dupe himself about them. . . . Beneath all his protective histrionism, his mind possessed a certain desperate integrity which should command respect." [5]

The quality which Lady Blessington and others among his contemporaries saw as a weakness was Byron's real strength: that sensitive response to the impression of the moment without regard to any "system" or principle of unity or consistency. Byron defined the term "mobility" as "an excessive susceptibility of immediate impressions—at the same time without *losing* the past." [6] As his "versified Aurora Borealis . . . flashes o'er a waste and icy clime," he throws the cold light of truth on human smugness. He has been accused, he says of

A tendency to under-rate and scoff
    At human power and virtue, and all that.

But, he replies,

I say no more than hath been said in Dante's
Verse, and by Solomon and by Cervantes;

By Swift, by Machiavel, by Rochefoucault,
  By Fénélon, by Luther, and by Plato;
By Tillotson, and Wesley, and Rousseau,
  Who knew this life was not worth a potato.

     *   *   *   *   *   *   *   *   *

Newton (that proverb of the mind), alas!
  Declared, with all his grand discoveries
    recent,
That he himself felt only "like a youth
Picking up shells by the great ocean—Truth."
              (*Don Juan*, VII, 3–5)

In another digression he gives his answer to those
who are "hot for certainties":

'T is true we speculate both far and wide,
  And deem, because we *see*, we are *all-
    seeing:* . . .

"*Que scais-je?*" was the motto of Montaigne,
  As also of the first academicians:
That all is dubious which man may attain,
  Was one of their most favourite positions.
There's no such thing as certainty, that's plain
  As any of Mortality's conditions. . . .
            (*Don Juan*, IX, 16–17)

In his disinclination to claim a truth he did not
possess, and in his skepticism of absolutes, Byron
finds a more sympathetic audience in the twentieth
century than he found in the nineteenth. He gives
voice to an era that is confused by the increase of
knowledge and that no longer has confidence in
intellectual leaders who seek easy answers. Byron
had the strength to resist the demand for adherence
to some creed, for acceptance of some simple and
final interpretation of the only partly understood
universe. He was aware that to keep an open mind
on all subjects required courage.

The consequence is, being of no party,
  I shall offend all parties. . . .
            (*Don Juan*, IX, 26)

Keats complained of his friend Dilke—he was
nearer to Byron here than either realized—that he
was a man "who cannot feel he has a personal
identity unless he has made up his mind about
everything." That "Negative Capability" which
Keats so admired in Shakespeare he might also have
seen in Byron had he been able to look under
the latter's flippant manner—"that is, when a man
is capable of being in uncertainties, mysteries,
doubts, without any irritable reaching after fact
and reason."

It is easy to see why Byron has frequently been
called a romantic paradox. The polarities of his life,
opinions, and poetic productions are apparent
enough. He was a Deist and free-thinker haunted
by a Calvinistic sense of original sin. He espoused
the cause of oppressed peoples in every land and
yet was always conscious of his noble ancestry and
sometimes displayed a childish aristocratic pride.
He liked to think of himself as a Regency Dandy
and yet he was sincere in admiration of Shelley's
simplicity and unaffected manners. Occasionally
with strangers, but seldom with his friends, he
struck an attitude, though at bottom he had a
"desperate integrity" and a disarming self-honesty.
He was a leader of the Romantic revolution in
poetry who clung to the literary ideals of Alexander
Pope. He was a worshipper of the ideal whose
leanings toward realism kept his feet on the
ground.

But rightly seen, what appear to be contradictions are in the main only two sides of the same
coin. The central problem for Byron, as for most
of the Romantics, was to find a satisfying compromise between the demands of the real and the
ideal. But with the strong strain of eighteenth century common sense in his nature, Byron's attitude
toward the problem was different from that of most
other Romantics.

There· are several possible attitudes. One may
deny that there is any disparity between the real
and the ideal, either (a) by saying that the real
is ideal (and then he is not a Romantic at all but
has taken the so-called common sense view of Pope
and the eighteenth century adherents of the "chain
of being" philosophy, that seeming imperfections
are only a part of the plan, that "all that is, is
right"); or (b) by saying that the ideal is real, the
only reality, and that the world of sense is only an
appearance, an illusion through which the man of
perception (let us say the poet) must penetrate in
order to get a view of ultimate reality. This latter
alternative is the one chosen by all the idealists
from Plato to the present. With variations as to the
means of perceiving ideal reality, this was the solution to which many of the nineteenth century
poets (the so-called transcendental group) turned:
Wordsworth, Coleridge, Shelley. Some of them
were uneasy in that point of view, and like Wordsworth felt as they grew older that they could only
fitfully command the power to see the ideal vision
and so asked themselves:

Whither is fled the visionary gleam?
Where is it now, the glory and the dream?

This brought on a temporary melancholy, but their "will to believe" was too strong to permit them to rest there.

A second way of viewing the disparity between the real and the ideal is to see the gap as essentially unbridgeable: to come face to face with the necessity of dealing with the real world as real and ideal world as ideal, as a creation of the mind. Within this possibility are two kinds and many degrees of attitudes: (a) One may be sensible (or insensitive, if you choose to call it so) enough to accept the separation of reality and ideality and feel no particular urge to bridge the gap between them. Such a person is not a Romantic but more nearly what we would call a realist. Or (b) one may be so constituted as to long for the ideal with an uncompromising zeal, and may be consequently disappointed and unhappy because the real fails to measure up to it, yet be too clear-sighted to confuse the two. He may then vary his mental occupations between a dwelling upon the ideal, which is his only true love, and a melancholy or a bitterly mocking reflection upon how disgustingly short of the ideal the real is and must always be. In this last description of an attitude we come as near as can any generalization to fixing the place of Byron among the Romantics. Of course Byron seemed at times to be admiring the classical (or neo-classical) acceptance of the world as it is. But because he was a child of his age, and could not detach himself sufficiently from the romantic longing for what the world does not give, he could seldom achieve the Augustan calm he admired in his idol Pope.

In one mood, that which permeates *Childe Harold*, he displays the melancholy and despair which accompany the recognition of the failure of the real to match the ideal. In another, he presents the comedy, sometimes bitter, sometimes roguishly facetious, of the disparity between real and ideal. With a keen delight he tears away the mask of sentimentalism, of hypocritical self-deception, of mock-ideality, of wishful thinking, and shows the plain or ugly face of reality. This is the mood that dominates much, but by no means all, of *Don Juan*.

We have the feeling now that the satiric Byron found himself, for it is this aspect of his work that most appeals to us. The melancholy Byron belongs more to his own time, though he too may voice a modern (and universal) *Weltschmerz*. But both moods pervade *Don Juan* and alternate in Byron's poetry throughout his career. Professor Fairchild has phrased it most aptly: "Aspiration, melancholy, mockery—the history of a mind too idealistic to refrain from blowing bubbles, and too realistic to refrain from pricking them." [7]

It is a common supposition that Byron began his career as a melancholy Childe Harold, a gloomy egoist, a Conrad (*The Corsair*) brooding over his "one virtue and a thousand crimes." Some biographers have pictured him standing on the sidelines at one of the London balls in his years of fame, wrapped in somber disillusionment and despair, "the wandering outlaw of his own dark mind." But it is just as likely that his curled lip of scorn indicated that he was about to voice a facetious witticism more appropriate to *Don Juan* than to *Childe Harold*. Judging not only from his letters and the record of his conversations at the time but also from some of the poems he wrote early in his career, the satiric, realistic, mocking vein was strong in Byron from his Cambridge days, or before, until the end of his life. It only tended to be suppressed in his poetry after the success of the first two cantos of *Childe Harold* had fixed the pattern of his poetic production, and the flattering public demand for his tales of "pleasing woe" made it difficult for him to shatter the image of himself he had created. [8]

Though he had written some facetious and realistic (or cynical) verses before he ended his residence at Cambridge, only a very few were ventured upon the public, and those only in the privately printed volume *Fugitive Pieces*, intended to be circulated among friends. After that volume was suppressed and all but four copies destroyed because his parson friend John Becher objected that one of the poems ("To Mary") was "rather too warmly drawn," Byron retained only the more romantic, and less original, verses in his subsequent volumes. Many of the moods of *Childe Harold* appeared in *Hours of Idleness*, but no hint was given that the author possessed even at that time much of the mischievous good humor that later found expression in *Beppo*. Perhaps the *Edinburgh Review* critic would have been kinder to *Hours of Idleness* if its mawkishness had been leavened by the lively satire on sentimentalism from *Fugitive Pieces*: "To a Lady Who Presented to the Author a Lock of Hair Braided with His Own, and Appointed a Night in

December to Meet Him in the Garden." Some of the lines suggest the mood if not the maturity of *Don Juan*.

> Why should you weep, like *Lydia Languish*,
> And fret with self-created anguish?
> Or doom the lover you have chosen,
> On winter nights to sigh half frozen. . . .

Byron's next attempt, stimulated rather than initiated by the attack in the *Edinburgh*, was a Popean satire begun at Cambridge under the influence of his friend Hobhouse and encouraged by Francis Hodgson, a translator of Juvenal. *English Bards, and Scotch Reviewers* owes something to the Roman satirist, but more to Pope and Gifford. Byron had read and admired Pope at Harrow, as most schoolboys who had any interest in poetry did at the time. But his immediate model was William Gifford, whose clever satires in the *Anti-Jacobin* and in *The Maeviad* and *The Baviad* roused Byron to emulation and to admiration scarcely this side idolatry. He would now try a *Dunciad* of his own: "The cry is up, and scribblers are my game."

Having made a success in this genre, imitative though it was, Byron henceforth felt that this was his forte. It was a style that was generally respected by those he most respected, and it did not bring ridicule on him but praise and admiration, even from some whom his barbs had stung. It was small wonder then that he tried to follow up his success by writing, while he was in Greece, *Hints from Horace* and that whenever he felt the urge to satiric expression he turned to the Popean couplet even when the subject and treatment were far from Pope.

Byron continued throughout his life to have a dual concept of poetry. On the one hand was the poetry of serious moral purpose (as he conceived Pope's to be). This was a poetry that would castigate the errors of the age with stringent wit, would point out deviations from good sense and good taste in brilliant balanced couplets, and would attack the corruptions and injustices in society with Juvenalian fierceness modified by Popean good temper.[9] It was the goal Byron had aimed at in *English Bards, and Scotch Reviewers*. It is significant that he set himself the task in that poem, beyond judging the little wits and poetasters of the day, of bringing "the force of wit" to bear on "Vice" and "Folly" as well as on literary lapses. It is signif-

icant too that he admired most the virtues of his models that he felt he could not achieve: the objectivity and the verbal skill that the very nature of his own character and genius made it most difficult for him to attain.

In the middle of his career, after he had finished the fourth canto of *Childe Harold* and thought it his best, he wrote to Murray: "With regard to poetry in general, I am convinced, the more I think of it, that . . . *all* of us—Scott, Southey, Wordsworth, Moore, Campbell, I,—are all in the wrong, one as much as another; that we are upon a wrong revolutionary poetical system, or systems, not worth a damn in itself, and from which none but Rogers and Crabbe are free; and that the present and next generations will finally be of this opinion. I am the more confirmed in this by having lately gone over some of our classics, particularly *Pope*, whom I tried in this way,—I took Moore's poems and my own and some others, and went over them side by side with Pope's, and I was really astonished (I ought not to have been so) and mortified at the ineffable distance in point of sense, harmony, effect, and even *Imagination*, passion, and *Invention*, between the little Queen Anne's man, and us of the Lower Empire. Depend upon it, it is all Horace then, and Claudian now, among us; and if I had to begin again, I would model myself accordingly." [10]

The other concept of poetry that guided Byron's literary performance was the subjective Romantic one born of the impulse to "look in your heart and write." He adopted it perforce, impelled by both his temperament and his environment, but he continued to consider it second best and to speak disparagingly of it, as he did in the letter just quoted. Having a conviction of the lesser nature of the art he was practicing, he found a certain satisfaction in deprecating poetry in general: "If one's years can't be better employed than in sweating poesy, a man had better be a ditcher." [11] It is characteristic of Byron that he could not compromise with his concept of the ideal in writing. He would live in the world, but he would not bend his mind to call its imperfections ideal, even when it concerned his own performance. "If I live ten years longer," he told Moore, "you will see, however, that it is not over with me—I don't mean in literature, for that is nothing; and it may seem odd enough to say, I do not think it my vocation." [12] As late as 1821, when he had found in *Don Juan* a literary style that suited his genius far better than any imitation of Gifford or Pope, he wrote to Moore after the failure of the Neapolitan uprising had blighted his hopes for a similar revolt in the Romagna in which he could take an active part: "And now let us be literary;—a sad falling off, but it is always a consolation. If 'Othello's occupation be gone,' let us take to the next best; and, if we cannot contribute to make mankind more free and wise, we may amuse ourselves and those who like it. . . . I have been scribbling at intervals. . . ." [13]

Even before he had fully accepted his own limitations, Byron found an outlet for his energies and his feelings in poetry of the Romantic category. "All convulsions end with me in Rhyme," [14] he wrote Moore in 1813. And again he spoke of poetry as "the lava of the imagination whose eruption prevents an earthquake." [15] His reluctance to publish *Childe Harold* was motivated as much by his anxiety that it would damage his claim as an Augustan wit, which he felt he had already staked out in *English Bards, and Scotch Reviewers,* as by his fear of revealing secrets of his private life and feelings. It would be an acknowledgment that he had enrolled himself in the camp of the Romantics who regarded poetry as nothing more than the safety valve of the emotions.

But the acclaim that greeted *Childe Harold,* together with the circumstances that led to the suppression of *English Bards* and the withdrawal of the manuscript of *Hints from Horace,* caused Byron to accept his role as a Romantic poet without ever giving up his conviction that the only ideal of poetry to which he could give full critical allegiance was that of the school of Pope. Swept along, however, by his phenomenal success in what he considered this lesser genre at a time when, frustrated in his ambition to be a political orator and statesman by the strait jacket of Whig politics, and pressed by the need for emotional relief for the impasses created by his fame and his passions, he succumbed to the poetry of self-expression as other men might to drugs or drink. But still he was from time to time stricken with remorse for having given up the ideal of poetic practice. Henceforth, except in these moments of critical contrition, he thought and spoke of poetry as a simple "lava of the imagination." While he was composing *The Bride of Abydos* he wrote Lady Melbourne: ". . . my mind has been from *late* and *later* events in such a state

of fermentation, that as usual I have been obliged to empty it in rhyme, and am in the very heart of another Eastern tale." [16]

Most of what Byron wrote henceforth grew directly or indirectly out of his personal need for emotional release, and through practice of this "inferior" art he became adept in voicing the pangs not only of himself but of his generation. Like "wild Rousseau" he "threw / Enchantment over passion, and from woe / Wrung overwhelming eloquence." In *Childe Harold,* in the Oriental and other tales, and also in shorter lyrics and in pieces with supposedly more objective themes like "The Prisoner of Chillon," personal catharsis of turbulent moods was the dominant motive for composition.[17] Likewise in his speculative dramas, *Manfred, Cain, Heaven and Earth,* and *The Deformed Transformed,* the driving force is always the poet's desire to work out a solution to his own deepest quandaries. And it might be said that whatever merit these poetic dramas have lies in the depth and sincerity of the personal revelation rather than in any resolution of a philosophical problem.

Fidelity to the mood of the moment was Byron's forte, and failure to acknowledge this has befuddled Byron criticism from the time the poems were published until the present day. There has been a persistent refusal to accept Byron's own frankest statements, and to recognize that honesty and self-honesty were almost an obsession with him. Somerset Maugham once wrote a story of a man who got a tremendous reputation for being a humorist merely by telling the simple truth about himself and others. So Byron acquired the reputation of being a great poseur because no one would believe that anyone would be as honest in literature as people may frequently be in private conversation.

Among his contemporaries, those who felt the strong spell of his passionate revelation of the romantic ego, but disapproved of the unconventional conduct or opinions of the hero, were constrained to apologize for Byron by saying that he was not drawing from his own experience but was only assuming a Satanic pose. A typical statement is that of one of the Cambridge "Apostle" editors of the *Athenaeum,* who wrote not long after Byron's death: "Among the states of feeling which he describes with so much intensity, we doubt whether any great proportion were really painted from his own feelings." [18] But recent biographical evidence shows convincingly that no writer was ever more patently autobiographical in the creations of his imagination. In fact, this became so much a habit of his mind and of his composition that even when he deliberately set out to write objectively, as in his historical dramas, in which he prided himself on fidelity to the written records of characters and events, he could not but make the major figures over into personalities like himself with problems that were his own.

Byron's supreme literary achievement, however, was developed almost by accident, though its ingredients had been long heated in the crucible of his own experience and literary practice. When he discovered in the Italian ottava rima the possibilities for both colloquial ease and rhetorical brilliance, for kaleidoscopic but natural shifts from serious to comic, he had found his métier and his medium. When he tried it out in *Beppo* he saw that it offered the freest outlet for all the thoughts and feelings of his mobile personality. The darker moods had already found adequate expression in the third and fourth cantos of *Childe Harold* and in *Manfred*. He had achieved something like calm again in Venice, which, he wrote Moore, "has always been (next to the East) the greenest island of my imagination." [19] At last, he felt freed by his self-exile from the necessity of fitting his life or his verse into an English pattern. By November, 1816, he was already willing to become a citizen of the world. If he could only arrange his financial affairs in England, he told Kinnaird, "you might consider me as *posthumous*, for I would never willingly dwell in the 'tight little Island.' " [20] He could now indulge in literature that facetious and satiric bent which had been largely confined to his letters since *Childe Harold* had diverted his talents into the single track of the "Romantic Agony."

When the success of *Beppo* encouraged him to continue the same style and manner in *Don Juan*, Byron was not fully conscious of the significance of the change that was being wrought not only in his poetic subject matter and style but also in his concept of the poetic function. While he was increasingly aware of the value of *Don Juan* as a production that possessed candor and life and truth more than any other literary work of the day, and while he defended it facetiously against the attacks of his squeamish friends in England, he never fully understood why it engrossed his loyalty more than any-

thing else he had written. The fact was that he had found a genre which satisfied his deepest feelings about the moral function of poetry and at the same time allowed the completest cathartic escape for his feelings, whether serious or comic.

It is true that by the very nature of the medium and the style he had adapted from the ottava rima mock-heroic poems of the Italians, Byron's work has less of the neat compactness of Pope's best couplets. But on the other hand, by following his own genius with a freedom of artistry that forgets art, Byron cuts deeper with his broadsword through the armor of conventional pretenses to the living flesh of the human condition than Pope ever does with his more pointed rapier. Byron swung wildly at times, but in more than half of *Don Juan* he did hit and the blow was crushing.

NOTES

1. Eliot's essay on "Byron" (*On Poetry and Poets*, 1961; the essay was first published in 1937) is an attempt to separate the good work from the bad, and he ends like most twentieth century critics by lauding *Don Juan*. He grants that in that poem Byron "has the cardinal virtue of being never dull." He praises Byron's "genius for digression," finds his banter and mockery "an admirable antacid to the high-falutin," and sees his ultimate virtue, as many others have, in his "reckless raffish honesty."

2. *The Works of Lord Byron, Letters and Journals*, ed. R. E. Prothero, IV, 237. Letter of June 1, 1818. (This edition is hereafter cited as *Letters and Journals*.)

3. *Letters and Journals*, V, 471. Letter of Nov. 3, 1821.

4. *Letters and Journals*, IV, 304–305. Letter of May 20, 1819.

5. Hoxie Neale Fairchild, *The Romantic Quest*, 1931, p. 362.

6. *The Works of Lord Byron, Poetry*, ed. E. H. Coleridge, VI, 600 (Hereafter cited as *Poetry*.)

7. *The Romantic Quest*, p. 370.

8. I have discussed this point in the Introduction to my edition of *Don Juan* (Riverside Edition, Houghton Mifflin, 1958). Byron himself was aware of the stamp that *Childe Harold* and other poems in that vein had put upon him. In 1817 he asked

Moore to assure Francis Jeffrey "that I was not, and, indeed, am not even *now*, the misanthropical, and gloomy gentleman he takes me for, but a facetious companion, well to do with those with whom I am intimate, and as loquacious and laughing as if I were a much cleverer fellow." (*Letters and Journals*, IV, 72–74.)

9. A close study of Byron's debt to the Roman satirists Horace and Juvenal has been made by Arthur Kahn (New York University doctoral dissertation). Aside from the obvious parallels in *Hints from Horace* and other poems in the Popean couplet, Kahn has found remarkable echoes of both the subject matter and the style of Horace, but many more and closer parallels with Juvenal in *Don Juan* particularly.

10. *Letters and Journals*, IV, 169. Letter of Sept. 15, 1817. Byron would have been flattered and pleased had he seen the note which Gifford, to whom Murray showed the letter, wrote on the manuscript: "There is more good sense, and feeling and judgment in this passage, than in any other I ever read, or Lord Byron wrote."

11. *Letters and Journals*, IV, 284. Letter of April 6, 1819.

12. *Letters and Journals*, IV, 62. Letter of Feb. 28, 1817.

13. *Letters and Journals*, V, 272. Letter of April 28, 1821.

14. *Letters and Journals*, II, 293. Letter of Nov. 30, 1813.

15. *Letters and Journals*, III, 405. Letter of Nov. 10, 1813, to Annabella Milbanke.

16. *Lord Byron's Correspondence*, ed. John Murray, I, 214. Letter of Nov. 4, 1813.

17. There is no doubt that Byron's deep hatred of personal restraint as well as of governmental tyranny made the story of Bonivard's imprisonment a subject congenial to him. The passionate interest it aroused in him is best seen in the "Sonnet on Chillon": "Eternal Spirit of the chainless Mind!"

18. *Athenaeum*, Jan. 23, 1828, p. 55.

19. *Letters and Journals*, IV, 7. Letter of Nov. 17, 1816.

20. *Lord Byron's Correspondence*, II, 24. Letter of Nov. 27, 1816.

Peter Thorslev

CHILDE HAROLD: THE BYRONIC HERO*

Even the casual reader of Byron's *juvenilia* can see that the earliest Byronic Hero did not spring full-grown and unprepared for from the mind of the young poet on his Grand Tour. Something like the poetic character of Childe Harold had already appeared in the early *Hours of Idleness*—in the figure of the eighteen-year-old student who fondly recalls his past "childhood" at Harrow, for instance, and the tombstone on which he was wont to lie and meditate on autumn evenings ("On a Distant View of Harrow"). Or in the figure who opines in "Childish Recollections" that he is a "Hermit" straying alone in the midst of crowds. The Gloomy Egoist

of the "Elegy on Newstead Abbey," the "last and youngest of a noble line," views with poetic melancholy the "mouldering turrets" and the "damp and mossy tombs," and finds that even the grass "exhales a murky dew" from the "humid pall of life-extinguished clay." Still, Byron's first volumes, being only the subsidized publications of another poetizing young nobleman, were not notably successful, and it is probably safe to say that by 1812 few remembered the derivative *Hours of Idleness* or their traditional poetic characters. If Byron was remembered at all, it was as the author of *English Bards and Scotch Reviewers*, the free-swinging Giffordesque satire prompted by the poor reviews of his first publications, and these heroic couplets gave little promise of *Childe Harold*.

Scott was therefore expressing the views of the

* From *The Byronic Hero* by Peter L. Thorslev, Jr. The University of Minnesota Press, Minneapolis. © Copyright 1962 by the University of Minnesota.

general public when he said he was pleasantly surprised by *Childe Harold* I and II, since this was not
the kind or the quality of poetry which he had come
to expect of Byron. That the reading public was
favorably impressed is of course amply evident in
the fact that both poem and poet became legendary
and lionized almost in a matter of days. Of course
the character of the Childe is not the poem's only
interest, or even perhaps its chief interest: *Childe
Harold* is also a great poetic travelogue, a moving
rhetorical account of scenes and events described
with uncommon sensitivity and intensity. Even in
our anti-Byronic twentieth century a Donne enthusiast like H. J. C. Grierson writes, "As a descriptive
poem alone . . . *Childe Harold* is the greatest of its
kind, the noblest panoramic poem in our literature." [1] Our concern here is with heroes, however,
and not primarily with poetic description, and, as
is commonly acknowledged, Childe Harold is the
first important Byronic Hero, and the prototype of
all the rest.

It has been almost as commonly supposed, however, from Byron's day to our own, that Childe
Harold is in reality none other than Lord Byron
himself, or at least his conception of himself, and
this, of course, in spite of Byron's repeated protestations to the contrary, both in his letters and in a
long passage in the Preface to Cantos I and II, in
which he refers repeatedly to Harold as a "fictitious
character" and a "child of the imagination." Critics
and the public have goodnaturedly ignored his distinction, however, and have made the identification
of poet and poetic character the subject of endless
biographical and critical discussion. The fact is, of
course, that Byron was himself in part responsible
for this popular misconception of his poem.

In reality the first two cantos of the poem have
no less than three different poetic characters, none
of which is kept clearly distinct from the others.
There is first of all the Childe himself, who is largely
a traditional literary Romantic hero or an agglomeration of hero types. Second, there is in the first canto,
at least, a minstrel-narrator whose archaic diction
and occasional moralizing comment are in the tradition of Scott's romances or of Beattie's *Minstrel*.
Finally, there is Byron's own persona, who breaks
in with personal elegies, or with poetic diatribes
against war and tyranny, and who is not really
consistent in voice or character with the other two
persons in the poem. Byron does not really clear

up the confusion until the fourth canto, when he
drops the first and the second poetic characters, and
retains only the third.

Byron had both a precedent and an apology for
this confusion of poetic characters or voices. Sir
Walter Scott frequently confuses narrators in his
romances. In *Marmion,* for instance, he sets up as
the narrator of his story a moral harpist with the
characteristic attitudes of a pious Catholic late-
medieval minstrel, but frequently he drops this pose
for that of a nineteenth-century Scots Romantic
poet. The confusion is even more evident in Beattie's *The Minstrel,* one of Byron's acknowledged
models for *Childe Harold.* The ballad-minstrel persona of the first book with a "Gothic Harp" and a
medieval mind, who reports sympathetically the
facts and myths of the Child of Nature's rearing,
becomes in the second book a contemporary Scottish moral philosopher, at home in the Age of
Reason. Byron obviously chose to follow the pattern
of having a minstrel-narrator, for the sake of the
objectivity and impersonality of third-person description of his pilgrim. When Dallas, who was following the poem through the press, asked Byron
whom the "he" referred to in the closing elegy of
the second canto, Byron replied, somewhat piqued,
"The 'he' refers to 'Wanderer' and anything is better
than the *I I I I* always *I*" (*Works,* II, 161, note).

The minstrel-narrator is plainly in evidence in the
opening of the third-person description of the
Childe in Canto I. His archaisms and shocked moral
tone are clear in the second stanza:

> Whilome in Albion's isle there dwelt a youth,
> Who ne in Virtue's ways did take delight;
> But spent his days in riot most uncouth,
> And vexed with mirth the drowsy ear of Night.
> Ah me! in sooth he was a shameless wight,
> Sore given to revel and ungodly glee . . .[2]

But even in the first canto Byron is inconsistent.
The sentiments of the stanzas on the Convention of
Cintra, for instance, seem peculiarly unfit either for
the Childe or for the aged Minstrel, so in the next
stanza (27), the poet catches himself with a "So
deemed the Childe," and apologizes by noting that
although the Childe was not accustomed to such
reasoning, "here a while he learned to moralize."
(For the dissipated young cynic portrayed in the
first few stanzas, this is a transformation indeed.)
The Minstrel seems to breathe his last in the closing
stanza of this canto, however, when he tells us

that after this "one fytte of Harold's pilgrimage" we may find "some tidings" in a "future page, / If he that rhymeth now may scribble moe."

In the second canto, the Minstrel having disappeared, we are left for the most part with Byron's own persona. Even the literary Childe of the first canto—the young-old Wandering Jew or Hero of Sensibility with Gothic sins—seems largely to have been eclipsed. The canto opens with a long *vanitas vanitatis* passage including a malediction on Lord Elgin and all despoilers of Greek ruins, and then the poet continues: "But where is Harold? Shall I then forget / To urge the gloomy Wanderer o'er the wave? / Little recked he of all that Men regret . . ." (II, 16)—in the last line dissociating the literary Childe from the sentiments of the poet's persona in the prologue. Through most of the canto, then, the Childe is used only for occasional and casual asides (usually "So deemed the Childe"), or for easy transitions ("Then rode Childe Harold" into the next landscape).

The third and fourth cantos were of course written much later, in 1816–17, after Byron's four eventful years in England—the years of his greatest fame, and, after the scandalous separation, of his greatest ignominy. Byron must have grown as a man during those years, and certainly he grew considerably as a poet. Yet something of the same confusion of poetic characters persists in *Childe Harold*, at least through Canto III. The literary Childe appears again in this canto, but he, like his creator, has grown more mature. There was something adolescent about the hero of the first cantos, but the new figure is more like the traditional rebellious Romantic Hero. Like Byron, he has returned to society, but unable to resist Beauty and Fame, he has again been "burned," and has finally realized that he is "himself the most unfit / Of men to herd with Man," since "He would not yield dominion of his mind / To Spirits against whom his own rebelled, / Proud though in desolation . . ." (III, 12)—including for the first time, I believe, an echo of the Satan of *Paradise Lost*. The identification between the literary Childe and Byron's own persona is of course quite close in this canto, and in the Preface to Canto IV, Byron drops all pretense at keeping the two distinct:

> With regard to the conduct of the last canto, there will be found less of the pilgrim than in any of the preceding, and that slightly, if at all, separated from the author speaking in his own person. The fact is, that I had become weary of drawing a line which every one seemed determined not to perceive: like the Chinese in Goldsmith's *Citizen of the World*, whom nobody would believe to be a Chinese, it was in vain that I asserted, and imagined that I had drawn, a distinction between the author and the pilgrim; and the very anxiety to preserve this difference, and disappointment at finding it unavailing, so far crushed my efforts in composition, that I determined to abandon it [i.e., the "difference," not the "composition"] altogether—and have done so. (*Works*, II, 323)

It is still important to note, however, that throughout the poem and even in Canto IV Byron and his persona are two different beings. The latter is of course a fabrication, an achievement of the poet's imagination, comparable, I believe, to Beattie's Edwin, and an even more "literary" personality than Wordsworth's "I" of the *Prelude* of 1850. The Byron of this period was no solitary, for instance, as Harold most certainly is; Byron was always the most social of poets, and even a casual reading of his letters proves that he realized the fact. Perhaps the distinction between the poetic and the real personalities is nowhere more evident than in the matter of a sense of humor or a capacity for irony. It is this capacity which Harold notably lacks, and it is this capacity which Byron himself, as seen in his letters and in his conversations, was never without. One need only note the manner in which he refers, in a letter to his friend Hodgson, to some of the most passionate concerns of the first cantos:

> I have attacked De Pauw, Thornton, Lord Elgin, Spain, Portugal, the *Edinburgh Review*, travellers, Painters, Antiquarians, and others, so you see what a dish of Sour Crout Controversy I shall prepare for myself . . . *Vae Victis!* If I fall, I shall fall gloriously, fighting against a host. (*LJ*, II, 46–47)

This is not to say, of course, that these concerns were insincere, but the passage does demonstrate that Byron was even in 1812 capable of that mixture of irony, pathos, and bravado, largely missing in *Childe Harold*, but which was to make *Don Juan* his masterpiece.

These, then, are the three poetic characters in *Childe Harold*: The minstrel-narrator one need not be concerned with; he is a traditional poetical mouthpiece, and in any case he disappears after

Canto I. The Childe himself is at first largely a traditional figure, a combination of sometimes incongruous traits from the heroes most popular in the Romantic age. He is kept distinct from Byron's own persona, however, only occasionally in the first two cantos; the distinction largely disappears in the third canto, and it is nonexistent in the fourth. Of course the earlier picture of the Childe colors all the rest of the poem, and the composite figure of the later cantos, while gaining in depth of distinctive personality as the first great Hero of Sensibility in English Romantic literature, retains many of the features he had acquired in his first traditional appearances in Cantos I and II.

Childe Harold of the first two cantos is indeed an imaginary literary figure, however many details of ancestry or biography he may have acquired from Byron's personal life, and in spite of the fact that he has also taken a Grand Tour. In personality he is a compound of many distinct and even disparate elements of the heroes discussed in the last chapters. In age and in some of his attitudes he is a Child of Nature; in his appearance and with his burnt-out passions and secret sins he bears a resemblance to the Gothic Villain, especially to the sentimentalized villain of Gothic drama; and in his meditations and in his personal reactions toward man and nature he resembles most closely those eighteenth-century types, the Gloomy Egoist and the Man of Feeling.

Insofar as he is a Child of Nature, Harold belongs of course to the romanticized late eighteenth-century type; he has not the aggressive ebullience of a Belcour or a Hermsprong, but rather the tender sensibilities of Fleetwood, or of Beattie's Edwin. (As we have seen, this hero was already on the wane at the turn of the century, and it could therefore be expected that this would be the least important aspect of Harold's personality.) First, his tender age is repeatedly emphasized. He is a youth "of Albion's isle," "scarce a third" of whose days have "passed by"; a "youth so raw," "One who, 'twas said, still sighed to all he saw" (I, 2, 4, 33). Like Beattie's Edwin, the Childe is also accomplished in rude minstrelsy, and in moments of solitude he turns to his lute to compose impromptu songs for the consolation of his drooping spirits: "He seized his harp, which he at times could string, / And strike, albeit with untaught melody, /

When deemed he no strange ear was listening..." (I, 13).

Mostly, however, Harold is a Child of Nature in his attitude toward the natural world. Like Beattie's Edwin, or Fleetwood, or perhaps the poet *manqué* of *The Prelude*, he loves "To sit on rocks— to muse o'er flood and fell— / To slowly trace the forest's shady scene, / Where things that own not Man's dominion dwell..." (II, 25). In another passage Harold himself calls nature his mother, and himself her child:

Dear Nature is the kindest mother still!
Though always changing, in her aspect mild;
From her bare bosom let me take my fill,
Her never-weaned, though not her favoured
    child...   (II, 37)

(Two manuscript variations help to explicate the last enigmatic adjective: "her weakly child," or "her rudest child.") Finally, we find that as with most of the Children of Nature, Harold, too, is fond of his "mother" in her more sublime and terrible aspects. Beattie's Edwin "was a strange and wayward youth, / Fond of each gentle and each dreadful scene. / In darkness and in storm he found delight..." [3] So also Childe Harold exclaims:

Oh! she is fairest in her features wild,
Where nothing polished dares pollute her
    path:
To me by day or night she ever smiled,
Though I have marked her when none other
    hath,
And sought her more and more, and loved her
    best in wrath.   (II, 37)

These features of the Child of Nature seem somewhat incongruous in combination with characteristics of the next of Harold's prototypes—the Gothic Villain. Harold, as were the Gothic Villains, is of "lineage long" which was "glorious in another day" (I, 3). This resemblance is perhaps adventitious, but the same cannot be said of the Childe's haughty pride and cold reserve, his burnt-out passions, his secret sins, and his flashes of half-hidden remorse.

It is interesting to note first of all that in a variant reading of one manuscript Harold is given two of the Gothic Villain's most typical characteristics, the first, pride, almost a hallmark. We are told that

An evil smile just bordering on a sneer
Curled on his lip...

[He] deemed ne mortal wight his peer
To gentle dames still less could he be dear . . .
> (*Works*, II, 21, note)

The finished picture is less blatantly Gothic, but his relationship to his villain cousin of the drama or novel is nevertheless still clear:

Strange pangs would flash along Childe Har-
> old's brow,
As if the Memory of some deadly feud
Or disappointed passion lurked below:
But this none knew, nor haply cared to know;
For his was not that open, artless soul
That feels relief by bidding sorrow flow,
Nor sought he friend to counsel or condole,
Whate'er this grief mote be . . . (I, 8)

That Byron had ample literary precedent for giving Harold these past and secret sins and the attendant remorse has I think been proven in the preceding chapters. The glamour, the irresistible romance of a secret and sinful past was one of the prime attractions of the original Gothic Villain, and, as we have seen, the intensity of remorse, sentimentalized in the hero-villain of the Gothic drama, had carried over into the character of the Noble Outlaw, long before Byron began to write. It is especially interesting to note that Byron gave the Childe these secret sins in his first appearance in Canto I, presumably before Byron had any of the sins of the rumored incest or of his marriage on his conscience, and when, from the evidence of his letters and the testimony of his personal friends, he seems to have been "not sated . . . not cheerless . . . not unamiable," but "all a-quiver with youth and enthusiasm and the joy of great living." [4] This seems clear evidence for the conclusion that this aspect of the Byronic Hero, in its earliest manifestation, at least, was inspired by literature, not by life.

Of course Gothic Villains were passionate actors in sensationalistic drama, and Childe Harold is not; he is above all a "pilgrim," not in the sense of being a tourist, on the one hand, or as a real penitent, on the other, but as marked and cursed of sin, wandering over the face of Europe in an almost hopeless search for self-restoration, and fearing that this can never come about, even in death. In other words, Harold is Byron's first Cain or his Wandering Jew. Now this is not to say that the Cain or Ahasuerus stories gave much direct inspiration for *Childe Harold*; these stories were themselves crea-

tions of the Romantic Movement, and they illustrate typical themes—eternal remorse, wanderlust, ennui, and *Weltschmerz*—which *Childe Harold* also illustrates. In other words, these are classic themes of the Romantic literary tradition; they are by no means personal to Byron. And, as might be expected, Byron does not leave implicit this association of Harold with his fellow remorse-stricken wanderers. We are first told of the Childe that "life-abhorring Gloom / Wrote on his faded brow curst Cain's unresting doom" (I, 83), and later, the Childe himself names his malady:

It is that settled, ceaseless gloom
The fabled Hebrew Wanderer bore;
That will not look beyond the tomb,
But cannot hope for rest before.
> ("To Inez": I, following 84)

These are still not the most important of his prototypes, however: most of all in his meditations (and most of the poem is meditation), the Childe of the first two cantos is an eighteenth-century Gloomy Egoist, or a Man of Feeling.

One of the purposes which *Childe Harold* served was to furnish eager readers with an imaginary Grand Tour, and this at a time when Englishmen had been obliged for years to sit at home, through wars and rumors of wars on the Continent. Of course then, as now, the commonest tourist sites in Europe were ruins, tombs, and monuments of glories past. Childe Harold was therefore making a natural choice when he selected such sites as settings for his meditations, and they were given an especial poignancy for his readers by the fact that many of the conflicts commemorated were of recent wars, and wars in which Englishmen had taken a prominent part.

Yet the general elegiac tone of the first two cantos of the poem, and the recurring themes of *ubi sunt* and *sic transit*, are very much in the tradition of the Gloomy Egoists of the preceding century. There are many passages reminiscent of such poems as Hervey's *Meditations among the Tombs,* or passages one might imagine having come from a later and secularized Edward Young. Beckford's deserted mansion at Quinta da Monserrate provides a setting for one such meditation:

Here giant weeds a passage scarce allow
To Halls deserted, portals gaping wide:
Fresh lessons to the thinking bosom, how

Vain are the pleasaunces on earth supplied;
Swept into wrecks anon by Time's ungentled
        tide!   (I, 23)

There is a long meditation on a skull in the second
canto which reminds one not only of a Hervey or
Young, but perhaps also of Hamlet in the grave-
yard:

Look on its broken arch, its ruined wall,
Its chambers desolate, and portals foul:
Yes, this was once Ambition's airy hall,
The Dome of Thought, the Palace of the Soul:
Behold through each lack-lustre, eyeless hole,
The gay recess of Wisdom and of Wit . . .
                                             (II, 6)

The personal elegies which close each canto remind
one particularly of Young's *Night Thoughts*. At
the close of the first canto, in a long note, Byron
himself reminds the reader of Young's lines: "Insatiate archer! could not one suffice? / Thy shaft
flew thrice, and thrice my peace was slain . . ." [5]
The second canto closes with an echo of the same
passage: "All thou couldst have of mine, stern
Death! thou hast; / The Parent, Friend, and now
the more than Friend: / Ne'er yet for one thine
arrows flew so fast" (II, 96). Harold's elegies hold
out no Christian consolation of an immortality beyond the grave, however. The Pilgrim, in part a
follower of Young or of Hervey, is a secularized
Gloomy Egoist, closer to the classics (in theme, at
least) than to his ecclesiastic forebears of the previous century. In the long *vanitas vanitatis* passage
with which Canto II opens (reminiscent of Lucretius, perhaps, but also of the Preacher), Harold
can only conclude that man is a "Poor child of
Doubt and Death, whose hope is built on reeds." [6]

Finally, the Childe of the first two cantos, in
many of his poses, is a Man of Feeling. He is suffering from unrequited love; in spite of his often-
confessed preference for solitude and his dislike for
mankind, he is a humanitarian—sternly against war
and tyranny in all its forms; and in his meditations
on the natural world he adopts many of the attitudes characteristic of Mackenzie's Harvey (*The
Man of Feeling*) or of the sentimental heroes of
Mrs. Radcliffe's Gothic novels.

His unfortunate love affair is merely hinted at,
and never developed. We are told from the first
that he "Had sighed to many though he loved but
one, / And that loved one, alas! could ne'er be his"
(I, 5). He is impervious now to Cupid's arrows,

even while watching dark-eyed Spanish maids dancing in the moonlight: "For not yet had he drunk of
Lethe's stream; / And lately had he learned with
truth to deem / Love has no gift so grateful as his
wings" (I, 82).

Harold's affinity with the Man of Feeling is
shown more clearly in his prevailing human sympathy. He is solitary and antisocial, but as with the
typical Man of Feeling, more because of his exquisite sensibilities than because of anything basi-
cally misanthropic in his nature. Like most Romantic poetic personalities, he has been "fated," set
apart from other men, alienated from the social
world of which he would otherwise gladly be a
part:

Still he beheld, nor mingled with the throng;
But viewed them not with misanthropic hate:
Fain would he now have joined the dance, the
        song;
But who may smile that sinks beneath his fate?
                                             (I, 84)

Again, like most Men of Feeling, he cannot stand
war or violence, and he sympathizes with the
"rustic" who shrinks from viewing "his vineyard
desolate, / Blasted below the dun hot breath of
War" (I, 47). In his description of his first experiences with Spanish bullfights, he concludes that the
sport is barbaric, and his sympathies go out to the
gored horse and the dying bull, reserving nothing
but contumely for the "vulgar eyes" that watch
(I, 72–80).

Finally, the Childe of the first two cantos belongs
with the Man of Feeling in his attitude toward
external nature. One can quite imagine Harold joining Mrs. Radcliffe's Emily St. Aubert in enraptured
contemplation of the more rugged reaches of the
Pyrenees or of the mountain fastnesses around
Udolpho. As Professor Lovell has so thoroughly
demonstrated, the early Childe, at least, belongs
in that long and persistent tradition of landscape
painters in English pre-Romantic literature. [7] The
scenes are carefully sketched and balanced, with
just the proper tinting, and just that note of the
fearful-lovely sublime which so attracted painters
and poets through the latter half of the eighteenth
century. One of the more famous of the scenes
serves to illustrate the point (note the "harmonizing" blue of the sky, and the definition of the sublime in the last line):

Monastic Zitza! from thy shady brow,
Thou small, but favoured spot of holy ground!
Where'er we gaze—around—above—be-
　　low,—
What rainbow tints, what magic charms are
　　found!
Rock, river, forest, mountain, all abound,
And bluest skies that harmonise the whole:
Beneath, the distant Torrent's rushing sound
Tells where the volumed Cataract doth roll
Between those hanging rocks, that shock yet
　　please the soul.　　　　　　　　(II, 48)

The traditional literary figure of Childe Harold
in Cantos I and II is indeed, then, a potpourri or
an agglomeration of the characteristics of the heroes
discussed in the last two chapters: the Child of
Nature; the Gothic Villain (unregenerate, as in the
novel, or remorseful, as in the drama or in Scott's
romances); the accursed Wanderer; the Gloomy
Egoist, meditating on ruins, death, or the vanity of
life; and the Man of Feeling, suffering from a lost
love, or philanthropically concerned with the suffering caused by war or oppression.

That such a literary character could not but contain some incongruities is perhaps obvious enough,
but I think it is highly probable that the very
breadth of the selection of heroic characteristics accounts in large part for the poem's immediate and
astounding acclaim. Here was a poetic character
who combined in his person many or most of the
characteristics the age found attractive: though suffering from "misfortuned" love and from the ennui
of spent passions and remorse, at the same time
he could appreciate the beauties of natural scenery
and could moralize with the best of the meditative
egoists on the passage of fame and glory and on
the vanity of life. In a preceding chapter I noted
that Scott's *Rokeby* was a very treasure trove of
Romantic hero types, offering a virile Child of Nature, a youthful Man of Feeling (given to solitary
walks and musical extemporizing), and no less than
two Gothic Villain-Heroes. But here, in the person
of Childe Harold, Byron has rolled all of these into
one, and added to boot the characteristics of a
meditative moralist. Such a hero could not fail to
attract in the Romantic age. This, then, is the character of the Childe Harold of the first two cantos:
he is striking, if largely traditional, and he was
vastly popular, even if somewhat inconsistent.

The Childe of Cantos III and IV is in some ways
a different person. Like the verse of the later poems,
he is less rhetorical, and more poetic; less traditional, and far more personal. The important transformation, as has been commonly noticed, is that
the Childe becomes assimilated to Byron's own persona, although some colors of the original portrait
remain, not only in the mind of the reader, but in
sporadic passages of the later poems. The scandalous "past" of the Childe has become actual, and
the "exile" of the Harold of Canto III has become
real, not merely a literary device. In other words,
the new figure is not so far from the old but that
many of his sentiments fit into the traditional pattern set in the first two cantos. There is, however,
less of cynicism, and more of suffering; less of sin
and guilt, and more of being sinned against. In a
word, there is less of the Gothic Villain and more
of the first important English Hero of Sensibility.

But let me first admit that there are passages in
the later cantos in which the suffering becomes too
personal to remain literary, in which the emotion
is too specific to be generalized and made objective.
The most offensive of these is the famous "appeal
to Nemesis":

　　if calmly I have borne
Good, and reserved my pride against the hate
Which shall not whelm me, let me not have
　　worn
This iron in my soul in vain—shall *they* not
　　mourn?

. 　. 　. 　. 　. 　. 　. 　. 　. 　. 　. 　. 　.

Not in the air shall these my words disperse,
Though I be ashes; a far hour shall wreak
The deep prophetic fulness of this verse,
And pile on human heads the mountain of my
　　curse!

. 　. 　. 　. 　. 　. 　. 　. 　. 　. 　. 　. 　.

That curse shall be Forgiveness . . .
Have I not suffered things to be forgiven?
　　　　　　　　　　　　　　(IV, 131–135)

Such a passage is not only too personal, but too
petty and vindictive. One could perhaps maintain
that this sentiment is in the "Christian" tradition,
as does Professor G. Wilson Knight, who goes so
far as to call these stanzas "Promethean," and points
to them as the source of Shelley's innovation in the
Prometheus legend—the Christian ideal of forgiveness which Prometheus exhibits toward Zeus.[8] In
the Alexandrine above there is probably an echo of
St. Paul: "If thine enemy hunger, feed him; if he
thirst, give him to drink: for in so doing thou shalt
heap coals of fire on his head" (Romans 12.19–20).

But the sentiment remains inconsistent in *Childe Harold*—and, one might add, in the New Testament. It is far more characteristic of the Byronic Hero to say:

> Meantime I seek no sympathies, nor need—
> The thorns which I have reaped are of the tree
> I planted,—they have torn me,—and I bleed:
> I should have known what fruit would spring
>   from such a seed.   (IV, 10)

But enough has been written on the autobiographical in *Childe Harold* III and IV. Comparatively little in these cantos is so strictly personal as the passage just quoted, but that little has been much exaggerated by those critics and biographers who are legitimately more concerned with the poet's life than with his work. What I am more interested to point out here is that the Childe becomes in these cantos one of a long line of Heroes of Sensibility, a line which begins in the Romantic movement and continues through the remainder of the nineteenth century.

In an earlier chapter I defined the Hero of Sensibility as having emerged from a union of a secularized Gloomy Egoist with the ethically uncommitted Man of Feeling. His essential characteristics are that he is always passive, not acting but being acted upon (as was Harvey, the *Man of Feeling*); that he is given to prolonged, intense, and sometimes even morbid self-analysis, especially of his emotional states (as was Parson Yorick, or the later Werther); that since he is always egocentrically self-concerned, the whole world becomes colored with his own particular ennui and world-weariness (as is the case certainly with Edward Young's persona, and is pre-eminently the case with Werther); and finally, that most of these characteristics stem from his peculiar psychic malady of *Weltschmerz*: the tension in his personality that results from the conflict of two contradictory drives, one toward total commitment, toward loss of self in a vision of absolutes, the other toward a skeptical and even aggressive assertion of self in a world which remains external and even alien.

Perhaps Rousseau's St. Preux (or Rousseau himself) was the first of these Romantic Heroes of Sensibility. Certainly Werther belongs to this line of development; his anguished cry for self-commitment I have cited earlier as a prime expression of *Weltschmerz*. Faust himself, with his lonely and discouraged search for absolutes, and his subsequent resolve that "The highest, lowest forms my soul shall borrow, / Shall heap upon itself their bliss and sorrow / And thus, my own sole self to all their selves expand..." [9] belongs in part in the same tradition.

That the later Childe Harold has the first of these characteristics of the Hero of Sensibility needs really no proof, I suppose. He is certainly passive, intensely self-analytic, and given to projecting his peculiar ennui and suffering on the whole world of his vision. He is one of those "Wanderers o'er Eternity / Whose bark drives on and on, and anchored ne'er shall be" (III, 70); one of those, in their "aspirations to be great," whose "destinies o'erleap their mortal state," and "claim a kindred with the stars" (III, 78). But he is also the first great English victim of the Romantic malady of *Weltschmerz*.

It has long been recognized that in the third canto Childe Harold has Wordsworthian visions of an ordered and ensouled natural universe. E. H. Coleridge pointed this out in his edition of the poems, and every other Byron scholar or critic has noticed and commented upon it:[10]

> I live not in myself, but I become
> Portion of that around me; and to me
> High mountains are a feeling, but the hum
> Of human cities torture...
>
>   the soul can flee
> And with the sky—the peak—the heaving
>   plain
> Of Ocean, or the stars, mingle—and not in
>   vain.
> .   .   .   .
> Are not the mountains, waves, and skies, a part
> Of me and of my Soul, as I of them?
> .   .   .   .
> Then stirs the feeling infinite, so felt
> In solitude, where we are *least* alone;
> A truth, which through our being then doth
>   melt,
> And purifies from self...   (III, 72, 75, 90)

This is the vision of the absolute "truth" to which the Hero of Sensibility longs to commit himself; it implies a loss of personal identity (it "purifies from self"), as does perhaps all religious or mystic commitment, and it was the "escape" of most of the Romantic generation, from Blake through Wordsworth and Shelley to Emerson or Whitman.

The Byronic Hero of Sensibility feels too positive

a sense of identity to be able so to commit himself, however. In one sense, since this self-assertion frustrates any total commitment, it brings about what Professor Lovell calls the "failure of a quest," and it is the disappointment of this failure which Werther expresses when he says, "When we hurry toward it . . ., everything is as before, and we stand in our poverty, in our own narrowness, and our soul languishes for the refreshment which has eluded our grasp." [11] Childe Harold feels at times the same disappointment:

> Could he have kept his spirit to that flight
> He had been happy; but this clay will sink
> Its spark immortal, envying it the light
> To which it mounts, as if to break the link
> That keeps us from yon heaven which woos us
>   to its brink.   (III, 14)

Still, it is not all disappointment and frustration; it is also in a sense a return to life: ". . . for waking Reason deems / Such over-weening phantasies unsound, / And other voices speak, and other sights surround" (IV, 7). There is certainly a note of defiance in the tone of this affirmation of the reasoning self, and this, perhaps, is Byron's final answer to all forms of Romantic mysticism:

> Yet let us ponder boldly—'tis a base
> Abandonment of reason to resign
> Our right of thought—our last and only place
> Of refuge; this, at least, shall still be mine:
> Though from our birth the Faculty divine
> Is chained and tortured—cabined, cribbed,
>   confined,
> And bred in darkness, lest the Truth should
>   shine
> Too brightly on the unpreparéd mind,
> The beam pours in—for Time and Skill will
>   couch the blind.   (IV, 127)

The same tone of skeptical self-assertion and humanistic self-reliance forms the keynote of *Manfred* and *Cain*, and this, I believe, is Byron's last word, and the typical stance of the Byronic Hero. This is also, after all, the position of the narrator-persona of *Don Juan*, although in that case the vision of the cosmic tragedy of human self-assertion in an alien universe has been reinforced by the resurgence of Byron's capacity for "Romantic" irony. *Don Juan* illustrates that life must be conceived as tragedy (as Yeats says), and the human predicament may be an absurdity (as Sartre says), but the poem also asserts that life is infinitely varied, intensely exciting, and at times even invigoratingly comic.

This is to anticipate a resolution of the conflict, however, which the Hero of Sensibility in *Childe Harold* never achieves. The tension remains, and in the closing stanzas of Canto IV the mood again returns, and Harold longs once more for that obliviousness of self, that annihilation of the ego:

> I love not Man the less, but Nature more,
> From these our interviews, in which I steal
> From all I may be, or have been before,
> To mingle with the Universe . . .   (IV, 178)

But in the splendid rhetoric of the address to the sea which follows—"Roll on, thou deep and dark blue Ocean—roll"—this first English Hero of Sensibility gives a vivid impression of a natural world impersonal and alien, totally indifferent to man and all his aspirations.

This agonized Hero of Sensibility was Byron's legacy to the literature of the age which succeeded him—not the healthy, ironic but life-affirming message of his great satire. Until almost the end of the century, both in England and on the Continent, Byron was remembered primarily as the author of *Childe Harold*, not of *Don Juan*. The agonized Hero of Sensibility appears again and again in the literature of the succeeding age: sometimes morbidly analytic of his own emotional and spiritual states, and in his *Weltschmerz* longing for some engagement to absolute truth which will rid him of his painful self-consciousness; longing to "mingle with the universe," but being continually frustrated in this desire by the reassertion of his skeptical, sometimes cynical, and sometimes remorseful ego. This hero and his central problem reappear in the poetry of De Musset, for instance, or in Pushkin's *Eugene Onegin*, and certainly this problem of commitment, this intense and longdrawn self-analysis, the agonized passiveness (some kind of "engagement" being necessary for action) reappear in England as the dominant traits of heroes in Arnold's *Empedocles*, in much of Tennyson's work (see *The Ancient Sage*, or passages of *In Memoriam*), especially clearly in Clough's *Dipsychus*, and even in Pater's *Marius*.

But I think it is not going too far to say that the climax of this hero's passion, and perhaps of his poetry, appears in Byron's *Childe Harold* III and IV.

NOTES

1. "Lord Byron: Arnold and Swinburne," The Warton Lecture on English Poetry, printed in *Proceedings of the British Academy, 1919–1920* (London, 1920), p. 444.

2. Canto I, stanza 2. References hereafter will be in the text. For obvious typographical reasons, I am using Arabic numerals for stanza numbers.

3. *The Minstrel,* in *The Poetical Works of James Beattie,* Aldine ed. (London, n.d.), p. 46.

4. E. H. Coleridge, in his introduction to *Childe Harold* (in *Works,* II, xiv).

5. "Night One," in *Poetical Works* (London, 1854), p. 5.

6. II, 3. The two stanzas following 3, beginning "Yet if, as holiest men have deemed, there be / A land of souls beyond that sable shore . . .," were written at the request of R. C. Dallas (Byron's "editor" of Cantos I and II) to replace a rabidly anticlerical and antireligious stanza in the original manuscript. They are superior as poetry, but not consistent with the frankly skeptical tone of the rest of the canto.

7. Ernest J. Lovell, *Byron: The Record of a Quest* (Austin: University of Texas Press, 1949), especially Chap. IV, "Byron and the Picturesque Tradition."

8. In *Byron: The Christian Virtues* (New York: Oxford University Press, 1953), pp. 249f. It is worth noting in this connection, since Knight points to this passage as having influenced Shelley, that both Shelley and Hobhouse were strongly against Byron's printing of this "appeal to Nemesis": see *LJ,* IV, 259 and note, and *Lord Byron's Correspondence,* ed. John Murray (London: John Murray, 1922), II, 69, note. Needless to say, Professor Knight does not note the possible echo of St. Paul's epistle in this passage.

9. *Faust I,* 1771–1773; translation of Bayard Taylor (1870), as in *Faust,* World Classics ed. (Oxford: Oxford University Press, 1932), p. 55.

10. Manfred Eimer, in his *Byron und der Kosmos,* in *Anglistische Forschungen,* XXXIV (Heidelberg, 1912), built an entire *Weltanschauung* for Byron largely on the basis of these passages. The most thorough study of the whole matter is in Professor Lovell's study (note 7 above).

11. *Die Leiden des jungen Werthers,* ed. Max Herrman, in Goethe's *Werke,* Jubiläumsausgabe (Stuttgart: 1902–12), XVI, 30 (see the chapter above on the Hero of Sensibility). In reference to Lovell, it is only fair to say that although he considers this a "failure of a quest" on Byron's part, he also makes it an important basis for Byron's "modernity": see the last chapter of his study (note 7 above): "The Contemporaneousness of Byron." For a similar attitude, see P. E. More, "The Wholesome Revival of Byron," *Atlantic Monthly,* LXXXII (1898), 801–809, and the essays by Willis W. Pratt ("Byron and Some Current Patterns of Thought") and Leslie Marchand ("Byron and the Modern Spirit") in *The Major English Romantic Poets,* ed. Clarence Thorpe, *et al.* (Carbondale: Southern Illinois University Press, 1957), pp. 149–168.

Paul Trueblood

BYRON AS SATIRIST*

The chief institutions which Byron satirizes in his *Don Juan* are war, despotism, and marriage. Let us

---

* From *The Flowering of Byron's Genius* by Paul G. Trueblood. Copyright 1945 by Paul G. Trueblood (Stanford, CA: Stanford University Press, 1945; reissued New York, Russell & Russell, 1962).

examine his satire of these institutions in order to see if his purpose coincides with the two major objectives which we have noted in his satire of individuals and of England.

War, declares Byron (IV, cv), is the result of the "wild instinct of gore and glory" of "those blood-hounds," the militarists. And, in consequence, the earth has known "those sufferings Dante saw in hell alone."

Cantos VII and VIII of *Don Juan* contain Byron's most vigorous and extended satiric treatment of war. On the day on which Byron finished these two cantos, August 8, 1822, he wrote to Thomas Moore:

> These contain a full detail (like the storm in Canto Second) of the siege and assault of Ismail, with much of sarcasm on those butchers in large business, your mercenary soldiery. . . . . With these things and these fellows, it is necessary, in the present clash of philosophy and tyranny, to throw away the scabbard.[1]

The first reference in Canto VII to the mercenary soldier is in his description (xviii) of the Russian army:

> Then there were foreigners of much renown,
>   Of various nations, and all volunteers;
> Not fighting for their country or its crown,
>   But wishing to be one day brigadiers;
> Also to have the sacking of a town;
>   A pleasant thing to young men of their years.

A few stanzas farther on in the same canto he ridicules (lxiv) the mercenary soldier as one whose "high, heroic bosom burn'd for cash and conquest." And again he inveighs against the mercenary soldiery who slay millions "for their ration" (VIII, lxviii). Their lust for slaughter and love of plunder draw Byron's scathing denunciation (VIII, cii–ciii and cxxiv–cxxix).

All through the description of the siege of Ismail Byron emphasizes the callousness and heartlessness of war. A soldier's reward for the sacrifice of his life on the battlefield is "three lines" in a bulletin (VII, xx). Apropos of this, Byron wonders if "a man's name in a *bulletin* may make up for a *bullet in* his body?" (VII, xxi). Byron condemns (VII, xxxi) the callousness which is displayed in the perfunctory listing in the gazettes of the names of the war dead. There is also the unknown soldier whose name receives not even the meager honor of mention in a "gazette of slaughter" (VII, xxxi and xxxiv; also VIII, xviii).

The indiscriminate ruthlessness of war, which inflicts suffering upon innocent noncombatants as well as participants, evokes Byron's sarcasm (VII, xxiii):

> The Russians, having built two batteries on
>   An isle near Ismail, had two ends in view;
> The first was to bombard it, and knock down

> The public buildings and the private too,
> No matter what poor souls might be undone.
>   The city's shape suggested this, 'tis true;
> Form'd like an amphitheatre, each dwelling
> Presented a fine mark to throw a shell in.

Byron epitomizes in a single line (VII, xli) the thoroughgoing destruction wrought by war:

> For war cuts up not only branch, but root.

Like some of the poets of the First World War, Byron portrays (VIII, xii–xiii) the sheer, brutal horror of war:

> Three hundred cannon threw up their emetic,
>   And thirty thousand muskets flung their pills
> Like hail, to make a bloody diuretic.
>   Mortality! thou hast thy monthly bills:
> Thy plagues, thy famines, thy physicians, yet tick,
>   Like the death-watch, within our ears the ills
> Past, present, and to come;—but all may yield
> To the true portrait of one battle-field;
>
> There the still varying pangs, which multiply
>   Until their very number makes men hard
> By the infinities of agony,
>   Which meet the gaze, whate'er it may regard—
> The groan, the roll in dust, the all-white eye
>   Turn'd back within its socket,—these reward
> Your rank and file by thousands, while the rest
> May win perhaps a riband at the breast!

The ugly picture continues (xix–xx), complete in every bloody detail:

> Juan and Johnson join'd a certain corps,
>   And fought away with might and main, not knowing
> The way which they had never tried before,
>   And still less guessing where they might be going;
> But on they march'd, dead bodies trampling o'er,
>   Firing, and thrusting, slashing, sweating, glowing,
> But fighting thoughtlessly enough to win,
> To their *two* selves, *one* whole bright bulletin.
>
> Thus on they wallow'd in the bloody mire
>   Of dead and dying thousands,—sometimes gaining
> A yard or two of ground, which brought them nigher
>   To some odd angle for which all were straining;
> At other times, repulsed by the close fire,
>   Which really poured as if all hell were raining

Instead of heaven, they stumbled backwards
    o'er
A wounded comrade, sprawling in his gore.

The crimes of depredation and rapine and plunder which follow the taking of a besieged city do not escape Byron (VIII, lxxxiii and lxxxviii):

The city's taken—only part by part—
    And death is drunk with gore: there's not a
      street
Where fights not to the last some desperate
    heart
    For those for whom it soon shall cease to
      beat.
Here War forgot his own destructive art
    In more destroying Nature; and the heat
Of carnage, like the Nile's sun-sodden slime,
Engender'd monstrous shapes of every crime.

  . . . .
  . . . .

The bayonet pierces and the sabre cleaves,
    And human lives are lavish'd everywhere,
As the year closing whirls the scarlet leaves
    When the stripp'd forest bows to the bleak
      air,
And groans; and thus the peopled city grieves,
    Shorn of its best and loveliest, and left bare;
But still it falls in vast and awful splinters,
As oaks blown down with all their thousand
    winters.

And Byron concludes this picture of war's horror and desolation with this stanza (cxxiii) in which he hints at all the dark horrors and unnatural crimes which ensue when an assaulted city is taken:

All that the mind would shrink from of excesses;
    All that the body perpetrates of bad;
All that we read, hear, dream, of man's
    distresses;
    All that the devil would do if run stark mad;
All that defies the worst which pen expresses;
    All by which hell is peopled, or as sad
As hell—mere mortals who their power
    abuse—
Was here (as heretofore and since) let loose.

Byron satirizes military leaders and officers also. He takes Suwarrow as a typical example and gives us in one stanza (VII, lviii) a vivid sketch of Suwarrow and an ironic epitome of the "noble art of killing." Great military leaders, he says (VII, lxviii), "for one sole leaf" of the imaginary laurel tree of fame have not hesitated to set flowing an "unebbing sea" of "blood and tears." Such a one was Suwarrow (lxxvii):

—who but saw things in the gross,
Being much too gross to see them in detail,
Who calculated life as so much dross,
    And as the wind a widow'd nation's wail—

Byron denounces not only the military leaders but also the idle and wealthy noncombatants who sit at home dining and drinking while the youth of the land give up their lives on the battlefield. During the last war, he says (XIII, liii, liv),

            the News abounded
More with these dinners than the kill'd or
    wounded;—

As thus: "On Thursday there was a grand
    dinner;
    Present, Lords A. B. C."—Earls, dukes, by
    name
Announced with no less pomp than victory's
    winner:
    Then underneath, and in the very same
Column: date, "Falmouth. There has lately
    been here
    The Slap-dash regiment, so well known to
    fame,
Whose loss in the late action we regret:
The vacancies are fill'd up—see Gazette."

This stanza is comparable with the withering irony of a poem of the First World War, "Base Details," by Siegfried Sassoon.

Again Byron's satire of the institution of war has a truly modern ring when he brands (XII, v–vi) the great financiers as the actual war lords of Europe:

Who hold the balance of the world? Who reign
    O'er congress, whether royalist or liberal?
Who rouse the shirtless patriots of Spain?
    (That make old Europe's journals squeak and
      gibber all).
Who keep the world, both old and new, in pain
    Or pleasure? Who make politics run glibber
      all?
The shade of Buonaparte's noble daring?—
Jew Rothschild, and his fellow-Christian,
    Baring.

Those, and the truly liberal Lafitte,
    Are the true lords of Europe. Every loan
Is not a merely speculative hit,
    But seats a nation or upsets a throne.

In the closing stanzas of Canto VII Byron provides a vigorous unmasking of war. He facetiously suggests that there may have been some romance in Homeric warfare but that any romantic element has long since vanished. At any rate, if the Ancients had more glory in their warfare, "still we moderns equal you in blood" (lxxx). There is fine irony in his invoking (lxxxii) of the shades of illustrious warriors of the past:

Oh, ye great bulletins of Bonaparte!
  Oh, ye less grand long lists of kill'd and
      wounded!
Shade of Leonidas, who fought so hearty,
  When my poor Greece was once, as now,
      surrounded!
Oh, Caesar's Commentaries! now impart, ye
  Shadows of glory! (lest I be confounded),
A portion of your fading twilight hues,
So beautiful, so fleeting, to the Muse.

Byron strips the tinsel and the sentiment from war and reveals its naked deformity (lxxxiv):

Medals, rank, ribands, lace, embroidery, scarlet,
  Are things immortal to immortal man,
As purple to the Babylonian harlot:
  An uniform to boys is like a fan
To women; there is scarce a crimson varlet
  But deems himself the first in Glory's van.
But Glory's glory; and if you would find
What that is—ask the pig who sees the wind!

He continues his exposure of the true nature of that ambiguous institution, sometimes called "murder" and other times "glory" (VII, xxvi), in the opening stanza of Canto VIII:

Oh, blood and thunder! and oh, blood and
      wounds!
  These are but vulgar oaths, as you may
      deem,
Too gentle reader! and most shocking sounds:
  And so they are; yet thus is Glory's dream
Unriddled, and as my true Muse expounds
  At present such things, since they are her
      theme,
So be they her inspirers! Call them Mars,
Bellona, what you will—they mean but wars.

On the battlefield, Byron observes, "courage does not glow so much as under a triumphal arch" (VIII, xxi). War, he declares (xlii), is "hell" in spite of what people say

  Of glory, and all that immortal stuff
Which daily fills a regiment (besides their pay,
  That daily shilling which makes warriors
      tough)—

Byron emphasizes (I, cxxxii) the senselessness of war and its total lack of constructive benefit for mankind:

This is the patent age of new inventions
  For killing bodies, and for saving souls,
All propagated with the best intentions;
  Sir Humphry Davy's lantern, by which coals
Are safely mined for in the mode he mentions,
  Timbuctoo travels, voyages to the Poles,
Are ways to benefit mankind, as true,
Perhaps, as shooting them at Waterloo.

He continues this emphasis in the following stanza in which he points to the tremendous price paid and the insignificant gain—the drying up of a single tear is of more importance than the shedding of seas of gore (VIII, iii):

History can only take things in the gross;
  But could we know them in detail, perchance
In balancing the profit and the loss,
  War's merit it by no means might enhance,
To waste so much gold for a little dross,
  As hath been done, mere conquest to
      advance.
The drying up a single tear has more
Of honest fame, than shedding seas of gore.

"One life saved," Byron avows (IX, xxxiv),

          is a thing to recollect
  Far sweeter than the greenest laurels sprung
From the manure of human clay, though deck'd
  With all the praises ever said or sung:

Nor does Byron neglect to ridicule the blind mob spirit and hysteria which accompany war. He impugns (VIII, xxxviii) that

      odd impulse, which in wars or creeds
Makes men, like cattle, follow him who leads.

And, finally, Byron shows himself not entirely a pacifist, for he justifies one kind of war, "defence of freedom, country, or of laws." All other war he denounces (VII, xl) as "mere lust of power." Wars, he says, "except in freedom's battles," are nothing but "a child of Murder's rattles" (VIII, iv), and continues (v):

And such they are—and such they will be
      found:
  Not so Leonidas and Washington,
Whose every battle-field is holy ground,
  Which breathes of nations saved, not worlds
      undone.
How sweetly on the ear such echoes sound!
  While the mere victor's may appal or stun
The servile and the vain, such names will be
A watchword till the future shall be free.

It has been demonstrated, then, that Byron in *Don Juan* satirizes the institution of war most vigorously. He condemns its mercenary aspect, its callousness and heartlessness, its indiscriminate ruthlessness, its sheer horror and sordidness, its meaningless brutality, its ambiguous and anomalous glory, its entire lack of constructive value, its enormous cost, its senselessness and futility, the ignorance from which it springs, and the hysteria by which it is nurtured. Only wars of liberation and wars waged in defense of country are justifiable.

This is Byron's mature attitude toward war.[2] He proves himself to be one of the greatest of satirists of war in English poetry. He is comparable with Shelley in this respect, and with Wordsworth in that poet's early writing. The attitude of these poets is far in advance of their age. It is like that of the leading British poets of the First World War—Hardy, Gibson, Sassoon, Owen, and others, who portray war in all its barbarity, senselessness, and futility.

Passing on now to Byron's satire of despotism, it is to be observed that he frequently contrasts *despotism* with *true kingship*. Byron minces no words in pronouncing judgment upon all despots. They are worse than barbarians, for they are not only the enemies of physical progress but the deadliest foes of Thought. He swears (IX, xxiii–xxiv) his plain, downright detestation of all despotism:

For me, I deem an absolute autocrat
Not a barbarian, but much worse than that.

And I will war, at least in words (and—should
    My chance so happen—deeds), with all who
    war
With Thought;—and of Thought's foes by far
    most rude,
    Tyrants and sycophants have been and are.
I know not who may conquer: if I could
    Have such a prescience, it should be no bar
To this my plain, sworn, downright detestation
Of every despotism in every nation.

This is Byron's war cry against all oppression. And how consistent and unrelenting was his warfare, both in words and deeds, against all that hampers individual and national freedom, we well know!

Despotism abounded in Byron's day. "Kings despotic," he asserts (IV, vi), have not become "obsolete" as have "true knights," "chaste dames," and other "fancies" of the age of chivalry. He holds despots responsible for the savagery of modern war-

fare; it is they who "employ all arts to teach their subjects to destroy" (VIII, xcii). Thousands slain scarce quench the insatiable thirst of tyrants for conquest. "Blood only serves to wash Ambition's hands!" (IX, lix). The human heart shudders at the horrors which "things call'd sovereigns" perpetrate (IX, lx). If modern despots differ in any respect from their predecessors it is in that they "*now* at least must *talk* of law before they butcher" (X, lxxiv).

But Byron foresees (XVI, x) a time when despotism will be obliterated from human society:

So perish every tyrant's robe piece-meal!

Byron hints (VI, xiii) the ultimate fate of all despots in his remarks about the Turkish Sultan:

His Highness, the sublimest of mankind,—
    So styled according to the usual forms
Of every monarch, till they are consigned
    To those sad hungry Jacobins the worms,
Who on the very loftiest kings have dined,—

Death, "the sovereign's sovereign," and the great "reformer," eventually levels even despots to the estate of their oppressed subjects (X, xxv):

And death, the sovereign's sovereign, though
    the great
    Gracchus of all mortality, who levels,
With his *Agrarian* laws, the high estate
    Of him who feasts, and fights, and roars, and
    revels,
To one small grass-grown patch (which must
    await
    Corruption for its crop), with the poor devils
Who never had a foot of land till now,—
Death's a reformer, all men must allow.

But Byron is not content to await the coming of the great "reformer"; he urges (VII, cxxxv) the people to rise against "earth's tyrants."

For I will teach, if possible, the stones
    To rise against earth's tyrants. Never let it
    Be said that we still truckle unto thrones;—

And he is confident (VIII, cxxxvii) that thrones and despots will become "the pleasant riddles of futurity" when men shall regard them as the "mammoth's bones" or "hieroglyphics on Egyptian stones," wondering "what old world such things could see." Another evidence that Byron looked upon despotism as a doomed institution is found in his expression, "the *setting* sun of tyranny" (XV, xxii).

Byron refuses to have any part in the perpetuation

of the institution of despotism. He will not lend his voice to "slavery's jackal cry" or become one of the "human insects" who are "catering for spiders"—the tyrants (IX, xxvi–xxvii). On the contrary, he very definitely reveals his interest in political reformation. It makes (XV, xcii) his

> blood boil like the springs of Hecla,
> To see men let these scoundrel sovereigns
>   break law.

And, finally, Byron contrasts (XII, lxxxiii) despotism with the only *true* kingship, constitutional possession of a throne; but even that is but a step toward the achievement of complete freedom:

> He saw, however, at the closing session,
>   That noble sight, when *really* free the
>   nation,
> A king in constitutional possession
>   Of such a throne as is the proudest station,
> Though despots know it not—till the
>   progression
>   Of freedom shall complete their education.
> 'Tis not mere splendour makes the show august
> To eye or heart—it is the people's trust.

It is easy to see that Byron's satire of despotism is motivated by his thoroughgoing and unqualified hatred of all that interferes with individual and national independence.'

Marriage is the third target of Byron's satire of institutions. But his satire of marriage differs in two important respects from his satire of war and despotism. In the case of marriage it is the abuses in the institution which he attacks and not the institution itself. Furthermore, marriage is the one of the three institutions which had most injured Byron. Hence his satire of it reflects the bias of his personal experience.

Byron recognizes that one of the common causes of marital infelicity is the marriage of youth with age; he has Juan fall in love (I, cvii) with the young and beautiful Julia, who is married to a man more than twice her years. It is the perfunctory and mercenary nature of much of the marriage in Byron's own class of society against which he inveighs (I, lxv).

> Alfonso was the name of Julia's lord,
>   A man well looking for his years, and who
> Was neither much beloved nor yet abhorr'd:
>   They lived together as most people do,
> Suffering each other's foibles by accord,
>   And not exactly either *one* or *two*;

Byron also ridicules (I, lxiv) the tendency in "the moral North" to parade matrimonial difficulties in the courtroom:

> Happy the nations of the moral North!
>   Where all is virtue, and the winter season
> Sends sin, without a rag on, shivering forth
>   ('Twas snow that brought St. Anthony to
>   reason);
> Where juries cast up what a wife is worth,
>   By laying whate'er sum, in mulct, they please
>   on
> The lover, who must pay a handsome price,
> Because it is a marketable vice.

Most marriage, Byron avers (XI, lxxix), is of the "lawful, awful wedlock" variety which has as its prosaic obligation the regular "peopling" of the earth. It is this kind of marriage—this "marketable vice"—of which he paints an extended picture in his description of the "marriage market" in Canto XII, stanzas xxxi–xxxvii. Young women are usually sold to the highest bidder by their ambitious and mercenary mothers.

The fate of the young unmarried man is much the same, for he has an awkward time of it (XII, lviii) in trying to please the ladies who have such "separate" aims, the single ladies "wishing to be double" and the married ones "to save the virgins trouble." The young man's fate is often thus (lx):

> Perhaps you'll have a letter from the mother,
>   To say her daughter's feelings are trepann'd;
> Perhaps you'll have a visit from the brother,
>   All strut, and stays, and whiskers, to demand
> What "your intentions are?"—One way or other
>   It seems the virgin's heart expects your
>   hand:
> And between pity for her case and yours,
> You'll add to Matrimony's list of cures.

Byron is obviously sincere when he deplores (III, v) the fact that marriage and love are so frequently antithetical:

> 'Tis melancholy, and a fearful sign
>   Of human frailty, folly, also crime,
> That love and marriage rarely can combine,
>   Although they both are born in the same
>   clime;
> Marriage from love, like vinegar from wine—
>   A sad, sour, sober beverage—by time
> Is sharpen'd from its high celestial flavour,
> Down to a very homely household savour.

And he points out (XV, xli) the reason for this antithesis; marriage, as he had encountered it in

society and in his own personal experience, was too
frequently regarded as the end of romance and the
beginning of a prosaic, devitalized, passionless relationship, shorn of all joyousness and zest:

> Love's riotous, but marriage should have quiet,
> And being consumptive, live on a milk diet.

"For instance," he says, "passion in a lover's glorious," but "in a husband is pronounced uxorious"
(III, vi).

Byron's own unfortunate marital experience colors all his view of marriage. Marriage is without
romance; there's something in "domestic doings"
which is incompatible with "wooings" and no one
"cares for matrimonial cooings" (III, viii). All
"comedies," he observes, are "ended as a marriage"
(III, ix). The poets do not write of marriage but of
courtship (III, ix); as for exceptions (x):

> The only two that in my recollection
>   Have sung of heaven and hell, or marriage,
>   are
> Dante and Milton, and of both the affection
>   Was hapless in their nuptials, for some bar
> Of fault or temper ruin'd the connexion
>   (Such things, in fact, it don't ask much to
>   mar);
> But Dante's Beatrice and Milton's Eve
> Were not drawn from their spouses, you
>   conceive.

There are frequent veiled allusions to his own
unhappy marital experience in his satire of marriage. In the description of Lambro's return (III, li)
is one of the more obvious allusions to his own
experience. His disillusionment is even more evident
in his ironical comparison of Eastern polygamy with
Western monogamy; he suggests (V, clviii) that the
East might learn a lesson from the West:

> Why don't they knead two virtuous souls for
>   life
> Into that moral centaur, man and wife?

Another gibe of this nature is his remark (VI,
lxxiii) that Juan, in his female disguise in the
harem, lay as fast asleep beside Dudu as ever "husband by his mate in holy matrimony snores away."
And several others in this ironic vein are as follows:
marriage like war is inevitably followed by "discord" (VII, xlix); Haidée was "as pure as Psyche
ere she grew a wife—" (III, lxxiv); "Chaste dames"
are among the "fancies" of an earlier time which
now are "obsolete" (IV, vi); and among the various

kinds of love is a third sort (IX, lxxvi) which flour-
ishes in "every Christian land," namely,

> when chaste matrons to their other ties,
> Add what may be call'd *marriage in disguise.*

There are many others, too numerous to mention.

Byron indulges in a bantering commentary (XV,
xxxv–xxxvi) on Rapp, the Harmonist, and his views
of marriage. Why, asks Byron, did Rapp call a
"state sans wedlock . . . . Harmony?" Apparently,
he regarded marriage and harmony as incompatible.

Another characteristic of marriage in Byron's conception of the institution was servitude or bondage.
Speaking of the wedding ring, he denounces it (IX,
lxx) as the symbol of bondage and "the damn'dest
part of matrimony." And again (III, vii):

> The same things cannot always be admired,
> Yet 'tis "so nominated in the bond,"
> That both are tied till one shall have expired.

Thus Byron's attack on marriage is directed
against its mercenary aspect, its perfunctoriness, its
want of romance and love and consequent infidelity,
and its bondage. But that he was able to conceive
of the true marital happiness of two sincerely devoted persons can be readily substantiated by his
attitude toward Teresa Guiccioli as well as his own
emphasis of the distinction between true marriage
and loveless wedlock in his poetry and in his conversations. He said to Lady Blessington:

> Were the Contessa Guiccioli and I married,
> we should, I am sure, be cited as an example
> of conjugal happiness, and the domestic and
> retired life we lead would entitle us to respect;
> but our union, wanting the legal and religious
> part of the ceremony of marriage, draws on us
> both censure and blame. She is formed to make
> a good wife to any man to whom she at-
> tached herself. She is fond of retirement—is
> of a most affectionate disposition—and noble-
> minded and disinterested to the highest degree
> . . . . When passion is replaced by better feel-
> ings—those of affection, friendship, and confi-
> dence—when, in short, the *liaison* has all of
> marriage but its forms, then it is that we wish
> to give it the respectability of wedlock.[4]

And at another time Byron, speaking of marriage,
said to her:

> If people like each other so well as not to be
> able to live asunder, this is the only tie that can
> assure happiness—all others entail misery.[5]

Byron states definitely his position with regard to marriage in a stanza (XII, xv) from *Don Juan* in which he grants that love and marriage may exist together, "and *should* ever"; but, unfortunately, marriage may also exist without love—and all too frequently does:

Is not all love prohibited whatever,
　Excepting marriage? which is love, no doubt,
After a sort; but somehow people never
　With the same thought the two words have
　　help'd out.
Love may exist *with* marriage, and *should* ever,
　And marriage also may exist without;

Byron reveals his esteem for true marriage in contradistinction to the intrigues and petty passions "of the common school" (IV, xvii) when he refers (XIV, xcv) to "the marriage state" as "the best or worst of any." It was because he did have a sincere regard for real love that he was so keenly alert to the notorious abuses in the institution of marriage and attacked them so relentlessly.

We may say, then, that Byron's satire of marriage is motivated by the same strong feelings which evoked his satire of other institutions—his love of liberty and his detestation of insincerity. He denounces war because it is not only barbarous but irrational and futile. He despises despotism because it is incompatible with individual and national liberty. And he pours out sarcasm upon marriage because to him it spells hypocrisy and bondage.

Closely associated with Byron's satire of institutions, in fact an extension of the same, is his satire of modern society in general. He satirizes his own epoch with its confusion, uncertainty, and unrest.[6] It is an age, he declares (XIV, lxxxiv), which is mad:

Shut up the world at large, let Bedlam out;
　And you will be perhaps surprised to find
All things pursue exactly the same route,
　As now with those of *soi-disant* sound mind.

It is an age of iron-handed despotism and seething unrest. Byron takes us across Europe, in his description of Juan's journey from Russia to England (X, lviii ff.), pointing out the oppression and misery which exist in the various European countries. Poland and Warsaw he mentions as famous for "yokes of iron" (X, lviii). Germany he refers to (X, lx) as the country

whose somewhat tardy millions
Have princes who spur more than their postilions.

Holland, "that water land of Dutchmen and of ditches," is a country where the common people have only a "cordial," since the "good government" has deprived them of all else (X, lxiii).

He denounces the servile attitude of the Irish toward the English king (XI, xxxviii),[7] and praises Greece and Spain as the only two nations "strongly stinging to be free" from despotism and oppression (IX, xxviii). He stigmatizes the Congress of Verona with this line: "I have seen a Congress doing all that's mean" (XI, lxxxiv).[8]

This modern age, Byron reiterates, is not a heroic one. It possesses no sublimity. For this reason a poet is hard put to sing its praises. A poet is obliged to color with nature "manners that are artificial." Gone are the days when "men made the manners"; quite the opposite is now true (XV, xxv–xxvi):

But "laissez aller"—knights and dames I sing,
　Such as the times may furnish. 'Tis a flight
Which seems at first to need no lofty wing,
　Plumed by Longinus or the Stagyrite:
The difficulty lies in colouring
　(Keeping the due proportions still in sight)
With nature manners which are artificial,
And rend'ring general that which is especial.

The difference is, that in the days of old
　Men made the manners; manners now make
　　men—
Pinn'd like a flock, and fleeced too in their fold,
　At least nine, and a ninth beside of ten.
Now this at all events must render cold
　Your writers, who must either draw again
Days better drawn before, or else assume
The present, with their common-place costume.

It is an age, he insists (VI, lvi), of "Corinthian Brass," which was, he adds, "a mixture of all metals, but the brazen uppermost."[9]

There is a Rousseauistic flavor to Byron's condemnation of modern society. He denounces society (IV, xxviii) as

these thick solitudes
Call'd social, haunts of Hate, and Vice, and
　Care;

Society, he avows (V, xxv), destroys whatever altruistic feeling is latent in men's hearts:

Society itself, which should create
　Kindness, destroys what little we had got:

To feel for none is the true social art
Of the world's stoics—men without a heart.

He gives fuller expression to this theme in Canto VIII (lxi–lxii) where he contrasts the natural, simple, and noble life of Daniel Boone, and other American frontiersmen, with the "savage" life of modern men:

Of all men, saving Sylla the man-slayer,
    Who passes for in life and death most lucky,
Of the great names which in our faces stare,
    The General Boon, back-woodsman of Kentucky,
Was happiest amongst mortals anywhere;
    For killing nothing but a bear or buck, he
Enjoy'd the lonely, vigorous, harmless days
Of his old age in wilds of deepest maze.

Crime came not near him—she is not the child
    Of solitude; Health shrank not from him—
    for
Her home is in the rarely trodden wild,
    Where if men seek her not, and death be
    more
Their choice than life, forgive them, as beguiled
    By habit to what their own hearts abhor—
In cities caged. The present case in point I
Cite is, that Boon lived hunting up to ninety;

He extols (VIII, lxv–lxvi) the natural life of these people with its freedom from the accompaniments of modern civilization—war, disease, and greed:

He was not all alone: around him grew
    A sylvan tribe of children of the chase,
Whose young, unawaken'd world was ever
    new,
    Nor sword nor sorrow yet had left a trace
On her unwrinkled brow, nor could you view
    A frown on Nature's or on human face;
The free-born forest found and kept them free,
And fresh as is a torrent or a tree.

And tall, and strong, and swift of foot were
    they,
    Beyond the dwarfing city's pale abortions,
Because their thoughts had never been the prey
    Of care or gain: the green woods were their
    portions;
No sinking spirits told them they grew grey,
    No fashion made them apes of her distortions;
Simple they were, not savage; and their rifles,
Though very true, were not yet used for trifles.

And he satirizes (lxvii) the corruption, ambition, and artificiality of modern life in his praise of natural life:

Motion was in their days, rest in their slumbers
    And cheerfulness the handmaid of their toil;
Nor yet too many nor too few their numbers;
    Corruption could not make their hearts her
    soil;
The lust which stings, the splendour which
    encumbers,
    With the free foresters divide no spoil;
Serene, not sullen, were the solitudes
Of this unsighing people of the woods.

Byron concludes his sweeping satire of modern society, with all its "sweet" consequences of war, disease, ambition, lust, oppression, and discontent, in these words (VIII, lxviii):

So much for Nature:—by way of variety,
    Now back to thy great joys, Civilisation!
And the sweet consequence of large society,
    War, pestilence, the despot's desolation,
The kingly scourge, the lust of notoriety,
    The millions slain by soldiers for their ration,
The scenes like Catherine's boudoir at threescore,
With Ismail's storm to soften it the more.

To recapitulate briefly the objects of Byron's satire in *Don Juan* . . . , Byron's satire, whether of individuals, nations, institutions, or modern society in general, is consistently directed against all insincerity and all which obstructs individual and national freedom.

NOTES

1. R. E. Prothero, *The Works of Lord Byron: Letters and Journals* (London, 1898–1902), VI, 101 (to Thomas Moore. Pisa, August 8, 1822.)

2. In his poem, "The Devil's Drive" (1814), Byron first gave satiric expression to what later became a frequent theme—the horror of war.

3. See also Byron's "Age of Bronze," which contains vigorous denunciation of "Legitimacy."

4. Countess of Blessington, *A Journal of the Conversations of Lord Byron with the Countess of Blessington* (London, 1834), pp. 115–16.

5. *Ibid.*, pp. 141–42.

6. Byron's most concentrated satirical attack on his age is in his "Age of Bronze." See *Poetical Works* (Oxford University Press, 1928), pp. 165–73.

7. Cf. Byron's "The Irish Avatar," stanza xiv.

8. See Byron's "The Age of Bronze," in *Poetical Works*, p. 169.

9. *Ibid.*

Carlos Baker

AN INTRODUCTION TO SHELLEY*

The argument which this book develops is that Shelley was primarily a philosophical and psychological poet with a strong if unorthodox ethical bias, an almost single-minded devotion to a set of esthetic ideals which he felt to be of the greatest utility to the inner life of man and to the progress of society, a conviction that in origin and effect the world's greatest poetry has been inspirational and in the best sense "visionary," and a belief, often enough reiterated to be taken as Shelleyan gospel, that the world's leading poets are great not so much because they have been artists as because they have been "philosophers of the very loftiest power." At any point in his mature career, Shelley would have been prepared to defend with eloquence, determination, and a mass of historical documentation culled from his extraordinarily wide reading, any or all of these biases, devotions, and convictions— because they were the very life-blood of his own effort as a writer.

Shelley's reputation has been distinguished by what may be called its regular variability. He has been praised as a resolute foe of political oppression, a prophet of far-off social events, an optimistic and altruistic idealist, a deliverer with a message of brotherly love, a noble rhetorician, a reviver of Platonism in a materialistic age, a romantic individualist, and a Newton among poets. He has been attacked as a falsetto screamer, a sentimental Narcissus, a dream-ridden escapist, an immoral free-love cultist with a highly inflammable nature, and, particularly in the present age, as the weakling author of the lyric called "The Indian Serenade." The remarkable aspect of these labels is that they regularly reappear: none of them is peculiar to any one age, although "The Indian Serenade" used to be liked, and understood, better than it is today. Shelley was praised or blamed in his own time for nearly all these virtues and faults, and each succeeding generation has had the battle to fight over again. There is hardly a poet in the history of English literature who has been the victim of so many attacks and so many defenses. No permanent peace is likely, nor is any single interpretation of the man or his work likely to gain universal acceptance. If all the lovers and haters of Shelley are not extremists, a sufficient number of hardy perennials is born into each generation to keep the colors flying. To achieve a balanced and judicious estimate of the only really important aspect of Shelley, his career as writer, in the midst of these periodic jostlings and fluctuations, one needs, above all, to understand his premises, his aims, and his achievements, and to keep as clear as may be from the two extremes. For all all the romantic poets Shelley has been taken for what, primarily, he was not, and praise or blame has been showered on him for what, only secondarily, he was.

What Shelley was has been either dimly com-

---

* Excerpts from "Introduction" to Carlos Baker, *Shelley's Major Poetry: The Fabric of a Vision* (copyright 1948 © 1976 by Princeton University Press: Princeton Paperback, 1966), pp. 10–18. Reprinted by permission of Princeton University Press.

prehended or separately and atomistically demonstrated: a sensitive and profoundly serious philosophical and psychological poet, the author of
three or four poems which, judged according to
their own and some other laws, are great, and of
large numbers of experimental, exploratory, and
only partially successful poems in which he tried
to employ and develop symbols of a sufficient magnitude and tensile strength to absorb the inner
stress he laid upon them. The anthologies have
tended to reprint numbers of little lyrics which
Shelley never cared to print in his own lifetime and
which were most often by-products of his main effort, sometimes ignoring the poems on which he
spent his greatest care, or again, on the assumption
that he was primarily a lyric poet, lifting shorter
songs from the longer works and exhibiting them
alone and out of context, a device which is excused
by the space-limits of anthology-makers but which
seems like trying to give an audience the central
idea of *The Tempest* by quoting, without further
comment, the song "Full Fathom Five."

It is a limited and partial, and therefore misrep-
resentative view of Shelley which sees him only as
Ariel, floating down or exuberantly diving through
waves of moonlit song, raising in the spirit those
tempests of emotion which, though meaningless, are
exceedingly beautiful. The lazy-mindedness of such
a view consists in the failure to work back of
the Arielism of Shelley into the stringently self-
disciplined ethical and metaphysical thinker who
employed the lyric as servant to his own particular
brand of white magic. For Shelley, like Prospero
in the mantle of invisibility, or like the poet in his
own lyric, "The Skylark," was often hidden in the
very light of his own thought: a manipulator of
large conceptions whose fundamental operations
no one quite understood. Often he rose like Ariel
to sport among the clouds or coast upon the western wind or ascend as near as could be to the sun;
it was at such times that he produced his most harmonious music, a music elicited by his ecstatic delight in moving swiftly among the timeless objects
of his thought. Behind the ascensions of Ariel, however, there lay always the directive brain of Prospero, author of all the visions, wielder of the power.

A clear majority of Shelley's poems belong to
the classification of inspirational literature, a kind
somewhat out of critical fashion in the present age

but not therefore to be ignored. The structural
method on which most of his lyrics and longer
poems have been built is characteristic of inspirational literature: an ascension from the quiet exposition of the opening stanzas to a kind of bursting climax at which the internal pressure apparently
becomes too great to be any longer withheld. From
what it is possible to learn of Shelley's writing
habits, it would not appear that in the act of composition he paid more than cursory attention to the
final order of the subdivisions of his poems. But in
the arrangement of what he had written (as in
Adonais, where nearly every one of the really
memorable stanzas comes in the last third of the
poem) Shelley seems intentionally to have placed
the most inspired and potentially inspiring passages
near the end of acts or scenes in order to emphasize
the ascensional structure. Even if one doubts that
this order was intentional, the fact remains that it
was the characteristic order in Shelley's poetry.

Shelley placed great value on such passages, and
believed that they were not the result of what he
called labor and study. "The toil and the delay recommended by critics," said he, could mean only
that one must make careful observation of his
inspired moments, and fill up "the spaces between
their suggestions by the intertexture of conventional
expressions." In *Adonais,* which Shelley called a
highly wrought piece of art, the intertexture of conventional expressions (derived from Milton, Bion,
and Moschus) comes chiefly in the first two-thirds
of the poem, and the product of Shelley's "inspired
moments" appears at the end. Perhaps Shelley's
main effort as poet consisted in the attempt not to
bridge but to close the gaps between his inspired
moments, and thus to eliminate the need of "conventional" expressions. In this effort he was no
more successful than most poets of his stamp,
and he was led by his experience to complain of
the "limitedness of the poetical faculty itself." But
he rarely stopped trying, being constituted as he
was, to remove the limits and to make the inspired
moment a permanent condition.

Keats once sought to persuade Shelley that "an
artist must serve Mammon." Shelley must be "more
of an artist, and load every rift" of his subject with
ore. Keats was thinking of Spenser's Cave of Mammon in the *Faerie Queene,* within whose rough
vault

        the ragged breaches hung
Embost with massy gold of glorious gift,
And with rich metall loaded every rift.

Shelley's work from about 1820 onwards shows that he was making some such attempt as Keats advised, so that in time his thinking on the art of poetry might have led him, not to devalue the importance of inspiration, but to pay greater attention to the importance of "toil and delay." The real and heart-breaking toil in Shelley was expended upon the working-out of the vision which lay behind his greatest poems, and in the development of symbols which could bear the burden he placed upon them. Under the surface of *Epipsychidion* and *Adonais* lies a tremendously complex substructure of symbolism, and when one has explored some of its reaches he knows where Shelley's hardest effort was expended. If the fabric of the poetry is full of "ragged breaches"—syntactic disorders, obscurities, images carelessly thrown down or so changeable and various that they are scarcely caught before they are bewilderingly superseded by others—it is partly because he was more deeply concerned with perception and conception than with expression.

Yet Shelley has not been taken seriously as a philosophical poet, and one often gathers from the remarks of his critics, whether inimical or worshipful, that his philosophy does not matter. Yet it does matter—and vitally so—because it is always either the central matter of his poetry, or the frame of reference in terms of which his poetry has been written. That is the chief reason why the present book contains an account, made as precise as possible for each of the periods of his career, of his philosophical development, and of the subtle or sweeping changes which took place in his reading of the world. Shelley has not been taken seriously as a moralist, on the grounds that anyone who abandoned his first wife and ran off with another woman is scarcely to be trusted as an ethical teacher. Yet this foolish and certainly reprehensible act, committed before Shelley had succeeded in the difficult process of growing up emotionally, was paid for a dozen times over, and is pertinent to the problem of Shelley's worth as an ethical teacher only in the fact that his knowledge of human beings and of the human situation was clearly deepened and broadened as a result of his unfortunate experiences. Shelley has not been taken

seriously as a psychological poet because it has not been generally understood that one of his major attempts was to present, by the use of a particular kind of symbolic language, his analyses of certain states of mind known to, but not often consciously recognized by, the thinking part of humankind.

Because the fundamentals of his poetic effort have been obscured—through careless or unsympathetic reading, through blind and breathless adulation, through the not inconsiderable difficulty of a great part of the major poetry, or through the fact that his spectacularly "romantic" life has tended to overshadow his achievement as a writer —Shelley has remained, in the century and a quarter since his death, a figure much talked about but seldom seen in his true light. Many of his biographers have sought to read his poetry as if it were literal or nearly literal autobiography, a mistake which this book seeks to adjust and to correct. Shelley is sometimes "autobiographical" in the very particularized sense that he uses his poetry as the vehicle for analysis of states of mind in which he has been interested. With the greatest rarity he will write of his own physical experience, as in the opening section of *Julian and Maddalo*. But in the main he is far more "objective" than has generally been believed, and the literalistic reading of his poetry will not hit the point, as many of the chapters in the present volume show.

Shelley was in fact one of the most literary poets who ever lived, and his poetry displays a striking combination of objective philosophical and psychological interests and a heavy dependence on antecedent literatures. His preoccupation with states of mind leads him to search for a special language through which they can be dramatically projected, and he arrives at a symbolic literary language developed from many traditional sources and refashioned into a mode of expression peculiarly his own. He once complained that when he tried to speak to other men in the language of poetry, they misunderstood him, as if he had been a visitor to an unknown country. Yet the explorer of Shelley's sources can nearly always trace his semiprivate language back to its origins, and its origins are almost invariably found, not in the events of his life, but in the events of his reading. With the help of earlier source-hunters, and through an extensive independent study of Shelley's reading, it has been possible in the present volume to discover the origins of most of his symbolic figures, to use that knowledge in the interpretation of the poems, and thus to provide a topographical map of Shelley's realms of gold.

If the study of Shelley's poetry is not necessarily a means of grace, the study of his source books is one of the means to an education. Among the important matters in the following pages are the proofs of Shelley's indebtedness to, and his imaginative reworking of, Greek literature (Plato, Aeschylus, Sophocles), Renaissance literature (Dante, Petrarch, Spenser, Shakespeare, and Milton), and the poetry of his own day (Wordsworth, Coleridge, Byron, and Keats). Though it is outside the scope of this book to provide an exhaustive study of Shelley's use of his forebears and his contemporaries, enough is included to show in broad outline, yet with necessary emphases, Shelley's direct relationship to the great tradition of western letters.

The definition of what Shelley was can be clarified by attention to what, primarily, he was not. He was not primarily an epic poet, though the internal dimensions of his four best poems, *Prometheus Unbound, Epipsychidion, Adonais,* and *The Triumph of Life,* are of an epic magnitude. He was not primarily a dramatic poet. Deeply interested in the analysis of character, and particularly of what he calls "the most interesting situations of the human mind," he read, admired, and imitated Shakespeare, Calderon, and Goethe. He wrote one tragedy, *The Cenci,* which with some editorial revision and directorial reemphasis, could be made into a highly effective stage-play. But he recognized in himself a deficiency in strictly literary architectonics, and he had not, as the first-line modern dramatist must have, a fundamental interest in the projection of character through action. He was not primarily a lyric poet. Though he was often most eloquent and memorable in the lyric mode, his greatest effort was expended on the arrangement, clarification, and development of his vision rather than on the hymning of it. He was not primarily a craftsman in the sense of being interested deeply in and unremittingly devoted to the finer details of structure and texture. On rare occasions, chiefly in the latter part of his life, he develops controlling metaphors whose logical complexities and multiple ramifications show that he took sometimes the craftsman-philosopher's delight in that process of

verbal and ideological intensification on which modern criticism rightly, though sometimes too exclusively, insists. But his characteristic texture is loosely woven of many strings, as if he hoped that through the veil of language his readers might discern the complex and many-faceted vision on which, rather than on verbal patternings, his texture was based.

Secondarily, of course, Shelley was all these kinds of poet at one time or another in his writing life. The variety of his experimental work is one of the most remarkable aspects of his brief career. But whatever the form he essayed, the fundamental dynamic of his writing remained the same. He belongs primarily to the class of psychological and philosophical poets which he describes in the peroration to his *Defence of Poetry.* He sought, first, "to measure the circumference and sound the depths of human nature with a comprehensive and all-penetrating spirit." He attempted, in the second place, to be the "hierophant" or philosophic interpreter of the great vision of supernal beauty and love—a vision which he knew to be "unapprehended" by the majority of men and only "approximated" in perception and expression by the poet himself, yet a vision absolutely necessary to the moral progress and mental well-being of the benighted world of men. Knowledge of the circumference and the depths of human nature led in Shelley's view to knowledge of self. Knowledge of the great vision meant knowledge of the moral law of love. To these two concepts, self-knowledge and knowledge of what he thought of as God, his career as poet was dedicated.

To understand Shelley's means, one may look to his ends. He began, at one end, as a didactic allegorical poet and ended by writing symbolic mythological poetry of an impressively high order. He began as an imitator of eighteenth-century forms, and the early work is full of obvious creaking machines which served him as the vehicles for a materialistic, necessitarian ideology and a black-and-white ethic. He ended as the formulator of an idealistic vision by which he measured the mundane world and found it wanting, but a vision whose very complexity and many-sidedness indicate that he had come to a kind of answer, as tentative as all such answers must be, to the perennial ethical and metaphysical problems. When he began to find himself as a poet, somewhere in the latter part of 1818, he entered the line that begins with Dante and continues through Milton and Blake. As ultimately developed and refined, his vision employs traditional symbols in an unconventional fashion for the ethical end of man's redemption and salvation. If Shelley's vision is less firmly grounded and detailed than Dante's, less Hebraically majestic than Milton's, and less spectacular than Blake's, it is somewhat easier than Dante's to grasp in its totality, less heavily weighted with theology than Milton's, and less insistently arbitrary than Blake's. Shelley's place as philosophic poet may be defined in terms of the myth-makers of classical, Renaissance and modern times. His place as a psychological poet is beside Wordsworth and Keats. Like them he took self-knowledge as the key to the understanding of man, and like them he came, by tortuous ways, to an understanding of man's place in the cosmic scheme. A century and a quarter of readers have not been wrong in asserting the indubitable charm of Shelley's Arielism; the error has lain in supposing that he had nothing else to offer.

F. R. Leavis

SHELLEY*

If Shelley had not received some distinguished attention in recent years (and he has been differed over by the most eminent critics) there might, perhaps, have seemed little point in attempting a restatement of the essential critical observations—the essential observations, that is, in the reading and appreciation of Shelley's poetry. For they would seem to be obvious enough. Yet it is only one incitement out of many when a critic of peculiar authority, contemplating the common change from being "intoxicated by Shelley's poetry at the age of fifteen" to finding it now "almost unreadable," invokes for explanation the nature of Shelley's "ideas" and, in reference to them, that much-canvassed question of the day, "the question of belief or disbelief":

> "It is not so much that thirty years ago I was able to read Shelley under an illusion which experience has dissipated, as that because the question of belief or disbelief did not arise I was in a much better position to enjoy the poetry. I can only regret that Shelley did not live to put his poetic gifts, which were certainly of the first order, at the service of more tenable beliefs—which need not have been, for my purposes, beliefs more acceptable to me."

This is, of course, a personal statement; but perhaps if one insists on the more obvious terms of literary criticism—more strictly critical terms—in which such a change might be explained, and suggests that the terms actually used might be found unfortunate in their effect, the impertinence will not be unpardonable. It does, in short, seem worth endeavouring to make finally plain that, when one dissents from persons who, sympathizing with Shelley's revolutionary doctrines and with his idealistic ardours and fervours—with his "beliefs," exalt him as a poet, it is strictly the "poetry" one is criticizing. There would also appear to be some reason for insisting that in finding Shelley almost unreadable one need not be committing oneself to a fashionably limited taste—an inability to appreciate unfashionable kinds of excellence or to understand a use of words that is unlike Hopkins's or Donne's.

It will be well to start, in fact, by examining the working of Shelley's poetry—his characteristic modes of expression—as exemplified in one of his best poems.

---

* From *Revaluation* by F. R. Leavis. Copyright 1936, Chatto and Windus Ltd. Reprinted by permission of the publisher.

Thou on whose stream, mid the steep sky's
　　commotion,
Loose clouds like earth's decaying leaves are
　　shed,
Shook from the tangled boughs of Heaven and
　　Ocean,

Angels of rain and lightning: there are spread
On the blue surface of thine aëry surge,
Like the bright hair uplifted from the head

Of some fierce Maenad, even from the dim
　　verge
Of the horizon to the zenith's height,
The locks of the approaching storm.

The sweeping movement of the verse, with the accompanying plangency, is so potent that, as many
can testify, it is possible to have been for years
familiar with the Ode—to know it by heart—without asking the obvious questions. In what respects
are the "loose clouds" like "decaying leaves"? The
correspondence is certainly not in shape, colour or
way of moving. It is only the vague general sense
of windy tumult that associates the clouds and the
leaves; and, accordingly, the appropriateness of the
metaphor "stream" in the first line is not that it
suggests a surface on which, like leaves, the clouds
might be "shed," but that it contributes to the
general "streaming" effect in which the inappropriateness of "shed" passes unnoticed. What again, are
those "tangled boughs of Heaven and Ocean"?
They stand for nothing that Shelley could have
pointed to in the scene before him; the "boughs,"
it is plain, have grown out of the "leaves" in the
previous line, and we are not to ask what the tree
is. Nor are we to scrutinize closely the "stream"
metaphor as developed: that "blue surface" must
be the concave of the sky, an oddly smooth surface
for a "surge"—if we consider a moment. But in this
poetic surge, while we let ourselves be swept along,
there is no considering, the image doesn't challenge
any inconvenient degree of realization, and the
oddness is lost. Then again, in what ways does the
approach of a storm ("loose clouds like earth's
decaying leaves," "like ghosts from an enchanter
fleeing") suggest streaming hair? The appropriateness of the Maenad, clearly, lies in the pervasive
suggestion of frenzied onset, and we are not to ask
whether her bright hair is to be seen as streaming
out in front of her (as, there is no need to assure
ourselves, it might be doing if she were running
before a still swifter gale: in the kind of reading

that got so far as proposing to itself this particular
reassurance no general satisfaction could be ex-
acted from Shelley's imagery).

Here, clearly, in these peculiarities of imagery
and sense, peculiarities analysable locally in the
mode of expression, we have the manifestation of
essential characteristics—the Shelleyan characteristics as envisaged by the criticism that works on
a philosophical plane and makes judgments of
a moral order. In the growth of those "tangled
boughs" out of the leaves, exemplifying as it does a
general tendency of the images to forget the status
of the metaphor or simile that introduced them
and to assume an autonomy and a right to propagate, so that we lose in confused generations and
perspectives the perception or thought that was
the ostensible *raison d'être* of imagery, we have a
recognized essential trait of Shelley's: his weak
grasp upon the actual. This weakness, of course,
commonly has more or less creditable accounts
given of it—idealism, Platonism and so on; and
even as unsentimental a judge as Mr. Santayana
correlates Shelley's inability to learn from experience with his having been born a "nature pre-
formed," a "spokesman of the *a priori*," "a dogmatic, inspired, perfect and incorrigible creature." [1]
It seems to me that Mr. Santayana's essay, admirable
as it is, rates the poetry too high. But for the
moment it will be enough to recall limitations that
are hardly disputed: Shelley was not gifted for
drama or narrative. Having said this, I realize that
I had forgotten the conventional standing of *The
Cenci*; but controversy may be postponed: it is at
any rate universally agreed that (to shift tactfully
to positive terms) Shelley's genius was "essentially
lyrical."

This predicate would, in common use, imply a
special emotional intensity—a vague gloss, but it
is difficult to go further without slipping into terms
that are immediately privative and limiting. Thus
there is certainly a sense in which Shelley's poetry
is peculiarly emotional, and when we try to define
this sense we find ourselves invoking an absence of
something. The point may be best made, perhaps,
by recalling the observation noted above, that one
may have been long familiar with the *Ode to the
West Wind* without ever having asked the obvious
questions; questions that propose themselves at the
first critical inspection. This poetry induces—depends for its success on inducing—a kind of atten-

tion that doesn't bring the critical intelligence into play: the imagery feels right, the associations work appropriately, if (as it takes conscious resistance not to do) one accepts the immediate feeling and doesn't slow down to think.

Shelley himself can hardly have asked the questions. Not that he didn't expend a great deal of critical labour upon his verse. "He composed rapidly and attained to perfection by intensive correction. He would sometimes write down a phrase with alterations and rejections time after time until it came within a measure of satisfying him. Words are frequently substituted for others and lines interpolated." The *Ode to the West Wind* itself, as is shown in the repository[2] of fragments the preface to which supplies these observations, profited by the process described, which must be allowed to have been in some sense critical. But the critical part of Shelley's creative labour was a matter of getting the verse to feel right, and feeling, for Shelley as a poet, had—as the insistent concern for "rightness," the typical final product being what it is, serves to emphasize—little to do with thinking (though Shelley was in some ways a very intelligent man).

We have here, if not sufficient justification for the predicate "essentially lyrical," certainly a large part of the reason for Shelley's being found essentially poetical by the succeeding age. He counted, in fact, for a great deal in what came to be the prevailing idea of "the poetical"—the idea that had its latest notable statement in Professor Housman's address, *The Name and Nature of Poetry*. The Romantic conceptions of genius and inspiration[3] developed (the French Revolution and its ideological background must, of course, be taken into account) in reaction against the Augustan insistence on the social and the rational. When Wordsworth says that "all good poetry is the spontaneous overflow of powerful feelings" he is of his period, though the intended force of this dictum, the force it has in its context and in relation to Wordsworth's own practice, is very different from that given it when Shelley assents, or when it is assimilated to Byron's "poetry is the lava of the imagination, whose eruption prevents an earthquake."[4] But Byron was for the young Tennyson (and the Ruskin parents)[5] the poet, and Shelley (Browning's "Sun-treader") was the idol of the undergraduate Tennyson and his fellow Apostles, and, since the poetry of "the

age of Wordsworth" became canonical, the assent given to Wordsworth's dictum has commonly been Shelleyan.

The force of Shelley's insistence on spontaneity is simple and unequivocal. It will be enough to recall a representative passage or two from the *Defence of Poetry*:

> "for the mind in creation is as a fading coal, which some invisible influence, like an inconstant wind, awakes to transitory brightness; this power arises from within, like the colour of a flower which fades and changes as it is developed, and the conscious portions of our nature are unprophetic either of its approach or its departure."

"Inspiration" is not something to be tested, clarified, defined and developed in composition,

> "but when composition begins, inspiration is already on the decline, and the most glorious poetry that has ever been communicated to the world is probably a feeble shadow of the original conceptions of the poet. . . . The toil and delay recommended by critics can be justly interpreted to mean no more than a careful observation of the inspired moments, and an artificial connexion of the spaces between their suggestions, by the intertexture of conventional expressions; a necessity only imposed by the limitedness of the poetical faculty itself. . . ."

The "poetical faculty," we are left no room for doubting, can, of its very nature, have nothing to do with any discipline, and can be associated with conscious effort only mechanically and externally, and when Shelley says that Poetry

> "is not subject to the control of the active powers of the mind, and that its birth and recurrence have no necessary connexion with consciousness or will"

he is not saying merely that the "active powers of the mind" are insufficient in themselves for creation —that poetry cannot be written merely by taking thought. The effect of Shelley's eloquence is to hand poetry over to a sensibility that has no more dealings with intelligence than it can help; to a "poetic faculty" that, for its duly responsive vibrating (though the poet must reverently make his pen as sensitive an instrument as possible to "observe" —in the scientific sense—the vibrations), demands that active intelligence shall be, as it were, switched off.

Shelley, of course, had ideas and ideals; he wrote philosophical essays, and it need not be irrelevant to refer, in discussing his poetry, to Plato, Godwin and other thinkers. But there is nothing grasped in the poetry—no object offered for contemplation, no realized presence to persuade or move us by what it is. A. C. Bradley, remarking that "Shelley's ideals of good, whether as a character or as a mode of life, resting as they do on abstraction from the mass of real existence, tend to lack body and individuality," adds: "But we must remember that Shelley's strength and weakness are closely allied, and it may be that the very abstractness of his ideal was a condition of that quivering intensity of aspiration towards it in which his poetry is unequalled." [6] That is the best that can be respectably said. Actually, that "quivering intensity," offered in itself apart from any substance, offered instead of any object, is what, though it may make Shelley intoxicating at fifteen makes him almost unreadable, except in very small quantities of his best, to the mature. Even when he is in his own way unmistakably a distinguished poet, as in *Prometheus Unbound*, it is impossible to go on reading him at any length with pleasure; the elusive imagery, the high-pitched emotions, the tone and movement, the ardours, ecstasies and despairs, are too much the same all through. The effect is of vanity and emptiness (Arnold was right) as well as monotony.

The force of the judgment that feeling in Shelley's poetry is divorced from thought needs examining further. Any suspicion that Donne is the implied criterion will, perhaps, be finally averted if for the illuminating contrast we go to Wordsworth. Wordsworth is another "Romantic" poet; he too is undramatic; and he too invites the criticism (Arnold, his devoted admirer, made it) that he lacks variety. "Thought" will hardly be found an assertive presence in his best poetry; in so far as the term suggests an overtly active energy it is decidedly inappropriate. "Emotion," his own word, is the word most readers would insist on, though they would probably judge Wordsworth's emotion to be less lyrical than Shelley's. The essential difference, however—and it is a very important one—seems, for present purposes, more relevantly stated in the terms I used in discussing[7] Wordsworth's "recollection in tranquillity." The process covered by this phrase was one of emotional discipline, critical exploration of experience, pondered valuation and

maturing reflection. As a result of it an organization is engaged in Wordsworth's poetry, and the activity and standards of critical intelligence are implicit.

An associated difference was noted in the sureness with which Wordsworth grasps the world of common perception. The illustration suggested was *The Simplon Pass* in comparison with Shelley's *Mont Blanc*. The element of Wordsworth in *Mont Blanc* (it is perceptible in these opening lines) serves only to enhance the contrast:

> The everlasting universe of things
> Flows through the mind, and rolls its rapid
>   waves,
> Now dark—now glittering—now reflecting
>   gloom—
> Now lending splendour, where from secret
>   springs
> The source of human thought its tribute brings
> Of waters—with a sound but half its own,
> Such as a feeble brook will oft assume
> In the wild woods, among the mountains lone,
> Where waterfalls around it leap for ever,
> Where woods and winds contend, and a vast
>   river
> Over its rocks ceaselessly bursts and raves.

The metaphorical and the actual, the real and the imagined, the inner and the outer, could hardly be more unsortably and indistinguishably confused. The setting, of course, provides special excuse for bewildered confusion; but Shelley takes eager advantage of the excuse and the confusion is characteristic—what might be found unusual in *Mont Blanc* is a certain compelling vividness. In any case, Wordsworth himself is explicitly offering a sense of sublime bewilderment, similarly inspired:

> Black drizzling crags that spake by the wayside
> As if a voice were in them, the sick sight
> And giddy prospect of the raving stream,
> The unfettered clouds and region of the
>   heavens,
> Tumult and peace, the darkness and the
>   light—
> Were all like workings of one mind, the features
> Of the same face . . .

He is, of course, recollecting in tranquillity; but the collectedness of those twenty lines (as against Shelley's one hundred and forty) does not belong merely to the record; it was present (or at least the movement towards it was) in the experience, as those images, "one mind," "the same face"—epitomizing, as they do, the contrast with Shelley's ecstatic dissipation—may fairly be taken to testify.

This comparison does not aim immediately at a judgment of relative value. *Mont Blanc* is very interesting as well as idiosyncratic, and is not obviously the product of the less rare gift. There are, nevertheless, critical judgments to be made—judgments concerning the emotional quality of Wordsworth's poetry and of Shelley's: something more than mere description of idiosyncrasy is in view. What should have come out in the comparison that started as a note on Wordsworth's grasp of the outer world is the unobtrusiveness with which that "outer" turns into "inner": the antithesis, clearly, is not altogether, for present purposes, a simple one to apply. What is characteristic of Wordsworth is to grasp surely (which, in the nature of the case, must be delicately and subtly) what he offers, whether this appears as belonging to the outer world—the world as perceived, or to inner experience. He seems always to be presenting an object (wherever this may belong) and the emotion seems to derive from what is presented. The point is very obviously and impressively exemplified in *A slumber did my spirit seal,* which shows Wordsworth at his supreme height. Here (compare it with the *Ode to the West Wind,* where we have Shelley's genius at its best; or, if something more obviously comparable is required, with Tennyson's *Break, break, break*) there is no emotional comment—nothing "emotional" in phrasing, movement or tone; the facts seem to be presented barely, and the emotional force to be generated by them in the reader's mind when he has taken them in—generated by the two juxtaposed stanzas, in the contrast between the situations or states they represent.

Shelley, at his best and worst, offers the emotion in itself, unattached, in the void. "In itself" "for itself"—it is an easy shift to the pejorative implications of "for its own sake"; just as, for a poet with the habit of sensibility and expression described, it was an easy shift to deserving them. For Shelley is obnoxious to the pejorative implications of "habit": being inspired was, for him, too apt to mean surrendering to a kind of hypnotic rote of favourite images, associations and words. "Inspiration," there not being an organization for it to engage (as in Wordsworth, whose sameness is of a different order from Shelley's, there was), had only poetical habits to fall back on. We have them in their most innocent aspect in those favourite words: *radiant, aërial,*

odorous, daedal, faint, sweet, bright, winged, -inwoven, and the rest of the fondled vocabulary that any reader of Shelley could go on enumerating. They manifest themselves as decidedly deplorable in *The Cloud* and *To a Skylark,* which illustrate the dangers of fostering the kind of inspiration that works only when critical intelligence is switched off. These poems may be not unfairly described as the products of switching poetry on.[8] There has been in recent years some controversy about particular points in *To a Skylark,* and there are a score or more points inviting adverse criticism. But this need hardly be offered; it is, or should be, so plain that the poem is a mere tumbled out spate ("spontaneous overflow") of poeticalities, the place of each one of which Shelley could have filled with another without the least difficulty and without making any essential difference. They are held together by the pervasive "lyrical emotion," and that this should be capable of holding them together is comment enough on the nature of its strength.

Cheaper surrenders to inspiration may easily be found in the collected Shelley; there are, for instance, gross indulgences in the basest Regency album taste.[9] But criticism of Shelley has something more important to deal with than mere bad poetry; or, rather, there are badnesses inviting the criticism that involves moral judgments. It must have already appeared (it has virtually been said) that surrendering to inspiration cannot, for a poet of Shelley's emotional habits, have been very distinguishable from surrendering to temptation. The point comes out in an element of the favoured vocabulary not exemplified above: *charnel, corpse, phantom, liberticide, aghast, ghastly* and so on. The wrong approach to emotion, the approach from the wrong side or end (so to speak), is apparent here; Shelley would clearly have done well not to have indulged these habits and these likings: the viciousness and corruption are immediately recognizable. But viciousness and corruption do not less attend upon likings for tender ("I love Love"),[10] sympathetic, exalted and ecstatic emotions, and may be especially expected to do so in a mind as little able to hold an object in front of it as Shelley's was.

The transition from the lighter concerns of literary criticism to the diagnosis of radical disabilities and perversions, such as call for moral comment, may be conveniently illustrated from a favourite anthology-piece, *When the lamp is shattered*:

When the lamp is shattered
The light in the dust lies dead—
    When the cloud is scattered
The rainbow's glory is shed.
    When the lute is broken,
Sweet tones are remembered not;
    When the lips have spoken,
Loved accents are soon forgot.

    As music and splendour
Survive not the lamp and the lute,
    The heart's echoes render
No song when the spirit is mute:—
    No song but sad dirges,
Like the wind through a ruined cell;
    Or the mournful surges
That ring the dead seaman's knell.

When hearts have once mingled
Love first leaves the well-built nest;
    The weak one is singled
To endure what it once possessed.
    O Love! who bewailest
The frailty of all things here,
    Why choose you the frailest
For your cradle, your home, and your bier?

    Its passions will rock thee
As the storms rock the ravens on high;
    Bright reason will mock thee,
Like the sun from a wintry sky.
    From thy nest every rafter
Will rot, and thine eagle home
    Leave thee naked to laughter,
When leaves fall and cold winds come.

The first two stanzas call for no very close attention—to say so, indeed, is to make the main
criticism, seeing that they offer a show of insistent
argument. However, reading with an unsolicited
closeness, one may stop at the second line and ask
whether the effect got with "lies dead" is legitimate.
Certainly, the emotional purpose of the poem is
served, but the emotional purpose that went on
being served in that way would be suspect. Leaving
the question in suspense, perhaps, one passes to
"shed"; "shed" as tears, petals and coats are shed,
or as light is shed? The latter would be a rather
more respectable use of the word in connexion with
a rainbow's glory, but the context indicates the
former. Only in the vaguest and slackest state of
mind—of imagination and thought—could one so
describe the fading of a rainbow; but for the right
reader "shed" sounds right, the alliteration with
"shattered" combining with the verse-movement to
produce a kind of inevitability. And, of course,
suggesting tears and the last rose of summer, it

suits with the general emotional effect. The nature
of this is by now so unmistakable that the complete
nullity of the clinching "so," when it arrives—of the
two lines that justify the ten preparatory lines of
analogy—seems hardly worth stopping to note:

The heart's echoes render
No song when the spirit is mute.

Nor is it surprising that there should turn out to be
a song after all, and a pretty powerful one—for
those who like that sort of thing; the "sad dirges,"
the "ruined cell," the "mournful surges" and the
"dead seaman's knell' being immediately recognizable as currency values. Those who take pleasure
in recognizing and accepting them are not at the
same time exacting about sense.

The critical interest up to this point has been to
see Shelley, himself (when inspired) so unexacting
about sense, giving himself so completely to sentimental banalities. With the next stanza it is much
the same, though the emotional *clichés* take on a
grosser unction and the required abeyance of
thought (and imagination) becomes more remarkable. In what form are we to imagine Love leaving
the well-built nest? For readers who get so far as
asking, there can be no acceptable answer. It would
be unpoetically literal to suggest that, since the
weak one is singled, the truant must be the mate,
and, besides, it would raise unnecessary difficulties.
Perhaps the mate, the strong one, is what the weak
one, deserted by Love, whose alliance made possession once possible, now has to endure? But the
suggestion is frivolous; the sense is plain enough—
enough, that is, for those who respond to the sentiment. Sufficient recognition of the sense depends
neither on thinking, nor on realization of the metaphors, but on response to the sentimental common-
places: it is only when intelligence and imagination
insist on intruding that difficulties arise. So plain is
this that there would be no point in contemplating
the metaphorical complexity that would develop if
we could take the tropes seriously and tried to
realize Love making of the weak one, whom it (if
we evade the problem of sex) leaves behind in the
well-built nest, a cradle, a home and a bier.

The last stanza brings a notable change; it alone
in the poem has any distinction, and its personal
quality, characteristically Shelleyan, stands out
against the sentimental conventionality of the rest.
The result is to compel a more radical judgment on

the poem than has yet been made. In "Its passions will rock thee" the "passions" must be those of Love, so that it can no longer be Love that is being apostrophized. Who, then, is "thee"? The "frailest" —the "weak one"—it would appear. But any notion one may have had that the "weak one," as the conventional sentiments imply, is the woman must be abandoned: the "eagle home," to which the "well-built nest" so incongruously turns, is the Poet's. The familiar timbre, the desolate intensity (note particularly the use of "bright" in "bright reason"), puts it beyond doubt that Shelley is, characteristically, addressing himself—the "pardlike Spirit beautiful and swift," the "Love in desolation masked," the "Power girt round with weakness."

Characteristically: that is, Shelley's characteristic pathos is self-regarding, directed upon an idealized self in the way suggested by the tags just quoted.[11] This is patently so in some of his best poetry; for instance, in the *Ode to the West Wind*. Even there, perhaps, one may find something too like an element of luxury in the poignancy (at any rate, one's limiting criticism of the Ode would move towards such a judgment); and that in general there must be dangers and weakness attending upon such a habit will hardly be denied. The poem just examined shows how gross may be, in Shelley, the corruptions that are incident. He can make self-pity a luxury at such level that the conventional pathos of album poeticizing, not excluding the banalities about (it is plainly so in the third stanza) the sad lot of woman, can come in to gratify the appetite.

The abeyance of thought exhibited by the first three stanzas now takes on a more sinister aspect. The switching-off of intelligence that is necessary if the sentiments of the third stanza are to be accepted has now to be invoked in explanation of a graver matter—Shelley's ability to accept the grosser, the truly corrupt, gratifications that have just been indicated. The antipathy of his sensibility to any play of the critical mind, the uncongeniality of intelligence to inspiration, these clearly go in Shelley, not merely with a capacity for momentary self-deceptions and insincerities, but with a radical lack of self-knowledge. He could say of Wordsworth, implying the opposite of himself, that

> he never could
> Fancy another situation
> From which to dart his contemplation
> Than that wherein he stood.

But, for all his altruistic fervours and his fancied capacity for projecting his sympathies, Shelley is habitually—it is no new observation—his own hero: Alastor, Laon, The Sensitive Plant

> (It loves, even like Love, its deep heart is full,
> It desires what it has not, the Beautiful)

and Prometheus. It is characteristic that he should say to the West Wind

> A heavy weight of hours has chained and
>   bowed
> One too like thee: tameless, and swift, and
>   proud,

and conclude:

> Be thou, Spirit fierce,
> My spirit! Be thou me, impetuous one!

About the love of such a nature there is likely at the best to be a certain innocent selfishness. And it is with fervour that Shelley says, as he is always saying implicitly, "I love Love." Mr. Santayana acutely observes: "In him, as in many people, too intense a need of loving excludes the capacity for intelligent sympathy." Perhaps love generally has less in it of intelligent sympathy than the lover supposes, and is less determined by the object of love; but Shelley, we have seen, was, while on the one hand conscious of ardent altruism, on the other peculiarly weak in his hold on objects—peculiarly unable to realize them as existing in their own natures and their own right. His need of loving (in a sense that was not, perhaps, in the full focus of Mr. Santayana's intention) comes out in the erotic element that, as already remarked in these pages, the texture of the poetry pervasively exhibits. There is hardly any need to illustrate here the tender, caressing, voluptuous effects and suggestions of the favourite vocabulary and imagery. The consequences of the need, or "love," of loving, combined, as it was, with a notable lack of self-knowledge and a capacity for ecstatic idealizing, are classically extant in *Epipsychidion*.

The love of loathing is, naturally, less conscious than the love of Love. It may fairly be said to involve a love of Hate, if not of hating: justification enough for putting it this way is provided by *The Cenci*, which exhibits a perverse luxury of insistence, not merely upon horror, but upon malignity. This work, of course, is commonly held to require noting as, in the general account of Shelley, a remarkable exception: his genius may be essentially lyrical, but he can, transcending limitations, write great drama. This estimate of *The Cenci* is certainly a remarkable instance of *vis inertiae*—of the power of conventional valuation to perpetuate itself, once established. For it takes no great discernment to see that *The Cenci* is very bad and that its badness is characteristic. Shelley, as usual, is the hero—here the heroine; his relation to Beatrice is of the same order as his relation to Alastor and Prometheus, and the usual vices should not be found more acceptable because of the show of drama.

Nor is this show the less significantly bad because Shelley doesn't know where it comes from—how he is contriving it. He says in his *Preface* that an idea suggested by Calderon is "the only plagiarism which I have intentionally committed in the whole piece." Actually, not only is the "whole piece" Shakespearian in inspiration (how peculiarly dubious an affair inspiration was apt to be for Shelley we have seen), it is full of particular echoes of Shakespeare—echoes protracted, confused and woolly; plagiarisms, that is, of the worst kind. This Shakespearianizing, general and particular is—and not the less so for its unconsciousness—quite damning. It means that Shelley's drama and tragedy do not grow out of any realized theme; there is nothing grasped at the core of the piece. Instead there is Beatrice-Shelley, in whose martyrdom the Count acts Jove—with more than Jovian gusto:

> I do not feel as if I were a man,
> But like a fiend appointed to chastise
> The offences of some unremembered world.
> My blood is running up and down my veins;
> A fearful pleasure makes it prick and tingle:
> I feel a giddy sickness of strange awe;
> My heart is beating with an expectation
> Of horrid joy.

The pathos is of corresponding corruptness. The habits that enable Shelley to be unconscious about this kind of indulgence enable him at the same time to turn it into tragic drama by virtue of an unconscious effort to be Shakespeare.

There are, of course, touches of Webster: Beatrice in the trial scene is commonly recognized to have borrowed an effect or two from the White Devil. But the Shakespearian promptings are everywhere, in some places almost ludicrously assorted, obvious and thick. For instance, Act III, Sc. ii starts (stage direction: "Thunder and the sound of a storm") by being at line two obviously Lear. At line eight Othello comes in and carries on for ten lines; and he reasserts himself at line fifty. At line fifty-five Hamlet speaks. At line seventy-eight we get an effect from *Macbeth,* to be followed by many more in the next act, during which, after much borrowed suspense, the Count's murder is consummated.

The quality of the dramatic poetry and the relation between Shelley and Shakespeare must, for reasons of space, be represented—the example is a fair one—by a single brief passage (Act V, Sc. iv, l. 48):

> O
> My God! Can it be possible I have
> To die so suddenly? So young to go
> Under the obscure, cold, rotting, wormy
>   ground!
> To be nailed down into a narrow place;
> To see no more sweet sunshine; hear no more
> Blithe voice of living thing; muse not again
> Upon familiar thoughts, sad, yet thus lost—
> How fearful! to be nothing! Or to be . . .
> What? Oh, where am I? Let me not go mad!
> Sweet Heaven, forgive weak thoughts! If there
>   should be
> No God, no Heaven, no Earth in the void
>   world;
> The wide, gray, lampless, deep, unpeopled
>   world!

This patently recalls Claudio's speech in *Measure for Measure* (Act III, Sc. i):

> Ay, but to die, and go we know not where;
> To lie in cold obstruction and to rot;
> This sensible warm motion to become
> A kneaded clod; and the delighted spirit
> To bathe in fiery floods, or to reside
> In thrilling region of thick-ribbed ice;
> To be imprisoned in the viewless winds,
> And blown with restless violence round about
> The pendent world; or to be worse than worst
> Of those that lawless and incertain thoughts
> Imagine howling:—'tis too horrible!
> The weariest and most loathed worldly life
> That age, ache, penury, and imprisonment
> Can lay on nature is a paradise
> To what we fear of death.

The juxtaposition is enough to expose the vague, generalizing externality of Shelley's rendering. Claudio's words spring from a vividly realized particular situation; from the imagined experience of a given mind in a given critical moment that is felt from the inside—that is lived—with sharp concrete particularity. Claudio's "Ay, but to die . . ." is not insistently and voluminously emotional like Beatrice's ("wildly")

O

My God! Can it be possible . . .

but it is incomparably more intense. That "cold obstruction" is not abstract; it gives rather the essence of the situation in which Claudio shrinkingly imagines himself—the sense of the warm body (given by "cold") struggling ("obstruction" takes an appropriate effort to pronounce) in vain with the suffocating earth. Sentience, warmth and motion, the essentials of being alive as epitomized in the next line, recoil from death, realized brutally in the concrete (the "clod" is a vehement protest, as "clay," which "kneaded" nevertheless brings appropriately in, would not have been). Sentience, in the "delighted spirit," plunges, not into the delightful coolness suggested by "bathe," but into the dreadful opposite, and warmth and motion shudder away from the icy prison ("reside" is analogous in working to "bathe"). The shudder is there in "thrilling," which also—such alliteration as that of "thrilling region" and "thick-ribbed" is not accidental in a Shakespearian passage of this quality—gives the sharp reverberating report of the ice as, in the intense cold, it is forced up into ridges or ribs (at which, owing to the cracks, the thickness of the ice can be seen).

But there is no need to go on. The point has been sufficiently enforced that, though this vivid concreteness of realization lodged the passage in Shelley's mind, to become at the due moment "inspiration," the passage inspired is nothing but wordy emotional generality. It does not grasp and present anything, but merely makes large gestures towards the kind of effect deemed appropriate. We are told emphatically what the emotion is that we are to feel; emphasis and insistence serving instead of realization and advertising its default. The intrusion of the tag from Lear brings out the vague generality of that unconscious set at being Shakespeare which Shelley took for dramatic inspiration.

Inspection of *The Cenci*, then, confirms all the worst in the account of Shelley. Further confirmation would not need much seeking; but, returning to the fact of his genius, it is pleasanter, and more profitable, to recall what may be said by way of explaining how he should have been capable of the

worst. His upbringing was against him. As Mr. Santayana says: "Shelley seems hardly to have been brought up; he grew up in the nursery among his young sisters, at school among the rude boys, without any affectionate guidance, without imbibing any religious or social tradition." Driven in on himself, he nourished the inner life of adolescence on the trashy fantasies and cheap excitements of the Terror school. The phase of serious tradition in which, in incipient maturity, he began to practise poetry was, in a subtler way, as unfavourable: Shelley needed no encouragement to cultivate spontaneity of emotion and poetical abeyance of thought. Then the state of the world at the time must, in its effect on a spirit of Shelley's sensitive humanity and idealizing bent, be allowed to account for a great deal—as the sonnet, *England in 1819*, so curiously intimates:

An old, mad, blind, despised, and dying
    king,—
Princes, the dregs of their dull race, who flow
Through public scorn,—mud from a muddy
    spring,—
Rulers who neither see, nor feel, nor know,
But leech-like to their fainting country cling,
Till they drop, blind in blood, without a
    blow,—
A people starved and stabbed in the untilled
    field,—
An army, which liberticide and prey
Makes as a two-edged sword to all who
    wield,—
Golden and sanguine laws which tempt and
    slay;
Religion Christless, Godless—a book sealed;
A Senate,—Time's worst statute unrepealed,—
Are graves, from which a glorious Phantom
    may
Burst, to illumine our tempestuous day.

The contrast between the unusual strength (for Shelley) of the main body of the sonnet and the pathetic weakness of the final couplet is eloquent. Contemplation of the actual world being unendurable, Shelley devotes himself to the glorious Phantom that may (an oddly ironical stress results from the rime position) work a sudden miraculous change but is in any case as vague as Demogorgon and as unrelated to actuality—to which Shelley's Evil is correspondingly unrelated.

The strength of the sonnet, though unusual in kind for Shelley, is not of remarkably distinguished quality in itself; the kindred strength of *The Mask* of *Anarchy* is. Of this poem Professor Elton says:[12] "There is a likeness in it to Blake's [gift] which has often been noticed; the same kind of anvil-stroke, and the same use of an awkward simplicity for the purposes of epigram." The likeness to Blake is certainly there—much more of a likeness than would have seemed possible from the characteristic work. It lies, not in any assumed broadsheet naïveté or crudity such as the account cited might perhaps suggest, but in a rare emotional integrity and force, deriving from a clear, disinterested and mature vision.

> When one fled past, a maniac maid,
> And her name was Hope, she said:
> But she looked more like Despair,
> And she cried out in the air:
>
> "My father Time is weak and gray
> With waiting for a better day;
> See how idiot-like he stands,
> Fumbling with his palsied hands!
>
> "He has had child after child,
> And the dust of death is piled
> Over every one but me—
> Misery, oh, Misery!"
>
> Then she lay down in the street,
> Right before the horses' feet,
> Expecting, with a patient eye,
> Murder, Fraud, and Anarchy.

These stanzas do not represent all the virtue of the poem, but they show its unusual purity and strength. In spite of "Murder, Fraud, and Anarchy," there is nothing of the usual Shelleyan emotionalism —no suspicion of indulgence, insistence, corrupt will or improper approach. The emotion seems to inhere in the vision communicated, the situation grasped: Shelley sees what is in front of him too clearly, and with too pure a pity and indignation, to have any regard for his emotions as such; the emotional value of what is presented asserts itself, or rather, does not need asserting. Had he used and developed his genius in the spirit of *The Mask of Anarchy* he would have been a much greater, and a much more readable, poet.

But *The Mask of Anarchy* is little more than a marginal throw-off, and gets perhaps too much stress in even so brief a distinguishing mention as this. The poetry in which Shelley's genius manifests itself characteristically, and for which he has his place in the English tradition, is much more closely related to his weaknesses. It would be perverse to

end without recognizing that he achieved memorable things in modes of experience that were peculiarly congenial to the European mind in that phase of its history and are of permanent interest. The sensibility expressed in the *Ode to the West Wind* is much more disablingly limited than current valuation allows, but the consummate expression is rightly treasured. The Shelleyan confusion appears, perhaps, at its most poignant in *The Triumph of Life*, the late unfinished poem. This poem has been paralleled with the revised *Hyperion*, and it is certainly related by more than the *terza rima* to Dante. There is in it a profounder note of disenchantment than before, a new kind of desolation, and, in its questioning, a new and profoundly serious concern for reality:

> . . . their might
> Could not repress the mystery within,
> And for the morn of truth they feigned, deep night
>
> Caught them ere evening . . .
>
> For in the battle Life and they did wage,
> She remained conqueror . . .
>
> "Whence camest thou? and whither goest thou?
> How did thy course begin?" I said, "and why?
>
> "Mine eyes are sick of this perpetual flow
> Of people, and my heart sick of one sad
>   thought—
> Speak!"
>
>   as one between desire and shame
> Suspended, I said—"If, as it doth seem,
> Thou comest from the realm without a name
>
> "Into this valley of perpetual dream,
> Show whence I came and where I am, and
>   why—
> Pass not away upon the passing stream."

But in spite of the earnest struggle to grasp something real, the sincere revulsion from personal dreams and fantasies, the poem itself is a drifting phantasmagoria—bewildering and bewildered. Vision opens into vision, dream unfolds within dream, and the visionary perspectives, like those of the imagery in the passage of *Mont Blanc*, shift elusively and are lost; and the failure to place the various phases or levels of visionary drift with reference to any grasped reality is the more significant because of the palpable effort. Nevertheless, *The Triumph of Life* is among the few things one can still read and go back to in Shelley when he has become, generally, "almost unreadable."

Shelley's part in the later notion of "the poetical" has been sufficiently indicated. His handling of the medium assimilates him readily, as an influence, to the Spenserian-Miltonic line running through *Hyperion* to Tennyson. Milton is patently present in *Alastor*, the earliest truly Shelleyan poem; and *Adonais*—

> Afar the melancholy thunder moaned,
> Pale Ocean in unquiet slumber lay

—relates him as obviously to *Hyperion* as to *Lycidas*. Indeed, to compare the verse of *Hyperion*, where the Miltonic Grand Style is transmuted by the Spenserianizing Keats, with that of *Adonais* is to bring out the essential relation between the organ resonances of *Paradise Lost* and the pastoral melodizing[13] of *Lycidas*. Mellifluous mourning in *Adonais* is a more fervent luxury than in *Lycidas*, and more declamatory ("Life like a dome of many-coloured glass"—the famous imagery is happily conscious of being impressive, but the impressiveness is for the spell-bound, for those sharing the simple happiness of intoxication); and it is, in the voluptuous self-absorption with which the medium enjoys itself, rather nearer to Tennyson.

NOTES

1. See the essay on Shelley in *Winds of Doctrine*.

2. *Verse and Prose from the Manuscripts of Percy Bysshe Shelley*. Edited by Sir John C. E. Shelley-Rolls, Bart., and Roger Ingpen.

3. See *Four Words* (now reprinted in *Words and Idioms*), by Logan Pearsall Smith.

4. *Letters and Journals*, ed. R. E. Prothero, vol. III, p. 405 (1900). (I am indebted for this quotation to Mr. F. W. Bateson's *English Poetry and the English Language*.)

5. "His ideal of my future,—now entirely formed in conviction of my genius,—was that I should enter at college into the best society, take all the best prizes every year, and a double first to finish with; marry Lady Clara Vere de Vere; write poetry as good as Byron's, only pious; preach sermons as good as Bossuet's, only Protestant; be made, at forty, Bishop of Winchester, and at fifty, Primate of England." *Praeterita*, vol. i, p. 340 (1886).

6. *Oxford Lectures on Poetry*, p. 167.

7. See p. 170 above.

8. Poesy's unfailing river
   Which through Albion winds forever
   Lashing with melodious wave
   Many a sacred Poet's grave . . .
   Lines Written Among the Euganean Hills.

9. See, for instance, the poem beginning, "That time is dead for ever, child."

10. See the last stanza of "Rarely, rarely comest thou."

11. Cf. Senseless is the breast, and cold,
    Which relenting love would fold;
    Bloodless are the veins and chill
    Which the pulse of pain did fill;
    Every little living nerve
    That from bitter words did swerve
    Round the tortured lips and brow,
    Are like sapless leaflets now,
    Frozen upon December's brow.
    Lines Written Among the Euganean Hills.

12. *Survey of English Literature, 1780–1830*, Vol. II, p. 202.

13. O Golden tongued Romance, with serene lute!
    Fair plumed Syren, Queen of far-away!
    Leave melodizing on this wintry day,
    Shut up thine olden pages, and be mute:
    Keats. *Sonnet: on sitting down to read King Lear once again.*

Kathleen Raine

A DEFENCE OF SHELLEY'S POETRY*

Shelley is at the present time perhaps the least understood of the major English poets. Reasons for this are not far to seek: the positivist philosophers who have so strongly influenced the climate of modern critical opinion are fond of applying to all that cannot (following the scientific method) be perceived by the senses or subjected to quantitative measurement the term "meaningless." But in fact their philosophy precludes the notion of meaning by definition, since meaning can never be "positive," being precisely that in any word or image which communicates a mental, and therefore immeasurable, attribute. Shelley, most Platonic of poets, becomes, in such terms, the most open to the charge of being "meaningless" precisely in so far as he is most rich in that quality. Emptied of meaning, poetic figures stand only for their physical terms; and Shelley's richly metaphorical poetry, read as merely descriptive, or "imagist" verse, seems superficial precisely to those readers who have least understood it. The beauty of metrical form and symbolic image speak immediately to the imagination, or not at all; to the discursive reason "meaningless," beauty is, to that higher faculty, meaning itself.

Not that Shelley was unlearned; quite the contrary. But his learning belongs to that old European civilization which has, in the course of a single generation, been all but submerged in the modern tide. One universe of knowledge has been replaced by another; and while this can be seen by those who work in the field of the sciences as an advance, we who belong to the other culture are aware of what has been lost. It is not among the scientists but, paradoxically, in the world of philosophy and the arts that the new barbarism is to be found; for these are the modes in which the old knowledge

found its expression. It seems unlikely that in the new world which is replacing what C. S. Lewis called "old western" civilization poetry will have any place at all; for poetry is a language of analogy whose terms establish relations of a mental character and within an inmaterial order which is for the positivist mentality as if non-existent. Those poets who best survive the change of background are necessarily the least poetic, or whose work contains the most alloy of the unpoetic—the passionate but unimaginative Donne with his conceptual "conceits"; the Augustans; poets who are, or who appear to be, concerned chiefly with the image (fulfilling the shallow requirements of the poetic theory of T. E. Hulme, which met the needs of a generation who had lost the old values but who still wanted to keep poetry of a sort); the pious "metaphysical" poets rather than metaphysical poetry. Even the relatively less learned and more sensuous Keats has suffered less than has Shelley by the disappearance of the universe of reference implicit in his poetry.

Shelley's work is poetry itself, as Mozart's is music itself; and the critic who does not recognize this can tell us nothing but his own inability to discern the very thing he pretends to evaluate. Between Milton and Yeats, Shelley is most perfectly the thing itself. Yeats, who devoted many years to the study of Blake, confessed that after all his greater poetic debt (Blake as a prophet is another matter) was to Shelley. He has taken, again and again, from Shelley, images, phrases, ideas essentially poetic in the sense in which certain themes and melodies are essentially musical. To say "poetic" is not to say "æsthetic"; for poetry is, for both these poets, a mode of thought, or even more a kind of consciousness, in whose expression mythological themes, images, ideas, language and music are indivisible; a synthesis perhaps more continuous and consistent in Shelley's work than in any other English poetry. In this lies the secret of his power to delight those who are able to respond with the whole of the mind

* From *Defending Ancient Springs* by Kathleen Raine, © Oxford University Press 1967. Reprinted by permission of Oxford University Press.

and its "quick elements, Will, Passion/Reason, Imagination"; and doubtless also of the inability of these critics to appreciate his genius whose thought is conceptual. Shelley is too "difficult" for such readers, but in a way they themselves cannot recognize, because he calls not for a degree but for a kind of understanding they do not possess.

"Poetry in the general sense may be defined as the expression of the imagination," Shelley wrote in his *Defence of Poetry*; poetry

> awakens and enlarges the mind itself by rendering it the receptacle of a thousand unapprehended combinations of thought. Poetry lifts the veil from the hidden beauty of the world, and makes familiar objects be as if they were not familiar. Poetry enlarges the circumference of the imagination by replenishing it with thoughts of ever new delight, which have the power of attracting and assimilating to their own nature all other thoughts, and which form new intervals and interstices whose void for ever craves fresh food.

To perceive these intervals and interstices (as with musical quarter-tones and unfamiliar harmonies) discursive thought cannot help us.

Such poetry, speaking as it does to "minds extended and enlarged," supposes, however, an extremely high level of culture both in the poet and in those to whom he addresses himself. Shelley's command of the English and the two classical languages (besides French, German, Italian and Spanish) was the natural heritage of his class and his excellent education. To read in Greek the works of Homer and the Athenian dramatists, of Plato and Proclus and the neo-Platonists, was as natural to him as to Coleridge. He belonged to a world and a class in which a man of culture measured himself against the whole of knowledge—a knowledge still given its unity by the spiritual orientation of the civilization from which it had arisen. But culture is more than education, than learning. It consists also, and above all, in a certain refinement in the quality of response, something which cannot be defined or measured but which is, within any civilized society, wordlessly communicated. Shelley was, in this sense, the inheritor of the fine essence of that now almost extinct English culture of which an aristocratic class and the universities of Oxford and Cambridge were once the custodians.

Shelley's poetry can best be understood in terms of his own definitions and principles, as he sets

these down in his *Defence of Poetry*. Not that this essay is more than an indication of the context, the universe of reference, of the poetry: it contains little or nothing which is "original"; rather it is a recall to order, to the Platonic tradition, an eloquent descant upon those first principles also set forth by Coleridge in his *Biographia Literaria*. Shelley's emphasis is in some important respects different, especially perhaps in his closer adherence to Plato's view of the relation of the arts to politics.

First of all attributes of poetry Shelley names "a certain rhythm or order" with which (following Plato) he associates "mimetic representation." This mimesis of the poet is the reverse of naturalistic imitation, for "language and gesture, together with plastic or pictorial imitation, become the image of the combined effect of those objects and his apprehension of them." Thus poetry is the expression at once of object and response; in the savage or the child, to natural objects, in the civilized man to "higher objects." Above all mimesis is an "approximation to the beautiful," "an echo of the eternal music." A perception of the approximation to these originals Shelley calls "taste," a term whose disappearance from the vocabulary of modern criticism is to be regretted.[1]

This rhythmic sense of form is his own most outstanding natural gift, and so seemingly spontaneous is his lyricism that it appears (like all supreme art) effortless; and an examination of his notebooks (upon which Neville Rodgers has written discerningly in his *Shelley at Work*) suggests that when he composed, lyric form often preceded words. We can see whole stanzas blocked out, like a musical score, with only a word or a phrase here and there, to be filled in later, as if in an instantaneous perception of the lyric form which is antecedent to the words, drawing them towards itself like particles of iron into a magnetic field. At others times no doubt words and metre came together. He wrote at astonishing speed, "Laon and Cythna" in six months, "The Witch of Atlas" in three days. He entrusted himself to that *enthusiasm* of which Plato speaks in the *Ion*, by whose inspiration the poets compose their lyrics "which they could not do when in their sober minds." Shelley himself wrote that "Poets are the Hierophants of an unapprehended inspiration, compelled to serve the power which is seated in the throne of their own soul. . . . I appeal to the greatest poets of the present day, whether it is not an error to assert that the finest passages of poetry are produced by labour or study": and he cites Milton's "unpremeditated song," adding that "Milton conceived the *Paradise Lost* as a whole before he executed its portions." That this was so of his own work, the evidence of his manuscripts suggests. It is Plotinus (whose tractate *Concerning the Beautiful* Shelley certainly knew, probably in the original, and in any case in Thomas Taylor's translation, one of the seminal works of the Romantic movement) who most clearly has stated the Platonic view of the precedence of the idea, or whole, of any work, over its parts; instancing a building, whose form as a whole exists in the mind of the architect, the stones of which it is constructed being fitted to a pre-existing form. To those critics who know only of discursive thought such rapid composition appears to be something abnormal; yet it seems to be the normal mode of poets who write from the "other" mind, from the imagination, abnormal only to those who laboriously imitate such spontaneous productions without what Plato in the *Ion* calls the inspiration of the Muses. We no longer speak of the Muse but the empirical fact remains, that true poets, when inspired, can accomplish what they could not accomplish, as Plato puts it "in their sober minds"; works "inspired" by the enthroned power of which Shelley speaks present themselves as wholes. Blake had written of poetic inspiration in similar terms, saying that portions of his *Milton* were written "from immediate dictation, twelve or sometimes twenty or thirty lines at a time without Premeditation and even against my Will . . . and an immense Poem Exists, which seems to be the Labour of a Long Life, all produc'd without Labour or Study"—Shelley's very words. Yeats, a laborious composer, was perhaps a little envious of Shelley's virtuosity, for he wrote in *A Vision* "he was subject to an automatism which he mistook for poetical invention, especially in his longer poems." But most of these are juvenilia. It is on the work written after he was twenty-five that his reputation rests.

In thus entrusting himself to *enthusiasm,* he had himself experienced what Plato describes, that magical and apparently spontaneous generation of poetic form which comes about when the inspiring spirit descends upon the poet. Such spontaneity is at once the expression of the energizing of imaginative thought, and the evidence of it. Shelley was, at the same time, skilled in traditional prosody, using

with apparently equal ease the Spenserian stanza, *terza rima,* the strophe and antistrophe of the Greek chorus, the structural elaboration of the Pindaric ode, besides a whole range of new and lovely lyric forms. That power enthroned in the poet's soul can, it seems, make use of whatever technical knowledge the poet has at his command. In this respect Shelley was a perfected instrument: not, however, through laborious imitation, but rather by ready imaginative assimilation of poetic forms of every kind, and his long and deep familiarity with the whole range of poetic literature.

Shelley has been most misunderstood by readers schooled in the positivist criticism of which T. E. Hulme's Imagism is an early expression, and which in Cambridge has found the kind of scorched earth upon which it thrives. Such readers look in Shelley's symbolic images for the kind of naturalistic description we find at its best in John Clare. A storm-cloud, it was proclaimed, does not resemble "a Maenad's hair"; whereas Hopkins's "silk-sack" is an image fit and worthy of the fullest admiration, because some clouds do look like silk sacks. John Holloway, who had looked at more kinds of cloud than one, and who had presumably also asked himself what happens to the hair of those "possessed," has pointed out that Shelley's image is, even visually, exact: a thunder-cloud on the Mediterranean often does send out strange points and ragged fringes of vapour, "the locks of the approaching storm." Nature is a mirror that reflects back to the observer whatever he is capable of discerning or chooses to notice. Turner is not less a painter of "nature" than is Stubbs, but of light not of animals; and Shelley's "nature" is (following perhaps, as has been said by others, his interest in chemistry and allied sciences) seen rather in terms of light, flux and transmutation than of Dr. Johnson's stone, more apt to the boot than to the eye. "Nature-poetry" is no less a convention than any other selection we may care to make from our environment; and has become, in England, an extremely meagre one; admirers who see in D. H. Lawrence's garden-tortoises a novel and expanded vision have seldom read (for example) St. John Perse's *Vents* or *Amers.* No poet has more beautifully described than has Shelley, in the volatile alchemy he shares with his contemporary Turner, landscapes real or imaginary; but even when this is so, his description is at all times a means not an end. Shelley's second mark of poetry is not vivid imagery, but a language "vitally metaphorical; that is, it marks the before unapprehended relations of things, and perpetuates their apprehension." When in the course of time these metaphors have ceased to be vital, and become mere abstractions and "signs for portions or classes of thought" they cease to be poetic, and new poets must discover new relations, must extend and explore those "intervals and interstices whose void ever craves fresh food." Shelley was a Berkeleyan immaterialist; and there is already implicit in what might appear simple description the relationship, itself mysterious, "between existence and perception." He makes his Ahasuerus, embodiment of knowledge itself, declare that

> . . . Thought
> Alone, and its quick elements, Will, Passion,
> Reason, Imagination, cannot die;
> They are what that which they regard appears,
> The stuff whence mutability can weave
> All that it hath dominion o'er, worlds, worms,
> Empires and superstitions. . . .

To perceive is already to create; and there is, alike in Shelley's imaginary and his earthly paradises, that quality of primary reality we occasionally experience in dreams or waking visions, in which thought and its object (landscapes, figures, or enactments) seem one and indivisible. In "that Elysian light" nature itself is perceived as if it were itself a region of imagination. Word and image have, in such poetry, that unity and correspondence Coleridge experienced when in writing "Kubla Khan" "all the images rose up before him as *things,* with the parallel production of their correspondent expressions," as if both alike from the same creative ground, the primary imagination itself. Those enchanted landscapes are not reflections of nature but immediate creations of that mental ground of which natural forms are themselves images, "idle shadows/Of thought's eternal flight." Therefore it is that in reading such poetry what we experience seems more real than reality; it comes from the source.

There is in Shelley's poetry a congruity between his lyricism and his themes. AE [George Russell] wrote of the inappropriateness of employing lyrical speech (which is the natural expression of the exalted imagination) for material of a discursive kind. Such poetry is factitious, an imitation of poetry more or less ingenious. But in Shelley both form and substance belong to the kind of thought, the level of consciousness to which lyrical rhythms and symbolic metaphor are alike native.

Besides the metaphorical essence diffused throughout Shelley's imaginative descriptive writing there are more complex symbolic figures. In his handling of mythological themes he stands with Spenser, Milton, Blake, Coleridge, and the Keats of "Hyperion," above all English poets except Shakespeare. Yeats may be right in finding his figure of Prometheus lacking in life, a mouthpiece of propaganda; but those female soul-figures the Witch of Atlas and the Lady of the Sensitive Plant, Ahasuerus, mask of Hermetic wisdom; or even those winged and living boats of the poet's interior journeys, and the rivers and seas on which they move, are informed with the life of the mystery in which they originate. In many passages (as in the last chorus of "Hellas" the ancient doctrine of the Great Year) some theme of traditional symbolism is explicit; more often, as in the "Ode to the West Wind" the metaphorical sense of his neo-Platonic symbolic language of wind, sea, seed, lyre, image and reflection, storm-inspired cloud, is all implicit, and unapparent to the untaught reader; but, yielding to our growing understanding, "acts otherwise than in a lyre, and produces not melody alone, but harmony."

Shelley must have known, besides the Platonic tradition in which he was learned, something of Indian, Cabalistic, and Hermetic works expressing the same metaphysical gnosis, found also in the plays of Calderón, whom he admired. He calls the truth of poetry "eternal truth"; in either case the order of truth is metaphysical. This truth, he says, belongs not to the poet himself but to his inspirers: "The persons in whom this power resides may often, as far as regards many portions of their nature, have little correspondence with the spirit of good of which they are the ministers" and may even be "themselves perhaps the most sincerely astonished at its manifestations." In this Shelley is nearer to Plato than was Blake, who blamed the philosopher who "made Socrates say that Poets and Prophets do not know or Understand what they write or Utter; this is a most Pernicious Falsehood. If they do not, pray is an inferior kind to be call'd Knowing?" Shelley, like Yeats, believed that "the poet may embody truth, but cannot know it." This must be so, for those who understand that "the deep truth is imageless."

An example will illustrate Shelley's metaphorical richness; and I choose one of his most characteristic poems, the "Ode to a Skylark" because, through its deceptive simplicity and the lightness of its vesture, the subtlety and strength of the internal structure of this poem has often been overlooked.

No poem is more suffused with "the Elysian light" wherein nature is apprehended as a region of the imagination, nor is there in this poem any point at which we can draw a distinction between the physical and the metaphysical objects of the poet's discourse. The metaphorical character of the whole lies in the perfect fusion of the two terms of the metaphor, which because of its very perfection may pass unnoticed. This assimilation of object and apprehension is established in the first stanza when the "blithe spirit" of the singer is said not to be a bird; the source of the song of which the bird is only the instrument is of a more mysterious kind. Like the poet the bird is the "hierophant of an unapprehended inspiration"; for "heaven or near it" is not a mere synonym for the sky; like Shakespeare's lark who sings at "heaven's gate" the bird's nearness to heaven lies in the immediacy of the song's inspiration: the ground from which it springs is not the material earth but "thought and its quick elements." The lark is less symbol of imaginative creation than itself an immediate expression of "the stuff whence mutability can weave."

There is in the phrase "unpremeditated art" used in the fifth line of the poem an implicit allusion to Milton's "unpremeditated song." Blake's lark too, which in his poem, *Milton,* "leads the choir of day" is equated with the poet who was, for Blake as for Shelley, the type of the "inspired man." It is tempting to wonder what of Blake's work Shelley might have seen; for Godwin, or perhaps Mary Shelley herself (of whose mother Mary Wollstonecraft Blake had been a friend) might well have possessed some of his illuminated books. Does the image of the eagle struggling with a serpent, which Shelley uses in "The Revolt of Islam" as an image of revolution, bear only an accidental resemblance to the emblem used in the same sense, of *The Marriage of Heaven and Hell?* Had Shelley read Blake's defence of free love (written perhaps with Mary Wollstonecraft herself in mind) the "Visions of the Daughters of Albion"? Blake's Urizen and that God-simulating Satan whose image his Milton casts down is uncommonly like Shelley's Jupiter. Had he even met Blake himself (who outlived Shelley by five years) in London? Shelley is, whether he knew it or not, Blake's spiritual successor; and his skylark has its prototype in Blake's whose "Nest is at the Gate of Los," spirit of prophecy. Perhaps both poets, supremely admiring Milton, chose the lark as the bird who in "L'Allegro" sings "From his watchtower in the skies." Shelley's skylark can, in any case, be seen as his tribute to Milton as the defender and exemplar of the Platonic doctrine of poetic inspiration.

Shelley's verse-form is itself a beautiful example of mimesis. Anyone who has listened attentively to the soaring lark will recognize in the delicate hesitant poise of each stanza upon its prolonged floating last line, the lark-song with its extended trill. The reiteration, too, of the verses has this mimetic quality; but in content these lovely musical variations are not a mere series of fragile images strung out on a slender thread. This reflection on the nature of inspiration owes its unity to the interior structure of the metaphysical idea which the images explore, each following from the last with the inevitability of a Socratic discourse.

First the poet seeks to identify the singer; the "blithe spirit" who is not a bird is called, in the third verse, "an unbodied joy," which "floats and runs" with the freedom of its mental being, on the clouds, like one of Blake's bright forms who, likewise, are often vested in "a cloud of fire," element of the spirit and of "the enjoyments of genius." A famous passage in the *Hermetica,* certainly known to Shelley, as it was to Blake and to Coleridge, describes this power of the soul to travel wherever it will, to be in those very places of which it thinks; a power which no body, however fine, can possess. "Command it to fly into Heaven, and it will need no Wings, neither shall anything hinder it; not the fire of the Sun, nor the Aether, nor the turning of the Spheres, not the bodies of any of the other Stars. . . ."

The bird song which the sensual ear receives as sound, consciousness experiences, more intimately, as "a joy." To this theme of joy the poet returns until he has, not by statement but by repeated reimmersion in the experience of song, established the identity of song-spirit-joy; as the Hindu metaphysicians equate *sit-chit-ananda, being-life-joy,* the primary reality; making joy not an attribute of spirit, but its essential nature. The divine rapture exceeds any pleasures compassable in natural terms, those of love, or wine. Like the Vedantic definition of the divine principle by a series of negations the poet rejects all apprehensible objects, all desire for known or knowable satisfactions: the joy "ignorant of pain" (and by implication the spirit itself) can only have its being in another principle than this world of duality, in an eternal order untouched by death. The poem ends, like the "Ode to the West Wind," with an invocation—the poet aspires to draw his music from that immortal source which no human virtue, knowledge or art can approach.

A series of metaphors suggest what cannot be defined, the mystery of the emergence of the song, whether of art or of nature, from the "blue deep" where the bird soars to "heaven or near it." The singer, bird or poet, is a minute centre through which the unmanifest issues into the temporal world. Again we think of Blake's timeless moment in which "the poet's work is done," of his minute flower centres in which "eternity expands," and of his lark whose "little throat labours with inspiration." Shelley's metaphors are a star, in daylight invisible but nevertheless present; the moon which from a "lonely cloud" diffuses light which fills all space; rain falling from the sky, as heaven nourishes earth. Each image metaphorically embodies the idea the poet is exploring, the flowing of the created from the uncreated; as Blake, again, describes how the work of creation flows forth "like visible out of the invisible." Implicit in both poets is the teaching of the Perennial Philosophy that every natural effect has a spiritual cause.

"A poet hidden / In the light of thought" is a mediator, like bird or star, between the seen and the unseen; here conceived as the specifically human power of giving form to immaterial thought, the "higher objects" of poetic mimesis.

What objects are the fountains
    Of thy happy strain?
What fields, or waves, or mountains?
    What shapes of sky or plain?
What love of thine own kind? What ignorance
    of pain?

Here the figure—in itself beautiful—of the bird which perceives a world unlike the human, is the vesture of Shelley's deeper thought on the higher, and invisible, objects of the poet; the Platonic ideas,

discovered perhaps in that Garden of the Muses of whose "fountains" Plato writes. Blake's lark too nests near a "fountain," a nesting-place improbable in nature, but symbolically inevitable for the bird who, like the poet, "winged, light and volatile," visits Plato's heavenly gardens.

As the poet embodies thought, "a high-born maiden / In a palace tower" gives form to love. The maiden is called "high-born" in the same sense as in Michelangelo's sonnet (translated by Wordsworth) the soul is called "heavenly-born":

Heaven-born, the Soul a Heavenward course
    must hold.

Heaven-born love is, like thought, one of the channels through which the eternal beauty may enter the world. With this introduction of the theme of love comes a change of key; the action of the poem moves down from the "blue deep" of the uncreated to the "dell of dew," the world of generation. Here the image of light is not star but "a glow-worm golden," a fallen star, a star generated, as Plato describes the descent of souls as stars into earthly life. As the souls descend into generation they become, in Porphyry's words, "drenched in moisture." Blake too uses the symbolism of dew in this sense, and also "dell" and "valley" as the physical world. Yet even in the "dell of dew" the light continues to shine as the poet, fallen child of Paradise, continues to scatter the "aerial hue" of Elysium in the darkness of this world. As the glow-worm echoes the "poet hidden," so the rose of love echoes the "high-born maiden"; and again Shelley uses an image Blake had used before him in the same sense, and in the same passage of *Milton* as his lark:

. . . the Flowers put forth their precious
    Odours
And none can tell how from so small a centre
    comes such sweets.

So the poem which to a superficial reading seems so slight proves to be, like the grace of Botticelli or Yeats's "little song about a rose" the delicate veil of thought which soars towards the bounds of the knowable, evoked rather than defined by images of star and cloud and fragrance of rain on flower. As Edgar Wind has somewhere said, this lightness of touch is ever the mark of supreme artistry. Where beauty is greatest, there we should look also for the greatest depth of meaning.

The same richly metaphorical internal structure is to be found no less in poems whose outer vesture is occasional; as in the deceptively simple poem "To Jane: the Recollection." Here the little pool in a pine-forest in which reflections are interfused with "an elysian glow" not perceptible in the real objects, is like "the waves' intenser day" of the "Ode to the West Wind," the microcosm of imagination. In the "intenser" medium of consciousness all that is reflected from nature becomes "more than truth," transmuted into the higher mode of existence. Freed from every "unwelcome thought" which effaces its images like the "envious wind" that ruffles the surface of the woodland pool, consciousness itself manifests, in moments of peace and love, its radical nature as the mirror of paradise. The true poet, when he seems to be describing some experience purely personal, is never, in reality (as with so many modern writers of verse) doing so; the personal occasion is merely another image, or symbolic term, by whose means he is enabled to discover some aspect of the eternal harmony. West wind, skylark, or Shelley and Jane Williams walking in a pine-wood, may according to Coleridge's definition of the symbol, themselves "abide as a living part in that Unity" of which they are representative, but never are themselves the subject of the poem, by definition an expression of the imagination, never of the personality.

Shelley's third mark of the poet is that of legislator or prophet; "for he not only beholds intensely the present as it is, and discovers these laws according to which present things ought to be ordered, but he beholds the future in the present, and his thoughts are the germs of the flower and fruit of latest time." Legislator more than prophet: for Shelley belonged to the ruling class, the class of Walpole and of Pitt, and in the natural course of things would have succeeded to his father's seat in Parliament. Even in exile the sense of political responsibility remained with Shelley, as it did with Byron (to whose genius the liberation of Greece is a monument perhaps more enduring than his poetry). A very high proportion of Shelley's early prose writings are on immediate political issues. That he was a liberal and a republican is not in any way surprising, though it is difficult now to sympathize with his enthusiasm for the ideas and ideals of Rousseau and Godwin and that contemporary ferment of atheist humanism whose nihilistic

term our age has seen. But it would be difficult even for those who still might share his political faith to read without embarrassment his doctrinaire proclamations of the advent of Utopia as soon as those vaguely called "tyrants" should be overthrown. Yeats wrote that "the justice of 'Prometheus Unbound' is a vague propagandist emotion and the women that await its coming are but clouds"; perhaps in "The Triumph of Life" we see the beginnings of political maturity. But Shelley understood that the poet, whose politics are those of eternity, has for that very reason a responsibility towards the politics of time. His political concern is an aspect of his greatness. He was not a poet, as Keats was, of private feelings and introspective imaginings; even more than Coleridge and Wordsworth (spectators rather than actors in the politics of their time) he understood the responsibility Plato lays upon the poets for their moral influence in society. In terms which the present time might do well to consider he castigated obscenity, "which is ever blasphemy against the divine beauty in life, which becomes, from the very vest which it assumes, more active if less disgusting: it is a monster for whom the corruption of society brings forth new food, which it devours in secret." The connexion of poetry and public morals is more observable in drama than in any other form; "And it is indisputable that the highest perfection of human society has ever corresponded with the highest dramatic excellence; and that the corruption or the extinction of the drama in a nation where it has once flourished is a mark of corruption of manners, and an extinction of the energies which sustain the soul of social life." Prophet of freedom as he was he would have assumed as of course that in the good city censorship is necessary for the protection of society, indeed of freedom itself; for he believed (as Ireland and Russia at the present time believe but not, apparently, the Anglo-Saxon nations) that people are changed by what they read and see, "become what they behold," and that its spiritual food can nourish or poison a nation.

Shelley gives a strange reason for holding poetry superior to the plastic arts: language only "has relation to thoughts alone," "to that imperial faculty whose throne is curtained within the invisible nature of man." Language is "a more direct representation of the actions and passions of our internal being, and is susceptible of more various and delicate combinations than colour, form or motion, and is more plastic and obedient to the control of that faculty of which it is the creation." For Shelley (and of this his political sense was an aspect) man's thoughts were of all things the fittest subject of poetry. For what reason, at the present time, sensations or tenuous personal emotions are regarded as more "poetic" than the more specifically human ideas of truth, justice, freedom, honour, and (in the spiritual sense) love, ideas of which humanity becomes capable only as a social being, it would be pointless here to discuss. Suffice it to recollect that these were the principal themes of the poetry of the Athenian dramatists not because the ancient Greeks had "no sense of natural beauty" (an opinion whose untruth can be seen by any student who visits Delphi and Sounion and Epidaurus, the most beautiful natural sites in the world) but because to those same Greeks things of the mind were held to be of a higher order than things of the senses, as alone belonging to man's unique nature and creation, to the god-imposed "know thyself" of Delphic Apollo. It is precisely in those energies of the mind which are at the present time so apathetically regarded, the "ideas" which man alone is capable of conceiving, that the ancient Greeks found the highest degree of beauty. A poetry of ideas is the most aristocratic order of poetry; for only the educated man is capable of any distinct notion of ideas; and in a demotic society therefore not likely to flourish. At the same time such poetry has the greatest potential power of civilizing and transforming unbred mankind. Shelley's poetry of ideas (when not on the level of the "vague propaganda" of his juvenilia) is, at its best, as impassioned, subtle and beautiful as that of Aeschylus; as in "Epipsychidion," "Adonais," "Prometheus Unbound," or in "Hellas." "Plato was essentially a poet," Shelley believed, "the truth and splendour of his imagery and the melody of his language are the most intense it is possible to conceive"; but it is especially Plato's "harmony in thought" which entitles him to be called a poet; a quality Shelley himself possessed in a high degree—it is this "harmony in thought" which establishes the structural ordering of the "Ode to a Skylark." Conversely Shakespeare, Dante and Milton "are philosophers of the very greatest power." "A poem is the very image of life expressed in its eternal truth," Shelley believed; and the "deep truth" of imagination—"imageless" likewise

—is not different in kind from that of the traditional metaphysics, called in the ancient world philosophy.

Shelley, Yeats objected, "lacked the vision of evil." A child of Paradise, the mistakes of his own tragic young life were all made through this obliviousness. He was bedevilled, besides, by the mistaken notions of his time on the innate virtue of "natural man." Shelley had not yet learned, as Blake had, in the bitter world of experience, wherein lay the error of "Paine and Voltaire with some of the Ancient Greeks" (all Shelley's false gods) who say "we will live in Paradise and Liberty. You may do so in spirit, but not in the Mortal Body, as you pretend. . . . While we are in the world of Mortality we Must Suffer." His mistakes were those of the same generosity, disinterestedness, and lack of self-knowledge which sent out young idealists of a later generation to be killed in the Spanish civil war in the name of an ideology insufficiently examined just because generous youth wants a cause to live and die for; an easier way, to be sure, than the long arduous way of perfection, or than to "wither into truth" with those who have, in Yeats's phrase, "awakened from the common dream." Had he lived he must have applied to those current opinions too hastily assumed the critical discernment with which he wrote that "Euripides, Lucan, Tasso, Spenser, have frequently affected a moral aim, and the effect of their poetry is diminished in exact proportion to the degree in which they compel us to admit to this purpose." Of none of these is Shelley's criticism so true as of himself.

But if Shelley had not the Christian "vision of evil" (as Blake had, and Shakespeare and Dante) and imagined Paradise to be more easily realizable "on earth as it is in heaven" than it really is, he certainly had the Platonic vision of that golden country itself, and of the radical innocence and beauty, likewise, of all human souls, however disfigured by outward personality; as his Witch of Atlas could see

Where in bright bowers immortal forms abide
Beneath the weltering of the restless tide.

He is the poet of apokatastasis, of the restitution of all things to their essential perfection. In his belief that this possibility lies latent in man and in all creation, Shelley has the unanimous teaching of tradition, both pre-Christian and Christian, with him; besides the interior assent of every spirit not quite dead. Nor was he wrong in believing that love is the transforming principle which alone can bring this about, uniting what is divided, transforming ("And that with little change of shape or hue") the hateful into the beautiful. Perhaps Shelley's "love" was too restricted, being, above all, that of lovers. But the glimpse of "the Elysian light" given to those in love is not therefore illusory. In "To Jane: the Recollection" it is the presence of the beloved which trans-substantiates the world:

> There seemed from the remotest seat
>   Of the white mountain waste,
> To the soft flower beneath our feet
>   A magic circle traced,—
> A spirit interfused around,
>   A thrilling silent life,—
> To momentary peace it bound
>   Our mortal nature's strife;—
> And still I felt the centre of
>   The magic circle there,
> Was one fair form that filled with love
>   The lifeless atmosphere.

Love is the agent of apokatastasis; a truth the Christian church itself acknowledges in the sacramental nature of marriage. His vision of the harmonious co-existence of all things in the state of Paradise (to which love, in whatever form, gives access) he has perhaps communicated (in "Prometheus Unbound" especially) more perfectly than has any other English poet; as C. S. Lewis wrote in an essay in which he contrasts (to the entire advantage of the former) Shelley with Dryden. We can no more object that such poetic evocation of the state of beatitude itself lacks "the sense of evil" than we can make the objection to Mozart's D-minor quartet. It might be said that the arts exist, finally, for no other end than the holding before us of images of Paradise.

No stupider judgement was ever passed upon Shelley than by Arnold who called him an "ineffectual angel." There spoke the school-inspector who believes that "good" is something done by busy people. Giving men material goods and material aid can not make them better, only better off; the effect of poetry is to change us permanently in our nature; a transmutation by no means ineffectual. It would be hard to name a poet whose political and social propaganda—to put it at its lowest—has more effectively changed public opinion and altered the course of history. More far-reaching is the transforming power of poetry itself. Only those lacking in all sensibility to a poetry which speaks to the soul in its own language and of its native place and state can read Shelley unchanged.

NOTES

1. The Japanese Nō plays, completely stylized as they are, are a perfect instance of mimesis in Shelley's sense.

John L. Mahoney

NO BETTER REALITY: NEW DIMENSIONS IN HAZLITT'S AESTHETICS

"If poetry is a dream, the business of life is much the same. If it is a fiction, made up of what we wish things to be, and fancy that they are, because we wish them so, there is no other or better reality. Ariosto has described the loves of Angelica and Medoro: but was not Medoro, who carved the name of his mistress on the barks of trees, as much en- *amoured of her charms as he? Homer has celebrated the anger of Achilles: but was not the hero as mad as the poet? Plato banished the poets from his Commonwealth, lest their descriptions of the natural man should spoil his mathematical man, who was to be without passions and affections, who was neither to laugh nor weep, to feel sorrow nor*

anger, to be cast down nor elated by any thing. This was a chimera, however, which never existed but in the brain of the inventor; and Homer's poetical world has outlived Plato's philosophical Republic."

"On Poetry in General" (V, 3) [1]

Overriding all the special emphases and techniques of William Hazlitt's practice, and yet seldom adequately stressed in studies of the great nineteenth century English theorist, is what may be described as a new explicit and implicit manifesto for poetry and for the arts in general.[2] The most profound themes of the manifesto, the uniqueness and autonomy of poetry and its power to represent reality in fresh and original ways, were, of course, articulated by contemporaries like Wordsworth and Shelley, but Hazlitt's distinctive formulation of these and his expression of quite new emphases stand as major contributions to aesthetics and criticism. Roy Park, who so perceptively traces the struggle of poetry to liberate itself from the intimidations of scientific abstraction and to replace in stature a philosophy and theology whose credibility had been drastically eroded, describes succinctly the special problem confronted by Hazlitt. That problem, he contends, is "whether poetry is poetry, or whether it is explicable only within the framework of a more general metaphysic." [3] In a word, does poetry have its own *raison d'être,* a unique inspiration, methodology, and effect, or is it the servant of another master?

Students of the problem are, of course, familiar with Wordsworth's memorable attempt in the *Preface to the Lyrical Ballads, 1800,* to assert the uniqueness of poetry and its ability to express those deeper and more spiritual truths that transcend the world of fact and particularity to which science addresses itself. Poetry for Wordsworth does not exist to serve the cause of science or philosophy or history; indeed it is greater than all of these in its wondrous power to move beyond the limitations that impede their progress and to express the mysterious and the intangible. Poetry's object, he says, and he echoes Aristotle's answer to Plato, is "truth, not individual and local, but general, and operative; not standing upon external testimony, but carried alive into the heart by passion; truth which is its own testimony, which gives competence and confidence to the tribunal to which it appeals, and receives them from the same tribunal." Poetry,

with its own special goals and methodology, is greater than science, for its mode of dealing with truth is to render it immediate and realizable to the human heart; while science, no less concerned with truth, nevertheless deals with it in more detached and dispassionate ways. Although both poet and man of science share a pleasure in knowledge, "the knowledge of the one cleaves to us as a necessary part of our existence, our natural and unalienable inheritance; the other is a personal and individual acquisition, slow to come to us, and by no habitual and direct sympathy connecting us with our fellow-beings." [4]

Shelley also shares the Wordsworthian and the general Romantic preoccupation with new questions at the beginning of the nineteenth century: What is poetry in its essence? Is it simply a more pleasant form of expressing the truths of philosophy and theology? Is its metaphorical and symbolic mode simply an adornment of the deeper truths of hard knowledge? Although a more exuberant document than Wordsworth's *Preface,* Shelley's *Defence of Poetry* is no less unqualified and confident in its critique of reason and didacticism and its defense of poetry as a form of inspired knowledge which must become the source of man's salvation in an increasingly materialistic world. The document rings with oft-quoted phrases and sentences that attest to the new theme of the autonomy of Poetry. "Poetry" is for him " 'the expression of the imagination': and poetry is connate with the origin of man." The Poet "participates in the eternal, the infinite, and the one; as far as relates to his conceptions, time and place and number are not," and poets as a class are "the unacknowledged legislators of the world." With an extraordinary concern for the ethical dimension of poetry, he argues that the "great instrument of moral good is the imagination; and poetry administers to the effect by acting upon the cause. Poetry enlarges the circumference of the imagination by replenishing it with thoughts of ever new delight, which have the power of attracting and assimilating to their own nature all other thoughts, and which form new intervals and interstices whose void forever craves fresh food." [5]

The new mission of poetry is clearly set at the beginning of the nineteenth century, then, and Hazlitt, although less evangelical in his mode of expression, is no less urgent in his need to talk about the mission and its implications not just for specific writings, but for criticism and for life itself. Although the new critic must be a person of strong feeling interested in describing his response to the work of art and although the act of criticism must be the record of an emotional encounter rather than a process of clinical analysis of texts and application of pre-established rules, some of Hazlitt's most urgent questions revolve around the meaning of poetry itself. He seems consistently interested in poetry's basic roots, its connections with life, the peculiar mode through which it represents life, and the special character of its impact on human personality. Too often the reader will remember popular Hazlitt terminology like "gusto" or the more superficial manner in which he uses metaphor or evocation to express a critical response, and will miss the deeper thrust of a methodology that takes him to the seminal questions suggested above. In fact, Hazlitt does have, in spite of his gospel of emotional strength in art, a remarkable capacity to stand back at times from immediate response and to isolate the larger and essential issues that are ultimately grounded in aesthetics.

Poetry, indeed art in general, is for Hazlitt intimately related to experience and to human experience in particular. "All art is built upon nature; and the tree of knowledge lifts its branches to the clouds, only as it has struck its roots deep into the earth" (XVIII, 77). Although intensely personal, it is a vision of life and not simply a vehicle for the artist's ingenuity or self-expression. Quite the contrary, the artist, in a constant struggle to minimize the claims of the ego, strives to capture with as much intensity as possible the essential reality that surrounds him.

Like many of his contemporaries, Hazlitt begins with the presumption that poetry is no ordinary gift, no simply elegant way of dealing with the everyday. Citing Bacon as his authority, he sees poetry as having something divine in it. It is, he says, "strictly the language of the imagination; and the imagination is that faculty which represents objects, not as they are in themselves, but as they are moulded by other thoughts and feelings, into an infinite variety of shapes and combinations of power. This language is not the less true to nature, because it is false in point of fact; but so much the more true and natural, if it conveys the impression which the object under the influence of passion

makes on the mind" (V, 3–4). Unlike history, which "treats, for the most part, of the cumbrous and uneasy masses of things, the empty cases in which the affairs of the world are packed "(V, 1–2), poetry, in the spirit of Juvenal, is dedicated to the principle that nothing human can be foreign to it. It is not "a branch of authorship: it is 'the stuff of which our life is made' " (V, 1–2). It moves beyond mere recital of objects and facts, mere delineation of natural feelings; indeed it becomes true poetry only when the heightening power of imagination charges objects, facts, and feelings with a new and powerful life. Poetry of this kind becomes the most emphatic of all languages, a language that symbolically translates those yearnings and desires of the human mind that make man essentially what he is and that make poetry a vital part of life for both artist and audience.

Not only is poetry the language of imagination and passion and not only does it draw its sustenance from life; it is addressed to life and achieves its unique effects only as it touches human beings in vital ways. Not a mere source of escape and entertainment or a vehicle for instructive platitudes, it is a vision of the essential dimension of experience; it is purposeful in the best sense. It "comes home to the bosoms and businesses of men; for nothing but what so comes home to them in the most general and intelligible shape, can be a subject for poetry" (V, 1). Poetry's ability to capture truth imaginatively and to render it vivid to the human spirit is truly a formative process by which experience is nourished and broadened, a process that is educative in the richest sense of the word. Hazlitt stressed how central this process is to poetry on many occasions, notably when he argued that poetry can be detected "wherever a movement of imagination or passion is impressed on the mind, by which it seeks to prolong and repeat the emotion, to bring all other objects into accord with it, and to give the same movement of harmony, sustained and continuous, or gradually varied according to the occasion" (V, 12).

Certainly no genre is more exemplary of literature's moral force than tragedy, which was the model of Hazlitt's much discussed criterion of sympathy or disinterestedness.[6] By providing the spectacle of the great man confronting his essential limitedness, it replaces mere selfishness with imaginary sympathy and gives us an interest and involvement in humanity itself, evoking those intellectual, imaginative, and emotional facets of human response. Hazlitt's metaphor is an apt one; tragedy "opens the chambers of the human heart. It leaves nothing indifferent to us that can affect our common nature" (IV, 200). Again he speaks of tragedy as the most impassioned poetry and traces its moral force with brilliant and telling imagery. On the one hand, he captures the power and shattering impact of the catastrophe on the reader or spectator, pointing up how "tragedy strives to carry on the feeling to the utmost point of sublimity and pathos." On the other hand, he quickly distinguishes true tragedy from the drama of terror that leaves one horrified or without hope. He is reminiscent of Aristotle in the discussion of cartharsis in the *Poetics* as he analyzes the peculiar psychological technique of the dramatist who can purge the force of great suffering by provoking and tapping the rich resources of mind and heart to come to terms with it. Great tragedy "loses the sense of present suffering in the imaginary exaggeration of it; exhausts the terror or pity by an unlimited indulgence of it; grapples with impossibilities in its desperate impatience of restraint; throws us back upon the past, forward into the future; brings every moment of our being or object of nature in startling review before us." It is precisely in tragedy's power to move us beyond our own feelings, to stir us to share emotionally and imaginatively the predicament of the hero or heroine that its great power resides. Its conclusion may bring a spectacle of death or great loss, but "in the rapid whirl of events, lifts us from the depths of woe to the highest contemplations on human life" (V, 5).

Examples could be multiplied, but they would add little to a point already strikingly clear, Hazlitt's critical preoccupation with poetry as a unique form of representing what is essential in experience, its reliance on the symbolic language of the imagination to penetrate the human heart and to open it up to the rich possibilities of human life. This truly moral dimension was always his first concern and was the occasion for many of his most searching observations on how the morality of art renders futile the strident demands that art be more overtly didactic in its method. He continually stressed that the most moral writers do not pretend to inculcate any message and that preaching in art weakens that art irreparably. The great English novelists, for example, vividly capture human manners and leave the audience to draw the inferences. The writer of comedy, Hazlitt argued, ought simply "to open the volume of nature and the world for his living materials, and not take them out of his ethical common-place book" (VI, 157). Drama, without becoming moralistic, can reveal good and evil not as fictions, but as realities in a real world; by committing itself freely to nature, "it is its own voucher for the truth of the inferences it draws, for its warnings, or its examples." It "brings out the higher, as well as the lower principles of action, in the most striking and convincing points of view; satisfies us that virtue is not a mere shadow; clothes it with passion, imagination, reality, and, if I may so say, translates morality from the language of theory into that of practice" (VI, 157).

Hazlitt turned to all kinds of literature to illustrate his belief in the moral force of art. He was touched by the garden scene at Shallow's country seat in Shakespeare's *Henry IV*, by the dialogue between Shallow and Silence on the death of old Double with its happy combination of wisdom and foolishness. The scenes are superior for him because they draw from "the stuff we are made of" and deeply affect us by their stunning revelation of "*what a little thing is human life,* what a poor forked creature man is" (IV, 283). *Coriolanus*, with its dramatic moral that the poor and humble shall be made poorer and the great shall further strengthen themselves at the expense of others, reveals "the logic of the imagination and the passions; which seek to aggrandize what excites admiration, and to heap contempt upon misery," and he concludes that "what men delight to read in books, they will put in practice in reality" (V, 349–350). *King Lear* is almost the perfect play because it reminds us how closely poetry touches the most interesting aspects of life and further illustrates that the man with a contempt for poetry is a man with a contempt for himself and humanity. It clarifies the essential superiority of poetry to painting since our strongest memories relate to emotions and not to faces. But, above all, and here Hazlitt seems to be at his psychological and critical best in describing the moral effect of the play, it actually engages the full range of the human spirit. In lines that clearly seem to anticipate Keats's "The excellence of every Art is its intensity, capable of making all disagreeables evaporate, from their being in close relationship with Beauty and Truth. Examine 'King Lear,' and you will find this exemplified throughout," he proceeds to examine the special ways in which the play engages us. What makes a great tragedy like *King Lear* bearable and constructive for us is a certain balance of pleasure and pain so that "in proportion to the greatness of the evil, is our sense and desire of the opposite good excited," and "our sympathy with actual suffering is lost in the strong impulse given to our natural affections, and carried away with the swelling tide of passion, that gushes from and relieves the heart" (IV, 271–272). Shakespeare's lack of explicit religious enthusiasm or moral concern stands apart from the strong religious zeal that is so much a part of Milton's poetry. Milton was never indifferent as an artist and would never take as much delight in conceiving an Iago as an Imogen. He wrote with the ideals of the Hebrew theocracy and the perfect Commonwealth as fixed points of his sensibility, "with a hand just warm from the touch of the ark of faith." His sympathetic powers were always secondary to his larger purposes; his "religious zeal infused its character into his imagination; so that he devotes himself with the same sense of duty to the cultivation of his genius, as he did to the exercise of virtue, or the good of his country" (V, 56–57). As with Shakespeare and Milton, so also with lesser lights like Sheridan and Steele. While the comedies of Steele were written not to imitate life but to reform the morals of the age, Sheridan, especially in an almost perfect comedy like *The School for Scandal*, uses the firm but light touch to carry on his satire. Hazlitt notes that "every thing in them *tells;* there is no labor in vain." The spirit of *The School for Scandal* is not preachy but open and generous. It seems unaffected by the moralistic strictures of Jeremy Collier and reveals a generosity and openness "that relieves the heart as well as clears the lungs" (VI, 165).

Despite Hazlitt's deep commitment to the autonomy and self-authenticating character of poetry, to poetry's ability to teach imaginatively and emotionally, he sensed a twofold decline. The Neoclassic preoccupation with art as a vehicle for rather overt moral instruction and the contemporary concern with art as self-revelation have taken a serious toll. He saw his own time as critical, didactic, paradoxical, and romantic in the bad sense of the term; it lacked the essentially dramatic quality that great

art requires, and consequently no great comedies and tragedies are being written. The French Revolution is obviously a major source of the problem as Englishmen have become a nation of newsmongers and politicians. They have become public creatures, arguing national questions, the rise of stocks, the fighting of battles, the fate of kingdoms. "We participate in the general progress of intellect, and the large vicissitudes of human affairs; but the hugest private sorrow looks dwarfish and puerile. In the sovereignty of our minds, we make mankind our quarry; and in the scope of our ambitious thoughts, hunt for prey through the four quarters of the world. In a word, literature and civilization have abstracted man from himself so far, that his existence is no longer *dramatic*, and the press has been the ruin of the stage, unless we are greatly deceived" (XVII, 304–305).

Yet the roots go even deeper, and, in a manner that reminds us of Wordsworth's complaints in the *Preface to the Lyrical Ballads*, Hazlitt speaks of the problem of the audience of poetry itself, a loss of taste and of the ability to respond with the full range of human sensibility. Like Wordsworth, he believes that although artists may still be intimidated by a certain traditionalism and a sense of the burden of past greatness, there is an equally serious problem in the state of public taste. Wordsworth spoke of the great national events and the increasing accumulation of men in cities as contributing factors to the blunting of the sensibilities of the audience for poetry. Hazlitt, deeply convinced that "no single mind can move in direct opposition to the vast machine of the world around it" and that the "public taste hangs like a millstone round the neck of all original genius that does not conform to established and exclusive models" (V, 96), finds no audience for the artist who would cut a deeper vein of feeling, who would confront men and women with their deepest selves through the symbolic and charged language of poetry. Something basic has been lost, the capacity to imagine greatly, to feel freely and passionately, to involve the self in the great objects of nature, to believe in myth as a conduit of the mysteries of the universe. Hazlitt argues that there can never be another Jacob's dream unless a revolution in taste is effected, unless artists and audiences recapture the primitive sense of wonder. The heavens have gone farther away as the increase of knowledge and the quite necessary development and refinement of civilization have challenged the province of poetry and constructed mechanisms that lead us safely but insipidly from the cradle to grave. "The heroes of the fabulous ages rid the world of monsters and giants. At present we are less exposed to the vicissitudes of good and evil, to the incursions of wild beasts, of 'bandit fierce,' or to the unmitigated fury of the elements. . . . But the police spoils all, and we now hardly so much as dream of a midnight murder. Macbeth is only tolerated in this country for the sake of the music; and in the United States of America, where the philosophical principles of government are carried still further in theory and practice, we find that Beggar's Opera is hooted from the stage" (V, 9–10).

And yet Hazlitt, like Wordsworth and Shelley, refused to despair over the contemporary scene. Indeed he spoke and wrote with even greater urgency about the mission of literature and the arts in such a world, about their power to renovate the sensibility and to create a new freshness and readiness of response. In a larger sense he positioned literature at the heart of any system, formal or informal, of liberal education, the only kind of education that can educe the richest possibilities of man's complex nature by providing the fullest range of what is great and noble in human history. Whether arguing with his customary enthusiasm that "Books govern the world better than kings or priests" (XVII, 21) or more philosophically that tragedy "is the refiner of the species; a discipline of humanity" (IV, 200), his stance is clear and firm. Education liberates man from his primitive barbarism, from his intense preoccupation with his own narrow views and prejudices, and literature is the key to any such education. "The habitual study of poetry and works of imagination is one chief part of a well-grounded education. A taste for liberal arts is necessary to complete the character of a gentleman. Science alone is hard and mechanical. It exercises the understanding upon things out of ourselves while it leaves the affections unemployed, or engrossed with our own immediate, narrow interests" (IV, 200).

To the new task of proclaiming the autonomy and power of literature Hazlitt summoned not only the artist himself but the critic. He also must liberate himself from older notions concerning his role as a servant of the preacher or the philosopher and establish himself as the proclaimer of the unique values of art and as the articulate and passionate spokesman of the distinctive emotional and imaginative encounter which is the core of the aesthetic experience itself. In short, he must possess something of that divine spark possessed by the artist himself.

Hazlitt did not view himself as a seer or lawgiver promulgating rules for the work of art and testing plays, poems, and novels by these rules. The older image of the self-conscious critic, aware of the tradition and weighing art in the context of that tradition, held little appeal for him. Neither, it would seem, did the more contemporary image of the systematic, analytic critic, working closely with texts and their implications, bringing to bear as he proceeds the tools of anthropology, history, sociology, linguistics, and a host of other disciplines. He was generally most unhappy with the idea of criticism as a negative activity, as a process of discovering and pointing up the failings of artists and writers. Verbal critics, as he calls them, are "mere word-catchers, fellows that pick out a word in a sentence and a sentence in a volume, and tell you it is wrong"; they are determined "to set you down lower than their opinion of themselves" (VIII, 226). In *A View of the English Stage* he took an interesting line as he discussed some of his fellow critics: "We are aware that there is a class of connoisseurs whose envy it might be prudent to disarm, by some compromise with their perverted taste; who are horror-struck at grace and beauty, and who can only find relief and repose in the consoling thoughts of deformity and defect; whose blood curdles into poison at deserved reputation, who shudder at every temptation *to admire*, as an unpardonable crime, and shrink from whatever gives delight to others, with more than monkish self-denial" (V, 195).

He was impatient with the modern tendency toward elaborate analysis and explication, toward a fascination with multiple interpretations so the "critic does nothing now-a-days who does not try to torture the most obvious expression into a thousand meanings, and enter into a circuitous explanation of all that can be urged for or against its being in the best or worst style possible. His object indeed is not to do justice to his author, whom he treats with very little ceremony, but to do himself homage, and to show his acquaintance with all the topics and resources of criticism" (VIII, 214). Historical, philosophical, and formalistic critics do not fare much better; he spoke of the "cavillers" for whom "the author must be reduced to a class, all the living or dead examples of which must be characteristically and pointedly *differenced* from one another; the value of this class of writing must be developed and ascertained in comparison with others; the principles of taste, the elements of our sensations, the structure of the human faculties, all must undergo a strict scrutiny and revision" (VIII, 217).

The tendency in his own time toward sensational criticism has had, in Hazlitt's mind, very bad effects. A host of talented, but shallow, critics seek the shocking and the spectacular effect, in the hope of gathering around them a special clique of followers. To these critics the basic values of a work of art are of relatively minor importance compared to "keeping up the character of the work and supplying the town with a sufficient number of grave or brilliant topics for the consumption of the next three months!" (VIII, 216).

Most troubling are the obscurantist critics, the *"Occult School-vere-adapti,"* as he described them. The obvious, the simply beautiful and delightful, all of these are secondary to those who "discern no beauties but what are concealed from superficial eyes, and overlook all that are obvious to the vulgar part of mankind. . . . If an author is utterly unreadable, they can read him for ever; his intricacies are their delight, his mysteries are their study." Preferring Sir Thomas Browne to Dr. Johnson's *Rambler* and Burton's *Anatomy of Melancholy* to all the writers of the Georgian Age, they hoard works of great genius as their special treasure which "is of no value unless they have it all to themselves" (VIII, 225).

There is a similar freshness in Hazlitt's attempt to define and describe in new ways the proper operation of the critical mind as it deals with life and literature as evolving phenomena. Much as he admired Samuel Johnson, he nevertheless criticized him as essentially an unpoetical mind and hence as incapable of dealing adequately with the major challenges of imaginative works of art. Johnson's basic cast of mind dominated his critical instincts; his ideas were too determined by rule and system. His was a consecutive mind capable of grasping general principles and the main flow of human events, but it "could not shew how the nature of man was modified by the workings of passion, or the infinite fluctuations of thought and accident" (IV, 175). His criticism is not just wrong-headed; it is dangerous. In a sense it was part of the mind of his age, which was in doubt about poetry, ambivalent about imaginative literature and its possibilities for the enlargement of the intellectual and emotional capacities of human beings. His analysis of Johnson and indeed of the dominant eighteenth century attitude toward the arts is both penetrating and fascinating. Johnson lacks "any particular fineness of organic sensibility" and "that intenseness of passion, . . . seeking to exaggerate whatever excites the feelings of pleasure or pain in the mind." Consequently aesthetic considerations are consistently subservient, and "he would be for setting up a foreign jurisdiction over poetry, and making criticism a kind of Procrustes' bed of genius, where he might cut down the imagination to matter-of-fact, regulate the passions according to reason, and translate the whole into logical diagrams and rhetorical declamation" (IV, 176).

Hazlitt was heartened by later developments in Reynolds's *Discourses* which take a larger view of the genius of the artist and of his ability to stir response in a reader or viewer. In a brief but perceptive statement he provides a summary of Reynolds's critical career, especially of the critic's development from early traditional criticism to the more venturesome and imaginative spirit of the later work, the spirit which underlies his statement that genius in a traditionally lesser form of art is to be preferred to feebleness and insipidity in a greater form (VIII, 122).

If Hazlitt operated within any tradition of criticism, it was the more personal, individualistic one inaugurated in large part by Wordsworth although even here the attempt to categorize him is dangerous. His philosophical and critical roots, were, to be sure, in British empirical psychology and in the complicated Anglo-Scottish aesthetics of the eighteenth century with its emphasis on sensation, individual response, taste, genius, and a host of other ideas, yet he everywhere moved beyond a more strictly psychological orientation to develop a critical posture that was unique.

Hazlitt was the most personal of critics, eager to cut through the stultifying abstractions of rules, the maze of elaborate analysis to provide open, unencumbered response. Indeed for him criticism becomes before all else the record of a sensitive man's encounter with a work of art. "I say what I think: I think what I feel" (V, 175) almost typifies his credo. How to communicate that record with a minimum of academic jargon, of dilettantish pretentiousness, became the consistent struggle. How to find a language, direct or metaphorical, to convey the sense of the critic's sympathetic experience of the great work of art became the continuing challenge.

It was this personal, individual dimension that marked most of his critical writing, the sense that Hazlitt was articulating his own artistic temperament rather than associating himself with a particular school. He quite consciously separates himself from contemporary criticism and defines a new and higher ground as he contends that a "genuine criticism should, as I take it, reflect the colors, the light and shade, the soul and body of a work:— here we have nothing but its superficial plan and elevation, as if a poem were a piece of formal architecture. We are told something of the plot or fable, or the moral, and of the observation of the three unities of time, place, and action; and perhaps a word or two is added on the dignity of the persons or the boldness of the style; but we no more know, after reading one of these complacent *tirades*, what the essence of the work is, what passion has been touched, or how skillfully, what tone and movement the author's mind imparts to his subject or receives from it, than if we had been reading a homily or a gazette. That is, we are left quite in the dark as to feelings of pleasure or pain to be derived from the genius of the performance or the manner in which it appeals to the imagination" (VIII, 217). In his essay "On Genius and Common Sense" he expresses the essence of this conviction: "In art, in taste, in life, in speech, you decide from feeling, and not from reason; that is, from the impression of a number of things on the mind, which impression is true and well-founded, through you may not be able to account for it in the several particulars" (VIII, 31).

Hazlitt takes great pains to emphasize feeling and taste not as mere subjective whimsies, but as informed and educated powers. Mere enthusiasm is not enough to produce great criticism; it must, he contended, be tempered by reason and knowledge. Not everyone can conform to the new image of the critic. Only the "most refined understandings" (XVIII, 46) can operate successfully in matters of

taste. Criticism as a profession has little room for democracy, for the tyranny of popular taste which stands to threaten the citadel of artistic excellence. Only "the opinion of the greatest number of well-informed minds" (XX, 386) can become a true standard of taste.

The critic must be free of the tyranny of both past and present, must be open to all kinds of expression as he pursues his task with great catholicity of taste. Hence Hazlitt ranged from Old English literature to Elizabethan drama to Renaissance painting, to the work of his contemporaries. Prefacing his observations on Elizabethan literature, he says, "If I can do anything to rescue some of these writers from hopeless obscurity, and to do them right, without prejudice to well-deserved reputation, I shall have succeeded in what I chiefly propose." He would "bring out their real beauties to the eager sight 'draw the curtain of Time, and shew the picture of Genius,' restraining my admiration within reasonable bounds!" (VI, 176).

Veneration of the merely contemporary was, he felt, a major problem; too many critics have proceeded from the premise that the post-Restoration years represent a literary Eden and have regarded all previous literature as Gothic, as lacking the elegance and sophistication of true art. Even where homage is paid to Old English literature, "it is more akin to the rites of superstition, than the worship of true religion." (VI, 179).

At the same time he had little patience with the nostalgists, with those drawn to the art of the past as a bulwark of values they have inherited and now choose to set as standards—who are uneasy with the new literature of complex emotion and imaginative complexity. Modern literature must be confronted, must be dealt with openly and honestly. "There is a change in the world, and we must conform to it" is his challenge (XVI, 218).

At his best Hazlitt, the theorist and critic of finely tuned intuition and strong feeling, brings to his work a genuine sense of the dominant thrust of a work of art, of that special quality that touches life so closely that it stirs the imagination and moves the heart. It is his image of the critic, passionately intelligent, broadly informed, and richly sympathetic that stands out so sharply in early nineteenth century English. His task was nothing less than a new justification of the arts and a sharing of their beauties with those readers and spectators for whom the arts are an intimate part of life itself.

NOTES

1. All quotations from Hazlitt in this essay are from *The Complete Works of William Hazlitt,* ed. P. P. Howe (London, 1930–1940). Quotations will be followed by parentheses with the volume numbers in Roman numerals and the page numbers in Arabic.

2. See especially W. J. Bate, *Criticism: The Major Texts* (Harcourt Brace Jovanovich, Inc., 1970), pp. 281–292 and Roy Park, *Hazlitt and the Spirit of the Age* (Clarendon Press, Oxford, 1971).

3. Park, p. 1.

4. *Criticism: The Major Texts,* pp. 340–341.

5. The same, pp. 429–435.

6. See W. P. Albrecht, "Hazlitt's Preference for Tragedy," *PMLA,* LXXI (December 1956), 1042–1051 and Sylvan Barnet and W. P. Albrecht, "More on Hazlitt's Preference for Tragedy," *PMLA,* LXIII (September 1958), 443–445.

Cleanth Brooks

KEATS'S SYLVAN HISTORIAN: HISTORY WITHOUT FOOTNOTES[1]*

There is much in the poetry of Keats which suggests that he would have approved of Archibald MacLeish's dictum, "A poem should not mean/ But be." There is even some warrant for thinking that the Grecian urn (real or imagined) which inspired the famous ode was, for Keats, just such a poem, "palpable and mute," a poem in stone. Hence it is

the more remarkable that the "Ode" itself differs from Keats's other odes by culminating in a statement—a statement even of some sententiousness in which the urn itself is made to say that beauty is truth, and—more sententious still—that this bit of wisdom sums up the whole of mortal knowledge.

This is "to mean" with a vengeance—to violate the doctrine of the objective correlative, not only by stating truths, but by defining the limits of truth. Small wonder that some critics have felt that the unravished bride of quietness protests too much.

T. S. Eliot, for example, says that "this line ['Beauty is truth,' etc.] strikes me as a serious blemish on a beautiful poem; and the reason must be either that I fail to understand it, or that it is a statement which is untrue." But even for persons who feel that they do understand it, the line may still constitue a blemish. Middleton Murry, who, after a discussion of Keats's other poems and his letters, feels that he knows what Keats meant by "beauty" and what he meant by "truth," and that Keats used them in senses which allowed them to be properly bracketed together, still, is forced to conclude: "My own opinion concerning the value of these two lines *in the context of the poem itself* is not very different from Mr. T. S. Eliot's." The

---

[1] This essay had been finished some months before I came upon Kenneth Burke's brilliant essay on Keats's "Ode" ("Symbolic Action in a Poem by Keats," *Accent,* Autumn, 1943). I have decided not to make any alterations, though I have been tempted to adopt some of Burke's insights, and, in at least one case, his essay has convinced me of a point which I had considered but rejected—the pun on "breed" and "Brede."

I am happy to find that two critics with methods and purposes so different should agree so thoroughly as we do on the poem. I am pleased, for my part, therefore, to acknowledge the amount of duplication which exists between the two essays, counting it as rather important corroboration of a view of the poem which will probably seem to some critics overingenious. In spite of the common elements, however, I feel that the emphasis of my essay is sufficiently different from Burke's to justify my going on with its publication.

*From *The Well-Wrought Urn* copyright 1947 and renewed 1975 by Cleanth Brooks. Reprinted by permission of Harcourt Brace & Company.

troubling assertion is apparently an intrusion upon the poem—does not grow out of it—is not dramatically accommodated to it.

This is essentially Garrod's objection, and the fact that Garrod does object indicates that a distaste for the ending of the "Ode" is by no means limited to critics of notoriously "modern" sympathies.

But the question of real importance is not whether Eliot, Murry, and Garrod are right in thinking that "Beauty is truth, truth beauty" injures the poem. The question of real importance concerns beauty and truth in a much more general way: what is the relation of the beauty (the goodness, the perfection) of a poem to the truth or falsity of what it seems to assert? It is a question which has particularly vexed our own generation—to give it I. A. Richards' phrasing, it is the problem of belief.

The "Ode," by its bold equation of beauty and truth, raises this question in its sharpest form—the more so when it becomes apparent that the poem itself is obviously intended to be a parable on the nature of poetry, and of art in general. The "Ode" has apparently been an enigmatic parable, to be sure: one can emphasize *beauty* is truth and throw Keats into the pure-art camp, the usual procedure. But it is only fair to point out that one could stress *truth* is beauty, and argue with the Marxist critics of the 'thirties for a propaganda art. The very ambiguity of the statement, "Beauty is truth, truth beauty" ought to warn us against insisting very much on the statement in isolation, and to drive us back to a consideration of the context in which the statement is set.

It will not be sufficient, however, if it merely drives us back to a study of Keats's reading, his conversation, his letters. We shall not find our answer there even if scholarship does prefer on principle investigations of Browning's ironic question, "What porridge had John Keats." For even if we knew just what porridge he had, physical and mental, we should still not be able to settle the problem of the "Ode." The reason should be clear: our specific question is not what did Keats the man perhaps want to assert here about the relation of beauty and truth; it is rather: was Keats the poet able to exemplify that relation in this particular poem? Middleton Murry is right: the relation of the final statement in the poem to the total context is all-important.

Indeed, Eliot, in the very passage in which he attacks the "Ode" has indicated the general line which we are to take in its defense. In that passage, Eliot goes on to contrast the closing lines of the "Ode" with a line from *King Lear*, "Ripeness is all." Keats's lines strike him as false; Shakespeare's, on the other hand, as not clearly false, and as possibly quite true. Shakespeare's generalization, in other words, avoids raising the question of truth. But is it really a question of truth and falsity? One is tempted to account for the difference of effect which Eliot feels in this way: "Ripeness is all" is a statement put in the mouth of a dramatic character and a statement which is governed and qualified by the whole context of the play. It does not directly challenge an examination into its truth because its relevance is pointed up and modified by the dramatic context.

Now, suppose that one could show that Keats's lines, *in quite the same way*, constitute a speech, a consciously riddling paradox, put in the mouth of a particular character, and modified by the total context of the poem. If we could demonstrate that the speech was "in character," was dramatically appropriate, was properly prepared for—then would not the lines have all the justification of "Ripeness is all"? In such case, should we not have waived the question of the scientific or philosophic truth of the lines in favor of the application of a principle curiously like that of dramatic propriety? I suggest that some such principle is the only one legitimately to be invoked in any case. Be this as it may, the "Ode on a Grecian Urn" provides us with as neat an instance as one could wish in order to test the implications of such a maneuver.

It has seemed best to be perfectly frank about procedures: the poem is to be read in order to see whether the last lines of the poem are not, after all, dramatically prepared for. Yet there are some claims to be made upon the reader too, claims which he, for his part, will have to be prepared to honor. He must not be allowed to dismiss the early characterizations of the urn as merely so much vaguely beautiful description. He must not be too much surprised if "mere decoration" turns out to be meaningful symbolism—or if ironies develop where he has been taught to expect only sensuous pictures. Most of all, if the teasing riddle spoken finally by the urn is not to strike him as a bewildering break in tone, he must not be too much disturbed to have the element of paradox latent in the poem emphasized, even in those parts of the poem which have none of the energetic crackle of wit with which he usually associates paradox. This is surely not too much to ask of the reader—namely, to assume that Keats meant what he said and that he chose his words with care. After all, the poem begins on a note of paradox, though a mild one: for we ordinarily do not expect an urn to speak at all; and yet, Keats does more than this: he begins his poem by emphasizing the apparent contradiction.

The silence of the urn is stressed—it is a "bride of quietness"; it is a "foster-child of silence," but the urn is a "historian" too. Historians tell the truth, or are at least expected to tell the truth. What is a "Sylvan historian"? A historian who is like the forest rustic, a woodlander? Or, a historian who writes histories of the forest? Presumably, the urn is sylvan in both senses. True, the latter meaning is uppermost: the urn can "express / A flowery tale more sweetly than our rhyme," and what the urn goes on to express is a "leaf-fring'd legend" of "Tempe or the dales of Arcady." But the urn, like the "leaf-fring'd legend" which it tells, is covered with emblems of the fields and forests: "Over-wrought, / With forest branches and the trodden weed." When we consider the way in which the urn utters its history, the fact that it must be sylvan in both senses is seen as inevitable. Perhaps too the fact that it is a rural historian, a rustic, a peasant historian, qualifies in our minds the dignity and the "truth" of the histories which it recites. Its histories, Keats has already conceded, may be characterized as "tales"—not formal history at all.

The sylvan historian certainly supplies no names and dates—"What men or gods are these?" the poet asks. What it does give is action—of men *or* gods, of godlike men or of superhuman (though not daemonic) gods—action, which is not the less intense for all that the urn is cool marble. The words "mad" and "ecstasy" occur, but it is the quiet, rigid urn which gives the dynamic picture. And the paradox goes further: the scene is one of violent love-making, a Bacchanalian scene, but the urn itself is like a "still unravish'd bride," or like a child, a child "of silence and slow time." It is not merely like a child, but like a "foster-child." The exactness of the term can be defended. "Silence and slow time," it is suggested, are not the true parents, but foster-parents. They are too old, one feels, to have

borne the child themselves. Moreover, they dote upon the "child" as grandparents do. The urn is fresh and unblemished; it is still young, for all its antiquity, and time which destroys so much has "fostered" it.

With Stanza II we move into the world presented by the urn, into an examination, not of the urn as a whole—as an entity with its own form—but of the details which overlay it. But as we enter that world, the paradox of silent speech is carried on, this time in terms of the objects portrayed on the vase.

The first lines of the stanza state a rather bold paradox—even the dulling effect of many readings has hardly blunted it. At least we can easily revive its sharpness. Attended to with care, it is a statement which is preposterous, and yet true—true on the same level on which the original metaphor of the speaking urn is true. The unheard music is sweeter than any audible music. The poet has rather cunningly enforced his conceit by using the phrase, "ye soft pipes." Actually, we might accept the poet's metaphor without being forced to accept the adjective "soft." The pipes might, although "unheard," be shrill, just as the action which is frozen in the figures on the urn can be violent and ecstatic as in Stanza I and slow and dignified as in Stanza IV (the procession to the sacrifice). Yet, by characterizing the pipes as "soft," the poet has provided a sort of realistic basis for his metaphor: the pipes, it is suggested, are playing very softly; if we listen carefully, we can hear them; their music is just below the threshold of normal sound.

This general paradox runs through the stanza: action goes on though the actors are motionless; the song will not cease; the lover cannot leave his song; the maiden, always to be kissed, never actually kissed, will remain changelessly beautiful. The maiden is, indeed, like the urn itself, a "still unravished bride of quietness"—not even ravished by a kiss; and it is implied, perhaps, that her changeless beauty, like that of the urn, springs from this fact.

The poet is obviously stressing the fresh, unwearied charm of the scene itself which can defy time and is deathless. But, at the same time, the poet is being perfectly fair to the terms of his metaphor. The beauty portrayed is deathless because it is lifeless. And it would be possible to shift the tone easily and ever so slightly by insisting more heavily on some of the phrasings so as to give them a darker implication. Thus, in the case of "thou canst not leave / Thy song," one could interpret: the musician cannot leave the song even if he would: he is fettered to it, a prisoner. In the same way, one could enlarge on the hint that the lover is not wholly satisfied and content: "never canst thou kiss, / ... yet, do not grieve." These items are mentioned here, not because one wishes to maintain that the poet is bitterly ironical, but because it is important for us to see that even here the paradox is being used fairly, particularly in view of the shift in tone which comes in the next stanza.

This third stanza represents, as various critics have pointed out, a recapitulation of earlier motifs. The boughs which cannot shed their leaves, the unwearied melodist, and the ever-ardent lover reappear. Indeed, I am not sure that this stanza can altogether be defended against the charge that it represents a falling-off from the delicate but firm precision of the earlier stanzas. There is a tendency to linger over the scene sentimentally: the repetition of the word "happy" is perhaps symptomatic of what is occurring. Here, if anywhere, in my opinion, is to be found the blemish on the ode—not in the last two lines. Yet, if we are to attempt a defense of the third stanza, we shall come nearest success by emphasizing the paradoxical implications of the repeated items; for whatever development there is in the stanza inheres in the increased stress on the paradoxical element. For example, the boughs cannot "bid the Spring adieu," a phrase which repeats "nor ever can those trees be bare," but the new line strengthens the implications of speaking: the falling leaves are a gesture, a word of farewell to the joy of spring. The melodist of Stanza II played sweeter music because unheard, but here, in the third stanza, it is implied that he does not tire of his song for the same reason that the lover does not tire of his love—neither song nor love is consummated. The songs are "for ever new" because they cannot be completed.

The paradox is carried further in the case of the lover whose love is "For ever warm and still to be enjoy'd." We are really dealing with an ambiguity here, for we can take "still to be enjoy'd" as an adjectival phrase on the same level as "warm"— that is, "still virginal and warm." But the tenor of the whole poem suggests that the warmth of the love depends upon the fact that it has not been enjoyed—that is, "warm and still to be enjoy'd" may mean also "warm because still to be enjoy'd."

But though the poet has developed and extended his metaphors furthest here in this third stanza, the ironic counterpoise is developed furthest too. The love which a line earlier was "warm" and "panting" becomes suddenly in the next line, "All breathing human passion far above." But if it is above all breathing passion, it is, after all, outside the realm of breathing passion, and therefore, not human passion at all.

(If one argues that we are to take "All breathing human passion" as qualified by "That leaves a heart high-sorrowful and cloy'd"—that is, if one argues that Keats is saying that the love depicted on the urn is above only that human passion which leaves one cloyed and not above human passion in general, he misses the point. For Keats in the "Ode" is stressing the ironic fact that all human passion does leave one cloyed; hence the superiority of art.)

The purpose in emphasizing the ironic undercurrent in the foregoing lines is not at all to disparage Keats—to point up implications of his poem of which he was himself unaware. Far from it: the poet knows precisely what he is doing. The point is to be made simply in order to make sure that we are completely aware of what he is doing. Garrod, sensing this ironic undercurrent, seems to interpret it as an element over which Keats was not able to exercise full control. He says: "Truth to his main theme [the fixity given by art to forms which in life are impermanent] has taken Keats farther than he meant to go. The pure and ideal art of this 'cold Pastoral,' this 'silent form,' has a cold silentness which in some degree saddens him. In the last lines of the fourth stanza, especially the last three lines ... every reader is conscious, I should suppose, of an undertone of sadness, of disappointment." The undertone is there, but Keats has not been taken "farther than he meant to go." Keats's attitude, even in the early stanzas, is more complex than Garrod would allow: it is more complex and more ironic, and a recognition of this is important if we are to be able to relate the last stanzas to the rest of the "Ode." Keats is perfectly aware that the frozen moment of loveliness is more dynamic than is the fluid world of reality only because it is frozen. The love depicted on the urn remains warm and young because it is not human flesh at all but cold, ancient marble.

With Stanza IV, we are still within the world depicted by the urn, but the scene presented in this stanza forms a contrast to the earlier scenes. It emphasizes, not individual aspiration and desire, but communal life. It constitutes another chapter in the history that the "Sylvan historian" has to tell. And again, names and dates have been omitted. We are not told to what god's altar the procession moves, nor the occasion of the sacrifice.

Moreover, the little town from which the celebrants come is unknown; and the poet rather goes out of his way to leave us the widest possible option in locating it. It may be a mountain town, or a river town, or a tiny seaport. Yet, of course, there is a sense in which the nature of the town—the essential character of the town—is actually suggested by the figured urn. But it is not given explicitly. The poet is willing to leave much to our imaginations; and yet the stanza in its organization of imagery and rhythm does describe the town clearly enough; it is small, it is quiet, its people are knit together as an organic whole, and on a "pious morn" such as this, its whole population has turned out to take part in the ritual.

The stanza has been justly admired. Its magic of effect defies reduction to any formula. Yet, without pretending to "account" for the effect in any mechanical fashion, one can point to some of the elements active in securing the effect: there is the suggestiveness of the word "green" in "green altar" —something natural, spontaneous, living; there is the suggestion that the little town is caught in a curve of the seashore, or nestled in a fold of the mountains—at any rate, is something secluded and something naturally related to its terrain; there is the effect of the phrase "peaceful citadel," a phrase which involves a clash between the ideas of war and peace and resolves it in the sense of stability and independence without imperialistic ambition— the sense of stable repose.

But to return to the larger pattern of the poem: Keats does something in this fourth stanza which is highly interesting in itself and thoroughly relevant to the sense in which the urn is a historian. One of the most moving passages in the poem is that in which the poet speculates on the strange emptiness of the little town which, of course, has not been pictured on the urn at all.

The little town which has been merely implied by the procession portrayed on the urn is endowed with a poignance beyond anything else in the poem. Its streets "for evermore / Will silent be," its desolation forever shrouded in a mystery. No one in the figured procession will ever be able to go back to the town to break the silence there, not even one to tell the stranger there why the town remains desolate.

If one attends closely to what Keats is doing here, he may easily come to feel that the poet is indulging himself in an ingenious fancy, an indulgence, however, which is gratuitous and finally silly; that is, the poet has created in his own imagination the town implied by the procession of worshipers, has given it a special character of desolation and loneliness, and then has gone on to treat it as if it were a real town to which a stranger might actually come and be puzzled by its emptiness. (I can see no other interpretation of the lines, "and not a soul to tell/ Why thou art desolate can e'er return.") But, actually, of course, no one will ever discover the town except by the very same process by which Keats has discovered it: namely, through the figured urn, and then, of course, he will not need to ask why it is empty. One can well imagine what a typical eighteenth-century critic would have made of this flaw in logic.

It will not be too difficult, however, to show that Keats's extension of the fancy is not irrelevant to the poem as a whole. The "reality" of the little town has a very close relation to the urn's character as a historian. If the earlier stanzas have been concerned with such paradoxes as the ability of static carving to convey dynamic action, of the soundless pipes to play music sweeter than that of the heard melody, of the figured lover to have a love more warm and panting than that of breathing flesh and blood, so in the same way the town implied by the urn comes to have a richer and more important history than that of actual cities. Indeed, the imagined town is to the figured procession as the unheard melody is to the carved pipes of the unwearied melodist. And the poet, by pretending to take the town as real—so real that he can imagine the effect of its silent streets upon the stranger who chances to come into it—has suggested in the most powerful way possible its essential reality for him—and for us. It is a case of the doctor's taking his own medicine: the poet is prepared to stand by the illusion of his own making.

With Stanza V we move back out of the enchanted world portrayed by the urn to consider the urn itself once more as a whole, as an object. The shift in point of view is marked with the first line of the stanza by the apostrophe, "O Attic shape . . ." It is the urn itself as a formed thing, as an autonomous world, to which the poet addresses these last words. And the rich, almost breathing world which the poet has conjured up for us contracts and hardens into the decorated motifs on the urn itself: "with brede/ Of marble men and maidens overwrought." The beings who have a life above life—"All breathing human passion far above"— are marble, after all.

This last is a matter which, of course, the poet has never denied. The recognition that the men and maidens are frozen, fixed, arrested, has, as we have already seen, run through the second, third, and fourth stanzas as an ironic undercurrent. The central paradox of the poem, thus, comes to conclusion in the phrase, "Cold Pastoral." The word "pastoral" suggests warmth, spontaneity, the natural and the informal as well as the idyllic, the simple, and the informally charming. What the urn tells is a "flowery tale," a "leaf-fring'd legend," but the "sylvan historian" works in terms of marble. The urn itself is cold, and the life beyond life which it expresses is life which has been formed, arranged. The urn itself is a "silent form," and it speaks, not by means of statement, but by "teasing us out of thought." It is as enigmatic as eternity is, for, like eternity, its history is beyond time, outside time, and for this very reason bewilders our time-ridden minds: it teases us.

The marble men and maidens of the urn will not age as flesh-and-blood men and women will: "When old age shall this generation waste." (The word "generation," by the way, is very rich. It means on one level "that which is generated"—that which springs from human loins—Adam's breed; and yet, so intimately is death wedded to men, the word "generation" itself has become, as here, a measure of time.) The marble men and women lie outside time. The urn which they adorn will remain. The "Sylvan historian" will recite its history to other generations.

What will it say to them? Presumably, what it says to the poet now: that "formed experience," imaginative insight, embodies the basic fundamental perception of man and nature. The urn is beautiful, and yet its beauty is based—what else

is the poem concerned with?—on an imaginative perception of essentials. Such a vision is beautiful but it is also true. The sylvan historian presents us with beautiful histories, but they are true histories, and it is a good historian.

Moreover, the "truth" which the sylvan historian gives is the only kind of truth which we are likely to get on this earth, and, furthermore, it is the only kind that we *have* to have. The names, dates, and special circumstances, the wealth of data—these the sylvan historian quietly ignores. But we shall never get all the facts anyway—there is no end to the accumulation of facts. Moreover, mere accumulations of facts—a point our own generation is only beginning to realize—are meaningless. The sylvan historian does better than that: it takes a few details and so orders them that we have not only beauty but insight into essential truth. Its "history," in short, is a history without footnotes. It has the validity of myth—not myth as a pretty but irrelevant make-belief, an idle fancy, but myth as a valid perception into reality.

So much for the "meaning" of the last lines of the "Ode." It is an interpretation which differs little from past interpretations. It is put forward here with no pretension to novelty. What is important is the fact that it can be derived from the context of the "Ode" itself.

And now, what of the objection that the final lines break the tone of the poem with a display of misplaced sententiousness? One can summarize the answer already implied thus: throughout the poem the poet has stressed the paradox of the speaking urn. First, the urn itself can tell a story, can give a history. Then, the various figures depicted upon the urn play music or speak or sing. If we have been alive to these items, we shall not, perhaps, be too much surprised to have the urn speak once more, not in the sense in which it tells a story—a metaphor which is rather easy to accept—but, to have it speak on a higher level, to have it make a commentary on its own nature. If the urn has been properly dramatized, if we have followed the development of the metaphors, if we have been alive to the paradoxes which work throughout the poem, perhaps then, we shall be prepared for the enigmatic, final paradox which the "silent form" utters. But in that case, we shall not feel that the generalization, unqualified and to be taken literally, is meant to march out of its context to compete with the scientific and philosophical generalizations which dominate our world.

"Beauty is truth, truth beauty" has precisely the same status, and the same justification as Shakespeare's "Ripeness is all." It is a speech "in character" and supported by a dramatic context.

To conclude thus may seem to weight the principle of dramatic propriety with more than it can bear. This would not be fair to the complexity of the problem of truth in art nor fair to Keats's little parable. Granted; and yet the principle of dramatic propriety may take us further than would first appear. Respect for it may at least insure our dealing with the problem of truth at the level on which it is really relevant to literature. If we can see that the assertions made in a poem are to be taken as part of an organic context, if we can resist the temptation to deal with them in isolation, then we may be willing to go on to deal with the world-view, or "philosophy," or "truth" of the *poem as a whole* in terms of its dramatic wholeness: that is, we shall not neglect the maturity of attitude, the dramatic tension, the emotional *and* intellectual coherence in favor of some statement of theme abstracted from it by paraphrase. Perhaps, best of all, we might learn to distrust our ability to represent any poem adequately by paraphrase. Such a distrust is healthy. Keats's sylvan historian, who is not above "teasing" us, exhibits such a distrust, and perhaps the point of what the sylvan historian "says" is to confirm us in our distrust.

Earl Wasserman

ODE TO A NIGHTINGALE*

I

Of all Keats' poems, it is probably the "Ode to a Nightingale" that has most tormented the critic. The "Ode on a Grecian Urn" may trouble (unnecessarily, I think) because of the identification of beauty and truth, but even an uncritical reading of that ode leaves one with the sense that the poet himself, at any rate, has arrived at the end of his making with all passion spent. Through the poet's engagement in the struggle the poetic storm appears to have been hushed into a calm that gives him a new resolution, a firmer grasp of values than he had before his shipwrecked journey in search of a Northwest Passage. But in any reading of the "Ode to a Nightingale" the turmoil will not down. Forces contend wildly within the poem, not only without resolution, but without possibility of resolution; and the reader comes away from his experience with the sense that he has been in a

> wild Abyss,
> The Womb of nature and perhaps her Grave,
> Of neither Sea, nor Shore, nor Air, nor Fire,
> But all these in their pregnant causes mixt
> Confusedly.

It is this turbulence, I suspect, that has led Allen Tate to believe the ode "at least tries to say everything that poetry can say." [1] But I propose it is the "Ode on a Grecian Urn" that succeeds in saying what poetry can say, and that the other ode attempts to say all that the *poet* can. For the first is self-contained art: it develops out of its initial situation by an inner compulsion, and works out its own destiny in terms of its inherent drama, its own grammar and symbols. Its dynamic force lies within itself and is released and exploited by factors that are the property of poetry alone, and of this poem in particular: rhythm, tempo, rhyme, syntax, grammatical gesture, the self-impelled movement of the images. It therefore satisfies Coleridge's definition of a legitimate poem: "one, the parts of which mutually support and explain each other; all in their proportion harmonizing with, and supporting the purpose and known influences of metrical arrangement." [2] But the second poem is synthetically fashioned: instead of operating within its own framework, it functions only because the poet intervenes and cuts across the grain of his materials to make them vibrant. The first is the poetic cosmos; the second is the poet's chaos. The first is the work of art; the second the workings of art. By these large generalizations I do not mean to imply a value judgment, but simply to put the two poems into different categories, despite their very great similarities in subject matter, procedure, and conceptual intent. What value judgments we make must take into consideration these categorical differences.

Many of our difficulties in interpreting the "Ode to a Nightingale" no doubt arise from a foresight born of long familiarity. Coming to the poem with a previous acquaintance in mind, we tend to read into each part the total intent. For example, we probably are inclined to think of the nightingale as an "immortal bird" even in the first stanza, and consequently contribute to the symbol considerably more than its activity at the moment justifies. But Keats' poetry is seldom static, and the nightingale does not have a fixed value throughout the poem: meaning lies not only in a symbol or a situation, but often more significantly in the direction being taken by any of the materials. The poetry is, in other words, dramatic and evolutionary, and we must read not only what is explicitly enacted but also what is implied by the abstract pattern made by the development of Keats' materials—their becomingness. The nightingale, for example, not only embodies a series of increasing symbolic values but also, by this act, traces out a sequentiality which is itself symbolic.

If, now, we search the poem for its most embracing active elements, we find that the two major actors are the poet and the nightingale, and that the poem elaborates a series of relationships of these two as a consequence of three proposals made by the poet. What I intend first, therefore, is not to observe the dramatic interaction of these elements, but to examine independently the courses taken by each of the dramatic threads of which the ode is woven, in order to discover what meaning may reside in the following abstract patterns: (1) the three proposals whereby the poet seeks to ease the pain of his "happiness"; (2) the symbolic significances of the nightingale; and (3) the capacities of the poet for intense experience.

II

The conflict out of which the ode is born is a recurrent one in Keats' poetry and is the inevitable result of the oxymoronic ontology within which he thinks. The poet's self has been caught up in empathic ecstasy so completely that he is "too happy." The absorption into essence—the fellowship divine which constitutes "happiness"—has been greater than is destined for mortal man, and the result is heartache and painful numbness. The ideal condition towards which Keats always strives because it is his ideal, is one in which mortal and immortal, dynamism and stasis, the Dionysian and the Apollonian, beauty and truth, are one. And in the "Ode on a Grecian Urn" and "La Belle Dame Sans Merci" he had traced mortal man's momentary ascent to, and his inevitable eviction from, this condition. But if, in his aspirations towards the conditions of heaven's bourne, man is unable to draw heaven and earth together into a stable union—and it is part of Keats' scheme of things that he must be unable while he is mortal—then he is torn between the two extremes, grasping after both but at home in neither. Even in the ode on the urn, where the material and the ethereal did for a moment coalesce, they quickly separated out of their volatile union. Therefore,

O that our dreamings all of sleep or wake
Would all their colours from the Sunset take:
From something of material sublime,
Rather than shadow our own Soul's daytime
In the dark void of Night. For in the world
We jostle. . . .

. . . Oh never will the prize,
High reason, and the lore of good and ill
Be my award.   Things cannot to the will
Be settled, but they ease us out of thought.
Or is it that Imagination brought
Beyond its proper bound, yet still confined,—
Lost in a sort of Purgatory blind,
Cannot refer to any standard law
Of either earth or heaven?—It is a flaw
In happiness to see beyond our bourn—
It forces us in Summer skies to mourn:
It spoils the singing of the Nightingale. [3]

If man could confine his aspirations to this physical world, to "something of material sublime," he might find a degree of content; but it is of his very nature that, unless he limits himself to the "level chambers" of mere revelry, he can no more renounce his quest for the ideal than Endymion can renounce his quest for Cynthia. Peona may convincingly describe the rewards of the world, but Endymion must still yearn for an immortality of passion and a love that makes "Men's being mortal, immortal." Once mortal man has glimpsed into heaven's bourne, the physical loses its splendor and charm: awakening from a vision of Cynthia, Endymion found that

> deepest shades
> Were deepest dungeons; heaths and sunny
>   glades
> Were full of pestilent light,

and that

> all the pleasant hues
> Of heaven and earth had faded. [4]

The fellowship with essence leaves only discontent with human life and spoils the singing of the nightingale.

It is inevitable, then, that men who are not merely brutish should strain to become "More happy than betides mortality" [5] and consequently be "too happy to be glad." [6] Man must always seek to ease the burden of the mystery; and since the mystery does not lie in the conceptual world, where an act of will can seize only the outward nature of things, it teases us "out of thought," tempting man to dodge conception until he is struggling against his mortal bonds. He must agonize to burst the bars that keep his spirit in. [7] Yet, man is of the earth—"For in the world / We jostle"—and he is bound to its nature, which is not perfectible: "The nature of the world will not admit of it—the inhabitants of the world will correspond to itself." [8] There can be no heaven on earth. Consequently, the heavenward flight of an earth-bound mortal must necessarily leave him in a gulf between the two worlds, one dead, the other powerless to be born. Striving to interknit his brain "With the glory and grace of Apollo," Keats had found that

> To thee my soul is flown,
> And my body is earthward press'd.
> It is an awful mission,
> A terrible division;
> And leaves a gulph austere
> To be fill'd with worldly fear.
> Aye, when the soul is fled
> To high above our head,
> Affrighted do we gaze
> After its airy maze,

> As doth a mother wild,
> When her young infant child
> Is in an eagle's claws—
> And is not this the cause
> Of madness? [9]

To look at these passages in another way, Keats is here examining the consequences of the act of ecstasy, the most intense empathic entrance into essence; for since "happiness" lies in the oxymoronic nature of heaven's bourne, it can be experienced only by the annihilation of self. Yet, while man is mortal the projection of self cannot be complete because the spirit cannot wholly leave behind the sensory substance in which it is encased; the effort to nourish life's self by its proper pith must torment the sensory clay. By attempting to gain "happiness," one is brought beyond his proper bound, and yet, being mortal, he is still confined to the earthly; and thus he is left with no standards to which to refer, or rather, with two conflicting sets of standards.

It is precisely in this maddening "Purgatory blind" that is neither earth nor heaven, and from which both seem without their pleasant hues, that the "Ode to a Nightingale" has its being. It is a poem without any standard law to which to refer, oscillating between heaven and earth and never able to reconcile them. The ode begins after the point that had been attained in the third stanza of the "Ode on a Grecian Urn." That poem, by enacting the ascent to a condition of happiness, could then salvage from the shattered momentary experience the meaning that the extra-human ascent has in the context of human existence; the "Ode to a Nightingale," however, by beginning with the dissolution itself, can only trace its further disintegration. It is necessary to recognize clearly this initial condition of the poet, for the significance of the entire poem is dependent upon it. Because the poem begins after the height of the empathic experience and traces the further journey homeward to habitual self, we are to look for irreconcilables, not harmonies; for patterns flying apart, not coming together; for conflicting standards.

Briefly, we are to read it by an inversion of the perspectives that give the "Ode on a Grecian Urn" its meaning. Or, better, we are to recognize the irony whereby Keats translates the experience with the nightingale into the terms of one who is being drawn back to the mortal world, and not one who, as in the other ode, is progressing towards the bourne of heaven. The thematic materials of the two odes, we shall see, are the same; but what blends organically in the "Ode on a Grecian Urn" disintegrates in this ode; what is seen in its immortal aspects in the former is seen in its mortal aspects in the latter.

This inversion is easily illustrated in the opening lines of the ode, for they establish the pattern that the poem is to follow. The pleasure thermometer that Keats outlined in *Endymion* is a series of increasing intensities that result in one's selflessly becoming assimilated into essence. As the experiences become more exquisite one is more free of his physical self and the dimensional world until at last he lives in essence. These two apparently contradictory acts—extremely vigorous sensation and the destruction of the self which experiences the sensations—are, nevertheless, a single and indivisible act; and in the "Ode on a Grecian Urn" the poet was absorbed into the life within the frieze in proportion as his own passions grew into ecstasy.

But let us now invert this movement. As we retreat from passionate selflessness, the two elements separate out of their organic union into strong emotion and a loss of self. And if then we evaluate these two, not as they carry us towards the dynamic stasis of heaven, but as they appear within the framework of merely mortal experience, the powerful emotion becomes only painfully exquisite sensation, and the selflessness only a swooning unresponsiveness. A drowsy numbness that pains the senses, paradoxical though it may seem, probably has some sound basis in psychological fact; but simply to psychologize the statement without reference to Keats' ideological system will not open the poem to us. It is necessary to see that in the dissolution of ecstasy into heartache and numbness the oxymoronic nature of Keats' ideal has begun to disintegrate into its component parts and that the poet's interpretation of his experience is being distorted by his translation of it into the concepts of the mortal world. What should be thrilling intensity is an intensity of the wrong kind—only the ache of the heart and the pain of the senses; what should be ecstatic selflessness is the wrong kind of selflessness—only drowsy numbness, a slipping Lethe-wards, something comparable to drinking hemlock or a dull opiate. And instead of blending mystically, intensity and selflessness struggle against each other irreconcilably.

Ideally, intensities enthrall the self; here the ideal is inverted: numbness pains the sense. In this dichotomy and inversion are contained all the workings of the poem, for the poet's effort to resolve his inner conflict by seeking ease will further split the elements of the poem into tense contrarieties.

In the first stanza there are two of these conflicts: the one we have been examining that fractures the poet's "happiness" into pain and numbness; and the antithesis of the two empathies, the poet's and the nightingale's, an antithesis of two "happinesses" that determine the structure of the stanza. The poet's heart aches, we are told, not because he envies the happiness of the nightingale—envy being the reverse of empathy; but because he has himself entered too deeply into the empathic happiness of the nightingale—is "too happy in thine happiness." For such selfless participation in essence is not designed for mortal man. He has ascended the pleasure thermometer as high as merely human powers permit, but there is nothing to fix his intensity there, nothing to remove its temporality, no heaven's bourne into which to empty it. The consequence is a drowsy ache like that of Porphyro, who, about to rise "Beyond a mortal man impassion'd far," complains to the sleeping Madeline, the "completed form" with whom he is to blend and so become mortally immortal:

> Open thine eyes, for meek St. Agnes' sake,
> Or I shall drowse beside thee, so my soul doth ache.

For Porphyro, too, what should be an impassioned selflessness threatens to become its human correlative, a drowsiness and an ache. The nightingale, on the other hand, is as self-annihilated as the poet, for it has entered into the essence of nature, the sense of its empathic indwelling being reinforced by its being a "Dryad," a nymph whose life is that of the tree she inhabits. Yet this empathy allows it to sing, not with mortal pain, but in "full-throated ease." The setting of the ode is mid-May, as stanza five will make clear, and yet the song the bird sings is one of summer, that period in the temporal world when the inner essence of nature comes to fruition and becomes manifest. The summer of which the bird sings is the full and timeless essence of nature, while spring is only that essence operating in the temporal context of becoming. Nevertheless, although it is spring, the bird is so absorbed into nature's inwardness that it knows its perfection, which, in the temporal world, is the point towards which and from which nature is always moving, but which, in the immortal, is fixed and change-less. The nightingale, then, is like Pan, to whom

> Broad leaved fig trees even now foredoom
> Their ripen'd fruitage. . . .
> The chuckling linnet its five young unborn,
> To sing for thee . . .
> . . . pent up butterflies
> Their freckled wings; yea, the fresh budding
>   year
> All its completions.[10]

For, being a firmament reflected in a sea, Pan is one with the heart of nature, and nature belongs to him, not in its becoming, its spring, but in its full and changelessly vital being, its "completions"—its summer. In another sense, too, this empathic union with nature is complete: the bird is deep *in* nature—among the shadows of the plot of trees; and nature itself is saturated with the sound of the bird—the plot of beechen green has taken on the quality of the bird to become "melodious." And yet, the nightingale is able to attain this perfect "hap-piness" in ease, whereas such spiritual projection by the poet—his happiness *in* the nightingale's—produces pain.

Only in the central two lines of the first stanza (5–6) are the three elements of the ode—the poet, the nightingale, and nature—integrated, although not harmoniously. The bird has entered into the essence of nature, and the poet into the essence of the bird. The empathic relationships embodied in these two lines are precisely those attained in the third stanza of the "Ode on a Grecian Urn"; for there the three symbols had attained "happiness" in arriving at a condition in which love is forever warm and still to be enjoyed, and the poet had re-vealed his absorption into their happiness by the ecstasy of his exclamations: "More happy, happy love!" But the first stanza of the ode to a nightin-gale sharply juxtaposes the two empathies, pivoting them on these two central lines: the weighty and sluggish movement of the opening four lines con-veys the dull ache of the poet's unnatural strain; the exhausting flow of the last four lines, the natural ease with which the bird participates in essence.

We now have the seminal elements of the poem. The opposition of pain and numbness in the poet must seek out a resolution. The juxtaposition of the two empathies excites the instability of the poet's condition, for the perfection of the nightingale's happiness underscores the uneasiness of the poet's, which must now fall apart into the two incom-patible elements of which it is compacted: spirit and matter, heaven and earth, the immortal and the mortal. The poem will now develop by two criss-crossing movements: the enervation of the poet's passion as he seeks ease from pain; and the in-creasing intensity of the bird's symbolic values. As the poet moves downward from the bird towards mortality in an effort to capture the bird's ease, he will see the bird as symbolizing proportionately higher levels of meaning. The first stanza therefore appropriately ends on the word "ease," which, like the word "ecstasy" (the antonym of "ease") at the end of the first stanza of the "Ode on a Grecian Urn," contains the motive of what is to follow. Ease appears to belong to the bird's empathy; and the poet, being misguided, will seek to capture it to resolve the pain-numbness conflict of his own empathy.

The condition created in the first stanza also con-tains in itself the proposals whereby the poet will vainly strive to free his happiness from pain. In the drinking of the hemlock, the deep draught of the opiate, the slipping Lethe-wards, the earthiness and warmth of the bird's singing of summer, and the full-throated ease—in all these is foreshadowed the desire for forgetfulness by drinking the warm and mature earthiness of wine. Transformed by the theme of wine, the beechen green will become the country green; the melodious plot, Provençal song; and the shadows numberless, the deep-delved earth. Second, that the light-winged Dryad is sing-ing a song of essence suggests the proposal to fly to heaven's bourne on the "viewless wings of Poesy." And finally, the drowsy numbness, the poi-sonous hemlock, the Lethe-ward movement, and the sense of shadowy darkness anticipate the proposal of death. The elements of the entire drama are, therefore, inherent in the opening stanza: it creates an unstable situation—the conflict within the poet—which must seek out a resolution; it dramati-cally contrasts this instability with the ideal happi-ness of the nightingale to give it depth and mean-ing; it thereby sets in motion two countercurrents; and it contains implicitly the three stages of the course these countercurrents will take. The poem will now proceed, not with dramatic inevitability, but by a series of jolting transformations whereby the three elements of the ode—the poet, the nightingale, and nature—will be shaken into a succession of different relationships.

III

To turn now to the first of the dramatic strands: the proposals whereby the poet will seek to free his "happiness" of mortal pain and to experience what appears to him to be the ease of the nightingale—wine, poesy, and death. In Keats' system of symbolic perceptions, wine had come to represent to him sensuous pleasure for its own sake. It seemed to promise a sensuous intensity, it is true, but one that, instead of leading to a self-annihilation through the projection of self into essence, leads only to a forgetfulness of self. It is, then, a false sort of self-destruction, for it ends only in that self-destruction and not in an interknitting with life's proper pith. "Happy" boughs symbolize sensory fellowship with essence, for in them lies "happiness," the power of beckoning man to essence; but wine symbolizes this sensuous act as merely mortal man would interpret it, for to him the pleasure seems to be its own end. When, for example, the Indian Maiden followed Bacchus and his crew she experienced the entire range of earthly pleasures and yet was "Sick hearted, weary":

> I've been a ranger
> In search of pleasure throughout every clime:
> Alas! 'tis not for me! [11]

For there is a difference between pleasure and "happiness," just as it is possible to be "too happy to be glad." Keats may have painted a glamorous and appealing picture of dance and Provençal song, but this mere gaiety was worthless in his scheme of values:

> The Muse should never make the spirit gay;
> Away, bright dulness, laughing fools away.[12]

In "The Eve of St. Agnes" the baron and his guests are all those who are so deep in the revelries of the world that the pleasures of the senses are ends in themselves, and therefore these creatures are confined to the "level chambers" of life. They are "Drown'd all in Rhenish and the sleepy mead"; they are the "bloated wassaillers" who, because of their concern with mere sensuous delight, "will never heed" the passage of Porphyro and Madeline into the mystery of the elfin-storm. The satyrs and sileni, followers of Bacchus, seeing only the physical beauty of Hermes' nymph, made her immortality grow pale by the "love-glances of their unlovely eyes"—their delight in the sensuous without even a recognition of the essence that lies in the sensuous. Finally, the Corinthian world which appears at the wedding of Lamia and Lycius—the "herd" with "common eyes"—luxuriates in the riches of the senses: "the cold full sponge to pleasure press'd," the fragrant oils. And the enthrallment by the wine, instead of leading to a sensuous fellowship with essence, makes the world-guests in the magic palace oblivious not only to human pain but also to the mystery in whose presence they stand: the mystery was,

> Now, when the wine has done its rosy deed,
> And every soul from human trammels freed,
> No more so strange; for merry wine, sweet wine,
> Will make Elysian shades not too fair, too divine.   (II. 209–12)

In the ode, then, wine is a symbol of the misguided effort to engage in the sensory essence of nature without pain; a beguiling hope of penetrating to the inwardness of the sensory in such a way as to be at ease in empathy; a worldly illusion that fellowship with sensuous essence is only a distracting pleasure. At first glance the proposal seems especially appropriate to the poetic situation that has been created. The ease of the nightingale appears to arise out of the perfect interpenetration of its essence with that of nature. The bird sings of the soul of nature, "of summer"; and nature is inhabited by the soul of the bird—the bird is within the shadows, and the plot is "melodious" with the bird's spirit, its song. So, too, the wine has been cooled *in* the depths of earth, and *in* it is the taste of the country green. Superficially, it appears that it is in the essence of earthiness, and that the essence of earthiness is in it. Moreover, like the ease of the bird, only pleasures are contained in the wine: a "sunburnt mirth" and the "warm South" which holds out the false promise of being the same completeness of nature into which the bird, in singing of summer, has insight. The parallelism of the nightingale and the wine is, of course, a false parallelism and suggests itself to the poet only because he is facing earthward. Wine has the illusory appearance of being a means of gaining the bird's easeful empathy only because he is looking on outward forms and is negligent of spiritual values.

There is no need to linger over the significance and appropriateness of the second proposal. "I am certain of nothing," Keats wrote, "but of the holiness of the Heart's affections and the truth of Imagination—What the imagination seizes as Beauty must be truth." [13] The imagination functions by projecting the self into the beauty, the vital essence of its objective, and thereby sees that essence in terms of its eternal being in heaven's bourne. The imagination, therefore, allows a pre-enactment, an earthly rehearsal, of the "happiness" to come. Ideally, then, poesy should provide a true happiness, a perfect fellowship with essence without a mortal heartache. The imagination does not merely look on outer forms but penetrates to the central life of what it deals with, just as the nightingale is able to sing of summer, the central life of nature. The poet, therefore, is

> the man who with a bird,
> Wren or Eagle, finds his way to
> All its instincts; he hath heard
> The Lion's roaring, and can tell
> What his horny throat expresseth,
> And to him the Tiger's yell
> Comes articulate and presseth
> On his ear like mother-tongue. [14]

To the sight of the poet

> The husk of natural objects opens quite
> To the core: and every secret essence there
> Reveals the elements of good and fair;
> Making him see, where Learning hath no
>   light. [15]

But again the metaphysical premises of the ode go awry. Poesy, which should open up the essence of nature and make it one with the poet's self, fails to function as it ideally should; and once again what should lead to the bourne of heaven is transformed into the merely mundane: "I cannot see what flowers are at my feet." The husk of natural objects refuses to open to the core.

It is fairly clear why wine and the poetic imagination should have appeared appropriate means of resolving the painful numbness into an easy empathy, but it may not be equally clear why these two proposals should finally suggest death. These first two proposals, it will be noticed, are approxi-

mately the same as the initial stages of a procedural pattern that had become a fixed part of Keats' ways of thinking. The aspiration towards a selfless, spaceless immortality of passion which Keats saw as the promised post-mortal life, and which he agonized to capture in this present existence, had fashioned for itself a clearly marked route which he once called the pleasure thermometer. The first two stages on that route—entrance into the essence of nature and art, or the exertion of the intensities of the senses and of the imagination—are here symbolized by wine (falsely) and by poetry (ineffectually). And if Keats is once again molding a poem into the pattern of his spiritual epistemology, as we have seen him do repeatedly, he should then seek mystical union with essence through love. Indeed, there is reason to believe that something of the original pattern of the pleasure thermometer still lingers in Keats' mind. For the poet addresses death in terms of love: he has been half in love with death; and in tenderly worded poetry, addressing him by "soft names," he has, like a lover, begged him to take up the poet's spirit.

But it is possible to see even more clearly why Keats now conceives of death instead of love as the last and highest stage of the pleasure thermometer. In the sonnet "Why did I laugh to-night?" he could not gain from heaven or hell or his own heart an explanation of the laugh. What meaning, he is asking, does this moment of joy have in the total design of his life, its pleasures and sufferings? To what end are being shaped the apparently fortuitous gladnesses and pains to which we are subjected in this life? The answer lies in the Mystery alone: "O Darkness! Darkness! ever must I moan, / To question Heaven and Hell and Heart in vain." Now, Keats was no "Godwin perfectibility Man." The full measure of happiness is not to be found in this world, nor could it ever be; and mortal man is therefore made to suffer:

> suppose a rose to have sensation, it blooms on a beautiful morning it enjoys itself—but there comes a cold wind, a hot sun—it cannot escape it, it cannot destroy its annoyances— they are as native to the world as itself: no more can man be happy in spite, the worldly elements will prey upon his nature. [16]

Even granted such earthly happiness, man "is mortal and there is still a heaven with its Stars above his head." Were there earthly perfectibility, "the whole troubles of life which are now frittered away in a series of years, would the[n] be accumulated for the last days of a being who instead of hailing its approach, would leave this world as Eve left Paradise." The pain that lies in mortal pleasures, the melancholy that has her shrine in the temple of delight, the burning forehead and the parching tongue that attend upon human passions—these must have a meaning and a function in the total scheme of one's being.

On the other hand, Keats could not accept what he understood to be the Christian scheme: "The common cognomen of this world among the misguided and superstitious is 'a vale of tears' from which we are to be redeemed by a certain arbitrary interposition of God and taken to Heaven—What a little circumscribed straightened notion!" Pain is not to be overcome in this life, nor is pain a penalty for sin, from which we are to be redeemed by happiness in a future state. There must be, Keats felt, a closer interconnection of experience than this. The burning forehead must come with the passion, and it must therefore have a part to play in the progress towards the bourne of heaven; for the future is not the inverse of the present, but the present divested of its mutability. Existence is a continuum, part of which endures pain and mutability; but since it is a continuum, all that occurs in this life is functionally progressive towards the next. Therefore (to return to the sonnet), although the poet knows the utmost blisses of his worldly existence, yet would he "on this very midnight cease" because

> Verse, Fame, and Beauty are intense indeed,
> But Death intenser—Death is Life's high
>   meed.

We can now see the position of death in the pleasure thermometer. Nature, art, and love are increasing intensities, and in proportion as they enthrall the spirit they interknit it with essence. But the "Richer entanglements, enthralments far / More self-destroying," Keats has said, lead by degrees "To the chief intensity," which is beyond even love. Death, then, is not an event which divides two existences, but the meeting point at which the ladder of intensities enters heaven's bourne. It is the final intensity at the very verge of immortal life that shatters the "fragile bar / That keeps us from our homes ethereal" and places

us in Intensity itself, where at last life's self is perpetually nourished by its own essence. Because death is the climax of these "*richer* entanglements"—indeed is the one whereby the self is totally enthralled—"now more than ever seems it *rich* to die." In his sonnet "Bright star!" we have seen, Keats longed for the steadfastness of the star, but not its lone splendor; he wished for its unchangeableness, but only if it would be fused with an intensity of passion:

> yet still steadfast, still unchangeable,
> Pillow'd upon my fair love's ripening breast,
> To feel for ever its soft fall and swell,
> Awake for ever in a sweet unrest,
> Still, still to hear her tender-taken breath,
> And so live ever. . . .

This, of course, is the oxymoronic condition of heaven's bourne experienced on earth—the becomingness of "ripening," the mutability of the passionate fall and swell, caught up in a changeless foreverness. Keats then continues,

> And so live ever—or else swoon to death.

His meaning is not that if he cannot capture on earth an immortality of passion he may as well not exist at all, but that death, the last earthly intensity, is an alternative and final source of an immortality of passion. That this is his intent is clear in an earlier version of the last line:

> Half-passionless, and so swoon on to death.

It is, therefore, towards death that all our earthly existence is leading. The intensities of pain and pleasure reach their final earthly degree in death; thus death is "Life's high meed," for it raises us to the ultimate Intensity, which is without degree, and it gives a meaning to our mortal experiences, even a random laugh.

In constructing in the ode another version of the pleasure thermometer, Keats has substituted for love the last earthly degree beyond love; and the progress from wine to poesy to death—the absorption of the sensuous, the imaginative, and finally the total spiritual self—should, unless the poet is beguiled, lead to one's capture in heaven's bourne and therefore to a "happiness" with ease. But once again the poet has mistaken Duessa for Fidessa: in desiring release from pain he has proposed a false view of death. The death that shatters the bar to admit the self into immortality is an intensity, an exquisite experience; but the poet here, although it seems *rich* to die, has limited his vision to the physical and sensory world, and from that perspective he asks only for an easeful death, a cessation with no pain. This is the worldly inverse of death in its immortal aspect, and because the poet is facing earthward instead of heavenward, such a view of death reveals, not an absorption of self into the immortal spirit of life, but only a physical decay. In a merely worldly framework, death is release from pain and eventuates in one's becoming a sod, a part of inanimate nature. The design that underlies the three proposals is drawn from the pleasure thermometer, but the scale of intensities is grotesquely distorted by being seen through the eyes of, let us say, the baron and his fellow revelers, or the guests in Lamia's palace. The axis on which Keats' universe rotates has been bent awry, and his entire scheme of things is being shaken apart.

IV

Each of these three proposals for empathic union brings about a reorientation of relationships among the poet, the nightingale, and the world of physical reality; and with each of these transformations the nightingale appears to take on additional degrees of symbolic value. The nightingale with whom the poem begins is, we have seen, an embodiment of the perfect empathy which the poet seeks. But the description reveals only that the bird has succeeded where the poet fails: each attains the same degree of empathic happiness, except that it is commensurate with the bird's capacity and so much beyond the poet's that it leads to an unpleasant separation of its components, a painful swooning of the senses. It is not in any way implied that the bird belongs to an order of things different from that of the poet, but only that the two are experiencing the same kind of "happiness" with contrary results.

Now in each successive transformation the nightingale seems to the poet to rise in the scale of values. When the poet proposes to release himself from the pain of his ecstasy by becoming one with the sensuous essence of physical nature, he finds (in stanza three) that the bird is now outside the context of physical nature: it has never known the weariness, the fever, and the fret which are inextricable from the world of extensions. But this is only a negative distinction; we know only that the nightingale now seems to belong to an order of things which is not the poet's.

(Before we follow this movement further, it will be necessary to clear away, parenthetically, one textual crux The line "Already with thee! tender is the night" (35) has generally been read as meaning that the poet finally succeeds in becoming united with the nightingale, and that he then finds the night to be tender. But such a reading can lead only to inconsistencies, if not to nonsense. The problem of the poet is not to get *to* the nightingale; he was, indeed, already absorbed into the bird's soul when the poem opened. His problem is how to convert that painful happiness into a happiness with ease, and something has happened meanwhile that has been dissolving the empathic union. The successive efforts of the poet to relieve the pain separate him farther from the symbol, and the whole dramatic direction of the poem is towards a further divorce, not towards a reunion. Moreover, there would be no meaning in the poet's complaint that "here there is no light" and that he cannot see the flowers at his feet, for if he is with the bird he should be able to see into essence as vividly as the bird can sing of summer, and he should be as much in the presence of the Queen-Moon as he supposes the bird is.

(I am convinced, therefore, that Mr. Clyde S. Kilby[17] is right in suggesting that the exclamation mark after "thee" is not terminal—although I would not accept his proposal that it should be removed in our reading of the line. The exclamation mark must be introduced only to underscore the word "thee" and thereby to emphasize the contrast between "with thee" and "here" (38), which, like the "Here" of line 24, designates the physical world. Indeed, in one manuscript version (E), the line does read: "Already with thee tender is the night"; and the exclamation mark seems to have been introduced to transfer the emphasis from "with," where the meter would normally place it, to "thee." The night is tender with the nightingale, but it leaves the poet in blind darkness. None of the proposals, then, not even poesy, succeeds in returning the poet to empathic union with the nightingale.)

To continue with the symbolic significance of the nightingale. With the second proposal, the bird, which had been distinguished from the mutable world, is now discovered to be in the presence of ideality. Not only is the nightingale distinct from the mutable world by never having been related to its inherent principle, decay; the night, the darkness in which the mystery resides, is tender with the nightingale, and to the bird the ideal Queen-Moon is on her throne, pouring out the light of complete illumination. The moon, as Endymion discovered, is "that completed form of all completeness," the perfection of beauty-truth in its ultimate being; and when he is bathed in its light, his

> dazzled soul
> Commingling with her argent spheres did roll
> Through clear and cloudy.[18]

In the presence of the moon, "On some bright essence could I lean, and lull / Myself to immortality." [19] In stanza four the nightingale, then, has apparently risen to a higher level of symbolic meaning, for it is not merely distinguished from the mutable, but is perhaps ("haply") partaking of ultimate truth, the "completeness" towards which all becoming tends and which draws one to an immortality. Moreover, the nightingale experiences the ideal with a perfection that earthly man cannot, for to it the Queen-Moon is not "sans merci."

However, only in the last transformation does the full symbolic meaning of the nightingale come about. It appears now to be experiencing the intensity of ecstasy, not merely a happiness with ease; it is not merely penetrating into the essence of nature—singing "of summer"—but pouring forth its spiritual essence, engaging in that total projection of spiritual self which Keats understood to be the condition of man only in heaven's bourne. Moreover, the bird is also singing a "high requiem," a song for the departed spirit. It is, then, in ecstatic union with spirit, for it is giving up its soul—its song—as mortal man will do only upon his death, and his soul-song is about the soul. The bird that originally appeared to be in fellowship with the essence of nature is now one with spiritual essence, or Essence itself. A requiem, however, is a mass that invites repose for the soul, and therefore suggests something antithetical to the vibrant restlessness of the bird's ecstasy. But the bird, indeed, is in ecstasy and yet is singing a requiem, fusing these two qualities, for the oxymoronic condition of heaven of which it sings is a vibrant repose—the rise and fall of passion fused with the star's steadfastness, an immortality of passion, beauty which is

identical with truth. Having outlined the pleasure thermometer in *Endymion,* Keats described love, the highest mortal means of fellowship with essence, as an "ardent listlessness." [20] Briefly, the nightingale has appeared to be a mortal creature, has risen out of mortality, has come into the presence of beauty-truth, and has at last become a vision of beauty-truth itself—and hence is an "immortal Bird." The movement is comparable to that of the first three stanzas of the "Ode on a Grecian Urn," where the figures in the frieze rose from merely human passions to the conditions of heaven and at last experienced a love that is forever warm and still to be enjoyed—a condition that corresponds to the ecstasy-requiem of the nightingale.

V

The two movements we have been tracing—the false pleasure thermometer of proposals, and the ascending values of the nightingale—do not, however, give to the poem its dramatic impetus. Considered dramatically, both are inert, at no point compelling a development. Although the three proposals are implicit in the first stanza, it is not inherently inevitable that wine lead to poesy and death, and the proposals do not causally give rise to the nightingale's symbolic significances. At best, Keats can only arrange the proposals in a hierarchic order and parallel the hierarchy with ascending symbolic meanings. What gives to the poem its dramatic tension—although not a dramatic inevitability, an inner compulsion—is that the poet himself cuts across these two ascending patterns. Only in the poet himself are the nightingale and the proposals related to each other, and he imparts to them a series of dramatic tensions by following, not a corresponding ascending path, as in the "Ode on a Grecian Urn," but one of decreasing capacity for sensuous intensity. The consequence is that at no point can the three strands be in harmonious relationship, and the poem unfolds, not organically, but by an episodic series of three transformations, each transformation supplying a new layer of ironic meanings. The melody of the "Ode on a Grecian Urn" is harmonic; that of the "Ode to a Nightingale," contrapuntal.

At the opening of the poem, we have seen, the poet is at the height of his empathic power, for his enthrallment by essence is more intense than his senses can bear. His ecstatic absorption cannot possibly rise higher and is already disintegrating into an intensity which is pain and a selflessness which is numbness. The effort to release himself from that pain by seeking the apparent ease of the nightingale must inevitably bring about a weakening of intensity, for it is Keats' basic assumption everywhere that "happiness," no matter how briefly it is experienced, is exquisite and ecstatic, not easeful. In making his first proposal in stanza two, therefore, the poet expresses himself by an optative exclamation: "O, for a draught of vintage!" The passion is still great, and the excited, overflowing energy of the entire stanza helps support the intensity; but it is somewhat weaker than that of the first stanza and is moving towards a release from the ecstatic pain. The frozen intensity of stanza one seems to have become a fluid violence.

In the fourth stanza, where he offers his second proposal, the poet feels now only the passionate power of the promissory, or the resolute: "for I will fly to thee" (31); and the movement from the optative to the promissory conveys a progressive enervation, a decreasing capacity for penetration into essence. The entire movement now comes to a close with the merely declarative form of stanza six, which proposes the final intensity: "Now more than ever seems it rich to die" (55). With this ebbing of passionate power there is also introduced a note of weak uncertainty and confusion. The poet is at first emotionally absorbed in his wish for wine and then is determined to fly on the wings of poesy; but already his self-confidence and assurance have begun to evaporate amidst a series of qualifications: he believes that perhaps—"haply"— the Queen-Moon is on her throne, he gropes about in bewildering darkness in stanza five, he is only *half* in love with death, it merely *seems* rich to die, and he can only speculate that *perhaps* the same song was heard by Ruth.

Since only the intense passion of ecstasy allows penetration into essence, the quest for ease that brings about these decreasing levels of emotional power necessarily filters the poet's essence out of the nightingale's, exactly as the poet of the "Ode on a Grecian Urn" withdrew from his absorption in the happiness of the figures in the frieze. The restless need for ease is destroying the very empathy which the poet is trying to make easeful, for it is not destined that the mortal clay be in

comfort in the bourne of heaven. Consequently, although the poet in the first stanza is *in* the nightingale's happiness, he is separated out of the symbol in the second. The poet and the nightingale now occupy the same plane, but they are distinct from each other, not empathically united, and the poet hopes to fade away *with* the bird. By stanza four they are on different levels: the bird is in the presence of the moon, but "here there is no light"; and therefore the poet now can only plan to fly *to* the nightingale. We can now see all the more clearly the inconsistency of assuming that in stanza four the poet succeeds in returning to the company of the bird, for that had already been his position in stanzas two and three, and the assumption would disrupt the progressiveness of the poet's withdrawal and destroy the meaning of the pattern.

At length, in stanza six, the poet and the nightingale have moved to opposite poles—heaven and earth—the bird addressing a spiritual song to spirit, and the poet having become a sod. The dissolution of the empathic projection is finally completed in the last stanza, where, like the poet of the ode on the Grecian urn and like the knight-at-arms, the poet is once again fully within his own individual identity: he is tolled "back *from* thee *to* my sole self." The experience of the poem is over, and it remains only for the "unpoeted" mortal to speculate on it. This drama of the poet's withdrawal and retreat, like the empathic movement in the "Ode on a Grecian Urn," has been enacted by both observable dramatic gesture and the implication of dramatic gesture through modal forms.

VI

We have dealt thus far with the increasing significances of the nightingale as though this movement were self-contained and as though the bird truly does take on greater values in its own right. But actually the nightingale is static throughout the first seven stanzas: hidden in the shadows of the trees, it continues to sing a thrilling song. It is only the descending series of intensities within the poet that gives to the nightingale its progressive meanings, for as the poet moves downward from his sensuous elevation the nightingale *seems* proportionately higher. For example, when he is merely *with* the bird spiritually in stanzas two and three, it seems unrelated to the mutable world, since the poet himself is at this moment outside the mutable world because of his still-lingering absorption into essence. But when the poet slips down to the dark world of things, the same nightingale appears to him to have risen to the presence of the Queen-Moon; and only when the poet contemplates becoming a sod does the nightingale therefore appear to be immortal. The downward movement of the poet "etherealizes" the nightingale, just as his increasing ecstasy "etherealized" the figures in the frieze of the urn.

The motivation for both of the inert sequences in the "Ode to a Nightingale" arises, then, from the poet himself: as he is drawn farther from his empathic union with the symbol, he calls upon increasingly more potent means of return, and the bird, although remaining static, appears more glorious as the poet's frame of reference is more mundane. The result is that the three strands run entirely different dramatic courses and can never come together into any resolution. At every point the nightingale outdistances the proposals: when the poet plans to ease his empathic pain with the sensuous intoxication of earthiness, the nightingale appears to belong to an order of things wholly distinct from the world of mutability; when he plans to perceive into the inwardness of nature, the nightingale is already in the presence of the light that comes from the ideal completed form of all completeness; and when he seeks release through what should be the greatest intensity, death, the nightingale is found to belong to the immortal order of things.

At the same time that the nightingale is outdistancing the false proposals, the poet himself is moving in the opposite direction, dropping counter to the intensities of his proposals and becoming progressively more remote from the symbol with which he seeks an untroubled spiritual union. By the first of his proposals for escaping mutability he hopes to participate in the vital pleasure and essential beauty of nature; by the second, to perceive into the essence of nature, but he fails; and by the third, to escape the mutable wholly, only to find that he is the insensate physical stuff of nature. In other words, with each advance up the false scale of intensities, the poet finds ironically that he is proportionately more insensate and that his attempt to free himself from the pains of the physical is binding him more inextricably to the physical.

His progress is from a participation in the life of nature (to drink the earthiness of the earth-stored wine), to an unsuccessful attempt to perceive its vitality (to see into the essence of what lies at his feet), to a discovery that by his wish for death he is to become the unvital material of nature (to become the very sod that lies beneath his feet). From the perspective of the mortal world—which is the poet's perspective throughout the poem—easeful self-annihilation is to be experienced only in becoming incapable of sensation: a sod.

Yet, all the while that he is sinking earthward, his proposals are false hopes in the other direction. And while his soul is fleeing heavenward although his "body is earthward pressed," the ironic knowledge is growing that it is the nightingale, not the poet, who is progressing to heaven's bourne. Because the poet's point of view is only mortal; the progress of the figures on the urn's frieze towards heaven, when translated into mortal terms, is only a movement from town to altar; the apotheosis of the nightingale, when placed in the context of mutability, turns out to be the poet's becoming a sod.

Here, indeed, is a Purgatory blind with no standard laws of either earth or heaven, a terrible division of currents running at cross purposes. The consequence is that within the first six stanzas the poem has completely inverted itself: the ease of the nightingale's happiness, which the poet wishes for himself, rises until it becomes a pleasure-pain selflessness, an ecstasy-requiem. And the poet's numb pain has fallen away with the contemplation of "easeful Death" and of the loss of his now "quiet breath" to become "no pain"—indeed, no sensation at all, for now he has ears in vain and has become a sod. In the broadest sense, the bird's ease has become the poet's, the poet's pain has become the bird's—but with a very real difference. The poet's striving for heaven's bourne can become painless only if, in terms of mortal man, he becomes a senseless sod, for in these terms to be selfless means to be without existence. But the bird's apparently easy empathy, when seen from the perspective of this world, turns out really to be intensity itself, an ardent listlessness, beauty-truth.

If now we reconsider the three strands we have been examining we shall notice that they are, in their general outlines, precisely the same three with which Keats wove the "Ode on a Grecian

Urn" and "La Belle Dame Sans Merci." We have already observed that the three proposals are false correspondences to the pleasure thermometer of intensities. The weakening of the poet's passion and his increasing separation from the happiness of the nightingale are the inverse of empathic absorption; and, by a series of transformations, the nightingale rises to an oxymoronic heaven. These are not arbitrary themes, but the three cardinal principles of Keats' mind: his aspiration is to ascend to a condition of beauty-truth which is to be found in heaven's bourne; the pleasure thermometer is the means; and self-annihilation is the condition.

However, in both the "Ode on a Grecian Urn" and "La Belle Dame Sans Merci" these strands were not only interdependent but even inextricable from each other. In the ballad, the knight-at-arms ascended the pleasure thermometer concurrently with his increasing selflessness and thereby arrived at the elfin grot; and in the ode on the urn the emergence of the pleasure thermometer is identical with the immergence of the poet's consciousness. In the present poem the three elements are flying apart, and not only run counter to each other but are so distributed that each belongs to a different referent. The three proposals turn out to be a distorted, mundane interpretation of the pleasure thermometer; the poet's empathy, instead of increasing proportionately with the proposals, becomes less until he is wholly self-contained. And out of the crisscrossing of these two themes, it is the nightingale, not the poet, who has attained the condition of heaven. The thematic elements of the three poems are the same; but the "Ode to a Nightingale" is the obverse of the other two, a chaos to their cosmos.

VII

Having examined the three strands separately, we are now in a position to see how they are brought together in the poem, and thus to enter the poetic chaos of stanzas two through six, where the elements of a cosmos struggle "in their pregnant causes mixt Confusedly." We are not to expect that the poetic factors will reinforce each other with a nice organicism, as they do in the "Ode on a Grecian Urn." Because the poem takes place in a lawless purgatory, the elements of these stanzas will stand in ironic and illogical contradiction to each other, convulsively tossing us back and forth from nightingale to poet, from heaven to earth. They will thwart every effort at reconciliation and leave us no center of reference. Images and statements will alter in value metamorphically before our eyes and turn out to be their own converses as their referents are interchanged. And therefore the best that an explication of these stanzas can do is to set in action the bewildering oscillations.

The chaotic turmoil begins slowly, for the unit made up of stanzas two and three and motivated by the suggestion of wine has the outward appearance of a controlled structure. The first stanza of the poem had nicely juxtaposed two equal units (1–4, 7–10) to contrast the conditions of the two happinesses, one sluggishly painful, the other flowing and unruffled; and the two moods had been interlinked by the two central lines (5–6), which relate the nightingale to the essence of nature, and the poet to this essence through the essence of the nightingale, the central symbol.

This same outward form, precise, balanced, and controlled, determines the structure of stanzas two and three. Stanza two, (11–18) attempts to capture a mood resembling that of the second half of stanza one, and in tempo has nearly the same breathless, unimpeded emotional sweep. Stanza three (23–30), by means of the monotonous series (weariness, fever, fret; few, sad, last gray; pale, spectre-thin, dies; etc.) and by the dull parallelisms (where men, where palsy, where youth, where but to think, where beauty) catches something similar to the sluggish, weighty movement of the opening lines of stanza one. It is needless to underscore the other obvious contrasts between stanzas two and three: the dance opposed to the palsy and weariness; the coolness and the warm South opposed to the fever; the green floral countryside, the blushful wine, and the purple-stained mouth opposed to the leaden eyes, the pallor, and gray hairs; mirth opposed to sorrow; Provençal song opposed to groaning. These two conflicting stanzas are brought together centrally by the last two lines of stanza two and the first two lines of stanza three, which, like the central lines of stanza one, interrelate the world, the poet, and the nightingale. By this grouping, stanzas two and three, taken together, repeat the structural pattern of stanza one but invert its order; and the general, superficial impression is that the poetic world is still harmonious and intelligibly ordered.

But the forces of dissolution inherent in the poet's being "too happy" are at work even within the apparent orderliness. Not only is the proposal of the second stanza vain, since it ends in self-forgetfulness instead of self-involvement; insofar as it implies an enthrallment of the senses, it is the least intense degree of the pleasure thermometer. And yet, it is conveyed in a rhapsodic mode and with a torrential tempo; and the description is a miracle of sensuous abundance. The result is that the stanza is an organic poetic unity perfect in itself but inconsistent with the total poem. Moreover, there is a violent inconsistency in the poet's struggle in the two stanzas that make up this unit. In his present position he is with the nightingale, above the level of the mutable world, and "yet still confined" because his pain results from his being drawn earthward by his own mortal nature. From this elevated position he looks down upon the world from two inconsistent perspectives—those of heaven and earth.

Illogically, he hopes to saturate himself with the joyous and intoxicating vitality of the earth in order to free himself from the earth. He turns his back on the truth that in the world melancholy has her shrine in the temple of delight; and he hopes to split these two factors—to "unperplex bliss from its neighbour pain"—so that by being absorbed in intoxicating delight he may overcome the melancholy and decay. The fact that the wine has been deep in the earth and contains the essence of earth is a beguiling parallel to the bird, who is intimate with nature's essence and whose essence is permeating physical nature; and the illusion leads the poet to the illogical hope of similarly engaging in all the brightness of nature in order, paradoxically, to fade with the nightingale into the forest dim. Equally illogically, he hopes that by fading and dissolving he will escape the very world in which all things fade and dissolve—the world in which all men grow gray and die. And in the hope of plunging downward into the rich materials of the senses in order to cut himself off from mutability, he finds that he is indeed "Here, where men sit and hear each other groan" and that the bird, now having become distinct from him, belongs to an order of things totally unrelated to the world of mutability.

In the next unit of two stanzas, four and five, motivated by the proposal to reach the bourne of heaven on the wings of Poesy, the neat structural pattern is fractured, and the themes become disordered and disproportionate. The proposal for union with the nightingale comes in the first four lines; the nightingale's status is described in the next three; and the remaining lines and all of stanza five are a long lament on the darkness of the poet in contrast to the illumination in which the nightingale exists. The sense of pattern has been shattered as the poet, in a confusing darkness, turns the direction of the poem upon his own bewilderment. But this disorder is the lawless Purgatory blind that arises from the increasing separation of poet and nightingale and the consequent oscillation between the standards of heaven and earth, which are moving farther apart.

The nightingale is now in the presence of the mystery, and the darkness of that mystery is being illuminated for it. The mystery, we recall, is "of haggard seeming, but a boon indeed." It can be a terrifying darkness, like the darkness the poet felt when he sought a reason for his own laughter—the darkness of ignorance within the mystery. But the night is tender with the nightingale; the bird lives in the mystery in comfort, and the Queen-Moon, the immortal ideal, illuminates that darkness. For the poet, however, there is no light into the mystery, except for the chance heaven-sent flashes lighting up the glooms and winding mossy ways that are our paths through this world of darkness. These dark worldly paths are very different from the shadows numberless in which the nightingale has his being, and from the dark green-recessed woods into which Hermes and the nymph fled. While the nightingale finds light in the ultimate mystery, the poet's passionate strength has so weakened that he cannot even perceive the sensuous essence, or vital principle of nature. The setting (and date of composition) of the poem is mid-May, the time to which the hawthorn belongs; but the fast-fading violets belong to April and are now disappearing, and the musk-rose is mid-May's eldest child, to be born in June. To read literally the poet's complaint that he cannot see the flowers would be meaningless, for not all the flowers are there to be perceived by the external senses. Were the poet able to "see" these flowers, he would, like Pan, be penetrating to nature's central principle, its full essence, and would be overcoming the temporality of the mortal world in which the inwardness of nature becomes manifest only fragmentarily. He would be able to see the sweets with which the season-making month impregnates nature. But the husk of nature will not open quite to the core, and, being now only a weak mortal, the poet can only guess at this inwardness as he moves about in the darkness that surrounds all earthly existence.

The nightingale and the poet have now been completely divorced, one failing to do in the physical world what the other is succeeding in doing in the immortal; only a flight *to* the nightingale could possibly reunite them. Yet, there is a curious relationship between the tone with which the poet describes the nightingale and the tone with which he describes his own blindness. The tense optative force of stanzas two and three has weakened, and the splendor of the nightingale in the light of the moon and the cluster of stars is described with a degree of awe, a hushed and regal astonishment. The floral scene in stanza five is equally splendid, and also seems surrounded by a quiet wonder; but it is the converse of awe—rather, a blind bewilderment, an astonishment that confuses.

It would be pointless to search for the initial pattern in stanza six, for the pattern has been destroyed. Bird, poet, death, and earth are mingled confusedly, and the purgatorial storm is raging wildly; and yet the turmoil of the elements takes place in the most subdued of all the stanzas, the poet's passions having fallen into something very near lethargy, although his proposal is itself the greatest intensity. The darkness that began to make its appearance in stanza four has now become complete; and the shadow of death that has hovered over the entire poem, impalpably prefigured in hemlock, Lethe, the desire to fade and dissolve, the deathliness of stanza three, and the embalmed darkness, has now become the central theme. The whole first movement of the poem is attaining its climax in stanza six.

Out of the nebulous confusion the polar extremes of the poem are about to appear vividly. In seeking ease from pain, the poet, capable of thinking only in terms of the physical world, calls upon death, which seems to his myopic vision easeful, and asks that his "quiet breath"—his now unimpassioned soul—be taken up into the air. Out of this desire arises a larger vision, a parallel but very different truth: the nightingale is also giving up its soul—its song. But in pouring out its soul into the air, just as the poet hopes to give up his "quiet breath," the nightingale is not easeful: the soul it pours out is an ecstasy-requiem, an emotionally tense, and sensorily perceptible, song of rest for the spirit, a beauty-truth. In effect, when the poet merely wishes for death, he finds again that the nightingale has greatly outdistanced him in the opposite direction, for it is eternally dying in its earthly existence; its life on earth is a continuous giving-up of its soul.

Conversely, from the point of view of earthly existence, death for the poet can mean only having ears in vain and becoming a sod. In a sense, the nightingale is the symbol of the poet's soul, and the poet is only the earthly self: death is both the heavenward flight of the soul and the material decay of mortal man's identity. Ironically, although poet and nightingale have been moving farther apart since their union in the first stanza, only in the last line of stanza six, when they have moved to their opposite poles, do they once again act directly upon each other: the sod which is the poet is present amidst the high requiem of the bird. And with further irony, one aspect of the poet's wish has now become a reality; the interpenetration of nightingale and nature in stanza one suggested the interpenetration of wine and nature, and now at last the poet is in earth and is himself earth. An interpenetration that brings ease has at last come about, but it is possible with respect to the world only if man no longer is vital. However, in the very act of myopically perceiving his outer death as merely his becoming a sod, the poet has gained a greater vision, for he now sees the bird, not merely as in the presence of beauty-truth, but as the very symbol of beauty-truth.

The first movement of the poem has reached its height by thrusting to their opposite poles the nature and the aspiration of earthly man. Keats saw as the terrible and maddening tension in man the heavenward flight of his soul while his body must be "earthward press'd." This division, which he symbolized in the "Ode on a Grecian Urn" as the altar and the town, which can never learn the reason for its desolation by soul, is here symbolized by the nightingale and the sod, which is insensible of the spirit-song.

VIII

In the "Ode on a Grecian Urn," it will be recalled, the filtering out of the component parts of of heaven's bourne led the poet to question, not the meaning of that divorce, but the meaning of the work of art that temporarily had led him to an immortality of passion, no matter how briefly. Keats' poetic mind is working here in the same fashion. As each effort to attain the state of the nightingale has brought him farther back to his sole self, so each transformation of relationships has put the bird farther from his reach, until finally, now that matter and spirit are at opposite poles, he must ask the meaning of this symbolic bird, who is all that remains to the poet of his experience, and who with apparent incongruity sings ecstatically a song of repose for the spirit although it does so wholly in this world of mutable things. Out of these apparent contradictions arises the full meaning of the nightingale. In the "Ode on a Grecian Urn," upon observing the separation of the senses and the soul outside the realm of art, Keats concluded that therefore art speaks to man of a realm where the two are forever and harmoniously one. What he concludes here is that the nightingale is an immortal bird. Now, of course, nightingales are born and do die; and obviously Keats' statement that the bird is immortal cannot make sense literally. It must be immortal in another fashion. What has been impressed upon the poet by his striving is that man is mortal with respect to earth; he must die out of earth, and if he is immortal it is only with respect to heaven. In the poem every effort of the poet to achieve a perfect spiritual state brought him closer to the insensate clay so long as he considered himself only in the context of his earthly being. Man, then, is mortal in the sense that his earthly existence is a movement towards a future immortality.

But the nightingale, the vision has revealed, pours out its ecstasy-requiem while it exists on earth. It has its heaven on earth, it experiences beauty-truth here, as man cannot. Being born *for* death, man is therefore mortal; not being born *for* death, the bird is immortal (not designed for death) with respect to the world, as man can be immortal only with respect to his postmortal existence. The full meaning of man is not completed in this world; but the nightingale, by experiencing beauty-truth here, completes its total purpose within the physical world and therefore is immortal with respect to it.

The nightingale, therefore, like the urn, remains in the midst of other woe than ours, although to the poet the experience has taken place in a "passing night." The nightingale's earthly existence being its own end and therefore not designed that it might lead to a death, the symbolic bird is outside the context of time and space within which the poet has his earthly being. And this symbolic nightingale, being itself a manifestation of beauty-truth, a heaven on earth, may therefore address not only man's senses but also his spirit, and may address to his sense-spirit a song that is both ecstasy and repose, both dynamic and static: a song, that is, that partakes of the oxymoronic nature of heaven's bourne. Hence man's earthly existence is filled with a hunger for its future spiritual fulfillment, but the nightingale is experiencing here the fullness of meaning that man can experience only hereafter: no hungry generations tread it down. In a sense, the nightingale is the urn, for both embody the experience that beauty is truth and truth beauty; and in this sense both are immortal, for death is not their vital principle, as it is the vital principle of man, driving him progressively closer to a future condition when he, too, will experience forever a beauty which is truth and a truth which is beauty.

IX

With the revelation that man is mortal because his earthly existence is a compulsion towards a future life which will give him a meaning, and with the converse revelation that the nightingale fulfills its meaningfulness in the world and is therefore immortal, the ode has reached a climax beyond which the initial movement cannot rise. All the potentialities that lay in the poet's being too happy in the bird's happiness have been released when the poet becomes a sod to the high requiem of the "immortal" bird. It will be recalled that a similar condition arose in the "Ode on a Grecian Urn," which attained its climax in the third stanza; and that there the poem could progress to a meaning only by the poet's then transforming the "ethereal" scene on the frieze into a vision of a worldly sacrificial procession moving from town to altar. Only when the insight gained from the experience with a heaven's bourne of trees, pipers, and lovers was translated into the context of the mortal world in which life is a passage to a future heaven, could the full meaning of the urn be discovered.

The mode of poetic procedure in the two odes is remarkably similar, for in stanza seven of the "Ode to a Nightingale" there is a similar transmutation of the imagery as the poet searches for the meaningfulness of the experience. Up to this point the only elements of the drama have been the poet, the nightingale, and nature; but since the drama is completed at the end of stanza six by the antipodal positions to which poet and nightingale are at last driven, only by bringing his experience to bear upon a new frame of reference—the worldly frame of reference made up of emperor and clown, Ruth, and magic casements—can the poet hope to give the vision dimensions of value to man. Since the bird is not born *for* death and therefore sings a song which is of the oxymoronic nature of heaven's bourne, all men at all times—from emperor to clown—had available this knowledge of beauty-truth, this promise of a futurity when the intense passions of this world will exist without mutability and outside dimensions and selfhood. And this knowledge can be gained from the nightingale's song, which is its soul, exactly as it can be learned from the artistic vision that has been captured on the urn and that is its soul. Or, to seek a special symbol of man's inherent yearning: the Biblical Ruth, sick for home—that home ethereal, from which she is kept by only "a fragile bar"—perhaps took into her heart the ecstasy-requiem of the nightingale as she stood amid the alien corn of this world (although it is not alien to the nightingale); for the nightingale's song is the ecstatic repose of that home for which she yearned and from which man is temporarily exiled. Ruth is all mortals who have had the spiritual aspiration for the meaning of life and have realized that in this alien world they cannot attain the full purpose of their being. (Is there not a strong suggestion that here the Biblical name serves also as a personification of "ruth" and in this sense encompasses all mortality?)

In the world of decay the nightingale creates this vision by living its heaven on earth, and thereby gives man a glimpse of the promise that the future holds out. It makes magic the casements ("magic" is proleptic in line 69) just as the magic union of Porphyro and Madeline opened the doors of the castle; and it opens them to the mystery, the elfin storm, for the beauty-truth song it sings is itself the mystery which permeates human life. The nightingale, like Pan, is a "firmament reflected in a sea"—a heaven on earth; and therefore, like Pan, it is the "opener of the mysterious doors / Leading to universal knowledge." It appears probable that Keats first wrote "ruthless seas" instead of "perilous seas"; and the original word more closely corresponds to the haggard-seeming of the elfin storm, which nevertheless is a boon indeed. Because the bird's song is the mystery, the perception of its meaning will open the casements into lost fairy lands, the same fairy lands of the elfin grot which are without time, space, and identity.

For the moment it appears that the poem will follow the same course as the "Ode on a Grecian Urn" after all and that the poet will pluck from his experience some conviction of a future existence for man which corresponds to the earthly "dying" of the nightingale. Keats seems to have gained insight into the nature of heaven through the "etherealizing" of the nightingale's song, to have translated that insight into the texture of human existence, and to be about to synthesize thesis and antithesis. But if he should conclude with a clear affirmation of values, he would be working contrary to the course of his materials. At best, the conflicts within the first six stanzas permit only irresolutions. Having no standard law of either heaven or earth, shifting his perspective violently from one to the other without possibility of finding a center, the poet can only guess that *perhaps* this is the meaning of the nightingale's song, for he can see only from the perspective of the "passing night" of mortal man's life, the blindness that surrounds all temporal existence before man himself can become immortal.

Because the poem cannot, therefore, reach a resolution, there must be yet another transmutation of the *données*. In stanza seven the experience of the first six stanzas had been reviewed in universal worldly terms; the translation of the "immortal" bird into the framework of the world of universal man had suggested the possibility of a meaning. But since the poem cannot arrive at a meaning, the poet once again transmutes his materials so that they appear in the texture, not of human universals, but of transiency, the world of dimensions and empty physical realities, the world in which a nightingale's song is only a song. To achieve this last metamorphosis, the poem pivots on the word "forlorn" and violently inverts itself with a terrible confusion of standards. The fairy lands are "forlorn" because they must be lost to man so long as he is in the mortal world. They are the mystery, but they cannot be peopled by mortals, for human existence involves an ignorance of the mystery even though the mystery is the central principle of man's life. But the word suddenly reverses its own value as it is torn from a context of universal man and applied to a particular man in a particular place and at a particular time. That the fairy lands are forlorn—deserted, lost—is a "good," a boon indeed; but the poet's frame of reference throughout the poem persists in being mortal, and suddenly it is the poet himself who, by contemplating the mystery, is forlorn—lost to the mortal world. To step beyond "the bourn of care / Beyond the sweet and bitter world" is

O horrible! to lose the sight of well remember'd
        face,
Of Brother's eyes, of Sister's brow.[21]

The consequence is the poet's realization that in the mortal world to contemplate the mystery, to seek to enter into it, is to be lost to the world. And now that the poet is fully out of his vision and is once again only a creature of the mutable world, along with the transmutation of the values of "forlorn" everything in the vision reappears as its opposite, the mutable world being the inverse of the vision.

This reversal of standards is brilliantly caught up in the ambiguity of the word "toll." The recollection of his isolation from man as a result of travelling "Beyond the sweet and bitter world" summons the poet back to his own self so that he is once again self-contained, no longer participating in essence, and therefore merely a mortal. But the tolling of the bell is both a summons of his soul back to his self and also the announcement of a death. The nightingale lives its death, dying being its true living; the poet has found that, from an earthly point of view, his own death is merely to become a meaningless sod. And yet there has been a death, for only during the vision has his soul truly been "living," as the nightingale has truly been

"living" by pouring forth its soul on earth. Now that his soul has returned to his self, the poet has "died" back into life. Or, to establish clearer standards, if we assume that true "life" is experiencing the condition of heaven's bourne, then the nightingale "lives" on earth but the poet cannot; and the poet's return to this world is therefore a "dying" that is announced by the same death-knell that summons him back to what most men call "life."

The first seven stanzas have taken place outside the context of time and space, but the poet's return to physical reality thaws the static scene, shakes time and space into activity: the bird now moves through space, which has until now been an irrelevant factor in the poem. And yet the irony lies in the fact that it was the poet who was striving to move to the nightingale, but that it is the nightingale who eventually moves. Consequently the enthusiastic "Away! away!" of stanza four, which announced the poet's hope for reunion with the symbol, is sadly echoed in the words "Adieu! adieu!" which recognize the futility of the aspiration, release the tension of the vision, and send the now physical bird through a spatial world. The ecstasy-requiem of the bird's song, now that it is being heard by only sensory ears, is merely the sad sweetness, the melancholy joy, that, according to the "Ode to Melancholy," characterizes the experience of beauty in the physical world—a "plaintive anthem." The poet had hoped to fade away from the mutable world into the shadows numberless in order to avoid the inherent fadingness of mortal man; but in the physical, spatial inversion of the vision it is the bird's song, the poet finds, that "fades." To the poet the night was "passing," but now the bird, who seemed fixed in darkness, passes.

And at last the final irony: the poet who had hoped for death that he might truly live—only to find that this death can have no meaning in the world—and who had discovered it is the visionary bird who has this true life even within the confines of the physical world, now discovers that in the spatial fabric of things it is the bird's song that becomes "buried" in the next valley glades. But such a series of inversions is inevitable. Because the elements of the poem are in irreconcilable conflict with each other, the poet's return to the spatial world can only turn his vision topsy-turvy and leave him with the same confusion of standards. Was it a true perception into the beauty-

truth that is to come—a penetration into that immortality that man calls "death"? or was it only
a fiction of the inventive faculty? "Do I wake or
sleep?" The poet knows only that perhaps the same
song was heard by Ruth. If it was the same, he
has had a vision; if not, only a waking dream. Very
early in his career Keats had asked:

> Can death be sleep, when life is but a dream,
> And scenes of bliss pass as a phantom by?
> The transient pleasures as a vision seem,
> And yet we think the greatest pain's to die.
>
> How strange it is that man on earth should
>   roam,
> And lead a life of woe, but not forsake
> His rugged path; nor dare he view alone
> His future doom which is but to awake.[22]

X

Until now we have been examining mainly the
ironic conflicts in the poem, such as the series of
tauntingly irreconcilable interpretations and values
of the death that begins with the burial of the
wine in the "deep-delved earth" and ends with the
bird's song "buried deep" in the valley glades—
that begins with the poet's desire to fade from
fadingness and ends with the fading of the song of
the bird that a moment before was seen as immortal. And yet there is an over-all framework
dominating the entire poem that, although it does
not reconcile these contradictions, gives them a
comprehensive relationship and imparts to them a
design. The aspiration for fellowship with essence,
Keats wrote, shadows "our own Soul's daytime / In
the dark void of Night." It is noticeable that in
stanzas one to three and in stanza eight there is
no suggestion of darkness, and that the darkness
which begins in stanza four grows thicker until
the concluding stanza. In the opening stanza the
poet seems able to see the green of the beech trees,
and in the last stanza, after the passing of the
metaphoric night, he observes the scene over which
the nightingale passes. The opening and close of
the poem, then, take place in the material world,
the soul's daytime.

But the core of the poem is the search for the
mystery, the unsuccessful quest for light within its
darkness, both spatial (the forest) and temporal
(the night); and that quest leads only to an increasing darkness, or a growing recognition of how

impenetrable the mystery is to mortals. There is no
light for the poet in the verdurous glooms of the
world; he cannot see into the embalmed darkness;
surrounded by darkness, he can only listen to the
soul-song of the nightingale; his quest for death is
the desire for the midnight of his life, instead of
his soul's daytime; and at last he recognizes that
mortal life is itself a "passing night." The "passing
night" is ambivalent, for if the poet has had a true
vision, he has seen momentarily into the "good"
darkness, and if his is only a waking dream, it is the
existence of man that is a transitory moment of
dark ignorance; but the "good" darkness, spatial
and temporal, is the persistent and proper condition
of the nightingale's existence. Suddenly, when the
poet has returned fully into himself, the darkness is
gone; there is light, but no insight into the mystery.

On the other hand, until the last stanza the
nightingale is also in darkness—among "shadows
numberless" and in the "forest dim." But this is far
from the agonizing darkness in which the poet
gropes for standards, for this is also the darkness of
the mystery—the green-recessed woods into which
Hermes and the nymph fled. And yet this darkness
is not cruel to the nightingale. The bird is not tormented by it as the poet is, for here there is the
light of the ideal, the visionary power of penetration
into the mystery. And for this reason the bird is
encouraged to pass from the "shadows numberless"
of the plot to the richer darkness of the "forest
dim," the deeper heart of the mystery.

There are, then, two kinds of darkness and two
kinds of light in the poem, just as there are two
kinds of death, two kinds of fading: the poet is in
the darkness of ignorance and bewilderment, the
nightingale in the darkness of the mystery; light to
the poet is only a return from the mystery, a withdrawal into the physical world to which his faculties
are adequate, but to the nightingale light is the
illumination of the mystery. Against the backdrop
of these "good" and "bad" darknesses and "good"
and "bad" lights, the incessant ironies and clashes
within the poem take on their consistency. For example, the poet's desire to fade into the dim forest
is a desire to penetrate into the mystery and hence
avoid the "bad" fadingness. But this pattern of
metaphysical chiaroscuro gives the poem only a
consistency, not a resolution.

And the poet can end only with the unreconciled
standards of a Purgatory blind. Has he glimpsed

into the beauty-truth to come, or is it all a fiction? There is nothing in the experience to give him an answer. If we distort the emphasis slightly by underscoring the supposition that the experience was only a fiction, we may say that early in May, 1819, Keats had uttered his Everlasting No. In the previous month he had written "La Belle Dame Sans Merci," his Center of Indifference. But late in May, 1819, Keats was spirited strong enough to elicit from these shattering visions the Everlasting Yea of his "Ode on a Grecian Urn."

NOTES

1. *On the Limits of Poetry* (New York, 1948), 168.
2. *Biographia Literaria*, ed. Shawcross, II. 10.
3. "To J. H. Reynolds, Esq.," 67–85.
4. *Endymion*, I. 691–94.
5. *Ibid.*, IV. 859.
6. *Ibid.*, 819.
7. *Ibid.*, II. 185–86.
8. Letter to George and Georgiana Keats, February 14–May 3, 1819.
9. "God of the Meridian."
10. *Endymion*, I. 251–60.
11. *Ibid.*, IV. 269, 274–76.
12. "The Eve of St. Agnes," stanza 5, variant.
13. Letter to Bailey, November 22, 1817.
14. "Where's the Poet?"
15. "The Poet" ("At morn, at noon, at Eve, and Middle Night").
16. Letter to George and Georgiana Keats, February 14–May 3, 1819.
17. *Explicator*, V (1947), no. 27.
18. *Endymion*, I. 594–96.
19. *Ibid.*, III. 172–73.
20. *Ibid.*, I. 825.
21. "Lines Written in the Highlands after a Visit to Burns's Country," 29–30, 33–34.
22. "On Death."

Stuart Sperry

TO AUTUMN*

The fallacy of using any single work, such as *The Fall of Hyperion*, either to predict or limit the shape of Keats's career or the direction of his evolution, had he lived, is nowhere better demonstrated than in the lyric he transcribed the same day he announced the final abandonment of *Hyperion*—the ode "To Autumn." As John Middleton Murry long ago observed, the two works are almost total contrasts in tone and spirit.[1] With its struggle for ascent through doubt and self-questioning to a point of visionary comprehensiveness above the human world, the longer work is fired with a Miltonic ardor and intensity. In its condensed but unhurried perfection, its contemplation of the actual, the ode is much closer to Shakespeare. The two works, to be certain, share one supreme concern: their common involvement with process. However as treatments of that theme they differ immeasurably. *Hyperion* fails through the inability to evolve a framework for transcending process, for reconciling man to the knowledge of sorrow and loss. "To Autumn" succeeds through its acceptance of an order innate in our experience—the natural rhythm of the seasons. It is a poem that, without ever stating it, inevitably suggests the truth of "ripeness is all" by developing, with a richness and profundity of implication, the simple perception that ripeness is fall.

The perfection of the ode lies chiefly in the care and subtlety of patterning within its three-part structure. The patterns are ones that partly connect "To Autumn" with the odes of the spring and partly mark a new development and vary in complexity. As critics have often pointed out, the three stanzas successively proceed from the last growth of late

* From *Keats the Poet* by Stuart M. Sperry (copyright © 1973 by Princeton University Press), pp. 336–342. Reprinted by permission of Princeton University Press.

summer through the fullness of high autumn to the spareness of an early winter landscape, just as they suggest the progress of a single day through to its close in sunset. As Bush, among others, has noted, the imagery of the first stanza is mainly tactile, that of the second mainly visual, that of the last chiefly auditory.[2] In these and other respects the ode displays a deliberate symmetry and balance the earlier odes do not possess. At the same time it makes a more even and practiced use of devices developed in its predecessors. The personification of the season, introduced at the beginning of the first stanza in a way reminiscent of the opening of the "Urn," is developed in the second into a full series of tableaux, and then is briefly and elegiacally revived at the outset of the third before the ode returns us to the simple sounds and images of the natural landscape. There remains, too, but in a more subtle way, the pattern of lyric questioning, from the submerged "how" of the first stanza, to the rhetorical "who" at the outset of the second, to the more imperative "where" at the commencement of the third, that marks the gradual emergence into consciousness of the recognition the season both epitomizes and expresses. One must add, following Bate's observation that " 'To Autumn' is so uniquely a distillation," [3] that the ode is Keats's last and most mature comment on the nature of the poetic process. For its whole development, from the imagery of ripening and storing in the first stanza, through that of winnowing and slow extraction in the second, to the subtle, thin, and tenuous music with which the poem rises to its close, represents his final adaptation of his favorite metaphor for poetic creation. The analogy Shelley makes explicit in his "Ode to the West Wind" is not less moving or real because it is left implicit in Keats's hymn. If the "wild West Wind" and its "mighty harmonies" express Shelley's sense of a universal force of spiritual creativity, the autumnal sounds that are borne away on "the light wind" that "lives or dies" at the end of Keats's ode converge to produce a music that is poignantly natural.

The ironies that pervade the odes of the spring are by no means missing in "To Autumn." However they are now resolved within an image that transcends them—the image of autumn itself. Virtually from its beginning the ode compels us to conceive of the season in two different ways: as a conventional setting or personified abstraction that has been depicted poetically and pictorially from time immemorial with a fixed nature and identity of its own;[4] and as a seasonal interval, a mere space between summer and winter that can never be abstracted from the larger cycle of birth and death.

> Season of mists and mellow fruitfulness,
>   Close bosom-friend of the maturing sun;
> Conspiring with him how to load and bless
>   With fruit the vines that round the thatch-
>   eves run.   (1–4)

The homely, welcoming personifications seem to proclaim a role that is familiar and established. Nevertheless, as B. C. Southam has observed, the opening line, with its allusion both to "mists" and "mellow fruitfulness," already points to different and contrasting aspects of the year.[5]

While the first stanza concentrates upon the natural world through images of growth and process, the second stanza shifts to a more artful and stylized conception by presenting autumn as a figure captured and framed within a series of perspectives that are recognizably conventional. However the two conceptions of autumn, as process and abstraction, continually modify and interpenetrate each other. To take only one example, there is the depiction in the second stanza of autumn

> sitting careless on a granary floor,
>   Thy hair soft-lifted by the winnowing wind;
> Or on a half-reap'd furrow sound asleep,
>   Drows'd with the fume of poppies, while
>   thy hook
>   Spares the next swath and all its twined
>   flowers.   (14–18)

The picture is more than an intermingling of activity and stasis. For a moment the figure of the season is involved with and actually worked upon by the very processes she emblemizes, even while she remains careless and impervious to the changes they imply. Such juxtapositions convey a sense of irony of the most delicate and subtle kind.

Throughout the ode the play of irony is developed by the way in which the major patterns alternate and run counter to each other. In the first stanza the sense of process and maturing is carried forward by such active verbs as "load," "bend," "fill," "swell," "plump," "set budding." At the same time another pattern of words, concentrated near the end of the stanza, suggests the contradictory idea of a repletion that has already been attained: "fruit*fulness*," "all," "more, / And still more," "later," "never," "e[v]er." In the second stanza, which, as Bate has written, is "something of a reverse or mirror image of the first,"[6] autumn is personified in a series of fixed poses—as thresher, reaper, gleaner, watcher—that, in their immobility, suggest an ideal of completion. Nevertheless the effect is in a measure counterbalanced by a sustained use of partitives—"oft[en]," "Sometimes," "care*less*," "half," "next," "sometimes," "last," "hours by hours"—as well as by the movement and diversity implied by such different positioning prepositions and adverbs as "amid," "abroad," "across."

It is in the last stanza that these various oppositions achieve a resolution unlike any in the odes of the spring. The questioning with which the stanza begins becomes more direct and pressing, forcing into conscious recognition[7] the knowledge that has all the while been growing latently throughout the ode:

> Where are the songs of Spring? Ay, where are they?
> *Think not* of them, thou has thy music too.
> (23–24)

The awareness of impermanence and ultimately of death is no less moving because it must be momentarily suppressed in a way that makes us recognize the impossibility of any direct confrontation. Still, such awareness is not finally rejected but rather tempered and reflected in the light of the "soft-dying day," where the imagery of the spring ("bloom," "rosy") is briefly reborn amid the tonalities of autumn, just as it is echoed in the "wailful choir" of gnats that "mourn" and in the distant "bleat[ing]" of the lambs. For it is, in the end, the *music* of autumn that works within the poem its saving mediation, that gathers together and resolves the various antinomies within a larger movement. It is a music that is alternately "borne *aloft*" or "*sinking*" as the "light wind *lives* or *dies*." It composes itself from the sounds of the "*small* gnats" as well as from those of "*full-grown* lambs," from the "*loud*" bleating of the sheep to the "*soft*" treble of the robin. It draws together the song of the redbreast, as Arnold Davenport has noted, "character-

istically a winter bird," and the call of the swallow, "proverbially the bird of summer [who] leaves the country when summer is over."[8] It combines the cadences of change and continuity, of life and death. It rises from earth, "*from* hilly bourn" and "*from* a garden croft" to ascend "*in* the skies." In its gradual withdrawal and attenuation ("treble," "whistles," "twitter"), it suggests the inevitable end of a natural cycle of growth, maturity and distillment in a ghostly and ethereal dissipation.

One aspect of the ode, especially of its final stanza, deserves to be commented on in more detail: the way it returns for a major element of its technique to the early verse, to sonnets like "How Many Bards" and "After Dark Vapours." The connection is suggested by Reuben Brower's remark that "To Autumn" reveals "how a succession of images, becoming something more than mere succession, imperceptibly blends into metaphor."[9] For the final stanza of the ode remains the most perfect expression of the poet's habit of cataloguing (though the latter term now seems crude and inadequate to describe the effect "To Autumn" achieves). The beginning of the stanza deliberately eschews the invitation to conscious reflection, avoiding the moral sentiment or epitaph that constitutes the chief resolution of a whole tradition of the pastoral mode. Instead the stanza gains its end by offering us one more succession of precise impressions, a series of images that extends its texture of associations and reverberations as it unfolds. It elaborates a music that is entirely earthly and natural, yet filled with further implications. It never removes us from the characteristic world of Keats's poetry, a world of

> leaves
> Budding—fruit ripening in stillness—autumn suns
> Smiling at eve upon the quiet sheaves.
> ("After Dark Vapours," 9–11)

Yet it imperceptibly creates a further range of meaning, the final awareness, if not of "a Poet's death," of a settled ripeness of experience we strive to articulate within such set terms as "maturity" or "resignation" or "acceptance." It preserves decorum by remaining to the last a poetry of sensation; yet it leaves us with a full sense of the ultimate values. It takes us as far as we have any right to require toward a poetry of thought.

NOTES

1. The contrast between the two works is the culmination of Murry's seminal study, *Keats and Shakespeare* (London, 1925). He juxtaposes the abandonment of *Hyperion* and the composition of the ode to assert his major thesis: "Shakespeare had triumphed in Keats' soul" (p. 168).

2. *John Keats: His Life and Writings* (New York, 1966), p. 177.

3. *John Keats* (Cambridge, Mass., 1963), p. 581. I am indebted to all the discussions cited in the footnotes to this chapter but particularly to Bate's, which is reprinted in his *Keats: A Collection of Critical Essays* (Englewood Cliffs, N.J., 1964), pp. 155–60.

4. In his chapter on "To Autumn" in *Keats and the Mirror of Art* (Oxford, 1967), pp. 232–43, Ian Jack has collected a sizable number of instances from both literature and painting.

5. The line, Southam argues, looks forward to the "spectral, disembodied, chill feature of the season's end" even while it "glances at Autumn in her first capacity, fecund and beneficent" and thus anticipates a central progression in the ode ("The Ode 'To Autumn,'" *Keats-Shelley Journal,* IX [1960], 93).

6. *John Keats,* p. 582.

7. See James Lott's interesting and subtle reading of the ode in "Keats's *To Autumn*: The Poetic Consciousness and the Awareness of Process," *Studies in Romanticism,* IX (1970), 71–81. Lott's argument is that the ode records a change from unthinking empathy with natural process to a consciousness of time and the speaker's separation from the season.

8. "A Note on 'To Autumn,'" *John Keats: A Reassessment,* ed. Kenneth Muir (Liverpool, 1958), p. 99.

9. *The Fields of Light* (New York, 1951), p. 39.

Index of Authors, Titles, and First Lines*

* Authors' names are in **boldface** type; titles in *italics;* and first lines in roman.